Contents

The National Garden Scheme

A company limited by guarantee. Registered in England & Wales. Charity No. 1112664. Company No. 5631421

Registered & Head Office: Hatchlands Park, East Clandon, Guildford, Surrey, GU4 7RT.
01483 211535 www.ngs.org.uk

© The National Garden Scheme 2022

Published by Constable, an imprint of Little, Brown Book Group, Carmelite House, 50 Victoria Embankment, London EC4Y 0DZ. An Hachette UK Company www.hachette.co.uk www.littlebrown.co.uk

CLARENCE HOUSE

As we all become increasingly aware of the need to lead our lives more sustainably, our gardens provide the most immediate and simplest examples of the benefits that can be achieved. Gardens are our domestic link with Nature: selecting and tending garden plants from one season to the next introduces us to the wider needs of the natural plant kingdom. At the same time, our gardens enable us to encourage and co-exist with wildlife, large and small, offering them a refuge and home that is all too often hard to find.

The thousands of people who open their gardens in support of the National Garden Scheme offer a wonderful opportunity for anyone to explore and find out about what sustainability really means. The seemingly limitless variety of their gardens demonstrates our relationship with Nature in myriad ways. Village gardens look out to, and often merge with, neighbouring farmland and countryside in a way that immediately increases their appeal, while a small garden plot in the city is an oasis which connects others in order to provide the urban landscape with a vital green lung.

The owners of these private plots, who open their gates and welcome visitors, want to share the benefits and they are often leading the way towards more sustainable living. They grow certain plants to encourage wildlife, from birds to butterflies; they grow others for the produce they will eat themselves – or make available to their visitors – on a more durable, seasonal basis.

As we steer a sometimes erratic course away from the Coronavirus pandemic, from which the National Garden Scheme made a remarkable recovery in 2021, it is heartening to witness that the appetite for a gentler style of gardening, in tune with the natural rhythms of the world, has never been greater. The warm-hearted community of people who open their gardens are uniquely placed to spread the word. The charitable impact of their activities from the funds they raise is plain for all to see in the annual donations to nursing and health charities, which returned to £3 million in 2021. I am certain that in the coming years the impact of their support for sustainable gardening will become equally significant. Both are to be celebrated and, as Patron, I would like to thank everyone involved in the National Garden Scheme.

Chairman's message

2021 saw the National Garden Scheme achieve a remarkable recovery from the impact of Covid-19 and even though I write this as the Omicron variant is causing continued concern, I am confident that 2022 will see us able to welcome visitors to our gardens and continue to provide vital support to our nursing and health beneficiaries.

We have some exciting new gardens opening, including for the very first time, gardens in Northern Ireland and the Channel Islands. They join the ranks of others who have supported us loyally for many years and I want to say an enormous thank you to them all. Your gardens are what the National Garden Scheme is all about and they give a positive message as we emerge from the dark clouds of Covid-19.

Our Patron, The Prince of Wales, writes eloquently in his Foreword about the need for us all to garden sustainably and the role our gardens can play in illustrating sustainability and I heartily concur with what he says. The National Garden Scheme is the largest franchise in the world of gardens that are open to visitors and our ability to set a powerful example is immense.

Charles and I have opened our garden in Clapham for many years and we know the vibrant diversity of gardens that can be discovered in towns and cities up and down the country. In his article about Small Urban Gardens, our Chief Executive George Plumptre sets out that it is an important priority for the National Garden Scheme to expand the diversity of our portfolio of gardens.

Within walking distance of our London street we know gardens whose planting and style originates in Jamaica, in India and in Japan and I am excited about attracting an ever-widening audience to open for the National Garden Scheme. We know this will attract a similar diversity of visitors and help us to achieve the Vision of the National Garden Scheme: that everyone has access to gardens and values the benefit to their health, wellbeing and enjoyment of life.

Rupert Tyler

Rupert Tyler

Discover the nation's best gardens

The National Garden Scheme gives visitors unique access to exceptional private gardens and raises impressive amounts of money for nursing and health charities through admissions, teas and cake.

Thanks to the generosity of garden owners, volunteers and visitors we have donated over £63 million to nursing and health charities since we were founded in 1927. In 2021, despite the continuing challenges we all faced from the COVID-19 pandemic, we made total donations of over £3 million.

Originally established to raise funds for district nurses, we are now the most significant charitable funder of nursing in the UK and our beneficiaries include Macmillan Cancer Support, Marie Curie, Hospice UK and The Queen's Nursing Institute. Year by year, the cumulative impact of the grants we give grows incrementally, helping our beneficiaries make their own important contribution to the nation's health and care and strengthening the partnerships that we have with them all.

The National Garden Scheme doesn't just open beautiful gardens for charity – we are passionate about the physical and mental health benefits of gardens too. We fund projects which promote gardens and gardening as therapy, and in 2017 launched our annual Gardens and Health Week to raise awareness of the topic. We also support charities doing amazing work in gardens and health and give grants for community gardening projects. Our funding also supports the training of gardeners and offers respite to horticultural workers who have fallen on difficult times.

With over 3,500 gardens opening across England, Wales, Northern Ireland and the Channel Islands in 2022, we hope you enjoy exploring our beautiful gardens this year. Each inspiring space not only provides a unique glimpse into hidden horticultural delights but also the chance to support the health and wellbeing of thousands.

Below The Laundry, Denbigh

© Joe Wainwright

YOUR GARDEN VISITS HELP CHANGE LIVES

In 2021 the National Garden Scheme donated over **£3 million** to our beneficiaries, providing critical support to nursing and health charities following a year of crisis.

Marie Curie
£525,000

Macmillan
Cancer Support
£500,000

Hospice UK
£500,000

Carers Trust
£425,000

The Queen's
Nursing Institute
£395,000

Parkinson's UK
£212,500

Your visits helped us
to donate over
£3 million
to charity in 2021

※ Perennial £115,000
※ Maggie's £100,000
※ Horatio's Garden £75,000
※ WRAGS £65,000
※ ABF The Soldiers' Charity £60,000
※ National Botanic Garden, Wales £20,000
※ Professional Gardeners' Trust £20,000
※ Garden Museum £10,000

Thank you!

To find out more visit **ngs.org.uk/beneficiaries**

A partner for all seasons

After every long, cold winter, gardens return to bloom, reminding us that all things come and go.

We are collectively emerging from a difficult past year, in which the enjoyment of outdoor spaces acted as a much-needed tonic to our physical and mental health. And as we enter a hopefully more positive period, these spaces will blossom in celebration with us.

As wealth managers, we are more accustomed to volatility than most. We pursue growth for our clients through rises and falls, and know that difficult times are, more often than not, followed by good.

Through both, we're delighted to sponsor the National Garden Scheme, facilitating access to exquisite gardens, and supporting their incredible fundraising for nursing and health charities.

With investment your capital is at risk.

Know where life can take you.

investecwin.co.uk

Tips on using your Handbook

This book lists all the gardens opening for the National Garden Scheme between January 2022 and early 2023. It is divided up into county sections, each including a map, calendar of opening dates and details of each garden, listed alphabetically.

Symbols explained

NEW Gardens opening for the first time this year or re-opening after a long break.

♦ Garden also opens on non-National Garden Scheme days. (Gardens which carry this symbol contribute to the National Garden Scheme either by opening on a specific day(s) and/or by giving a guaranteed contribution.)

♿ Wheelchair access to at least the main features of the garden.

🐕 Dogs on short leads welcome.

✽ Plants usually for sale.

⑴⑴ Card payments accepted.

NPC Plant Heritage National Plant Collection.

🛏 Gardens that offer accommodation.

☕ Refreshments are available, normally at a charge, subject to Covid-19 guidelines.

🪑 Picnics welcome.

D Garden designed by a Fellow, Member, Pre-registered Member, or Student of The Society of Garden Designers.

🚌 Garden accessible to coaches. Coach sizes vary so please contact garden owner or County Organiser in advance to check details.

Group Visits Group Organisers may contact the County Organiser or a garden owner direct to organise a group visit to a particular county or garden. Otherwise contact the National Garden Scheme office on 01483 211535.

Children must be accompanied by an adult.

Photography is at the discretion of the garden owner; please check first. Photographs must not be used for sale or reproduction without prior permission of the owner.

Funds raised In most cases all funds raised at our open gardens comes to the National Garden Scheme. However, there are some instances where income from teas or a percentage of admissions is given to another charity.

Toilet facilities are not usually available at gardens.

If you cannot find the information you require from a garden or County Organiser, call the National Garden Scheme office on 01483 211535.

There are many ways to book and enjoy a visit to our gardens...

Cashless payments and online booking

)))

Pre-booking available

Many gardens accept card payments. Look for the cashless symbol in the garden listing on our website.

For over 2,000 gardens you can purchase tickets online in advance, as well as purchasing them on the gate on the day. Look for the Pre-booking available symbol in the garden listing.

Pre-booking essential

The **Pre-booking essential** symbol in the garden listing means you need to pre-book your visit. You will also see either:

Book now

A book now button which allows you to book your tickets through the National Garden Scheme

OR

Owner Info

If there is no book now button, you will need to book your tickets direct with the Garden Owner. Click on the Owner Info tab to find their contact details

Special Events

Some gardens offer Special Events which may include a tour, an exclusive visit or a meal. These must be pre-booked, and sell out fast. Visit **ngs.org.uk/special-events** to book your ticket and sign up to receive the latest updates.

Open by arrangement

Over 1,100 gardens invite you to visit By Arrangement – so that you can visit on a date to suit you. Contact the Garden Owner to discuss availability and book your visit.

Dame Mary Berry
President of the National Garden Scheme
INVITES YOU TO

party in the world's greatest

glasshouse

TEMPERATE HOUSE, KEW GARDENS
THURSDAY 26TH MAY, 2022 | 6.30PM-9.30PM

Join us for an exclusive evening of fine wines, delicious food, and live music within the magnificent setting of the iconic Temperate House and explore the vast collection of 10,000 plants, after hours.

Tickets are limited and entrance is by pre-booked ticket only. For more information and to book tickets visit ngs.org.uk/kew

Photo credit © Marianne Majerus

All funds raised in aid of the National Garden Scheme.   Sponsored by

The impact of our donations to nursing

Since our inception the National Garden Scheme has developed an efficient fundraising formula which allows us to donate over 80% of money raised at our open gardens to nursing and health beneficiaries. Despite the ongoing restrictions and uncertainty that continued throughout the early months of 2021, severely curtailing garden opening activities, we were still able to announce donations of over £3 million to our beneficiary charities in 2021.

The lion's share, £2,557,500, went to some of the UK's best-loved nursing and health charities, many of which have provided vital support to the NHS and communities across the UK throughout the COVID-19 pandemic. National Garden Scheme funding has allowed these charities to continue the provision of critical services including the weekly provision of one million items of PPE to the hospice network and bereavement counselling for patients, families and staff.

National Garden Scheme Chairman Rupert Tyler said: "At a time when the collective activities and contributions of our beneficiaries in supporting the national endeavour continued to put unbearable pressure on many aspects of their work, we were delighted to be able to continue our support in such a meaningful way."

Here are some of the incredible things our donations have supported in 2021:

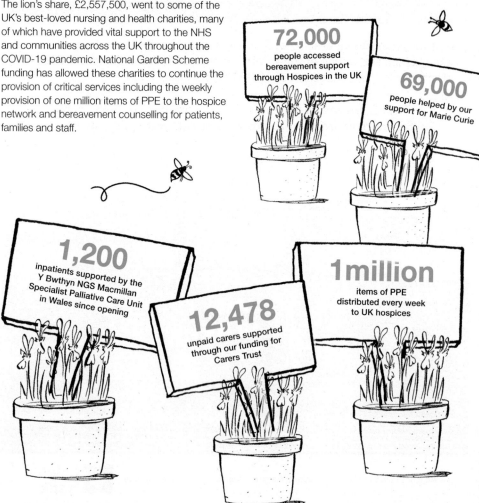

72,000
people accessed
bereavement support
through Hospices in the UK

69,000
people helped by our
support for Marie Curie

1,200
inpatients supported by the
Y Bwthyn NGS Macmillan
Specialist Palliative Care Unit
in Wales since opening

12,478
unpaid carers supported
through our funding for
Carers Trust

1million
items of PPE
distributed every week
to UK hospices

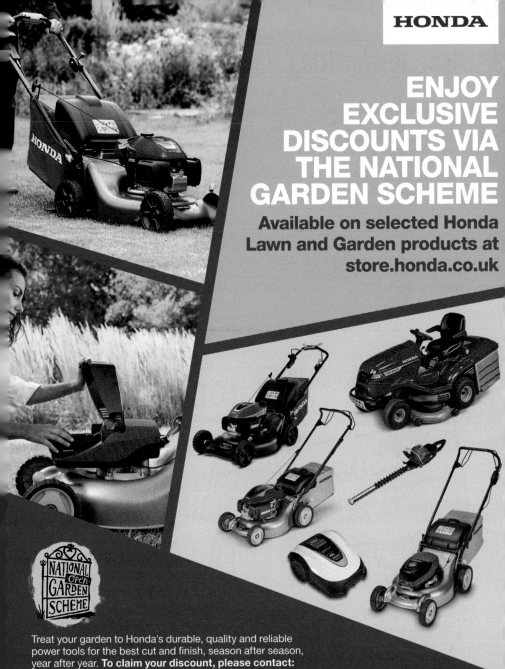

HONDA

ENJOY EXCLUSIVE DISCOUNTS VIA THE NATIONAL GARDEN SCHEME

Available on selected Honda Lawn and Garden products at store.honda.co.uk

NATIONAL Open **GARDEN SCHEME**

Treat your garden to Honda's durable, quality and reliable power tools for the best cut and finish, season after season, year after year. **To claim your discount, please contact:** joanne.beattie@honda-eu.com

HONDA | ENGINEERING FOR *Life*

store.honda.co.uk

Gardens and health: people and communities

We have championed and supported the concept that access to gardens and practical gardening are good for people's health and wellbeing since 2016. The report we commissioned from the Kings Fund – *Gardens and health: Implications for policy and practice*, remains a key reference for the understanding, assessment and development of the links between gardens, gardening and health. And our annual Gardens and Health campaign ensures that we raise awareness of the benefits of gardens and gardening to a growing audience of gardeners and garden visitors alike.

In addition, we continue to make substantial donations to specific charities for health-related garden projects. We have committed to support the building of all eleven Horatio's Gardens in NHS Spinal Injury Units across the UK and make annual donations to Maggie's to add to their portfolio of gardens at their cancer support centres.

Passionate about the physical and mental health benefits of gardens, we also fund projects that promote gardens and gardening as therapy and support charities doing amazing work through community gardening projects. Our funding also supports the training of gardeners and, through our support for Perennial, offers respite to horticultural workers and their families who have fallen on difficult times.

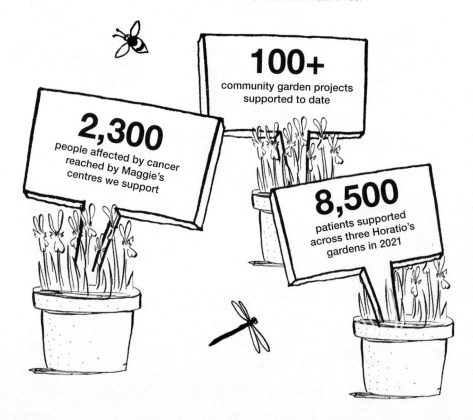

100+
community garden projects
supported to date

2,300
people affected by cancer
reached by Maggie's
centres we support

8,500
patients supported
across three Horatio's
gardens in 2021

Opposite page: Patients enjoying horticultural therapy with Horatio's Garden staff at Stoke Mandeville

Our Great British Garden Party

Last summer people up and down the country, and as far away as Houston, USA, hosted Great British Garden Parties to support some of the UK's best-loved nursing and health charities. From afternoon tea to paella parties, plant sales to street parties, cake stalls to evening events, there were a multitude of creative interpretations of what a Great British Garden Party can be.

"It's been a wonderfully creative and exciting Great British Garden Party season," says Chief Executive, George Plumptre. "Along with some great themes and fundraising activities – from guess the name of the calf, to raffles and bring and buy sales – we've been supported by young helpers, staunch supporters and lots of new friends. Together we raised almost £40,000."

"I love hosting friends and family and the National Garden Scheme's campaign gave me a great reason to get everyone together and enjoy tea and treats in the sun, for a great cause! The best part of the day was seeing family I hadn't caught up with for ages. It's a great way to make the most of the British summer whilst raising funds and awareness for the brilliant nursing charities." – Alice.

A chance meeting with a friend on a dog walk led Claire and Charles to host a Great British Garden Party last summer. "It seemed such a brilliant idea and having been a nurse myself years ago, I liked the idea of raising money for nursing charities. Despite torrential rain hampering our preparations, our visitors did not let it dampen their enjoyment and together we raised over £1,600!"

Emma, a 24-year-old gardening enthusiast who grows fruit, vegetables and cut flowers on two veg patches in Cheshire, hosted a Great British Garden Party plant sale and raised £630. "I sold home grown produce, fresh flowers and plants from the garden. We also had 'guess the name of the calf', as well as cakes and refreshments. It was great to see so many familiar faces and share our garden."

You too can get involved!

Sign up to host your own Great British Garden Party event in 2022 at **ngs.org.uk/gardenparty**

Join the
Great British
Garden Party

Everyone is invited!

This is your opportunity to help us to raise money for some of the best loved nursing and health charities. Host an event this summer: afternoon tea, prosecco by candlelight, a plant and produce sale – the choice is yours. Invite friends and families and gather together in support of some great causes including Marie Curie, Macmillan Cancer support, The Queen's Nursing Institute, Hospice UK, Carer's Trust and Parkinson's UK.

Joining the Great British Garden Party this year could not be simpler. Just visit ngs.org.uk/gardenparty (or scan the QR code) to sign up and find out more.

In partnership with

talking tables

plan it. host it. love it.

The fascination of our urban gardens

The National Garden Scheme has long been renowned for opening the gates of gorgeous country gardens all over England and Wales. But in recent years the presence of small urban gardens has been steadily growing and as our Chief Executive George Plumptre describes: what they might lack in size is more than made up for by the fascination of what can be achieved in a garden of limited space, in their impact within an urban landscape, and by their familiarity for visitors with similar gardens of their own.

Below: 28a Worcester Road, Walthamstow

Gardens in the countryside very often perpetuate the cherished picture of the 'English garden' with which the National Garden Scheme is so strongly associated. But it is often in our towns and cities that we can celebrate the wonderful diversity of gardens in Britain, many inspired by the plants and gardening styles of different countries and cultures around the world, from the Caribbean to South America, from Japan and Australia to India and Africa. We want the gardens that open in support of the National Garden Scheme to include and showcase all the gardening enthusiasts and styles to be found in Britain and we know that we will discover many of them in our urban settings.

Above: 190 Barnet Road, Barnet **Below:** 81 Coombe Lane, Bristol; 81 Baston Road, Bromley

I know from visiting myself that there is the real fascination of 'what lies behind' as you approach many urban gardens for the first time. From parking on the street to in many cases accessing the garden through the house, perhaps passing on the way a small front garden which sets the tone for what to expect, you emerge into what is likely to be a haven of calm which might stretch away for a surprising distance. You will probably notice that any trees have been carefully selected for appropriate size and seasonal interest, ideally with spring or early summer blossom, autumn berries and interesting foliage that changes through the year.

In the countryside it is generally easy for wildlife to survive, to find a home, to move about and to raise young. In the harsh reality of an urban setting, it is far more difficult, and gardens are – literally – a vital lifeline. The smallest single tree will immediately attract small birds, mammals such as hedgehogs will find food and shelter, and a tiny pond will soon be teeming with aquatic life from small fish to frogs and damsel flies.

Many small urban gardens open together in groups and there is something very cheering about following a small map to discover a selection of gardens dotted around a network of streets, as we did last summer in Birmingham's Bournville, originally built as a late-Victorian model village by the Cadbury family for the workers at their chocolate factory. The selection of gardens on offer in such groups demonstrate the range of personal taste and gardening styles that we all find so fascinating as visitors.

Although teeming with people, towns and cities can be unfriendly places to live and opening your garden can immediately create a strong sense of local community. One friend told me about opening her garden in London's Clapham for the first time; among the visitors were lots of people she passed regularly when walking to the bus or underground on the way to work, but never spoke to. Now they were in her garden, chatting and socialising in a way that few other activities would encourage.

Many large towns and cities enjoy a particular type of microclimate in which exotic and tender plants will thrive. The garden square on which we live in London very rarely experiences either a frost or low winter temperatures. This, with the shelter of buildings and towering plane trees, as well as high summer temperatures is celebrated and enjoyed by echiums which you would be more likely to see in Cornwall or the Scilly Isles, and a selection of choice and tender shrubs and small trees – many from Australasia.

In the 1980s there were just 30 gardens opening in support of the National Garden Scheme within the area of Greater London encircled by the M25. In 2022 there will be more than 260 gardens opening in the same area. In the group that opens together in historic Spitalfields most gardens are a few square metres in size, while in Walthamstow Mark and Emma Luggie will open their amazing mini-jungle at 28A Worcester Road for the very first time. We hope that we can achieve a similar growth in garden numbers in towns and cities up and down the country and we look forward to recruiting and welcoming new gardeners this year and beyond.

Below: Bournville Village, Birmingham

The National Garden Scheme are looking for new gardens

Join a community of like-minded individuals passionate about gardens and open your garden to raise money for vital nursing and health charities.

Our garden portfolio is diverse: from gorgeous country estates to tropical urban extravaganzas, gardens planted for wildlife and allotments. So, whatever its size or style, if your garden has quality, character and interest we'd love to hear from you.

Call us on 01483 211 535 or email hello@ngs.org.uk

Our Community Gardens Awards

In addition to our annual donations to nursing and health charities, the National Garden Scheme grants awards to help community gardening projects, celebrating with the presentation of a special plaque on completion of the work.

It began in 2011 when we set up an award scheme in memory of Elspeth Thompson, the much-loved garden writer and journalist who died in 2010. Elspeth was a great friend and supporter of the National Garden Scheme; she also wrote an admired 'Urban Gardener' column in the *Sunday Telegraph* that often celebrated community gardens.

In 2020 we gave out £97,210 to 44 projects bringing the number of projects supported to-date to over 100, with a total amount donated of £217,156.

Unfortunately, the COVID-19 pandemic impacted heavily on our Community Gardens Award programme and the ability of the gardens to carry out the work that the money has been donated for. Because of this, our Trustees decided to allow the existing 2020 projects to run over into 2021 and for new applications for 2022 funding to open at the end of 2021.

Despite the restrictions, many of the community gardens have now completed the work funded by us in 2020 and throughout England and Wales have received commemorative plaques to acknowledge completion of their projects. From women's refuge groups and social inclusion projects to health and wellness community gardens and therapeutic horticultural projects, the diversity of community gardens that we support is helping thousands of people across the country.

We look forward to receiving applications in 2022. Visit **ngs.org.uk/cga-application** for information.

Above: County Organiser for Berkshire, Heather Skinner presents the National Garden Scheme Community Gardens Award plaque to the New Leaf Project – an allotment project which uses gardening to help local people with mental health

Opposite: Twigs community garden – a delightful 2-acre garden created and maintained by volunteers. Open for the National Garden Scheme in May

Below: Volunteers from Grange Farm Community Garden in Chigwell – an allotment project which is maintained by adults with learning disabilities. Open for the National Garden Scheme in July

OUR FUTURE IS BOTANIC.

**PLANTS AND FUNGI ARE
VITAL TO THE FUTURE
OF FOOD, CLEAN AIR,
AND MEDICINE**

JOIN | DONATE | DISCOVER

Royal Botanic Gardens
Kew

Titan arum

COBRA

One of the UK's largest range of lawnmowers

Create a lawn that is the envy of your neighbours with a new lawnmower from Cobra. At the heart of these powerful, stylish mowers is a choice of either electric, cordless or petrol engines powered by Briggs & Stratton, Honda, Kohler and more.

Cobra have over 65 lawnmowers in their portfolio including a comprehensive range of powerful 40V and Twin 40V cordless models including the 'Which?' award winning Cobra MX51S80V cordless lawnmower. Whatever your gardening needs, Cobra has a lawnmower for you.

Best Buy
Which?
Lawnmowers May 2021

80VMAX LITHIUM-ION

POWERED BY BRIGGS & STRATTON

Expertly Powered By
COBRA

Model Shown: Cobra MX51S80V

For your nearest dealer visit: **www.cobragarden.co.uk** or call: **0115 986 6646**   *Promotional prices only at participating dealers*

Pass on your love of gardens
with a gift in your will

Leaving a gift to the National Garden Scheme will help us ensure that everyone can experience the joy of garden visiting and inspire a passion for gardens in future generations.

Scan for more information

For more information or to speak to a member of our team call **01483 211535** email **giftinwill@ngs.org.uk** or visit **ngs.org.uk/giftinwill**

BEDFORDSHIRE

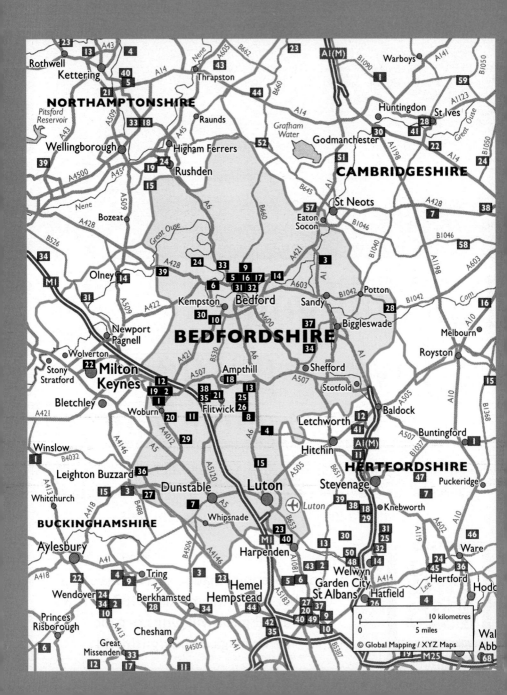

Rothwell
Kettering
Thrapston

NORTHAMPTONSHIRE
Pitsford Reservoir
Raunds
Wellingborough
Higham Ferrers
Rushden
Nene
Bozeat
Olney
Kempston
Bedford
Newport Pagnell
Wolverton
Stony Stratford
Milton Keynes
Bletchley
Woburn
Flitwick
Winslow
Leighton Buzzard
Whitchurch
Dunstable
BUCKINGHAMSHIRE
Aylesbury
Tring
Wendover
Berkhamsted
Princes Risborough
Chesham
Great Missenden

Warboys
Huntingdon
St Ives
Godmanchester
Grafham Water
CAMBRIDGESHIRE
St Neots
Eaton Socon
Potton
Sandy
Biggleswade
Melbourn
Royston
BEDFORDSHIRE
Ampthill
Shefford
Stotfold
Letchworth
Baldock
Buntingford
Hitchin
Luton
Stevenage
Puckeridge
Whipsnade
Knebworth
Ware
Harpenden
Welwyn Garden City
Hertford
Hemel Hempstead
St Albans
Hatfield
Hodd
Wal Abb

HERTFORDSHIRE

Luton

| 0 | 10 kilometres |
| 0 | 5 miles |

© Global Mapping / XYZ Maps

The Birthplace of John Bunyan, it is little wonder the county of Bedfordshire inspired the author of Pilgrim's Progress.

Dear Visitor, we are delighted to welcome you to the National Garden Scheme in Bedfordshire. Your visits make a huge difference, and thanks to your generosity and that of our garden owners and volunteers, we raised nearly 40K in 2021 for our nursing and health, and gardening charities.

We begin the open garden season in February with snowdrops followed by spring bulbs in March and April. You can enjoy beautiful plantings and inspirational designs at numerous gardens throughout the summer, some of which have been featured in national magazines and on television. There are also themed gardens such as the alpine garden, the serene Japanese garden and the meandering Texan dry riverbed garden, as well as several walled gardens. A trio of 18th century gardens designed by Capability Brown – Southill Park, Luton Hoo, and The Walled Garden at Luton Hoo– are also open for the National Garden Scheme. We will conclude the year with an enchanting celebration of Diwali themed evening of lights.

Thank you for your support to the National Garden Scheme, and we look forward to welcoming you to our gardens in Bedfordshire in 2022.

Volunteers

County Organiser
Indi Jackson
01525 713798
indi.jackson@ngs.org.uk

County Treasurer
Colin Davies
01525 712721
colin.davies@ngs.org.uk

Press Officer
Lucy Debenham
lucy.debenham@ngs.org.uk

Facebook & Twitter
Lucy Debenham
(as above)

Booklet Co-ordinators
Indi Jackson
(as above)

Alex Ballance
alexballance@yahoo.co.uk

Photography
Venetia Barrington
venetiajanesgarden@gmail.com

Talks Co-ordinator
Indi Jackson
(as above)

Assistant County Organisers
Geoff & Davina Barrett
geoffanddean@gmail.com

Alex Ballance
(as above)

Julie Neilson
julieneilson@outlook.com

f @bedfordshire.ngs

@NGSBeds

@ngsbedfordshire

Left: Old Church House

OPENING DATES

All entries subject to change. For latest information check www.ngs.org.uk Map locator numbers are shown to the right of each garden name.

February

Snowdrop Festival

Thursday 24th
The Swiss Garden 37

Sunday 27th
◆ King's Arms Garden 18

March

Sunday 27th
NEW Keech Hospice Care 15

April

Saturday 23rd
22 Elmsdale Road 10

Sunday 24th
22 Elmsdale Road 10

May

Sunday 1st
Townsend Farmhouse 38

Monday 2nd
Townsend Farmhouse 38

Sunday 8th
The Old Rectory, Wrestlingworth 28

Saturday 14th
Secret Garden 33

Sunday 15th
◆ The Manor House, Stevington 24

Saturday 21st
Church Farm 8

Sunday 22nd
Church Farm 8

Saturday 28th
Steppingley Village Gardens 35

Sunday 29th
Steppingley Village Gardens 35

June

Saturday 4th
69 Mill Lane 25
70 Mill Lane 26

Sunday 5th
69 Mill Lane 25
70 Mill Lane 26
Southill Park 34

Friday 10th
Ash Trees 1

Saturday 11th
Ash Trees 1
88 Castlehill Road 7

Sunday 12th
Ash Trees 1
192 Kimbolton Road 16
NEW 194a Kimbolton Road 17

Saturday 18th
22 Elmsdale Road 10

Sunday 19th
Barton le Clay Gardens 4
22 Elmsdale Road 10

Saturday 25th
Bedford Heights 5
Hollington Farm 13

Sunday 26th
Hollington Farm 13
NEW Turvey Village Gardens 39

July

Saturday 2nd
Aspley Guise Gardens 2
NEW 1 Linton Close 22

Sunday 3rd
Aspley Guise Gardens 2
NEW 1 Linton Close 22

Saturday 9th
88 Castlehill Road 7
NEW Eversholt Gardens 11
4 St Andrews Road 31

Sunday 10th
NEW Eversholt Gardens 11

Sunday 17th
Lindy Lea 21
Royal Oak Cottage 30

Saturday 23rd
NEW Old Church House 27

Sunday 24th
NEW 26 Bridge End 6
Luton Hoo Hotel Golf & Spa 23
NEW Old Church House 27

Sunday 31st
Lake End House 19

August

Friday 5th
◆ The Walled Garden 40

Wednesday 10th
Flaxbourne Farm 12

Sunday 14th
NEW Rose Cottage 29

Sunday 21st
Lake End House 19

Sunday 28th
NEW 15 Douglas Road 9

September

Sunday 4th
Flaxbourne Farm 12

Sunday 11th
Howbury Hall Garden 14

Saturday 17th
22 Elmsdale Road 10
40 Leighton Street 20

Sunday 18th
22 Elmsdale Road 10
NEW Keech Hospice Care 15

October

Saturday 29th
Townsend Farmhouse 38

Sunday 30th
◆ King's Arms Garden 18

February 2023

Sunday 26th
◆ King's Arms Garden 18

By Arrangement

Arrange a personalised garden visit with your club, or group of friends, on a date to suit you. See individual garden entries for full details.

1c Bakers Lane	3
NEW 26 Bridge End	6
Church Farm	8
22 Elmsdale Road	10
Lake End House	19
NEW 1 Linton Close	22
The Old Rectory, Wrestlingworth	28
1a St Augustine's Road	32
Secret Garden	33

The National Garden Scheme searches the length and breadth of England, Channel Islands, Northern Ireland and Wales for the very best private gardens

THE GARDENS

1 ASH TREES

Green Lane, Aspley Guise, Milton Keynes, MK17 8EN. John & Teresa. *Green Ln is off Wood Ln. Yellow signs indicate where to turn. Some on-road parking in Wood Ln. Disabled or mobility issue parking only at house.* **Fri 10, Sat 11, Sun 12 June (10-4.30). Adm £5, chd free. Home-made teas.**
Medium sized, secluded village garden, walled in with borrowed treescape and hidden in a private lane. Herbaceous borders, shrubs, trees, bulbs, and fruit inc apricot and peach. There is a unique garden arch sculpture created for a Hampton Court show garden. Seats in quiet spots amongst the plants. Children and wheelchairs welcome as are dogs on leads. Garden is flat with reasonable access for wheels and walkers.

& 🐕 ✿ ☕))

GROUP OPENING

2 ASPLEY GUISE GARDENS

Spinney Lane, Aspley Guise, Milton Keynes, MK17 8JT. Alex Ballance. *SE of Milton Keynes. 1½ m from M1 J13. Follow rd to Aspley Guise Sq, turn up Woburn Ln, L into Spinney Ln, R into Village Hall car park. Gardens are signed from there. Blue Badge parking only outside individual gardens.* **Sat 2, Sun 3 July (1-5). Combined adm £7, chd free. Home-made teas at Aspley Guise Village Hall.**

DAWNEDGE LODGE
Phil & Lynne Wallace.

GLADE HOUSE
Alex Ballance.

HOLLYDALE, WOBURN LANE
Gill & Simon Cockle.

Three colourful gardens that are well-stocked with a wide range of different plants, displayed in a variety of planting styles. There are herbaceous borders and shrubs galore, plus vegetable and herb gardens, chickens, a wildlife pond and greenhouses. Home-made teas, plant sale, locally handmade craft stalls, horticultural art and honey. Parking and WC at Village Hall. Partial wheelchair access to parts of

Glade House and Hollydale gardens. Dawnedge Lodge is accessible but with some steps.

& 🐕 ✿ ☕))

3 1C BAKERS LANE

Tempsford, Sandy, SG19 2BJ. Juliet & David Pennington, 01767 640482, juliet.pennington01@gmail.com. *1m N of Sandy on A1 & Station Rd is on the E side. Bakers Ln is 300 yds down Station Rd on L.* **Visits by arrangement for groups of 5 to 20. Adm £6, chd free.**
This is a garden for all seasons with interesting and unusual plants. It comes to life with a winter border planted with colourful cornus and evergreen shrubs underplanted with snowdrops and hellebores with gravel areas carpeted with miniature cyclamen. It develops through the seasons culminating in early autumn with a spectacular show of sun-loving herbaceous plants. Plant sale: exotic and unusual plants. No refreshments but visitors are welcome to bring a picnic to enjoy in the garden. Sorry no dogs.

& ✿

GROUP OPENING

4 BARTON LE CLAY GARDENS

Manor Road, Barton-Le-Clay, Bedford, MK45 4NR. David Pilcher. *Old A6 through Barton-le-Clay Village, Manor Rd is off Bedford Rd. Parking in paddock.* **Sun 19 June (2-5). Combined adm £6, chd free. Home-made teas.**

THE MANOR HOUSE
David Pilcher.

WAYSIDE COTTAGE
Nigel Barrett.

Two gardens in the attractive village of Barton-le-Clay surrounded by beautiful Bedfordshire countryside. The gardens are beautifully landscaped with picturesque stream and bridge over a natural river. At the Manor House, colourful stream side planting inc an abundance of arum lilies and a sunken garden with lily pond. A well-stocked pond with a fountain and waterfalls and a variety of outbuildings nestled within the old walled garden create a tranquil scene at Wayside Cottage. Partial wheelchair access, 2ft wide bridges.

& 🐕 ✿ ☕))

Hollington Farm
VenetiaJane

Church Farm, Pulloxhill

5 BEDFORD HEIGHTS
Brickhill Drive, Bedford, MK41 7PH. Graham A Pavey, www.grahamapavey.co.uk. *Park in main car park & not at Travelodge.* **Sat 25 June (10-2). Adm £5, chd free. Light refreshments.** Originally built by Texas Instruments, a Texan theme runs throughout the building and gardens. The entrance simulates an arroyo or dry riverbed, and is filled with succulents and cacti, plus a mixture of grasses and herbaceous plants, many of which are Texan natives. There are also three courtyard gardens, where less hardy plants thrive in the almost frost-free environment. No wheelchair access to two of the courtyards but can be viewed from a viewing platform.

&. 🚐 ☕))

6 NEW 26 BRIDGE END
Bromham, Bedford, MK43 8LP. Roger & Sue Taylor, 07866 225126, taylorroger73@gmail.com. *The garden is a very short walk from Bromham Mill in the direction of The Swan pub.* **Sun 24 July (12.30-5). Adm £5, chd free. Visits also by arrangement May to Oct for groups of 5 to 15.** Secluded, wildlife friendly garden, gently sloping down to a semi wild area. There is a good selection of trees and shrubs and herbaceous borders planted for colour throughout the summer. Visitors are invited to bring their own picnic. This garden is not suitable for wheelchairs.

7 88 CASTLEHILL ROAD
Totternhoe, Dunstable, LU6 1QG. Chris & Carole Jell. *Middle End. Turn R off B489 Aston Clinton rd. Fronting main rd approx ½ m through village. Garden is in the centre of the village.* **Sat 11 June, Sat 9 July (2-6). Adm £6, chd free. Home-made teas.** Diverse planting managed in a natural and artistic way, creating a feel of peace and beauty and a wildlife haven. Roses, clematis, shrubs, trees and perennials are arranged in glorious disarray with a gentle plea for chaos. Sloping on limestone and clay, created and evolved by the owners over 40 yrs, this garden enjoys its own microclimate. Views of Chiltern Hills from the front garden. This garden is not suitable for wheelchairs.

❀ ☕))

8 CHURCH FARM
Church Road, Pulloxhill, Bedford, MK45 5HD. Keith & Sue Miles, 07941 593152. *Parking by kind permission of The Cross Keys Pub, Pulloxhill High Street, MK45 5HB (approx 500yds from garden). Yellow signs from the Cross Keys to Church Rd, past parish church.* **Sat 21, Sun 22 May (2-5). Adm £6, chd free. Refreshments at The Cross Keys, pre booking advised. Visits also by arrangement Apr to Oct for groups of up to 20. Adm £10, inc refreshments.** Mixed colourful planting to the rear of the house inc a long sunny border of drought tolerant plants and large topiary subjects. Beyond the farmyard

a small kitchen garden and wildflower orchard incorporating a rose walk and views to the wider countryside. Livestock may be present in adjoining fields so sorry, no dogs.

❀ ☕))

9 NEW 15 DOUGLAS ROAD
Bedford, MK41 7YF. Peter & Penny Berrington. *B660 Kimbolton Rd, turn into Avon Drive, R into Tyne Crescent, & Douglas Rd on R.* **Sun 28 Aug (2-5). Adm £5, chd free. Light refreshments.** This medium sized town garden has a series of outdoor rooms, separated by hedges, fences and arches. There is seating for visitors to relax and enjoy the peace and seclusion. A circular cottage garden with a central decorative fire pit, separated by plum and apple trees from vegetables and herbs grown in raised beds. The pond is home to newts, snails and 'Brickhill' frogs. Wheelchair access to most parts of the garden.

&. 🐐 ❀ ☕))

10 22 ELMSDALE ROAD
Wootton, Bedford, MK43 9JN. Roy & Dianne Richards, 07733 222495, roy.richards60@ntlworld.com. *Follow signs to Wootton, turn R at The Cock Pub, follow to Elmsdale Rd.* **Sat 23, Sun 24 Apr, Sat 18, Sun 19 June, Sat 17, Sun 18 Sept (1.30-5). Adm £5, chd free. Home-made teas. Visits also by arrangement Mar to Oct for groups of 10 to 30.** Topiary garden greets visitors before

they enter a genuine Japanese Feng Shui garden inc bonsai. Large collection of Japanese plants, Koi pond, lily pond and a Japanese Tea House. The garden was created from scratch by the owners about 20 yrs ago and has many interesting features inc Japanese lanterns and the Kneeling Archer terracotta soldier from China.

GROUP OPENING

11 NEW EVERSHOLT GARDENS
Eversholt, Milton Keynes, MK17 9DS. Car park in field next to Tyrells End Farm. **Sat 9, Sun 10 July (2-5). Combined adm £6, chd free.**

NEW THE THATCH
Rosemary & Martin Kennedy.

NEW TYRELLS END FARM
Nathalie Muller & Robert Berkeley.

'Eversholt Gardens' contains a lovely circular 1km walk taking in three ends of Eversholt, two country gardens, a beautiful small vegetable plot and atmospheric church yard. Picturesque village green opposite large pond area surrounded by wooded paths, overlooked by the church.

12 FLAXBOURNE FARM
Salford Road, Aspley Guise, MK17 8HZ. Paul Linden, www.flaxbournegardens.com. From village centre take Salford Rd, go over the railway line & 250 yds on L. **Wed 10 Aug, Sun 4 Sept (2-5). Adm £6, chd free. Light refreshments.**
An entertaining and fun garden, lovingly developed with numerous water features, a windmill, romantic bridges, small moated castle, lily pond, herbaceous borders and Greek temple ruin. Children will enjoy exploring the intriguing nooks and crannies, discovering a grotto, crocodiles and a crow's nest. There is also a large Roman arched stone gateway.

13 HOLLINGTON FARM
Flitton Hill, Maulden, Bedford, MK45 2BE. Susan & John Rickatson. Off A507 between Clophill & Ampthill- take Silsoe/ Flitton then bear R & follow yellow signs. **Sat 25, Sun 26 June (12-5.30). Adm £6, chd free. Home-made teas.**
Two acre country garden. Semi formal near house with small parterre, pergola, pond and borders. Planting is massed perennials, shrubs and roses. Outer areas are wilder with mature trees. There is an option to walk through a wildflower farm meadow with views over Mid Beds. A good variety of plants for sale. Wheelchair access, some steps and slopes.

14 HOWBURY HALL GARDEN
Howbury Hall Estate, Renhold, Bedford, MK41 0JB. Julian Polhill & Lucy Copeman, www.howburyfarmflowers.co.uk. Leave A421 at A428/Gt Barford exit towards Bedford. Entrance to house & gardens ½m on R. Parking in field. **Sun 11 Sept (2-5). Adm £6, chd free. Home-made teas.**
A late Victorian garden designed with mature trees, sweeping lawns and herbaceous borders. The large walled garden is a working garden, where one half is dedicated to growing a large variety of vegetables whilst the other is run as a cut flower business. In the woodland area, walking towards the large pond, the outside of a disused ice house can be seen. Gravel paths and lawns may be difficult for smaller wheels.

15 NEW KEECH HOSPICE CARE
Great Bramingham Lane, Luton, LU3 3NT. Nikki Samsa, www.keech.org.uk. Approx 4m N of Luton town centre on A6. From Luton head towards Bedford on A6. At r'about for Bramingham, go straight over, stay on A6. Immed after the r'about take L turn to the hospice. **Sun 27 Mar, Sun 18 Sept (2-5). Adm £5, chd free. Cream teas.**
Keech Hospice Care has a wildlife garden behind the hospice buildings, with areas designed by Alan Titchmarsh for the benefit of patients, families, visitors and staff. The garden inc a pond, mature trees, hedgerows and wildlife habitats alongside more traditional areas. A memorial pathway winds through the area, passing a children's play area. Our wildlife

garden consists of a large pond, bug hotels and bee accommodation. Our courtyard garden is a colourful and peaceful design. Both gardens offer the perfect place for patients, families and staff to enjoy being outside and contribute towards their wellbeing.

16 192 KIMBOLTON ROAD
Bedford, MK41 8DP. Tricia Atkinson. On B660 between Brickhill Drive & Avon Drive nr pedestrian crossing. **Sun 12 June (2-5). Combined adm with 194a Kimbolton Road £5, chd free. Home-made teas at 194a Kimbolton Road.**
⅓ acre cottage garden specialising in many varieties of roses. There are also vegetable and soft fruit patches and an orchard. The garden inc over 90 roses. Wheelchair access with care. Some gravel.

17 NEW 194A KIMBOLTON ROAD
Bedford, MK41 8DP. Fern Mirto. On B660 between Brickhill Drive & Avon Drive nr pedestrian crossing (next door to 192). **Sun 12 June (2-5). Combined adm with 192 Kimbolton Road £5, chd free. Home-made teas.**
Cottage style planting, mature shrubs and perennials and pond. A town garden with a relaxed ambience incorporating innovative upcycled planting ideas.

18 ◆ KING'S ARMS GARDEN
Brinsmade Road, Ampthill, Bedford, MK45 2PP. Ampthill Town Council. Free parking in town centre. Entrance opp Old Market Place, down King's Arms Yard. **For NGS: Sun 27 Feb, Sun 30 Oct (2-4). Adm £4, chd free. Light refreshments. 2023: Sun 26 Feb.**
Small woodland garden of about 1½ acres created by plantsman, the late William Nourish. Trees, shrubs, bulbs and many interesting collections throughout the year. Since 1987, the garden has been maintained by 'The Friends of the Garden' on behalf of Ampthill Town Council. Charming woodland garden with mass plantings of snowdrops and early spring bulbs. Beautiful autumn colours in October. Halloween themed opening.

19 LAKE END HOUSE

Mill Lane, Woburn Sands, Milton Keynes, MK17 8SP. Mr & Mrs G Barrett, 07831 110959, Geoffanddean@gmail.com. *From A5130, turn into Weathercock Ln, to Burrows Close & to Mill Ln.* Sun 31 July, Sun 21 Aug (2-5). Adm £6, chd free. Light refreshments. Visits also by arrangement for groups of 10 to 40.

A large 3 acre lake created on a brown field site, provides a wonderful watery centrepiece for this extensive modern garden. The modern house (not open) overlooks the lake, while on the other side, a Japanese themed garden with a tea house, red wooden bridge, small pond and cloud-pruned trees. The planting is naturalistic around the lake with willows, alders, cornuses providing sanctuary for waterfowl.

20 40 LEIGHTON STREET

Woburn, MK17 9PH. Ron & Rita Chidley. *500yds from centre of village L side of rd. Very limited on rd parking outside house.* Sat 17 Sept (2-5). Adm £5, chd free. Home-made teas.

Large cottage style garden in three parts. There are several 'rooms' with interesting features to explore and many quiet seating areas. There are perennials, climbers, vegetables, shrubs, trees and two ponds with fish. In late summer and autumn there is an abundance of colour from dahlias, fuchsias and grasses and late flowering roses. Many pots of unusual and tender plants.

21 LINDY LEA

Ampthill Road, Steppingley, Bedford, MK45 1AB. Roy & Linda Collins. *Next to Steppingley Hospital. Park in hospital car park.* Sun 17 July (2-5). Adm £5, chd free. Home-made teas.

Set within an acre, this garden is a haven for wildlife with two water features, cottage garden style perennial plantings, variety of shrubs and mature trees. There is also a vegetable garden and a sunny terrace furnished with pots and climbers. Wheelchair access to some paths may be difficult to negotiate.

22 NEW 1 LINTON CLOSE

Heelands, Milton Keynes, MK13 7NR. Pat & John Partridge, 01908 220571, pip1941@icloud.com. *From H4 Dansteed Way, take Stainton Drive, Linton Close is 3rd R.* Sat 2, Sun 3 July (12-5). Adm £4, chd free. Visits also by arrangement May to Sept for groups of up to 6.

Town garden developed over 30 years from heavy clay and builder's rubble. Gravel garden with sedum and dwarf conifer collection at the front. The back garden is planted with hardy evergreen shrubs for structure and seasonal plantings of bulbs, geraniums, lavender, clematis, roses, herbs and pots, provide year-round interest and colour.

23 LUTON HOO HOTEL GOLF & SPA

The Mansion House, Luton Hoo, Luton, LU1 3TQ. Luton Hoo Hotel Golf & Spa, www.lutonhoo.co.uk. *Approx 1m from J10 M1, take London Rd A1081 signed Harpenden for approx 1/2 m - entrance on L for Luton Hoo Hotel Golf & Spa.* Sun 24 July (11-3). Adm £6, chd free. Light refreshments. Pre-booking essential, please visit www.ngs. org.uk for information & booking. Visitors wishing to have lunch/ formal afternoon tea at the hotel must book in advance directly with the hotel.

The gardens and parkland designed by Capability Brown are of national historic significance and lie in a conservation area. Main features - lakes, woodland and pleasure grounds, Victorian grass tennis court and late C19 sunken rockery. Italianate garden with herbaceous borders and topiary garden. Wheelchair access gravel and grass paths.

24 ♦ THE MANOR HOUSE, STEVINGTON

Church Road, Stevington, Bedford, MK43 7QB. Kathy Brown, www.kathybrownsgarden.com. *Off A428 through Bromham. If using SatNav please enter entire address, not just postcode.* For NGS: Sun 15 May (11-4). Adm £8, chd free. Pre-booking essential, please visit www.ngs.org.uk for information & booking. Home-made teas. For other opening times and information, please visit garden website.

The Manor House Garden has many different rooms, inc six art inspired gardens. Early roses and wisteria along with several different Clematis montana festoons the walls and pergolas; foxgloves, poppies and peonies providing colour down below. Elsewhere avenues of white stemmed birches, gingko, eucalyptus, and metasequoia leads the eye to further parts of the garden. 85% wheelchair access. Disabled WC.

25 69 MILL LANE

Greenfield, Bedford, MK45 5DG. Pat Rishton. *On R of Mill In near the end.* Sat 4, Sun 5 June (1-5). Combined adm with 70 Mill Lane £5, chd free. Light refreshments.

Deceptively long back garden, recently re-loved from neglect with most of the planting less than 3 yrs old. Old English Rose border with perennials, a white border in shade and a hot border in full sun. The waterlily pond leads to the fruit area then onto an arch with Rambling Rector screening a woodland area. All planting has to survive deer, badger, rabbits and two granddaughters.

26 70 MILL LANE

Greenfield, Bedford, MK45 5DF. Lesley Arthur. *At the end of Mill Ln, on the L* Sat 4, Sun 5 June (1-5). Combined adm with 69 Mill Lane £5, chd free.

This is a split level garden, near to where the old Greenfield mill was situated. The planting is cottage style, with a small pond. The banks of the River Flit, which flows through the garden, are left to allow nettles and comfrey to grow for the benefit of wildlife. There are two fruit trees, a small vegetable plot and a second pond on the other side of the river.

National Garden Scheme gardens are identified by their yellow road signs and posters. You can expect a garden of quality, character and interest, a warm welcome and plenty of home-made cakes!

22 Elmsdale Road

26 Bridge End

27 NEW OLD CHURCH HOUSE

Grove, Leighton Buzzard, LU7 0QU. **Rob King.** *Off the B488 S of Leighton Buzzard. Take the turning signed for Grove Church. Garden at end of a narrow single track lane, caution as tight blind bend half way down.* **Sat 23, Sun 24 July (1-5). Adm £5, chd free. Home-made teas.**
This varied and colourful, sunny garden surrounds a pretty converted C13 church. There is a small wildflower meadow and many generously sized herbaceous borders and island beds, filled with a wide variety of cottage garden plants. Beautiful views across open pasture. Plenty of places to sit and relax with home-made refreshments, then enjoy walk on the adjacent canal footpath. Garden accessed via gravel driveway

28 THE OLD RECTORY, WRESTLINGWORTH

Church Lane, Wrestlingworth, Sandy, SG19 2EU. **Josephine Hoy,** 01767 631204, hoyjosephine@hotmail.co.uk. *The Old Rectory is at the top of Church Ln, which is well signed, behind the church.* **Sun 8 May (12-5). Adm £7, chd free. Visits also by arrangement Apr to June for groups of up to 20.**
4 acre garden full of colour and interest. The owner has a free style of gardening sensitive to wildlife. Beds overflowing with tulips, alliums, bearded iris, peonies, poppies, geraniums and much more. Beautiful mature trees and many more planted in the last 30 yrs inc a large selection of betulas. Gravel gardens, box hedging and clipped balls, woodland garden and wildflower meadows. Wheelchair access may be restricted to grass paths.

29 NEW ROSE COTTAGE

South End, Milton Bryan, Milton Keynes, MK17 9HS. **Pete & Veronica Langford.** *Pond Lane is opposite the Red Lion pub. Walk down pond lane for 100 yds, look L over the pond & Rose cottage is the white house.* **Sun 14 Aug (2-5). Adm £5, chd free.**
This garden is situated in the pretty village of Milton Bryan, opposite a romantic village pond. Colourful flower borders wrap around the house with a summerhouse in the garden. Through the bottom gate is another garden with raised beds, roses, wild flower strip of about 50 metres, two plum trees, two pear trees and two apple trees.

30 ROYAL OAK COTTAGE

46 Wood End Road, Kempston Rural, Bedford, MK43 9BB. Teresa & Mike Clarke. *From Wood End Lane turn L at the Cross Keys, no 46 is on the L after 400yds.* Sun 17 July (11.30-5.30). Adm £5, chd free. Home-made teas.
³/₄ acre garden created on the land of an old beer house, with wildlife in mind. Shallow wildlife ponds support amphibians.The wildflower meadows are Austrian scythed in August. Herbaceous beds, a small oriental garden, cornfield borders to the vegetable plot, blue and white borders around a very old renovated piggery. Agapanthus and blue hydrangeas are a patio speciality in July. The grass paths through the meadows are mostly even and flat and a solid path runs the length of the garden. Also access to motorised scooters.

& ✿ ➎ ⋅))

31 4 ST ANDREWS ROAD

Bedford, MK40 2LJ. Amanda Dimmock. *Bedford. Off Park Avenue.* Sat 9 July (10-4). Adm £3.50, chd free. Light refreshments.
An elegant, multi-functional urban garden set within a semi-formal layout featuring clipped beech hedges softened by colourful shrubs and perennials and a rose pergola. Focal points have been created to be enjoyed from both within the garden as well from the house.

 ➎ ⋅))

32 1A ST AUGUSTINE'S ROAD

Bedford, MK40 2NB.
Chris Bamforth Damp, 01234 353730/01234 353465, chrisdamp@mac.com. *St Augustine's Rd is on L off Kimbolton Rd as you leave the centre of Bedford.* Visits by arrangement for groups of up to 30. Adm £5, chd free. Home-made teas.
A colourful town garden with herbaceous borders, climbers, a greenhouse and pond. Planted in cottage garden style with traditional flowers, the borders overflow with late summer annuals and perennials inc salvias and rudbeckia. The pretty terrace next to the house is lined with ferns and hostas. The owners also make home-made chutneys and preserves which can be purchased on the day. The garden is wheelchair accessible.

& ✿ ➎ ⋅))

33 SECRET GARDEN

4 George Street, Clapham, Bedford, MK41 6AZ. Graham Bolton, 07746 864247, bolton_graham@hotmail.com. *Clapham Village High St. R into Mount Pleasant Rd then L into George St. 1st white Bungalow on R.* Sat 14 May (2-5.30). Adm £3.50, chd free. Light refreshments. Visits also by arrangement Apr & May for groups of 6 to 15.
Profiled in the RHS The Garden, alpine lovers can see a wide collection of alpines in two small scree gardens, front and back of bungalow plus pans. Planting also inc dwarf salix, rhododendrons, daphnes, acers, conifers, pines, hellebores and epimediums. Two small borders of herbaceous salvias, lavenders and potentillas. Alpine greenhouse with rare varieties and cold frames with plants for sale.

✿ ➎ ⋅))

34 SOUTHILL PARK

Southill, nr Biggleswade, SG18 9LL. Mr & Mrs Charles Whitbread. *In the village of Southill, 5m from the A1.* Sun 5 June (2-5). Adm £6, chd free. Home-made teas.
Southill Park first opened its gates to NGS visitors in 1927. A large garden with mature trees and flowering shrubs, herbaceous borders, a formal rose garden, sunken garden, ponds and kitchen garden. It is on the south side of the 1795 Palladian house. The parkland was designed by Lancelot 'Capability' Brown. A large conservatory houses the tropical collection.

& ✿ ✿ ➎ ⋅))

Top Barn, Steppingley Village Gardens

GROUP OPENING

35 STEPPINGLEY VILLAGE GARDENS

Steppingley, Bedford, MK45 5AT. *Follow signs to Steppingley, pick up yellow signs from village centre.* **Sat 28, Sun 29 May (2-5). Combined adm £7, chd free. Home-made teas. Classic Car show on Sunday 29th.**

NEW THE HAVEN
Rachel & Jim Farnsworth.

MIDDLE BARN
John & Sally Eilbeck.

37 RECTORY ROAD
Bill & Julie Neilson.

TOP BARN
Tim & Nicky Kemp.

TOWNSEND FARMHOUSE
Hugh & Indi Jackson.
(See separate entry)

Steppingley is a picturesque Bedfordshire village on the Greensand Ridge, close to Ampthill, Flitwick and Woburn. Although a few older buildings survive, most of Steppingley was built by the 7th Duke of Bedford between 1840 and 1872. Five gardens in the village offer an interesting mix of planting styles and design to include pretty courtyards, cottage garden style perennial borders, ponds, a Victorian well, glasshouses, an orchard, vegetable gardens, a herb garden, wildlife havens and country views. Livestock inc chickens, ducks and fish.

You can make a difference! Join our Great British Garden Party fundraising campaign and raise money for some of the best-loved nursing and health charities. Visit ngs.org.uk/gardenparty to find out how you can get involved

37 THE SWISS GARDEN

Old Warden Aerodrome, Old Warden, Biggleswade, SG18 9ER. The Shuttleworth Trust, www.shuttleworth.org/explore/swiss-garden/. *2m W of Biggleswade.* Signed from A1 & A600. **Thur 24 Feb (10-5). Adm £15, chd free. Light refreshments at the Runway Cafe.** This enchanting garden was created in the 'Swiss Picturesque' style for the 3rd Lord Ongley in the early C19 and reopened in July 2014 after a major HLF-funded restoration. Serpentine paths lead to cleverly contrived vistas, many of which focus on the thatched Swiss Cottage. Beautiful wrought-iron bridges, ponds, sweeping lawns and the magnificent Pulhamite-lined Grotto Fernery have all been given a new lease of life by this landmark restoration. The pathways in the Swiss Garden are firm and even, with minimal gradients, and most are suitable for access by wheelchair users.

38 TOWNSEND FARMHOUSE

Rectory Road, Steppingley, Bedford, MK45 5AT. Hugh & Indi Jackson. *Follow directions to Steppingley village and pick up yellow signs from village centre.* **Sun 1, Mon 2 May (2-5). Adm £6, chd free. Home-made teas. Evening opening Sat 29 Oct (5.30-8.30). Adm £10, chd £2. Entry inc light refreshment. Pre-booking essential, please visit www.ngs.org.uk for information & booking. Opening with Steppingley Village Gardens on Sat 28, Sun 29 May.** Country garden with tree lined driveway and many perennial borders. Pretty cobbled courtyard with a glasshouse and a Victorian well 30 metres deep, viewed through a glass top. Colourful display of tulips and spring bulbs in early May and a spectacular evening of lanterns, diya lamps and flower rangoli in late October.

GROUP OPENING

39 NEW TURVEY VILLAGE GARDENS

High Street, Turvey, Bedford, MK43 8EP. *Follow arrow signs from village centre. Parking in field behind Chantry House.* **Sun 26 June (2-5). Combined adm £7, chd free. Cream teas in medieval church of All Saints.**

NEW CHANTRY HOUSE
Sheila & Anthony Ormerod.

NEW 7 THE GREEN
Paul & Rosemary Gentry.

NEW HOLMWOOD HOUSE
Richard & Judith Bray.

The historic village of Turvey lies beside the River Ouse and is recorded in Domesday Book of 1086 as a parish in the Hundred of Willey. Three gardens in the village offer a varied mix of design and interest. Chantry House is a 1½ acre garden, approached by a drive bounded by mature yew and box cloud hedges where the medieval church of All Saints overlooks the garden at this point. A south facing lawn is flanked by high rose covered walls and interspersed by herbaceous beds. A courtyard leads to the white garden and north lawn. Holmwood is a historic mid Victorian house (not open) set in gardens of approx 1 acre. The garden at the rear includes a long red border, a cottage border and lawn with two ancient fruit trees. 7 The Green is an informal village garden. A wide terrace with comfortable seating and a myriad (100 plus) of planted pots overlooks a central lawn and flowerbeds which slope down to flowering cherries and a view of pasture and mature trees. Wheelchair access via gravel paths and few shallow distanced steps. 500 metres walk from car park to Holmwood House.

40 ♦ THE WALLED GARDEN

Luton, LU1 4LF. Luton Hoo Estate, www.lutonhooestate.co.uk. *From A1081 turn at West Hyde Road After 100 metres turn L through black gates, follow signs to Walled Garden.* **For NGS: Fri 5 Aug (11-3). Adm £6, chd free. Light refreshments at Woodyard Coffee Shop. Visit lutonhooestate.co.uk to book your tickets. For other opening times and information, please visit garden website.** The 5 acre Luton Hoo Estate Walled Garden was designed by Capability Brown and established by noted botanist and former Prime Minister, Lord Bute in the late 1760s. The Walled Garden is now the focus of an incredible volunteer project and continues to be researched, restored, repaired and re-imagined for the enjoyment of all. Unique service buildings inc a vinery, fernery and propagation houses. Exhibition of Victorian tools. Uneven surfaces reflecting the age and history of the site.

Chantry House, Turvey Village Gardens

BERKSHIRE

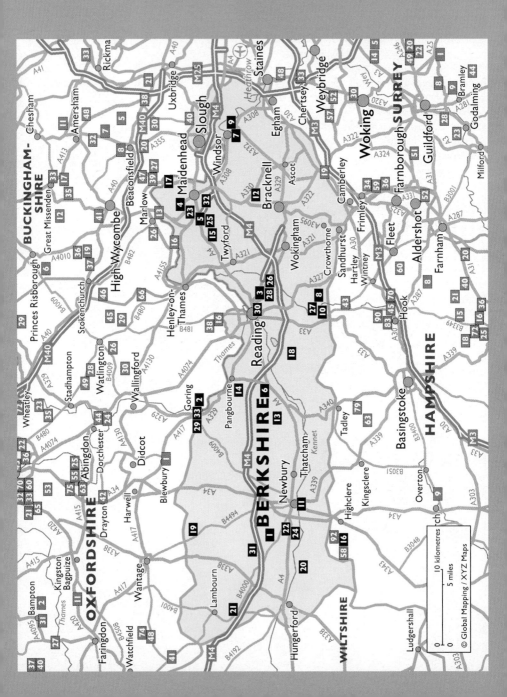

The Royal County of Berkshire offers a wonderful mix of natural beauty and historic landmarks that are reflected in the portfolio of gardens opening for the National Garden Scheme.

Our gardens come in all shapes, sizes and styles, from urban oases and community plots, to village gems and country house landscapes. We are delighted to welcome seven gardens opening for the first time this year. They include private gardens at Brookside Cottage in Swallowfield Village, Chaddleworth in Streatley, 68 Church Road and 61 Sutcliffe Avenue in Earley, The Old Rectory Burghfield and Wembury in Maidenhead, along with the community garden at Watlington House in Reading.

In addition to our open days, thirteen gardens offer opportunities for private visits 'By Arrangement' and you can contact the garden openers directly to organise them. Also, if you are involved in a club or society and would like to know more about the talks we offer (in person or on-line), please contact Angela at angela.oconnell@icloud.com.

So while some gardens may capture your interest due to their designers or their historic setting, most have evolved thanks to the efforts of their enthusiastic owners. None more so than Sarah and Sal Pajwani at St Timothee in Pinkneys Green, whose lovely garden was voted 'The Nation's Favourite Garden' in 2021 by readers of 'The English Garden' - many congratulations to them. We hope that all NGS gardens offer moments of inspiration and pleasure, and look forward to welcoming you soon.

Volunteers

County Organiser
Heather Skinner
01189 737197
heather.skinner@ngs.org.uk

County Treasurer
Hugh Priestley
01189 744349 Fri – Mon
hughpriestley@aol.com

Booklet Co-ordinator
Heather Skinner
(as above)

Talks & Group Visits
Angela O'Connell
01252 668645
angela.oconnell@icloud.com

Assistant County Organisers
Claire Fletcher
claire.fletcher@ngs.org.uk

Carolyn Foster
01628 624635
candrfoster@btinternet.com

Angela O'Connell
(as above)

Graham O'Connell
01252 668645
graham.oconnell22@gmail.com

Rebecca Thomas
01491 628302
rebecca.thomas@ngs.org.uk

Bob Weston,
01635 550240
bob.weston@ngs.org.uk

f @BerksNationalGardenScheme
𝕏 @BerksNGS

Left: Wembury

OPENING DATES

All entries subject to change. For latest information check www.ngs.org.uk

Map locator numbers are shown to the right of each garden name.

Extended openings are shown at the beginning of the month.

February

Snowdrop Festival

Wednesday 9th
◆ Welford Park   31

March

Saturday 12th
Stubbings House   25

Sunday 13th
Stubbings House   25

April

Sunday 10th
Rookwood Farm
House   22

Sunday 24th
Odney Club   17
The Old Rectory,
Farnborough   19

Wednesday 27th
NEW The Old Rectory,
Burghfield   18
Rooksnest   21

May

**Every day from
Tuesday 10th to
Saturday 14th**
NEW 61 Sutcliffe
Avenue   26

Wednesday 4th
Malverleys   16

Saturday 7th
Stubbings House   25

Sunday 8th
Stubbings House   25

Saturday 14th
Thurle Grange   29
Wynders   33

Sunday 15th
Thurle Grange   29
Wynders   33

Sunday 22nd
The Old Rectory,
Farnborough   19
Rookwood Farm
House   22

Wednesday 25th
7 The Knapp   28

68 Church Road

June

**Every Tuesday and
Thursday from
Tuesday 7th**
NEW 68 Church Road   3

**Every day from
Tuesday 7th to
Saturday 11th**
NEW 61 Sutcliffe
Avenue   26

Every Wednesday
7 The Knapp   28

Wednesday 1st
Eton College Gardens   7

Sunday 5th
Stockcross House   24

Saturday 11th
7 The Knapp   28

Sunday 19th
NEW Chaddleworth   2
St Timothee   23

Wednesday 22nd
Rooksnest   21

Tuesday 28th
NEW Wembury   32

Wednesday 29th
Malverleys   16
The Old Rectory,
Farnborough   19

July

**Every Tuesday
and Thursday**
NEW 68 Church Road   3

Friday 1st
NEW Wembury   32

Sunday 3rd
Island Cottage   11
Swallowfield Village
Gardens   27
NEW Watlington House,
Geoff Hill Memorial
Garden   30

Wednesday 6th
Malverleys   16

Thursday 7th
Lower Lovetts Farm   15
St Timothee   23

Saturday 16th
Jealott's Hill Community
Landshare   12

Sunday 17th
Deepwood Stud Farm   5

August

**Every Tuesday
and Thursday to
Tuesday 16th**
NEW 68 Church Road   3

**Every day from
Tuesday 23rd to
Saturday 27th**
NEW 61 Sutcliffe
Avenue   26

Tuesday 2nd
NEW Wembury   32

Thursday 4th
St Timothee   23

Sunday 7th
King's Copse House   13

Wednesday 10th
The Old Rectory,
Farnborough   19

Wednesday 17th
NEW The Old Rectory,
Burghfield   18

Sunday 28th
Stockcross House   24

September

Tuesday 6th
NEW Wembury   32

Sunday 11th
Rookwood Farm
House   22

By Arrangement

Arrange a personalised garden visit on a date to suit you. See individual garden entries for full details.

Boxford House   1
NEW 68 Church Road   3
Compton Elms   4
Deepwood Stud Farm   5
Farley Hill Place
Gardens   8
Handpost   10
Island Cottage   11
Lower Bowden Manor   14
The Old Rectory
Inkpen   20
Rooksnest   21
St Timothee   23
Stockcross House   24
7 The Knapp   28

THE GARDENS

1 BOXFORD HOUSE
Boxford, Newbury, RG20 8DP.
Tammy Darvell, Head
Gardener, 07802 883084,
tammydarvell@hotmail.com. *4m
NW of Newbury. Directions will be
provided on booking.* **Visits by
arrangement May to Aug for
groups of 10 to 30. Adm £10.
Guided tour & refreshments inc.**
Beautiful large family garden
extensively developed over the past
10 yrs. Emphasis on roses and
scent throughout the 5 acre main
garden. Old and new orchards,
laburnum tunnel, formal and colourful
herbaceous borders. Handsome
formal terraces, pond, water features
and garden woodland areas. Inviting
cottage garden and productive
vegetable gardens.

2 NEW CHADDLEWORTH
Streatley, Reading, RG8 9PR.
Susan & Simon Carter,
07711 420586, www.
chaddleworthbedandbreakfast.
com. *Just off A329 leaving Streatley
towards Wallingford. From T-lights
in Streatley take A329 towards
Wallingford. Pass L turn for A417.
Take next R signed Cleeve Court,
then Chaddleworth is 1st on R along
lane.* **Sun 19 June (10-5). Adm
£4.50, chd free. Home-made teas.**
Chaddleworth's gardens surround
the house on all four sides with a
variety of garden styles. Several
lawned areas with different borders,
small herbaceous, ornamental
grasses, wildflower area, wild orchids,
vegetable garden, rose path, small
cutting garden. Mostly wheelchair
accessible with some gravel.

3 NEW 68 CHURCH ROAD
Earley, Reading, RG6 1HU.
Pat Burton, 07809 613850,
patsi777@virginmedia.com. *E
of Reading. Off A4 at Shepherd's
House Hill, turn into Pitts Ln, into
Church Rd, across r'about, 4th
property on L.* **Every Tue and
Thur 7 June to 16 Aug (2-5).
Adm £5, chd free. Pre-booking
essential, please visit www.ngs.
org.uk for information & booking.
Home-made teas. Visits also
by arrangement June to Aug for**
groups of 5 to 20.
A fascinating urban garden with
changing elements throughout the
seasons. Different areas showcase
a variety of interesting plants,
pergola, outdoor dining room and
small summerhouse. The working
greenhouse is home to alpines grown
year-round and seen as specimen
plants in the garden. A living roof
covers the pergola. Tiered areas of
hostas and an abundance of summer
bedding.

4 COMPTON ELMS
Marlow Road, Pinkneys Green,
Maidenhead, SL6 6NR. Alison
Kellett, kellettaj@gmail.com.
*Situated at end of gravel road
located opp & in between The
Arbour & The Golden Ball Pub &
Kitchen on the A308.* **Visits by
arrangement Mar & Apr for
groups of 15 to 40. Adm £10, chd
free. Light refreshments inc.**
A delightful spring garden set
in a sunken woodland, lovingly
recovered from clay pit workings.
The atmospheric garden is filled with
snowdrops, primroses, hellebores and
fritillaria, interspersed with anemone
and narcissi under a canopy of ash
and beech.

5 DEEPWOOD STUD FARM
Henley Road, Stubbings, nr
Maidenhead, SL6 6QW. Mr &
Mrs E Goodwin, 01628 822684,
ed.goodwin@deepwood.co. *2m W
of Maidenhead. M4 J8/9 take A404M
N. 2nd exit for A4 to Maidenhead.
L at 1st r'about on A4130 Henley,
approx 1m on R.* **Sun 17 July (2-5).
Adm £5, chd free. Home-made
teas. Visits also by arrangement
Mar to Oct for groups of 10+.**
4 acres of formal and informal
gardens within a stud farm, so
great roses! Small lake with Monet
style bridge and three further water
features. Several neo-classical follies
and statues. Walled garden with
windows cut in to admire the views
and horses. Woodland walk and
enough hanging baskets to decorate
a pub! Partial wheelchair access.

6 ◆ ENGLEFIELD HOUSE GARDEN
Englefield, Theale, Reading,
RG7 5EN. Lord & Lady
Benyon, 01189 302504,
peter.carson@englefield.co.uk,
www.englefieldestate.co.uk. *6m
W of Reading. M4 J12. Take A4
towards Theale. 2nd r'about take
A340 to Pangbourne. After ⅙ m
entrance on the L.* **For opening
times and information, please
phone, email or visit garden
website.**
The 12 acre garden descends
dramatically from the hill above the
historic house through woodland
where mature native trees mix with
rhododendrons and camellias. Drifts
of spring and summer planting are
followed by striking autumn colour.
Stone balustrades enclose the lower
terrace with lawns, roses and mixed
borders. A stream meanders through
the woodland. Open every Monday
from Apr-Sept (10am-6pm) and
Oct-Mar (10am-4pm). Please check
the Englefield Estate website for any
changes before travelling. Wheelchair
access to some parts of the garden.

7 ETON COLLEGE GARDENS
Eton, nr Windsor, SL4 6DB. Eton
College. *½ m N of Windsor. Parking
signed off B3022, Slough Rd. Walk
from car park across playing fields
to entry. Follow signs for tickets &
maps which are sold at gazebo nr
entrance.* **Wed 1 June (12-4.30).
Adm £6, chd free. Home-made
teas in the Fellows Garden.**
A rare chance to visit a group of
central College gardens surrounded
by historic school buildings, inc
Luxmoore's garden on a small island
in the Thames reached across two
attractive bridges. Also an opportunity
to explore the fascinating Eton
College Natural History Museum,
the Museum of Eton Life and a small
group of other private gardens.

*During 2020 – 2021
National Garden Scheme
funding supported over
1,400 Queen's Nurses
to deliver virtual and
hands-on, community
care across England, Wales
and Northern Ireland*

8 FARLEY HILL PLACE GARDENS

Church Road, Farley Hill, Reading, RG7 1TZ. Tony & Margaret Finch, 01189 762544, tony.finch7@btinternet.com. *From M4 J11, take A33 S to Basingstoke. At T-lights turn L for Spencers Wood, B3349. Continue 2m, turn L through Swallowfield towards Farley Hill. Garden ½m on R.* **Visits by arrangement May to Sept for groups of 15+. Adm £6. Teas & light refreshments.**
A 4 acre, C18 cottage garden. 1½ acre walled garden with year-round interest and colour. Well-stocked herbaceous borders, large productive vegetable areas with herb garden, dahlia and cutting flower beds. Enjoy wandering around the garden. Victorian glasshouse recently renovated and small nursery. Plants, lovely cut flowers and produce for sale. Partial wheelchair access, no steps. Disabled WC.

SPECIAL EVENT

9 ◆ FROGMORE HOUSE & GARDEN

Windsor, SL4 1LU. Her Majesty The Queen. *1m SE of Windsor. Entrance via Park Street gate into Long Walk.* **A late summer opening date to be confirmed, please visit www.ngs.org.uk for information.**
A late summer opening date to be confirmed, please visit www.ngs.org.uk in 2022 for information. The private royal garden at Frogmore House on the Crown Estate at Windsor. This landscaped garden, in 30 acres with notable trees, lawns, flowering shrubs and C18 lake, is rich in history. Largely the creation of Queen Charlotte in the 1790s, it has over 4,000 trees and shrubs. The historic plantings inc tulip trees and redwoods, along with Queen Victoria's Tea House, remain key features today. The Royal Mausoleum is closed due to long term restoration. Please note Windsor traffic may be halted around 11am for Guard change.

10 HANDPOST

Basingstoke Road, Swallowfield, Reading, RG7 1PU. Faith Ramsay, 07801 239937, faith@mycountrygarden.co.uk, www.mycountrygarden.co.uk.

From M4 J11, take A33 S. At 1st T-lights turn L on B3349 Basingstoke Rd. Follow road for 2¾m, garden on L, opp Barge Ln. Parking for 10 cars max. **Visits by arrangement Apr to Sept for groups of 15 to 30. Adm £6.50, chd free. Home-made teas on request.** Donation to Thrive.
4 acre designer's garden with many areas of interest. Features inc two lovely long herbaceous borders attractively and densely planted in six colour sections, a formal rose garden, an old orchard with a grass meadow, pretty pond and peaceful wooded area. Large variety of plants, trees and a productive fruit and vegetable patch.

11 ISLAND COTTAGE

West Mills, Newbury, RG14 5HT. Karen Swaffield, karen@lockisland.com. *7m from M4 J13. Park in town centre car parks. Walk past St Nicholas Church or between Côte Restaurant & Holland & Barrett to canal. 200yds to Swing Bridge & follow signs. Limited side road parking.* **Sun 3 July (2-5). Adm £4, chd free. Home-made teas. Visits also by arrangement May to Sept for small groups.**
A pretty, small waterside garden set between the River Kennet and the Kennet and Avon Canal. Interesting combinations of colour and texture to look at rather than walk through, although visitors are welcome to do that too! A deck overlooks a sluiceway towards a lawn and border. Started from scratch in 2005 and mostly again after the floods of 2014. Being simplified for 2022 for manageability!

12 JEALOTT'S HILL COMMUNITY LANDSHARE

Wellers Lane, at junction of Penfurzen Lane, Warfield, Bracknell, RG42 6BQ. Jealott's Hill Community Landshare, www.jealottshilllandshare.org.uk. *Enter Wellers Ln off the A330, 1st gateway on R at junction with Penfurzen Ln.* **Sat 16 July (1-4). Adm £4.50, chd free. Home-made teas.**
Jealott's Hill Community Landshare is an inspirational 6 acre multi-purpose community garden, tended by the local community. The site offers various horticultural activities as well as creating a haven for wildlife, amongst a developed sensory garden, vineyard, a 450 tree orchard,

wildlife pond and crop areas. Plant sales, site tours and refreshments. Wheelchair access to most of the site from level car park, please phone 07867 695931 with any queries. Disabled WC.

13 KING'S COPSE HOUSE

Bradfield Gate, Nr Reading, RG7 6JR. Mr & Mrs J Wyatt. *11 W of Reading. M4 J12, A4 to Theale. At 2nd r'about take 3rd exit A340 towards Pangbourne, then soon 1st L. After 1¼m turn L to Bradfield Southend. In village turn R on Hungerford Ln, after ½m L on Cock Ln.* **Sun 7 Aug (2-5). Adm £5, chd free. Home-made teas.**
A beautiful, formal landscaped garden set in 4 acres, recently renovated to a high standard to incorporate some original and rare specimens together with new plantings. Orchard, large fish pond, secret rose garden, herbaceous borders and lovely views over the Pang Valley. Walks through 40 acre SSSI ancient woodland. WWII Air Raid Shelter.

14 LOWER BOWDEN MANOR

Bowden Green, Pangbourne, RG8 8JL. Juliette & Robert Cox-Nicol, 07552 217872, robert.cox-nicol@orange.fr. *1½m W of Pangbourne. Directions provided on booking.* **Visits by arrangement Apr to Oct for groups of up to 50. Adm £6, chd free. Home-made teas by prior request.**
A 3 acre designer's garden with stunning views and where structure predominates. Specimen trees show contrasting bark and foliage. A marble 'Pan' plays to a pond with boulders and boulder-shaped evergreens. Versailles planters with standard topiaries line a rill. A stumpery leads to the orchard's carpet of daffodils and later a wave of white hydrangeas. Some gravel, but most areas accessible. Dogs welcome on leads.

15 LOWER LOVETTS FARM

Knowl Hill Common, Knowl Hill, RG10 9YE. Richard Sandford. *5m W of Maidenhead. Turn S off A4 at Knowl Hill Church into Knowl Hill Common. Past pub & across common to T-junction. Turn L down dead end lane.* **Thur 7 July (10.30-4). Adm £15, chd free. Pre-**

Stockcross House

booking essential, please visit www.ngs.org.uk for information & booking. Two hour timed slots start promptly with talk at 10.30am or 2pm.

Enjoy a Talk & Walk in this fascinating large modern organic kitchen garden (60 x 30 metres) with a wildflower meadow and herbaceous border. Wide variety of vegetables and fruit grown for year-round home consumption and nutritional value. Flowers grown for eating or herbal teas. Lots of interesting growing techniques and tips. The visit inc an outdoor talk by Richard Sandford who shares fascinating information about this amazing garden and how his plant-based diet influences his growing methods. You are then welcome to walk around. Sorry, no teas or WC. Visitors welcome to bring refreshments.

SPECIAL EVENT

16 MALVERLEYS

Fullers Lane, East End, Newbury, RG20 0AA. *A34 S of Newbury, exit signed for Highclere. Directions provided on booking.* **Wed 4 May, Wed 29 June, Wed 6 July (10.30-5). Adm £17.50, chd free. Pre-booking essential, please visit www.ngs.org.uk for information & booking. Two hour timed slots start promptly at 10.30am, 1pm or 3pm with guided tour by Head Gardener. Tea or coffee inc.**

10 acres of dynamic gardens which have been developed over the last 10 yrs to inc magnificent mixed borders and a series of contrasting yew hedged rooms, hosting flame borders, a cool garden, a pond garden and new stumpery. A vegetable garden with striking fruit cages sit within a walled garden, also encompassing a white garden. Meadows open out to views over the parkland.

17 ODNEY CLUB

Odney Lane, Cookham, SL6 9SR. John Lewis Partnership. *3m N of Maidenhead. Off A4094 S of Cookham Bridge. Signs to car park in grounds.* **Sun 24 Apr (1-5). Adm £5, chd free. Light refreshments.**

This 120 acre site is beside the Thames with lovely riverside walks. A favourite with Stanley Spencer who featured our magnolia in his work. Lovely wisteria, specimen trees, side gardens, spring bedding and ornamental lake. The John Lewis Partnership Heritage Centre will be open, showcasing the textile archive and items illustrating the history of John Lewis and Waitrose. Light refreshments from 1-5pm (Guide Dogs only indoors). Dogs on leads. Wheelchair access with some gravel paths.

& 🐕 ☕ 🎪 »)

18 NEW THE OLD RECTORY, BURGHFIELD

The Hatch, Burghfield, Reading, RG30 3TH. www.theoldrectory.com. *5m SW of Reading. Turn S off A4 to Burghfield village, R after Hatch Gate Inn. Street parking in The Hatch. Entrance on R.* **Wed 27 Apr, Wed 17 Aug (10.30-4). Adm £5, chd free. Pre-booking essential, please visit www.ngs. org.uk for information & booking. Home-made teas. Two hour timed slots at 10.30am or 2pm.**
A 4 acre garden set around an attractive Georgian house (not open). Colourful double herbaceous borders recently replanted to reflect the seasons, featuring tulips in April and dahlias in late summer. A pretty pool garden, woodland area and terraced lawns with mature trees inc a stunning cedar of Lebanon. Mostly accessible with some uneven ground and gravel paths.

19 THE OLD RECTORY, FARNBOROUGH

nr Wantage, OX12 8NX. Mr & Mrs Michael Todhunter. *4m SE of Wantage. Take B4494 Wantage-Newbury road, after 4m turn E at sign for Farnborough. Approx 1m to village, Old Rectory on L.* **Sun 24 Apr, Sun 22 May (2-5); Wed 29 June, Wed 10 Aug (11-4.30). Adm £5, chd free. Home-made teas. Donation to Farnborough PCC.**
In a series of immaculately tended garden rooms, inc herbaceous borders, arboretum, secret garden, roses, vegetables and bog garden, there is an explosion of rare and interesting plants, beautifully combined for colour and texture. With stunning views across the countryside, it is the perfect setting for the 1749 rectory (not open), once home of John Betjeman, in memory of whom John Piper created a window in the local church.

20 THE OLD RECTORY INKPEN

Lower Green, Inkpen, RG17 9DS. Mrs C McKeon, 01488 668793, claremckeon@gmail.com. *4m SE of Hungerford. From centre of Kintbury at the Xrds, take Inkpen Rd. After ½m turn R, then go approx 3m (passing Crown & Garter Pub, then Inkpen Village Hall on L). Next to St Michaels Church.* **Visits by arrangement May to Sept for groups of 10 to 20. Adm £10, chd free. Light refreshments inc.**
On a gentle hillside with lovely countryside views, the Old Rectory offers a peaceful setting for this pretty 2 acre garden. Enjoy strolling through the formal and walled gardens, herbaceous borders, pleached lime walk and wildflower meadow (some slopes).

Odney Club

21 ROOKSNEST

Ermin Street, Lambourn
Woodlands, RG17 7SB.
Rooksnest Estate, 07787 085565,
gardens@rooksnest.net. *2m S
of Lambourn on B4000. From
M4 J14, take A338 Wantage Rd,
turn 1st L onto B4000 (Ermin St).
Rooksnest signed after 3m.* **Wed
27 Apr, Wed 22 June** (11-4). **Adm
£5, chd free. Light refreshments.
Last entry 3.30pm. Visits also
by arrangement Apr to June for
groups of 20+.**
Approx 10 acre, exceptionally fine
traditional English garden. Rose
garden, herbaceous garden, pond
garden, herb garden, fruit, vegetable
and cutting garden and glasshouses.
Many specimen trees and fine shrubs,
orchard and terraces. Garden mostly
designed by Arabella Lennox-Boyd.
Most areas have step-free wheelchair
access, although surface consists of
gravel and mowed grass.

22 ROOKWOOD FARM HOUSE

Stockcross, Newbury,
RG20 8JX. The Hon Rupert &
Charlotte Digby, 01488 608676,
charlotte@rookwoodhouse.co.uk,
www.rookwoodhouse.co.uk. *3m W
of Newbury. M4 J13, A34(S). After
3m exit for A4(W) to Hungerford. At
2nd r'about take B4000 towards
Stockcross, after approx ³/₄ m turn R
into Rookwood.* **Sun 10 Apr, Sun 22
May, Sun 11 Sept** (11-5). **Adm £5,
chd free. Home-made teas & light
refreshments.**
This exciting valley garden, a work
in progress, has elements all visitors
can enjoy. A rose covered pergola,
fabulous tulips, giant alliums, and
a recently developed jungle garden
with cannas, bananas and echiums.
A kitchen garden features a parterre
of raised beds, which along with
a bog garden and colour themed
herbaceous planting, all make
Rookwood well worth a visit. WC
available.

23 ST TIMOTHEE

Darlings Lane, Pinkneys Green,
Maidenhead, SL6 6PA. Sarah
& Sal Pajwani, 07976 892667,
pajwanisarah@gmail.com. *1m N of
Maidenhead. M4 J8/9 to A404M. 3rd
exit onto A4 to Maidenhead. L at 1st
r'about to A4130 Henley Rd. After
½ m turn R onto Pinkneys Drive. At
Pinkneys Arms Pub, turn L into Lee
Ln, follow NGS signs.* **Sun 19 June**
(11-4). **Adm £6, chd free. Talk
& Walk events on Thur 7 July,
Thur 4 Aug** (2-4). **Adm £15. Pre-
booking essential, please visit
www.ngs.org.uk for information &
booking. Home-made teas. Visits
also by arrangement May to Aug
for groups of 10 to 50. Talks about
the garden also offered.**
A 2 acre country garden planted for
year-round interest with a variety
of different colour themed borders
each featuring a wide range of hardy
perennials, shrubs and ornamental
grasses. Also inc a box parterre,
wildlife pond and rose terrace
together with areas of long grass
and beautiful mature trees, all set
against the backdrop of a 1930s
house. Talk & Walk events inc tea
and cake. 7th July - Key ideas used
to create a beautiful and easy garden
that's teeming with wildlife, 4th
Aug - Key plants and easy ways to
keep the garden colourful and full of
interest from spring right through to
autumn. Overall and regional winner,
The English Garden's The Nation's
Favourite Gardens 2021.

24 STOCKCROSS HOUSE

Church Road, Stockcross,
Newbury, RG20 8LP.
Susan & Edward Vandyk,
07836 727212, Info@
stockcrosshousegarden.co.uk,
www.stockcrosshousegarden.
co.uk. *3m W of Newbury. M4 J13,
A34(S). After 3m exit A4(W) to
Hungerford. At 2nd r'about take
B4000, 1m to Stockcross, 2nd L
into Church Rd.* **Sun 5 June, Sun
28 Aug** (12-5). **Adm £5, chd free.
Home-made teas. Visits also
by arrangement Apr to Sept for
groups of 10 to 20.**
Romantic 2 acre garden set around a
former rectory (not open). Deep mixed
borders with emphasis on strong,
complementary colour combinations.
Large orangery, wisteria and clematis
clad pergola, folly with pond reflecting
the church tower. Croquet lawn and
pavilion. Naturalistic planting and
pond on lower level. Small stumpery.
Kitchen garden. Plants from garden
for sale. Partial wheelchair access
with some gravelled areas.

25 STUBBINGS HOUSE

Stubbings Lane, Henley
Road, Maidenhead,
SL6 6QL. Mr & Mrs D Good,
www.stubbingsnursery.co.uk.
*From A404(M) W of Maidenhead,
exit at A4 r'about & follow signs to
Maidenhead. At the small r'about
turn L towards Stubbings. Take the
next L onto Stubbings Ln.* **Sat 12,
Sun 13 Mar, Sat 7, Sun 8 May** (10-
4). **Adm £4, chd free.**
Parkland garden accessed via
adjacent retail nursery. Set around
C18 Grade II listed house (not
open), home to Queen Wilhelmina
of Netherlands in WW2. Large lawn
with ha-ha and woodland walks.
Notable trees inc historic cedars
and araucaria. March brings an
abundance of daffodils and in May a
60 metre wall of wisteria. Attractions
inc a C18 icehouse and access to
adjacent NT woodland. Wheelchair
access to a level site with firm gravel
paths.

26 NEW 61 SUTCLIFFE AVENUE

Earley, Reading, RG6 7JN. Sue &
Dave Wilder. *3m SE of Reading. On
Wokingham Rd (A329), from E, pass
Showcase Cinema, then L at Co-op
(Meadow Rd), then R into Sutcliffe
Ave. If coming from W, turn R at
Co-op.* **Daily Tue 10 May to Sat 14
May, Tue 7 June to Sat 11 June,
Tue 23 Aug to Sat 27 Aug** (10-4).
**Adm £3.50, chd free. Pre-booking
essential, please visit www.ngs.
org.uk for information & booking.
Home-made teas. Two hour
timed slots at 10am or 2pm.**
A characterful urban wildlife friendly
garden, offering the relaxing sense
of a walk in the countryside. An
inviting path winds past wildflower
islands, through a rose covered arch,
to a cutting garden and small pond.
Features inc tree trunks creatively
recycled and a chicken run. Partial
wheelchair access.

'In 2021 the National Garden
Scheme donated & £500,000
to Marie Curie enabling us to
continue providing our vital
services and be there, caring
for people on the frontline of
the Coronavirus pandemic'
Marie Curie

GROUP OPENING

27 SWALLOWFIELD VILLAGE GARDENS

The Street, Swallowfield, RG7 1QY. *5m S of Reading. From M4 J11 take A33 S. At 1st T-lights turn L on B3349 signed Swallowfield. In the village follow signs for parking. Buy tickets & map in Swallowfield Medical Practice car park, opp Crown Pub.* Sun 3 July (2-5.30). Combined adm £8, chd free. Home-made teas at Brambles.

5 BEEHIVE COTTAGE
Ray Tormey.

BRAMBLES
Sarah & Martyn Dadds.

NEW BROOKSIDE COTTAGE
Jackie & Graham King.

5 CURLYS WAY
Carolyn & Gary Clark.

THE FIRS
Harmi Kandohla & Mark Binns.

LAMBS FARMHOUSE
Eva Koskuba.

NORKETT COTTAGE
Jenny Spencer.

PRIMROSE COTTAGE
Hilda Phillips.

RUSSETTS
Roberta Stewart.

WESSEX HOUSE
Val Payne.

This year Swallowfield is offering at least 10 gardens to visit. A number are in the village itself or just outside, so there is a mix of walking to some, with those in different directions needing a car or bicycle to reach them comfortably. Whilst each provides its own character and interest, they all nestle in countryside by the Blackwater and Loddon rivers with an abundance of wildlife and lovely views. The garden owners, many of whom are members of the local Horticultural Society, are always happy to chat and share their enthusiasm and experience. Plants for sale. Wheelchair access to many gardens, however some have gravel drives, slopes and uneven ground.

 ♿ ✳ 🍵 ›))

28 7 THE KNAPP

Earley, Reading, RG6 7DD. Mrs Ann McKie, 07881 451708, annmckie@hotmail.co.uk. *A329 from Wokingham to Reading. Turn L into Aldbourne Ave just before junction with B3350 & 1st L into The Knapp.* Every Wed 25 May to 29 June (10.30-3.30). Sat 11 June (10.30-3.30). Adm £4, chd free. Pre-booking essential, please visit www.ngs.org.uk for information & booking. Home-made teas. Two hour timed slots at 10.30am or 1.30pm. Visits also by arrangement May & June for groups of 5 to 20.
A mature suburban garden, surrounded by trees and divided into rooms with lawns, island beds, mixed borders, gravel area, pond and an area with natural planting and beehives. The garden provides interest most of the yr, but the highlights are the rhododendrons and roses, particularly rambling roses over gazebos and arches.

🍵

29 THURLE GRANGE

Rectory Road, Streatley, Reading, RG8 9QH. David Juster. *From Streatley, N on A329 Wallingford Rd. Fork L onto A417 Wantage Rd, then fork L again along Rectory Rd. Past golf course, downhill & after stables, Thurle Grange is on R. Parking will be signed.* Sat 14, Sun 15 May (10-4). Combined adm with Wynders £6, chd free. Home-made teas at Wynders.
Recently developed 1 acre garden set around attractive country house (c1900, not open) with lovely views across peaceful valley. Centred upon a splendid catalpa tree with a mix of formal and informal successional planting for year-round interest. Features inc rose filled parterre, wildflower area, yew avenue and richly planted herbaceous borders. Wheelchair access over gravel.

♿ 🍵

30 NEW WATLINGTON HOUSE, GEOFF HILL MEMORIAL GARDEN

44 Watlington Street, Reading, RG1 4RJ. Watlington House Trust, www.watlingtonhouse.org.uk. *Reading town centre. Limited car parking on site via South St. Public car parks at Oracle & Queen's Rd, approx 10 min walk.* Sun 3 July (10.30-5). Adm £4, chd free. Light refreshments.

King's Copse House

An attractive walled garden at Watlington House, a Grade II* property, recreated since 2012 using archival research on site of previous car park. Clipped panel-pleached hornbeam, box hedging and pruned fruit trees give formal structure within a quadrangle design. Featuring a shade walk, knot garden and colourful herbaceous planting, it is a calm oasis in a bustling town. Wheelchair access via gravel topped paths, but no access to buildings and WC.

 ♿ ❀ ☕ »))

31 ◆ WELFORD PARK

Welford, Newbury, RG20 8HU. **Mrs J H Puxley, 01488 608691, snowdrops@welfordpark.co.uk, www.welfordpark.co.uk.** *6m NW of Newbury. M4 J13, A34(S). After 3m exit for A4(W) to Hungerford. At 2nd r'about take B4000, after 4m turn R signed Welford. Entrance on Newbury-Lambourn road.* **For NGS: Wed 9 Feb (11-4). Adm £8, chd £4. Light refreshments. For other opening times and information, please phone, email or visit garden website.**
One of the finest natural snowdrop woodlands in the country, approx 4 acres, along with a wonderful display of hellebores throughout the garden and winter flowering shrubs. This is an NGS 1927 pioneer garden on the River Lambourn set around Queen Anne House (not open). Also the stunning setting for Great British Bake Off 2014 - 2019. Dogs welcome on leads. Coach parties please book in advance.

♿ 🐕 🚌 ☕

32 NEW WEMBURY

Altwood Close, Maidenhead, SL6 4PP. Carolyn Foster. *W side of Maidenhead, S of A4. M4 J8/9, then A404M J9B, 3rd exit to A4 to Maidenhead, R at 1st r'about, 2nd L onto Altwood Rd, then 5th R, follow NGS signs.* **Tue 28 June, Fri 1 July, Tue 2 Aug, Tue 6 Sept (10.30-4). Adm £4, chd free. Pre-booking essential, please visit www.ngs. org.uk for information & booking. Home-made teas. Two hour timed slots at 10.30am or 2pm.**
A wildlife friendly, plant lover's cottage garden with borders generously planted with bulbs, perennials, grasses and shrubs for successional interest for every season. Productive vegetable garden and greenhouses. Many pots and baskets with seasonal annuals and tender perennials especially salvias.

❀ ☕

33 WYNDERS

Rectory Road, Streatley, Reading, RG8 9QA. Marcus & Emma Francis. *From Streatley, N on A329 Wallingford Rd. Fork L onto A417 Wantage Rd, then fork L again along Rectory Rd. After golf course, down hill & parking will be signed. Wynders is on L after stables.* **Sat 14, Sun 15 May (10-4). Combined adm with Thurle Grange £6, chd free. Home-made teas.**
Magnificent views combined with generous and varied planting across ¾ acre surrounded by open countryside. Grass borders, formal garden, orchard, wildflower meadow, roses, shrub borders, ferns and vegetable plots. Classic cars on display for non-gardeners. Something for everyone. Partial wheelchair access over gravel drive, please call 07920 712571 in advance for reserved parking.

♿ 🐕 ❀ ☕ »))

Our 2021 donations mean that 1,200 inpatients were supported by the Y Bwthyn NGS Macmillan Specialist Palliative Care unit in Wales since opening

Chaddleworth

BUCKINGHAMSHIRE

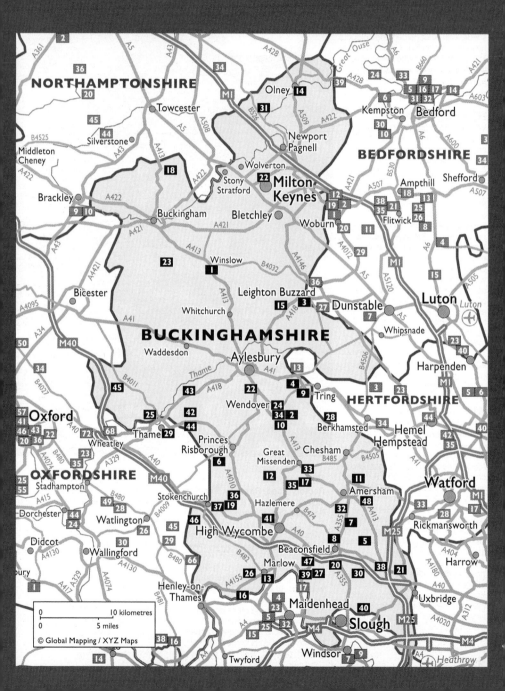

Buckinghamshire has a beautiful and varied landscape; edged by the River Thames to the south, crossed by the Chiltern Hills, and with the Vale of Aylesbury stretching to the north.

This year Buckinghamshire will hold four group openings, many of which can be found in villages of thatched or brick and flint cottages.

Many Buckinghamshire gardens have been used as locations for films and television, with the Pinewood Studios nearby and excellent proximity to London.

We also boast historical gardens including Ascott, Cowper and Newton Museum Gardens, Hall Barn, and Stoke Poges Memorial Gardens (Grade I listed).

Most of our gardens offer homemade tea and cakes to round off a lovely afternoon, visitors can leave knowing they have enjoyed a wonderful visit and helped raise money for nursing and health charities at the same time.

Volunteers

County Organiser
Maggie Bateson
01494 866265
maggiebateson@gmail.com

County Treasurer
Tim Hart
01494 837328
timgc.hart@btinternet.com

Publicity
Sandra Wetherall
01494 862264
sandracwetherall@gmail.com

Social Media
Stella Vaines
07711 420621
stella@bakersclose.com

Talks
Janice Cross
01494 728291
janice.cross@ngs.org.uk

Booklet Co-ordinator
Maggie Bateson
(as above)

Assistant County Organisers
Janice Cross
(as above)

Judy Hart
01494 837328
judy.elgood@gmail.com

Mhairi Sharpley
01494 782870
mhairisharpley@btinternet.com

Stella Vaines
(as above)

🔲 @BucksNGS
🔲 @BucksNGS
🔲 @national_garden_scheme_bucks

Left: 20 Whitepit Lane

OPENING DATES

All entries subject to change. For latest information check www.ngs.org.uk

Extended openings are shown at the beginning of the month.

Map locator numbers are shown to the right of each garden name.

March

Sunday 20th
Higher Denham
 Gardens   21

Wednesday 23rd
Montana   28

April

Sunday 10th
Long Crendon
 Gardens   25

Sunday 17th
Overstroud Cottage   33

Monday 18th
Aston Clinton Gardens   4

Wednesday 20th
Montana   28

Saturday 23rd
Orchard House   32

Sunday 24th
Abbots House   1

May

Monday 2nd
◆ Ascott   3
Turn End   42

Tuesday 10th
Red Kites   36

Saturday 14th
Horatio's Garden   22

Sunday 15th
Overstroud Cottage   33

Wednesday 18th
Montana   28

Sunday 22nd
Higher Denham
 Gardens   21
Lindengate   24

Sunday 29th
Tyringham Hall   43

Monday 30th
Glebe Farm   18

June

**Every Sunday from
Sunday 12th**
11 The Paddocks   34

Sunday 5th
Abbots House   1
Aston Clinton Gardens   4
Canal Cottage   9

Thursday 9th
Bowers Farm   7

Saturday 11th
Acer Corner   2
◆ Cowper & Newton
 Museum Gardens   14

Sunday 12th
Acer Corner   2
Bledlow Manor   6
◆ Cowper & Newton
 Museum Gardens   14
Cublington Gardens   15
Long Crendon
 Gardens   25
Overstroud Cottage   33

Thursday 16th
Lords Wood   26

Saturday 18th
St Michaels Convent   38
Woodside   48

Sunday 19th
18 Brownswood Road   8
Woodside   48

Wednesday 22nd
Montana   28

Saturday 25th
Old Park Barn   31

Sunday 26th
Old Park Barn   31
◆ Stoke Poges
 Memorial Gardens   40
Tythrop Park   44

Wednesday 29th
The Walled Garden,
 Wormsley   46

July

Sunday 3rd
Fressingwood   17
Overstroud Cottage   33
11 The Paddocks   34

Tuesday 12th
Red Kites   36

Saturday 16th
8 Claremont Road   13

Sunday 17th
Chiltern Forage Farm   12
8 Claremont Road   13

Wednesday 20th
Montana   28

Saturday 23rd
8 Claremont Road   13

Sunday 24th
8 Claremont Road   13
NEW Wadzana   45

August

Wednesday 3rd
Danesfield House   16

Sunday 28th
◆ Nether Winchendon
 House   29

Monday 29th
◆ Ascott   3

September

Sunday 11th
Lindengate   24
NEW Old Keepers   30

October

Saturday 15th
Acer Corner   2

Sunday 16th
Acer Corner   2

By Arrangement

Arrange a personalised garden visit on a date to suit you. See individual garden entries for full details.

Abbots House   1
Acer Corner   2
Beech House   5
18 Brownswood Road   8
Cedar House   10
Chesham Bois House   11
Danesfield House   16
Glebe Farm   18
11a Green Lane   19
Hall Barn   20
Kingsbridge Farm   23
Magnolia House   27
Montana   28
Old Park Barn   31
Orchard House   32
11 The Paddocks   34
Peterley Corner
 Cottage   35
Red Kites   36
Robin Hill   37
The Shades   39
1 Talbot Avenue   41
Tyringham Hall   43
20 Whitepit Lane   47
Wind in the Willows,
 Higher Denham
 Gardens   21
Woodside   48

'The National Garden Scheme donated £500,000 to Hospice UK in 2021, enabling us to continue supporting over 200 hospices in the UK who have been at the forefront of the battle against COVID-19.' *Hospice UK*

THE GARDENS

1 ABBOTS HOUSE

10 Church Street, Winslow, MK18 3AN. Mrs Jane Rennie, 01296 712326, jane@renniemail.com. *9m N of Aylesbury. A413 into Winslow. From town centre take Horn St & R into Church St, L fork at top. Entrance through door in wall, Church Walk. Parking in town centre & adjacent streets.* Sun 24 Apr, Sun 5 June (12.30-5.30). Adm £4.50, chd free. Home-made teas. Visits also by arrangement Apr to July for groups of up to 20.
Behind red brick walls a ¾ acre garden on four different levels, each with unique planting and atmosphere. Lower lawn with white wisteria arbour and pond, upper lawn with rose pergola and woodland, pool area with grasses, Victorian kitchen garden and wild meadow. Spring bulbs in wild areas and woodland is a major feature in April, remaining areas peak in June/July. Water feature, sculpture and many pots. Rennie's Winslow Cider and Cider Lush available. Partial wheelchair access due to steps to garden levels. Guide dogs and medical-aid dogs only.
&. ✿ ☕ ☕

2 ACER CORNER

10 Manor Road, Wendover, HP22 6HQ. Jo Naiman, 07958 319234, jo@acercorner.com, www.acercorner.com. *3m S of Aylesbury. Follow A413 into Wendover. L at clock tower r'about into Aylesbury Rd. R at next r'about into Wharf Rd, continue past schools on L, garden on R.* Sat 11, Sun 12 June, Sat 15, Sun 16 Oct (2-5). Adm £4, chd free. Home-made teas. Visits also by arrangement May to Oct for groups of up to 20.
Garden designer's garden with Japanese influence and large collection of Japanese maples. The enclosed front garden is Japanese in style. Back garden is divided into three areas; patio area recently redesigned in the Japanese style, densely planted area with many acers and roses, also a corner which inc a productive greenhouse and interesting planting.
🐴 ✿ ☕ ☕

3 ✦ ASCOTT

Ascott, Wing, Leighton Buzzard, LU7 0PP. The National Trust, info@ascottestate.co.uk, www.ascottestate.co.uk. *2m SW of Leighton Buzzard, 8m NE of Aylesbury. Via A418. Buses: 150 Aylesbury - Milton Keynes, 250 Aylesbury & Milton Keynes. Access is via the visitors entrance.* For NGS: Mon 2 May, Mon 29 Aug (1-5). Adm £7, chd £3. Light refreshments. (NT members are required to pay to enter the gardens on NGS days). For other opening times and information, please email or visit garden website.
Combining Victorian formality with early C20 natural style and recent plantings to lead it into the C21. A completed garden designed by Jacques and Peter Wirtz and also a Richard Long sculpture. Terraced lawns with specimen and ornamental trees, panoramic views to the Chilterns. Naturalised bulbs, mirror image herbaceous borders and impressive topiary inc box and yew sundial. Ascott House is closed on NGS Days. Tickets are available via the website ngs.org.uk or can be purchased on entry. Please contact the Estate Office to reserve a wheelchair.
&. ✿ ☕ 🚃 ⦿)

GROUP OPENING

4 ASTON CLINTON GARDENS

Green End Street, Aston Clinton, Aylesbury, HP22 5JE. *3m E of Aylesbury. From Aylesbury take A41 E. At large r'about, continue straight (signed Aston Clinton). Continue onto London Rd. L at The Bell Pub, parking on Green End St & side roads.* Mon 18 Apr, Sun 5 June (2-5). Combined adm £4, chd free. Home-made teas at The Lantern Cottage. Open nearby Canal Cottage on 5 June.

101 GREEN END STREET
Sue Lipscomb.

THE LANTERN COTTAGE
Jacki Connell.

These two lovely cottage gardens, one well established and the other having recently undergone a radical redesign by its new owner, share a basis of seasonal interest underpinned by evergreens and perennial planting. At The Lantern Cottage, spring hellebores and an abundance of tulips give way to an early summer display of roses, peonies, bearded iris, alliums and climbers inc various clematis, wisteria and akebia. A wide selection of salvias and herbaceous perennials, mostly raised from seed and cuttings. Pelargoniums provide year-round colour in the conservatory and the greenhouse is always full! At No.101, the new owner took up residence in autumn 2015, quickly establishing raised beds for vegetable production, a number of fruit trees and a variety of soft fruits. There is also a wildlife pond, an arbour overlooking the Victorian greenhouse, plus herbaceous borders, ornamental grasses surrounding a red kite sculpture and varied container planting. Wildlife is encouraged to visit.
✿ ☕

5 BEECH HOUSE

Long Wood Drive, Jordans, Beaconsfield, HP9 2SS. Sue & Ray Edwards, 01494 875580, raychessmad@hotmail.com. *From A40, L to Seer Green & Jordans for approx 1m, turn into Jordans Way on R, Long Wood Dr 1st L. From A413, turn into Chalfont St Giles, straight ahead until L signed Jordans, 1st L Jordans Way.* Visits by arrangement Apr to Sept. Adm £4, chd free.
2 acre plantsman's garden built up over the last 34 yrs with a wide range of flowering and foliage plants in a variety of habitats to provide a show and enjoyment all yr. Many bulbs, perennials, shrubs, roses and grasses provide continuous show. Trees planted for their foliage, ornamental bark and autumn display. Two flowering meadows are always a popular feature. Wheelchair access dependent upon weather conditions.
&. 🐴 🚗

Our 2021 donations mean that 12,478 unpaid carers have been supported through funding for Carers Trust

6 BLEDLOW MANOR

Off Perry Lane, Bledlow, nr
Princes Risborough, HP27 9PA.
Lord & Lady Carrington,
www.carington.co.uk/gardens/.
*9m NW of High Wycombe, 3m SW
of Princes Risborough. ½m off
B4009 in middle of Bledlow village.
For SatNav use postcode HP27 9PA.*
**Sun 12 June (2-5). Adm £7, chd
free. Light refreshments.**
8 acres of gardens revitalised during
2020/21. Highlights inc the walled
kitchen garden criss-crossed by
paths with vegetables, fruit, herbs
and flowers. The sculpture garden,
the replanted Granary garden with
fountain and borders, as well as
the individual paved gardens and
parterres divided by yew hedges
and more. The Lyde water garden
formed out of old cress beds fed by
numerous springs. Partial wheelchair
access via steps or sloped grass to
enter gardens.

7 BOWERS FARM

Magpie Lane, Coleshill, HP7 0LU.
John & Linda Daly. *2m S of
Amersham & 3m N of Beaconsfield.
Magpie Ln is off A355, by Harte
& Magpies Pub.* **Thur 9 June
(12.30-5). Adm £5, chd free. Light
refreshments.**
An established 5 acre garden that has
undergone significant renovation over
the past 5-6 yrs with trees, perennials,
annuals and bulbs; creating a variety
of planting spaces inc herbaceous
beds, ponds, kitchen and cutting
garden, new bulb meadow, small
woodland and open parkland areas.

8 18 BROWNSWOOD ROAD

Beaconsfield, HP9 2NU.
John & Bernadette
Thompson, 07879 282191,
tbernadette60@gmail.com. *From
New Town turn R into Ledborough
Ln, L into Sandleswood Rd, 2nd
R into Brownswood Rd.* **Sun 19
June (2-5). Adm £4, chd free.
Visits also by arrangement Mar to
Oct for groups of 10 to 20. Thur
afternoons only.**
A plant filled garden designed
by Barbara Hunt. A harmonious
arrangement of arcs and circles
introduces a rhythm that leads
through the garden. Sweeping box
curves, gravel beds, brick edging
and lush planting. A restrained use
of purples and reds dazzle against a
grey and green background. There

has been considerable replanning and
replanting during the winter.

9 CANAL COTTAGE

11 Wharf Row, Buckland Road,
Buckland, Aylesbury, HP22 5LJ.
Angela Hale. *4m E of Aylesbury.
On the A41 exit at Aston Clinton/
Wendover. Down Lower Icknield
Way onto Buckland Rd. Park along
road & walk over white bridge.
Garden is signed.* **Sun 5 June
(2-6). Adm £3.50, chd free. Light
refreshments. Open nearby Aston
Clinton Gardens.**
A peaceful garden celebrates what
can be achieved in a long narrow
strip behind a cottage (not open).
Recently landscaped to create
rooms and feeding places for wildlife.
Open deep borders of perennials
welcome the visitor. Shaped lawns
lead you through a shady rose arbour
undergrown with a variety of ferns.
Final room is a pond, seating area
with Mediterranean terracing and
many pots.

10 CEDAR HOUSE

Bacombe Lane, Wendover,
HP22 6EQ. Sarah Nicholson,
01296 622131,
sarahhnicholson@btinternet.com.
*5m SE Aylesbury. From Gt
Missenden take A413 into Wendover.
Take 1st L before row of cottages,
house at top of lane. Parking for 10
cars only.* **Visits by arrangement
Feb to Sept for groups of 10 to
30. Adm £5, chd free. Home-
made teas.**
A plantsman's garden in the Chiltern
Hills with a great variety of trees,
shrubs and plants. A sloping lawn
leads to a natural swimming pond
with wild flowers inc native orchids.
A lodge greenhouse and a good
collection of half-hardy plants in
pots. Local artist's sculptures can be
viewed. Picnics welcome on prior
request. Wheelchair access over
gentle sloping lawn.

11 CHESHAM BOIS HOUSE

85 Bois Lane, Chesham Bois,
Amersham, HP6 6DF. Julia
Plaistowe, 01494 726476,
plaistowejulia@gmail.com,
cheshamboishouse.co.uk. *1m N
of Amersham-on-the-Hill. Follow
Sycamore Rd (main shopping centre
road of Amersham), which becomes*

*Bois Ln. Do not use SatNav once in
lane as you will be led astray.* **Visits
by arrangement Mar to Aug for
groups of 6+. Adm £5, chd free.
Home-made teas.**
3 acre beautiful garden with
primroses, daffodils and hellebores
in early spring. Interesting for most of
the yr with lovely herbaceous borders,
rill with small ornamental canal, walled
garden, old orchard with wildlife pond,
and handsome trees some of which
are topiaried. It is a peaceful oasis.
Wheelchair access via gravel at front
of house.

12 CHILTERN FORAGE FARM

Speen, Princes Risborough,
HP27 0SU. Emma Plunket.
Directions provided on booking. **Sun
17 July (2.30-4). Adm £5, chd free.
Pre-booking essential, please
email emma@plunketgardens.
com for information & booking.
Light refreshments.**
Pre-booked tour only at 2.30pm or
4.00pm (limited numbers) of this project
under development in attractive AONB
setting. Pasture being restored to native
hay meadows and planted with fruit
trees and soft fruit. Tips for planting,
creation of wildlife habitats and spotting
butterflies in sunny weather.

13 8 CLAREMONT ROAD

Marlow, SL7 1BW. Andi Gallagher.
*No parking at garden, but short
walk from all town car parks. From
town centre walk S on High St, L on
Institute Rd, L on Beaufort Gardens
& R on Claremont Rd.* **Sat 16, Sun
17, Sat 23, Sun 24 July (2-5). Adm
£4, chd free.**
Paintings, prints and pots to see and
buy in this small town garden owned
by an artist gardener. The unusual
house was built in 2015. Gravel paths
divide the rectangular beds filled with
herbaceous perennials, grasses and
ferns. A cow trough water feature
and owner's ceramics add surprise.
A gate leads to a deliberate wild area
with fruit trees and art studio with
garden related paintings.

14 ♦ COWPER & NEWTON
MUSEUM GARDENS

Orchard Side, Market Place,
Olney, MK46 4AJ. Cowper
and Newton Museum,
01234 711516, house-manager@
cowperandnewtonmuseum.org.uk,

www.cowperandnewtonmuseum. org.uk. *5m N of Newport Pagnell. 12m S of Wellingborough. On A509. Please park in public car park in East St.* **For NGS: Sat 11, Sun 12 June (11-4.30). Adm £3.50, chd free. Home-made teas. For other opening times and information, please phone, email or visit garden website.**
The tranquil Flower Garden of C18 poet William Cowper, who said 'Gardening was of all employments, that in which I succeeded best', has plants introduced prior to his death in 1800, many mentioned in his writings. The Summer House Garden with Cowper's 'verse manufactory', now a Victorian Kitchen Garden, has new and heritage vegetables organically grown, also a herb border and medicinal plant bed. Features inc lacemaking demonstrations and local artists painting live art on both days. Georgian dancers on Sun 12 June. Wheelchair access on mostly hard paths.

43 High Street, Long Crendon Gardens

GROUP OPENING

15 CUBLINGTON GARDENS
Cublington, Leighton Buzzard, LU7 0LF. *5m SE Winslow, 5m NE Aylesbury. From Aylesbury take A413 Buckingham Rd. After 4m at Whitchurch, turn R to Cublington.* **Sun 12 June (2-6). Combined adm £5, chd free. Home-made teas in Biggs Pavilion, Orchard Ground, Stewkley Road.**

CHERRY COTTAGE, 3 THE WALLED GARDEN
Gwyneira Waters.

LARKSPUR HOUSE
Mr & Mrs S Jenkins.

1 STEWKLEY ROAD
Tom & Helen Gadsby,
www.structuredgrowth.co.uk.

A group of diverse gardens in this attractive Buckinghamshire village listed as a conservation area. Larkspur House garden uses a variety of plants and hard landscaping to create distinct areas. Through an Art Nouveau inspired gate there is a large orchard and wildflower meadow. 1 Stewkley Road has a strong focus on homegrown food with an idyllic organic kitchen garden, small orchard and courtyard garden. Cherry Cottage is an enclosed small modern garden

interestingly planted and designed with ease of accessibility in mind. Partial wheelchair access to some gardens.

16 DANESFIELD HOUSE
Henley Road, Marlow, SL7 2EY. Danesfield House Hotel, 01628 891010, amoorin@danesfieldhouse.co.uk, www.danesfieldhouse.co.uk. *3m from Marlow. On the A4155 between Marlow & Henley-on-Thames. Signed on the LH-side Danesfield House Hotel & Spa.* **Wed 3 Aug (10.30-3.30). Adm £5, chd free. Visits also by arrangement in Aug.**
The gardens at Danesfield were completed in 1901 by Robert Hudson, the Sunlight Soap magnate

who built the house. Since the house opened as a hotel in 1991, the gardens have been admired by several thousand guests each yr. However, in 2009 it was discovered that the gardens contained outstanding examples of pulhamite in both the formal gardens and the waterfall areas. The 100 yr old topiary is also outstanding. Part of the grounds inc an Iron Age fort. Tour with Head Garderner, Dan Lawrence at 10.30am or 1.30pm only (max 25 per tour). Tours must be pre-booked and lunch and afternoon tea must be pre-booked by contacting Alex Moorin on amoorin@danesfieldhouse. co.uk or 01628 891010. Wheelchair access on gravel paths through parts of the garden.

17 FRESSINGWOOD
Hare Lane, Little Kingshill, Great
Missenden, HP16 0EF. John
& Maggie Bateson. *1m S of Gt
Missenden, 4m W of Amersham.
From the A413 at Chiltern Hospital,
turn L signed Gt & Lt Kingshill. Take
1st L into Nags Head Ln. Turn R
under railway bridge, then L into New
Rd & continue to Hare Ln.* **Sun 3
July (2-5.30). Adm £4.50, chd free.
Home-made cake & elderflower
cordial.**
Thoughtfully designed and structured
garden with year-round colour
and many interesting features inc
herbaceous borders, a shrubbery with
ferns, hostas, grasses and hellebores.
Small formal garden, pergolas with
roses and clematis. A variety of
topiary and small garden rooms. A
central feature incorporating water
with grasses. Large bonsai collection.

18 GLEBE FARM
Lillingstone Lovell,
Buckingham, MK18 5BB. Mr
David Hilliard, 01280 860384,
thehilliards@talk21.com,
www.glebefarmbarn.co.uk. *Off*

*A413, 5m N of Buckingham &
2m S of Whittlebury. From A5 at
Potterspury, turn off A5 & follow
signs to Lillingstone Lovell.* **Mon 30
May (1.30-5). Adm £4, chd free.
Home-made teas. Visits also by
arrangement in June for groups of
5 to 10. Mons or Fris only.**
A large cottage garden with an
exuberance of colourful planting
and winding gravel paths, amongst
lawns and herbaceous borders on
two levels. Ponds, a wishing well,
vegetable beds, a knot garden, a
small walled garden and an old tractor
feature. Everything combines to make
a beautiful garden full of surprises.

19 11A GREEN LANE
Radnage, High Wycombe,
HP14 4DJ. Ms Jo Dudley,
07710 484434,
jo5456@hotmail.com. *Turn off
A40 Stokenchurch to Radnage &
follow signs to village hall. Park at
village hall (use postcode HP14
4DF). Walk through the gap in the
hedge to 11a Green Ln opp.* **Visits
by arrangement Mar to Oct for
groups of 5 to 30. Adm £4, chd**

free. Home-made teas.
Year-round interest in this ⅔ acre of
relaxed cottage garden planting with
a nod to prairie style, augmented by
local artist sculptures. White border,
hot border, wildflower meadow and
woodland walk. Productive no dig
vegetable garden with greenhouses
and fruit cage. A double pond water
feature with bog garden. Lots of
places to sit and enjoy.

20 HALL BARN
Windsor End, Beaconsfield,
HP9 2SG. Mrs Farncombe,
01494 677788,
garden@thefarncombes.com.
*½ m S of Beaconsfield. Lodge gate
300yds S of St Mary & All Saints'
Church in Old Town centre. Please
do not use SatNav.* **Visits by
arrangement to individual visitors as well as
groups. Adm £5, chd free. Home-
made teas provided for groups
of 10+.**
Historical landscaped garden laid
out between 1680-1730 for the poet
Edmund Waller and his descendants.
Features 300 yr old cloud formation

Robin Hill

yew hedges, formal lake and vistas ending with classical buildings and statues. Wooded walks around the grove offer respite from the heat on sunny days. One of the original NGS garden openings of 1927. Gravel paths, but certain areas can be accessed by car for those with limited mobility.

GROUP OPENING

21 HIGHER DENHAM GARDENS
Higher Denham, UB9 5EA. *6m E of Beaconsfield. Turn off A412, approx ½m N of junction with A40 into Old Rectory Ln. After 1m enter Higher Denham straight ahead. Tickets available for all gardens at community hall, 70yds into the village.* **Sun 20 Mar, Sun 22 May (2-5). Combined adm £6, chd free. Home-made teas in village hall. Donation to Higher Denham Community CIO (Garden Upkeep Fund).**

9 LOWER ROAD
Mrs Patricia Davidson.
Open on Sun 22 May

5 SIDE ROAD
Jane Blyth.
Open on all dates

WIND IN THE WILLOWS
Ron James, 07740 177038,
r.james@company-doc.co.uk.
Open on all dates
Visits also by arrangement Mar to Sept for groups of 10+.

At least three gardens will open in 2022 in the delightful Misbourne chalk stream valley, two will open in March and three in May. Wind in the Willows has over 350 shrubs and trees, informal woodland and wild gardens inc riverside and bog plantings and a collection of 80 hostas and 12 striped roses in 3 acres. A new water lily pond has been created within the river. 'Really different' was a typical visitor comment. The garden at 5 Side Road is medium sized with lawns, borders and shrubs, and many features which children will love. This yr a big conifer has been removed and the area replanted for greater interest. Opening in May, 9 Lower Road is a small garden backing onto the river. Recently professionally designed on concentric circles, it is now maturing and has new shrubs. In May the owner of Wind in the Willows will lead optional guided tours of the

garden starting at 2.30pm and 4pm. Tours generally last approx 1 hour. Partial wheelchair access to each garden.

22 HORATIO'S GARDEN
National Spinal Injuries Centre (NSIC), Stoke Mandeville Hospital, Mandeville Road, Stoke Mandeville, Aylesbury, HP21 8AL. Amy Moffett, www.horatiosgarden.org.uk. *The closest car park to Horatio's Garden at Stoke Mandeville Hospital is Car Park B, opp Asda. Free parking on open day.* **Sat 14 May (2-5). Adm £5, chd free. Home-made teas in the garden room.**
Opened in Sept 2018, Horatio's Garden at the National Spinal Injuries Centre, Stoke Mandeville Hospital is designed by Joe Swift. The fully accessible garden for patients with spinal injuries has been part funded by the NGS. The beautiful space is cleverly designed to bring the sights, sounds and scents of nature into the heart of the NHS. Everything is high quality and carefully designed to bring benefit to patients who often have lengthy stays in hospital. The garden features a contemporary garden room, designed by Andrew Wells as well as a stunning Griffin Glasshouse. We also have a wonderful wildflower meadow. Please come along and meet the Head Gardener and volunteer team and taste our delicious tea and home-made cake! The garden is fully accessible, having been designed specifically for patients in wheelchairs or hospital beds.

23 KINGSBRIDGE FARM
Steeple Claydon, MK18 2EJ. Mr & Mrs Tom Aldous, 01296 730224. *3m S of Buckingham. Halfway between Padbury & Steeple Claydon. Xrds signed to Kingsbridge Only.* **Visits by arrangement Mar to July for groups of 6+. Adm £6, chd free. Home-made teas in our cosy, converted barn.**
Stunning and exceptional 6 acre garden, ever evolving! Main lawn is enclosed by softly curving, colour themed herbaceous borders with gazebo, topiary, clipped yews, pleached hornbeams leading to ha-ha and countryside beyond. A natural stream with bog plants and nesting kingfishers, meanders serenely through shrub and woodland gardens

with many walks. A garden always evolving, to visit again and again.

24 LINDENGATE
The Old Allotment Site, Dobbies Garden Centre, Aylesbury Road, Wendover, HP22 6BD. Lindengate Charity, www.lindengate.org.uk. *4m SE of Aylesbury on A413. Turn into Dobbies Garden Centre, Lindengate on LHS.* **Sun 22 May, Sun 11 Sept (1-5). Adm £5, chd free. Home-made teas.**
Lindengate Mental Health Charity is located at a stunning 5 acre site in Buckinghamshire, where nature breathes new life into anyone who is struggling with their wellbeing. The garden lends itself to supporting people in recovering from a range of common mental health needs. The natural beauty and richness of the site help to restore and heal, whilst specialised gardening, conservation, construction, cooking, and nature based art and crafts activities provide focus and purpose. Add to this the community of volunteers and staff who nurture a supportive, inclusive and safe environment and you have a recipe for success. A selection of homegrown produce and crafts will be available for sale. Wheelchair access throughout the garden.

In 2021 the National Garden Scheme donation helped support Perennial's caseworkers, who helped over 250 people and their families in crisis to receive a wide range of support including emergency food parcels and accommodation, energy payments and expert advice and information

GROUP OPENING

25 LONG CRENDON GARDENS

Long Crendon, HP18 9AN. *2m N of Thame. Park in the village not at individual gardens apart from Lopemead Farm, which is approx 1m S of the village.* Sun 10 Apr, Sun 12 June (2-6). Combined adm £6, chd free. Home-made teas.

BAKER'S CLOSE
Mr & Mrs Peter Vaines.
Open on Sun 10 Apr

BARRY'S CLOSE
Mr & Mrs Richard Salmon.
Open on Sun 10 Apr

NEW **BRINDLES**
Sarah Chapman.
Open on Sun 12 June

COP CLOSE
Sandra & Tony Phipkin.
Open on Sun 12 June

25 ELM TREES
Carol & Mike Price.
Open on Sun 12 June

NEW **43 HIGH STREET**
James & Laura Solyom.
Open on Sun 12 June

LOPEMEDE FARM
Wendy Thompson & Briony Rixon.
Open on Sun 12 June

MANOR HOUSE
Mr & Mrs West.
Open on Sun 10 Apr

TOMPSONS FARM
Mr & Mrs T Moynihan.
Open on Sun 10 Apr

Four gardens will open on Sun 10 Apr. Barry's Close, spring flowering trees, borders and water garden. Baker's Close 1000's of daffodils, tulips and narcissi, shrubs and wild area. Manor House, a large garden with views to the Chilterns, two ornamental lakes, a variety of spring bulbs and shrubs. Tompsons Farm, a large woodland garden with lake and newly planted borders. Five gardens will also open on Sun 12 June. A formal courtyard garden at Lopemede Farm with raised beds, vegetables and flower borders. Cop Close with mixed borders, and cutting garden. 25 Elm Trees, featuring herbaceous borders, roses and clematis. Brindles is a totally organic garden with natural swimming pool, beehives, roses and vegetable garden. 43 High Street is a recently planted cottage front garden designed by a local garden designer. Partial wheelchair access.

26 LORDS WOOD

Frieth Road, Marlow Common, SL7 2QS. Mr & Mrs Messum, www.messums.com. *1½m NW Marlow. From Marlow turn off the A4155 at Platts Garage into Oxford Rd & Chalkpit Ln towards Frieth for 1½m, 100yds past the Marlow Common road turn L down a made up bridlepath & follow parking signs.* Thur 16 June (11-4). Adm £5, chd free. Home-made teas.
'An outpost of Old Bloomsbury in Marlow Woods' was how diarist Frances Partridge described Lords Wood. James and Alex Strachey entertained many of the Bloomsbury Group inc Lytton Strachey and Dora Carrington. The 5 acres surrounding the house (not open) showcase sculpture, water features, extensive mature borders, flower and herb gardens, orchard, and woodland walks with spectacular views over the Chilterns. Partial wheelchair access; gravel paths, steep slopes and open water.

27 MAGNOLIA HOUSE

Grange Drive, Wooburn Green, Wooburn, HP10 0QD. Elaine & Alan Ford, 01628 525818, lanforddesigns@gmail.com. *On A4094 2m SW of A40 between Bourne End & Wooburn. From Wooburn Church, direction Maidenhead, Grange Drive is on L before r'about. From Bourne End, L at 2 mini r'abouts, then 1st R.* Visits by arrangement Mar to July for groups of up to 30. Combined visit with The Shades. Light refreshments.
½ acre garden with mature trees inc large magnolia. Cacti, fernery, stream, ponds, greenhouses, aviary, 10,000 snowdrops, hellebores, bluebells and over 60 varieties of hosta. Child friendly. Constantly being changed and updated. Partial wheelchair access.

28 MONTANA

Shire Lane, Cholesbury, HP23 6NA. Diana Garner. *3m NW of Chesham. From Wigginton turn R after Champneys, 2nd R onto Shire Ln. From Cholesbury Common, turn on Cholesbury Rd by cricket club, take 1st L onto Shire Ln. Montana is ½m down Shire Ln on LH-side.* Limited parking. Wed 23 Mar, Wed 20 Apr, Wed 18 May, Wed 22 June, Wed 20 July (11-2). Adm £4, chd free. Pre-booking essential, please phone 01494 758347 or email montana@cholesbury. net for information & booking. Home-made teas. Visits also by arrangement Mar to July for groups of up to 35.
A peaceful large country garden planted with rare trees, unusual flowering shrubs and perennials under planted with thousands of bulbs; kitchen garden edged by sweet peas; shade loving plants and small meadow. A gate leads to a mixed deciduous wood with level paths, a large fernery planted in an old clay pit and an avenue of daffodils and acers. Lots of seats to enjoy the atmosphere. Small apiary. An un-manicured garden high in the Chiltern Hills. Surrounding fields have been permanent pasture for more than 100 yrs. Covered open barn for teas in wet weather. The majority of paths in the garden and wood are wheelchair friendly.

29 ♦ NETHER WINCHENDON HOUSE

Nether Winchendon, Near Aylesbury, HP18 0DY. Mr Robert Spencer Bernard, 01844 290101, Contactus@ netherwinchendonhouse.com, www.nwhouse.co.uk. *6m SW of Aylesbury, 6m from Thame. Approx 4m from Thame on A418, turn 1st L to Cuddington, turn L at Xrds, downhill turn R & R again to parking by house.* For NGS: Sun 28 Aug (2-5.30). Adm £4, chd free. Cream teas at church. For other opening times and information, please phone, email or visit garden website.
Nether Winchendon House has fine and rare trees, set in a stunning landscape surrounded by parkland with 7 acres of lawned grounds running down to the River Thame. A Founder NGS Member (1927). Enchanting and romantic Mediaeval and Tudor House, one of the most romantic of the historic houses of England and Grade I listed. Picturesque small village with an interesting church.

30 NEW OLD KEEPERS

Village Lane, Hedgerley, SL2 3UY.
Rob Cooper. *Garden located up drive
opp Kiln Ln. Parking in village hall.* **Sun
11 Sept (11-4). Adm £4, chd free.
Pre-booking essential, please visit
www.ngs.org.uk for information &
booking. Tea in village hall.**
Recently established, 1½ acre garden
combining beautiful perennial borders
that peak in late summer, an orchard,
meadow and woodland edge gardens,
surrounding a Grade II listed former
brickmaker's cottage (not open).

31 OLD PARK BARN

Dag Lane, Stoke Goldington,
MK16 8NY. Emily & James
Chua, 01908 551092,
emilychua51@yahoo.com. *4m N
of Newport Pagnell on B526. Park
on High St. A short walk up Dag Ln.
Disabled parking for four cars near
garden via Orchard Way.* **Sat 25,
Sun 26 June (1.30-5). Adm £5, chd
free. Home-made teas. Visits also
by arrangement June & July for
groups of 10 to 40.**
A garden of almost 3 acres made
from a rough field over 20 yrs ago.
Near the house (not open) a series
of terraces cut into the sloping site
create the formal garden with long
and cross vistas, lawns and deep
borders. The aim is to provide interest
throughout the yr with naturalistic
planting and views borrowed from the
surrounding countryside. Beyond is a
wildlife pond, meadow and woodland
garden. Partial wheelchair access.

32 ORCHARD HOUSE

Tower Road, Coleshill, Amersham,
HP7 0LB. Mr & Mrs Douglas Livesey,
jane.livesey88@btinternet.com. *From
Amersham Old Town take the A355 to
Beaconsfield. Appox ¾ m along this
road at top of hill, take 1st R into Tower
Rd. Parking in cricket club grounds.*
**Sat 23 Apr (2-5). Adm £5, chd free.
Home-made teas in the barn. Visits
also by arrangement in Apr.**
The 5 acre garden inc several
wooded areas with eco bug hotels
for wildlife. Two ponds with wild
flower planting, large avenues of silver
birches, a bog garden with board
walk and a wildflower meadow. There
is a cut flower garden and a dramatic
collection of spring bulbs set amongst
an acer glade. Wheelchair access
with sloping lawn in rear garden.

33 OVERSTROUD COTTAGE

The Dell, Frith Hill, Gt Missenden,
HP16 9QE. Mr & Mrs Jonathan
Brooke. *½ m E Gt Missenden. Turn
E off A413 at Gt Missenden onto
B485 Frith Hill to Chesham Rd. White
Gothic cottage set back in lay-by
100yds uphill on L. Parking on R at
church.* **Sun 17 Apr, Sun 15 May,
Sun 12 June, Sun 3 July (2-5).
Adm £4, chd free. Cream teas at
parish church.**
Artistic chalk garden on two levels.
Collection of C17/C18 plants
inc auriculas, hellebores, bulbs,
pulmonarias, peonies, geraniums,
dahlias, herbs and succulents. Many
antique species and rambling roses.
Potager and lily pond. Blue and white
ribbon border. Cottage was once C17
fever house for Missenden Abbey.
Features inc a garden studio with
painting exhibition (share of flower
painting proceeds to NGS).

34 11 THE PADDOCKS

Wendover, HP22 6HE. Mr &
Mrs E Rye, 01296 623870,
pam.rye@talktalk.net. *5m from
Aylesbury on A413. From Aylesbury
turn L at mini r'about onto Wharf
Rd. From Gt Missenden turn L at the
Clock Tower, then R at mini r'about
onto Wharf Rd.* **Every Sun 12 June
to 3 July (11-4.30). Adm £4. Visits
also by arrangement June & July
for groups of 10 to 25. Donation to
Bonnie People in South Africa.**
Small peaceful garden with mixed
borders of colourful herbaceous
perennials, a special show of David
Austin roses and a large variety of
spectacular named Blackmore and
Langdon delphiniums. A tremendous
variety of colour in a small area. The
White Garden with a peaceful and
shady arbour, and The Magic of
Moonlight created for the BBC.

Old Keepers

35 PETERLEY CORNER COTTAGE

Perks Lane, Prestwood, Great Missenden, HP16 0JH. Dawn Philipps, 01494 862198, dawn.philipps@googlemail.com. *Turn into Perks Ln from Wycombe Rd (A4128), Peterley Corner Cottage is 3rd house on the L.* **Visits by arrangement May to Aug for groups of 10 to 30. Adm £5, chd free. Light refreshments.**
A 3 acre mature garden inc an acre of wild flowers and indigenous trees. Surrounded by tall hedges and a wood, the garden has evolved over the last 30 yrs. There are many specimen trees and mature roses inc a Paul's Himalaya Musk. A large herbaceous border runs alongside the formal lawns with other borders like heathers and shrubs. A more recent addition is an enclosed potager.

&. ☕))

36 RED KITES

46 Haw Lane, Bledlow Ridge, HP14 4JJ. Mag & Les Terry, 01494 481474, lesterry747@gmail.com. *4m S of Princes Risborough. Off A4010 halfway between Princes Risborough & West Wycombe. At Hearing Dogs sign in Saunderton turn into Haw Ln, then 3/4 m on L up the hill.* **Tue 10 May, Tue 12 July (2-5). Adm £5, chd free. Home-made teas. Visits also by arrangement May to Sept for groups of 20+.**
This Chiltern hillside garden of 1½ acres is planted for year-round interest and has superb views. Lovingly and beautifully maintained, there are several different areas to relax in, each with their own character. Wildflower orchard, mixed borders, pond, vegetables, woodland area and a lovely hidden garden. Many climbers used in the garden which changes significantly through the seasons.

☕

37 ROBIN HILL

Water End, Stokenchurch, High Wycombe, HP14 3XQ. Caroline Renshaw & Stuart Yates, 07957 394134, Info@cazrenshawdesigns.co.uk. *2m from M40 J5 Stokenchurch. Turn off A40 just S of Stokenchurch towards Radnage, then 1st R to Waterend & then follow signs.* **Visits by arrangement June to Sept for groups of 10 to 20. Adm £4.50, chd free. Home-made teas.**

1½ acre informal and relaxed country garden at the start of The Chiltern Hills, open to the views over its own wildflower meadow. The garden is full of planting with shrubs, perennials and grass borders, new and established trees, and lots of places to sit and enjoy the views. Wind your way through the paths in the meadow and you can also visit the chickens in the large cherry orchard. Wheelchair access over mainly flat and lawned garden, but no paths.

&. 🐕 ✿ Ⓓ ☕))

38 ST MICHAELS CONVENT

Vicarage Way, Gerrards Cross, SL9 8AT. Sisters of the Church. *15 min walk from Gerrards Cross Stn. 10 mins from East Common buses. Parking in nearby street, limited parking at St Michael's.* **Sat 18 June (2-4.30). Adm by donation. Tea.**
Recently acquired garden, having been neglected for many yrs, is now being developed by the Community as a place for quiet, reflection and to gaze upon beauty. Inc a walled garden with vegetables, labyrinth and pond, a shady woodland dell and a recently built chapel. Colourful borders, beds and mature majestic trees. Come and see how the garden is developing and growing!

&. ☕ 🪑))

39 THE SHADES

High Wycombe, HP10 0QD. Pauline & Maurice Kirkpatrick, 01628 522540. *On A4094 2m SW of A40 between Bourne End & Wooburn. From Wooburn Church, direction Maidenhead, Grange Drive is on L before r'about. From Bourne End, L at 2 mini r'abouts, then 1st R.* **Visits by arrangement Mar to July for groups of up to 30. Combined visit with Magnolia House. Light refreshments at Magnolia House.**
The Shades drive is approached through mature trees, areas of shade loving plants, beds of shrubs, 60 various roses and herbaceous plants. The rear garden with natural well surrounded by plants, shrubs and acers. A green slate water feature and scree garden with alpine plants completes the garden. Partial wheelchair access.

&. ☕

40 ◆ STOKE POGES MEMORIAL GARDENS

Church Lane, Stoke Poges, Slough, SL2 4NZ. Buckinghamshire Council, 01753 523744, memorial. gardens@buckinghamshire.gov. uk, www.southbucks.gov.uk/ stokepogesmemorialgardens. *1m N of Slough, 4m S of Gerrards Cross. Follow signs to Stoke Poges & from there to the Memorial Gardens. Car park opp main entrance, disabled visitor parking in the gardens. Weekend disabled access through churchyard.* **For NGS: Sun 26 June (1-4.30). Adm £5, chd free. Home-made teas. For other opening times and information, please phone, email or visit garden website.**
Unique 22 acre Grade I registered garden constructed 1934-9. Rock and water gardens, sunken colonnade, rose garden, 500 individual gated gardens, beautiful mature trees and newly landscaped areas. Guided tours every hour. Guide dogs only.

&. ✿ 🚌 ☕))

41 1 TALBOT AVENUE

Downley, High Wycombe, HP13 5HZ. Mr Alan Mayes, 01494 451044, alan.mayes2@btopenworld.com. *From Downley T-lights off West Wycombe Rd, take Plomer Hill turn off, then 2nd L into Westover Rd, then 2nd L into Talbot Ave.* **Visits by arrangement May to Sept for groups of up to 15. Adm £4, chd free.**
A Japanese garden, shielded from the top garden level by Shoji screens. A winding path leads you over a traditional Japanese bridge by a pond and waterfall and invites you through a moongate to reveal a purpose-built tea house, all surrounded by traditional Japanese planting inc maples, cherry blossom trees, azaleas and rhododendrons. Ornamental grasses and bamboo complement the hard landscaping with feature cloud tree and checkerboard garden path.

 ☕))

42 TURN END

Townside, Haddenham, Aylesbury, HP17 8BG. Margaret & Peter Aldington, turnendgarden@gmail.com, www.turnend.org.uk. *3m NE of Thame, 5m SW of Aylesbury. Exit A418 to Haddenham. Turn at Rising Sun Pub into Townside. Street*

parking very limited. Please park with consideration for residents. See Turn End website for parking info for this event. **Mon 2 May (2-5). Adm £4.50, chd free. Home-made teas.** Grade II registered series of garden rooms, each with a different planting style enveloping architect's own Grade II* listed house (not open). Dry garden, formal box garden, sunken gardens, mixed borders around curving lawn, all framed by ancient walls and mature trees. Bulbs, irises, wisteria, roses, ferns and climbers. Courtyards with pools, pergolas, secluded seating and Victorian coach house. Open artist's studio with displays and demonstrations.

43 TYRINGHAM HALL
Upper Church Street, Cuddington, Aylesbury, HP18 0AP. Mrs Sherry Scott MBE, 01844 291526, philandsherryscott@gmail.com. R at Cuddington Xrd (Upper Church St), 100 metres Tyringham Hall on RH-bend. **Sun 29 May (2-5). Adm £5, chd free. Home-made teas. Visits also by arrangement May to Sept.** Medieval house that will be partly open. A large garden with extensive lawns, water garden with underground springs, vegetable garden, tennis court and swimming pool. Colourful varieties of flowers are planted around the garden with mature trees offering shade where needed. Many seating areas around the garden. Parking at garden for wheelchair visitors only.

44 TYTHROP PARK
Kingsey, HP17 8LT. Nick & Chrissie Wheeler. 2m E of Thame, 4m NW of Princes Risborough. Via A4129, at T-junction in Kingsey turn towards Haddenham, take L turn on bend. Parking in field on L. **Sun 26 June (2-5.30). Adm £7, chd free. Home-made teas.** 10 acres of garden surrounds a C17 Grade I listed manor house (not open). This large and varied garden blends traditional and contemporary styles, featuring pool borders rich in grasses with a green and white theme, walled kitchen and cutting garden with large greenhouse at its heart, box parterre, deep mixed borders, water feature, rose garden, wildflower meadow and many old trees and shrubs.

45 NEW WADZANA
8 Lynnens View, Oakley, HP18 9LQ. Wendy & Peter Hopcroft, www.wadzanaartandgarden.co.uk. Within 8m of Oxford, Bicester & Thame. 6m from M40. The village is halfway between Bicester & Thame on the B4011. Oxford Rd starts at B4011 in Oakley. Wadzana is on Oxford Rd leaving Oakley. For SatNav use HP18 9RD. **Sun 24 July (1-5). Adm £4, chd free. Home-made teas.** A young, but surprisingly mature garden divided into individually themed areas, formal, herb, meadow, stumpery. Views over neighbouring fields gives sense of space. Extensive vegetable garden and greenhouse. 40ft pergola leads to golf practice area and beyond. Seating for teas near fountain and pond with fish, and also the opportunity to enjoy Wendy's art. Wheelchair access to main part of garden.

SPECIAL EVENT

46 THE WALLED GARDEN, WORMSLEY
Wormsley, Stokenchurch, High Wycombe, HP14 3YE. Wormsley Estate. Leave M40 at J5. Turn towards Ibstone. Entrance to estate is ¼m on R. NB: 20mph speed limit on estate. Please do not drive on grass verges. **Wed 29 June (10-3). Adm £7, chd free. Pre-booking essential, please visit www.ngs. org.uk for information & booking. Home-made teas.** The Walled Garden at Wormsley Estate is a 2 acre garden providing flowers, vegetables and tranquil contemplative space for the family. For many yrs the garden was neglected until Sir Paul Getty purchased the estate in the mid-1980s. In 1991 the garden was redesigned and has changed over the yrs, but remains true to the original brief. Wheelchair access to grounds, but no WC facilities.

47 20 WHITEPIT LANE
Flackwell Heath, High Wycombe, HP10 9HS. Trevor Jones, 01628 524876, trevorol4969@gmail.com. ¾m E Flackwell Heath, 4m High Wycombe. From M40 J3 (W bound exit only) take 1st L, 300yds T-junction turn R, 300yds turn L uphill to centre of Flackwell Heath, turn L ¾m, garden 75yds on R past mini r'about. **Visits by arrangement May to Sept for groups of up to 6. Adm £7, chd free. Teas inc.** The front garden has a seaside type landscape with timber groynes and a rock pool. The rear garden is long and thin with colour from Apr to Oct, containing many unusual plants with steps and bridges over two ponds. Amongst the plants are a large banana, an albizia, grevilleas, callistemons, abutilon, salvias and several alstroemerias. The beds are filled with mixed shrubs and herbaceous plants. Many rare and unusual plants and a garden railway.

48 WOODSIDE
23 Willow Lane, Amersham, HP7 9DW. Elin & Graham Stone. On A413, 1m SE from Old Amersham, between Barley Ln & Finch Ln. The garden is the last but one on the RHS. Limited parking, please park with consideration to neighbours. **Sat 18, Sun 19 June (2-5). Adm £4, chd free. Pre-booking essential, please phone 07592 367434 or email glsimagesuk@gmail.com for information & booking. Light refreshments & delicious home-made cakes. Visits also by arrangement in June for groups of up to 15.** A small cottage garden, created on south facing slope, integrating a circular lawn, lily pond, gravel paths and steps to a curved clematis and rose pergola. Rose beds and abundant humped borders. In contrast, a secret naturally arching woodland path winds past a stumpery/fernery, a shade area and wildlife hedging leading to a kitchen garden and bee hotel. Hidden seating areas abound. Artist's Studio. Features inc dragon flies, wildlife habitat, seasonal potted decorative plants and an 8 monthly composting process.

CAMBRIDGESHIRE

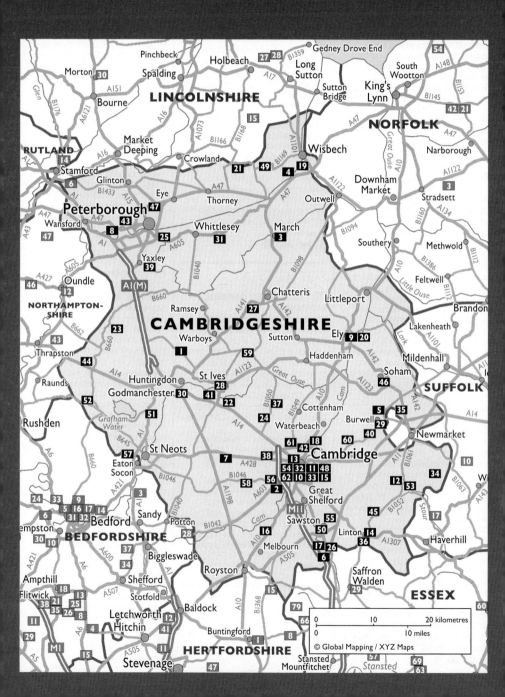

Historic cathedral cities, wide open skies and unique fenland landscapes combine to make Cambridgeshire special.

Our generous gardeners invite you to come and take a closer look at gardens to delight and surprise.

From the splendid city gardens to parkland magnificence and rural idylls in isolated hamlets the county has something to suit all tastes.

Stroll around our group gardens and be inspired by their diversity and interest. Explore spaces planned for the dry East Anglian climate and others on rich fenland soil. See the contemporary and the historic; small town courtyards, large country gardens and those maintained for wildlife and the environment. Be inspired by innovative and creative ideas and talk to our enthusiastic and knowledgeable gardeners.

Some are open by arrangement where your host will happily share plant knowledge, anecdotes and plant passions with you - so long as you have time to listen!

Begin the year with a visit to our snowdrop gardens in February. Later enjoy a summer afternoon with friends and family. Relax and unwind with good tea and cake in the surroundings of a beautiful garden. End with the spectacular autumn tree colour changes.

Whenever you visit, you can be sure that you will receive a warm welcome and a memorable day out.

Volunteers

County Organiser
Jenny Marks 07956 049257
jenny.marks@ngs.org.uk

Deputy County Organiser
Pam Bullivant 01353 667355
pam.bullivant@ngs.org.uk

County Treasurer
Position vacant – for details please
contact Jenny Marks (as above)

Booklet Coordinator
Jenny Marks (As above)

Publicity
Penny Miles 07771 516448
penny.miles@ngs.org.uk

Social Media
Hetty Dean
hetty.dean@ngs.org.uk

Assistant County Organisers
Russell Dean 07801 383454
russell.dean@ngs.org.uk

Jacquie Latten-Quinn
07941 279571
jacqui.quinn@ngs.org.uk

Penny Miles (As above)

Jane Pearson 07890 080303
Jane.pearson@ngs.org.uk

Barbara Stalker 07800 575100
barbara.stalker@ngs.org.uk

Annette White 01638 730876
annette323@btinternet.com

Claire Winfrey 01733 380216
claire@winfrey.co.uk

 National Garden Scheme Cambs @GardenCambs cambsngs

Left: Isaacsons

OPENING DATES

All entries subject to change. For latest information check www.ngs.org.uk

Extended openings are shown at the beginning of the month.

Map locator numbers are shown to the right of each garden name.

February

Snowdrop Festival

Saturday 12th
Caldrees Manor 6

Saturday 19th
Landwade Hall 35

Sunday 20th
Clover Cottage 14
Landwade Hall 35

Sunday 27th
Clover Cottage 14

March

Sunday 6th
Clover Cottage 14

Sunday 27th
Kirtling Tower 34

April

Sunday 3rd
Barton Gardens 2
Netherhall Manor 46

Sunday 24th
Churchill College 13
Staploe Gardens 57

Saturday 30th
28 Houghton Road 28

May

Every Friday, Saturday and Sunday from Friday 6th
23A Perry Road 51

Sunday 1st
Chaucer Road Gardens 10
28 Houghton Road 28
Netherhall Manor 46

Monday 2nd
Chaucer Road Gardens 10
28 Houghton Road 28

Saturday 7th
28 Houghton Road 28

Sunday 8th
◆ Docwra's Manor 16
28 Houghton Road 28
NEW Milton Hall 43

Saturday 14th
NEW East Anglia Children's Hospital Milton 18

Sunday 15th
◆ Ferrar House 23
NEW Linton Gardens 36

Saturday 21st
28 Houghton Road 28

Sunday 22nd
28 Houghton Road 28

Saturday 28th
NEW Fenstanton 22
28 Houghton Road 28

Sunday 29th
Cambourne Gardens 7
NEW Fenstanton 22
28 Houghton Road 28
Island Hall 30

June

Every Friday, Saturday and Sunday
23A Perry Road 51

Saturday 4th
67 Main Street 39
NEW The Manor House 40

Sunday 5th
Barton Gardens 2
Cottage Garden 15
Duxford Gardens 17
38 Kingston Street 33
NEW The Manor House 40

Monday 6th
Abbots Ripton Hall 1

Saturday 11th
Beaver Lodge 3
NEW East Anglia Children's Hospital Milton 18
◆ The Manor, Hemingford Grey 41
Staploe Gardens 57

Sunday 12th
Beaver Lodge 3
Clover Cottage 14
Ely Open Gardens 20
◆ The Manor, Hemingford Grey 41
Molesworth & Brington Gardens 44
The Old Rectory 49
Staploe Gardens 57

Tuesday 14th
Abbots Ripton Hall 1

Saturday 18th
NEW Juniper House 31
NEW Marmalade Lane, Cohousing Community Garden 42

Sunday 19th
Clover Cottage 14
Green End Farm 24
Hinxton Gardens 26
NEW Juniper House 31
Madingley Hall 38

Monday 20th
Abbots Ripton Hall 1

Wednesday 22nd
Wild Rose Cottage 60

Saturday 25th
Twin Tarns 59

Sunday 26th
Burwell Village Gardens 5
NEW Church Lane House 12
Isaacson's 29
Kirtling Tower 34
Twin Tarns 59

Tuesday 28th
Abbots Ripton Hall 1

July

Every Friday, Saturday and Sunday
23A Perry Road 51

Daily from Monday 11th
Robinson College 54

Saturday 2nd
Bramley Cottage 4
38 Norfolk Terrace Garden 48

Sunday 3rd
Bramley Cottage 4
King's College Fellows' Garden and Provost's Garden 32
38 Norfolk Terrace Garden 48
Sawston Gardens 55
Toft Gardens 58

Monday 4th
Abbots Ripton Hall 1

Saturday 9th
NEW East Anglia Children's Hospital Milton 18
Wolfson College Garden 62

Saturday 16th
Preachers Passing 52

Sunday 17th
Preachers Passing 52

Sunday 24th
Christ's College 11

Saturday 30th
Little Oak 37

Sunday 31st
Little Oak 37

August

Every Friday, Saturday and Sunday
23A Perry Road 51

Daily to Friday 12th
Robinson College 54

Saturday 6th
Little Oak 37

Sunday 7th
Little Oak 37
Netherhall Manor 46

Wednesday 10th
◆ Elgood's Brewery Gardens 19

Saturday 13th
Beaver Lodge 3

Sunday 14th
Beaver Lodge 3

Milton Hall

© James Fennell

By Arrangement

Arrange a personalised garden visit with your club, or group of friends, on a date to suit you. See individual garden entries for full details.

Our 2021 donations mean that 750 people living with Parkinson's were supported

THE GARDENS

◻ ABBOTS RIPTON HALL
Abbots Ripton, PE17 2PQ.
The Lord & Lady De Ramsey,
www.abbotsriptonhall.co.uk. *2m
N of Huntingdon. On B1090.* Mon 6,
Tue 14, Mon 20, Tue 28 June, Mon
4 July (2-4). Adm £10. Pre-booking
essential, please visit www.ngs.
org.uk for information & booking.
8½ acres of quintessential English
garden with 5 acre lake developed
since 1937 with much work done
recently by the current owners. 150yd
'cottage' double border, mixed borders,
old shrub roses garden, Victorian rose
arch walk. Tender Mediterranean grey
border. Bog garden, fine collection of
trees, inc 60 different oaks. Many follies,
each with its own character. Over 1600
plant species. Wheelchair access some
gravel paths, stream.
&

GROUP OPENING

◻ BARTON GARDENS
High Street, Barton, Cambridge,
CB23 7BG. *4m SW of Cambridge.
Barton is on A603 Cambridge to
Sandy Rd, close to J12 M11.* Sun 3
Apr (1-5). Combined adm £5, chd
free. Sun 5 June (1-5). Combined
adm £6, chd free. Home-made
teas at The Six Houses.

FARM COTTAGE
Dr R M Belbin.
Open on all dates

11 KINGS GROVE
Mrs Judith Bowen.
Open on all dates

2 MAILES CLOSE
Mr Patrick Coulson.
Open on Sun 5 June

31 NEW ROAD
Drs D & M Macdonald.
Open on Sun 5 June

THE SIX HOUSES
Perennial.
Open on all dates
(See separate entry)

Varied group of large and small
gardens reflecting a wide range
of gardening styles, from a large,
landscaped cottage garden inc
themed woodland walk to a small
complex featuring gardens created
and tended by professional retired
gardeners. Magnificent spring
bulb displays feature in the April
opening. In June, enjoy abundant
displays of herbaceous planting in
all five gardens, many also featuring
vegetable and fruit growing in their
designs, as well as magnificent
specimen trees. Wheelchair access,
some gardens have gravel paths.
& 🐕 ✿ ☕ »)

◻ BEAVER LODGE
Henson Road, March,
PE15 8BA. Mr & Mrs
Nielson-Bom, 07455 495592,
beaverbom@gmail.com. *A141
to Wisbech rd into March, L into
Westwood Ave, at end, R into
Henson Rd, property on R opp
school playground.* Sat 11, Sun 12
June, Sat 13, Sun 14 Aug (10-4).
Adm £3, chd free. Home-made
teas. **Visits also by arrangement
May to Nov for groups of up to 20.**
An impeccable oriental garden with
more than 120 large and small
bonsai trees, acers, pagodas, oriental
statues, water features and pond
with koi carp, creating a peaceful
and relaxing atmosphere. The garden
is divided into different rooms, one
with a Mediterranean feel inc tree
ferns, lemon trees, bougainvilleas
and a great variety of plants and
water fountain. Plenty of sitting areas.
The garden contains water features,
Oriental statues and a pagoda.
🐎 ✿ 🚙 ☕ ♿

◻ BRAMLEY COTTAGE
Barton Road, Wisbech St Mary,
Wisbech, PE13 4RP. Jim &
Mel Wakefield, 01945 410554,
melaniewright061@btinternet.com.
*Coming towards Wisbech St Mary
from Wisbech, 1st house on R
following a sweeping R bend.* Sat 2
July (12-4); Sun 3 July (11-4). Adm
£5, chd free. Light refreshments.

Abbots Ripton Hall

Visits also by arrangement Apr to Sept for groups of 10+. No machinery will be on show if in the evenings.

It is an adult garden with structures of a rose arch and a wisteria and laburnum arch. It has various quirky pieces that we like. The garden can also be viewed from a platform giving an aerial view of the garden and surrounding fields. On display also will be a selection of vintage horticultural machinery and hand tools.

GROUP OPENING

5 BURWELL VILLAGE GARDENS

Burwell, CB25 0BB. *10m NE of Cambridge, 4m NW of Newmarket via the B1102/B1103.* **Sun 26 June (12-5.30). Combined adm with Isaacsons £6, chd free. Home-made teas at Silver Birches.**

3 ROMAN CLOSE
Mrs Dove.

SILVER BIRCHES
Jeremy & Sally Lander.

[NEW] **8 SILVER STREET**
Mr David & Mrs Frances Watt.

[NEW] **SPRING VIEW**
Colin Smith.
[NPC]

New this year, 8 Silver street is a small garden full of interest with colourful planting, hanging baskets, small waterfalls and two ponds. Some perennials, mixed shrubs and many annuals raised from cuttings every year. Isaacson's, the oldest house in garden is warmed and sheltered by the medieval walls of the C14 house Burwell, is richly diverse in format and planting, with unusual and rare plants. There are "Theatres" (Auricula, Pinks), hints of Snowdonia, the Mediterranean, a French Potager, Anglesey Abbey and much else. 3 Roman Close is a small, newly established garden, which won the Burwell village garden competition for best diversity of planting in 2020. Cottage garden planting, pretty and full borders with roses and many other perennials and annuals. Pots and hanging baskets. Silver Birches is a 400' long garden on the edge of the Fens, divided into separate 'compartments', an informal flower garden with seating, lawns and a small pond, a wooded area with silver birches, and coppiced hazel, A gate

leads to an orchard with chickens. Beyond is a vegetable garden, and finally a wooden jetty onto the 'Catchwater Drain'. Spring View houses the National Collection of Yucca, a huge diversity of forms and sizes, demonstrates drought tolerant planting with other species as well. A specialist plantsman's garden.

6 CALDREES MANOR

2 Abbey Street, Ickleton, CB10 1SS. *In the centre of Ickleton on Abbey Street. From M11 J10, A505 E, then through Duxford village, signed Ickleton. From Saffron Walden, via Gt Chesterford.* **Sat 12 Feb, Sat 29 Oct (10.30-4). Adm £7, chd free. Walk and Talk with Head Gardener Sat 12 Feb (9-10.30am), Sat 29 Oct (9-10.30am). Adm £15. Pre-booking essential, please visit www.ngs.org.uk for information & booking.**

C19 Manor House with extensive formal gardens, lakes and streams, over 150 varieties of Acer palmatum, many specimen trees, a Japanese garden, orchard, woodland walks, wildlife garden and wildflower meadows as well as snowdrops in late winter. The garden has been designed to peak in spring and autumn. Wheelchair access some gravel, and a few steps.

GROUP OPENING

7 CAMBOURNE GARDENS

Great Cambourne, CB23 6AH. *8m W of Cambridge on A428. From A428: take Cambourne junction into Great Cambourne. From B1198, enter village at Lower Cambourne & drive through to Great Cambourne. Follow NGS signs via either route to start at any garden.* **Sun 29 May (11-5). Combined adm £6, chd free. Home-made teas at 13 Fenbridge. Coffee & biscotti at 43 Monkfield Lane.**

13 FENBRIDGE
Lucinda & Tony Williams.

14 GRANARY WAY
Jackie Hutchinson.

88 GREENHAZE LANE
Darren & Irette Murray.

[NEW] **128 JEAVONS LANE**
Mr Tim Smith, 07884007338, headmansmith@yahoo.co.uk.
Visits also by arrangement.

8 LANGATE GREEN
Steve & Julie Friend.

5 MAYFIELD WAY
Debbie & Mike Perry.

43 MONKFIELD LANE
Tony & Penny Miles.

A unique and inspiring modern group, all created from new build in just a few years. This selection of six demonstrates how imagination and gardening skill can be combined in a short time to create great effects from unpromising and awkward beginnings. The grouping inc foliage gardens with collections of carnivorous pitcher plants and hosta; a suntrap garden for play, socialising and colour; gardens with ponds, a vegetable plot and many other beautiful borders showing their owners' creativity and love of growing fine plants well. Cambourne is one of Cambridgeshire's newest communities, and this grouping showcases the happy, vibrant place our village has become. Superb examples beauty and creativity in a newly built environment.

8 CASTOR HOUSE

Peterborough Rd, Castor, Peterborough, PE5 7AX. Ian & Claire Winfrey, 017333 80216, ian@winfrey.co.uk, www.castorhousegardens.co.uk. *4m W of Peterborough. House on main Peterborough Rd in Castor. Parking in paddock off Water Ln.* **Sat 20, Sun 21 Aug (2-5). Adm £7.50, chd free. Home-made teas. Visits also by arrangement July to Sept for groups of 20 to 50.**

12 acres for all seasons to explore, italianate spring fed ponds and stream gardens, 60+ different roses, peony and prunus walk, colour themed borders, vibrant tropical and late season plantings, potager, stumpery, hydrangea walk, woodland plants areas, mature woodland walks with large wildlife pond with views to enjoy.

'National Garden Scheme donations have funded four of our gardens in regional NHS spinal injury centres supporting nearly 8,500 patients and their visitors.' Horatio's Garden

9 38 CHAPEL STREET
Ely, CB6 1AD. Peter & Julia
Williams, 01353 659161,
peterrcwilliams@btinternet.com.
*Bungalow, 100 yds L along
Chapel St from Downham Rd,
end. Entering Ely from Cambridge
(A10), pass Cathedral Green (on
your R) take 1st L (Downham Rd)
towards Ely College. Chapel St is
1st R. Alternatively enter Chapel
St from Lynn Rd (300yds).* **Visits
by arrangement Mar to Oct.
Individuals or groups up to
20. Adm £5, chd free. Home-
made teas. Open with Ely Open
Gardens on Sun 12 June.**
Approx 1/2 acre, level, with many
unusual plants. Year-round interest.
Secluded back garden with well-
stocked colourful rockery, herbaceous
borders raised vegetable beds, soft
fruit and fruit trees (inc quince, fig);
pergolas with climbing roses. Front
garden has a wide variety of roses,
flowering prunus, philadelphus,
judas tree. Side borders contain a
range of hellebores, herbaceous and
numerous salvias.

ᕦ ✿ ☕

GROUP OPENING

10 CHAUCER ROAD GARDENS
Cambridge, CB2 7EB. *1m S of
Cambridge. Off Trumpington Rd
(A1309), nr Brooklands Ave junction.
Parking available at MRC Psychology
Dept on Chaucer Rd.* **Sun 1, Mon
2 May (2-5). Combined adm £7,
chd free. Home-made teas at
Upwater Lodge.**

11 CHAUCER ROAD
Mark & Jigs Hill.

16 CHAUCER ROAD
Mrs V Albutt.

UPWATER LODGE
Mr & Mrs George
Pearson, 07890 080303,
jmp@pearson.co.uk.
**Visits also by arrangement May
to Sept. Garden tour on request.**

11 Chaucer Road is a 3/4 acre
Edwardian garden that has changed
rapidly over the ensuing 110 yrs. A
rock garden with pond and large
weeping Japanese maple dates from
about 1930. 16 Chaucer Road is
an artist's garden, full of surprises,
and attractions for children. Upwater
Lodge is an Edwardian academic's
house with 7 acres of grounds. It has
mature trees, fine lawns, old wisterias,

and colourful borders. There is a
small, pretty potager with a selection
of fruits, and a well maintained grass
tennis court. A network of paths
through a wooded area lead down to
a dyke, water meadows and a small
flock of rare breed sheep. Enjoy a
walk by the river and watch the punts
go by. Buy home-made teas and sit
in the garden or take them down to
enjoy a lazy afternoon with ducks,
geese, swans and heron on the
riverbank. Cakes made with garden
fruit where possible. Swings and
climbing ropes. Plant stall possible
but please email to check. Wheelchair
access some gravel areas and grassy
paths with fairly gentle slopes.

ᕦ ☕))

---

11 CHRIST'S COLLEGE
St. Andrew's Street,
Cambridge, CB2 3BU. Christ's
College, 01223 334926,
reservations@christs.cam.ac.uk,
www.christs.cam.ac.uk/college-
gardens. *Fellows' Garden, College
grounds main site. In central
Cambridge. Public parking available
at Grand Arcade car park, Corn
Exchange Street CB2 3QF.* **Sun 24
July (2-6). Adm £6, chd free. Tea.**
Situated in the centre of the College
grounds, the Fellows' Garden of over
2 acres features informal borders,
shrubs, trees and winding paths. On
the east side of the garden stands
an enormous Plantanus x hispanica,
thought to be over 200 yrs old. Other
features: Milton's Mulberry Tree
(Morus nigra) and the C18 swimming
pool. Large salvia and iris collections
in a separate courtyard.

ᕦ 🛏 ☕))

12 [NEW] CHURCH LANE HOUSE
Church Lane, Westley Waterless,
CB8 0RL. Dr Lucy Crosby. *5m S of
Newmarket. Located on the L side
corner of Church Ln.* **Sun 26 June
(2-5). Adm £5, chd free. Home-
made teas.**
Set in just under an acre, our garden
offers a wildlife pond, herbaceous
borders, Victorian style greenhouse
and kitchen garden, orchard and
wildflower meadow. There are
borders dedicated to cut flowers and
dye plants. This is a family friendly
garden, shared with chickens, guinea
pigs and fish with plenty of seating
areas to take in the views. Wheelchair
access is mostly via lawns.

ᕦ ✿ ☕))

13 CHURCHILL COLLEGE
Storey's Way, Cambridge,
CB3 0DS. University of
Cambridge, www.chu.cam.ac.uk/
about/grounds-gardens/. *1m from
M11 J13. 1m NW of Cambridge city
centre. Turn into Storeys Way from
Madingley Rd. Parking on site.* **Sun
24 Apr (2-5). Adm £3.50, chd free.**
42 acre site designed in 1960s
for foliage and form, to provide
year-round interest in peaceful and
relaxing surrounds with courtyards,
large open spaces and specimen
trees. 10m x 5m orchid house,
herbaceous plantings. Beautiful
grouping of Prunus Tai Haku (great
white cherry) trees forming striking
canopy and drifts of naturalised bulbs
in grass around the site. The planting
provides a setting for the impressive
collection of modern sculpture. Walk
through trees and around the sports
fields. National collection of plants
named after Sir Winston Churchill.
Wheelchair access to the greenhouse
is restricted.

ᕦ NPC ☕))

14 CLOVER COTTAGE
50 Streetly End, West Wickham,
CB21 4RP. Mr Paul & Mrs
Shirley Shadford, 01223 893122,
shirleyshadford@live.co.uk. *3m
from Linton, 3m from Haverhill & 2m
from Balsham. From Horseheath turn
L, from Balsham turn R, thatched
cottage opp triangle of grass next
to old windmill.* **Sun 20, Sun 27
Feb, Sun 6 Mar (2-4). Adm £3,
chd free. Sun 12, Sun 19 June
(12-5). Adm £3.50, chd free.
Light refreshments. Visits also by
arrangement Feb to June.**
In winter find a flowering cherry tree,
borders of snowdrops, aconites, iris
reticulata, hellebores and miniature
narcissus throughout the packed
small garden which has inspiring
ideas on use of space. Pond and
arbour, raised beds of fruit and
vegetables. In summer arches of
roses and clematis, hardy geraniums,
delightful borders of English roses
and herbaceous plants. Snowdrops,
hellebores and spring flowering bulbs
for sale for the snowdrop festival,
plants also for sale in June.

✿ 🚗 ☕

COTTAGE GARDEN

79 Sedgwick Street, Cambridge, CB1 3AL. Rosie Wilson, 07805 443818, liccycat@icloud.com. *Cambridge City. Off Mill Rd, S of the railway bridge.* **Sun 5 June (2-6). Adm £3.50, chd free. Home-made teas. Open nearby 38 Kingston Street. Visits also by arrangement June to Aug for groups of 5 to 20.**
Small, long, narrow and planted in the cottage garden style with over 40 roses some on arches and growing through trees. Particularly planned to encourage wildlife with small pond, mature trees and shrubs. Perennials and some unusual plants interspersed with sculptures. Wheelchair access, some narrow paths.

16 ♦ DOCWRA'S MANOR

2 Meldreth Road, Shepreth, Royston, SG8 6PS. Mrs Faith Raven, www.docwrasmanorgarden.co.uk. *8m S of Cambridge. ½m W of A10. Garden is opp the War Memorial in Shepreth. King's Cross-Cambridge train stop 5 min walk.* **For NGS: Sun 8 May (2-5). Adm £5, chd free. Home-made teas.** 2½ acres of choice plants in a series of enclosed gardens. Tulips and Judas trees. Opened for the NGS for more than 50 yrs. The garden is featured in great detail in a book published 2013 'The Gardens of England' edited by George Plumptre. Unusual plants. Wheelchair access to most parts of the garden, gravel paths. Guide dogs only.

GROUP OPENING

DUXFORD GARDENS

Duxford, CB22 4RP. *Most gardens are close to the centre of the village of Duxford. S of the A505 between M11 J10 & Sawston.* **Sun 5 June (2-6). Combined adm £7, chd free. Cream teas. Sun 14 Aug (2-6). Combined adm £6, chd free. Home-made teas.**

BUSTLERS COTTAGE
John & Jenny Marks.
Open on Sun 5 June

2 GREEN STREET
Mr Bruce Crockford.
Open on Sun 5 June

5 GREEN STREET
Jenny Shaw.
Open on Sun 5 June

16 ICKLETON ROAD
Claire James.
Open on Sun 14 Aug

26 PETERSFIELD ROAD
Robert & Josephine Smit.
Open on Sun 5 June

ROBYNET HOUSE
Gordon Lister
Open on Sun 14 Aug

NEW 3 ST JOHN'S STREET
Dr Celia Duff.
Open on Sun 5 June

31 ST PETER'S STREET
Mr David Baker.
Open on Sun 5 June

Eight village gardens of different sizes and characters. In June, six gardens open: Bustlers Cottage has an acre of cottage garden inc vegetable garden and recently planted hedges. Close by, 31 St Peter's Street on a steep slope is filled with colour and surprises, also has a dry rockery in front of the house. 5 Green Street's walled garden contains lawn, pergolas, various beds and vegetables. The innovative green walls in the garden at 26 Petersfield Road are vibrant with colour. New this year is 3 St John's Street, a recently planted small garden which also provides for lots of hedgehog care and features a large wildlife pond. The tiny, charming 2 Green Street, always full of colour and interest, makes the group complete. In August the sunny aspect at 16 Ickleton Road has interesting, unusual planting, always a work in progress, the knowledgable owner enjoys experimenting with plants. The big, beautiful garden at Robynet House is full of colourful dahlias and at its best this month. Wheelchair access, some gravel paths and a few steps, mostly avoidable.

In the first six months of operation at Maggie's Southampton, which was part funded by the National Garden Scheme, the team has supported people affected by cancer more than 2,300 times

Pampisford Allotments

© Simon Baylis

18 NEW **EAST ANGLIA CHILDREN'S HOSPICE MILTON**
Church Lane, Milton, Cambridge, CB24 6AB. Tina Burkett, www.each.org.uk. *3m N of Cambridge. Turn off Milton High St onto Fen Rd, immed turn L down Church Ln & follow the rd where it ends in the Hospice grounds.* **Sat 14 May, Sat 11 June, Sat 9 July (12-4). Adm £5, chd free. Pre-booking essential, please visit www.ngs.org.uk for information & booking. Light refreshments.**
Small secluded garden within the 2 acre grounds of EACH's Milton Children's Hospice. Inc both formal and informal planting developed and maintained entirely by volunteers. Evergreens, ornamental trees, shrubs, grasses and perennials provide year-round interest with sparkling display of spring flowers and bulbs. Feature inc unusual wisteria trained canopy. Children's playground.

  ♿ ❀ 🍵

19 ♦ **ELGOOD'S BREWERY GARDENS**
North Brink, Wisbech, PE13 1LW. Elgood & Sons Ltd, www.elgoods-brewery.co.uk. *1m W of town centre. Leave A47 towards Wisbech Centre. Cross river to North Brink. Follow river & brown signs to brewery & car park beyond.*

For NGS: **Wed 10 Aug (11.30-4.30). Adm £5, chd free. Light refreshments.**
Approx 4 acres of peaceful garden featuring 250 yr old specimen trees providing a framework to lawns, lake, rockery, herb garden and maze. Wheelchair access to Visitor Centre and most areas of the garden.

  ♿ ❀ 🚐 🍵

GROUP OPENING

20 **ELY OPEN GARDENS**
Ely, CB7 4DL. www.elyopengardens.com. *14m N of Cambridge. Parking at Barton Rd, Tower Rd, (adjacent to 42 Cambridge Rd); the Grange Council Offices. All in easy reach of most gardens. Map on website or from elyopengardens.com.* **Sun 12 June (12-6). Combined adm £8, chd free.**

THE BISHOP'S HOUSE
The Bishop of Ely.

42 CAMBRIDGE ROAD
Mr & Mrs J Switsur.

12 CHAPEL STREET
Ken & Linda Ellis.

9 CHIEFS STREET
Amanda Seamark.

5B DOWNHAM ROAD
Mr Christopher Cain.

NEW **1 MERLIN DRIVE**
Dr Chris Wood.

NEW **1 ROBINS CLOSE**
Mr Brian & Mrs Ann Mitchell.

A delightful and varied group of gardens in an historic Cathedral city: The Bishop's House, adjoining Ely Cathedral, has mixed planting and formal rose garden bordered by wisteria. Local artist displays and sells work. 9 Chiefs Street, is divided into areas, inc developing borders, an all weather play area, mini allotment and chickens. 12 Chapel Street, a small town garden, shows varied gardening interests, from alpines to herbaceous plants and shrubs and a railway! 38 Chapel St has year-round interest and is bursting with unusual and interesting planting. 42 Cambridge Road, a secluded town garden, has colourful herbaceous borders, roses, shrubs, vegs and trees. 5b Downham Road shows how careful planting in a small, challenging, interestingly shaped area has created a tranquil garden. 1 Merlin Drive and 1 Robins Close are modern estate gardens, new this year. The former has a small collection of subtropical plants, and ferns. The latter has raised beds and a small dry garden. Wheelchair access to areas of most gardens.

  ♿ ❀ 🍵))

The Manor House

21 FENLEIGH

Inkerson Fen, off Common Rd, Throckenholt, PE12 0QY. Jeff & Barbara Stalker, 07800 575100, barbara.stalker@ngs.org.uk. *Half way between Gedney Hill & Parson Drove. Postcode for SatNavs PE12 0QY. Please email for further directions.* **Visits by arrangement May to Aug for groups of up to 30. Adm £4, chd free. Light refreshments.**

A fish pond dominates this large garden surrounded with planting. Patio with pots and raised beds, Undercover BBQ area. Small wooded area, polytunnels and corners of the garden for wildlife.

GROUP OPENING

22 NEW FENSTANTON

Huntingdon, PE28 9JW. *Public car park next to the Church, a 2 min walk away from both gardens.* **Sat 28, Sun 29 May (12-5). Combined adm £5, chd free. Home-made teas in United Reform Church garden & green.**

5 CHURCH LANE
Mrs Jan Stone.

THE MANOR HOUSE
Lynda Symonds & Nigel Ferrier.

Two contrasting gardens, one large and one small, set around the oldest houses in the village, one of which was once owned by Lancelot Capability Brown. Whilst in Fenstanton why not visit Brown's memorial in the Parish Church and the grave stone of the Country's most famous landscape gardeners.

23 ◆ FERRAR HOUSE

Little Gidding, Huntingdon, PE28 5RJ. Mrs Susan Capp, www.ferrarhouse.co.uk. *Take Mill Rd from Great Gidding (turn at Fox & Hounds) then after 1m turn R down single track lane. Car Park at Ferrar House.* **For NGS: Sun 15 May (10.30-5). Adm £5, chd free. Home-made teas.**

A peaceful garden of a Retreat House with beautiful uninterrupted views across meadows and farm land. Adjacent to the historic Church of St John's, it was here that a small religious community was formed in the C17. The poet T. S. Eliot visited in 1936 and it inspired the 4th of his Quartets named Little Gidding. Lawn and walled flower beds with a walled vegetable garden. Games on the lawn. Traditional wooden garden games, tea and home-made cakes, plant stall. History talks in Church. WC accessible at Ferrar House.

24 GREEN END FARM

Over Road, Longstanton, Cambridge, CB24 3DW. Sylvia Newman, www.sngardendesign.co.uk. *From A14 take direction of Longstanton, at r'about take 2nd exit, at next r'about turn L (this shows a dead end on the sign) Garden 200 metres on L.* **Sun 19 June (11-4). Adm £5, chd free. Home-made teas.**

A developing garden that's beginning to blend well with the farm. An interesting combination of new and established spaces executed with a design eye. An established orchard with beehives; two wildlife ponds. An outside kitchen and social space inc pool, productive kitchen and cutting garden. Doves, chickens, bees and sheep complete the picture!

25 6 HEMINGFORD CRESCENT

Stanground, Peterborough, PE2 8LL. Michael & Nick Mitchell, 07880 871763, michaelandnick64@gmail.com. *S side of city centre. 10 mins drive from A1M. Take Whittlesey Rd B1092. Coming out of town look for Apple Green petrol stn on L. Turn into Coneygree Rd. Follow rd round, Hemingford Crescent is 6th turning on L.* **Visits by arrangement June to Aug for groups of 5 to 25. Adm £4, chd free.**

Medium sized city garden. Inspired by our travels to Morocco, Egypt and India. Mixture of exotic planting, shrubs and perennials. Various seating areas inc an outside dining area and an enclosed moroccan/egyptian room. Raised beds and pond area. Michael is an artist and his work is available for viewing.

GROUP OPENING

26 HINXTON GARDENS

High Street, Hinxton, CB10 1QY. *Most gardens are on or close to Hinxton High Street. Accessible via A1301.* **Sun 19 June (2-5). Combined adm £6, chd free. Home-made teas.**

NEW THE GRANGE, 8 HUNTS LANE
Amanda Cliffe.

2 HALL FARM BARNS
Ivan Yardley.

NEW HALL FARM BARNS, 10 HUNTS LANE
Anita Excell.

25 HIGH STREET
Steve Trudgill.

MANOR HOUSE
Sara Varey.

MILLER'S COTTAGE
Sue & Chris Elliott.

A group of six village gardens of varying sizes inc cottage gardens, with traditional planting, a garden belonging to a C15 Manor House with planting appropriate to the era. Millers Cottage, next to the old water mill, with narrow riverside garden and planting appropriate to its position, three barn conversion gardens one with tropical dry planting, and the others with very different cottage garden planting. Delicious teas and selection of plants for sale. Wheelchair access, some gravel paths, a few steps, and narrow entrances, but mainly navigable.

27 HORSESHOE FARM

Chatteris Road, Somersham, Huntingdon, PE28 3DR. Neil & Claire Callan, 01354 693546, nccallan@yahoo.co.uk. *9m NE of St Ives, Cambs. Easy access from the A14. Situated on E side of B1050, 4m N of Somersham Village. Parking for 8 cars on the drive.* **Visits by arrangement May to July. For individuals or any number up to 20. Adm £4, chd free. Home-made teas.**
This ³⁄₄ acre plant-lovers' garden has a large pond with summerhouse and decking, bog garden, alpine troughs, mixed rainbow island beds with over 30 varieties of bearded irises, water features, a small hazel woodland area, wildlife meadow, secret corners and a lookout tower for wide Fenland views and bird watching.

28 28 HOUGHTON ROAD

St Ives, PE27 6RH. Julie Pepper, 07788 657568. *On A1123, western edge of St Ives. Garden on the L as you enter St Ives from Huntingdon.* **Sat 30 Apr, Sun 1, Mon 2, Sat 7, Sun 8, Sat 21, Sun 22, Sat 28, Sun 29 May (11-5). Adm £3.50, chd free. Pre-booking essential, please visit www.ngs.org. uk for information & booking. Light refreshments. Gluten free options available. Visits also by arrangement Apr & May for groups of up to 10.**
Step into the peace and tranquillity of Acer heaven, created by designer Julie. Among more than 90 Acers, of which there are 52 varieties, you will also find a patio area set out as a room for outside dining and relaxation. There is much use of dramatic accent planting, punctuated with sculpture, artifacts, water feature, seating areas, bonsai, hostas, trees, ferns and other interesting plants. Plants for sale and refreshments.

29 ISAACSON'S

6 High Street, Burwell, CB25 0HB. Dr Richard & Dr Caroline Dyer, richard@familydyer.com. *10m NE of Cambridge, 4m NW of Newmarket. Behind a tall yew hedge with topiary, & grass triangle, at the S end of the village where Isaacson Rd turns off the High St. Approx 400 yds S of the church.* **Sun 26 June (12-5.30). Combined adm with Burwell Village Gardens £6, chd free. Home-made teas. Visits also**

by arrangement Mar to July for groups of 8 to 20. Visit times 4pm or 6pm.
Warmed and sheltered by the mediaeval walls of a C14 house (the oldest in Burwell) the garden is richly diverse in format and planting. There are 'theatres' (auricula, pinks), hints of Snowdonia, the Mediterranean, and a French potager, Anglesey Abbey in the snowdrop season and much else. Throughout there are many interesting, unusual and rare plants. Around each corner a new vista surprises.

30 ISLAND HALL

Godmanchester, PE29 2BA. Grace Vane Percy, 01480 459676, enquire@islandhall.com, www.islandhall.com. *1m S of Huntingdon (A1). 15m NW of Cambridge (A14). In centre of Godmanchester next to free Mill Yard car park.* **Sun 29 May (10.30-4.30). Adm £5, chd free. Home-made teas in the 'Fisherman's Lodge' on the Island set within the grounds.**
3 acre grounds. Tranquil riverside setting with mature trees. Chinese bridge over Saxon mill race to embowered island with wild flowers. Garden restored in 1983 to mid C18 formal design, with box hedging, clipped hornbeams, parterres, topiary, good vistas over borrowed landscape and C18 wrought iron and stone urns. The ornamental island has been replanted with Princeton elms (ulmus americana). Mid C18 mansion (not open).

31 NEW JUNIPER HOUSE

Cross Drove Coates, Whittlesey, Peterborough, PE7 2HJ. Mrs Jeni Cairns, 07541 229447, jenicairns@btinternet.com, www.juniperhouseemporium.com. *Please stay on A605 until you reach Coates village green and turn up S green, R off S green, L onto lane follow signs, please be aware of uneven road surfaces.* **Sat 18, Sun 19 June (10-5). Adm £4, chd free. Home-made teas. Visits also by arrangement June & July for groups of 5 to 30.**
Artist and designer Jeni Cairns has been creating a garden for enjoyment and nature over the past 13 yrs, It was previously the home of her Grandparents for 60 yrs. Jeni is passionate about plants and learning as much as possible through

experimentation and creativity. She takes inspiration from her garden to create her sculptures and decorative metal work.

32 KING'S COLLEGE FELLOWS' GARDEN AND PROVOST'S GARDEN

Queen's Road, Cambridge, CB2 1ST. Provost & Scholars of King's College, tinyurl.com/kingscol. *In Cambridge, the Backs. Entry by gate at junction of Queen's Rd & West Rd or at King's Parade. Parking at Lion Yard, short walk, or some pay & display places in West Rd & Queen's Rd.* **Sun 3 July (2-5). Adm £6, chd free. Home-made teas.**
Fine example of a Victorian garden with rare specimen trees. Rond Pont entrance leads to a small woodland walk, herbaceous and sub-tropical borders, rose pergola, kitchen/allotment garden and orchard. The Provost's garden opens with kind permission, offering rare glimpse of an Arts and Crafts design. Chance to view the new wildflower meadow created on the former Great Lawn. Wheelchair access, gravel paths.

33 38 KINGSTON STREET

Cambridge, CB1 2NU. Wendy & Clive Chapman. *Central Cambridge. Off Mill Rd, W of railway bridge.* **Sun 5 June (2-6). Adm £3, chd free. Open nearby Cottage Garden.**
A tiny courtyard garden with contrasts between deep shade and sunlit areas. Raised beds and pots of various sizes with a range of perennial and annual planting. Small step into garden.

34 KIRTLING TOWER

Newmarket Road, Kirtling, CB8 9PA. The Lord & Lady Fairhaven. *6m SE of Newmarket. From Newmarket head towards village of Saxon Street, through village to Kirtling, turn L at war memorial, signed to Upend, entrance is signed on the L.* **Sun 27 Mar, Sun 26 June (11-4). Adm £6, chd free. Light refreshments.**
Surrounded by a moat, formal gardens and parkland. In the spring there are swathes of daffodils narcissi crocus muscari, chionodoxa and tulips. Closer to the house are vast lawn areas. Secret and Cutting Gardens. In the summer the Walled Garden

has superb herbaceous borders with anthemis hemerocallis, geraniums and delphiniums. The Victorian Garden is filled with peonies. Views of surrounding countryside. A Classic car display will be in attendance. The Arcadia Recorder Group will be playing in the walled garden. A variety of plant and craft stalls on both dates as well as a display of Stonework from the Fairhaven Stoneyard. Selection of delicious hot and cold food, sandwiches, cakes, tea and coffee. Many of the paths and routes around the garden are grass - they are accessible by wheelchairs, but can be hard work if wet.

35 LANDWADE HALL
Landwade Road, Exning, CB8 7NH. Executors of the late Mr. Simon Gibson. *3m N of Newmarket. From A142 take the turning off r'about to Snailwell past Turners, round a sharp L bend, approx ½ m on R is Landwade Hall.* Sat 19, Sun 20 Feb (10-2). Adm £7.50, chd free. Pre-booking essential, please visit www.ngs.org.uk for information & booking.
4 acre garden with small C15 church. Moat with foundations of the original house. 101 years of snowdrops, aconites and daffodils. A delight in early spring. Wheelchair access to grassed areas (approx 50%) may be hard work on damp ground.

🚺🐕🐶🍵🪑 »))

GROUP OPENING

36 NEW LINTON GARDENS
Mill Lane, Linton, Cambridge, CB21 4JY. Henry & Sarah Bennett. *From A1307 turn into Linton High St and follow signs to car park. Most of the gardens accessible from Church Ln, Mill Ln & Green Ln, which are close to each other.* Sun 15 May (2-6). Combined adm £10, chd £10. Home-made teas at The Old Guildhall.

NEW **94 HIGH STREET**
Rosemary Wellings.

NEW **LINTON HOUSE**
Steve Meeks.

NEW **MILLICENT HOUSE**
Sue Anderson.

NEW **THE OLD GUILDHALL**
Bill Bickerstaff.

NEW **QUEENS HOUSE**
Michael & Alison Wilcockson.

NEW **THE SHRUBBERY**
Henry & Sarah Bennett.

NEW **SUMMERFIELD HOUSE**
Ray & Bridget Linsey.

Seven gardens in the middle of Linton. The largest, Linton House, has the river Granta flowing through, and a pretty bridge. A rose walk, huge trees, and interesting planting, as well as a mulberry tree older than the house. Next door is The Old Guildhall where, in marked contrast with the opulence of its neighbour, there is a romantic and tranquil garden of curves and trees.Queens House near the top of the High Street has a hedged formal garden with statuary which reflects the age and feel of the Grade II* listed house, as well as other pretty areas, full of colour. The Shrubbery is an Edwardian garden with an unusual number of mature trees, separate well defined spaces, and interesting ponds. Summerfield House is an immaculate garden with a plantsman's collection of herbaceous perennials and shrubs, sympathetic hard landscaping and a pleached lime wall. Next door is Millicent House which has a long-established garden again with some unusual planting. 94 High Street is the smallest garden, a secret garden, full of herbs and other edible plants, as well as surprising artefacts. It was substantially worked on during the lockdowns, and is found behind the owner's art gallery

37 LITTLE OAK
66 Station Road, Willingham, Cambridge, CB24 5HG. Mr & Mrs Eileen Hughes, www.littleoak.org.uk/garden. *4m N of A14 J29 nr Cambridge. Easy to find on the main rd in the village. Driveway parking for disabled use only.* Sat 30, Sun 31 July, Sat 6, Sun 7 Aug (1-5). Adm £5, chd free. Light refreshments.
Michael and Eileen welcome you to our 1 acre garden. Featuring a 50' Laburnum Walk with perennial borders, ponds, Cottage Garden, fruit cage, kitchen garden/greenhouses/growing tunnels, orchard, Mediterranean and rose garden, coppice and chickens. Teas and home-made cakes. Picnics Welcome. Weather permitting, Michael will demonstrate woodturning using a pole lathe throughout afternoon

openings. Main garden is wheelchair accessible.

🚺🌸🍵🪑

38 MADINGLEY HALL
Cambridge, CB23 8AQ. University of Cambridge, 01223 746222, reservations@madingleyhall.co.uk, www.madingleyhall.co.uk. *4m W of Cambridge. 1m from M11 J13. Located in the centre of Madingley village. Entrance adjacent to mini r'about.* Sun 19 June (2.30-5.30). Adm £6, chd free. Home-made teas at St Mary Magdalene Church, in the grounds of Madingley Hall.
C16 Hall (not open) set in 8 acres of attractive grounds landscaped by Capability Brown. Features inc landscaped walled garden with hazel walk, alpine bed, medicinal border and rose pergola. Historic meadow, topiary, mature trees and wide variety of hardy plants.

🐕🌸🛏️🍵 »))

39 67 MAIN STREET
Yaxley, Peterborough, PE7 3LZ. Mrs Karen Woods, 07787 864426, karenandstevewoods@yahoo.co.uk. *S of Peterborough, approx 3m from J16 on A1. On entering Yaxley, turn R into Dovecote Lane. At the bottom, turn L onto Main St. Find us approx 1m on R.* Sat 4 June (11-4). Adm £4, chd free. Visits also by arrangement May to Sept.
1 acre working organic cottage garden providing something for the kitchen and vase year-round. Seasonal cut flowers grown in raised beds and traditional borders. Allotment style vegetable garden. Paddock with fruit trees and views over the fen to the rear. Chickens for eggs. We enjoy working alongside the wildlife that we share our garden with.

🍵🪑

The National Garden Scheme searches the length and breadth of England and Wales for the very best private gardens

40 NEW THE MANOR HOUSE

Lower End, Swaffham Prior, Cambridge, CB25 0HT. Mr Adrian & Mrs Catherine Dickens. *Between Cambridge & Newmarket. 3m from NT Anglesey Abbey. From W, Exit J35 at Quy onto B1102 for Swaffhams & Anglesey Abbey. After 4m 1st L into Swaffham Prior, past churches to Lower End. From East, B1102, 1st R into Rogers Road. L at end.* **Sat 4, Sun 5 June (10-6). Adm £7, chd free. Home-made teas. Picnics in adjacent paddocks welcome.**

4 acre formal/informal garden surrounding partly dry moated Manor House (not open). Traditional areas, mature trees, small arboretum, orchard, 30metre herbaceous bed. Picket fenced vegetable garden/ feature greenhouse. Fruit cage. Part reconfigured in 2016 by Thomas Hoblyn, (will be visiting) to inc grass border, alpine bed and low maintenance planting. Far reaching views. Picnics in Paddock. Wheelchair access sloping gravel drive access. Some further slopes but all areas accessible with some pushing!

♿ 🐎 D ☕ 🍽))

41 ♦ THE MANOR, HEMINGFORD GREY

Hemingford Grey, PE28 9BN. Mrs D S Boston, 01480 463134, diana_boston@hotmail.com, www.greenknowe.co.uk. *4m E of Huntingdon. Off A1307. Parking for NGS opening day ONLY in field off double bends between Hemingford Grey & Hemingford Abbots. This will be signed. Entrance to garden via small gate off river towpath.* **For NGS: Sat 11, Sun 12 June (11-5). Adm £6, chd free. Home-made teas in the garden on NGS weekend only. For other opening times and information, please phone, email or visit garden website.**

Garden designed by author Lucy Boston, surrounds C12 manor house on which Green Knowe books based (house open by appt). 3 acre 'cottage' garden with topiary, snowdrops, old roses, extensive collection of irises inc Dykes Medal winners and Cedric Morris varieties, herbaceous borders with mainly scented plants. Meadow with mown paths. Enclosed by river, moat and wilderness. Late May splendid show of irises followed by the old roses. Care is taken with the planting to start the year with a large variety of snowdrops and to extend the flowering season through to the first frosts with colour from unusual annuals. The garden is interesting even in winter with the topiary. Gravel paths, wheelchairs are encouraged to go on the lawns.

♿ 🐎 ✿ �"☕))

42 NEW MARMALADE LANE, COHOUSING COMMUNITY GARDEN

09 Marmalade Lane, Orchard Park, Cambridge, CB4 2ZE. Cambridge Cohousing Ltd, www.cambridge-k1.co.uk/. *Please arrive at the Common House & take a seat outside. A guide will conduct you. Please arrive by public transport, parking on site for disabled visitors. We are very close to Orchard Park East Bus Stop, Mere Rd bus stop. Cambridge North Stn is a short taxi or bus ride.* **Sat 18 June (10-4). Adm £5, chd free. Pre-booking essential, please visit www.ngs.org.uk for information & booking. Home-made teas.**

Community Garden owned, created and looked after by residents. A path circumnavigates the main garden.

♿ ☕ 🍽

43 NEW MILTON HALL

Milton Park, Milton, Peterborough, PE6 7AG. Lady Isabella Naylor-Leyland. *Please use entrance off A47, shared with Peterborough (Milton) Golf Club.* **Sun 8 May (10.30-5.30). Adm £8, chd free. Home-made teas.**

20 acres of pleasure grounds laid out by Humphry Repton in 1791 inc lake, mature trees, extensive lawns, hard gravel paths, historic orangery. Enclosed walled Italian garden and kitchen garden. Teas served in orangery all day. Garden level, with hard gravel surfaced paths.

♿ 🐎 ✿ ☕))

GROUP OPENING

44 MOLESWORTH & BRINGTON GARDENS

Molesworth, Huntingdon, PE28 0QD. *10m W of Huntingdon. A14 W for Molesworth & Brington exit at J16 onto B660.* **Sun 12 June (2-6). Combined adm £5, chd free. Home-made teas at Molesworth.**

MOLESWORTH HOUSE
John Prentis.

YEW TREE COTTAGE
Christine & Don Eggleston.

Molesworth House is an old rectory garden with everything that you'd both expect and hope for, given its Victorian past. There are surprising corners to this traditional take on a happy and relaxed, yet also formal garden. Yew Tree Cottage, informal garden approx 1 acre, complements the C16 building (not open) and comprises flower beds, lawns, vegetable patch, boggy garden, copses and orchard. Plants in pots and hanging baskets.

♿ 🐎 ✿ ☕

Milton Hall

© Simon Baylis

45 MUSIC MAZE AND GARDEN

Troy Green, 2a Nine Chimneys Lane, Balsham, Cambridge, CB21 4ES. Mr Jim & Mrs Hilary Potter, 01223 891211, hppotter@btinternet.com, www.musicmaze.org. *In centre of Balsham just off High St. 3m E of A11, 12m S of Newmarket & 10m SE of Cambridge. Car parking in the High St or the Church car park. 2 disabled spaces in Nine Chimneys Ln.* **Visits by arrangement Mar to Oct. £10 per person for groups of up to 24 people, min £100. Personally conducted tour by Jim and Hilary lasting 2 hours with interval for tea, biscuits and a chat.**

Formal front garden with a great variety of flowering plants, shrubs and raised vegetable beds. Peaceful and spacious rear parkland with Hedge Maze - fun for all ages. Wildflower meadow, butterflies, many mature and new trees, lawns, modern sculptures and a large duck pond. Hard paths around formal garden area. Limited wheelchair access to parkland but fine in dry weather with a good driver.

46 NETHERHALL MANOR

Tanners Lane, Soham, CB7 5AB. Timothy Clark, 01353 720269, timothy.r.clark@btinternet.com. *6m Ely, 6m Newmarket. Enter Soham from Newmarket, Tanners Ln 2nd R 100yds after cemetery. Enter Soham from Ely, Tanners Ln 2nd L after War Memorial.* **Sun 3 Apr, Sun 1 May, Sun 7, Sun 14 Aug (2-5). Adm £3, chd free. Visits also by arrangement Apr to Aug for groups of 5 to 15.**

Elegant garden 'touched with antiquity'. Good Gardens Guide 2000. Unusual garden appealing to those with historical interest in individual collections of plant groups: March-old primroses, daffodils, Victorian double flowered hyacinths and first garden hellebore hybrids. May-old English tulips, Crown Imperials. Aug-Victorian pelargonium, heliotrope, calceolaria, dahlias. Author-Margery Fish's Country Gardening and Mary McMurtrie's Country Garden Flowers Historic Plants 1500-1900. The only bed of English tulips on display in the country. Author's books for sale. Featured on Gardeners' World three times. Wheelchair access flat garden with two optional steps. Lawns.

47 THE NIGHT GARDEN

37 Honeyhill, Paston, Peterborough, PE4 7DR. Andrea Connor, 07801 987905, andrea.connors@ntlworld.com, www.gardenofsanctuary.co.uk. *From A47 Soke Parkway at J19. Take exit N on Topmoor Way. R at next r'about (3rd exit) to Paston Ridings, over the speed humps. Take 4th L to Honeyhill. 1st R into car park. No.37 at top L corner.* **Evening opening Tue 16, Wed 17, Thur 18 Aug (7.30-10). Adm £6, chd free. Light refreshments in garden, or house if weather inclement. Tea, coffee, wine, cake and biscuits. Visits also by arrangement July to Oct for groups of 10 to 20.**

Designed with mental wellbeing and relaxation in mind The Night Garden is a magical space in which to unwind at the end of the day, gently easing your mood as the lights appear, leaving your spirits uplifted by the full spectacle as night falls. Best viewed in the evening, relax at dusk and watch the transformation as the light fades and the myriad of solar lights build to an illumination festival of colour.

48 38 NORFOLK TERRACE GARDEN

Cambridge, CB1 2NG. John Tordoff & Maurice Reeve. *Central Cambridge. A603 East Rd turn R into St Matthews St to Norfolk St, L into Blossom St & Norfolk Terrace is at the end.* **Sat 2, Sun 3 July (11-6). Adm £3, chd free. Home-made teas.**

A small, paved courtyard garden in Moroccan style. Masses of colour, backed by oriental arches. An ornamental pool done in patterned tiles.The garden won third prize in the 2018 Gardener's World national competition. It is also inc in the book 'The Secret Gardens of East Anglia'.The owners' previous, London garden, was named by BBC Gardeners' World as 'Best Small Garden in Britain'. There will also be a display of recent paintings by John Tordoff and handmade books by Maurice Reeve.

49 THE OLD RECTORY

312 Main Road, Parson Drove, Wisbech, PE13 4LF. Helen Roberts. *SW of Wisbech. From Peterborough on A47 follow signs to Parson Drove L after Thorney Toll.*

From Wisbech follow the B1166 through Leverington Common. **Sun 12 June (11-4). Adm £5, chd free. Home-made teas.**

After parking in our field walk through the wildflower meadow and paddocks, past the long pond and then enter the main walled cottage style garden under our new moon gate. No hills but lovely open Fen views. A classical Georgian house and trying to make a classical English garden!

50 NEW PAMPISFORD ALLOTMENTS

Brewery Road, Pampisford, CB22 3EW. Mr Graeme Udall, 01223 833682, graemeudall@btinternet.com. *5m SE of Cambridge. From A505 turn onto Town Lane, Pampisford, allotment ¼ m on R. From London Rd Sawston take Brewery Rd Pampisford Allotment 300yds on L.* **Sun 14 Aug (11-4.30). Adm £5, chd free. Home-made teas in the garden of 47 Brewery Road, Pampisford opposite the allotments. Visits also by arrangement in Aug.**

A big organic, bee friendly allotment with a large variety of traditional vegetables together with a free range chicken area. Visitors will have the opportunity to discuss all aspects of preparing and planting up an allotment. Allotment paths are grassed and uneven. Guide dogs only.

51 23A PERRY ROAD

Buckden, St Neots, PE19 5XG. David & Valerie Bunnage, 01480 810553, d.bunnage@btinternet.com. *5m S of Huntingdon on A1. From A1 Buckden r'about take B661, Perry Rd approx 300yds on L.* **Every Fri, Sat and Sun 6 May to 28 Aug (2-5). Adm £4, chd free. Pre-booking essential, please visit www.ngs.org.uk for information & booking. Visits also by arrangement May to Aug.**

Approx 1 acre garden of many garden designs inc japanese interlinked by gravel paths. Plantsmans garden 155 acers and unusual shrubs. Quirky garden with interesting features some narrow paths not suitable for wheelchairs. Regret no dogs. WC. Coaches welcome.

52 PREACHERS PASSING
55 Station Road, Tilbrook, Huntingdon, PE28 0JT. Keith & Rosamund Nancekievill. *Tilbrook 4½m S of J16 on A14. Station Rd in Tilbrook can be accessed from the B645 or B660. Preachers Passing faces the small bridge over the River Til at a sharp bend in Station Rd with All Saints church behind it.* Sat 16, Sun 17 July (10.30-5). Adm £5, chd free. Home-made teas. ³/4 acre garden fits into its pastoral setting. Near the house, parterre, courtyard and terrace offer formality; but beyond, prairie planting leads to a wildlife pond, rock gardens, meadow, stumpery, rose garden and copse. Enjoy different views from arbour, honeysuckle-covered swing or scattered benches. Deciduous trees and perennials give changing colour. Here are open spaces and hidden places.

53 QUERCUS
Bradley Road, Burrough Green, Newmarket, CB8 9NH. Dulce Threlfall, 01638 508470, thedulcethrelfall@gmail.com. *5m S of Newmarket. First house on L entering Burrough Green from Newmarket immed after 30 speed limit.* Visits by arrangement Apr to Sept for groups of 10 to 30. Adm £10, chd free. Home-made teas inc in price.
There are 7 different areas in this renovated, replanted, redesigned and evolving 1½ acre garden. Mirrored mixed borders, roses, shade plants, vegetables, orchard, interesting trees, greenhouse. Recently completed large natural swimming pool with decking and eating area. Many lovely aquatic plants and wildlife. Wheelchair access to all garden.

54 ROBINSON COLLEGE
Grange Road, Cambridge, CB3 9AN. Warden and Fellows, www.robinson.cam.ac.uk/about-robinson/gardens/national-gardens-scheme. *Garden at main Robinson College site, report to Porters' Lodge. There is only on-street parking.* Mon 11 July to Fri 12 Aug, Mon 5 Sept to Sat 31 Dec (exc Sun 25 and Mon 26 Dec). Weekdays (10-4), weekends (2-4). Adm £5, chd free. Pre-booking essential, please visit www.ngs.org.uk for information & booking. 10 original Edwardian gardens are

linked to central wild woodland water garden focusing on Bin Brook with small lake at heart of site. This gives a feeling of park and informal woodland, while at the same time keeping the sense of older more formal gardens beyond. Central area has a wide lawn running down to the lake framed by many mature stately trees with much of the original planting intact. More recent planting inc herbaceous borders and commemorative trees. Please take ticket to Porters' Lodge on arrival and collect guidebook. No picnics. Children must be accompanied at all times. NB from time to time some parts, or occasionally all, of Robinson College gardens may be closed for safety reasons involving work by contractors and our maintenance staff. Please report to Porters' Lodge on arrival for information. Ask at Porters' Lodge for wheelchair access.

GROUP OPENING

55 SAWSTON GARDENS
Sawston, CB22 3HY. *5m SE of Cambridge. Midway between Saffron Walden & Cambridge on A1301.* Sun 3 July (1-5). Combined adm £6, chd free. Home-made teas in Mary Challis Garden, 68 High Street. served from 1.30-4.00pm.

BROOK HOUSE
Mr Ian & Mrs Mia Devereux.

NEW 34 CAMBRIDGE ROAD
Mrs Mary Hollyhead.

♦ MARY CHALLIS GARDEN
A M Challis Trust Ltd, 01223 560816, chair@challistrust.org.uk, www.challistrust.org.uk.

11 MILL LANE
Tim & Rosie Phillips.

22 ST MARY'S ROAD
Ann & Mike Redshaw.

5 gardens in this large South Cambs. village. Brook House has many delightful features in 1½ acres of a grade II listed house, inc a pond with expansive patio and pergolas, and a large walled kitchen garden with greenhouse, raised beds and herbaceous borders. 11 Mill Lane is an attractive C16/C19 house with an impressive semi-circular front lawn edged with roses and mixed borders, and a secluded sun-dappled garden at the rear. A large wildlife-friendly family garden at 22 St Mary's Road

has colour themed borders, pond, fruit trees, gravel beds, raised salad beds and beehives, and good views over SSSI meadows. 34 Cambridge Road features a long rear garden, with meticulously maintained lawns, colourful borders, mature trees and shrubs, small pond and fruit and vegetable plots. The 2 acre Mary Challis Garden, maintained by volunteers, opens on four days every week, with lawns, wildflower meadow, herbaceous borders, orchard, vegetable beds, vinehouse and beehives. Nearly all parts of the gardens are accessible by wheelchair.

56 THE SIX HOUSES
33-45 Comberton Road, Barton, Cambridge, CB23 7BA. Perennial. Sun 18 Sept (1-5). Adm £5, chd free. Home-made teas. Opening with Barton Gardens on Sun 3 Apr, Sun 5 June.
Gardens surrounding small bungalow complex housing retired gardeners. Individual gardens at each bungalow. Communal garden with specimen trees, naturalised bulbs and gorgeous herbaceous borders.

GROUP OPENING

57 STAPLOE GARDENS
Staploe, St Neots, PE19 5JA. 07702 707880, caroline-falling@hotmail.co.uk. *Great North Rd in western part of St Neots. At r'about just N of the Coop store, exit westwards on Duloe Rd. Follow this under the A1, through the village of Duloe & on to Staploe.* Sun 24 Apr (1-5). Sat 11, Sun 12 June (1-5). Home-made teas at Falling Water House. Combined adm £6, chd free. Visits also by arrangement May to Oct. For groups of 5+.

FALLING WATER HOUSE
Caroline Kent.

OLD FARM COTTAGE
Sir Graham & Lady Fry.

Old Farm Cottage: Formal and terraced beds with rose, lavender, lawns, surrounding thatched house (not open), leading to 3 acres of orchard, wildflower meadow, woodland and pond maintained for wildlife. Ginkgo, loquat and manuka trees grown from seed. Cherry blossom brightens the spring, and

in summer bees and butterflies are attracted to the flower-beds and meadow. Falling Water House: a mature woodland garden, partly reclaimed from farmland 10 yrs ago and constructed around several century old trees inc three Wellingtonia. Kitchen garden potager, courtyard and herbaceous borders, planted to attract bees and wildlife, through which meandering paths have created hidden vistas. Wheelchair access, Old Farm Cottage has uneven ground and one steep slope.

GROUP OPENING

58 TOFT GARDENS
Toft, Cambridge, CB23 2RY. *8m W of Cambridge. Park on main road or near church & follow yellow signs.* Sun 3 July (12-5). Combined adm £5, chd free. Home-made teas.

21 COMBERTON ROAD
Mr Sheppard.
NEW **THE GIG HOUSE**
Jane Tebbit.
NEW **MANOR COTTAGE**
Mrs Mary Paxman.
OLD FARM
Kay Brown.

The Gig House: cottage garden with roses, clematis, perennials, cut flower beds and vegetables. Also plants for natural dyes, dry beds, wild flowers, a small wildlife pond, tiny orchard and plenty of places to sit. Manor Cottage: cottage garden extended and developed by the current owner over 30 yrs. Herbaceous borders, vegetable garden, greenhouse and orchard covering an acre, as well as a paddock and two wooded areas. Borders extended and replanted in 2020 when various grasses, salvias and alliums were added. Old Farm: south facing cottage garden with island beds and grass paths. Further area with vegetable beds, flower cutting beds and a small wild grass area with wild flowers and trees. Also a living roof on garden room. 21 Comberton Road: the basic concept was conceived before moving in, calling on a wide range of sources and experiences. Four zones in 0.18 acres, 123 taxa, 450 plants; one afternoon to view this newly planted garden.

59 TWIN TARNS
6 Pinfold Lane, Somersham, PE28 3EQ. Michael & Frances Robinson, 07938 174536, mikerobinson987@btinternet.com. *Easy access from the A14. 4m NE of St Ives. Turn onto Church St. Pinfold Ln is next to the church. Please park on Church Street as access is narrow & limited.* Sat 25, Sun 26 June (1-6). Adm £5, chd free. Cream teas. Visits also by arrangement May to Sept for groups of up to 30.
1 acre wildlife garden with formal borders, kitchen garden and ponds, large rockery, mini woodland, wildflower meadow (June/July). Topiary, rose walk, greenhouses. Character oak bridge, veranda and treehouse. Adjacent to C13 village church.

60 WILD ROSE COTTAGE
Church Walk, Lode, Cambridge, CB25 9EX. Mrs Joy Martin, 07565 694662, joymartin123@outlook.com. *From A14 take the rd towards Burwell turn L into Lode & park on L after 150 metres next to the Shed Walk straight on between thatched cottages to the archway of Wild Rose Cottage.* Evening opening Wed 22 June (6-8). Adm £5, chd free. Wine and home made elderflower is available by donation on the evening opening. Visits also by arrangement Apr to Oct.
A real cottage garden overflowing with plants. Gardens within gardens of abundant vegetation, roses climbing through trees, laburnum tunnel, a daffodil spiral which becomes a daisy spiral in the summer. Circular vegetable garden and wildlife pond. Described by one visitor as a garden to write poetry in! It is a truly wild and loved garden where flowers in the vegetable circle are not pulled up! Geese, a dog, circular vegetable garden, wild life pond, and wild romantic garden! Food and drink available at 'The Shed'.

61 THE WINDMILL
10 Cambridge Road, Impington, CB24 9NU. Pippa & Steve Temple, 07775 446443, mill.impington@ntlworld.com, www.impingtonmill.org. *2½ m N of Cambridge. Off A14 at J32, B1049 to Histon, L into Cambridge Rd at*

T-lights, follow Cambridge Rd round to R, the Windmill is approx 400yds on L. Visits by arrangement Apr to Oct for groups of up to 50. Adm £5, chd free. Light refreshments inc coffee/tea/wine and nibbles by arrangement.
A previously romantic wilderness of 1½ acres surrounding windmill, now filled with bulbs, perennial beds, pergolas, bog gardens, grass bed and herb bank. Secret paths and wild areas with thuggish roses maintain the romance. Millstone seating area in smouldering borders contrasts with the pastel colours of the remainder of the garden. Also 'Pond Life' seat, 'Tree God' and amazing compost area! The Windmill - an C18 smock on C19 tower on C17 base on C16 foundations - is being restored. Guide dogs only.

62 WOLFSON COLLEGE GARDEN
Barton Road, Cambridge, CB3 9BB. Wolfson College. *On SW side of Cambridge. From M11 J12, take A603 into Cambridge. Wolfson College is approx 2m from J12, on L.* Sat 9 July (12-4). Adm £5, chd free. Light refreshments.
Wolfson garden is comprised of mixed garden rooms over a 10 acre site. We have year-round interest and always something to see and find interest in. We have a small amount of themed gardens from exotic to Chinese and winter gardens, bringing plants from all over the world to create a enticing visual that you will want to take a piece home for yourself. We have a team of four gardeners and so we are able to teach and inspire about what we do well when visitors come to see us. Cosy rooms of mixed planting, lots of topiary to find within borders. Courtyards with fine lawns and mature trees. Sir Vivian Fuchs garden, home once to the Artic explorer. herbaceous pot designs and seasonally planted beds. Formal mixed with the informal around beautiful buildings. Ramps and lowered curbs are onsite and use of disabled facilities in the porters lodge. All paths are wide enough for disabled access.

CHESHIRE & WIRRAL

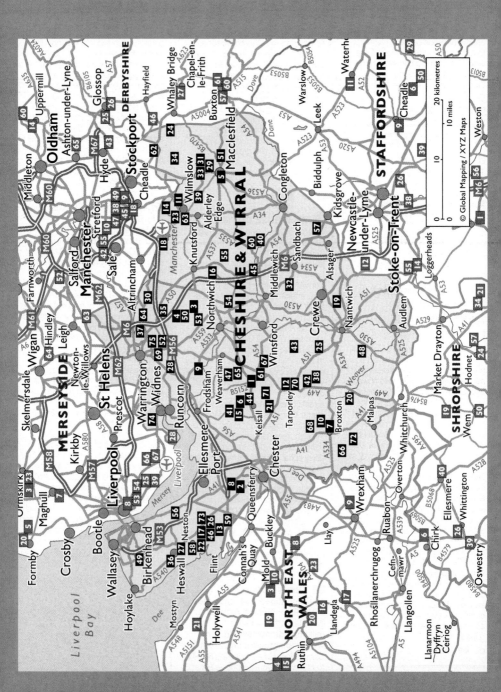

The area of Cheshire and Wirral comprises what are now the four administrative regions of West Cheshire and Chester, East Cheshire, Warrington and Wirral, together with gardens in the south of Greater Manchester, Trafford and Stockport.

The perception of the area is that of a fertile county dominated by the Cheshire Plain, but to the extreme west it enjoys a mild maritime climate, with gardens often sitting on sandstone and sandy soils and enjoying mildly acidic conditions.

A large sandstone ridge also rises out of the landscape, running some 30-odd miles from north to south. Many gardens grow ericaceous-loving plants, although in some areas, the slightly acidic soil is quite clayey. But the soil is rarely too extreme to prevent the growing of a wide range of plants, both woody and herbaceous.

As one travels east and the region rises up the foothills of the Pennine range, the seasons become somewhat harsher, with spring starting a few weeks later than in the coastal region.

As well as being home to one of the RHS's major shows, the region's gardens include two National Garden Scheme 'founder' gardens in Arley Hall and Peover Hall, as well as the University of Liverpool Botanic Garden at Ness.

Below: 45 Needham Drive

f @National Garden Scheme Cheshire & Wirral CheshireWirrNGS

Volunteers

County Organiser
Janet Bashforth
07809 030525
jan.bashforth@ngs.org.uk

County Treasurer
Andrew Collin
01513 393 614
andrewcollin@btinternet.com

Booklet Co-ordinator
John Hinde
0151 353 0032
johnhinde059@gmail.com

Booklet Advertising
Linda Enderby
07949 496747
linda.enderby@ngs.org.uk

Social Media & Publicity
Jacquie Denyer
jacquie.denyer@ngs.org.uk

Assistant County Organisers
Sue Bryant
0161 928 3819
suewestlakebryant@btinternet.com

Jean Davies
01606 892383
mrsjeandavies@gmail.com

Sandra Fairclough
0151 342 4645
sandrafairclough51@gmail.com

Richard Goodyear
01270 528944
richard.goodyear@ngs.org.uk

Juliet Hill
01829 732804
t.hill573@btinternet.com

Romy Holmes
01829 732053
romy@bowmerecottage.co.uk

Mike Porter
01925 753488
porters@mikeandgailporter.co.uk

OPENING DATES

All entries subject to change. For latest information check www.ngs.org.uk

Map locator numbers are shown to the right of each garden name.

February

Snowdrop Festival

Saturday 19th
Briarfield 13

Sunday 20th
Briarfield 13

Sunday 27th
Bucklow Farm 16

April

Saturday 2nd
Adswood 2

Sunday 3rd
Adswood 2
Parm Place 53

Monday 11th
◆ Arley Hall & Gardens 4

Saturday 16th
Poulton Hall 56

Sunday 17th
Long Acre 38
Poulton Hall 56

Saturday 23rd
Adswood 2

Sunday 24th
Adswood 2
Hill Farm 32

May

Sunday 1st
All Fours Farm 3
Laskey Farm 37
10 Statham Avenue 64

Monday 2nd
All Fours Farm 3
Framley 26
Laskey Farm 37
10 Statham Avenue 64

Thursday 5th
◆ Cholmondeley Castle
Gardens 20

Saturday 7th
Hathaway 29

Sunday 8th
◆ Abbeywood Gardens 1
Briarfield 13
Hathaway 29
Tirley Garth Gardens 71

Saturday 14th
Brooke Cottage 14
64 Carr Wood 18

Sunday 15th
Brooke Cottage 14
◆ Mount Pleasant 44
Sandymere 61
◆ Stonyford Cottage 65
Tirley Garth Gardens 71

Saturday 21st
NEW Bankhead 7
Holmecroft 34

Sunday 22nd
Holmecroft 34
Manley Knoll 41
NEW 45 Needham Drive 45

Wednesday 25th
10 Statham Avenue 64

Saturday 28th
The Old Parsonage 50

Sunday 29th
Delfan 22
Hill Farm 32
The Old Parsonage 50
Rowley House 60
Tattenhall Hall 68
Tiresford 70
Tirley Garth Gardens 71

June

Saturday 4th
Laskey Farm 37
◆ Peover Hall Gardens 55

Sunday 5th
Laskey Farm 37
◆ Peover Hall Gardens 55

Saturday 11th
Ashmead 5
NEW Bankhead 7
NEW 9 Chalfield Close 19
Drake Carr 24
Mayfield House 42
One House Walled
Garden 51

10 Statham Avenue 64

Sunday 12th
Ashmead 5
Bucklow Farm 16
NEW 9 Chalfield Close 19
Drake Carr 24
Hill Farm 32
Mayfield House 42
One House Walled
Garden 51
10 Statham Avenue 64

Saturday 18th
Ashmead 5
NEW Dial House 23
18 Highfield Road 31
NEW Longcroft 39
Stretton Old Hall 66
Willaston Grange 73

Sunday 19th
Ashmead 5
Hall Lane Farm 28
18 Highfield Road 31
Long Acre 38
NEW 45 Needham Drive 45
15 Park Crescent 52
Stretton Old Hall 66
NEW The Wonky
Garden 74

Saturday 25th
All Fours Farm 3
Holmecroft 34
The Homestead 35

Sunday 26th
All Fours Farm 3
Burton Village
Gardens 17
Clemley House 21
Holmecroft 34
The Homestead 35
24 Old Greasby Road 49
Parm Place 53

Wednesday 29th
10 Statham Avenue 64

July

Saturday 2nd
◆ Bluebell Cottage
Gardens 9

Sunday 3rd
Ashton Grange 6
◆ Bluebell Cottage
Gardens 9
NEW 5 Pennys Lane 54

Sunday 10th
Rowley House 60

10 Statham Avenue 64

Sunday 12th
Ashmead 5
Bucklow Farm 16
NEW 9 Chalfield Close 19
Drake Carr 24
Hill Farm 32
Mayfield House 42
One House Walled
Garden 51
10 Statham Avenue 64

Saturday 16th
Inglewood 36
Laskey Farm 37
NEW The Old Byre 48

Sunday 17th
Inglewood 36
Laskey Farm 37
NEW The Old Byre 48
NEW The Wonky
Garden 74

Saturday 23rd
5 Gayton Lane 27
Milford House Farm 43

Sunday 24th
The Firs 25
5 Gayton Lane 27
Norley Bank Farm 47
Rose Brae 58

Thursday 28th
The Firs 25

Saturday 30th
The Birches 8
21 Scafell Close 62
Stretton Old Hall 66

Sunday 31st
The Birches 8
Norley Bank Farm 47
21 Scafell Close 62
Stretton Old Hall 66

August

Sunday 28th
Laskey Farm 37

Monday 29th
Laskey Farm 37

September

Sunday 4th
◆ Mount Pleasant 44
NEW The Wonky
Garden 74

Tuesday 13th
◆ Ness Botanic
Gardens 46

Sunday 18th
◆ Abbeywood Gardens 1

Saturday 24th
Thorncar 69

October

Sunday 9th
◆ The Lovell Quinta
Arboretum 40

February 2023

Sunday 26th
Bucklow Farm 16

By Arrangement

Arrange a personalised garden visit with your club, or group of friends, on a date to suit you. See individual garden entries for full details.

During 2020 – 2021 National Garden Scheme funding supported over 1,400 Queen's Nurses to deliver virtual and hands-on, community care across England, Wales and Northern Ireland

THE GARDENS

❶ ◆ ABBEYWOOD GARDENS
Chester Road, Delamere, Northwich, CW8 2HS. The Rowlinson Family, 01606 889477, info@abbeywoodestate.co.uk, www.abbeywoodestate.co.uk. *11m E of Chester. On the A556 facing Delamere Church.* For NGS: Sun 8 May, Sun 18 Sept (9-5). Adm £6, chd free. Restaurant in Garden. For other opening times and information, please phone, email or visit garden website. Superb setting near Delamere Forest. Total area 45 acres inc mature woodland, new woodland and new arboretum all with connecting pathways. Approx 4½ acres of gardens surrounding large Edwardian house. Vegetable garden, exotic garden, chapel garden, pool garden, woodland garden, lawned area with beds.

& 🐎 ✿ ♿ 🚌 ☕

❷ ADSWOOD
Townfield Lane, Mollington, CH1 6LB. Ken & Helen Black, 01244 851327, keneblack@outlook.com, www.kenblackclematis.com. *3m N of Chester. From Wirral take A540 towards Chester. Cross A55 at r'about, past Wheatsheaf pub, turn L into Overwood Lane. At T junction*

turn R into Townfield Lane. Parking will be signed. Sat 2, Sun 3, Sat 23, Sun 24 Apr (10-4). Adm £5, chd free. Pre-booking essential, please visit www.ngs.org.uk for information & booking. Home-made teas. Pls note the garden will be closed between 12 - 2 pm. Visits also by arrangement Apr to July for groups of 6 to 20. Refreshments available on request.
A cottage garden with a wide range of perennials, climbers and English roses.The garden has over 150 varieties of clematis, providing colour throughout the year. There are several seating areas inc a garden pavilion. Book on April dates for tours of early spring flowered clematis - as featured on Gardeners' World. Packs of young clematis to start your own collection can be purchased. There are no steps but the front drive and some of the garden paths are gravelled and side access to the garden is quite narrow.

& 🐎 ✿ ♿ ☕))

❸ ALL FOURS FARM
Colliers Lane, Aston by Budworth, Northwich, CW9 6NF. Mr & Mrs Evans, 01565 733286. *M6 J19, take A556 towards Northwich. Turn immed R, past The Windmill pub. Turn R after approx 1m, follow rd, garden on L after approx 2m. Direct access available for drop off & collection for those with limited mobility.* Sun 1, Mon 2 May, Sat 25,

Sun 26 June (10-4). Adm £5, chd free. Home-made teas. Visits also by arrangement May & June for groups of 20+.
A traditional and well established country garden with a wide range of roses, hardy shrubs, bulbs, perennials and annuals. You will also find a small vegetable garden, pond and greenhouse as well as vintage machinery and original features from its days as a working farm. The garden is adjacent to the family's traditional rose nursery. The majority of the garden is accessible by wheelchair.

& ✿ ♿ ☕

National Garden Scheme gardens are identified by their yellow road signs and posters. You can expect a garden of quality, character and interest, a warm welcome and plenty of home-made cakes!

4 ◆ ARLEY HALL & GARDENS
Arley, Northwich, CW9 6NA.
Viscount Ashbrook,
01565 777353, enquiries@
arleyhallandgardens.com,
www.arleyhallandgardens.com.
*10m from Warrington. Signed from
J9 & 10 (M56) & J19 & 20 (M6)
(20 min from Tatton Park, 40 min
to Manchester). Please follow the
brown tourist signs.* **For NGS: Mon
11 Apr (10-4.30). Adm £10, chd
£4. All refreshments available.**
**For other opening times and
information, please phone, email or
visit garden website.**
Within Arley's 8 acres of formal
garden there are many different
areas, each with its own distinctive
character. Beyond the Chapel is The
Grove, a well established arboretum
and a woodland walk of about
another 6 or 7 acres. Gardens are
wheelchair accessible, however parts
of the estate have cobbles which
can prove a little difficult for manual
wheelchairs.

5 ASHMEAD
2 Bramhall Way, off Gritstone
Drive, Macclesfield, SK10 3SH.
Peter & Penelope McDermott. *1m
W of Macclesfield. Turn onto Pavilion
Way, off Victoria Rd , then immed L
onto Gritstone Drive. Bramhall Way
first on R.* **Sat 11, Sun 12, Sat 18,
Sun 19 June (1-5). Adm £4, chd
free. Home-made teas.**
⅛ acre suburban cottage garden,
featuring plant packed mixed borders,
rock gardens, kitchen garden, island
beds, water feature, pond. The
garden demonstrates how small
spaces can be planted to maximum
effect to create all round interest.
Extensive range of plants favoured
for colours, texture and scent. Pots
used in a creative way to extend and
enhance borders.

6 ASHTON GRANGE
Grange Road, Ashton Hayes,
Chester, CH3 8AE. Martin &
Kate Slack, 01829 759172,
kateslack1@icloud.com. *8m E of
Chester. Grange Rd is a single track
road off B5393, by the village sign
at N end of Ashton Hayes.* **Sun 3
July (12-4.30). Adm £6, chd free.
Home-made teas. Visits also
by arrangement May to Aug for
groups of 10 to 30.**
Ashton Grange has a traditional
country house garden with sweeping

lawns, herbaceous borders, kitchen
garden and unusual trees. You
can also wander through mature
woodlands, see tree carvings, visit
the wildflower meadow with lovely
views and sit by a large wildlife
pond. The garden, meadows and
woodlands open to visitors extend
to approximately 12 acres. Picnics
welcome. Wheelchair access to most
parts of the garden but woodland
paths could be difficult. Limited
parking for wheelchair users.

7 NEW BANKHEAD
Old Coach Road, Barnhill, Chester,
CH3 9JL. Simon & Sian Preston.
*10 m S of Chester. End of Old Coach
Rd at the junction with A534.* **Sat 21
May, Sat 11 June (12-4). Adm £7,
chd free. Light refreshments.**
Two acres of terraced gardens
developed from Victorian times with
spectacular views south and west
over the Dee valley towards the
Welsh hills. Rose garden, herbaceous
borders, large pond with Japanese
style garden, rhododendrons and
azaleas. Small orchard and vegetable
garden. Shetland ponies and
chickens.

8 THE BIRCHES
Grove Road, Mollington, Chester,
CH1 6LG. Martin Bentley & Colin
Williams. *3m N of Chester. From
the A540 Parkgate Rd turn onto
Coal Pit Lane & follow around until
it becomes Grove Rd. Pass riding
stables on R, gardens approx ¼ m
further on R.* **Sat 30, Sun 31 July
(12-5). Adm £5, chd free. Home-
made teas. Wine.**
½ acre of gardens comprising
of front night garden with pale/
white herbaceous borders. Back
garden split into 5 distinct areas:
Koi and wildlife pond with two large
herbaceous borders, grasses and
tropical border with fernery, orchard
with hens and bees, vegetable garden
and a wildlife stream with bog plants
and sunken garden. Level garden with
lawn or pathways to most areas.

**9 ◆ BLUEBELL COTTAGE
GARDENS**
Lodge Lane, Dutton, WA4 4HP.
Sue Beesley, 01928 713718,
info@bluebellcottage.co.uk,
www.bluebellcottage.co.uk. *5m
NW of Northwich. From M56 (J10)
take A49 to Whitchurch. After 3m*

*turn R at T-lights towards Runcorn/
Dutton on A533. Then 1st L. Signed
with brown tourism signs from A533.*
**For NGS: Sat 2, Sun 3 July (10-5).
Adm £5, chd free. Home-made
teas. For other opening times and
information, please phone, email or
visit garden website.**
South facing country garden wrapped
around a cottage on a quiet rural
lane in the heart of Cheshire. Packed
with thousands of rare and familiar
hardy herbaceous perennials, shrubs
and trees. Unusual plants available
at adjacent nursery. The opening
dates coincide with the peak of
flowering in the herbaceous borders.
Picnics welcome in the meadow area
adjacent to the car park. Some gravel
paths. Wheelchair access to 90% of
garden. WC is not fully wheelchair
accessible.

10 BOLESWORTH CASTLE
Tattenhall, CH3 9HQ. Mrs
Anthony Barbour, 01829 782210,
dcb@bolesworth.com,
www.bolesworth.com. *8m S of
Chester on A41. Enter through
Broxton gate on Bolesworth Hill Rd
using postcode CH3 9HN.* **Visits
by arrangement Apr & May for
groups of 6 to 30. Adm £5, chd
free.**
Set on top of a sandstone ridge,
a collection of rhododendrons,
azaleas, camellias and specimen
shrubs and trees planted in the
90s and undergoing restoration
and development with exciting new
planting. Well-stocked herbaceous
borders within the castle garden,
dotted with unusual and rare trees
planted over a period of 25 yrs by
Anthony Barbour now looking at their
best for autumn colour.

11 BOLLIN HOUSE
Hollies Lane, Wilmslow,
SK9 2BW. Angela Ferguson &
Gerry Lemon, 07828 207492,
fergusonang@doctors.org.uk.
*From Wilmslow past stn & proceed
to T-junction. Turn L onto Adlington
Rd. Proceed for ½ m, then turn R
into Hollies Lane (just after One Oak
Lane). Drive to the end of Hollies
Lane & follow yellow signage.
Park on Browns Lane (other side
Adlington Rd) or Hollies Lane.* **Visits
by arrangement May & June for
groups of 8 to 30. Small groups
with 5 cars or fewer may park at
the house. Adm £5, chd free. Tea**

The Wonky Garden

and cake or scones, cold drinks also available.

Our garden has established deep borders full of perennials, a wildflower meadow and a new formal area with parterres and central water feature. The meadow, with its annual and perennial wildflower areas (with mown pathways and benches), attracts lots of bees, buzzing insects and butterflies. Bollin House is in an idyllic location with the garden, orchard and meadow dropping into the Bollin valley. The River Bollin flows along this valley and on the opp side the fields lead up to views of Alderley Edge. Ramps to gravel lined paths to most of the garden. Some narrow paths through borders. Mown pathways in the meadow.

 ♿ ✿ ☕

🔢 BOWMERE COTTAGE

Bowmere Road, Tarporley, CW6 0BS. Romy & Tom Holmes, 01829 732053, romy@bowmerecottage.co.uk. *10m E of Chester. From Tarporley High St (old A49) take Eaton Rd* signed *Eaton. After 100 metres take R fork into Bowmere Rd, Garden 100 metres on L.* **Visits by arrangement June & July for groups of up to 30. Adm £5, chd free. Home-made teas.**

A colourful and relaxing 1 acre country style garden around a Grade II listed house. Lawns are surrounded by 3 well-stocked herbaceous and shrub borders and rose covered pergolas. There are 2 plant filled courtyard gardens and a small vegetable garden. Shrubs and rambling roses, clematis, hardy geraniums and a wide range of mostly hardy plants make this a very traditional English garden.

✿ 🚗 ☕ 🔊

🔢 BRIARFIELD

The Rake, Burton, Neston, CH64 5TL. Liz Carter, 07711 813732, carter.burton@btinternet.com. *9m NW of Chester. Turn off A540 at Willaston-Burton Xrds T-lights & follow rd for 1m to Burton village* centre. **Sat 19, Sun 20 Feb (11-4). Sun 8 May (1-5). Home-made teas in the church just along the lane from the garden on May 8th only. Adm £5, chd free. Opening with Burton Village Gardens on Sun 26 June. Visits also by arrangement Feb to Sept. Park in the village and walk up the lane.**

Tucked under the south facing side of Burton Wood the garden is home to many specialist and unusual plants, some available in plant sale. This 2 acre garden is on two sites, a short walk along an unmade lane. Shrubs, colourful herbaceous, bulbs, alpines and water features compete for attention as you wander through 4 distinctly different gardens. Always changing, Liz can't resist a new plant! Erythronium 'Elizabeth' raised at Briarfield. Erythronium are a feature of the garden in April and May. Rare and unusual plants sold (70% to NGS) from the drive each Friday from 9am to 5pm, Feb to Oct. Check updates on Briarfield Gardens Facebook.

✿ 🚗 ☕

BROOKE COTTAGE

Church Road, Handforth, SK9 3LT.
Barry & Melanie Davy. *1m N of Wilmslow. Centre of Handforth, behind Health Centre. Turn off Wilmslow Rd at St Chads, follow Church Rd round to R. Garden last on L. Parking in Health Centre car park.* **Sat 14, Sun 15 May (12-5). Adm £4.50, chd free. Home-made teas.**
A chance to see this plant-filled garden in spring. Shady woodland area of ferns, azaleas, rhododendrons, camellias, magnolia, erythroniums, trilliums, arisaema and foxgloves. Patio with many hostas, daylilies and pond. Borders with grasses, perennials, euphorbia, alliums and tulips. Anthriscus, aquilegia, persicaria and astrantia create meadow effect popular with insects. Featured in RHS 'The Garden' magazine.

ID BROOKLANDS

Smithy Lane, Mouldsworth, CH3 8AR. Barbara & Brian Russell-Moore, 01928 740413, wbrm1@netscape.co.uk. *1½m N of Tarvin. 5½m S of Frodsham. Smithy Lane is off B5393 via A54 Tarvin/Kelsall rd or the A56 Frodsham/Helsby rd.* **Visits by arrangement May to Sept for groups of 6 to 30. Adm £5, chd free. Home-made teas.**
Repeat visitors will see major changes in the garden as we seek to develop a lower maintenance format – less perennials and more shrubs. We plan to plant more lilies, and late season hydrangeas while being less ruthless on self-sown poppies and *Verbena bonariensis*. The hens will still provide the eggs for all the afternoon tea cakes!!

ID BUCKLOW FARM

Pinfold Lane, Plumley, Knutsford, WA16 9RP. Dawn & Peter Freeman. *2m S of Knutsford. M6 J19, A556 Chester. L at 2nd set of T-lights. In 1¼m, L at concealed Xrds. 1st R. From Knutsford A5033, L at Sudlow Lane, becomes Pinfold Lane.* **Sun 27 Feb (12.30-4). Adm £3.50, chd free. Light refreshments. Sun 12 June (1.30-5). Adm £4.50, chd free. Cream teas. Mulled wine in Feb. Cream teas in June. 2023: Sun 26 Feb. Donation to Knutsford Methodist Church.**

Country garden with shrubs, perennial borders, rambling roses, herb garden, vegetable patch, meadow, wildlife pond/water feature and alpines. Landscaped and planted over the last 30 yrs with recorded changes. Free range hens. Carpet of snowdrops and spring bulbs. Leaf, stem and berries to show colour in autumn and winter. Cobbled yard from car park, but wheelchairs can be dropped off near gate.

GROUP OPENING

ID BURTON VILLAGE GARDENS

Burton, Neston, CH64 5SJ. 07711 813732. *9m NW of Chester. Turn off A540 at Willaston-Burton Xrds T-lights & follow road for 1m to Burton. Maps given to visitors. Buy your ticket at first garden & keep it for entry to other gardens.* **Sun 26 June (11-5). Combined adm £6, chd free. Home-made teas in the Sport and Social Club behind the village hall.**

BRIARFIELD
Liz Carter.
(See separate entry)

♦ **BURTON MANOR WALLED GARDEN**
Friends of Burton Manor Gardens CIO, 0151 336 6154, www.burtonmanorgardens.org.uk.

NEW THE COACH HOUSE
Jane & Mike Davies, 0151 353 0074, burtontower@googlemail.com.

TRUSTWOOD
Peter & Lin Friend, 0151 336 7118, lin@trustwoodbnb.uk, www.trustwoodbnb.uk.
Visits also by arrangement Apr to Aug for groups of up to 20. Very limited parking is available on site.

Our exciting new garden, The Coach House, has stunning views of the Welsh hills. The recently revitalised garden is full of colour with herbaceous borders, a cut flower area plus a productive fruit and vegetable patch The wooded hillside is work in progress. Briarfield's sheltered site, to the south of Burton Wood (NT), is home to many unusual plants, some available in the plant

sale at the house. The 1½ acre main garden invites exploration not only for its variety of plants but also for the imaginative use of ceramic sculptures. Period planting with a splendid vegetable garden surrounds the restored Edwardian glasshouse in Burton Manor's walled garden. Paths lead past a sunken garden and terraces to views across the Cheshire countryside. Trustwood is a relaxed country garden, a haven for wildlife with emphasis on British native trees planted along the drive and the use of insect friendly plants. Chickens roam in the woodland. Plant sales at 2 gardens. Free car parks. Briarfield & The Coach House are too hilly for wheelchairs, with steep slopes and steps.

IB 64 CARR WOOD

Hale Barns, Altrincham, WA15 0EP. Mr David Booth. *10m S of Manchester city centre. 2m from J6 M56: Take A538 to Hale Barns. L at 'triangle' by church into Wicker Lane & L at mini r'about into Chapel Lane & 1st R into Carr Wood.* **Sat 14 May (1.30-6.30). Adm £5, chd free. Home-made teas.**
⅔ acre landscaped, south facing garden overlooking Bollin valley laid out in 1959 by Clibrans of Altrincham. Gently sloping lawn, woodland walk, seating areas and terrace, extensive mixed shrub and plant borders. Ample parking on Carr Wood. Wheelchair access to terrace overlooking main garden.

ID NEW 9 CHALFIELD CLOSE

Crewe, CW2 6TJ. Tracy Jones, www.manorfarmbotanics.com. *From Nantwich ypass/A51 head SE, at the r'about take the 1st exit onto Crewe Rd/A534, turn R onto Laidon Ave, turn L onto Fuller Drive & R onto Chalfield Close.* **Sat 11, Sun 12 June (10-4). Adm £4, chd free. Light refreshments.**
This is a fascinating garden set in a ⅓ of an acre and has been cleverly developed over the last 6 yrs where the owner runs practical herbalist workshops using plants from the garden, under the name Manor Farm Botanicals. Tinctures, teas and balms are also made using the healing herbs. www.manorfarmbotanics.com.

20 ◆ CHOLMONDELEY CASTLE GARDENS
Cholmondeley, Malpas, SY14 8AH. The Cholmondeley Gardens Trust, 01829 720203, eo@chol-estates.co.uk, www.cholmondeleycastle.com. *4m NE of Malpas Sat Nav SY14 8ET. Signed from A41 Chester-Whitchurch rd & A49 Whitchurch-Tarporley rd.* **For NGS: Thur 5 May (10-4). Adm £8.50, chd £4.**
For other opening times and information, please phone, email or visit garden website.
70 acres of romantically landscaped gardens with fine views and eye-catching water features, which still manages to retain its intimacy. Beautiful mature trees form a background to millions of spring bulbs and superb plant collections inc magnolias, rhododendrons and camellias. Largest display of daffodils. Magnificent magnolias. One of the finest features of the gardens are its trees, many of which are rare and unusual, Cholmondeley Gardens is home to over 40 county champion trees. 100m long double mixed herbaceous border and Rose Garden with 250 roses. Fresh coffee, lunches and cakes daily with locally sourced products located in the heart of the Gardens. Partial wheelchair access.

21 CLEMLEY HOUSE
Well Lane, Duddon Common, Tarporley, CW6 0HG. Sue & Tom Makin, 07790 610586, s_makingardens@yahoo.co.uk. *8m SE of Chester, 3m W of Tarporley. A51 from Chester towards Tarporley. 1m after Tarvin turn off, at bus shelter, turn L into Willington Rd. After community centre, 2nd L into Well Lane, 3rd house.* **Sun 26 June (1-5). Adm £6, chd free. Home-made teas. Home grown organic fruits used in jams & cakes. Gluten free available by prior arrangement.**
2 acre organic, wildlife friendly, gold award winning cottage garden. Orchard, 2 wildlife ponds, perennial wildflower meadow, fruit and vegetable areas, badger sett, rose pergola and veranda, gazebo, shepherd's hut, summerhouse, barn owl and many other nest and bat boxes. Drought tolerant gravel garden and shade garden. New wild areas. Year-round interest. Run on vegan principles. 'Frogwatch' charity volunteers transport migrating amphibians to the safety of our ponds when they are found on the roads in early spring. Butterflies, bees, dragonflies etc are plentiful in their season. The garden is a clear example of how an oasis for wildlife can be beautiful. Gravel paths may be difficult to use but most areas are flat and comprise grass paths or lawn.

22 DELFAN
Burton Road, Little Neston, Neston, CH64 4AF. Chris Sullivan. *10m NW of Chester situated between Neston & Ness Gardens. M53 J4, follow signs M56 & A5117 (signed N Wales). Turn onto A540 follow signs for Hoylake. Garden is 1m past Ness Gardens, nr to Marshlands Rd. Parking at St Michael's Church.* **Sun 29 May (1-4). Adm £4, chd free.**
The garden is surrounded by mature trees. Spring borders with camellias and rhododendrons, followed by herbaceous borders offering colour and variety of planting. The borders provide fragrance with roses climbing up obelisks. A tender plant area and fern bed sit amongst the cottage garden plants. Late summer colour is provided by echinaceas, heleniums and dahlias.

Sandymere
© Joe Wainwright

23 NEW **DIAL HOUSE**
62 Carrwood Road, Wilmslow,
SK9 5DN. Eileen & Malcolm
MacAulay. *From A538 turn into
Kings Rd. At the end turn R onto
Carrwood Rd, which is unadopted
at this end of the road, Dial House is
the 3rd house on the R.* Sat 18 June
(10.30-4.30). Adm £4.50, chd free.
Home-made teas. Open nearby
Longcroft. Home made cakes will
also be available.
The design has been described as
the best and probably only modernist
domestic garden in the county. It is
not contemporary, nor a pastiche
of earlier historical styles, but one
that is unashamedly inspired by
1930s modernism in general and
the paintings of Piet Mondrian in
particular. The layout with its clean
lines and hard edges both horticultural
and architectural is a brave choice.

24 **DRAKE CARR**
Mudhurst Lane, Higher Disley,
SK12 2AN. Alan & Joan Morris.
*8m SE of Stockport, 12m NE of
Macclesfield. From A6 in Disley
centre turn into Buxton Old Rd, go
up hill 1m & turn R into Mudhurst*

*Lane. After ⅓ m park on layby or
grass verge. No parking at garden.
Approx 150 metre walk.* Sat 11, Sun
12 June (11-5). Adm £5, chd free.
Home-made teas. Home-made
gluten-free cakes available.
½ acre cottage garden in beautiful
rural setting with natural stream
running into wildlife pond with many
native species. Surrounding C17
stone cottage, the garden, containing
borders, shrubs and vegetable plot, is
on several levels divided by grassed
areas, slopes and steps. This blends
into a boarded walk through bog
garden, mature wooded area and
stream-side walk into a wildflower
meadow.

25 **THE FIRS**
Old Chester Road, Barbridge,
Nantwich, CW5 6AY. Richard &
Valerie Goodyear, 07775 924929,
richard.goodyear@ngs.org.uk.
*3m N of Nantwich on A51. After
entering Barbridge turn R at Xrds
after 100 metres. The Firs is 2nd
house on L.* Sun 24, Thur 28 July
(11-4). Adm £4.50, chd free.
Light refreshments. **Visits also
by arrangement May to July for**

groups of 10+.
Canalside garden set idyllically by a
wide section of the Shropshire Union
Canal with long frontage. Garden
alongside canal with varied trees,
shrubs and herbaceous beds, with
some wild areas. All leading down
to an observatory and Japanese
torii gate at the end of the garden.
Usually have nesting friendly swans
with cygnets May to September that
occupy a small area of the garden.

26 **FRAMLEY**
Hadlow Road, Willaston,
Neston, CH64 2US. Mrs
Sally Reader, 07496 015259,
sllyreader@yahoo.co.uk. *½ m S
of Willaston village centre. From
Willaston Green, proceed along
Hadlow Rd, crossing the Wirral
Way. Framley is the next house on
R. From Chester High Rd, proceed
along Hadlow Rd toward Willaston.
Framley is third house on L.* Mon
2 May (10-4). Adm £5, chd free.
Home-made teas. **Visits also
by arrangement May & June for
groups of up to 12.**
This 5 acre garden holds many
hidden gems. Comprising extensive

Longcroft

mature wooded areas, underplanted with a variety of interesting and unusual woodland plants - all at their very best in spring. A selection of deep seasonal borders surround a mystical sunken garden, planted to suit its challenging conditions. Wide lawns and sandstone paths invite you to discover what lies around every corner. Please phone ahead for parking instructions for wheelchair users - access around much of the garden although the woodland paths may be challenging.

&. ✿ ☕))

27 5 GAYTON LANE
Gayton, Wirral, CH60 3SH. Stuart & Maggie Watson. *From the 'Devon Doorway' r'about in Heswall follow the A540 towards Chester. Gayton Lane is 1st turning on L. No. 5 is 3rd entrance on L.* **Sat 23, Sun 24 July (1-4). Adm £4, chd free. Light refreshments.**
1/3 acre suburban garden stocked with a variety of shrubs and perennials. Roses and clematis are accompanied by a large selection of colourful pots. You may even find a few hidden fairy houses.

🐈 ☕))

28 HALL LANE FARM
Hall Lane, Daresbury, Warrington, WA4 4AF. Sir Michael & Lady Beverley Bibby. *Leave M56 at J11, head towards Warrington take 2nd R turn into Daresbury village go around sharp bend then take L into Daresbury Lane. Entrance on L after 100 yds.* **Sun 19 June (12.30-4.30). Adm £5, chd free.**
The 2 acres of private formal garden originally designed by Arabella Lennox-Boyd are arranged in a 'gardens within gardens' style to create a series of enclosed spaces each with their own character and style. The gardens inc a vegetable garden, orchard, Koi pond, as well as lawns and a treehouse.

Ⓓ ☕))

29 HATHAWAY
1 Pool End Road, Tytherington, Macclesfield, SK10 2LB. Mr & Mrs Cordingley. *2m N of Macclesfield, 1/2m from The Tytherington Club. From Stockport follow A523 to Butley Ash, R on A538 Tytherington. From Knutsford follow A537 at A538, L for Tytherington. From Leek follow A523 at A537 L & 1st R A53.* **Sat 7, Sun 8 May (10-4). Adm £4, chd**

free. Teas/coffee/cordial & cakes. SW facing garden of approx 1/5 acre, laid out in two parts. Lawn area surrounded by mature, colourful perennial borders. Rose arbour. Our small pond has now become a large one, located in the lawn, with goldfish. Larger patio. Small mature wooded area with winding paths on a lower level. Front, laid to lawn with 2 main borders separated by a small grass area. Good wheelchair access to most of garden except wood area.

&. ☕

30 213 HIGHER LANE
Lymm, WA13 0RN. Mark Stevenson, 07470 715007, mjs.stevenson@btinternet.com. *From M56 J7 follow the signs for Lymm A56. The garden is approx 300 metres from the Jolly Thresher pub towards Lymm on R.* **Visits by arrangement Apr to Oct for groups of 5 to 20. Adm £4, chd free. Cream teas.**
Established on an acre of grounds, segregated into various planting schemes. Herbaceous borders, specimen rhododendrons, hydrangeas, ferns and grasses, gingers and subtropical plants, along with so much more. A pond complete with fish and waterfalls surrounded by Japanese acers with far reaching views across fields and woodland. Many rare and unusual plants and shrubs with wooded pathways. 70% of the garden is accessible to wheelchair users.

&. 🐈 ☕

31 18 HIGHFIELD ROAD
Bollington, Macclesfield, SK10 5LR. Mrs Melita Turner. *3m N of Macclesfield. A523 to Stockport. Turn R at B5090 r'about signed Bollington. Pass under viaduct. Take next R (by Library) up Hurst Lane. Turn R into Highfield Rd. Property on L. Park on wider road just past it.* **Sat 18, Sun 19 June (10-4.30). Adm £4.50, chd free. Home-made teas.**
This small terraced garden packed with plants was designed by Melita and has evolved over the past 14 yrs. This plantswoman is a plantaholic and RHS Certificate holder. An attempt has been made to combine formality through structural planting with a more casual look influenced by the style of Christopher Lloyd. Some minor changes for 2022.

🐈 ✿ ☕))

32 HILL FARM
Mill Lane, Moston, Sandbach, CW11 3PS. Mrs Chris & Mr Richard House, 01270 526264, housecr2002@yahoo.co.uk. *2m NW of Sandbach. From Sandbach town centre take A533 towards Middlewich. After Fox Pub take next L (Mill Lane) to a canal bridge & turn L. Hill Farm 400m on L.* **Sun 24 Apr, Sun 29 May, Sun 12 June (11-5). Adm £5, chd free. Light refreshments. Visits by arrangement May to Sept. Adm £5, chd free. Home-made teas.**
The garden extends to approx 1/2 acre and is made up of a series of gardens inc a formal courtyard with a pond and vegetable garden with south facing wall. An orchard and meadow were established about 3 yrs ago. A principal feature is a woodland garden which supports a rich variety of woodland plants. This was extended in April 2020 to include a pond and grass/herbaceous borders. A level garden, the majority of which can be accessed by wheelchair.

&. ☕))

33 HILLTOP

Flash Lane, Prestbury, SK10 4ED. Martin Gardner, 07768 337525, hughmartingardner@gmail.com, www.yourhilltopwedding.com. *2m N of Macclesfield. A523 to Stockport. Turn R at B5090 r'about signed Bollington, after ½m turn L at Cock & Pheasant pub into Flash Lane. At bottom of lane turn R into cul-de-sac. Hilltop Country House signed on R.* **Visits by arrangement May to July for groups of 10 to 20. Adm £6, chd free. Tea/Coffee & a cake £2 per person.** Interesting country garden of approx 4 acres. Woodland walk, parterre, herb garden, herbaceous borders, dry stone walled terracing, lily ponds with waterfall. Wisteria clad 1693 house (not open), ancient trees, orchard with magnificent views to Pennines and to the west. Partial wheelchair access, disabled WC, easy parking.

34 HOLMECROFT

Wood Lane North, Adlington, SK10 4PF. Iain & Karen Reddy, 07595 893793, iainreddy@mac.com. *6m N of Macclesfield. From Poynton head towards Macclesfield, turn L opp Starbucks. Stay on Street Lane until T-junction. Turn L until Minors Arms pub, Holmcroft is opp pub car park.* **Sat 21, Sun 22 May, Sat 25, Sun 26 June (12-5). Adm £5, chd free. Home-made teas. Gluten-free options. Visits also by arrangement May to Sept.** The garden is cottage style with mature shrubs, trees and perennial borders. 4 sections inc a pond garden, small courtyard, pot display, cottage garden beds and front shrub garden, approx ½ acre. The gardens are on multiple levels. Wheelchair access to most of the garden - sloping gravel path links upper and lower levels in the rear garden. Some uneven steps.

35 THE HOMESTEAD

2 Fanners Lane, High Legh, Knutsford, WA16 0RZ. Janet Bashforth, 01925 349895, janbash43@sky.com. *J20 M6/J9 M56 at Lymm interchange take A50 for Knutsford, after 1m turn R into Heath Lane then 1st R into Fanners Lane. Follow parking signs.* **Sat 25, Sun 26 June (11-5). Adm £4.50, chd free. Home-made teas. Visits also by arrangement May to Aug**

for groups of 10 to 40. This compact gem of a garden has been created over the last 6 yrs by a keen gardener and plantswoman. Enter past groups of liquidambar and white stemmed birch. Colour themed areas with many perennials, shrubs and trees. Past topiary and obelisks covered with many varieties of clematis and roses, enjoy the colours of the hot border, a decorative greenhouse and pond complete the picture. Further on there is a small pond with water lilies and iris. Many types of roses and clematis adorn the fencing along the paths and into the trees.

36 INGLEWOOD

4 Birchmere, Heswall, CH60 6TN. Colin & Sandra Fairclough. *6m S of Birkenhead. From A540 Devon Doorway/Clegg Arms r'about go through Heswall. ¼m after Tesco, R into Quarry Rd East, 2nd L into Tower Rd North & L into Birchmere.* **Sat 16, Sun 17 July (1-4). Adm £5, chd free. Home-made teas.** Beautiful ½ acre garden with stream, large koi pond, 'beach' with grasses, wildlife pond and bog area. Brimming with shrubs, bulbs, acers, conifers, rhododendrons, herbaceous plants and hosta border. Interesting features inc hand cart, antique mangle, wood carvings, bug hotel and Indian dog gates leading to a secret garden. Lots of seating to enjoy refreshments. Live music may be available.

37 LASKEY FARM

Laskey Lane, Thelwall, Warrington, WA4 2TF. Howard & Wendy Platt, 07740 804825, howardplatt@lockergroup.com, www.laskeyfarm.com. *2m from M6/M56. From M56/M6 follow directions to Lymm. At T-junction turn L onto the A56 in Warrington direction. Turn R onto Lymm Rd. Turn R onto Laskey Lane.* **Sun 1, Mon 2 May, Sat 4, Sun 5 June, Sat 16, Sun 17 July, Sun 28, Mon 29 Aug (11-4). Adm £5, chd £1. Home-made teas. Open nearby 10 Statham Avenue Sun 1, Mon 2 May. Visits also by arrangement May to Sept for groups of 12 to 50. Combined visits with 10 Statham Avenue and afternoon teas by arrangement.** 1½ acre garden inc herbaceous and rose borders, vegetable area, a greenhouse, parterre and a maze showcasing grasses and prairie style

planting. Interconnected pools for wildlife, specimen koi and terrapins form an unusual water garden which features a swimming pond There is a treehouse plus a number of birds and animals. Most areas of the garden may be accessed by wheelchair.

38 LONG ACRE

Wyche Lane, Bunbury, CW6 9PS. Margaret & Michael Bourne, 01829 260944, mjbourne249@tiscali.co.uk. *3½m SE of Tarporley. In Bunbury village turn into Wyche Lane by Nags Head pub car park, garden 400yds on L.* **Sun 17 Apr, Sun 19 June (2-5). Adm £5, chd free. Home-made teas. Visits also by arrangement Apr to June for groups of 10+. Donation to St Boniface Church Flower Fund and Bunbury Village Hall.** Plantswoman's garden of approx 1 acre with unusual and rare plants and trees inc Kentucky Coffee Tree, Scadiopitys, Kalapanax Picta and others. Pool garden, exotic conservatory with bananas, anthuriums and medinilla, herbaceous, greenhouses with Clivia in spring and Disa orchids in summer. Spring garden with camellias, magnolias, bulbs; roses and lilies in summer.

39 NEW LONGCROFT

Oak Road, Mottram St Andrew, Macclesfield, SK10 4RA. Janette & Paul Hopkin, 01625 828764, pehopkin@gmail.com. *3.9 m from centre of Wilmslow. From Wilmslow A34 take turning onto A538 to Prestbury. After 1.8 m slight R onto Wilmslow Old Rd. L onto Priest Lane then 1st R onto Oak Rd. 100 yds on right.* **Sat 18 June (10.30-4.30). Adm £7, chd free. Visits also by arrangement June & July.** This 1½ acre country garden has long views to the hills. It has formal and informal spaces made up of mixed borders, many shrub roses, hard landscaping, artworks, wild parts inc ponds, a small woodland and wildflower meadow. An enclosed vegetable garden with greenhouse and raised beds is productive and also ornamental. Many places to sit and enjoy make for a relaxing visit. Gravel and grass paths but there are no steps.

5 Pennys Lane

40 ◆ THE LOVELL QUINTA ARBORETUM

Swettenham, CW12 2LF.
Tatton Garden Society,
01565 831981, admin@
tattongardensociety.org.uk,
www.lovellquintaarboretum.co.uk.
*4m NW of Congleton. Turn off A54
N 2m W of Congleton or turn E off
A535 at Twemlow Green, NE of
Holmes Chapel. Follow signs to
Swettenham. Park at Swettenham
Arms. What3words app - twins.
sheds.keepers.* **For NGS: Sun 9
Oct (1.30-4). Adm £5, chd free.
For other opening times and
information, please phone, email or
visit garden website.**
This 28 acre arboretum has been
established since 1960s and contains
around 2,500 trees and shrubs, some
very rare. National Collections of
Pinus and Fraxinus. A large selection
of oak, a private collection of hebes
plus autumn flowering, fruiting and
colourful trees and shrubs. A lake
and waymarked walks. Autumn
colour, winter walk and spring bulbs.
Refreshments at the Swettenham
Arms during licenced hours or by
arrangement. Care required but
wheelchairs can access much of the
arboretum on the mown paths.
 NPC

41 MANLEY KNOLL

Manley Road, Manley,
WA6 9DX. Mr & Mrs James
Timpson, 07854 661989,
Thomas.leese@hotmail.co.uk,
www.manleyknoll.com. *3m N of
Tarvin. On B5393, via Ashton &
Mouldsworth. 3m S of Frodsham, via
Alvanley.* **Sun 22 May (12-5). Adm
£5, chd free. Light refreshments.
Visits also by arrangement May to
Aug for groups of 10 to 30.**
Arts & Crafts garden created early
1900s. Covering 6 acres, divided
into different rooms encompassing
parterres, clipped yew hedging,
ornamental ponds and herbaceous
borders. Banks of rhododendron and
azaleas frame a far-reaching view of
the Cheshire Plain. Also a magical
quarry/folly garden with waterfall and
woodland walks.

42 MAYFIELD HOUSE

Moss Lane, Bunbury Heath,
Tarporley, CW6 9SY.
Mr & Mrs J France Hayhurst,
jeanniefh@me.com. *Off A49 on
Tarporley/Whitchurch Rd. Moss Lane
is opp School Lane which leads to
Bunbury village. There's a yellow
speed camera (30 mph) across the
road from the house.* **Sat 11, Sun 12
June (1-5.30). Adm £5, chd free.
Light refreshments. Visits also
by arrangement May to Sept for
groups of 10 to 30.**
A thoroughly English mature
garden with a wealth of colour
and variety throughout the year. A
background of fine trees, defined
areas bordered by mixed hedging,
masses of rhododendrons, azaleas,
camellias,hydrangeas and colourful
shrubs. Clematis and wisteria festoon
the walls in early summer. Easy
access and random seating areas.
Small lake with an island and broad
lawns with glades of foxgloves.
Garden statuary, large pond with fish,
swimming pool. Gravel drive. Very
wide wrought iron gates lead to the
garden and it is entirely navigable.

43 MILFORD HOUSE FARM

Long Lane, Wettenhall, Winsford, CW7 4DN. Chris & Heather Pope, 07887 760930, hclp@btinternet.com. *3m E of Tarporley. From A51 at Alpraham turn into Long Lane. Proceed for 2½ m to St David's Church on L. Milford House Farm is 150 metres further on L. Park at church. Limited mobility parking at house.* Sat 23 July (12-5). Adm £4, chd free. Home-made teas in marquee at garden. Visits also by arrangement July & Aug for groups of 6 to 25.

A large country garden created over 20 yrs with lawn, herbaceous borders, trees, perennials and annuals. Modern walled garden for vegetables, fruit, greenhouse, shed, flowers, shrubs and various pots. Orchard with fruit, native and ornamental trees, large wildlife pond with toads and newts. Gardened on organic lines to increase biodiversity and attract wildlife. All areas are flat Good views over borders, lawn, orchard. Picnics in orchard. New for 2022 -openings by arrangement can include woodland walks (weather dependent). Walled garden has gravel and flags. Church fully accessible for WC.

44 ◆ MOUNT PLEASANT

Yeld Lane, Kelsall, CW6 0TB. Dave Darlington & Louise Worthington, 01829 751592, louisedarlington@btinternet.com, www.mountpleasantgardens.co.uk. *8m E of Chester. Off A54 at T-lights into Kelsall. Turn into Yeld Lane opp Farmers Arms pub, 200yds on L. Do not follow SatNav directions.* For NGS: Sun 15 May, Sun 4 Sept (11-4). Adm £7, chd £5. Cream teas. For other opening times and information, please phone, email or visit garden website.

10 acres of landscaped garden and woodland started in 1994 with impressive views over the Cheshire countryside. Steeply terraced in places. Specimen trees, rhododendrons, azaleas, conifers, mixed and herbaceous borders; 4 ponds, formal and wildlife. Vegetable garden, stumpery with tree ferns, sculptures, wildflower meadow and Japanese garden. Bog garden, tropical garden. Sculpture trail and exhibition.

45 NEW 45 NEEDHAM DRIVE

Cranage, Crewe, CW4 8FB. Darrell & Claire Jackson, 07515 949131, clairejackson56@hotmail.com. *1m outside Holmes Chapel off A50 towards Knutsford.* Sun 22 May, Sun 19 June (12-5). Adm £4, chd free. Light refreshments. Visits also by arrangement May to Aug for groups of 5 to 20.

This small, walled garden has been designed and built on varying levels by the owners over 20 yrs in reclaimed brick and natural stone materials to maximise its irregular shape. Features inc raised pond, potting shed and ornamental vegetable garden with 2 active beehives. Planting is abundant, with many varieties chosen for their wildlife benefits. Winner of Daily Mail garden of the year.

46 ◆ NESS BOTANIC GARDENS

Neston Road, Ness, Neston, CH64 4AY. The University of Liverpool, 0151 795 6300, nessgdns@liverpool.ac.uk, www. liverpool.ac.uk/ness-gardens. *10m NW of Chester. Off A540. M53 J4, follow signs M56 & A5117 (signed N Wales). Turn onto A540 follow signs for Hoylake. Ness Gardens is signed locally. 487 bus takes visitors travelling from Liverpool, Birkenhead etc.* For NGS: Tue 13 Sept (10-5). Adm £7.50, chd £3.50. For other opening times and information, please phone, email or visit garden website.

Looking out over the dramatic views of the Dee estuary from a lofty perch on the Wirral peninsula, Ness Botanic Gardens boasts 64 acres of landscaped and natural gardens overflowing with horticultural treasures. With a delightfully peaceful atmosphere, a wide array of events taking place, plus a café and gorgeous open spaces it's a great fun-filled day out for all the family. National Collections of Sorbus and Betula. Herbaceous borders, Rock Garden, Mediterranean Bank, Potager and conservation area. Wheelchairs are available free to hire (donations gratefully accepted) but advance booking is highly recommended.

47 NORLEY BANK FARM

Cow Lane, Norley, Frodsham, WA6 8PJ. Margaret & Neil Holding, 07828 913961, neil.holding@hotmail.com. *From the Tigers Head pub in the centre*

of Norley village keep the pub on L, carry straight on through the village for approx 300 metres. Cow Lane is on the R. Sun 24, Sun 31 July (11-5). Adm £5, chd free. Home-made teas. Some allergy free refreshments available. Visits also by arrangement July & Aug.

A garden well-stocked with perennials, annuals and shrubs that wraps around this traditional Cheshire farmhouse. There is an enclosed cut flower and nursery garden surrounding a greenhouse and just beyond the house a vegetable garden. Wander past this to a large wildlife pond with a backdrop of further planting. All set in about 2 acres. Free range hens, donkeys and Coloured Ryeland sheep.

48 NEW THE OLD BYRE

Sound Lane, Sound, Nantwich, CW5 8BE. Gill Farrington. *11m from J16 from Nantwich signs for A530 Whitchurch. At Sound School take 1st R Wrenbury Heath Rd at Xds turn L for parking, 0.3m to garden. Visitors with limited mobility turn R to park at garden.* Sat 16, Sun 17 July (10-4). Adm £4, chd free. Home-made teas.

5 acre working smallholding. 4 acres used for grazing and beehives, the rest is garden with a large cider apple orchard, wildlife pond, vegetable and cutting garden patch, herbaceous borders poultry and sheep. We aim to be wildlife friendly and re-use, and recycle everything we can hence some weedy and untidy areas where items are stored ready to be re-used or incorporated into a new project. We produce up to 2 tons of cider apples a year which are used by a local cider maker just 3 miles away. Homemade crafts using recycled materials will be on sale including yarn made from the fleece of our Ouessant sheep.

49 24 OLD GREASBY ROAD

Upton, Wirral, Merseyside, CH49 6LT. Lesley Whorton & Jon Price, 07905 775750, wlesley@hotmail.co.uk. *Approx 1m from J2A M53 (Upton bypass). M53 J2 follow Upton sign. At r'about (J2A) straight on to Upton bypass. At 2nd r'about, turn L by Upton Cricket Club. 24 Old Greasby Rd is on L.* Sun 26 June (11-4). Adm £4, chd free. Home-made teas. Visits also by arrangement June & July for groups of 10 to 30.

A multi-interest and surprising suburban garden. Both front and rear gardens incorporate innovative features designed for climbing and rambling roses, clematis, underplanted with cottage garden plants with a very productive kitchen garden. Garden transformed from a boggy, heavily-clayed and flood-damaged suburban garden to a peaceful and productive location.

✻ 🍵))

50 THE OLD PARSONAGE
Arley Green, Northwich, CW9 6LZ. The Hon Rowland & Mrs Flower, www.arleyhallandgardens.com. *5m NNE of Northwich. 3m NNE of Great Budworth. M6 J19 & 20 & M56 J10. Follow signs to Arley Hall & Gardens. From Arley Hall notices to Old Parsonage which lies across park at Arley Green (approx 1m).* **Sat 28, Sun 29 May (2-5). Adm £5, chd free. Home-made teas.** 2 acre garden in attractive and secretive rural setting in secluded part of Arley Estate, with ancient yew hedges, herbaceous and mixed borders, shrub roses, climbers, leading to woodland garden and unfenced pond with gunnera and water plants. Rhododendrons, azaleas, meconopsis, cardiocrinum, some interesting and unusual trees. Wheelchair access over mown grass, some slopes and bumps and rougher grass further away from the house.

♿ 🐕 ✻ 🍵))

51 ONE HOUSE WALLED GARDEN
2 Edinboro Cottages, Wildboarclough, Rainow, SK11 0AD. Louise Baylis. *2½ m NE of Macclesfield. Just off A537 Macclesfield to Buxton rd. 2½ m from Macclesfield stn.* **Sat 11, Sun 12 June (10-5). Adm £5, chd free. Home-made teas at One House Lodge, Buxton New Road, Rainow.** An historic early C18 walled kitchen garden, hidden for 60 yrs and restored by volunteers. This romantic and atmospheric garden has a wide range of vegetables, flowers and old tools. There is an orchard with friendly pigs, a wildlife area and pond, and a traditional greenhouse with ornamental and edible crops. There is a free rural life exhibition next to the car park.

🐕 ✻ 🍵 🪑

52 15 PARK CRESCENT
Appleton, Warrington, WA4 5JJ. Linda & Mark Enderby, 07949 496 747, lmaenderby@outlook.com. *2½ m S of Warrington. From M56 J10 take A49 towards Warrington for 1½ m. At 2nd set of lights turn R into Lyons Lane , then 1st R into Park Crescent. No.15 is last house on R.* **Sun 19 June (11.30-5). Adm £5, chd free. Light refreshments. Prosecco. Visits also by arrangement June to Aug for groups of 10 to 53.** An abundant garden containing many unusual plants, trees and a mini orchard. A cascade, ponds and planting encourage wildlife. There are raised beds, many roses in various forms and herbaceous borders. The garden has been split into distinct areas on different levels each with their own vista drawing one through the garden. Some unusual plants and a good example of planting under a lime tree in clay soil and shade.

🐕 ✻ 🚗 🍵))

Manley Knoll

© Joe Wainwright

'In 2021 the National Garden Scheme donated £500,000 to Marie Curie enabling us to continue providing our vital services and be there, caring for people on the frontline of the Coronavirus pandemic.'
Marie Curie

53 PARM PLACE

High Street, Great Budworth, CW9 6HF. Jane Fairclough, 01606 891131, janefair@btinternet.com. *3m N of Northwich. Great Budworth on E side of A559 between Northwich & Warrington, 4m from J10 M56, also 4m from J19 M6. Parm Place is W of village on S side of High St.* **Sun 3 Apr, Sun 26 June (1-5). Adm £5, chd free. Visits also by arrangement Apr to Aug for groups of 10 to 30. Donation to Great Ormond Street Hospital.**
Well-stocked ½ acre plantswoman's garden with stunning views towards S Cheshire. Curving lawns, parterre, shrubs, colour coordinated herbaceous borders, roses, water features, rockery, gravel bed with some grasses. Fruit and vegetable plots. In spring large collection of bulbs and flowers, camellias, hellebores and blossom.
♿ 🐾 🚐

54 NEW 5 PENNYS LANE

Lach Dennis, Northwich, CW9 7SJ. Simon & Heather Hayes, 07787 445379, sihayes@aol.com. *Just off A556 Northwich. M6 J19, take A556 N Wales/Chester. After 4 ¾ m turn L into Pennys Lane. No. 5 is 200 yds on L, we're first set of cottages. Access to garden is via a track signed Clay Bank Farm.* **Sun 3 July (11-5). Adm £5, chd free. Home-made teas. Visits also by arrangement May to Aug for groups of 10+.**
An English cottage garden with an eclectic mix of plants. Set over ⅓ acre, the garden has been split into several 'rooms'. These inc a fern garden, 'hot-bed', stumpery and borders filled with perennials, shrubs, roses and azaleas. There is an allotment inc an area for cut flowers, and greenhouse. There is even a Secret Garden! All areas are flat with just 2 steps to a small patio. Access to the garden is via a gravel drive. If in doubt phone in advance to discuss disabled access.
♿ 🌼 ☕))

55 ♦ PEOVER HALL GARDENS

Over Peover, Knutsford, WA16 9HW. Mr & Mrs Brooks, 01565 654107, bookings@peoverhall.com, www.peoverhall.com. *4m S of Knutsford. Do not rely on SatNav. From A50/Holmes Chapel Rd at Whipping Stocks pub turn onto Stocks Lane. Follow R onto Grotto Ln ¼ m turn R onto Goostrey Ln. Main entrance on R on bend through white gates.* **For NGS: Sat 4, Sun 5 June (2-5). Adm £5, chd free. Home-made cakes & cream teas. For other opening times and information, please phone, email or visit garden website.**
The extensive formal gardens to Peover Hall feature a series of 'garden rooms' filled with clipped box, water garden, Romanesque loggia, warm brick walls, unusual doors, secret passageways, beautiful topiary work and walled gardens, rockery, rhododendrons and pleached limes. Peover Hall, a Grade II* listed

Parm Place

© Joe Wainwright

Elizabethan family house dating from 1585, provides a fine backdrop. The Grade I listed Carolean Stables which are of significant architectural importance will be open to view. Partial wheelchair access to garden - wheelchair users please ask the car-park attendant for parking on hard standing rather than on the grass.

&. ♞ ✿ ⌂ ☕

56 POULTON HALL
Poulton Lancelyn, Bebington, Wirral, CH63 9LN. The Poulton Hall Estate Trust & Poulton Hall Walled Garden Charitable Trust, www.poultonhall.co.uk. *2m S of Bebington. From M53, J4 towards Bebington; at T-lights R along Poulton Rd; house 1m on R.* **Sat 16, Sun 17 Apr (2-5). Adm £6, chd free. Cream teas.**
3 acres, lawns fronting house, wildflower meadow. Surprise approach to walled garden, with reminders of Roger Lancelyn Green's retellings, Excalibur, Robin Hood and Jabberwocky. Scented sundial garden for the visually impaired. Memorial sculpture for Richard Lancelyn Green by Sue Sharples. Rose, nursery rhyme, witch, herb and oriental gardens and new Memories Reading room. Level gravel paths. Separate wheelchair access (not across parking field). Disabled WC.

&. ♞ ✿ ☕

57 ◆ RODE HALL
Church Lane, Scholar Green, ST7 3QP. Randle & Amanda Baker Wilbraham, 01270 873237, enquiries@rodehall.co.uk, www.rodehall.co.uk. *5m SW of Congleton. Between Scholar Green (A34) & Rode Heath (A50).* **For opening times and information, please phone, email or visit garden website.**
Nesfield's terrace and rose garden with stunning view over Humphry Repton's landscape is a feature of Rode, as is the woodland garden with terraced rock garden and grotto. Other attractions inc the walk to the lake with a view of Birthday Island complete with heronry, restored ice house, working 2 acre walled kitchen garden and Italian garden. Fine display of snowdrops in Feb and bluebells in May. Snowdrop walks in February 11-4pm, Tues - Sat (Closed Mons). Bluebell walks in May. Summer: Weds and Bank Hol Mons until end of Sep, 11-5. Courtyard

Kitchen offering wide variety of refreshments.

♞ ✿ ⌂ ☕

58 ROSE BRAE
Earle Drive, Parkgate, Neston, CH64 6RY. Joe & Carole Rae. *11m NW of Chester. From A540 take B5134 at the Hinderton Arms towards Neston. Turn R at the T-lights in Neston & L at the Cross onto Parkgate Rd, B5135. Earle Drive is ½m on R.* **Sun 24 July (1-4.30). Adm £5, chd free. Home-made teas.**
An all season, half acre garden comprising bulbs, trees, shrubs, perennials and climbers. In July roses, clematis, hydrangeas, phlox and agapanthus predominate together with ferns, grasses, flowering trees, topiary, an unmown bulb lawn and a formal pool with water lilies.

✿ ☕ ♪))

59 ROSEWOOD
Old Hall Lane, Puddington, Neston, CH64 5SP. Mr & Mrs C E J Brabin, 0151 353 1193, angela.brabin@btinternet.com. *8m N of Chester. From A540 turn down Puddington Lane, 1½m. Park by village green. Walk 30yds to Old Hall Lane, turn L through archway into garden.* **Visits by arrangement for groups of up to 30. Parking restricted. Adm £3, chd free. Tea.**
Year-round garden; thousands of snowdrops in Feb, camellias in autumn, winter and spring. Rhododendrons in April/May and unusual flowering trees from March to June. Autumn cyclamen in quantity from Aug to Nov. Perhaps the greatest delight to owners are 2 large *Cornus capitate*, flowering in June. Bees kept in the garden. Honey sometimes available.

&. ✿ ⌂ ☕

60 ROWLEY HOUSE
Forty Acre Lane, Kermincham, Holmes Chapel, CW4 8DX. Tim & Juliet Foden. *3m ENE from Holmes Chapel. J18 M6 to Holmes Chapel, then take A535 (Macclesfield). Take R turn in Twemlow (Swettenham) at Yellow Broom restaurant. Rowley House ½m on L.* **Sun 29 May, Sun 10 July (10-4.30). Adm £5, chd free. Home-made teas.**
Our aim is to give nature a home and create a place of beauty. There is a formal courtyard garden and informal gardens featuring rare trees, and

herbaceous borders, a pond with swamp cypress and woodland walk with maples, rhododendrons, ferns and shade-loving plants. Beyond the garden there are wildflower meadows, natural ponds and a wood with ancient oaks. Also wood sculptures by Andy Burgess. Many unusual plants and trees, also many areas dedicated to wildlife.

♞ ☕

61 SANDYMERE
Middlewich Road, Cotebrook, CW6 9EH. Sir John Timpson. *5m N of Tarporley. On A54 approx 300yds W of T-lights at Xrds of A49/A54.* **Sun 15 May (12-4). Adm £7, chd free. Home-made teas.**
16 landscaped acres of beautiful Cheshire countryside with terraces, walled garden, extensive woodland walks and an amazing hosta garden. Turn each corner and you find another gem with lots of different water features inc a new rill built in 2014, which links the main lawn to the hostas. Partial wheelchair access.

&. ✿ ☕ ♪))

62 21 SCAFELL CLOSE
High Lane, Stockport, SK6 8JA. Lesley & Dean Stafford, 01663 763015, lesley.stafford@live.co.uk. *High Lane is on A6 SE of Stockport towards Buxton. From A6 take Russell Ave then Kirkfell Drive. Scafell Close on R.* **Sat 30, Sun 31 July (1-4.30). Adm £4, chd free. Light refreshments. Tea/coffee and cakes. Visits also by arrangement July & Aug for groups of 10+.**
⅓ acre landscaped suburban garden. Colour themed annuals border the lawn featuring the Kinder Ram statue in a heather garden, passing into vegetables, soft fruits and fruit trees. Returning perennial pathway leads to the fishpond and secret terraced garden with modern water feature and patio planting. Finally visit the blue front garden. Partial wheelchair access.

&. ♞ ✿ ☕ ♪))

More than 1,200 people have been cared for at Y Bwthyn NGS Macmillan Specialist Palliative Care Unit, a unit that would simply not have been built without the National Garden Scheme funding

63 68 SOUTH OAK LANE

Wilmslow, SK9 6AT. Caroline Melliar-Smith, 01625 528147, caroline.ms@btinternet.com. ³⁄₄ m SW of Wilmslow. From M56 (J6) take A538 (Wilmslow) R into Buckingham Rd. From centre of Wilmslow turn R onto B5086, 1st R into Gravel Lane, 4th R into South Oak Lane. **Visits by arrangement June & July for groups of up to 15. Adm £5, chd free.**

With year-round colour, scent and interest, this attractive, narrow, hedged cottage garden has evolved over the years into 5 natural 'rooms'. The owner's passion for unusual plants is reflected in the variety of shrubs, trees, flower borders and pond, creating havens for wildlife. Share this garden with its varied history from the 1890s. Some rare and unusual hardy, herbaceous and shade loving plants and shrubs.

64 10 STATHAM AVENUE

Lymm, WA13 9NH. Mike & Gail Porter, 01925 753488, porters@mikeandgailporter.co.uk. Approx 1m from J20 M6 /M56 interchange. From M/way follow B5158 to Lymm. Take A56 Booth's Hill Rd, L towards Warrington, turn R on to Barsbank Lane, pass under Bridgewater canal, after 50 metres turn R on to Statham Ave. No 10 is 100 metres on R. **Sun 1, Mon 2, Wed 25 May, Sat 11, Sun 12, Wed 29 June (11-4). Adm £5, chd free. Home-made teas. Enjoy home-made cakes or try Gail's famous meringues with fresh fruit and cream. Open nearby Laskey Farm Sun 1, Mon 2 May. Visits also by arrangement May to July for groups of 10 to 40. Combined visits with Laskey Farm (1 mile away) can be arranged.**

Peaceful, pastel shades in early summer. Beautifully structured ¹⁄₄ acre south facing garden carefully terraced and planted rising to the Bridgewater towpath. Hazel arch opens to clay paved courtyard with peach trees. Rose pillars lead to varied herbaceous beds and quiet shaded areas bordered by fuchsias, azaleas and rhododendrons. Wide variety of plants and shrubs. Interesting garden buildings. A treasure hunt/quiz to keep the children occupied. Delicious refreshments to satisfy the grown ups.

65 ◆ STONYFORD COTTAGE

Stonyford Lane, Oakmere, CW8 2TF. Janet & Tony Overland, 01606 888970, info@ stonyfordcottagegardens.co.uk, www.stonyfordcottagegardens. co.uk. 5m SW of Northwich. From Northwich take A556 towards Chester. ³⁄₄ m past A49 junction turn R into Stonyford Lane. Entrance ¹⁄₂ m on L. **For NGS: Sun 15 May (11.30-4). Adm £4.50, chd free. Home-made cakes, lunches and cream teas available. For other opening times and information, please phone, email or visit garden website.**

Set around a tranquil pool this Monet style landscape has a wealth of moisture loving plants, inc iris and candelabra primulas. Drier areas feature unusual perennials and rarer trees and shrubs. Woodland paths meander through shade and bog plantings, along boarded walks, across wild natural areas with views over the pool to the cottage gardens. Unusual plants available at the adjacent nursery. Open Tues - Fri, Apr - Oct 10-5pm. Plant Nursery, Tea room. Some gravel paths.

66 STRETTON OLD HALL

Stretton, Tilston, Malpas, SY14 7JA. Stephen Gore Head Gardener, 07800 602225, Strettonoldhallgardens@hotmail. com. 5m N of Malpas. From Chester follow A41, Broxton r'about follow signs for Stretton Water Mill, turn L at Cock o Barton. 2m on L. **Sat 18, Sun 19 June, Sat 30, Sun 31 July (10-5). Adm £7, chd free. Home-made teas. Visits also by arrangement Mar to Oct for groups of 10+.**

5 acre Cheshire countryside garden with a planting style best described as controlled exuberance with a definite emphasis upon perennials, colour, form and scale. Divided into several discrete and individual gardens inc stunning herbaceous borders, scree garden, walled kitchen garden and glasshouse. Wildflower meadows, wildlife walk around the lake with breathtaking vistas in every direction. Regional Winner, The English Garden's The Nation's Favourite Gardens 2021

67 SUNNYSIDE FARM

Shop Lane, Little Budworth, CW6 9HA. Mike & Joan Smeethe, 01829 760618, joan.ann.smeethe@btinternet.com. 4m NE of Tarporley. On A54 1m E of T-lights at A54/A49 junction. Turn off A54 into Shop Lane opp Shrewsbury Arms pub. After 30yds take farm track on R & continue to end. Parking at house. **Visits by arrangement June to Sept. Adm £5, chd free. Home-made teas.**

A plant lover's and beekeeper's atmospheric country garden. Wildlife and child friendly, the 5 acres encompass oak woodland, wildflower meadow, pool garden, potager and fruit garden, orchard with beehives, long border with naturalistic planting and cottage garden. With a wealth of unusual plants and interesting colour schemes this is a constantly evolving garden. Always something new. Wheelchair access to most parts of the garden.

68 TATTENHALL HALL

High Street, Tattenhall, Chester, CH3 9PX. Jen & Nick Benefield, Chris Evered & Jannie Hollins, 01829 770654, janniehollins@gmail.com. 8m S of Chester on A41. Turn L to Tattenhall, through village, turn R at Letters pub, past War Memorial on L through sandstone pillared gates. Park on rd or in village car park. **Sun 29 May (2-5). Adm £5, chd free. Home-made teas. Visits also by arrangement Apr to July.**

Plant enthusiasts' garden around Jacobean house (not open). 4¹⁄₂ acres, wildflower meadows, interesting trees, large pond, stream, walled garden, colour themed borders, succession planting, spinney walk with shade plants, yew terrace overlooking meadow, views to hills. Glasshouse and vegetable garden. Wildlife friendly, sometimes untidy garden, interest year-round, continuing to develop. Partial wheelchair access due to gravel paths, cobbles and some steps.

69 THORNCAR

Windmill Lane, Appleton, Warrington, WA4 5JN. Mrs Kath Carey, 01925 267633, john.carey516@btinternet.com. *South Warrington. From M56 J10 take A49 towards Warrington for 1½ m. At 2nd set of T-lights turn L into Quarry Lane, as the rd swings R it becomes Windmill Lane. Thorncar is 4th house on R.* **Sat 24 Sept (10.30-4). Adm £4, chd free. Visits also by arrangement Jan to Oct for groups of up to 20.**
⅓ acre plantwoman's suburban garden planted since 2011 within the framework of part of an older garden to provide year-round interest. Each month has its plants of interest. The plants grown have to survive in poor sandy soil with no watering even during hot spells.

&. ❀

70 TIRESFORD

Tarporley, CW6 9LY. Susanna Posnett, 07989 306425. *Tiresford is on A49 Tarporley bypass. It is adjacent to the farm on R leaving Tarporley in the direction of Four Lane Ends T-lights.* **Sun 29 May (2-5). Adm £5, chd free. Home-made teas. Ice-Cream.**
Established 1930s garden undergoing a major restoration project to reinstate it to its former glory. Fabulous views of both Beeston and Peckforton Castles offer a wonderful backdrop in which to relax and enjoy a delicious tea. This year we hope to realise our long term plan to recreate the kitchen garden and to repair the fountain amongst the new hot borders of the sunken garden. The house has been transformed into a stylish 6 bedroom B&B. There is parking for wheelchair users next to the house and access to a disabled WC in the house.

&. 🐏 ❀ 🚐 ☕ ⁣))

71 TIRLEY GARTH GARDENS

Mallows Way, Willington, Tarporley, CW6 0RQ. *2m N of Tarporley. 2m S of Kelsall. Entrance 500yds from village of Utkinton. At N of Tarporley take Utkinton rd.* **Sun 8, Sun 15, Sun 29 May (1-5). Adm £5, chd free. Home-made teas.**
40 acre garden, terraced & landscaped, designed by Thomas Mawson who is considered the leading exponent of garden design in early C20. It is the only Grade II* Arts & Crafts garden in Cheshire that remains complete and in excellent condition. The gardens are an important example of an early

C20 garden laid out in both formal and informal styles. By early May the garden is bursting into flower with almost 3000 rhododendron and azalea, many 100 yrs old. Art Exhibition by local Artists.

🚐 ☕

72 THE WELL HOUSE

Wet Lane, Tilston, Malpas, SY14 7DP. Mrs S H French-Greenslade, 01829 250332. *3m NW of Malpas. On A41, 1st R after Broxton r'about, L on Malpas Rd through Tilston. House on L.* **Visits by arrangement Feb to Sept. Adm by donation. Pre-booked refreshments for small groups only.**
1 acre cottage garden, bridge over natural stream, spring bulbs, perennials, herbs and shrubs. Triple ponds. Adjoining ¾ acre field made into wildflower meadow; first seeding late 2003. Large bog area of kingcups and ragged robin. February for snowdrop walk. Victorian parlour and collector's items on show. Dogs on leads only.

🐕 🚐 ☕

73 WILLASTON GRANGE

Hadlow Road, Willaston, Neston, CH64 2UN. Mr & Mrs M Mitchell. *On A540 (Chester High Rd) take the B5151 into Willaston. From the village green in the centre of Willaston turn onto Hadlow Rd, Willaston Grange is ½ m on L.* **Sat 18 June (12-4.30). Adm £5, chd free. Home-made teas.**
Willaston Grange is an Arts & Craft property. 12 yrs ago the house and gardens had been derelict for 3 yrs. After months of detailed planning, the significant restoration work began. The gardens extend to 6 acres with a small lake, wide range of mature and rare tree species, herbaceous border, woodland and vegetable gardens, orchard and magical treehouse. The fully restored Arts & Crafts house provides the perfect backdrop for a summer visit, along with afternoon tea and live music. Most areas accessible by wheelchair.

&. 🐏 ❀ ☕ ⁣))

74 NEW THE WONKY GARDEN

Ditton Community Centre, Dundalk Road, Widnes, WA8 8DF. Mrs Angela Hayler, 07976 373979, thewonkygarden@gmail.com. *From the Widnes exit of the A533 turn L (Lowerhouse La) then L at the r'about. The Community*

Centre is ½ a mile up on the R. The garden is behind the Centre. **Sun 19 June, Sun 17 July, Sun 4 Sept (11-4). Adm £5, chd free. Light refreshments. Visits also by arrangement June to Sept for groups of 5 to 20.**
The flower garden is our show garden, the focus for horticultural/flower therapy and nature based activities. It has large herbaceous borders, trees and shrubs, with planting focussing on the senses and wildlife. We grow masses of edibles and cut flowers in the allotment garden and greenhouses. The children's 'explorify' garden nestles between the two and is used to support young families. The garden is designed and managed by a wonderful group of volunteers. We support many community groups and individuals of all ages and abilities including schools colleges and work experience. Our focus is on supporting physical and mental health, isolation and loneliness. An accessible path (1.5m wide) extends from the car park through the herbaceous and children's nature garden.

&. ❀ 🚐 ☕ ⁣))

75 WOODSIDE

6 Sunbury Gardens, Appleton, Warrington, WA4 5QE. Mrs Margaret & Mr Peter Wilkinson, 01925 269919, marg.wilkinson43@gmail.com. *M56, J10 r'about take A49 signed Warrington to T- lights just past golf club. Turn R into Lyons Lane. R at next r'about into Longwood Rd. Sunbury Gardens is second rd on L.* **Visits by arrangement June to Aug for groups of 5 to 10. Adm £5, chd free. Light refreshments.**
Woodside garden is positioned adjacent to a deciduous woodland area. This acts as a backdrop to a small suburban garden on 2 levels of beds packed with shrubs interspersed with perennials to create an artistic colour blend. Many clematis on trellis and obelisks give height to this flagged garden. More design is achieved with large pots of bananas, palms and tree ferns plus hostas and flowers.

❀ ☕

CORNWALL

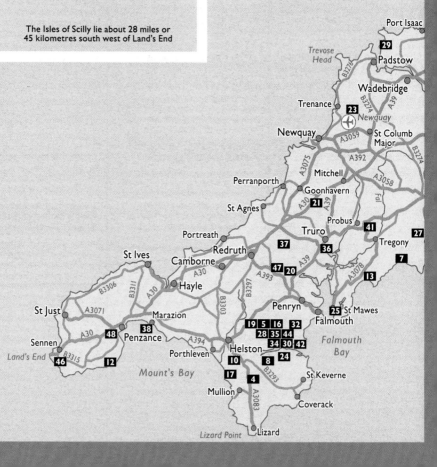

ISLES OF SCILLY

Tresco
St Martin's
Bryher
Hugh Town
St Mary's
St Agnes

The Isles of Scilly lie about 28 miles or
45 kilometres south west of Land's End

Port Isaac

29

Trevose
Head

Padstow

Wadebridge

Trenance
23
Newquay

Newquay
St Columb
Major

Perranporth

Mitchell

Goonhavern

St Agnes
21

Probus

Portreath
Truro
41
27

Redruth
37
Tregony

St Ives
36
7

Camborne
47 **20**
13

Hayle
Penryn
25 St Mawes
Falmouth

St Just
19 **5** **16** **32**
Marazion
28 **35** **44**
Falmouth
Bay
48 Penzance
34 **30** **42**
Sennen
Helston
24

Land's End
8
46 **12**
Porthleven
10

Mount's Bay
17
St Keverne
4

Mullion
Coverack

Lizard Point
Lizard

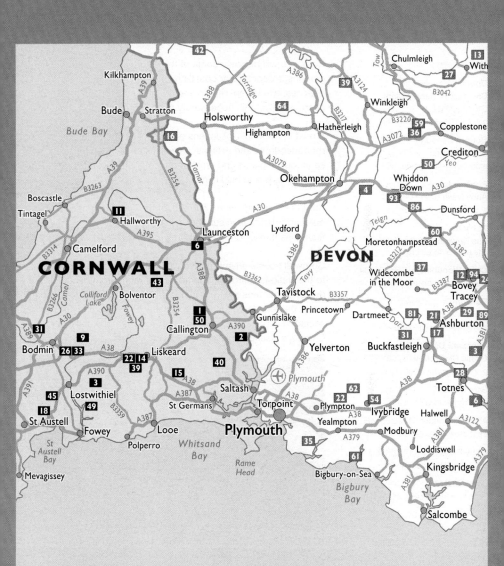

Cornwall has some of the most beautiful natural landscapes to be found anywhere in the world.

Here, you will discover some of the country's most extraordinary gardens, a spectacular coastline, internationally famous surfing beaches, windswept moors and countless historic sites. Cornish gardens reflect this huge variety of environments particularly well.

A host of National Collections of magnolias, camellias, rhododendrons and azaleas, as well as exotic Mediterranean semitropical plants and an abundance of other plants flourish in our acid soils and mild climate.

Surrounded by the warm currents of the Gulf Stream, with our warm damp air in summer and mild moist winters, growth flourishes throughout most of the year.

Cornwall boasts an impressive variety of beautiful places open to the National Garden Scheme. These range from beautifully-designed gardens centred on ancient manor houses, to moorland water gardens, gardens with epic sea views, a serene and secluded Japanese garden and the world-famous collection at Caerhays Castle.

Volunteers

County Organiser
Christopher Harvey Clark
01872 530165
suffree2012@gmail.com

County Treasurer
Marie Tolhurst
marie.tolhurst@ngs.org.uk

Photographer
Abby Nash 07904 068290
abby.nash@ngs.org.uk

Publicity
Sue Newton 01726 813829
sue.newton@ngs.org.uk

Claire Woodbine 01208 821339
claire.woodbine@ngs.org.uk

Booklet Co-ordinator
Claire Vickers 07494 448255
claire.vickers@ngs.org.uk

Assistant County Organisers
Ginnie Clotworthy 01208 872612
ginnieclotworthy@hotmail.co.uk

Sara Gadd 07814 885141
sara@gartendesign.co.uk

Alison O'Connor 01726 882460
tregoose@tregoose.co.uk

Libby Pidcock 01208 821303
libby.pidcock@ngs.org.uk

Laura Tucker
laura.tucker@ngs.org.uk

Claire Woodbine 01208 821339
claire.woodbine@ngs.org.uk

�facebook @CornwallNGS
📷 @ngs_cornwall

Right: Lower Penbothidnow

OPENING DATES

All entries subject to change. For latest information check www.ngs.org.uk

Extended openings are shown at the beginning of the month.

Map locator numbers are shown to the right of each garden name.

April

Every Tuesday
Riverside Cottage 36

Saturday 2nd
◆ Trewidden Garden 48

Saturday 23rd
◆ Chygurno 12

Sunday 24th
Anvil Cottage 1
◆ Chygurno 12
The Lodge 26
Pinsla Garden 33
Windmills 50

Monday 25th
◆ Pencarrow 31

Tuesday 26th
Pinsla Garden 33

Wednesday 27th
Pinsla Garden 33

Saturday 30th
◆ Lamorran House 25

May

Every Tuesday
Riverside Cottage 36

Every day
Waye Cottage 49

Sunday 1st
Ethnevas Cottage 16

Saturday 7th
NEW Greenwith Meadow 20

Sunday 8th
◆ Boconnoc 3
East Down Barn 15

NEW Greenwith Meadow 20
NEW Lower Penbothidnow 28
South Lea 40

Tuesday 10th
Pinsla Garden 33

Wednesday 11th
South Bosent 39

Thursday 12th
South Bosent 39

Saturday 14th
NEW ◆ Trevince Estate Gardens 47

Sunday 15th
Crugsillick Manor 13
◆ The Japanese Garden 23
Navas Hill House 30
NEW Port Navas Chapel 34
Trebartha Estate Garden and Country Garden at Lemarne 43

Monday 16th
◆ The Japanese Garden 23

Tuesday 24th
Pinsla Garden 33

Wednesday 25th
Pinsla Garden 33

Sunday 29th
NEW Cardinham Gardens 9

June

Every day
Waye Cottage 49

Wednesday 1st
Gardens Cottage 18
Kestle Barton 24

Thursday 2nd
Gardens Cottage 18
Kestle Barton 24

Friday 3rd
Kestle Barton 24

Saturday 4th
Kestle Barton 24

Sunday 5th
Kestle Barton 24

Tuesday 7th
Kestle Barton 24

Wednesday 8th
Kestle Barton 24

Thursday 9th
Kestle Barton 24

Friday 10th
Kestle Barton 24

Saturday 11th
Kestle Barton 24

Sunday 12th
Caervallack 8
Kestle Barton 24

Tuesday 14th
Kestle Barton 24
Pinsla Garden 33

Wednesday 15th
Kestle Barton 24
Pinsla Garden 33
South Bosent 39

Thursday 16th
◆ Caerhays Castle 7
Kestle Barton 24
South Bosent 39

Friday 17th
Kestle Barton 24

Saturday 18th
Kestle Barton 24

Sunday 19th
Kestle Barton 24
Trenarth 44
Trethew 45

Tuesday 21st
Kestle Barton 24

Wednesday 22nd
Kestle Barton 24

Thursday 23rd
Kestle Barton 24

Friday 24th
Dove Cottage 14
9 Higman Close 22
Kestle Barton 24

Saturday 25th
Dove Cottage 14
NEW Higher Balstyle 21
9 Higman Close 22
Kestle Barton 24

Sunday 26th
Kestle Barton 24

Tuesday 28th
Kestle Barton 24
Pinsla Garden 33

Wednesday 29th
Kestle Barton 24
Pinsla Garden 33

Thursday 30th
Kestle Barton 24

July

Friday 1st
Kestle Barton 24

Saturday 2nd
Kestle Barton 24
◆ Roseland House 37
NEW Suffree Farm 41

Sunday 3rd
Anvil Cottage 1
NEW Cardinham Gardens 9
Kestle Barton 24
◆ Roseland House 37
South Lea 40
NEW Suffree Farm 41
Windmills 50

Tuesday 5th
Kestle Barton 24

Wednesday 6th
Gardens Cottage 18
Kestle Barton 24

Thursday 7th
Gardens Cottage 18
Kestle Barton 24

Friday 8th
Kestle Barton 24

Saturday 9th
Dove Cottage 14
9 Higman Close 22
Kestle Barton 24

Sunday 10th
Dove Cottage 14
9 Higman Close 22
Kestle Barton 24

Tuesday 12th
Kestle Barton 24
Pinsla Garden 33

Wednesday 13th
Kestle Barton 24
Pinsla Garden 33
South Bosent 39

Thursday 14th
Kestle Barton 24
South Bosent 39

Friday 15th
NEW Cartmell House 11
Kestle Barton 24

Saturday 16th
◆ Chygurno 12
Kestle Barton 24

Sunday 17th
◆ Chygurno 12
Kestle Barton 24
NEW Lower
  Penbothidnow 28

Tuesday 19th
Kestle Barton 24

Wednesday 20th
Kestle Barton 24

Thursday 21st
Kestle Barton 24

Friday 22nd
Kestle Barton 24

Saturday 23rd
Kestle Barton 24

Sunday 24th
Byeways 6
Kestle Barton 24

Tuesday 26th
Kestle Barton 24
Pinsla Garden 33

Wednesday 27th
Kestle Barton 24
Pinsla Garden 33

Thursday 28th
Kestle Barton 24

Friday 29th
Kestle Barton 24

Saturday 30th
Kestle Barton 24

Sunday 31st
Dove Cottage 14
9 Higman Close 22
Kestle Barton 24

August

Monday 1st
Dove Cottage 14
9 Higman Close 22

Tuesday 2nd
Kestle Barton 24

Wednesday 3rd
Kestle Barton 24

Thursday 4th
Kestle Barton 24

Friday 5th
Kestle Barton 24

Saturday 6th
Kestle Barton 24

Sunday 7th
Kestle Barton 24

Tuesday 9th
Kestle Barton 24
Pinsla Garden 33

Wednesday 10th
Kestle Barton 24
Pinsla Garden 33

Thursday 11th
Kestle Barton 24

Friday 12th
Dove Cottage 14
9 Higman Close 22
Kestle Barton 24

Saturday 13th
Dove Cottage 14
9 Higman Close 22
Kestle Barton 24

Sunday 14th
Kestle Barton 24

Tuesday 16th
◆ Bonython Manor 4
Kestle Barton 24

Wednesday 17th
Kestle Barton 24
South Bosent 39

Thursday 18th
Kestle Barton 24
South Bosent 39

Friday 19th
Kestle Barton 24

Saturday 20th
Kestle Barton 24

Sunday 21st
Kestle Barton 24

Tuesday 23rd
Kestle Barton 24
Pinsla Garden 33

Wednesday 24th
Kestle Barton 24
Pinsla Garden 33

Thursday 25th
Kestle Barton 24

Friday 26th
Kestle Barton 24

Saturday 27th
Kestle Barton 24

Sunday 28th
Kestle Barton 24

Tuesday 30th
Kestle Barton 24

Wednesday 31st
Gardens Cottage 18
Kestle Barton 24

September

Thursday 1st
Gardens Cottage 18
Kestle Barton 24

Friday 2nd
Kestle Barton 24

Saturday 3rd
Ash Barn 2
Kestle Barton 24

Sunday 4th
Ash Barn 2
Kestle Barton 24
Trethew 45

Tuesday 6th
Kestle Barton 24

Wednesday 7th
Kestle Barton 24

Thursday 8th
Kestle Barton 24

Friday 9th
Kestle Barton 24

Saturday 10th
Kestle Barton 24

Sunday 11th
Kestle Barton 24

Tuesday 13th
Kestle Barton 24

Wednesday 14th
Kestle Barton 24
South Bosent 39

Thursday 15th
Kestle Barton 24
South Bosent 39

Friday 16th
Kestle Barton 24

Saturday 17th
Kestle Barton 24

Sunday 18th
Kestle Barton 24
NEW Towan House 42

Tuesday 20th
Kestle Barton 24

Wednesday 21st
Kestle Barton 24

Thursday 22nd
Kestle Barton 24

Friday 23rd
Kestle Barton 24

Saturday 24th
Kestle Barton 24

Sunday 25th
Byeways 6
Kestle Barton 24

Tuesday 27th
Kestle Barton 24

Wednesday 28th
Kestle Barton 24

October

Sunday 2nd
Trebartha Estate Garden
and Country Garden at
  Lemarne 43

By Arrangement

Arrange a personalised
garden visit with your
club, or group of friends,
on a date to suit you. See
individual garden entries
for full details.

THE GARDENS

Greenwith Meadow

🚹 ANVIL COTTAGE

South Hill, PL17 7LP. Geoff &
Barbara Clemerson, 01579 362623,
gcclemerson@gmail.com. *3m
NW of Callington. Head N on
A388 from Callington centre.
After ½ m L onto South Hill Rd
(signed South Hill), straight on for
3m. Gardens on R just before St
Sampson's Church.* **Sun 24 Apr,
Sun 3 July (1-5). Combined adm
with Windmills £6, chd free.
Home-made teas. Gluten free
refreshments available. Visits
also by arrangement May to Aug
for groups of 10 to 30. Donation to
Cornwall Air Ambulance.**
Essentially, this is a plantsman's
garden. Winding paths lead through a
series of themed rooms with familiar,
rare and unusual plants. Steps lead
up to a raised viewpoint looking west
towards Caradon Hill and Bodmin
Moor, and other paths take you on a
circular route through a rose garden,
hot beds, a tropical area, and a secret
garden.

🔟 ASH BARN

Callington, PL17 8BP. Mary
Martin. *3m E of Callington. Leaving
Callington on A390 (Tavistock
direction) take 1st R signed
Harrowbarrow. Turn R at T junction
in village then 1m down hill to
Glamorgan Mill. Parking on L.* **Sat 3,
Sun 4 Sept (10-5). Adm £5, chd
free. Home-made teas.**
Terraced 3 acre woodland garden, full
of magnolias, camellias and fruit trees,
underplanted with old roses, shrubs
and Tamar Valley narcissi. Intensive
herbaceous planting provides interest
for most of the year, and contrasts
with box and holly topiary. Narrow,
uneven paths and steps reflect the
wild wood atmosphere. There is
also a quarry edge, so no dogs or
unsupervised children.

🔟 ◆ BOCONNOC

Lostwithiel, PL22 0RG.
Fortescue Family, 01208 872507,
events@boconnoc.com,
www.boconnoc.com. *Off A390
between Liskeard & Lostwithiel.
From East Taphouse follow signs to
Boconnoc. (SatNav does not work
well in this area).* **For NGS: Sun
8 May (2-5). Adm £6, chd free.**

**Light refreshments in stable
yard. For other opening times and
information, please phone, email or
visit garden website.**
20 acres surrounded by parkland
and woods with magnificent trees,
flowering shrubs and stunning views.
The gardens are set amongst mature
trees which provide the backcloth
for exotic spring flowering shrubs,
woodland plants, with newly planted
magnolias and a fine collection of
hydrangeas. Bathhouse built in 1804,
obelisk built in 1771, house dating
from Domesday, deer park and C15
church.

🔟 ◆ BONYTHON MANOR

Cury Cross Lanes, Helston,
TR12 7BA. Mr & Mrs Richard
Nathan, 01326 240550,
sbonython@gmail.com,
www.bonythonmanor.co.uk.
*5m S of Helston. On main A3083
Helston to Lizard Rd. Turn L at Cury
Cross Lanes (Wheel Inn). Entrance
300yds on R.* **For NGS: Tue 16
Aug (2-4.30). Adm £9, chd £2.
Tea, coffee, fruit juices and
home-made cakes. For other
opening times and information,
please phone, email or visit garden
website.**
Magnificent 20 acre colour garden
inc sweeping hydrangea drive
to Georgian manor (not open).
Herbaceous walled garden, potager

with vegetables and picking flowers;
3 lakes in valley planted with
ornamental grasses, perennials and
South African flowers. A 'must see'
for all seasons colour.

🔟 BUCKS HEAD HOUSE GARDEN

Trengove Cross, Constantine,
TR11 5QR. Deborah Baker,
07801 444916,
deborah.fwbaker@gmail.com,
www.instagram.com/bucks_head_
garden. *5m SW of Falmouth. A394
towards Helston, L at Edgcumbe
towards Gweek/Constantine.
Proceed for 0.8 m then L towards
Constantine. Further 0.8m, garden
on L at Trengove Cross.* **Visits by
arrangement Apr to July Fridays
1-4 pm. (Combined opening with
The gARTen garden £8.50). Adm
£5, chd free. Tea.**
Enchanting cottage and woodland
gardens of native and rare trees,
shrubs and perennials, encouraging
biodiversity. The site of 1½ acres
is on a south facing Cornish hillside
with panoramic views. Protected by
essential windbreaks, the inspiring
collection of plants has been chosen
to create a calm and tranquil retreat.
During the summer months art works
will be on display. Wheelchair access
to lower garden and to woodland.

6 BYEWAYS

Dunheved Road, Launceston, PL15 9JE. Tony Reddicliffe. *Launceston town centre. 100yds from multi-storey car park past offices of Cornish & Devon Post into Dunheved Rd, 3rd bungalow on R.* Sun 24 July, Sun 25 Sept (1-5). Adm £5, chd free. Light refreshments.

Small town garden developed over 11 yrs by enthusiastic amateur gardeners. Herbaceous borders, rockery. Tropicals inc bananas, gingers and senecio. Stream and water features. Roof garden. Japanese inspired tea house and courtyard with bridge. Fig tree and Pawlonia lark area giving secluded seating. Living pergola. Wildflower planting. New this year is a sunken garden area with water feature.

SPECIAL EVENT

7 ◆ CAERHAYS CASTLE

Caerhays Estate, Gorran, St Austell, PL26 6LY. Charles Williams, 01872 501310, enquiries@caerhays.co.uk, www.caerhays.co.uk. *Please follow brown signs to Caerhays Estate.* For NGS: Thur 16 June (11-4.30). Adm £65. Pre-booking essential, please visit www.ngs.org.uk for information & booking. Buffet lunch served with wine in the castle. For other opening times and information, please phone, email or visit garden website.

Caerhays Castle and estate has over 140 acres of woodland garden, which are recognised by English Heritage Listed Grade II*. It is home to one of the UK's National Magnolia Collections and is also famous for its unusual and rare camellias inc *Camellia x williamsii*. The garden also features many rhododendrons and hydrangea. The plants within this garden are like nothing else you will ever see, they are huge and spectacular in colour. A limited number of tickets have been made available for this extremely special one-day event. There will be a warm welcome at 11am, followed by a private guided tour with the owner, Charles Williams. Following the tour, there will be a light buffet lunch served around 1pm, inc wines served in the dining halls of the Castle and kindly hosted by Charles & Lizzie Williams. In the afternoon there will be the opportunity to explore further the wider grounds and parkland of the estate entirely at your own leisure.

---

8 CAERVALLACK

St Martin, Helston, TR12 6DF. Matt Robinson & Louise McClary, 01326 221130, mat@build-art.co.uk. *5m SE of Helston. Go through Mawgan village, over 2 bridges, past Gear Farm shop; go past turning on L, garden next farmhouse on L. Parking is in field opp entrance.* Sun 12 June (1.30-4.30). Adm £5, chd free. Tea & home-made cakes; scones, clotted cream & jam.

Romantic garden arranged into rooms, the collaboration between an artist and an architect. Colour and form of plants against architectural experiments in cob, concrete and shaped hedges and topiary. Grade II listed farmhouse and orchard. Roses and wisteria a speciality. 25 yrs in the making. Arts & Crafts cob walls and paving; heroic 54ft pedestrian footbridge; 5 sided meditation studio, cast concrete ponds and amphitheatre; coppice and wildflower meadow; mature orchard and vegetable plot.

GROUP OPENING

9 NEW CARDINHAM GARDENS

Cardinham, Bodmin, PL30 4BN. *5m NE of Bodmin. Signs in Cardinham village, garden map outside parish hall, opp. church.* Sun 29 May, Sun 3 July (11-5). Combined adm £6, chd free. Home-made teas in Cardinham Parish Hall, opp Cardinham Church. Teas from 2pm to 5pm.

NEW THE BEECHES
Rosemary Rowe.
Open on Sun 3 July

NEW HAYGROVE COTTAGE
Loveday Sutton.
Open on Sun 3 July

NEW MADDERHAY
Susan Edward-Collins.
Open on Sun 3 July

THE OLD SCHOOL HOUSE
Mrs Libby Pidcock.
Open on Sun 29 May

PINSLA GARDEN
Mark & Claire Woodbine.
Open on all dates
(See separate entry)

The rural parish of Cardinham on the SW side of Bodmin Moor has a wide range of eco-systems as the moorland merges into woodland and ancient

---

downs and meadows. May 29th group opening has 2 gardens, The Old School House, a classic cottage garden with beehives, vegetables, flowers, pond and espaliers, and Pinsla Garden with naturalistic planting, stone circle and vegetable garden in peaceful woodland. On July 3rd there are 4 gardens to enjoy. Madderhay with its soft palette of flowers and scented roses clambering over arches, overlooking rolling countryside. Haygrove Cottage at 200m has spectacular views across the valley. It is an informal cottage garden, encouraging wildlife with pond, meadow, vegetables, and flowers. The Beeches is a small rural idyll being adapted for easier maintenance, with shrubs, colourful containers, roses and climbers. Pinsla Garden will show continuous colour with seasonal planting. Parking and gardens map at Parish Hall. Madderhay only open from 2pm to 5pm.

---

10 CARMINOWE VALLEY GARDEN

Tangies, Gunwalloe, TR12 7PU. Mr & Mrs Peter Stanley, 01326 565868, stanley.m2@sky.com. *3m SW of Helston. A3083 Helston-Lizard rd. R opp main gate to Culdrose. 1m downhill, garden on R.* Visits by arrangement May & June for groups of 5+. Adm £5, chd free. Cream teas.

Overlooking the beautiful Carminowe valley towards Loe Pool this abundant garden combines native oak woodland, babbling brook and large natural pond with more formal areas. wildflowers, mown pathways, shrubberies, orchard. Enclosed cottage garden, spring colours and roses early summer provide huge contrast. Gravel paths, slopes.

---

11 NEW CARTMELL HOUSE

Trelash, Warbstow, Launceston, PL15 8RL. Katie Webb. *North Cornwall. From A39 take turning to Otterham, follow road for 2m into Trelash. From A395 turn at pub to Warbstow, follow rd 1m, then1st L, then R, then L.* Fri 15 July (9-4). Adm £4.50, chd free. Pre-booking essential, please visit www.ngs. org.uk for information & booking. Home-made teas.

A 2 acre garden, once an empty field, now a wildlife haven. The garden is full

of different areas inc a Mediterranean style courtyard, a cottage garden full of flowers, fruit and vegetable garden and places to sit. Paths lead you through a ³⁄₄ acre young woodland to a large willow dome, a ³⁄₄ acre meadow and an orchard. Birds, mammals, amphibians, insects, and reptiles are encouraged here. Lots of places to sit around the garden. Wheelchair access to refreshments over slate chippings. Garden can be accessed via grass ramp. There are steps and some paths and gateways are narrow.

12 ◆ CHYGURNO
Lamorna, TR19 6XH. Dr & Mrs Robert Moule, 01736 732153, rmoule010@btinternet.com. *4m S of Penzance. Off B3315. Follow signs for The Lamorna Cove Hotel. Garden is at top of hill, past Hotel on L.* **For NGS: Sat 23, Sun 24 Apr, Sat 16, Sun 17 July (2-5). Adm £5, chd free. For other opening times and information, please phone or email.**
Beautiful, unique, 3 acre cliffside garden overlooking Lamorna Cove. Planting started in 1998, mainly southern hemisphere shrubs and exotics with hydrangeas, camellias and rhododendrons. Woodland area with tree ferns set against large granite outcrops. Garden terraced with steep steps and paths. Plenty of benches so you can take a rest and enjoy the wonderful views.

13 CRUGSILLICK MANOR
Ruan High Lanes, Truro, TR2 5LJ. Dr Alison Agnew & Mr Brian Yule, 07538 218201, alisonagnew@icloud.com. *On Roseland Peninsula. Turn off A390 Truro-St Austell rd onto A3078 towards St Mawes. Approx 5m after Tregony turn 1st L after Ruan High Lanes towards Veryan, garden is 200yds on R. Limited parking.* **Sun 15 May (11-5). Adm £5, chd free. Tea, coffee, soft drinks, cakes and light lunches. Visits also by arrangement May to Oct for groups of 12 to 40. We can also provide tea and cakes.**
2 acre garden, substantially re-landscaped and planted, mostly over last 10 yrs. To the side of the C17/C18 house, a wooded bank drops down to walled kitchen garden and hot garden. In front, sweeping yew hedges and paths define oval lawns

and broad mixed borders. On a lower terrace, the focus is a large pond and the planting is predominantly exotic flowering trees and shrubs. Wheelchair access to the central level of the garden, the house and cafe. Garden is on several levels connected by fairly steep sloping gravel paths.

14 DOVE COTTAGE
Lantoom, Dobwalls, Liskeard, PL14 4LR. Becky Martin. *Do not use postcode for SatNav. In Dobwalls at double mini r'about take road to Duloe, About 20 metres after end-of-speed-limit sign turn L at football club. Follow concrete track.* **Fri 24, Sat 25 June, Sat 9, Sun 10, Sun 31 July, Mon 1, Fri 12, Sat 13 Aug (1-5). Combined adm with 9 Higman Close £6, chd free.**
Two very different, modestly-sized enclosed gardens. The three owners have between them over 100 yrs of professional horticultural experience. Replanted from scratch in 2017 showing what can be achieved in 5 yrs. Separate areas with different types of planting. Emphasis on colour. Narrow winding paths, shady pergola,

deck with tropical planting, tiny sunroom, lush foliage area.

15 EAST DOWN BARN
Menheniot, Liskeard, PL14 3QU. David & Shelley Lockett, 07803 159662. *S side of village nr cricket ground. Turn off A38 at Hayloft restaurant/railway stn junction & head towards Menheniot village. Follow NGS signs from sharp LH bend as you enter village.* **Sun 8 May (1-5). Adm £4, chd free. Home-made teas. Visits also by arrangement Apr & May for groups of 20+.**
Garden laid down between 1986-1991 with the conversion of the barn into a home and covers almost ¹⁄₂ acre of east sloping land with stream running north-south acting as the easterly boundary. 3 terraces before garden starts to level out at the stream. Garden won awards in the early years under the stewardship of the original owners. Ducks are in residence in the stream so regret no dogs.

Cartmell House

16 ETHNEVAS COTTAGE

Constantine, Falmouth, TR11 5PY.
Lyn Watson & Ray Chun,
01326 340076. *6m SW of Falmouth.
Nearest main rds A39, A394. Follow
signs for Constantine. At lower
village sign, at bottom of winding hill,
turn off on private lane. Garden ¾ m
up hill.* **Sun 1 May (1-5). Adm £5,
chd free. Home-made teas. Visits
also by arrangement Mar to June.**
Isolated granite cottage in 2 acres.
Intimate flower and vegetable garden.
Bridge over stream to large pond
and primrose path through semi-wild
bog area. Hillside with grass paths
among native and exotic trees.
Many camellias and rhododendrons.
Mixed shrubs and herbaceous beds,
wildflower glade, spring bulbs. A
garden of discovery with hidden
delights.

17 GARDEN COTTAGE

Gunwalloe, Helston, TR12 7QB.
Dan & Beth Tarling, 01326 241906,
beth@gunwalloe.com,
www.gunwalloecottages.co.uk.
*Just beyond Halzephron Inn
at Gunwalloe. Cream cottage
with green windows.* **Visits by
arrangement Mar to Oct. Adm £5,
chd £5. Cream teas.**
Coastal cottage garden. Small garden
with traditional cottage flowers,
vegetable garden, greenhouse and
meadow with far reaching views.
Artistically planted spring bulbs.
Instagram: seaview_gunwalloe.
Garden featured in Country Living
magazine.

18 GARDENS COTTAGE

Prideaux, St Blazey, PL24 2SS.
Sue & Roger Paine, 07786 367610,
sue.newton@btinternet.com. *1m
from railway Xing on A390 in St Blazey.
Turn into Prideaux Rd opp Gulf petrol
station on A390 in St Blazey (signed
Luxulyan). Proceed ½ m. Turn R
(signed Luxulyan Valley and Prideaux)
and follow signs.* **Wed 1, Thur 2
June, Wed 6, Thur 7 July, Wed 31
Aug, Thur 1 Sept (2-5). Adm £5,
chd free. Home-made teas. Visits
also by arrangement May to Sept
for groups of 12 to 30. Limited
parking - maximum of 9 cars.**
Set in a tranquil location on the edge
of Luxulyan valley, work commenced
on creating a 1½ acre garden from
scratch in winter 2015. The aim
has been to create a garden that's
sympathetic to its surrounding
landscape, has year-round interest
with lots of colour, is productive and
simply feels good to be in. Check our
Facebook page for special events - @
gardenscottageprideaux.

19 NEW THE GARTEN GARDEN

Lower Treculliacks House,
Constantine, Falmouth,
TR11 5QW. Dr Sara Gadd & Dr
Daro Montag, 07814 885141,
sara@gartendesign.co.uk, www.
gardendesignincornwall.co.uk.
*1½ m N of Gweek, 1m NW of
Constantine. A394 Falmouth-
Helston. At Edgcumbe go to
Gweek. Take 2nd L after 1½ m at
staggered Xrds. On R after 150m.
From Constantine go to Brill.
Take Rame road. After 1m go L
to Seworgan. 400m, garden on
L.* **Visits by arrangement Apr
to July for groups of up to 20.**

The gARTen Garden

Friday mornings only. (Combined opening with Bucks Head House £8.50). Adm £5, chd free. Light refreshments. Teas are help-yourself from outside of the tea cabin in the coppice. An honesty box is provided. Teas can be taken anywhere in the garden to enjoy!.

Ecologically, organically and artistically executed, embracing ecosystems, home, work, play, children, plants, food, wildlife and animals. Granite terrace with spring bulb displays, tranquil oriental-style pond garden with sarracenia border, acers, tree ferns and fern rockery, short bamboo walk, small coppice with cedar tea house, willow circle, glasshouse and vegetable garden, active design studio. Wheelchair access to both sides of the garden. Small steps to negotiate. Surfaces are all uneven.In winter the lower areas of the garden are boggy.

&. ❀ ☕ 🍽 »))

20 NEW GREENWITH MEADOW

Greenwith, Perranwell Station, Truro, TR3 7LS. Kathy Atkins, 01872 862772. *In Perranwell village go up hill signed Greenwith. At Xrds go straight on & garden is the 2nd on R. Parking further up on road, well tucked in or in Silverhill Rd on R.* **Sat 7, Sun 8 May (12-5). Adm £4, chd free.** Visits also by arrangement Apr to July.

Smallish garden made in the last 6 yrs by artist owner. Flower borders, roses, gravel garden, small meadow areas, and wildlife pond. Many sitting areas and lots of plants in containers.

❀

21 NEW HIGHER BALSTYLE

Zelah, Truro, TR4 9JJ. Jonathan McCulloch. *From the Hawkins Arms, head west. After the bus stop turn R, after 200yds turn R on sharp LH bend.* **Sat 25 June (10-4). Adm £5, chd free. Light refreshments.**

A new garden created by the owner since 2016, from an overgrown market garden. The front garden is laid to lawn with a 'Cornish' spring shrubbery and an orchard. The rear garden has a developing border and a productive walled vegetable garden. A 3 acre woodland was planted in 2021. A wheelchair can access the borders and front garden, but not the woodland.

&. 🐕 ☕

22 9 HIGMAN CLOSE

Dobwalls, Liskeard, PL14 4LW. Jim Stephens & Sue Martin. *3m W of Liskeard. From double mini-r'about in Dobwalls village take road to Duloe, take 2nd R onto Treheath Road, then 1st R into Higman Close.* **Fri 24, Sat 25 June, Sat 9, Sun 10, Sun 31 July, Mon 1, Fri 12, Sat 13 Aug (1-5). Combined adm with Dove Cottage £6, chd free.**

Two very different, modestly-sized enclosed gardens. The three owners have between them over a 100 yrs of professional horticultural experience. A restless, constantly changing, unapologetically busy garden, full of good plants but also colour, scent and surprises. Sue's glasshouse is overflowing with cacti and succulents, some over 35 yrs old.

❀

23 ◆ THE JAPANESE GARDEN

St Mawgan, TR8 4ET. Natalie Hore & Stuart Ellison, 01637 860116, info@japanesegarden.co.uk, www.japanesegarden.co.uk. *6m E of Newquay. St Mawgan village is directly below Newquay Airport. Follow brown & white road signs on A3059 and B3276.* **For NGS: Sun 15, Mon 16 May (10-6). Adm £5, chd £2.50. Pre-booking essential, please phone 01637 860116, email info@japanesegarden. co.uk or visit http://www. japanesegarden.co.uk for information & booking.** For other opening times and information, please phone, email or visit garden website.

Discover an oasis of tranquillity in a Japanese-style Cornish garden, set in approx 1 acre. Spectacular Japanese maples and azaleas, symbolic teahouse, koi pond, bamboo grove, stroll woodland, zen and moss gardens. A place created for contemplation and meditation. Adm free to gift shop, bonsai and plant areas. Featured in BBC2 Big Dreams Small Spaces.Refreshments available in village a short walk from garden. 90% wheelchair accessible, with gravel paths.

&. ❀

24 KESTLE BARTON

Manaccan, Helston, TR12 6HU. Karen Townsend, 01326 231811, info@kestlebarton.co.uk, www.kestlebarton.co.uk. *Leave Helston on A3083 towards Lizard. At the R'about take 1st exit onto B3293 & follow signs towards St Keverne;* after Trelowarren turn L and follow the brown signs for appprox 4m. **Every Tue to Sun 1 June to 28 Sept (10.30-5). Adm by donation.** Modest Tea Room in garden. Cash only honesty box. Tea/coffee, cakes, ice creams, apple juice from our own orchards.

A delightful garden near Frenchmans Creek, on the Lizard, which is the setting for Kestle Barton Gallery; wildflower meadow, Cornish orchard with named varieties and a formal garden with prairie planting in blocks by James Alexander Sinclair. It is a riot of colour in summer and continues to delight well into late summer. Parking, honesty box tea hut. Art Gallery. Good wheelchair access and reasonably accessible WC. Dogs on leads welcome.

&. 🐕 🚻 ☕ 🍽

25 ◆ LAMORRAN HOUSE

Upper Castle Road, St Mawes, Truro, TR2 5BZ. Robert Dudley-Cooke, 01326 270800, info@lamorrangarden.co.uk, www.lamorrangarden.co.uk. *A3078, R past garage at entrance to St Mawes. ¾m on L. ¼m from castle if using passenger ferry service.* **For NGS: Sat 30 Apr (11-4). Adm £6.50, chd free. Home-made teas.** For other opening times and information, please phone, email or visit garden website.

4 acre subtropical garden overlooking Falmouth Bay. Designed by owner in an Italianate/Cote d'Azur style. Extensive collection of Mediterranean and subtropical plants inc large collection of palms *Butia capitata/ Butia yatay* and tree ferns. Reflects both design and remarkable microclimate. Beautiful collection of Japanese azaleas and tender rhododendrons. Italianate garden with many water features. Champion trees. Large collection of Southern hemisphere plants.

🐕 🚗 ☕

26 THE LODGE

Fletchersbridge, Bodmin, PL30 4AN. Mr Tony Ryde. *2m E of Bodmin. From A38 at Glynn Crematorium r'about take rd towards Cardinham & continue down to hamlet of Fletchersbridge. Park at Stable Art on R. Short walk to garden 1st R over river bridge.* **Sun 24 Apr (12-5.30). Adm £5, chd free. Cream teas. Open nearby Pinsla Garden.**

3 acre riverside garden created since 1998, specialising in trees and shrubs chosen for their flowers, foliage and form, and embracing a Gothic lodge remodelled in 2016, once part of the Glynn estate. Water garden with ponds, waterfalls and abstract sculptures. magnolias, azaleas, rhododendrons, camellias, cornus, prunus and late spring bulbs star in April. Wheelchair access to gravelled areas around house and along Lside of garden.

&. ✿ ☕

27 ◆ THE LOST GARDENS OF HELIGAN

Pentewan, St Austell, PL26 6EN. Heligan Gardens Ltd, 01726 845100, heligan.reception@heligan.com, www.heligan.com. *5m S of St Austell. From St Austell take B3273 signed Mevagissey, follow signs.* **For opening times and information, please phone, email or visit garden website.**

Lose yourself in the mysterious world of The Lost Gardens where an exotic sub-tropical jungle, atmospheric Victorian pleasure grounds, an interactive wildlife project and the finest productive gardens in Britain all await your discovery. Wheelchair access to Northern gardens. Armchair tour shows video of unreachable areas. Wheelchairs available at reception free of charge.

&. ✿ ✱ 🚌 NPC ☕

28 NEW LOWER PENBOTHIDNOW

Penbothidno Lane, Constantine, Falmouth, TR11 5AU. Dorothy Livingston, 07809 200385, Dorothy.livingston@me.com. *Signs point downhill on Fore St ⅓ m & top of lane, opp Save the Children Shop at bottom of Fore St - 200 metres at end of lane. Park by church or on street. Disabled parking only at property.* **Sun 8 May, Sun 17 July (2-6). Adm £6, chd free. Home-made teas. Outside seating. WC**

in studio available. **Visits also by arrangement Mar to Oct for groups of up to 10. Please call or WhatsApp.**

Hillside garden of about 2 acres with different areas planted in different styles and plant selections, ranging from formal to wildflower meadow. Surrounded by field and woods. Colour year-round with high point for shrubs and trees in late spring and with herbaceous border, hydrangeas and flowering shrubs in July/August. Lots of seating areas. Plenty to interest a plantsperson. Spring and summer shrubs and flowering trees. Formal garden with clipped hedges and wisteria. Tree fern grove. Southern hemisphere plants Summer herbaceous border, lawns and sculpture. Wheelchair can access drive and main lawns and see over or into most areas of the garden inc the formal garden.

&. ✿ ☕))

29 NEW MALIBU

Tristram Cliff, Polzeath, Wadebridge, PL27 6TP. Nick Pickles, 07944 414006, nickdpickles@gmail.com. *Travel via Pityme/Rock/Trebetherick past Oystercatcher pub on L. Take 2nd L signposted Tristram Caravan Park/ Cracking Crab Restaurant. Then L signposted Tristram Cliff, up to end house. Free parking for coast & beach.* **Visits by arrangement for groups of up to 20. 10 to 4pm. Adm £4, chd free. Cream teas, coffee, cakes & light lunches offered by prior agreement.**

Just yards away from the Coast Path with stunning views over the beach and Pentire headland, Malibu consists of a sheltered compact garden to the rear and a general interest front garden. An interesting mix of features, different rockeries and strong focus on succulents, ferns and herbaceous plants. Greenhouse with many plants make this a rounded garden experience. We welcome dogs on leads. Wheelchairs can access the front garden only with ease. Ground floor WC available.

&. ✿ ✱ ☕ ⛩

30 NAVAS HILL HOUSE

Bosanath Valley, Mawnan Smith, Falmouth, TR11 5LL. Aline & Richard Turner. *1½ m from Trebah & Glendurgan Gdns. Head for Mawnan Smith, pass Trebah & Glendurgan Gdns then follow yellow signs. Don't follow SatNav which suggests*

you turn R before Mawnan Smith - congestion alert! **Sun 15 May (2-5). Adm £5, chd free. Home-made teas on the veranda/terrace. 'All you can eat' £5.00. Open nearby Port Navas Chapel.**

8½ acre elevated valley garden with paddocks, woodland, kitchen garden and ornamental areas. The ornamental garden consists of 2 plantsman areas with specialist trees and shrubs, walled rose garden, water features and rockery. Young and established wooded areas with bluebells, camellia walks and young large leafed rhododendrons. Seating areas with views across wooded valley. Parking is in Nibbs car park opp the garden, then a 2 min walk up the drive. There are limited disabled parking places near the house which must be pre booked via alineturner@btinternet.com. Partial wheelchair access, some gravel and grass paths.

&. ✿ ☕))

31 ◆ PENCARROW

Washaway, Bodmin, PL30 3AG. Molesworth-St Aubyn Family, 01208 841369, info@pencarrow.co.uk, www.pencarrow.co.uk. *4m NW of Bodmin. Signed off A389 & B3266. Free parking.* **For NGS: Mon 25 Apr (10-5). Adm £7.50, chd free. Cream teas. For other opening times and information, please phone, email or visit garden website.**

50 acres of tranquil, family-owned Grade II* listed gardens. Superb specimen conifers, azaleas, magnolias and camellias galore. Many varieties of rhododendron give a blaze of spring colour; blue hydrangeas line the mile-long carriage drive throughout the summer. Discover the Iron Age hill fort, lake, Italian gardens and granite rock garden. Dogs welcome, café and children's play area. Gravel paths, some steep slopes.

&. ✿ ✱ 🚌 ☕

32 PENWARNE

Mawnan Smith, Falmouth, TR11 5PH. Mrs R Sawyer, penwarnegarden@gmail.com. *1m outside Mawnan Smith towards Mabe Burnthouse & Falmouth.* **Visits by arrangement Mar to June for groups of 10 to 20. Adm £6, chd free.**

Originally planted in the late C19, this 12 acre garden inc extensive plantings of camellias, rhododendrons

and azaleas. Special features inc large magnolias and a number of fine mature trees inc copper beech, handkerchief tree and Himalayan cedar. The walled garden, believed to be the site of a medieval chapel, houses herbaceous planting, climbing roses and fruit trees. Historic house and gardens with many mature specimens.

33 PINSLA GARDEN
Glynn, Nr Cardinham, Bodmin, PL30 4AY. Mark & Claire Woodbine, www.pinslagarden.wordpress .com. *3½ m E of Bodmin. From A30 or Bodmin take A38 towards Plymouth, 1st L at r'about, past Crematorium & Cardinham woods turning. Go towards Cardinham village, up steep hill, 2m on R.* **Sun 24, Tue 26, Wed 27 Apr, Tue 10, Tue 24, Wed 25 May, Tue 14, Wed 15, Tue 28, Wed 29 June, Tue 12, Wed 13, Tue 26, Wed 27 July, Tue 9, Wed 10, Tue 23, Wed 24 Aug (9-5). Adm £4, chd free. Opening with Cardinham Gardens on Sun 29 May, Sun 3 July (11-5).**
Surround yourself with deep nature. Pinsla is a tranquil cottage garden buzzing with insects enjoying the sheltered sunny edge of a wild wood. Lose yourself in a colourful tapestry of naturalistic planting. There are lots of unusual planting combinations, cloud pruning, intricate paths, garden art and a stone circle. Sorry, no teas but you are welcome to bring your own thermos. Partial wheelchair access as some paths are narrow and bumpy.

34 NEW PORT NAVAS CHAPEL
Port Navas, Constantine, Falmouth, TR11 5RQ. Keith Wilkins & Linda World, 01326 341206, keithwilkins47@gmail.com. *From the direction of Constantine, we are the 2nd driveway on R after the 'Port Navas' sign.* **Sun 15 May (11.30-2.30). Adm £5, chd free. Open nearby Navas Hill House. Visits also by arrangement Mar to Nov for groups of up to 20.**
Japanese style garden set in ¾ acre of woodland, next to the old Methodist Chapel, with ornamental ponds and waterfalls, rock formations, Tsukubai water feature, lanterns, woodland stream and geodesic dome. Teas available between 2pm-5pm at Navas Hill House, 4 mins away by car (1.1 miles).

35 ◆ POTAGER GARDEN
High Cross, Constantine, Falmouth, TR11 5RF. Mr Mark Harris, 01326 341258, enquiries@potagergarden.org, www.potagergarden.org. *5m SW of Falmouth. From Falmouth, follow signs to Constantine. From Helston, drive through Constantine and continue towards Falmouth.* **For opening times and information, please phone, email or visit garden website.**
Potager has emerged from the bramble choked wilderness of an abandoned plant nursery. With mature trees which were once nursery stock and lush herbaceous planting interspersed with fruit and vegetables Potager Garden aims to demonstrate the beauty of productive organic gardening. There are games to play, hammocks to laze in and boules and badminton to enjoy. Potager café serving vegetarian food all day.

36 RIVERSIDE COTTAGE
St. Clement, Truro, TR1 1SZ. Billa & Nick Jeans. *1½ m SE of Truro. From Trafalgar r'about on A39 in Truro, follow signs for St Clement, up St Clement Hill. R at top of hill, continue to car park by river; Riverside Cottage is first cottage on L.* **Every Tue 5 Apr to 31 May (10-4). Adm by donation. Tea, coffee & cakes.**
Small wildlife friendly cottage garden overlooking beautiful Tresillian River. Wildflower areas, soft fruit and raised bed vegetable patch. Old apple trees, sloping grassy paths and steps and plenty of seats affording places to rest to enjoy views down river. Sadly not suitable for wheelchairs.

Malibu

37 ◆ ROSELAND HOUSE
Chacewater, TR4 8QB. Mr &
Mrs Pridham, 01872 560451,
charlie@roselandhouse.co.uk,
www.roselandhouse.co.uk. *4m
W of Truro. At end of main street
in Truro. Park in village car park
(100yds) or on surrounding rds.*
For NGS: Sat 2, Sun 3 July (1-5).
Adm £5, chd free. Home-made
teas. For other opening times and
information, please phone, email or
visit garden website.
The 1 acre garden is a mass of
summer colour when the National
Collection of *Clematis viticella* is
at its peak in July, other climbing
plants abound lending both foliage
and scent, the conservatory and
greenhouses are also full of unusual
and interesting plants. Two ponds
and a Victorian conservatory. Some
slopes.

   🚻 ❀ NPC ☕ 🎪

38 ◆ ST MICHAEL'S MOUNT
Marazion, TR17 0HS.
James & Mary St Levan,
www.stmichaelsmount.co.uk.
*2½m E of Penzance. ½m from
shore at Marazion by Causeway;
otherwise by motor boat.* For
opening times and information,
please visit garden website.
Infuse your senses with colour and
scent in the unique sub-tropical
gardens basking in the mild climate
and salty breeze. Clinging to granite
slopes the terraced beds tier steeply
to the ocean's edge, boasting tender
exotics from places such as Mexico,
the Canary Islands and South Africa.
Laundry lawn, mackerel bank,
pill box, gun emplacement, tiered
terraces, well, tortoise lawn. Walled
gardens, seagull seat.

   ❀ 🚗 ☕ 🎪

39 SOUTH BOSENT
Liskeard, PL14 4LX. Adrienne
Lloyd & Trish Wilson. *2½m W of
Liskeard. From r'about at junction
of A390 & A38 take turning to
Dobwalls. At mini-r'about R to Duloe,
after 1¼m at Xrds turn R. Garden
on L after ¼m.* Wed 11, Thur 12
May, Wed 15, Thur 16 June, Wed
13, Thur 14 July, Wed 17, Thur
18 Aug, Wed 14, Thur 15 Sept
(2-5.30). Adm £5, chd free. Home-
made teas.
This garden is an example of work in
progress currently being developed
from farmland. The aim is to create
a combination of interesting plants
coupled with habitat for wildlife over a

total of 9½ acres. There are several
garden areas, woodland gardens, a
meadow, ponds of varying sizes, inc
new rill and waterfall. In spring, the
bluebell wood trail runs alongside the
stream. Regret no wheelchair access
to bluebell wood due to steps.

   ♿ 🚻 ❀ ☕ 🎪

40 SOUTH LEA
Pillaton, Saltash, PL12 6QS. Viv
& Tony Laurillard, 01579 350629,
tonyandviv.laurillard@gmail.com.
*Opp Weary Friar pub. 4m S of
Callington. Signed from r'abouts
on A388 at St Mellion & Hatt, & on
A38 at Landrake. Roadside parking.
Please do not park in pub car park.*
Sun 8 May, Sun 3 July (1-5). Adm
£5, chd free. Home-made teas.
Visits also by arrangement May to
July for groups of 10+.
In the front a path winds through
interesting landscaping with a small
pond and unusual planting. Tropical
beds by front door with palms,
cannas, etc. The back garden, with
views over the valley, is a pretty
picture in May with spring bulbs
and clematis, with attractive mixed
borders in July. Lawns are separated
by a fair sized fish pond and the
small woodland area is enchanting
in spring. Plenty of seating. Due to
steps, wheelchair access only to front
dry garden and rear terrace, from
which much of garden can be viewed.

   ♿ 🚻 🚗 ☕

41 NEW SUFFREE FARM
Probus, Truro, TR2 4HZ. Chris &
Wendy Harvey Clark. *1m south of
centre of Probus. Take A3078 (Tregony/
St Mawes) turning off the A390 Probus
bypass. After 600 yds layby on R of
road. Through layby down gravel track.
Parking in field round bend.* Sat 2,
Sun 3 July (2-6). Adm £5, chd free.
Home-made teas.
Cornish farmhouse surrounded
by two acre garden overlooking
beautiful wooded valley. Borders,
Mediterranean garden, wildflower
areas, woodland plantation, Shetland
ponies and pigs.

   ♿ 🚻 ☕ 🎪

42 NEW TOWAN HOUSE
Old Church Road, Mawnan
Smith, Falmouth, TR11 5HX.
Mr Dave & Mrs Tessa Thomson,
01326 250378. *On entering
Mawnan Smith, fork L at the Red
Lion pub. When you see the gate to
Nansidwell, turn R into Old Church*

*Rd. Continue until you see the sign
for parking.* Sun 18 Sept (2-5). Adm
£5, chd free. Home-made teas.
Visits also by arrangement Apr to
Sept for groups of 5 to 20.
Towan House is a coastal garden with
some unusual plants and views to St
Mawes, St Anthony Head lighthouse
and beyond with easy access to the
SW coast path overlooking Falmouth
Bay. It is approximately ¼ acre and
divided into 2 gardens, one exposed
to the north and east winds, the other
sheltered allowing tropical plants to
flourish such as 'Hedychium' and
cannas.

   ❀ ☕ 🎪

43 TREBARTHA ESTATE GARDEN AND COUNTRY GARDEN AT LEMARNE
Trebartha, nr Launceston,
PL15 7PD. The Latham Family. *6m
SW of Launceston. North Hill, SW of
Launceston nr junction of B3254 &
B3257. No coaches.* Sun 15 May,
Sun 2 Oct (2-5). Adm £8, chd free.
Home-made teas.
Historic landscape gardens featuring
streams, cascades, rocks and
woodlands, inc fine trees, bluebells,
ornamental walled garden and
private modern country garden at
Lemarne. Ongoing development of
C19 American garden and C18 fish
ponds. Allow at least 1 hour for a
circular walk. Some steep and rough
paths, which can be slippery when
wet. Stout footwear advised. October
opening for autumn colour.

   🚻 ☕

44 TRENARTH
High Cross, Constantine,
Falmouth, TR11 5JN. Lucie
Nottingham, 01326 340444,
lmnottingham@btinternet.com,
www.trenarthgardens.com. *6m SW
of Falmouth. Main rd A39/A394 Truro
to Helston, follow Constantine signs.
High X garage turn L for Mawnan,
30yds on R down dead end lane,
Trenarth is ½m at end of lane.* Sun
19 June (2-5). Adm £5, chd free.
Home-made teas. Visits also
by arrangement Feb to Nov for
groups of up to 30.
4 acres round C17 farmhouse in
peaceful pastoral setting. Year-round
and varied. Emphasis on tender,
unusual plants, structure and form.
C16 courtyard, listed garden walls,
holm oak avenue, yew rooms,
vegetable garden, traditional potting
shed, orchard, palm and gravel area
with close planting inc agapanthus,

agave and dierama, woodland area with children's interest. Circular walk down ancient green lane via animal pond to Trenarth Bridge, returning through woods. Abundant wildlife. Bees in tree bole, lesser horseshoe bat colony, swallows, wildflowers and butterflies. Family friendly, children's play area, the Wolery, and plenty of room to run, jump and climb.

45 TRETHEW

Lanlivery, nr Bodmin, PL30 5BZ. Ginnie & Giles Clotworthy. *3 m W of Lostwithiel. On rd between Lanlivery and Luxulyan. Signed from both villages and A390. Do not use SatNav.* Sun 19 June (12-6); Sun 4 Sept (12-5). Adm £5, chd free. Home-made teas.

Series of profusely planted and colourful areas surrounding an ancient Cornish farmhouse. Features include terracing with wisteria and rose covered pergola, gazebo and herbaceous borders within yew and beech hedges, all overlooking orchard with old fashioned roses and pond beyond. Magnificent views. This is a garden on a hill with flat areas around the house. Parking is in field with uneven drive and some gravel.

46 TREVILLEY

Sennen, Penzance, TR19 7AH. Patrick Gale & Aidan Hicks, 01736 871808, trevilley@btinternet.com. *For walkers, Trevilley lies on footpath from Trevescan to Polgigga & Nanjizal. Trevilley is a signed unmade track just outside Trevescan. If you get to the white house, confusingly called Trevilley Farmhouse, you need to reverse!* Visits by arrangement June & July for groups of 6 to 30. Adm £6, chd free.

Eccentric, romantic and constantly evolving garden, as befits the intense creativity of its owners, carved out of an expanse of concrete farmyard over 20 yrs. Inc elaborate network of decorative cobbling, pools, container garden, vegetable garden, shade garden, the largely subtropical mowhay garden and both owners' studios but arguably its glory is the westernmost walled rose garden in England. Dogs are welcome on leads and there's direct access to fields where they can let off steam. The garden visit can form the climax of enjoying the circular coast path walk

from Land's End to Nanjizal and back across the fields. The rose garden is accessible by wheelchair though much of its surface is uneven due to decorative cobbling. Beyond that lie narrow paths and steps.

47 NEW ◆ TREVINCE ESTATE GARDENS

Gwennap, Redruth, TR16 6BA. Richard & Trish Stone, 01209 822725, info@trevince.co.uk, www.trevince.co.uk. *From A30 turn off at Scorrier A3047, then take B3298 past St Day & through Carharrack. After 1m turn L into Gwennap.* For NGS: Sat 14 May (10-5). Adm £8, chd £2. Light lunches, cakes and cream teas. For other opening times and information, please phone, email or visit garden website.

A haven for garden lovers and curious souls. An old family estate garden, reimagined for modern times. A no-dig productive walled garden is at the heart of the space. A woodland walk with a collection of large leaved rhododendrons among old oaks. Includes several 30 yr old conifers planted as a a living conservation seed bank. Wheelchairs can access the walled garden and Pond Garden. All terrain wheelchairs can also access the Shrubbery and Oriental Glade.

48 ◆ TREWIDDEN GARDEN

Buryas Bridge, Penzance, TR20 8TT. Mr Alverne Bolitho - Richard Morton, Head Gardener, 01736 364275/363021, contact@trewiddengarden.co.uk, www.trewiddengarden.co.uk. *2m W of Penzance. Entry on A30 just before Buryas Bridge. Postcode for SatNav is TR19 6AU.* For NGS: Sat 2 Apr (10.30-5.30). Adm £8, chd free. For other opening times and information, please phone, email or visit garden website.

Historic Victorian garden with magnolias, camellias and magnificent tree ferns planted within ancient tin workings. Tender, rare and unusual exotic plantings create a riot of colour thoughout the season. Water features, specimen trees and artefacts from Cornwall's tin industry provide a wide range of interest for all. Last entry is 4:30pm.

49 WAYE COTTAGE

Lerryn, nr Lostwithiel, PL22 0QQ. Malcolm & Jennifer Bell, 01208 872119, lerrynbells@gmail.com. *4m S of Lostwithiel along north river bank. Parking usually available at property or in village car park. Garden 10 minute level stroll along riverbank/ stepping stones.* Daily Sun 1 May to Thur 30 June (10-5). Adm £5, chd free. Visits also by arrangement May & June. Garden/ other clubs welcome.

An enchanting cottage garden on the footprint of an old market garden - many interesting plants, enticing paths, secluded seats and stunning river views. New grass garden. 'Magical! The perfect place for a botanical recharge and horticultural inspiration.' Reproduced courtesy of Cornwall Life magazine. Garden groups very welcome. Pretty, tidal village. Lovely walks. Refreshments/ light lunches available in shop and pub on village green.

50 WINDMILLS

South Hill, Callington, PL17 7LP. Sue & Peter Tunnicliffe, 01579 363981, tunnicliffesue@gmail.com. *3m NW of Callington. Head N from Callington A388, after about ½ m turn L onto South Hill Rd (signed South Hill). Straight on for 3m, gardens on R just before church.* Sun 24 Apr, Sun 3 July (1-5). Combined adm with Anvil Cottage £6, chd free. Home-made teas. Gluten free cakes available. Visits also by arrangement May to Aug for groups of 10 to 30. Donation to Cornwall Air Ambulance.

Next to medieval church and on the site of an old rectory there are still signs in places of that long gone building. A garden full of surprises, formal paths and steps lead up from the flower beds to extensive vegetable and soft fruit area. More paths lead to a pond, past a pergola, and down into large lawns with trees and shrubs and chickens.

Our 2021 donations mean that 12,478 unpaid carers have been supported through funding for Carers Trust

CUMBRIA

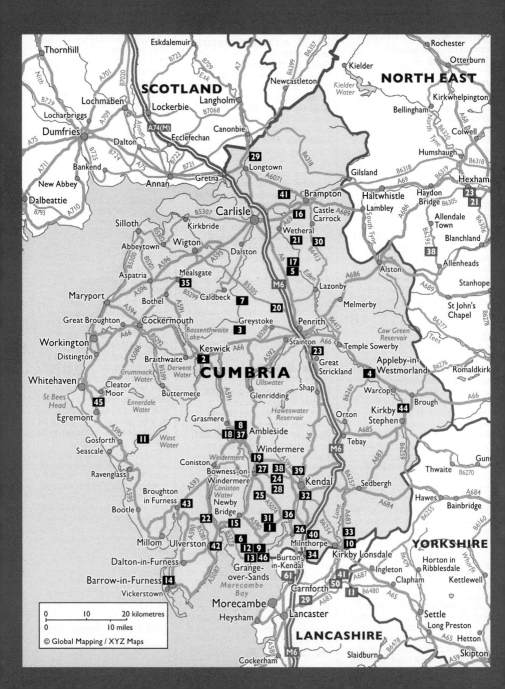

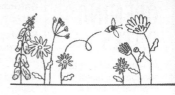

CUMBRIA is where Wordsworth `wandered lonely as a cloud' before finding his `host of golden daffodils'. A county where part has been a UNESCO World Heritage Site since 2017.

It offers mountains, fells, lakes, tarns, waterfalls and a rugged coastline softened by estuaries and rolling open country spaces through which rivers, streams and becks wander and hurry on their way to the sea.

Amongst all of this natural beauty are our gardens, offering havens of tranquillity, panoramic views of distant lakes and mountains - family gardens flourishing alongside stately homes set in their vast estates.

It is a county of contrasts in scale and interest, where a visit to some of our gardens will offer colour, relaxation, evidence of love and care and perhaps an idea or two to take back home. Perhaps even a plant or two to create a corner of our county in your own patch.

Below: Chapelside

© Fiona Lea

 @CumbriaNGS

 @CumbriaNGS

Volunteers

County Organisers

North
Alannah Rylands
01697 320413
alannah.rylands@ngs.org.uk

South
Sue Sharkey
07811 710248
ewebank85@gmail.com

County Treasurer
Derek Farman
01539 444893
derek@derejam.myzen.co.uk

Publicity –
Publications & Special Interest
Carole Berryman
01539 443649
carole.berryman@outlook.com

Publicity – Social Media
Gráinne Jakobson
01946 813017
grainne.jakobson@ngs.org.uk

Booklet Co-ordinator
Cate Bowman
01228 573903
cate.bowman@ngs.org.uk

Assistant County Organisers
Carole Berryman (as above)

Cate Bowman (as above)

Bruno Gouillon
01539 532317
brunog45@hotmail.com

Linda & Alec Greening
01524 781624
greening@ngs.org.uk

Gráinne Jakobson (as above)

Christine Davidson
07966 524302
christine.davidson@ngs.org.uk

OPENING DATES

All entries subject to change. For latest information check www.ngs.org.uk

Extended openings are shown at the beginning of the month.

Map locator numbers are shown to the right of each garden name.

February

Snowdrop Festival

Every Saturday from Saturday 19th
Summerdale House | 40

March

Every Saturday
Summerdale House | 40

Sunday 20th
◆ Dora's Field | 8
◆ High Close Estate & Arboretum | 18
◆ Holehird Gardens | 19
◆ Rydal Hall | 37

April

Every Saturday
Summerdale House | 40

Saturday 9th
Bishop's House | 2

Sunday 24th
Summerdale House | 40

May

Every Saturday
Summerdale House | 40

Sunday 1st
Low Fell West | 25
NEW ◆ Netherby Hall | 29

Monday 2nd
Low Fell West | 25

Sunday 8th
◆ Rydal Hall | 37

Saturday 14th
Bishop's House | 2

Sunday 15th
Chapelside | 3
Matson Ground | 27

Saturday 28th
Galesyke | 11

Sunday 29th
Chapelside | 3
Galesyke | 11
Grange over Sands Hidden Gardens | 13

June

Every Saturday
Summerdale House | 40

Sunday 5th
Abi and Tom's Garden Plants | 1
◆ Hutton-In-The-Forest | 20
NEW The Old Vicarage | 31
Quarry Hill House | 35
◆ Rydal Hall | 37
Yewbarrow House | 46

Saturday 11th
Coombe Eden | 5
Hazel Cottage | 17

Sunday 12th
Chapelside | 3
Coombe Eden | 5
Hayton Village Gardens | 16
Hazel Cottage | 17
Low Crag | 24
Middle Blakebank | 28
8 Oxenholme Road | 32
Summerdale House | 40

Wednesday 15th
Church View | 4

Saturday 18th
Whetstone Croft & Cottage | 43

Sunday 19th
Crumble Cottages | 6
Haverthwaite Lodge | 15
Whetstone Croft & Cottage | 43

Saturday 25th
Woodend House | 45

Sunday 26th
Chapelside | 3
Eden Mount Gardens | 9
Ivy House | 21
Woodend House | 45

July

Saturday 2nd
Park House | 33
Summerdale House | 40

Sunday 3rd
NEW 27 Haverigg Gardens | 14
Park House | 33
Ulverston Gardens | 42
Yewbarrow House | 46

Thursday 7th
◆ Holehird Gardens | 19
Larch Cottage Nurseries | 23

Sunday 10th
Chapelside | 3
Winton Park | 44

Saturday 16th
Deer Rudding | 7

Sunday 17th
◆ Rydal Hall | 37

Saturday 23rd
Coombe Eden | 5
Hazel Cottage | 17

Sunday 24th
Coombe Eden | 5
Crumble Cottages | 6
Hazel Cottage | 17
NEW Sidegarth | 38

Sunday 31st
Grange over Sands Hidden Gardens | 13
Newlands | 30

August

Sunday 7th
Rose Croft | 36
Yewbarrow House | 46

Thursday 11th
Larch Cottage Nurseries | 23

Sunday 14th
Grange Fell Allotments | 12
Ivy House | 21

Sunday 21st
Fell Yeat | 10

September

Sunday 4th
Middle Blakebank | 28
Yewbarrow House | 46

Thursday 8th
Larch Cottage Nurseries | 23

Wednesday 14th
Church View | 4

October

Saturday 15th
Bishop's House | 2

Sunday 23rd
Low Fell West | 25

By Arrangement

Arrange a personalised garden visit with your club, or group of friends, on a date to suit you. See individual garden entries for full details.

Chapelside | 3
Church View | 4
Crumble Cottages | 6
Deer Rudding | 7
Elder Cottage, Grange over Sands Hidden Gardens | 13
Galesyke | 11
Grange Fell Allotments | 12
Haverthwaite Lodge | 15
Ivy House | 21
Low Fell West | 25
Lower Rowell Farm & Cottage | 26
Matson Ground | 27
Middle Blakebank | 28
Pear Tree Cottage | 34
Quarry Hill House | 35
Rose Croft | 36
Sprint Mill | 39
Tithe Barn | 41
Woodend House | 45
Yewbarrow House | 46

Our 2021 donations mean that 8,500 patients have been supported across three Horatio's gardens

THE GARDENS

❶ ABI AND TOM'S GARDEN PLANTS

Halecat, Witherslack, Grange-Over-Sands, LA11 6RT. Abi & Tom Attwood, *20 mins from Kendal. From A590 turn N to Witherslack. Follow brown tourist signs to Halecat. Rail Grange-over-sands 5m, Bus X6 2m, NCR 70.* **Sun 5 June (10-5). Combined adm with The Old Vicarage £6, chd free. Light refreshments.**
The 1 acre nursery garden is a fusion of traditional horticultural values with modern approaches to the display, growing and use of plant material. Our full range of perennials can be seen growing alongside one another in themed borders be they shady damp corners or south facing hot spots. The propagating areas, stock beds and family garden, normally closed to visitors, will be open on the NGS day. More than 1,000 different herbaceous perennials are grown in the nursery, many that are excellent for wildlife. For other opening times and information please phone, e-mail or visit our website. Sloping site that has no steps but steep inclines in places.

❷ BISHOP'S HOUSE

Ambleside Road, Keswick, CA12 4DD. Mrs Alison Newcome. *Turn off the A591, signed to Castlerigg Manor. House is on L just before St Johns Church.* **Sat 9 Apr, Sat 14 May, Sat 15 Oct (2-5). Adm £5, chd free. Home-made teas.**
The garden is approx 1 acre and comprises a mixture of woodland garden, small rockery, herbaceous bed, pond, orchard area, trees and shrubs. The garden was completely recreated, apart from the mature trees which were already here, about 10 yrs ago. It continues to grow and mature with each year that passes. There have been ongoing innovations as situations have prompted. Gravel paths.

❸ CHAPELSIDE

Mungrisdale, Penrith, CA11 0XR. Tricia & Robin Acland, 017687 79672, rtacland@gmail.com. *12m W of Penrith. On A66 take minor rd N signed Mungrisdale. After 2m, sharp bends, garden on L immed after tiny church on R. Use church car park at foot of our short drive. On C2C Reivers 71, 10 cycle routes.* **Sun 15, Sun 29 May, Sun 12, Sun 26 June, Sun 10 July (1-5). Adm £4, chd free. Visits also by arrangement May to July.**
1 acre windy garden below fell, round C18 farmhouse and outbuildings. Fine views. Tiny stream, large pond. Herbaceous, gravel, alpine, damp and shade areas, bulbs in grass. Wide range of plants, many unusual. Relaxed planting regime. Run on organic lines. Art constructions in and out, local stone used creatively. Featured in leading magazines and several books.

❹ CHURCH VIEW

Bongate, Appleby-in-Westmorland, CA16 6UN. Mrs H Holmes, 01768 351397, engcougars@btinternet.com, www.sites.google.com/site/engcougars/church-view. *0.4m SE of Appleby town centre. A66 W take B6542 for 2m St Michael's Church on L garden opp. A66 E take B6542 & continue to Royal Oak Inn, garden next door, opp church.* **Wed 15 June, Wed 14 Sept (1-4.30). Adm £4, chd free. Visits also by arrangement May to Sept for groups of up to 30.**
It's all about the plants! Less than ½ acre of garden but with layers of texture, colour and interest in abundance, this is a garden for plantaholics. Plant combinations are at the heart of the design. With self-contained vistas and maximum use of planting space, the garden photographs very well and has been a subject for many local and national publications and photographers over recent years.

❺ COOMBE EDEN

Armathwaite, Carlisle, CA4 9PQ. Belinda & Mike. *8m SE of Carlisle. Turn off A6 just S of High Hesket signed Armathwaite. Continue to bottom of hill where garden can be found on R turn for Lazonby.* **Sat 11, Sun 12 June, Sat 23, Sun 24 July (12-5). Combined adm with Hazel Cottage £5, chd free. Home-made teas at Hazel Cottage.**
A garden of traditional and contemporary beds. Steep banks down to stream with pretty Japanese style bridge. Large rhododendrons give a breathtaking show late May/early June. New formal garden and vegetable areas added 2020.

❻ CRUMBLE COTTAGES

Beckside, Cartmel, LA11 7SP. Sarah Byrne & Stewart Cowe, 015395 34405, sarah@crumblecottages.co.uk, www.crumblecottages.co.uk. *1m from Cartmel up past the racecourse. Please note car SatNav brings you directly here however mobile phone SatNav take you up the wrong lane.* **Sun 19 June, Sun 24 July (10.30-4). Adm £5, chd £1. Home-made teas. Ice cream and home made raspberry sauce. Visits also by arrangement Apr to Oct for groups of 10+.**
The gardens inc wildflower meadows, 1½ acre water gardens built just over 6 years ago to improve the biodiversity of the area, walled kitchen gardens which have a Grade II listed wall with 7 bee boles. Cut flower and butterfly borders. Ornamental planting around the house divided into a number of planting styles. All areas designed to encourage wildlife. We now have hedgehogs! Wheelchair access to ornamental areas by house and outlying areas of garden but only by a wheelchair that can cope with uneven ground.

❼ DEER RUDDING

Hesket Newmarket, Wigton, CA7 8HU. Mrs Lynne Carruthers, deer.rudding@gmail.com. *Located off the road from Millhouse to Haltcliff Bridge, not in Hesket Newmarket. From Penrith J41 M6 take B5305 6.8m, L to Hesket Newmarket 2.2m, at Millhouse L to Haltcliffe Bridge by village hall, continue 1m, R over cattle grid.* **Sat 16 July (10-4). Adm £5, chd free. Light refreshments at Millhouse Village Hall. Visits also by arrangement Apr to Aug. Tuesdays only.**
Set in the lee of the Northern Fells on the bank of the Caldew and enjoying views into the wider landscape, notably Carrock Fell. The garden extends to 8 acres and surrounds a former Cumbrian farmhouse and outbuildings. Mixed shrub and perennial borders, woodland and meadow grass areas, extensive rockery and stone walls built by Cumbrian champion waller, Steve Allen of Tebay. The rockery and meadow areas are very attractive in May and June.

8 ♦ DORA'S FIELD

Rydal, Ambleside, LA22 9LX. National Trust, www.nationaltrust.org.uk. *1½ m N of Ambleside. Follow A591 from Ambleside to Rydal. Dora's Field is next to St Mary's Church.* **For NGS: Sun 20 Mar (10-4.30). Adm by donation. Open nearby High Close Estate & Arboretum. For other opening times and information, please visit garden website.**

Named for Dora, the daughter of the poet William Wordsworth. Wordsworth planned to build a house on the land but, after her early death, he planted the area with daffodils in her memory. Now known as Dora's field the area is renowned for its spring display of daffodils and bluebells. The impact of the pandemic and reduced resource means some areas will look more wild than normal. However, paths are still accessible and you will still be able to enjoy the spring colour. Please visit www.ngs.org.uk to make your donation. 20 March; Wordsworth's Daffodil Legacy.

GROUP OPENING

9 EDEN MOUNT GARDENS

Eden Mount, Grange-Over-Sands, LA11 6BZ. Dr Ian & Pauline Wilson. *Please park on Eden Mount Road as there is no parking near the gardens.* **Sun 26 June (11-4). Combined adm £5, chd free. Light refreshments.**

THE COTTAGE
Dr Ian & Pauline Wilson.

EDENHURST
Mr & Mrs P Bowe.

ENDCLIFFE
Mr & Mrs John Barker.

GREY GABLE
Mr Peter Stas.

NEW GROVE HOUSE
Mr & Mrs Melissa Harrington.

The Cottage: Hidden from view with wide gravel paths and a number of steps. Lovely changing views over Morecambe Bay. Endcliffe: Compact garden, mostly hard landscaped with planted borders, container plants and pebble art feature. Edenhurst: Sloping front garden with large patio. Limestone rockeries and walkways, 3 pools, a waterfall, stream, fountain and fish. Small rear garden, large variety of plants, flowers and roses. Grey Gable: South facing front garden with a terrace overlooking island beds, stocked with trees, shrubs and perennials. Small pond, arbour and feature rockery with exposed limestone bedrock. At the side of the house there are raised beds and at the back is a secluded decking area. The house enjoys extensive views across Morecambe Bay. Grove House: Victorian layout of front terrace with limestone above a sloping lawn and hedged kitchen side lawn. Collection of David Austen roses, cottage garden borders, orchard border, wild area and stone circle garden feature.

10 FELL YEAT

Casterton, Kirkby Lonsdale, LA6 2JW. Mrs A E Benson. *1m E of Casterton Village. On the rd to Bull Pot. Leave A65 at Devils Bridge, follow A683 for 1m, take the R fork to High Casterton at golf course, straight across at 2 sets of Xrds, house on L, ¼ m from no-through-rd sign.* **Sun 21 Aug (12-5). Adm £4, chd free.**

1 acre garden with many unusual trees and shrubs. A developing wood is becoming the dominant feature, along with a small meadow, which has orchids. As the garden has matured the emphasis has been increasingly on wildlife habitat, creating a wilder feel and home to birds of prey. Explore the fernery and maturing stumpery and new grotto house with rocks and ferns. Large collection of hydrangeas. Adjoining nursery specialising in ferns, hostas, hydrangeas and many unusual plants.

11 GALESYKE

Wasdale, CA20 1ET. Christine & Mike McKinley, 01946 726267, mckinley2112@sky.com. *In Wasdale valley, between Nether Wasdale village and the lake. From Gosforth, follow signs to Nether Wasdale & then to lake, approx 5m. From Santon Bridge follow signs to Wasdale then to lake, approx 2¼ m.* **Sat 28, Sun 29 May (10-5). Adm £4, chd free. Cream teas. Visits also by arrangement May to Aug.**

4 acre woodland garden with spectacular views of the Wasdale fells.The River Irt runs through the garden and both banks are landscaped. You can cross over the river via a picturesque mini suspension bridge. The garden has an impressive collection of rhododendrons and azaleas that light up the woodlands in springtime.

12 GRANGE FELL ALLOTMENTS

Fell Road, Grange-Over-Sands, LA11 6HB. Mr Bruno Gouillon, 01539 532317, brunog45@hotmail.com. *Opp Grange Fell Golf Club. Rail 1.3m, Bus 1m X6, NCR 70.* **Sun 14 Aug (11.30-3.30). Adm £5, chd free. Light refreshments. Visits also by arrangement Apr to Sept.**

The allotments are managed by Grange Town Council. Opened in 2010, 30 plots are now rented out and offer a wide selection of gardening styles and techniques. The majority of plots grow a mixture of vegetables, fruit trees and flowers. There are a few communal areas where local fruit tree varieties have been donated by plot holders with herbaceous borders and annuals.

GROUP OPENING

13 GRANGE OVER SANDS HIDDEN GARDENS

Grange-Over-Sands, LA11 7AF. Bruno Gouillon. *Off Kents Bank Rd, 3 gardens on Cart Lane then last garden up Carter Rd for Shrublands. Rail 1.4m; Bus X6; NCR 70.* **Sun 29 May, Sun 31 July (11-4). Combined adm £5, chd free. Light refreshments. Donation to St Mary's Hopsice.**

21 CART LANE
Veronica Cameron.

ELDER COTTAGE
Bruno Gouillon & Andrew Fairey, 01539 532317, brunog45@hotmail.com. **Visits also by arrangement Mar to Sept.**

HAWTHORNE COTTAGE
Mrs Carroll & Mr John Ashton.

SHRUBLANDS
Jon & Avril Trevorrow.

4 very different gardens hidden down narrow lanes off the road south out of Grange. Off Kents Bank Road, 3 gardens on Cart Lane all back onto

the railway embankment, providing shelter from the wind but also creating a frost pocket. The garden at 21 Cart Lane is a series of rooms designed to create an element of surprise with fruit and vegetables in raised beds. Elder Cottage is an organised riot of fruit trees, vegetables, shrubby perennials and herbaceous plants. Productive and peaceful. Hawthorne Cottage has been redesigned and replanted over the last 2 yrs to create a garden with colour and interest. Up the hill on Carter Road Shrublands is a ¾ acre garden situated on a hillside overlooking Morecambe Bay. Visitors with mobility issues can access Shrublands & 21 Cart Ln, but can only view Elder Cottage from the roadside & Hawthorne Cottage from the gate.

♿ 🐐 ❄ ☕ ⊕))

⒕ NEW 27 HAVERIGG GARDENS
North Scale, Walney, Barrow-In-Furness, LA14 3TH. Jo & Brendan Sweeney. *North end of Walney Island. A590 to Walney Island, R at end of the bridge, continue on through N Scale. We are the last road before the airport. Additional parking at N Scale Community Centre.* **Sun 3 July (11-4). Adm £4, chd free. Home-made teas.**
Relaxing 300ft cottage style garden backing on to sheep fields with views to Blackcombe and the Coniston hills. Designed to be wildlife friendly and cope with the exposed site and salt laden winds for which Walney is renowned. Wildlife pond, woodland area, mini-wildflower meadow, vegetable and fruit beds, summerhouses and seating areas; plus a slate scree front garden. Live Brass Band.

♿ 🐐 ☕ ⛱

⒖ HAVERTHWAITE LODGE
Haverthwaite, LA12 8AJ. David Snowdon, 015395 30022, office@dstrust.org.uk. *100yds off A590 at Haverthwaite. Turn S off A590 opp Haverthwaite railway stn. Bus 6, NCR 70 Parking on the roadside at the top of the drive. No vehicle access on the drive except for those with mobility aids.* **Sun 19 June (11-4). Adm £5, chd free. Light refreshments. Visits also by arrangement Mar to Oct for groups of up to 30. Refreshments only available on 19 June.**
Traditional Lake District garden that has been redesigned and replanted.

A series of terraces lead down to the River Leven and wooded area. Inc a rose garden, cutting garden, dell area, rock terrace, herbaceous borders and many interesting mature shrubs. Although unsuitable for wheelchairs or those using mobility aids, visitors

may view the garden from the terrace. In a stunning setting the garden is surrounded by oak woodland and was once a place of C18 and C19 industry. A wonderful display of hellebores and spring flowers.

🐐 🚗 ☕

Deer Rudding

Church View

GROUP OPENING

🔟 HAYTON VILLAGE GARDENS

Hayton, Brampton, CA8 9HR.
Facebook.HaytonOpenGardens.
5m E of M6 J43 at Carlisle, ½m S of A69. 3m W of Brampton. Signed to Hayton off A69. Narrow roads: Please park one side only. If able, park less centrally leaving space for less able nr pub. Tickets sold in east of village (Townhead), west & middle with map. Map also avail on FB. **Sun 12 June (12-6). Combined adm £5, chd free. Home-made teas at Hayton Village Primary School with live music. Cold refreshments in one of the gardens outside if suitable. Donation to Hayton Village Primary School.**

ARNWOOD
Joanne Reeves-Brown.

ASH TREE FARM
Mr & Mrs J Dowling.

BECK COTTAGE
Fiona Cox.

BRACKENHOW
Johnny & Susan Tranter.

CHESTNUT COTTAGE
Mr Barry Brian.

HAYTON C OF E PRIMARY SCHOOL
Hayton C of E Primary School, www.hayton.cumbria.sch.uk.

NEW HEMPGARTH
Sheila & David Heslop.

KINRARA
Tim & Alison Brown, Facebook.KinraraOpenGardens.

MILLBROOK
M & J Carruthers.

THE PADDOCK
Phil & Louise Jones.

TOWNHEAD COTTAGE
Chris & Pam Haynes.

WEST GARTH COTTAGE
Debbie Jenkins, www.westgarth-cottage-gardens.co.uk.

NEW WHITE HOUSE COTTAGE
Mr Chris Potts.

A valley of gardens of varied size and styles all within ½m, mostly of old stone cottages. Smaller and larger cottage gardens, courtyards and containers, steep wooded slopes, lawns, exuberant borders, frogs, pools, colour and texture throughout. Home-made teas and live music at the school where the children annually create gardens within the main school garden (RHS award). Gardens additional to those listed also generally open or visible. Two of the gardens, Westgarth Cottage and Kinrara, are designed by artist/s and an architect with multiple garden design experience. Accessibility ranges from full to none. Note that gardens are spread out & some walking needed to see all. Come early or late for easier parking.

 ♿ ❊

17 HAZEL COTTAGE
Armathwaite, Carlisle, CA4 9PG.
Mr D Ryland & Mr J Thexton.
*8m SE of Carlisle. Turn off A6
just S of High Hesket signed
Armathwaite, after 2m house facing
you at T-junction 1¼m walk from
Armathwaite railway station.* **Sat
11, Sun 12 June, Sat 23, Sun
24 July (11-5). Combined adm
with Coombe Eden £5, chd free.
Home-made teas.**
Flower arrangers and plantsman's
garden. Extending to approx 5 acres.
Inc mature herbaceous borders,
pergola, ponds and planting of
disused railway siding providing
home to wildlife. Many variegated
and unusual plants. Varied areas,
planted for all seasons, south facing,
some gentle slopes, ever changing.
Abandoned railway cutting now a
woodland walk. Various animals
around garden. Only partial access,
small steps to WC area . Main garden
planted on gentle slope.
♿ ✿ �car ☕ ♿

**18 ◆ HIGH CLOSE ESTATE &
ARBORETUM**
Loughrigg, Ambleside, LA22 9HH.
National Trust, 015394 37623,
neil.winder@nationaltrust.org.
uk, www.nationaltrust.org.uk.
*Ambleside (A593) to Skelwith Bridge
signed for High Close, turn R & head
up hill until you see a white painted
stone sign to 'Langdale', turn L, High
Close on L.* **For NGS: Sun 20 Mar
(10-4.30). Adm by donation. Open
nearby Dora's Field. For other
opening times and information,
please phone, email or visit garden
website.**
Originally planted in 1866 by Edward
Wheatley-Balme, High Close was
designed in the fashion of the day
using many of the recently discovered
'exotic' conifers and evergreen shrubs
coming into Britain from the Americas.
Today the garden works in partnership
with the Royal Botanic Gardens
Edinburgh and International Conifer
Conservation Programme, preserving
endangered Conifers species. The
impact of the pandemic and reduced
resource means some areas will look
more wild than normal. However, paths
are still accessible and you will still be
able to enjoy the spring colour. Please
visit www.ngs.org.uk to make your
donation. Guided walk at 11am, tree
trail and chat to our volunteers. Small
cafe in house part of the YHA (please
check with YHA for opening times).
🐕

19 ◆ HOLEHIRD GARDENS
Patterdale Road, Windermere,
LA23 1NP. Lakeland Horticultural
Society, 015394 46008, enquiries@
holehirdgardens.org.uk,
www.holehirdgardens.org.uk.
*1m N of Windermere. On A592,
Windermere to Patterdale rd.* **For
NGS: Sun 20 Mar (10-4); Thur 7
July (10-5). Adm £5, chd free.
Self-service hot drinks available.
For other opening times and
information, please phone, email or
visit garden website. Donation to
Plant Heritage.**
Run by volunteers of the Lakeland
Horticultural Society to promote
knowledge of gardening in Lakeland
conditions. On fellside overlooking
Windermere, the 12 acres provide
interest year-round. 4 National
Collections (astilbe, daboecia,
polystichum, meconopsis). Lakeland
Collection of hydrangeas. Walled
garden has colourful mixed borders
and island beds. Alpine beds and
display houses. Wheelchair access
limited to walled garden and beds
accessible from drive.
♿ ✿ [NPC] ☕

20 ◆ HUTTON-IN-THE-FOREST
Penrith, CA11 9TH. Lord &
Lady Inglewood, 017684 84449,
info@hutton-in-the-forest.co.uk,
www.hutton-in-the-forest.co.uk.
*6m NW of Penrith. On B5305, 2m
from exit 41 of M6 towards Wigton.*
**For NGS: Sun 5 June (10-5).
Adm £7, chd free. Home-made
teas. For other opening times and
information, please phone, email or
visit garden website.**
Hutton-in-the-Forest is surrounded on
two sides by distinctive yew topiary
and grass terraces - which to the
S lead to C18 lake and cascade.
1730s walled garden is full of old fruit
trees, tulips in spring, roses and an
extensive collection of herbaceous
plants in summer.
♿ 🐕 ✿ 🚗 ☕ 🪑 🔊

21 IVY HOUSE
Cumwhitton, CA8 9EX.
Martin Johns & Ian Forrest,
01228 561851,
martinjohns193@btinternet.com.
*6m E of Carlisle. At the bridge at
Warwick Bridge on A69 take turning
to Great Corby & Cumwhitton.
Through Great Corby & woodland
until you reach a T-junction Turn
R.* **Sun 26 June, Sun 14 Aug
(1-5). Adm £5, chd free. Light
refreshments. Visits also by**

arrangement Apr to Sept.
Approx 2 acres of sloping fellside
garden with meandering paths
leading to a series of 'rooms': pond,
fern garden, gravel garden with
assorted grasses, herbaceous beds
and vegetable garden. Copse with
meadow leading down to beck. Trees,
shrubs, ferns, bamboos, evergreens
and perennials planted with emphasis
on variety of texture and colour. WC
available.
🐕 🚗 ☕

**23 LARCH COTTAGE
NURSERIES**
Melkinthorpe, Penrith,
CA10 2DR. Peter Stott,
www.larchcottage.co.uk. *From N
leave M6 J40 take A6 S. From S
leave M6 J39 take A6 N signed off
A6.* **Thur 7 July, Thur 11 Aug, Thur
8 Sept (1-4). Adm £4, chd free.
Light refreshments in La Casa
Verde.**
We are pleased to open our gardens
and chapel for 3 days this year in
support of the NGS. The gardens
inc lawns, flowing perennial borders,
rare and unusual shrubs, trees,
small orchard and a kitchen garden.
A natural stream runs into a small
lake - a haven for wildlife and birds.
At the head of the lake stands a
small frescoed chapel designed and
built by Peter for family use. Larch
Cottage has a Japanese Dry garden,
ponds and Italianesque columned
garden specifically for shade plants,
the Italianesque tumbled down walls
are draped in greenery acting as a
backdrop for the borders filled with
stock plants. Newly designed and
constructed lower gardens and
chapel. Accessible to wheelchair users
although the paths are rocky in places.
♿ ✿ ☕

*In 2021 the National
Garden Scheme donation
helped support Perennial's
caseworkers, who helped over
250 people and their families
in crisis to receive a wide
range of support including
emergency food parcels and
accommodation, energy
payments and expert advice
and information*

24 LOW CRAG

Crook, Kendal, LA8 8LE. Chris Dodd & Liz Jolley. *Turn off B5284 opp Sun Inn. Pass Ellerbeck Farm on R, continue for ¼ m. Take the 3rd drive on L. Steep drive to large, flat yard. Note - SatNav takes you to Ellerbeck Farm.* **Sun 12 June (10-5). Adm £4, chd free. Light refreshments.**
A relaxed, wildlife friendly 2 acre farmhouse garden, designed and maintained on organic principles. Transitions from a formal garden, featuring yew hedges and herbaceous planting, through to a wildlife pond, arboretum, small vegetable garden, and an orchard, and out to meadows and the greater landscape. Long views with seating and viewpoints throughout. No press coverage thanks. Some steep slopes and steps

25 LOW FELL WEST

Crosthwaite, Kendal, LA8 8JG. Barbie & John Handley, 015395 68297, barbie@handleyfamily.co.uk. *4½ m S of Bowness. Off A5074, turn W just S of Damson Dene Hotel. Follow lane for ½ m.* **Sun 1 May (1-5); Mon 2 May (10-2); Sun 23 Oct (11-5). Adm £5, chd free. Light refreshments. Visits also by arrangement. Nearest coach access on A5074, half a mile from the garden.**
This 2 acre woodland garden in the tranquil Winster Valley has extensive views to the Pennines. The four season garden, restored since 2003, inc expanses of rock planted sympathetically with grasses, unusual trees and shrubs, climaxing for autumn colour. There are native hedges and areas of plant rich meadows. A woodland area houses a gypsy caravan and there is direct access to Cumbria Wildlife Trust's Barkbooth Reserve of Oak woodland, bluebells and open fellside. Wheelchair access to much of the garden, but some rough paths and steep slopes.

26 LOWER ROWELL FARM & COTTAGE

Milnthorpe, LA7 7LU. John & Mavis Robinson & Julie & Andy Welton, 015395 62270. *Approx 2m from Milnthorpe, 2m from Crooklands. Signed to Rowell off B6385, Milnthorpe to Crooklands Rd. Garden ½ m up lane on L.* **Visits by arrangement Feb to July for groups of 10 to 30. Refreshments by arrangement.**
Approx 1¼ acre garden with views to Farleton Knott and Lakeland hills. Unusual trees and shrubs, plus perennial borders. Architectural pruning, retro greenhouse, polytunnel with tropical plants, cottage gravel garden and vegetable plot. Fabulous display of snowdrops in spring followed by other spring flowers, with colour most of the year. Wildlife ponds and 2 friendly pet hens.

27 MATSON GROUND

Windermere, LA23 2NH. Matson Ground Estate Co Ltd, 07831 831918, sam@matsonground.co.uk. *⅔ m E of Bowness. Turn N off B5284 signed Heathwaite. From E 100yds after Windermere Golf Club, from W 400yds after Windy Hall Rd. Rail 2½ m; Bus 1m, 6, 599, 755, 800; NCR 6 (1m).* **Sun 15 May (1-5). Adm £6.50, chd free. Home-made teas. Visits also by arrangement for groups of 5+.**
2 acres of mature, south facing gardens. A good mix of formal and informal planting including topiary features, herbaceous and shrub borders, wildflower areas, stream leading to a large pond and developing arboretum. Rose garden, rockery, topiary terrace borders, ha-ha. Productive, walled kitchen garden c 1862, a wide assortment of fruit, vegetables, cut flowers, cobnuts and herbs. Greenhouse.

28 MIDDLE BLAKEBANK

Underbarrow, Kendal, LA8 8HP. Mrs Hilary Crowe, 07713 608963, hfcmbb@aol.com. *Lyth Valley between Underbarrow & Crosthwaite. E off A5074 to Crosthwaite. The garden is on Broom Lane, a turning between Crosthwaite & Underbarrow signed Red Scar & Broom Farm.* **Sun 12 June, Sun 4 Sept (11-4). Adm £5, chd free. Home-made teas. Visits also by arrangement Apr to Oct for groups of 10 to 20.**
The garden extends to 4½ acres and overlooks the Lyth Valley with extensive views south to Morecambe Bay and east to the Howgills. We have orchards, a wildflower meadow and more formal garden with a range of outbuildings. Over the last 8 years the garden has been developed with plantings that provide varying colour and texture all year. Some parts of the garden are accessed by steps. We enjoy providing home made cakes and sandwiches - under cover in large barn if necessary!

29 NEW ◆ NETHERBY HALL

Longtown, Carlisle, CA6 5PR. Mr Gerald & Mrs Margo Smith, 01228 792732, info@netherbyhall.co.uk, netherbyhall.co.uk/. *Take Junction 44 from the M6 & follow the A7 to Longtown. Take Netherby road and follow it for about 2m. Netherby Hall is on L.* **For NGS: Sun 1 May (10-3). Adm £6, chd free. The tea room will be open in the Orangery serving tea, coffee and cakes. For other opening times and information, please phone, email or visit garden website.**
Netherby Hall's 36 acres consists of a 1½ acre walled kitchen garden which produces fruit, vegetables and herbs for the Pentonbridge Inn restaurant, with herbaceous borders, a Victorian pleasure ground, woodlands with many fine specimen trees, lawns with azaleas and rhododendrons and a wildflower meadow, all set in more than 200 acres of designed landscape bordering the River Esk. Ample parking. Carriage paths allow access around the Victorian pleasure rounds & around the walled garden.

30 NEWLANDS

Cumrew, CA8 9DD. Mr Colin & Mrs Teresa Clark. *Approach the village via B6413 or use SatNav postcode. On arrival in Cumrew, park considerately on village street & walk up gravelled lane by red telephone box. House is last (2nd) on L.* **Sun 31 July (10-4). Adm £3, chd free.**
A newish and developing garden with spectacular views, nestled on the edge of the Pennines. Garden areas inc a small, young but well-stocked orchard with quince, medlar, pears, damson, plum, apples and cherry. Long borders are filled with colourful perennials, with brilliant colours in Jul/Aug. Shrubbery, ferns, alpines and ericaceous beds and a well-stocked vegetable garden with greenhouse. Newly established pond and gravel garden. Mostly level. Access to the garden is via the gravel area. Lawns and solid paths are easily accessible thereafter. Single step can be bypassed.

31 NEW THE OLD VICARAGE

Church Road, Witherslack,
Grange-Over-Sands, LA11 6RS.
Mr Alaisdhair & Mrs Mary
MacPhie. *On Church Rd between
Dean Barwick School & the church
green. Follow brown signs to Halecat
until final L turn sign where instead
of turning L carry on past the school.
First building on L 100 yds after
school. Enter through white gate.*
**Sun 5 June (11-4.30). Combined
adm with Abi and Tom's Garden
Plants £6, chd free. Home-made
teas.**
1 acre garden on edge of ancient
woodland with old and newer
specimen trees including magnificent
Cedrus libani from the original
Georgian planting. Beech and walnut
surrounding well mown lawns and
a bog garden with stepping stones.
Shrubbed, flowering and herbaceous
beds. Woodland walk along limestone
pavement to attractive fernery. Close
to Halecat Garden and Nursery
Centre approx 800 yds. One level
from driveway and then over lawned
areas and gravel paths.

© Richard Jakobson

32 8 OXENHOLME ROAD

Kendal, LA9 7NJ. Mr John & Mrs
Frances Davenport. *SE Kendal.
From A65 (Burton Rd, Kendal/Kirkby
Lonsdale) take B6254 (Oxenholme
Rd). No.8 is 1st house on L beyond
red post box.* **Sun 12 June
(10-5). Adm £4, chd free. Light
refreshments.**
Artist and potter's garden of approx
½ acre of mixed planting designed
for year-round interest, inc two linked
small ponds. Roses, grasses and
colour themed borders surround
the house, with a gravel garden at
the front, as well as a number of
woodland plant areas, vegetable and
fruit areas and sitting spaces. John
is a ceramic artist and Frances is
a painter. Paintings and pots are a
feature of the garden display. We offer
tea/coffee and biscuits/cakes to eat
at seating around garden. Garden
essentially level, but access to WC is
up steps.

33 PARK HOUSE

Barbon, Kirkby Lonsdale,
LA6 2LG. Mr & Mrs P Pattison.
*2½ m N of Kirkby Lonsdale. Off A683
Kirkby Lonsdale to Sedburgh rd.
Follow signs into Barbon Village.* **Sat
2, Sun 3 July (10.30-4). Adm £5,**

chd free. Cream teas.
Romantic Manor House (not open).
Extensive vistas. Formal tranquil pond
encased in yew hedging. Meadow
with meandering pathways, water
garden filled with bulbs and ferns.
Formal lawn, gravel pathways,
cottage borders with hues of soft
pinks and purples, shady border,
kitchen garden. An evolving garden
to follow.

34 PEAR TREE COTTAGE

Dalton, Burton-in-Kendal,
LA6 1NN. Linda & Alec
Greening, 01524 781624,
greening@ngs.org.uk. *5m from J35
& J36 of M6. From northern end of
Burton-in-Kendal (A6070) turn E into
Vicarage Lane & continue approx
1m.* **Visits by arrangement June
& July for groups of 15+. Adm
£4.50, chd free. Refreshments by
prior arrangement.**
⅓ acre cottage garden in a delightful
rural setting. A peaceful and relaxing
garden, harmonising with its
environment and incorporating many
different planting areas, from packed
herbaceous borders and rambling
roses, to wildlife pond, bog garden,
rock garden and gravel garden. A

plantsperson's delight, inc over 200
different ferns, and many other rare
and unusual plants.

35 QUARRY HILL HOUSE

Boltongate, Mealsgate,
Wigton, CA7 1AE. Mr Charles
Woodhouse & Mrs Philippa Irving,
01697 371225/ 07785 934 377,
cfwoodhouse@btinternet.com.
*⅓m W of Boltongate, 6m SSW of
Wigton, 13m NW of Keswick, 10m
E Cockermouth. M6 J41, direction
Wigton, through Hesket Newmarket,
Caldbeck, & Boltongate on B5299,
entrance gates Quarry Hill House drive
on R. On A595 Carlisle to Cockermouth
turn L for Boltongate, Ireby.* **Sun 5
June (1-5.30). Adm £5, chd free.
Home-made teas. Visits also by
arrangement May to July. Donation
to Cumbria Community Foundation:
Quarry Hill Grassroots Fund.**
3 acre parkland setting, country
house (not open), woodland garden
with marvellous views of Skiddaw,
Binsey and the Northern Fells and
also the Solway and Scotland. Trees,
some very old and many specimen,
shrubs, herbaceous borders, potager
vegetable garden.

Park House

36 ROSE CROFT
Levens, Kendal, LA8 8PH.
Enid Fraser, 07976 977018,
enidfraser123@btinternet.com.
Approx 4m from J36 on M6. From J36 take A590 toward Barrow. R turn Levens, L at pub, follow rd to garden on L. From A6, into Levens, past shop, bear L, over Xrds, downhill. L turn signed 'PV Dobson'. Garden on R after Dobsons. **Sun 7 Aug (1-4.30). Adm £4, chd free. Light refreshments. Visits also by arrangement June to Sept for groups of up to 30.**
Gardening on a steep slope with wildlife in mind. Naturalistic plantings, perennials and grasses pouring away from the top terrace, shrubs, rose arches and silver birches for supporting structure. August sees the peak of this colourful drama: set against the views that dominate the westerly scene beyond the summerhouse, past the sown wildflowers and lawn which fold into the garden-bounding stream.

37 ♦ RYDAL HALL
Ambleside, LA22 9LX. Diocese of Carlisle, 01539 432050, gardens@rydalhall.org, www.rydalhall.org. *2m N of Ambleside. E from A591 at Rydal signed Rydal Hall. Bus 555, 599, X8, X55; NCR 6.* **For NGS: Sun 20 Mar, Sun 8 May, Sun 5 June, Sun 17 July (9-4). Adm by donation. Light refreshments in tea shop on site. For other opening times and information, please phone, email or visit garden website.**
Forty acres of park, woodland and gardens to explore. The formal Thomas Mawson garden has fine examples of herbaceous planting, seasonal displays and magnificent views of the Lakeland Fells. Enjoy the peaceful atmosphere created in the Quiet Garden with informal planting around the pond and stunning views of the waterfalls from The Grot, the UK's first viewing station. Partial wheelchair access, top terrace only.

38 NEW SIDEGARTH
Staveley, Kendal, LA8 9NN. Susy Rayner. *From the Crook Rd (B5284) take the Staveley turning. Drive 1m down road and turn L. 1st house on the R.* **Sun 24 July (10.30-4). Adm £5, chd free. Light refreshments.**
Large, country garden with extensive views. Formal box edged beds

surround the house. Steps and paths lead to long borders with mixed planting. The formal garden paths lead to a sculptural ball surrounded by grasses, a pergola walkway with wisteria and clematis provides a quiet spot to view the garden. 6 acres of woodland with a mass of spring bluebells and summer ferns. Some hard surfaces around perimeter of house, gravelled and lawned paths in garden. Woodland walk not suitable for wheelchair access.

39 SPRINT MILL
Burneside, Kendal, LA8 9AQ. Edward & Romola Acland, 01539 725168 or 07806 065602, mail@sprintmill.uk. *2m N of Kendal. From Burneside follow signs towards Skelsmergh for ½m, then L into drive of Sprint Mill. Or from A6, about 1m N of Kendal follow signs towards Burneside, then R into drive.* **Visits by arrangement Mar to Sept for groups of up to 30. Adm £4, chd free. Light refreshments.**
Unorthodox organically run garden, the wild and natural alongside provision of owners' fruit, vegetables and firewood. Idyllic riverside setting, 5 acres to explore including wooded riverbank with hand-crafted seats. Large vegetable and soft fruit area, following no dig and permaculture principles. Hand tools prevail. Historic water mill with original turbine. The 3 storey building houses owner's art studio and personal museum, inc collection of old hand tools associated with rural crafts. Goats, hens, ducks, rope swing, very family friendly. Short walk to our flower rich hay meadows. Access for wheelchairs to some parts of both garden and mill.

40 SUMMERDALE HOUSE
Cow Brow, Nook, Lupton, LA6 1PE. David & Gail Sheals, www.summerdalegardenplants.co.uk. *7m S of Kendal, 5m W of Kirkby Lonsdale. From J36 M6 take A65 towards Kirkby Lonsdale, at Nook take R turn Farleton. Location not signed on highway. Detailed directions available on our website.* **Every Sat 19 Feb to 2 July (11-4.30). Sun 24 Apr, Sun 12 June (11-4.30). Home-made teas on Sundays only. Adm £5, chd free.**
1½ acre part-walled country garden set around C18 former vicarage. Several defined areas are created by hedges, each with its own

theme and linked by intricate cobbled pathways. Relaxed natural planting in a formal structure. Rural setting with fine views across to Farleton Fell. Large collections of auricula, primulas and snowdrops. Adjoining RHS Gold Medal winning nursery. Auricula display during season.

41 TITHE BARN
Laversdale, Irthington, Carlisle, CA6 4PJ. Mr Gordon & Mrs Christine Davidson, 01228 573090, christinedavidson7@sky.com. *8m N E of Carlisle. ½m from Carlisle Lake District Airport. From 6071 turn for Laversdale, from M6 J44 follow A689 Hexham/Brampton/ Airport. Follow NGS signs.* **Visits by arrangement June & July for groups of up to 30. Home-made teas.**
Set on a slight incline, the thatched property has stunning views of the Lake District, Pennines and Scottish Border hills. Planting follows the cottage garden style, the surrounding walls, arches, grottos and quirky features have all been designed and created by the owners. There is a peaceful sitting glade beside a rill and pond. This property also offers self-catering accommodation (sleeps 2) within the grounds of the garden.

GROUP OPENING

42 ULVERSTON GARDENS
Hamilton Grove, Oubas Hill, Ulverston, LA12 7LB. Martin & Helen Cooper. *Hamilton Grove, where directions to other gardens will be available, is on the A590 as you approach Ulverston from the east; Rail Ulverston; Bus 6, X6; NCR70.* **Sun 3 July (10-5). Combined adm £5, chd free. Light refreshments available at several of the gardens. Excellent picnic sites at Hamilton Grove.**
Hamilton Grove, and several other gardens in and around the historic market town of Ulverston, with its canal and lighthouse monument to Sir John Barrow. Details of other gardens, after an earlier local garden festival, will be available on the day at Hamilton Grove. All will surprise. Hamilton Grove has a sloping garden from a large terrace down to what was the canal feeder, when the canal was opened in 1796. Mixed perennial and annual planting and a large

collection of scented pelargonium. Lovely countryside views and up to the lighthouse monument.

43 WHETSTONE CROFT & COTTAGE
Woodland, Broughton-In-Furness, LA20 6AE. John & Elaine Hudson, Rob Wilson & Iain Speak. *On the A593, approx 2m N of Broughton-in-Furness. Follow NGS signs through yard to park.* **Sat 18, Sun 19 June (12-5). Adm £5, chd free. Home-made teas.**
Two different, tranquil, south facing cottage gardens overlooking the Woodland valley. Herbaceous borders bursting with cottage garden favourites, mature flowering shrubs, azaleas, herb beds, stoop garden, courtyard and shrubbery surrounding C18 farmhouse and barns. Easy access to renowned traditional hay meadows including eyebright, orchids, yellow rattle and oxeye daisies.

44 WINTON PARK
Appleby Road, Kirkby Stephen, CA17 4PG. Mr Anthony Kilvington, www.wintonparkgardens.co.uk. *2m N of Kirkby Stephen. On A685 turn L signed Gt Musgrave/Warcop (B6259). After approx 1m turn L as signed.* **Sun 10 July (11-4). Adm £6, chd free. Light refreshments.**
5 acre country garden bordered by the banks of the River Eden with stunning views. Many fine conifers, acers and rhododendrons, herbaceous borders, hostas, ferns, grasses, heathers and several hundred roses. Four formal ponds plus rock pool. Partial wheelchair access.

45 WOODEND HOUSE
Woodend, Egremont, CA22 2TA. Grainne & Richard Jakobson, 019468 13017, gmjakobson22@gmail.com. *2m S of Whitehaven. Take the A595 from Whitehaven towards Egremont. On leaving Bigrigg take 1st turn L. Go down hill, garden at bottom on R opp Woodend Farm.* **Sat 25, Sun 26 June (11-5). Adm £4, chd free. Home-made teas. Visits also by arrangement May to Sept for groups of up to 25.**
A small interesting garden tucked away in a small hamlet. Meandering gravel paths lead around the garden with imaginative, colourful planting and quirky features. Take a look around a productive, organic potager, wildlife pond, mini spring and summer meadows and sit in the pretty summerhouse. Designed to be beautiful throughout the year and wildlife friendly. Mini-quiz for children. Live Blues and Jazz in the garden. The gravel drive and paths are difficult for wheelchairs but more mobile visitors can access the main seating areas in the rear garden.

46 YEWBARROW HOUSE
Hampsfell Road, Grange-over-Sands, LA11 6BE. Jonathan & Margaret Denby, 077 333 22349, jonathan@bestlakesbreaks.co.uk, www.yewbarrowhouse.co.uk. *¼m from town centre. Proceed along Hampsfell Rd passing a house called Yewbarrow to brow of hill then turn L onto a lane signed 'Charney Wood/ Yewbarrow Wood' & sharp L again. Rail 0.7m, Bus X6, NCR 70.* **Sun 5 June, Sun 3 July, Sun 7 Aug, Sun 4 Sept (11-4). Adm £5, chd free. Light refreshments. Visits also by arrangement May to Sept for groups of 10+.**
'More Cornwall than Cumbria' according to Country Life, a colourful 4 acre garden filled with exotic and rare plants, with dramatic views over Morecambe Bay. Outstanding features include the Orangery; the Japanese garden with infinity pool, the Italian terraces and the restored Victorian kitchen garden. Dahlias, cannas and colourful exotica are a speciality. Find us on youTube.

Netherby Hall

DERBYSHIRE

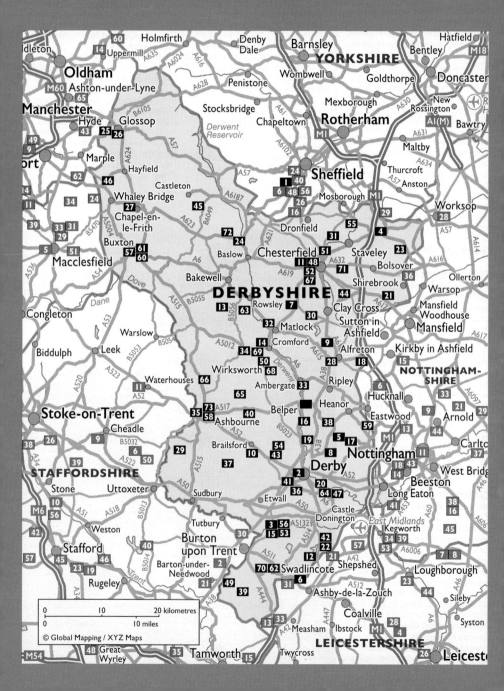

Derbyshire is the county where the Midlands meets the North, and visitors are attracted to the rugged hills of the High Peak, the high moorlands near Sheffield and the unspoilt countryside of the Dales.

There are many stately homes in the county with world famous gardens, delightful private country gardens, and interesting small cottage and town gardens.

Some of the northern gardens have spectacular views across the Peak District; their planting reflecting the rigours of the climate and long, cold winters. In the Derbyshire Dales, stone walls give way to hedges and the countryside is hilly with many trees, good agricultural land and very pretty villages.

South of Derby the land is much flatter, the architecture has a Midlands look with red brick replacing stone and softer planting in the gardens.

The east side of Derbyshire is different again, reflecting the recent past with small pit villages, and looking towards the rolling countryside of Nottinghamshire. There are fast road links with other parts of the country via the M1 and M6, making a day trip to a Derbyshire garden a very easy choice.

Below: The Lilies

Volunteers

County Organiser
Peter Gardner 01335 372001
peter.gardner@ngs.org.uk

County Treasurer
Robert Little 01283 702267
robert.little@ngs.org.uk

Social Media
Tracy Reid 07932 977314
tracy.reid@ngs.org.uk,

Booklet Co-ordinator
Malcolm & Wendy Fisher
0115 9664 322
wendy.fisher111@btinternet.com

Dave & Valerie Booth 01283 221167
valerie.booth1955@gmail.com

Group Visit Co-ordinator
Pauline Little 01283 702267
plittle@hotmail.co.uk

Assistant County Organisers
Gill & Colin Hancock 01159 301061
gillandcolinhancock@gmail.com

Jane Lennox 07939 012634
jane@lennoxonline.net

Pauline Little (See above)

Christine & Vernon Sanderson
01246 570830
christine.r.sanderson@uwclub.net

Kate & Peter Spencer 01629 822499
pandkspencer@gmail.com

Jean Gardner 01335 372001
jean.gardner@ngs.org.uk

Paul & Kathy Harvey 01629 822218
pandk.harvey@ngs.org.uk

OPENING DATES

All entries subject to change. For latest information check www.ngs.org.uk

Map locator numbers are shown to the right of each garden name.

February

Snowdrop Festival

Saturday 12th
The Dower House — 22

Sunday 13th
The Dower House — 22

Sunday 20th
10 Chestnut Way — 15

March

Saturday 19th
◆ Cascades Gardens — 14

Saturday 26th
Chevin Brae — 16

April

Wednesday 13th
334 Belper Road — 5

Monday 18th
◆ The Burrows Gardens — 10

Friday 22nd
◆ Cascades Gardens — 14

Sunday 24th
◆ Old English Walled Garden, Elvaston Castle Country Park — 47
The Paddock — 51

May

Sunday 1st
12 Ansell Road — 1
Barlborough Gardens — 4

Monday 2nd
12 Ansell Road — 1

Sunday 8th
Littleover Lane Allotments — 36

Tuesday 10th
NEW Brierley Farm — 7

Sunday 15th
Fir Croft — 24
◆ Meynell Langley Trials Garden — 43
NEW 26 Stiles Road — 64
27 Wash Green — 68

Saturday 21st
Longford Hall Farm — 37

Sunday 22nd
Askew Cottage — 3
334 Belper Road — 5
10 Chestnut Way — 15

Saturday 28th
12 Ansell Road — 1

Sunday 29th
12 Ansell Road — 1
Broomfield Hall — 8
◆ The Burrows Gardens — 10
13 Chiltern Drive — 17
Fir Croft — 24
Highfield House — 28
Rectory House — 54

June

Saturday 4th
The Holly Tree — 32
Longford Hall Farm — 37
The Smithy — 60
12 Water Lane — 69

Sunday 5th
Highfields House — 29
The Holly Tree — 32
12 Water Lane — 69

Monday 6th
The Smithy — 60

Saturday 11th
The Dower House — 22
◆ Melbourne Hall Gardens — 42

Sunday 12th
The Dower House — 22
Fir Croft — 24
◆ Melbourne Hall Gardens — 42
Walton Cottage — 67
13 Westfield Road — 70

Wednesday 15th
◆ Bluebell Arboretum and Nursery — 6

Saturday 18th
Holmlea — 33

Sunday 19th
12 Ansell Road — 1
334 Belper Road — 5
◆ The Burrows Gardens — 10
NEW 88 Church Street West — 18
Holmlea — 33
◆ Meynell Langley Trials Garden — 43

Friday 24th
330 Old Road — 48

Saturday 25th
12 Ansell Road — 1
◆ Calke Abbey — 12
Elmton Gardens — 23
NEW The Limes — 35
330 Old Road — 48

Sunday 26th
Elmton Gardens — 23
High Roost — 26
NEW 25 Melbourne Close — 41
Moorfields — 44
Old Shoulder of Mutton - 7 Main Street — 49

July

Saturday 2nd
Barlborough Gardens — 4

Sunday 3rd
Barlborough Gardens — 4
Candlemas Cottage — 13
8 Curzon Lane — 20
Hill Cottage — 30
The Lilies — 34
58A Main Street — 39

Tuesday 5th
◆ Renishaw Hall & Gardens — 55

Saturday 9th
NEW Nether Moor House — 45
New Mills School — 46

Sunday 10th
New Mills School — 46
The Old Vicarage — 50

Wednesday 13th
◆ Bluebell Arboretum and Nursery — 6
Spingles — 61

Saturday 16th
Askew Cottage — 3
Longford Hall Farm — 37

---

22 Pinfold Close — 53
Repton Allotments — 56

Sunday 17th
◆ The Burrows Gardens — 10
8 Curzon Lane — 20
58A Main Street — 39
◆ Meynell Langley Trials Garden — 43

Friday 22nd
The Smithy — 60

Saturday 23rd
◆ Cascades Gardens — 14
Stanton in Peak Gardens — 63
26 Windmill Rise — 74

Sunday 24th
The Paddock — 51
Stanton in Peak Gardens — 63
26 Windmill Rise — 74

Saturday 30th
12 Ansell Road — 1
Byways — 11
NEW 92 Springfield Road — 62

Sunday 31st
12 Ansell Road — 1
Byways — 11

August

Sunday 7th
Barlborough Gardens — 4
8 Curzon Lane — 20
9 Main Street — 38
◆ Old English Walled Garden, Elvaston Castle Country Park — 47
15 Windmill Lane — 73

Saturday 13th
Ashbourne Road and District Allotments Ltd — 2
Wild in the Country — 72

Sunday 14th
Ashbourne Road and District Allotments Ltd — 2
The Lilies — 34

Monday 15th
◆ Tissington Hall — 66

Wednesday 17th
◆ Bluebell Arboretum and Nursery — 6

Saturday 20th
Chevin Brae — 16

Cascades Gardens

THE GARDENS

🏠 12 ANSELL ROAD

Ecclesall, Sheffield, S11 7PE. Dave Darwent, 01142 665881, dave@poptasticdave.co.uk. *Approx 3m SW of City Centre. Travel to Ringinglow Rd (88 bus), then Edale Rd (opp Ecclesall C of E Primary School). 3rd R - Ansell Rd. No 12 on L ¾ way down, solar panel on roof.* **Sun 1, Mon 2, Sat 28, Sun 29 May (11.30-5.30); Sun 19, Sat 25 June (3-7); Sat 30, Sun 31 July (11.30-5.30). Adm £3.50, chd free. Light refreshments. Vegan & gluten free options available. Visits also by arrangement May to Aug for groups of up to 20. By arrangement adm inc drinks & home-made cakes.**

Now in its 94th year since being created by my grandparents, this is a suburban mixed productive and flower garden retaining many original plants and features as well as the original layout. A book documenting the history of the garden has been published and is on sale to raise further funds for charity. Original rustic pergola with 90+ year old roses. Then and now pictures of the garden in 1929 and 1950's vs present.

🏠 ASHBOURNE ROAD AND DISTRICT ALLOTMENTS LTD

Mackworth Road, Derby, DE22 3BL. Elaine Crick, www.araa.org.uk. *From Kedleston Rd turn onto Cowley St which becomes Mackworth Rd. From Ashbourne Rd turn onto Merchant St which becomes Mackworth Rd.* **Sat 13, Sun 14 Aug (10.30-2.30). Adm £5, chd free. Home-made teas.**

This beautiful allotment site is nestled quietly between two main roads leading into Derby city. It boasts of being over 100 yrs old with plots of all differing shapes and sizes. It houses a giant cockerel made from sheet metal and recycled tools, as well as a Growing Academy, packed polytunnels, starter plots, a Centenary Allotment and is the 'home' of Radio Derby's Potty Plotters. The site has plots for you to venture onto and enthusiastic plot holders to chat to. There are 12 starter plots to inspect and main plots filled with flowers, vegetables and fruits in varying stages of growth and production. Bees to view and allotmenty things to buy. The main grass paths are flat and accessible with care.

♿ 🐕 ❀ ☕ ⋙

🏠 ASKEW COTTAGE

23 Milton Road, Repton, Derby, DE65 6FZ. Louise Hardwick, 07970 411748, louise.hardwick@hotmail.co.uk, www.hardwickgardendesign. co.uk. *6m S of Derby. From A38/A50 junction S of Derby. Follow signs to Willington then Repton on B5008. In Repton turn 1st L then bear sharp R into Milton Rd.* **Sun 22 May (1-5.30). Sat 16 July (1-5.30). Home-made teas. Sat 17 Sept (1-5.30). Adm £4, chd free. Teas at 10 Chestnut Way in May and September. Visits also by arrangement May to Oct for groups of 10 to 25.**

The owner, a professional garden designer, has used curved paths and a variety of structural hedges to enclose spaces, each with a distinct feel. The planting within the borders changes as areas are altered and new combinations tried. Features inc a circle of meadow grass with a border of cloud-pruned box hedge and mixed perennial planting, trained apple trees and a small wildlife pool.

🐕 ☕ ⋙

Map of landmarks up to 55m away which can be seen from garden. Seven water features. Wide variety of unique-recipe home-made cakes with takeaway service available. New winter garden.

❀ ☕

The Paddock

GROUP OPENING

4 BARLBOROUGH GARDENS

Chesterfield Road, Barlborough, Chesterfield, S43 4TR. Christine Sanderson, 07956 203184, christine.r.sanderson@uwclub.net, www.facebook.com/barlboroughgardens. *7m NE of Chesterfield. Off A619 midway between Chesterfield & Worksop. ½m E M1, J30. Follow signs for Barlborough then yellow NGS signs. Parking available in village.* **Sun 1 May, Sat 2, Sun 3 July, Sun 7 Aug (11.30-4.30). Combined adm £5, chd free. Sun 11 Sept (11.30-4.30). Combined adm £4.50, chd free. Refreshments at The Hollies (all dates) & at Raisewells House (selected dates)** Visits also by arrangement May to Aug for groups of 10 to 30. By arrangement adm price inc private tour of two gardens and refreshments.

CLARENDON
Neil & Lorraine Jones.
Open on Sun 1 May, Sat 2, Sun 3 July

THE HOLLIES
Vernon & Christine Sanderson, www.facebook.com/barlboroughgardens.
Open on all dates

LINDWAY
Thomas & Margaret Pettinger.
Open on all dates

RAISWELLS HOUSE
Mr Andrew & Mrs Rosie Dale.
Open on Sat 2 July, Sun 7 Aug

Barlborough is an attractive historic village and a range of interesting buildings can be seen all around the village centre. The village is situated close to Renishaw Hall for possible combined visit. Map detailing location of all gardens is issued with admission ticket. For more information visit our Facebook page - see details above. Barlborough Gardens celebrated 10 years of opening for National Garden Scheme in 2021. The Hollies inc an area influenced by the Majorelle Garden in Marrakech. This makeover was achieved using upcycled items together with appropriate planting. It was featured in an episode of TVs "Love Your Garden". Partial wheelchair access at The Hollies.

5 334 BELPER ROAD

Stanley Common, DE7 6FY. Gill & Colin Hancock, 01159 301061, gillandcolinhancock@gmail.com. *7m N of Derby. 3m W of Ilkeston. On A609, ¾m from Rose & Crown Xrds (A608). Please park in field up farm drive.* **Wed 13 Apr (12-4); Sun 22 May, Sun 19 June (11-4). Adm £4, chd free. Home-made teas.** Visits also by arrangement Mar to July for groups of 5 to 40. By arrangement adm inc refreshments.
Beautiful country garden with many attractive features inc a laburnum tunnel, rose wisteria domes, old workmen's hut, wildlife pond and more. Take a walk through the 10 acres of woodland and glades to a ½ acre lake. Organic vegetable garden. See Snowdrops and Hellebores in February, cowslips in April and wild orchids in June. Newly planted rose meadow. Plenty of seating to enjoy home-made cakes. Children welcome with plenty of activities to keep them entertained. Abundant wildlife. Paths round wood lake and some of the garden not suitable for wheelchairs.

6 ♦ BLUEBELL ARBORETUM AND NURSERY

Annwell Lane, Smisby, Ashby de la Zouch, LE65 2TA. Robert & Suzette Vernon, 01530 413700, sales@bluebellnursery.com, www.bluebellnursery.com. *1m NW of Ashby-de-la-Zouch. Arboretum is clearly signed in Annwell Lane (follow brown signs), ¼m S, through village of Smisby off B5006, between Ticknall & Ashby-de-la-Zouch. Free parking.* **For NGS: Wed 15 June, Wed 13 July, Wed 17 Aug (9-4). Adm £5, chd free. For other opening times and information, please phone, email or visit garden website.**
Beautiful 9 acre woodland garden with a large collection of rare trees and shrubs. Interest throughout the yr with spring flowers, cool leafy areas in summer and sensational autumn colour. Many information posters describing the more obscure plants. Adjacent specialist tree and shrub nursery. Please be aware this is not a wood full of bluebells, despite the name. The woodland garden is fully labelled and the staff can answer questions or talk at length about any of the trees or shrubs on display. Rare trees and shrubs. Educational signs. Woodland. Arboretum. Please wear sturdy, waterproof footwear during or after wet weather. Full wheelchair access in dry, warm weather however grass paths can become wet and inaccessible in snow or after rain.

7 NEW BRIERLEY FARM

Mill Lane, Brockhurst, Ashover, Chesterfield, S45 0HS. Anne & David Wilkinson, 07831 598396, annelwilkinson@btinternet.com. *6m SW of Chesterfield, 4m NE of Matlock. 1½m NW of Ashover. From the A632 turn W into Alicehead Rd, L into Swinger Ln, 2nd L into Brockhurst Ln & R into Mill Ln. Brierley Farm is the only house on the L.* **Tue 10 May (11-4). Adm £6. Home-made teas.** Visits also by arrangement Mar to Sept for groups of 15 to 30.
This 5 acre site features a 2 acre garden and lawns and 3 acre woodland with paths. The sloping garden leads down to a bridge crossing a stream into the woodland. A high water table feeds three linked ponds and areas of bog garden. Raised stone-walled beds feature bulbs, hellebore, geum and rhododendron in the spring followed by seasonal perennial and annual flowering plants into the autumn.

8 BROOMFIELD HALL

Morley, Ilkeston, DE7 6DN. Derby College, www.facebook.com/BroomfieldPlantCentre. *4m N of Derby. 6m S of Heanor on A608.* **Sun 29 May, Sun 11 Sept (10-4). Adm £5, chd free. Light refreshments in a pop-up volunteer run cafe.**
25 acres of constantly developing educational Victorian gardens/woodlands maintained by volunteers and students. Herbaceous borders, walled garden, themed gardens, rose garden, potager, prairie plantings, Japanese garden, tropical garden, winter garden, plant centre. Light entertainment, cacti, carnivorous, bonsai, fuchsia specialists and craft stalls. Most of garden is accessible to wheelchair users and we are all on hand to help.

9 NEW **72 BURNSIDE AVENUE**
Shirland, Alfreton, DE55 6AE.
A & S Wilson-Hunt, 07856 900022,
sandrawh16@gmail.com. 2½ m
from Alfreton. 3½ m from Clay Cross
on A61. From the A61 turn onto
Hallfieldgate Lane, onto Byron St.
R onto Burnside Ave. Follow the
road & garden is last bungalow on
L. What3words app - relate.rivers.
mostly. **Visits by arrangement
July to Sept for groups of up
to 6. Adm £4, chd free. Light
refreshments.**
Delightful small cottage garden with
tropical planting. Bananas, cannas,
tree ferns, palms and bamboos and
succulents. Clematis, acers, shrubs
and phlox mix with ferns, hostas and
dahlias to ensure all year interest.
Greenhouse, hanging baskets, shady
planting, sedum roof. Level garden
with paved seating area offering a
peaceful haven to enjoy refreshments.
🐾 ❀ 🍵 •))

10 ♦ **THE BURROWS GARDENS**
Burrows Lane, Brailsford,
Ashbourne, DE6 3BU.
Mrs N M Dalton, 01335 360745,
enquiries@burrowsgardens.com,
www.burrowsgardens.com. 5m
SE of Ashbourne; 5m NW of Derby.
A52 from Derby: turn L opp sign
for Wild Park Leisure 1m before
village of Brailsford. ¼ m & at grass
triangle head straight over through
wrought iron gates. **For NGS: Mon
18 Apr, Sun 29 May, Sun 19 June,
Sun 17 July, Mon 29 Aug (11-4).
Adm £5, chd free. Home-made
teas. For other opening times and
information, please phone, email or
visit garden website.**
Immaculate lawns show off exotic
rare plants and trees, mixing with old
favourites in this outstanding garden.
A wide variety of styles from temple to
Cornish, Italian to English, gloriously
designed and displayed. This is a
must see garden. Most of garden
accessible to wheelchairs.
♿ ❀ 🚗 🍵 🏕

11 **BYWAYS**
7A Brookfield Avenue, Brookside,
Chesterfield, S40 3NX. Terry
& Eileen Kelly, 07414 827813,
telkel1@aol.com. 1½ m W of
Chesterfield. Follow A619 from
Chesterfield towards Baslow.
Brookfield Ave is 2nd R after
Brookfield Sch. Please park on
Chatsworth Rd (A619). **Sat 30, Sun
31 July (11.30-4.30). Adm £3.50,**

chd free. Light refreshments inc
gluten free option. Visits also by
arrangement July & Aug for groups
of 10 to 25. Donation to Ashgate
Hospice.**
Previous winners of the Best Back
Garden over 80 sqm, Best Front
Garden, Best Container Garden and
Best Hanging Basket in Chesterfield
in Bloom. Well established perennial
borders inc helenium, monardas,
phlox, grasses, acers, giving a
very colourful display. Rockery and
many planters containing acers,
pelargoniums, ferns, hostas and
fuchsias. Also a greenhouse with a
display of pelargoniums.
❀ 🍵

12 ♦ **CALKE ABBEY**
Ticknall, DE73 7LE. National
Trust, 01332 863822,
calkeabbey@nationaltrust.org.uk,
www.nationaltrust.org.uk/calke.
10m S of Derby. On A514 at Ticknall
between Swadlincote & Melbourne. For
SatNav use DE73 7JF. **For NGS: Sat
25 June, Sat 24 Sept (9-4.30). Adm
£6.50, chd £3.25. For other opening
times and information, please phone,
email or visit garden website.**
With peeling paintwork and
overgrown courtyards, Calke Abbey
tells the story of the dramatic decline
of a country-house estate. The
productive kitchen garden, impressive
collection of glasshouses, garden
buildings and tunnels hint at the work
of past gardeners, while today the
flower garden, herbaceous borders
and auricula theatre providing
stunning displays all year. Restaurant
at main visitor facilities for light
refreshments and locally sourced
food. House is also open. Electric
buggy available for those with mobility
problems. Tramper also available to
book for 2 hours. Please call 01332
863822 to book.
♿ 🐾 ❀ 🚗 🍵

13 **CANDLEMAS COTTAGE**
Alport Lane, Youlgrave, Bakewell,
DE45 1WN. Jane Ide. 3½ m S of
Bakewell. From A6: pass playing
fields on L, then Youlgrave Garage
on R. From A515: through village
& straight on at church/George
pub Xrds. Blue house directly opp
Youlgrave Primary Sch. **Sun 3 July
(11.30-4.30). Adm £3.50, chd free.
Home-made teas.**
A recently established plantswoman's
contemporary cottage garden in
the heart of the Peak National Park,
featuring rose beds and wisteria

arch, winter garden, green garden,
long mixed border, specimen trees,
kitchen garden and pollinator's patch.
Gardened to maximise benefits to
wildlife and humans, with carefully sited
seating areas in shade and sunshine.
🐾 ❀ 🍵 •))

14 ♦ **CASCADES GARDENS**
Clatterway, Bonsall, Matlock,
DE4 2AH. Alan & Alesia Clements,
07967 337404, alan.clements@
cascadesgardens.com,
www.cascadesgardens.com. 5m
SW of Matlock. From Cromford A6
T-lights turn towards Wirksworth.
Turn R along Via Gellia, signed
Buxton & Bonsall. After 1m turn R up
hill towards Bonsall. Garden entrance
at top of hill. Park in village car park.
**For NGS: Sat 19 Mar, Fri 22 Apr,
Sat 23 July, Sat 3 Sept (12-4).
Adm £7, chd £3. Home-made
teas. For other opening times and
information, please phone, email or
visit garden website.**
The Meditation Garden: Fascinating 4
acre peaceful garden in spectacular
natural surroundings with woodland,
cliffs, stream, pond and limestone
quarry. Inspired by Japanese gardens
and Buddhist philosophy, secluded
garden rooms for relaxation and
reflection. Beautiful landscape with a
wide collection of unusual perennials,
conifers, shrubs and trees. Bonsai
centre and Nursery. Plants for sale.
Hellebore month in March. Mostly
wheelchair accessible. Gravel paths,
some steep slopes.
♿ 🐾 ❀ 🚗 🚍 🍵

15 **10 CHESTNUT WAY**
Repton, DE65 6FQ. Robert &
Pauline Little, 01283 702267,
rlittleq@gmail.com,
www.littlegarden.org.uk. 6m S of
Derby. From A38/A50, S of Derby,
follow signs to Willington, then Repton.
In Repton turn R at r'about. Chestnut
Way is ¼ m up hill, on L. **Sun 20 Feb
(11-3). Adm £4, chd free. Sun 22
May, Sat 17 Sept (1-5.30). Adm £5,
chd free. Home-made teas. Home-
made soup available in Feb. Visits
also by arrangement Feb to Oct for
groups of 5+. By Arrangement fee
includes refreshments and garden
tour.**
A large and wonderfully diverse
garden with lots of separate areas
of interest and thoughtful planting
throughout. Much admired by visitors
who enjoy the many benches to sit
and soak up the atmosphere. Our
unusual sculptures and renowned

home-made teas make for a memorable visit. Overflowing borders and a surprise round every corner. Look out for pop-up openings. Come in May for the best selection of plants for sale from the garden. Special interest in viticella clematis, organic vegetables, woodland/shade plants and composting. Level garden, good solid paths to main areas. Some grass/bark paths.

16 CHEVIN BRAE
Milford, Belper, DE56 0QH. Dr David Moreton, 07778 004374, davidmoretonchevinbrae@gmail.com. *1½ m S of Belper. Coming from S on A6 turn L at Strutt Arms & cont up Chevin Rd. Park on Chevin Rd. After 300 yds follow arrow to L up Morrells Lane. After 300 yds Chevin Brae on L with silver garage.* Sat 26 Mar, Sat 20 Aug (1-5). Adm £3, chd £2.50. Home-made teas. Visits also by arrangement Feb to Oct.
A large garden, with swathes of daffodils in the orchard a spring feature. Extensive wildflower planting along edge of wood features aconites, snowdrops, wood anemones, fritillaries and dog tooth violets. Other parts of garden will have hellebores and early camelias. During the summer the extensive flower borders and rose trellises give much colour. Large kitchen garden and fruit cages. Tea and home-made cakes, pastries and biscuits, many of which feature fruit and jam from the garden.

17 13 CHILTERN DRIVE
West Hallam, Ilkeston, DE7 6PA. Jacqueline & Keith Holness. *Approx 7m NE of Derby. From A609, 2m W of Ilkeston, nr The Bottle Kiln, take St Wilfreds Rd. Take 1st R onto Derbyshire Av, Chiltern Drive is 3rd turning on L.* Sun 29 May (11.30-4.30). Adm £3, chd free. Home-made teas. Gluten free options available.
Ours is a plant lover's garden, every corner brimming with plants, many rare and unusual. Paris, beesia, schefflera, podophyllum, to name but a few. There's a pretty summerhouse, a small pond and fernery, together with over 50 different acers, over 30 varieties of hosta, many ferns and some well hidden lizards! As the garden has matured the acers have now given the garden a real woodland feel.

18 NEW 88 CHURCH STREET WEST
Pinxton, Nottingham, NG16 6PU. Rosemary Ahmed. *Pinxton is located approx 1m from junction 28 of the M1. At motorway island take the B6019 towards Alfreton & take the first turning on L Alfreton Rd, garden will be sign posted from there.* Sun 19 June (1-5). Adm £3.50, chd free. Light refreshments.
Plantwomens garden on various levels, developed over 25 yrs from rough grass to inc collections of hardy geraniums, agaves, ferns, persicaria and grasses. The garden has a quirky mix of salvage items collected by the owner. A wildflower lawn is a work in progress, a small rockery, upcycled garden room, mixed borders and a large patio with pot displays.

19 COXBENCH HALL
Alfreton Road, Coxbench, Derby, DE21 5BB. Mr Brian Ballin, 01332 880200, office@coxbench-hall.co.uk, www.coxbench-hall.co.uk. *4m N of Derby close to A38. After passing thru Little Eaton, turn L onto Alfreton Rd for 1m, Coxbench Hall is on L next to Fox & Hounds pub between Little Eaton & Holbrook. From A38, take Kilburn turn & go towards Little Eaton.* Sun 11 Sept (2.30-5.30). Adm £3, chd free. Light refreshments. Home-made diabetic & gluten free cakes. Visits also by arrangement for groups of up to 15.
Formerly the ancestral home of the Meynell family, the gardens reflect the Georgian house standing in 4½ acres of grounds most of which is accessible and wheelchair friendly. The garden has two fishponds connected by a stream, a sensory garden for the sight impaired, a short woodland walk through shrubbery, rockery, raised vegetable beds, an orchard and seasonal displays in the mainly lawned areas. Our Gardens are developed to inspire our residents from a number of sensory perspectives- different colours, textures and fragrances of plants. We grow vegetables next to the C18 potting shed, have a veteran (500-800 year old) yew tree, are developing a rhododendron garden and have woodland walks. Most of garden is lawned or block paved inc a block paved path around the edges of the main lawn. Regret no wheelchair

access to woodland area.

20 8 CURZON LANE
Alvaston, Derby, DE24 8QS. John & Marian Gray, 01332 601596, maz@curzongarden.com, www.curzongarden.com. *2m SE of Derby city centre. From city centre take A6 (London Rd) towards Alvaston. Curzon Lane on L, approx ½ m before Alvaston shops.* Sun 3, Sun 17 July, Sun 7 Aug (12-5). Adm £3.50, chd free. Light refreshments. Visits also by arrangement July & Aug for groups of up to 30.
Mature garden with lawns, borders packed full with perennials, shrubs and small trees, tropical planting and hot border. Ornamental and wildlife ponds, greenhouse with different varieties of tomato, cucumber, peppers and chillies. Well-stocked vegetable plot. Gravel area and large patio with container planting.

21 DOVECOTE COTTAGE
Stony Houghton, Mansfield, NG19 8TR. Rachel Hayes, 01623 811472, rachelhayes_@hotmail.com. *Between Rotherham Rd & Water Lane opp the phone box.* Visits by arrangement May to Aug for groups of 5 to 20. Adm £5. Light refreshments.
Wildlife friendly, mature garden set in a rural location. A variety of evergreens, foliage plants and cottage garden favourites with Spring and Autumn highlights. The garden is on different levels with steps and slopes and is not suitable for wheelchairs. Two local cafes within 5 mins drive. Dogs welcome. Limited parking.

Around 1,050 people living with Parkinson's - and their families - have been helped by Parkinson's nurses thanks to funding from the National Garden Scheme

22 THE DOWER HOUSE

Church Square, Melbourne, DE73 8JH. William & Griselda Kerr, 01332 864756, griseldakerr@btinternet.com. *6m S of Derby. 5m W of exit 23A M1. 4m N of exit 13 M42. When in Church Square, turn R just before the church by a blue sign giving church service times. Gates are then 50 yds ahead.* **Sat 12, Sun 13 Feb (10-3.30). Adm £4, chd free. Sat 11, Sun 12 June (10-5). Adm £5, chd free. Light refreshments (served outside) are weather dependant. Visits also by arrangement Jan to Nov for groups of 10 to 20.**
Beautiful view of Melbourne Pool from balustraded terrace running length of 1829 house. Garden drops steeply by paths and steps to lawn with herbaceous borders and bank of some 60 shrubs. Numerous paths lead to different areas of the garden, providing different planting opportunities inc a bog garden, glade, shrubbery, grasses, herb and vegetable garden, rose tunnel, orchard and small woodland. Hidden paths and different areas for children to explore and various animals such as a bronze crocodile and stone dragon to find. They should be supervised by an adult at all times due to the proximity of water.

Wheelchair access to top half of the garden only. Shoes with a good grip are highly recommended as slopes are steep. No parking within 50 yards.

GROUP OPENING

23 ELMTON GARDENS

Elmton, Worksop, S80 4LS. *2m from Creswell, 3m from Clowne, 5m from J30, M1. From M1 J30 take A616 to Newark. Follow approx 4m. Turn R at Elmton signpost. At junction turn R, the village centre is in ½m.* **Sat 25, Sun 26 June (1-5). Combined adm £5, chd free. Cream teas at the Old Schoolroom next to the church. Food also available all day at the Elm Tree Inn.**

THE BARN
Mrs Anne Merrick, annemerrick.nutbrook@outlook.com. **Visits also by arrangement in June.**

NEW THE COTTAGE
Judith Maughan & Roy Reeves.

ELM TREE COTTAGE
Mark & Linda Hopkinson.

ELM TREE FARM
Angie & Tim Caulton.

PEAR TREE COTTAGE
Geoff & Janet Cutts.

PINFOLD
Nikki Kirsop & Barry Davies.

NEW ROSE COTTAGE
Andrew & Ruth Saxton.

Elmton is a lovely little village situated on a stretch of rare unimproved Magnesian limestone grassland with quaking grass, bee orchids and harebells all set in the middle of attractive, rolling farm land. It has a pub, which serves food all day, a church and a village green with award winning wildlife conservation area and newly restored Pinfold. Garden opening coincides with Elmton Well Dressing, with three well dressings on display. There is a brass band and a local history exhibition. The very colourful but different open gardens have wonderful views. They show a range of gardening styles, themed beds and have a commitment to fruit and vegetable growing. Elmton received a gold award and was voted best small village for the 7th time and best wildlife and conservation area in the East Midlands in Bloom competition in 2019.

The Hollies, Barlborough Gardens

© Amanda McConnell

24 FIR CROFT
Froggatt Road, Calver,
S32 3ZD. Dr S B Furness,
www.alpineplantcentre.co.uk. *4m
N of Bakewell. At junction of B6001
with A625 (formerly B6054), adjacent
to Froggat Edge Garage.* **Sun 15,
Sun 29 May, Sun 12 June (2-5).
Adm by donation.**
Massive scree with many varieties.
Plantsman's garden; rockeries;
water garden and nursery; extensive
collection (over 3000 varieties)
of alpines; conifers; over 800
sempervivums, 500 saxifrages and
350 primulas. Many new varieties not
seen anywhere else in the UK. Huge
new tufa wall planted with many rare
Alpines and sempervivums. Access to
part of garden only.

⅋ ✻ ➢

25 GAMESLEY FOLD COTTAGE
10 Gamesley Fold, Glossop,
SK13 6JJ. Mrs G M Carr,
01457 867856,
gcarr@gamesleyfold.co.uk,
www.gamesleyfold.co.uk. *2m W of
Glossop. Off A626 Glossop/Marple
Rd nr Charlesworth. Turn down
lane directly opp St. Margaret's
School, white cottage at the bottom.
Car parking in the adjacent field if
weather is dry.*
**Visits by arrangement Apr to July.
Any group size. Adm £4. Light
refreshments.**
Old fashioned cottage garden with
rhododendrons, herbaceous borders
with candelabra primulas, cottage
garden perennial flowers and herbs
also a plant nursery selling a wide
variety of these plus wildflowers.
Small ornamental fish pond and
an orchard. Lovely views of the
surrounding countryside and plenty
of seats available to relax and enjoy
tea and cakes. Garden planted to be
in keeping with the great age of the
house, 1650.

✻ ➢ ☕ ✏

26 HIGH ROOST
27 Storthmeadow Road,
Simmondley, Glossop,
SK13 6UZ. Peter & Christina
Harris, 01457 863888,
harrispeter448@gmail.com. *¾m
SW of Glossop. From Glossop
A57 to M/CL at 2nd r'about, up
Simmondley Ln nr top R turn.
From Marple A626 to Glossop,
in Chworth R up Town Ln past
Hare & Hound pub 2nd L.* **Sun 26
June (12-4). Adm £3, chd free.
Light refreshments. Visits also**

**by arrangement May to July for
groups of up to 40. Donation to
Donkey Sanctuary.**
Garden on terraced slopes, views
over fields and hills. Winding paths,
archways and steps explore different
garden rooms packed with plants,
designed to attract wildlife. Alpine
bed, gravel gardens; vegetable
garden, water features, statuary,
troughs and planters. A garden
which needs exploring to discover
its secrets tucked away in hidden
corners. Craft stall, children's garden
quiz and lucky dip.

🐕 ✻ ➢ ☕

27 HIGHER CROSSINGS
Crossings Road, Chapel-
en-le-Frith, High Peak,
SK23 9RX. Malcolm & Christine
Hoskins, 01298 812970,
malcolm275@btinternet.com. *Turn
off B5470 N from Chapel-en-le-Frith
on Crossings Rd signed Whitehough/
Chinley. Higher Crossings is 2nd
house on R beyond 1st xrds. Park
best before xrds on Crossings
Rd or L on Eccles Rd.* **Visits by
arrangement May to Sept for
groups of 15 to 30. Adm £4, chd
free. Light refreshments.**
Nearly 2 acres of formal terraced
country garden, sweeping lawns
and magnificent Peak District views.
Rhododendrons, acers, azaleas,
hostas, herbaceous borders,
Japanese garden. Mature specimen
trees and shrubs leading through
a dell. Beautiful stone terrace and
sitting areas. Garden gate leading into
meadow. Tea and biscuits or home-
made cakes available (not included in
admission price). Wheelchair access
around the house and upper terrace
and gravel garden.

⅋ ☕

28 HIGHFIELD HOUSE
Wingfield Road, Oakerthorpe,
Alfreton, DE55 7AP. Paul &
Ruth Peat & Janet & Brian
Costall, 01773 521342,
highfieldhouseopengardens@
hotmail.co.uk,
www.highfieldhouse.weebly.com.
*Rear of Alfreton Golf Club. A615
Alfreton-Matlock Rd.* **Sun 29 May
(10.30-5). Adm £3, chd free.
Home-made teas. Visits also
by arrangement Feb to July for
groups of 15+. Entry price inc
refreshments for by arrangement
only groups.**
Lovely country garden of approx 1
acre, incorporating a shady garden,

woodland, pond, laburnum tunnel,
orchard, herbaceous borders and
vegetable garden. Fabulous AGA
baked cakes and lunches. Groups
welcome by appointment (inc 16th
-24th February for Snowdrops with
afternoon tea or lunch inside by the
fire). Lovely walk to Derbyshire Wildlife
Trust nature reserve to see Orchids in
June. Some steps, slopes and gravel
areas.

⅋ 🐕 ✻ ➢ 🚌 ☕ ♪)

29 HIGHFIELDS HOUSE
Shields Lane, Roston, Ashbourne,
DE6 2EF. Sarah Pennell. *6m SW of
Ashbourne. From Ashbourne: Follow
A515 S, after 3m turn R onto B5033.
After 2m turn L at grass triangle
onto Lid Lane & follow signs. Turn
L at Roston Inn & follow signs.* **Sun
5 June (1-5). Adm £4, chd free.
Home-made teas.**
A countryside garden with extensive
views. Colourful mixed borders,
patio, small pond, greenhouse
and vegetable plot with fruit trees.
Summerhouse area. polytunnel and a
short walk through field to the brook
and willow area. Many quiet areas
to sit and shade/woodland border.
Garden crafts. Partial wheelchair
access. Some gravel paths.

⅋ 🐕 ✻ ☕ 🪑

30 HILL COTTAGE
Ashover Road, Littlemoor,
Ashover, nr Chesterfield,
S45 0BL. Jane Tomlinson &
Tim Walls, 07946 388185,
lavenderhen@aol.com. *Littlemoor.
1.8m from Ashover village, 6.3m
from Chesterfield & 6.1m from
Matlock. Hill Cottage is on Ashover
Rd (also known as Stubben Edge
Ln). Opp the end of Eastwood Ln.*
**Sun 3 July (10.30-4.30). Adm £4,
chd free. Home-made teas. Visits
also by arrangement June to Sept
for groups of up to 15.**
Hill Cottage is a lovely example of
an English country cottage garden.
Whilst small, the garden has full,
colourful and fragrant mixed borders
with hostas and roses in pots
along with a heart shaped lawn. A
greenhouse full of chillies and scented
pelargoniums and a small vegetable
patch. Views over a pastoral
landscape to Ogston reservoir. A
wide variety of perennials and annuals
grown in pots and containers.

✻ ☕ ♪)

31 HILLSIDE
286 Handley Road, New Whittington, Chesterfield, S43 2ET. Mr E J Lee, 01246 454960, eric.lee5@btinternet.com. *3m N of Chesterfield. Between B6056 & B6052.* **Visits by arrangement Apr to Oct. Adm £4, chd free. Light refreshments.**
Part of the ⅓ of an acre site, slopes steeply but there are handrails for all the steps. There is a Japanese feature showcasing Japanese plants and a tree trail with 60 named trees, both small and large. There is a Himalayan bed with 40 species grown from wild collected seeds and an Asian area with bamboos, acers and a Chinese border. Other attractions are pools, streams and bog gardens.

32 THE HOLLY TREE
21 Hackney Road, Hackney, Matlock, DE4 2PX. Carl Hodgkinson. *½ m NW of Matlock, off A6. Take A6 NW past bus stn & 1st R up Dimple Rd. At T-junction, turn R & immed L, for Farley & Hackney. Take 1st L onto Hackney Rd. Continue ¾ m.* **Sat 4, Sun 5 June (11-4.30). Adm £4, chd free. Home-made teas.**
In excess of 1½ acres and set on a steeply sloping south facing site, sheltering behind a high retaining wall. It contains a bog garden, herbaceous borders, pond, vegetable plot, fruit trees and shrubs, honeybees and chickens. Extensively terraced with many paths and steps. Spectacular views across the Derwent valley.

33 HOLMLEA
Derby Road, Ambergate, Belper, DE56 2EJ. Bill & Tracy Reid. *On the A6 in Ambergate - between Belper & Matlock. Bungalow set slightly back from the rd between petrol station & St Anne's Church. Additional parking at Anila Restaurant opp The Hurt Arms on the A6.* **Sat 18, Sun 19 June, Sat 10, Sun 11 Sept (11-4). Adm £4, chd free. Light refreshments.**
Large garden with something for everyone. Formal garden, kitchen garden, fruit trees, greenhouses, herbaceous borders, and a gravel garden. A path from the vegetable garden leads you to the riverside area with signal box/summerhouse, boules court, canal lock water feature and riverside walk. Lots for children to

see and do. Dogs welcome - please be aware free ranging poultry in all areas. Wheelchair route around main features of the garden. Unfortunately the Riverside Walk is not suitable for wheelchairs.

34 THE LILIES
Griffe Grange Valley, Grange Mill, Matlock, DE4 4BW. Chris & Bridget Sheppard, www.thelilies.com. *On A5012 Via Gellia Rd 4m N Cromford. 1st house on R after junction with B5023 to Middleton. From Grange Mill, 1st house on L after IKO Grangemill (Formerly Prospect Quarry).* **Sun 3 July, Sun 14 Aug (10.30-4). Adm £4, chd free. Light lunches served 11.30am to 2pm. Tea, coffee and cake served all day.**
1 acre garden gradually restored over the past 16 years situated at the top of a wooded valley, surrounded by wildflower meadow and ash woodland. Area adjacent to house with seasonal planting and containers. Mixed shrubs and perennial borders many raised from seed. Three ponds, vegetable plot, barn conversion with separate cottage style garden. Natural garden with stream developed from old mill pond. Walks in large wildflower meadow and ash woodland both SSSI's. Handspinning demonstration and natural dyeing display using materials from the garden and wool from sheep in the meadow. Locally made crafts for sale. Partial wheelchair access. Steep slope from car park, limestone chippings at entrance, some boggy areas if wet.

35 NEW THE LIMES
Belle Vue Road, Ashbourne, DE6 1AT. Adam & Karen Noble, limevue@peakbreaks.co.uk. *2nd house on the L as you enter Belle Vue Rd. Note the tall curved wall & cobbled driveway. Enter via the wooden pedestrian gate. Parking in town car parks or further along Belle Vue Rd.* **Sat 25 June (1-7); Fri 9 Sept (1-5). Adm £3.50, chd free. Light refreshments.**
A secret garden overlooking the roof tops of Ashbourne town centre. Designed as a series of rooms cascading down multiple levels. Bask on the sun deck. Float through the scent garden, down past the hidden loungers to the fish pond, home to large friendly koi and onward to

the main borders with cottage style planting, shade planting and a large prairie border.

36 LITTLEOVER LANE ALLOTMENTS
19 Littleover Lane, Normanton, Derby, DE23 6JF. Mr David Kenyon, 07745 227230, davidkenyon@tinyworld.co.uk, littleoverlaneallotments.org.uk. *On Littleover Ln, opp the junction with Foremark Avenue. Just off the Derby Outer Ring Road (A5111). At the Normanton Park r'about turn into Stenson Rd then R into Littleover Ln. The Main Gates are on the L as you travel down the rd.* **Sun 8 May, Sun 4 Sept (11-3.30). Adm £5, chd free. Light refreshments. Visits also by arrangement Apr to Oct for groups of 5 to 30.**
A large private allotment site in SW Derby. About 170 plots, many cultivated to a high standard. If you are interested in growing your own you should find help, advice and inspiration. Many plot holders practice organic methods and some cultivate unusual and heritage vegetables. On site disabled parking available. All avenues have been stoned but site is on a slope and extensive (12 acres) so some areas may not be accessible.

37 LONGFORD HALL FARM
Longford, Ashbourne, DE6 3DS. Liz Wolfenden, Longfordhallfarmholidaycottages.com. *Use the drive which has Longford Hall Farm sign at the entrance off Long Lane.* **Sat 21 May, Sat 4 June, Sat 16 July (1.30-5.30). Adm £5, chd free. Home-made teas.**
The front garden is mainly shrubs, hydrangeas, roses, ferns, grasses and hostas beds. These surround a modern pond and fountain. There are on going projects in this garden. The walled garden has large traditional herbaceous perennial borders, landscaped rill and small orchard. Most of the garden is on one level.

38 9 MAIN STREET
Horsley Woodhouse, Derby, DE7 6AU. Ms Alison Napier, 01332 881629, ibhillib@btinternet.com. *3m SW of Heanor. 6m N of Derby. Turn off*

A608 Derby to Heanor Rd at Smalley, towards Belper, (A609). Garden on A609, 1m from Smalley turning. **Sun 7 Aug (1.30-4.30). Adm £3.50, chd free. Cream teas. Visits also by arrangement Apr to Sept for groups of 5+.**
⅓ acre hilltop garden overlooking lovely farmland view. Terracing, borders, lawns and pergola create space for an informal layout with planting for colour effect. Features inc large wildlife pond with water lilies, bog garden and small formal pool. Emphasis on carefully selected herbaceous perennials mixed with shrubs and old fashioned roses. Gravel garden for sun loving plants and scree garden, both developed from former drive. Please ensure you bring your own carrier bags for the plant stall. Wide collection of homegrown plants for sale. All parts of the garden accessible to wheelchairs. Wheelchair adapted WC.

39 58A MAIN STREET
Rosliston, Swadlincote, DE12 8JW. Paul Marbrow, 01283 362780, paulmarbrow@hotmail.co.uk. *Rosliston. if exiting the M42, J11 onto the A444 to Overseal follow signs Linton then Rosliston. From A38, exit to Walton on Trent, then follow Rosliston signs.* **Sun 3, Sun 17 July (11.30-5). Adm £4, chd free. Light refreshments. Visits also by arrangement June to Aug for groups of 5 to 30. On site parking by arrangement only.**
½ acre garden formed from a once open field over the last few years. The garden has developed into themed areas and is changing and maturing. Japanese, arid beach, bamboo grove with ferns etc. The 100 sq metre indoor garden for cacti, exotic and tender plants, is now becoming established as a mini Eden. There are also vegetable gardens. Areas are easily accessible, although some are only for the sure of foot, advice signs will be situated on non suitable routes.

40 MEADOW COTTAGE
1 Russell Square, Hulland Ward, Ashbourne, DE6 3EA. Michael Halls, 01335 372064, mvaehalls@gmail.com. *5m E of Ashbourne. There is a lane between & on the same side as the 2 garages in Hulland Ward. Meadow Cottage is just down the lane to the R.* **Visits**

by arrangement Apr to Aug for groups of up to 30. Adm £6, chd free. Home-made teas.
Created from what was a field in 1995, this garden faces south and is on a sloping site. There is a wooded area, a wildflower orchard, herbaceous and vegetable areas. The soil is heavy clay so roses do well here. At 750' above sea level, growing seasons are later and shorter. The lawns are all original meadow. There are bees and hens too. The access to the garden is over a gravel area and the slope is significant down the garden but can be mastered with care.

41 NEW 25 MELBOURNE CLOSE
Mickleover, Derby, DE3 9LG. Marie Wilton, marie-mmt@hotmail.com. *3m from Derby city centre. W from Royal Derby Hospital. At 2nd set of T-lights past hosp take R filter lane onto Western Rd, 2nd R onto Brisbane Rd. Melbourne Close is 3rd R but no parking. Park on nearby roads.* **Sun 26 June (1-5). Adm £3.50, chd free. Tea. Visits also by arrangement May to July for groups of up to 12. Tea, coffee and cake.**
Suburban cottage style garden developed over the past three years. Mixed colour themed borders and beds with an emphasis on structure and texture. A small wildlife pond under development. Mediterranean style gravel area with olive tree, lavender and herbs. Seasonal planting in containers and hanging baskets together with climbing plants over archways. Bamboos in pots provide interest and privacy.

42 ◆ MELBOURNE HALL GARDENS
Church Square, Melbourne, Derby, DE73 8EN. Melbourne Gardens Charity, 01332 862502, info@melbournehall.com, www.melbournehall.com. *6m S of Derby. At Melbourne Market Place turn into Church St, go down to Church Sq. Garden entrance across visitor centre next to Melbourne Hall tea room.* **For NGS: Sat 11, Sun 12 June (1-5). Adm £8, chd £5. Sitooterie - Coffee/Ice Cream Takeaway - Melbourne Hall Courtyard. For other opening times and information, please phone, email or visit garden website.**

A 17 acre historic garden with an abundance of rare trees and shrubs. Woodland and waterside planting with extensive herbaceous borders. Meconopsis, candelabra primulas, various Styrax and Cornus kousa. Other garden features inc Bakewells wrought iron arbour, a yew tunnel and fine C18 statuary and water features. 300yr old trees, waterside planting, feature hedges and herbaceous borders. Fine statuary and stonework. Don't forget to visit our pigs, alpacas, goats and various other animals in their garden enclosures. Gravel paths, uneven surface in places, some steep slopes.

43 ◆ MEYNELL LANGLEY TRIALS GARDEN
Lodge Lane (off Flagshaw Lane), Kirk Langley, Ashbourne, DE6 4NT. Robert & Karen Walker, 01332 824358, enquiries@meynell-langley-gardens.co.uk, www.meynell-langley-gardens.co.uk. *4m W of Derby, nr Kedleston Hall. Head W out of Derby on A52. At Kirk Langley turn R onto Flagshaw Ln (signed to Kedleston Hall) then R onto Lodge Ln. Follow Meynell Langley Gardens signs.* **For NGS: Sun 15 May, Sun 19 June, Sun 17 July, Sun 21 Aug, Sun 18 Sept (10-4.30). Adm £5, chd free. For other opening times and information, please phone, email or visit garden website.**
Completely re-designed during 2020 with new glasshouse and patio area incorporating water rills and small ponds. New wildlife and fish ponds also added. Displays and trials of new and existing varieties of bedding plants, herbaceous perennials and vegetable plants grown at the adjacent nursery. Over 180 hanging baskets and floral displays. Adjacent tea rooms serving lunches and refreshments daily. Level ground and firm grass and some hard paths.

'In the first six months of operation at Maggie's Southampton, which was part funded by the National Garden Scheme, the team has supported people affected by cancer more than 2,300 times.' *Maggie's*

44 MOORFIELDS

261 Chesterfield Road, Temple Normanton, Chesterfield, S42 5DE. Peter, Janet & Stephen Wright. *4m SE of Chesterfield. From Chesterfield take A617 for 2m, turn on to B6039 through Temple Normanton, taking R fork signed Tibshelf, B6039. Garden ¼ m on R. Limited parking.* **Sun 26 June (1-5). Adm £3.50, chd free. Light refreshments.**
Two adjoining gardens each planted for seasonal colour. The larger one has mature, mixed island beds and borders, a gravel garden to the front, a small wildflower area, large wildlife pond, orchard, soft fruit beds and vegetable garden. The smaller gardens of No. 257 feature herbaceous borders and shrubs both back and front. Extensive views to mid Derbyshire.

🌺 ☕

45 NEW NETHER MOOR HOUSE

Granby Road, Bradwell, Hope Valley, S33 9HU. Anna & Rod Smallwood, 07973 738846, annamsmallwood@gmail.com. *15m W of Sheffield on the B6049 off the Hope Valley (A6187). From N via A6187 & B6049 R at playing field (Gore Ln), up Smalldale. From S via B6049 L at playing field, (Town Ln) up Smalldale. Turn L onto Granby Rd. Park on L side of rd, well tucked in.* **Sat 9 July (10.30-4.30). Adm £5, chd free. Visits also by arrangement Feb to June for groups of 6 to 20.**
A country garden with views of Hope Valley. Mature trees. Front terraces with colourful planting and box hedges, below lawn and colourful borders, unusual plants. Japanese patio garden: small pond, pools of planting, massive arches, mix of Japanese and traditional plants. At the back, a long border, sloping grass, sculptures, wild flowers, fruit and vegetables. Sit and take in the views. Snowdrops, hellebores, daffodils, peonies, Japanese Tai Haku, ginkgo and handkerchief trees, rambling and shrub roses.

🐎 Ⓓ 🪑))

46 NEW MILLS SCHOOL

Church Lane, New Mills, High Peak, SK22 4NR. Mr Craig Pickering, 07774567635, cpickering@newmillsschool.co.uk, www.newmillsschool.co.uk. *12m NNW of Buxton. From A6 take A6105 signed New Mills, Hayfield. At C of E Church turn L onto Church Lane. Sch on L. Parking on site.* **Sat 9, Sun 10 July (1.30-4.30). Adm £4, chd free. Visits also by arrangement July & Aug for groups of 15 to 50.**
Mixed herbaceous perennials/shrub borders, with mature trees and lawns and gravel border situated in the semi rural setting of the High Peak inc a Grade II listed building with four themed quads. The school was awarded highly commended in the School Garden 2019 RHS Tatton Show and won the Best High School Garden and the People's Choice Award. Hot and cold beverages and cakes are available. Ramps allow wheelchair access to most of outside, flower beds and into Grade II listed building and library.

♿ 🌺 🚗 ☕

47 ◆ OLD ENGLISH WALLED GARDEN, ELVASTON CASTLE COUNTRY PARK

Borrowash Road, Elvaston, Derby, DE72 3EP. Derbyshire County Council, 01629 533870, www.derbyshire.gov.uk/elvaston. *4m E of Derby. Signed from A52 & A50. Car parking charge applies.* **For NGS: Sun 24 Apr, Sun 7 Aug (12-4). Adm £2.50, chd free. Home-made teas. For other opening times and information, please phone or visit garden website.**
Come and discover the beauty of the Old English walled garden at Elvaston Castle. Take in the peaceful atmosphere and enjoy the scents and colours of all the varieties of trees, shrubs and plants. Summer bedding and large herbaceous borders. After your visit to the walled garden take time to walk around the wider estate featuring romantic topiary gardens, lake, woodland and nature reserve. Estate gardeners on hand during the day. Delicious home-made cakes available.

♿ 🐕 🌺 ☕

48 330 OLD ROAD

Brampton, Chesterfield, S40 3QH. Christine Stubbs & Julia Stubbs. *Approx 1½ m from town centre. 50 yds from junc with Storrs Rd. 1st house next to grazing field; on-road parking available adjacent to tree-lined roadside stone wall.* **Fri 24, Sat 25 June (10.30-5). Adm £4, chd free. Home-made teas.**
Deceptive ⅓ acre plot of mature trees, landscaped lawns, orchard and cottage style planting. Unusual perennials, species groups such as astrantia, lychnis, thalictrum, heuchera and 40+ clematis. Acers, actea, hosta, ferns and acanthus lie within this interesting garden. Through a hidden gate, another smaller plot of similar planting, with delphinium, helenium, Echinacea, acers and hosta. Winner Chesterfield in Bloom Best Large Garden.

🌺 🚗 ☕

49 OLD SHOULDER OF MUTTON - 7 MAIN STREET

Walton on Trent, DE12 8LY. Sarah & Mark Smith, 07710 903385, mark_and_sarah@live.co.uk. *Off the A38 at the Barton/Walton junction. Parking available at The White Swan pub. Garden 2 min walk from there.* **Sun 26 June (11-4). Adm £4, chd free. Home baked sausage rolls again by popular demand, as well as a selection of home made cakes. Visits also by arrangement in July for groups of 10+.**
Delightful herbaceous borders fill this formerly neglected pub garden. From the topiary courtyard garden, step up past pleached limes to the cottage garden idyll scented by delicate roses. The abundant herbaceous borders with careful colour arrangements delight the eye. Walk past the lush shade border to explore the pond and beyond.

🌺 ☕))

50 THE OLD VICARAGE

The Fields, Middleton by Wirksworth, Matlock, DE4 4NH. Jane Irwing, 01629 825010, irwingjane@gmail.com. *Garden located behind church on Main St & nr school. Travelling N on A6 from Derby turn L at Cromford, at top of hill turn R onto Porter Ln, at T-lights, turn R onto Main St. Park on Main St near DWT. Walk through churchyard. No parking at house.* **Sun 10 July (11-5); Sun 18 Sept (11-4). Adm £4, chd free. Home-made teas at the house with limited seating in kitchen and fernery if raining. Visits also by arrangement May to Sept for groups of up to 30.**
Glorious garden with mixed flowering borders and mature trees in gentle valley with fantastic views to Black Rocks. All-season interest. Acid loving plants such as camellias and rhododendrons are grown in pots in courtyard garden. Tender ferns and exotic plants grown in fernery. Beyond is the orchard, fruit garden, vegetable patch and greenhouse, the home of honey bees, doves and

Ashbourne Road and District Allotments Ltd

© Amanda McConnell

hens. Spectacular Rambling Rector rose over front of house late June to early July.

51 THE PADDOCK

12 Manknell Rd, Whittington Moor, Chesterfield, S41 8LZ. Mel & Wendy Taylor, 01246 451001, debijt9276@gmail.com. *2m N of Chesterfield. Whittington Moor just off A61 between Sheffield & Chesterfield. Parking available at Victoria Working Mens Club, garden signed from here.* **Sun 24 Apr, Sun 24 July (11-5). Adm £3.50, chd free. Cream teas. Visits also by arrangement Apr to Sept for groups of 10+.**
½ acre garden incorporating small formal garden, stream and koi filled pond. Stone path over bridge, up some steps, past small copse, across the stream at the top and back down again. Past herbaceous border towards a pergola where cream teas can be enjoyed.

52 PARK HALL

Walton Back Lane, Walton, Chesterfield, S42 7LT. Kim Staniforth, 07785 784439, kim.staniforth@btinternet.com. *2m SW of Chesterfield centre. From town on A619 L into Somersall Lane. On A632 R into Acorn Ridge. Park on field side only of Walton Back Lane.* **Visits by arrangement Apr to July for groups of 10+. Minimum group charge £50. Adm £6, chd free. Light refreshments.**
Romantic 2 acre plantsmans garden, in a stunningly beautiful setting surrounding C17 house (not open) four main rooms, terraced garden, parkland area with forest trees, croquet lawn, sunken garden with arbours, pergolas, pleached hedge, topiary, statuary, roses, rhododendrons, camellias, several water features. Runner-up in Daily Telegraph Great British Gardens Competition 2018. Two steps down to gain access to garden.

53 22 PINFOLD CLOSE

Repton, DE65 6FR. Mr & Mrs O Jowett, 01283 701964. *6m S of Derby. From A38, A50 J, S of Derby follow signs to Willington then Repton. Off Repton High St turn L into Pinfold Lane, Pinfold Close 1st L.* **Sat 16 July (12-5). Adm £2.50, chd free. Visits also by arrangement Apr to Sept for groups of 5 to 20.**
Small garden with an interest in tropical plants. Palms, gingers, cannas and bananas. Mainly foliage plants. Changes over the last year inc construction of a Safari Breeze Hut and repositioning of pond.

The National Garden Scheme searches the length and breadth of England, Channel Islands, Northern Ireland and Wales for the very best private gardens

54 RECTORY HOUSE
Kedleston, Derby, DE22 5JJ.
Helene Viscountess Scarsdale. *5m NW Derby. A52 from Derby turn R Kedleston sign. Drive to village turn R. Brick house standing back from road on sharp corner.* **Sun 29 May (2-5). Adm £5, chd free. Home-made teas.**
The garden is next to Kedleston Park and is of C18 origin. Many established rare trees and shrubs also rhododendrons, azaleas and unusual roses. Large natural pond with amusing frog fountain. Primulas, gunneras, darmeras and lots of moisture loving plants. The winding paths go through trees and past wildflowers and grasses. New woodland with rare plants. An atmospheric garden. A sphere of Cumbrian slate built by Jo Smith, Kirkcudbrightshire. Lily fountain in tea courtyard area.

55 ◆ RENISHAW HALL & GARDENS
Renishaw, Sheffield, S21 3WB.
Alexandra Hayward,
01246 432310,
enquiries@renishaw-hall.co.uk,
www.renishaw-hall.co.uk. *10m from Sheffield city centre. By car: Renishaw Hall only 3m from J30 on M1, well signed from junction r'about.* **For NGS: Tue 5 July (10.30-4). Adm £8, chd £3.50. Light refreshments at the kiosk. For other opening times and information, please phone, email or visit garden website.**
Renishaw Hall and Gardens boasts 7 acres of stunning gardens created by Sir George Sitwell in 1885. The Italianate gardens feature various rooms with extravagant herbaceous borders. Rose gardens, rare trees and shrubs, National Collection of Yuccas, sculptures, woodland walks and lakes create a magical and engaging garden experience. Wheelchair route around garden.

56 REPTON ALLOTMENTS
Monsom Lane, Repton, Derby, DE65 6FX. **Mr A Topping.** *From Willington, L at r'about in Repton then L into Monsom Lane, at bottom of hill.* **Sat 16 July (1-5.30). Adm by donation. Refreshments available at Askew Cottage, Milton Road.**
Set on the edge of Repton with lovely views over the Derbyshire countryside. There are about 20 plots

growing many types of vegetables and flowers too, a Community Garden is a new addition and now includes a large communal polytunnel. Mainly grass paths.

57 NEW RIVERSVALE LODGE
Riversvale, Buxton, SK17 6UZ.
Dena Lewis, 01298 70504,
lewis.riversvale@btinternet.com.
½m from Buxton town centre just off the A53 to Leek. turn R off St John's Rd down Gadley Lane. This becomes single track so cars need to park at the top of the lane. It is a short walk down to the garden, following the NGS signs. **Visits by arrangement Apr to Sept for groups of up to 15. Adm £4.50, chd free. Adm inc tea/coffee and cake.**
My garden is small but full of plants collected over nearly 30 years. The aim is for interest throughout the seasons, based on foliage, texture and unusual plants which will flourish at over 1000 ft. A wide range of insects has resulted. The site provides a clay loam soil and a range of aspects so that many plant groups thrive.

58 40 ST OSWALD'S CRESCENT
Ashbourne, DE6 1FS. **Anne McSkimming, 01335 342235, anneofashbourne@hotmail.com.** *From centre of Ashbourne, Shaw Croft car park, go along Park St. L into Park Ave then 2nd R into St Oswald's Crescent. Follow rd til you see signs. Park on rd.* **Visits by arrangement May to July for groups of up to 8. Adm £4, chd free. Light refreshments.**
Small enclosed town garden, developed by a plantswoman, from scratch 9 years ago. Trees, lots of shrubs, perennials, climbers. Some unusual specimens. Wide and narrow beds. Plenty of colour and interest throughout the season. A few steps lead up to a level garden. Can be slippery in places.

59 NEW SHIPLEY WOODSIDE COMMUNITY GARDEN
Hassock Lane South,
Shipley, Heanor, DE75 7JE.
Kay Kearton, 07939 556277,
kkearton2@gmail.com,
www.seag.uk. *Situated in Shipley between Ilkeston & Heanor. The*

Community Garden is off a main rd approx 200 yrds from Shipley Garden Centre on the opp side of the rd. There is gate & grass verge signage & bus stops adjacent. Bike park available. **Wed 7 Sept (1-4). Home-made teas. Sat 10 Sept (10-2). Adm £4, chd free. Visits also by arrangement Apr to Oct for groups of 5 to 25. Not available on weekends.**
Shipley Woodside Community Garden is on a 1½ acre site and reflects the ethics of Earth Care, People Care and Fair Share. We offer a sensory and cut flower garden, Friendship Bench, Wildlife Pond, Raised beds, Children's natural play area, Food forest and orchard, Wildflower meadow, butterfly bank, a bird hide and beehives. Shed-quarters and picnic area will be open displaying local crafts and art work. We operate an honesty library and by arrangement a presentation on bee keeping. A scavenger hunt and bug hunting activities are available for children as well as refreshments and homemade pizza using our garden produce.

60 THE SMITHY
Church Street, Buxton, SK17 6HD.
Roddie & Kate MacLean. *200 metres S of Buxton Market Place, in Higher Buxton. Located on access-only Church St, which cuts corner between B5059 & A515. Walk S from Buxton Market Place car park. Take slight R off A515, between Scriveners Bookshop & The Swan Inn.* **Sat 4 June (10-6); Mon 6 June (2-8); Fri 22 July (10-6). Adm £3.50, chd free.**
Architect-designed small oasis of calm in the town centre, subliminally inspired by Geoff Hamilton. Created from a sloping lawn into terraces, following the party walls of former houses on the site, demolished into themselves in 1930s - hence the garden is elevated above Church St. Herbaceous borders, wildlife pond, octagonal greenhouse, raised vegetable beds. Alliums in June; sweet peas in July.

61 SPINGLES
1 Nunbrook Grove, Buxton, SK17 7AU. **Sue & Geoff Ashby.** *All main roads bring you into town centre. 5 mins walk from Springs shopping centre car park. Signed from side of Aldi, under railway bridge, 2 L turns to Nunbrook Grove. Ltd on street parking nr house.* **Wed**

13 July (11-6). Adm £3, chd free. **Home-made teas. Gluten free options available.**
We invite you to visit our beautiful gardens created by us from a blank canvas. Front garden a mix of white yellow and purple back garden a haven of pastel colours with roses and clematis and much more. Various seating around the garden so come and relax with some home baking, inc gluten free, tea/coffee. We also sell plants. 2 steps to garden. Our garden is also open for the Buxton Garden Trail held in July.

62 NEW **92 SPRINGFIELD ROAD**
Swadlincote, DE11 0BX. Stephen & Marcia Baillie, 07450 608151, mcbaillie@hotmail.co.uk. *5m E of Burton on Trent off A511. Follow signs for Swadlincote. Turn R into Springfield Road & follow signs.* **Sat 30 July (1-5). Adm £3.50, chd free. Light refreshments. Visits also by arrangement June to Aug for groups of 5 to 10.**
Visit our unique sculpture garden, a garden with a difference. Throughout our garden we have various hand made metal sculptures using recycled materials. From a paved patio seating area with pots, baskets and raised borders full of shrubs, perennials and annuals, pass the raised koi pond to the underground air raid shelter, greenhouse, rockery and upper terrace.

GROUP OPENING

63 **STANTON IN PEAK GARDENS**
Stanton-In-The-Peak, Matlock, DE4 2LR. *At the top of the hill in Stanton in Peak, on the rd to Birchover. Stanton in Peak is 5m S of Bakewell. Turn off the A6 at Rowsley, or at the B5056 & follow signs up the hill.* **Sat 23, Sun 24 July (1-5). Combined adm £5, chd free. Home-made teas at 2 Haddon View. At Woodend a pop-up pub serves real ale from the barrel.**

2 HADDON VIEW
Steve Tompkins.

HARE HATCH COTTAGE
Bill Chandler.

WOODEND COTTAGE
Will Chandler.

Stanton in Peak is a hillside, stone village with glorious views, and is a Conservation Area in the Peak District National Park. Three gardens are open. Steve's garden at 2 Haddon View is at the top of the village and is one tenth acre crammed with plants. Follow the winding path up the garden with a few steps. There are cacti flowering in the greenhouse, lots of pots, herbaceous borders, three wildlife ponds with red and pink water lilies, a koi pond, rhododendrons and a cosy summerhouse. Just down the hill is Woodend where Will has constructed charming, roadside, stone follies on a strip of raised land along the road. The hidden, rear garden has diverse planting, and an extended vegetable plot. All with breathtaking views. A pop-up 'pub' will have draught beer from a local brewery. Nearby is Hare Hatch where Bill's garden wraps around the cottage. This is carefully designed to get the best of every planting opportunity, with a little bit of everything!

64 NEW **26 STILES ROAD**
Alvaston, Derby, DE24 0PG.
Mr Colin Summerfield & Karen Wild. *Off A6. 2m SE of Derby city centre. From city take A6 (London Rd) towards Alvaston. At Blue Peter Island take L into Beech Ave 1st R into Kelmore Rd & 1st L into Stiles Rd.* **Sun 15 May (1-5). Adm £3, chd free. Home-made teas.**
Small town garden with lawn and paved areas, two ponds, stream, fruit and veg area, summerhouse, seating areas, mini woodland walk. Clematis, Azaleas, Acers, Wisterias and mixed borders. Aubretia wall on the front garden.

65 **TILFORD HOUSE**
Hognaston, Ashbourne, DE6 1PW. Mr & Mrs P R Gardner, 01335 372001, peter.gardner@ngs.org.uk. *5m NE of Ashbourne. A517 Belper to Ashbourne. At Hulland Ward follow signs to Hognaston. Downhill (2m) to bridge. Roadside parking 100 metres.* **Visits by arrangement May to July for groups of 6 to 30. Adm £6, chd free. Light refreshments.**
A 1½ acre streamside English country garden. Woodland, wildlife areas, alpine beds and ponds lie alongside colourful seasonal planting. Beds and borders are a mixture of

herbaceous plants and shrubs in this plantsman's garden. Sit and relax with tea and cake whilst listening to the continuous sounds of the birds.

66 ♦ **TISSINGTON HALL**
Tissington, Ashbourne, DE6 1RA. Sir Richard & Lady FitzHerbert, 07836 782439, sirrichard@tissingtonhall.co.uk, www.tissingtonhall.co.uk. *4m N of Ashbourne. E of A515 on Ashbourne to Buxton Rd in centre of the beautiful Estate Village of Tissington.* **For NGS: Mon 15, Mon 22, Mon 29 Aug (12-3). Adm £7, chd £3.50. Light refreshments at award winning Herbert's Fine English Tearooms. Tel 01335 350501. For other opening times and information, please phone, email or visit garden website.**
Large garden celebrating over 85yrs in the National Garden Scheme, with stunning rose garden on west terrace, herbaceous borders and 5 acres of grounds. Edward & Vintage Sweetshop, Andrew Holmes Butchers and Onawick Candle workshop also open in the village. Wheelchair access advice from ticket seller. Please seek staff and we shall park you nearer the gardens.

67 **WALTON COTTAGE**
Matlock Road, Walton, Chesterfield, S42 7LG. Neil & Julie Brown, 07968 128313, jmbrown.waltoncottage@gmail.com. *3m from Chesterfield. 6½m from Matlock. On A632 Matlock to Chesterfield main rd. From Chesterfield 1m after junction near garage with T-lights. From Matlock 1m after B5057 junction.* **Sun 12 June (11-4). Adm £4, chd free. Light refreshments. Visits also by arrangement in June for groups of up to 20.**
A large garden that has both formal and informal areas, inc woodland, orchard, kitchen garden and sweeping lawns with views over Chesterfield.

Hill Cottage

68 27 WASH GREEN
Wirksworth, Matlock,
DE4 4FD. Mr Paul & Mrs
Kathy Harvey, 07811 395679,
pandkharvey@btinternet.com.
⅓m E of Wirksworth centre. From
Wirksworth centre, follow B5035
towards Whatstandwell. Cauldwell
St leads over railway bridge to Wash
Green, 200 metres up steep hill on
L. Park in town or uphill from garden
entry. **Sun 15 May, Sun 28 Aug (11-
4). Adm £4, chd free. Home-made
teas. Gluten free cakes available.
Visits also by arrangement Apr to
Oct for groups of up to 30.**
Secluded 1 acre garden, with
outstanding 360 degree views. Inner
enclosed area has topiary, pergola
and lawn surrounded by mixed
borders, with paved seating area.
The larger part of the garden has
sweeping lawns, with large borders,
beds, large wildlife pond and bog
garden, areas of woodland and
specimen trees. A quarter of the plot
is a productive fruit and vegetable
garden with polytunnel. Drop off at
property entry for wheelchair access.
The inner garden has flat paths with
good views of whole garden.

69 12 WATER LANE
Middleton, Matlock, DE4 4LY.
Hildegard Wiesehofer,
07809 883393,
wiesehofer@btinternet.com.
Approx 2½m SW of Matlock.
1½m NW of Wirksworth, 8m from
Ashbourne. From Derby: at A6 &
B5023 intersection take Road to
Wirksworth. Follow NGS signs.
From Ashbourne take Matlock rd
to Middleton. Follow signs. Park on
main rd. Limited parking in Water
Lane. **Sat 4, Sun 5 June, Sun 28,
Mon 29 Aug (11-5). Adm £4, chd
free. Home-made teas. Gluten
free options available. Visits also
by arrangement June to Aug for
groups of 10+. Home-made teas
are £3.50 per person, payable in
advance.**
Small, eclectic hillside garden on
different levels, created as a series of
rooms. Each room has been designed
to capture the stunning views over
Derbyshire and Nottinghamshire.
Mini woodland walk, ponds, eastern
and 'infinity' garden. Emphasis is
on holistic, sustainable and organic
principles. Glorious views and short
distance from High Peak Trail,
Middleton Top and Engine House.

70 13 WESTFIELD ROAD
Swadlincote, DE11 0BG.
Val & Dave Booth, 07891 436632,
valerie.booth1955@gmail.com. 5m
E of Burton-on-Trent, off A511. Take
A511 from Burton-on-Trent. Follow
signs for Swadlincote. Turn R into
Springfield Rd, take 3rd R into Westfield
Rd. **Sun 12 June, Sun 28 Aug (1-5).
Adm £3.50, chd free. Home-made
teas. Visits also by arrangement May
to Aug for groups of 5+.**
A deceptive country-style garden in
Swadlincote, a real gem. The garden
is on two levels of approx ½ acre.
Packed herbaceous borders designed
for colour. Shrubs, baskets and tubs.
Lots of roses. Greenhouses, raised-
bed vegetable area, fruit trees and
two ponds. Free range chicken area.
Plenty of seating to relax and take
in the wonderful planting from two
passionate gardeners.

71 NEW WHITE ROSE COTTAGE
220 Top Road, Calow,
Chesterfield, S44 5TE. David
Mcgowan, 07792 289 383,
mcgdavid@live.co.uk. A632
Chesterfield to Bolsover Road.
Directly opposite White Hart Pub &
Dining. **Visits by arrangement July
to Sept for groups of up to 6. Wed
to Sat only (am/pm not evenings).
Adm £3.50, chd free.**
Originally the wheelwright's cottage
(c. 1862), approx ⅓ acre, cottage
garden to front; south-facing to rear:
lawns and Italian terrace with sound
of running water, white, pink and
blue borders – dahlias, penstemons,
phlox. Greenhouse and polytunnel.
Hidden 'Tai Chi' garden in the style
of a Japanese stroll garden, - foliage
plants, grasses, hostas, ferns and
complete with a Zen garden.

72 WILD IN THE COUNTRY
Hawkhill Road, Eyam, Hope Valley,
S32 5QQ. Mrs Gill Bagshawe,
www.wildinthecountryflowers.co.uk.
In Eyam, follow signs to public car
park. Located next to Eyam Museum
& opp public car park on Hawkhill
Rd. **Sat 13 Aug (11-4). Adm £3,
chd free.**
A rectangular plot devoted totally to
growing flowers and foliage for cutting.
Sweet pea, rose, larkspur, cornflower,
nigella, ammi. All the florist's favourites
can be found here. There is a tea
room, a village pub and several cafes
in the village to enjoy refreshments.

73 15 WINDMILL LANE
Ashbourne, DE6 1EY. Jean Ross &
Chris Duncan. Take A515 (Buxton
Rd) from the market place & at the
top of the hill turn R into Windmill
Lane; house by 4th tree on L. **Sun 7
Aug (1.30-5). Adm £3, chd free.**
Landscaped and densely-planted
town garden providing ideas others
may wish to develop. Using a limited
palette (mainly white, pink, mauve
and burgundy) and emphasising leaf
shape and colour, the key aims in
establishing this garden were all-year
interest; low maintenance; no grass;
attraction of pollinators; and growing
some soft fruit, peas and beans.
Extensive views. A few steps.

74 26 WINDMILL RISE
Belper, DE56 1GQ. Kathy
Fairweather. From Belper Market
Place take Chesterfield Rd towards
Heage. Top of hill, 1st R Marsh Lane,
1st R Windmill Lane, 1st R Windmill
Rise - limited parking on Windmill
Rise - disabled mainly. **Sat 23, Sun
24 July (11.30-4.30). Adm £4, chd
free. Light refreshments. Gluten
free & vegan options available.**
Behind a deceptively ordinary façade,
lies a real surprise. A lush oasis,
much larger than expected, with
an amazing collection of rare and
unusual plants. A truly plant lovers'
organic garden divided into sections:
woodland, Japanese, secret garden,
cottage, edible, ponds and small
stream. Many seating areas, inc a
new summerhouse in which to enjoy
a variety of refreshments. Home made
delicious cakes and light lunches
available.

National Garden Scheme
gardens are identified
by their yellow road
signs and posters. You
can expect a garden of
quality, character and
interest, a warm welcome
and plenty of home-made
cakes!

DEVON

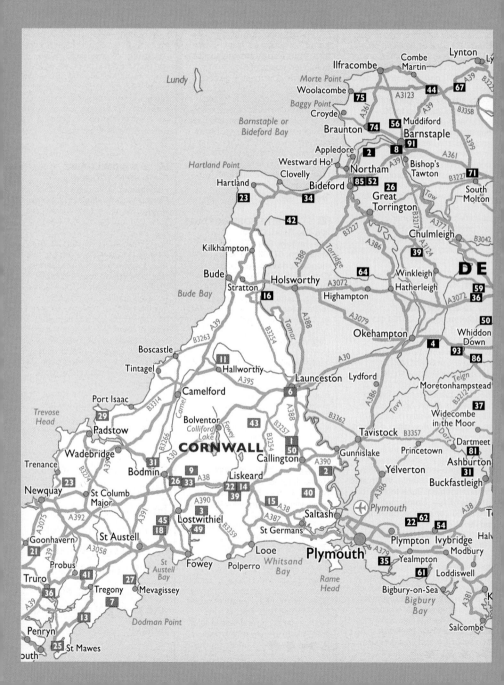

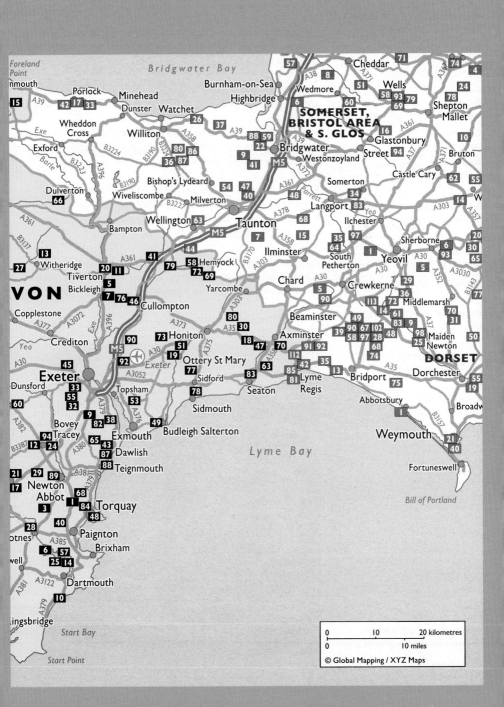

Volunteers

County Organiser & Central Devon
Miranda Allhusen 01647 440296
Miranda@allhusen.co.uk

County Treasurer
Nigel Hall 01884 38812
nigel.hall@ngs.org.uk

Publicity
Brian Mackness 01626 356004
brianmackness@clara.co.uk

Cath Pettyfer 01837 89024
cathpettyfer@gmail.com

Paul Vincent 01803 722227
paul.vincent@ngs.org.uk

Booklet Co-ordinator
Anne Sercombe 01626 438698
anne.sercombe@ngs.org.uk

Talks
Julia Tremlett 01392 832671
jandjtremlett@hotmail.co.uk

Assistant County Organisers

East Devon
Penny Walmsley 01404 831375
walyp_uk@yahoo.co.uk

Exeter
Jenny Phillips 01392 254076
jennypips25@hotmail.co.uk

Exmoor
Anna Whinney 01598 760217
annawhinney@yahoo.co.uk

North Devon
Jo Hynes 01805 804265
hynesjo@gmail.com

North East Devon
Jill Hall 01884 38812
jill22hall@gmail.com

Plymouth Position vacant

South Hams
Sally Vincent 01803 722227
sallyvincent14@gmail.com

South West Devon
Naomi Hindley 01364 654902
naomi.hindley@ngs.org.uk

Torbay
Michelle Fairley 01626 879576
grosvenorgreengardens@gmail.com

West Devon
Alex Meads 01822 615558
ameads2015@outlook.com

Devon is a county of great contrasts in geography and climate, and therefore also in gardening.

The rugged north coast has terraces clinging precariously to hillsides so steep that the faint-hearted would never contemplate making a garden there. But here, and on the rolling hills and deep valleys of Exmoor, despite a constant battle with the elements, National Garden Scheme gardeners create remarkable results by choosing hardy plants that withstand the high winds and salty air.

In the south, in peaceful wooded estuaries and tucked into warm valleys, gardens grow bananas, palms and fruit usually associated with the Mediterranean.

Between these two terrains is a third: Dartmoor, 365 square miles of rugged moorland rising to 2000 feet, presents its own horticultural demands. Typically, here too are many National Garden Scheme gardens.

In idyllic villages scattered throughout this very large county, in gardens large and small, in single manors and in village groups within thriving communities – gardeners pursue their passion.

Below: Quince Honey Farm

 @Devon NGS
 @DevonNGS
 @ngsdevon

OPENING DATES

All entries subject to change. For latest information check www.ngs.org.uk

Extended openings are shown at the beginning of the month.

Map locator numbers are shown to the right of each garden name.

February

Snowdrop Festival

Friday 4th
Higher Cherubeer 39

Friday 11th
Higher Cherubeer 39

Saturday 12th
The Mount, Delamore 62

Sunday 13th
The Mount, Delamore 62

Saturday 19th
Higher Cherubeer 39

Saturday 26th
NEW Ashley Court 5

Sunday 27th
East Worlington House 27

Monday 28th
Houndspool 43

March

Every Saturday and Sunday from Saturday 12th
Haldon Grange 32

Tuesday 1st
Houndspool 43

Sunday 6th
East Worlington House 27

Sunday 20th
Bickham House 9

Saturday 26th
Monkscroft 59
Samlingstead 75

Sunday 27th
Heathercombe 37

Monkscroft 59
Upper Gorwell House 91

Monday 28th
Houndspool 43

Tuesday 29th
Houndspool 43

Wednesday 30th
Haldon Grange 32

April

Every Saturday and Sunday
Haldon Grange 32

Friday 1st
Holbrook Garden 41

Saturday 2nd
Holbrook Garden 41

Sunday 3rd
High Garden 38
Holbrook Garden 41

Friday 8th
Sidbury Manor 77
Torview 89

Saturday 9th
Brendon Gardens 15
Torview 89

Sunday 10th
Andrew's Corner 4
Brendon Gardens 15
Sidbury Manor 77
Torview 89

Friday 15th
NEW Ashley Court 5

Saturday 16th
Bickham House 9
Coombe Meadow 21
NEW Goodwill Gardens 29

Sunday 17th
Andrew's Corner 4
Bickham House 9
Coombe Meadow 21
NEW Goodwill Gardens 29
Kia-Ora Farm & Gardens 46

Monday 18th
Andrew's Corner 4
NEW Goodwill Gardens 29
Haldon Grange 32
Kia-Ora Farm & Gardens 46

Saturday 23rd
South Wood Farm 80

Sunday 24th
St Merryn 74
South Wood Farm 80
Whitstone Farm 94

Wednesday 27th
Haldon Grange 32

Saturday 30th
NEW Goodwill Gardens 29
Greatcombe 31

May

Every Saturday and Sunday
Haldon Grange 32

Every Thursday and Friday from Thursday 12th
NEW Quince Honey Farm 71

Sunday 1st
Andrew's Corner 4
Chevithorne Barton 20
Coombe Meadow 21
NEW Goodwill Gardens 29
Greatcombe 31
High Garden 38
Kia-Ora Farm & Gardens 46
Mothecombe House 61
Upper Gorwell House 91

Monday 2nd
Andrew's Corner 4
Coombe Meadow 21
Greatcombe 31
Haldon Grange 32
Kia-Ora Farm & Gardens 46

Sunday 8th
Bickham House 9
Heathercombe 37

Monday 9th
Houndspool 43

Tuesday 10th
Houndspool 43

Wednesday 11th
Haldon Grange 32

Saturday 14th
Kentlands 45
Kilmington (Shute Road) Gardens 47
Spitchwick Manor 81

Sunday 15th
Heathercombe 37
Kentlands 45

Kilmington (Shute Road) Gardens 47
Spitchwick Manor 81
Upper Gorwell House 91

Tuesday 17th
Avenue Cottage 6

Wednesday 18th
Avenue Cottage 6

Friday 20th
Moretonhampstead Gardens 60

Saturday 21st
NEW Blundell's School Gardening Project 11
Bradford Tracey House 13
NEW Goodwill Gardens 29
Heathercombe 37
Moretonhampstead Gardens 60
The Old Vicarage 66

Sunday 22nd
Bickham House 9
NEW Blundell's School Gardening Project 11
Bradford Tracey House 13
NEW Goodwill Gardens 29
Heathercombe 37
Kia-Ora Farm & Gardens 46
Moretonhampstead Gardens 60
The Old Vicarage 66
St Merryn 74
NEW Spring Lodge 82

Tuesday 24th
Heathercombe 37

Wednesday 25th
Haldon Grange 32
Heathercombe 37

Thursday 26th
Heathercombe 37

Friday 27th
Heathercombe 37

Saturday 28th
Abbotskerswell Gardens 1
Andrew's Corner 4
◆ Cadhay 19
Dunley House 24
NEW Goodwill Gardens 29
Heathercombe 37
Lewis Cottage 50
Shutelake 76
Springfield House 83

Sunday 29th

Abbotskerswell Gardens	1
Andrew's Corner	4
The Bridge Mill	16
◆ Cadhay	19
Dunley House	24
NEW Goodwill Gardens	29
Heathercombe	37
Lewis Cottage	50
Shutelake	76

Monday 30th

◆ Cadhay	19

Tuesday 31st

Heathercombe	37

June

Every Saturday and Sunday to Sunday 12th

Haldon Grange	32

Every Thursday and Friday

NEW Quince Honey Farm	71

Wednesday 1st

Heathercombe	37

Thursday 2nd

NEW Ashley Court	5
Brocton Cottage	17
Greatcombe	31
Haldon Grange	32
Heathercombe	37
Little Ash Bungalow	51

Friday 3rd

Brocton Cottage	17
Greatcombe	31
Haldon Grange	32
Heathercombe	37

Saturday 4th

Brocton Cottage	17
◆ Goren Farm	30
Greatcombe	31
Heathercombe	37
Higher Cherubeer	39
Higher Orchard Cottage	40
Pounds	69
Whiddon Goyle	93

Sunday 5th

Brocton Cottage	17
Chevithorne Barton	20
◆ Goren Farm	30
Greatcombe	31
Heathercombe	37
High Garden	38

Higher Orchard Cottage	40
Kia-Ora Farm & Gardens	46
Upper Gorwell House	91
Whiddon Goyle	93

Friday 10th

Bramble Torre	14
Marshall Farm	55
◆ Marwood Hill Garden	56

Saturday 11th

Bovey Tracey Gardens	12
Bramble Torre	14
Brendon Gardens	15
◆ Goren Farm	30
Heathercombe	37
Languard Place	48

Sunday 12th

Bickham House	9
Bovey Tracey Gardens	12
Bramble Torre	14
Brendon Gardens	15
◆ Docton Mill	23
◆ Goren Farm	30
Hayne	36
Heathercombe	37
Languard Place	48
Marshall Farm	55
NEW Mill House	58
Regency House	72

Monday 13th

NEW Mill House	58
Regency House	72

Tuesday 14th

Heathercombe	37
NEW Mill House	58
Regency House	72

Wednesday 15th

Heathercombe	37

Thursday 16th

Heathercombe	37

Friday 17th

Heathercombe	37
Sidbury Manor	77

Saturday 18th

Harbour Lights	34
Heathercombe	37
Littlefield	53
NEW Parracombe Gardens	67
Spitchwick Manor	81
Teignmouth Gardens	88
NEW West Clyst Barnyard Gardens	92

Sunday 19th

Harbour Lights	34

Heathercombe	37
Kia-Ora Farm & Gardens	46
Littlefield	53
NEW Parracombe Gardens	67
St Merryn	74
Spitchwick Manor	81
Teignmouth Gardens	88
NEW West Clyst Barnyard Gardens	92

Tuesday 21st

Heathercombe	37

Wednesday 22nd

Heathercombe	37

Thursday 23rd

Heathercombe	37

Friday 24th

Greatcombe	31
Heathercombe	37

Saturday 25th

Greatcombe	31
Halscombe Farm	33
Heathercombe	37
Lewis Cottage	50
Musbury Barton	63
Stone Farm	85
Treetops	90

Sunday 26th

Bickham House	9
Greatcombe	31
Halscombe Farm	33
Heathercombe	37
Lewis Cottage	50
Musbury Barton	63
Stone Farm	85
Treetops	90

Tuesday 28th

Heathercombe	37

Wednesday 29th

Heathercombe	37

Thursday 30th

Heathercombe	37

July

Every Thursday and Friday

NEW Quince Honey Farm	71

Friday 1st

Heathercombe	37

Saturday 2nd

Heathercombe	37
Springfield House	83

Sunday 3rd

Chevithorne Barton	20
Foxhole Community Garden	28
Heathercombe	37
High Garden	38
Kia-Ora Farm & Gardens	46

Saturday 9th

Backswood Farm	7
East Woodlands Farmhouse	26
Samlingstead	75

Sunday 10th

Backswood Farm	7
Bickham House	9
East Woodlands Farmhouse	26
Upper Gorwell House	91

Saturday 16th

East Cornworthy Gardens	25

Sunday 17th

East Cornworthy Gardens	25
Hole Farm	42
Kia-Ora Farm & Gardens	46

Friday 22nd

Greatcombe	31

Saturday 23rd

Am Brook Meadow	3
Coombe Meadow	21
Greatcombe	31
Kentisbury Gardens	44

Sunday 24th

Am Brook Meadow	3
Bickham House	9
Coombe Meadow	21
Greatcombe	31
Kentisbury Gardens	44
Kentlands	45

Saturday 30th

Houndspool	43
The Old School House	65
Squirrels	84

Sunday 31st

Houndspool	43
Kia-Ora Farm & Gardens	46
The Old School House	65
Squirrels	84
Whitstone Farm	94

West Clyst Barnyard

THE GARDENS

GROUP OPENING

1 ABBOTSKERSWELL GARDENS

Abbotskerswell, TQ12 5PN. *2m SW of Newton Abbot town centre. A381 Newton Abbot/Totnes rd. Sharp L turn from NA, R from Totnes. Field parking at Fairfield. Maps available at all gardens & at Church House.* **Sat 28, Sun 29 May (1-5). Combined adm £7, chd free. Home-made teas. Teas available from 2pm. Maps and tickets from 1pm.**

ABBOTSFORD
Wendy & Phil Grierson.

ABBOTSKERSWELL ALLOTMENTS
Tasha Mundy.

1 ABBOTSWELL COTTAGES
Jane Taylor.

BRIAR COTTAGE
Peggy & David Munden.

FAIRFIELD
Brian Mackness.

NEW 1 FORDE CLOSE
Ann Allen.

NEW THE POTTERY
Mr D & Mrs B Dubash.

7 WILTON WAY
Mr Vernon & Mrs Cindy Stunt.

16 WILTON WAY
Katy & Chris Yates.

For 2022, Abbotskerswell offers 8 gardens plus the village allotments, ranging from very small to large they offer a wide range of planting styles and innovative landscaping. Cottage gardens, terracing, wildflower areas specialist plants and an arboretum. Two new gardens and changes to others from 2020. Ideas for every type and size of garden. Visitors are welcome to picnic in the field or arboretum at Fairfield. Sales of plants, garden produce, jams and chutneys and other creative crafts. Disabled access to 3 gardens. Partial access to most others.

2 32 ALLENSTYLE DRIVE

Yelland, Barnstaple, EX31 3DZ. Steve & Dawn Morgan, 01271 861433, fourhungrycats@aol.com, www.devonsubtropicalgarden.rocks. *5m W of Barnstaple. From Barnstaple take B3233 towards Instow. Through Bickington & Fremington. L at Yelland sign into Allenstyle Rd. 1st R into Allenstyle Dr. Light blue bungalow. From Bideford go past Instow on B3233.* **Sun 28 Aug, Sun 4, Sun 11 Sept (12-5). Adm £4, chd free. Light refreshments. Visits also by arrangement Aug & Sept for groups of up to 20.**

Our garden is 30m x 15m and is packed full of all our favourite plants. See our huge bananas, cannas, colocasias, delicate and scented tropical passion flowers, prairie planting, a wildlife pond and 2 large greenhouses. Relax and inhale the heady scents of the ginger lilies and rest awhile in the many seating areas.
✿ ☕ ᐳᐳ

3 AM BROOK MEADOW

Torbryan, Ipplepen, Newton Abbot, TQ12 5UP. Jennie & Jethro Marles. *5m from Newton Abbot on A381. Leaving A381 at Causeway Cross go through Ipplepen village, heading towards Broadhempston. Stay on Orley Rd for ¾m. At Poole Cross turn L signed Totnes, then turn 2nd L into field parking.* **Sat 23, Sun 24 July (2-6.30). Adm £6, chd free. Home-made teas.**

Country garden developed over past 16 yrs to encourage wildlife. Perennial native wildflower meadows, large ponds with ducks and swans, streams and wild areas covering 10 acres are accessible by gravel and grass pathways. Formal courtyard garden with water features and herbaceous borders and prairie-style planting together with poultry and bees close by. Wheelchair access to most gravel path areas is good, but grass pathways in larger wildflower meadow are weather dependent.
♿ ✿ ☕ 🎋

4 ANDREW'S CORNER

Skaigh Lane, Belstone, EX20 1RD. Robin & Edwina Hill, 01837 840332, edwinarobinhill@outlook.com, www.andrewscorner.garden. *3m E of Okehampton. Signed to Belstone from A30. In village turn L, signed Skaigh. Follow NGS signs. Garden approx ½m on R. Visitors may be dropped off at house, parking in nearby field.* **Sun 10, Sun 17, Mon 18 Apr, Sun 1, Mon 2, Sat 28, Sun 29 May (2-5). Adm £5, chd free. Home-made teas. Visits also by arrangement Feb to Oct. Coaches have to be parked in village car park.**

Join us as we enter our 51st year of opening and take a walk on the wild side in this tranquil moorland garden. April openings highlight magnolias, trillium and the lovely erythroniums. Early May the maples, rhododendrons and unusual shrubs provide interest, late May brings the flowering davidia, cornus, embothrium and the spectacular blue poppies. Wheelchair access difficult when wet.
♿ 🐴 ✿ ☕ ᐳᐳ

5 NEW ASHLEY COURT

Ashley, Tiverton, EX16 5PD. Tara Fraser & Nigel Jones, 07768 878015, hello@ashleycourtdevon.co.uk, www.ashleycourtdevon.co.uk. *1m S of Tiverton on the Bickleigh road (A396). Turn off the A396 to Ashley & then immediately L. Take the drive to the L of Ashley Court Lodge Cottage (don't go up Ashley Back Lane where the SatNav will direct you).* **Sat 26 Feb, Fri 15 Apr, Thur 2 June, Wed 14 Sept (11-4.30). Adm £6, chd free. Speciality teas inc many delicious vegan recipes & cakes containing fruits and vegetables from the walled kitchen garden.**

Ashley Court is a small Regency country house with an historically interesting walled kitchen garden currently undergoing restoration. The garden is unusually situated in a deep valley and has a frost window and the remains of several glasshouses and cold frames. View the apple loft, root stores, stable buildings, woodland walk and lawns, borders and beautiful mature trees. A single concrete path runs the whole length of the kitchen garden, providing a view down over the whole.
♿ 🐴 ✿ 🚗 🛏 ☕ ᐳᐳ

6 AVENUE COTTAGE

Ashprington, Totnes, TQ9 7UT. Mr Richard Pitts & Mr David Sykes, 01803 732769, richard.pitts@btinternet.com, www.avenuecottage.com. *3m SW of Totnes. A381 Totnes to Kingsbridge for 1m; L for Ashprington, into village then L by pub. Garden ¼m on R after Sharpham Estate sign.* **Tue 17, Wed 18 May, Tue 2, Wed 3 Aug (10.30-**

4.30). **Adm £5, chd free. Pre-booking essential, please visit www.ngs.org.uk for information & booking. Home-made teas. Visits also by arrangement Apr to Sept for groups of up to 25.**
11 acres of mature and young trees and shrubs. Once part of an C18 landscape, the neglected garden has been cleared and replanted over the last 30 yrs. Good views of Sharpham House and River Dart. Azaleas and hydrangeas are a feature.

7 BACKSWOOD FARM
Bickleigh, Tiverton, EX16 8RA. Andrew Hughes, 01884 855005, andrew@backswood.co.uk. *2m SE of Tiverton. Take A396 off the A361. Turn L to Butterleigh opp Tesco, L at mini r'about, after 150 yds turn R up Exeter Hill for 2m then 1st R to Bickleigh. After 500 yds turn 1st R into farm entrance.* **Sat 9, Sun 10 July (2-5). Adm £6, chd free. Home-made teas in the Sheep Barn. Gluten & dairy free options available. Visits also by arrangement Apr to Aug.**
This newly created 2 acre nature garden provides many uniquely designed homes for wildlife. Wander through the flower meadow visiting individually designed areas,

structures, water features and ponds. Seating areas afford stunning views towards Exmoor and Dartmoor. Both native and herbaceous plants have been chosen to benefit insect and bird life. A Photographic Exhibition will be open each day. WC available.

GROUP OPENING

8 BARNSTAPLE WORLD GARDENS
Anne Crescent, Little Elche, Barnstaple, EX31 3AF. *31 Anne Cres L off Old Torrington Rd into Phillips Ave then follow signs: 21 Becklake Close from A3125 turn into Roundswell on Westermoor Way then signs: 25 Elmfield Rd from B3233 L at Bickington PO.* **Sun 7 Aug (11-4). Combined adm £5, chd free. Light refreshments. Japanese snacks, teas and cakes.**

31 ANNE CRESCENT
Mr Gavin Hendry.

21 BECKLAKE CLOSE
Karen & Steve Moss.

25 ELMFIELD ROAD
Nigel & Carol Oates.

Explore 3 very different spaces, one focusing on everything Japanese,

one on tropical plants, and one to interest the plantsman. 31 Anne Crescent: N Devon's Little Elche. Small urban L-shaped tropical garden complete with wide variety of palms, agaves, bananas, cacti, tree ferns and delightful pond loaded with a wide variety of colourful koi. 21 Becklake Close: All things Japanese. 25 Elmfield Rd: Front: mixed borders and gravel area containing hardy palms and Mount Etna Broom. Rear: L shaped patio leading to lawn edged by mixed borders of unusual plants. The overall impression is of a colourful but calm place, enhanced by the sound of the stream trickling past the end of the garden. A garden to attract those interested in plants with a difference.

During 2020 – 2021 National Garden Scheme funding supported over 1,400 Queen's Nurses to deliver virtual and hands-on, community care across England, Wales and Northern Ireland

Heddon Hall, Parracombe Gardens

Higher Cherubeer

© Carole Drake

⑨ BICKHAM HOUSE

Kenn, Exeter, EX6 7XL. Julia Tremlett, **01392 832671, jandjtremlett@hotmail.com.** *6m S of Exeter, 1m off A38. Leave A38 at Kennford Services, follow signs to Kenn, 1st R in village, follow lane for ¾ m to end of no through rd. Only use SatNav once you are in the village of Kenn.* **Sun 20 Mar, Sat 16, Sun 17 Apr, Sun 8, Sun 22 May, Sun 12, Sun 26 June, Sun 10, Sun 24 July, Sun 14, Sun 21 Aug, Sat 3, Sun 4 Sept (1.30-5). Adm £6, chd free. Home-made teas. Visits also by arrangement Mar to Aug.** 6 acres with lawns, borders, mature trees. Formal parterre with lily pond. Walled garden with colourful profusion of vegetables and flowers. Palm tree avenue leading to millennium summerhouse. Late summer colour with dahlias, crocosmia, agapanthus etc. Cactus and succulent greenhouse. Pelargonium collection. Lakeside walk. WC, disabled access.

& 🐎 ✳ 🚗 🛏 ☕ 🪑

⑩ ◆ BLACKPOOL GARDENS

Dartmouth, TQ6 0RG. Sir Geoffrey Newman, **01803 771801, beach@blackpoolsands.co.uk, www.blackpoolsands.co.uk.** *3m SW of Dartmouth. From Dartmouth follow brown signs to Blackpool Sands on A379. Entry tickets, parking, WCs & refreshments available at Blackpool Sands. Sorry, no dogs permitted.* **For opening times and information, please phone, email or visit garden website.** Carefully restored C19 subtropical plantsman's garden with collection of mature and newly planted tender and unusual trees, shrubs and carpet of spring flowers. Paths and steps lead gradually uphill and above the Captain's Seat offering fine coastal views. Recent plantings follow the southern hemisphere theme with callistemons, pittosporums, acacias and buddlejas.

🔢 NEW BLUNDELL'S SCHOOL GARDENING PROJECT

Blundells Road, Tiverton, EX16 4DN. Harry Flower. *From Tiverton: Continue up Blundells Rd, take 1st R into School. Follow parking signs over mini r'about and park on signed field.* **Sat 21, Sun 22 May (1-4). Adm £5, chd free. Pre-booking essential, please visit www.ngs.org.uk for information & booking. Cream teas.**

Pupils of the school have created an area of vegetable production to supply the school kitchens and have created a wildlife pond, cut flower beds, chicken run and an area of wildflowers with outdoor seating area. Also open - the Headmaster's Garden and other areas of the grounds. Pupils will be on hand to talk about the different projects they are undertaking in the garden. Fairly steep gravel and grass paths.

&. ✿ ☕ 🪑))

GROUP OPENING

🔢 BOVEY TRACEY GARDENS

Bovey Tracey, TQ13 9NA. *6m N of Newton Abbot. Take A382 to Bovey Tracey. Car parking at town car parks or on some roads for Ashwell, Green Hedges & 11 St Peter's Close & on roads for 4 gardens S of town.* **Sat 11, Sun 12 June (1.30-5.30). Combined adm £7, chd free. Home-made teas at Gleam Tor. Wine at Ashwell.**

ASHWELL
TQ13 9EJ. Jeanette Pearce.

5 BRIDGE COTTAGES
TQ13 9DR. Cath Valentine.

FOOTLANDS
TQ13 9JX. Jon & Helen Elliott.

GLEAM TOR
TQ13 9DH. Gillian & Colin Liddy.

GREEN HEDGES
TQ13 9LZ. Alan & Linda Jackson.

2 REDWOODS
TQ13 9YG. Mrs Julia Mooney.

11 ST PETER'S CLOSE
TQ13 9ES. Pauline & Keith Gregory.

Nestling in the Dartmoor foothills, Bovey Tracey offers a wide range of gardens. Colourful 11 St Peter's Close has a mini railway and art exhibition, while Ashwell's steeply sloping, stone-walled acre has a vineyard, orchard, vegetables, mixed borders, wildflower areas and extensive views. Green Hedges is packed full of interest – colourful borders, shade plants, organic vegetables, greenhouses and a stream. There's lots to enjoy at Gleam Tor - long herbaceous border, white garden, wildflower meadow, prairie planting, interesting 'memory patio' (and Colin's legendary cakes for tea), and at Footlands, recently redesigned, with unusual and colourful shrubs, conifers, young trees, perennials and grasses. 2 Redwoods has mature trees, a Dartmoor leat, a fernery, a sunny gravel garden and acid loving shrubs, while 5 Bridge Cottages is a productive, imaginatively designed and quirky cottage garden within an historical pottery site. Partial wheelchair access, none at St Peter's Close, Ashwell or Green Hedges.

&. ✿ ☕))

🔢 BRADFORD TRACEY HOUSE

Witheridge, Tiverton, EX16 8QG. Elizabeth Wilkinson. *20 mins from Tiverton. Postcode will get you to thatched lodge at bottom of drive which has 2 bouncing hares on the top.* **Sat 21, Sun 22 May (1.30-5). Adm £6, chd free. Tea and cake served takeaway style to enjoy in the garden.**

A pleasure garden set around a Regency hunting lodge combining flowers with grasses, shrubs and huge trees in a natural and joyful space. It is planted for productivity and sustainability giving harvests of wonderful flowers, fruits, herbs and vegetables (and weeds!). There are beautiful views over the lake, forest walks, deep blowsy borders, an ancient wisteria and an oriental treehouse garden.

✿ ☕ 🪑))

🔢 BRAMBLE TORRE

Dittisham, nr Dartmouth, TQ6 0HZ. Paul & Sally Vincent, www.rainingsideways.com. ¾m *from Dittisham. Leave A3122 at Sportsman's Arms. Drop down into village, at Red Lion turn L to Cornworthy. Continue* ¾m, *Bramble Torre straight ahead. Follow signs to car park.* **Fri 10, Sat 11, Sun 12 June (2-5). Adm £5, chd free. Cream teas.**

Set in 30 acres of farmland in the beautiful South Hams, the 3 acre garden follows a rambling stream through a steep valley: lily pond, herbaceous borders, roses, camellias, lawns and shrubs, a formal herb and vegetable garden. All are dominated by a huge embothrium glowing scarlet in late spring against a sometimes blue sky! Well behaved dogs on leads welcome. Partial wheelchair access, parts of garden very steep and uneven. Tea area with wheelchair access and excellent garden view.

&. 🐕 ✿ ☕

GROUP OPENING

🔢 BRENDON GARDENS

Brendon, Lynton, EX35 6PU. 01598 741343, lalindevon@yahoo.co.uk. *1m S of A39 N Devon coast rd between Porlock and Lynton.* **Sat 9, Sun 10 Apr, Sat 11, Sun 12 June (11-4.30). Combined adm £5, chd free. Higher Tippacott Farm serves light lunches, home-made cakes, inc gluten free & cream teas. WC. Visits also by arrangement Apr to Sept.**

HALL FARM
Karen Wall.

HIGHER TIPPACOTT FARM
Angela & Malcolm Percival.

Stunning part of Exmoor National Park. Excellent walking along river and through village; map available online or pick up from gardens. Hall Farm: C16 longhouse set in 2 acres of tranquil mature gardens, with lake and wild area beyond. Idyllic setting with views. Black swans, rare Whitebred Shorthorn cattle, bees and chickens. Higher Tippacott Farm: 950ft altitude on moor, facing south overlooking its own valley with stream and pond. Interesting planting in areas on various levels with lawns and paths. Young fruit trees in meadow. Vegetable patch with sea glimpse. Lovely views along valley and towards high moorland. Plants, produce, books and bric-a-brac for sale. Display of vintage telephones and toys.

🐕 ✿ ☕))

'In 2021 the National Garden Scheme donated £500,000 to Marie Curie enabling us to continue providing our vital services and be there, caring for people on the frontline of the Coronavirus pandemic.' *Marie Curie*

16 THE BRIDGE MILL
Mill Rd, Bridgerule,
Holsworthy, EX22 7EL. Rosie
& Alan Beat, 01288 381341,
rosie@thebridgemill.org.uk,
www.thebridgemill.org.uk. *In
Bridgerule village on R Tamar
between Bude & Holsworthy.
Between the chapel by river bridge
& church at top of hill. Garden is at
bottom of hill opp Short & Abbott
agricultural engineers. See website
for detailed directions.* **Sun 29 May
(11-5). Adm £4, chd free. Home-
made teas in garden with friendly
ducks if fine or in stable if wet.
Plenty of dry seating. Visits also
by arrangement May & June for
groups of 15+.**
One acre organic gardens around mill
house and restored working water
mill. Cottage garden style planting;
herb garden with medicinal and dye
plants; productive fruit and vegetable
garden, and wild woodland and water
garden by mill. 16 acre smallholding:
lake and riverside walks, wildflower
meadows, friendly livestock, sheep,
ducks and hens. The historic water
mill was restored to working order in
April 2012 and in 2017 was awarded
a plaque by the Society for the
Protection of Ancient Buildings. For
other opening times and information,
please see website. Wheelchair
access to some of gardens plus
accessible WC.
& ✿ ☕ 🛆

17 BROCTON COTTAGE
Pear Tree, Ashburton, Newton
Abbot, TQ13 7QZ. Mrs Naomi
Hindley. *¼m from A38. Leave A38
at Princetown turning and turn R at
end of slip road. Parking is restricted
so if possible park by Shell garage
& walk up road to thatched house.*
**Thur 2, Fri 3, Sat 4, Sun 5 June
(2-5). Adm £5, chd free. Home-
made teas.**
1.3 acres recovered from neglect,
starting to look wonderful. Orchard,
woodland, ponds and productive
areas linked to established and
newly planted herbaceous borders
and shrubberies. Views over Devon
countryside. Dogs on leads only
please. Lunches available at Dartmoor
Lodge Hotel and Furzeleigh Hotel
nearby, also in Ashburton town
centre. There is wheelchair access
to the main terrace, one of the
greenhouses and to the wildlife pond
at the bottom of the garden.
& 🐄 ✿ ☕ 🛆))

18 ✦ BURROW FARM GARDENS
Dalwood, Axminster, EX13 7ET.
Mary & John Benger,
01404 831285, enquiries@
burrowfarmgardens.co.uk,
www.burrowfarmgardens.co.uk.
*3½m W of Axminster. From A35
turn N at Taunton Xrds then follow
brown signs.* **For opening times and
information, please phone, email or
visit garden website.**
This beautiful 13 acre garden
has unusual trees, shrubs and
herbaceous plants. Traditional
summerhouse looks towards lake
and ancient oak woodland with
rhododendrons and azaleas. Early
spring interest and superb autumn
colour. The more formal Millennium
garden features a rill. Anniversary
garden featuring late summer
perennials and grasses. Café, nursery
and gift shop with range of Garden
Ironwork. Various events inc spring
and summer plant fair and open air
theatre held at garden each yr. Visit
events page on website for more
details. Winner of the Public Gardens
category of The English Garden's The
Nation's Favourite Gardens 2021.
& 🐄 ✿ 🚗 ☕

19 ✦ CADHAY
Ottery St Mary, EX11 1QT. Rupert
Thistlethwayte, 01404 813511,
jayne@cadhay.org.uk,
www.cadhay.org.uk. *1m NW of
Ottery St Mary. On B3176 between
Ottery St Mary & Fairmile. From E exit
A30 at Iron Bridge. From W exit A30 at
Patteson's Cross, follow brown signs
for Cadhay.* **For NGS: Sat 28, Sun
29, Mon 30 May, Sun 28, Mon 29
Aug (2-5). Adm £5, chd £1. Cream
teas. For other opening times and
information, please phone, email or
visit garden website.**
Tranquil 2 acre setting for Tudor
manor house. 2 medieval fish ponds
surrounded by rhododendrons,
gunnera, hostas and flag iris. Roses,
clematis, lilies and hellebores
surround walled water garden. 120ft
herbaceous border walk informally
planted. Magnificent display of dahlias
throughout. Walled kitchen gardens
have been turned into allotments and
old apple store is now a tea room.
Gravel paths.
& 🐄 🚗 ☕

20 CHEVITHORNE BARTON
Chevithorne, Tiverton,
EX16 7QB. Head Gardener,
chevithornebarton.co.uk. *3m NE
of Tiverton. Follow yellow signs from*

A361, A396 or Sampford Peverell.
**Sun 1 May, Sun 5 June, Sun 3
July, Sun 7 Aug (2.30-5.30). Adm
£6, chd free. Light refreshments.**
Walled garden, summer borders
and Robinsonian inspired woodland
of rare trees and shrubs. In spring,
garden features a large collection
of magnolias, camellias, and
rhododendrons with grass paths
meandering through a sea of bluebells.
Home to National Collection of
Quercus (Oaks). From time to time
within the gardens are a flock of Jacob
sheep and rare breed woodland pigs.
Lanning Roper's favourite garden
(Country Life 1969). Recently planted
collection of birches and witch hazels.
Orchard of West country apples and
recently added mazzards.
🐄 NPC ☕))

21 COOMBE MEADOW
Ashburton, Newton Abbot,
TQ13 7HU. Angela & Mike
Walker, 07775 627237,
coombemeadow2016@gmail.com.
*Opp Waterleat. Enter Ashburton
town centre, turn onto North St.
After Victoria Inn, bear R at junction,
do not cross bridge to Buckland in
the Moor. Follow signs.* **Sat 16, Sun
17 Apr, Sun 1, Mon 2 May, Sat 23,
Sun 24 July (11-4). Adm £4.50,
chd free. Light refreshments.
Visits also by arrangement Mar
to Sept for groups of 5 to 20.
Maximum 8 cars.**
This lost garden, by a beautiful
Dartmoor stream was overgrown and
neglected. Since 2016 its mature
magnolias, camellias, azaleas and
other trees have been rescued.
Paths and ponds have been cleared,
archaeology preserved, borders
created, bridges and terraces repaired
and over 15,000 bulbs planted. The
meadows contain wild daffodils and
bluebells, so in spring the garden is
a kaleidoscope of colour. Wheelchair
access to front and rear patios only.
& ☕))

22 DERRYDOWN
Sparkwell, Plymouth, PL7 5DF.
Peter & Ann Tremain,
07940 543707,
anntremain1942@gmail.com. *From
Treby Arms in Sparkwell, 100yds
on, take RH fork. Derrydown is 2nd
property on R, a bungalow on the
corner.* **Visits by arrangement Apr
to Sept for groups of up to 25.
Adm £5, chd free. Cream teas.**
Newly created ½ acre with raised
beds, quirky fish pond. Pagoda

with kiwi and grape vines. Water harvesting and rill. Lawn surrounded by hydrangeas and herbaceous. 2020 new plot added with a 50ft circular lawn, frog pond, berry hedge, wild meadows, flowers, moon gates, double glazed greenhouses. Rain water harvesting and upcycling. Panoramic views. Children's quiz. By arrangement min group size 4 with a max of 25. Dogs on leads.

& ✿ ♨

23 ◆ DOCTON MILL
Lymebridge, Hartland, EX39 6EA. **Lana & John Borrett, 01237 441369, docton.mill@btconnect.com, www.doctonmill.co.uk.** *8m W of Clovelly. Follow brown tourist signs on A39 nr Clovelly.* **For NGS: Sun 12 June (10-4.30). Adm £5, chd free. Cream teas and light lunches available all day. For other opening times and information, please phone, email or visit garden website.**
Situated in stunning valley location. Garden surrounds original mill pond and the microclimate created within the wooded valley enables tender species to flourish. Recent planting of herbaceous, stream and summer garden give variety through the season.

🐕 ✿ ♨

24 DUNLEY HOUSE
Bovey Tracey, TQ13 9PW. **Mr & Mrs F Gilbert.** *2m E of Bovey Tracey on rd to Hennock. From A38 going W turn off slip rd R towards Chudleigh Knighton on B3344, in village follow yellow signs to Dunley House. From A38 eastwards turn off on Chudleigh K slip rd L and follow signs.* **Sat 28, Sun 29 May, Sat 15, Sun 16 Oct (2-5). Adm £6, chd free. Home-made teas.**
9 acre garden set among mature oaks, sequoiadendrons and a huge liquidambar started from a wilderness in mid eighties. Rhododendrons, camellias and over 40 different magnolias. Arboretum, walled garden with borders and fruit and vegetables, rose garden and new enclosed garden with lily pond. Large pond renovated 2016 with new plantings. Woodland walk around perimeter of property.

& 🐕 ✿ ♨ ⋙

GROUP OPENING

25 EAST CORNWORTHY GARDENS
East Cornworthy, Totnes, TQ9 7HQ. *Leave A3122 at Sportsman's Arms to Dittisham. At Red Lion L to Totnes. Continue 1m following signs to East Cornworthy.* **Sat 16, Sun 17 July (2-5). Combined adm £6, chd free. Cream teas at Rivendale.**

BLACKNESS BARN
Andrew & Karen Davis.

BROOK
John & Michelle Pain.

RIVENDALE FARM
Simon & Lesley Stubbs.

TOAD HALL
Denis & Jacky Kerslake.

East Cornworthy is a small hamlet nestling in a valley just outside the village of Dittisham near the River Dart where 4 beautiful gardens will be opening their gates in July. Surrounded by rolling hills, with Dartmoor in the distance, you can enjoy woodland walks, streams, ponds as well as interesting planting and magnificent mixed borders in sun and shade in these very different gardens. A Devonshire cream tea will complete the afternoon.

✿ ♨

Mothecombe House

26 EAST WOODLANDS FARMHOUSE

Alverdiscott, Newton Tracey, Barnstaple, EX31 3PP. Ed & Heather Holt, 07342 632211, heatherholtexmoor@gmail.com. *5m NE of Great Torrington, 5m S of Barnstaple, off B3232. From Grt Torrington turn R into single track rd before Alverdiscott; & from Barnstaple turn L after Alverdiscott. 1m down rd R fork at Y-junction.* **Sat 9, Sun 10 July (2-5). Adm £5, chd free. Home-made teas. Gluten free cakes available. Visits also by arrangement July & Aug for groups of 10+.**

East Woodlands is a beautiful RHS inspired and designed garden full of rooms packed with plants, shrubs and trees. Enjoy the spectacular bamboos, flowing grasses, colourful roses, Mediterranean, Japanese, cottage and bog gardens (unfenced pond), all set in an acre looking out over N Devon countryside. Occasional live music. Lots of seating areas and teas served in vintage crockery. Partial wheelchair access.

&. ✿ ☕ ›))

27 EAST WORLINGTON HOUSE

East Worlington, Witheridge, Crediton, EX17 4TS. Barnabas & Campie Hurst-Bannister. *In centre of E Worlington, 2m W of Witheridge. From Witheridge Square R to E Worlington. After 1½m R at T-junction in Drayford, then L to Worlington. After ½m L at T-junction. 200 yds on L. Parking nearby, disabled parking at house.* **Sun 27 Feb, Sun 6 Mar (1.30-5). Adm £4, chd free. Cream teas in thatched parish hall next to house.**

Thousands of purple crocuses feature in this 2 acre garden, set in a lovely position with views down the valley to the Little Dart river. These spectacular crocuses have spread over many years through the garden and into the neighbouring churchyard. Walks from the garden across the river and into the woods. Dogs on leads please.

&. ☕ ☕

28 FOXHOLE COMMUNITY GARDEN

Dartington, Totnes, TQ9 6EB. Zoe Jong, www. foxholecommunitygarden.org. uk. *On the Dartington Estate near the Foxhole Centre at Old School Farm.* **Sun 3 July, Sun 18 Sept (10-3). Adm £4, chd free. Home-made teas.**

Beautiful community garden and orchard on the Dartington Estate. Since 2016 it has been developed to provide a garden space for all abilities. Garden tour at 11am and 1pm presenting organic, no-dig low maintenance principles. Raised vegetable beds, orchard, herb, wildlife, wildflower, cutting flower, pond and potager planting areas. Full of colour, produce and wildlife. Parking directly outside the garden, main area of the garden accessible by wheelchair as is the WC.

&. ☕ ✿ ☕ ☕ ⌓ ›))

29 NEW GOODWILL GARDENS

Bickington, Newton Abbot, TQ12 6JY. Michael Hext. *Nr to Granny Pats Tiny Farmshop & Nursery on old A38 Liverton to Bickington rd. Past Welcome Stranger pub next to layby on R before Bickington.* **Sat 16, Sun 17, Mon 18, Sat 30 Apr, Sun 1, Sat 21, Sun 22, Sat 28, Sun 29 May, Sat 27, Sun 28 Aug, Sat 3, Sun 4 Sept (11-4.30). Adm £4, chd free. Light refreshments on the decking area.**

A small nursery and smallholding with a large wild flower area also shrubs herbaceous perennials beds, flowers full of insects and birds no-dig vegetable and soft fruit area, large cut flower area, sweetpeas, dahlias and lots more. Small wildflower meadow in apple orchard with pet geese, pigs and hens and polytunnels. The garden, which was started in 1990 on a steep site, is now laid out in terraces.

☕ ✿ ☕

30 ◆ GOREN FARM

Broadhayes, Stockland, Honiton, EX14 9EN. Julian Pady, 01404 881335, gorenfarm@hotmail.com, www.goren.co.uk/pages/ open-days. *6m E of Honiton, 6m W of Axminster. Go to Stockland television mast. Head 100 metres N signed from Ridge Cross, head E towards ridge.* **For NGS: Sat 4, Sun 5, Sat 11, Sun 12 June (11-7). Adm £5, chd £2. Home-made teas. Groups of more than 4 are asked to book their cream teas in advance. The farm has a licence to serve cider. For other opening times and information, please phone, email or visit garden website.**

Wander through 50 acres of natural species rich wildflower meadows.

Easy access footpaths. Dozens of varieties of wild flowers and grasses. Thousands of orchids from early June and butterflies in July. Stunning views of Blackdown Hills. Georgian house and walled gardens. In August it's late season and the meadows are setting seed, ready to be mown. Butterflies, beetles and many other insects are in abundance on the grasses and wild flower seed heads. Café, pick your own and farm shop. Nature trail with species information signs and picnic tables. Visit the cider museum, walled gardens and greenhouses. Various music events are held throughout the summer. Visit website for more details. Partial wheelchair access to meadows. Dogs welcome on a lead only, please clean up after your pet.

&. ☕ ☕ ⌓ ›))

31 GREATCOMBE

Holne, Newton Abbot, TQ13 7SP. Robbie & Sarah Richardson. *4m NW Ashburton via Holne Bridge & Holne village. 4m NE Buckfastleigh via Scorriton. Narrow lanes. Large car park adjacent to garden.* **Sat 30 Apr, Sun 1, Mon 2 May, Thur 2, Fri 3, Sat 4, Sun 5, Fri 24, Sat 25, Sun 26 June, Fri 22, Sat 23, Sun 24 July, Fri 19, Sat 20, Sun 21 Aug (1-5). Adm £5, chd free. Home-made teas.**

An oasis of a garden hidden in a Dartmoor valley with a fast growing reputation for its unusual planting and colour schemes (and home-made teas) set in 2 acres and evoking a deep sense of tranquillity. Moorland stream, spring flowering shrubs and bulbs, summer climbers, perennial borders, wide variety of hydrangeas and grasses, a haven for pollinators. Art, plants and metalwork for sale. Artist's studio featuring brightly coloured acrylic paintings, prints and cards all available to purchase along with ornamental metal plant supports in all sizes and shapes and 'Made by Robbie' metal artefacts.

☕ ✿ ☕

32 HALDON GRANGE

Dunchideock, Exeter, EX6 7YE. Ted Phythian, 01392 832349, judithphythian@yahoo.com. *5m SW of Exeter. From A30 through Ide village to Dunchideock 5m. L to Lord Haldon, Haldon Grange is next L. From A38 (S) turn L on top of Haldon Hill follow Dunchideock signs, R at village centre to Lord Haldon.* **Every Sat and Sun 12 Mar to 12 June (1-5). Wed 30 Mar, Mon 18, Wed 27**

Apr, Mon 2, Wed 11, Wed 25 May, Thur 2, Fri 3 June (1-5). Adm £6, chd free. Home-made teas. Our visitors are welcome to bring a picnic. Visits also by arrangement Mar to June.

Peaceful, well established 12 acre garden some dating back to 1770s. This hidden gem boasts one of the largest collections of rhododendrons, azaleas, magnolias and camellias. Interspersed with mature and rare trees and complemented by a lake and cascading ponds. 5 acre arboretum, large lilac circle, wisteria pergola with views over Exeter and Woodbury complete this family run treasure. Plants are on sale, also teas and home bakes. Please bring cash. On site car parking. WC available, alcohol wipes and hand gel is provided. Strictly no dogs. Wheelchair access to main parts of garden.

33 HALSCOMBE FARM
Halscombe Lane, Ide, Exeter, EX2 9TQ. Prof J Rawlings, jgshayward@tiscali.co.uk. *From Exeter go through Ide to mini r'about take 2nd exit and continue to L turn into Halscombe Lane.* Sat 25, Sun 26 June (2-5). Adm £5, chd free. Home-made teas. Visits also by arrangement May to Sept.

Donation to The Friends of Exeter Cathedral.

Farmhouse garden created over last 9 yrs. Large collection of old roses and peonies, long and colourful mixed borders, productive fruit cage and vegetable garden all set within a wonderful borrowed landscape.

34 HARBOUR LIGHTS
Horns Cross, Bideford, EX39 5DW. Brian & Faith Butler, 01237 451627, brian.nfu@gmail.com, harbourlightsgarden.org. *8m W of Bideford, 3m E of Clovelly. On main A39, so easy to find & access, between Bideford and Clovelly, halfway between Hoops Inn & Bucks Cross. There will be a union jack flag & yellow arrow signs at the entrance.* Sat 18, Sun 19 June (11-5). Adm £4.50, chd free. Cream teas, cakes, light lunches, wine all available. Visits also by arrangement June to Aug for groups of 12+.

½ acre colourful garden with Lundy views. A garden of wit, humour, unusual ideas, installation art, puzzles, volcano and many surprises. Water features, shrubs, foliage area, grasses in an unusual setting, fernery, bonsai and polytunnel, plus masses of colourful plants. You will never have

seen a garden like this! Free leaflet. We like our visitors to leave with a smile! Child friendly. A 'must visit' unique and interactive garden with intriguing artwork of various kinds, original plantings and ideas.

35 THE HAVEN
Wembury Road, Hollacombe, Wembury, South Hams, PL9 0DQ. Mrs S Norton & Mr J Norton, 01752 862149, suenorton1@hotmail.co.uk. *20mins from Plymouth city centre. Use A379 Plymouth to Kingsbridge Rd. At Elburton r'about follow signs to Wembury. Parking on roadside. Bus stop nearby on Wembury Rd. Route 48 from Plymouth.* Visits by arrangement Mar to May for groups of up to 20. Adm £4.50, chd free. Cream teas.

½ acre sloping plantsman's garden in South Hams AONB. Tearoom and seating areas. 2 ponds. Substantial collection of large flowering Asiatic and hybrid tree magnolias. Large collection of camellias inc *Camellia reticulata*. Rare dwarf, weeping and slow growing conifers. Daphnes, early azaleas and rhododendrons, spring bulbs and hellebores. Wheelchair access to top part of garden.

Lukesland

36 HAYNE
Zeal Monachorum, Crediton, EX17 6DE. Tim & Milla Herniman, www.haynedevon.co.uk. ½ m S of Zeal Monachorum. From Zeal Monachorum, keeping church on L, drive through village. Continue on this road for ⅓ m, garden drive is 1st entrance on R. Sun 12 June (2-6). Adm £5, chd free. Home-made teas.

In the magical walled garden exciting new planting blends with the beautiful tree peonies, mature wisteria, purple and white, and rambling wild roses in combination with a more modern Piet Oudolf style perennial planting surrounding the recently renovated grade II* farm buildings. Extensive vegetable and cut flower planting adds to the scene. Magic, mystery and soul by the spadeful! Live jazz band. Disabled WC. Wheelchair access to walled garden through orchard.

37 HEATHERCOMBE
Manaton, nr Bovey Tracey, TQ13 9XE. Claude & Margaret Pike Woodlands Trust, 01626 354404, gardens@pike.me.uk, www.heathercombe.com. 7m NW of Bovey Tracey. From Bovey Tracey take scenic B3387 to Haytor/ Widecombe. 1.7m past Haytor Rocks (before Widecombe hill) turn R to Hound Tor & Manaton. 1.4m past Hound Tor turn L at Heatree Cross to Heathercombe. Sun 27 Mar, Sun 8, Sun 15 May (1.30-5.30). Every Tue to Sun 21 May to 5 June (1.30-5.30). Every Tue to Sun 11 June to 3 July (11-5.30). Adm £6, chd free. Pre-booking essential, please visit www.ngs.org.uk for information & booking. Self service tea and coffee. Do bring a picnic. **Visits also by arrangement Apr to Oct. Donation to Rowcroft Hospice.**

Tranquil secluded valley with streams running through woods, ponds and lake - 30 acres of spring/summer interest with many sculptures and new developments - daffodils, extensive bluebells, large displays of rhododendrons, many unusual specimen trees, cottage gardens, orchard, wildflower meadow, bog/ fern/woodland gardens and woodland walks. 2 miles of mainly level sandy paths with many benches. Disabled reserved parking close to tea room & WC.

38 HIGH GARDEN
Chiverstone Lane, Kenton, EX6 8NJ. Chris & Sharon Britton, www.highgardennurserykenton. wordpress.com. 5m S of Exeter on A379 Dawlish Rd. Leaving Kenton towards Exeter, L into Chiverstone Lane, 50yds along lane Sun 3 Apr, Sun 1 May, Sun 5 June, Sun 3 July, Sun 4 Sept (12-5). Adm £5, chd free. Home-made teas.

Stunning garden of over 4 acres. Huge range of trees, shrubs, perennials, grasses, climbers and exotics planted over past 14 yrs Great use of foliage to give texture and substance as well as offset the floral display. 70 metre summer herbaceous border. Over 40 individual mixed beds surrounded by meandering grass walkways. Exciting new formal plantings. Large range of plants from adjoining plantsman's nursery. Donation made to NGS from sales of teas and plants. Slightly sloping site but the few steps can be avoided.

Musselbrook Cottage Garden

39 HIGHER CHERUBEER

Dolton, Winkleigh, EX19 8PP. **Jo & Tom Hynes, 01805 804265, hynesjo@gmail.com.** *2m E of Dolton. From A3124 turn S towards Stafford Moor Fisheries, take 1st R, garden 500m on L.* **Fri 4, Fri 11, Sat 19 Feb (2-5); Sat 4 June (2.30-5.30). Adm £5, chd free. Home-made teas. 2023: Fri 3, Fri 10, Sat 18 Feb. Visits also by arrangement Feb to Oct for groups of 10+. Excluding August.**
1¾ acre country garden with gravelled courtyard and paths, raised beds, alpine house, lawns, herbaceous borders, woodland beds with naturalised cyclamen and snowdrops, kitchen garden with large greenhouse and orchard. Winter openings for National Collection of cyclamen species, hellebores and over 400 snowdrop varieties.

40 HIGHER ORCHARD COTTAGE

Aptor, Marldon, Paignton, TQ3 1SQ. **Mrs Jenny Saunders, 01803 551221.** *1m SW of Marldon. A380 Torquay to Paignton. At Churscombe Cross r'about R for Marldon, L towards Berry Pomeroy, take 2nd R into Farthing Lane. Follow for exactly 1m. Turn R at NGS sign & follow signs for parking.* **Sat 4, Sun 5 June (11-5). Adm £5, chd free. Light refreshments from 2pm provided by Marldon Garden Club if weather permits. Outside seating only. Visits also by arrangement Apr to Sept for groups of up to 20. Limited parking so please phone to discuss.**
2 acre garden with generous colourful herbaceous borders, wildlife pond, specimen trees, productive vegetable beds and grass path walks through wildflower meadows in lovely countryside. Sculpture and art installations by local artists add excitement at every turn.

41 HOLBROOK GARDEN

Sampford Shrubs, Sampford Peverell, EX16 7EN. **Martin Hughes-Jones & Susan Proud, 07741 192915, holbrookgarden.com.** *From M5 J27 follow signs to Tiverton Parkway. At top of slip rd off A361 follow brown sign to Holbrook Garden. Cash payment only for entry.* **Fri 1, Sat 2, Sun 3 Apr, Thur 1, Fri 2,**

Sat 3 Sept (11-5). Adm £5, chd free. Light refreshments. Home made cakes. Donation to MSF UK (Medecin sans Frontieres).
Ask our visitors - "Heaven for bumble bees", "sun shining through layers of plants", "an immersive experience", "inspiring", "exciting plants", "magical, artistic, free flowing paradise", "cleverly planted but looks so natural". Productive vegetable garden and polytunnel. If you like 'neat and tidy' then this garden may not be for you. Amazing display of Snakeshead fritillaries in early April. See ngs.org.uk and holbrookgarden.com for pop-up openings.

42 HOLE FARM

Woolsery, Bideford, EX39 5RF. **Heather Alford.** *11m SW of Bideford. Follow directions for Woolfardisworthy, signed from A39 at Bucks Cross. From village follow NGS signs from school for approx 2m.* **Sun 17 July, Sun 11 Sept (2-6). Adm £5, chd free. Home-made teas in converted barn. Room to sit and have a cup of tea even if its raining!.**
3 acres of exciting gardens with established waterfall, ponds, vegetable and bog garden. Terraces and features, inc round house, have all been created using natural stone from original farm quarry. Peaceful walks through Culm grassland and water meadows border the River Torridge and host a range of wildlife. Home to a herd of pedigree native Devon cattle.

43 HOUNDSPOOL

Ashcombe Road, Dawlish, EX7 0QP. **Mr & Mrs Edward Bourne.** *3m from Dawlish centre, 3-4m from A380. From A380 exit at Ashcombe Cross (2.8m) or Great Haldon Café (3.8m), follow signs to Ashcombe. Garden is adjacent to Whetman Plants International nursery.* **Mon 28 Feb, Tue 1, Mon 28, Tue 29 Mar, Mon 9, Tue 10 May, Sat 30, Sun 31 July, Mon 12, Tue 13 Sept (2-5). Adm £5, chd free. Light refreshments. Open nearby The Old School House on Sat 30 & Sun 31 July.**
Formerly a market garden, now a private pleasure garden developed over past 43 yrs. The garden is very much a work in progress, the owners aiming to make it as labour saving as possible indulging in their

love of trees, shrubs, herbaceous, water, fruit/vegetables and flowers, providing year-round interest. Dogs on leads. Children welcome. If social restrictions apply please feel free to wander around at your leisure. Gravel paths may cause a little difficulty for some wheelchairs but motorised wheelchairs should have no problem accessing most of the garden.

GROUP OPENING

44 KENTISBURY GARDENS

Kentisbury, Barnstaple, EX31 4NT. **Jerry & Jenny Burnett.** *9m N of Barnstaple, midway between Barnstaple & Lynton. From Barnstaple take A39 to Lynton & follow signs at Kentisbury Ford. From Blackmoor Gate follow signs. From Combe Martin & Ilfracombe turn R at Easter Close Cross and follow signs on B3229.* **Sat 23, Sun 24 July (12-5). Combined adm £5, chd free. Home-made teas at South Sandpark, Kentisbury EX31 4NT.**

LITTLE LEY
Jerry & Jenny Burnett.

SPRING COTTAGE
Nerys Cadvan-Jones.

Kentisbury is situated high in the N Devon countryside a few miles inland from the dramatic coastline and bordering Exmoor National Park. These 2 gardens make good use of the landscape and views, providing a variety of planting and garden habitats. Little Ley is a large country garden with pond, stream, mature trees and shrubs and a productive fruit and vegetable area. The large herbaceous borders peak in late summer giving a fantastic display of vibrant colour. Spring Cottage is a pretty cottage garden with colourful flower borders, shrubs, climbers and small trees giving year-round interest. Devon banks, a stream and stone walls afford varying views and conditions for planting and the growing collection of hardy geraniums.

45 KENTLANDS

Whitestone, Exeter, EX4 2JR. David & Gill Oakey, 01392 811585, david.oakey3@hotmail.co.uk. *NW of Exeter midway between Exwick & Tedburn St Mary. Follow NGS signs from centre of Whitestone village.* **Sat 14, Sun 15 May, Sun 24 July, Sun 11 Sept (10.30-4). Adm £5, chd free. Home-made teas. Light lunches. Visits also by arrangement Apr to Sept for groups of up to 20.**

2 acre secluded garden south facing with distant views from Exeter to E Devon. New beds for 2022 for increasing salvia collection. Newly erected summerhouse looks down on the garden. Patio area has pond with amazing collection of goldfish. Perennials, shrubs and salvias. A greenhouse houses orchids and alpines, productive vegetable area, polytunnel, variety of seasonal vegetables and amazing sweet peas. Sloping garden.

 ﺙ ⚘ ☕))

46 KIA-ORA FARM & GARDENS

Knowle Lane, Cullompton, EX15 1PZ. Mrs M B Disney, www.kia-orafarm.co.uk. *On W side of Cullompton & 6m SE of Tiverton. M5 J28, through town centre to r'about, 3rd exit R, top of Swallow Way turn L into Knowle Lane, garden beside Cullompton Rugby Club.* **Sun 17, Mon 18 Apr, Sun 1, Mon 2, Sun 22 May, Sun 5, Sun 19 June, Sun 3, Sun 17, Sun 31 July, Sun 14, Sun 28, Mon 29 Aug, Sun 11, Sun 25 Sept (2-5.30). Adm £4, chd free. Home-made teas. Teas, plants & sales not for NGS.**

Charming, peaceful 10 acre garden with lawns, lakes and ponds. Water features with swans, ducks and other wildlife. Mature trees, shrubs, rhododendrons, azaleas, heathers, roses, herbaceous borders and rockeries. Nursery avenue, novelty crazy golf. Stroll leisurely around and finish by sitting back, enjoying a traditional home-made Devonshire cream tea or choose from the wide selection of cakes!

 ﺙ ⚘ ☖ ☕

GROUP OPENING

47 KILMINGTON (SHUTE ROAD) GARDENS

Kilmington, Axminster, EX13 7ST. www.kilmingtonvillage.com. *1½ m W of Axminster. Signed off A35.*

Sat 14, Sun 15 May (1.30-5). Combined adm £6. Home-made teas at Breach.

BETTY'S GROUND
Mary-Anne Driscoll.

BREACH
Judith Chapman & BJ Lewis, 01297 35159, jachapman16@btinternet.com. Visits also by arrangement Apr to Oct for groups of 8+.

SPINNEY TWO
Paul & Celia Dunsford.

Set in rural E Devon in AONB yet easily accessed from A35, 3 gardens just under 1m apart. Spinney Two: ½ acre garden planted for year-round colour, foliage and texture. Mature oaks and beech. Spring bulbs, hellebores, shrubs; azaleas, camellias, cornus, pieris, skimmias, viburnums. Roses, acers, flowering trees, clematis and other climbers. Vegetable patch. Breach: 3+ acres with woodland, partially underplanted with rhododendrons, camellia and hydrangea; rose bed, variety of trees and shrubs, wildflower area, colourful borders, vegetable garden and fruit trees. Two ponds, one in bog garden. Betty's Ground, Haddon Corner: 1½ acres, a third of which was designed and replanted 6 yrs ago. Remaining two thirds has been restored, replanted in places and continues to evolve. Good selection of mature trees inc beautiful Wisteria walk. Beds both formal and relaxed inc woodland area all united by repeated perennial planting.

 ﺙ ⚘ ☕

48 LANGUARD PLACE

Middle Warberry Road, Torquay, TQ1 1RS. Alison & Steve Dockray. *From Babbacombe Rd opp St Matthias Church, turn into Higher Warberry Rd, then L into Middle Warberry Rd. Approx 800yds up hill to junction on R. Languard Place is on the corner.* **Sat 11, Sun 12 June (1-5.30). Adm £5, chd free. Light refreshments. Teas, coffees and cakes available in the garden.**

This small level south facing cottage style organic garden is a plantsman's delight. Enjoy the herbaceous borders packed with roses, clematis and many unusual perennials. Archways and paths lead to a separate Japanese style area with natural wildlife pond and gazebo, acers

and bamboos. There's a productive greenhouse, vegetable and fruit areas and a wisteria arch. Limited wheelchair access.

 ⚘ ☕

49 LEE FORD

Knowle Village, Budleigh Salterton, EX9 7AJ. Mr & Mrs N Lindsay-Fynn, 01395 445894, crescent@leeford.co.uk, www.leeford.co.uk/. *3½ m E of Exmouth. For SatNav use postcode EX9 6AL.* **Visits by arrangement Mar to Sept for groups of 10 to 40. Tea and cake served in conservatory. Donation to Lindsay-Fynn Trust.**

Extensive, formal and woodland garden, largely developed in 1950s, but recently much extended with mass displays of camellias, rhododendrons and azaleas, inc many rare varieties. Traditional walled garden filled with fruit and vegetables, herb garden, bog garden, rose garden, hydrangea collection, greenhouses. Ornamental conservatory with collection of pot plants. Direct access to Pedestrian route and National Cycle Network route 2 which follows old railway linking Exmouth to Budleigh Salterton. Garden ideal destination for cycle clubs or rambling groups. See website for pop-up openings. Formal gardens are lawn with gravel paths. Moderately steep slope to woodland garden on tarmac with gravel paths in woodland.

 ﺙ ☖ ☕

50 LEWIS COTTAGE

Spreyton, nr Crediton, EX17 5AA. Mr & Mrs M Pell and Mr R Orton, 07773 785939, rworton@mac.com, www.lewiscottageplants.co.uk. *5m NE of Spreyton, 8m W of Crediton. From Hillerton X keep stone X to your R. Drive approx 1½ m, Lewis Cottage on L, drive down farm track. From Crediton follow A377 N. Turn L at Barnstaple X junction, then 2m from Colebrooke Church.* **Sat 28, Sun 29 May, Sat 25, Sun 26 June (12-5). Adm £5, chd free. Home-made teas. Visits also by arrangement May to Sept for groups of 12 to 24. Max coach size 27 seater by prior arrangement.**

4 acre garden located on SW facing slope in rural mid Devon. Evolved primarily over last 30 yrs, harnessing and working with the natural landscape. Using informal

planting and natural formal structures to create a garden that reflects the souls of those who garden in it, it is an incredibly personal space that is a joy to share. Spring camassia cricket pitch, rose garden, large natural dew pond, woodland walks, bog garden, hornbeam rondel, winter garden, hot and cool herbaceous borders, fruit and veg garden, outdoor poetry reading room and plant nursery selling plants mostly propagated from the garden.

🐐 ✳ ☕ 🔊

51 LITTLE ASH BUNGALOW
Fenny Bridges, Honiton, EX14 3BL. Helen & Brian Brown, 01404 850941, helenlittleash@hotmail.com, www.facebook.com/littleashgarden. *3m W of Honiton. Leave A30 at 1st turn off from Honiton 1m, Patteson's Cross from Exeter ½ m and follow NGS signs.* **Thur 2 June, Sun 14 Aug (1-5). Adm £5, chd free. Light refreshments. Visits also by arrangement May to Oct for groups of 10+. Easy access and parking for coaches.**
Country garden of 1½ acres, packed with different and unusual herbaceous perennials, trees, shrubs and bamboos. Designed for year-round interest, wildlife and owners' pleasure. Naturalistic planting in colour coordinated mixed borders, highlighted by metal sculptures, providing foreground to the view. Natural stream, pond and damp woodland area, mini wildlife meadows and raised gravel/alpine garden. Regional Winner, The English Garden's The Nation's Favourite Gardens in 2021 Grass paths.

⚒ 🐐 ✳ 🚗 ☕ 🔊

52 LITTLE WEBBERY
Webbery, Bideford, EX39 4PS. Mr & Mrs J A Yewdall, 01271 858206, jyewdall1@icloud.com. *2m E of Bideford. From Bideford (East the Water) along Alverdiscott Rd, or from Barnstaple to Torrington on B3232. Take rd to Bideford at Alverdiscott, pass through Stoney Cross.* **Visits by arrangement Apr to Sept. Adm £5, chd free. Home-made teas.**
Approx 3 acres in valley setting with pond, lake, mature trees, 2 ha-has and large mature raised border. Large walled kitchen garden with yew and box hedging inc rose garden, lawns with shrubs and rose and clematis trellises. Vegetables and greenhouse and adjacent traditional cottage

garden. Partial wheelchair access.

⚒ 🐐 ☕

53 LITTLEFIELD
Parsonage Way, Woodbury, Exeter, EX5 1HY. Bruno Dalbiez & Caryn Vanstone. *Please park cars in the village and follow signs to a narrow driveway shared with Summer Lodge. Access to driveway from Parsonage Way, opp the stone cross on junction with Pound Lane.* **Sat 18, Sun 19 June (11-4). Adm £4, chd £1. Cream teas. Made with the owners home-made organic jams.**
½ acre eco-garden. Rescued from derelict land in 2009/10, only 13m wide, 150m long, divided into herbaceous, shrub and tree planting, with large vegetable area, fruit and orchard with chickens and beehive. Plantsperson's garden - stocked with large range of varieties, in colourful combinations. Sculptures, unusual ironwork, wildlife pond all add charm and interest. Managed using permaculture techniques. Large displays showing photos, and telling the story of the garden's development since 2009. Other displays introduce the visitor to the key ideas of permaculture and high-sustainability gardening, with wildlife and healthy ecosystems at its heart. The entire garden can be accessed in a wheelchair, but be aware that most paths are gravel and can be soft.

⚒ ✳ ☕ 🔊

54 ♦ LUKESLAND
Harford, Ivybridge, PL21 0JF. Mrs R Howell and Mr & Mrs J Howell, 01752 691749, lorna.lukesland@gmail.com, www.lukesland.co.uk. *10m E of Plymouth. Turn off A38 at Ivybridge. 1½ m N on Harford rd, E side of Erme valley. Beware of using SatNavs as these can be very misleading.* **For opening times and information, please phone, email or visit garden website.**
24 acres of flowering shrubs, wild flowers and rare trees with pinetum in Dartmoor National Park. Beautiful setting of small valley around Addicombe Brook with lakes, numerous waterfalls and pools. Extensive and impressive collections of camellias, rhododendrons, azaleas and acers; also spectacular *Magnolia campbellii* and huge *Davidia involucrata*. Superb spring and autumn colour. Open Suns, Weds and BH (11-5) 13 March - 12 June and

2 Oct - 13 November. Adm £7.50, under 16s free. Group discount for parties of 20+. Group tours available by appointment. Children's trail.

🐐 ✳ 🚗 🚌 ☕

55 MARSHALL FARM
Ide, nr Exeter, EX2 9TN. Jenny Tuckett. *Between Ide and Dunchideock. Drive through Ide to top of village r'about, straight on for 1½ m. Turn R onto concrete drive, parking in farmyard at rear of property.* **Fri 10, Sun 12 June (1-5). Adm £4, chd free. Home-made teas. Donation to Devon Air Ambulance.**
Garden approached along lane lined with homegrown lime, oak and chestnut trees. A country garden created approx 1967. One acre featuring wildflower gardens, gravel beds, pond, parterre garden and a vegetable and cutting garden. Wildlife ponds set in old orchard. Stunning views of Woodbury, Sidmouth gap and Haldon.

✳ ☕

56 ♦ MARWOOD HILL GARDEN
Marwood, EX31 4EB. Dr J A Snowdon, 01271 342528, info@marwoodhillgarden.co.uk, www.marwoodhillgarden.co.uk. *4m N of Barnstaple. Signed from A361 & B3230. Look out for brown signs. See website for map & directions.* **Coach & Car park. For NGS: Fri 10 June (10-4.30). Adm £7, chd free. Garden Tea Room offers selection of light refreshments throughout the day, all home-made or locally sourced delicious food to suit most tastes. For other opening times and information, please phone, email or visit garden website.**
Marwood Hill is a very special private garden covering an area of 20 acres with lakes and set in a valley tucked away in N Devon. From early spring snowdrops through to late autumn there is always a colourful surprise around every turn. National Collections of astilbe, iris ensata and tulbaghia, large collections of camellia, rhododendron and magnolia. Winner of MacLaren Cup at rhododendron and camellia show RHS Rosemoor. Partial wheelchair access.

⚒ 🐐 ✳ 🚗 NPC ☕ 🛆 🔊

57 MIDDLE WELL

Waddeton Road, Stoke Gabriel, Totnes, TQ9 6RL. Neil & Pamela Millward, 01803 782981, neilandpamela@talktalk.net. *A385 Totnes towards Paignton. Turn off A385 at Parkers Arms, Collaton St. Mary. After 1m, turn L at Four Cross.* **Sun 7 Aug (11-5). Adm £6, chd free. Home-made teas. Visits also by arrangement Apr to Oct. Large (52-seater) coaches have to park 300m away.**

Tranquil 2 acre garden plus woodland and streams contain a wealth of interesting plants chosen for colour, form and long season of interest. Many seating places from which to enjoy the vistas. Interesting structural features (rill, summerhouse, pergola, cobbling, slate bridge). Heady mix of exciting perennials, shrubs, bulbs, climbers and specimen trees. Vegetable garden. Child friendly. Architectural features offset by striking planting. Regional Finalist, The English Garden's The Nation's Favourite Gardens 2021. Mostly accessible by wheelchair.

&. ✖ 🚗 ☕

58 NEW MILL HOUSE

Whitehall, Hemyock, Cullompton, EX15 3UQ. Vanessa Worrall. *1m from Hemyock centre. Travel towards Culmstock from Hemyock turn 1st R, over 2 bridges Garden is 1st on the R.* **Sun 12, Mon 13, Tue 14 June (10-4). Adm £6, chd free. Home-made teas. Open nearby Regency House.**

A delightful ramshackle cottage garden wraps the front of the house. Lupins, oriental poppies, geraniums and pops of alliums crowd the beds. The back garden has a wonderful perennial border with an orchard of apple and pear trees in a meadow of grasses, oxeye daisies, wildflowers and camassias. The Mill leat is bordered with hydrangeas, specimen trees and rhododendrons. The garden is owned by artist Vanessa Worrall who will be opening her studio to coincide with the garden opening.

✖ ☕))

59 MONKSCROFT

Zeal Monachorum, Crediton, EX17 6DG. Mr Ken & Mrs Jane Hogg. *Lane opp church. Parking in farmyard.* **Sat 26, Sun 27 Mar (12-5). Adm £5, chd free. Home-made teas.**

Pretty, medium sized garden of oldest cottage in village. Packed with spring colours, primroses, daffodils, tulips, magnolias and camellias. Views to far hills. New exotic garden. Also tranquil fishing lake with daffodils and wildflowers in beautiful setting, home to resident kingfisher. Steep walk to lake approx 20mins, or 5mins by car. Dogs on leads welcome. WC at lake.

🐑 ✖ ☕

GROUP OPENING

60 MORETONHAMPSTEAD GARDENS

Moretonhampstead, TQ13 8PW. *12m W of Exeter, 12m N of Newton Abbot. Signs from the Xrd of A382 and B3212. On E slopes of Dartmoor National Park. Parking at both gardens.* **Fri 20, Sat 21, Sun 22 May, Sat 3, Sun 4 Sept (1-5). Combined adm £6, chd free. Home-made teas at both gardens.**

MARDON
Graham & Mary Wilson.

SUTTON MEAD
Edward & Miranda Allhusen, 01647 440296, miranda@allhusen.co.uk.
Visits also by arrangement Apr to Sept.

2 large gardens on edge of moorland town. One in a wooded valley, the other higher up with magnificent views of Dartmoor. Both have mature orchards and year-round vegetable gardens. Substantial rhododendron, azalea and tree planting, croquet lawns, summer colour and woodland walks through hydrangeas and acers. Mardon: 4 acres based on its original Edwardian design. Long herbaceous border and formal granite terraces, stunning grasses. Fernery and colourful bog garden beside stream fed pond with its thatched boathouse. Arboretum. Sutton Mead: also 4 acres, shrub lined drive. Lawns surrounding granite lined pond with seat at water's edge. Unusual planting, dahlias, grasses, bog garden, rill fed round pond, secluded seating and gothic

concrete greenhouse. Sedum roofed summerhouse. Enjoy the views as you wander through the woods. Dogs on leads welcome. Teas are a must.

🐑 ✖ 🚗 ☕))

61 MOTHECOMBE HOUSE

Mothecombe, Holbeton, Plymouth, PL8 1LA. Mr & Mrs J Mildmay-White, www.flete.co.uk. *12m E of Plymouth. From A379 between Yealmpton & Modbury turn S for Holbeton. Continue 2m to Mothecombe.* **Sun 1 May (11-5). Adm £6, chd £3. Home-made teas.**

Queen Anne House (not open) with Lutyens additions and terraces set in private estate hamlet. Walled gardens, orchard with spring bulbs and magnolias, camellia walk leading through bluebell woods to streams and pond. Mothecombe Garden is managed for wildlife and pollinators. Bee garden with 250 lavenders in 16 varieties. New project to manage adjacent 6 acre meadow as a traditional wildflower pasture. Sandy beach at bottom of garden, unusual shaped large *Liriodendron tulipifera*. Lunches at The Schoolhouse, Mothecombe village. Gravel paths, two slopes.

&. 🐑 ☕))

62 THE MOUNT, DELAMORE

Cornwood, Ivybridge, PL21 9QP. Mr & Mrs Gavin Dollard. *Please park in car park for Delamore Park Offices not in village. From Ivybridge turn L at Xrds in Cornwood village keep pub on L, follow wall on R to sharp R bend, turn R.* **Sat 12, Sun 13 Feb (10-3.30). Adm £4.50, chd free.**

Welcome one of the first signs of spring by wandering through swathes of thousands of snowdrops in this lovely wood. Closer to the village than to Delamore Gardens, paths meander through a sea of these lovely plants, some of which are unique to Delamore and which were sold as posies to Covent Garden market as late as 2002. The Cornwood Inn in the village is now community owned and open, serving excellent food. Main house and garden open for sculpture exhibition every day in May.

🐑 ✖ 🚗 🍽))

63 MUSBURY BARTON

Musbury, Axminster, EX13 8BB.
Lt Col Anthony Drake. *3m S of
Axminster off A358. Turn E into village,
follow yellow arrows. Garden next to
church, parking for 12 cars, otherwise
park on road in village.* **Sat 25, Sun 26
June (1.30-5). Adm £5, chd free.**
This 6 acre garden surrounds a
traditional Devon longhouse. It is
planted with much imagination. There
are many rare and unusual things to
see. Over 2000 rose bushes in beds,
some of them edged with local stone.
A steep valley in which a stream
tumbles through the garden. Visit
the avenue of horse chestnuts and
the arboretum with interesting trees.
Enjoy the many vantage points in this
unusual garden with a surprise round
every corner.

64 MUSSELBROOK COTTAGE GARDEN

Sheepwash, Beaworthy, EX21 5PE.
Richard Coward, 01409 231677,
coward.richard@sky.com. *1.3m
N of Sheepwash. Satnav may be
misleading. A3072 to Highampton.
Through Sheepwash. L on track
signed Lake Farm. A386 S of Merton
take rd to Petrockstow. Up hill opp,
eventually L. After 350 yds turn R
down track signed Lake Farm.* **Visits
by arrangement Apr to Oct for
groups of up to 24. Adm £4.50,
chd free. Tea, coffee and cakes
provided on request.**
1 acre naturalistic/wildlife/plantsman's
garden of all season interest. Rare/
unusual plants on sloping site. 12
ponds (koi, lilies), stream, Japanese
garden, Mediterranean garden,
wildflower meadow, clock golf,
massed bulbs. Ericaceous plants inc
camellias, magnolias, rhododendrons,
acers, hydrangeas. Dierama,
crocosmia, many grasses. Superb
autumn colour. Aquatic nursery
inc waterlilies. Planting extremely
labour intensive as ground is full of
rocks. A mattock soon became my
indispensable tool, even for planting
bulbs. The aquatic plant nursery can
be visited by separate arrangement.

Burrow Farm Gardens

Marwood Hill Garden

65 THE OLD SCHOOL HOUSE
Ashcombe, Dawlish, EX7 0QB.
Vanessa Hurley. *From A38 at Kennford take A380 towards Torquay. Turn off onto B3192 signed to Teignmouth, take 1st exit off r'about follow windy road for 1½m 1st R after church and follow signs.* Sat 30 July (1-5); Sun 31 July (1.30-5). Adm £5, chd free. Light refreshments. Home-made cakes for sale.
The Old School House is part of Ashcombe Estate. Created by Queen's Nurse Vanessa and husband Chaz. It is an artistic palette of colour with a hint of the theatrical. Set in over ½ acre there is a variety of plants, shrubs, vines, bananas and trees attracting insects and wildlife plus an interesting array of quirky recycled materials. Dawlish water stream circles around the pretty garden. There are gravelled areas to entrances and some uneven ground. Some disabled parking outside house.
&♿ ☕ ❀ 🐕

66 THE OLD VICARAGE
West Anstey, South Molton,
EX36 3PE. Tuck & Juliet Moss,
01398 341604,
julietm@onetel.com. *9m E of South Molton. From S Molton go E on B3227 to Jubilee Inn. From Tiverton r'about take A396 7m to B3227 then L to Jubilee Inn. Follow NGS signs to garden.* Sat 21, Sun 22 May, Sat 13, Sun 14 Aug (12-5). Adm £5, chd £2. Cream teas. Visits also by arrangement Apr to Sept for groups of 10 to 40.
Croquet lawn leads to multi-level garden overlooking 3 large ponds with winding paths, climbing roses and overviews. Brook with waterfall flows through garden past fascinating summerhouse built by owner. Benched deck overhangs first pond. Features rhododendrons, azaleas and primulas in spring and large collection of wonderful hydrangeas in August. A wall fountain is mounted on handsome, traditional dry wall above house. Access by path through kitchen garden. A number of smaller standing stones echoing local Devon tradition have been added as entertainment.
🐕 🐕 🚌 ☕ 🔊

GROUP OPENING

67 NEW PARRACOMBE GARDENS
Parracombe, Barnstaple,
EX31 4QJ. *Parracombe. Off A39 between Blackmore Gate & Lynton. Car parking at Heddon Hall EX31 4QL.* Sat 18, Sun 19 June (12.30-5.30). Combined adm £6, chd free. Home-made teas at the Coronation Playing Field.

HEDDON HALL
Mr & Mrs de Falbe.
NEW **LAUREL HOUSE**
Lesley Brownlee.
NEW **LITTLECLOSE**
Julia Holtom.
NEW **PARADISE VILLA**
Andy Full.

NEW ROCK COTTAGE

Kevin & Val Green.

NEW SOUTH HILL HOUSE

Alison Smith.

Set in the historic village of Parracombe with its Norman motte and bailey castle, ancient church and a pottery, the 6 varied gardens are all within walking distance. A larger garden at Heddon Hall has a stunning walled garden laid out by Penelope Hobhouse, a natural rockery leading to bog garden and many rare plants, all in a spectacular valley setting. Laurel House is a small garden packed with successional planting and landscape features. Paradise Villa and Rock Cottage & Pottery feature flower, fruit and vegetable gardens. South Hill House has a walled front garden and a charming cobbled courtyard leading to the rear garden with herbaceous borders and mature trees set beside the River Heddon. Littleclose has a terraced garden with unusual plants, lovely roses and a developing orchard. Partial wheelchair access. Accessible tea area and WC. Lunches available at the Fox & Goose (booking advised 01598 763239).

68 ◆ PLANT WORLD

St Marychurch Road, Newton Abbot, TQ12 4SE. Ray Brown, 01803 872939, info@plant-world-seeds.com, www.plant-world-gardens.co.uk. *2m SE of Newton Abbot. 1½m from Penn Inn turn-off on A380. Follow brown tourist signs at end of A380 dual carriageway from Exeter.* **For opening times and information, please phone, email or visit garden website.**

The 4 acres of landscape gardens with fabulous views have been called Devon's 'Little Outdoor Eden'. Representing 5 continents, they offer an extensive collection of rare and exotic plants from around the world. Superb mature cottage garden and Mediterranean garden will delight the visitor. Attractive viewpoint café, picnic area and shop. Open April 1st to end of Sept (9.30-5.00).

69 POUNDS

Hemyock, Cullompton, EX15 3QS. Diana Elliott, 01823 680802, shillingscottage@yahoo.co.uk, www.poundsfarm.co.uk. *8m N of*

Honiton. M5 J26. From ornate village pump, nr pub & church, turn up rd signed Dunkeswell Abbey. Entrance ½m on R. Park in field. Short walk up to garden on R. **Sat 4 June (12-4). Adm £5, chd free.**

Cottage garden of lawns, colourful borders and roses, set within low flint walls with distant views. Slate paths lead through an acer grove to a swimming pool, amid scented borders. Beyond lies a traditional ridge and furrow orchard, with a rose hedge, where apple, pear, plum and cherries grow among ornamental trees. Further on, an area of raised beds combine vegetables with flowers for cutting. Some steps, but most of the garden accessible via sloping grass, concrete, slate or gravel paths.

70 PROSPECT HOUSE

Lyme Road, Axminster, EX13 5BH. Peter Wadeley. *½m uphill from centre of Axminster. Just before service station.* **Sat 20, Sun 21 Aug (1.30-5). Adm £10, chd free. Pre-booking essential, please visit www.ngs.org.uk for information & booking. Home-made teas. Tea & cake included in adm.**

1 acre garden hidden behind stone walls with extended views over the Axe valley. 200 varieties of salvia plus echinacea, helenium, helianthus, crocosmia and grasses, among mature trees and shrubs such as cornus, grevillia, cestrum, viburnum, calycanthus and acers.

71 NEW QUINCE HONEY FARM

Aller Cross, South Molton, EX36 3RD. Wallace Family, 01769 572401, hello@quincehoneyfarm.co.uk, quincehoneyfarm.co.uk/. *50 metres from the Aller Cross r'about, heading S into South Molton from the A361 N Devon link road.* **Every Thur and Fri 12 May to 29 July (9.30-5). Visits also by arrangement May to July. Arranged visits include a walk and talk by the Head Gardener, Pip Howard.**

The Nectar Gardens are designed specifically for bees, other pollinators and the local wildlife, a place where nectar and pollen are maximised. All the planting is bee and pollinator friendly, and all the features were designed to provide a habitat for various wildlife. The garden itself is the largest wildlife garden in the UK that is open to the public. Book a talk

on an open day, ring or email. Full wheelchair access throughout.

72 REGENCY HOUSE

Hemyock, EX15 3RQ. Mrs Jenny Parsons, 07772 998982, jenny.parsons@btinternet.com, www.regencyhouse hemyock.co.uk. *8m N of Honiton. M5 J26. From Catherine Wheel pub & church in Hemyock take Dunkeswell-Honiton Rd. Entrance ½m on R. Please do not drive on the long, uncut grass alongside the drive. Disabled parking (only) at house.* **Sun 12, Mon 13, Tue 14 June, Sat 15, Sun 16 Oct (2.30-5.30). Adm £6, chd free. Home-made teas on terrace. Visits also by arrangement June to Oct for groups of up to 30. No coach access.**

5 acre plantsman's garden approached across private ford. Many interesting and unusual trees and shrubs. Visitors can try their hand at identifying plants with the plant list or have a game of croquet. Plenty of space to eat your own picnic. Walled vegetable and fruit garden, lake, ponds, bog plantings and sweeping lawns. Horses, Dexter cattle and Jacob sheep. See www.ngs.org.uk for pop-up openings. Gently sloping gravel paths give wheelchair access to the walled garden, lawns, borders and terrace, where teas are served.

73 NEW RUSSET HOUSE

Talaton, Exeter, EX5 2RL. Liz & Alan Franklin, www.russethouse.uk. *16m NE Exeter. Exit A30 onto B3177 signed Fenny Bridges & brown signs for Escot. Follow Escot signs. At Escot, straight on 1½m to Talaton. Park in village.* **Fri 2, Sun 4 Sept (1-5). Adm £4, chd free. Home-made teas.**

¾ acre garden with extensive views created since 2019. Mature orchard with 70 varieties, wildflower banks and perennial planting supports beehives and pollinators. Walled back garden, meandering path through trees, shrubs, roses, clematis and perennials. Past the pond, a productive raised bed vegetable/soft fruit garden with a greenhouse and potting shed. Patio seating areas filled with many pots.

74 ST MERRYN
Higher Park Road, Braunton, EX33 2LG. Dr W & Mrs Ros Bradford, 01271 813805, ros@st-merryn.co.uk. *5m W of Barnstaple. On A361, R at 30mph sign, then at mini r'about, R into Lower Park Rd, then L into Seven Acre Lane, at top of lane R into Higher Park Rd. Pink house 200 yds on R.* **Sun 24 Apr, Sun 22 May, Sun 19 June (2-5.30). Adm £4.50, chd free. Cream teas. Visits also by arrangement Apr to Sept for groups of up to 20.**

1 acre garden which has been renovated and developed over the last 46 yrs with foliage, flowers, scent, colour-themed borders. Sheltered seating. Artist-owner hopes to lead the visitor around the garden using the winding paths to the thatched summerhouse, ponds, sculptural bonfire, hens, and swimming pool. Earth removed in the construction of the Art Gallery has been used to construct a grassy knoll.

75 SAMLINGSTEAD
Near Roadway Corner, Woolacombe, EX34 7HL. Roland & Marion Grzybek, 01271 870886, roland135@msn.com. *1m outside Woolacombe. Stay on A361 all the way to Woolacombe. Passing through town head up Chalacombe Hill, L at T-junction, garden 150metres on L.* **Sat 26 Mar, Sat 9 July (11-3.30). Adm £5, chd free. Cream teas in 'The Swallows' a purpose built out-building. Hot sausage rolls and cakes, tea and coffee and cold soft drinks will also be available. Visits also by arrangement Mar to Aug for groups of up to 30.**

Garden is within 2 mins of N Devon coastline and Woolacombe AONB. 6 distinct areas; cottage garden at front, patio garden to one side, swallows garden at rear, meadow garden, orchard and field (500m walk with newly planted hedgerow). Slightly sloping ground so whilst wheelchair access is available to most parts of garden certain areas may require assistance.

76 SHUTELAKE
Butterleigh, Cullompton, EX15 1PG. Jill & Nigel Hall, 01884 38812, jill22hall@gmail.com. *3m W of Cullompton; 3m S of Tiverton. Follow signs for Silverton from Butterleigh village. Take L fork 100yds after entrance to Pound Farm. Car park sign on L after 150yds.* **Sat 28, Sun 29 May (11.30-4.30). Adm £6, chd free. Light refreshments in the studio barn if inclement. Snack lunches & cakes inc GF/Veg. Visits also by arrangement May to Sept for groups of 10 to 20.**

Shutelake is a working farm and the garden melds subtly with the surrounding landscape,not least in the way its terraces complement the tumbling Devon countryside. Formal close to the old house, even with a sense of the Italianate. Terrace borders full of warm perennials in summer. Beyond a natural pond teeming with wildlife feeds the Burn stream. Wander along woodland paths and enjoy the sculptures.

77 SIDBURY MANOR
Sidmouth, EX10 0QE. Lady Cave, www.sidburymanor.com. *1m NW of Sidbury. Sidbury village is on A375, S of Honiton, N of Sidmouth.* **Fri 8, Sun 10 Apr, Fri 17 June (2-5). Adm £6, chd free. Cream teas.**

Built in 1870s this Victorian manor house built by owner's family and set within E Devon AONB comes complete with 20 acres of garden inc substantial walled gardens, extensive arboretum containing many fine trees and shrubs, a number of champion trees, and areas devoted to magnolias, rhododendrons and camellias. Partial wheelchair access.

GROUP OPENING

78 SIDMOUTH GARDENS
Coulsdon Road, Sidmouth, EX10 9JP. *Byes Reach From Exeter on A3052 turn R at lights, Sidford Rd A375. ½m turn L into Coulsdon Rd. Fairpark on A3052, at signpost 'Sidmouth' turn R on B3174. 1½m R onto Broadway. First L Knowle Drive.* **Sat 13, Sun 14 Aug (1.30-5). Combined adm £5, chd free. Home-made teas. Gluten free, lactose free cakes available.**

BYES REACH
26 Coulsdon Road, Sidmouth, EX10 9JP. Lynette Talbot & Peter Endersby, 01395 578081, latalbot01@gmail.com. **Visits also by arrangement May to Aug for groups of 5 to 20.**

Coach can access street and park nearby. Teas can be pre-ordered for group.

FAIRPARK
Knowle Drive, Sidmouth, EX10 8HP. Helen & Ian Crackston.

Situated on Jurassic Coast World Heritage Site, Sidmouth has fine beaches, beautiful gardens and magnificent coastal views. 2 contrasting ¼ acre gardens 1m apart. Byes Reach: Potager style vegetable garden, colour-themed herbaceous borders, rill, ferns, rockery, hostas. Spring colour of fruit blossom, spring bulbs - tulips, erythroniums and alliums. 20m arched walkway. Seating in secluded niches each with views of garden. Front hot border. Fairpark lies behind a 12ft red brick wall, terraces, rockery, impressionist palette of colour, texture, many acers, small woodland and greenhouse, grasses, raised beds and willow sculptures. Seating areas to enjoy home-made treats.

79 SILVER STREET FARM
Prescott, Uffculme, Cullompton, EX15 3BA. Alasdair & Tor Cameron, www.camerongardens.co.uk. *Signs will guide you from A38 between M5 and Wellington.* **Sat 10 Sept (1-5). Adm £6, chd free. Home-made teas.**

A plantsman's garden in rural setting, alive with scent, colour and dynamic planting. Roses, herbs and perennials, enormous herbaceous borders with meandering paths, an eclectic collection of plants and shrubs. Designed with the family and surrounding landscape at its heart by Alasdair Cameron as a haven for people who love to nurture and be playful with their plants. Embracing the agricultural setting it encourages birds and insects and crafts a magical family space. Seating areas.

80 SOUTH WOOD FARM
Cotleigh, Honiton, EX14 9HU. Professor Clive Potter, Southwoodfarmgarden@gmail.com. *3m NE of Honiton. From Honiton head N on A30, take 1st R past Otter Valley Field Kitchen layby. Follow for 1m. Go straight over Xrds and take first L. Entrance after 1m on R.* **Sat 23, Sun 24 Apr (2-5). Adm £6, chd free. Home-made teas.**

Visits also by arrangement May to Sept for groups of 15+.

Designed by renowned Arne Maynard around C17 thatched farmhouse, country garden exemplifying how contemporary design can be integrated into a traditional setting. Herbaceous borders, roses, yew topiary, knot garden, wildflower meadows, orchards, lean-to greenhouses and a mouthwatering kitchen garden create an unforgettable sense of place. Rare opportunity to visit spring garden in all its glory with 5000 bulbs inc 2500 tulips and hundreds of camassias in flower meadow. Regional Finalist, The English Garden's The Nation's Favourite Gardens 2019. Gravel pathways, cobbles and steps.

& 🐕 🍵))

81 SPITCHWICK MANOR
Poundsgate, Newton Abbot, TQ13 7PB. Mr & Mrs P Simpson. *4m NW of Ashburton. Princetown rd from Ashburton through Poundsgate, 1st R at Lodge. From Princetown L at Poundsgate sign. Past Lodge. Park after 300yds at Xrds.* Sat 14, Sun 15 May, Sat 18, Sun 19 June (11-4.30). Adm £6, chd free. Home-made teas.

6½ acre garden with extensive beautiful views. Mature garden undergoing refreshment. A variety of different areas; lower walled garden with glasshouses, formal rose garden with fountain, camellia walk with small leat and secret garden with Lady Ashburton's plunge pool built 1763. 2.6 acre vegetable garden sheltered by high granite walls housing 9 allotments and lily pond. Mostly wheelchair access.

& 🐕 ✿ 🍵

82 NEW SPRING LODGE
Kenton, Exeter, EX6 8EY. David & Ann Blandford. *Between Lyson and Oxton. Head for Lyson then Oxton.* Sun 22 May, Sun 21 Aug (10-5). Adm £4, chd free. Pre-booking essential, please visit www.ngs.org.uk for information & booking. Tea.

Originally part of the Georgian pleasure gardens to Oxton House, the garden at Spring Lodge boasts a hermit's cave, dramatic cliffs and a stream which runs under the house. Built in the quarry of the big house this ½ acre garden is on many levels, with picturesque vistas and lush planting. Restricted parking so pls pre book.

🐕 ✿ 🍵

83 SPRINGFIELD HOUSE
Seaton Road, Colyford, EX24 6QW. Wendy Pountney, 01297 552481. *Starting on A3052 coast rd, at Colyford PO take Seaton Rd. House 500m on L. Ample parking in field.* Sat 28 May, Sat 2 July, Sat 6 Aug (10.30-5). Adm £5, chd free. Home-made teas. Visits also by arrangement Feb to Oct for groups of up to 30. Refreshments by arrangement.

1 acre garden with mainly new planting. Numerous beds, majority of plants from cuttings and seed keeping cost to minimum, full of colour spring to autumn. Vegetable garden, fruit cage and orchard with ducks and chickens. Large formal pond. Wonderful views over River Axe and bird sanctuary, which is well worth a visit, path leads from the garden.

& 🐕 ✿ 🚐 🍵

84 SQUIRRELS
98 Barton Road, Torquay, TQ2 7NS. Graham & Carol Starkie, 01803 329241, calgra@talktalk.net. *5m S of Newton Abbot. From Newton Abbot take A380 to Torquay. After ASDA store on L, turn L at T-lights up Old Woods Hill. 1st L into Barton Rd. Bungalow 200yds on L. Also could turn by B&Q. Parking nearby.* Sat 30, Sun 31 July (2-5). Adm £5, chd free. Light refreshments. Visits also by arrangement in Aug.

Plantsman's small town environmental garden, landscaped with small ponds and 7ft waterfall. Interlinked through abutilons to Japanese, Italianate, Spanish, tropical areas. Specialising in fruit inc peaches, figs, kiwi. Tender plants inc bananas, tree fern, brugmansia, lantanas, oleanders. Collection of fuchsia, dahlias, abutilons, bougainvillea. Environmental and Superclass Gold Medal Winners. 27 cleverly hidden rain water storage containers. Advice on free electric from solar panels and solar hot water heating and fruit pruning. 3 sculptures. Many topiary birds and balls. Huge 20ft Torbay palm. 9ft geranium. 15ft abutilons. New Moroccan and Spanish courtyard with tender succulents etc.

✿ 🚐 🍵

85 STONE FARM
Alverdiscott Rd, Bideford, EX39 4PN. Mr & Mrs Ray Auvray, 01237 421420, rayauvray@icloud.com. *1½m from Bideford towards Alverdiscott. From Bideford cross river using Old Bridge and turn L onto Barnstaple Rd. 2nd R onto Manteo Way and 1st L at mini r'about.* Sat 25, Sun 26 June, Sat 27, Sun 28 Aug (2-5). Adm £4, chd free. Home-made teas. Visits also by arrangement May to Aug for groups of 10+. Tours of our organic farms can also be arranged.

1 acre country garden with striking herbaceous borders, dry stone wall terracing, white garden, hot garden and dahlia beds. Extensive fully organic vegetable gardens with polytunnels and newly created ¼ acre walled garden, together with an orchard with traditional apples and pears. Farm walks to see our herd of rare breed organic Devon cattle, GOS pigs and Lleyn and Devon Longwool sheep flocks. Some gravel paths but wheelchair access to whole garden with some help.

& 🐕 ✿ 🍵

86 ♦ STONE LANE GARDENS
Stone Farm, Chagford, TQ13 8JU. Stone Lane Gardens Charitable Trust, 01647 231311, admin@stonelanegardens.com, www.stonelanegardens.com. *Halfway between Chagford & Whiddon Down, close to A382. 2.3m from Chagford, 1½m from Castle Drogo, 2½m from A30 Whiddon Down via Long Lane.* For NGS: Sat 8, Sat 15 Oct (10-6). Adm £5, chd £2.50. Light refreshments in small tea room and tea garden. For other opening times and information, please phone, email or visit garden website.

Outstanding and unusual 5 acre arboretum and water garden on edge of Dartmoor National Park. Beautiful National Collection of Betula species with lovely colourful peeling bark, from dark brown, reds, orange, pink and white. Interesting underplanting. Meadow walks and lovely views. Summer sculpture exhibition situated in the garden. Tripadvisor award winner. Near to NT Castle Drogo and garden. RHS Partner Garden. Partial wheelchair access to the gardens.

& 🐕 ✿ NPC 🍵 🧺))

87 STONELANDS HOUSE

Stonelands Bridge, Dawlish, EX7 9BL. Mr Kerim Derhalli (Owner) Mr Saul Walker (Head Gardener), 07815 807832, saulwalkerstonelands@outlook.com. *Outskirts of NW Dawlish. From A380 take junction for B3192 & follow signs for Teignmouth, after 2m L at Xrds onto Luscombe Hill, further 2m main gate on L.* **Visits by arrangement Apr to July for groups of 10 to 20. Home-made teas available as part of the tour for an extra fee. Adm £7, chd free.**

Beautiful 12 acre pleasure garden surrounding early C19 property designed by John Nash. Mature specimen trees, shrubs and rhododendrons, large formal lawn, recently landscaped herbaceous beds, vegetable garden, woodland garden, orchard with wildflower meadow and river walk. An atmospheric and delightful horticultural secret! Wheelchair access to lower area of gardens, paths through woodland, meadow and riverside walk may be unsuitable.

&. 🐕 Ⓓ ☕ 🛆

GROUP OPENING

88 TEIGNMOUTH GARDENS

Cliff Road, Teignmouth, TQ14 8TW. *½m from Teignmouth town centre. 5m E of Newton Abbot. 11m S of Exeter. Purchase ticket for all gardens at first garden visited, a map will be provided showing location of gardens and parking.* **Sat 18, Sun 19 June (11-5). Combined adm £7, chd free. Home-made teas at High Tor, Cliff Road.**

BERRY COTTAGE
Alan & Irene Ward.

7 COOMBE AVENUE
Stewart & Pat Henchie.

NEW 21 GORWAY
Mrs Christine Richman.

GROSVENOR GREEN GARDENS
Michelle & Neal Fairley.

26 HAZELDOWN ROAD
Mrs Ann Sadler.

HIGH TOR
Gill Treweek.

LOWER COOMBE COTTAGE
Tim & Tracy Armstrong.

NEW LOWER HOLCOMBE HOUSE
Joanne Sparks.

THE ORANGERY
Teignmouth Town Council, teignmouthorangery.wordpress.com.

9 THE ROWDENS
Mr Michael Brown.

SEA VISTA
Mr Tim & Mrs Shirley Williams.

65 TEIGNMOUTH ROAD
Mr Terry Rogers.

6 YANNON TERRACE
Stuart Barker & Grahame Flynn.

The picturesque coastal town of Teignmouth has 2 new gardens joining this large group, plus the beautifully restored Orangery, built in 1842. A wide range of garden styles and sizes to be explored this year from very small but inspiring manicured gardens to large wildlife havens. Features include Mediterranean courtyards, Japanese garden, greenhouses, pollinator friendly planting, exotic plants, streams and ponds, fruit and vegetable beds and stunning sea views from several of the gardens. Home-made teas can be enjoyed from the large bee and butterfly friendly garden at High Tor, overlooking the sea. If you plan to see all 13 gardens, you may wish to start on Sat. Tickets are valid for both days. Partial wheelchair access at some gardens.

&. ❀ ☕

89 TORVIEW

44 Highweek Village, Newton Abbot, TQ12 1QQ. Ms Penny Hammond, penny.hammond2@btinternet.com. *On N of Newton Abbot accessed via A38. From Plymouth: A38 to Goodstone, A383 past Hele Park, L onto Mile End Rd. From Exeter: A38 to Drumbridges then A382 past Forches X signed at r'about. R at top of hill. Locally take Highweek signs.* **Fri 8, Sat 9, Sun 10 Apr (12-5). Adm £5, chd free. Home-made teas. Visits also by arrangement Apr to Oct for groups of 12 to 25.**

Owned by two semi-retired horticulturalists: Mediterranean formal front garden with wisteria clad Georgian house, small alpine house. Rear courtyard with tree ferns, pots/troughs, lean-to 7m conservatory with tender plants and climbers. Steps to 30x20m walled garden - flowers, vegetables and trained fruit. Shade tunnel of woodlanders. Many rare/unusual plants.

❀ ☕))

90 TREETOPS

Broadclyst, Exeter, EX5 3DT. Geoffrey & Margaret Gould. *From Exeter direction on B3181 drive through Broadclyst past school, next turn R. Follow signs.* **Sat 25, Sun 26 June, Sun 21 Aug (1-5). Adm £4, chd free. Home-made teas.**

Previously an orchard this 1 acre cottage garden, which is still evolving, is bordered by a forest and set within a beautiful borrowed landscape. Incorporating an avenue of Olivia Austin roses and an old restored brick path surrounded by borders featuring traditional and unusual cottage garden plants and a pond.

&. 🐕 ☕

91 UPPER GORWELL HOUSE

Goodleigh Rd, Barnstaple, EX32 7JP. Dr J A Marston, www.gorwellhousegarden.co.uk. *¾m E of Barnstaple centre on Bratton Fleming rd. Drive entrance between 2 lodges on L coming uphill (Bear Street) approx ¾m from Barnstaple centre. Take R fork at end of long drive. New garden entrance to R of house up steep slope.* **Sun 27 Mar, Sun 1, Sun 15 May, Sun 5 June, Sun 10 July, Sun 25 Sept (2-6). Adm £6, chd free. Cream teas. Visitors are welcome to bring their own picnics.**

Created mostly since 1979, this 4 acre garden overlooking the Taw estuary has a benign microclimate which allows many rare and tender plants to grow and thrive, both in the open and in walled garden. Several strategically placed follies complement the enclosures and vistas within the garden. Mostly wheelchair access but some very steep slopes at first to get into garden.

&. 🐕 ❀ ☕ 🛆))

GROUP OPENING

92 NEW WEST CLYST BARNYARD GARDENS

Westclyst, Exeter, EX1 3TR. *From Pinhoe take B3181 towards Broadclyst. At Westclyst T-lights continue straight past speed camera 1st R onto Private Road*

Am Brooke Meadow

© Carole Drake

over M5 bridge, R into West Clyst Barnyard. **Sat 18, Sun 19 June (1-5). Combined adm £5, chd free. Home-made teas.**

NEW **6 WEST CLYST BARNYARD**
Alan & Toni Coulson.

7 WEST CLYST BARNYARD
Malcolm & Ethel Hillier.

These gardens have been planted in farmland around a converted barnyard of a medieval farm. There are 2 gardens with a wildflower meadow, wildlife ponds, bog garden, David Austin roses, magnolias and many trees and shrubs. Cars may be driven to the gate of No 7 for disabled access to the gardens but then please park in the car park.

♿ 🐕 🌼 ☕))

---

93 WHIDDON GOYLE
Whiddon Down, Okehampton, EX20 2QJ. Mr &Mrs Lethbridge.
From Whiddon Down, follow signs

for Okehampton, take 2nd exit at r'about. Whiddon Goyle is on L, signed. **Sat 4, Sun 5 June (11-4). Adm £5, chd free. Light refreshments.**
Whiddon Goyle enjoys stunning views over Dartmoor and sits 1000 ft above sea level. Built in 1930s and cleverly designed to protect its 2 acre garden against the Dartmoor weather. It enjoys many features including a rockery, croquet lawn, rose garden herbaceous borders, ponds, small vegetable and flower plot along with a pair of majestic monkey puzzle trees. Access is via a gravelled driveway on a slope.

♿ 🐕 🌼 ☕))

---

94 WHITSTONE FARM
Whitstone Lane, Bovey Tracey, TQ13 9NA. Katie & Alan Bunn, 01626 832258, klbbovey@gmail.com. *½ m N of Bovey Tracey. From A382 turn towards hospital (sign opp golf range), after ⅓ m L at swinging sign 'Private road leading to Whitstone'. Follow NGS signs.* **Sun 24 Apr, Sun**

31 July, Sun 14 Aug (1.30-4.30). Adm £6, chd free. Pre-booking essential, please visit www.ngs. org.uk for information & booking. Light refreshments. Tea and home-made cakes, gluten free option. Visits also by arrangement Apr to Sept for groups of up to 25. Pre booking essential for all openings. Mini bus and small coach access.**
Nearly 4 acres of steep hillside garden with stunning views of Haytor and Dartmoor. Snowdrops start in January followed by bluebells throughout the garden. Arboretum planted 40 yrs ago, over 200 trees from all over the world inc magnolias, camellias, acers, alders, betula, davidias and sorbus. Always colour in the garden and wonderful tree bark. Major plantings of rhododendrons and cornus. Late flowering eucryphia (National Collection) and hydrangeas. Display of architectural and metal sculptures and ornaments. Partial access to lower terraces for wheelchair users.

♿ NPC 🛏 ☕

DORSET

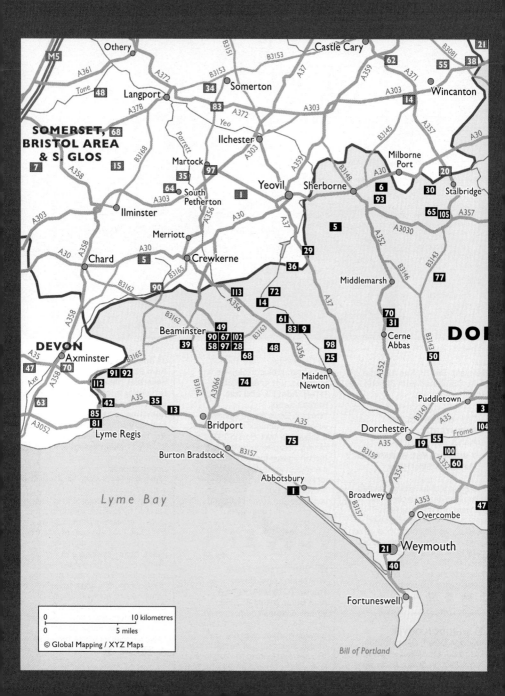

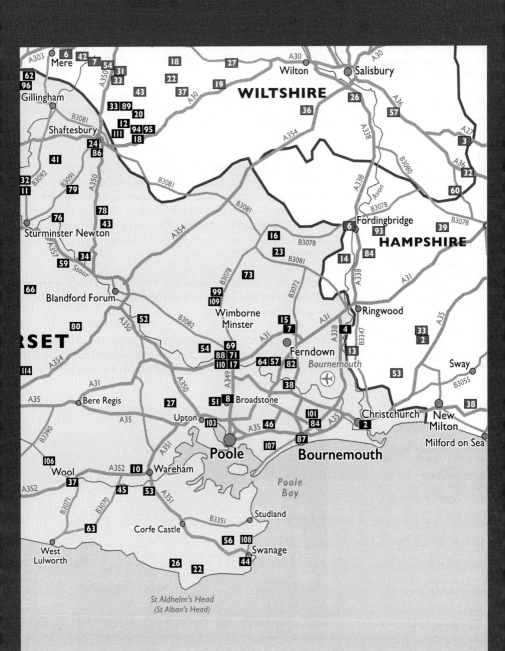

Volunteers

County Organiser
Alison Wright 01935 83652
alison.wright@ngs.org.uk

County Treasurer
Richard Smedley 01202 528286
richard@carter-coley.co.uk

Publicity & Social Media
Alison Wright (as above)

Booklet Editor
Alison Wright (as above)

Events Organiser
Trish Neale 01308 863790
trish.neale@ngs.co.uk

Photographers
Elena Librandi 07539 410423
elena.librandi@ngs.org.uk

Tony Leonard 07711 643445
tony.leonard@ngs.org.uk

Assistant County Organisers

Central East/ Wimborne
Tony Leonard 07711 643445
tony.leonard@ngs.org.uk

Central East/Poole
Phil Broomfield 07810 646123
phil.broomfield@ngs.org.uk

North East
Alexandra Davies 01747 860351
alex@theparishhouse.co.uk

North Central
Caroline Renner 01747 811140
croftfarm12@gmail.com

South East
Mary Angus 01202 872789
mary@gladestock.co.uk

North West
Annie Dove 01300 345450
anniedove1@btinternet.com

South Central
Helen Hardy 01929 471379
helliehardy@hotmail.co.uk

Fiona Johnston 07702 077200
fiona.johnston@ngs.org.uk

South West/Bridport
Christine Corson 01308 863923
christine.corson@ngs.org.uk

West Central
Alison Wright (as above)

◼ @NGS.Dorset

◼ @DorsetNGS

◉ @dorset_national_garden_scheme

Dorset is not on the way to anywhere. We have no cathedral and no motorways. The county has been inhabited forever and the constantly varying landscape is dotted with prehistoric earthworks and ancient monuments, bordered to the south by the magnificent Jurassic Coast.

Discover our cosy villages with their thatched cottages, churches and pubs. Small historic towns including Dorchester, Blandford, Sherborne, Shaftesbury and Weymouth are scattered throughout, with Bournemouth and Poole to the east being the main centres of population.

Amongst all this, we offer the visitor a wonderfully diverse collection of gardens, found in both towns and deep countryside. They are well planted and vary in size, topography and content. In between the larger ones are the tiniest, all beautifully presented by the generous garden owners who open for the National Garden Scheme. Most of the county's loveliest gardens in their romantic settings also support us.

Each garden rewards the visitor with originality and brings joy, even on the rainiest day! They are never very far away from an excellent meal and comfortable bed.

So do come, discover and explore what the gardens of Dorset have to offer with the added bonus of that welcome cup of tea and that irresistible slice of cake, or a scone laden with clotted cream and strawberry jam!

Above: Hooke Farm

OPENING DATES

All entries subject to change. For latest information check www.ngs.org.uk

Extended openings are shown at the beginning of the month.

Map locator numbers are shown to the right of each garden name.

February

Snowdrop Festival

Every day from Wednesday 23rd to Sunday 27th
Lawsbrook 59

Friday 11th
The Old Vicarage 79

Sunday 13th
The Old Vicarage 79

March

Wednesday 2nd
Knitson Old Farmhouse 56

Wednesday 9th
Knitson Old Farmhouse 56

Saturday 12th
Manor Farm, Hampreston 64

Sunday 13th
Manor Farm, Hampreston 64

Sunday 20th
Frankham Farm 29
Herons Mead 37
22 Holt Road 46
The Old Vicarage 79

April

Wednesday 6th
◆ Edmondsham House 23
Knitson Old Farmhouse 56

Saturday 9th
◆ Cranborne Manor Garden 16
Ivy House Garden 50

Sunday 10th
NEW The Hideaway 38
Ivy House Garden 50

Wednesday 13th
◆ Edmondsham House 23
Knitson Old Farmhouse 56

Thursday 14th
Horn Park 49

Sunday 17th
Herons Mead 37

Monday 18th
◆ Edmondsham House 23

Wednesday 20th
◆ Edmondsham House 23

Saturday 23rd
Chideock Manor 13

Sunday 24th
Broomhill 9
NEW ◆ Carey's Secret Garden 10
Chideock Manor 13
Frankham Farm 29
NEW The Hideaway 38
The Old Vicarage 79

Wednesday 27th
◆ Edmondsham House 23

Saturday 30th
NEW Kings Barrow 53
NEW White Cliff Manor 108

May

Sunday 1st
22 Avon Avenue 4
Herons Mead 37
Holworth Farmhouse 47
NEW Kings Barrow 53
The Manor House, Beaminster 67
NEW White Cliff Manor 108

Monday 2nd
Holworth Farmhouse 47
The Manor House, Beaminster 67
Mayfield 69
Wolverhollow 112

Tuesday 3rd
Wolverhollow 112

Wednesday 4th
Knitson Old Farmhouse 56

Saturday 7th
NEW Julia's House Children's Hospice 51
NEW Lower Silton 62
NEW Silton House 96
NEW 49 Stirling Road 101

Sunday 8th
NEW Julia's House Children's Hospice 51
The Old Rectory, Litton Cheney 75

Wednesday 11th
Knitson Old Farmhouse 56
The Old Rectory, Litton Cheney 75

Saturday 14th
NEW Falconers 27
NEW Russell-Cotes Art Gallery & Museum 87

Sunday 15th
NEW Falconers 27
Knowle Cottage 58
Mayfield 69
The Pines 82
Wincombe Park 111

Wednesday 18th
Wincombe Park 111

Saturday 21st
Edwardstowe 24
NEW Harcombe House 35
The Pines 82
NEW 49 Stirling Road 101

Sunday 22nd
Edwardstowe 24
NEW Harcombe House 35
22 Holt Road 46
The Old Rectory, Pulham 77
The Old Vicarage 79

Tuesday 24th
◆ Keyneston Mill 52

Saturday 28th
The Secret Garden and Serles House 88
Staddlestones 99

Sunday 29th
Annalal's Gallery 2
Manor Farm, Hampreston 64
Mayfield 69
Staddlestones 99

June

Thursday 2nd
Horn Park 49

Saturday 4th
The Grange 32
NEW Kings Barrow 53
The Manor House, Beaminster 67
NEW White Cliff Manor 108

Sunday 5th
Frankham Farm 29
The Grange 32
Holworth Farmhouse 47
NEW Kings Barrow 53
The Manor House, Beaminster 67
Mayfield 69
NEW White Cliff Manor 108

Tuesday 7th
NEW Eastington Farm 22
Encombe House 26
◆ Holme for Gardens 45

Wednesday 8th
Knitson Old Farmhouse 56
Old Down House 73
NEW Shute House 95

Saturday 11th
NEW Hooke Farm 48
Little Benville House 61
Manor Farm, Stourton Caundle 65
Old Down House 73
Philipston House 80
The Secret Garden and Serles House 88
Wagtails 105

Sunday 12th
22 Avon Avenue 4
NEW Carraway Barn 11
Dorchester Gardens 19
NEW Hooke Farm 48
Little Benville House 61
Manor Farm, Hampreston 64
Manor Farm, Stourton Caundle 65
Old Down House 73
Rampisham Gardens 83
Utopia 104
Wagtails 105

Wednesday 15th
NEW Ellerslie 25
Farrs 28
Knitson Old Farmhouse 56

*More than 1,200 people
have been cared for
at Y Bwthyn NGS
Macmillan Specialist
Palliative Care Unit, a
unit that would simply
not have been built
without the National
Garden Scheme funding*

THE GARDENS

1 ◆ ABBOTSBURY GARDENS
Abbotsbury, Weymouth, DT3 4LA.
Ilchester Estates, 01305 871387,
info@abbotsbury-tourism.co.uk,
www.abbotsburygardens.co.uk.
*8m W of Weymouth. From B3157
Weymouth-Bridport, 200yds W of
Abbotsbury village.* **For opening
times and information, please
phone, email or visit garden
website.**
30 acres, started in 1760 and
considerably extended in C19.
Much recent replanting. The
maritime microclimate enables
this Mediterranean and southern
hemisphere garden to grow rare and
tender plants. National Collection
of Hoherias (flowering Aug in NZ
garden). Woodland valley with ponds,
stream and hillside walk to view the
Jurassic Coast. Open all year except
for Christmas week. Featured in
Country Life and on Countrywise and
Gardeners' World. Partial wheelchair
access, some very steep paths and
rolled gravel but we have a selected
wheelchair route with sections of
tarmac hard surface.
&. 🐕 ⚘ ♿ NPC 🍵

2 ANNALAL'S GALLERY
25 Millhams Street, Christchurch,
BH23 1DN. Anna & Lal Sims,
www.annasims.co.uk. *Town centre.
Park in Saxon Square PCP - exit
to Millhams St via alley at side of
church.* Sun 29 May, Sun 26 June,
Sun 24 July, Sun 7, Sun 28 Aug,
Sun 11 Sept, Sun 4, Sun 11 Dec
(2-4). Adm £3, chd free.
Enchanting 150 yr old cottage, home
of two Royal Academy artists. 32ft
x 12½ ft garden on 3 patio levels.
Pencil gate leads to colourful scented
Victorian walled garden. Sculptures
and paintings hide among the flowers
and shrubs. Unusual studio and
garden room.

3 NEW ◆ ATHELHAMPTON
HOUSE & GARDENS
Athelhampton, Dorchester,
DT2 7LG. Giles Keating,
01305 848363,
enquiries@athelhampton.co.uk,
www.athelhampton.co.uk. *5m
E of Dorchester signed off A35 at
Puddletown.* **For opening times and
information, please phone, email or
visit garden website.**
The gardens date from 1891 and
include the Great Court with 12 giant
yew topiary pyramids overlooked by
two terraced pavilions. This glorious

Grade I architectural garden is full of
vistas and surprises with spectacular
fountains and the River Piddle flowing
through it. Wheelchair map to guide
you around the gardens. There are
accessible toilets in Visitor Centre.
Please see our Accessibility Guide on
our website.
&. 🐕 ⚘ ♿ ♨ 🍵 🧺

4 22 AVON AVENUE
Avon Castle, Ringwood,
BH24 2BH. Terry & Dawn
Heaver, 01425 473970,
dawnandterry@yahoo.com,
dawnandterry@yahoo.com. *Past
Ringwood from E A31 turn L after
garage, L again into Matchams Ln,
Avon Castle 1m on L. A31 from west
turn R into Boundary Ln, then L into
Matchams Ln, Avon Ave ½ m on R.*
Sun 1 May, Sun 12 June, Sun 17
July, Sun 28 Aug (12-5). Adm £5,
chd free. Home-made teas. Visits
also by arrangement May to Sept.
Japanese themed water garden
featuring granite sculptures, ponds,
waterfalls, azaleas, rhododendrons
cloud topiary and a collection of
goldfish and water lilies. Children
must be under parental supervision
due to large, deep water pond. No
dogs please.
⚘ 🍵

SPECIAL EVENT

5 [NEW] BEMBURY FARM

Bembury Lane, Thornford, Sherborne, DT9 6QF. Sir John & Lady Garnier, 01935 873551, dodie.garnier32@gmail.com. *Bottom of Bembury Lane, N of Thornford village. 6m E of Yeovil, 3m W of Sherborne on Yetminster road. Follow signs in village. Parking in field.* Wed 22 June, Wed 6 July (2-4). Adm £20, chd free. Pre-booking essential, please visit www.ngs.org.uk for information & booking. Home-made teas. Visits also by arrangement May to Sept for groups of 10+.
Created and developed since 1996 this peaceful garden has lawns and large herbaceous borders informally planted with interesting perennials around unusual trees, shrubs and roses. Large collection of clematis; also a pretty woodland walk, wildflower corner, lily pond, oak circle, yew hedges with peacock, clipped hornbeam round kitchen garden and plenty of seating to sit and reflect. A limited number of tickets have been made available for these 2 special event days, including a private tour of the gardens and grounds. On arrival Sir John & Lady Garnier will provide an introductory talk on the gardens. Please arrive promptly at 2pm. Home-made teas served from 3pm.

&. 🐎 ✿ ☕))

6 BLACK SHED

Blackmarsh Farm, Dodds Cross, Sherborne, DT9 4JX. Paul & Helen Stickland, blackshedflowers.blogspot.com/. *From Sherborne, follow A30 towards Shaftesbury. Black Shed approx 1m E at Blackmarsh Farm, on L, next to The Toy Barn. Large car park shared with The Toy Barn.* Sun 24 July, Sun 28 Aug (1-5). Adm £5, chd free.
Over 200 colourful and productive flower beds growing a sophisticated selection of cut flowers and foliage to supply florists and the public, for weddings, events and occasions throughout the seasons. Traditional garden favourites, delphiniums, larkspur, foxgloves, scabious and dahlias alongside more unusual perennials, foliage plants and grasses, creating a stunning and unique display. A warm welcome and generous advice on creating your own cut flower garden is offered. Easy access from gravel car park. Wide grass pathways enabling access for wheelchairs. Gently sloping site.

7 BROOK VIEW CARE HOME

Riverside Road, West Moors, Ferndown, BH22 0LQ. Charles Hubberstey, www.brookviewcare.co.uk. *Past village shops, L into Riverside Rd, Brook View Care Home is on R after 100 metres. Parking onsite or nearby roads.* Sat 20, Sun 21 Aug (11-5). Adm £3.50, chd free. Home-made teas.
Our colourful and vibrant garden is spread over two main areas, one warm and sunny, the other cooler and shadier. A cool fountain area, games lawn and mixed borders, then walking past our greenhouse leads to the fruit and vegetable gardens. Produce is eagerly used by the kitchen, and residents will help out with the production of the bedding plants, all expertly managed by our gardener.

&. 🐎 ☕ 🛋))

8 10 BROOKDALE CLOSE

Broadstone, BH18 9AA. Michael & Sylvia Cooper. *Located just 100yds from centre of Broadstone, Brookdale Close is on Higher Blandford Rd, with additional parking in next road, Fairview Cres.* Sat 20, Sun 21 Aug (2-5). Adm £4, chd free. Home-made teas.
Host garden for BBC Gardeners' World August 2021, described as 'a work of art and utterly gorgeous'. Our 75ftx 50ft wildlife friendly garden, with hidden pond and tumbling waterfall, offers a dazzling display of colour, with a seamless transition from cottage to tropical, with a different perspective at every turn.

✿ ☕

9 BROOMHILL

Rampisham, Dorchester, DT2 0PU. Mr & Mrs D Parry, 01935 83266, carol.parry2@btopenworld.com. *11m NW of Dorchester. From Dorchester A37 Yeovil, 9m L Evershot. From Yeovil A37 Dorchester, 7m R Evershot. Follow signs. From Crewkerne A356, 1½ m after Rampisham Garage L Rampisham. Follow signs.* Sun 24 Apr, Sun 10 July, Thur 11 Aug (2-5). Adm £5, chd free. Home-made teas. Opening with Rampisham Gardens on Sun 12 June. Visits also by arrangement May to Aug for groups of 8+.
Once a farmyard now a delightful, tranquil garden set in 2 acres. Clipped box, island beds and borders planted with shrubs, roses, grasses, masses of unusual perennials and choice

annuals to give vibrancy and colour into the autumn. Lawns and paths lead to a less formal area with large wildlife pond, meadow, shaded areas, bog garden, late summer border. Orchard and vegetable garden. Gravel entrance, the rest is grass, some gentle slopes.

&. 🐎 ✿ 🛋 ☕ 🛏

10 [NEW] ◆ CAREY'S SECRET GARDEN

Wareham, BH20 7PG. Simon Constantine, hello@careyssecretgarden.co.uk, www.careyssecretgarden.co.uk. *We send out the exact location once you have booked a ticket. (it's within a 3m radius of Wareham, 11m from Poole & 19m from Dorchester).* For NGS: Sun 24 Apr (10-3.30). Adm £7.50, chd £2.75. Pre-booking essential, please email hello@careyssecretgarden.co.uk or visit https://www.careyssecretgarden.co.uk for information & booking. Light refreshments in the walled garden. Please feel free to bring along your own re-usable cup to help us reduce waste. For other opening times and information, please email or visit garden website.
Behind a 150 yr old wall, situated just outside of Wareham, sits 3 ½ acres in the midst of transformation. Left untouched for more than 40 yrs, this garden is about to flourish again, with a focus on permaculture and rewilding. Further bookings can be made for year-round visits at www.careyssecretgarden.co.uk - open Thurs- Sat (10am - 4pm). Those with mobility issues are welcome to contact us in advance and we can tailor your visit to your needs accordingly.

&. ✿ 🛋))

11 [NEW] CARRAWAY BARN

Carraway Lane, Marnhull, Sturminster Newton, DT10 1NJ. Catherine & Mark Turner, 07905 960281, Carrawaybarn.ngs@gmail.com. *From Shaftesbury A30 & B3092. ½ m after The Crown turn R into Carraway Lane. From Sturminster Newton B3092 2.8m turn L into Carraway Lane. Bear R behind 1st house, until in large courtyard.* Sun 12, Thur 16, Sun 19 June (2-5). Adm £6, chd free. Pre-booking essential, please visit www.ngs.org.uk for information & booking. Visits also by arrangement in June

for groups of up to 20.
Set in 2 acres, around C19 former barn. In recent years, a natural swimming pond, large shrub border, waterfall and wildflower area (with beehives) have been created. Shady woodland walks, a white border of hydrangeas, hostas and ferns lead to the beautiful established walled garden, where deep borders are planted with roses, peonies, alliums, geraniums and topiary, encircling a water lily pond. Partial wheelchair access; gravelled courtyard and walled garden, gently sloping lawns.

  🚫 ✿ 🍵))

🄲 NEW CASTLE RINGS
Donhead St. Mary, Shaftesbury, SP7 9BZ. Michael Thomas. *2 m N of Shaftesbury. A350 Shaftesbury/ Warminster road, past Wincombe Business Park. 1st R signed Wincombe & Donhead St Mary.* **Sun 21 Aug (2-5). Adm £5, chd free. Home-made teas at village hall in centre of Donhead St Mary.**
Small, long garden in two parts laid out beside an Iron Age hillfort with spectacular views. A formal area with

colourful planting and pots is followed by a paved area with more pots and steps leading through informal planting. Topiary, roses and clematis on tripods.

🄱 CHIDEOCK MANOR
Chideock, Bridport, DT6 6LF. Mr & Mrs Howard Coates, 07885 551795, deirdrecoates9@gmail.com. *2m W of Bridport on A35. In centre of village turn N at church. The Manor is ¼m along this rd on R.* **Sat 23, Sun 24 Apr, Sat 18, Sun 19 June (2-5). Adm £10, chd free. Cream teas. Visits also by arrangement for groups of 10 to 30.**
6/7 acres of formal and informal gardens. Bog garden beside stream and series of ponds. Yew hedges and mature trees. Lime and crab apple walks, herbaceous borders, colourful rose and clematis arches, fernery and nuttery. Walled vegetable garden and orchard. Woodland and lakeside walks. Fine views. Partial wheelchair access.

  🚫 🐕 🚗 🍵

SPECIAL EVENT

🄸 NEW CORSCOMBE HOUSE
Corscombe, DT2 0NU. James Bartos. *3½m W of Beaminster. Do not follow Sat Nav. Corscombe House is next to the church. On A356 take southern of 2 signed turnings E to Corscombe, then R signed to the church; or on A37 turn W signed to Corscombe, then L signed to the church.* **Sun 3 July (2-4). Adm £20, chd free. Pre-booking essential, please visit www.ngs.org.uk for information & booking.**
Strong architectural hedges define multiple rooms on different levels with yew columns, parterre and cool beds in the lower garden. Reflecting pool and hot beds in the upper garden. Wildflower meadow and orchard. Part walled vegetable garden and secret garden with Mediterranean planting and lemons in pots. A limited number of tickets have been made available for this special one day event. There will be an introductory talk on the history and development of the gardens on arrival and guidance given on exploring the gardens and grounds.

🐕

Carey's Secret Garden

15 COTTESMORE FARM

Newmans Lane, West Moors, Ferndown, BH22 0LW. Paul & Valerie Guppy, 07413 925372, paulguppy@googlemail.com. *1m N of West Moors. Off B3072 Bournemouth to Verwood rd. Car parking in owner's field.* **Visits by arrangement July & Aug. Visits from 2pm-5pm. Adm £5, chd free. Home-made teas.**

Gardens of over an acre, created from scratch over 20 yrs. Wander through a plantsman's tropical paradise of giant gunneras, bananas, towering bamboos and over 100 palm trees, into a floral extravaganza. Large borders and sweeping island beds overflowing with phlox, heliopsis, helenium and much more combine to drown you in scent and colour. Wheelchair users please ask on arrival to make use of level route through main drive gate to avoid steps.

16 ◆ CRANBORNE MANOR GARDEN

Cranborne, BH21 5PP. Viscount Cranborne, 01725 517289, info@cranborne.co.uk, www.cranborne.co.uk. *10m N of Wimborne on B3078. Enter garden via Cranborne Garden Centre, on L as you enter top of village of Cranborne.* **For NGS: Sat 9 Apr, Sat 9 July (9.30-5). Adm £6.50, chd £1. Light refreshments. For other opening times and information, please phone, email or visit garden website. Donation to other charities.**

Beautiful and historic garden laid out in C17 by John Tradescant and enlarged in C20, featuring several gardens surrounded by walls and yew hedges: blue and white garden, cottage style and mount gardens, water and wild garden. Many interesting plants, with fine trees and avenues. Mostly wheelchair access.

17 DEANS COURT

Deans Court Lane, Wimborne Minster, BH21 1EE. Sir William Hanham, 01202 849314, info@deanscourt.org, www.deanscourt.org. *Pedestrian entrance (no parking) is on Deans Court Lane, BH21 1EE. Vehicle entrance via Poole Road (BH21 1QF).* **Wed 22 June, Wed 20 July (11-5). Adm £5, chd free. Donation to Friends of Victoria Hospital, Wimborne.**

13 acres of peaceful, partly wild gardens in ancient monastic setting with mature specimen trees, Saxon fish pond, herb garden, orchard and apiary beside River Allen close to town centre. First Soil Association accredited garden, within C18 serpentine walls. The Permaculture system has been introduced here with chemical free produce supplying the Deans Court café (open) nearby. For disabled access, please contact us in advance of visiting to help us understand your specific needs regarding accessibility, and work out the best plan. Follow signs within grounds for disabled parking closer to gardens. Deeper gravel on some paths. See website extended description re access.

18 NEW DONHEAD HALL

Donhead St Mary, Shaftesbury, SP7 9DS. Paul & Penny Brewer. *4m E of Shaftesbury. A30 towards Shaftesbury. In Ludwell turn R opp brown sign to Tollard Royal. Follow rd for ³⁄₄ m and bear R at T-junction. Donhead Hall 50 yds on L on corner of Watery Lane, cream gates.* **Sun 2 Oct (2-5). Adm £7, chd free. Home-made teas.**

Walled garden overlooking deer park. The house and garden are built into the side of a hill with uninterrupted views to Cranborne Chase. Martin Lane Fox designed the terracing and advised on the landscaping of the gardens which are on 4 different levels. Large mixed borders and specimen trees, kitchen garden with glasshouses.

GROUP OPENING

19 DORCHESTER GARDENS

Fordington, Dorchester, DT1 1ED. msomerville162@gmail.com. *Nr to Salisbury Fields, St Georges Church & Fordington Green, accessed by a lane leading to the large park, Salisbury Fields, between 10 &12 South Walks Rd. Follow signs to parking.* **Sun 12 June, Sun 10 July (2-5). Combined adm £5, chd free. Cream teas in Bean on the Green Cafe.**

6 SOUTH WALKS ROAD
Paul Cairnes.

8 SOUTH WALKS ROAD
Mrs Margaret Somerville.

18 SOUTH WALKS ROAD
Sandra Manfield.

18 South Walks Road: Tiny Victorian front garden with mature olive trees: back garden, a corridor of stunning Japanese acers and other exotic trees leading into the park. 6 South Walks Rd: Large mid C20 walled garden, with ongoing restoration. Peonies, magnolias, climbing and shrub roses, *Wisteria sinensis* and a water feature. 8 South Walks Road: Small, sheltered garden. Upper level *Heptacodium miconoides*; lower courtyard garden with mature climbers, inc *Hydrangea seemanii* and species camellias. Cream teas at the Bean on the Green. Follow signs.

20 EAST END FARM

Barkers Hill, Semley, Shaftesbury, SP7 9BJ. Celia & Piers Petrie. *From A350 take exit to Semley & continue to church. Take turning next to church towards Tisbury then 1st R to Barkers Hill. Continue along lane (1m) continue up hill East End Farm on R.* **Sun 19 June (2-5). Adm £5, chd free. Home-made teas.**

Exquisite wildflower meadow started 20 yrs ago. 2 acres on spectacular site with views to Pyt House. Orchids, yellow rattle, grass vetchling, ragged robin, agrimony, meadow cranesbill, various vetches, amongst many other species. Very pretty and relaxed garden with wild areas. Wheelchair access to garden only but views from garden to wildflower meadow.

21 NEW 23 EAST WYLD ROAD

Weymouth, DT4 0RP. Jenny & Charles Stiling. *From A354 Weymouth Relief Road take B3157 Granby Way then B3158 Radipole Lane, in ½ m turn L into East Wyld Rd, house is on the L.* **Sun 10, Sat 16 July (12.30-5). Adm £4.50, chd free.**

A real plantsperson's suburban garden full of an array of floral colour. A meandering pathway draws you through a long garden filled with water features, sitting places and many unusual plants. Patio and seating areas near the house and a lovely summerhouse at the end of the garden with terracing.

SPECIAL EVENT

22 NEW EASTINGTON FARM

Worth Matravers, Swanage, BH19 3LF. Rachel James. *In Corfe Castle village take the R turn signed Kingston. Take the 2nd R signed Worth Matravers. Eastington Farm is 650 metres on L, long gravel drive & parking at the end of the field.* Tue 7 June (10.30-5). Combined adm with Encombe House £120. Pre-booking essential, please visit www.ngs. org.uk for information & booking. Please arrive on time at 10.30am for tea, coffee and light refreshments. The garden has been created over the last 25 yrs and sits within dry Purbeck stone walls with views to the sea. It is divided into different garden rooms with planting themes, all surrounding the C16/17 house. These include more formal yew hedge pyramids, lonicera balls and cloud topiary alongside soft floral planting, with an orchard of wild flowers, and a working vegetable garden. A buffet lunch with wine will be provided at nearby Encombe House. Please arrive there between 12.30 and 1pm.

🍵 ♿

23 ◆ EDMONDSHAM HOUSE

Edmondsham, Wimborne, BH21 5RE. Mrs Julia Smith, 01725 517207, julia.edmondsham@homeuser.net. *9m NE of Wimborne. 9m W of Ringwood. Between Cranborne & Verwood. Edmondsham off B3081. Wheelchair access and disabled parking at West front door.* For NGS: Every Wed 6 Apr to 27 Apr (2-5). Mon 18 Apr (2-5). Every Wed 5 Oct to 26 Oct (2-5). Adm £4, chd £1. Tea, coffee, cake and soft drinks, 3.30 to 4.00 p.m. in Edmondsham House, Weds. only. For other opening times and information, please phone or email. Donation to Prama Care.
6 acres of mature gardens, grounds, views, trees, rare shrubs, spring bulbs and shaped hedges surrounding C16/C18 house, much to explore inc C12 church adjacent to garden. Large Victorian walled garden is productive and managed organically (since 1984) using 'no dig' vegetable beds. Wide herbaceous borders planted for seasonal colour. Traditional potting shed, cob wall, sunken greenhouse. Coaches by appointment only. Some grass and gravel paths.

♿ ♿ 🚌 🍵

24 EDWARDSTOWE

50-52 Bimport, Shaftesbury, SP7 8BA. Mike & Louise Madgwick. *Park in town's main car park. Walk along Bimport (B3091) 500 metres, Edwardstowe last house on L.* Sat 21, Sun 22 May (10.30-4.30). Adm £4, chd free.
Parts of the garden were extensively remodelled during 2018, a new greenhouse and potting shed have been added, along with changing pathways and the vegetable garden layout. Long borders have been replanted in places with trees managed letting in more light.

🐓 ♿ 🔊

SPECIAL EVENT

25 NEW ELLERSLIE

Cattistock, Dorchester, DT2 0JL. Sue & David Orr. *From Maiden Newton 1st house on L after cricket ground. Parking through gate in field on L before the house (signed).* Wed 15 June, Wed 24 Aug (11-12.30). Adm £20. Pre-booking essential, please visit www.ngs.org.uk for information & booking. Open nearby Farrs, Beaminster 2.30-4.30pm.
A large restored C19 walled garden with formal lawn and paths with box/yew features on 3 sides framed by densely planted borders, north and south facing beds with coordinating cool tones, the west facing longer border divided by a water feature and warm colours. All planted for year-round colour. The 4th side is a wide terrace with 2 rose borders and further planting against the house. Ancient wisteria around the house itself. Outside the walls - mown grass, large fruit cage, cutting bed, fruit trees and a recently planted terraced area with specimen trees for autumn colour.

♿

SPECIAL EVENT

26 ENCOMBE HOUSE

Kingston, Corfe Castle, Wareham, BH20 5LW. James & Arabella Gaggero. *Drive through Corfe turn R to Kingston. Turn R at The Scott Arms. Drive past church, 300yds 2nd turning L. Turn onto tarmac driveway signed Encombe. Follow signs for parking.* Tue 7 June (10.30-5). Combined adm with Eastington Farm £120, chd free. Pre-booking essential, please visit www.ngs.

org.uk for information & booking. Light buffet lunch with wines.
The historic Encombe House and Estate is nestled within a unique stunning valley in the Purbeck hills. The garden has been extensively redeveloped since 2009, with a modern, sympathetic design for the garden by Tom Stuart-Smith. The main garden to the south of the house includes large sweeping borders filled with grasses and perennials, alongside extensive lawns, lake and deep herbaceous beds. A limited number of tickets have been made available for this special one day event and private tour of the gardens and grounds. Following your visit to Eastington Farm pls make your way to Encombe where there will be a light buffet lunch, hosted by the owners, James & Arabella Gaggero. After lunch an introductory talk will be given and then there will be the opportunity to explore the gardens accompanied by the owners and gardening team.

D ♿

27 NEW FALCONERS

89 High Street, Lytchett Matravers, Poole, BH16 6BJ. Hazel & David Dent. *6m W from Poole. Garden is past village hall at end of High St, on L. No parking at the garden, please park considerately in the village.* Sat 14, Sun 15 May (10.30-4.30). Adm £3.50, chd free. Drinks & home-made cakes.
Behind the gate of 150 yr old Falconers Cottage lies a ¼ acre mature garden with some interesting plants. The characterful cottage and garden have been cared for and enhanced by the current custodians. As you wander round the many aspects, inc pond, herbaceous bed, climbers and vegetable plot, you will find restful areas to sit and enjoy this garden in spring.

🐓 ♿ 🔊

You can make a difference! Join our Great British Garden Party fundraising campaign and raise money for some of the best-loved nursing and health charities. Visit ngs.org. uk/gardenparty to find out how you can get involved

Athelhampton House & Gardens

SPECIAL EVENT

28 FARRS

3, Whitcombe Rd, Beaminster, DT8 3NB. John Makepeace, 01308 862204, info@johnmakepeacefurniture.com, www.johnmakepeacefurniture.com. *Southern edge of Beaminster. On B3163. Car parking in the Square or Yarn Barton Car Park, or side streets of Beaminster.* **Wed 15 June, Wed 24 Aug (2.30-4.30). Adm £40. Pre-booking essential, please visit www.ngs.org.uk for information & booking. Cream teas in the house or garden, weather dependent. Open nearby Ellerslie, Cattistock 11-12.30pm. Visits also by arrangement June to Sept for groups of 12 to 24. Donation to V & A.**
Enjoy several distinctive walled gardens, rolling lawns, sculpture and giant topiary around one of Beaminster's historic town houses. John's inspirational grasses garden, Jennie's riotous potager with an oak fruit cage. Glasshouse, straw bale studio, geese in orchard. Remarkable trees, planked and seasoning in open sided barn for future furniture commissions. A limited number of tickets have been made available for these two special afternoon openings, hosted by John and Jennie Makepeace. There will be a warm welcome from John at 2.30pm in the main rooms of the house, with a talk on his furniture design and recent commissions. This will be followed by the opportunity to wander through the beautiful walled gardens. At 3.30pm, Jennie will give a talk on plants and this will be followed by a cream tea served in the house. Some gravel paths, alternative wheelchair route through orchard.

  ♿ ✿ 🚌 🚗 ☕

29 FRANKHAM FARM

Ryme Intrinseca, Sherborne, DT9 6JT. Susan Ross MBE, 07594 427365, neilandsusanross@gmail.com. *3m S of Yeovil. Just off A37 - turn next to Hamish's signed to Ryme Intrinseca, go over small bridge and up hill, drive is on L.* **Sun 20 Mar, Sun 24 Apr, Sun 5 June, Sun 16 Oct (12-5). Adm £6, chd free. Light refreshments.**
3½ acre garden, created since 1960 by the late Jo Earle for year-round interest. This large and lovely garden is filled with a wide variety of well grown plants, roses, unusual labelled shrubs and trees. Productive vegetable garden. Clematis and other climbers. Spring bulbs through to autumn colour, particularly oaks. Sorry, no dogs. Ramp available for the two steps to the garden. Modern WCs including disabled.

  ♿ 🚗 🚌 ☕ 🔊

30 FRITH HOUSE

Stalbridge, DT10 2SD. Mr & Mrs Patrick Sclater, 01963 250809, rosalynsclater@btinternet.com. *5m E of Sherborne. Between Milborne Port & Stalbridge. From A30 1m, follow sign to Stalbridge. From Stalbridge 2m and turn W by PO.* **Visits by arrangement May to July for groups of 10+. Adm £5, chd free. Home-made teas.**
Approached down a long drive with fine views. 4 acres of garden around Edwardian house and self-contained hamlet. Range of mature trees, lakes and flower borders. House terrace edged by rose border and featuring Lutyensesque wall fountain and game larder. Well-stocked kitchen gardens. Woodland walks with masses of bluebells in spring. Garden with pretty walks set amidst working farm. Accessible gravel paths.

  ♿ ☕ 🔊

31 GILLANS

Minterne Parva, nr Dorchester, DT2 7AP. Robert & Sabina ffrench Blake, 01300 342077, sfb@gillans.net. *N of Cerne Abbas off A352, plenty of parking. Signed off main road - 200 yds to gate on L.* **Visits by arrangement Mar to Oct for groups of 5+. Adm £6, chd free. Teas served with biscuits, coffee and squash also available.**
Hidden 5 acre garden set in deep valley beside ponds and River Cerne; surrounded by ancient trees with borrowed landscape. Spring bulbs and blossom with species magnolia and cornus. Carpets of primroses around camellias and rhododendrons. Steep paths, stout footwear recommended! Partially replanted over past 6yrs. Formal beds, pots, climbing roses, wisteria and productive vegetable garden surround house. Dogs on leads.

32 THE GRANGE

Burton Street, Marnhull, Sturminster Newton, DT10 1PS. Francesca Pratt. *8m SW from Shaftesbury take A30 and B3092 to Marnhull, turn R into Sodom Lane. From S B3092 to Marnhall turn L into Church St & follow NGS signs.* **Sat 4, Sun 5 June (2-5). Adm £5, chd free. Home-made teas.**
This will be the second year of the newly laid out terrace and twin borders where a new planting scheme for 2022 is planned. The woodland area continues to develop.

33 GROVE HOUSE

Semley, Shaftesbury, SP7 9AP. Judy & Peter Williamson, 07976 391723, judy@judywilliamson.net. *A350 turn to Semley. Grove House approx ½m on L just before railway bridge. From Semley village leave pub on R go under railway bridge (approx ⅓m) Grove House 2nd on R.* **Visits by arrangement June to Aug for groups of up to 20. Adm £10, chd free.**
Classic English garden divided into rooms. Yew hedges and topiary. Rose garden. Large herbaceous border. Late summer hot garden with grasses. Lawns. Mown walks through specimen trees. Several good places to eat nearby.

34 HANFORD SCHOOL

Child Okeford, Blandford Forum, DT11 8HN. Rory & Georgina Johnston. *From Blandford take A350 to Shaftesbury; 2m after Stourpaine turn L for Hanford. From Shaftesbury take A350 to Poole; after Iwerne Courtney turn R to Hanford. NGS signage from A350 & A357.* **Sun 26 June (2-4.30). Adm £5, chd free. Home-made teas.**
Perhaps the only school in England with a working kitchen garden growing quantities of seasonal vegetables, fruit and flowers for the table. The rolling lawns host sports matches, gymnastics, dance and plays while ancient cedars look on. The stable clock chimes the hour and the chapel presides over it all. Teas in Great Hall (think Hogwarts). What a place to go to school or visit. Several steps/ramp to main house. No wheelchair access to WC.

35 NEW HARCOMBE HOUSE

Pitman's Lane, Morcombelake, Bridport, DT6 6EB. John & Rachael Willmott. *4m W of Bridport - do not follow SatNav. A35 from Bridport: R to Whitchurch Canonicorum just past The Artwave Gallery. Immed R, bear L into Pitmans Lane. Approx 800m, park in paddock on L.* **Sat 21, Sun 22 May, Sat 13, Sun 14 Aug (1-6). Adm £5, chd free. Home-made teas.**
Landscaped into hillside 500ft above the Char Valley with spectacular views across Charmouth and Lyme Bay. Steeply sloping site comprises ¾ acre formal garden and ½ acre wild garden. The beautiful ¾ acre garden has been rediscovered, restored and replanted in natural and relaxed style over last 15 yrs with an abundance of shrubs and perennials, many unusual and visually stunning. Majestic rhododendrons and azaleas complement spring bulbs and bluebells in a blaze of colour in May/June and in Aug the beautiful hydrangeas and eucryphia are the stars of the garden. Challenging for the less mobile visitor and definitely unsuitable for wheelchairs and buggies.

SPECIAL EVENT

36 NEW HARVARD FARM

Closworth Road, Halstock, Yeovil, BA22 9SZ. Dilly & Tim Hobson. *About 5m S of Yeovil on A37 turn westwards to Closworth. (Do not take previous signs to Halstock). Harvard is approx 1m beyond Closworth.* **Wed 22 June (2.30-4.30). Adm £30, chd free. Pre-booking essential, please visit www.ngs.org.uk for information & booking. Home made teas inc in adm.**
Created from farm yards in 1993, on a very exposed site, by planting shelter belts, demolishing buildings and removing concrete. Now mature but always changing, features include the Millennium Mount, an apple tunnel, artwork by Tim Hobson and different topiary styles. Jake Hobson, founder of Niwaki, has introduced a Japanese influence to evergreens which contrasts well with English planting. A limited number of tickets have been made available for this special one day event. Please arrive on time at 2.30pm for an introductory talk on the history and development of the gardens and guidance given on exploring the gardens and grounds.

37 HERONS MEAD

East Burton Road, East Burton, Wool, BH20 6HF. Ron & Angela Millington, 01929 463872, ronamillington@btinternet.com. *6m W of Wareham on A352. Approaching Wool from Wareham, turn R just before level Xing into East Burton Rd. Herons Mead ¾m on L.* **Sun 20 Mar, Sun 17 Apr, Sun 1 May, Sun 18 Sept (2-5). Adm £4, chd free. Home-made teas. Visits also by arrangement Mar to Sept for groups of 10 to 25.**
½ acre plantlover's garden full of interest from spring (bulbs, many hellebores, pulmonaria, fritillaries) through abundant summer perennials, old roses scrambling through trees and late seasonal exuberant plants amongst swathes of tall grasses. Wildlife pond and plants to attract bees, butterflies, etc. Tiny woodland. Cacti. Small wheelchairs can gain partial access - as far as the tea house.

38 NEW **THE HIDEAWAY**
37 Markham Avenue, Bournemouth, BH10 7HL. Mr Tony Wetherall. *Cul-de-sac location with limited parking outside the property.* **Sun 10, Sun 24 Apr (2-6). Adm £3, chd free. Home-made teas.**
A small English style front and back garden, with a hint of the cottage feel. The initial layout was planned in 2005, and despite some smaller changes has remained to plan. The front garden is a nautical spring garden with an assortment of bulbs arranged within neat borders. The back garden has a more classical themed design. This is a bungalow property with a level tarmac driveway linking the front and back gardens. Access to the back garden is through the side gate.

39 **HIGHER BRIMLEY COOMBE FARM**
Stoke Abbott, Beaminster, DT8 3JZ. Linda & Will Bowditch. *1m W of Stoke Abbott. On B3162, 2m S of Broadwindsor, 5.7m N of Bridport.* **Thur 8, Sun 11 Sept (2-5). Adm £5, chd free. Cream teas.**
This is a new garden of just over an acre, planted over the last 5 yrs to give year-round interest. Rose and herbaceous borders surround the house and new prairie styled planting blends into the orchard where mown paths wind through the long grass. It is an open site at 500ft on Lewesdon Hill with stunning views across Marshwood Vale to the sea. Garden to front is grass and flat, other areas are sloped so help with wheelchair may be required.

40 **6 HILLCREST ROAD**
Weymouth, DT4 9JP. Helen & Michael Toft. *Via Weymouth take A345 towards Portland, L at Rylands Lane, last L at bottom of hill 3rd bungalow on R. Via Bridport take B13156 to W'mth follow signs to Portland, L at A345, R at Rylands Lane.* **Sat 16, Sun 17 July (1-5). Adm £4, chd free. Home-made teas.**
A suburban garden with the sea at the end, allows the cultivation of some exotic plants inc Strelitzia, Banana and *Cobaea scandens*. Fish pond, greenhouse, mature fruit trees, vegetable patch and soft fruit. Hot bed nearest the house is balanced by white bed at bottom of lawn. Other beds with colour themes and a long grass/wildflower patch at the end.

41 **HILLTOP**
Woodville, Stour Provost, Gillingham, SP8 5LY. Josse & Brian Emerson, www.hilltopgarden.co.uk. *7m N of Sturminster Newton, 5m W of Shaftesbury. On B3092 turn E at Stour Provost Xrds, signed Woodville. After 1¼m thatched cottage on R. On A30, 4m W of Shaftesbury, turn S opp Kings Arms. 2nd turning on R signed Woodville, 100 yds on L.* **Every Sun 17 July to 31 July (2-6). Every Sun 14 Aug to 21 Aug (2-6). Adm £3.50, chd free. Home-made teas.**
Summer at Hilltop is a gorgeous riot of colour and scent, the old thatched cottage barely visible amongst the flowers. Unusual annuals and perennials grow alongside the traditional and familiar, boldly combining to make a spectacular display, which attracts an abundance of wildlife. Always something new, the unique, gothic garden loo a great success.

42 NEW ◆ **HOGCHESTER FARM**
Axminster Road, Charmouth, Bridport, DT6 6BY. Mr Rob Powell. *A35 Charmouth Rd, follow dual carriageway and take turning at signs for Hogchester Farm.* **For NGS: Sat 25 June, Sat 16 July (9-6). Adm £4, chd £1. Café on hillside offering tea, coffee, soft drinks, cakes and light refreshments.**
Hogchester Farm is a collaboration between those seeking connection with nature and themselves through conservation therapy and the arts. The 75 acre old dairy farm has been largely gifted to nature which has helped to preserve the overflowing abundance of natural life. Having worked closely with the Dorset Wildlife Trust, Hogchester Farm has been able to preserve wild meadows and wilding areas which are filled with local flora and fauna including wild orchids, foxgloves and primroses. The farm offers something for everyone, making a great family day out with a treasure hunt for children in the wild meadow area, many animals including rare breed sheep, goats, pigs and horses, as well as horticulture based therapy for general mental health and well-being.

43 **THE HOLLOW, BLANDFORD FORUM**
Tower Hill, Iwerne Minster, Blandford Forum, DT11 8NJ. Sue Le Prevost. *Between Blandford & Shaftesbury. Follow signs on A350 to Iwerne Minster. Turn off at Talbot Inn, continue straight to The Chalk, bear R along Watery Lane for parking in Parish Field on R. 5 min uphill walk to house.* **Sat 18, Sun 19, Wed 22 June (2-5). Adm £4, chd free. Home-made cakes and gluten-free available.**
Hillside cottage garden built on chalk, about ⅓ acre with an interesting variety of plants in borders that line the numerous sloping pathways. Water features for wildlife and well placed seating areas to sit back and enjoy the views. Productive fruit and vegetable garden in converted paddock with raised beds and greenhouses. A high maintenance garden which is constantly evolving. Use of different methods to plant steep banks.

44 **THE HOLLOW, SWANAGE**
25 Newton Road, Swanage, BH19 2EA. Suzanne Nutbeem, 01929 423662, gdnsuzanne@gmail.com. *½m S of Swanage town centre. From town follow signs to Durlston Country Park. At top of hill turn R at red postbox into Bon Accord Rd. 4th turn R into Newton Rd.* **Every Wed 6 July to 31 Aug (2-5.30). Adm £4, chd free. Visits also by arrangement July & Aug.**
Come and wander round a dramatic sunken former stone quarry, a surprising garden at the top of a hill above the seaside town of Swanage. Stone terraces, with many unusual shrubs and grasses, form a beautiful pattern of colour and foliage attracting butterflies and bees. Pieces of mediaeval London Bridge lurk in the walls. Steps have elegant handrails. WC available. Exceptionally wide range of plants including cacti and airplants.

45 ◆ **HOLME FOR GARDENS**
West Holme Farm, Wareham, BH20 6AQ. Simon Goldsack, 01929 554716, simon@holmefg.co.uk, www.holmefg.co.uk. *Easy to find on the B3070 road to Lulworth 2m out of Wareham.* **For NGS: Tue 7 June, Tue 13 Sept (10-4.30).**

Russell Cotes Art Gallery & Museum

Adm £6, chd free. Cream teas in The Orchard Café. For other opening times and information, please phone, email or visit garden website.

Extensive formal and informal gardens strongly influenced by Hidcote Manor and The Laskett. The garden is made up of distinct rooms separated by hedges and taller planting. Extensive collection of trees, shrubs, perennials and annuals sourced from across the UK. Spectacular wildflower meadows. Grass amphitheatre, Holme henge garden, lavender avenue, cutting garden, pear tunnel, hot borders, white borders, ornamental grasses, unusual trees and shrubs. Grass paths are kept in good order and soil is well drained so wheelchair access is reasonable except immediately after heavy rain.

46 22 HOLT ROAD

Branksome, Poole, BH12 1JQ. Alan & Sylvia Lloyd, 01202 387509, alan.lloyd22@ntlworld.com. 2½ m W of Bournemouth Square, 3m E of Poole Civic Centre. From Alder Rd turn into Winston Ave, 3rd R into Guest Ave, 2nd R into Holt Rd, at end of cul-de-sac. Park in Holt Rd or in Guest Ave. **Sun 20 Mar, Sun 22 May, Sun 24 July (2-5). Adm £3.50, chd free. Home-made teas. Visits also by arrangement Mar to Oct for groups of 10+.**

¾ acre walled garden for all seasons. Garden seating throughout the diverse planting areas, inc Mediterranean courtyard garden and wisteria pergola. Walk up slope beside rill and bog garden to raised bed vegetable garden. Return through shrubbery and rockery back to waterfall cascading into a pebble beach. Partial wheelchair access.

47 HOLWORTH FARMHOUSE

Holworth, Dorchester, DT2 8NH. Anthony & Philippa Bush, 01305 852242, bushinarcadia@yahoo.co.uk. 7m E of Dorchester. 1m S of A352. Follow signs to Holworth. Through farmyard with duckpond on R. 1st L after 200yds of rough track. Ignore No Access signs. **Sun 1, Mon 2 May, Sun 5 June, Sun 10 July (2-5). Adm £5, chd free. Home-made teas. Visits also by arrangement May to Sept.**

Escape briefly from the cares and pressures of the world. Visit this unusual garden tucked away in an area of extraordinary peace and tranquillity chosen by the monks of Milton Abbey. The garden was created 37 years ago and is constantly evolving. New projects every year. Many mature and unusual trees and shrubs, numerous borders with seats to ponder and reflect. Vegetables, water and wild spaces. Beautiful unspoilt views. Many birds and butterflies.

Shute Farm

48 NEW HOOKE FARM

Hooke, Beaminster, DT8 3NZ. Julia Hailes MBE & Jamie Macdonald, www.juliahailes.com. *Coming from Crewkerne, Yeovil or Dorchester, turn R at church & R again after 500 yds, just before pond. From Beaminster or Bridport turn left at Hooke woods, past Hooke Court & L after pond.* **Sat 11, Sun 12 June (10.30-5.30). Adm £8, chd £4. Locally sourced lunch, cream teas & refreshments throughout the day.**

Hooke Farm has been transformed into a wildlife haven with bird boxes, bat caves, butterflies and bee-friendly wildflower meadows. The landscaping project includes a series of ponds in a wetland area, orchard trees, woodland planting all interlinked with mown paths through swaying grass. There are standing stones, a stilted henhouse, a giant throne and driftwood stags. There will be talks and guided tours on both afternoons, covering different aspects of wilding and environmentally friendly gardening. This will include butterflies, moths, reptiles, weed control, tree

maintenance, grassland management and how to attract insects and birds. We are peat-free. There are areas of the garden that cannot be accessed by wheelchairs but there's still plenty to see if you can manage slopes.

49 HORN PARK

Tunnel Rd, Beaminster, DT8 3HB. Mr & Mrs David Ashcroft, 01308 862212, angieashcroft@btinternet.com. *1½m N of Beaminster. On A3066 from Beaminster, L before tunnel (see signs).* **Thur 14 Apr, Thur 2 June (2.30-4.30). Adm £5, chd free. Home-made teas. Visits also by arrangement Apr to Oct.**

Large plantsman's garden with magnificent views over Dorset countryside towards the sea. Many rare and mature plants and shrubs in terrraced, herbaceous, rock and water gardens. Woodland garden and walks in bluebell woods. Good amount of spring interest with magnolia, rhododendron and bulbs which are followed by roses and

herbaceous planting, wildflower meadow with 164 varieties inc orchids.

50 IVY HOUSE GARDEN

Piddletrenthide, DT2 7QF. Bridget Bowen, 07586 377675, beepeebee66@icloud.com. *9m N of Dorchester. On B3143. In middle of Piddletrenthide village, opp Village Stores.* **Sat 9, Sun 10 Apr (2-5). Adm £5, chd free. Home-made teas. Visits also by arrangement Apr & May for groups of 12+.**

A steep and challenging ½ acre garden with fine views, set on south facing site in the beautiful Piddle valley. Wildlife friendly garden with mixed borders, ponds, propagating area, large vegetable garden, fruit cage, greenhouses and polytunnel, chickens and bees, plus a nearby allotment. Daffodils, tulips and hellebores in quantity for spring openings. Come prepared for steep terrain and a warm welcome! Run on organic lines with plants to attract birds, bees and other insects.

Insect friendly plants usually for sale. Honey and hive products available. Beekeeper present to answer queries. We hope to hold a live music event in the garden over the weekend.

✿ ☕

51 NEW JULIA'S HOUSE CHILDREN'S HOSPICE
135 Springdale Road, Broadstone, BH18 9BP. Liz Thompson. *From Broadstone turn L at T-lights on Lower Blandford Rd. ½ m on L. Parking not available on site.* **Sat 7, Sun 8 May (10.30-3.30). Adm £4, chd free. Light refreshments.**
Julia's House Children's Hospice provides respite care for children with life-threatening or limiting conditions. Our garden has been designed so the children can experience and enjoy different sensory elements and is cared for by our volunteer gardeners. Explore how our children use the garden. Tours of the hospice may be available.

♿ ✿ ☕ ♪))

52 ◆ KEYNESTON MILL
Tarrant Keyneston, Blandford Forum, DT11 9HZ. Julia & David Bridger, 01258 786022, enquiries@keynestonmill.com, www.keynestonmill.com. *From Blandford or Wimborne take B3082. Turn into Tarrant Keynston village and continue right through to Xrds, we are straight ahead.* **For NGS: Tue 24 May, Tue 13 Sept (2-5). Adm £5, chd free. Home-made teas. For other opening times and information, please phone, email or visit garden website.**
Keyneston Mill is the creative home of Parterre Fragrances - a 50 acre working estate dedicated to fragrant and aromatic plants. Enjoy the gardens, each compartment featuring plants from a different perfume family eg. floral, fern and citrus. Enjoy a walk around the river meadow and the perfume crop fields where we grow the ingredients for our perfumes, and see the exhibition and distillery. Open all year-round. Compacted gravel paths in floral garden, lawns elsewhere. Wheelchair access to bistro-café and WCs. Dogs on leads welcome in the gardens.

♿ 🐕 ✿ ☕ ♪))

53 NEW KINGS BARROW
Grange Road, Wareham, BH20 5AJ. Janet Triniman. *2nd gateway on R on Grange Rd. If you get to the Springfield Hotel you have passed us. On Isle of Purbeck. A351 from Wareham towards Swanage. Turn Rat filter lane with brown sign to Springfield Hotel. 200yds on bend turn R into Kings Barrow.* **Sat 30 Apr, Sun 1 May, Sat 4, Sun 5 June (1-5). Adm £5, chd free. Home-made teas.**
Several acres of garden built around a structure of mature hedges and trees. The lawn edged with herbaceous borders dominates and via an avenue of yews leads to a woodland walk encompassing an ancient Barrow. A walled garden is split into a vegetable patch, cutting patch and party area. Roses abound throughout and swathes of bluebells are visible in spring. An orchard completes the garden.

✿ ☕ ♪))

54 ◆ KINGSTON LACY
Wimborne Minster, BH21 4EA. National Trust, 01202 883402, kingstonlacy@nationaltrust.org.uk, www.nationaltrust.org.uk/kingston-lacy. *2½ m W of Wimborne Minster. On Wimborne-Blandford rd B3082.* **For opening times and information, please phone, email or visit garden website.**
35 acres of formal garden, incorporating parterre and sunk garden planted with Edwardian schemes during spring and summer. 5 acre kitchen garden and allotments. Victorian fernery containing over 35 varieties. Rose garden, mixed herbaceous borders, vast formal lawns and Japanese garden restored to Henrietta Bankes' creation of 1910. National Collection of *Convallaria* and *Anemone nemorosa*. Snowdrops, blossom, bluebells, autumn colour and Christmas light display. Deep gravel on some paths but lawns suitable for wheelchairs. Slope to visitor reception and South lawn. Dogs allowed in some areas of woodland.

♿ ✿ 🐕 NPC ☕

55 ◆ KINGSTON MAURWARD GARDENS AND ANIMAL PARK
Kingston Maurward, Dorchester, DT2 8PY. Kingston Maurward College, 01305 215003, events@kmc.ac.uk, www.morekmc.com. *1mile E of Dorchester. Off A35. Follow brown Tourist Information signs.* **For opening times and information, please phone, email or visit garden website.**
Stepping into the grounds you will be greeted with 35 impressive acres of formal gardens. During the late spring and summer months, our National Collection of penstemons and salvias display a lustrous rainbow of purples, pinks, blues and whites, leading you on through the ample hedges and stonework balustrades. An added treat is the Elizabethan walled garden, offering a new vision of enchantment. Open early Jan to mid Dec. Hours will vary in winter depending on conditions - check garden website or call before visiting. Partial wheelchair access only, gravel paths, steps and steep slopes. Map provided at entry, highlighting the most suitable routes.

♿ 🚗 NPC ☕

56 KNITSON OLD FARMHOUSE
Corfe Castle, Wareham, BH20 5JB. Rachel Helfer, 01929 421681, rjehelfer@gmail.com. *Purbeck. Between Corfe Castle & Swanage. Follow the A351 3m E from Corfe Castle. Turn L signed Knitson. After1m fork R. We are on L after ¼ m.* **Wed 2, Wed 9 Mar (1-4); Wed 6, Wed 13 Apr, Wed 4, Wed 11 May, Wed 8, Wed 15 June, Wed 6, Wed 13 July, Wed 3, Wed 10 Aug, Wed 7, Wed 14 Sept (12-4.30); Wed 5, Wed 12 Oct, Wed 9, Wed 16 Nov, Wed 7 Dec (1-4). Home-made teas. Wed 14 Dec (1-4). Light refreshments. Adm £4, chd free. Visits also by arrangement Mar to Dec for groups of 8 to 25.**
Mature cottage garden nestled at base of chalk downland. Herbaceous borders, rockeries, climbers and shrubs, evolved and designed over 60yrs for year-round colour and interest. Large wildlife friendly kitchen garden for self sufficiency. Historical stone artefacts are used in the garden design. Ancient trees and shrubs are retained as integral to garden design. Over 20 varieties of fruits and many vegetables all year-round are the basis for a sustainable lifestyle. Garden is on a slope, main lawn and tea area are level but there are uneven, sloping paths.

♿ 🐕 ✿ ☕ 🍽 ♪))

57 ◆ KNOLL GARDENS

Hampreston, Wimborne,
BH21 7ND. Mr Neil Lucas,
01202 873931,
enquiries@knollgardens.co.uk,
www.knollgardens.co.uk. 2½ m W
of Ferndown. ETB brown signs from
all directions approaching Wimborne.
Large car park. For NGS: Fri 23
Sept (10-5). Adm £6.95, chd £4.95.
Light refreshments. For other
opening times and information,
please phone, email or visit garden
website.
A unique, naturalistic and calming
garden, renowned for its whispering
ornamental grasses, it also surprises
and delights with an abundance of
show-stopping flowering perennials.
A stunning backdrop of trees and
shrubs add drama to this wildlife and
environmentally-friendly garden. On
site nursery selling quality plants, with
expert advice readily available. Some
slopes. Various surfaces inc gravel,
paving, grass and bark.

&. ✿ 😊 NPC ☕ 😊

58 KNOWLE COTTAGE

No.1, Shorts Lane, Beaminster,
DT8 3BD. Claire & Guy Fender.
Near St Mary's Church. Park in
main square of Beaminster or in
main town car park and walk down
Church Lane and R onto single track
Shorts Lane. Entry is through blue
gates after 1st cottage on L. Sun 15
May, Sat 10 Sept (11-3.30). Adm
£5, chd free.
Large 1½ acre garden with 35 metre
long south facing herbaceous border
with year-round colour. Formal rose
garden within a circular floral planting
is bound on 3 sides by lavender.
Small orchard and vegetables in
raised beds in adjacent walled area,
with whole garden leading to small
stream, and bridge to pasture. Beds
accessed from level grass, slope
not suitable for wheelchairs. Picnics
welcome. Limited outside seating
available. Dogs welcome on leads.

&. 🐕 ☕ 🍴))

59 LAWSBROOK

Brodham Way, Shillingstone,
DT11 0TE. Clive Nelson,
07771 658846, cne70bl@aol.com,
www.facebook.com/Lawsbrook.
5m NW of Blandford. To Shillingstone
on A357. Turn up Gunn Lane (past
Wessex Ave on L & Everetts Lane
on R) then turn R at next opportunity
as road bends to L. Lawsbrook
250 metres on R. Daily Wed 23
Feb to Sun 27 Feb (10-4). Sun

6 Nov (10-4). Adm £4, chd free.
Light refreshments. Visits also by
arrangement Feb to Nov.
Open for over 10 yrs for NGS. Garden
inc over 130 different tree species
spread over 6 acres. Native species
and many unusual specimens inc
Dawn redwood, Damyio oak and
Wollemi pine. Extensive snowdrop
display at Feb opening, wonderful
autumn colour in November. You can
be assured of a relaxed and friendly
day out, with guided tour included
if desired. Children's activities, all
day teas/cakes and dogs are very
welcome. Gravel path at entrance,
grass paths over whole garden.

&. 🐕 ✿ 😊 ☕ 🍴))

60 LEWELL LODGE

West Knighton, Dorchester,
DT2 8RP. Rose & Charles Joly.
3m SE of Dorchester. Turn off A35
onto A352 towards Wareham, take
West Stafford bypass, turn R for
West Knighton at T junction. ¾ m
turn R up drive after village sign. Fri
17 June (2-5). Adm £6, chd free.
Home-made teas.
Elegant 2 acre classic English garden
designed by present owners over
last 25 yrs, surrounding Gothic
Revival house. Double herbaceous
borders enclosed by yew hedges
with old fashioned roses. Shrub beds
edged with box and large pyramided
hornbeam hedge. Crab apple tunnel,
box parterre and pleached hornbeam
avenue. Large walled garden, many
mature trees and woodland walk.
Garden is level but parking is on
gravel and there are gravel pathways.

&. ☕))

61 LITTLE BENVILLE HOUSE

Benville Lane, Corscombe,
Dorchester, DT2 0NN. Jo & Gavin
Bacon. 2½ m (6mins) from Evershot
village on Benville Lane. Benville
may be approached from A37, via
Evershot village. House is on L ½ m
after Benville Bridge. Alternatively
from A356, Dorchester to Crewkerne
road, 1m down on R. Sat 11, Sun
12 June (11-5). Adm £8, chd £4.
Wine & light refreshments served
on terrace or in kitchen & barn
if wet.
Contemporary garden, with
landscape interventions by Harris
Bugg Studio within a varied ecological
ANOB and historic landscape off
Benville Lane, mentioned in Thomas
Hardy's Tess. Within the curtilage
there are new herbaceous borders,
woodland planting, walled vegetable

and cutting garden, cloud pruned
topiary, ha-ha, ornamental and
productive trees and moat which is
a listed Ancient Monument. Bring
a tennis racquet and appropriate
footwear and try the tennis court and
enjoy the view.

✿ ☕))

62 NEW LOWER SILTON

Silton, Gillingham, SP8 5AQ. Jenny
Peel. Between Bourton & Milton on
Stour. From Bourton take B3081
towards Gillingham. Under A303 &
continue ¼ m to next L bend. Turn L
before following bend & Lower Silton
is before you. Sat 7 May (2-5).
Combined adm with Silton House
£8, chd free.
Wonderful recently recovered 25
acre bluebell wood with emerging
colonies of early purple orchid. Large
developing arboretum with many
varieties of interesting trees in the
fields alongside. Ponds with black
neck swans and ducks protected by
fencing.

🐕))

SPECIAL EVENT

63 NEW LULWORTH CASTLE HOUSE

Lulworth Park, East Lulworth,
Wareham, BH20 5QS. James
& Sara Weld, 01935 83652,
alison.wright@ngs.org.uk. In the
village of E Lulworth enter through
the main entrance to Lulworth
Castle and Park & follow the signs.
Wed 15 June (11.30-3). Adm
£100. Pre-booking essential,
please visit www.ngs.org.uk for
information & booking. Visits also
by arrangement in June.
Large coastal garden next to Lulworth
Castle with views to the sea. Pleasure
grounds surround a walled garden filled
with roses and perennials, behind which
sits a working kitchen garden with fruit
cages. In front of the house a scented
pathway leading to a wildflower
meadow, lavender labyrinth and Islamic
garden with rills and fountains. A limited
number of tickets have been made
available for this special one day event
and private tour of the gardens and
grounds of Lulworth Castle House,
which have not previously been open
to the public. Kindly hosted by the
owners, James & Sara Weld, light
refreshments will be served on arrival
at 11.30. This will be followed by an
introductory talk and the opportunity
to view the gardens accompanied by

the owners and gardening team. Buffet lunch to be served at 1pm, after which there will be the chance to further explore the gardens and grounds at your own leisure.

&

64 MANOR FARM, HAMPRESTON
Wimborne, BH21 7LX. Guy & Anne Trehane, 01202 574223, anne.trehane@live.co.uk. *2½ m E of Wimborne, 2½ m W of Ferndown. From Canford Bottom r'about on A31, take exit B3073 Ham Lane. ½ m turn R at Hampreston Xrds. House at bottom of village.* **Sat 12 Mar (10-1). Light refreshments. Sun 13 Mar (1-4); Sun 29 May, Sun 12 June, Sun 17 July, Sun 7 Aug (1-5). Home-made teas. Adm £5, chd free. Visits also by arrangement May to Aug for groups of 15 to 40.**
Traditional farmhouse garden designed and cared for by 3 generations of the Trehane family through over 100 yrs of farming and gardening at Hampreston. Garden is noted for its herbaceous borders and rose beds within box and yew hedges. Mature shrubbery, water and bog garden. Open for hellebores in March. Dorset Hardy Plant Society sales at openings. Hellebores for sale in March.

& ❈ ☕))

65 MANOR FARM, STOURTON CAUNDLE
Stourton Caundle, DT10 2JW. Mr & Mrs O S L Simon. *6m E of Sherborne, 4 m W of Sturminster Newton. From Sherborne take A3030. At Bishops Caundle, L signed Stourton Caundle. After 1½ m, L opp Trooper Inn in middle of village.* **Sat 11, Sun 12 June (2-5.30). Combined adm with Wagtails £10, chd free.**
C17 farmhouse and barns with walled garden in middle of village. Mature trees, shrubberies, herbaceous borders, lakes and vegetable garden. Lovingly created over last 50 yrs by current owners. Wheelchair access to lower areas of garden, steps to top areas of garden.

& 🐕 ❈ ☕

66 MANOR HOUSE FARM
Ibberton, Blandford Forum, DT11 0EN. Fiona Closier, www.instagram.com/ thefloristwithin/?hl=en. *Off A357 between Blandford Forum & Sturminster Newton. From A357 at Shillingstone take road to Okeford Fitzpaine. Follow signs for Belchalwell & Ibberton. Continue through Belchalwell to Ibberton.* **Sat 18, Sun 19 June (2-5). Adm £5, chd free. Home-made teas.**
Set in the lee of Bulbarrow Hill, this 1½ acre partially terraced garden has formal yew and beech hedging interspersed with topiary, lawn, and many abundantly filled herbaceous borders. Native trees, 2 spring-fed ponds attracting wildlife, and walled kitchen garden also give many areas of interest. Orchard area left to meadow with spring bulbs. Partial wheelchair access in dry weather due to steps,slopes and steep grass areas. No ground floor level disabled WC.

& ❈ 🚗 ☕

67 THE MANOR HOUSE, BEAMINSTER
North St, Beaminster, DT8 3DZ. Christine Wood. *200yds N of town square. Park in the square or public car park, 5 mins walk along North St from the square. Limited disabled parking on site.* **Sun 1, Mon 2 May (11-5). Sat 4, Sun 5 June, Sat 2 July (11-5). Home-made teas in Coach House garden. Adm £7, chd £2. Sorry, no teas for May dates but do bring a picnic.**
Set in heart of Beaminster, 16 acres of stunning parkland with mature specimen trees, lake and waterfall, The Manor House looks forward again to welcoming old and new visitors to enjoy this peaceful garden a haven for wildlife with a woodland walk, wildflower meadow and walled garden 'serendipity'. Ornamental ducks, black swans, pigmy goats, chickens and guinea pigs. Partial wheelchair access.

& 🐕 ❈ ☕ 🪑))

68 ♦ MAPPERTON GARDENS
Mapperton, Beaminster, DT8 3NR. The Earl & Countess of Sandwich, 01308 862645, office@mapperton.com, www.mapperton.com. *6m N of Bridport. Off A356/A3066. 2m SE of Beaminster off B3163.* **For opening times and information, please phone, email or visit garden website.**
Terraced valley gardens surrounding Tudor/Jacobean manor house. On upper levels, walled croquet lawn, orangery and Italianate formal garden with fountains, topiary and grottoes.

Below, C17 summerhouse and fishponds. Lower garden with shrubs and rare trees, leading to woodland and spring gardens. Partial wheelchair access (lawn and upper levels).

& ❈ 🚗 ☕ 🪑

69 MAYFIELD
4 Walford Close, Wimborne Minster, BH21 1PH. Mr & Mrs Terry Wheeler, 01202 849838, t.w@live.co.uk. *½ m N of Wimborne town centre. B3078 out of Wimborne, R into Burts Hill, 1st L into Walford Close.* **Mon 2, Sun 15, Sun 29 May, Sun 5 June (2-5). Adm £3.50, chd free. Home-made teas. Visits also by arrangement May & June for groups of 8 to 25.**
Town garden of approx ¼ acre. Front: formal hard landscaping planted with drought-resistant shrubs and perennials. Back garden contrasts with a seductive series of garden rooms containing herbaceous perennial beds separated by winding grass paths and rustic arches. Pond, vegetable beds and greenhouses containing succulents and vines. Garden access is across a pea-shingle drive. If this is manageable, wheelchairs can access the back garden provided they are no wider than 65cms.

& 🐕 ❈ 🚗 ☕))

70 ♦ MINTERNE GARDEN
Minterne House, Minterne Magna, Dorchester, DT2 7AU. Lord & Lady Digby, 01300 341370, enquiries@minterne.co.uk, www.minterne.co.uk. *2m N of Cerne Abbas. On A352 Dorchester-Sherborne road.* **For opening times and information, please phone, email or visit garden website.**
As seen on BBC Gardeners' World and voted one of the 10 prettiest gardens in England by The Times. Famed for their display of historic rhododendrons, azaleas, Japanese cherries and magnolias in April/ May when the garden is at its peak. Small lakes, streams and cascades offer new vistas at each turn around the 1m horseshoe shaped gardens covering 23 acres. The season ends with spectacular autumn colour. Snowdrops in Feb. Spring bulbs, blossom and bluebells in April. Over 200 acers provide spectacular autumn colour in Sept/Oct.

🐕 🚗 ☕

Harvard Farm

71 ◆ MUSEUM OF EAST DORSET

23-29 High Street, Wimborne Minster, BH21 1HR. Museum of East Dorset, 01202 882533, info@museumofeastdorset.co.uk, www.museumofeastdorset.co.uk. *Wimborne town centre. Wimborne is just off A31. From W take B3078, from E take B3073 towards town centre. From Poole and Bournemouth enter town from S on A341.* **For opening times and information, please phone, email or visit garden website.**

Discover a real gem tucked away in the centre of Wimborne. The walled garden, with its path leading from the back door to the mill stream, is 100 metres long. Colourful herbaceous borders and old varieties of apple and pear trees line the path further down. Groups are asked to pre-book. There is a separate admission charge to visit the new Museum of East Dorset. Wheelchair access throughout the site.

&. 🚐 ☕

SPECIAL EVENT

72 NORWOOD HOUSE

Corscombe, Dorchester, DT2 0PD. Mr & Mrs Jonathan Lewis, 07836 600185, jonathan.lewis@livegroup.co.uk. *Equidistant between Halstock & Corscombe. 1m from Fox Inn towards Halstock. 1m from national speed limit sign leaving Halstock towards Corscombe. Parking in field off the main drive.* **Evening opening Fri 17, Fri 24 June (5-8.30). Adm £45. Pre-booking essential, please visit www.ngs.org.uk for information & booking.**

Our garden is hidden away in a stunning West Dorset valley surrounded by our small family estate. We started our landscaping adventure from scratch in 2011. Today the glorious purple, pink and white borders surround the house and lawns. Many varieties of geranium and other perennials, grasses, shrubs and rockery. Lake, woodland and wild flower walks thoroughly recommended, weather permitting. This year a limited number of tickets have been made available for 2 exclusive evening events, with classical music being played in the garden near the main terrace. There will be food and wine served, whilst you take in the ambience and enjoy the garden, meadows, lake and woodland walks. We can assist wheelchair users to access the gardens only some parts of which are inaccessible.

&. ❄ 🚐 🏠 ☕

73 OLD DOWN HOUSE
Horton, Wimborne,
BH21 7HL. Dr & Mrs Colin
Davidson, 07765 404248,
pipdavidson59@gmail.com.
*7½ m N of Wimborne. Horton Inn
at junction of B3078 with Horton
Rd, pick up yellow signs leading
up through North Farm. No garden
access from Matterley Drove. 5min
walk to garden down farm track.*
**Wed 8, Sat 11, Sun 12 June
(2-5). Adm £4, chd free. Home-
made teas in garden with some
undercover areas available. Visits
also by arrangement in June.**
Nestled down a farm track, this ¾
acre garden on chalk, surrounds
C18 farmhouse. Stunning views over
Horton Tower and farmland. Cottage
garden planting with formal elements.
Climbing roses clothe pergola and
house walls along with stunning
Wisteria sinensis and banksian rose.
Mainly walled potager, well-stocked.
Chickens. Interesting and unusual
locally grown plants for sale.

74 NEW OLD GRANARY COTTAGE
West Milton, Bridport,
DT6 3TN. Hugo Grenville,
www.hugogrenville.com. *Just as
you come into West Milton, opp the
very 1st house, turn sharp L signed
Porton & Loscombe; proceed up
hill 500 yds & at the Xrds turn R.*
**Evening opening Fri 5 Aug (5.30-
8). Wine. Sat 6 Aug (12-6). Home-
made teas. Adm £5, chd £3.**
The garden at Old Granary Cottage is
perhaps best described as a painter's
garden. Perched on the top of a hill,
and overlooking the valley of West
Milton, it has been created by Hugo
Grenville to be an inspiration for his
painting, a blaze of pink and yellow,
violet and red, silhouetted against the
bluish-greens of the south Dorset hills.

75 THE OLD RECTORY, LITTON CHENEY
Litton Cheney, Dorchester,
DT2 9AH. Richard & Emily Cave.
*9m W of Dorchester. 1m S of A35,
6m E of Bridport. Small village in the
beautiful Bride Valley. Park in village
and follow signs.* **Sun 8, Wed 11
May, Sun 3 July (11-5). Adm £6,
chd free. Home-made teas.**
Steep paths lead to beguiling 4
acres of natural woodland with many
springs, streams, 2 pools one a
natural swimming pool planted with

native plants. Formal front garden,
designed by Arne Maynard, with
pleached crabtree border, topiary and
soft planting including tulips, peonies,
roses and verbascums. Walled
garden with informal planting, kitchen
garden, orchard and 350 rose bushes
for a cut flower business.

76 THE OLD RECTORY, MANSTON
Manston, Sturminster Newton,
DT10 1EX. Andrew & Judith
Hussey, 01258 474673,
judithhussey@hotmail.com.
*6m S of Shaftesbury, 2½ m N
of Sturminster Newton. From
Shaftesbury, take B3091. On
reaching Manston, past Plough Inn,
L for Child Okeford on R-hand bend.
Old Rectory last house on L.* **Sun 19,
Wed 22 June (2-5). Adm £6, chd
free. Home-made teas. Visits also
by arrangement May to July for
groups of 10 to 40.**
Beautifully restored 5 acre garden.
South facing wall with 120ft
herbaceous border edged by old brick
path. Enclosed yew hedge flower
garden. Wildflower meadow marked
with mown paths and young plantation
of mixed hardwoods. Well maintained
walled Victorian kitchen garden with
new picking flower section. Large new
greenhouse also installed. Knot garden
now well established.

77 THE OLD RECTORY, PULHAM
Dorchester, DT2 7EA. Mr &
Mrs N Elliott, 01258 817595,
gilly.elliott@hotmail.com. *13m N
of Dorchester. 8m SE of Sherborne.
On B3143 turn E at Xrds in Pulham.
Signed Cannings Court.* **Sun 22
May, Thur 16 June, Thur 7 July,
Sun 7 Aug (2-5). Adm £8, chd free.
Tea. Visits also by arrangement
Apr to Sept for groups of 10 to 40.**
4 acres formal and informal gardens
surround C18 rectory, splendid views.
Yew pyramid allées and hedges,
circular herbaceous borders with late
summer colour. Exuberantly planted
terrace, purple and white beds. Box
parterres, mature trees, pond, fernery,
ha-ha, pleached hornbeam circle. 10
acres woodland walks. Flourishing
extended bog garden with islands;
awash with primulas and irises in
May. Interesting plants for sale. Mostly
wheelchair access.

78 THE OLD SCHOOL HOUSE
The Street, Sutton Waldron,
Blandford Forum, DT11 8NZ.
David Milanes. *Turn into Sutton
Waldron from A350, continue for
300 yds, 1st house on L in The
Street. Entrance past house through
gates in wall.* **Sun 19, Wed 22 June
(2-5.30). Adm £4.50, chd free.
Home-made teas.**
Small village garden laid out in last
8 yrs with planting of hedges into
rooms inc orchard, secret garden
and pergola walkway. Recent
addition of raised bed for growing
vegetables. Strong framework of
existing large trees, beds are mostly
planted with roses and herbaceous
plants. Pleached hornbeam screen.
A designer's garden with interesting
semi-tender plants close to house.
Level lawns.

79 THE OLD VICARAGE
East Orchard, Shaftesbury,
SP7 0BA. Miss Tina Wright,
01747 811744, tina_lon@msn.com.
*4½ m S of Shaftesbury, 3½ m N of
Sturminster Newton. Between 90
degree bend & layby with defibrillator
red phone box. Parking is on the opp
corner towards Hartgrove.* **Fri 11,
Sun 13 Feb, Sun 20 Mar, Sun 24
Apr, Sun 22 May, Sun 14 Aug (2-
5). Adm £4, chd free. Cream teas.
Visits also by arrangement Jan to
Nov. Any number greater than 1.**
1.7 acre wildlife garden with hundreds
of different snowdrops, crocus and
hellebores and other winter flowering
shrubs. Followed by other bulbs
inc large swathes of narcissi and
hundreds of tulips, camassias and
alliums. A wonderful stream meanders
down to a pond and there are lovely
reflections from the swimming pond,
the first to be built in Dorset. Tree
viewing platform allows you to look
over garden and to the wider area.
Grotto, old Victorian man pushing
his lawn mower which his owner
purchased brand new in 1866.Pond
dipping, swing and other children's
attractions. Cakes inc gluten free,
diabetic and vegans are also catered
for. Not suitable for wheelchairs if
very wet.

80 PHILIPSTON HOUSE

Winterborne Clenston, Blandford Forum, DT11 0NR. Mark & Ana Hudson. *2 km N of Winterborne Whitechurch & 1 km S of Crown Inn in Winterborne Stickland. Park in signed track/field off road, nr Bourne Farm Cottage. Enter garden from field.* **Sat 11, Sat 25 June (2-5.30). Adm £5, chd free. Cream teas £5 - please bring cash.**
Charming 2 acre garden with lovely views in Winterborne valley. Many unusual trees, rambling roses, wisteria, mixed borders and shrubs. Sculptures. Rose parterre, walled garden, swimming pool garden, vegetable garden. Stream with bridge over to wooded shady area with cedarwood pavilion. Orchard with mown paths planted with spring bulbs. Sorry, no WC available. Dogs welcome on leads, pls clear up after them. Wheelchair access is good providing it is dry.
&. ♞ ☕

81 NEW 1 PINE WALK

Lyme Regis, DT7 3LA. Mrs Erika Savory. *Please park in Holmbush Car Park at top of Cobb Rd.* **Fri 9, Sat 10, Sun 11 Sept (11-4). Adm £5, chd £1. Home-made teas.**
Unconventional ½ acre, multi level garden above Lyme Bay, adjoining NT's Ware Cliffs. Abundantly planted with an exotic range of shrubs, cannas, gingers and magnificent ferns. Apart from a rose and hydrangea collection, planting reflects owner's love of Southern Africa inc staggering succulents and late summer colour explosion featuring drifts of salvias, dahlias, asters, grasses and rudbeckia.
☕

82 THE PINES

15 Longacre Drive, Ferndown, BH22 9EE. Ian Gallimore. *½ m from centre of Ferndown. R off A348 towards Poole, Longacre Drive is almost opp M&S Foodhall.* **Sun 15, Sat 21 May (2-6). Adm £4, chd free. Light refreshments.**
Suburban garden. Heavily planted with mostly perennials, trees and exotic type plants to give a secluded and private feel. 2 ponds, seating areas and outdoor kitchen/BBQ area.
❄ ☕ ꜙ)

GROUP OPENING

83 RAMPISHAM GARDENS

Dorchester, DT2 0PU. 01935 83652, alison.wright@ngs.org.uk. *11m NW of Dorchester. From Dorchester A37 Yeovil, 9m L to Evershot. From Yeovil A37 Dorchester, 7m R Evershot, follow signs. From Crewkerne A356, 1½ m after Rampisham Garage L to Rampisham.* **Sun 12 June (11-5). Combined adm £8, chd £4. Home-made teas.**

BROOMHILL
Mr & Mrs D Parry.
(See separate entry)

THE CURATAGE
Mr & Mrs Tim Hill.

NEW **LITTLE UPHALL**
Esther Jeanes.

NEW **THE OLD RECTORY**
Mr & Mrs Peter Thomas.

PUGIN HALL
Mr & Mrs Tim Wright, 01935 83652, wright.alison68@yahoo.com. **Visits also by arrangement May to July for groups of 10 to 50.**

NEW **1 ROSE COTTAGE**
Trevor & Sarah Ball.

NEW **2 ROSE COTTAGE**
Florence Drake.

NEW **THATCHERS REST**
David & Carole Angel.

This beautiful historic village will host an open garden day for a wide variety of gardens, with 8 gardens opening this year. These will include some larger gardens with perennial borders, roses and shrubs, as well as an old walled garden more recently developed as a flower garden with topiary, standard trees and soft floral planting. Included this year for the first time are some new cottage gardens with an array of floral colour, fruit trees and vegetables. Within these cottage gardens the village will host a number of attractions that will be open to the public. There will be a number of items for sale, including woodturning, Blue Bowl gifts, local landscape paintings by artist Esther Jeanes, Capreolus Smokery open for the day and plants for sale at Broomhill. The village church with aspects designed by Pugin will be open with floral arrangements.
&. ♞ ❄ ☕ ꜙ)

84 25 RICHMOND PARK AVENUE

Bournemouth, BH8 9DL. Barbara Hutchinson & Mike Roberts, 01202 531072, barbarahutchinson@tiscali.co.uk. *2½ m NE Bournemouth town centre. From T-lights at junction with Alma Rd & Richmond Park Rd, head N on B3063 Charminster Rd, 2nd turning on R into Richmond Park Ave.* **Sun 19 June, Sun 3, Sun 31 July (2-5). Adm £4, chd free. Home-made teas. Visits also by arrangement June & July for groups of 10 to 30.**
Beautifully designed town garden with pergola leading to canopy over raised decking. Cascading waterfall connects 2 wildlife ponds enhanced with domed acers. Circular lawn with colourful herbaceous border planted to attract bees and butterflies. Fragrant south facing courtyard garden at front, sparkling with vibrant colour and Mediterranean planting. Partial wheelchair access.
&. ♞ ❄ ꞕ ☕

85 NEW ROMAN HOUSE

Roman House, 5 St Andrews Meadow, Lyme Regis, DT7 3NS. Samantha & John Pennington. *In a quiet cul-de-sac less than a mile from the centre of town. Turn off A35 onto B3165 to Lyme R. Thru Uplyme & turn L into Haye Lane (NGS arrows). St Andrews Meadow on R after junction. No parking at house; please use local roads or town car parks.* **Sat 13, Sun 14 Aug (1-5). Adm £4.50, chd free. Home-made teas in the garden.**
Evolved over 22 yrs this small town garden has a sub-tropical twist. Bordered by a stream the trickle of water can be heard whilst perusing the borders. The planting is loose and informal attracting many species of insects around a charming little garden studio. There are terraced cut flower beds, raised beds for vegetables in a gravel garden, several herbaceous borders and a lawned area.
❄ ☕

Our 2021 donations mean that 72,000 people accessed bereavement support through hospices in the UK

Holworth Farmhouse

86 ROSEBANK

8 Love Lane, Shaftesbury,
SP7 8BG. **Nigel & Shouanna
Hawkins.** *Park in town's main car
park. Walk along Bimport, take 3rd
L opp hospital sign into Magdalene
Lane. Continue past hospital into
Love Lane. Reserved disabled
parking in drive.* **Sat 18, Sun 19
June (11-4.30). Adm £4, chd free.**
Delightful small garden living up to
its name, 106 rose plants have been
bedded in during the last 4 yrs,
transforming the front garden into
box-edged flower beds with rose
arches and peonies. The back garden
is in cottage style, planted with many
varieties of herbaceous perennials
and tea roses. A pergola shades an
alpine rockery and a herbaceous
border. Wheelchair access around
garden. Slope near entrance.

&

87 NEW RUSSELL-COTES ART GALLERY & MUSEUM

East Cliff, Bournemouth,
BH1 3AA. **Sarah Newman,**
www.russellcotes.com.
*Bournemouth's East Cliff Promenade.
Situated next to the Royal Bath Hotel,
2 mins walk from Bournemouth Pier.
The closest car park is Bath Road Sth.
Parking also available on the cliff top.*
**Sat 14 May, Sat 18 June (2-5). Adm
£4, chd free. Light refreshments at
Museum Café.**
A sub-tropical garden sited on the cliff
top, overlooking the sea, full of a wide
variety of plants from around the globe.
East Cliff Hall was the home of Sir
Merton and Lady Annie Russell-Cotes.
The garden was restored allowing for
modern access with areas retaining
original 1901 design conceived by the
founders such as the ivy clad grotto
and Japanese influence. The Russell-
Cotes Café serves a delicious range of
light lunches, teas, coffees, and cakes.
Some gravel paths and no wheelchair
access to terrace.

& ☕

88 THE SECRET GARDEN AND SERLES HOUSE

47 Victoria Road, Wimborne,
BH21 1EN. **Phil Broomfield.** *Centre
of Wimborne. On B3082 W of town,
very near hospital, Westfield car park
300yds. Off road parking close by.*
**Sat 28 May, Sat 11 June (10-4).
Adm £4, chd free. Home-made
teas. Donation to Wimborne Civic
Society and The Arts' Society.**
The home of the late Ian Willis, who
lived here for just under 40 yrs. The
Executors of Ian's estate have kindly
offered to open up his home and
garden for the NGS, in his memory.
Alan Titchmarsh described this
amusingly creative garden as 'one of
the best 10 private gardens in Britain'.
The ingenious use of unusual plants
complements the imaginative treasure
trove of garden objects d'art. Period
Victorian house also open with Gothic
conservatory. Oriental summerhouse
and Indian summer room to view.
Wheelchair access to garden only.
Narrow steps may prohibit wide
wheelchairs.

& ✿ 🚐 ☕

89 SEMLEY GRANGE

Semley, Shaftesbury, SP7 9AP. Mr & Mrs Reid Scott. *From A350 take turning to Semley continue along road & under railway bridge. Take 1st R up Sem Hill. Semley Grange is 1st on L - parking on green.* **Sun 3 July (1-5). Adm £5, chd free. Light refreshments.**
Large garden recreated in last 10 yrs. Herbaceous border, lawn and wildflower meadow intersected by paths and planted with numerous bulbs. The garden has been greatly expanded by introducing many standard weeping roses, new mixed borders, pergolas and raised beds for dahlias, underplanted with alliums. Numerous fruit and ornamental trees introduced over last 10 yrs.

&. ✿ 🍽))

90 SHADRACK HOUSE

Shadrack Street, Beaminster, DT8 3BE. Mr & Mrs Hugh Lindsay, 01308 863923, christine.corson@ngs.org.uk. *Centre of Beaminster. Within 5 mins walk of 21A The Square.* **Visits by arrangement May to Sept for groups of 5 to 10. Opening together with 21A The Square. Adm £5.50, chd free.**
Delightful small mature garden, hidden behind high walls, with abundance of roses, clematis, shrubs, and climbers galore. Entrance through garden gates below the house, with views over to the church. There are several cafes, pubs and a restaurant within The Square. Beaminster Festival end of June, beginning of July.

✿

91 NEW 1 SHEEPWASH GREEN

Fishpond Bottom, Bridport, DT6 6NP. A.R. Edwards, www.ambra-edwards.com. *From B3165 Crewkerne Rd, take fingerpost turning to Fishpond. At junction, sharp R, downhill, to Fishpond Bottom. Parking at church or on lane sides.* **Sun 3 July (11-5). Combined adm with Sheepwash Mead £6, chd free. Home-made teas at Sheepwash Mead.**
Adventurously planted small modern garden designed as a writer's retreat by Chelsea gold medallist Ruth Willmott. Inspired by the curves of the surrounding landscape, it aims to offer a sense of seclusion while guiding your gaze to the sea. Terraced into distinct areas, including a gravel garden, green garden, flower meadow and newly planted grass parterre. Ambra Edwards is an award-winning writer and garden historian. Signed copies of her books will be on sale.

🐾 ✿ D 🍽

92 NEW SHEEPWASH MEAD

Fishpond, Bridport, DT6 6NP. Mike & Wendy Mann. *From B3165 Crewkerne road, take finger post turning to Fishponds. At junction, sharp R, downhill to Fishpond Bottom. Parking at church, on lane sides, limited disabled parking.* **Sun 3 July (11-5). Combined adm with 1 Sheepwash Green £6, chd free. Home-made teas.**
An adventurously planted modern garden of 1½ acres, created from a blank paddock in just 5 yrs, featuring many interesting perennials, climbers and billowing ornamental grasses. Colourful raised beds lead to an ancient olive tree; a pergola walk divides the formal and informal areas and frames a glorious view to the sea. Many attractive trees including birch, white mulberry and walnut. Partially accessible.

&. 🐾 ✿ 🍽

93 ◆ SHERBORNE CASTLE

New Rd, Sherborne, DT9 5NR. Mr E Wingfield Digby, www.sherbornecastle.com. *½ m E of Sherborne. On New Rd B3145. Follow brown signs from A30 & A352.* **For opening times and information, please visit garden website.**
40+ acres. Grade I Capability Brown garden with magnificent vistas across surrounding landscape, inc lake and views to ruined castle. Herbaceous planting, notable trees, mixed ornamental planting and managed wilderness are linked together with lawn and pathways. Short and long walks available. Partial wheelchair access, gravel paths, steep slopes, steps.

&. 🐾 �car 🍽 ⛩

94 NEW SHUTE FARM

Donhead St Mary, SP7 9DG. John & Caroline David. *5m E of Shaftesbury. Take A350 towards Warminster from Shaftesbury. Turn R at 1st turning outside of Shaftesbury, signed Wincombe & Donhead St Mary. At Donhead St Mary, turn R at T-junction. 1st house on L opp tel box.* **Sat 25, Sun 26 June (2-5). Adm £6, chd free. Home-made teas.**
Charming cottage garden around thatched house. Plenty to see and explore. Small stream, pond, kitchen garden and wildflower area. Neat and tidy flower beds change to a wild garden as they join the fields. Magnificent views over the Donheads.

🐾 🚗 🍽))

SPECIAL EVENT

95 NEW SHUTE HOUSE

Donhead St. Mary, Shaftesbury, SP7 9DG. John & Suzy Lewis. *2½ m E of Shaftesbury. 2m from the Dorset & Wiltshire border, follow navigation using post code, house on left in centre of village, parking in field.* **Wed 8 June (11.30-3). Adm £75. Pre-booking essential, please visit www.ngs.org.uk for information & booking. Light lunch served with wine.**
Sir Geoffrey Jellicoe, one of our finest landscape architects, was commissioned in 1969 to create a water garden for Lady Anne and Captain Michael Tree. The result was Shute House Gardens; his favourite and some say his finest work. The River Nadder rises at the top of the garden and is diverted into canals, waterfalls, rills and mysterious pools through a series of atmospheric garden 'rooms'. A limited number of tickets have been made available for this special one day event, which includes a talk and private guided tour with the garden owner, Suzy Lewis. A light lunch will be served with wine after your visit. Wheelchair access to the main front garden, although pathways and the woodland walkway would limit access to certain parts of the garden.

&. ✿ 🍽

96 NEW SILTON HOUSE

Church Road, Silton, Gillingham, SP8 5PR. Sandra Menzies & David Desborough. *Silton House is just next to Silton Church, parking in the church car park.* **Sat 7 May (2-5). Combined adm with Lower Silton £8, chd free. Home-made teas.**
Large garden divided into rooms. Topiary and yew hedges, Pleached lime walk extending to garden wall against which is an herbaceous and shrub border. Vegetable and flower garden though arch in wall with orchard beyond. Gravel garden with box edged flowerbeds against house, lawn extending to enclosed swimming pool garden.

&. 🍽))

97 21A THE SQUARE

Beaminster, DT8 3AU. Christine Corson, 01308 863923, christine.corson@ngs.org.uk. *6m N of Bridport. 6m S of Crewkerne on B3162. 5 mins walk from public car park.* **Visits by arrangement May to Sept for groups of 5 to 10. Opening together with Shadrack House. Adm £5.50, chd free.** 2 town gardens, within walking distance of each other, one 5 yrs old, started from scratch, the other is well established, both with lovely views and both quite large for town gardens. 21A is a plantaholic and flower arranger's garden which says all. There is something to pick all year-round. Wide collection of shrubs, trees, roses and borders. Awarded 1st prize in Medium Gardens category in the 2021 Melplash Show. Very wheelchair friendly, house and garden flat, and ramp from house into garden.

&

98 STABLE COURT

Chalmington, Dorchester, DT2 0HB. Jenny & James Shanahan, 01300 321345, jennyshanahan8@gmail.com. *From A37 travel towards Cattistock & Chalmington for 1½ m. R at triangle to Chalmington. ½ m house on R, red letter box at gate. From Cattistock take 1st turn R then next L at triangle.* **Wed 22, Sun 26 June (2-5.30). Adm £6, chd free. Home-made teas. Visits also by arrangement May to Sept for groups of up to 20.** This exuberant garden was begun in 2010. Extending to about 1½ acres, it is naturalistic in style with a shrubbery, gravel garden, wild garden and pond where many trees have been planted & which are maturing wonderfully. Overflowing with roses scrambling up trees, over hedges and walls. More formal garden closer to house with lawns and herbaceous borders. Lovely views over Dorset countryside. Exhibition of paintings in studio. Gravel path partway around garden, otherwise the paths are grass, not suitable for wheelchairs in wet weather.

& 🐕 ❀ ☕ 🍽

99 STADDLESTONES

14 Witchampton Mill, Witchampton, Wimborne, BH21 5DE. Annette & Richard Lockwood, 01258 841405, richardglockwood@yahoo.co.uk. *5m N of Wimborne off B3078. Follow signs through village and park in sports field, 7 min walk to garden, limited disabled parking near garden.* **Sat 28, Sun 29 May (2-5). Adm £4.50, chd free. Home-made teas. Visits also by arrangement Apr to Sept.** A beautiful setting for a cottage garden with colour themed borders, pleached limes and hidden gems, leading over chalk stream to shady area which has some unusual plants. Plenty of areas just to sit and enjoy the wildlife. Wire bird sculptures by local artist. Wheelchair access to 1st half of garden.

& ❀ ☕

SPECIAL EVENT

100 STAFFORD HOUSE

West Stafford, Dorchester, DT2 8AD. Lord & Lady Fellowes. *2m E of Dorchester in Frome Valley. Follow signs to West Stafford from the West, 1st house on L before you get to the village, green park railings and gate.* **Fri 1 July (10-12). Adm £50, chd free. Pre-booking essential, please visit www.ngs.org.uk for information & booking.** Home-made elevenses including cake and biscuits in a gardening theme. The gardens at Stafford House inc a river walk and tree planting in the style of early C19 Picturesque. Humphry Repton prepared landscape proposals for the garden and the designs were later implemented, they were also included in his famous Red Books. A limited number of tickets have been made available for this special private morning opening, hosted by Lord and Lady Fellowes. The morning will inc special home-made elevenses which will be served underneath the turkey oak tree planted in 1633 on the main terrace. There will then be the opportunity to explore the grounds and gardens, finishing at 12pm.

 ☕

101 NEW 49 STIRLING ROAD

Bournemouth, BH3 7JH. Mr John Stapleton. *Approx 2 m N of Bournemouth town centre. From A338 take A347 towards Winton/*
Charminster. Stay on A347 until you can take a R onto Berkeley Rd. Then take 1st L. **Sat 7, Sat 21 May (2.30-5). Adm £4, chd free. Home-made teas.** A family garden of several parts, focused on being nature friendly with a view to sustainable living. Pond with waterfall, orchard area and well tended vegetable garden. Unfortunately, not wheelchair friendly due to stepped entrance and multiple stepped decking area.

❀ ☕

102 NEW TREYFORD

16 Woodswater Lane, Beaminster, DT8 3DU. Fiona Johnston. *Signed off the A3066 Bridport - Beaminster - Crewkerne & B3163 Dorchester-Beaminster - Broadwindsor roads. Parking best in Hollymoor Lane.* **Sat 16 July (10.30-4.30). Adm £4.** A recently developed garden with some original features. Herbaceous borders have been enlarged to create a diverse range of interesting and unusual plantings.This includes a large collection of salvias. The owner has concentrated on increasing the plant stock which has led to an abundance of colour and form all year-round, attracting pollinators. Raised beds contribute to a sustainable lifestyle.

❀))

103 ◆ UPTON COUNTRY PARK

Upton, Poole, BH17 7BJ. BCP Council, 01202 127770, uptoncountrypark@ bcpcouncil.gov.uk, www.uptoncountrypark.com. *3m W of Poole town centre. On S side of A35/A3049. Follow brown signs.* **For opening times and information, please phone, email or visit garden website.** Over 65 hectares of award winning parkland inc formal gardens, walled garden, woodland and shoreline. Maritime microclimate offers a wonderful collection of unusual trees, vintage camellias and stunning roses. Home to Upton House, Grade II* listed Georgian mansion. Regular special events, art gallery and tea rooms. Car parking pay + display (cash or card), free entry to the park. Open 8am - 6pm (winter) and 8am - 9pm (summer). www.facebook.com/uptoncountrypark. Easy access for wheelchair users.

& 🐕 🚻 ☕ 🍽

104 UTOPIA

Tincleton, Dorchester,
DT2 8QP. Nick & Sharon
Spiller, 07970 971983,
sharspiller@hotmail.co.uk. *Take
signs to Tincleton from Dorchester,
Puddletown. Pick up garden signs in
the village.* **Sun 12 June (2-5). Adm
£4.50, chd £3. Light refreshments.
Visits also by arrangement May to
Aug for groups of up to 10.**
Approximately ½ acre of secluded,
peaceful garden made up of
several rooms inspired by different
themes. Inspiration is taken from
Mediterranean and Italian gardens,
woodland space, water gardens
and the traditional country vegetable
garden. Seating is scattered
throughout to enable you to sit and
enjoy the different spaces and take
advantage of both sun and shade.

105 WAGTAILS

Stourton Caundle, Sturminster
Newton, DT10 2JW. Sally & Nick
Reynolds. *6m E of Sherborne.
From Sherborne take A3030. At
Bishops Caundle, L signed Stourton
Caundle. After 1½ m in village on R
as descending hill, 5 houses before
Trooper Inn.* **Sat 11, Sun 12 June
(2-5.30). Combined adm with
Manor Farm, Stourton Caundle
£10, chd free.**

Contemporary Arne Maynard
inspired garden of almost 3 acres,
with wildflower meadows, orchards,
kitchen garden and lawns, linked by
a sweeping mown pathway, studded
with topiary, divided by box, yew and
beech hedging. Landscaped and
planted over last 10 yrs by current
owners, and still a work in progress,
with further changes planned for
2022. Wheelchair access over
majority of garden and orchards over
lawn grade paths. Gentle slopes.

106 NEW ◆ THE WALLED GARDEN

Moreton, Dorchester, DT2 8RH.
Kelsi Dean-Bluck,
01929 405685, info@
thewalledgardenmoreton.co.uk,
walledgardenmoreton.co.uk/.
*In the village of Moreton, near
Crossways. Look for the brown
signs out on the main road.* **For
opening times and information,
please phone, email or visit garden
website.**
The Walled Garden is a beautiful
5 acre landscaped formal garden
situated in Moreton, Dorset. The
village is close to the historic market
town of Dorchester and situated on
the River Frome. A wide variety of
perennial plants sit in the borders,
which have been styled in original

Georgian and Victorian designs.
Sculpture from various local artists,
family area and play park, animal area,
and plant shop, plus on site cafe.

107 WESTERN GARDENS

24A Western Ave, Branksome
Park, Poole, BH13 7AN. Mr
Peter Jackson, 01202 708388,
pjbranpark@gmail.com. *3m W of
Bournemouth. From S end Wessex
Way (A338) at gyratory take The
Avenue, 2nd exit. At T-lights turn R
into Western Rd then at bottom of
hill L. At church turn R into Western
Ave.* **Sun 26 June, Sun 7 Aug (2-5).
Adm £5, chd free. Home-made
teas. Visits also by arrangement
Apr to Sept for groups of 20+.**
'This secluded and magical 1acre
garden captures the spirit of warmer
climes and begs for repeated visits'
(Gardening Which?). Created over
40 yrs it offers enormous variety
with rose, Mediterranean courtyard
and woodland gardens, herbaceous
borders and cherry tree and camellia
walk. Lush foliage and vibrant flowers
give year-round colour and interest
enhanced by sculpture and topiary.
Plants and home-made jams and
chutneys for sale. Wheelchair access
to ¾ garden.

Carraway Barn

108 NEW WHITE CLIFF MANOR

Whitecliff Road, Swanage, BH19 1RL. James & Semra Sinclair-Taylor. *Enter Swanage on the Ulwell road. Whitecliff Rd is on the L at the junction with Washpond Lane.* **Sat 30 Apr (2-5). Home-made teas. Sun 1 May (11.30-2.30). Light refreshments. Sat 4, Sun 5 June (2-5.30). Home-made teas. Adm £4, chd free.**

A walled garden of just under an acre terraced and divided into rooms by yew hedges. There are vegetable gardens, an orchard, mature mulberry trees and ancient tower. From the garden there are views of the sea, the cliffs, the Isle of Wight (on a clear day) and a large wildlife pond in the field below. Shrub roses in the meadow garden.

109 WHITE HOUSE

Newtown, Witchampton, Wimborne, BH21 5AU. Mr Tim Read, 01258 840438, tim.read@catralex.com. *5m N of Wimborne off B3078. Travel through village of Witchampton towards Newtown for 800m. Pass Crichel House's castellated gates on L. White House is a modern house sitting back from road on L after further 300m.* **Sat 2, Sun 3 July (2-5). Adm £4, chd free. Light refreshments. Visits also by arrangement May to Sept for groups of up to 10.**

1½ acre garden set on different levels, with a Mediterranean feel, planted to encourage wildlife and pollinators. Wildflower border, pond surrounded by moisture loving plants, prairie planting of grasses and perennials, orchard. Chainsaw sculptures of birds of prey. Reasonable wheelchair access to all but the top level of the garden.

110 ◆ WIMBORNE MODEL TOWN & GARDENS

16 King Street, Wimborne, BH21 1DY. Wimborne Minster Model Town Ltd Registered Charity No 298116, 01202 881924, info@wimborne-modeltown.com, www.wimborne-modeltown.com. *2 mins walk from Wimborne town centre & the Minster Church. Follow Wimborne signs from A31; from Poole/Bournemouth follow Wimborne signs on A341; from N follow Wimborne signs B3082/*

B3078. Public parking opp in King St car park. **For opening times and information, please phone, email or visit garden website.**

Attractive garden surrounding intriguing model town buildings, inc original 1950s miniature buildings of Wimborne. Herbaceous borders, rockery, perennials, shrubs and rare trees. Miniature river system inc bog garden and other water features. Sensory area inc vegetable garden, grasses, a seasonally fragrant and colourful border, wind and water features. Plentiful seating. Open 27 March - 31 October (10am - 5pm). Seniors discount; groups welcome. Tea room, shop, crazy golf, miniature dolls' house collection, 00 gauge model railway, Wendy Street play area.

111 WINCOMBE PARK

Shaftesbury, SP7 9AB. John & Phoebe Fortescue, 01747 852121, pacfortescue@gmail.com, www.wincombepark.com. *2m N of Shaftesbury. A350 Shaftesbury to Warminster, past Wincombe Business Park, 1st R signed Wincombe & Donhead St Mary. ¾m on R.* **Sun 15, Wed 18 May (2-5). Adm £6, chd free. Home-made teas. Dairy and gluten free options available. Visits also by arrangement May & June for groups of 10+.**

Extensive mature garden with sweeping panoramic views from lawn over parkland to lake and enchanting woods through which you can wander amongst bluebells. Garden is a riot of colour in spring with azaleas, camellias and rhododendrons in flower amongst shrubs and unusual trees. Beautiful walled kitchen garden. Partial wheelchair access only, slopes and gravel paths.

112 WOLVERHOLLOW

Elsdons Lane, Monkton Wyld, DT6 6DA. Mr & Mrs D Wiscombe. *4m N of Lyme Regis. Monkton Wyld is signed from A35 approx 4m NW of Charmouth off dual carriageway. Wolverhollow is next to church.* **Mon 2, Tue 3 May, Mon 7, Mon 8 Aug (11.30-4.30). Adm £5, chd free. Home-made teas.**

Over 1 acre of informal mature garden on different levels. Lawns lead past borders and rockeries down to a shady lower garden. Numerous paths take you past a variety of

uncommon shrubs and plants. A managed meadow has an abundance of primulas growing close to stream. A garden not to be missed! Cabin in meadow area from which vintage, retro and other lovely things can be purchased.

113 NEW WYKE FARM

Chedington, Beaminster, DT8 3HX. Alex & Robert Appleby, wykefarm.com. *Take the turning from the A356, opp The Winyards Gap Inn, away from Chedington, signposted to Halstock. Drive 1m down the lane and we are the first farm entrance on the L.* **Sat 18, Sun 19 June (9.30-5). Adm £8, chd free.**

The farm house garden was planted when the building of the house was finished in 2005. There are herbaceous borders and lawns around the house. There is a rose garden that leads to a woodland garden, then a more formal courtyard garden that leads through the barn to a kitchen garden. At the front of the house there are wildflower meadows which we have been establishing for about 15 yrs. The paths are gravel.

114 YARDES COTTAGE

Dewlish, Dorchester, DT2 7LT. Christine & Ross Robertson, 07774 855152, christine.m.robertson@hotmail.com. *9m NE of Dorchester. From A35 Puddletown/A354 junction, take B3142 & immed turn R onto Long Lane. Follow road around bend to R, then turn R through Dewlish to garden. Disabled parking only.* **Thur 30 June, Sat 2 July (1-5). Adm £5, chd free. Cream teas. Visits also by arrangement June & July for groups of up to 10.**

Country cottage garden of 1½ acres bordering the Devil's Brook, having a wealth of different planting areas inc woodland, stream, small lake, extensive lawns fringed with formal herbaceous borders, vegetable and soft fruit areas. Much of the planting encourages insect life and supports our bees and hens. Yardes Cottage honey for sale.

ESSEX

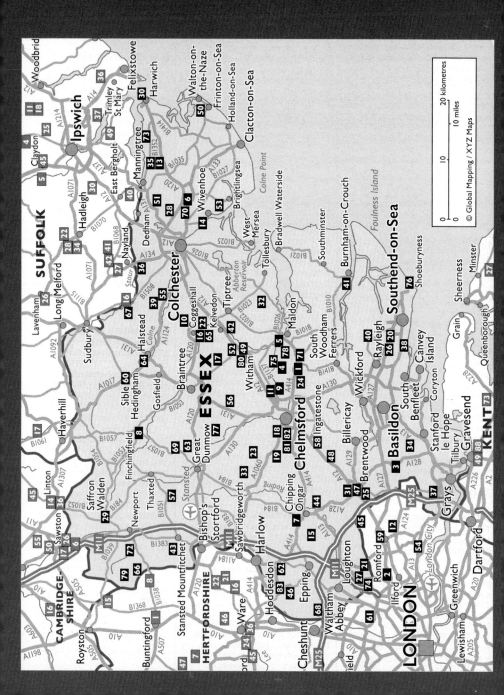

Close to London but with its own unique character, Essex is perhaps England's best kept secret - with a beautiful coastline, rolling countryside and exquisite villages. It is a little known fact that over seventy per cent of Essex is rural. There are wide horizons, ancient woodlands and hamlets pierced by flint church spires.

A perfect mix of villages, small towns, coast line and riverside settings enables Essex to provide some of the most varied garden styles in the country.

Despite its proximity to London, Essex is a largely rural county, its rich, fertile soil and long hours of sunshine make it possible to grow a wide variety of plants and our garden owners make the most of this opportunity. We have some grand country estates, small town gardens and much in between.

Our year starts with snowdrop gardens in February, runs through tulip gardens in the spring and makes the most of the high summer months with gardens full of roses and colourful perennials. Our visiting season extends into late summer when many gardens feature more exotic and tropical planting schemes making September a good time to explore.

Recent months have shown that, more than ever, visiting a garden provides huge benefits to mind and body. And whether you wish to visit as part of a group or club, with family, friends or on your own, you will be sure of a warm welcome. Our garden owners are usually on hand to talk about their garden to ensure you leave with a little more knowledge and lots of inspiration.

We look forward to sharing our gardens with you.

Volunteers

County Organiser
Susan Copeland
01799 550553
susan.copeland@ngs.org.uk

County Treasurer
Richard Steers
07392 426490
steers123@aol.com

Publicity & Social Media Co-ordinator
Debbie Thomson
07759 226579
debbie.thomson@ngs.org.uk

Publicity & Social Media Assistant Co-ordinator
Alan Gamblin 07720 446797
alan.gamblin@ngs.org.uk

Booklet Co-ordinator and Publicity Assistant
Doug Copeland 01799 550553
doug.copeland@ngs.org.uk

Assistant County Organisers
Tricia Brett 01255 870415
tricia.brett@ngs.org.uk

Avril & Roger Cole-Jones
01245 225726
randacj@gmail.com

Lesley Gamblin 07801 445299
lesley.gamblin@ngs.org.uk

Linda & Frank Jewson
01992 714047
linda.jewson@ngs.org.uk

Frances Vincent 07766 707379
frances.vincent@ngs.org.uk

Talks
Ed Fairey 07780 685634
ed@faireyassociates.co.uk

County Photographer
Caroline Cassell 07973 551196
caroline.cassell@ngs.org.uk

 @EssexNGS   **@EssexNGS**   **@essexngs**

Left: Ace Gardeners at Grange Farm Community Garden

OPENING DATES

All entries subject to change. For latest information check www.ngs.org.uk

Extended openings are shown at the beginning of the month.

Map locator numbers are shown to the right of each garden name.

January

Sunday 23rd
◆ Green Island — 28

February

Snowdrop Festival

Saturday 12th
Horkesley Hall — 36

Wednesday 16th
Dragons — 19

Thursday 17th
Dragons — 19

Sunday 20th
Grove Lodge — 29
Longyard Cottage — 46

Sunday 27th
Grove Lodge — 29

March

Saturday 12th
Beth Chatto's Plants & Gardens — 6

April

Every Thursday
Barnards Farm — 3

Every Thursday and Friday
Feeringbury Manor — 22

Friday 8th
◆ Beeleigh Abbey Gardens — 5

Sunday 17th
Peacocks — 58

Saturday 23rd
Loxley House — 47
Writtle University College — 82

Sunday 24th
Ulting Wick — 75

Friday 29th
Scrips House — 65
Ulting Wick — 75

May

Every Thursday
Barnards Farm — 3

Every Thursday and Friday
Feeringbury Manor — 22

Sunday 1st
NEW Bucklers Farmhouse — 10
Furzelea — 24

Monday 2nd
Heyrons — 33

Friday 6th
Bassetts — 4

Saturday 7th
◆ Green Island — 28
39 Wakering Avenue — 76

Sunday 8th
Bassetts — 4
The Old Vicarage — 57
1 Whitehouse Cottages — 78

Saturday 14th
14 Clifton Terrace — 14

Sunday 15th
14 Clifton Terrace — 14
NEW The Old Rectory — 56
Peacocks — 58

Wednesday 18th
NEW Appledore, 46 Hopping Jacks Lane — 1

Saturday 21st
NEW May Cottage — 50
Moverons — 53
79 Royston Avenue — 61

Sunday 22nd
NEW Appledore, 46 Hopping Jacks Lane — 1
NEW Laurel Cottage — 43
Moverons — 53
79 Royston Avenue — 61

Saturday 28th
Fairfield — 20

Sunday 29th
Chippins — 13
Fairfield — 20
Fairwinds — 21
The Gates — 25
Horkesley Hall — 36
Rookwoods — 60
Silver Birches — 68

Tuesday 31st
Caynton Cottage — 11

June

Every Thursday
Barnards Farm — 3

Every Thursday and Friday
Feeringbury Manor — 22

Wednesday 1st
Caynton Cottage — 11

Thursday 2nd
Caynton Cottage — 11

Friday 3rd
Grove Lodge — 29

Saturday 4th
Isabella's Garden — 38

Sunday 5th
Furzelea — 24
Isabella's Garden — 38
NEW Jankes House — 39
Sheepcote Green Gardens — 66
37 Turpins Lane — 74

Tuesday 7th
8 Dene Court — 18

Wednesday 8th
Oak Farm — 55

Friday 10th
NEW Bucklers Farmhouse — 10

Sunday 12th
NEW Bucklers Farmhouse — 10
Peacocks — 58
NEW Walnut Tree Cottage — 77

Friday 17th
8 Dene Court — 18
Havendell — 32

Saturday 18th
Havendell — 32

Sunday 19th
Oak Farm — 55
The Old Vicarage — 57
Peacocks — 58
1 Whitehouse Cottages — 78

Saturday 25th
NEW May Cottage — 50
18 Pettits Boulevard, RM1 — 59

Sunday 26th
Barnards Farm — 3
Clunes House — 15
Fudlers Hall — 23
18 Pettits Boulevard, RM1 — 59
Writtle Gardens — 81

Tuesday 28th
8 Dene Court — 18

Wednesday 29th
Keeway — 41

July

Every Thursday
Barnards Farm — 3

Every Thursday and Friday
Feeringbury Manor — 22

Friday 1st
9 Malyon Road — 49

Saturday 2nd
NEW Chine House — 12
Keeway — 41
9 Malyon Road — 49
Miraflores — 52

Sunday 3rd
Chippins — 13
262 Hatch Road — 31
Havendell — 32
2 Hope Cottages — 35
9 Malyon Road — 49
Miraflores — 52
Peacocks — 58
37 Turpins Lane — 74
Wychwood — 83

Wednesday 6th
Little Myles — 44
Long House Plants — 45
Oak Farm — 55

Friday 8th
8 Dene Court — 18
Ulting Wick — 75

'In 2021 the generous donation from the National Garden Scheme helped 12,000 unpaid carers to access the support they need, with 50 more receiving crisis grants to support those in dire need.'

Carers Trust

THE GARDENS

1 NEW APPLEDORE, 46 HOPPING JACKS LANE
Danbury, CM3 4PJ. Gerry & Lynne Collins, 01245 221341, lynnemorley@ymail.com, www. lynnemorleygardendesign.co.uk. *Danbury, Essex. From Eves Corner small public car park, take the narrow one way road into Hopping Jacks Lane. Garden is approx 400 metres on the R opp Simmons Way. RHS Hyde Hall is within 4m of garden.* **Wed 18 May (2-5); Sun 22 May (11-5); Wed 19 Oct (2-5); Sun 23 Oct (11-5). Adm £4, chd free. Tea, coffee and cakes. Visits also by arrangement May to Oct for groups of up to 12.**
Tranquil village garden featuring mature trees, shady paths, sunny lawn and borders. Paths circulate around the garden leading to a moon gate framing our secret garden, where you can sit and relax a while. Planting inc a growing collection of over 40 Japanese Acers with Ferns and Hostas providing the understorey. Dahlias in the borders and Acers in flaming foliage provide autumn interest.

2 254 ASHURST DRIVE
Barkingside, IG6 1EW. Maureen Keating, 07984 646374. *2m S of Chigwell. Nearest tube: Barkingside on Central Line approx 8 mins walk. Bus: 150 stops outside Tesco's on Cranbrook Rd. go round R side of Tescos car park. Keep R, alleyway leads to Ashurst Drive.* **Sun 24 July (11-4). Adm £3.50. Light refreshments. Visits also by arrangement July & Aug for groups of 10 to 20.**
Bird friendly colour filled town garden with interesting nooks and crannies each telling a story. Contains seven water features, six seating areas, waterfall, pond and stream, model village and vibrant planting all in 40 ft square area! Regret, garden unsuitable for children.

3 BARNARDS FARM
Brentwood Road, West Horndon, CM13 3FY. Bernard & Sylvia Holmes & The Christabella Charitable Trust, 01268 454075, vanessa@barnardsfarm.eu, www.barnardsfarm.eu.

What3words app - tulip.folds.statue. 5m S of Brentwood. On A128 1½m S of A127 Halfway House flyover. From Junction continue S on A128 under the railway bridge. Garden on R just past bridge. Please use postcode CM13 3FY **Every Thur 7 Apr to 1 Sept (11-4.30). Adm £8.50, chd free. Sun 26 June, Sun 4 Sept (1-5). Adm £12, chd free. Pre-booking essential, please visit www.ngs.org.uk for information & booking. Light refreshments. Visits also by arrangement for groups of 30+. Refreshments can normally be provided by arrangement.**
So much to explore! Climb the Belvedere for the wider view and take the train for a woodland adventure. Spring bulbs and blossom, summer beds and borders, ponds, lakes and streams, walled vegetable plot. 'Japanese garden', sculptures grand and quirky enhance and delight. See the new Talia-May Avenue and Angel sculptures. Sorry, no dogs except guide dogs. Barnards Miniature Railway rides (BMR): Separate charges apply. Sunday extras: Bernard's Sculpture tour 2.30pm Car collection. 1920s Cycle shop. Archery. Model T Ford Rides. Collect loyalty points on Thur visits and earn a free Sun or Thur entry. Season Tickets available Aviators welcome (PPO). Picnics welcome. Wheelchair accessible WC Golf Buggy tours available.

4 BASSETTS
Bassetts Lane, Little Baddow, Chelmsford, CM3 4BZ. Mrs Margaret Chalmers, 079401 79572, magschalmers@btinternet.com. *1m down Tofts Chase which becomes Bassetts Ln. Big yellow house on L, wooden gates, red brick wall. From Spring Elms Ln go down Bassetts Ln ½m. House on R.* **Fri 6, Sun 8 May (10.30-5). Adm £5, chd free. Visits also by arrangement May to Oct.**
2 acre garden, tennis court, swimming pool surrounding an early C17 house with plants for year-round interest set on gently sloping ground with lovely distant views of the Essex countryside. Shrub borders and mature ornamental trees, an orchard and two natural ponds. Many places to sit and relax. No refreshments but bring a picnic and enjoy the views! Please check wheelchair access with garden owner 01245 226768.

5 ♦ BEELEIGH ABBEY GARDENS
Abbey Turning, Beeleigh, Maldon, CM9 6LL. Christopher & Catherine Foyle, 07506 867122, www. visitmaldon.co.uk/beeleigh-abbey. *1m NW of Maldon. Leaving Maldon via London Road take 1st R after Cemetery into Abbey Turning.* For NGS: **Fri 8 Apr (10.30-4.30). Adm £7, chd £2.50. Home-made teas.** For other opening times and information, please phone or visit garden website.
3 acres of secluded gardens in rural historic setting. Mature trees surround variety of planting and water features, woodland walks under planted with bulbs leading to tidal river, cottage garden, kitchen garden, orchard, wildflower meadow, rose garden, wisteria walk, magnolia trees, lawn with 85yd long herbaceous border. Scenic backdrop of remains of C12 abbey incorporated into private house (not open). Refreshments inc hot and cold drinks, cakes and rolls. Wheelchair access, gravel paths, some gentle slopes and some steps. Large WC with ramp and handlebars.

6 ♦ BETH CHATTO'S PLANTS & GARDENS
Elmstead Market, Colchester, CO7 7DB. Beth Chatto's Plants & Gardens, 01206 822007, customer@bethchatto.co.uk, www.bethchatto.co.uk. *¼m E of Elmstead Market. On A133 Colchester to Clacton Rd in village of Elmstead Market.* For NGS: **Sat 12 Mar (10-4); Sat 24 Sept (10-5). Adm £10.45, chd free. Light refreshments at Chatto's inc sandwiches, pastries, cakes, hot & cold beverages.** For other opening times and information, please phone, email or visit garden website.
Internationally famous gardens, inc dry, damp, shade, reservoir and woodland areas. The result of over 60 yrs of hard work and application of the huge body of plant knowledge possessed by Beth Chatto and her husband Andrew. Visitors cannot fail to be affected by the peace and beauty of the garden. Beth is renowned internationally for her books, her gardens and her influence on the world of gardening and plants. Please visit website for up to date visiting details and pre-booking Picnic area available in the adjacent field. Disabled WC & parking. Wheelchair access around all of the gardens - on gravel or

grass (concrete in Nursery, Welcome Centre & Gardener's shop areas).

7 BLAKE HALL
Bobbingworth, CM5 0DG.
Mr & Mrs H Capel Cure,
www.blakehall.co.uk. *10m W of Chelmsford. Just off A414 between Four Wantz r'about in Ongar & Talbot r'about in North Weald. Signed on A414.* **Sun 4 Sept (10.30-4). Adm £6, chd free. Home-made teas in C17 barn.**
25 acres of mature gardens within the historic setting of Blake Hall (not open). Arboretum with broad variety of specimen and spectacular ancient trees. Lawns overlooking countryside. Plenty of late summer/early autumn colour - one of our favourite times of year in the gardens. Teas served from Essex Barn. Some gravel paths.

8 BRICK HOUSE
The Green, Finchingfield, Saffron Walden, CM7 4JS. Mr Graham & Mrs Susan Tobbell. *9m NW of Braintree. Brick House in the centre of the picturesque village of Finchingfield, at the Xrds of the B1053 & B1057 in rural NW Essex.* **Sat 16 July (2-6). Adm £6, chd**

free. Light refreshments. Tea, coffee, soft drinks, bottled water, a variety of cakes, strawberries and cream.
This recently renovated period property and garden covers 1½ acres, with a brook running through the middle. The garden features contemporary sculptures, and several distinct planting styles; most notably a hidden scented cottage-style garden, a crinkle-crankle walled area with an oriental feel and some rather glorious high summer herbaceous borders inspired by the New Perennial Movement. Modern marble sculptures by Paul Vanstone add drama and contrast to the soft landscaping. Garden is professionally designed to be a calming space.

9 BROOKFIELD
Church Road, Boreham, CM3 3EB. Bob & Linda Taylor. *4m NE Chelmsford. Take B1137 Boreham village, turn R into Church Rd at Lion Inn. In approx ¼m turning on R after The Chase marked 58-76 Church Rd. Pedestrians & disabled access only - please park & walk down.* **Sun 4 Sept (11-5). Adm £5, chd free. Home-made teas.**
A large garden with a long wall border and perennial island beds glowing with

late summer colour, inc dahlias and roses. Other highlights are a vegetable garden with raised beds and a soft fruit area, a pond and a shrub bank. The garden opens out into a landscaped meadow surrounded with many trees and a woodland area. Over 3 acres to explore. Wheelchair access to main part of garden. Partial access to meadow.

10 NEW BUCKLERS FARMHOUSE
Buckleys Lane, Coggeshall, Colchester, CO6 1SB. Ann Bartleet. *1½m E of Coggeshall. 1m N of A120 via Salmons Lane.* **Sun 1 May, Fri 10, Sun 12 June (1.30-5.30). Adm £6, chd free. Home-made teas.**
Traditional country garden, with blowsy borders, yew hedges, topiary and a little knot garden. A very tranquil, magical place, with two ponds and a pool - is it just for the reflections or can you swim in it? In the spring we have about 1,000 tulips. Later, there is a terrace full of succulents, almost no room for sitting! This 2 acre garden has been created by the owners over the last 50 yrs. There is gravel, but about 50% of the garden is accessible with a wheelchair.

Bucklers Farmhouse

1 CAYNTON COTTAGE
Church Road, Boreham, Chelmsford, CM3 3EF. Les & Lynn Mann. *4m NE Chelmsford. Take B1137 Boreham Village, turn into Church Rd at the Lion Inn. 50mtrs on L.* **Tue 31 May, Wed 1, Thur 2 June (1-5). Adm £4, chd free. Home-made teas.**

A traditional cottage garden designed and planted by the owners since 2013 from a neglected and overgrown plot surrounding a C15 thatched cottage (not open). Planted with a good selection of shrubs and perennials for maximum all year interest with a small wildlife pond and dry stream. It is ever changing as the plants grow and mature to fill the space, with new features added each season.

✿ ☕

2 NEW CHINE HOUSE
Hornchurch, RM11 1HA. Mrs Lily Crosby. *Close to the Osborne Rd entrance of Hylands Park, Hornchurch on the same side of the rd as Hylands Park.* **Sat 2 July (11-4). Adm £5, chd free. Home-made teas.**

Our suburban garden in Havering is approx. ¼ acre. Laid to lawn with flower beds containing annuals, perennials, shrubs, roses and trees. There is a small pond with goldfish, a vegetable plot and seating areas to rest and enjoy the variety of plants. Over the last 28 yrs we have planted whatever we fancy so this garden is a mix of vibrant colours and plants. We hope you will enjoy your visit.

♿ ✿ ☕

3 CHIPPINS
Heath Road, Bradfield, CO11 2UZ. Kit & Ceri Leese, 01255 870730, ceriandkit@gmail.com. *3m E of Manningtree. Take A137 from Manningtree Station, turn L opp garage. Take 1st R towards Clacton. At Radio Mast turn L into Bradfield continue through village. Bungalow is opp primary school.* **Sun 29 May (11-4). Sun 3 July (11-4), open nearby 2 Hope Cottages. Adm £4, chd free. Home-made teas. Visits also by arrangement May to July for groups of 5 to 35. Small sketching classes can be offered by arrangement.**

Artist's and plantaholics' paradise packed with interest. Spring heralds hostas, aquilegia and irises. Inc meandering stream, wildlife pond and Horace the Huge! Vast range of colourful summer perennials in large mixed borders, featuring day lilies. Over one hundred pots and hanging baskets! Exotic border with cannas and dahlias. Studio in conservatory with paintings and etching press. Kit is a landscape artist and printmaker, pictures always on display. Afternoon tea with delicious homemade cakes is also available for small parties (min of 5) on specific days if booked in advance.

♿ ✿ 🚗 ☕ 🔊

4 14 CLIFTON TERRACE
Wivenhoe, Colchester, CO7 9DY. Mr Michael & Mrs Liz Taylor Jones. *Clifton Terrace turning on R off Wivenhoe High St opp Greyhound Pub, beside Concord estate agents. On R of Clifton Terrace is the public car park & WC. Clifton Terrace ends in our front garden situated just above the station platform.* **Sat 14, Sun 15 May (12-5). Adm £4, chd free.**

A very long, narrow garden alongside the railway station. Near house: herbaceous border, shrubs, lawn and roses. Slope down to station footpath: ground cover shrubs. Beyond the lawn: vegetable garden and small orchard, treehouse in walnut tree and swing. Continue to part of old coppiced Wivenhoe Woods. Beyond a wildlife pond, natural woodland continues to rhododendrons, bamboos and a second pond. Unfortunately no refreshments will be served.

🐕 ✿ 🪑

Walnut Tree Cottage

15 CLUNES HOUSE
Mill Lane, Toot Hill, Ongar,
CM5 9SF. Dr Hugh & Mrs Elaine
Taylor. *4m from J7 M11 & 4m from
the Towns of Ongar & Epping. The
garden is at the end of Mill Ln in
Toot Hill.* **Sun 26 June, Sun 24
July (10.30-4). Adm £6, chd free.
Home-made teas.**
This is a beautiful, and interesting
traditional country garden with
wonderful views over the Essex
countryside. A pergola with roses,
clematis and wisteria leads into a
woodland walk and pond surrounded
by herbaceous borders and sculpture.
A path through the wildlife meadow
takes you into the orchard and a small
holding with pigs and sheep, ending
at the kitchen garden and cut flower
beds. Original World War II air raid
shelter. The garden is adjacent to the
'Essex Way' long distance walking trail.

16 NEW COGGESHALL HAMLET ALLOTMENTS
Kelvedon Road, Coggeshall,
Colchester, CO6 1RJ. Denise
Brodie. *From A12 N/S take
Kelvedon/Feering exit. Turn L/R onto
B1024 past Kelvedon stn. Continue
for approx 2½ m - Allotments on R
From A120 take Coggeshall exit.* **Sun
7 Aug (10.30-3). Combined adm
with Scrips House £10, chd free.
Light refreshments. Home-made
cold drinks available. Individual
garden adm £4.**
Next to the River Blackwater and
surrounded by open countryside the
allotments have been established on
this tranquil site for over many years.
With 35 plots the friendly allotment
community grows a wide range of
vegetables, flowers and fruit. The
site is a haven for bees and wildlife.
Differing size plots, eclectic mix of
sheds, diverse growing methods
make an entertaining visit. Partial
wheelchair access on grass paths.

17 CRESSING TEMPLE COMMUNITY GARDEN
Witham Road, Cressing,
Braintree, CM77 8PD. Rebecca
Ashbey, 07747 670058,
rebecca.ashbey@essex.gov.uk,
www.thefriendsofcressingtemple.
org. *Between Braintree & Witham on
B1018. Follow brown tourist signs to
Cressing Temple Historic monument
Ample on-site parking.* **Visits by
arrangement Apr to Sept.**
In 2016, The Friends of Cressing

Temple developed unused land to
create the Community Garden with
growing areas, polytunnels and beds.
Educational resource for volunteers
to learn new skills, share experiences
and tasks. Garden produces fresh
fruit and vegetables for visitors.
Demonstrations of environment
friendly gardening and sustainable
horticulture. Guided tours of the Tudor
walled garden. Community shop open
selling produce, home made cakes,
homemade craft items and willow
products for your garden made from
willow grown on site.

18 8 DENE COURT
Chignall Road, Chelmsford,
CM1 2JQ. Mrs Sheila Chapman,
01245 266156. *W of Chelmsford
(Parkway). Take A1060 Roxwell
Rd for 1m. Turn R at T-lights into
Chignall Rd. Dene Court 3rd exit on
R. Parking in Chignall Rd.* **Tue 7,
Fri 17, Tue 28 June, Fri 8, Sat 16
July (2-5). Wed 27 July (2-5). Fri 5
Aug (2-5). Tue 16 Aug (2-5), open
nearby Dragons. Wed 24 Aug (2-
5). Sun 4 Sept (2-5), open nearby
Dragons, see details below.
Adm £3.50, chd free. Visits also
by arrangement June to Sept for
groups of 10 to 40.**
Beautifully maintained and designed
compact garden (250sq yds). Owner
is well-known RHS gold medal-
winning exhibitor (now retired).
Circular lawn, long pergola and walls
festooned with roses and climbers.
Large selection of unusual clematis.
Densely-planted colour coordinated
perennials add interest from June to
Sept in this immaculate garden.

19 DRAGONS
Boyton Cross, Chelmsford,
CM1 4LS. Mrs Margot
Grice, 01245 248651,
margot@snowdragons.co.uk. *3m
W of Chelmsford. On A1060. ½ m W
of The Hare Pub.* **Wed 16, Thur 17
Feb (11-3). Light refreshments.
Wed 27 July, Tue 16 Aug, Sun
4 Sept (2-5). Home-made teas.
Open nearby 8 Dene Court.
Adm £5, chd free. Visits also by
arrangement Feb to Oct for groups
of 10+.**
A plantswoman's ¾ acre garden,
planted to encourage wildlife.
Sumptuous colour-themed borders
with striking plant combinations,
featuring specimen plants, fernery,
clematis and grasses. Meandering

paths lead to ponds, patio, scree
garden and small vegetable garden.
Two summerhouses, one overlooking
stream and farmland.

20 FAIRFIELD
5 Fairfield Road, Leigh-On-Sea,
SS9 5RZ. Rob & Gwen Evison.
*Follow A127 towards Southend
past Rayleigh Weir. At Progress
Rd T-lights turn L. At the end turn
R at the T-lights along Rayleigh Rd
A1015. Fairfield Road is approx
1m on the L.* **Sat 28, Sun 29 May
(12-5). Adm £4, chd free. Light
refreshments.**
A lovingly kept garden divided into
different areas. A seating area with
climbing plants and topiary leads
to a lawn with numerous beds
filled with roses, alliums, irises and
peonies. Rose covered arch leads
to a secluded woodland area, young
birch and maple trees and many
woodland plants inc camellias and
rhododendrons. Living evergreen
arches lead to a magical secret
garden. Most of the garden is
wheelchair accessible. There are a
few shallow steps.

21 FAIRWINDS
Chapel Lane, Chigwell
Row, IG7 6JJ. Sue & David
Coates, 07731 796467,
scoates@forest.org.uk. *2m SE of
Chigwell, Grange Hill Tube turn R at
exit, 10 mins walk uphill. Car: Nr M25
J26. From N Circular Waterworks
r'about, signed Chigwell. Fork R
for Manor/Lambourne Rd. Park in
Lodge Close Car Park. Space for 2
disabled cars to park by the house.*
**Sun 29 May (2-5). Adm £5, chd
free. Home-made teas. Visits also
by arrangement Mar to Oct for
groups of 10 to 25.**
Gravelled front garden and three
differently styled back garden spaces
with planting changes every year.
Established wildflower meadow in
main lawn. Meander, sit, relax and
enjoy. Beyond the rustic fence, lies
the wildlife pond and vegetable plot.
Planting influenced by Beth Chatto,
Penelope Hobhouse, Christopher
Lloyd and Piet Oudolf. Happy insects
in bee house, bug houses, log piles,
meadow and sampling the spring
pollen. Newts in pond. There be
dragons a plenty!! Wheelchair access
wood chip paths in woodland area
may require assistance.

22 FEERINGBURY MANOR

Coggeshall Road, Feering, CO5 9RB. Mr & Mrs Giles Coode-Adams, 01376 561946, seca@btinternet.com. *Between Feering & Coggeshall on Coggeshall Rd, 1m from Feering village.* **Every Thur and Fri 1 Apr to 29 July (10-4). Every Thur and Fri 1 Sept to 14 Oct (10-4). Adm £6, chd free. Visits also by arrangement for groups of up to 20. Donation to Feering Church.**

There is always plenty to see in this peaceful 10 acre garden with two ponds and river Blackwater. Jewelled lawn in early April then spectacular tulips and blossom lead on to a huge number of different and colourful plants, many unusual, culminating in a purple explosion of michaelmas daisies in late Sept. No wheelchair access to arboretum, steep slope.

&. 🐴

23 FUDLERS HALL

Fox Road, Mashbury, CM1 4TJ. Mr & Mrs A J Meacock, 01245 231335. *7m NW of Chelmsford. Chelmsford take A1060, R into Chignal Rd. ½m L to Chignal St James approx 5m, 2nd R into Fox Rd signed Gt Waltham. Fudlers From Gt Waltham. Take Barrack Lane for 3m.* **Sun 26 June, Sun 10 July (2-5). Adm £6, chd free. Cream teas. Visits also by arrangement in July.**

An award winning, romantic 2 acre garden surrounding C17 farmhouse with lovely pastoral views, across the Chelmer Valley. Old walls divide garden into many rooms, each having a different character, featuring long herbaceous borders, ropes and pergolas festooned with rambling old fashioned roses. Enjoy the vibrant hot border in late summer. Yew hedged kitchen garden. Ample seating. Wonderful views across Chelmer Valley. 2 new flower beds, many roses. 500yr old yew tree. gravel farmyard and 30ft path to gardens, all of which is level lawn.

&. 🚗 🍵

24 FURZELEA

Bicknacre Road, Danbury, CM3 4JR. Avril & Roger Cole-Jones, 01245 225726, randacj@gmail.com. *4m E of Chelmsford, 4m W of Maldon A414 to Danbury. At village centre S into Mayes Ln. 1st R. Past Cricketers Pub, L on to Bicknacre Rd. Use NT car park on L. Garden 50 metres on R. Or parking 200 m past on L. Use*

NT Common paths from back of car park. **Sun 1 May, Sun 5 June, Sun 10 July, Sun 18 Sept (11-5). Adm £6, chd free. Home-made teas. Visits also by arrangement Apr to Sept for groups of 15+.**

Country garden of nearly one acre that has evolved overtime to showcase the seasons by titillating the senses with colour, scent, texture and form. Paths, steps and archways lead you onwards through intimate spaces and flowing lawns. Clipped box hedges edge flower beds of tulips in spring, roses, hemerocallis and other herbaceous plants in summer, dahlias, grasses, salvias and exotics in autumn. Black and White garden plus exotics and many unusual plants add to the Visitors interest. International garden tour visitors voted us the best garden in their recent tours of East Anglia. Opp Danbury Common (NT), short walk to Danbury Country Park and Lakes and short drive to RHS Hyde Hall.

✻ 🚗 🍵 ♪))

25 THE GATES

London Road Cemetery, London Road, Brentwood, CM14 4QW. Ms Mary Yiannoullou, www.frontlinepartnership.org. *At the rear of the cemetery. Enter the Cemetery (opp Tesco Express). Drive to the rear of the cemetery where you will see our site on L. Limited parking within but plenty in the surrounding rds.* **Sun 29 May (11-3.30). Adm £4, chd free. Home-made teas in the Tea House.**

A horticultural project that offers local citizens, inc vulnerable adults, an opportunity to develop new skills within a horticultural setting. Greenhouses and allotments for raising bedding plants, educational workshops and growing fruit and vegetables. Walks through the Woodland Dell and Sensory area. Large variety of plants and produce for sale. Enjoy the mosaic garden, visit the apiary and relax in the various seating areas around the site. All areas are accessed via slopes and ramps.

&. ✻ 🍵 ♪))

26 30 GLENWOOD AVENUE

Leigh-On-Sea, SS9 5EB. Joan Squibb, 07543 031772, squibb44@gmail.com. *Follow A127 towards Southend. Past Rayleigh Weir. At Progress Rd T-lights turn L. At next T-lights turn L down Rayleigh Rd A1015. Past shops*

turn 2nd L into Glenwood Ave. *Garden halfway down on R.* **Sun 4 Sept (10.30-4). Adm £4, chd free. Light refreshments. £3 for tea and slice of cake. Visits also by arrangement July to Sept for groups of up to 12.**

Nestled next to the busy A127 lies a beautifully transformed town garden. Home-made raised beds with tulips in spring, dahlias and roses in the summer. From a corridor, you emerge into an open garden giving a vista of colour, inspiration and peaceful harmony, with many different scents to savour. Hanging baskets bloom in the fruit trees and along the fences. A paved area allows one to enjoy the view of the garden as does a deck at the back where herbs and some vegetables live alongside the flowers. A peaceful vista, to sit in and restore the batteries. Vegetables are also grown in raised beds.

🍵

27 NEW GRANGE FARM COMMUNITY GARDEN

High Road, Chigwell, IG7 6DP. Mrs Sally Panrucker, 07809 151020, spanrucker@vaef.org.uk. *Turn off High Rd onto Grange Farm Ln, the Grange Farm Centre is aprox 500 metres on the L (plenty of free parking).* **Thur 21 July (10.30-3). Adm £4, chd free. Light refreshments. Visits also by arrangement in July.**

An allotment project maintained by a group of adults with learning disabilities set within the beautiful grounds of The Grange Farm Centre, adjoining Chigwell Meadows. All staff and volunteers are trained using the THRIVE therapeutic approach to gardening. We encourage members to be fully involved in all aspects of gardening: choosing plants and long term planning. Range of goods for sale, inc hanging baskets, planters, home-made jams and pickles all grown and made by our members. Meet our wonderful Ace Gardeners who will be proud to tell you about the lovely community garden that they have helped develop.

&. 🐴 ✻ 🚗 🍵 🪑

28 ◆ GREEN ISLAND

Park Road, Ardleigh, CO7 7SP. Fiona Edmond, 01206 230455, greenislandgardens@gmail.com, www.greenislandgardens.co.uk. *3m NE of Colchester. From Ardleigh village centre, take B1029 towards Great Bromley. Park Rd is 2nd on R*

after level crossing. *Garden is last on L.* **For NGS: Sun 23 Jan (10-5). Adm £8. Sat 7 May (10-5); Sat 8 Oct (10-4). Adm £8, chd £2.50. Home-made cakes, scones, sandwiches and baguettes, Cream teas or full afternoon teas to order Picnics only in car park area. 2023: Sun 22 Jan. For other opening times and information, please phone, email or visit garden website. Donation to Plant Heritage.**

A garden for all seasons, highlights inc bluebells, azaleas, autumn colour, winter hamamelis and snowdrops. A plantsman's paradise. Carved within 20 acre mature woodland are huge island beds, Japanese garden, terrace, gravel, seaside and water gardens, all packed with rare and unusual plants. Bluebells Bazaar weekend 7/8 May, Autumn colour weekend 8/9 Oct, Snowdrops 22 Jan 2023. National collections of Hamamelis cvs and Camellias (autumn and winter flowering). January-Hamamelis, February-snowdrops, May-bluebells, azaleas, acers and rhododendrons. Summer-water gardens, island beds and tree lilies. Oct/Nov-Stunning autumn colour. Flat and easy walking /pushing wheelchairs. Ramps at entrance and tearoom. Disabled parking and WC.

29 GROVE LODGE
3 Chater's Hill, Saffron Walden, CB10 2AB. Chris Shennan, 01799 522271. *Approx 10 mins walk from town centre. Facing The Common on E side, about 100 yds from the turf maze. Note: Chater's Hill is one way.* **Sun 20 Feb (2-5). Home-made teas. Sun 27 Feb (2-5); Sorry, no refreshments available. Fri 3 June (2-5). Home-made teas. Adm £5, chd free. Visits also by arrangement Jan to Oct for groups of 5+. Afternoons preferred.**

A large walled garden close to the town centre with unusually high biodiversity (e.g. 17 species of butterfly recorded), close to the turf maze and Norman castle. Semi-woodland on light free-draining chalk soil allows bulbs, hellebores and winter-flowering shrubs to thrive. Two ponds, topiary, orchard and small vegetable garden blend some formality with informal areas where wildlife thrives. A profusion of snowdrops, other bulbs and spring blossom A town (walled) garden with unusually high biodiversity. Wheelchair access via fairly steep drive leading to terrace from which the garden may be viewed.

GROUP OPENING

30 HARWICH GARDENS
Harwich, CO12 3NH. *Centre of Old Harwich. Car park on Wellington Rd, CO12 3DT within 50 metres of St Helens Green. Street parking available.* **Sun 17 July (10.30-4). Combined adm £5, chd free. Teas, coffees, cakes and light refreshments available all day at 8 St. Helens Green.**

63 CHURCH STREET
Sue & Richard Watts.

30 KINGS HEAD STREET
Jane Monahan.

QUAYSIDE COURT
Dave Burton.

8 ST HELENS GREEN
Frances Vincent.

Four gardens all within walking distance in the historical town of Harwich. 8 St Helens Green, just 100m from the sea. A small town garden, with dahlias, hydrangeas mixed with perennials, small fruit trees and pots. 63 Church Street is a long, narrow walled courtyard with shrubs, climbers, perennials and a small vegetable garden packed into the garden. Architectural features inc an Elizabethan window with original glass. Quayside Court, a community garden, unusually boasts a sunken garden hidden from view at the end of the car park which features a pond, vegetable patch, roses and climbers. 30 Kings Head Street. This garden is at the back of what was the Ebenezer Chapel built by the Methodists in 1820 and more recently used as a chandlery but converted into a house in 2017. The garden was started in 2018, made from a concrete car park and is a work in progress. Already it boasts shrubs, perennials and some vegetables. It is a patch of peace in historic Harwich. Tickets and light refreshments available at 8 St Helens Green.

31 262 HATCH ROAD
Pilgrims Hatch, Brentwood, CM15 9QR. Mike & Liz Thomas. *2m N of Brentwood town centre. On A128 N toward Ongar turn R onto Doddinghurst Rd at mini-r'about (to Brentwood Centre) After the Centre turn next L into Hatch Rd. Garden 4th on R.* **Sun 3, Sun 17 July (11.30-4.30). Adm £5, chd free. Tea and cakes.**

A formal frontage with lavender. An eclectic rear garden of around an acre divided into 'rooms' with themed borders, several ponds, three greenhouses, fruit and vegetable plots and oriental garden. There is also a secret white garden, spring and summer wildflower meadows,Yin and Yang borders, a folly and an exotic area. There is plenty of seating to enjoy the views and a cup of tea and cake.

32 HAVENDELL
Beckingham Street, Tolleshunt Major, CM9 8LJ. Malcolm & Val. *5m E of Maldon 3m W of Tiptree. From B1022 take Loamy Hill rd. At the Xrds L into Witham Rd. Follow NGS signs.* **Fri 17, Sat 18 June, Sun 3 July (10.30-4). Sun 17 July (11-4.30). Home-made teas on 17 July only. Adm £4, chd free.**

This beautiful and tranquil garden will amaze and inspire you as you walk among the herbaceous and shrub borders. Meandering paths and seating areas entice you to take time out in a garden that surrounds you with nature in all its splendour. The many scented roses allowing all of your senses to be aroused. Exotic sub- tropical plants and over 50 hostas. WC available.

In 2021 the National Garden Scheme donation helped support Perennial's caseworkers, who helped over 250 people and their families in crisis to receive a wide range of support including emergency food parcels and accommodation, energy payments and expert advice and information

33 HEYRONS

High Easter, Chelmsford, CM1 4QN. Mr Richard Wollaston, 01245 231428, richard.wollaston@gmail.com. ½ m outside High Easter towards Good Easter. Via High Easter through village. Turn L down hill. ¼ m on R. Via Good Easter. After 2m on L halfway up hill before the village. Via Leaden Roding. After 2m turn L over bridge. ¼ m on L. **Mon 2 May (11-5). Adm £5, chd free. Pre-booking essential, please visit www.ngs.org.uk for information & booking. Light refreshments. Visits also by arrangement May to Sept for groups of 10 to 35.**

An informal garden of four parts created for family enjoyment within and around an ancient restored farmyard. An Essex barn and red brick farm buildings surround an intensely planted walled garden. A terraced area with mature trees, herbaceous and shady beds leads up to a rose garden. Beyond is an open area with grass tennis court, big skies, a small meadow and fine views over Essex countryside. Wheelchair access gravel driveway, small curb, shallow steps into farmyard, ramp available. Please email/call to arrange drop off or onsite parking.

& ❀ 🍵))

34 HILLDROP

Laindon Road (B1007), Horndon-On-The-Hill, Stanford-le-Hope, SS17 8QB. John Little & Fiona Crummay, www.grassroofcompany.co.uk. Just N of Horndon on the Hill. 80m E of junction B1007 & Lower Dunton Rd. **Sun 10 July (10-5). Adm £5, chd free. Light refreshments inc veggie/vegan snacks.**

Since building our turf roof house in 1995 we have trialled waste materials in our 4 acre garden to mimic brownfield habitat, one of the most undervalued places for wildlife. These are now our most beautiful and diverse habitats for plants and insects. Several green roofs and lots of ideas to create biodiverse habitats, especially for solitary bees. Views across the Thames Estuary to Kent. The 4 acre garden features a self build timber house with green roof, 6 other green roofs, 3 ponds, brownfield landscapes to create plant diversity and solitary bee habitats. New area created this year, using local sand and gravel from A13 widening work to trial climate change plant species. Some wheelchair friendly paths and grass paths that may be accessible depending on rabbit damage. Garden is on a slight slope.

& ❀ 🍵))

35 2 HOPE COTTAGES

Heath Road, Bradfield, Manningtree, CO11 2UZ. Martin Ford. 3m E of Manningtree. 9m W of Harwich. Take A137 from Manningtree Station. Turn L opp garage. Take 1st R towards Clacton. At Radio Mast turn L into Bradfield continue through village. Garden is opp just past the Primary School. **Sun 3 July (11-4), open nearby Chippins. Sun 7 Aug (11-4). Adm £4, chd free.**

This is a tranquil, country style garden overlooking the serene open countryside. The beautifully planted garden reflects the owner's love of trees. In early summer the rich variety of roses and peonies, give the garden a soft, romantic feel. Followed later with splashes of vibrant colour from dahlias, salvias, agapanthus and sweet peas. Unfortunately no refreshments will be served.

&

36 HORKESLEY HALL

Vinesse Road, Little Horkesley, Colchester, CO6 4DB. Mr & Mrs Johnny Eddis, 07808 599290, pollyeddis@hotmail.com, www.airbnb.co.uk/rooms/ 10354093. 6m N of Colchester City Centre. 2m W of A134, 10 mins from

Sandy Lodge

A12. At the grass triangle with tree in middle, turn into Little Horkesley Church car park to the very far end - access is via low double black gates at the far end. **Sat 12 Feb (2-4); Sun 29 May (2-5). Adm £6, chd free. Home-made teas. Visits also by arrangement Feb to Oct for groups of 10+.**
Magical setting with 8 acres of romantic garden surrounding classical house. Parkland setting with major 20ft high sculpture of balancing stones. Exceptional trees inc vast gingko. 2 yr old planting of over 50 varieties of iris from disbanded National Collection. Walled garden, and a wonderful traditional English garden setting. Charming enclosed swimming pool garden to relax with teas. Excellent Plant Stall. Partial wheelchair access to some areas, gravel paths and slopes but easy access to tea area with lovely views over lake and garden.
&. 🐎 ✿ 🚗 🚐 ☕ 🔊

37 61 HUMBER AVENUE
South Ockendon, RM15 5JW.
Mr & Mrs Kasia & Greg Purton-Dmowski, 07711 721629, kasia.purtondmowski@gmail.com.
M25 - J30/31 or A13 - exit to Lakeside. J31/M25 to Thurrock Services, or Grays from A13, at r'about take exit onto Ship Ln to Aveley, turn R then 2nd exit at r'about onto Stifford Rd/B1335, take Foyle Dr to Humber Ave. **Visits by arrangement May to Sept for groups of 5 to 20. Gluten Free refreshments available.**
A suburban garden close to Nature Reserve, 30m x 14m space featuring an old cherry tree from the orchard of the famous Belhus Mansion. The garden features abundant large borders planted heavily with herbaceous plants, small trees, roses, lilies, and ornamental grasses with oriental senses mixed with a traditional English feel with shady areas with hostas, tree ferns and Japanese style plants. The owners are interested in design and are members of Sogetsu International School, original arrangements will be on display during open day.
&. 🐎 ✿ ☕

38 ISABELLA'S GARDEN
42 Theobalds Road, Leigh-On-Sea, SS9 2NE. Mrs Elizabeth Isabella Ling-Locke, 01702 714424, ling_locke@yahoo.co.uk. *Take A13 towards Southend on Sea. As you pass Welcome to Leigh-on-Sea sign, turn R at T-lights onto Thames Drive then L onto Western Road, carry on 0.6m then R onto Theobalds Rd.* **Sat 4, Sun 5 June, Sat 16, Sun 17 July (12-4.30). Adm £4, chd free. Cream teas. Visits also by arrangement June to Aug for groups of 10 to 25.**
This enchanting town garden is bursting with a profusion of colour from early Spring through to the Autumn months. Roses, clematis, agapanthus, herbaceous plants, alpines and pots with unusual succulents fill every corner of this garden. There is a wildlife pond. Lilies and water features as well as other garden ornaments which are to be found hiding within the shrubbery and throughout the garden. This garden is situated in the town of Leigh on Sea, and just a 5 min walk from the cockle sheds of old Leigh and Leigh railway station. Cakes made by Broadway Belles, the local WI. Wheelchair access most of the garden is accessible, there are steps near to the house.
&. ☕ 🔊

39 NEW JANKES HOUSE
Jankes Green, Wakes Colne, Colchester, CO6 2AT. Bridget Marshall. *8m NW of Colchester. From A1124 Halstead Road turn R at Wakes Colne opp. village shop to Station Rd. Take 2nd R after station entrance into Jankes Ln. House signed. Parking on grass verge.* **Sun 5 June (2-5). Adm £5, chd free. Light refreshments.**
½ acre Traditional English country garden with amazing rural views. Garden has been artistically created by owner. Beautiful mixed borders featuring roses, clematis and architectural shrubs. Camassia in wild grass area. Many young specimen trees. Dry garden. Delightful pond and patio area. Vegetable garden and small orchard. Intimate places to sit and relax. Garden Owner's artistic cards and home-made preserves for sale. Wheelchair access to whole garden.
&. ✿ ☕ 🔊

40 KAMALA
262 Main Road, Hawkwell, Hockley, SS5 4NW. Karen Mann, 07976 272999, karenmann10@hotmail.com.
3m NE of Rayleigh. From A127 at Rayleigh Weir take B1013 towards Hockley. Garden on L after White Hart Pub & village green. **Sat 30 July, Sun 21 Aug (12-5.30). Adm £6, chd free. Home-made teas. Visits also by arrangement in Aug.**
Spectacular herbaceous borders which sing with colour as displays of salvia are surpassed by Dahlia drifts. Gingers, Brugmansia, various bananas, bamboos and canna add an exotic note. Grasses sway above the blooms, giving movement. Rest in the rose clad pergola while listening to the two Amazon Parrots in the aviary. The garden features an RHS accredited Dahlia named "Jake Mann". Trees and shrubs inc Acers, Catalpa aurea, Cercis 'Forest Pansy' and a large unusual Sinocalycanthus (Chinese Allspice) a stunning, rare plant with fantastic flowers. Featured on Gardeners' World August 2021.
☕ 🔊

41 KEEWAY
Ferry Road, Creeksea, nr Burnham-on-Crouch, CM0 8PL. John & Sue Ketteley, 01621 782083, sueketteley@hotmail.com. *2m W of Burnham-on-Crouch. B1010 to Burnham on Crouch. At town sign take 1st R into Ferry Rd signed Creeksea & Burnham Golf Club & follow NGS signs.* **Wed 29 June, Sat 2 July (2-5). Adm £5, chd free. Home-made teas with refills £5. Visits also by arrangement June & July.**
Large, mature country garden with stunning views over the River Crouch. Formal terraces surround the house with steps leading to sweeping lawns, mixed borders packed full of bulbs and perennials, formal rose and herb garden with interesting water feature. Further afield there are wilder areas, paddocks and lake. A productive greenhouse, vegetable and cutting gardens complete the picture.
&. ✿ ☕

In 2021 the National Garden Scheme donated £3 million to our beneficiary charities

42 KELVEDON HALL

Kelvedon, Colchester, CO5 9BN. Mr & Mrs Jack Inglis, 07973 795955, v_inglis@btinternet.com. *Take Maldon Rd direction Great Braxted from Kelvedon High St. Go over R Blackwater bridge & bridge over A12 At T-junction turn R onto Kelvedon Rd. Take 1st L, single gravel road, oak tree on corner.* **Visits by arrangement Apr to June for groups of 20 to 40. Adm £7.50, chd free. Home-made teas in the Courtyard Garden or in the Pool Walled Garden - weather permitting.**

Varied 6 acre garden surrounding a gorgeous C18 house. A blend of formal and informal spaces interspersed with modern sculpture. Pleached hornbeam and yew and box topiary provide structure. A courtyard walled garden juxtaposes a modern walled pool garden, both providing season long displays. Herbaceous borders offset an abundance of roses around the house. Lily covered ponds with a wet garden. Topiary, sculpture, tulips and roses.

✤ Ⓓ ☕

43 NEW LAUREL COTTAGE

88 The Street, Manuden, Bishop's Stortford, CM23 1DS. Mr Stewart Woskett. *Approx 3m N of Bishop's Stortford. From B/S along Rye St At the Mountbatten Restaurant r'about continue straight on to Hazelend Rd. In ½m turn L to stay on Hazelend Rd. Continue past Yew Tree pub. Gdn is last Cottage on R.* **Sun 22 May, Sun 24 July (1-5). Adm £5, chd free. Pre-booking essential, please visit www.ngs.org.uk for information & booking. Light refreshments.**

Romantic, quintessential thatched cottage garden. Features intimate pathways meandering through borders with an abundance of cottage garden favourites and 1or 2 surprises. Full of rustic charm and an ancient Yew tree. Tranquil seating areas to sit and enjoy fragrant, colourful borders. Hidden treasures enhance this characterful and quirky garden. Created in just 4 years from a very neglected plot. Parking at Community Centre car park adjacent to cottage and playing field.

☕

44 LITTLE MYLES

Ongar Road, Stondon Massey, CM15 0LD. Judy & Adrian Cowan. *1½m SE of Chipping Ongar. Off A128 at Stag Pub, Marden Ash, towards Stondon Massey. Over bridge, 1st house on R after 'S' bend. 400yds Ongar side of Stondon Church.* **Wed 6, Wed 13 July (2-5). Adm £5, chd free. Home-made teas.**

A 3 acre romantic garden that has shifted its emphasis to providing an abundance of nectar-rich flowers for struggling bees and butterflies. The Herb garden full of vipers bugloss and roses. Meandering paths past full borders, themed hidden gardens, hornbeam pergola, sculptures and tranquil benches. Crafts and handmade herbal cosmetics for sale. Explorers sheet and map for children. New expanded flower meadow full of colourful nectar-rich flowers for bees and butterflies. Gravel paths. No disabled WC available.

♿ ✤ ☕

45 LONG HOUSE PLANTS

Church Road, Noak Hill, Romford, RM4 1LD. Tim Carter, 01708 371719, tim@thelonghouse.net, www.longhouse-plants.co.uk. *3½m NW of J28 M25. J28 M25 take A1023 Brentwood. At 1st T-lights, turn L to South Weald after 0.8m turn L at T junction. After 1.6m turn L, over M25 after ½m turn R into Church Rd, nursery opp church. Disabled Car Parking.* **Wed 6 July, Wed 3 Aug, Wed 7 Sept (11-4). Adm £6, chd £3. Home-made teas. Visits also by arrangement July to Sept for groups of 25+.**

A beautiful garden - yes, but one with a purpose. Long House Plants has been producing homegrown plants for more than 10 years - here is a chance to see where it all begins! With wide paths and plenty of seats carefully placed to enjoy the plants and views. It has been thoughtfully designed so that the collections of plants look great together through all seasons. Paths are suitable for wheelchairs and mobility scooters. Disabled WC in nursery. Two small cobbled areas not suitable.

♿ ✤ 🚗 ☕

46 LONGYARD COTTAGE

Betts Lane, Nazeing, Waltham Abbey, EN9 2DA. Jackie & John Copping, 07780 802863, jackie.70@icloud.com. *Opposite red telephone box.* **Sun 20 Feb (11-4). Adm £4, chd free. Home-made teas. Visits also by arrangement Feb to Oct for groups of 6 to 30.**

Longyard Cottage is an interesting ¾ of an acre garden situated within yards of an SSSI site, a C11 Church, a myriad of footpaths and a fine display of snowdrops and spring bulbs. This conceptual garden is based on a 'journey' and depicted through the use of paths which take you through 3 distinct areas, with its own characteristics. It's a tactile garden with which you can engage or simply sit and relax. Snowdrops during February.

✤ ☕

47 LOXLEY HOUSE

49 Robin Hood Road, Brentwood, CM15 9EL. Robert & Helen Smith. *1m N of Brentwood town centre. On A128 N towards Ongar turn R onto Doddinghurst Rd at mini r'about. Take the 1st rd on L into Robin Hood Rd. 2 houses before the bend on L.* **Sat 23 Apr, Sat 23 July (11-3). Adm £4, chd free. Home-made teas.**

On entering the rear garden you will be surprised and delighted by this town garden. A colourful patio with pots and containers. Steps up onto a lawn with new circular beds surrounded by hedges, herbaceous borders, trees and climbers. Two water features, one a Japanese theme and another with ferns in a quiet seating area. The garden is planted to offer colour throughout the seasons.

☕ ♪)

48 MALTINGS COTTAGE,

172 High Street, Ingatestone, CM4 9EZ. Richard & Susan Martin. *Leave A12 on B1002 exit to Ingatestone. Maltings Cottage is on High Street B1002. Parking at Station Car Park CM4 0BW 8 mins walk. Disabled parking please contact owner to reserve space on driveway.* **Sat 17 Sept (12.30-4.30). Adm £4, chd free. Tea.**

The garden echoes the look and feel of a traditional cottage garden reflecting the character of the property. Rear courtyard surrounded by large structural plants inc banana plants, dahlias, cannas and Japanese

anemones. Dry and Shade area beds. Front garden has a modern slant with pleached hornbeams and wildflower meadow planting using cosmos, zinnia, echinacea and lupin.

49 9 MALYON ROAD

Witham, CM8 1DF. Maureen & Stephen Hicks. *Car park at bottom of High St opp Swan Pub, 5 min walk from car park cross High St by pedestrian crossing onto River Walk, follow path, take 1st R turn into Luard Way, Malyon Rd straight ahead.* Fri 1, Sat 2, Sun 3, Fri 15, Sat 16, Fri 29, Sat 30, Sun 31 July (10.30-5). Adm £4, chd free. Home-made teas. Opening with Witham Town Gardens on Sun 17 July (11-4.30).

Large town garden with mature trees and shrubs made up of a series of garden rooms. Flower beds, pond, summerhouse and greenhouse giving all year interest. Plenty of places to sit and relax with paths that take you on a tour of the garden. A quiet hidden place not expected in a busy town. Our garden is a hidden oasis, where you can escape from the hustle and bustle of busy life. On the edge of town, close to the Witham's rambling Town River Walk. Wheelchair access, but there is a step down into part of the garden.

50 NEW MAY COTTAGE

19 Walton Road, Kirby-Le-Soken, Frinton-On-Sea, CO13 0DU. Julie Abbey, 07885 875822, jools.abbey@hotmail.com. *Kirby-Le-Soken, Essex, CO13 0DU. May Cottage is on the B1034, 2m before Walton on Naze.* Sat 21 May, Sat 25 June (11-4). Adm £5, chd free. Light refreshments. Tea/coffee and cake. Visits also by arrangement May to Sept for groups of 5 to 20. Adm £7 inc tea/coffee and cake.

Come and enjoy my garden at May Cottage, a quintessential English country garden and although relatively small, there is much to see. Follow paths down to the Bakers Oven, a building which is over one hundred years old. Through a picket gate and you enter a secret garden with a twisting path, an area which was only planted in 2020.

51 MAYFIELD FARM

Hungerdown Lane, Ardleigh, CO7 7LZ. Ed Fairey & Jennifer Hughes, 07780 685634, ed@faireyassociates.co.uk. *3½m NE of Colchester. From Ardleigh village centre continue on the A137 to Manningtree. 3rd R, Tile Barn Lane. R again Hungerdown Lane. 500yds garden on R.* Visits by arrangement Feb to Sept for groups of 10+. Adm £10, chd free. Home-made teas. Open every Monday: Adm inc tea and cake and guided tour with the Garden Owner.

Mayfield Farm is a seven acre garden which only a few years ago was largely a field with a huge glasshouse and polytunnels. Now filled with many beautiful beds and borders, we have also created a secret garden and planted yew hedging for topiary. Over two hundred thousand bulbs have been planted in the garden during the past three years to create a wonderful spring display. Always a new and exciting project being undertaken! Mostly flat but areas of gravel, grass and paddock for parking.

52 MIRAFLORES

Witham, CM8 2LJ. Yvonne & Danny Owen. *Please DO NOT go via Rowan Way, go to Forest Rd as there is rear access only to garden. Access is ONLY by rear gate at the top The Spinney, off of FOREST RD, CM8 2TP. Please follow yellow signs. PLEASE do not park in The Spinney as this is a private parking area.* Sat 2, Sun 3 July (2-5). Adm £4, chd free. Home-made teas.

An award-winning, cottage garden described as a 'Little Bit of Heaven'. A blaze of colour with roses, clematis, pergola, rose arch, triple fountain with box hedging and deep herbaceous borders. See our 'Folly', exuberant and cascading hanging baskets...find our Secret Door. Featured in Garden Answers, Amateur Gardening and Essex Life. Tranquil seating areas inc summerhouse. Cakes (inc gluten free), teas, coffee, soft drinks, herbal teas are available.

53 MOVERONS

Brightlingsea, CO7 0SB. Lesley & Payne Gunfield, lesleyorrock@me.com, www.moverons.co.uk. *7m SE of Colchester. At old church turn R signed Moverons Farm. Follow lane and garden signs for approx 1m. Beware some SatNavs take you the wrong side of the river.* Open garden with Sculpture Exhibition. Sat 21, Sun 22 May (10.30-5). Adm £5, chd free. Home-made teas. Visits also by arrangement May to Sept for groups of 10+.

Tranquil 4 acre garden in touch with its surroundings and enjoying stunning estuary views. A wide variety of planting in mixed borders to suit different growing conditions. Courtyard, large natural ponds, sculptures and barn for rainy day teas! Our Reflection pool garden has been completely redeveloped. Magnificent trees some over 300yrs old give this garden real presence. Most of the garden is accessible by wheelchair via grass and gravel paths, There are some steps and bark paths.

54 23 NEW ROAD

Dagenham, RM10 9NH. John Seaman, 07504 712818, echinopsis100@gmail.com. *Leave A13 at the junction signed for A1306 - Dagenham & Hornchurch. Go around the r'about following it off at the 4th exit. Then follow the 2nd r'about straight onwards.* Sun 31 July, Mon 1, Sun 14, Mon 15 Aug (11-5). Adm £4, chd free. Visits also by arrangement July to Sept for groups of 5 to 10.

This is an exotic garden, themed on the foothills of the Himalayas in India. This garden will be like no other you may have seen before despite its modest size. It is filled with exquisite tropical plants inc canna, gingers and bananas. A feast for the eyes filled with good ideas for vertical space. An extravaganza of plants in all shapes, colour and form.

'National Garden Scheme donations have funded four of our gardens in regional NHS spinal injury centres supporting nearly 8,500 patients and their visitors.'
Horatio's Garden

55 OAK FARM

Vernons Road, Wakes Colne, Colchester, CO6 2AH. Ann & Peter Chillingworth. *Vernons Road off A1124 between Ford Street & Chappel. From Colchester, 3rd R after Ford St; Oak Farm is 200 metres up lane on R. From Halstead, 2nd L after viaduct in Chappel.* **Wed 8, Sun 19 June, Wed 6, Wed 20 July, Wed 7 Sept (2-5). Adm £5, chd free. Home-made teas.**
Informal farmhouse garden of about 1 acre on an exposed site with extensive views south and west across the Colne Valley. Shrubberies, lawned borders and shady spots where people can enjoy refreshments. Look out for the secret garden. On-going projects inc the rose avenue, Mediterranean bed and prairie garden. Wheelchair access although there are some steps in places, access can be gained to most of the garden.

ૐ ☕ ☕

56 NEW THE OLD RECTORY

Boreham Road, Great Leighs, Chelmsford, CM3 1PP. Pauline & Neil Leigh-Collyer. *Approx ½ m outside the village of Great Leighs. From Boreham village (J19 off A12) turn into Waltham Rd & travel about 5m, Garden on L. From Great Leighs travel on Boreham Rd for ¾ m, garden on R. Garden is found via the post code.* **Sun 15 May, Sun 21 Aug (12-4.30). Adm £7, chd free. Light refreshments. Tea, coffee & home-made cakes.**
Wander around 4 acres of mature gardens surrounded by open countryside. Aspects inc herbaceous borders, a delightful courtyard, lake, fountain, sweeping lawns, arched walkways and many specimen trees. Beautiful wisteria clothing house. Many seating areas to enjoy alternative vistas. Extensive car parking available on grass off the main road. Main areas accessible for wheelchairs. Some areas limited by gravel paths and steps.

ૐ ☕ »)

57 THE OLD VICARAGE

Church End, Broxted, CM6 2BU. Ruth & Adam Tidball. *3m S of Thaxted. From Thaxted on the B1051, take Broxted turning. Just before next junction, turn R into field for parking.* **Sun 8 May, Sun 19 June (12-5). Adm £6, chd free. Light refreshments.**

Victorian former vicarage surrounded by three acres of formal gardens, one acre woodland garden and seven acre hay meadow. Deep mixed borders. Rose garden with perennial underplanting. Many rare and special plants and trees. Alpine and succulent rockeries, series of ponds providing habitat for ornamental goldfish and native wildlife. Views across the meadow to church and beyond.

ૐ ☕ ☕ ☕ ⌂ »)

58 PEACOCKS

Main Road, Margaretting, CM4 9HY. Phil Torr, 07802 472382, phil.torr@btinternet.com. *Margaretting Village Centre. From village Xrds go 75yds in the direction of Ingatestone, entrance gates will be found on L set back 50ft from road frontage.* **Sun 17 Apr, Sun 15 May, Sun 12, Sun 19 June, Sun 3 July (11-4). Adm £5. Visits also by arrangement Apr to Sept for groups of 15+. Donation to St Francis Hospice.**
10 acre varied garden ideal for picnics with several seating areas. Mature native and specimen trees. Restored horticultural buildings. A series of garden rooms inc Walled Paradise Gardens, Garden of Reconciliation, Alhambra fusion. Long herbaceous/ mixed border. Sunken dell and waterfall. Temple of Antheia on the banks of a lily lake. Large areas for wildlife inc woodland walk, nuttery and orchard. Traditionally managed large wildflower meadow. Picnics are encouraged. Display of old Margaretting postcards. Garden sculpture. Winner of the Daily Mail National Garden Competition 2021. Most of garden wheelchair accessible.

ૐ ☕ ☕ ⌂

59 18 PETTITS BOULEVARD, RM1

Rise Park, Romford, RM1 4PL. Peter & Lynn Nutley. *From M25 take A12 towards London, turn R at Pettits Lane junction then R again into Pettits Blvd or Romford Stn then 103 or 499 bus to Romford Fire Stn & follow NGS signs.* **Sat 25, Sun 26 June, Sat 3, Sun 4 Sept (1-5). Adm £4, chd free. Home-made teas.**
The garden is 80ft x 23ft on three levels with an ornamental pond, patio area with shrubs and perennials, many in pots. Large eucalyptus tree leads to a woodland themed area

with many ferns and hostas. There are agricultural implements and garden ornaments giving a unique and quirky feel to the garden. Tranquil seating areas situated throughout.

ૐ ☕ ☕ ☕

60 ROOKWOODS

Yeldham Road, Sible Hedingham, CO9 3QG. Peter & Sandra Robinson, 07770 957111, sandy1989@btinternet.com, www.rookwoodsgarden.com. *8m NW of Halstead. Entering Sible Hedingham from direction of Haverhill on A1017 take 1st R just after 30mph sign. Coming through SH from the Braintree direction turn L just before the 40mph leaving the village.* **Sun 29 May (11-5). Adm £6, chd free. Home-made teas. Visits also by arrangement May to Sept.**
Rookwoods is a tranquil garden where you can enjoy a variety of mature trees; herbaceous borders; a shrubbery; pleached hornbeam rooms; a work-in-progress wildflower bed; a buttercup meadow, and an ancient oak wood. There is no need to walk far, you can come and linger over tea, under a dreamy wisteria canopy while enjoying views across the garden. Beehive. Wildflower garden. Meadow to walk through leading to Ancient Oak Wood. Mature Foxglove tree. Terrace with views across garden. Wheelchair access gravel drive.

ૐ ☕ ☕ ⌂ ☕ ⌂ »)

61 79 ROYSTON AVENUE

Chingford, E4 9DE. Paul & Christine Lidbury. *From A406 Crooked Billet r'about take A112 towards Chingford. Continue ½ m, across T-lights (Morrison's), Royston Ave is 3rd turn on R. Bus 97, 158, 215, 357 (Leonard Rd or Ainslie Wood Rd stops).* **Sat 21, Sun 22 May (12-5). Adm £4, chd free. Home-made teas. Pimm's and home-made beer tastings.**
A 55 x 19ft urban garden with over 600 different varieties of plants - a great many in containers, inc collections of hostas, acers, heucheras and sempervivums. An oasis for local birds and wildlife with two small ponds and insect habitats with further interest provided by ornaments, sculptures and artwork, where words of gardening wisdom abound. Not suitable for young children.

☕ ☕ »)

62 69 RUNDELLS - THE SECRET GARDEN
Harlow, CM18 7HD. Mr & Mrs K Naunton, 01279 303471, k_naunton@hotmail.com. *3m from J7 M11. A414 exit T-lights take L exit Southern Way, mini r'about 1st exit Trotters Rd leading into Commonside Rd, after shops on left 3rd L into Rundells.* **Sat 16 July (2-5). Adm £4, chd free. Home-made teas. Visits also by arrangement for groups of 5 to 10.**
Featured on Alan Titchmarsh's first 'Love Your Garden' series ('The Secret Garden') 69, Rundells is a very colourful, small town garden packed with a wide variety of shrubs, perennials, herbaceous and bedding plants in over 200 assorted containers. Hard landscaping on different levels has a summerhouse, various seating areas and water features. Steep steps. Access to adjacent allotment open to view. Various small secluded seating areas. A small fairy garden has been added to give interest for younger visitors. The garden is next to a large allotment and this is open to view with lots of interesting features inc a bee apiary. Honey and other produce for sale (conditions permitting).

63 ST HELENS
High Street, Stebbing, CM6 3SE. Stephen & Joan Bazlinton, 01371 856495, jbazlinton@gmail.com. *3m E of Great Dunmow. Leave Gt Dunmow on B1256. Take 1st L to Stebbing, at T-junction turn L into High St, garden 2nd on R.* **Visits by arrangement Apr to July. Adm £8, chd free. Home-made teas.**
A garden established over 40 years from a bog-ridden, cricket-bat plantation into a gently sloping woodland garden. Springs and ponds divide the garden into different areas with various shrubs and perennial planting. Partial wheelchair access.

64 SANDY LODGE
Howe Drive, Hedingham Road, Halstead, CO9 2QL. Emma & Rick Rengasamy, 07899 920002, emmarengasamy@gmail.com. *8m NE of Braintree. Turn off Hedingham Rd into Ashlong Grove. Howe Drive is on L. Please park in Ashlong Grove & walk up Howe Drive. Winners of the Ideal Home magazine Best Readers Garden Award 2021* **Sun 11 Sept (11-5). Adm £4.50, chd free. Home-made teas. Visits also by arrangement June to Sept for groups of 10 to 30.**
A stunning garden with views over Halstead, there is something to see every day. ¾ acre created over 10 years. Enter to our gravel Bee Border, walk through the Winter Wedding border and Woodlands Walk to the meadow. Stroll across to double borders and long border with flowing prairie planting up towards cabin and BBQ. Lots of seating. Featured in Garden Gate is Open https://thegardengateisopen.blog/. Winners of the Ideal Home magazine Best Readers Garden Award 2021

'National Garden Scheme funding helped support the provision of horticultural-related assistance to soldiers, veterans and their immediate families, providing education, training and employment opportunities along with supporting the recovery, health and wellbeing of individuals.'
ABF The Soldiers' Charity

Mayfield Farm

Coggeshall Hamlet Allotment

SHEEPCOTE GREEN HOUSE
Jilly & Ross McNaughton,
www.thehabitatgarden.co.uk.
WAGGON AND HORSES
Jenny & Peter Milledge.

Four quite different - yet equally
charming - gardens of varying size,
offering inspiration and delight!
The first three gardens neighbour
one another, while the Waggon
and Horses is just a short stroll up
the leafy footpath. April Cottage
boasts a well-established, colourful
cottage garden, filmed in 2020 with
Alan Titchmarsh for the Love Your
Garden Series. Appletree Cottage
is a compact cottage garden of
fragrant roses, clematis, honeysuckle
with annuals and perennial beds.
Sheepcote Green House is an
atmospheric, old country garden, set
in the three acre grounds of a former
farmhouse, currently undergoing a
gentle reawakening with wildlife in
mind. The Waggon and Horses is a
$\frac{1}{4}$ acre garden offering rural views
and mixed planting incorporating
rhubarb and soft fruit amongst flowers
grown for perfume and pollinators. All
enjoy an idyllic setting in a hamlet in
the ancient countryside of North West
Essex. Homegrown plant sale on the
green. Partial wheelchair access due
to gravel, narrow paths and uneven
surfaces.

&. ✿ 🚗 ☕))

65 SCRIPS HOUSE
Cut Hedge Lane, Coggeshall,
CO6 1RL. Mr James & Mrs Sophie
Bardrick. *From A12 N/S take
Kelvedon/Feering exit. Turn L/R
passed Kelvedon stn. Continue for
2m turn L into Scrips Rd. From A120
take Coggeshall exit. Drive through
village towards Kelvedon. Turn R up
Scrips Rd.* Fri 29 Apr (10.30-3.30).
Adm £7, chd free. Sun 7 Aug
(10.30-3.30). Combined adm with
Coggeshall Hamlet Allotments
£10, chd free. Home-made teas.
Individual garden adm £7 on 7
Aug.
A large garden with further paddocks
inc a mature woodland with a
memorial avenue of fastigiate oaks.
The garden is divided into smaller
areas including a walled pool garden
and a Spring garden. A pleached
lime walk leads to a white garden
flanked by two 30m herbaceous
borders. There is an ornamental
pond with ducks, an ample
vegetable garden and fruit cage, an
orchard and a chicken run. Picnics

Welcome. Wheelchair access most
areas accessible with a fairly strong
wheelchair pusher.

&. ✿ ☕ 🛏))

GROUP OPENING

**66 SHEEPCOTE GREEN
GARDENS**
Sheepcote Green, Clavering,
Saffron Walden, CB11 4SJ. *Midway
between Clavering & Langley. Take
lane signed 'Sheepcote Green'
on the Clavering to Langley Lower
Green road. Park on the green at the
end of the lane.* Sun 5 June (12-5).
Combined adm £8, chd free.
Home-made teas and savouries
on the lawn at Sheepcote Green
House.

APPLETREE COTTAGE
Judy & Adrian Wilson-Smith.

APRIL COTTAGE
Anne & Neil Harris.

67 SHRUBS FARM
Lamarsh, Bures, CO8 5EA. Mr &
Mrs Robert Erith, 01787 227520,
bob@shrubsfarm.co.uk,
www.shrubsfarm.co.uk. *1¼m from
Bures. On rd to Lamarsh, the drive
is signed to Shrubs Farm.* Visits
by arrangement May to Oct for
groups of 6+. Adm £8, chd free.
Home-made teas in barn £7
per head. Payment for numbers
agreed on day before visit. Wine
& canapes by arrangement.
2 acres with shrub borders, lawns,
roses and trees. 50 acres parkland
with wildflower paths and woodland
trails. Over 60 species of oak. Superb
10m views over Stour valley. Ancient
coppice and pollards inc largest
goat (pussy) willow (*Salix caprea*) in
England. Wollemi and Norfolk pines,
and banana trees. Full size black
rhinoceros. Display of Bronze Age
burial urns. Large grass maze. Guided
Tour to inc garden, park and ancient
woodland, historic items including
Bronze Age Burial Urns and painting

of the Stour valley 200 years ago. Restored C18 Essex barn is available for refreshment by prior arrangement. Wheelchair access some ground may be boggy in wet weather.

♿ 🐂 ☇ ⛾

68 SILVER BIRCHES
Quendon Drive, Waltham Abbey, EN9 1LG. Frank & Linda Jewson, 01992 714047, linda.jewson@ngs.org. *M25, J26 to Waltham Abbey. At T-lights by McD turn R to r'about. Take 2nd exit to next r'about. Take 3rd exit (A112) to T-lights. L to Monkswood Av follow ngs signage.* **Sun 29 May, Sun 4 Sept (11.30-5.30). Adm £5, chd free. Visits also by arrangement May to Sept for groups of 5 to 15.**
The garden boasts three lawns on the two levels. This surprisingly secluded garden has many mixed borders packed with colour. Mature shrubs and trees create a short woodland walk. Crystal clear water flows through a shady area of the garden. Chimney Pots for sale. Wheelchairs are able to visit the garden, but there are areas which would not be suitable.

♿ ✧ ⛾

69 SNARES HILL COTTAGE
Duck End, Stebbing, CM6 3RY. Pete & Liz Stabler, 01371 856565, petestabler@gmail.com. *Between Dunmow & Bardfield. On B1057 from Great Dunmow to Great Bardfield, ½ m after Bran End on L.* **Visits by arrangement Mar to Sept for groups of 8 to 40. Adm £6, chd free. Home-made teas.**
A 'quintessential English Garden' - Gardeners' World. Our quirky 1½ acre garden has surprises round every corner and many interesting sculptures. A natural swimming pool is bordered by romantic flower beds, herb garden and Victorian folly. A bog garden borders woods and leads to silver birch copse, beach garden and 'Roman' temple. Classic cars. Shepherds Hut natural swimming pond.

☇ ⛾

70 SPRING COTTAGE
Chapel Lane, Elmstead Market, CO7 7AG. Mr Roger & Mrs Sharon Sciachettano. *3m from Colchester. Overlooking village green N of A133 through Elmstead Market. Parking limited adjacent to cottage, village car park nearby on S side of A133.*

Sat 27, Sun 28 Aug (1.30-4). Adm £4, chd free. Home-made teas. We provide a gluten free chocolate cake.
From Acteas to Zauscherenias and Aressima to Zebra grass we hope our large variety of plants will please. Our award winning garden features a range of styles and habitats e.g. woodland dell, stumpery, Mediterranean area, perennial borders and pond. Our C17 thatched cottage and garden show case a number of plants found at the world famous Beth Chatto gardens ½ m down the road. In late summer we can promise colour and scent to delight the senses and a range of unusual species to please the plant enthusiast. We also have a productive vegetable patch.

✧ ⛾

71 2 SPRING COTTAGES
Conduit Lane, Woodham Mortimer, Maldon, CM9 6SZ. Sharon & Michael Cox, 07841 867908, sharoncox799@gmail.com. *From Danbury continue on A414 towards Maldon for 1½ m until you come to Oak Corner r'about, 1st L continuing on A414. 200 yds take 1st R into Conduit Ln.* **Fri 22, Sun 24 July (10.30-4.30). Adm £4, chd free. Home-made teas. Visits also by arrangement in July for groups of 5 to 20.**
A small pretty terraced cottage garden, featuring many different levels, each area exhibiting good use of space and varied planting. Plenty of seating in a relaxed quiet setting. The garden has been developed to encourage wildlife, with an abundance of bee, butterfly, bird houses water feature and lilly pond.

⛾

72 STRANDLANDS
off Rectory Road, Wrabness, Manningtree, CO11 2TX. Jenny & David Edmunds, 01255 886260, strandlands@outlook.com. *1km along farm track from the corner of Rectory Rd. If using a SatNav, the post code will leave you at the corner of Rectory Rd. Turn onto a farm track, signed to Woodcutters Cottage & Strandlands, & continue for 1km.* **Visits by arrangement May to June for groups of 10 to 20. Adm inc light refreshments. Adm £7.50, chd free.**
Cottage surrounded by 4 acres of land bordering beautiful and unspoilt Stour Estuary. One acre of decorative garden: formal courtyard with yew,

box and perovskia hedges, lily pond summerhouse and greenhouse; 2 large island beds, secret 'moon garden', madly and vividly planted 'Madison' garden, 3 acres of wildlife meadows with groups of native trees, large wildlife pond, also riverside bird hide. View the Stour Estuary from our own bird hide. Grayson Perry's 'A House for Essex' can be seen just one field away from Strandlands. Wheelchair access mostly accessible and flat although parking area is gravelled.

♿ ✧ ⛾

74 37 TURPINS LANE
Chigwell, IG8 8AZ. Fabrice Aru & Martin Thurston, 0208 5050 739, martin.thurston@talktalk.net. *Between Woodford & Epping. Tube: Chigwell, 2m from North Circular Rd at Woodford, follow the signs for Chigwell (A113) through Woodford Bridge into Manor Rd & turn L, Bus 275 & W14.* **Sun 5 June, Sun 3 July (11-6.30). Adm £4, chd free. Visits also by arrangement May to Oct for groups of up to 10.**
An unexpected hidden, magical, part-walled garden showing how much can be achieved in a small space. An oasis of calm with densely planted rich, lush foliage, tree ferns, hostas, topiary and an abundance of well maintained shrubs complemented by a small pond and 3 water features designed for year-round interest. Featured on BBC Gardeners' World and ITV Good Morning Britain.

The National Garden Scheme searches the length and breadth of England, Channel Islands, Northern Ireland and Wales for the very best private gardens

75 ULTING WICK
Crouchmans Farm Road, Maldon, CM9 6QX. Mr & Mrs B Burrough, 01245 380216, philippa.burrough@btinternet.com, www.ultingwickgarden.co.uk. *3m NW of Maldon. Take R turning to Ulting off B1019 as you exit Hatfield Peverel by a green. Garden on R after 2 M.* Sun 24, Fri 29 Apr, Fri 8 July, Mon 29 Aug, Fri 9 Sept (2-5). Adm £7.50, chd free. Home-made teas. Visits also by arrangement Feb to Oct for groups of 15+. Room for parking for one coach. Donation to All Saints Ulting Church.

Listed black barns provide backdrop for vibrant and exuberant planting in 8 acres. Thousands of colourful tulips, flowing innovative spring planting, herbaceous borders, pond, mature weeping willows, kitchen garden, dramatic late summer beds with zingy, tender, exotic plant combinations. Drought tolerant perennial and mini annual wildflower meadows. Woodland. Many plants propagated in-house. Lots of unusual plants for sale. Beautiful dog walks along the River Chelmer from the garden. Regional Winner, The English Garden's The Nation's Favourite Gardens 2021 Some gravel around the house but main areas of interest are accessible for wheelchairs.

♿ 🐴 ✿ 🚗 🍵

76 39 WAKERING AVENUE
Shoeburyness, Southend-On-Sea, SS3 9BE. Wendy Adlington. *Shoeburyness 3m E of Southend Town Centre on A13. Roadside parking available on Wakering Ave & surrounding roads.* Sat 7 May, Sat 16 July (11-4). Adm £4, chd free. Home-made teas. Vegan and Gluten Free Cakes available.

A small well-established town garden with an interesting use of space creating several garden rooms. Seating areas capture the sun as it moves across the garden. Lush green foliage of palm and cordyline contrast with established ceanothus and silver birch. Wisteria clambers over the pergola while arum and calla lilies, Californian poppies, nigella and bluebells fill the pots and beds.

✿ 🍵))

77 [NEW] WALNUT TREE COTTAGE
Cobblers Green, Felsted, Dunmow, CM6 3LX. Mrs Susan Monk. *B1417 brings you into Felsted from both ends of the village then turn into a Causeway End Rd, ½m down the road you will see a yellow sign on your L to turn R into the paddock.* Sun 12 June (11-4). Adm £5, chd free. Home-made teas.

A traditional cottage garden framed by wonderful views over the Essex countryside and planted with well-stocked flower borders and lawns that slop gently down to a natural pond. A productive garden borders the well maintained paddock where chickens and guinea fowl roam. Large patio and other seating areas provide a place to relax and appreciate the garden. Wheelchair access, there is a path that makes most of the garden accessible.

♿ 🍵 🪑

78 1 WHITEHOUSE COTTAGES
Blue Mill Lane, Woodham Walter, CM9 6LR. Mrs Shelley Rand, 07799 848772, shelley@special-p.co.uk. *In between Maldon & Danbury, short drive from A12. From A414 Danbury, turn L at The Anchor & continue into the village. Directly after the white village gates at the far end of the village, turn R into Blue Mill Lane.* Sun 8 May, Sun 19 June, Sun 17 July (10-3.30). Adm £4. Home-made teas. Visits also by arrangement May to Aug for groups of 20 to 60. Refreshments inc in adm £8.

Nestled betwixt farmland in rural Essex, is our small secret garden, that has a wonderful charm and serenity to it. Set in 3½ acres, mostly paddocks, a little plot of loveliness wraps around our Victorian cottage, and roses smother the porch in June. A meandering lawn takes you through beds and borders softly planted with a cottage feel, a haven for wildlife and people alike. Dean Harris a local artist blacksmith will have a pop-up forge on site making and selling metal plant accessories on the day of your visit. Parking available a short walk up the lane near The Cats pub, and for those who might struggle to walk there's parking at the property in the paddock.

🍵))

79 WICKETS
Langley Upper Green, Saffron Walden, CB11 4RY. Susan & Doug Copeland, 01799 550553, susan.copeland@ngs.org.uk. *7m W of Saffron Walden, 10m N of Bishops Stortford. At Newport take B1038 After 3m turn R at Clavering, signed Langley. Upper Green is 3m further on. At cricket green turn R. House 200m on R.* Visits by arrangement June & July for groups of 20+.

Rejuvenate your spirits in this wonderfully floral garden with fine rural views. Billowing Borders inc roses and summer colour. Wildflower meadow with shepherd's hut, orchard and small prairie/pond area. Lily pond with 'Monet' bridge sheltered by silver birch. Mediterranean courtyard. Parterre enclosed by espalier apples. Specimen trees abound. Wonderful views over open countryside. Sit and relax in our Shepherd's Hut, far from the madding crowd. Perhaps the ultimate romantic garden? Wheelchair access, gravel drive.

♿ 🐴 ✿ 🚗 🍵))

GROUP OPENING

80 WITHAM TOWN GARDENS
Witham, CM8 1NB. 01376 514931, whitechat@sky.com. *Witham is on B1038 approx 8m from Chelmsford & 10m from Colchester. A map will be available at all gardens with locations & parking details.* Sun 17 July (11-4.30). Combined adm £6, chd free. Home-made teas.

9 MALYON ROAD
Maureen & Stephen Hicks.
(See separate entry)

13 STEVENS ROAD
Robin & Isobel Norton.

A warm welcome awaits you at our two contrasting town gardens in Witham. 13 Stevens Road is an established garden full of plants inc many Salvia, Sanguisorba and Thalictrum. From the lawn the garden slopes down to a secluded shaded area and stream. The paved patio is a welcoming area to sit and enjoy home-made cakes, tea and soft drinks as well as an opportunity to purchase home-made jam. Malyon Road is a large town garden with mature trees and shrubs laid out in a series of garden rooms. Flower beds, pond and summerhouse give year-round interest. Plenty of places to sit and relax with paths taking you on a

tour of the garden. Partial wheelchair access at Stevens Road and Malyon Road. Plant Sales at Malyon Road.

GROUP OPENING

81 WRITTLE GARDENS
Chelmsford, CM1 3NA. *Writtle can be approached from 3 directions. From the A1060, A1016 & A414 follow the yellow signs to the Village. A local map showing the gardens open in the village will be available at each house.* **Sun 26 June (1-5). Combined adm £5, chd free.**

8 THE GREEN
CM1 3DU. Andrea Johnson.

53 LONG BRANDOCKS
CM1 3JL. Roger & Margaret Barker.

65 ONGAR ROAD
CM1 3NA. Doug & Jean Pinkney.

13 ROMANS WAY
Mr Peter & Mrs Anne Pegg.

Four contrasting, colourful and interesting gardens to enjoy in the delightful village of Writtle. 8 The Green offers creatively planted borders and a tapestry of colour, texture and form, with perennials, shrubs, ornamental trees, annuals and alpines, and a south-facing summerhouse. The garden at 65 Ongar Road will transport visitors to tropical destinations, with its colour and 'summer living' features. 53 Long Brandocks is a plantsman's garden with a wealth of unusual shrubs, clematis, daylilies, and some exotic herbaceous plants. There is also a selection of trees including catalpas and acers. At 13 Romans Way the back garden, originally part of an old orchard, often surprises visitors by its size for a village garden, with a long vista towards distant willow trees on the banks of the River Wid. No refreshments are offered at these gardens, but Writtle offers a number of pubs and cafes, inc the renowned Tiptree Tea Room in Lordship Rd. The ancient and traditional village of Writtle, with its delightful Norman church, village green and pond, dates back to pre-Roman times, and was featured in the Doomsday Book.

Laurel Cottage

82 WRITTLE UNIVERSITY COLLEGE
Writtle, CM1 3RR. Writtle University College, www.writtle.ac.uk. *4m W of Chelmsford. On A414, nr Writtle village.* **Sat 23 Apr (10-3). Adm £5, chd free. Light refreshments in The Garden Room (main campus) & The Lordship tea room (Lordship campus).**
Writtle University college has 15 acres of informal lawns with naturalized bulbs and wildflowers. Large tree collection, mixed shrubs, herbaceous border, dry/ Mediterranean borders, seasonal bedding and landscaped glasshouses. All gardens have been designed and built by our students studying a wide range of horticultural courses. Wheelchair access some gravel, however majority of areas accessible to all.

83 WYCHWOOD
Epping Road, Roydon, CM19 5DW. Mrs Madeleine Paine. *At Tylers Cross r'about head in the direction of Roydon. Garden on R approx 400 metres from the r'about. Parking is available in Redrick's nursery next to garden.* **Sun 3 July (12-5.30). Adm £5, chd free. Home-made teas.**
A garden approx. $\frac{3}{4}$ acre with a large pond, attracting much wildlife, as well as the owners resident ducks. Free ranging chickens roam in the shrubbery and budgerigar aviary. There are numerous features inc vegetable and fruit plot, mixed shrub and herbaceous borders, 1920's summerhouse and Scandinavian cabin. Old fashioned style roses are a particular feature of the garden. Lake fully stocked with fish and inhabited by resident and wild ducks. Sit in the Norwegian hut and enjoy your refreshments.

GLOUCESTERSHIRE

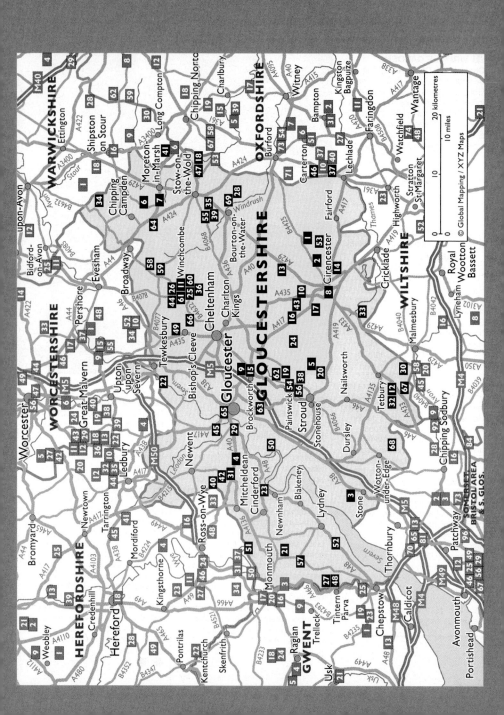

Gloucestershire is one of the most beautiful counties in England, spanning as it does a large part of the area known as the Cotswolds as well as the Forest of Dean and Wye and Severn Valleys.

The Cotswolds is an expanse of gently sloping green hills, wooded valleys and ancient, picturesque towns and villages; it is designated as an area of Outstanding Natural Beauty, and its quintessentially English charm attracts many visitors.

Like the county itself many of the gardens that open for the National Garden Scheme are simply quite outstanding. There are significant gardens which open for the public as well, such as Kiftsgate and Bourton House. There are also some large private gardens which only open for us, such as Daylesford and Charlton Down House.

There are however many more modest private gardens whose doors only open on the National Garden Scheme open day, such as Bowling Green Road in Cirencester with over 300 varieties of Hemerocallis. This tiny garden has now opened for over 40 years. The National collection of Rambling Roses is held at Moor Wood and that of Juglans and Pterocarya at Upton Wold.

Several very attractive Cotswold villages also open their gardens and a wonderful day can be had strolling from cottage to house marvelling at both the standard of the gardens and the beauty of the wonderful buildings, only to pause for the obligatory tea and cake!

Volunteers

County Organiser
Vanessa Berridge
01242 609535
vanessa.berridge@ngs.org.uk

County Treasurer
Pam Sissons
01242 573942
pam.sissons@ngs.org.uk

Social Media
Mandy Bradshaw
01242 512491
mandy.bradshaw@ngs.org.uk

Publicity
Ruth Chivers
01452 542493
ruth.chivers@ngs.org.uk

Booklet Coordinator
Vanessa Graham
07595 880261
vanessa.graham@ngs.org.uk

Assistant County Organisers
Valerie Kent
01993 823294
valerie.kent@ngs.org.uk

Sally Oates
01285 841320
sally.oates@ngs.org.uk

Colin & Verena Olle
01452 863750
colin.olle@ngs.org.uk

Rose Parrott
07853 164924
rosemary.parrott@ngs.org.uk

Gareth & Sarah Williams
01531 821654
dgwilliams84@hotmail.com

f @gloucestershirengs
@Glosngs

Left: Sheepehouse Cottage

OPENING DATES

All entries subject to change. For latest information check www.ngs.org.uk

Map locator numbers are shown to the right of each garden name.

January

Sunday 30th
Home Farm — 31

February

Snowdrop Festival

Sunday 6th
Trench Hill — 62

Sunday 13th
Home Farm — 31
Trench Hill — 62

Saturday 19th
Cotswold Farm — 16

Sunday 20th
Cotswold Farm — 16

March

Sunday 6th
Home Farm — 31

Sunday 20th
Trench Hill — 62

Sunday 27th
◆ The Coach House Garden — 14

April

Sunday 3rd
Highnam Court — 29
Home Farm — 31

Saturday 9th
South Lodge — 57

Sunday 10th
NEW Sheepehouse Cottage — 56
Upton Wold — 64

Monday 11th
◆ Kiftsgate Court — 34

Sunday 17th
Trench Hill — 62

Monday 18th
Trench Hill — 62

Tuesday 19th
Barnsley House — 2

Wednesday 20th
NEW Kemble House — 33

Saturday 23rd
The Gate — 25

Sunday 24th
Blockley Gardens — 6
Charlton Down House — 12

Tuesday 26th
Wortley House — 68

Thursday 28th
NEW Lords of the Manor Hotel — 39
Ready Token House — 53

Friday 29th
Ready Token House — 53

May

Sunday 1st
Eastcombe and Bussage Gardens — 20
Greenfields, Brockweir Common — 27
Highnam Court — 29
Home Farm — 31
Ramblers — 52
Trench Hill — 62

Monday 2nd
Eastcombe and Bussage Gardens — 20

Wednesday 4th
Daylesford House — 18

Wednesday 11th
Downton House — 19

Thursday 12th
Downton House — 19

Saturday 14th
South Lodge — 57

Sunday 15th
◆ Stanway Fountain & Water Garden — 59

Saturday 21st
Charingworth Court — 11

Sunday 22nd
Charingworth Court — 11
20 Forsdene Walk — 21

Wednesday 25th
Lower Farm House — 40

Thursday 26th
Richmond Painswick Retirement Village — 54

Saturday 28th
Forthampton Court — 22
Pasture Farm — 47
Richmond Painswick Retirement Village — 54

Sunday 29th
Forthampton Court — 22
Pasture Farm — 47
NEW Tuffley Gardens — 63

June

Wednesday 1st
Hookshouse Pottery — 32

Thursday 2nd
Hookshouse Pottery — 32

Friday 3rd
Hookshouse Pottery — 32
The Old Vicarage — 45

Saturday 4th
Hookshouse Pottery — 32
The Old Vicarage — 45

Sunday 5th
Highnam Court — 29
Hookshouse Pottery — 32
The Old Vicarage — 45

Monday 6th
Berkeley Castle — 3

Tuesday 7th
Rockcliffe — 55

Wednesday 8th
Trench Hill — 62

Thursday 9th
Richmond Painswick Retirement Village — 54

Saturday 11th
Cotswold Farm — 16
Richmond Painswick Retirement Village — 54

Sunday 12th
Charlton Down House — 12
Cotswold Chase Gardens — 15
Cotswold Farm — 16
The Gables — 23
Hodges Barn — 30
Stanton Village Gardens — 58
Weir Reach — 65

Monday 13th
Hodges Barn — 30

Wednesday 15th
NEW Oak House — 44
Trench Hill — 62
Weir Reach — 65

Friday 17th
Hookshouse Pottery — 32

Saturday 18th
Berrys Place Farm — 4
Chedworth Gardens — 13
NEW Oak House — 44

Sunday 19th
Berrys Place Farm — 4
Bisley Gardens — 5
Blockley Gardens — 6
Chedworth Gardens — 13
20 Forsdene Walk — 21

Wednesday 22nd
Berrys Place Farm — 4
Brockworth Court — 9
◆ Oxleaze Farm — 46
Trench Hill — 62

Thursday 23rd
Ready Token House — 53

Friday 24th
Ready Token House — 53

Saturday 25th
Little Orchard — 38
Perrywood House — 50
South Lodge — 57

Sunday 26th
Little Orchard — 38
The Manor — 41
Moor Wood — 43
Perrywood House — 50
NEW Westaway — 66

Tuesday 28th
Wortley House — 68

Wednesday 29th
NEW Langford Downs Farm — 37
Rockcliffe — 55
Trench Hill — 62
NEW Westaway — 66

July

Friday 1st
Hookshouse Pottery — 32

Sunday 3rd
Awkward Hill Cottage — 1
◆ Cerney House Gardens — 10

*Our 2021 donations
mean that 750
people living with
Parkinson's were
supported*

Blockley Allotments, Blockley Gardens

THE GARDENS

◘ AWKWARD HILL COTTAGE

Awkward Hill, Bibury,
GL7 5NH. Mrs Victoria
Summerley, 01285 740289,
v.summerley@hotmail.com,
www.awkwardhill.co.uk. *No parking
at property, best to park in village &
walk past Arlington Row up Awkward
Hill, or up Hawkers Hill from
Catherine Wheel pub.* Sun 3 July,
Sun 4 Sept (2-6). Adm £5, chd
free. Home-made teas. Visits also
by arrangement July & Aug for
groups of 10 to 30. No children.
An ever-evolving country garden in
one of the most beautiful villages in
the Cotswolds, designed to reflect
the local landscape and encourage
wildlife. Planting is both formal and
informal, contributing year-round
interest with lots of colour and
texture. Pond and waterfall, beehives,
chickens. Lots of seating areas.
Wonderful views over neighbouring
meadow and woodland, small pond
with jetty, 2 sunny terraces and plenty
of places to sit and relax, both in sun
and shade.

🐕 ❀ ☕))

◙ BARNSLEY HOUSE

Barnsley, Cirencester,
GL7 5EE. Calcot Health &
Leisure Ltd, 01285 740000,
reception@barnsleyhouse.com,
www.barnsleyhouse.com. *4m NE
of Cirencester. From Cirencester,
take B4425 to Barnsley. House
entrance on R as you enter village.*
Tue 19 Apr (10-3). Adm £5, chd
free. Home-made teas.
The beautiful garden at Barnsley
House, created by Rosemary Verey,
is one of England's finest and most
famous gardens inc knot garden,
potager garden and mixed borders
in her successional planting style.
The house also has an extensive
kitchen garden which will be open
with plants and vegetables available
for purchase. Narrow paths mean
restricted wheelchair access but
happy to provide assistance.

♿ 🚗 🚌 ☕

◛ BERKELEY CASTLE

Berkeley, GL13 9PJ.
Charles Berkeley,
www.berkeley-castle.com. *Halfway
between Bristol & Gloucester,
10mins from J13 &14 of M5. Follow
signs to Berkeley from A38 & B4066.
Visitor entrance L off Canonbury
St, just before town centre.* Mon
6 June (11-5). Adm £6, chd £3.
Pre-booking essential, please
phone 01453 810303, email info@
berkeley-castle.com or visit
http://www.berkeley-castle.
com for information & booking.

Light refreshments in The Walled
Garden. Delicious home-made
cakes, light lunches and locally-
sourced items.
Unique historic garden of a keen
plantsman, with far-reaching views
across the River Severn. Gardens
contain many rare plants which thrive
in the warm microclimate against the
stone walls of this medieval castle.
Woodland, historic trees and stunning
terraced borders. The admission price
does not include entrance into the
castle.

🚗 ☕ 🛋

◜ BERRYS PLACE FARM

Bulley Lane, Churcham,
Gloucester, GL2 8AS. Anne
Thomas, 07950 808022,
gary.j.thomas1953@gmail.com.
*6m W of Gloucester. A40 towards
Ross. Turning R into Bulley Lane at
Birdwood.* Sat 18, Sun 19, Wed 22
June (11-5). Adm £4, chd free.
Light refreshments. Ploughman's
lunches, cakes and cream tea.
Country garden, approx 2 acres,
surrounded by farmland and old
orchards. Lawns and large sweeping
mixed herbaceous borders with over
100 roses. Formal kitchen garden and
beautiful rose arbour leading to lake
and summerhouse with a variety of
water lilies and carp. All shared with
ducks.

♿ ❀ 🚗 🚌 ☕))

Kemble House

GROUP OPENING

5 BISLEY GARDENS

Wells Road, Bisley, Stroud, GL6 7AG. *Gardens & car park well signed in Bisley village. Gardens on S edge of village at head of Toadsmoor Valley, N of A419 Stroud to Cirencester road.* Sun 19 June (2-6). Combined adm £5, chd free. Home-made teas at Paulmead.

PAULMEAD
Judy & Philip Howard and Tom & Emma Howard.

PAX
Mr David Holden & Mr Ramesh Mootoo.

WELLS COTTAGE
Mr & Mrs Michael Flint, 01452 770289, bisleyflints@gmail.com.

3 beautiful gardens with differing styles. Paulmead: 1 acre landscaped garden constructed in stages over last 25 yrs. Terraced in 3 main levels. Natural stream garden, herbaceous and shrub borders, formal vegetable garden, summerhouse overlooking pond. Unusual treehouse. Development of new garden around hen house, inc ha-ha. Pax: Small box and yew topiary garden comprising 3 rooms with Arts & Crafts inspired planting, in a hidden away location, with great views. Wells Cottage: Just under 1 acre, terraced on several levels with formal topiary and beautiful views over the valley. Much informal planting of trees and shrubs to give colour and texture. Lawns and herbaceous borders. Collection of grasses. Formal pond area. Rambling roses on chain pergola. Vegetable garden with raised beds.

GROUP OPENING

6 BLOCKLEY GARDENS

Blockley, Moreton in Marsh, GL56 9DB. *3m NW of Moreton-in-Marsh. Just off the Morton-in-Marsh to Evesham road A44.* Sun 24 Apr, Sun 19 June (2-6). Combined adm £7, chd free. Home-made teas at St George's Hall.

BLOCKLEY ALLOTMENTS
Blockley and District Allotment Association, blockleyallotments. wixsite.com/blockleyallotments. Open on Sun 19 June

CHURCH GATES
Mrs Brenda Salmon. Open on all dates

COLEBROOK HOUSE
Mr & Mrs G Apsion, admin@colebrookhousegardens. com, www.instagram.com/ colebrook_house_gardens. Open on all dates
Visits also by arrangement Apr to Aug for groups of 10 to 25. We ask visitors please not to bring their dogs.

ELM HOUSE
Chris & Val Scragg. Open on all dates

THE MANOR HOUSE
Zoe Thompson. Open on Sun 19 June

PORCH HOUSE
Mr & Mrs Johnson. Open on Sun 24 Apr

SNUGBOROUGH MILL
Rupert & Mandy Williams-Ellis, 01386 701310, rupert.williams-ellis@talk21.com. Open on Sun 19 June

WOODRUFF
Paul & Maggie Adams. Open on all dates

This popular historic hillside village has a great variety of high quality, well-stocked gardens - large and small, old and new. Blockley Brook, an attractive stream which flows right through the village, graces some of the gardens; these inc gardens of former water mills, with millponds attached. From some gardens there are wonderful rural views. Children welcome but close supervision is essential. Regional finalist in The English Garden's The Nation's Favourite Gardens 2021.

7 ◆ BOURTON HOUSE GARDEN

Bourton-on-the-Hill, GL56 9AE. Mr & Mrs R Quintus, 01386 700754, info@bourtonhouse.com, www.bourtonhouse.com. *2m W of Moreton-in-Marsh. On A44.* For NGS: Sun 14 Aug (10-5). Adm £8, chd free. Light refreshments & home-made cakes in Grade I Listed C16 Tithe Barn. For other opening times and information, please phone, email or visit garden website.
Award winning 3 acre garden featuring imaginative topiary, wide herbaceous borders with many rare, unusual and exotic plants, water features, unique shade house and many creatively planted pots. Fabulous at any time of year but magnificent in summer months and early autumn. Walk in 7 acre pasture with free printed guide to specimen trees available. 70% access for wheelchairs. Disabled WC.

8 25 BOWLING GREEN ROAD

Cirencester, GL7 2HD. Mrs Sue Beck, 01285 653778, zen155198@zen.co.uk. *On NW edge of Cirencester. Take A435 to Spitalgate/Whiteway T-lights, turn into The Whiteway (Chedworth turn), then 1st L into Bowling Green Rd, garden in bend in rd between Nos 23 & 27.* Visits by arrangement July & Aug for groups of up to 20. Adm £3.50, chd free. Refreshments on request for small groups.
Welcome to this naturalistic garden, increasingly designed by plants themselves, where you can wander at will in a mini-jungle of curvaceous clematis, gorgeous grasses, romantic roses, heavenly hemerocallis and plentiful perennials, glimpsing a graceful giraffe, friendly frogs and a unicorn. Rated by visitors as an amazing hidden gem with a unique atmosphere. View The Chatty Gardener's blog, https:// thechattygardener.com/plants-and-more/how-to-grow-hemerocallis/ on growing Hemerocallis and the garden owner having a daylily cultivar registered by UK Hybridizer to mark her 40th Anniversary of opening for NGS.

In the first six months of operation at Maggie's Southampton, which was part funded by the National Garden Scheme, the team has supported people affected by cancer more than 2,300 times

9 BROCKWORTH COURT

Court Road, Brockworth, GL3 4QU. Tim & Bridget Wiltshire, 01452 862938, timwiltshire@hotmail.co.uk. *6m E of Gloucester. 6m W of Cheltenham. Adj St Georges Church on Court Rd. From A46 turn into Mill Lane, turn R, L, R at T junctions. From Ermin St, turn into Ermin Park, then R at r'about then L at next r'about.* Wed 22 June (2-5.30). Adm £6, chd free. Home-made teas. Visits also by arrangement Apr to Oct for groups of 5 to 30.
This intense yet informal tapestry style garden beautifully complements the period manor house which it surrounds. Organic, naturalistic, with informal cottage-style planting areas that seamlessly blend together. Natural fish pond, with Monet bridge leading to small island with thatched Fiji house. Kitchen garden once cultivated by monks. Views to Crickley and Coopers Hill. Adjacent Norman church (open). Historic tithe barn, manor house visited by Henry VIII and Anne Boleyn in 1535. Partial wheelchair access.

10 ◆ CERNEY HOUSE GARDENS

North Cerney, Cirencester, GL7 7BX. Mr N W Angus & Dr J Angus, 01285 831300, janet@cerneygardens.com, www.cerneygardens.com. *4m NW of Cirencester. On A435 Cheltenham rd turn L opp Bathurst Arms, follow rd past church up hill, then go straight towards pillared gates on R (signed Cerney House).* For NGS: Sun 3 July (10-7). Adm £5, chd £1. For other opening times and information, please phone, email or visit garden website.
A romantic English garden for all seasons. There is a secluded Victorian walled garden featuring herbaceous borders overflowing with colour. Early in the year we have a wonderful display of snowdrops, in spring we feature a magnificent display of tulips and during the summer the rambling romantic roses come to life. Enjoy our woodland walk, extended nature trail and new medicinal herb garden. Dogs welcome. Walled garden accessible for electric wheelchairs. Gravel paths and inclines may not suit manual wheelchairs.

11 CHARINGWORTH COURT

Broadway Road, Winchcombe, GL54 5JN. Susan & Richard Wakeford, 07791 353779, susanwakeford@gmail.com, www. charingworthcourtcotswolds garden.com. *8m NE of Cheltenham. 400 metres N of Winchcombe town centre on B4632. Limited parking along Broadway Rd. Town car parks in Bull Lane (short stay) and all day parking (£1) in Back Lane. Map on our website.* Sat 21, Sun 22 May (11-6). Adm £5, chd free. Home-made teas. Visits also by arrangement Apr to July for groups of 10 to 30. Refreshments on request.
Artistically and lovingly created 1½ acre garden surrounding restored Georgian/Tudor house (not open). Relaxed country style with Japanese influences, large pond, sculpture and walled vegetable/flower garden, created over 25 yrs from a blank canvas. Mature copper beech trees, Cedar of Lebanon and Wellingtonia; and younger trees replacing an earlier excess of *Cupressus leylandii*. Partial access due to gravel paths which can be challenging but several areas accessible without steps. Some disabled parking next to house.

12 CHARLTON DOWN HOUSE

Charlton Down, Tetbury, GL8 8TZ. Neil & Julie Record, mjtingay@yahoo.com. *From Tetbury, take A433 towards Bath for 1½m; turn R (north) just before the Hare & Hounds, then R again after 200yds into Hookshouse Lane. Charlton Down House is 600yds on R.* Sun 24 Apr, Sun 12 June (11-5); Thur 7, Thur 14, Thur 28 July, Thur 4, Thur 18, Thur 25 Aug (1-5). Adm £6, chd free. Home-made teas. Visits also by arrangement Apr to Aug for groups of 15 to 35.
Extensive country house gardens in 180 acre equestrian estate. Formal terraces, perennial borders, walled topiary garden, enclosed cut flower garden and large glasshouse. Newly planted copse. Rescue animals. Ample parking. Largely flat terrain; most garden areas accessible.

GROUP OPENING

13 CHEDWORTH GARDENS

Chedworth, Cheltenham, GL54 4AN. *7m NE of Cirencester. Off Fosseway, A429 between Stow-on-the-Wold (12m) & Cirencester. Park & Ride in field by village hall (signed). Tickets available from village hall.* Sat 18, Sun 19 June (10-5). Combined adm £7.50, chd free. Home-made teas at Chedworth Village Hall. Donation to Chedworth & District Horticultural Society.
Varied collection of country gardens, nestling throughout the mile long Chedworth Valley with tributary of River Coln running below. Stunning views. Featuring lots of ideas to inspire. Teas and lunches served in village hall throughout the day. WC available plus plant sales and stalls.

14 ◆ THE COACH HOUSE GARDEN

Church Lane, Ampney Crucis, Cirencester, GL7 5RY. Mr & Mrs Nicholas Tanner, 01285 850256, mel@thegenerousgardener.co.uk, www.thegenerousgardener.co.uk. *3m E of Cirencester. Turn into village from A417, immed before Crown of Crucis Inn. Over hump-back bridge, parking to R on cricket field (weather permitting) or signed nearby field. Disabled parking near house.* For NGS: Sun 27 Mar (2-5). Adm £6, chd free. Home-made teas. For other opening times and information, please phone, email or visit garden website.
Approx 1½ acres, full of structure and design. Garden is divided into rooms inc rill garden, gravel garden, rose garden, herbaceous borders, pleached lime allee and potager. Created over last 30+ yrs by present owners and constantly evolving. New potting shed and greenhouse and wildlife pond added since 2018. Visitors welcome during mid March - mid May (groups of 15+), please see above website. Garden Lecture Days, workshops and Specialist Plant Sales held during the year.

GROUP OPENING

15 COTSWOLD CHASE GARDENS

Spinners Road, Brockworth, Gloucester, GL3 4LR. *Follow signs off Ermin Street.* **Sun 12 June (2-5). Combined adm £5, chd free. Home-made tea and cake at MidGlos Bowls Club.**

A group of small gardens all recently created on a new development. A wide range of designs, planting and imaginative ideas that show what can be achieved in a short space of time. The Chase is rich in open spaces which have been tastefully landscaped, with many foot/cycle paths, a sports field, children's play areas and three wildlife friendly balancing ponds. Lots of places to walk, take in the vistas (e.g. Coopers Hill) and view some new gardens. Parking, tickets, maps and WCs at MidGlos Bowls Club.

16 COTSWOLD FARM

Duntisbourne Abbots, Cirencester, GL7 7JS. John & Sarah Birchall, 01285 821837, garden@birchall.org.uk, www.cotswoldfarmgardens.org.uk. *5m NW of Cirencester off old A417. From Cirencester L signed Duntisbourne Abbots Services, R and R underpass. Drive ahead. From Gloucester L signed Duntisbourne Abbots Services. Pass Services. Drive L.* **Sat 19, Sun 20 Feb (11-3). Light refreshments. Sat 11, Sun 12 June, Sat 3, Sun 4 Sept (2-5). Home-made teas. Adm £7.50, chd free. Visits also by arrangement Feb to Sept. Donation to A Rocha.**

This beautiful Arts & Crafts garden overlooks a quiet valley on descending levels with terraces designed by Norman Jewson in the 1930s. Enclosed by Cotswold stone walls and yew hedges, the garden has year-round interest inc a snowdrop collection with over 80 varieties. The terraces, shrub garden, herbaceous borders and bog garden are full of scent and colour from spring to autumn. Rare orchid walks. Picnics welcome. Wheelchair access to main terrace only (no wheelchair access to WCs).

17 DAGLINGWORTH HOUSE

Daglingworth, Cirencester, GL7 7AG. David & Henrietta Howard, 07970 122122, ettajhoward@gmail.com. *3m N of Cirencester off A417/419. House with blue gate beside church in centre of Daglingworth, at end of No Through Road.* **Visits by arrangement Apr to Sept. For individuals and groups up to 20. Adm £7, chd free. Light refreshments on request.**

Walled garden, temple, grotto, and pools. Classical garden of 2½ acres, with humorous contemporary twist. Hedges, topiary shapes, herbaceous borders. Pergolas, grass garden, wildflower meadow, woodland, cascade and mirror canal. Sunken garden. Pretty Cotswold village setting beside church. Visitor comment: 'It breaks every rule of gardening - but it's wonderful!'.

Oxleaze Farm

18 DAYLESFORD HOUSE

Daylesford, GL56 0YG. **Lord & Lady Bamford.** *5m West of Chipping Norton. Off A436 between Stow-on-the-Wold & Chipping Norton.* **Wed 4 May (1-5). Adm £6, chd free. Home-made teas.**
Magnificent C18 landscape grounds created 1790 for Warren Hastings, greatly restored and enhanced by present owners under organic regime. Lakeside and woodland walks within natural wildflower meadows. Large formal walled garden, centred around orchid, peach and working glasshouses. Trellised rose garden. Collection of citrus within period orangery. Secret garden, pavilion formal pools. Very large garden with substantial distances. The owners of Daylesford House have specifically requested that photographs are NOT taken in their garden or grounds. No dogs allowed other than guide dogs. Teas cash only. Partial wheelchair access.

19 DOWNTON HOUSE

Gloucester St, Painswick, GL6 6QN. **Ms Jane Kilpatrick, 01452 813861, info@janekilpatrick.co.uk.** *4m N of Stroud. Entry to garden is via Hollyhock Lane only. Please note: NO cars in lane, park in Stamages Lane village car park off A46 below church, or in Churchill Way, 1st L off Gloucester St B4073.* **Wed 11, Thur 12 May (1-4.30). Adm £5, chd free.** Home-made teas. **Visits also by arrangement in Feb for groups of 8 to 20. Snowdrop talk by authors of The Galanthophiles (2018) on weekdays.**
Plant historian and author's walled ⅓ acre garden in heart of historic Painswick. Planted for year-round foliage colour and interest with particular focus on plants that thrive on thin limey soil in a changing climate. Many rare and unusual trees, shrubs and herbaceous plants associated with owner's interest in plant introductions from China.

The National Garden Scheme searches the length and breadth of England, Channel Islands, Northern Ireland and Wales for the very best private gardens

The Manor House, Blockley Gardens

GROUP OPENING

20 EASTCOMBE AND BUSSAGE GARDENS

Eastcombe, Stroud, GL6 7EB. *3m E of Stroud. Maps available on the day from Eastcombe Village Hall GL6 7EB & Redwood GL6 8AZ. On street parking only. Tickets valid Sun & Mon due to length of trail (2 miles).* Sun 1, Mon 2 May (1.30-5.30). Combined adm £8, chd free. Light refreshments at Eastcombe Village Hall. Ice creams at Hawkley Cottage.

BREWERS COTTAGE
Jackie & Nick Topman.

CADSONBURY
Natalie & Glen Beswetherick.

NEW **17 FARMCOTE CLOSE**
John & Sheila Coyle.

20 FARMCOTE CLOSE
Ian & Dawn Sim.

21 FARMCOTE CLOSE
Mr & Mrs Robert Bryant.

HAMPTON VIEW
Geraldine & Mike Carter.

HAWKLEY COTTAGE
Helen & Gerwin Westendorp.

12 HIDCOTE CLOSE
Mr K Walker.

HIGHLANDS
Helen & Bob Watkinson.

NEW **1 JASMINE COTTAGE**
Mrs June Gardiner.

1 THE LAURELS
Andrew & Ruth Fraser.

MARYFIELD AND MARYFIELD COTTAGE
Margaret & Mike Thomas.

REDWOOD
Heather Collins.

VALLEY VIEW
Mrs Rebecca Benneyworth.

YEW TREE COTTAGE
Andy & Sue Green.

Medium and small gardens in a variety of styles and settings within this picturesque, hilltop village location with its spectacular views of the Toadsmoor Valley. In addition, one large garden is located in the bottom of the valley, approachable only on foot as are some of the other gardens. Full descriptions of each garden and those with wheelchair access can be found on the National Garden Scheme website. Please

show any pre-booked tickets at village hall or Redwood. WC at village hall and Hawkley Cottage. Please be prepared to wear a mask when entering a small garden. Plants for sale at village hall and some gardens.

🐕 ❀ 🍵 ᵒ))

21 20 FORSDENE WALK

Coalway, Coleford, GL16 7JZ. Pamela Buckland, 01594 837179. *From Coleford take Lydney/Chepstow Rd at T-lights. L after police station ½m up hill turn L at Xrds then 2nd R (Old Road) straight on at minor Xrds then L into Forsdene Walk.* Sun 22 May, Sun 19 June (2-5). Adm £3.50, chd free. Light refreshments. Visits also by arrangement May to Sept for groups of up to 20.
Corner garden filled with interest and design ideas to maximise smaller spaces. A series of interlinking colour themed rooms, some on different levels. Packed with perennials, grasses and ferns. A pergola, small man-made stream, fruit and vegetables and pots in abundance on gravelled areas.

❀ 🍵

22 FORTHAMPTON COURT

Forthampton, Tewkesbury, GL19 4RD. Alan & Anabel Mackinnon. *W of Tewkesbury. From Tewkesbury A438 to Ledbury. After 2m turn L to Forthampton. At Xrds go L towards Chaceley. Go 1m turn L at Xrds.* Sat 28, Sun 29 May (12.30-4.30). Adm £6, chd free. Home-made teas.
Charming and varied garden surrounding N Gloucestershire medieval manor house (not open) within sight of Tewkesbury Abbey. Inc borders, lawns, roses and magnificent Victorian vegetable garden. Disabled drop off at entrance, some gravel paths and uneven areas.

♿ ❀ 🍵 ᵒ))

23 THE GABLES

Riverside Lane, Broadoak, Newnham on Severn, GL14 1JE. Bryan & Christine Bamber, 01594 516323, bryanbamber21@gmail.com. *1m NE of Newnham on Severn. Park in White Hart pub overspill car park, to R of pub when facing river. Please follow signs to car park. Walk, turning R along rd towards Gloucester for approx 250yds. Access through*

marked gate. Sun 12 June, Sun 21 Aug (11-5). Adm £4, chd free. Light refreshments. Visits also by arrangement May to Aug for groups of 10+.
Large flat ¾ acre garden with formal lawns, colourful herbaceous borders from May to September, rose beds, shrubberies, hidden long border, mini stumpery with hostas, bamboos, grasses, wildflower meadow with soft fruits and fruit trees, wildlife pond created autumn 2020, allotment size productive potager vegetable plot with herbaceous borders, greenhouse and composting bin area. Disabled parking info available at entrance. Partial wheelchair access but all areas of garden visible.

♿ 🍵

24 ♦ THE GARDEN AT MISERDEN

Miserden, nr Stroud, GL6 7JA. Mr Nicholas Wills, 01285 821303, estate.office@miserden.org, www.miserden.org. *6m NW of Cirencester. Leave A417 at Birdlip, drive through Whiteway & follow signs for Miserden.* For NGS: Fri 22 July (10-5). Adm £9, chd free. Light refreshments at The Garden Café. For other opening times and information, please phone, email or visit garden website.
Winner of Historic Houses Garden of the Year, this timeless walled garden designed in the C17 still retains a wonderful sense of peace and tranquillity. Known for its magnificent mixed borders and Lutyens' Yew Walk and quaint grass steps; there is also an ancient mulberry tree, enchanting arboretum and stunning views across the Golden Valley. There will also be a selection of beautiful sculptures as the garden is hosting the Cotswold Sculptors Association 'Creating Spaces 2022' exhibition. Routes around the garden are gravel or grass, there are alternative routes to those that have steps. Disabled WC at the café.

♿ ❀ 🚗 🍵 ᵒ))

National Garden Scheme gardens are identified by their yellow road signs and posters. You can expect a garden of quality, character and interest, a warm welcome and plenty of home-made cakes!

25 THE GATE
80 North Street, Winchcombe,
GL54 5PS. Vanessa Berridge
& Chris Evans, 01242 609535,
vanessa.berridge@sky.com.
*Winchcombe is on B4632 midway
between Cheltenham & Broadway.
Parking behind Library in Back Lane,
50 yds from The Gate. Entry via Cowl
Lane.* Sat 23 Apr (2-6). Adm £3.50,
chd free. Home-made teas. Visits
also by arrangement Apr to Sept
for groups of 5 to 20.
Compact cottage-style garden
planted with bulbs in spring, and with
summer perennials, annuals, climbers
and herbs in the walled courtyard
of C17 former Coaching Inn. Also a
separate, productive, walled kitchen
garden with espaliers and other fruit
trees.

26 GREEN BOUGH
Market Lane, Greet,
Winchcombe, GL54 5BL. Mary
& Barry Roberts, 07966 528646,
barryandmary@gmail.com.
*1¼ m N of Winchcombe. From
Winchcombe take B4078. After
railway bridge, R into Becketts Lane,
immed L into Market Lane. Garden
on R at Mill Lane junction.* Visits
by arrangement Apr to Sept for
groups of up to 20. Home-made
teas on request. Adm £3.50, chd
free.
Compact country garden, densely
planted for all seasons starting in early
spring with massed bulbs, flowers,
shrubs and trees surrounding the
house. Many of the plants are either
grown from seed or propagated
from cuttings by the owner, to give
generous drifts of colour in wide
mixed borders and in pots and
planters on the terraces.

27 GREENFIELDS, BROCKWEIR COMMON
Brockweir, Chepstow, NP16 7NU.
Jackie Healy, 07747 186302,
jackie@greenfields.garden,
www.greenfields.garden. *Located
in Wye valley midway between
Chepstow & Monmouth. A446 from
M'mouth. Go thru Llandogo, L to
Brockweir. From Chepstow, thru
Tintern, R to B'weir. Go over bridge,
pass pub up hill, 1st L, follow lane
to fork, L at fork. 1st property on
R. No coaches.* Sun 1 May (1-5).
Adm £5, chd free. Sun 28 Aug
(12-5). Combined adm with The
Patch £8, chd free. Home-made

teas. All visits and refreshments
subject to weather. Visits also
by arrangement Apr to Aug for
groups of up to 40.
1½ acre plant person's gem of
a garden set in the beautiful Wye
Valley AONB. Many mature trees
and numerous rare/unusual plants
and shrubs, all planted as discrete
gardens within a garden. Greenfields
is the passion and work of Head
Gardener, Jackie, who has a long
interest in the propagation of
plants. Featured in Garden Answers
magazine. Mostly wheelchair access.

28 GREENFIELDS, LITTLE RISSINGTON
Cheltenham, GL54 2NA. Mrs
Diana MacKenzie-Charrington. *On
Rissington Rd between Bourton-on-
the-Water & Little Rissington, opp
turn to Grt Rissington (Leasow Lane).
SatNav using postcode does not
take you to house.* Sun 3 July (2-5).
Adm £5, chd free. Home-made
teas.
The honey coloured Georgian
Cotswold stone house sits in 2
acres of garden, created by current
owners over last 20 yrs. Lawns are
edged with borders full of flowers
and flowering bulbs. A small pond
and stream overlook fields. Bantams
roam freely. Mature apple trees in
wild garden, greenhouse in working
vegetable garden. Sorry no dogs.
Partial wheelchair access.

29 HIGHNAM COURT
Highnam, Gloucester,
GL2 8DP. Mr R J Head,
01684 292875 (Mike Bennett),
mike.highnamcourt@gmail.com,
www.HighnamCourt.co.uk. *2m
W of Gloucester. On A40/A48
junction from Gloucester to Ross or
Chepstow. At this r'about take exit at
3 o'clock if coming from Gloucester
direction. Do NOT go into Highnam
village.* Sun 3 Apr, Sun 1 May, Sun
5 June, Sun 3 July, Sun 7 Aug,
Sun 4 Sept (11-4.30). Adm £5, chd
free. Light refreshments. Visits
also by arrangement.
40 acres of Victorian landscaped
gardens surrounding magnificent
Grade I house (not open), set out by
artist Thomas Gambier Parry. Lakes,
shrubberies and listed Pulhamite
water gardens with grottos and
fernery. Exciting ornamental lakes,
and woodland areas. Extensive 1
acre rose garden and many features,

inc numerous wood carvings.
Some gravel paths and steps into
refreshment area. Disabled WC
outside.

30 HODGES BARN
Shipton Moyne, Tetbury,
GL8 8PR. Mr & Mrs N Hornby,
www.hodgesbarn.com. *3m S of
Tetbury. On Malmesbury side of
village.* Sun 12, Mon 13 June (2-6).
Adm £7, chd free. Home-made
teas at the Pool House.
Very unusual C15 dovecote converted
into family home. Cotswold stone
walls host climbing and rambling
roses, clematis, vines, hydrangeas
and together with yew, rose and
tapestry hedges create formality
around house. Mixed shrub and
herbaceous borders, shrub roses,
water garden, woodland garden
planted with cherries and magnolias.
Vegetable and picking flower garden.

31 HOME FARM
Newent Lane, Huntley, GL19 3HQ.
Mrs T Freeman, 01452 830210,
torillfreeman@gmail.com. *4m S of
Newent. On B4216 ½ m off A40 in
Huntley travelling towards Newent.*
Sun 30 Jan, Sun 13 Feb, Sun 6
Mar, Sun 3 Apr, Sun 1 May (11-4).
Adm £3.50, chd free. 2023: Sun
29 Jan, Sun 12 Feb. Visits also by
arrangement Jan to Apr.
Set in elevated position with
exceptional views. 1m walk through
woods and fields to show carpets of
spring flowers. Enclosed garden with
fern border, sundial and heather bed.
White and mixed shrub borders. Stout
footwear advisable in winter. Two
delightful cafés within a mile.

32 HOOKSHOUSE POTTERY
Hookshouse Lane,
Tetbury, GL8 8TZ. Lise
& Christopher White,
www.hookshousepottery.co.uk.
*2½ m SW of Tetbury. Follow signs
from A433 at Hare & Hounds Hotel,
Westonbirt. Alternatively take A4135
out of Tetbury towards Dursley
& follow signs after ½ m on L.*
Daily Wed 1 June to Sun 5 June
(11-5.30). Fri 17 June, Fri 1 July
(1.30-5.30). Adm £5, chd free.
Home-made teas.
Garden offers a combination of
long perspectives and intimate
corners. Planting inc wide variety of

perennials, with emphasis on colour interest throughout the seasons. Herbaceous borders, new woodland garden and flower meadow, water garden containing treatment ponds (unfenced) and flowform cascades. Sculptural features. Kitchen garden with raised beds, orchard. Run on organic principles. Pottery showroom with hand thrown woodfired pots inc frost proof garden pots. Art and craft exhibition (Jun 1st to 5th) inc garden furniture and sculptures. Garden games and treehouse. Mostly wheelchair accessible.

🚻 🐕 ✿ 🚗 ☕ 🪑 •))

33 NEW KEMBLE HOUSE
Kemble, Cirencester, GL7 6AD. Jill Kingston. *Approaching Kemble on the A429 from Cirencester, turn L onto School Rd then R onto Church Rd, pass Kemble Church on L. Kemble House is the next house on L.* Wed 20 Apr (2-5). Adm £5, chd free.

A landscaped garden with many tall lime trees. Herbaceous borders line the lawns. The main one in front of the house is a grass tennis court that was laid in the 1880s. There is a walled garden with many fruit trees and two rose gardens. Two paddocks surround the property with Hebridean sheep. •))

34 ◆ KIFTSGATE COURT
Chipping Campden, GL55 6LN. Mr & Mrs J G Chambers, 01386 438777, info@kiftsgate.co.uk, www.kiftsgate.co.uk. *4m NE of Chipping Campden. Adj to Hidcote NT Garden.* For NGS: Mon 11 Apr, Mon 15 Aug (2-6). Adm £9.50, chd £3. Home-made teas. For other opening times and information, please phone, email or visit garden website.

Magnificent situation and views, many unusual plants and shrubs, tree peonies, hydrangeas, abutilons, species and old-fashioned roses

inc largest rose in England, *Rosa filipes* Kiftsgate. Regional Finalist, The English Garden's The Nation's Favourite Gardens 2019.

✿ 🚗 🛏 ☕

35 NEW KIRKHAM FARM
Upper Slaughter, Cheltenham, GL54 2JS. Ms Liz Wills. *On road between Lower Slaughter & Lower Swell. Opp farm buildings on roadside. 1½ m W of Fosseway A429 & SW of Stow on the Wold.* Sun 3 July (11-5). Adm £6, chd free. Home-made teas.

A country garden overlooking lovely views with several mixed borders that always have a succession of colour. Gravel gardens, trees and shrubs and a hidden pool garden, raised beds, cutting beds and a developing wildflower bank give plenty of interest. Teas are served in our beautifully restored stone barn. The majority of the garden is accessible.

🚻 🐕 ☕

Kirkham Farm

36 LANE'S COTTAGE
Winchcombe, GL54 5BA.
Norman & Zoe Carter,
lanescottage@trelowen.com,
lanescottagegarden.blogspot.
com. *1m S of entrance to Sudeley
Castle. From Cheltenham on B4632,
turn R after church down Vineyard
St, after 200yds bear R and follow
road for 1m.* **Visits by arrangement
Apr to Aug for groups of 5 to 10.
Parking limited to 5 cars. Adm £8,
chd free. Tea or coffee and home-
made cake inc in adm.**
This 2½ acre triangular garden
was planted in 2018 in the grounds
of a listed cottage. Different easily
maintained landscaped areas with
wildlife habitat. The garden has
interest and colour year-round with
orchard, woodland, spring bulbs,
wildflower areas, cloud trees,
perennial borders and prairie planting.
In spring camasia/daffodil/tulip/allium,
summer poppy/wildflowers/various
perennials.

37 [NEW] **LANGFORD DOWNS
FARM**
Langford, Lechlade,
GL7 3QL. Mr & Mrs Gavin
MacEchern, 07778 355 115,
caroline@macechern.com. *Access
from A361 via layby behind copse -
6m from Burford towards Lechlade
on the R OR 2m from Lechlade
towards Burford on the L.* **Wed 29
June (2-6). Adm £7, chd free.
Home-made teas. Visits also
by arrangement June & July for
groups of 15 to 20.**
Cotswold house built in 2009 and
new garden created from blank
canvas. Extensive tree planting. Good
sized garden comprising mixed tree,
shrub and herbaceous borders.
Traditional hedges comprising arches
and windows, Cotswold pond, Walnut
walk, spiral and mature vegetable
garden. Bug hotels and hedgehog
piles. 'Mrs Bennet's Walk' and year-
round interest. All areas wheelchair
friendly.

38 LITTLE ORCHARD
Slad, Stroud, GL6 7QD. Rod &
Terry Clifford, 01452 813944,
terryclifford.tlc@gmail.com. *2m
from Stroud, 10 m from Cheltenham.
Last property on L in Slad village
before leaving 30mph speed limit
travelling from Stroud to Birdlip on
B4070. SatNav may not bring you
directly to property. Parking on verge*

opp. **Sat 25, Sun 26 June (10.30-
5). Adm £5, chd free. Home-made
teas. Cider tasting available.
Visits also by arrangement May to
Sept for groups of 5 to 30.**
1 acre garden created from
wilderness on a challenging, steeply
sloping site using many reclaimed
materials, stonework and statuary.
Multiple terraces and garden rooms
enhanced with different styles of
planting and water features to
complement the natural surroundings.
Many seating areas with stunning
views of the Slad Valley. Access into
adjoining Nature Reserve. Children's
Trail. Cidery. Wheelchair access
possible but challenging due to the
severity of slopes and steps. Please
phone for further details.

39 [NEW] **LORDS OF THE MANOR
HOTEL**
Upper Slaughter, Cheltenham,
GL54 2JD. Mike Dron (Head
Gardener), 01451 820243,
reservations@lordsofthemanor.
com, www.lordsofthemanor.com.
*From Fosse way follow signs for the
Slaughters from close to Bourton-
on-the-Water (toward Stow). From
B4077 (Stanway Hill road) coming
from Tewkesbury direction, follow
signs 2m after Ford village.* **Thur
28 Apr (10-3). Adm £7, chd £5.
Refreshments are available from
the hotel, from light snacks to
afternoon tea. Pre booking may
be necessary.**
Classic Cotswold country garden
with a very English blend of formal
and informal, merging beautifully with
the surrounding landscape. Beautiful
walled garden, established wildflower
meadow, the River Eye. The herb
garden and stunning bog garden
were designed by Julie Toll around
2012. Wildlife garden, croquet lawn,
courtyard and Victorian skating pond.
Mostly wheelchair access but steps
within walled garden and bog garden.

40 LOWER FARM HOUSE
Cliffords Mesne, Newent,
GL18 1JT. Gareth & Sarah
Williams. *2m S of Newent. From
Newent, follow signs to Cliffords
Mesne & Birds of Prey Centre
(1½m). Approx ½m beyond Centre,
turn L at Xrds (before church).* **Wed
25 May (2-5.30). Adm £5, chd free.
Light refreshments.**
2½ acre garden, inc woodland,
stream and large natural lily pond with

rockery and bog garden. Herbaceous
borders, pergola walk, terrace with
ornamental fishpond, kitchen and
herb garden; collections of irises,
hostas and peonies. Many interesting
and unusual trees and shrubs inc
magnolias and cornus. Some gravel
paths.

41 THE MANOR
Little Compton, Moreton-
In-Marsh, GL56 0RZ. Reed
Foundation (Charity),
www.reedbusinessschool.co.uk/.
*Next to church in Little Compton.
½m from A44 or 2m from A3400.
Follow signs to Little Compton, then
yellow NGS signs.* **Sun 26 June,
Sun 21 Aug (2-5). Adm £6, chd
free. Home-made teas. Donation
to another charity.**
Extensive Arts & Crafts garden with
meadow and arboreta. Footpaths
around our fields, playground between
car park and garden. Croquet, and
tennis free to play. Children and dogs
welcome. One ramp in main part of
the garden. Rock garden, tennis court
lawn and meadow not accessible
by wheelchair. Disabled drop-off at
entrance.

42 [NEW] **MONKS SPOUT
COTTAGE**
Glasshouse Hill, May Hill,
Longhope, GL17 0NN. Nigel &
Jane Jackson, 07767 858295,
monksspout@icloud.com. *1m
from NT May Hill, in the hamlet
of Glasshouse. Access via lane
(which is also a public footpath
called the Wysis Way) immed
adjacent to Glasshouse Inn.* **Visits
by arrangement Feb to Sept for
groups of up to 30. Adm £7.50,
chd free. Home-made teas.**
The ⅔ acre garden is adjacent
to Castle Hill Wood which is the
backdrop for a mix of herbaceous
borders, lawns and ponds, with
greenhouse, stream and large display
of insectivorous plants, mostly planted
outside but some in the greenhouse.
With several mature trees and recently
planted acers, there is a mix of shade
and sun creating both damp and
dry planting opportunities. Garden
sculptures. Adjacent public footpaths
through the wood (not part of the
garden) where visitors can see the
remains of a ringwork castle dating
from C12.

43 MOOR WOOD

Woodmancote, GL7 7EB. Mr & Mrs Henry Robinson, 01285 831397, henry@moorwoodhouse.co.uk, www.moorwoodroses.co.uk. *3½ m NW of Cirencester. Turn L off A435 to Cheltenham at N Cerney, signed Woodmancote 1¼ m; entrance in village on L beside lodge with white gates.* **Sun 26 June (2-6). Adm £5, chd free. Home-made teas. Visits also by arrangement in June for groups of up to 25.**

2 acres of shrub, orchard and wildflower gardens in beautiful isolated valley setting. Holder of National Collection of Rambler Roses. June 20th to 30th is usually the best time for the roses.

44 NEW OAK HOUSE

Greenway Lane, Gretton, Cheltenham, GL54 5ER. Paul & Sue Hughes, 01242 603990, ppphug@gmail.com. *In centre of Gretton. Signed Gretton from B4077, approx 3m from A46 Teddington Hands r'about. Greenway Lane 300m R past railway bridge. Parking on main road with short walk to garden.* **Wed 15, Sat 18 June (11-5). Adm £5, chd free. Home-made teas. Visits also by arrangement Apr to Sept for groups of up to 20. Tea and cake by prior arrangement.**

A one acre secret garden divided into rooms. Gradually developed over the last 30 yrs. Many places to sit and enjoy the scent of honeysuckle, philadelphus and over 50 varieties of roses. Wildflower meadow, gazebo and summerhouse. Formal lily pond and small wildlife pond. Some quirky features. You may see a fairy. Wheelchair access from top drive.

45 THE OLD VICARAGE

Murrells End, Hartpury, GL19 3DF. Mrs Carol Huckvale. *5m NW of Gloucester. From Over r'about on A40 N Gloucester bypass, take A417 NW to Hartpury (Ledbury Rd). After Maisemore, turn L at signs for Hartpury College. House 1m on R. Follow signs for parking.* **Fri 3, Sat 4, Sun 5 June (1-4.30). Adm £5, chd free. Home-made teas.**

Tranquil garden of about 2 acres, with yew oval, mature trees, steps to croquet lawn, mixed borders around main lawn, potager, fruit trees. Work in progress developing wildflower meadow area and dry, shady woodland walk.

46 ◆ OXLEAZE FARM

Between Eastleach & Filkins, Lechlade, GL7 3RB. Mr & Mrs Charles Mann, 07786 918502, chipps@oxleaze.co.uk, www. oxleaze.co.uk/oxleaze-garden. *5m S of Burford, 3m N of Lechlade off A361 to W (signed Barringtons). Take 2nd L then follow signs.* **For NGS: Wed 22 June (3-7). Adm £6, chd free. Home-made teas, and wine. For other opening times and information, please phone, email or visit garden website.**

Set among beautiful traditional farm buildings, plantsperson's good size garden created by owners over 35 yrs. Year-round interest; mixed borders, vegetable potager, decorative fruit cages, pond/bog garden, bees, potting shed, meadow, and topiary for structure when the flowers fade. Garden rooms off central lawn with corners in which to enjoy this organic Cotswold garden. Groups welcome by arrangement. Mostly wheelchair access.

47 PASTURE FARM

Upper Oddington, GL56 0XG. Mr & Mrs John LLoyd, 01451 830203, ljmlloyd@yahoo.com. *3m W of Stow-on-the-Wold. Just off A436, midway between Upper & Lower Oddington.* **Sat 28, Sun 29 May (11-6). Adm £6, chd free. Home-made teas. Visits also by arrangement in June.**

Informal country garden developed over 30 yrs by current owners. Mixed borders, topiary, orchard and many species of trees. Gravel garden and rambling roses in 'the ruins'. A concrete garden and wildflower area leads to vegetable patch. Large spring-fed pond with ducks. Also bantams, chickens, black Welsh sheep and a Kunekune pig. Public footpath across 2 small fields arrives at C11 church, St Nicholas, with doom paintings, set in ancient woodlands. Truly worth a visit. See Simon Jenkins' Book of Churches. Mostly wheelchair access.

48 THE PATCH

Hollywell Lane, Brockweir, Chepstow, NP16 7PJ. Mrs Immy Lee, 07801 816340, immylee1@hotmail.com. *6.7m N of Chepstow & 10.6m S of Monmouth, off A466, across Brockweir Bridge.* **Sun 28 Aug (12-5). Combined adm with Greenfields, Brockweir Common £8, chd free. Home-made teas.**

Visits also by arrangement May to July. Possibility of combining arrangements with Greenfields. Rural ¼ acre garden with far reaching views across the Wye Valley, containing 60+ repeat flowering roses and a variety of shrubs and perennials, providing interest year-round. The garden open day is in combination with Greenfields. The gardens are linked by an easy drive or a 15 min stony walk along the Offa's Dyke path. Ample parking at both gardens. Partial wheelchair access.

49 PEAR TREE COTTAGE

58 Malleson Road, Gotherington, nr Cheltenham, GL52 9EX. Mr & Mrs E Manders-Trett, 01242 674592, mmanderstrett@gmail.com. *4m N of Cheltenham. From A435, travelling N, turn R into Gotherington 1m after Bishop's Cleeve bypass at garage. Garden on L 100yds past Shutter Inn.* **Visits by arrangement Feb to June for groups of up to 30. Adm £6, chd free. Tea/coffee and cake available.**

Mainly informal country garden of approx ½ acre with pond and gravel garden. Herbaceous borders, trees and shrubs surround lawns and seating areas. Wild garden and orchard lead to greenhouses, vegetable garden and beehives. Spring bulbs, early summer perennials and shrubs particularly colourful. Gravel drive and several shallow steps can be overcome for wheelchair users with prior notice.

50 PERRYWOOD HOUSE

Longney, Gloucester, GL2 3SN. Gill & Mike Farmer. *7m SW of Gloucester, 4m W of Quedgeley. From N: R off B4008 at Tesco r'about. R at next r'about then R at 2nd mini r'about, then signed. From S: L off A38 at Moreton Valence to Epney/Longney, over canal bridge, R at T junction then signed.* **Sat 25, Sun 26 June (11-5). Adm £5, chd free. Home-made teas.**

1 acre plant lover's garden in the Severn Vale surrounded by open farmland. Established over 20 yrs, an informal country garden with mature trees and shrubs, small pond, colourful herbaceous borders and containers. Plenty of places to sit and enjoy the garden. Lots of interesting plants for sale. All areas accessible with level lawns and gravel drives. Disabled parking available.

51 RADNORS
Wheatstone Lane, Lydbrook, GL17 9DP. Mrs Mary Wood, 01594 861690, mary.wood37@btinternet.com. *From Lydbrook, go through village towards the R Wye. At the T junction turn L into Stowfield Rd. Wheatstone Ln (300m) is 1st turning L after the white cottages. Radnors is at end of lane.* **Visits by arrangement Apr to Oct for groups of up to 10. Adm £4, chd free. Light refreshments.**
5 acre hillside woodland garden in AONB on bank above the River Wye. Focus on wildlife with naturalistic planting and weeds, some left for specific insects/birds. It has many paths, a wooded area, wildflower area, flower beds and borders, lawns, stumpery, fernery, vegetable beds and white garden. Of particular interest is the path along a disused railway line, and the summer dahlias.

52 RAMBLERS
Lower Common, Aylburton, Lydney, GL15 6DS. Jane & Leslie Hale. *1½ m W of Lydney. Off A48 Gloucester to Chepstow Rd. From Lydney through Aylburton, out of de-limit turn R signed Aylburton Common, ¾ m along lane.* **Sun 1 May (1.30-5). Adm £5, chd free. Home-made teas.**

Peaceful medium sized country garden with informal cottage planting, herbaceous borders and small pond looking through hedge windows onto wildflower meadow and mature apple orchard. Some shade loving plants and topiary. Large productive vegetable garden. Past winner of The English Garden magazine's Britain's Best Gardener's Garden competition.

53 READY TOKEN HOUSE
Ready Token, Cirencester, GL7 5SX. Mark & Tabitha Mayall. *Hamlet between Bibury and Poulton. From Cirencester take Roman Road.* **Thur 28, Fri 29 Apr, Thur 23, Fri 24 June, Thur 8, Fri 9 Sept (10-5). Adm £7, chd free. Home-made teas.**
Nature-friendly garden with formal and informal herbaceous borders and mixed topiary; 300 yr old wisteria-clad country house and mature trees, set in 60 acres of rewilded parkland, with mown pathways through wildflower meadows for walks with stunning views to Vale of the White Horse; Roman sunken garden, well, pond, lake, orchard, organic vegetable garden with raised beds, greenhouse.

54 RICHMOND PAINSWICK RETIREMENT VILLAGE
Stroud Road, Painswick, Stroud, GL6 6UL. Richmond Villages/bupa. *Roughly 5m E of Stroud. Just outside Painswick village.* **Thur 26, Sat 28 May, Thur 9, Sat 11 June (9-3). Adm £5, chd free. Light refreshments.**
Situated on the southern slopes of Painswick this 4 acre retirement village boasts formal lawns and borders planted for year-round interest. A varied mix of herbaceous and perennial planting, with many areas of interest inc wildflower meadow and fruit trees that combine to attract an abundance of wildlife. The gardens are a blaze of colour throughout. Car parking, WC, cafe serving tea/coffee plus light bites, and a restaurant. There are gentle slopes in wildflower meadow and around some areas of the village.

55 ROCKCLIFFE
Upper Slaughter, Cheltenham, GL54 2JW. Mr & Mrs Simon Keswick, www.rockcliffegarden.co.uk. *2m from Stow-on-the-Wold. 1½ m from Lower Swell on B4068 towards Cheltenham. Leave Stow-on-the-Wold on B4068 through Lower Swell. Continue on B4068 for 1½ m.*

1 Jasmine Cottage, Eastcombe and Bussage Gardens

Rockcliffe is well signed on R. **Tue 7, Wed 29 June (10-5). Adm £7.50, chd free. Home-made teas. Donation to Kate's Home Nursing.** Large traditional English garden of 8 acres inc pink garden, white and blue garden, herbaceous borders, rose terrace, large walled kitchen garden and greenhouses. Pathway of topiary birds leading up through orchard to stone dovecot. 2 wide stone steps through gate, otherwise good wheelchair access. Sorry no dogs.

56 NEW ▶ SHEEPEHOUSE COTTAGE
Stepping Stone Lane, Painswick, Stroud, GL6 6RX. Mr Russ & Mrs Jackie Herbert, 01452 813229, sheepehouse@hotmail.com. *3m N of Stroud off the A46 in Painswick. From A46 turn into Stamages Ln (signed Painswick Car Park). Pass car park, keep straight on Stamages Ln/Stepping Stone Ln to bottom of hill and climb until you find parking signs.* **Sun 10 Apr, Sun 14 Aug (11-5). Adm £5, chd free. Home-made teas. Visits also by arrangement May to Sept for groups of up to 8.** Lovely country, hillside garden with outstanding views across the Cotswolds. Variety of mixed borders and garden 'rooms' including perennials, herbaceous and evergreens. New cottage garden with formal pond and arbour. Wildflower orchard with mown paths and many bulbs leading into small wooded area with paths. Greenhouse and raised vegetable beds. Wildlife pond. Much of garden can be seen from the level paved access around house. All areas wheelchair accessible pushing across grass but with some steep slopes.

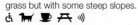

57 SOUTH LODGE
Church Road, Clearwell, Coleford, GL16 8LG. Andrew & Jane MacBean, 01594 837769, southlodgegarden@btinternet. com, www.southlodgegarden. co.uk. *2m S of Coleford. Off B4228. Follow signs to Clearwell. Garden on L of castle driveway. Please park on rd in front of church or in village. No parking on castle drive.* **Sat 9 Apr, Sat 14 May, Sat 25 June (1-5). Adm £4.50, chd free. Home-made teas. Visits also by arrangement Apr to June for groups of 15+.** Peaceful country garden in 2 acres with stunning views of surrounding countryside. High walls provide

a backdrop for rambling roses, clematis, and honeysuckles. Organic garden with large variety of perennials, annuals, shrubs and specimen trees with year-round colour. Vegetable garden, wildlife and formal ponds. Rustic pergola planted with English climbing roses and willow arbour in gravel garden. Gravel paths and steep grassy slopes. Assistance dogs only.

GROUP OPENING

58 STANTON VILLAGE GARDENS
Stanton, nr Broadway, WR12 7NE. 01386 584659, susanhughes83@hotmail.co.uk. *3m S of Broadway. Off B4632, between Broadway (3m) & Winchcombe (6m).* **Sun 12 June (2-6). Combined adm £7.50, chd free. Home-made teas in several gardens around the village. Ice cream trike in village. Visits also by arrangement in June. Donation to Village charities.** A selection of gardens open in this picturesque, unspoilt Cotswold village. Many houses border the street with long gardens hidden behind. Gardens vary, from houses with colourful herbaceous borders, established trees, shrubs and vegetable gardens to tiny cottage gardens. Some also have attractive, natural water features fed by the stream which runs through the village. Plants for sale and book stall. Free parking. Church also open. The Mount Inn open for lunch. An NGS visit not to be missed in this gem of a Cotswold village. Gardens not suitable for wheelchair users due to gravel drives.

59 ♦ STANWAY FOUNTAIN & WATER GARDEN
Stanway, Cheltenham, GL54 5PQ. The Earl of Wemyss & March, 01386 584528, office@stanwayhouse.co.uk, www.stanwayfountain.co.uk. *9m NE of Cheltenham. 1m E of B4632 Cheltenham to Broadway rd on B4077 Toddington to Stow-on-the-Wold rd.* **For NGS: Sun 15 May, Sun 14 Aug (2-5). Adm £7, chd £2.50. Home-made teas in Stanway Tea Room. For other opening times and information,**

please phone, email or visit garden website. 20 acres of planted landscape in early C18 formal setting. The restored canal, upper pond and fountain have recreated one of the most interesting Baroque water gardens in Britain. Striking C16 manor with gatehouse, tithe barn and church. The garden features Britain's highest fountain at 300ft, and it is the world's highest gravity fountain. It runs at 2.45pm and 4.00pm for 30 mins each time. Partial wheelchair access in garden, some flat areas, able to view fountain and some of garden. House is not suitable for wheelchairs.

60 ♦ SUDELEY CASTLE & GARDENS
Winchcombe, GL54 5JD. Lady Ashcombe, 01242 604244, enquiries@sudeley.org.uk, www.sudeleycastle.co.uk. *8m NE Cheltenham, 10 m from M5 J9. SatNavs use GL54 5LP. Free parking.* **For NGS: Fri 23 Sept (10.30-3). Adm £10, chd £6. For other opening times and information, please phone, email or visit garden website.** Sudeley Castle features 10 magnificent gardens, each with its own unique style and design. Surrounded by striking views of the Cotswold Hills, each garden reflects the fascinating 1000 yr history of the Castle. This series of elegant gardens is set among the Castle and atmospheric ruins and inc a Knot garden, Queen's garden and Tudor physic garden. Sudeley Castle remains the only private castle in England to have a queen buried within the grounds - Queen Katherine Parr, the last and surviving wife of King Henry VIII – who lived and died in the castle. A circular route around the gardens is wheelchair accessible although some visitors may require assistance from their companion.

During 2020 – 2021 National Garden Scheme funding supported over 1,400 Queen's Nurses to deliver virtual and hands-on, community care across England, Wales and Northern Ireland

61 TREE HILL

76 Gretton Road, Winchcombe, Cheltenham, GL54 5EL. Mark Caswell. ½ m N of Winchcombe. Leave Winchcombe via North St, straight ahead onto Gretton Rd for ½ m. Sun 28 Aug (10-4). Adm £4, chd free.

Stepping into this garden is akin to stepping into another world. As one visitor remarked 'this is unlike any English garden I have ever seen.' On this small and modest plot one finds huge leaves, tall exotic plants jostling for light with the small and the delicate. Created with a passion for the exotic landscapes of the Caribbean which was inspired by a visit to Barbados.

))))

62 TRENCH HILL

Sheepscombe, GL6 6TZ. Celia & Dave Hargrave, 01452 814306, celia.hargrave@btconnect.com. 1½ m E of Painswick. From Cheltenham A46 take 1st turn signed Sheepscombe, follow for approx 1½ m. Or from the Butcher's Arms in Sheepscombe (with it on R) leave village and take lane signed for Cranham. Sun 6, Sun 13 Feb (11-4.30); Sun 20 Mar, Sun 17, Mon 18 Apr, Sun 1 May (11-6). Every Wed 8 June to 29 June (2-6). Sun 17 July, Sun 28 Aug, Sun 18 Sept (11-6). Adm £5, chd free. Home-made teas. 2023: Sun 12, Sun 19 Feb. Visits also by arrangement Feb to Sept for groups of up to 35. All groups using a coach must consult with garden owners prior to visit.

Approx 3 acres set in small woodland with panoramic views. Variety of herbaceous and mixed borders, rose garden, extensive vegetable plots, wildflower areas, plantings of spring bulbs with thousands of snowdrops and hellebores, woodland walk, 2 small ponds, waterfall and larger conservation pond. Interesting wooden sculptures, many within the garden. Run on organic principles. Children's play area. Mostly wheelchair access but some steps and slopes.

&. ❁ 🚐 🍵

GROUP OPENING

63 NEW TUFFLEY GARDENS

Stroud Road, Gloucester, GL4 0DT. Martyn & Jenny Parker. 3m S Gloucester. Follow arrows off St. Barnabas R'about. Sun 29 May (11-4). Combined adm £5, chd free.

Home-made teas in St Barnabas Church Hall.

A number of suburban gardens of different styles and sizes, some corner plots, lawned or gravelled, each with their own personality. Some have ponds or water features, others have specimen and fruit trees on land once a huge orchard prior to housing. Close to Robinswood Hill Country park, 250 acres of open countryside with viewpoint, pleasant walks and waymarked nature trails.

❁ 🍵

64 UPTON WOLD

Moreton-in-Marsh, GL56 9TR. Mr & Mrs I R S Bond, 01386 700667, uptonwold@btinternet.com, www.uptonwold.co.uk. 4½ m W of Moreton-in-Marsh on A44. From Moreton/Stow ½ m past A424 turn R opp Deer Sign to road into fields then L at mini Xrds. From Evesham 1m past B4081 C/Campden Xrds turn L at end of stone wall to road into fields then as above. Sun 10 Apr (10-5). Adm £14, chd free. Home-made teas. Visits also by arrangement.

One of the secret gardens of the Cotswolds, Upton Wold has commanding views, yew hedges, herbaceous walk, vegetable, pond and woodland gardens, labyrinth. An abundance of unusual and interesting plants, shrubs and trees. National Collections of juglans and pterocarya. A garden of interest to any garden and plant lover. 2 Star award from GGG.

❁ 🚌 NPC 🍵

65 WEIR REACH

The Rudge, Maisemore, Gloucester, GL2 8HY. Sheila & Mark Wardle, weirreach@gmail.com. 3m NW of Gloucester. Turn into The Rudge by White Hart Pub. Parking 100m from garden. Sun 12, Wed 15 June (11-5). Adm £4, chd free. Home-made teas. Visits also by arrangement in June for groups of 10 to 30.

Country garden by River Severn. Approx 2 acres, half cultivated with herbaceous beds and mixed borders plus fruit and vegetable cages. Clematis and acers, stone ornaments, small sculptures, bonsai collection. Planted rockery with waterfall and stream connect 2 ponds. Large specimen koi pond borders patio. Meadow with specimen and fruit trees leading to river and country views.

❁ 🍵))))

66 NEW WESTAWAY

Stockwell Lane, Cleeve Hill, Cheltenham, GL52 3PU. Liz & Ian Ramsay, 01242 672676, lizmramsay@gmail.com. Off the B4632 Cheltenham to Winchcombe road at Cleeve Hill. Sun 26, Wed 29 June (1-5). Adm £5, chd free. Home-made teas. Visits also by arrangement June & July for groups of 10 to 20.

Hillside 1½ acre garden situated on the Cotswold escarpment with spectacular views across the Severn Vale. Interesting solutions to the challenges of gardening on a gradient, reflecting the local topography. Mixed shrub and herbaceous borders, bog garden, orchard, small arboretum and several wildflower areas. Landscaping includes extensive terracing with grass banks.

❁ 🍵))))

67 ♦ WESTONBIRT SCHOOL GARDENS

Tetbury, GL8 8QG. Holfords of Westonbirt Trust, 01666 881373, jbaker@holfordtrust.com, www.holfordtrust.com. 3m SW of Tetbury. Please enter through main school gates on A433 - some SatNavs will send you via a side entrance where there will be no access - main school gates only please. For NGS: Sun 10 July (11-4.30). Adm £5, chd free. Tea. For other opening times and information, please phone, email or visit garden website.

28 acres. Former private garden of Robert Holford, founder of Westonbirt Arboretum. Formal Victorian gardens inc walled Italian garden now restored with early herbaceous borders and exotic border. Rustic walks, lake, statuary and grotto. Rare, exotic trees and shrubs. Beautiful views of Westonbirt House open with guided tours to see fascinating Victorian interior on designated days of the year. There are gravelled paths in some areas, grass in others and wheelchair users are limited to downstairs part of the house due to evacuation protocols.

&. 🚐 🍵))))

68 WORTLEY HOUSE

Wortley, Wotton-Under-Edge, GL12 7QP. Simon & Jessica Dickinson, 01453 843174, jessica@wortleyhouse.co.uk. On Wortley Rd 1m south of Wotton-under-Edge. Grand entrance on L

as you enter Wortley coming from Wotton. **Tue 26 Apr, Tue 28 June (2-5). Adm £15, chd free. Pre-booking essential, please visit www.ngs.org.uk for information & booking. Home-made teas included in the admission price. Visits also by arrangement Apr to Sept for groups of up to 30.**
A diverse garden of over 20 acres created during the last 30 yrs by the current owners. Includes walled garden, pleached lime avenues, nut walk, potager, ponds, Italian garden, shrubberies and wildflower meadows. Strategically placed follies, urns and statues enhance extraordinary vistas throughout, and the garden is filled with plants, arbours, roses through trees and up walls, and herbaceous borders. The stunning surrounding countryside is incorporated into the garden with views up the steep valley that are such a feature in this part of Gloucestershire. Picnics are allowed, and a map and plant list are available. Wheelchair access to most areas, golf buggy also available.

GROUP OPENING

69 WYCK RISSINGTON GARDENS

Cheltenham, GL54 2PN. *Nr Stow-on-the-Wold & Bourton-on-the-Water. 1m from Fosse Way A429.* Sun 4 Sept (1-5). Combined adm £9, chd free. Home-made teas in village hall. **Donation to St Laurence's Church Fabric Fund.**

NEW ANSELLS BARN
Andrew & Elizabeth Ransom.

GREENFIELDS FARM
Graham Wild.

LAURENCE HOUSE
Mr & Mrs Robert Montague, 01451 822275.
Visits also by arrangement.

MACES COTTAGE
Tim & Pippa Simon.

An unspoilt Cotswold village off the beaten track set round a village green and its pond. The gardens are within easy reach of convenient parking and this popular group reopening provides an enjoyable afternoon in a perfect Cotswold setting. Gardens included are at various stages of maturity. The much admired Laurence House garden has new features such as a wildlife pond. Greenfields Farm is completely redesigned under its new owners to include a stunning Japanese Garden. Maces Cottage has fine borders and old fruit trees, and like Greenfields, has wonderful views over the Windrush Valley. Ansell's Barn is wholly new, with an emphasis on grasses, fruit trees and sculpture. Plants, garden produce, and an exhibition in the church of native species growing on the village green. The walk between gardens allows you to appreciate the beauty of the historic buildings grouped around the village green. Wheelchair access available at all gardens and WC in village hall.

Monk's Spout Cottage

HAMPSHIRE

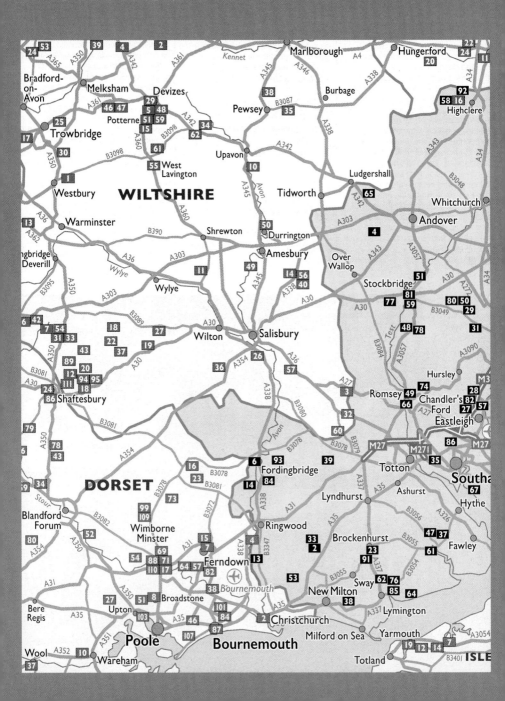

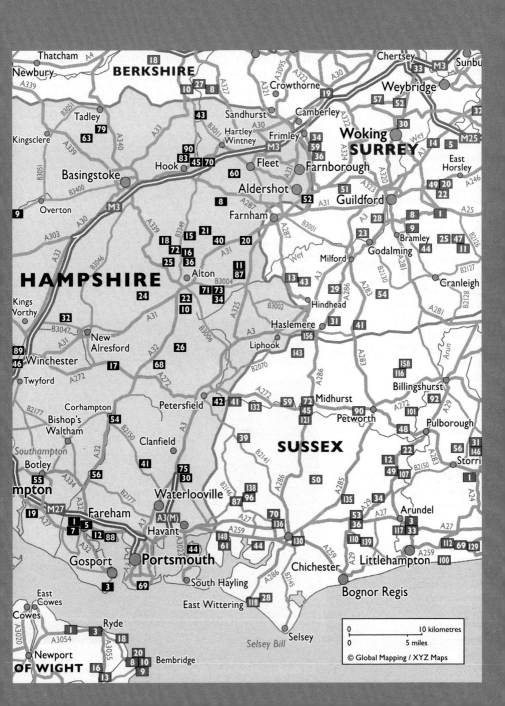

Volunteers

County Organiser
Mark Porter 07814 958810
markstephenporter@gmail.com

County Treasurer
Fred Fratter 01962 776243
fred@fratter.co.uk

Publicity
Pat Beagley 01256 764772
pat.beagley@ngs.org.uk

Social Media - Facebook
Mary Hayter 07512 639772
mary.hayter@ngs.org.uk

Social Media - Twitter
Louise Moreton 07943 837993
louise.moreton@ngs.org.uk

Booklet Co-ordinator
Mark Porter (as above)

Assistant County Organisers

Central
Sue Cox 01962 732043
suealex13@gmail.com

Central West
Kate Cann 01794 389105
kategcann@gmail.com

East
Linda Smith 01329 833253
linda.ngs@btinternet.com

North
Cynthia Oldale 01420 520438
c.k.oldale@btinternet.com

North East
Lizzie Powell 01420 23185
lizziepowellbroadhatch@gmail.com

North West
Adam Vetere 01635 268267
adam.vetere@ngs.org.uk

South
Barbara Sykes 02380 254521
barandhugh@aol.com

South West
Elizabeth Walker 01590 677415
elizabethwalker13@gmail.com

West
Jane Wingate-Saul 01725 519414
jane.wingatesaul@ngs.org.uk

Hampshire is a large, diverse county. The landscape ranges from clay/gravel heath and woodland in the New Forest National Park in the south west, across famous trout rivers – the Test and Itchen – to chalk downland in the east, where you will find the South Downs National Park.

Our open gardens are spread right across the county and offer a very diverse range of interest for both the keen gardener and the casual visitor.

We have a large number of gardens with rivers running through them such as those in The Island and Bere Mill; gardens with large vegetable kitchen gardens such as Bramdean House; and seven new gardens will open for the very first time.

You will be assured of a warm welcome by all our garden owners and we hope you enjoy your visits.

Below: Appleyards

 @HampshireNGS @HantsNGS @hantsngs

OPENING DATES

All entries subject to change. For latest information check www.ngs.org.uk

Extended openings are shown at the beginning of the month.

Map locator numbers are shown to the right of each garden name.

February

Snowdrop Festival

Sunday 6th
◆ Chawton House 22

Saturday 12th
Little Court 50

Sunday 13th
Bramdean House 17

Monday 14th
Little Court 50

Sunday 20th
Little Court 50

Monday 21st
Little Court 50

Saturday 26th
Pilley Hill Cottage 62

Sunday 27th
Pilley Hill Cottage 62

March

Thursday 3rd
Little Court 50

Saturday 5th
Pilley Hill Cottage 62

Sunday 6th
Pilley Hill Cottage 62

Sunday 13th
Bere Mill 9

Wednesday 30th
Beechenwood Farm 8

April

Every Wednesday
Beechenwood Farm 8

Sunday 3rd
Durmast House 33

Saturday 9th
The Island 49

Sunday 10th
Bramdean House 17
The Island 49
Old Thatch & The Millennium Barn 60

Friday 15th
Crawley Gardens 29

Sunday 17th
Pylewell Park 64
28 St Ronan's Avenue 69
Terstan 81
Twin Oaks 82

Monday 18th
Crawley Gardens 29
Twin Oaks 82

Wednesday 20th
Abbotsfield 2

Thursday 21st
Appleyards 6

Friday 22nd
Appleyards 6

Saturday 23rd
Appleyards 6

Sunday 24th
Appleyards 6
◆ Spinners Garden 76
Tylney Hall Hotel 83

Friday 29th
Bluebell Wood 16

Saturday 30th
Bluebell Wood 16

May

Every Wednesday
Beechenwood Farm 8

Sunday 1st
The Cottage 27
Walhampton 85

Monday 2nd
Beechenwood Farm 8
Bere Mill 9
The Cottage 27
Pylewell Park 64

Wednesday 4th
Abbotsfield 2

Saturday 7th
Brick Kiln Cottage 18

Sunday 8th
The Cottage 27
The House in the Wood 47

Monday 9th
The Cottage 27

Thursday 12th
Tanglefoot 80

Saturday 14th
◆ Alverstoke Crescent Garden 3
146 Bridge Road 19
21 Chestnut Road 23

Sunday 15th
Brick Kiln Cottage 18
146 Bridge Road 19
21 Chestnut Road 23
Tanglefoot 80

Wednesday 18th
Abbotsfield 2
Little Court 50

Sunday 22nd
How Park Barn 48
Tylney Hall Hotel 83

Saturday 28th
Amport & Monxton Gardens 4
Bisterne Manor 13
Ferns Lodge 38
'Selborne' 71
NEW Winchester College 89

Sunday 29th
Amport & Monxton Gardens 4
Crookley Pool 30
Ferns Lodge 38
Manor House 54
Romsey Gardens 66
28 St Ronan's Avenue 69
'Selborne' 71
Shalden Park House 72
Spitfire House 77
NEW Winchester College 89

June

Every Wednesday to Wednesday 8th
Beechenwood Farm 8

Wednesday 1st
Abbotsfield 2

Thursday 2nd
Appleyards 6
Bere Mill 9

Friday 3rd
Appleyards 6

Saturday 4th
Appleyards 6
Twin Oaks 82

Sunday 5th
Appleyards 6
Bramdean House 17
108 Heath Road 42
South View House 75
Twin Oaks 82

Wednesday 8th
Spitfire House 77

Thursday 9th
Tanglefoot 80

Saturday 11th
Froyle Gardens 40
Manor Lodge 55
1 Povey's Cottage 63

Sunday 12th
Cranbury Park 28
Froyle Gardens 40
Manor House 54
Manor Lodge 55
1 Povey's Cottage 63
Tanglefoot 80

Monday 13th
Heckfield Place 43

Tuesday 14th
Heckfield Place 43
Little Court 50

Wednesday 15th
Little Court 50

Thursday 16th
Stockbridge Gardens 78

Saturday 18th
5 Oakfields 57

Sunday 19th
Berry Cottage 10
Fritham Lodge 39
Longstock Park Water Garden 51
5 Oakfields 57
Stockbridge Gardens 78
Terstan 81
Tylney Hall Hotel 83

Friday 24th
Searles Lane Gardens 70

Yew Hurst

Saturday 25th
21 Chestnut Road   23
Searles Lane Gardens 70
NEW Yew Hurst   93

Sunday 26th
Binsted Place   11
21 Chestnut Road   23
Durmast House   33
Searles Lane Gardens 70
Tadley Place   79
Wicor Primary School
Community Garden   88
Woolton House   92
NEW Yew Hurst   93

Monday 27th
Binsted Place   11

Thursday 30th
Appleyards   6
Crawley Gardens   29

July

Every Tuesday
Old Swan House   59

Friday 1st
Appleyards   6

Saturday 2nd
Angels Folly   5
Appleyards   6
East Worldham Manor 34
26 Lower Newport
Road   52
'Selborne'   71

Sunday 3rd
Angels Folly   5
Appleyards   6
Bramdean House   17
Bumpers   21
Crawley Gardens   29
East Worldham Manor 34
26 Lower Newport
Road   52
'Selborne'   71

Saturday 9th
NEW Venards   84

Sunday 10th
Broadhatch House   20
Little Court   50

NEW Venards   84
1 Wogsbarne
Cottages   90

Monday 11th
Broadhatch House   20
1 Wogsbarne
Cottages   90

Tuesday 12th
Broadhatch House   20

Saturday 16th
Angels Folly   5
8 Birdwood Grove   12
21 Chestnut Road   23
NEW Hook Cross
Allotments   45

Sunday 17th
Angels Folly   5
Berry Cottage   10
8 Birdwood Grove   12
21 Chestnut Road   23
NEW Hook Cross
Allotments   45

Thursday 21st
Tanglefoot   80

Saturday 23rd
Fairweather's Nursery 37

Sunday 24th
Bleak Hill Nursery &
Garden   14
Fairweather's Nursery 37
Tanglefoot   80
Terstan   81

Monday 25th
Bleak Hill Nursery &
Garden   14

Saturday 30th
Twin Oaks   82

Sunday 31st
Twin Oaks   82

August

Wednesday 3rd
The Down House   32

Saturday 6th
NEW Church House   24

THE GARDENS

1 80 ABBEY ROAD
Fareham, PO15 5HW. Brian & Vivienne Garford, 01329 843939, vgarford@aol.com. *From M27 J9 take A27 E to Fareham for approx 2m. At top of hill, turn L at lights into Highlands Rd. Turn 4th R into Blackbrook Rd. Abbey Rd is 4th L.* Visits by arrangement May to Aug for groups of up to 30. Light refreshments. Wine for evening visits.
A small garden designed to use all the available space. Many unusual plants inc a large collection of herbs and native wildflowers. Interesting use of containers and other ideas for the smaller garden. Two ponds and tiny meadow help attract a wide range of wildlife. Living willow seat, summerhouse and trained grapevine.
✿ ➡ ☕ ⬤

2 ABBOTSFIELD
Bennetts Lane, Burley, Ringwood, BH24 4AT. Anne Blackman. *1m W of Burley village centre. Signed from village centre. Parking at Mill Lawn Car Park, then approx 400 metres walk to garden.* Wed 20 Apr, Wed 4, Wed 18 May, Wed 1 June (10.30-4.30). Adm £3.50, chd free. Home-made teas.
Accessible paths lead past numerous beds, containing shrubs and herbaceous perennials of a variety of leaf form and texture with seasonal accents of colour and a fish pond. Then through trees to a summerhouse, a tea shelter in wet weather. The circular route continues round to the kitchen garden with raised beds, then return to the start for tea and home-made cakes. Wheelchair access to most of the garden.
♿ ✿ ☕ ⬤

You can make a difference! Join our Great British Garden Party fundraising campaign and raise money for some of the best-loved nursing and health charities. Visit ngs.org.uk/gardenparty to find out how you can get involved

3 ◆ ALVERSTOKE CRESCENT GARDEN

Crescent Road, Gosport, PO12 2DH. Gosport Borough Council, www. alverstokecrescentgarden.co.uk. *1m S of Gosport. From A32 & Gosport follow signs for Stokes Bay. Continue alongside bay to small r'about, turn L into Anglesey Rd. Crescent Garden signed 50yds on R.* **For NGS: Sat 14 May (10-4). Adm by donation. Home-made teas. For other opening times and information, please visit garden website.**

Restored Regency ornamental garden designed to enhance fine crescent (Thomas Ellis Owen 1828). Trees, walks and flowers lovingly maintained by community and council partnership. A garden of considerable local historic interest highlighted by impressive restoration and creative planting. Adjacent to St Mark's churchyard, worth seeing together. Heritage, history and horticulture, a fascinating package. Plant sale. Green Flag Award.

GROUP OPENING

4 AMPORT & MONXTON GARDENS

Amport and Monxton, SP11 8AY. *3m SW of Andover. Turn off the A303 signed East Cholderton from the E, or Thruxton village from the W. Follow signs to Amport. Car parking in field next to Amport village green.* **Sat 28, Sun 29 May (2-5.30). Combined adm £6, chd free. Cream teas in a marquee on the village green, Amport.**

BRIDGE COTTAGE
John & Jenny Van de Pette.

CORNER COTTAGE, 15 SARSON
Ms Jill McAvoy.

FLEUR DE LYS
Ian & Jane Morrison.

WHITE GABLES
David & Coral Eaglesham.

Monxton and Amport are two pretty villages linked by Pill Hill Brook. Visitors have four gardens to enjoy. Bridge Cottage, a 2 acre haven for wildlife with the banks of the trout stream and lake planted informally with drifts of colour, a large vegetable garden, fruit cage, small mixed orchard and arboretum with specimen trees. Corner Cottage is a delightful cottage garden with a serpentine gravel path winding between gravel borders, clipped box hedging and old fashioned roses. Fleur de Lys is opening again with a series of rooms with glorious herbaceous borders, leading to a large orchard. A cottage style garden at White Gables with a collection of trees, along with old roses and herbaceous plants. Regrettably, for owners with dogs who visit Fleur De Lys, they must leave their dogs with house owners at the front gate. Very popular large plant sale at Bridge Cottage. Preserves and chutneys for sale, along with an artist selling cards (10% to NGS). As always choc ices for sale (100% to NGS). Amport has a lovely village green, come early and bring a picnic. No wheelchair access to White Gables and partial access to Corner Cottage.

5 ANGELS FOLLY

15 Bruce Close, Fareham, PO16 7QJ. Teresa & John Greenwood, 07545 242654, tgreenwood@ntlworld.com. *M27 W J10 under M27 bridge RH-lane, do U-turn. At r'about 3rd exit, across T-lights, Ist R Miller Drive, 2nd R Somervell Drive, 1st R Bruce Close (2 disabled spaces). Free parking at Fareham Leisure Centre.* **Sat 2, Sun 3, Sat 16, Sun 17 July (10.30-5). Adm £3.50, chd free. Home-made teas. Evening opening Fri 12 Aug (6-9). Adm £6, chd free. Wine. Visits also by arrangement July to Sept for groups of 5 to 25.**

The garden has a number of secluded areas each with their own character inc a Mediterranean garden, decking with raised beds and a seating area with a living wall. An arched folly, bench and fish pond leads to a raised planting bed and fireplace adjacent to a summerhouse. There is a wide range of colourful plants, hanging baskets and a lower secluded decked area with a planted gazebo and statue.

6 APPLEYARDS

Bowerwood Road, Fordingbridge, SP6 3BP. Bob & Jean Carr. *½m from Fordingbridge on B3078. After church & houses, 400yds on L as road climbs after bridge. Parking for 8 cars only. No parking on narrow road.* **Thur 21, Fri 22, Sat 23, Sun 24 Apr, Thur 2, Fri 3, Sat 4, Sun 5, Thur 30 June, Fri 1, Sat 2, Sun 3 July (12-6). Adm £5, chd free. Pre-booking essential, please phone 01425 657631 or email bob.carr. rtd@gmail.com for information & booking. Home-made teas. Visits also by arrangement Apr to July.**

2 acre sloping south facing garden, newly restored, overlooking pasture. 100+ trees, sloping lawns and paths though wooded sections with massed daffodils and bluebells in spring. Newly planted rhododendrons in wooded area. Herbaceous beds, two rose beds, shrubberies, two wildlife ponds, orchard, sloping rockery beds, soft fruit cages and greenhouse.

7 19 BARNWOOD ROAD

Fareham, PO15 5LA. Jill & Michael Hill, 07814 811956, Jillhillflowers@icloud.com. *M27 J9, A27 towards Fareham. At top of Titchfield Hill, L at T-lights, 4th R Blackbrook Rd, 4th R Meadow Bank. Barnwood Rd is off Meadow Bank. Please consider neighbours when parking.* **Visits by arrangement June & July for groups of 6 to 30. Adm £4, chd free. Home-made teas.**

Step through the gate to an enchanting garden, designed for peace with an abundance of floral colour and delightful features. Greek style courtyard leads to natural pond with bridge and beach garden, complemented by a thatched summerhouse and jetty, designed and built by owners. Secret pathways and hexagonal greenhouse. New raised beds in the front garden with standard olives, lavender and salvias.

8 BEECHENWOOD FARM

Hillside, Odiham, Hook, RG29 1JA. Mr & Mrs M Heber-Percy, 01256 702300, Beechenwood@gmail.com. *5m SE of Hook. Turn S into King St from Odiham High St. Turn L after cricket ground for Hillside. Take 2nd R after 1½m, modern house ½m.* **Every Wed 30 Mar to 8 June (2-5). Mon 2 May (2-5). Adm £5, chd free. Home-made teas. Visits also by arrangement Mar to June.**

2 acre garden in many parts. Lawn meandering through woodland with drifts of spring bulbs. Rose pergola with steps, pots with spring bulbs and later aeoniums. Fritillary and

cowslip meadow. Walled herb garden with pool and exuberant planting. Orchard inc white garden and hot border. Greenhouse and vegetable garden. Rock garden extending to grasses, ferns and bamboos. Shady walk to belvedere. 8 acre copse of native species with grassed rides. Assistance available with gravel drive and avoidable shallow steps.

9 BERE MILL
London Road, Whitchurch, RG28 7NH. Rupert & Elizabeth Nabarro, 07703 161074, rupertnab@gmail.com, www.beremillfarm.com. *9m E of Andover, 12m N of Winchester. In centre of Whitchurch, take London Rd at r'about. Uphill 1m, turn R 50yds beyond The Gables on R. Drop-off point for disabled at garden.* **Sun 13 Mar, Mon 2 May, Thur 2 June, Mon 29 Aug (1-5). Adm £7.50, chd free. Home-made teas. Visits also by arrangement Feb to Oct. Entry for private visits is subject to fixed fee of £400, plus teas.**
On the Upper Test with water meadows and wooded valleys, this garden offers herbaceous borders, bog and Mediterranean plants, as well as a replanted orchard and two small arboretums. Features inc early bulbs, species tulips, Japanese prunus, peonies, wisteria, irises, roses, and semi-tropical planting. At heart it aims to complement the natural beauty of the site and to incorporate elements of oriental garden design and practice. The working mill was where Portals first made paper for the Bank of England in 1716. Unfenced and unguarded rivers and streams. Wheelchair access unless very wet.

10 BERRY COTTAGE
Church Road, Upper Farringdon, Alton, GU34 3EG. Mrs P Watts, 01420 588318. *3m S of Alton off A32. Turn L at Xrds, 1st L into Church Rd. Follow road past Massey's Folly, 2nd house on R, opp church.* **Sun 19 June, Sun 17 July, Sun 21 Aug (2-5). Adm £4, chd free. Home-made teas. Visits also by arrangement May to Sept for groups of 10+.**
Organic cottage garden with year-round interest, designed and maintained by owner, surrounding C16 house (not open). Spring bulbs, roses, clematis and herbaceous

borders. The borders are colour themed and contain many unusual plants. Pond, bog garden and fernery. Close to Massey's Folly built by the Victorian rector inc 80ft tower with unique handmade floral bricks, C11 church and some of the oldest yew trees in the county.

11 BINSTED PLACE
River Hill, Binsted Road, Binsted, Alton, GU34 4PQ. Max & Catherine Hadfield. *At eastern edge of Binsted Village on Binsted Rd. 1m from Jolly Farmer Pub in Blacknest. 1½m from A325. Parking limited, but safe on-road parking outside the property.* **Sun 26 June (12-5.30); Mon 27 June (2-5.30). Adm £5, chd free. Home-made teas.**

Binsted Place, a C17 farmhouse with attractive local stone outbuildings, is surrounded by a series of garden rooms covering approx 1½ acres, enclosed by yew hedges and old walls. It is very traditional in style and inc many roses, pergolas, herbaceous borders, lily pond and a productive vegetable garden and orchards. Step-free disabled access to most of the garden.

Our 2021 donations mean that 69,000 people were helped by our support for Marie Curie

Winchester College

2 8 BIRDWOOD GROVE
Downend, Fareham, PO16 8AF. Jayne & Eddie McBride, 01329 280838, jayne.mcbride@ntlworld.com. *M27 J11, L lane slip to Delme r'about, L on A27 to Portchester, over 2 T-lights, completely around small r'about, Birdwood Grove 1st L. Sat 16, Sun 17 July (12.30-5).* Adm £3.50, chd free. Home-made teas. **Visits also by arrangement July & Aug for groups of up to 20.**
The subtropics in Fareham! This small garden is influenced by the flora of Australia and New Zealand and inc many indigenous species and plants that are widely grown down under. The four climate zones; arid, temperate, lush and fertile and, a shady fernery, are all densely planted to make the most of dramatic foliage, from huge bananas to towering cordylines. Wheelchair access over short gravel path. Not suitable for mobility scooters.
♿ 🐕 ✿ ☕

3 BISTERNE MANOR
Bisterne, Ringwood, BH24 3BN. Mr & Mrs Hallam Mills. *2½m S of Ringwood on B3347 Christchurch Rd, 500yds past church on L. Entrance signed Stable Family Home Trust on L (blue sign), just past lodge. Disabled parking signed.* Sat 28 May (1-5). Adm £5, chd free. Home-made teas.
Two spectacular gardens in one visit, linked by history. The original commercial walled garden to the C16 Manor House (not open) now used by the Stable Family Home Trust, a charity, founded in 1980, supporting adults with learning difficulties, will be open alongside the Manor garden providing a wonderful 4 acre combination. Wheelchair access to a level garden with wide gravel paths.
♿ 🐕 ✿ ☕

4 BLEAK HILL NURSERY & GARDEN
Braemoor, Bleak Hill, Harbridge, Ringwood, BH24 3PX. Tracy & John Netherway, www.bleakhillplants.co.uk. *2½m S of Fordingbridge. Turn off A338 at Ibsley. Go through Harbridge village to T-junction at top of hill, turn R for ¼m.* Sun 24 July (2-5); Mon 25 July (11-3); Sun 14 Aug (2-5); Mon 15 Aug (11-3); Mon 29 Aug (2-5). Adm £4, chd free. Home-made teas. No refreshments on 25 July & 15 Aug, welcome to bring a picnic.
Enjoy this ¾ acre garden, pass through the moongate to reveal the billowing borders contrasting against a seaside scene with painted beach huts and a boat on the gravel. Herbaceous borders fill the garden with colour wrapping around a pond and small stream. Greenhouses with cacti and *Sarracenias*. Vegetable patch and small wildflower meadow. New this yr will be a tropical border. No refreshments on 25 July and 15 Aug, welcome to bring a picnic. Small adjacent nursery.
✿ ☕ 🏖

5 BLOUNCE HOUSE
Blounce, South Warnborough, Hook, RG29 1RX. Tom & Gay Bartlam. *In hamlet of Blounce, 1m S of South Warnborough on B3349 from Odiham to Alton.* Sun 4 Sept (1-4). Adm £4, chd free. Home-made teas.
A 2 acre garden surrounding a classic Queen Anne house (not open). Mixed planting to give interest from spring to late autumn. Herbaceous borders with a variety of colour themes. In later summer an emphasis on dahlias, salvias and grasses.
♿ ☕ 🔊

6 BLUEBELL WOOD
Stancombe Lane, Bavins, New Odiham Road, Alton, GU34 5SX. Mrs Jennifer Ospici, www.bavins.co.uk. *On the corner of Stancombe Ln & the B3349 2½m N of Alton.* Fri 29, Sat 30 Apr (11-4). Adm £5, chd free. Light refreshments.
Unique 100 acre ancient bluebell woodland. If you are a keen walker you will have much to explore on the long meandering paths and rides dotted with secluded seats. Those who enjoy a more leisurely pace will experience the perfume of the carpet of blue, listen to the birdsong and watch the contrasting light through the trees nearer to the entrance of the woods. Refreshments will be served in an original rustic building and inc soups using natural woodland ingredients.
🐕 ☕

7 BRAMDEAN HOUSE
Bramdean, Alresford, SO24 0JU. Mr & Mrs E Wakefield, garden@bramdeanhouse.com. *4m S of Alresford; 9m E of Winchester; 9m W of Petersfield. In centre of village on A272. Entrance opp sign to the church. Parking is usually immed across the road from entrance.* Sun 13 Feb, Sun 10 Apr, Sun 5 June, Sun 3 July, Sun 7 Aug, Sun 4 Sept (2-4). Adm £7.50, chd free. Home-made teas. **Donation to Bramdean Church.**
Beautiful 5 acre garden best known for its mirror image herbaceous borders. Also carpets of spring bulbs, especially snowdrops and a large and unusual collection of plants and shrubs giving year-round interest. 1 acre walled garden featuring prize-winning vegetables, fruit and flowers. Small arboretum. Features inc a large collection of old fashioned sweet peas, an expansive collection of nerines and a boxwood castle. Home of the nation's tallest sunflower 'Giraffe'. Flowering cherries recently imported from Japan. Visits also by arrangement for groups of 5+ (non-NGS). No dogs, except guide dogs.
✿ ☕

8 BRICK KILN COTTAGE
The Avenue, Herriard, nr Alton, RG25 2PR. Barbara Jeremiah, 01256 381301, barbara@klca.co.uk. *4m NE of Alton. A339 Basingstoke to Alton, 7m out of Basingstoke turn L along The Avenue, past Lasham Gliding Club on R, then past church on L & take next track on L, one field later.* Sat 7, Sun 15 May (11.30-4). Adm £5, chd free. Home-made teas. **Visits also by arrangement Apr to June.**
Bluebell woodland garden in 2 acres with a perimeter woodland path inc treehouse, pebble garden, billabong, stumpery, ferny hollow, bug palace, waterpool, shepherd's hut and a traditional cottage garden filled with herbs. The garden is maintained using eco-friendly methods as a haven for wild animals, butterflies, birds, bees and English bluebells. New feature children's reading area. Wildlife friendly garden in a former brick works. A haven in the trees. Gallery of textiles.
🐕 ✿ ☕ 🔊

9 146 BRIDGE ROAD
Sarisbury Green, Southampton, SO31 7EJ. Audrey & Jonathan Crutchfield. *4m W of Fareham. On A27 between Chapel Rd & Glen Rd. Free car parking by kind permission of the United Reformed Church on Chapel Rd.* Sat 14, Sun 15 May (11.30-4.30). Adm £3.50, chd free.

Light refreshments.
A rambling, deceptively large, tranquil cottage garden that is accessed through a side gate and unexpectedly removed from the sometimes bustling A27. Creatively divided with rooms, richly filled borders, patios and lawns giving intense variety. These are interspersed with nooks, arbours, mirrors, statues and unexpected resting spots that offer promise, privacy and the chance to unwind and reflect.

& ✿ ☕ ⊲⊳

20 BROADHATCH HOUSE
Bentley, Farnham, GU10 5JJ.
Bruce & Lizzie Powell. *4m NE of Alton. Turn off A31 (Bentley bypass) through village, then L up School Ln. R to Perrylands, after 300yds drive on R.* Sun 10, Mon 11, Tue 12 July (2-5.30). Adm £5, chd free. Home-made teas.
3½ acre garden set in lovely Hampshire countryside with views to Alice Holt. Divided into different areas by yew hedges and walled garden. Focussing on as long a season as possible on heavy clay. Two reflective pools help break up lawn areas; lots of flower borders and beds; mature trees. Working greenhouses and vegetable garden. Old sunken garden redesigned in 2020. Wheelchair access with gravel paths and steps in some areas.

& ✿ 🚗 ☕ ⊲⊳

21 BUMPERS
Sutton Common, Long Sutton, Hook, RG29 1SJ. Stella Wildsmith, 07766 754993, sfw@staxgroup.com. *From village of Long Sutton, turn up Copse Ln, immed opp duck pond. Follow lane for 1½ m to top of steep hill, house on L.* Sun 3 July, Sun 4 Sept (2-6). Adm £5, chd free. Home-made teas. Visits also by arrangement May to Sept.
Large country garden with beautiful views spread over 2 acres with mixed herbaceous and shrub borders and laid out in a series of individual areas. Some interesting sculptures and water features with informal paths through the grounds and a number of places to sit and enjoy the views. Visitors with wheelchairs, please park at front of house.

& ✿ ☕

22 ◆ CHAWTON HOUSE
Chawton, Alton, GU34 1SJ.
Chawton House, 01420 541010, info@chawtonhouse.org, www.chawtonhouse.org. *2m S of Alton. Take the Gosport Rd opp Jane Austen's House museum towards St Nicholas Church. Property is at the end of this road on the L. Parking is signed at the end of the road & in Chawton village.* For NGS: Sun 6 Feb (10-3.30). Adm £6, chd free. Light refreshments. For other opening times and information, please phone, email or visit garden website.
Snowdrops and spring flowering bulbs are scattered through this 15 acre listed English landscape garden. Sweeping lawns, wilderness, terraces, fernery and shrubbery walk surround the Elizabethan manor house. The walled garden designed by Edward Knight surrounds a rose garden, borders, orchard, vegetable garden and 'Elizabeth Blackwell' herb garden based on her book 'A Curious Herbal' of 1737-39. Hot and cold drinks, wine, light lunches, cream teas, home-made cakes and local ice creams available in our tea shed on the main drive and in the Old Kitchen Tearoom at the house.

🐄 🦮 ☕ 🪑

23 21 CHESTNUT ROAD
Brockenhurst, SO42 7RF. Iain & Mary Hayter, www.21-chestnut-rdgardens.co.uk. *New Forest. Please use village car park. Leave M27 J2, follow Heavy Lorry Route. Mainline station less than 10 mins walk.* Sat 14, Sun 15 May, Sat 25, Sun 26 June, Sat 16, Sun 17 July, Sat 13, Sun 14 Aug (11.30-5.30). Adm £5, chd free. Home-made teas.
Creative ideas aplenty, from formal to mature cottage style, all planted with wildlife in mind. In the heart of the New Forest National Park our ⅓ acre garden offers ponds, pergolas, arches, statues, fruit and vegetable, in a restful oasis. Colour and scent combine artistically, all aimed to inspire garden owners. Various seating options around the garden for you to enjoy our home-made teas. Art exhibition of owners paintings with a donation to NGS from any sales made on open days. Plants, bug houses and bird boxes usually available to purchase. Fairy garden.

& 🐄 ✿ ☕ ⊲⊳

24 NEW CHURCH HOUSE
Trinity Hill, Medstead, Alton, GU34 5LT. Mr Paul & Mrs Alice Beresford, 01420 562592, pauljames2309@gmail.com. *5m WSW of Alton. From A31 Four Marks follow signs to Medstead for 1½ m to village centre, turn R into Church Ln/Trinity Hill. From N on A339, R at Bentworth Xrds & continue via Bentworth to Medstead.* Sat 6 Aug (1-6); Sun 7 Aug (1-5). Adm £5, chd free. Home-made teas. Visits also by arrangement Apr to Sept for groups of 8 to 30.
A colourful 1 acre garden, set within a wide variety of mature trees and shrubs. Long, sweeping, colour themed mixed borders give lots of ideas for planting in sun and shade. Contrasting features and textures throughout the garden are enhanced by interesting sculptures. Espaliered fruit trees, a woodland area, small greenhouse and roses in different settings all contribute to this much loved garden. Wheelchair access via gravel drive to flat lawned garden. No access to some paths and patio.

& ✿ ☕ ⊲⊳

25 CLOVER FARM
Shalden Lane, Shalden, Alton, GU34 4DU. Tom & Sarah Floyd, 01420 86294. *Approx 3m N of Alton in the village of Shalden. Take A339 out of Alton. After approx 2m turn R up Shalden Ln. At top, turn sharp R next to church sign.* Visits by arrangement June to Sept for groups of 20+. Adm £10, chd free. Tea & cake inc.
3 acre garden with far-reaching views. Herbaceous borders and sloping lawns down to reflection pond, wildflower meadow, lime avenue, rose and kitchen garden and ornamental grass area.

& 🐄 ✿ ☕

More than 1,200 people have been cared for at Y Bwthyn NGS Macmillan Specialist Palliative Care Unit, a unit that would simply not have been built without the National Garden Scheme funding

26 COLEMORE HOUSE GARDENS

Colemore, Alton, GU34 3RX. Mr & Mrs Simon de Zoete, 01420 588202, simondezoete@gmail.com. *4m S of Alton, off A32. Approach from N on A32, turn L in to Shell Ln, ¼ m S of East Tisted. Go under bridge, keep L until you see Colemore Church. Park on verge of church.* **Visits by arrangement May to Sept for groups of up to 40.**

4 acres in lovely unspoilt countryside, featuring rooms containing many unusual plants and different aspects with a spectacular arched rose walk, water rill, mirror pond, herbaceous and shrub borders. Newly designed by David Austin roses, an octagonal garden with 25 different varieties. Explore the interesting arboretum, grass gardens and thatched pavilion. Every yr the owners seek improvement and the introduction of new, interesting and rare plants. We propagate and sell plants, many of which can be found in the garden.

Some are unusual and not readily available elsewhere. For private visits, we endeavour to give a conducted tour and try to explain our future plans, rationale and objectives.

27 THE COTTAGE

16 Lakewood Road, Chandler's Ford, Eastleigh, SO53 1ES. Hugh & Barbara Sykes, 02380 254521, barandhugh@aol.com. *Leave M3 J12, follow signs to Chandler's Ford. At King Rufus on Winchester Rd, turn R into Merdon Ave, then 3rd road on L.* **Sun 1, Mon 2, Sun 8, Mon 9 May (1.30-5.30). Adm £4.50, chd free. Home-made teas. Visits also by arrangement Apr & May.**

The house was built in 1905, but the ¾ acre garden has been designed, planted and cared for since 1950 by two keen garden loving families. Azaleas, camellias, trilliums and erythroniums under old oaks and pines. Herbaceous cottage style borders with many unusual plants for year-round interest. Bog garden, ponds, kitchen garden. Bantams, bees and birdsong with over 30 bird species noted. Wildlife areas. NGS sundial for opening for 30 yrs. Childrens' quiz. 'A lovely tranquil garden', Anne Swithinbank. Hampshire Wildlife Trust Wildlife Garden Award. Honey from our garden hives for sale.

28 CRANBURY PARK

Otterbourne, nr Winchester, SO21 2HL. Mrs Chamberlayne-Macdonald. *3m NW of Eastleigh. Main entrance on old A33 at top of Otterbourne Hill by bus stop. Entrances also in Hocombe Rd (opp Nichol Rd), Chandlers Ford & next to Otterbourne Church.* **Sun 12 June (2-6). Adm £5, chd free. Home-made teas. Donation to St Matthew's Church, Otterbourne.**

Extensive pleasure grounds laid out in late C18 and early C19 by Papworth; fountains, rose garden, specimen trees and pinetum, lakeside walk and fern walk. Family carriages and collection of prams will be on view, also photos of King George VI, Eisenhower and Montgomery reviewing Canadian troops at Cranbury before D-Day. All dogs on leads please. Disabled WC.

GROUP OPENING

29 CRAWLEY GARDENS

Crawley, Winchester, SO21 2PR. F J Fratter, 01962 776243, fred@fratter.co.uk. *5m NW of Winchester. Between B3049 (Winchester - Stockbridge) & A272 (Winchester - Andover). Parking throughout village & in field at Tanglefoot.* **Fri 15, Mon 18 Apr, Thur 30 June, Sun 3 July (2-5.30). Combined adm £8, chd free. Home-made teas in the village hall.**

BAY TREE HOUSE
Julia & Charles Whiteaway. Open on all dates

LITTLE COURT
Mrs A R Elkington. Open on Fri 15, Mon 18 Apr (See separate entry)

PAIGE COTTAGE
Mr & Mrs T W Parker. Open on all dates

Trout Cottage, Stockbridge Gardens

TANGLEFOOT
Mr & Mrs F J Fratter.
Open on Thur 30 June, Sun 3 July
(See separate entry)

Crawley is a pretty period village nestling in chalk downland with thatched houses, C14 church and village pond. The spring gardens are Bay Tree House, Little Court and Paige Cottage; the summer gardens are Bay Tree House, Paige Cottage and Tanglefoot; providing varied seasonal interest with traditional and contemporary approaches to landscape and planting. Most of the gardens have beautiful country views and other gardens can be seen from the road. Bay Tree House has bulbs, wild flowers, a Mediterranean garden, pleached limes, a rill and contemporary borders of perennials and grasses. Little Court is a 3 acre country garden with carpets of spring bulbs and a large meadow. Paige Cottage is a 1 acre traditional English garden surrounding a period thatched cottage (not open) with bulbs and wild flowers in spring and old climbing roses in summer. Tanglefoot has colour themed borders, herb wheel, kitchen garden, Victorian boundary wall supporting trained fruit and a large wildflower meadow. Plants from the garden for sale at Little Court and Tanglefoot.

 ❂ 🏵 🚗 ☕))

30 CROOKLEY POOL
Blendworth Lane, Horndean,
PO8 0AB. Mr & Mrs Simon
Privett, 02392 592662,
jennyprivett@icloud.com. *5m S of Petersfield, 2m E of Waterlooville, off the A3. From Horndean up Blendworth Ln between bakery & hairdresser. Entrance 200yds before church on L with white railings. Parking in field.* Sun 29 May (1-4.30). Adm £6, chd free. Home-made teas. Visits also by arrangement May to Sept.
Here the plants decide where to grow. Californian tree poppies elbow valerian aside to crowd round the pool. Evening primroses obstruct the way to the door and the steps to wisteria shaded terraces. Hellebores bloom under the trees. Salvias, *Pandorea jasminoides, Justicia, Pachystachys lutea* and passion flowers riot quietly with tomatoes in the greenhouse. Not a garden for the neat or tidy minded, although this is a plantsman's garden full of unusual

plants and a lot of tender perennials. Bantams stroll throughout. Oil and watercolour paintings of flowers found in the garden will be on display and for sale in the studio. Access to all parts of the garden.

 ❂ 🏵 🚗 ☕

31 THE DEANE HOUSE
Sparsholt, Winchester,
SO21 2LR. Mr & Mrs Richard
Morse, 07774 863004,
chrissiemorse7@gmail.com. *3½m NW of Winchester. Turn off A3049 Stockbridge Rd, onto Woodman Ln, signed Sparsholt. Turn L at 1st cottage on L, white with blue gables, come to top of the drive.* Visits by arrangement Mar to Sept for groups of 10+. Adm £10, chd free. Home-made teas. Wine & canapés in evenings.
This beautiful 4 acre rural garden, nestling on a gentle slope, has been landscaped to draw the eye from one gentle terraced lawn to another with borders merging into the surrounding countryside. Featuring a good selection of specimen trees, a walled garden, prairie planting and herbaceous borders. Water features and sculptures. Sorry no dogs. Although the garden is on the side of a hill there is always a path to avoid steps. Plentiful parking.

 ❂ 🚗 🚌 ☕))

32 THE DOWN HOUSE
Itchen Abbas, SO21 1AX. Jackie
& Mark Porter, 07814 958810,
markstephenporter@gmail.com,
www.thedownhouse.co.uk. *5m E of Winchester on B3047. 5th house on R after the Itchen Abbas village sign, if coming on B3047 from Kings Worthy. 400yds on L after Plough Pub if coming on B3047 from Alresford.* Wed 3 Aug (12-5). Adm £5, chd free. Home-made teas. Visits also by arrangement Feb & Mar for groups of 6+.
A 2 acre garden laid out in rooms overlooking the Itchen Valley, adjoining the Pilgrim's Way. In winter, come and see the snowdrops, aconites and crocus, plus borders of dogwoods, willow stems and white birches. In summer, see the agapanthus, herbaceous perennials and potager. A garden of structure with pleached hornbeams, rope-lined fountain garden, yew lined avenue and walks in adjoining meadows.

 ❂ 🐕 🏵 ☕ 🏕))

33 DURMAST HOUSE
Bennetts Lane, Burley,
BH24 4AT. Mr & Mrs P E G
Daubeney, 01425 402132,
philip@daubeney.co.uk,
www.durmasthouse.co.uk. *5m SE of Ringwood. Off Burley to Lyndhurst Rd, nr White Buck Hotel, C10 road.* Sun 3 Apr, Sun 26 June (2-5). Adm £5, chd free. Cream teas. Visits also by arrangement Apr to Sept. Donation to Delhi Commonwealth Women's Association Medical Clinic (26 June only).
Designed by Gertrude Jekyll, Durmast has contrasting hot and cool colour borders, formal rose garden edged with lavender and a long herbaceous border. Many old trees, Victorian rockery and orchard with beautiful spring bulbs. Rare azaleas; Fama, Princeps and Gloria Mundi from Ghent. Features inc rose bowers with rare French roses; Eleanor Berkeley, Psyche and Reine Olga de Wurtemberg. Many old trees inc cedar and Douglas firs. Wheelchair access on stone and gravel paths.

 ❂ 🐎 🏵 🚗 🚌 ☕

34 EAST WORLDHAM MANOR
Worldham Hill, East Worldham,
Alton, GU34 3AX. Hermione Wood,
www.worldham.org. *2m SE of Alton on B3004 in East Worldham. Coming from Alton, turn R by village hall, signed car park.* Sat 2, Sun 3 July (2-5.30). Combined adm with 'Selborne' £6, chd free. Home-made teas.
A rambling double walled garden laid out in the 1870s with far-reaching views to the South Downs. Illustrates a substantial Victorian garden with fruit, vegetables and flower borders, rose garden, many shrubs, herbaceous plants, apple and pear orchard and large productive greenhouses. Gravel paths, some naturalised with white foxgloves and campanulas, wind through many parts of the garden.

 ❂ 🐕 🏵 ☕ 🏕

'The National Garden Scheme donated £500,000 to Hospice UK in 2021, enabling us to continue supporting over 200 hospices in the UK who have been at the forefront of the battle against COVID-19.' Hospice UK

35 ENDHOUSE

6 Wimpson Gardens,
Southampton, SO16 9ES.
Kevin Liles, 02380 777590,
k.liles@ntlworld.com,
www.gardenatendhouse.com.
*Exit M271 at J1 toward Lordshill. At
2nd r'about, turn R into Romsey Rd
towards Shirley. After ½ m turn R
at Xrds into Wimpson Ln, 3rd on R
Crabwood Rd (additional parking).
Wimpson Gardens 4th on R.* **Visits
by arrangement May to July for
groups of 8 to 15. Adm £3.50, chd
free. Home-made teas.**
Award-winning urban oasis of linked
garden areas inc small secret garden.
Best in spring and summer months,
but rich year-round plant interest with
tree ferns, palms, acers and wisteria.
Deep herbaceous borders planted
with hostas, grasses, agapanthus and
alstroemerias. Significant exhibition of
gallery quality sculpture and ceramics.
Please call Garden Owner or visit
www.ngs.org.uk for pop-up openings

36 FAIRBANK

Old Odiham Road, Alton,
GU34 4BU. Jane & Robin
Lees, 01420 86665,
j.lees558@btinternet.com. *1½ m
N of Alton. From S, past Sixth
Form College, then 1½ m beyond
road junction on R. From N, turn
L at Golden Pot & then 50yds turn
R. Garden 1m on L before road
junction.* **Visits by arrangement
May to Sept for groups of up to
30. Adm £4, chd free. Home-
made teas.**
The planting in this large garden
reflects our interest in trees, shrubs,
fruit and vegetables. A wide variety of
herbaceous plants provide colour and
are placed in sweeping mixed borders
that carry the eye down the long
garden to the orchard and beyond.
Near the house (not open), there are
rose beds and herbaceous borders,
as well as a small formal pond. There
is a range of acers, ferns and unusual
shrubs and 60 different varieties of
fruit, together with a large vegetable
garden. Wheelchair access with
uneven ground in some areas.

37 FAIRWEATHER'S NURSERY

Hilltop, Beaulieu, SO42 7YR.
Patrick Fairweather, 01590 612113,
info@fairweathers.co.uk,
www.fairweathers.co.uk. *Hilltop
Nursery. 1½ m NE of Beaulieu
village on B3054.* **Sat 23, Sun 24**

July (9.30-3). Adm £5, chd free.
Cream teas in Aline Fairweather's
garden next door.
Fairweather's hold a specialist
collection of over 400 agapanthus
grown in pots and display beds, inc
AGM award-winning agapanthus
trialled by the RHS. Patrick
Fairweather will give guided tours
of the nursery at 10am, 12pm and
2pm with demonstrations of how to
get the best from agapanthus and
companion planting. Agapanthus and
a range of other traditional and new
perennials for sale. Aline Fairweather's
garden (adjacent to the nursery) will
also be open with mixed shrub and
perennial borders containing many
unusual plants. Also open Patrick's
Patch at Fairweather's Garden Centre.

38 FERNS LODGE

Cottagers Lane, Hordle,
Lymington, SO41 0FE.
Sue Grant, 07860 521501,
sue.grant@fernslodge.co.uk,
www.fernslodge.co.uk. *Approx
5½ m W of Lymington. From Silver St
turn into Woodcock Ln, 100 metres
to Cottagers Ln, parking in field ½ m
on L. From A337 turn into Everton
Rd & drive approx 1½ m, Cottagers
Ln on R.* **Sat 28, Sun 29 May (2-5).
Adm £5, chd free. Home-made
teas & cream teas. Visits also
by arrangement May to Aug for
groups of 5 to 20.**
4 acres of wildlife garden inc a ½
acre cottage garden with a heady
mix of colour and scent surrounding
a Victorian lodge with winding
brick paths. Azalea, fig, sweet
pea, roses, agapanthus, salvia and
foxgloves jostle for attention. While
honeysuckle, clematis, passionflower
and jasmine lead you to the big
garden in restoration filled with
rhododendron, tree ferns and mature
trees of all description. Wheelchair
access to many areas.

39 FRITHAM LODGE

Fritham, SO43 7HH. Sir Chris &
Lady Powell. *6m N of Lyndhurst.
3m NW of M27 J1 (Cadnam). Follow
signs to Fritham.* **Sun 19 June (2-4).
Adm £5, chd free. Home-made
teas.**
A walled garden of 1 acre in the heart
of the New Forest, set within 18
acres surrounding a house that was
originally a Charles 1 hunting lodge
(not open). Herbaceous and blue
and white mixed borders, pergolas

and ponds. A box hedge enclosed
parterre of roses, fruit and vegetables.
Visitors will enjoy the ponies, donkeys,
sheep and old breed hens on their
meadow walk to the woodland and
stream.

GROUP OPENING

40 FROYLE GARDENS

Lower Froyle, Froyle, GU34 4LG.
www.froyle.com/ngs. *5m NE of
Alton. Access to Froyle from A31
between Alton & Farnham at Bentley,
or at Hen & Chicken Inn. Park at
Recreation Ground in Lower Froyle.
Map provided. Additional signed
parking in Upper Froyle.* **Sat 11, Sun
12 June (2-5.30). Combined adm
£10, chd free. Home-made teas
in Froyle Village Hall & picnics
welcome on the recreation
ground, Lower Froyle.**

ALDERSEY HOUSE
Nigel & Julie Southern.

BROCAS FARM
Harry & Lara Speir.

DAY COTTAGE
Nick & Corinna Whines,
www.daycottage.co.uk.

OLD BREWERY HOUSE
Vivienne & John Sexton.

OLD COURT
Sarah & Charlie Zorab.

WARREN COTTAGE
Gillian & Jonathan Pickering.

WELL LANE CORNER
Mark & Sue Lelliott.

You will certainly receive a warm
welcome as Froyle Gardens open
their gates this yr, enabling visitors to
enjoy a wide variety of gardens, which
have undergone development since
last yr and will be looking splendid.
Froyle is a beautiful village with many
old and interesting buildings, our
gardens harmonise with the
surrounding landscape and most
have spectacular views. The gardens
themselves are diverse with rich
planting. You will see greenhouses,
water features, vegetables, roses,
clematis and wildflower meadows.
Lots of ideas to take away with you,
along with plants to buy and delicious
teas served in the village hall. Close
by is a playground with a zip wire
where children can let off steam.
There is also an exhibition of richly

embroidered historic vestments in the Church in Upper Froyle (separate donation). No wheelchair access to Day Cottage and on request at Warren Cottage. Long drive to Old Court.

41 HAMBLEDON HOUSE
East Street, Hambledon, PO7 4RX. Capt & Mrs David Hart Dyke, 02392 632380, dianahartdyke@gmail.com. *8m SW of Petersfield, 5m NW of Waterlooville. In village centre, driveway leading to house in East St. Do not go up Speltham Hill even if advised by SatNav.* **Visits by arrangement Apr to Oct. Home-made teas.**
3 acre partly walled plantsman's garden for all seasons. Large borders filled with a wide variety of unusual shrubs and perennials with imaginative plant combinations culminating in a profusion of colour in late summer. Hidden, secluded areas reveal surprise views of garden

and village rooftops. Planting a large central area, which started in 2011, has given the garden an exciting new dimension.

42 108 HEATH ROAD
Petersfield, GU31 4EL. Mrs Karen Llewelyn, 01730 269541, k.llewelyn@btinternet.com. *A3 N & S take A272 exit signed Midhurst. Take 1st exit from r'about, 1st R into Pullens Ln (B2199) & then 6th road on R into Heath Rd.* **Sun 5 June, Sun 11 Sept (2-5.30). Adm £4, chd free. Home-made teas. Visits also by arrangement May to Sept.**
²/₃ acre garden close to town centre and Heath Pond. Greenhouse and succulent collection. Tropical plants, acers, small woodland walk. 30 metre long border with shade loving plants inc many hostas and ferns. Patio garden, seasonal pots and late summer herbaceous border. Mixed planted driveway borders. Lots to see. Wheelchair access after a 5 metre sloping gravel drive.

43 HECKFIELD PLACE
Heckfield, RG27 0LD. Heckfield Management Ltd, 01189 326868, enquiries@heckfieldplace.com, www.heckfieldplace.com. *9m S of Reading. 4½ m NW of Hartley Wintney on B3011. Two car parks, signed on the day.* **Mon 13, Tue 14 June (2-6). Adm £8, chd free. Pre-booking essential, please visit www.ngs.org.uk for information & booking. Home-made teas.**
Heckfield Place is a hotel on a 438 acre estate with an original 1927 NGS garden, now reopening with walled garden and pleasure grounds, inc two lakes and arboretum. Both tamed and gently wild, the garden was created by Head Gardener William Walker Wildsmith in the C19 and has been lovingly restored through years of diligent work. Pre-booked 2 hr timed slots for 30 visitors at 2pm, 3pm and 4pm. Home-made teas inc gluten free option which will also be nut free £4 (card payment on the day only). No dogs please. Wheelchair access to the upper walled garden on gravel pathway.

Wheatley House

© Leigh Clapp

44 THE HOMESTEAD

Northney Road, Hayling Island, PO11 0NF. Stan & Mary Pike, 02392 464888, jhomestead@aol.com, www.homesteadhayling.co.uk. *3m S of Havant. From A27 Havant & Hayling Island r'about, travel S over Langstone Bridge & turn immed L into Northney Rd. Car park entrance on R after Langstone Hotel.* **Sun 7 Aug (2-5.30). Adm £4, chd free. Home-made teas. Visits also by arrangement June to Sept for groups of 10+.**

1¼ acre garden surrounded by working farmland with views to Butser Hill and boats in Chichester Harbour. Trees, shrubs, colourful herbaceous borders and small walled garden with herbs, vegetables and trained fruit trees. Large pond and woodland walk with shade-loving plants. A quiet and peaceful atmosphere with plenty of seats to enjoy the vistas within the garden and beyond. A recently constructed look-out platform provides some different views of the garden. Wheelchair access with some gravel paths.

45 NEW HOOK CROSS ALLOTMENTS

Reading Road, Hook, RG27 9DB. Hook Allotment Association, hookallotments.co.uk/. *Northern edge of Hook village on B3349 Reading Rd, 900 metres N of A30 r'about. Concealed entrance track is on RHS at foot of hill opp a farm entrance, straight after turns to B & M Fencing & Searle's Ln.* **Sat 16, Sun 17 July (1-5). Adm £4, chd free. Light refreshments.**

5¼ acre community run allotments overlooking Hook village. More than 100 plots showcasing different vegetable, fruit and flower growing styles. Plot holder demonstrations of how to grow your own. Community orchard, wildflower meadow, beetle banks, wildlife friendly gardening information. Plants and refreshments for sale.

46 ♦ THE HOSPITAL OF ST CROSS

St Cross Road, Winchester, SO23 9SD. The Hospital of St Cross & Almshouse of Noble Poverty, 01962 851375, porter@hospitalofstcross.co.uk, www.hospitalofstcross.co.uk. *½m S of Winchester. From city*

centre take B3335 (Southgate St & St Cross Rd) S. Turn L immed before The Bell Pub. If on foot follow riverside path S from Cathedral & College, approx 20 mins. **For NGS: Sun 11 Sept (2-5). Adm £4, chd free. Light refreshments in the Hundred Men's Hall in the Outer Quadrangle. For other opening times and information, please phone, email or visit garden website.**

The Medieval Hospital of St Cross nestles in water meadows beside the River Itchen and is one of England's oldest almshouses. The tranquil, walled Master's Garden, created in the late C17 by Bishop Compton, now contains colourful herbaceous borders, old fashioned roses, interesting trees and a large fish pond. The Compton Garden has unusual plants of the type he imported when Bishop of London. Wheelchair access, but surfaces are uneven in places.

47 THE HOUSE IN THE WOOD

Beaulieu, SO42 7YN. Victoria Roberts. *New Forest. 8m NE of Lymington. Leaving the entrance to Beaulieu Motor Museum on R (B3056), take next R signed Ipley Cross. Take 2nd gravel drive on RH-bend, approx ½m.* **Sun 8 May (1.30-5). Adm £6, chd free. Cream teas.**

Peaceful 12 acre woodland garden with continuing progress and improvement. Very much a spring garden with tall, glorious mature azaleas and rhododendrons in every shade of pink, orange, red and white, interspersed with acers and other woodland wonders. A magical garden to get lost in with many twisting paths leading downhill to a pond and a more formal layout of lawns around the house (not open). Used in the war to train the Special Operations Executive.

48 HOW PARK BARN

Kings Somborne, Stockbridge, SO20 6QG. Kate & Chris Cann. *2m from Stockbridge, just outside Kings Somborne. A3057 from Stockbridge, turn R into Cow Drove Hill, then follow NGS signs.* **Sun 22 May (2-5). Adm £5, chd free. Home-made teas.**

2 acre country garden in elevated position with magnificent views over the Test Valley. Large borders

of naturalistic planting. Sweeping lawns with some slopes. Large natural wildlife pond, all in tranquil setting within the landscape of C17 listed barn (not open). Adjacent to the Clarendon and Test Ways. Gravel drive and some slopes, but wheelchair access to most of the garden.

49 THE ISLAND

Greatbridge, Romsey, SO51 0HP. Mr & Mrs Christopher Saunders-Davies. *1m N of Romsey on A3057. Entrance at bridge. Follow drive 100yds. Car park on RHS.* **Sat 9, Sun 10 Apr, Sat 6, Sun 7 Aug (1-5). Adm £5, chd free. Home-made teas.**

6 acres either side of the River Test. Fine display of daffodils, tulips, spring flowering trees and summer bedding. Main garden has herbaceous and annual borders, fruit trees, rose pergola, lavender walk and extensive lawns. An arboretum planted in the 1930s by Sir Harold Hillier contains trees and shrubs providing interest throughout the yr. Please Note: No dogs allowed. Disabled WC.

50 LITTLE COURT

Crawley, Winchester, SO21 2PU. Mrs A R Elkington, 01962 776365, elkslc@btinternet.com. *5m NW of Winchester. Between B3049 (Winchester - Stockbridge) & A272 (Winchester - Andover), 400yds from either pond or church.* **Sat 12, Mon 14, Sun 20, Mon 21 Feb (2-5); Thur 3 Mar, Wed 18 May, Tue 14, Wed 15 June, Sun 10 July (2-5.30). Adm £5, chd free. Home-made teas in Crawley Village Hall. Opening with Crawley Gardens on Fri 15, Mon 18 Apr. Visits also by arrangement Feb to Aug. Teas in the garden.**

This traditional walled, sheltered garden is open in all seasons, specially exciting in spring. There are many flower beds and climbers, a kitchen garden, colourful free range bantams, also a south facing natural wildlife field of English wild flowers and butterflies. Many informal seats both within the garden and to the surrounding countryside, each with a good view. A garden for all seasons and ages.

51 LONGSTOCK PARK WATER GARDEN
Leckford, Stockbridge, SO20 6EH. Leckford Estate Ltd, part of John Lewis Partnership, www.leckfordestate.co.uk. *4m S of Andover. From Leckford village on A3057 towards Andover, cross the river bridge & take 1st turning L signed Longstock.* **Sun 19 June (1-4). Adm £10, chd £2.**
Famous water garden with extensive collection of aquatic and bog plants set in 7 acres of woodland with rhododendrons and azaleas. A walk through the park leads to National Collections of *Buddleja* and *Clematis viticella*; arboretum and herbaceous border at Longstock Park Nursery. Refreshments at Longstock Park Farm Shop and Nursery (last orders at 3.30pm). Assistance dogs only.

&. ✽ 🚐 NPC 🍵 »))

52 26 LOWER NEWPORT ROAD
Aldershot, GU12 4QD. Mr & Mrs P Myles. *Parking is normally arranged with the factory opp 'Jondo' & the Salvation Army. Signage in place on the day if available. We are 100 metres away from the McDonalds drive through.* **Sat 2, Sun 3 July (11-4). Adm £3, chd free. Light refreshments.**
A T-shaped small town garden full of ideas, split into four distinct sections; a semi-enclosed patio area with pots and water feature; a free-form lawn with a tree fern, perennials, bulbs and shrubs and 200 varieties of hosta; secret garden with a 20ft x 6ft raised pond, exotic planting backdrop and African carvings; and a potager garden with vegetables, roses, cannas and plant storage and sales.

✽ 🍵

53 ♦ MACPENNYS WOODLAND GARDEN & NURSERIES
Burley Road, Bransgore, Christchurch, BH23 8DB. Mr & Mrs T M Lowndes, 01425 672348, office@macpennys.co.uk, www.macpennys.co.uk. *6m SE of Ringwood, 5m NE of Christchurch. From Crown Pub Xrd in Bransgore take Burley Rd, following sign for Thorney Hill & Burley. Entrance 1/2 m on R.* **For opening times and information, please phone, email or visit garden website.**
4 acre woodland garden originating from worked out gravel pits in the 1950s, offering interest year-round, but particularly late in spring and autumn. Attached to a large nursery that

offers for sale a wide selection of homegrown trees, shrubs, conifers, perennials, hedging plants, fruit trees and bushes. Tearoom offering home-made cakes, afternoon tea (pre-booking required) and light lunches, using locally sourced produce wherever possible. Nursery closed Christmas through to the New Year. Partial wheelchair access on grass and gravel paths. Can be bumpy with tree roots and, muddy in winter.

&. ➶ ✽ 🚐 🍵

54 MANOR HOUSE
Church Lane, Exton, SO32 3NU. Tina Blackmore. *Off A32, just N of Corhampton. Pass The Shoe Inn on your L, go to the end of the road to a T-junction, turn R & Manor House is immed on the L, just below the church.* **Sun 29 May, Sun 12 June (2-4.30). Adm £5, chd free. Home-made teas.**
An enchanting 1 acre mature walled garden set in the Meon Valley. Yew hedges and flint walls divide the garden into rooms. The white garden planted with hydrangeas and roses. Herbaceous borders with colourful cottage favourites; delphiniums, roses, geraniums and salvias. A secluded, highly productive walled vegetable garden, a parterre with fountain, woodland and meadow with wild flowers.

&. ✽ 🍵 »))

55 MANOR LODGE
Brook Lane, Botley, Southampton, SO30 2ER. Gary & Janine Stone. *6m E of Southampton. From A334 to the W of Botley village centre, turn into Brook Ln. Manor Lodge is 1/2 m on the R. Limited disabled parking. Continue past Manor Lodge to parking (signed).* **Sat 11, Sun 12 June (2-5). Adm £4, chd free. Home-made teas.**
Close to Manor Farm Country Park, this mid Victorian house (not open), set in over 1 1/2 acres is the garden of an enthusiastic plantswoman. A garden in evolution with established areas and new projects, a mixture of informal and formal planting, woodland and wildflower meadow areas. There are large established and new specimen trees, common and exotic perennials, planting combinations for extended seasonal interest. Fruit cages. Largely flat with hard paving, but some gravel and grass to access all areas.

&. ➶ ✽ 🍵

56 MEON ORCHARD
Kingsmead, North of Wickham, PO17 5AU. Doug & Linda Smith, 01329 833253, meonorchard@btinternet.com. *5m N of Fareham. From Wickham take A32 N for 1 1/2 m. Turn L at Roebuck Inn. Garden in 1/2 m. Park on verge or in field N of property.* **Sun 4 Sept (2-5.30). Adm £5, chd free. Home-made teas.**
2 acre garden designed and constructed by current owners. An exceptional range of rare, unusual and architectural plants inc National Collection of Eucalyptus. Dramatic foliage plants from around the world, see plants you have never seen before! Bananas, tree ferns, cannas, gingers, palms and perennials dominate July to Sep; streams and ponds, plus an extensive range of planters complete the display. Visitors are welcome to explore the 20 acre meadow and 1/2 m of the River Meon frontage attached to the garden. Extra big plant sale of the exotic and rare. Garden fully accessible by wheelchair, reserved parking.

&. ➶ ✽ 🚐 NPC 🍵 »))

In 2021 the generous donation from the National Garden Scheme helped 12,000 unpaid carers to access the support they need, with 50 more receiving crisis grants to support those in dire need

Alverstoke Crescent Garden

57 5 OAKFIELDS

Boyatt Wood, Eastleigh, SO50 4RP. Martin & Margaret Ward. *M3 J12, follow signs to Eastleigh. 3rd exit at r'about into Woodside Ave, 2nd R into Bosville, 2nd R onto Boyatt Ln, 1st R to Porchester Rise & 1st L into Oakfields.* Sat 18, Sun 19 June (2-5). Adm £4, chd free. Home-made teas.

A ⅓ acre garden full of interesting and unusual plants in predominately woodland beds and rambling roses cascading from birch trees. A pond with rockery, waterfall and flower beds formed from the intermittent winter streams, accommodate moisture loving plants. Colourful mixed herbaceous border and a terrace with architectural agapanthus and fuchsia. Wheelchair access over hard paths and some gravel.

58 THE OLD RECTORY

East Woodhay, Newbury, RG20 0AL. David & Victoria Wormsley, 07801 418976, victoria@wormsley.net. *6m SW of Newbury. Turn off A343 between Newbury & Highclere to Woolton Hill. Turn L to East End, continue ¾ m beyond East End. Turn R, garden opp St Martin's Church.* Visits by arrangement Apr to Oct for groups of 20+. Adm £10, chd free. Home-made teas.

A classic English country garden of about 2 acres surrounding a Regency former rectory (not open). Formal lawns and terrace provide tranquil views over parkland. A large walled garden with grass paths, full of interesting herbaceous plants inc topiary, roses and unusual perennials. A Mediterranean pool garden, wildflower meadow and fruit garden. Explore and enjoy.

59 OLD SWAN HOUSE

High Street, Stockbridge, SO20 6EU. Mr Herry Lawford, www.facebook.com/oldswanhouse. *9m W of Winchester. The entrance to the garden is in Recreation Ground Ln,* at the E end of the High St. Every Tue 5 July to 26 July (2-4.30). Adm £5, chd free. Home-made teas. Opening with Stockbridge Gardens on Thur 16, Sun 19 June.

This town garden is designed around seven areas defined by the sun at different times of the day. Planting is modern perennial with euphorbias, rosemary and box used extensively. Particular interest is provided by a grass and gravel garden and a small wildflower meadow. There is an ancient hazel under a brick and flint wall, a loggia hung with creeper, an orchard and a pond.

GROUP OPENING

60 OLD THATCH & THE MILLENNIUM BARN

Sprats Hatch Lane, Winchfield, Hook, RG27 8DD. www.old-thatch.co.uk. *3m W of Fleet. 1½ m E of Winchfield Stn, follow NGS signs. Sprats Hatch Ln is opp the Barley Mow Pub. Public*

car park at Barley Mow slipway is ½m from garden. Parking in field next to Old Thatch, if dry. Disabled parking on site. See garden website for further info. **Sun 10 Apr (2-6). Combined adm £4, chd free. Home-made teas. Pimms if hot & mulled wine if cool.**

THE MILLENNIUM BARN
Mr & Mrs G Carter.

OLD THATCH
Jill Ede.

Who could resist visiting Old Thatch, a chocolate box thatched cottage (not open), featured on film and TV, a smallholding with a 5 acre garden and woodland alongside the Basingstoke Canal (unfenced). A succession of spring bulbs, a profusion of wild flowers, perennials and homegrown annuals pollinated by our own bees and fertilised by the donkeys, who await your visit. Over 30 named clematis and rose cultivars. Children enjoy our garden quiz, adults enjoy tea and home-made cakes. Arrive by narrow boat! Trips on 'John Pinkerton' may stop at Old Thatch on NGS days www.basingstoke-canal.org.uk. Also Accessible Boating shuttle from Barley Mow wharf, approx every 45 mins. Signed parking for Blue Badge holders: please use entrance by the red telephone box. Paved paths and grass slopes give access to the whole garden.

& 🐕 ❀ 🍵

61 ◆ PATRICK'S PATCH
Fairweather's Garden Centre, High Street, Beaulieu, SO42 7YB. Patrick Fairweather, 01590 612307, info@fairweathers.co.uk, www.fairweathers.co.uk. *SE of New Forest at head of Beaulieu River. Leave M27 at J2 & follow signs for Beaulieu Motor Museum. Go up the one way High St & park in Fairweather's car park on the LHS.* **For opening times and information, please phone, email or visit garden website.**
Model kitchen garden with a full range of vegetables, trained top and soft fruit and herbs. Salads in succession used as an educational project for all ages. Maintained by volunteers, primary school children and a head gardener. We run a series of fun educational gardening sessions for children as well as informal workshops for adults. Open

daily by donation from dawn to dusk. Wheelchair access on gravelled site.
& ❀ 🍵

62 PILLEY HILL COTTAGE
Pilley Hill, Lymington, SO41 5QF. Steph & Sandy Glen, 01590 677844, stephglen@hotmail.co.uk. *New Forest. Pilley Hill Cottage is on the R as you come up Pilley Hill. Please park in school.* **Sat 26, Sun 27 Feb, Sat 5, Sun 6 Mar (1-4). Adm £4, chd free. Cream teas. Visits also by arrangement Feb to Apr.**
Entering via the creeper covered lych gate, the garden reveals itself via winding paths. Dogwood, cornus and ghost bramble bring winter colour among gnarled trees, but the stark structure of winter is softened as spring brings snowdrops, then masses of daffodils. Wild flowers are making a welcome debut in our little meadow strips and, green shoots of bog plants and ferns are jostling for attention.
🐕 ❀ 🍵 🍽))

63 1 POVEY'S COTTAGE
Stoney Heath, Baughurst, Tadley, RG26 5SN. Jonathan & Sheila Richards, 01256 850633, smrjrichards@sky.com. *Between villages of Ramsdell & Baughurst, 10 mins drive from Basingstoke. Take A339 out of Basingstoke, direction Newbury. Turn R off A339 towards Ramsdell, then 4m to Stoneyheath. Pass under overhead power cables, take next L into unmade road & Povey's is 1st on the R.* **Sat 11, Sun 12 June, Sat 20, Sun 21 Aug (1-5). Adm £4, chd free. Home-made teas. Visits also by arrangement June to Sept for groups of 15 to 30.**
Herbaceous borders, trees and shrubs, a small orchard, greenhouses, fruit cage, vegetable garden and a small wildflower meadow area. Beehives in one corner of the garden and chickens in another corner. A feature of the garden is an unusual natural swimming pond. Plant sale and home-made bee pottery for sale. See our Facebook page photos by searching 'One Poveys Cottage'. Wheelchair access across flat grassed areas, but no hard pathways.
& ❀ 🍵))

64 PYLEWELL PARK
South Baddesley, Lymington, SO41 5SJ. Lord Teynham. *Coast road 2m E of Lymington. From Lymington follow signs for Car Ferry to Isle of Wight, continue for 2m to South Baddesley.* **Sun 17 Apr, Mon 2 May (2-5). Adm £5, chd free.**
A large parkland garden laid out in 1890. Enjoy a walk along the extensive informal grass and moss paths, bordered by fine rhododendron, magnolia and azalea. Wild daffodils bloom at Easter and bluebells in May. Large lakes feature giant *Gunnera manicata*, lily pads and are home to magnificent swans. Distant views across the Solent to the Isle of Wight. Lovely day out for families and dogs. Bring your own tea or picnic and wellingtons! Old glasshouses and other outbuildings are not open to visitors. Wear suitable footwear for muddy areas. Pylewell House is private and its surrounding garden is not open for the NGS.
🐕))

65 REDENHAM PARK HOUSE
Redenham Park, Andover, SP11 9AQ. Lady Olivia Clark, 01264 772511, oliviaclark@redenhampark.co.uk. *Approx 1½m from Weyhill on the A342 Andover to Ludgershall road.* **Thur 22, Fri 23 Sept (2.30-5). Adm £6, chd free. Home-made teas & cream teas in the thatched pool house. Visits also by arrangement June to Oct for groups of up to 26.**
Redenham Park built in 1784. The garden sits behind the house (not open). The formal rose garden is planted with white flowered roses. Steps lead up to the main herbaceous borders, which peak in late summer. A calm green interlude, a gate opens into gardens with espaliered pears, apples, mass of scented roses, shrubs and perennial planting surrounds the swimming pool. A door opens onto a kitchen garden.
❀ 🚘 🍵

In 2021 the National Garden Scheme donated £3 million to our beneficiary charities

GROUP OPENING

66 ROMSEY GARDENS
Romsey, SO51 8LD. *Town Centre. Use Lortemore Place public car park SO51 8LD (free on Suns), which is directly next to King John's Garden. All gardens are within easy walking distance of each other.* Sun 29 May (10.30-4.30). Combined adm £7, chd free. Tea at King John's Garden and La Sagesse Convent.

KING JOHN'S GARDEN
Friends of King John's Garden & Test Valley Borough Council, www.facebook.com/ KingJohnsGarden/.
NEW LA SAGESSE CONVENT
Fiona Jenvey, 01794 830206, reception@ wisdomhouseromsey.co.uk, www.wisdomhouseromsey. org.uk/.

4 MILL LANE
Miss J Flindall.

THE NELSON COTTAGE
Margaret Prosser.

OLD THATCHED COTTAGE
Genevieve & Derek Langford.

King John's House is a fascinating listed C13 house (not open Sun) and the garden inc some pre-1700 period planting and a Victorian courtyard. The majestic C12 Romsey Abbey is the backdrop to 4 Mill Lane, a garden described by Joe Swift as 'the best solution for a long thin garden with a view'. The C15 listed Old Thatched Cottage on Mill Lane has a typical cottage garden with hollyhocks, wisteria and roses; it features a variety of shrubs, fruit cordons, rockery, water features, rain water harvesting and a small chicken coop. Nelson Cottage on Cherville St, formally a pub with a ½ acre garden, has a variety of perennial plants and shrubs with a wild grass meadow bringing the countryside into the town. Opening for the NGS for the first time La Sagesse Convent immediately to the south of Romsey Abbey has an unusual seven circuit meditation labyrinth, a rose garden and a walled garden. No wheelchair access at 4 Mill Lane.

67 NEW 15 ROTHSCHILD CLOSE
Southampton, SO19 9TE. Steve Campion, 07968 512773, Spcampion@talktalk.net. *3m from M27 J8. From M27 J8 follow A3025 towards Woolston. After cemetery r'about L to Weston, next r'about 2nd exit Rothschild Close.* Visits by arrangement July to Sept for groups of up to 15. Weekends preferred. Adm £3, chd free. Home-made teas.

Small, 8 metre x 8 metre, modern city garden incorporating family living with lush tropical foliage. A large range of unusual tropical style plants inc tree ferns, bananas, cannas, gingers and dahlias. The garden has flourished over the last 5 yrs into a tropical oasis with many plants grown from seeds and cuttings. Tropical plant enthusiasts do come to have a cuppa in the jungle!! Adjacent to the River Solent and Royal Victoria Country Park.

Bridge Cottage, Amport & Monxton Gardens

68 SAGES
Sages Lane, Privett,
Alton, GU34 3NP. Joanne
Edmonds, 07739 680052,
sagesprivett@gmail.com. *Turn
off A32 opp The Angel Hotel, then
Sages is ½ m down the road on the
L. Visits by arrangement in July
for groups of 20 to 40. Adm £5,
chd free.*
Newly developed 2½ acre garden
designed and maintained by
the owners set amongst mature
trees. Complementary planting
with sustainable drought tolerant
perennials and grasses, tranquil
Japanese style pond, secluded
woodland shade garden, modern
kitchen garden, charming courtyard
garden with raised pond, pots of
lilies and hydrangeas cascading over
tiered flint walls. Beautiful heated
Alitex greenhouse with tropical plants.
Wheelchair access via new sloping
path to upper levels.

69 28 ST RONAN'S AVENUE
Southsea, Portsmouth,
PO4 0QE. Ian & Liz Craig,
www.28stronansavenue.co.uk. *St
Ronan's Rd can be found off Albert
Rd. Follow signs from Albert Rd or
Canoe Lake on seafront. Parking in
Craneswater School. Sun 17 Apr,
Sun 29 May (2-6). Adm £3.50, chd
free. Home-made teas.*
Town garden 145ft x 25ft, 700 metres
from the sea. A mixture of tender,
exotic and dry loving plants, along
with more traditional inc king protea,
bananas, ferns, agaves, echeverias,
echium and puya. Wildflower area
and wildlife pond. Two different dry
gardens showing what can be grown
in sandy soil. Recycled items have
been used to create sculptures.

GROUP OPENING

70 SEARLES LANE GARDENS
Searles Lane, Hook, RG27 9EQ. *5
mins from J5 M3. Searles Ln is off
A30 (London Rd), N of Hook towards
Hartley Wintney. For disabled parking
only go to Searles Ln (RG27 9EQ).
Other parking nearby, approx ¼ m,
signed on the day. Fri 24, Sat 25,
Sun 26 June (2-5). Combined adm
£6.50, chd free. Home-made teas,
gluten and dairy free options at
Maple Cottage.*

CHERRY TREE BARN
Lois & Patrick Bellew.

MAPLE COTTAGE
John & Pat Beagley.

After a very successful 2021 we
are back with a few new things to
see: Maple Cottage is a ½ acre
cottage style garden with herbaceous
borders, vegetable plots and a
tiny, but very active wildlife pond
surrounded by hostas, astilbe,
sarracenia. The frogs and hedgehogs
do a good job on the slugs! The
neighbouring 1 acre contemporary
garden at Cherry Tree Barn is just 3
yrs old, the front just a yr. The area
around the thatched barn has been
planted with grasses, iris, salvia,
euphorbia, phlomis and knautia. Drifts
of oxeye daisies and other wildflowers
on bunds line the perimeter. Hard
landscaping inc terracing, decking,
pathways and Japanese influenced
Yatsuhashi bridge through the main
border. A small Japanese style garden
was constructed in 2021. The front
garden was redesigned and rebuilt to
inc a wide range of plants and trees
that set the buildings off beautifully.
The garden inc a small collection of
contemporary stone sculptures. Plant
sale at Maple Cottage, renowned for
high quality! Wheelchair access with
mainly grassed areas and avoidable
steps.

71 'SELBORNE'
Caker Lane, East Worldham,
Alton, GU34 3AE. Mary Trigwell-
Jones, www.worldham.org. *2m SE
of Alton. On B3004 at Alton end of
the village of East Worldham, nr The
Three Horseshoes pub. Please note:
'Selborne' is the name of the house.
It is not in the village of Selborne.
Parking signed. Sat 28, Sun 29 May
(2-5). Adm £4, chd free. Sat 2, Sun
3 July (2-5.30). Combined adm
with East Worldham Manor £6,
chd free. Sat 6, Sun 7, Mon 8 Aug
(2-5). Adm £4, chd free. Home-
made teas.*
Described as a 'happy garden', this
much-loved ½ acre mature cottage
style garden provides visitors with
surprises around every corner and
views across farmland. Productive
60 yr old orchard of named varieties,
densely planted borders, shrubs and
climbers, especially clematis. Metal
and stone sculptures enhance the
borders. Containers. Bug mansion.

Enjoy tea in the shade of the orchard.
Summerhouses and conservatory
provide shelter. Wheelchair access to
parts of the garden with some gravel
paths.

72 SHALDEN PARK HOUSE
The Avenue, Shalden, Alton,
GU34 4DS. Mr & Mrs Michael
Campbell. *4½ m NW of Alton.
B3349 from Alton or M3 J5 onto
B3349. Turn W at Kapadokya
Restaurant (formerly The Golden
Pot pub) signed Herriard, Lasham,
Shalden. Entrance ¼ m on L.
Disabled parking on entry. Sun 29
May (2-5). Adm £5, chd free.
Home-made teas.*
Large 4 acre garden to stroll around
with beautiful views. Herbaceous
borders inc kitchen walk and rose
garden, all with large scale planting
and foliage interest. Pond, arboretum,
kitchen garden and garden statuary.

73 SILVER BIRCHES
Old House Gardens,
East Worldham, nr Alton,
GU34 3AN. Jenny & Roger
Bateman, 07464 696245,
Jennyabateman@gmail.com.
*2m E of Alton off B3004. Turn L
signed Wyck & Binstead, then 1st
R into Old House Gardens. Visits
by arrangement May to Aug for
groups of 10 to 30. Adm £5, chd
free. Home-made teas.*
½ acre garden completely
redesigned by the owners over
the last 12 yrs. Winding paths lead
through shrub and herbaceous
borders to fish pond with stream,
rockery and summerhouse. Rose
garden with arbour. Planting designed
for year-round colour and interest
using foliage as well as flowers.
Many sitting areas and some unusual
plants. Partial wheelchair access.

'National Garden Scheme
donations have funded four
of our gardens in regional
NHS spinal injury centres
supporting nearly 8,500
patients and their visitors.'
Horatio's Garden

74 ◆ SIR HAROLD HILLIER GARDENS
Jermyns Lane, Ampfield, Romsey, SO51 0QA. Hampshire County Council, 01794 369318, info.hilliers@hants.gov.uk, www.hants.gov.uk/hilliergardens. *2m NE of Romsey. Follow brown tourist signs off M3 J11, or off M27 J2, or A3057 Romsey to Andover.* For opening times and information, please phone, email or visit garden website.
Established by the plantsman Sir Harold Hillier, this 180 acre garden holds a unique collection of 12,000 different hardy plants from across the world. It inc the famous Winter Garden, Magnolia Avenue, Centenary Border, Himalayan Valley, Gurkha Memorial Garden, Magnolia Avenue, spring woodlands, Hydrangea Walk, fabulous autumn colour, 14 National Collections and over 600 champion trees. The Centenary Border is one of the longest double mixed border in the country, a feast from early summer to autumn. Celebrated Winter Garden is one of the largest in Europe. Electric scooters and wheelchairs are available for hire (please pre-book). Accessible WC and parking. Registered assistance dogs only.
♿ ✿ ♿ NPC ☕

75 SOUTH VIEW HOUSE
60 South Road, Horndean, Waterlooville, PO8 0EP. James & Victoria Greenshields. *Between Horndean & Clanfield. From N A3 towards Horndean, R at T-junction to r'about. From S A3 B2149 to Horndean, continue on A3 N to r'about, 1st exit into Downwood Way, 3rd L into South Rd. House is 3rd on R. Park in road.* Sun 5 June, Sun 14 Aug (1-5). Adm £3.50, chd free. Light refreshments.
A fusion of traditional and contemporary designs across a ½ acre site. The formal cottage garden to the front inc a large herbaceous border, small woodland garden and formal topiary. The cleverly designed garden to the rear features pond, alpine garden, mini fruit orchard, chickens and greenhouse and, for entertaining, a patio with bar (not open) and a large summerhouse. Well worth a visit. Garden is accessed along a gravel drive on a gentle slope.
♿ ✿ ☕))

76 ◆ SPINNERS GARDEN
School Lane, Pilley, Lymington, SO41 5QE. Andrew & Vicky Roberts, www.spinnersgarden.co.uk. *New Forest. 1½m N of Lymington off A337.* For NGS: Sun 24 Apr (1.30-5). Adm £6, chd free. Cream teas. For other opening times and information, please visit garden website.
Peaceful woodland garden overlooking the Lymington valley with many rare and unusual plants. Drifts of trilliums, erythroniums and anemones light up the woodland floor in early spring. The garden continues to be developed with new plants added to the collections and the layout changed to enhance the views. The house was rebuilt in 2014 to reflect its garden setting. Andy will take groups of 15 on tours of the hillside with its woodland wonders and draw attention to the treats at their feet.
🐾 🐕 ♿ ☕))

77 SPITFIRE HOUSE
Chattis Hill, Stockbridge, SO20 6JS. Tessa & Clive Redshaw, 07711 547543, tessa@redshaw.co.uk. *2m from Stockbridge. Follow the A30 W from Stockbridge for 2m. Go past the Broughton/Chattis Hill Xrds, do not follow SatNav into Spitfire Ln, take next R to the Wallops & then immed R again to Spitfire House.* Sun 29 May (2-5); Wed 8 June (11-3). Adm £5, chd free. Home-made teas on 29 May only. Visits also by arrangement June & July for groups of up to 30.
A country garden situated high on chalk downland. On the site of a WW11 Spitfire assembly factory with Spitfire tethering rings still visible. This garden has wildlife at its heart and inc fruit and vegetables, a small orchard, wildlife pond, woodland planting and large areas of wildflower meadow. Wander across the downs to be rewarded with extensive views. Wheelchair access with areas of gravel and a slope up to wildflower meadow.
♿ 🐕 ♿ ☕

GROUP OPENING

78 STOCKBRIDGE GARDENS
Stockbridge, SO20 6EX. *9m W of Winchester. On A30, at the junction of A3057 & B3049. All gardens & parking on High St.* Thur 16, Sun 19 June (2-5). Combined adm £8,

chd free. Home-made teas at St Peter's Church, High St.

LITTLE WYKE
Mrs Mary Matthews.
THE OLD RECTORY
Robin Colenso & Chrissie Quayle.
OLD SWAN HOUSE
Mr Herry Lawford.
(See separate entry)
SHEPHERDS HOUSE
Kim & Frances Candler.
TROUT COTTAGE
Mrs Sally Milligan, sally@sallymilligan.co.uk.
Visits also by arrangement July to Sept for groups of 5 to 10.

Five gardens will open this yr in Stockbridge, offering a variety of styles and character. Little Wyke, next to the Town Hall has a long mature town garden with mixed borders and fruit trees. Trout Cottage is a small walled garden, which will inspire those with small spaces and little time to achieve tranquillity and beauty. Full of approx 180 plants flowering for almost 10 months of the yr. The Old Rectory has a partially walled garden with formal pond, fountain and planting near the house (not open) with a stream-side walk under trees, many climbing and shrub roses and a woodland area. Old Swan House, at the east end of the High St has modern mixed planting. There is a gravel grass garden and an orchard, as well as a pond. Shepherds House on Winton Hill with herbaceous borders, a new kitchen garden and a belvedere overlooking the pond. Plant sale at the church where teas can also be taken on the church lawn. Wheelchair access to all gardens. Gravel path at Shepherds House and driveway at Old Swan House.
♿ ✿ ☕))

79 TADLEY PLACE
Church Lane, Baughurst, Tadley, RG26 5LA. Lyn & Ronald Duncan. *10 mins drive from Basingstoke, nr Tadley.* Sun 26 June (2-5). Adm £6, chd free. Light refreshments.
Tadley Place is a Tudor manor house (not open) dating from the C15. The gardens surround the house and inc formal areas, a large kitchen garden and access to a fabulous bluebell wood with a pond.
 ☕))

Cherry Tree Barn, Searle Lane Gardens

© Marianne Majerus

80 TANGLEFOOT

Crawley, Winchester, SO21 2QB.
Mr & Mrs F J Fratter,
01962 776243, fred@fratter.co.uk.
*5m NW of Winchester. Between
B3049 (Winchester - Stockbridge) &
A272 (Winchester - Andover). Lane
beside Crawley Court (Arqiva). For
SatNav use SO21 2QA. Parking in
adjacent mown field.* **Thur 12, Sun
15 May, Thur 9, Sun 12 June, Thur
21 July (2-5.30). Sun 24 July (2-
5.30), open nearby Terstan. Adm
£5, chd free. Self service drinks
& biscuits. Opening with Crawley
Gardens on Thur 30 June, Sun 3
July.** Visits also by arrangement
May to July.
Developed by owners since 1976,
Tanglefoot's $\frac{1}{2}$ acre garden is a
blend of influences, from Monet-
inspired rose arch and small lily
pond to Victorian boundary wall with
trained fruit trees. Highlights inc a
raised lily pond, herbaceous bed (a

riot of colour later in the summer),
herb wheel, large productive kitchen
garden and unusual flowering plants.
In contrast to the garden, a 2 acre
field with views over the Hampshire
countryside has been converted
into walk-through spring and
summer wildflower meadows with
mostly native trees and shrubs. The
meadow contains plenty of ox-eye
daisy, bedstraw, scabious, vetch,
knapweed, bees, butterflies and
much more; it has delighted many
visitors. Visitors can picnic in the field,
but there are no facilities available.
Plants from the garden for sale.
Wheelchair access with narrow paths
in vegetable area.

♿ 🐕 ✱ ☕ ⍅

81 TERSTAN

Longstock, Stockbridge,
SO20 6DW. Penny Burnfield,
paburnfield@gmail.com, www.
pennyburnfield.wordpress.com.

*$\frac{3}{4}$ m N of Stockbridge. From
Stockbridge (A30) turn N to
Longstock at bridge. Garden $\frac{3}{4}$ m on
R.* **Sun 17 Apr, Sun 19 June (2-5).
Sun 24 July (2-5), open nearby
Tanglefoot. Sun 18 Sept (2-5).
Adm £5, chd free. Home-made
teas.** Visits also by arrangement
Apr to Sept for groups of 10+.
A garden for all seasons, developed
over 50 yrs into a profusely planted,
contemporary cottage garden in
peaceful surroundings. There is a
constantly changing display in pots,
starting with tulips and continuing with
many unusual plants. Features inc
gravel garden, water features, cutting
garden, showman's caravan and live
music. Wheelchair access with some
gravel paths and steps.

♿ 🐕 ✱ 🚗 ☕

82 TWIN OAKS

13 Oakwood Road, Chandler's Ford, Eastleigh, SO53 1LW. Syd & Sue Hutchinson, 02380 907517, syd@sydh.co.uk. *Leave M3 J12. Follow signs to Chandlers Ford onto Winchester Rd. After ½m turn R into Hiltingbury Rd. After approx ½m turn L into Oakwood Rd.* Sun 17, Mon 18 Apr, Sat 4, Sun 5 June, Sat 30, Sun 31 July, Sat 20, Sun 21 Aug (1-5). Adm £4, chd free. Home-made teas. Visits also by arrangement May to Aug for groups of up to 30.
Evolving suburban water garden. Enjoy spring colour from azaleas, rhododendrons and bulbs then summer colour from perennials, water lilies and tropical plants. A lawn meanders between informal beds and ponds and bridges lead to a tranquil pergola seating area overlooking a wildlife pond. A rockery is skirted by a stream and a waterfall tumbles into a large lily pond home to dragonflies. Aviary.

83 TYLNEY HALL HOTEL

Ridge Lane, Rotherwick, RG27 9AZ. Elite Hotels, 01256 764881, sales@tylneyhall.com, www.tylneyhall.co.uk. *3m NW of Hook. From M3 J5 via A287 & Newnham, M4 J11 via B3349 & Rotherwick.* Sun 24 Apr, Sun 22 May, Sun 19 June (10-5). Adm £5, chd free. Cream teas in the Chestnut Suite from 12pm.

Large garden of 66 acres with extensive woodlands and beautiful vista. Fine avenues of wellingtonias; rhododendrons and azaleas, Italian garden, lakes, large water and rock garden, dry stone walls originally designed with assistance of Gertrude Jekyll. Partial wheelchair access.

84 NEW VENARDS

Ringwood Road, North Gorley, Fordingbridge, SP6 2PJ. Nadine Sherborne. *Exit A338 onto Lawrence Ln, over cattle grid, then turn R at T-junction. Venards house is ½m on L, just before the ford.* Sat 9, Sun 10 July (10-3). Adm £5. Home-made teas.
Heart of the New Forest, established ³⁄₄ acre walled garden has undergone a loving revival over the past 5 yrs. Stunning Victorian herbaceous borders in rear garden beneath the ancient yew hedging are particularly beautiful. Large Victorian style greenhouse in well-stocked kitchen garden. Brook runs through the garden and, a newly planted wildflower meadow.

85 WALHAMPTON

Beaulieu Road, Walhampton, Lymington, SO41 5ZG. Walhampton School Trust Ltd, 07928 385694, d.hill@walhampton.com. *1m E of Lymington. From Lymington follow signs to Beaulieu (B3054) for 1m & turn R into main entrance*

at 1st school sign, 200yds after top of hill. Sun 1 May (2-6). Adm £5, chd free. Tea. Visits also by arrangement Mar to Oct for groups of 10 to 20. Donation to St John's Church, Boldre.
Glorious walks through large C18 landscape garden surrounding magnificent mansion (now a school). Visitors will discover three lakes, serpentine canal, climbable prospect mount, period former banana house and orangery, fascinating shell grotto, plantsman's glade and Italian terrace by Peto (c1907), drives and colonnade by Mawson (c1914) with magnificent views to the Isle of Wight. Exedrae and sunken garden, rockery, Roman arch, fountain and seating. Talks will be given at the fountain, every 30 mins to groups of 20 people by David Hill on the day. Wheelchair access with gravel paths and some slopes. Regret, no dogs allowed.

86 WESTWARD

11 Ridgemount Avenue, Bassett, Southampton, SO16 7FP. Russ & Jan Smith, 02380 767112, russjsmith@btinternet.com. *3m N of Southampton city centre. From end of M3 J14 continue down A33 to 2nd r'about & head back to M3. Ridgemount Ave 2nd on L.* Sat 13, Sun 14, Mon 15 Aug (1-5). Adm £4, chd free. Home-made teas. Visits also by arrangement June to Sept for groups of 10+.
Very colourful ¼ acre garden with diverse selection of planting in

Tanglefoot

summer inc lilies, heucheras, acers, clematis and hydrangeas. Many baskets and containers full of summer colour. Hosta border, vegetable garden, summerhouse, koi pond, waterfall and wildlife pond. Large collection of aeoniums, echeverias and cacti. New raised water feature in front garden. Wheelchair access through garage.

🔥 🐐 ✿ 🚐 🍵

87 WHEATLEY HOUSE

Wheatley Lane, between Binsted & Kingsley, Bordon, GU35 9PA. Mr & Mrs Michael Adlington, 01420 23113, adlingtons36@gmail.com. *4m E of Alton, 5m SW of Farnham. Take A31 to Bentley, follow sign to Bordon. After 2m, R at Jolly Farmer Pub towards Binsted, 1m L & follow signs to Wheatley.* Sat 20, Sun 21 Aug (1.30-5.30). Adm £5, chd free. Home-made teas. Visits also by arrangement May to Oct for groups of 10+.

Situated on a rural hilltop with panoramic views over Alice Holt Forest and the South Downs. The owner admits to being much more of an artist than a plantswoman, but has had great fun creating this 1½ acre garden full of interesting and unusual planting combinations. The sweeping mixed borders and shrubs are spectacular with colour throughout the season, particularly in late summer. The black and white border, now with bright red accents, is very popular with visitors. Plants for sale. Selection of home-made, local crafts in the barn and a variety of artwork and sculptures in the garden. Wheelchair access with care on lawns, good views of garden and beyond from terrace.

🔥 ✿ 🍵

88 WICOR PRIMARY SCHOOL COMMUNITY GARDEN

Portchester, Fareham, PO16 9DL. Louise Moreton, www.wicor.hants.sch.uk. *Halfway between Portsmouth & Fareham on A27. Turn S at Seagull Pub r'about into Cornaway Ln, 1st R into Hatherley Drive. Entrance to school is almost opp. Parking on site, pay at main gate.* Sun 26 June (12-4). Adm £3.50, chd free. Home-made teas.

As shown on BBC Gardeners' World in 2017. Beautiful school gardens tended by pupils, staff and community gardeners. Wander along Darwin's path to see the coastal

garden, Jurassic garden, orchard, tropical bed, stumpery, wildlife areas, allotments and apiary, plus one of the few camera obscuras in the south of England. Wheelchair access to all areas, flat ground.

🔥 🐐 ✿ 🍵))

89 NEW WINCHESTER COLLEGE

College Street, Winchester, SO23 9NA. The College, www.winchestercollege.org/. *Entrance to the College is via the Porter's Lodge on College St, a short walk from Winchester City Centre. Note there is very limited parking nr the college.* Sat 28 May (11-5); Sun 29 May (11-4). Adm £10, chd free. A selection of refreshments will be available on site.

See the gardens of C14 Winchester College. These inc the main quad with herb garden, herbaceous borders and splendid climbing hydrangea; War Cloister designed by Herbert Baker, 'Bethesda' a soft cottage style garden; 'Meads' a stunning walled cricket ground surrounded by magnificent plane trees; and the Warden's Garden with Regency border, chalk stream and wilder woodland area.

🍵))

90 1 WOGSBARNE COTTAGES

Rotherwick, RG27 9BL. Miss S & Mr R Whistler. *2½ m N of Hook. M3 J5, M4 J11, A30 or A33 via B3349.* Sun 10, Mon 11 July (2-5). Adm £4, chd free. Home-made teas.

Small traditional cottage garden with a 'roses around the door' look, much photographed for calendars, jigsaws and magazines. Mixed flower beds and borders. Vegetables grown in abundance. Ornamental pond and alpine garden. Views over open countryside to be enjoyed whilst you take afternoon tea on the lawn. The garden has been open for the NGS for more than 30 yrs. Wheelchair access with some gravel paths.

🔥 ✿ 🍵

91 WOODPECKERS CARE HOME

Sway Road, Brockenhurst, SO42 7RX. Mr Charles Hubberstey. *New Forest. Signed from A337. Sway Rd from village centre. past petrol stn, then school & Woodpeckers on R.* Sat 3, Sun 4 Sept (11-5). Adm £4, chd free. Home-made teas.

A vibrant and colourful garden surrounds our care home. We have active involvement from our residents who enjoy the wide paths, whether in a wheelchair or strolling on foot. The courtyard area, small orchard and woodland, all look particularly beautiful in spring and late summer with views through neighbouring fields. An amazing bug house, the woodpecker and vibrant plantings will wow you!

🔥 🐐 🍵 🪑))

92 WOOLTON HOUSE

Woolton Hill, Newbury, RG20 9TZ. Rosamond Brown. *8m S of Newbury. From A343 take road to Woolton Hill, keep L at Xrds. Continue through village, turn L on 1st lane after short downhill & sign to Woolton Hill Sports Ground (Fullers Ln) & immed R on 1st driveway.* Sun 26 June, Fri 23 Sept (2-5). Adm £8, chd free. Home-made teas.

Spectacular, contemporary walled garden set in 4 acres, designed by Pascal Cribier with influence of Mondrian and planted in blues and yellows, interspersed with vegetables. Unique red and green 'tramline' garden. Red courtyard picking garden and new walled sedum and cactus garden. Rose garden with majestic pond. Stunning use of colour and texture.

🚐 🍵))

93 NEW YEW HURST

Blissford, Fordingbridge, SP6 2JQ. Mr & Mrs Henry Richardson, Marie-anne@newforestfarm.co.uk. *From Fordingbridge B3078 towards Brook. After approx 1m take R turn to Blissford. Down hill to water splash & Yew Hurst is 3rd house on the L after splash.* Sat 25, Sun 26 June (2-6). Adm £3.50, chd free. Home-made teas.

Set in a glorious position in the New Forest this is the home of a keen gardener and plant lover. A small but perfectly formed garden has lots to offer as it wraps around the house (not open) with every part having been designed to take advantage of the space. Each area has been given a sense of purpose whilst there is a flow from one part to another.

 🐐 🍵

HEREFORDSHIRE

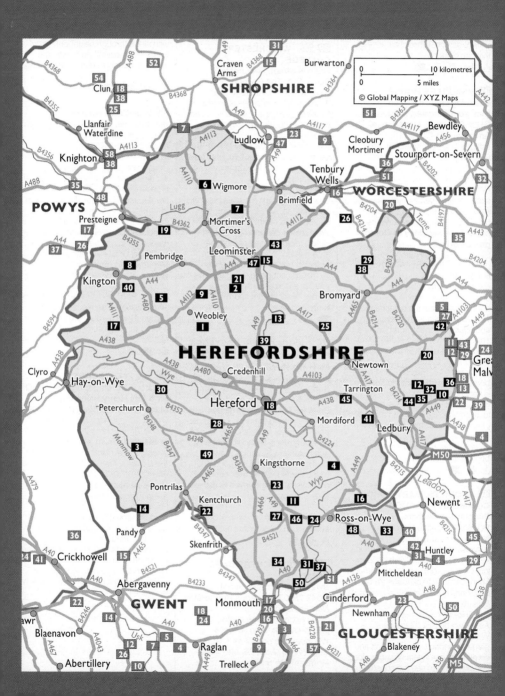

Herefordshire is essentially an agricultural county, characterised by small market towns, black and white villages, fruit and hop orchards, meandering rivers, wonderful wildlife and spectacular, and often remote, countryside (a must for keen walkers).

As a major region in the Welsh Marches, Herefordshire has a long and diverse history, as indicated by the numerous prehistoric hill forts, medieval castles and ancient battle sites. Exploring the quiet country lanes can lead to many delightful surprises.

For garden enthusiasts the National Garden Scheme offers a range of charming and interesting gardens ranging from informal cottage plots to those of grand houses with parterres, terraces and parkland. Widely contrasting in design and plantings they offer inspiration and innovative ideas.

National collections of Asters and Siberian Iris can be found at The Picton Garden and Aulden Farm, respectively; and, for Galanthophiles, Ivycroft will not disappoint. The numerous specialist nurseries offer tempting collections of rare and unusual plants.

You can always be sure of a warm welcome at a National Garden Scheme open garden.

Volunteers

County Organiser
Lavinia Sole
07880 550235
lavinia.sole@ngs.org.uk

County Treasurer
Angela Mainwaring
01981 251331
angela.mainwaring@ngs.org.uk

Booklet Coordinator
Chris Meakins
01544 370215
christine.meakins@btinternet.com

Booklet Distribution
Graham Sole
01568 797522
grahamsole3@gmail.com

Social Media
Naomi Grove
naomi.grove@ngs.org.uk

Assistant County Organisers
Sue Londesborough
01981 510148
slondesborough138@btinternet.com

Penny Usher
01568 611688
pennyusher@btinternet.com

🅕 @NGSHerefordshire
🅧 @HerefordNGS

Left: Lower Brook

OPENING DATES

All entries subject to change. For latest information check www.ngs.org.uk

Extended openings are shown at the beginning of the month.

Map locator numbers are shown to the right of each garden name.

January

Thursday 27th
Ivy Croft 21

February

Snowdrop Festival

Every Thursday
Ivy Croft 21

Sunday 13th
◆ The Picton Garden 36

Sunday 27th
◆ The Picton Garden 36

March

Every Thursday to Thursday 3rd
Ivy Croft 21

Saturday 19th
◆ Ralph Court Gardens 38

Sunday 20th
NEW Lower Brook 24
◆ The Picton Garden 36
◆ Ralph Court Gardens 38

Monday 21st
NEW Lower Brook 24

Saturday 26th
Wainfield 46

Sunday 27th
Whitfield 49

Wednesday 30th
Ivy Croft 21

April

Every Wednesday
Ivy Croft 21

Friday 1st
◆ Stockton Bury Gardens 43

Sunday 10th
Bury Court Farmhouse 6
Lower Hope 25
◆ The Picton Garden 36

Monday 11th
◆ Moors Meadow Gardens 29

Saturday 23rd
NEW Dinmore Gardens 13

Sunday 24th
NEW Dinmore Gardens 13
Lower House Farm 26

Saturday 30th
Aulden Farm 2
Coddington Vineyard 12
Ivy Croft 21

May

Every Wednesday
Ivy Croft 21

Sunday 1st
Aulden Farm 2
Coddington Vineyard 12
Ivy Croft 21
◆ The Picton Garden 36

Saturday 14th
NEW The Old Vicarage 35

Sunday 15th
NEW The Old Vicarage 35

Monday 16th
◆ Moors Meadow Gardens 29

Sunday 22nd
Lower Hope 25
Lower House Farm 26

Thursday 26th
Wainfield 46

Friday 27th
Kentchurch Court 22
NEW Millfield House 28
Wainfield 46

Saturday 28th
Sheepcote 41
Wainfield 46

Sunday 29th
NEW Millfield House 28
◆ The Picton Garden 36

June

Every Wednesday
Ivy Croft 21

Friday 3rd
Castle Moat House 9

Saturday 4th
Castle Moat House 9

Sunday 5th
◆ Caves Folly Nurseries 10
The Nutshell 31

Saturday 11th
Brockhampton Cottage 4
Grendon Court 16

Sunday 12th
Broxwood Court 5
Grange Court 15

Monday 13th
◆ Moors Meadow Gardens 29

Thursday 16th
NEW Uplands & Uplands Cottage 44

Friday 17th
NEW Uplands & Uplands Cottage 44

Saturday 18th
Byecroft 7
NEW New House Farm 30
NEW Uplands & Uplands Cottage 44

Sunday 19th
Byecroft 7
Lower House Farm 26
NEW New House Farm 30
◆ The Picton Garden 36

Tuesday 21st
Hillcroft 19

Wednesday 22nd
Hillcroft 19

Thursday 23rd
Hillcroft 19

Saturday 25th
◆ The Garden of the Wind at Middle Hunt House 14
◆ Hereford Cathedral Gardens 18
NEW New House Farm 30

Sunday 26th
◆ The Garden of the Wind at Middle Hunt House 14
Grange Court 15
The Hurst 20
NEW New House Farm 30
Old Colwall House 32

Monday 27th
Whitfield 49

July

Every Wednesday
Ivy Croft 21

Friday 1st
Kentchurch Court 22
Wainfield 46

Saturday 2nd
◆ Ralph Court Gardens 38
Wainfield 46

Sunday 3rd
Michaelchurch Court 27
◆ Ralph Court Gardens 38
The Vine 45

Monday 4th
◆ Moors Meadow Gardens 29

Wednesday 6th
The Laskett Gardens 23

Sunday 10th
◆ The Picton Garden 36
22 Westfield Walk 47

Tuesday 12th
NEW Cae Bach Hall 8

Wednesday 13th
NEW Cae Bach Hall 8

Friday 15th
Herbfarmacy 17

Saturday 16th
Herbfarmacy 17

Sunday 17th
Rhodds Farm 40

Thursday 21st
Herbfarmacy 17

Friday 22nd
Herbfarmacy 17

Saturday 23rd
NEW Arrow Cottage 1

Sunday 24th
NEW Arrow Cottage 1
Ivy Croft 21

August

Every Wednesday
Ivy Croft 21

Monday 1st
◆ Moors Meadow
Gardens 29

Friday 5th
NEW Millfield House 28

Sunday 7th
NEW Millfield House 28

Tuesday 16th
◆ The Picton Garden 36

Saturday 27th
◆ The Garden of the
Wind at Middle Hunt
House 14

Sunday 28th
◆ The Garden of the
Wind at Middle Hunt
House 14

September

Every Wednesday
Ivy Croft 21

Sunday 4th
Broxwood Court 5
Old Grove 34

Sunday 11th
Brockhampton Cottage 4
Grendon Court 16
Lower Hope 25

Sunday 18th
Ivy Croft 21

Tuesday 20th
◆ The Picton Garden 36

Friday 23rd
Kentchurch Court 22

October

**Every Wednesday
to Wednesday 12th**
Ivy Croft 21

Saturday 8th
◆ Ralph Court
Gardens 38

Sunday 9th
NEW Lower Brook 24
◆ Ralph Court Gardens
38

Monday 10th
NEW Lower Brook 24

Thursday 20th
◆ The Picton Garden 36

November

Saturday 12th
◆ Ralph Court Gardens
38

Sunday 13th
◆ Ralph Court Gardens
38

February 2023

Sunday 12th
◆ The Picton Garden 36

Sunday 26th
◆ The Picton Garden 36

By Arrangement

Arrange a personalised
garden visit with your
club, or group of friends,
on a date to suit you. See
individual garden entries
for full details.

Aulden Farm 2
Brighton House 3
Bury Court Farmhouse 6
Byecroft 7
Church Cottage 11
Coddington Vineyard 12
Hillcroft 19
Ivy Croft 21
Kentchurch Court 22
The Laskett Gardens 23
NEW Millfield House 28
The Old Corn Mill 33
Poole Cottage 37
Revilo 39
Shuttifield Cottage 42
Wainfield 46
Weston Hall 48
Whitfield 49
Woodview 50

New House Farm

THE GARDENS

1 **[NEW]** **ARROW COTTAGE**
Ledgemoor, Weobley, HR4 8RN.
Jim & Annie Manchester. *Take
the Tillington road from Hereford.
Pass two golf courses then signs for
Ledgemoor are on R. Approx 6m in
total.* **Sat 23, Sun 24 July (11-5).
Adm £5, chd free. Home-made
cakes, cheese scones, tea and
coffee.**
A 1½ acre garden with interesting
tulip trees, catalpa, ginkgo,
ornamental pears, many willows
and tall birches. A stream, a long
rill, two ponds and a dam. A large
productive no-dig vegetable garden.
An arboretum is being planned to
replace the vineyard and a wildflower
garden has been newly created.
There is unusual statuary throughout
in this peaceful rural garden. Long
rill, a stream, 2 ponds and statuary.
Wheelchair access uneven ground
and some steps.

2 **AULDEN FARM**
Aulden, Leominster, HR6 0JT. Alun
& Jill Whitehead, 01568 720129,
web@auldenfarm.co.uk,
www.auldenfarm.co.uk. *4m SW
of Leominster. From Leominster
take Ivington/Upper Hill rd, ¾m
after Ivington church turn R signed
Aulden. From A4110 signed Ivington,
take 2nd R signed Aulden.* **Sat 30
Apr, Sun 1 May (11-4). Adm £5,
chd free. Home-made teas. Open
nearby Ivy Croft. Visits also by
arrangement Apr to Sept.**
Informal country garden, thankfully
never at its Sunday best! 3 acres
planted with wildlife in mind.
Emphasis on structure and form,
with a hint of quirkiness, a garden
to explore with eclectic planting.
Irises thrive around a natural pond,
shady beds and open borders,
seats abound, feels mature but ever
evolving. Our own ice cream and
home-burnt cakes, Lemon Chisel a
speciality.

3 **BRIGHTON HOUSE**
Newton St. Margarets, Hereford,
HR2 0JU. Sue & Richard
Londesborough, 01981 510148,
slondesborough138@btinternet.
com. *17m SW of Hereford; 9m SE of
Hay on Wye. A465 S from Hereford,*
*R onto B4348, L to Vowchurch &
Michaelchurch Escley. After approx.
3m take 3rd L turn. From Hay
B4348, R to Vowchurch & as above.
Further directions from owner.*
**Visits by arrangement June to
Sept. Adm £5, chd free. Light
refreshments.**
A plantswoman's garden of just over
an acre, divided into several distinct
areas crammed with many unusual
and interesting species. Herbaceous
borders, ornamental and fruit trees,
kitchen garden, two small ponds.
The garden is planted to encourage
wildlife. Views to the Black Mountains.
Children's garden trail and play area.
Plants for sale propagated from the
garden.

4 **BROCKHAMPTON COTTAGE**
Brockhampton, HR1 4TQ. Peter
Clay. *8m SW of Hereford. 5m N
of Ross-on-Wye on B4224. In
Brockhampton take road signed to
B Crt nursing home, pass N Home
after ³⁄₄m, go down hill & turn L.
Car park 500yds downhill on L in
orchard.* **Sat 11 June, Sun 11 Sept
(11-4). Adm £5, chd free. Open
nearby Grendon Court. Picnic
parties welcome by the lake.**
Created from scratch in 1999 by
the owner and Tom Stuart-Smith,
this beautiful hilltop garden looks
south and west over miles of unspoilt
countryside. On one side a woodland
garden and 5 acre wildflower
meadow, on the other side a Perry
pear orchard and in valley below:
lake, stream and arboretum. The
extensive borders are planted with
drifts of perennials in the modern
romantic style. Allow 1½ hrs. Visit
Grendon Court (11-4) after your visit
to us. Regional Finalist, The English
Garden's The Nation's Favourite
Gardens 2021.

5 **BROXWOOD COURT**
Broxwood, nr Pembridge,
Leominster, HR6 9JJ. Richard
Snead-Cox & Mike & Anne Allen.
*From Leominster follow signs to
Brecon A44/A4112. After approx
8m, just past Weobley turn off, go
R to Broxwood/Pembridge. After
2m straight over Xrds to Lyonshall.
500yds on L over cattle grid.* **Sun 12
June, Sun 4 Sept (11-5.30). Adm
£5, chd free. Home-made teas.**
Impressive 29 acre garden and
arboretum, designed in 1859
by W. Nesfield. Magnificent yew

hedges, long avenue of cedars and
Scots pines. Spectacular view of
Black Mountains, sweeping lawns,
rhododendrons, gentle walks to
summerhouse, chapel and lakes.
Rose garden, mixed borders, rill,
gazebo, sculpted benches and
fountain. White and coloured
peacocks, ornamental duck. Wildlife
meadow in progress. Wheelchair
access some gravel, but mostly lawn.
Gentle slopes. Disabled WC.

6 **BURY COURT FARMHOUSE**
Ford Street, Wigmore,
Leominster, HR6 9UP. Margaret
& Les Barclay, 01568 770618,
l.barclay@zoho.com. *10m from
Leominster, 10m from Knighton,
8m from Ludlow. On A4110 from
Leominster, at Wigmore turn R just
after shop & garage. Follow signs to
parking & garden.* **Sun 10 Apr (2-5).
Adm £4, chd free. Home-made
teas. Visits also by arrangement
Feb to May and Sep to Oct for
groups of up to 25.** ³⁄₄ acre garden,
'rescued' since 1997, surrounds the
1820's stone farmhouse (not open).
The courtyard contains a pond, mixed
borders, fruit trees and shrubs, with
steps up to a terrace which leads to
lawn and vegetable plot. The main
garden (semi-walled) is on two levels
with mixed borders, greenhouse,
pond, mini-orchard , many spring
flowers, and wildlife areas. Year-
round colour. Mostly accessible for
wheelchairs by arrangement.

7 **BYECROFT**
Welshman's Lane, Bircher,
Leominster, HR6 0BP. Sue &
Peter Russell, 01568 780559,
peterandsuerussell@btinternet.
com, www.byecroft.weebly.com.
*6m N of Leominster. From
Leominster take B4361. Turn L
at T-junction with B4362. ¼m
beyond Bircher village turn R at war
memorial into Welshman's Ln, signed
Bircher Common.* **Sat 18, Sun 19
June (2-5.30). Adm £4, chd free.
Home-made teas. Visits also
by arrangement May to July for
groups of 10+.**
A compact garden stuffed full of
interesting and unusual plants chosen
not just for their flowers but also for
their foliage. Pergola smothered in
old-fashioned roses, herbaceous
borders full of things you may not
have seen before, formal pond, lots
of pots, vegetable garden, wildflower

orchard, soft fruit area. Sue and Peter take particular pride in their plant sales table. Wheelchair access, most areas accessible with assistance. Some small steps.

♿ ✿ 🚙 ☕

8 NEW CAE BACH HALL
Kington, HR5 3RH. Judith Weir. *Half way between Kington & Titley on B4355. B4355 from Kington. Travel 1½m to stone cottage on R.* **Tue 12, Wed 13 July (10-4). Adm £4. Pre-booking essential, please visit www.ngs.org.uk for information & booking. Home-made teas.** ⅓ acre garden with far reaching views and inc an aviary, rose garden, parterre, 30ft canal pond and wisteria arch. Several lawns, flower and shrub borders and seating. Tea, coffee and soft drinks. Home-made cakes and scones. There is also an art exhibition.

✿ ☕ ⁍))

9 CASTLE MOAT HOUSE
Dilwyn, Hereford, HR4 8HZ. Mr & Mrs T Voogd. *6m W of Leominster. A44, after 4m take A4112 to Dilwyn. Garden by the village green.* **Fri 3 June (10.30-4). Cream teas. Sat 4 June (10.30-4). Light refreshments. Adm £4, chd free.** A 2 acre plot consisting of a more formal cottage garden that wraps around the house. The remaining area is a tranquil wild garden with paths to a Medieval Castle Motte, part filled Moat and Medieval fish and fowl ponds. A haven for wildlife and people alike. The garden contains some steep banks and deep water, with limited access to Motte, Moat and ponds.

🐐 ☕ 🍽

10 ♦ CAVES FOLLY NURSERIES
Evendine Lane, Colwall, WR13 6DX. Wil Leaper & Bridget Evans, 01684 540631, bridget@cavesfolly.com, www.cavesfolly.com. *1¼m NE of Ledbury. Between Malvern & Ledbury. Evendine Ln, off Colwall Green.* **For NGS: Sun 5 June (2-5). Adm £3, chd free. Light refreshments. For other opening times and information, please phone, email or visit garden website.** Organic nursery and display gardens. Specialist growers of cottage garden plants, wild flowers, herbs and alpines. All plants are grown in peat free organic compost. This is not a manicured garden! It is full of drifts of

colour and wild flowers and a haven for wildlife. Wildflower meadow.

♿ ✿ 🚙 🚌 ☕ 🍽

11 CHURCH COTTAGE
Hentland, Ross-on-Wye, HR9 6LP. Sue Emms & Pete Weller, 01989 730222, sue.emms@mac.com, www.wyegardensbydesign.com. *6m from Ross-on-Wye. A49 from Ross. R turn Hentland/Kynaston. Sharp R to St Dubricius, narrow lane few passing places for ½m. Park at Church 150 metres to garden, can drop off at gate. Lane unsuitable for motor homes.* **Visits by arrangement May to Aug. We are happy to have small numbers. Adm £3, chd free.** Garden designer and plantswoman's ½ acre garden - feels much larger than it is! Series of garden rooms melting seamlessly into one another. Huge variety of plants, many of which are for sale, unusual varieties mixed with old favourites, providing interest over a long period. Wildlife pond, rose garden, potager, mixed borders, white terrace. Interesting plant combinations and design ideas to inspire.

✿ 🍽

12 CODDINGTON VINEYARD
Coddington, HR8 1JJ. Sharon & Peter Maiden, 01531 641817, sgmaiden@yahoo.co.uk, www.coddingtonvineyard.co.uk. *4m NE of Ledbury. From Ledbury to Malvern A449, follow brown signs to Coddington Vineyard.* **Sat 30 Apr, Sun 1 May (12-4). Adm £4, chd free. Home-made teas. Wine, home-made ice cream and our own apple juice available. Visits also by arrangement Feb to Oct for groups of 10+.** 5 acres inc 2 acre vineyard, listed farmhouse, threshing barn and cider mill. Garden with terraces, wildflower meadow, woodland with massed spring bulbs, large pond with wildlife, stream garden with masses of primula and hosta. Hellebores and snowdrops, hamamelis and parrottia. Azaleas followed by roses and perennials. Lots to see all year. In spring, the gardens are a mass of bulbs.

♿ 🐐 ✿ 🚙 🚌 ☕ ⁍))

GROUP OPENING

13 NEW DINMORE GARDENS
Dinmore, Hereford, HR1 3JR. *8m N of Hereford, 8m S of Leominster. From Hereford on A49, turn R at bottom of Dinmore Hill towards Bodenham, gardens 1m on L. From Leominster on A49, L onto A417, 2m turn R & through Bodenham, following NGS signs to garden.* **Sat 23, Sun 24 Apr (11-5). Combined adm £7.50, chd free. Home-made teas at Southbourne garden.**

NEW HILL HOUSE
Guy & Pippa Heath.

NEW PINE LODGE
Frank Ryding.

SOUTHBOURNE
Graham & Lavinia Sole.

3 neighbouring gardens with panoramic views over Bodenham Lakes to the Malvern Hills and Black Mountains. Hill House: New opening for 2022, a 2 acre garden on the lower slopes of Dinmore Hill, bordering the Bodenham Lake Nature Reserve. Pine Lodge: 2½ acres of woodland featuring most of Britain's native trees. Goblins are thought to live here! Southbourne: 2 acre, terraced garden with herbaceous beds, shrubs, pond and ornamental woodland. Tickets sold at Hill House.

 🐐 ☕ 🍽 ⁍))

In 2021 the National Garden Scheme donation helped support Perennial's caseworkers, who helped over 250 people and their families in crisis to receive a wide range of support including emergency food parcels and accommodation, energy payments and expert advice and information

⁴ ♦ THE GARDEN OF THE WIND AT MIDDLE HUNT HOUSE

Walterstone, Hereford, HR2 0DY. Rupert & Antoinetta Otten, 01873 860359, gardenofthewind@gmail.com, www.gardenofthewind.co.uk. *4m W of Pandy, 17m S of Hereford, 10m N of Abergavenny. A465 to Pandy, W towards Longtown, turn R at Clodock Church, 1m on R. Disabled parking available. SatNav may take you via a different route but indicates arrival at adjacent farm.* **For NGS: Sat 25, Sun 26 June, Sat 27, Sun 28 Aug (2-6). Adm £5, chd free. Home-made teas. For other opening times and information, please phone, email or visit garden website.**

A modern garden using swathes of herbaceous plants and grasses, surrounding stone built farmhouse and barns with stunning views of the Black Mountains. Special features: rose border, hornbeam alley, formal parterre and water rill and fountains, William Pye water feature, architecturally designed greenhouse and RIBA bridge, vegetable gardens. Carved lettering and sculpture throughout, garden covering about 4 acres. Garden seating throughout the site on stone, wood and metal benches inc some with carved lettering. Water rill and fountains. Partial wheelchair access but WC facilities not easily accessible due to gravel.

⁵ GRANGE COURT

Pinsley Road, Leominster, HR6 8NL. Leominster Area Regeneration Company, www.grangecourt.org. *Grange Court in the centre of Leominster, accessible by car via Church St but not Pinsley Rd via Etnam St. Short walk from Broad St & Etnam St car parks.* **Sun 12, Sun 26 June (10-5). Adm £5, chd free. Light refreshments.**

Set in the beautiful, tranquil Grange, Leominster's C17 market hall, Grange Court, has an ornate knot garden edged by the Saverne roses from our twin in France and the woodland garden to the front. Behind is the beautiful walled garden planted with a variety of roses, climbers and herbaceous flowers in the informal style of Marjory Fish. The Victorian Folly adds a little bit of kitsch! There will be a display of beautiful garden sculptures from the Metalsmiths,

Claudia Petley and Paul Shepherd. Open for visitors to see the various displays and the extraordinary exhibition of the history of Leominster in embroidery by Leominster in Stitches subject to Covid Restrictions. Wheelchair access, the gardens and building are fully accessible. We have accessible WC, baby-changing facilities and a walk-in shower available.

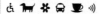

⁶ GRENDON COURT

Upton Bishop, Ross-on-Wye, HR9 7QP. Mark & Kate Edwards. *3m NE of Ross-on-Wye. M50, J3. Hereford B4224 'Moody Cow Pub', 1m open gate on R. From Ross. A40, B449, Xrds R Upton Bishop. 100yds on L by cream cottage.* **Sat 11 June, Sun 11 Sept (11-4). Adm £5, chd free. Picnics welcome in carpark field.**

A contemporary garden designed by Tom Stuart-Smith. Planted on two levels, a clever collection of mass-planted perennials and grasses of different heights, textures and colour give all yr interest. The upper walled garden with a sea of flowering grasses makes a highlight. Views of the new pond and valley walk. Opening in conjuction with Brockhampton Cottage. Wheelchair access possible but some gravel.

⁷ HERBFARMACY

The Field, Eardisley, Hereford, HR3 6NB. Paul Richards, www.herbfarmacy.com. *11m NW of Hereford. Take A438 from Hereford, turn onto A4112 to Leominster, then A4111 to Eardisley. In Eardisley turn L off A4111 by Tram Inn & tram R 3 times. Farm is at end of No Through Road on L.* **Fri 15, Sat 16, Thur 21, Fri 22 July (10-4). Adm £5, chd free. Light refreshments.**

A 4 acre organic herb farm overlooking the Wye valley with views to the Black Mountains. Featured on BBC Countryfile, crops are grown for use in herbal skincare and medicinal products. Colourful plots of Echinacea, Marshmallow, Mullein and Calendula will be on show as well as displays on making products. Light refreshments will be available along with a shop selling Herbfarmacy products. Wheelchair Access possible when dry with assistance but some ground rough and some slopes.

⁸ ♦ HEREFORD CATHEDRAL GARDENS

Hereford, HR1 2NG. Dean of Hereford Cathedral, 01432 374251, visits@herefordcathedral.org, www.herefordcathedral.org/garden-tours. *Centre of Hereford. Approach rds to the Cathedral are signed. Tours leave from information desk in the cathedral building or as directed.* **For NGS: Sat 25 June (10-3). Adm £5, chd free. Light refreshments on-site Cafe. For other opening times and information, please phone, email or visit garden website.**

A guided tour of late C15 historic award-winning gardens. Tours inc colourful courtyard garden, an atmospheric cloisters garden enclosed by C15 buildings, the Vicars Choral garden, with plants with ecclesiastical connections and roses, the private Dean's Garden and the Bishop's Garden with fine trees and an outdoor chapel for meditation in ancient surroundings. Partial wheelchair access. Tours can be adapted to suit individual needs. For more information please visit website.

⁹ HILLCROFT

Coombes Moor, Presteigne, LD8 2HY. Liz O'Rourke & Michael Clarke, 01544 262795, lorconsulting@hotmail.co.uk. *North Herefordshire, 10m from Leominster. Coombes Moor is under Wapley Hill on the B4362, between Shobdon & Presteigne. Garden on R just beyond Byton Cross when heading W* **Tue 21, Wed 22, Thur 23 June (11-5). Adm £4, chd free. Home-made teas. Visits also by arrangement June & July.**

The garden is part of a 5 acre site on the lower slopes of Wapley Hill in the beautiful Lugg Valley. The highlight in mid summer is the romantic Rose Walk, combining over sixty roses with mixed herbaceous planting set in an old cider apple orchard. In addition to the garden area around the house, there is a secret garden, wildflower meadow and a vegetable and fruit area. Tea, coffee and cold drinks along with delicious home-made cakes can be enjoyed in the garden or the conservatory.

20 THE HURST
Bosbury Road, Cradley, Malvern,
WR13 5LT. Clare Gogerty. *16m E
of Hereford, 11m W of Worcester.
'The Hurst' is situated directly on
the Bosbury Rd. From the junction
of A4103 & B4220, garden is 0.7m
towards Bosbury on the L. On-road
parking.* **Sun 26 June (12-4). Adm
£5, chd free. Home-made teas.**
A south facing country garden/
smallholding of 1½ acres with
ornamental garden, moon gate,
vegetable plot, polytunnel, cutting
garden, hens and orchard with a
stream and views of the Malvern
Hills. Mostly level but gently sloping
gravel and grass track to lower area.
Orchard not suitable for wheelchairs.

A productive smallholding. Plants for
sale. Tea and cake. Gently sloping
gravel and grass track to lower area.
Orchard not suitable for wheelchairs.

21 IVY CROFT
Ivington Green, Leominster,
HR6 0JN. Roger
Norman, 01568 720344,
ivycroft@homecall.co.uk,
www.ivycroftgarden.co.uk. *3m
SW of Leominster. From Leominster
take Ryelands Rd to Ivington. Turn R
at church, garden ¾m on R. From
A4110 signed Ivington, garden 1¾m
on L.* **Every Thur 27 Jan to 3 Mar
(10-4). Home-made teas. Every
Wed 30 Mar to 12 Oct (10-4).**

**Sat 30 Apr, Sun 1 May (11-4).
Home-made teas. Open nearby
Aulden Farm. Sun 24 July, Sun
18 Sept (11-4). Home-made teas.
Adm £5, chd free. Visits also by
arrangement.**
Now 25 yrs old, the garden shows
signs of maturity, inc some surprising
trees. A very wide range of plants is
displayed, blending with countryside
and providing habitat for wildlife. The
cottage is surrounded by borders,
raised beds, trained pear trees and
containers giving all year interest.
Paths lead to the wider garden inc
mixed borders, vegetables framed
with espalier apples. Snowdrops.
Partial wheelchair access.

Hereford Cathedral Gardens

22 KENTCHURCH COURT

Pontrilas, HR2 0DB. Mrs Jan Lucas-Scudamore, 01981 240228, joss@kentchurch-estate.com, www.kentchurchcourt.co.uk. *12m SW of Hereford. From Hereford A465 towards Abergavanny, at Pontrilas turn L signed Kentchurch. After 2m fork L, after Bridge Inn. Garden opp church.* **Fri 27 May, Fri 1 July, Fri 23 Sept (11-4.30). Adm £7.50, chd free. Home-made teas. Visits also by arrangement May to Oct. House tours available via enquiry@ kentchurch.co.uk.**

Kentchurch Court is sited close to the Welsh border. The large stately home dates to C11 and has been in the Scudamore family for over 1000yrs The deer-park surrounding the house dates back to the Knights Hospitallers of Dinmore and lies at the heart of an estate of over 5000 acres. Historical characters associated with the house inc Welsh hero Owain Glendower, whose daughter married Sir John Scudamore. The house was modernised by John Nash in 1795. First opened for NGS in 1927. Formal rose garden, traditional vegetable garden redesigned with colour, scent and easy access. Walled garden and herbaceous borders, rhododendrons and wildflower walk. Deer-park and ancient woodland. Extensive collection of mature trees and shrubs. Stream with habitat for spawning trout. Wheelchair access, some slopes, shallow gravel.

23 THE LASKETT GARDENS

Much Birch, Hereford, HR2 8HZ. Perennial, www.perennial.org.uk. *Approx 7m from Hereford; 7m from Ross. On A49, midway between Ross-on-Wye & Hereford, turn into Laskett Lane towards Hoarwithy. The drive is approx 350yds on L.* **Wed 6 July (10.30-4). Adm £10, chd free. Visits also by arrangement July & Aug.**

The Laskett Gardens are the largest private formal gardens to be created in England since 1945 consisting of 4 acres of stunning garden rooms inc rose and knot gardens, fountains, statuary, topiary and a Belvedere from which to view the gardens on high. Partial wheelchair access.

 ♿ ☕ ⚫))

24 NEW LOWER BROOK

Buckcastle, Bridstow, Ross-On-Wye, HR9 6QF. Mr & Mrs Steve Richards. *1m from Ross on Wye. From the Wilton r'about on A40 take A49 Hereford exit. Take 2nd turning R (towards Hoarwithy) then the 2nd turning on L (looks like straight on). Follow signs. Parking for 6 cars.* **Sun 20, Mon 21 Mar, Sun 9, Mon 10 Oct (11-4). Adm £5, chd free. Pre-booking essential, please visit www.ngs.org.uk for information & booking. Light refreshments. Tea, coffee, home-made cakes.**

A sloping, landscaped garden of 2 acres inc a mixture of hard landscaping, a waterfall, lawns, flower beds and 124 trees (some exotic species) and a similar number of shrubs. Particular highlights in spring are the daffodils, tulips and snowdrops while in the early autumn there is a blaze of colour from the trees. Some parts of the garden only accessible by steps.

25 LOWER HOPE

Lower Hope Estate, Ullingswick, Hereford, HR1 3JF. Mrs Clive Richards, www.lowerhopegardens.co.uk. *5m S of Bromyard. A465 N from Hereford, after 6m turn L at Burley Gate onto A417 towards Leominster. After approx 2m take 3rd R to Lower Hope. After ½m garden on L. Disabled parking available.* **Sun 10 Apr, Sun 22 May, Sun 11 Sept (2-5). Adm £7.50, chd £2. Light refreshments.**

The Laskett Gardens

Outstanding 5 acre garden with wonderful seasonal variations. Impeccable lawns with herbaceous borders, rose gardens, white garden, Mediterranean, Italian and Japanese gardens. Natural streams, man-made waterfalls, bog gardens. Woodland with azaleas and rhododendrons with lime avenue to lake with wild flowers and bulbs. Glasshouses with exotic plants and breeding butterflies. Wildflower lake. Tickets brought on the gate will be cash only. Wheelchair access to most areas.

26 LOWER HOUSE FARM
Vine Lane, Sutton, Tenbury Wells, WR15 8RL. Mrs Anne Durston Smith, 07891 928412, adskyre@outlook.com, www.kyre-equestrian.co.uk. *3m SE of Tenbury Wells; 8m NW of Bromyard. From Tenbury take A4214 to Bromyard. After approx 3m turn R into Vine Lane, then R fork to Lower House Farm.* **Sun 24 Apr, Sun 22 May, Sun 19 June (10-4). Adm £5, chd free. Home-made teas.** Award-winning country garden surrounding C16 farm-house (not open) on working farm. Herbaceous borders, roses, box-parterre, productive kitchen and cutting garden, spring garden, ha-ha allowing wonderful views. Wildlife pond. Walkers and dogs can enjoy numerous footpaths across the farm land. Home to Kyre Equestrian Centre with access to safe rides and riding events.

27 MICHAELCHURCH COURT
St Owen's Cross, Hereford, HR2 8LD. John & Kathy Handby. *7m N of Ross-on-Wye. On A4137 Hereford/Monmouth Rd, coming from St Owen's Cross in the direction of Hereford, take small, unmarked lane 200 yds on L, garden 1m on L.* **Sun 3 July (11-4). Adm £5, chd free. Light refreshments. Home-made cakes and tea/ coffee.** Early C17 house (not open), in open countryside near Norman church. Approx 2 acres inc large pond, brook with flower borders. Old-fashioned roses and herbaceous borders set amongst lawns, one long border backed by high wall covered with climbing roses, honeysuckle and wisteria. Long pergola covered with roses, honeysuckle, clematis and wisteria leads to sunken garden

with water feature and seating area. Climbing roses and hydrangeas cover house. Small arboretum. Winner of Harewood End Agricultural Society best kept garden competition. Small exhibition of the history of the property from its origins as a mill to becoming the centre of a farming community in the C19.

28 NEW MILLFIELD HOUSE
Eaton Bishop, Hereford, HR2 9QS. Angela & Richard Mainwaring, 01981 251331, angela.mainwaring@ngs.org.uk. *4m SW of Hereford. A465 W to B4349 Hay on Wye. Approx 2m L in Clehonger B4349 to Kingstone. l00yds after 40mph sign R into lane 'unsuitable for long or wide vehicles'. Follow yellow signs.* **Fri 27, Sun 29 May, Fri 5, Sun 7 Aug (11-5). Adm £5, chd free. Tea, coffee and cakes for visitors to help themselves. Visits also by arrangement May to Sept for groups of up to 20.** 1½ acre informal country garden shared with wildlife. The terrace and vegetable garden are enclosed by pergolas, espalier fruit trees and raised borders. Grass paths connect the open and woodland borders, ponds, and wildflower meadow while formal and native hedges and trees enclose and divide the different areas

29 ◆ MOORS MEADOW GARDENS
Collington, Bromyard, HR7 4LZ. Ros Bissell, 01885 410318/07942 636153, moorsmeadow@hotmail.co.uk, www.moorsmeadow.co.uk. *4m N of Bromyard, on B4214. ½m up lane follow yellow arrows.* **For NGS: Mon 11 Apr, Mon 16 May, Mon 13 June, Mon 4 July, Mon 1 Aug (10-5). Adm £7, chd £1.50. For other opening times and information, please phone, email or visit garden website.** 7 acre organic hillside garden with a vast amount of species, many rarely seen, an emphasis on working with nature to create a wildlife haven. With intriguing features and sculptures it is an inspiration to the garden novice as well as the serious plantsman. Wander through fernery, grass garden, extensive shrubberies, herbaceous beds, meadow, dingle, pools and kitchen garden. Resident Blacksmith. Huge range of unusual

and rarely seen plants from around the world. Unique home-crafted sculptures.

30 NEW NEW HOUSE FARM
Moccas, Hereford, HR2 9LA. Rachel Jenkins, newhousemoccas.farm. *Drive from Hereford on A438, turning L to Bredwardine, & L again to Moccas. At the Moccas Xrds, carry on towards Blakemere for 200 yds, & take a hidden farm track on R. New House is 100 yds down a farm track, around 200 yds E of Moccas Xrds.* **Sat 18, Sun 19, Sat 25, Sun 26 June (1.30-6). Adm £5, chd free. Cream teas.** Informal, wildlife friendly 1½ acre garden under development, surrounding C16 house and C17 barn, surrounded by cider apple orchards, comprising herb garden, white garden, woodland garden, wildflower meadows, herbaceous borders, ice age pond, plum walk, orchard fruit and vegetable garden, and over 100 different varieties of old roses. Over 100 varieties of old roses Ice age pond Herb garden White garden Fruit and vegetable garden Woodland garden Wildflower meadows.

31 THE NUTSHELL
Goodrich, Ross-on-Wye, HR9 6HG. Louise Short. *The garden is half way between Ross on Wye & Monmouth, close to the A40 & the Cross Keys pub.* **Sun 5 June (10-4). Adm £5, chd free. Light refreshments.** The Nutshell is a cottage garden in approx ½ an acre, created from scratch over the last 20 yrs. The garden is made up of different areas separated by herbaceous borders and rose arches.There is a lovely selection of plants used inc many peonys and an extensive collection of hostas. The owner has a keen interest in propagation with two polytunnels of plants available to purchase.

Around 1,050 people living with Parkinson's - and their families - have been helped by Parkinson's nurses thanks to funding from the National Garden Scheme

Church Cottage

32 OLD COLWALL HOUSE
Old Colwall, Malvern, WR13 6HF.
Mr & Mrs Roland Trafford-Roberts.
*3m NE of Ledbury. From Ledbury,
turn L off A449 to Malvern towards
Coddington. Signed from 2½m
along lane. Signed from Colwall &
Bosbury. Visitors will need to walk
from car park to garden.* **Sun 26
June (2-5). Adm £5, chd free.
Home-made teas.**
Early C18 garden on a site owned by
the Church till Henry VIII. Brick-walled
lawns on various levels. The heart
is the yew walk, a rare survival from
the 1700s: 100 yds long, 30ft high,
cloud clipped, and with a church
aisle-like quality inside. Later centuries
have brought a summerhouse, water
garden, and rock gardens. Fine trees,
inc enormous veteran yew; fine views.
Steep in places. C18 yew walk C18
walled gardens.

33 THE OLD CORN MILL
Aston Crews, Ross-on-
Wye, HR9 7LW. Mrs Jill
Hunter, 01989 750059,
mjhunterross@outlook.com,
www.theoldcornmillgarden.com.
*5m E of Ross-on-Wye. A40 Ross
to Gloucester. Turn L at T-lights
at Lea Xrds onto B4222 signed
Newent, Garden ½m on L.
Parking for disabled down drive.
For SatNavs use HR9 7LA* **Visits
by arrangement Feb to Oct for
groups of up to 50. Home-made
teas. Tea, coffee and cakes inc
in adm.**
Snowdrops in February, Daffodils in
March, Tulips in April, Orchids in May.
Do come and enjoy the calm of this
very natural valley garden. Pretty good
cakes too. Prize winning conversion
of a ruined C18 mill.

34 OLD GROVE
Llangrove, Ross-On-Wye,
HR9 6HA. Ken & Lynette Knowles.
*Between Ross & Monmouth. 2m off
A40 at Whitchurch. Disabled parking
at house otherwise follow signs for
parking in nearby field.* **Sun 4 Sept
(2-6). Adm £5, chd free. Home-
made teas.**
1½ acre garden plus two fields.
South west facing with unspoilt views.
Lots of mixed beds with plenty of late
summer colour and many unusual
plants. Large collection of dahlias
and salvias; wildlife pond; formal herb
garden; masses of pots; interesting

trees. Seating throughout. Wheelchair
access, gentle slopes, some steps
but accessible.

35 NEW THE OLD VICARAGE
Wellington Heath, Ledbury,
HR8 1NA. Gavin James. *Next door
to the Church. Leaving Ledbury on
the Bromyard Rd take 1st rd to your
R (Beggars Ash) proceed to the top
of the Hill & turn L onto Church Lane.*
**Sat 14, Sun 15 May (10.30-5).
Adm £7.50, chd free. Home-made
teas at Wellington Heath church.**
The Old Vicarage abuts the Church.
This 2½ acre garden is set in a
valley with formal lawns leading into
a wooded area. Wheelchair access,
gravel paths lead you round the
garden and are suitable for a powered
wheelchair.

36 ◆ THE PICTON GARDEN
Old Court Nurseries, Walwyn
Road, Colwall, WR13 6QE. Mr &
Mrs Paul Picton, 01684 540416,
oldcourtnurseries@btinternet.com,
www.autumnasters.co.uk. *3m W of
Malvern. On B4218 (Walwyn Rd) N
of Colwall Stone. Turn off A449 from
Ledbury or Malvern onto the B4218
for Colwall.* **For NGS: Sun 13, Sun
27 Feb, Sun 20 Mar (11-4); Sun
10 Apr, Sun 1, Sun 29 May, Sun
19 June, Sun 10 July, Tue 16
Aug, Tue 20 Sept, Thur 20 Oct
(11-5). Adm £4, chd free. 2023:
Sun 12, Sun 26 Feb. For other
opening times and information,
please phone, email or visit
garden website. Donation to Plant
Heritage.**
1½ acres west of Malvern Hills.
Bulbs and a multitude of woodland
plants in spring. Interesting perennials
and shrubs in Aug. In late Sept and
early Oct colourful borders display
the National Plant Collection of
Michaelmas daisies, backed by
autumn colouring trees and shrubs.
Many unusual plants to be seen, inc
more than 100 different ferns and
acers. Features raised beds and silver
garden. National Plant Collection
of autumn-flowering asters and an
extensive nursery that has been
growing them since 1906.

37 POOLE COTTAGE
Coppett Hill, Goodrich, Ross-on-
Wye, HR9 6JH. Jo Ward-Ellison
& Roy Smith, 07718 229813,
jo@ward-ellison.com. *5m from
Ross on Wye, 7m from Monmouth.
Above Goodrich Castle in Wye Valley
AONB. Goodrich signed from A40
or take B4234 from Ross.* **Visits
by arrangement July & Aug for
groups of up to 20. Parking at
garden limited to 5 cars only.
Adm £5, chd free. Home-made
teas.**
A modern country garden in
keeping with the local natural
landscape. Home to designer Jo
Ward-Ellison the 2 acre garden is
predominately naturalistic in style with
a contemporary feel. A long season
of interest with grasses and later
flowering perennials. Some steep
slopes, steps and uneven paths.
Features inc a small orchard, a pond
loved by wildlife and kitchen garden
with fabulous views.

38 ◆ RALPH COURT GARDENS
Edwyn Ralph, Bromyard,
Hereford, HR7 4LU. Mr &
Mrs Morgan, 01885 483225,
ralphcourtgardens@aol.com,
www.ralphcourtgardens.co.uk.
*From Bromyard follow the Tenbury
rd for approx 1m. On entering the
village of Edwyn Ralph take 1st
turning on R towards the church.*
**For NGS: Sat 19, Sun 20 Mar, Sat
2, Sun 3 July, Sat 8, Sun 9 Oct,
Sat 12, Sun 13 Nov (10-5). Adm
£10, chd £7. Light refreshments.
For other opening times and
information, please phone, email or
visit garden website.**
All tickets must be purchased
through the garden website or at
the gate. 12 amazing gardens set
in the grounds of a gothic rectory. A
family orientated garden with a twist,
incorporating an Italian Piazza, an
African Jungle, Dragon Pool, Alice
in Wonderland and the elves in their
conifer forest and our new section
'The Monet Garden'. These are just a
few of the themes within this stunning
garden. Overlooking the Malvern Hills
120 seater Licenced Restaurant.
Offering a good selection of daily
specials, delicious Sunday roasts,
Afternoon tea and our scrumptious
homemade cakes. All areas ramped
for wheelchair and pushchair access.
Some grass areas, without help can
be challenging during wet periods.

39 REVILO
Wellington, Hereford, HR4 8AZ.
Mrs Shirley Edgar, 01432 830189,
Shirleyskinner@btinternet.com. *6m
N of Hereford. On A49 from Hereford
turn L into Wellington village, pass
church on R. Then just after barn on
L, turn L up driveway in front of The
Harbour, to furthest bungalow.* **Visits
by arrangement Apr to Oct for
groups of up to 25.**
⅓ acre garden surrounding bungalow
inc mixed borders, meadow and
woodland areas, scented garden, late
summer bed, gravelled herb garden
and vegetable/fruit garden. Flower
arranger's garden. Wheelchair access
to all central areas of the garden from
the garage side.

40 RHODDS FARM
Lyonshall, HR5 3LW.
Richard & Cary Goode,
www.rhoddsfarm.co.uk. *1m E of
Kington. From A44 take small turning
S just E of Penrhos Farm, 1m E
of Kington. Continue 1m, garden
straight ahead (a little further than
SatNav sends you).* **Sun 17 July
(11-5). Adm £5, chd free. Home-
made teas available for visitors to
help themselves.**
Created by the owner, a garden
designer, over the past 16 yrs, the
garden contains an extensive range
of interesting plants. Formal garden
with dovecote and 100 white doves,
mixed borders, double herbaceous
borders of hot colours, large gravel
garden, three ponds, arboretum,
perennial and wildflower meadows
and 13 acres of woodland. A natural
garden that fits the setting with
magnificent views. Interesting and
unusual trees, shrubs and perennials.
A natural garden on a challenging site.
A number of sculptures by different
artists. No pesticides used.

41 SHEEPCOTE
Putley, Ledbury, HR8 2RD. Tim &
Julie Beaumont. *5m W of Ledbury
off the A438 Hereford to Ledbury Rd.
Passenger drop off; parking 200 yds.*
**Sat 28 May (12-5.30). Adm £5, chd
free. Light refreshments.**
⅓ acre garden taken in hand
from 2011 retaining many quality
plants, shrubs and trees from
earlier gardeners. Topiary holly, box,
hawthorn, privet and yew formalise
the varied plantings around the
croquet lawn and gravel garden;
beds with heathers, azaleas, lavender

surrounded by herbaceous perennials
and bulbs; small ponds; kitchen
garden with raised beds.

42 SHUTTIFIELD COTTAGE
Birchwood, Storridge,
WR13 5HA. Mr & Mrs David
Judge, 01886 884243,
judge.shutti@btinternet.com.
*15m E of Hereford. Turn L off
A4103 at Storridg opp the Church
to Birchwood. After 1¼m L down
steep tarmac drive. Please park on
roadside at the top of the drive but
drive down if walking is difficult (150
yards).* **Visits by arrangement Apr
to Sept. Adm £5, chd free. Home-
made teas.**
Superb position and views.
Unexpected 3 acre plantsman's
garden, extensive herbaceous borders,
primula and stump bed, many unusual
trees, shrubs, perennials, colour
themed for all year interest. Anemones,
bluebells, rhododendrons, azaleas
and camelias are a particular spring
feature. Large old rose garden with
many spectacular climbers. Small deer
park, vegetable garden and 20 acre
wood. Wildlife ponds, wild flowers and
walks in 20 acres of ancient woodland.

43 ◆ STOCKTON BURY GARDENS
Kimbolton, HR6 0HA. Raymond
G Treasure, 07880 712649,
twstockton@outlook.com,
www.stocktonbury.co.uk. *2m NE
of Leominster. From Leominster to
Ludlow on A49 turn R onto A4112.
Gardens 300yds on R.* **For NGS:
Fri 1 Apr (11-4.30). Adm £8.50,
chd free. Home-made teas
in Tithe Barn Cafe. For other
opening times and information,
please phone, email or visit garden
website.**
Superb, sheltered 4 acre garden with
colour and interest from April until
the end of September. Extensive
collection of plants, many rare and
unusual set amongst medieval
buildings. Features pigeon house,
tithe barn, grotto, cider press, auricula
theatre, pools, secret garden, garden
museum and rill, all surrounded by
unspoilt countryside. Garden museum
and Roman hoard. Home made
Teas, Light Refreshments, Wine in
Tithe Barn Cafe. Partial wheelchair
access. A fit able bodied companion
is advisable for wheelchair users.

44 NEW UPLANDS & UPLANDS COTTAGE
Burtons Lane, Wellington
Heath, Ledbury, HR8 1NF. Stuart
Atkinson, Kiel Shaw & Becky and
Mark Le Brocq. *For parking: drive
past Uplands Cottage & drive past
Upland & the car park will be signed
on L.* **Thur 16, Fri 17, Sat 18 June
(11-4). Adm £7.50, chd free.
Home-made teas.**
Uplands Cottage garden was
designed in the early 2000s. Now
an established garden, it has a vast
collection of plants and flowers
arranged in rooms after the style of
the Arts and Crafts. Uplands garden
has been created over the last 5
yrs and is evolving over time. The
extensive Kitchen Garden was begun
in 2020 and is central to the way of
life at Uplands. Uplands Cottage -
most of the garden is accessible as
long as the wheelchair can go through
gravel and over grass. Uplands is
accessible all areas.

45 THE VINE
Tarrington, HR1 4EX. Richard &
Tonya Price. *Between Hereford &
Ledbury on A438. On School Lane,
Tarrington village S of the A438. Park
as directed. Disabled parking only at
house.* **Sun 3 July (2-6). Adm £5,
chd free. Cream teas.**
Mature, traditional garden in peaceful
setting with stunning views of the
surrounding countryside. Consisting
of various rooms with mixed and
herbaceous borders. Secret garden
in blue/yellow/white, croquet lawn
with C18 summerhouse, temple
garden with ponds, herb and nosegay
garden, vegetable/cutting/soft fruit
garden around greenhouse in the
paddock. Cornus avenues with
obelisk and willow bower.

46 WAINFIELD
Peterstow, Ross-On-Wye,
HR9 6LJ. Nick & Sue Helme,
01989 730663. *From the A49
between Ross-on-Wye & Hereford.
Take the B4521 to Skenfrith/
Abergavenny. Wainfeild is 50yds on
R.* **Sat 26 Mar, Thur 26, Fri 27, Sat
28 May, Fri 1, Sat 2 July (10.30-4).
Adm £5, chd free. Home-made
teas. Visits also by arrangement
Feb to July for groups of 25 to 50.**
3 acre informal, wildlife garden inc
rose garden, fruit trees, climbing
roses and clematis. Delightful pond

with waterfall. Climbing roses, many different clematis and honeysuckle. In spring, tulips, bluebells, crocuses and grasses followed by lush summer planting. Fruit walk with naturalised cowslips all set in an open area of interesting, unusual mature trees and sculptures. Wheelchair access on uneven grass.

 ✿ ☕ ⋅))

47 22 WESTFIELD WALK

Leominster, HR6 8HD. Mr Vic & Mrs Sue Hamer. *Westfield Walk can be accessed from both Bargates Rd & Ryelands Rd.* **Sun 10 July (12-4.30). Adm £4, chd free. Home-made teas.**
A flower arranger's haven amongst the bustling town, this terraced garden is full of many unusual plants in various mixed borders and boasts a bog garden and large working vegetable and fruit area. Year-round colour is ensured with such a variety of flora and fauna on show. Plants for sale. Partial wheelchair access. Some steps and steeper slopes.

 ✿ ☕

48 WESTON HALL

Weston-under-Penyard, Ross-on-Wye, HR9 7NS. Mr P & Miss L Aldrich-Blake, 01989 562597, aldrichblake@btinternet.com. *1m E of Ross-on-Wye. On A40 towards Gloucester.* **Visits by arrangement Apr to Sept for groups of 5 to 30. Light refreshments by arrangement for modest extra charge. Adm £5, chd free.**
6 acres surrounding Elizabethan house (not open). Large walled garden with herbaceous borders, vegetables and fruit, overlooked by Millennium folly. Lawns and mature and recently planted trees and shrubs, with many unusual varieties. Orchard, ornamental ponds and lake. 4 generations in the family, but still evolving year on year. Wheelchair access to walled garden only.

&. ☕

49 WHITFIELD

Wormbridge, HR2 9BA. Mr & Mrs Edward Clive, 01981 570202, office@tamsinclive.co.uk, www.whitfield-hereford.com. *8m SW of Hereford. The entrance gates are off the A465 Hereford to Abergavenny rd, ½ m N of Wormbridge.* **Sun 27 Mar, Mon 27 June (2-5). Adm £5, chd free. Home-made teas. Visits also**

by arrangement Mar to July for groups of up to 25. Please call to discuss requirements.
Parkland, wild flowers, ponds, walled garden, many flowering magnolias (species and hybrids), 1780 ginkgo tree, 1½ m woodland walk with 1851 grove of coastal redwood trees. Dogs on leads welcome. Delicious teas. (June). Partial access to wheelchair users, some gravel paths and steep slopes.

&. 🐐 ✿ 🚗 ☕ ⋅))

50 WOODVIEW

Great Doward, Whitchurch, Ross-on-Wye, HR9 6DZ. Janet & Clive Townsend, 01600 890477, janetrtownsend@hotmail.com. *6m SW of Ross-on-Wye, 4m NE of Monmouth. A40 Ross/Mon*

At Whitchurch follow signs to Symonds Yat W, then to Doward Park campsite. Take forestry rd 1st L garden 2nd L - follow NGS signs. (Don't rely on SatNav). **Visits by arrangement Apr & May for groups of up to 25. Adm £5.50, chd free. Home-made teas.**
Formal and informal gardens approx 4 acres in woodland setting. Herbaceous borders, hosta collection, mature trees, shrubs and seasonal bedding. Gently sloping lawns. Statuary and found sculpture, local limestone, rockwork and pools. Woodland garden, wildflower meadow and indigenous orchids. Collection of vintage tools and memorabilia. Croquet, clock golf and garden games.

&. 🐐 ☕

Broxwood Court

HERTFORDSHIRE

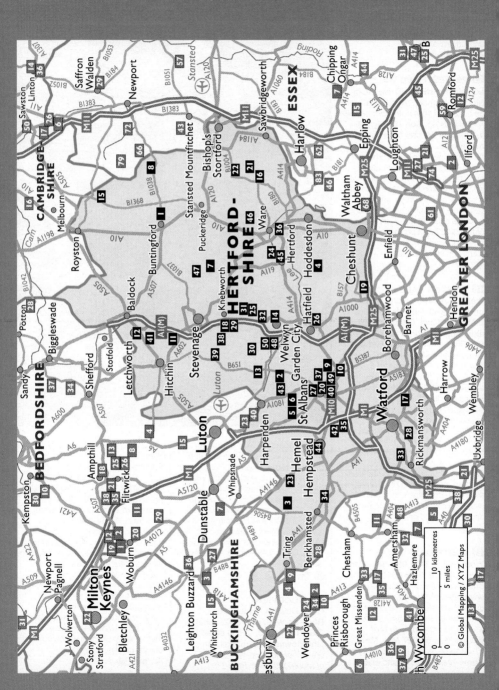

With its proximity to London, Hertfordshire became a breath of country air and a retreat for wealthy families wishing to escape the grime of the city – hence the county is peppered with large and small country estates, some of which open their garden gates for the National Garden Scheme.

We are immensely proud of our horticultural heritage. Our history of market gardening, which supplied vegetables, fruit, and cut flowers to London markets, dates back to the 1600s. We are home to historic houses whose gardens, parklands, and landscapes have associations with such celebrated names as Tradescant, Repton, Jekyll, and Lutyens. And our county is the birthplace of Ebenezer Howard's Garden City Movement.

Now Hertfordshire is very different and across our sprawling urban areas and tiny rural hamlets, we have gardens that offer everything from contemporary garden design to rewilded spaces, from wildflower meadows to productive potagers, from ancient woodlands to tropical oases. There is inspiration for everyone.

Many are open 'by arrangement' for private visits by groups of all sizes and we are happy to provide assistance in arranging group tours of multiple gardens.

Last year was a challenge for everyone involved with our open gardens, and a huge thank you goes to our garden owners and volunteers. Against all the odds Hertfordshire raised a record amount of money – over £100,000 – for our charities. We approach 2022 hopeful that there will be no disruption to our plans, but it is possible that there will be changes at short notice. Our website will always give you the latest information.

Below: Herts Mill House

f @HertfordshireNGS　**y** @HertfordshirNGS　**◎** @hertsngs

Volunteers

County Organisers
Bella Stuart-Smith 07710 099132
bella.stuart-smith@ngs.org.uk

Kate Stuart-Smith 07551 923217
kate.stuart-smith@ngs.org.uk

County Treasurer
Peter Barrett 01442 393508
peter.barrett@ngs.org.uk

Publicity
Kerrie Lloyd-Dawson 07736 442883
kerrie.lloyddawson@ngs.org.uk

Photography
Barbara Goult 07712 131414
barbara.goult@ngs.org.uk

Social Media - Facebook
Anastasia Rezanova
anastasia.rezanova@ngs.org.uk

Social Media - Twitter
Charly Denton-Woods
charlotte.denton-woods@ngs.org.uk

Social Media - Instagram
Rebecca Fincham
rebecca.fincham@ngs.org.uk

Radio
Lucy Swift 07808 737965
lucy.swift@ngs.org.uk

Booklet Coordinator
Janie Nicholas 07973 802929
janie.nicholas@ngs.org.uk

New Gardens
Julie Wise 07759 462330
julie.wise@ngs.org.uk

Group Tours
Sarah Marsh 07813 083126
sarah.marsh@ngs.org.uk

Assistant County Organisers
Vivien Arey 07880 726722
vivien.arey@ngs.org.uk

Tessa Birch 07721682481
tessa.birch@ngs.org.uk

OPENING DATES

All entries subject to change. For latest information check www.ngs.org.uk

Extended openings are shown at the beginning of the month.

Map locator numbers are shown to the right of each garden name.

February

Snowdrop Festival

Wednesday 2nd
8 Gosselin Road — 24

Friday 4th
8 Gosselin Road — 24

Saturday 5th
Walkern Hall — 47

Sunday 6th
Walkern Hall — 47

Tuesday 8th
◆ Benington Lordship — 7

Wednesday 9th
8 Gosselin Road — 24

Friday 18th
1 Elia Cottage — 16

Sunday 20th
1 Elia Cottage — 16

March

Saturday 19th
◆ Hatfield House West Garden — 26

Saturday 26th
Walkern Hall — 47

Sunday 27th
Amwell Cottage — 2
Walkern Hall — 47

April

Sunday 3rd
◆ St Paul's Walden Bury — 39

Sunday 10th
Alswick Hall — 1

Monday 18th
10 Cross Street — 12

May

Sunday 1st
Patchwork — 34
Pie Corner — 35
Serendi — 41

Sunday 8th
◆ Benington Lordship — 7

Sunday 15th
39 Firs Wood Close — 19
◆ St Paul's Walden Bury — 39

Saturday 21st
The Manor House, Ayot St Lawrence — 30

Sunday 22nd
The Manor House, Ayot St Lawrence — 30
43 Mardley Hill — 31
NEW The Pines — 36

Friday 27th
Railway Cottage — 37

Sunday 29th
Beesonend House — 6
28 Dale Avenue — 13
15 Gade Valley Cottages — 23
Railway Cottage — 37

June

Every day from Sunday 26th
42 Falconer Road — 17

Thursday 2nd
The Mill House — 32

Friday 3rd
The White Cottage — 50

Saturday 4th
Brent Pelham Hall — 8
The Mill House — 32

Sunday 5th
Brent Pelham Hall — 8
The Cherry Tree — 11
9 Tannsfield Drive — 44

Sunday 12th
Dovehouse Shott — 15
Morning Light — 33

◆ St Paul's Walden Bury — 39
Thundridge Hill House — 46

Tuesday 14th
◆ Ashridge House — 3

Wednesday 15th
◆ Ashridge House — 3

Thursday 16th
◆ Ashridge House — 3

Sunday 19th
Bayford Musical Gardens Day — 4
Serge Hill Gardens — 42

Friday 24th
28 Fishpool Street — 20
Foxglove Cottage — 21

Saturday 25th
Waterend House — 48

Sunday 26th
28 Fishpool Street — 20
NEW Gable House — 22
St Stephens Avenue Gardens — 40
Southdown Gardens — 43

July

Every day to Sunday 3rd
42 Falconer Road — 17

Friday 1st
NEW 16 Langley Crescent — 27
Pie Corner — 35

Saturday 2nd
NEW 16 Langley Crescent — 27

Sunday 3rd
Pie Corner — 35
9 Tannsfield Drive — 44

Friday 8th
Field End House — 18
NEW Manor Farmhouse — 29
14 Watling Street — 49

Saturday 9th
14 Watling Street — 49

Sunday 10th
Beesonend Gardens — 5
Field End House — 18
NEW Manor Farmhouse — 29

Friday 15th
102 Cambridge Road — 9

Sunday 17th
102 Cambridge Road — 9
15 Gade Valley Cottages — 23

Friday 22nd
Greenwood House — 25
Rustling End Cottage — 38

Saturday 23rd
Rustling End Cottage — 38

Sunday 24th
Greenwood House — 25
Morning Light — 33

Sunday 31st
35 Digswell Road — 14
12 Longmans Close — 28

August

Saturday 6th
NEW Terrace House Garden — 45

Sunday 7th
12 Longmans Close — 28

Sunday 21st
Patchwork — 34

September

Every day from Saturday 3rd to Sunday 11th
◆ The Celebration Garden — 10

Saturday 3rd
102 Cambridge Road — 9

Sunday 4th
St Stephens Avenue Gardens — 40

Sunday 11th
NEW The Pines — 36

Sunday 18th
Alswick Hall — 1

Wednesday 28th
8 Gosselin Road — 24

October

Wednesday 5th
8 Gosselin Road — 24

November

Sunday 6th

42 Falconer Road   17

By Arrangement

Arrange a personalised garden visit with your club, or group of friends, on a date to suit you. See individual garden entries for full details.

THE GARDENS

1 ALSWICK HALL

Hare Street Road, Buntingford, SG9 0AA. Mike & Annie Johnson, alswick_annie@yahoo.co.uk, www.alswickhall.com/gardens. *1m from Buntingford on B1038. From the S take A10 to Buntingford, drive into town & take B1038 E towards Hare Street Village. Alswick Hall is 1m on R.* **Sun 10 Apr, Sun 18 Sept (12-4). Adm £8, chd free. Home-made teas. Hog roast. Visits also by arrangement.**

Listed Tudor House with 5 acres of landscaped gardens set in unspoiled farmland. Two well established natural ponds with rockeries. Herbaceous borders, shrubs, woodland walk and wildflower meadow with a fantastic selection of daffodils, tulips, camassias and crown imperials. Later in the year enjoy the spectacular dahlia beds and late season planting. Formal beds, orchard and glasshouses. Licensed Bar, Hog Roast, Teas, delicious home-made cakes, plant stall and various other trade stands, children's entertainment. Good access for disabled with lawns and wood chip paths. Slight undulations.

♿ 🐴 ✿ 🚗 ☕))

2 AMWELL COTTAGE

Amwell Lane, Wheathampstead, AL4 8EA. Colin & Kate Birss. *½m S of Wheathampstead. From St Helen's Church, Wheathampstead turn up Brewhouse Hill. At top L fork (Amwell Lane), 300yds down lane, park in field opp.* **Sun 27 Mar (2-5). Adm £5, chd free. Home-made teas.**

Informal garden of approx 2½ acres around C17 cottage. Large orchard of mature apples, plums and pear laid out with paths. Extensive lawns with borders, framed by tall yew hedges and old brick walls. A large variety of roses, stone seats with views, woodland pond, greenhouse, vegetable garden with raised beds and fire-pit area. Wheelchair access, gravel drive.

♿ 🐴 ✿ 🚗 ☕))

3 ◆ ASHRIDGE HOUSE

Berkhamsted, HP4 1NS. E F Corporate Education Ltd, 01442 841027, events@ashridge.hult.edu, www.ashridgehouse.org.uk. *3m N of Berkhamsted. A4251, 1m S of Little Gaddesden.* **For NGS: Tue 14, Wed 15, Thur 16 June (9-6). Adm £5, chd £2.50. For other opening times and information, please phone, email or visit garden website.**

The gardens cover 190 acres forming part of the Grade II Registered Landscape of Ashridge Park. Based on designs by Humphry Repton in 1813 and modified by Jeffry Wyatville. A collection of small secluded gardens, as well as a large lawn area leading to avenues of trees. 2013 marked the 200th anniversary of Repton presenting Ashridge with the Red Book, detailing his designs for the estate. Once a monastic site then home to Henry VIII and his children. One of Repton's finest gardens with influences from the Bridgewater dynasty, comprising colourful formal bedding, a rosary, shrubberies, topiary, stunning rhododendrons and tree lined avenues leading to an arboretum.

♿ 🐴 ✿ 🚗 ☕))

GROUP OPENING

4 BAYFORD MUSICAL GARDENS DAY

Bayford, SG13 8PX. www.bayfordgardensday.org. *3m S of Hertford. Off B158 between Hatfield & Hertford. Free car parking.* **Sun 19 June (11.30-5). Combined adm £10, chd free. Light refreshments in gardens, village school and village hall.**

A popular biennial event held for over 30yrs. A variety of gardens from large, long established formal layouts to pretty cottage gardens. Live bands inc jazz, steel and brass add a festive backdrop, while visitors can enjoy a variety of ploughman's lunches, cream teas, BBQs and licensed bars. Stalls sell plants, local produce, cakes and ice-cream. Complementary transport around the village is also provided and there is ample free car parking. Bayford itself remains an oasis of countryside even though it is just 3m S of Hertford, and 10 mins from Potters Bar. The village has a station which is on the Stevenage to Moorgate line. Mentioned in the Doomsday book of 1086 as Begesford, the village today is fortunate to retain much of its old world charm, inc a fine church with C15 font. Please see website for more details. All proceeds are for charitable causes. People return year after year and many regard it as a great day out in the countryside. Wheelchairs are of course welcome but we would ask people to remember that garden surfaces can be difficult.

♿ 🐴 ✿ 🚗 🛏 ☕))

'National Garden Scheme funding helped support the provision of horticultural-related assistance to soldiers, veterans and their immediate families, providing education, training and employment opportunities along with supporting the recovery, health and wellbeing of individuals.'

ABF The Soldiers' Charity

GROUP OPENING

5 BEESONEND GARDENS

Harpenden, AL5 2AN. *1m S of Harpenden on A1081. After 1m turn R into Beesonend Ln, bear R into Burywick to T junction. Follow signs.* **Sun 10 July (2-5.30). Combined adm £6, chd free. Home-made teas.**

2 BARLINGS ROAD
Liz & Jim Machin.

7 BARLINGS ROAD
Chris & Paul Berendt.

Two gardens each reflecting their owner's individual interests. 2 Barlings Road is packed with perennials, shrubs and climbers and a formal pond to provide year-round structure and privacy. A courtyard suntrap and shade garden provide extra interest. 7 Barlings Road is a professionally landscaped garden designed for minimal maintenance and maximum impact with mature trees, climbers, water feature, children's play area, pagoda and plant-filled borders. Wheelchair access to Barlings Road, level gardens accessed via side paths.

6 BEESONEND HOUSE

Beesonend Lane, Harpenden, AL5 2AB. John & Sarah Worth. *Turn off A1081(turn R from Harpenden & L from St Albans). Keep L up Beesonend Lane, past cottages & derelict stables on the L. Beesonend House is on L next to white stones.* **Sun 29 May (11-5). Adm £5, chd free.**
Four garden areas. East garden lawn with herbaceous borders, pleached hedges, Japanese-themed border sitting under Eucalyptus tree. South garden laid lawn with herbaceous borders with semi-mature Lebanese cedar. South-West facing garden inc pond and orchard. North garden comprises circular lawn, pots, roses and herbaceous border. Vegetable garden with raised borders and a greenhouse.

7 ◆ BENINGTON LORDSHIP

Stevenage, SG2 7BS.
Mr & Mrs R Bott, 01438 869668, garden@beningtonlordship.co.uk, www.beningtonlordship.co.uk. *4m E of Stevenage. In Benington Village, next to church. Signs off A602.* **For NGS: Tue 8 Feb (11-4). Adm £7, chd £3. Light refreshments. Sun 8 May (2-5). Adm £7.50, chd free. For other opening times and information, please phone, email or visit garden website.**
7 acre site dating back to Saxon times which includes the ruin of a C12 Norman keep and C19 neo Norman folly. Garden comprises rose garden, walled kitchen garden with wildflower meadow, vegetables and bantams, orchard and lakes. Spectacular snowdrops, spring bulbs and herbaceous borders. Unspoilt panoramic views over surrounding parkland.

8 BRENT PELHAM HALL

Brent Pelham, Buntingford, SG9 0HF. Alex & Mike Carrell. *From Buntingford take the B1038 E for 5m. From Clavering take the B1038 W for 3m.* **Sat 4, Sun 5 June (2-5). Adm £6, chd free. Home-made teas in the Estate Office.**
Surrounding a beautiful Grade I listed property, the gardens consist of 12 acres of formal gardens, redesigned in 2007 by the renowned landscaper Kim Wilkie. With two walled gardens, a potager, walled kitchen garden, greenhouses, orchard and a new double herbaceous border, there is lots to discover. The further 14 acres of parkland boast lakes and wildflower meadows. All gardened organically. Access by wheelchair to most areas of the garden, inc paths of paving, gravel and grass.

9 102 CAMBRIDGE ROAD

St Albans, AL1 5LG. Anastasia & Keith, arezanova@gmail.com. *Nr Ashley Rd end of Cambridge Rd in The Camp neighbourhood on E side of city. S of A1057 (Hatfield Rd). Take the A1057 from A1(M) J3. Take A1081 from M25 J22.* **Evening opening Fri 15 July (5-8.30). Wine. Sun 17 July, Sat 3 Sept (2-5.30). Home-made teas. Adm £5, chd free. Friday: Wines and authentic home-made samosas. Sunday: Selection of teas, barista/coffee-shop coffee, home-made cakes.**

Visits also by arrangement May to Oct for groups of up to 20. Donation to Alzheimer's Research UK.
Contemporary space sympathetically redesigned in 2017 to keep as much of the existing plants, trees and shrubs in a 1930s semi's garden. Modern take on the classic garden in two halves: ornamental and vegetable. All-year interest gabion borders packed with perennials and annuals, central bed featuring a pond and a mature Japanese maple. Tea, coffee, barista coffee, cordial, and cake served. Dogs and photography welcome. All vegetables, annuals, and some perennials, grown from seed. 'Count the Frog' activity for children and young-at-heart.

10 ◆ THE CELEBRATION GARDEN

North Orbital Road, St Albans, AL2 1DH. Aylett Nurseries Ltd, 01727 822255, info@aylettnurseries.co.uk, www.aylettnurseries.co.uk. *The Celebration Garden is adjacent to Garden Centre. Aylett Nurseries is on the eastbound carriageway of A414, S of St Albans, between Park Street r'about & London Colney r'about. Turn L on entry & drive through green gates at end of car park.* **For NGS: Daily Sat 3 Sept to Sun 11 Sept (10-4). Adm by donation. Light refreshments in the café area adjacent to the garden. For other opening times and information, please phone, email or visit garden website.**
The Celebration Garden is sited next to our famous Dahlia Field. Dahlias are planted amongst other herbaceous plants and shrubs. We also have a wildflower border complete with insect hotel. The garden is open all year to visit, during the garden centre opening hours, but it is especially spectacular from July to early autumn when the Dahlias are in flower. Annual Autumn Festival held in September. Refreshments in our Seasons Café in the Garden Centre available year-round. Wheelchair access to the Celebration Garden via grass paths.

◧ THE CHERRY TREE

Stevenage Road, Little Wymondley, Hitchin, SG4 7HY. Patrick Woollard & Jane Woollard, 07952 655613, cherrywy@btinternet.com. *½ m W of J8 off A1M. Follow sign to Little Wymondley; under railway bridge & house is R at central island flower bed opp Bucks Head Pub. Parking in adjacent rds.* **Sun 5 June (11-5). Adm £4.50, chd free. Light refreshments. Visits also by arrangement June to Aug for groups of up to 15.**

The Cherry Tree is a secluded garden on several levels containing shrubs, trees and climbers, many of them perfumed. Much of the planting, inc exotics, is in containers that are cycled in various positions throughout the seasons. A heated greenhouse and summerhouse maintain tender plants in winter. The garden has been designed to be a journey of discovery as you ascend.

✿ 🍷))

◨ 10 CROSS STREET

Letchworth Garden City, SG6 4UD. Renata & Colin Hume, www.cyclamengardens.com. *Nr town centre. From A1(M) J9 signed Letchworth, across 2 r'abouts, R at 3rd, across next 3 r'abouts L into Nevells Rd, 1st R into Cross St.* **Mon 18 Apr (1-5). Adm £5, chd free. Home-made teas.**

A garden with mature fruit trees is planted for interest throughout the year. The structure of the garden evolved around three circles - two grass lawns and a wildlife pond. Mixed borders connect the different levels of the garden.

🐕 ✿ 🍷

◩ 28 DALE AVENUE

Wheathampstead, St Albans, AL4 8LS. Judy Shardlow, www.heartwoodgardendesign. co.uk. *Up Lamer Lane (B651) through Lower Gustard Wood, past the entrance to Mid Herts Golf Course. Turn L into The Slype, continuing then R into The Broadway & 1st R into Dale Avenue.* **Sun 29 May (12.30-4.30). Adm £5, chd free. Cream teas.**

A large country garden designed by Heartwood Garden Design, with sweeping central lawn and deep mixed borders with evergreen and perennial plants and grasses. It inc a large island bed with a stepping stone path to a lawned path beneath a large

Silver Birch. The border inc herbs, salvias, irises, agapanthus, lavender, eryngiums and many varieties of Harkness and David Austin roses.

🅳 🍷))

◪ 35 DIGSWELL ROAD

Welwyn Garden City, AL8 7PB. Adrian & Clare de Baat, 01707 324074, adrian.debaat@ntlworld.com, www.adriansgarden.org. *½ m N of Welwyn Garden City centre. From the Campus r'about in city centre take N exit just past the Public Library into Digswell Rd. Over the White Bridge, 200yds on L.* **Sun 31 July (2-5.30). Adm £5, chd free. Home-made teas. Visits also by arrangement July to Oct for groups of 5 to 20. £8 adm inc refreshments.**

Town garden of around a ⅓ acre with naturalistic planting inspired by the Dutch garden designer, Piet Oudolf. The garden has perennial borders plus a small meadow packed with herbaceous plants and grasses. The contemporary planting gives way to the exotic, inc a succulent bed and under mature trees, a lush jungle garden inc bamboos, bananas, palms and tree ferns. Daisy Roots Nursery will be selling plants. Grass paths and gentle slopes to all areas of the garden.

♿ ✿ 🍷))

◫ DOVEHOUSE SHOTT

Smiths End Lane, Barley, Royston, SG8 8LL. Stephen & Justine Marsh. *Barley, Herts. The drive starts beside The Hoops.* **Sun 12 June (11-4.30). Adm £5, chd free. Home-made teas. Gin bar.**

A lovely cottage garden with quirky features owned by the producer of Pinkster Gin. Masses of lupins and other perennials in the borders, a kitchen garden, orchard, lavender walks, roses and a wildlife meadow. Step free access to most areas.

♿ 🐕 ✿ 🍷))

◬ 1 ELIA COTTAGE

Nether Street, Widford, Ware, SG12 8TH. Margaret & Hugh O'Reilly, 01279 843324, hughoreilly56@yahoo.co.uk. *B1004 from Ware, Wareside to Widford past Green Man pub into dip at Xrd take R Nether St. 8m W of Bishop's Stortford on B1004 through Much Hadham at Widford sign turn L. B180 from Stanstead Abbots.* **Fri**

18, Sun 20 Feb (12.30-4.30). Adm £5, chd free. Light refreshments. Visits also by arrangement Mar to Sept.

A ⅓ acre garden reflecting the seasons. Early spring combines snowdrops, hellebores and crocus tommasinianus. Uneven garden with pond, cascade water features, stream with Monet-style bridge. Plenty of seats and two summerhouses. Garden quiz. Steep nature of garden means we are sorry no wheelchair access. NEW 2022: ½ acre land opposite, with snowdrops.

🍷

◭ 42 FALCONER ROAD

Bushey, Watford, WD23 3AD. Mrs Suzette Fuller, 077142 94170. *M1 J5 follow signs for Bushey. From London A40 via Stanmore towards Watford. From Watford via Bushey Arches, through to Bushey High St, turn L into Falconer Rd, opp St James church.* **Daily Sun 26 June to Sun 3 July (12-6). Evening opening Sun 6 Nov (7-9.30). Adm £3.50, chd free. Mulled Wine on 6 Nov. Visits also by arrangement May to Sept for groups of up to 10.**

Enchanting magical unusual Victorian style space. Bird cages and chimney pots feature, plus a walk through conservatory with many plants. Children so very welcome. Winter viewing for fairyland lighting, for all ages, bring a torch.

♿ 🍷

◮ FIELD END HOUSE

The Green, Park Lane, Old Knebworth, SG3 6QN. Sue & Paul Wood. *From J6 A1(M) Welwyn take B656 signed Codicote then follow NGS signs From J7 A1(M) Stevenage S exit take A602 to Knebworth. Follow NGS signs. Park in field short walk to garden.* **Evening opening Fri 8 July (5.30-9). Wine. Sun 10 July (2.30-5.30). Home-made teas. Combined adm with Manor Farmhouse £8, chd free.**

⅓ acre garden with views over countryside. Summer planting in the prairie style has been inc to withstand windy conditions. A curved grass meadow under mature lime trees looks out on to arable farmland with distant views. A sheltered corner with exotic planting affords an enticing place to sit. Large terrace with seating. Wheelchair access good in most areas of the garden.

♿ 🐕 ✿ 🍷))

19 39 FIRS WOOD CLOSE

Potters Bar, EN6 4BY. Val & Peter Mackie, Valmackie@gmail.com. *Potters Bar, High Street (A1000) fork R towards Cuffley, along the Causeway. Immed before the T-lights/Chequers pub, R down Coopers Lane Road. ½ m on L Firs Wood Close.* **Sun 15 May (11-5). Adm £5, chd free. Home-made teas. Visits also by arrangement.** Situated within Northaw Park, a 3 acre garden made up of a woodland area, a field inc a wildflower meadow and a more formal ½ acre around the house. Raised vegetable beds and Victorian greenhouse. Choice of seating areas include a breeze house, sunken fire pit area and colourful patio benches under the pergola covered with wisteria. Tranquil views up to Northaw village. Wheelchair access, flat access from road to back garden and then on grass.

20 28 FISHPOOL STREET

St Albans, AL3 4RT. Jenny & Antony Jay. *28 Fishpool St. is at the Cathedral end near The Lower Red Lion pub. Free parking on Sunday in the Boys School car park otherwise town parking.* **Evening opening Fri 24 June (6-8). Wine. Sun 26 June (2-5). Home-made teas. Adm £6, chd free.** Sculpted box and yew hedging and a C17 Tripe House feature strongly in this tranquil oasis set in the vicinity of St Albans Cathedral. Gravel paths lead to a lawn surrounded by late flowering sustainable herbaceous perennial borders and a relaxed woodland retreat. Imaginative planting in all areas offer unique perspectives. Plants are on sale. Not suitable for wheelchairs due to differing levels.

21 FOXGLOVE COTTAGE

Perry Green, Much Hadham, SG10 6EF. Jennifer & John Flexton, 07778 037044, jenniferflexton@hotmail.com. *6m SW of Bishops Stortford. Follow brown signs to Henry Moore Foundation. Foxglove is 4 mins walk from Hoops Inn Pub & Henry Moore Foundation SatNav postcode SG10 6EE Free Parking at Hoops Inn Pub.* **Evening opening Fri 24 June (6-8). Adm £4.50, chd free. Wine. Visits also by arrangement May to Sept for groups of 10+.**
A beautiful thatched cottage, in an idyllic setting on ⅔ of an acre, the epitome of English country charm. Colourful abundant successional planting and classic cottage garden plants fill the overflowing herbaceous borders. After an extensive renovation, a large Kew summerhouse is bordered by a cascading pond. Meander past the Wisteria pergola to the rose garden and greenhouse, and enjoy a seat along the way.

22 NEW GABLE HOUSE

Church Lane, Much Hadham, SG10 6DH. Tessa & Keith Birch. *Situated in the picturesque & historic village of Much Hadham. Follow signs to the church. Continue around the R bend & past several white cottages. Gable House driveway is immed on R. Please park in the High St.* **Sun 26 June (2-5.30). Adm £5, chd free. Home-made teas.**
Enjoy this colourful and walled village garden of just under an acre. Surrounding the house on 3 sides, the design is both formal and naturalistic, with structural clipped evergreens and wildlife friendly grassy areas. The planting displays abundant year-round borders, with an emphasis on strong colour and varied texture. Features inc a woodland walk and cuttings garden. Wheelchair access, level with easy access.

23 15 GADE VALLEY COTTAGES

Dagnall Road, Great Gaddesden, Hemel Hempstead, HP1 3BW. Bryan Trueman. *3m N of Hemel Hempstead. Follow B440 N from Hemel Hempstead. Through Water End. Go past turning for Great Gaddesden on L. Park in village hall car park on R. Gade Valley Cottages on R (short walk).* **Sun 29 May, Sun 17 July (1.30-5). Adm £4.50, chd free. Home-made teas.**
Medium sized sloping rural garden. Patio, lawn, borders and pond. Paths lead through a woodland area emerging by wildlife pond and sunny border. A choice of seating offers views across the beautiful Gade valley or quiet shady contemplation with sounds of rustling bamboos and bubbling water. Many acers, hostas and ferns in shady areas. Hemerocallis, dahlias, iris, crocosmia and phlox found in sun.

24 8 GOSSELIN ROAD

Bengeo, Hertford, SG14 3LG. Annie Godfrey & Steve Machin, www.daisyroots.com. *Take B158 from Hertford signed to Bengeo. Gosselin Rd 2nd R after White Lion Pub.* **Wed 2, Fri 4, Wed 9 Feb (1-3.30); Wed 28 Sept, Wed 5 Oct (1-4). Adm £5, chd free.** Owners of Daisy Roots nursery, garden acts as trial ground and show case for perennials and ornamental grasses grown there. Over 150 varieties of snowdrop in February, deep borders packed with perennials and grasses later in the year. Small front garden with lots of foliage interest. Regret no dogs.

25 GREENWOOD HOUSE

2a Lanercost Close, Welwyn, AL6 0RW. David & Cheryl Chalk. *1½ m E of Welwyn village, close to J6 on A1(M). Off B197 in Oaklands. Opp North Star pub turn into Lower Mardley Hill. Park here as limited at house (5min walk). Take Oaklands Rise to top of the hill & take L fork.* **Evening opening Fri 22 July (6-9). Wine. Sun 24 July (2-5). Home-made teas. Adm £5, chd free.** Secluded garden of ⅓ acre surrounds our contemporary home and backs on to a beautiful ancient woodland. Garden has been transformed in last 10 years, with mature trees providing a natural backdrop to the many shrubs and perennials which provide interest and colour throughout the seasons. Access to rear garden across pebble paths and some steps.

26 ◆ HATFIELD HOUSE WEST GARDEN

Hatfield, AL9 5HX. The Marquess of Salisbury, 01707 287010, r.ravera@hatfield-house.co.uk, www.hatfield-house.co.uk. *Pedestrian Entrance to Hatfield Park is opp Hatfield Railway Stn, from here you can obtain directions to the gardens. Free parking is available, please use AL9 5HX with a SatNav.* **For NGS: Sat 19 Mar (11-4). Adm £11, chd £4. For other opening times and information, please phone, email or visit garden website. Donation to another Charity.**
Visitors can enjoy the spring bulbs in the lime walk, sundial garden and view the famous Old Palace garden, childhood home of Queen Elizabeth I.

102 Cambridge Road

The adjoining woodland garden is at its best in spring with masses of naturalised daffodils and bluebells. Beautifully designed gifts, jewellery, toys and much more can be found in the Stable Yard shops. Visitors can also enjoy relaxing at the River Cottage Restaurant which serves a variety of delicious foods throughout the day. There is a good route for wheelchairs around the West garden and a plan can be picked up at the garden kiosk.

&♿☕️

27 NEW **16 LANGLEY CRESCENT**
St Albans, AL3 5RS. Jonathan Redmayne. ½ m S of St Albans city centre. J21a M25, follow B4630. At mini-r'about by King Harry Pub turn L. At big r'about turn R along A4147, then R at mini-r'about. Langley

Crescent is 2nd L. **Evening opening Fri 1 July (6-9). Wine. Sat 2 July (2.30-5.30). Home-made teas. Adm £4, chd free.**
A compact walled garden set on a slope with a wide range of unusual herbaceous perennials, shrubs and trees, both edible and ornamental, and a gentle ambience. The rear garden is divided into two parts; the lower section comprises extensive herbaceous beds including a collection of Phlomis and leads to a secluded area for quiet contemplation beside a wildlife pond surrounded by rambling roses. There will be a display by Peter Buckley, a local beekeeper. Access by wheelchair to most areas of the garden, inc paved paths, grass and brick terrace beside pond.

&✿☕️))

28 **12 LONGMANS CLOSE**
Byewaters, Watford, WD18 8WP. Mark Lammin, www.instagram. com/hertstinytropicalgarden. Leave M25 at J18 (A404) & follow signs for Rickmansworth/Croxley Green/Watford then follow A412 towards Watford & follow signs for Watford & Croxley Business Parks then follow the NGS signs. **Sun 31 July, Sun 7 Aug (2-6). Adm £4, chd free. Home-made teas.**
Hertfordshire's Tiny Tropical Garden. See how dazzling colour, scent, lush tropical foliage, trickling water and clever use of pots in a densely planted small garden can transport you to the tropics. Stately bananas and canna rub shoulders with delicate lily and roses amongst a large variety of begonia, hibiscus, ferns and houseplants in a tropical theme more often associated with warmer climes.

☕️))

29 NEW MANOR FARMHOUSE

Park Lane, Old Knebworth,
SG3 6QB. Alison & Cliff Ewer. *Opp the war memorial in Old Knebworth. From J6 A1(M) Welwyn take B656 signed Codicote then follow NGS signs. From J7 A1(M) Stevenage S exit take A602 to Knebworth. Follow NGS signs. Park in field short walk to garden.* **Evening opening Fri 8 July (5.30-9). Wine. Sun 10 July (2.30-5.30). Home-made teas. Combined adm with Field End House £8, chd free.**
Farm house country garden. Clipped circular hedging with roses and lavender in front. 28m Pergola with climbers and shady woodland paths. Sunny circular borders and raised veg beds. New wildlife pond built as lockdown project. Seating areas around the garden to enjoy the view and refreshments.

30 THE MANOR HOUSE, AYOT ST LAWRENCE

Welwyn, AL6 9BP. Rob & Sara Lucas. *4m W of Welwyn. 20 mins J4 A1M. Take B653 Wheathampstead. Turn into Codicote Rd follow signs to Shaws Corner. Parking in field, short walk to garden. A disabled drop-off point is available at the end of the drive.* **Sat 21, Sun 22 May (11-5). Adm £7.50, chd free. Home-made teas.**

A 6 acre garden set in mature landscape around Elizabethan Manor House (not open). 1 acre walled garden inc glasshouses, fruit and vegetables, double herbaceous borders, rose and herb beds. Herbaceous perennial island beds, topiary specimens. Parterre and temple pond garden surround the house. Gates and water features by Arc Angel. Garden designed by Julie Toll. Home-made cakes and tea/coffee. Produce for sale.

31 43 MARDLEY HILL

Welwyn, AL6 0TT. Kerrie & Pete, www.agardenlessordinary. blogspot.co.uk. *5m N of Welwyn Garden City. On B197 between Welwyn & Woolmer Green, on crest of Mardley Hill by bus stop for Arriva 300/301.* **Sun 22 May (1-5). Adm £5, chd free. Home-made teas.**
An unexpected garden created by plantaholics and packed with unusual plants. Focus on foliage and long season of interest. Constantly being developed and new plants sourced. Various areas: alpine bed; sunny border; deep shade; white-stemmed birches and woodland planting; naturalistic stream, pond and bog; chicken house and potted vegetables; potted exotics. Seating areas on different levels. Featured in Garden News and Garden Answers.

32 THE MILL HOUSE

31 Mill Lane, Welwyn, AL6 9EU. Sarah & Ian. *Old Welwyn. J6 A1M approx ¾ m to garden, follow yellow arrows to Welwyn Village.* **Evening opening Thur 2 June (4-8.30). Wine. Sat 4 June (2-6). Home-made teas. Adm £5, chd free.**
An abundant colourful display of roses, and summer perennials set off this Listed house with semi-walled garden bordered by a bridged millstream and race. Ancient apple and box trees under planted with a display of perennials and herbaceous plants set off a garden full of promise, within which nestles a box parterre, vegetable planters magnolia tree and colourful terrace. Regional Finalist, The English Garden's The Nation's Favourite Gardens 2021. Wheelchair access, some gravel and uneven paths.

33 MORNING LIGHT

7 Armitage Close, Loudwater, Rickmansworth, WD3 4HL. Roger & Patt Trigg. *From M25 J18 take A404 towards Rickmansworth, after ¾ m turn L into Loudwater Lane, follow bends, then turn R at T-junction & R again into Armitage Close.* **Sun 12 June, Sun 24 July (1-5.30). Adm £5, chd free. Pre-booking essential, please phone 01923 774293 or email roger@triggmail.org.uk for information & booking. Home-made teas. Visits also by arrangement Apr to Sept for groups of up to 20.**
South facing plantsman's garden, densely planted with mainly hardy and tender perennials and shrubs in a shady environment. Astilbes and phlox prominently featured. The garden inc island beds, pond, chipped paths and raised deck. Tall perennials can be viewed advantageously from the deck. Large conservatory (450 sq ft) stocked with sub-tropicals.

Elia Cottage

34 PATCHWORK

22 Hall Park Gate,
Berkhamsted, HP4 2NJ. Jean
& Peter Block, 01442 864731,
patchwork2@btinternet.com. *3m
W of Hemel Hempstead. Entering E
side of Berkhamsted on A4251, turn
L 200yds after 40mph sign.* **Sun 1
May, Sun 21 Aug (2-5). Adm £5,
chd free. Light refreshments.
Visits also by arrangement Apr to
Oct for groups of 5 to 30. Tea &
coffee by arrangement.**
¼ acre garden with lots of year-
round colour, interest and perfume,
particularly on opening days. Sloping
site containing rockeries, 2 small
ponds, herbaceous borders, island
beds with bulbs in Spring and dahlias
in Summer, roses, fuchsias, hostas,
begonias, patio pots and tubs galore
- all set against a background of
trees and shrubs of varying colours.
Seating and cover from the elements.
Traditional, labour intensive garden,
sloping site, many levels and views,
colourful, perfumed, Spring bulbs,
Roses, Fuchsias, Dahlias, shrubs and
trees, compost heaps.

🐕 ✿ ☕

35 PIE CORNER

Millhouse Lane, Bedmond,
WD5 0SG. Bella & Jeremy Stuart-
Smith, piebella1@gmail.com.
*Between Watford & Hemel
Hempstead. 1½m from J21 M25.
3m from J8 of M1. Go to the centre
of Bedmond. Millhouse Lane is
opp the shops. Entrance is 50m
down Millhouse Lane.* **Sun 1 May
(2-5). Home-made teas. Evening
opening Fri 1 July (5.30-8). Wine.
Sun 3 July (2-5). Home-made
teas. Adm £6, chd free. Visits also
by arrangement Apr to July for
groups of 15 to 30.**
A garden designed to complement
the modern classical house. Formal
borders near the house, pond and
views across lawn towards valley.
More informal shrub plantings with
bulbs edge the woodland. A dry
garden leads through new meadow
planting to the vegetable garden.
Enjoy blossom, bulbs, wild garlic,
bluebells and young rhododendron
planting in late spring. Plants &
produce in aid of Sunnyside Rural
Trust Wheelchair access to all areas
on grass or gravel paths except the
formal pond where there are steps.

♿ ✿ ☕ 🏕

36 NEW THE PINES

58 Hoe Lane, Ware, SG12 9NZ.
Peter Laing. *Approx ½m S of Ware
centre. At S (top) end of Hoe Lane,
close to Hertford Rugby Club (car
parking) and opp Pinewood School.
Look for prominent white gateposts
with lions.* **Sun 22 May, Sun 11
Sept (2-5.30). Adm £5, chd free.
Tea.**
Plantsman's garden with many
unusual plants, created by present
owner over 30 yrs. 1 acre, E/W axis
so much shade, sandy soil over chalk
but can grow ericaceous plants. Front
garden formal with fountain. Main
garden mature trees, herbaceous
borders and island beds. Features inc
gravel garden, pergola and obelisk
with moss rose "William Lobb".
Among many specimen trees, the rare
Kashmir cypress. Wheelchairs access
OK unless recent heavy rain.

♿ ☕ 🔊

37 RAILWAY COTTAGE

16 Sandpit Lane, St Albans,
AL1 4HW. Siobhan & Barry
Brindley, 07766 798949,
siobhanbrindley@yahoo.co.uk.
*½m N of St Albans city centre.
J21a M25, follow St Albans A5183.
Through town centre on A1081.
Please use on-street parking in
Battlefield, Lancaster, & Gurney
Court Rds.* **Evening opening Fri 27
May (5-8). Wine. Sun 29 May (2-5).
Home-made teas. Adm £4.50, chd
free. Visits also by arrangement
May to Aug for groups of 5 to 40.**
Sandwiched between a main road
and railway line, this urban cottage
garden is a hidden gem. Little paths
are bordered by plants and flowers
of all descriptions creating a mass of
colour and a haven for insects and
birds. There is seating throughout
the garden with an eclectic collection
of reclaimed items old and new.
Greenhouse, summerhouses and
water features.

🐕 ✿ 🚗 ☕ 🔊

38 RUSTLING END COTTAGE

Rustling End, Codicote,
SG4 8TD. Julie & Tim Wise,
www.rustlingend.com. *1m N of
Codicote. From B656 turn L into
'3 Houses Lane' then R to Rustling
End. House 2nd on L.* **Evening
opening Fri 22, Sat 23 July (5-
8.30). Adm £5, chd free. Wine.**
Meander through our wildflower
meadow to a cottage garden with
contemporary planting. Behind
lumpy hedges explore a garden

managed extensively. Natural planting
provides an environment for birds,
small mammals and insects. Our
terrace features drought tolerant low
maintenance plants. The lawn around
the pond is now a flowery mead and
an abundant floral vegetable garden
provides produce for the summer.
Hens in residence.

✿ ☕ 🔊

39 ◆ ST PAUL'S WALDEN BURY

Whitwell, Hitchin, SG4 8BP.
The Bowes Lyon family,
stpaulswalden@gmail.com,
www.stpaulswaldenbury.co.uk.
*5m S of Hitchin. On B651; ½m N
of Whitwell village. From London
leave A1(M) J6 for Welwyn (not
Welwyn Garden City). Pick up signs
to Codicote, then Whitwell.* **For
NGS: Sun 3 Apr, Sun 15 May, Sun
12 June (2-7). Adm £7.50, chd
free. Home-made teas. Payment
for refreshments only by cash.
For other opening times and
information, please email or visit
garden website. Donation to St
Paul's Walden Charity.**
Spectacular formal woodland
garden, Grade I listed, laid out 1720,
covering over 50 acres. Long rides
lined with clipped beech hedges
lead to temples, statues, lake and a
terraced theatre. Seasonal displays of
daffodils, cowslips, irises, magnolias,
rhododendrons, lilies. wild flowers are
encouraged. This was the childhood
home of the late Queen Mother.
Children welcome. Dogs on leads.
Pre-booking available online at ngs.
org.uk Good wheelchair access
to part of the garden. Steep grass
slopes in places.

♿ 🐕 🚗 ☕ 🏕 🔊

*'In the first six months
of operation at Maggie's
Southampton, which
was part funded by the
National Garden Scheme,
the team has supported
people affected by cancer
more than 2,300 times.'
Maggie's*

The Barn, Serge Hill Gardens

GROUP OPENING

40 ST STEPHENS AVENUE GARDENS

St Albans, AL3 4AD. *1m S of St Albans City Centre. From A414 take A5183 Watling St. At mini-r'about by St Stephens Church/King Harry Pub take B4630 Watford Rd. St Stephens Ave is 1st R.* **Sun 26 June, Sun 4 Sept (2.30-5.30). Combined adm £6, chd free. Home-made teas.**

20 ST STEPHENS AVENUE
Heather & Peter Osborne.

30 ST STEPHENS AVENUE
Carol & Roger Harlow.

Two gardens of similar size and the same aspect, developed in totally different ways. Number 20 is designed for year-round colour, fragrance and structure. Dense planting makes it impossible to see from one end of the garden to the other, enticing visitors to explore. Paths meander through and behind the colour coordinated borders, giving access to all parts. Varied plant habitats include cool shade, hot dry gravel and lush pondside displays. New borders are developed or areas replanted every year. Seating is in both sun and shade, a large conservatory provides shelter. Number 30 has a southwest facing gravelled front garden that has a Mediterranean feel. Herbaceous plants, such as sea hollies and achilleas, thrive in the poor, dry soil. Clipped box, beech and hornbeam in the back garden provide a cool backdrop for the strong colours of the herbaceous planting. A gate beneath a beech arch frames the view to the park beyond. Plants for sale at June opening only.

41 SERENDI

22 Hitchin Road, Letchworth Garden City, SG6 3LT. Valerie, 01462 635386, valerie.aitken@ntlworld.com. *1m from city centre. A1(M) J9 signed Letchworth on A505. At 2nd r'about take 1st exit Hitchin A505. Straight over T-lights. Garden 1m on R.* **Sun 1 May (11-5). Adm £5, chd free. Home-made teas. Visits also by arrangement Apr to Aug for groups of up to 30.**

A mass of tulips and other Spring bulbs, silver birch grove, a 'dribble of stones', rill, contemporary knot garden, dry area with allium. Many different areas within a well designed garden. Later in the year an abundance of roses climbing 5 pillars, perennials, grasses and dahlias. A greenhouse for over wintering and a Griffin glasshouse with brugmansia, ginger lily, tibochina and other plants. Regional Finalist, The English Garden's The Nation's Favourite Gardens. Wheelchair access, gravel entrance driveway and paths, can be difficult. Plenty of lawns.

GROUP OPENING

42 SERGE HILL GARDENS

Serge Hill Lane, Bedmond, WD5 0RT. sergehill@icloud.com. *½ m E of Bedmond. Go to Bedmond & take Serge Hill Lane, where you will be directed past the lodge & down the drive.* **Sun 19 June (12-5). Combined adm £12, chd free. Pre-booking essential, please visit www.ngs.org.uk for information & booking. Home-made teas at Serge Hill.**

THE BARN
Sue & Tom Stuart-Smith, www.tomstuartsmith.co.uk/our-work/toms-garden.

SERGE HILL
Kate Stuart-Smith.

Two large country gardens a short walk from each other. Tom and Sue Stuart-Smith's garden at The Barn has an enclosed courtyard with tanks of water, herbaceous perennials and shrubs tolerant of generally dry conditions. To the North there are views over the 5 acre wildflower meadow. The West Garden is a series of different gardens overflowing with bulbs, herbaceous perennials, and shrubs. There is also an exotic prairie planted from seed in 2011. Kate Stuart-Smith lives next door at Serge Hill, where there is a lovely walled garden with a large greenhouse, orderly rows of vegetables, and disorderly self-seeded annuals and perennials. The walls are crowded with climbers and shrubs. From here you emerge to a new meadow, a mixed border and a wonderful view looking Southwest over the ha-ha to the park and woods beyond. Pause to sit on the lawn in front of the house and enjoy home-made teas before visiting the outside stage and the ship that sails through the bunny walk. Country views, wildflower meadows, wildlife pond, greenhouses, vegetable gardens, walled garden, prairie planting. Plants & produce in aid of Sunnyside Rural Trust

GROUP OPENING

43 SOUTHDOWN GARDENS

Harpenden, AL5 1EL. *Exit M1 J9; turn R onto A5183 heading towards Redbourn; turn L at r'about towards Harpenden on B487; pass the White Horse Pub on the L; take 2nd exit at r'about onto Walkers Rd.* **Sun 26 June (1-6). Combined adm £7, chd free. Tea, coffee, cakes.**

4 COLESWOOD ROAD
Mrs Linzi Claridge, www.linziclaridgegardendesign.com.

5 COLESWOOD ROAD
Marilyn Couldridge.

8 KINGCROFT ROAD
Zia Allaway, www.ziaallaway.com.

Three gardens in close proximity to each other. All void of a lawn; instead showing an abundance of mixed planting. There is structure, varied planting, water features, pots, resting areas; making the most of each garden space.

The National Garden Scheme searches the length and breadth of England, Channel Islands, Northern Ireland and Wales for the very best private gardens

44 9 TANNSFIELD DRIVE

Hemel Hempstead, HP2 5LG. Peter & Gaynor Barrett, 01442 393508, peteslittlepatch@virginmedia.com, www.peteslittlepatch.co.uk. *Approx. 1m NE of Hemel Hempstead town centre & 2m W of J8 on M1. From M1 J8, cross r'about to A414 to Hemel Hempstead. Under footbridge, cross r'about then 1st R across dual c'way to Leverstock Green Rd. On to High St Green. L into Ellingham Rd then follow signs.* **Sun 5 June, Sun 3 July (1.30-4.30). Adm £4, chd free. Home-made teas.** Visits also by arrangement June to Aug for groups of 6 to 10. Please discuss refreshments when booking.

A town garden to surprise. Dense planting together with the ever-present sound of water, create an intimate and welcoming oasis of calm. Narrow paths divide, leading visitors on a voyage of discovery of the garden's many features. The owners regularly experiment with the planting scheme which ensures the 'look' of the garden changes from year to year. Dense planting together with simple water features, stone statues, metal sculptures, wall art and mirrors can be seen throughout the garden. As a time and cost saving experiment all hanging baskets are planted with hardy perennials most of which are normally used for ground cover.

✿ ☕ ⬤))

45 NEW TERRACE HOUSE GARDEN

35 Fanshawe Street, Bengeo, Hertford, SG14 3AT. Peter & Rosie Freeland. *1m from Hertford Town centre. Please park on nearby Elton Rd & not Fanshawe St due to limited parking.* **Sat 6 Aug (11-5). Adm £5, chd free.** Terraced garden with stunning views across the Beane Valley. Seven levels featuring a rockery, secluded pond, wisteria tunnel, orchard with wildflowers and more. Mixed-planting with an emphasis on late summer perennials and grasses intertwined with vivid annuals. Vegetable plantings also feature. Some steep steps with railings.

✿ ☕ ⬤))

46 THUNDRIDGE HILL HOUSE

Cold Christmas Lane, Ware, SG12 0UE. Christopher & Susie Melluish, 01920 462500, c.melluish@btopenworld.com. *2m NE of Ware. ¾m from Maltons off the A10 down Cold Christmas Ln, Xing bypass.* **Sun 12 June (11-**

5.30). Adm £5, chd free. Cream teas. **Visits also by arrangement May to Sept for groups of 15+.**

Well-established garden of approx 2½ acres; good variety of plants, shrubs and roses, attractive hedges. Visitors often ask for the unusual yellow-only bed. Several delightful places to sit. Wonderful views in and out of the garden especially down to the Rib Valley to Youngsbury, visited briefly by Lancelot 'Capability' Brown. 'A most popular garden to visit'. Fine views down to Thundridge Old Church.

♿ 🐕 ☕

47 WALKERN HALL

Walkern, Stevenage, SG2 7JA. Mrs Kate de Boinville. *4m E of Stevenage. Turn L at War Memorial as you leave Walkern, heading for Benington (immed after small bridge). Garden 1m up hill on R.* **Sat 5, Sun 6 Feb (12-4); Sat 26, Sun 27 Mar (12-5). Adm £5, chd free. Home-made teas. Warming home-made soup and cakes.**

Walkern Hall is essentially a winter woodland garden. Set in 8 acres, the carpet of snowdrops and aconites is a constant source of wonder in Jan/Feb. This medieval hunting park is known more for its established trees such as the tulip trees and a magnificent London plane tree which dominates the garden. Following on in March and April is a stunning display of daffodils. and other spring bulbs. There is wheelchair access but quite a lot of gravel. No disabled WC.

♿ ✿ 🚌 ☕ ⬤))

48 WATEREND HOUSE

Waterend Lane, Wheathampstead, St Albans, AL4 8EP. Mr & Mrs J Nall-Cain, 07736 880810, sj@nallcain.com. *2m E of Wheathampstead. Approx 10 mins from J4 of A1M. Take B653 to Wheathampstead, past Crooked Chimney Pub, after ½m turn R into Waterend Lane. Cross river, house is immed. on R.* **Evening opening Sat 25 June (5.30-9). Adm £15, chd £3. Pre-booking essential, please visit www.ngs.org.uk for information & booking. Wine, music & nibbles.** Visits also by arrangement Feb to Sept for groups of 18 to 20. We can give a guided tour of the garden, with home-made teas and cake.

A hidden garden of 4 acres sets off an elegant Jacobean Manor House (not open). Steep grass slopes and fine views of glorious countryside. Large quantities of spring bulbs, formal

flint-walled garden. Roses, peonies and irises in the summer. Formal beds and lots of colour throughout the year. Mature specimen trees, ponds, formal vegetable garden, bantams and Indian runner ducks. Meditation garden. Hilly garden. Wheelchair access to lower gardens only.

♿ ☕ ⬤))

49 14 WATLING STREET

St Albans, AL1 2PX. Phil & Becky Leach. *1m S of St Albans. Take A5183 up St Stephen's Hill & turn L at King Harry Pub. From A414 take A5183. No. 14 is off the main road, in cul-de-sac diagonally opposite St Stephen's Church (some parking in church car park).* **Evening opening Fri 8 July (6-9). Wine. Sat 9 July (2.30-5.30). Home-made teas. Adm £4, chd free.**

A vibrant garden replete with perennials grown from seed and striking foliage plants inc Chinese rice-paper plants, foxglove trees, chusan palms, cardoons, echium and honey flowers. Gravel garden out front leads to a back garden divided into separate beds (including bog garden, with giant rhubarb, ligularia and hosta) and which ends in a glade of bamboo shaded by maple trees. Wheelchair access, some gravel paths and raised patio area.

♿ ✿ ☕ ⬤))

50 THE WHITE COTTAGE

Waterend Lane, Wheathampstead, St Albans, AL4 8EP. Sally Trendell, 01582 834617, sallytrendell@me.com. *2m E of Wheathampstead. Approx 10 mins from J5 A1M Take B653 to Wheathampstead. Soon after Crooked Chimney pub turn R into Waterend Ln, garden 300yds on L. Parking in field opp.* **Evening opening Fri 3 June (5-9). Adm £5, chd free. Wine. Visits also by arrangement May to July for groups of 10 to 25.**

Idyllic riverside retreat of over an acre in rural setting adjacent to a ford over the River Lea which widens to form the garden boundary. A wildlife haven cottage garden straight out of 'The Wind in the Willows'. Please bring a picnic to enjoy on the riverbank.

♿ 🐕 🛋 ☕ 🪑 ⬤))

The Celebration Garden

ISLE OF WIGHT

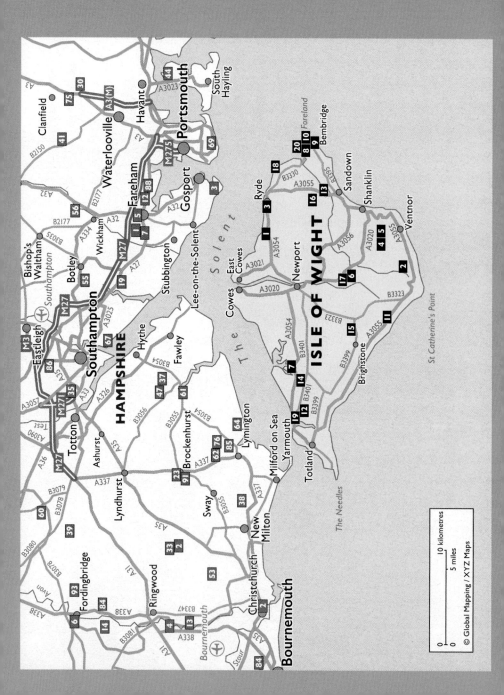

The island is a very special place to those who live and work here and to those who visit and keep returning. We have a range of natural features, from a dramatic coastline of cliffs and tiny coves to long sandy beaches.

Inland, the grasslands and rolling chalk downlands contrast with the shady forests and woodlands. Amongst all of this beauty nestle the picturesque villages and hamlets, many with gardens open for the National Garden Scheme. Most of our towns are on the coast and many of the gardens have wonderful sea views.

The one thing that makes our gardens so special is our climate. The moderating influence of the sea keeps hard frosts at bay, and the range of plants that can be grown is therefore greatly extended.

Conservatory plants are planted outdoors and flourish. Pictures taken of many island gardens fool people into thinking that they are holiday snaps of the Mediterranean and the Canaries.

Our gardens are very varied and our small enthusiastic group of garden owners are proud of their gardens, whether they are small town gardens or large manor gardens, and they love to share them for the National Garden Scheme.

Volunteers

County Organiser
Jennie Fradgley
01983 730805
Jennie.Fradgley@ngs.org.uk

County Treasurer
Jennie Fradgley (as above)

Publicity
Lindsay Becker
07803 824373
lindsay.becker@ngs.org.uk

Booklet Co-ordinator
Jennie Fradgley
(as above)

Assistant County Organisers
Jane Bland
01983 874592
jane.bland@ngs.org.uk

Mike Eastwood
01983 721060
mike@aristia.co.uk

Sally Parker
01983 612495
sallyparkeriow@btinternet.com

Below: Apple Trees

OPENING DATES

All entries subject to change. For latest information check www.ngs.org.uk

Map locator numbers are shown to the right of each garden name.

April

Sunday 10th
Northcourt Manor
Gardens 15

May

Sunday 15th
Morton Manor 13

Sunday 22nd
Goldings 12
Thorley Manor 19

June

Sunday 12th
NEW Darts 8
NEW Yew Tree Lodge 20

Saturday 25th
NEW Bluebell Cottage 4
NEW 3 Castle Lane 5
NEW East Cliff 10

July

Saturday 2nd
Ashknowle House 2

Sunday 3rd
Ashknowle House 2

Sunday 10th
◆ Nunwell House 16

Saturday 16th
NEW Dove Cottage 9

Sunday 17th
NEW Dove Cottage 9

Saturday 23rd
NEW Corris 6
NEW Oakdene 17

Sunday 24th
NEW Corris 6
NEW Oakdene 17

Saturday 30th
East Dene 11

Sunday 31st
East Dene 11

August

Saturday 13th
Blenheim House 3

Sunday 14th
Blenheim House 3
Crab Cottage 7

Sunday 21st
Morton Manor 13

September

Sunday 18th
Northcourt Manor
Gardens 15

By Arrangement

Arrange a personalised garden visit on a date to suit you. See individual garden entries for full details.

NEW Apple Trees 1
Crab Cottage 7
Morton Manor 13
Ningwood Manor 14
Northcourt Manor
Gardens 15
Salterns Cottage 18

THE GARDENS

1 NEW APPLE TREES

Ashlake Copse Road, Ryde, PO33 4EY. Mrs Ros Mulholland, 07711 598503, bella.mulholland35@gmail.com. *Approx ½ m from Fishbourne Ferry Terminal. At junction with the Ryde to Newport road, turn into Fishbourne Ln at the T-lights. Ashlake Copse Rd is 1st on the L, just before Fishbourne Garage. Apple Trees is 2nd house on R.* **Visits by arrangement May to Sept for groups of 5 to 20. Adm £5, chd free. Light refreshments.**
Newly designed gravel garden. Interesting seating areas, perennial planting, water features and vegetable garden. Wheelchair access over gravel paths.
♿ ☕ ⛱ ♪))

2 ASHKNOWLE HOUSE

Ashknowle Lane, Whitwell, Ventnor, PO38 2PP. Mr & Mrs K Fradgley. *4m W of Ventnor. Take the Whitwell Rd from Ventnor or Godshill. Turn into unmade lane next to Old Rectory. Field parking. Disabled parking at house.* **Sat 2, Sun 3 July (11.30-4.30). Adm £5, chd free. Home-made teas.**
The mature garden of this Victorian house (not open) has great diversity inc woodland walks, water features, colourful beds and borders. The large, well maintained kitchen garden is highly productive and boasts a wide range of fruit and vegetables grown in cages, tunnels, glasshouses and raised beds. Diversely planted and highly productive orchard inc protected cropping of strawberries, peaches and apricots. Propagation areas for trees, shrubs and crops.
🐕 ❄ ☕ ⛱

3 BLENHEIM HOUSE

9 Spencer Road (use Market St entrance), Ryde, PO33 2NY. David Rosewarne & Magie Gray. *Market St entrance behind Ryde Town Hall/ Theatre, off Lind St.* **Sat 13, Sun 14 Aug (11-4). Adm £4, chd free. Home-made teas.**
A garden developed over 17 yrs, exploring the decorative qualities and long term effects of pattern making with hard and soft landscaping, form, colour and texture. This terraced 116ft x 30ft sloping site is centred on a twisting red brick path that both reveals and hides interesting and contrasting areas of planting, creating intimate and secluded spaces that belie its town centre location.
☕ ⛱

4 NEW BLUEBELL COTTAGE

Clevelands Road, Wroxall, Ventnor, PO38 3DZ. Mr Ken & Mrs Lynn Orchard. *3m from Shanklin, 2m from Ventnor. From Whitely Bank mini r'about follow signs to Wroxall. From Ventnor follow signs to Wroxall. Turn at St John's Church to free car park opp Stenbury Hall Community Centre. Continue on foot.* **Sat 25 June (12-4). Combined adm with 3 Castle Lane £5, chd free. Home-made teas.**
Cottage garden front and back with tranquil sitting areas among the many varieties of colourful flowers, trees and shrubs. A mix of reality and quirky, magical moments to enjoy. Sit and have refreshments surrounded by colour.
🐕 ☕

5 NEW 3 CASTLE LANE
Wroxall, Ventnor, PO38 3DX. Mr Tony & Mrs Helen Wood. *At the bottom of Castle Ln, which leads off Castle Rd, on the N side of Wroxall. From Whitely Bank, follow main road into Wroxall, then turn L into Station Rd immed after the church. Park in the free car park on the R. Then on foot follow signs up Castle Rd.* Sat 25 June (12-4). Combined adm with Bluebell Cottage £5, chd free.

A ¾ acre, gently sloping windswept garden on heavy clay. There are: mixed borders, a variety of trees and shrubs, grasses, a tiny stream with bridges, a small pond and a Paul Sivell tree sculpture. Planting is mainly based on the 'if it survives, we'll have it' principle of gardening.

6 NEW CORRIS
Main Road, Rookley, Ventnor, PO38 3NF. Mr David & Mrs Helen Crook. *4m S of Newport. Leave Newport via Blackwater, turn R to Shanklin. Continue to Rookley village. Garden is located on the RHS at the end of main road, opp the established Holiday Park.* Sat 23, Sun 24 July (11-4). Combined adm with Oakdene £5, chd free. Light refreshments.

A medium sized mature village garden, featuring diverse, colourful borders around separate lawned areas. There are borders in the long front garden of the property; and in the rear garden, various pathways lead around different areas to view.

✿ ☕

7 CRAB COTTAGE
Mill Road, Shalfleet, PO30 4NE. Mr & Mrs Peter Scott, 07768 065756, mencia@btinternet.com. *4½m E of Yarmouth. At New Inn, Shalfleet, turn into Mill Rd. Continue 400yds to end of metalled road, drive onto unmade road through open NT gates. After 100yds pass Crab Cottage on L. Park opp on grass.* Sun 14 Aug (11-5). Adm £5, chd free. Home-made teas. Visits also by arrangement May to Sept.

1¼ acres on gravelly soil. Part glorious views across croquet lawn over Newtown Creek and Solent, leading through wildflower meadow to hidden water lily pond, secluded lawn and woodland walk. Part walled garden protected from westerlies with mixed borders, leading to terraced sunken garden with ornamental pool and pavilion, planted with exotics, tender

shrubs and herbaceous perennials. Croquet, plant sales and excellent tea and cake. Wheelchair access over gravel and uneven grass paths.

♿ 🐑 🚾 ☕

8 NEW DARTS
Darts Lane, Bembridge, PO35 5YH. Joanna Truman. *Up the hill from Bembridge Harbour, turn L after the Co-op down Love Ln & take 1st L. The house is painted grey.* Sun 12 June (12.30-5). Combined adm with Yew Tree Lodge £6, chd free.

Classic walled garden with roses, climbers, shrubs, two large raised vegetable beds and running water feature. Work in progress continues!

♿

9 NEW DOVE COTTAGE
Swains Lane, Bembridge, PO35 5ST. Mr James & Mrs Alex Hearn. *Head E on Lane End Rd, passing Lane End Court Shops on L. Take 3rd turning on L onto Swains Ln. Dove Cottage is on R.* Sat 16, Sun 17 July (11-4). Adm £4, chd free. Light refreshments.

An enclosed garden with lawn and woodland area. A central path leads through the woodland setting which has mature variagated shrubs and perennials, leading to the swimming pool area and tennis court.

☕

Corris

3 Castle Lane

10 NEW EAST CLIFF

Love Lane, Bembridge, PO35 5NH. Kate Cheshire. *Please visit www. ngs.org.uk closer to opening for parking information.* Sat 25 June (2-6). Adm £8, chd £2. Prosecco & Pimm's Tent.

The garden is situated in Bembridge overlooking the sea. It is on a 15 acre plot with the lawn and garden covering about 8 acres. The garden was designed by Arabella Lennox Boyd in 2016. She has created rooms within the garden, they inc a white rose garden and a walled cottage garden and to the rear of the house there are six large herbaceous beds. We also have a wildflower meadow.

11 EAST DENE

Atherfield Green, Ventnor, PO38 2LF. Marc & Lisa Morgan-Huws. *From A3055 Military Rd, turn into Southdown. At end of road turn L on to Atherfield Rd & the garden is ahead on the R.* Sat 30, Sun 31 July (11-5). Adm £4, chd free. Light refreshments.

Planted from 2 acres of farmland in the 1970s, the garden is structured around a variety of mature trees. Taken over by brambles and nettles prior to our arrival 7 yrs ago, the garden is continuing to be developed, whilst still being a haven for wildlife. Occupying a windswept coastal location with areas of woodland, fruit trees, mature pond and informal planting. Alpacas. Although the garden has level access, the ground is unmade.

12 GOLDINGS

Thorley Street, Thorley, Yarmouth, PO41 0SN. John & Dee Sichel. *E of Yarmouth. Follow directions for Thorley from Yarmouth/Newport road or from Wilmingham Ln. Then follow NGS signs. Parking shared with Thorley Manor.* Sun 22 May (2-5). Combined adm with Thorley Manor £5, chd free. Tea at Thorley Manor.

A country garden with many focuses of interest. A newly planted orchard already producing cider apples in large amounts. A small, but productive vegetable garden and a well maintained lawn with shrub borders and roses. A microclimate has been created by the adjustment of levels to create a series of terraced areas for planting.

13 MORTON MANOR

Morton Manor Road, Brading, Sandown, PO36 0EP. Mr & Mrs G Godliman, 07768 605900, patricia.godliman@yahoo.co.uk. *Off A3055 5m S of Ryde, just out of Brading. At Yarbridge T-lights turn into The Mall. Take next L into Morton Manor Rd.* Sun 15 May, Sun 21 Aug (11-4). Adm £4, chd free. Light refreshments. Visits also by arrangement Apr to Oct.

A colourful garden of great plant variety. Mature trees inc many acers with a wide variety of leaf colour. Early in the season a display of rhododendrons, azaleas and camellias and later hydrangeas and hibiscus. Ponds, sweeping lawns, roses set on a sunny terrace and much more to see in this extensive garden surrounding a picturesque C16 manor house (not open). Wheelchair access over gravel driveway.

14 NINGWOOD MANOR

Station Road, Ningwood, nr Newport, PO30 4NJ. Nicholas & Claire Oulton, 07738 737482, claireoulton@gmail.com. *Nr Shalfleet. From Newport, turn L opp the Horse & Groom Pub. Ningwood Manor is 300-400yds on the L. Please use 2nd set of gates.* **Visits by arrangement May to Aug for groups of up to 30. Light refreshments.**
A 3 acre, landscaped country garden divided into several rooms; a walled courtyard, croquet lawn, white garden and kitchen garden. They flow into each other, each with their own gentle colour schemes; the exception to this is the croquet lawn garden which is a riot of colour, mixing oranges, reds, yellows and pinks. Much new planting has taken place over the last few yrs. The owners have several new projects underway, so the garden is a work in progress. Features inc a vegetable garden with raised beds and a small summerhouse, part of which is alleged to be Georgian. Please inform us at time of booking if wheelchair access is required.

&. 🍷

15 NORTHCOURT MANOR GARDENS

Main Road, Shorwell, Newport, PO30 3JG. Mr & Mrs J Harrison, 01983 740415, john@northcourt.info, www.northcourt.info. *4m SW of Newport. On entering Shorwell from Newport, entrance at bottom of hill on R. If entering from other directions head through village in direction of Newport. Garden on the L, on bend after passing the church.* **Sun 10 Apr (12-4). Tea. Sun 18 Sept (12-5). Home-made teas. Adm £5, chd free. Visits also by arrangement Mar to Sept for groups of 8 to 45.**
15 acre garden surrounding large C17 manor house (not open). Boardwalk along jungle garden. Stream and bog garden. A large variety of plants enjoying the different microclimates. Large collection of camellias and magnolias. Woodland walks. Tree collection. Salvias and subtropical plantings for autumn drama. Productive walled kitchen garden. Some steep paths in places. Picturesque wooded valley around the house. Bathhouse and snail mount leading to terraces. 1 acre walled garden. The house celebrated its 406th yr anniversary. A plantsman' garden. Wheelchair access on main paths only, some paths are uneven and the terraces are hilly.

&. 🐐 🌾 🛏 🍷 •))

16 ◆ NUNWELL HOUSE

Coach Lane, Brading, PO36 0JQ. Mr & Mrs S Bonsey, 01983 407240, info@nunwellhouse.co.uk, www.nunwellhouse.co.uk. *3m S of Ryde. Signed off A3055 as you arrive at Brading from Ryde & turn into Coach Ln.* **For NGS: Sun 10 July (1-4.30). Adm £5, chd free. Home-made teas. For other opening times and information, please phone, email or visit garden website.**
6 acres of tranquil and beautifully set formal and shrub gardens and old fashioned shrub roses prominent. Exceptional Solent views over historic parkland and Brading Haven from the terraces. Small arboretum and walled garden with herbaceous borders. House developed over 5 centuries and full of architectural interest.

🌾 🚗 🍷

17 NEW OAKDENE

Main Road, Rookley, Ventnor, PO38 3NH. Mr Tim Marshall. *Oakdene is next to Rookley Old School on the Shanklin side & almost opp Niton Rd. Parking will be signed.* **Sat 23, Sun 24 July (11-4). Combined adm with Corris £5, chd free. Light refreshments at Corris.**
A village garden with a variety of features. Trees and shrubs, herbaceous and annual flowers, vegetable beds and glasshouse housing both annual and perennial, ornamental and food crops. Orchard and bees also kept and honey for sale. A nice display of historical photographs of the house, garden and the village. Wheelchair access via a concrete slope from the drive to the back garden.

&. 🌾 🍷

18 SALTERNS COTTAGE

Salterns Road, Seaview, PO34 5AH. Susan & Noël Dobbs, 01983 612132, sk.dobbs@icloud.com. *Enter Seaview from W via Springvale, Salterns Rd links the Duver Rd with Bluett Ave.* **Visits by arrangement Apr to Sept for groups of 8 to 30. Adm £5, chd free. Light refreshments.**
A glasshouse, a potager, exotic borders and fruit trees are some of the many attractions in this 40 metre x 10 metre plot. Salterns Cottage is a listed building built in 1640 and was bought in 1927 by Noël's grandmother Florence, married to Bram Stoker the author of Dracula. The garden was created by Susan in 2005 when she sold her school. Flooding and sandy soil poses a constant challenge to the planting. The greenhouse and potager all raised to cope with floods. Visitors welcome to see garden renovation in progress.

🌾 🍷 •))

19 THORLEY MANOR

Thorley, Yarmouth, PO41 0SJ. Mr & Mrs Anthony Blest. *1m E of Yarmouth. From Bouldnor take Wilmingham Ln, house ½m on L.* **Sun 22 May (2-5). Combined adm with Goldings £5, chd free. Tea.**
Mature informal gardens of over 3 acres surrounding manor house (not open). Garden set out in a number of walled rooms, perennial and colourful self-seeding borders, shrub borders, lawns, large old trees and an unusual island lawn, all seamlessly blending in to the surrounding farmland. The delightful cottage garden of Goldings is open a short walk away.

🐐 🌾 🍷

20 NEW YEW TREE LODGE

Love Lane, Bembridge, PO35 5NH. Jane Bland. *On the Bembridge circular one way system, take 1st L after Co-op into Love Ln. Darts is on the L, Yew Tree Lodge is facing you when Love Ln turns sharply to the R.* **Sun 12 June (12.30-5). Combined adm with Darts £6, chd free. Home-made teas.**
Yew Tree Lodge garden is flanked by mature oak trees and well established gardens, its main axis being north south. It is divided into separate areas which take into account available natural light and soil type. There have been gardening here for 10 yrs, during this time the garden has altered a great deal. As well as flowering plants there is a vegetable garden, fruit cages and a cool greenhouse. Paved path connecting the front and back gardens and paved access to decking area.

&. 🌾 🍷 •))

National Garden Scheme gardens are identified by their yellow road signs and posters. You can expect a garden of quality, character and interest, a warm welcome and plenty of home-made cakes!

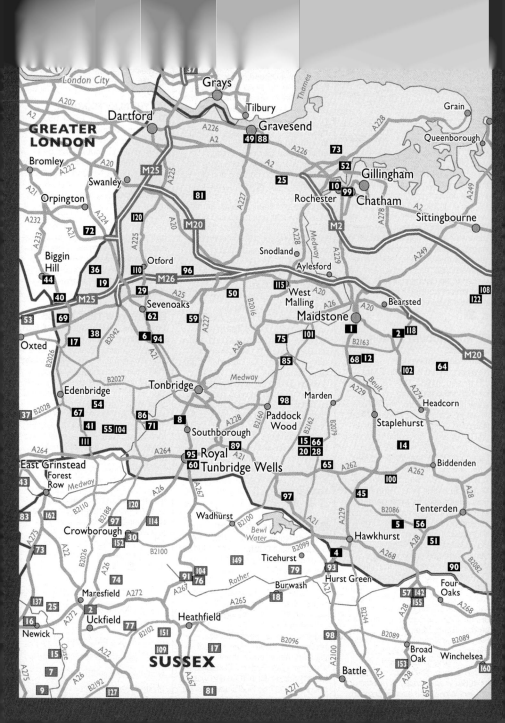

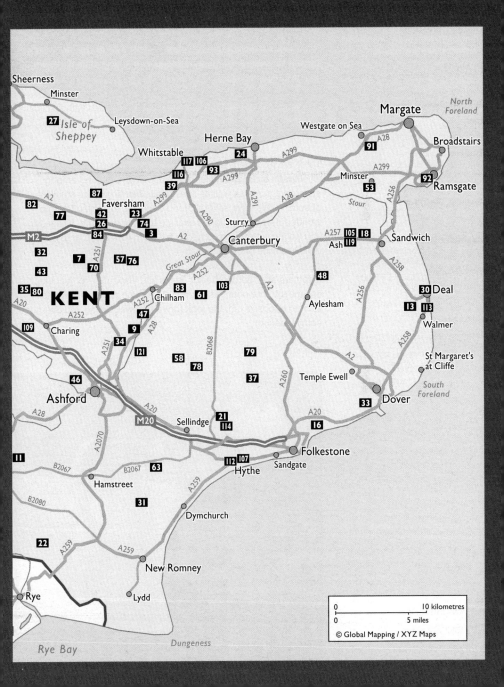

Volunteers

County Organiser
Jane Streatfeild 01342 850362
janestreatfeild@btinternet.com

County Treasurer
Andrew McClintock 01732 838605
andrew.mcclintock@ngs.org.uk

Publicity
Susie Challen
susie.challen@ngs.org.uk

Booklet Advertising
Nicola Denoon-Duncan
01233 758600
nicola.denoonduncan@ngs.org.uk

Booklet Co-ordinator
Ingrid Morgan Hitchcock
01892 528341
ingrid@morganhitchcock.co.uk

Booklet Distribution
Diana Morrish 01892 723905
diana.morrish@ngs.org.uk

Assistant County Organisers
Jacqueline Anthony 01892 518879
jacquelineanthony7@gmail.com

Marylyn Bacon 01797 270300
ngsbacon@ramsdenfarm.co.uk

Clare Barham 01580 241386
clarebarham@holepark.com

Pam Bridges
pam.bridges@ngs.co.uk

Mary Bruce 01795 531124
mary.bruce@ngs.org.uk

Liz Coulson 01233 813551
coulson.el@gmail.com

Kate Dymant 07766201806
katedymant@hotmail.co.uk

Andy Garland
andy.garland@bbc.co.uk

Jo Hammond
jo.hammond@ngs.org.uk

Virginia Latham 01303 862881
lathamvj@gmail.com

Diana Morrish (as above)

Nicola Talbot 01342 850526
nicola@falconhurst.co.uk

@KentNGS

@NGSKent

@nationalgardenschemekent

Famously known as 'The Garden of England', it is no wonder that over a quarter of Kent has been designated as Areas of Outstanding Natural Beauty.

The unique landscapes here offer ancient woodlands and rolling downs, as well as haunting marshes and iconic white cliffs along the 350-mile coastline.

Being the oldest county too means that Kent is filled with fascinating historic sites and buildings, several of which open their gardens for the NGS such as Ightham Mote and Sissinghurst Castle.

There are also many enchanting private gardens to explore, of all different sizes and styles. Inspiration can be found among expansive acres as well as in exquisite planting in the smallest of spaces. We have several group openings as well, offering a wonderful way to explore a seaside town or a country village. You will be warmly welcomed in all, often with a cup of tea and a delicious slice of cake!

If you are after garden design ideas and inspiration, or just want to escape into the countryside, there is a huge range of gardens in Kent to choose from. We look forward to welcoming you over the coming season.

Below: Dean House

OPENING DATES

All entries subject to change. For latest information check **www.ngs.org.uk**

Map locator numbers are shown to the right of each garden name.

Extended openings are shown at the beginning of each month.

January

Wednesday 19th
Spring Platt — 102

Sunday 23rd
Spring Platt — 102

Sunday 30th
Spring Platt — 102

February

Snowdrop Festival

By arrangement
The Old Rectory, Fawkham · 81

Thursday 3rd
Spring Platt — 102

Saturday 5th
Knowle Hill Farm — 64

Sunday 6th
Knowle Hill Farm — 64

Monday 7th
Knowle Hill Farm — 64

Wednesday 9th
Spring Platt — 102

Saturday 12th
Copton Ash — 26

Sunday 20th
Copton Ash — 26
◆ Doddington Place — 32
Frith Old Farmhouse — 43
◆ Goodnestone Park Gardens — 48

March

Sunday 6th
Haven — 53

Sunday 13th
◆ Godinton House & Gardens — 46
Stonewall Park — 104

Tuesday 15th
◆ Hever Castle & Gardens — 54

Sunday 20th
Copton Ash — 26

Sunday 27th
Copton Ash — 26
Godmersham Park — 47
◆ Great Comp Garden — 50
Haven — 53
◆ Mount Ephraim Gardens — 74
Potmans Heath House — 90

Thursday 31st
◆ Ightham Mote — 59

April

Every Sunday from Sunday 10th
Copton Ash — 26

Sunday 3rd
◆ Doddington Place — 32
Linton Park — 68

Sunday 10th
◆ Doddington Place — 32
◆ Hole Park — 56

Wednesday 13th
Oak Cottage and Swallowfields Nursery — 78

Thursday 14th
Oak Cottage and Swallowfields Nursery — 78

Friday 15th
Haven — 53

Monday 18th
Haven — 53

Saturday 23rd
Bilting House — 9
The Knoll Farm — 63

Sunday 24th
Balmoral Cottage — 5
Bilting House — 9
Eagleswood — 35
Frith Old Farmhouse — 43

Potmans Heath House — 90

Saturday 30th
Bishopscourt — 10
NEW Postillions — 89

May

Sunday 1st
◆ Boldshaves — 11
Copton Ash — 26
Goddards Green — 45
Haven — 53
NEW Postillions — 89

Monday 2nd
Haven — 53
NEW Postillions — 89

Sunday 8th
◆ Boughton Monchelsea Place — 12
Elgin House — 36
Frith Old Farmhouse — 43
Meadow Wood — 71
Stonewall Park — 104

Tuesday 10th
◆ Riverhill Himalayan Gardens — 94

Wednesday 11th
◆ Hole Park — 56

Saturday 14th
43 The Ridings — 93
The Silk House — 98

Sunday 15th
Balmoral Cottage — 5
◆ Godinton House & Gardens — 46
Ladham House — 65
The Orangery — 83

Tuesday 17th
◆ Scotney Castle — 97

Friday 20th
Avalon — 3

Saturday 21st
Avalon — 3
Bilting House — 9
Little Gables — 69

Sunday 22nd
◆ Belmont — 7
Bilting House — 9
Eagleswood — 35
Elgin House — 36
Frith Old Farmhouse — 43
Haven — 53
Little Gables — 69
43 The Ridings — 93
St Clere — 96

Whitstable Joy Lane Gardens — 116

Wednesday 25th
Great Maytham Hall — 51

Friday 27th
Oak Cottage and Swallowfields Nursery — 78

Saturday 28th
The Coach House — 23
NEW Dover Garden Trail — 33
Falconhurst — 41
Oak Cottage and Swallowfields Nursery — 78

Sunday 29th
The Coach House — 23
52 Cobblers Bridge Road — 24
Copton Ash — 26
NEW Dover Garden Trail — 33

June

Saturday 4th
Enchanted Gardens — 39
Falconhurst — 41
Topgallant — 107
Vergers — 112

Sunday 5th
Enchanted Gardens — 39
Haven — 53
Old Bladbean Stud — 79
Topgallant — 107
Tram Hatch — 109
Vergers — 112

Monday 6th
Haven — 53
Norton Court — 77

Tuesday 7th
Norton Court — 77

Wednesday 8th
18 Royal Chase — 95

Friday 10th
NEW Windmill Cottage — 118

Saturday 11th
142 Cramptons Road — 29
Elham Gardens — 37
Faversham Gardens — 42
Ivy Chimneys — 60
Little Gables — 69
Tankerton Gardens — 106
NEW Windmill Cottage — 118

Sunday 12th
◆ Boughton Monchelsea Place — 12
Brewery Farmhouse — 13

50 Pine Avenue

During 2020 – 2021 National Garden Scheme funding supported over 1,400 Queen's Nurses to deliver virtual and hands-on, community care across England, Wales and Northern Ireland

THE GARDENS

1 14 ANGLESEY AVENUE
Maidstone, ME15 9SH. Mike & Hazel Brett, 01622 299932, mhbrett06@gmail.com. *2m S of Maidstone. From Maidstone take A229 (bus routes 5 & 89) & after Swan pub 1st R into Anglesey Ave. Limited street parking.* **Visits by arrangement Apr to June for groups of up to 15. Adm £3.50, chd free. Light refreshments.** Plantsman's 120ft x 30ft garden with many unusual plants. Raised beds, rockeries and troughs accommodating alpine/rock garden plants. Herbaceous and shrub borders plus a shady woodland area at the end of the garden with hellebores, erythroniums, trilliums, anemones etc.

2 ARNOLD YOKE
Back Street, Leeds, Maidstone, ME17 1TF. Richard & Patricia Stileman, 07968 787950, richstileman@btinternet.com. *5m E of Maidstone. Fm M20 J8 take A20 Lenham R to B2163 to Leeds. Thru Leeds R into Horseshoes Ln, 1st R into Back St. House ¾ m on L. Fm A274 follow B2163 to Langley L into Horseshoes Ln 1st R Back St.* **Sun 19 June (2-6). Adm £5, chd free. Home-made teas. Visits also by arrangement May to Sept for groups of 10 to 20. By arrangement price inc tea & cake, & garden tour.** Recently redesigned ½ acre garden, adjacent to C15 Wealden Hall house with formal structure of box and yew embracing long mixed border, and centrally placed 'paradise garden' with water feature. Wheelchair access from the car park and around most parts of the garden.

3 AVALON
57 Stoney Road, Dunkirk, ME13 9TN. Mrs Croll, avalongarden8@gmail.com. *4m E of Faversham, 5m W of Canterbury, 2½m E of J7 M2. M2 J7 or A2 E of Faversham take A299, first L, Staplestreet, then L, R past Mt Ephraim, turn L, R. From A2 Canterbury, turn off Dunkirk, bottom hill turn R, Staplestreet then R, R. Park in side roads.* **Fri 20, Sat 21**

May, Fri 17, Sat 18, Sun 19 June, Fri 8, Sun 10 July, Fri 12, Sat 13, Sun 14 Aug (11-4). Adm £6, chd free. Visits also by arrangement June to Aug for groups of up to 12. ½ acre woodland garden, for all seasons, on north west slope, something round every corner, views of surrounding countryside. Collections of roses, hostas and ferns plus rhododendrons, shrubs, trees, vegetables, fruit, unusual plants, flowers for local shows. Planted by feeling, making it a reflective space and plant lovers garden. Plenty of seating for taking in the garden and resting from lots of steps.

4 NEW BADGERS
Bokes Farm, Horns Hill, Hawkhurst, Cranbrook, TN18 4XG. Bronwyn Cowdery, 01580 754178, cowderyfamily@btinternet.com. *On the border of Kent & East Sussex. In centre of Hawkhurst, follow A229 in the direction of Hurst Green. Pass the The Wealden Advertiser. At sharp L bend turn R up Horns Hill. Drive SLOWLY up Horns Hill.* **Visits by arrangement in Sept for groups of 10 to 25. Adm £5, chd free. Home-made teas. Covered area for teas** The garden comes into its own in September when the Tropical Garden is in full growth. There is also a walled Italian style garden, small Japanese area and woodland with ponds and a waterfall. The Tropical Garden has a wide variety of Palms, Bananas, Gingers, Eucomis, Gingers and Dahlias and has a network of paths threading through for you to explore and immerse yourself in the Tropics.

5 BALMORAL COTTAGE
The Green, Benenden, Cranbrook, TN17 4DL. Charlotte Molesworth, thepottingshedholidaylet@gmail. com. *Few 100 yds down unmade track to W of St George's Church, Benenden.* **Sun 24 Apr, Sun 15 May, Wed 15 June (12-5). Adm £6, chd £2.50. Refreshments available at Hole park (separate additional price).** An owner created and maintained garden now 33 yrs mature. Varied, romantic and extensive topiary form the backbone for mixed borders. Vegetable garden, organically managed. Particular attention to the needs of nesting birds and small mammals lend this artistic

plantswoman's garden a rare and unusual quality. No hot borders or dazzling dahlias here, where autumn exemplifies the 'season of mists and mellow fruitfulness'.

6 BEECHMONT HALL
Gracious Lane, Sevenoaks, TN13 1TH. Lene Hansen, 01732 461657, lene@netvigator.com. *There are four different 'Beechmonts' on this road. Please turn L after 'Little Beechmont' when coming from the Tonbridge Rd direction.* **Sat 25, Sun 26 June (10-4). Adm £12, chd free. Adm inc cream teas. Visits also by arrangement June & July.** Panoramic views across the Weald towards Ashdown Forest create a spectacular borrowed landscape for the sweeping curves of this award-winning modern garden. Lovingly created over the last decade it celebrates a passion for supporting local wildlife, the elegant elements of Japanese aesthetics and unusual plants (Buddha's Hand, Pseudolarix, Golden Elm and Wollemi pine amongst others). The garden is easily accessible from the car park.

7 ◆ BELMONT
Belmont Park, Throwley, Faversham, ME13 0HH. Harris (Belmont) Charity, 01795 890202, administrator@belmont-house.org, www.belmont-house.org. *4½m SW of Faversham. A251 Faversham-Ashford. At Badlesmere, brown tourist signs to Belmont.* **For NGS: Sun 22 May (12-5), open nearby Frith Old Farmhouse. Sun 3 July (12-5), open nearby Pheasant Barn. Adm £5, chd free. Home-made cakes. For other opening times and information, please phone, email or visit garden website.** Belmont House is surrounded by large formal lawns that are landscaped with fine specimen trees, a pinetum and a walled garden containing long borders, wisteria and large rose border. Across the drive there is a second walled kitchen garden, restored in 2001 to a design by Arabella Lennox-Boyd. Inc vegetable and herbaceous borders, hop arbours and walls trained with a variety of fruit. The gardens are open daily from 10 am - 6pm (dusk if earlier).

GROUP OPENING

8 BIDBOROUGH GARDENS
Bidborough, Tunbridge Wells, TN4 0XB. *3m N of Tunbridge Wells, between Tonbridge & Tunbridge Wells W off A26. Take B2176 Bidborough Ridge signed to Penshurst. Take 1st L into Darnley Drive, then 1st R into St Lawrence Ave, no. 2.* **Sun 3 July (1-5). Combined adm £6, chd free. Home-made teas at Boundes End. Gluten and dairy free cake available. Donation to Hospice in the Weald.**

BOUNDES END
Carole & Mike Marks, 01892 542233, carole.marks@btinternet.com, www.boundesendgarden.co.uk. Visits also by arrangement June to Aug for groups of up to 20.

NEW DARNLEY LODGE
Frances & Carl Stick.

SHEERDROP
Mr John Perry.

The Bidborough gardens (collect garden list from Boundes End, 2 St Lawrence Avenue) are in a small village at the heart of which are The Kentish Hare pub (book in advance), the church, village store and primary school. Partial wheelchair access, some gardens have steps.

  ♿ 🐕 ❄ ☕ 🔊

9 BILTING HOUSE
nr Ashford, TN25 4HA. Mr John Erle-Drax, 07764 580011, erle-drax@marlboroughgallery.com. *5m NE of Ashford. A28, 5m E from Ashford , 9m S from Canterbury. Wye 1½m.* **Sat 23, Sun 24 Apr, Sat 21, Sun 22 May (1.30-5.30). Adm £7, chd free. Home-made teas. Visits also by arrangement Apr to July for groups of 10 to 50.** 6 acre garden with ha-ha set in beautiful part of Stour Valley. Wide variety of rhododendrons, azaleas and ornamental shrubs. Woodland walk with spring bulbs. Mature arboretum with recent planting of specimen trees. Rose garden and herbaceous borders. Conservatory.

♿ 🐕 ❄ 🚗 ☕ 🔊

10 BISHOPSCOURT
24 St Margaret's Street, Rochester, ME1 1TS. Kelly Thomas (Head Gardener). *Central Rochester, nr castle & cathedral. On St Margaret's St at junction with Vines Lane.* **Sat 30 Apr, Sat 18 June (11-2). Adm £5, chd free. Home-made teas.** The residence of the Bishop of Rochester, this is a mature 1 acre historic walled garden within the heart of Rochester. Mature trees, lawns, yew hedges, rose garden, fountain, mixed herbaceous borders and a greenhouse next to a small vegetable garden. Child friendly. WC inc disabled.

♿ 🐕 ❄ ☕ 🔊

In 2021 the National Garden Scheme donated £500,000 to Marie Curie enabling us to continue providing our vital services and be there, caring for people on the frontline of the Coronavirus pandemic

Wye Gardens

1 ◆ BOLDSHAVES
Woodchurch, nr Ashford,
TN26 3RA. Mr & Mrs Peregrine
Massey, 01233 860283,
masseypd@hotmail.co.uk,
www.boldshaves.co.uk. *Between
Woodchurch & High Halden off
Redbrook St. From centre of
Woodchurch, with church on L &
Bonny Cravat/Six Bells Pub on R,
2nd L down Susan's Hill, then 1st
R after ½ m before L after a few
100 yrds to Boldshaves. Park as
indicated.* **Sun 1 May (2-6). Adm
£7.50, chd free. Home-made teas
In the Cliff Tea House (weather
permitting), otherwise in the
Barn. Donation to Kent Minds.**
7 acre garden developed over past 25
yrs, partly terraced, south facing, with
wide range of ornamental trees and
shrubs, walled garden, Italian garden,
Diamond Jubilee garden, camellia
dell, herbaceous borders (inc flame
bed, red borders and rainbow border),
vegetable garden, bluebell walks in
April, woodland and ponds; wildlife
haven renowned for nightingales and
butterflies. Home of the Wealden
Literary Festival. Grass paths.

**2 ◆ BOUGHTON
MONCHELSEA PLACE**
Church Hill, Boughton
Monchelsea, Maidstone,
ME17 4BU. Mr & Mrs Dominic
Kendrick, 01622 743120,
mk@boughtonplace.co.uk,
www.boughtonplace.co.uk. *4m SE
of Maidstone. From Maidstone follow
A229 S for 3½ m to T-lights at Linton
Xrds, turn L onto B2163, house 1m
on R; or take J8 off M20 & follow
Leeds Castle signs to B2163, house
5½ m on L. For Satnav use ME17
4HP.* **For NGS: Sun 8 May, Sun 12
June (2-5.30). Adm £5, chd £1.
Home-made teas. Cash payment
only. For other opening times and
information, please phone, email or
visit garden website.**
150 acre estate mainly park and
woodland, spectacular views over
own deer park and the Weald. Grade
I manor house (not open). Courtyard
herb garden, intimate walled gardens,
box hedges, herbaceous borders,
orchard. Planting is romantic
rather than manicured. Terrace
with panoramic views, bluebell
woods, wisteria tunnel, David Austin
roses, traditional greenhouse and
kitchen garden. Visit St. Peter's
Church next door to see the huge
stained glass Millennium Window

designed by renowned local artist
Graham Clark and the tranquil rose
garden overlooking the deer park of
Boughton Place.

3 BREWERY FARMHOUSE
182 Mongeham Road, Great
Mongeham, Deal, CT14 9LR.
Mr David & Mrs Maureen
Royston-Lee, 07966 202243,
david@davidroystonlee.com.
*On the corner of Mongeham Rd &
Northbourne Rd. Opp the village
green, with a white picket fence at
the front of the house, entrance to
the gardens are through the Brewery
yard at the back of the house -
entrance on Northbourne Rd.*
**Sun 12 June (10-4). Adm £6,
chd free. Light refreshments.
Visits also by arrangement June
& July for groups of up to 30.**
An established country walled garden
divided into a series of 'rooms'.
Roses, clematis, poppies abound in
herbaceous borders and against walls
and trellises.With water features, fruit
tree pergola and a chinese pagoda.

4 1 BRICKWALL COTTAGES
Frittenden, Cranbrook, TN17 2DH.
Mrs Sue Martin, 01580 852425,
sue.martin@talktalk.net,
www.geumcollection.co.uk.
*6m NW of Tenterden. E of A229
between Cranbrook & Staplehurst
& W of A274 between Biddenden
& Headcorn. Park in village & walk
along footpath opp school.* **Visits
by arrangement Apr to June for
groups of up to 30. Adm £5, chd
free. Home-made teas.**
The garden is a secluded oasis in the
centre of the village. It is filled with a
wide range of plants, inc many trees,
shrubs, perennials and over 100
geums which make up the National
Collection. In an effort to attract
more wildlife some areas of grass
have been left unmown, and a new
butterfly and moth 'meadow' was
created during lockdown to replace
the main nursery area. Some paths
are narrow and wheelchairs may not
be able to reach far end of garden.

5 CACKETTS FARMHOUSE
Haymans Hill, Horsmonden,
TN12 8BX. Mr & Mrs Lance
Morrish, 07831 432528,
diana.morrish@hotmail.co.uk.
Take B2162 from Horsmonden

*towards Marden. 1st R into Haymans
Hill, 200yds 1st L, drive immed
to R of Little Cacketts.* **Visits by
arrangement for groups of 10+.
Adm £7, chd free.**
1½ acre garden surrounding C17
farmhouse (not open). Walled garden,
bog garden and ponds, woodland
garden with unusual plants, bug
hotel. 4 acre hayfield with self planted
wildflowers.

6 69 CAPEL STREET
Capel-Le-Ferne, Folkestone,
CT18 7LY. John & Jenny Carter.
*Take B2011 from Folkestone towards
Dover. Past Battle of Britain Memorial
on R & then take first L into Capel
Street. 69 is 400yds on L.* **Sat 13,
Sun 14 Aug (11-4). Adm £4, chd
free. Light refreshments.**
A contemporary urban cottage
garden. A clever use of traditional
and modern planting providing
colour throughout the seasons. A
rectangular garden where straight
lines have been diffused by angles
and planting. Space is provided for
vegetables for self sufficiency. A quiet
location occasionally amplified by a
passing Spitfire. Walking distance to
the famous Battle of Britain Memorial
and pleasant walks along the White
Cliffs of Dover.

7 ◆ CHARTWELL
Mapleton Road, Westerham,
TN16 1PS. National
Trust, 01732 868381,
chartwell@nationaltrust.org.uk,
www.nationaltrust.org.uk/chartwell.
*4m N of Edenbridge, 2m S of
Westerham. Fork L off B2026 after
1½ m.* **For NGS: Wed 14 Sept
(10-5). Adm £8, chd free. For other
opening times and information,
please phone, email or visit garden
website.**
Informal gardens on hillside with
glorious views over Weald of Kent.
Water features and lakes together
with red brick wall built by Sir Winston
Churchill, former owner of Chartwell.
Lady Churchill's rose garden. Avenue
of golden roses runs down the centre
of a must see productive kitchen
garden. Hard paths to Lady Churchill's
rose garden and the terrace. Some
steep slopes and steps.

18 CHERRY TREE COTTAGE
Brookestreet, Ash, Canterbury,
CT3 2NP. Mrs Kate & Mr Neil
Dymant. *8m from Canterbury.
Turn off A257 into Hill's Court Rd
(opp side of bypass to Ash village),
continue ³/₄ m past Brookestreet
Farmhouse, garden entrance on L
after sharp L bend. Ample parking.*
**Fri 17 June, Fri 22, Sun 24 July
(11-5). Adm £6, chd free. Home-
made teas.**
1 acre garden managed completely
organically featuring a stream side
woodland garden, mixed borders,
gravel garden, ponds, orchards,
Japanese garden and formal
vegetable beds. Home to a wide
variety of wildlife. Most of the garden
is wheelchair accessible, fairly flat with
gravel paths except sloping woodland
garden.

ᕫ 🐄 ✻ ☕ 🪑

19 CHEVENING
nr Sevenoaks, TN14 6HG.
The Board of Trustees of the
Chevening Estate, 01732 744809,
info@cheveninghouse.com,
www.cheveninghouse.com. *4m
NW of Sevenoaks. Turn N off A25
at Sundridge T-lights on to B2211;
at Chevening Xrds 1¹/₂ m turn L.*
**Sun 12 June (2-5). Adm £8, chd
£1. Local teas, ice cream, Picnic
area. Visits also by arrangement
in June.**
The pleasure grounds of the Earls
Stanhope at Chevening House are
today characterised by lawns and
wooded walks around an ornamental
lake. First laid out between 1690 and
1720 in the French formal style, in the
1770s a more informal English design
was introduced. In the early C19
lawns, parterres and a maze were
established, a lake was created from
the ornamental canal and basin, and
many specimen trees were planted
to shade woodland walks. Expert-
guided group tours of the park and
gardens can sometimes be arranged
with the Estate Office when the house
is unoccupied. Gentle slopes, gravel
paths throughout.

ᕫ 🐄 ✻ ☕ 🪑))

20 CHURCH VIEW
Grovehurst Lane, Horsmonden,
Tonbridge, TN12 8BG. Mr & Mrs H
Tangen. *10m E of Tunbridge Wells.*
**Sun 17 July (12-5.30). Combined
adm with The Courtyard,
Horsmonden £8, chd free.**
Church View is a 1 acre south facing
sloping garden with spectacular

views across the Teise valley. Several
mixed herbaceous borders and raised
beds containing numerous bulbs,
shrubs and perennials, inc a wide
variety of plants attracting wildlife.
Woodland spring garden. Pond with
water feature set in rockery garden.
Terraced vegetable and fruit garden.
Several secluded seating areas.
Extensive country views. Wide variety
of plants attracting wildlife. Productive
fruit and vegetable garden.

21 CHURCHFIELD
Pilgrims Way, Postling,
Hythe, CT21 4EY. Chris &
Nikki Clark, 01303 863558,
coulclark@hotmail.com. *2m NW of
Hythe. From M20 J11 turn S onto
A20. 1st L after ¹/₂ m on bend take rd
signed Lyminge. 1st L into Postling.*
**Visits by arrangement Apr to
Sept. Adm £4, chd free.**
At the base of the Downs, springs
rising in this garden form the source
of the East Stour. Two large ponds
are home to wildfowl and fish and the
banks have been planted with drifts
of primula, large leaved herbaceous
bamboo and ferns. The rest of the
5 acre garden is a Kent cobnut platt
and vegetable garden, large grass
areas and naturally planted borders
and woodland. Postling Church open
for visitors.

🐄 ✻ 🚌 ☕ 🪑))

22 NEW CLIFF BARN
Knock Hill, Stone-in-Oxney,
Tenterden, TN30 7JX. Nicola &
James Denoon Duncan. *Between
Tenterden & Rye. Top of Knock Hill.*
**Sun 14 Aug (11-4.30). Adm £5,
chd free. Home-made teas.**
2 acre garden surrounding an C18
barn. Designed in 2013 by award
winning, Marian Boswall, and planted
by the owner. Positioned on the old
cliffs overlooking Romney Marsh
and the sea beyond. Hedges and
herbaceous borders, cottage garden,
new orchard, vegetable garden, large
wildlife pond and a walk to the edge
of the cliff to enjoy the unique views.
Gravel drive.

ᕫ 🅓 ☕ 🪑))

23 THE COACH HOUSE
Kemsdale Road, Hernhill,
Faversham, ME13 9JP. Alison
& Philip West, 07801 824867,
alison.west@kemsdale.plus.com.
*3m E of Faversham. At J7 of M2 take
A299, signed Margate. After 600
metres take 1st exit signed Hernhill,
take 1st L over dual carriageway to*

T-junction, turn R & follow yellow
NGS signs. **Sat 28, Sun 29 May
(11-6). Adm £6, chd free. Cream
teas. Visits also by arrangement
May to Sept.**
The ³/₄ acre garden has views over
surrounding fruit-producing farmland.
Sloping terraced site and island beds
with year-round interest, a pond
room, herbaceous borders containing
bulbs, shrubs, perennials and a
tropical bed. The different areas are
connected by flowing curved paths.
Unusual planting on light sandy soil
where wildlife is encouraged. Kent
Wild for Wildlife gold award winner
2019. Most of garden accessible to
wheelchairs but some slopes. Seating
available in all areas.

ᕫ 🐄 ✻ 🚌 ☕ 🪑))

**24 52 COBBLERS BRIDGE
ROAD**
Herne Bay, CT6 8NT. Mercy
Morris, www.home-plants.com. *10
mins walk from centre of Herne Bay.
Exit the A299 to Herne Bay. Cobblers
Bridge Rd can be accessed from
Sea St or Eddington Lane. Street
parking can be limited so allow time
to walk.* **Sun 29 May, Sun 28 Aug
(12-5). Adm £4, chd free. Pre-
booking essential, please phone
07860 537664, email mercy@
home-plants.com or visit
www.home-plants.com for
information & booking. Home-
made teas. Donation to Plant
Heritage.**
As you walk through the house
to the garden admire around 150
houseplants in a 1¹/₂ bedroom house;
from tiny airplants to philodendrons
and monsteras. A range of cacti,
succulents, tillandsia, tropical and
half-hardy plants. A further selection
of house plants are on view in the
greenhouse outside. Collection
of indoor plants suitable for most
homes.

✻ NPC ☕))

More than 1,200 people have
been cared for at Y Bwthyn
NGS Macmillan Specialist
Palliative Care Unit, a unit
that would simply not have
been built without the
National Garden Scheme
funding

The Old Rectory, Fawkham

25 ◆ COBHAM HALL

Cobham, DA12 3BL.
Mr D Standen (Bursar),
01474 823371,
www.cobhamhall.com. *3m W of
Rochester, 8m E of M25 J2. Ignore
SatNav directions to Lodge Ln.
Entrance drive is off Brewers Rd,
50 metres E from Cobham/Shorne
A2 junction.* **For NGS: Sun 14 Aug
(2-5). Adm £3.50, chd free. Cream
teas in the Gilt Hall. For other
opening times and information,
please phone or visit garden
website.**
1584 brick mansion (open for tours)
and parkland of historical importance,
now a boarding and day school for
girls. Some herbaceous borders,
formal parterres, drifts of daffodils,
C17 garden walls, yew hedges
and lime avenue. Humphry Repton
designed 50 hectares of park. Most
garden follies restored in 2009. Film
location for BBC's Bleak House series
and films by MGM and Universal. ITV
serial The Great Fire. CBBC filmed
serial 1 and 2 of Hetty Feather. Gravel
and slab paths through gardens.
Land uneven, many slopes. Stairs
and steps in Main Hall. Please call in
advance to ensure assistance.

&♿ 🐐 🚌 ☕

26 COPTON ASH

105 Ashford Road, Faversham,
ME13 8XW. Drs Tim & Gillian
Ingram, www.coptonash.plus.com.
*½ m S of A2, Faversham on A251.
On A251 Faversham to Ashford rd.
Opp J6 with M2. Park in
nearby laybys, single yellow lines are
Mon to Fri restrictions.* **Sat 12, Sun
20 Feb (12-4); Sun 20, Sun 27 Mar
(12-5). Every Sun 10 Apr to 1 May
(12-5). Sun 29 May (12-5); Sun
30 Oct (12-4). Adm £5, chd free.
Home-made teas. 2023: Sat 11,
Sun 19 Feb.**
Garden grown out of a love and
fascination with plants. Contains wide
collection inc many rarities and newly
introduced species raised from wild
seed. Special interest in woodland
flowers, snowdrops and hellebores
with flowering trees and shrubs of
spring. Refreshed Mediterranean
plantings to adapt to a warming
climate. Raised beds with choice
alpines and bulbs. Alpine and dryland
plant nursery. Gravel drive, shallow
step by house and some narrow
grass paths.

&♿ ❀ 🚌 ☕))

28 THE COURTYARD, HORSMONDEN

Grovehurst Lane, TN12 8BG.
Mr & Mrs Iain Stewart,
07860 804912,
georginacstewart@gmail.com,
www.capelcourtyard.co.uk.
*Between Horsmonden & Goudhurst.
From Horsmonden village,
follow yellow NGS signs towards
Goudhurst, leaving Gun & Spitroast
Pub on R. Approx 1m after
Horsmonden look for NGS signs
showing parking in field on L.* **Sun
17 July (12-5.30). Combined
adm with Church View £8, chd
free. Cream teas. Visits also by
arrangement in July.**
The Courtyard is a mid C19 Italianate
garden, forming a substantial part
of the Capel Manor estate built
for the Austen family (relatives
of the renowned Jane Austen)
of Horsmonden. The Courtyard
gardens cover several acres of formal
gardens and woodland inc a stunning
Mediterranean courtyard garden
using tranquil coloured planting with a
fountain at its centre. Amazing home-
made teas in The Courtyard with
plenty of seating. Most of the garden
can be viewed easily by wheelchair
but down towards, and within the
formal woodland, the paths are loose
gravel.

&♿ ❀ 🚌 🏠 ☕

You can make a difference! Join our Great British Garden Party fundraising campaign and raise money for some of the best-loved nursing and health charities. Visit ngs.org.uk/gardenparty to find out how you can get involved

27 THE COURTYARD, SHEERNESS

Elmley Road, Minster On Sea,
ME12 3SS. Kyle Ratcliffe. *Located
on The Isle of Sheppey, 11m from
the M2. From the A2500, travel past
the rugby club, over the small r'about
& turn immed R after the 2nd hand
car lot. Our garden is situated to the
rear of the 5th bungalow on the L.*
**Sun 26 June, Sun 24, Mon 25 July,
Sun 28 Aug (10.30-3). Adm £5,
chd free. Cream teas.**
A young garden and home created
in October 2016 by the BBC DIY
SOS team. This is our family garden
and smallholding which is enjoyed
by our four young children daily. Our
family garden has planted borders
and raised beds. Having raised flower
beds aids our two young sons who
are full-time wheelchair users, to enjoy
their garden too. Sensory based,
family focused garden. We are a
smallholding with a few hens, pigs,
sheep, honey bees and hives, a small
raised fish pond and a little pony. We
welcome all families - especially those
with children with special needs.
Tarmac and hard stone pathways
and drive.

&♿ 🐐 ☕

29 142 CRAMPTONS ROAD

Sevenoaks, TN14 5DZ. Mr Bennet
Smith. *3½ m from M25 J5. 1½ m
N of Sevenoaks, off Otford Rd
(A225) between Bat & Ball T-lights &
Otford. Access to garden via side/
rear passage. Limited parking in
Cramptons Rd.* **Sat 11, Sun 12
June (11-5). Adm £3.50, chd free.
Light refreshments.**
A very small, lush and leafy
plantsman's oasis. A tapestry of
plants selected for texture, elegance,
leaf shape, long-season interest or
rarity: wildlife-friendly umbellifers;
acers, sassafras, tetrapanax,
pseudopanax and Aesculus wangii.
Immerse yourself in plants and
discover what can be created
and combined in a tiny space. Kent Life
Garden Awards Finalist (September
2019), RHS The Garden (Oct. 2021).

❀ ☕))

GROUP OPENING

30 DEAL TOWN GARDENS

Deal, CT14 6EB. *Signs from all town car parks, maps & tickets at all gardens.* **Sun 26 June (11-5). Combined adm £5, chd free. Home-made teas at 53 Sandown Road.**

4 GEORGE ALLEY
Lyn Freeman & Barry Popple.

4 ROBERT STREET
Christine & Peter Hayes-Watkins.

8 ROBERT STREET
Gill & Nigel Walshe.

16 ST ANDREW'S ROAD
Martin Parkes & Paul Green.

NEW **5 ST PATRICK'S CLOSE**
Chris & Geoff Hobbs-East.

53 SANDOWN ROAD
Robin Green & Ralph Cade.

88 WEST STREET
Lyn & Peter Buller.

Start from any town car park (signs from here). 88 West Street: A non water cottage garden with perennials, shrubs, clematis and roses and shade garden. 4 George Alley: A pretty alley leads to a secret garden with courtyard, leading to a vibrant cottage garden with summerhouse. 4 Robert Street: A small walled garden divided into four areas. Bedding plants, perennials, shrubs, trees, mature bamboos and water feature. 8 Robert Street: A walled garden with an added bonus of a verge overflowing with colour. 16 St Andrew's Road: A tropical themed walled urban garden with large sun-drenched borders, lawn and family seating area. 53 Sandown Road: A south west facing garden with garden rooms for entertainment. Decking terraces surround the house with pots of summer flowering bulbs. 5 St Patrick's Close: South-facing, rented garden, featuring roses, herbs and scented flowers in a range of containers and pots. The summerhouse hosts a OO gauge railway which extends into the garden.
✿ ⚲

31 NEW DEAN HOUSE

Newchurch, Romney Marsh, TN29 0DL. Jaqui Bamford, 07480 150684, jaquibamford@gmail.com. *Between the village of Newchurch & New Romney. Leave B2067 at Bilsington Xrds SE towards New Romney. Continue for 2.9m to S bend. Garden on R after bend. From New Romney leave A259 NE onto St Marys Rd. Continue for 3.7m. Garden on L.* **Visits by arrangement July to Sept for groups of up to 12. Adm £7.50, chd free. Tea.**
A garden created over 20 yrs, from an old farmyard, featuring mature trees, shady areas, wildlife pond, paths, secluded sitting areas, sun-drenched gravel beds and herbaceous borders designed for pollinators. Extensive views across Romney Marsh. Visitors can explore the field next to garden maintained for wildlife. Collection of large cacti some over 40 yrs old. Cannas also a feature. Wheelchair must be operable on flat gravel and grass areas. Stepping stone paths and some seating will not be accessible.
ঙ 🐐 ☕ 🎪 »))

32 ♦ DODDINGTON PLACE

Church Lane, Doddington, Sittingbourne, ME9 0BB. Mr & Mrs Richard Oldfield, 01795 886101, enquiries@ doddingtonplacegardens.co.uk, www.doddingtonplacegardens. co.uk. *6m SE of Sittingbourne. From A20 turn N opp Lenham or from A2 turn S at Teynham or Ospringe (Faversham), all 4m.* **For NGS: Sun 20 Feb, Sun 3, Sun 10 Apr, Sun 25 Sept (11-5). Adm £9, chd £2.50. Home-made teas. For other opening times and information, please phone, email or visit garden website.**
10 acre garden, wide views; trees and cloud clipped yew hedges; woodland garden with azaleas and rhododendrons; Edwardian rock garden (not wheelchair accessible); formal garden with mixed borders. A flint and brick late C20 gothic folly; newly installed at the end of the Wellingtonia walk, a disused pinnacle from the southeast tower of Rochester Cathedral. Snowdrops in February. Chelsea Fringe Events. Wheelchair access possible to majority of gardens except rock garden.
ঙ 🐐 ✿ 🚗 ☕ »))

GROUP OPENING

33 NEW DOVER GARDEN TRAIL

Dover, CT17 9PU. *Tickets & maps will be available from all gardens - at CT15 5EH, CT15 7ER & CT17 9PU. Yellow signs in place.* **Sat 28 May (11-5); Sun 29 May (2-5). Combined adm £5, chd free. Home-made teas at Lacey Down and Windy Ridge.**

NEW **LACEY DOWN**
Wendy & Nick Smith.

NEW **2 QUEENS AVENUE**
Deborah Gasking.

NEW **WINDY RIDGE, DOVER ROAD**
Mr David & Mrs Marianne Slater.

Three very different gardens, from artist's long, narrow cottage garden to terraced garden on a south facing hillside inc planted garage roof, and a large well-established garden in ⅓ acre plot. All contain water features and use of recycled materials in many varied ways but that is where the similarity ends. Ideas for all sorts of gardening conundrum. None of the gardens are wheelchair accessible.
✿ ⚲

34 DOWNS COURT

Church Lane, Boughton Aluph, Ashford, TN25 4EU. Mr Bay Green. *4m NE of Ashford. From A28 Ashford or Canterbury, after Wye Xrds take next turn NW to Boughton Aluph Church signed Church Ln. Fork R at pillar box, garden only drive on R. Park in field. Disabled may park in drive.* **Sun 19, Sun 26 June (2-5.30). Adm £5, chd free.**
3 acre downland garden on alkaline soil with fine trees, mature yew and box hedges, mixed borders. Shrub roses and rose arch pathway, small parterre. Sweeping lawns and lovely views over surrounding countryside.
ঙ 🚗 »))

35 EAGLESWOOD

Slade Road, Warren Street, Lenham, ME17 2EG. Mike & Edith Darvill, 01622 858702, mike.darvill@btinternet.com. *E on A20 nr Lenham, L into Hubbards Hill for approx 1m then 2nd L into Slade Rd. Garden 150yds on R. Coaches permitted by prior arrangement.* **Sun 24 Apr, Sun 22 May (11-5), open nearby Frith Old Farmhouse. Sun**

Quex Gardens

9 Oct (11-5). Adm £5, chd free.
**Light refreshments. Visits also by
arrangement Apr to Oct for groups
of 5+. Donation to Demelza House
Hospice.**
2 acre plant enthusiasts garden. Wide
range of trees and shrubs (many
unusual), herbaceous material and
woodland plants grown to give year-
round interest.

36 ELGIN HOUSE
**Main Road, Knockholt, Sevenoaks,
TN14 7LH. Mrs Avril Bromley.** *Off
A21 between Sevenoaks/Orpington
at Pratts Bottom r'about, rd signed
Knockholt (Rushmore Hill) 3m on
R, follow yellow NGS signs. Main
Rd is continuation of Rushmore Hill.*
**Sun 8, Sun 22 May (1.30-5). Adm
£7.50, chd free. Home-made teas.**
Victorian family house surrounded
by a garden which has evolved over
the last 50 years. A new pergola
garden created in 2020. Bluebells and

green tree shoots on mature trees.
Rhododendrons, azaleas, wisteria,
camellias, magnolias, mature trees,
inc a magnificent cedar tree and
spacious lawns. This garden is on the
top of the North Downs.

GROUP OPENING

37 ELHAM GARDENS
**High Street, Elham, CT4 6TD.
www.elhamgardeningsociety.org.
uk.** *10m S of Canterbury, 6m N of
Hythe. Enter Elham from Lyminge (off
A20) or Barham (off A2). Car parking
in various locations as signposted
inc the Village Hall & weather
permitting, the Primary Sch Grounds
in New Rd.* **Sat 11, Sun 12 June
(12-4.30). Combined adm £7.50,
chd free. Home-made teas in the
Old Vicarage Garden, available
between 2.00-4.30.**
Elham has a thriving community of

amateur gardeners, many of whom
will open their gardens in this idyllic
setting. This picturesque village with
its beautiful Grade I listed St Mary's
church at its centre, is situated in
glorious countryside within the Elham
Valley Area of Outstanding Natural
Beauty. The Elham Food & Craft
Festival will be in The Square and
St Mary's Church between 11am -
2pm on Sunday 12 June with the
declaration of the winners of the
Elham Scarecrow competition. There
will be a plant stall in the Vicarage
Garden.

Our 2021 donations mean
that 72,000 people accessed
bereavement support
through hospices in the UK

38 ◆ EMMETTS GARDEN
Ide Hill, Sevenoaks, TN14 6BA.
National Trust, 01732 751507,
emmetts@nationaltrust.org.uk,
www.nationaltrust.org.uk/
emmetts-garden. *5m SW of
Sevenoaks. 1½ m S of A25 on
Sundridge-Ide Hill Rd. 1½ m N of
Ide Hill off B2042.* **For NGS: Wed
7 Sept (10-5). Adm £8, chd free.
For other opening times and
information, please phone, email or
visit garden website.**
5 acre hillside garden, with the highest
tree top in Kent, noted for its fine
collection of rare trees and flowering
shrubs. The garden is particularly
fine in spring, while a rose garden,
rock garden and extensive planting
of acers for autumn colour extend
the interest throughout the season.
Hard paths to the Old Stables for
light refreshments and WC. Some
steep slopes. Volunteer driven buggy
available for lifts up steepest hill.

39 ENCHANTED GARDENS
Sonoma House, Pilgrims Lane,
Seasalter, Whitstable, CT5 3AP.
Mrs Donna Richardson,
www.enchantedgardenskent.co.uk.
*2m from Whitstable Town.
Whitstable: At r'about, take exit onto
A290 Canterbury. At r'about, take
3rd exit onto A299 ramp London/
Faversham Merge onto A299.
Take slip rd offered on L, turn R for
Pilgrims Lane.* **Sat 4, Sun 5 June,
Sat 24, Sun 25 Sept (10.30-5).
Adm £5, chd free. Home-made
teas inc a variety of vegan home-
made cakes.**
It has taken 25 years to create
Enchanted Gardens from our
farmland to the traditional cottage
style garden it is today. I am
passionate about the loss of our
pollinating insects and am organic. I
have collections of roses, shrubs and
perennials in herbaceous borders
for all garden situations to provide
colour and interest from February
to December. Over 100 roses, 40+
peony, established natural habitats,
pond, bog garden, mature trees.

40 EUREKA
Buckhurst Rd, Westerham
Hill, TN16 2HR. Gordon &
Suzanne Wright, 01959 570848,
sb.wright@btinternet.com. *Park at
Westerham Heights Garden Centre
TN16 2HW off A233, 200m from*
Eureka. Parking at house for those
with walking difficulties. **Sat 18, Sun
19 June, Sat 9, Sun 10, Sat 30, Sun
31 July, Sat 20, Sun 21 Aug (11-4).
Adm £5, chd free. Home-made
teas. Visits also by arrangement for
groups of 15 to 30.**
Approx 1 acre garden with a blaze of
colourful displays in perennial borders
and the eight cartwheel centre beds.
Sculptures, garden art, chickens,
lots of seating and stairs to a viewing
platform. Many quirky surprises at
every turn. 100s of annuals in tubs
and baskets, a David Austin shrub
rose border and a free Treasure Trail
with prizes for all children. Garden
art inc 12ft Blacksmith's made red
dragon, a horse's head carved out
of a 200yr old yew tree stump and a
10ft dragonfly on a reed. Wheelchair
access to most of the garden.

41 FALCONHURST
Cowden Pound Road, Markbeech,
Edenbridge, TN8 5NR. Mr & Mrs
Charles Talbot, 01342 850526,
nicola@falconhurst.co.uk,
www.falconhurst.co.uk. *3m SE of
Edenbridge. B2026 at Queens Arms
pub turn E to Markbeech. 2nd drive
on R before Markbeech village.* **Sat
28 May, Sat 4 June (11-5). Adm
£6, chd free. Home-made teas.
Visits also by arrangement May &
June for groups of 12 to 40.**
4 acre garden with fabulous views
devised and cared for by the same
family for 170 yrs. Deep mixed borders
with old roses, peonies, shrubs and
a wide variety of herbaceous and
annual plants; ruin garden; walled
garden; interesting mature trees and
shrubs; kitchen garden; wildflower
meadows with woodland and pond
walks. Market garden, pigs, orchard
chickens; lambs in the paddocks.

GROUP OPENING

42 FAVERSHAM GARDENS
Faversham, ME13 8QN. *On edge
of town, short distance from A2 &
train stn. From M2 J6 take A251, L
into A2, R into The Mall. Start at No.
58.* **Sat 11 June (11-5). Combined
adm £6, chd free. Tea at The
Abbey Physic Community Garden
ME13 7BG 10.30-3.30.**

54 ATHELSTAN ROAD
Sarah Langton-Lockton OBE.

NEW 58 THE MALL
Jane Beedle.

19 NEWTON ROAD
Posy Gentles,
www.posygentles.co.uk.

NEW 12 NORMAN ROAD
Anne Vincent.

17 NORMAN ROAD
Mary & John Cousins.

5 distinctive walled gardens in historic
Faversham. Start at 58 The Mall, a
contemporary garden packed with
pollinators, created in 2018, with
materials reused in wire gabions to
create raised beds and a wildlife
haven. On to 54 Athelstan Road,
an 82ft walled garden packed with
unusual shrubs, hardy perennials,
vegetables and fruit. Next, 17 Norman
Road, a 90ft walled garden with
trees, shrubs, flowers and raised
vegetable beds, two ponds, patio,
pergola and a small greenhouse. 12
Norman Road is a newly created
wildlife garden dedicated to UK native
planting. 19 Newton Road, a long,
thin walled town garden in which
privacy and elements of surprise
have been created with planting and
turns in footpaths. There is exuberant
planting of perennials and roses, and
the group of maturing Chinese birch
provides scope for shade planting.

43 FRITH OLD FARMHOUSE
Frith Road, Otterden, Faversham,
ME13 0DD. Drs Gillian &
Peter Regan, 01795 890556,
peter.regan@cantab.net. *½ m off
Lenham to Faversham rd. From A20
E of Lenham N up Hubbards Hill,
follow signs Eastling;. after 4m L into
Frith Rd. From A2 in Faversham turn
S (Brogdale Rd); continue 7m (thro'
Eastling), R into Frith Rd Limited
parking - may be necessary to park
some distance away on roadside.*
**Sun 20 Feb (11-3); Sun 24 Apr,
Sun 8, Sun 22 May (11-4.30). Adm
£5, chd free. Home-made teas.
Visits also by arrangement Apr to
Sept for groups of up to 40.**
A riot of plants growing together as if
in the wild, developed over 40 years.
No neat edges or formal beds, but
several hundred interesting (and some
very unusual) plants. Trees and shrubs
chosen for year-round appeal. Special
interest in bulbs and woodland plants.
Visitor comments - 'one of the best
we have seen, natural and full of
treasures', 'a plethora of plants',

'inspirational', 'a hidden gem'. Altered habitat areas to increase the range of plants grown. Areas for wildlife. Unusual trees and shrubs.

44 GARDENVIEW
6 Edward Road, Biggin Hill, Westerham, TN16 3HL. Freda Davis, www.fredasgarden.co.uk. *Off A233, 7½ m S of Bromley, 3½ m N of Westerham. Edward Rd is located at the southern end of Main Rd, Biggin Hill by the pedestrian crossing. Parking available on rd. Buses 246 (Village Green Way stop) & 320 (Lebanon Gardens stop).* **Sun 24 July (12-4). Adm £5, chd free. Home-made teas.**
Full of interest with a wide variety of shrubs, small orchard, vegetable beds and tranquil seating areas with carefully situated statuary, this garden has been transformed into an oasis, where live music is performed with an art exhibition in the studio. Various musicians will entertain visitors during the main opening. Just a 4 inch step.

45 GODDARDS GREEN
Angley Road, Cranbrook, TN17 3LR. John & Linde Wotton, 01580 715507, jpwotton@gmail.com, www.goddardsgreengarden.com. *½ m SW of Cranbrook. On W of Angley Rd. (A229) at junction with High St, opp War Memorial.* **Sun 1 May, Sun 3 July (12-4). Adm £5, chd free. Home-made teas. Visits also by arrangement May to Sept for groups of 10 to 50.**
Gardens of about 5 acres, surrounding beautiful 500+yr old clothier's hall (not open), laid out in 1920s and redesigned since 1992 to combine traditional and modern planting schemes. fountain and rill, water garden, fern garden, mixed borders of bulbs, perennials, shrubs, trees and exotics; birch grove, grass border, pond, kitchen garden, meadows, arboretum and mature orchard. Some slopes and steps, but most areas (though not the toilets) are wheelchair accessible. Disabled parking is reserved near the house.

46 ♦ GODINTON HOUSE & GARDENS
Godinton Lane, Ashford, TN23 3BP. The Godinton House Preservation Trust. *1½ m W of Ashford. M20 J9 to Ashford. Take A20 towards Charing & Lenham, then follow brown tourist signs.* **For NGS: Sun 13 Mar, Sun 15 May, Fri 17 June, Fri 23 Sept (1-6). Adm £7, chd free. Pre-booking essential, please phone 01233 643854, email info@godintonhouse.co.uk or visit www.godintonhouse.co.uk for information & booking. Home-made teas. Ticket office serves takeaway refreshments, check website for tearoom opening times. For other opening times and information, please phone, email or visit garden website.**
12 acres complement the magnificent Jacobean house. Terraced lawns lead through herbaceous borders, rose garden and formal lily pond to intimate Italian garden and large walled garden with delphiniums, potager, cut flowers and iris border. March/April the 3 acre wild garden is a mass of daffodils, fritillaries, primroses and other spring flowers. Delphinium Festival (11 June - 26 June). Garden workshops and courses throughout the year. Partial wheelchair access to ground floor of house and most of gardens.

47 GODMERSHAM PARK
Godmersham, CT4 7DT. Mrs Fiona Sunley. *5m NE of Ashford. Off A28, midway between Canterbury & Ashford.* **Sun 27 Mar, Sun 12 June (1-5). Adm £5, chd free. Home-made teas in the Orangery. Donation to Godmersham Church.**
24 acres of restored wilderness and formal gardens set around C18 mansion (not open). Topiary, rose garden, herbaceous borders, walled kitchen garden and recently restored Italian and swimming pool gardens. Superb daffodils in spring and roses in June. Historical association with Jane Austen. Also visit the Heritage Centre. Deep gravel paths.

48 ♦ GOODNESTONE PARK GARDENS
Wingham, Canterbury, CT3 1PL. Julian Fitzwalter, 01304 840107, enquiries@goodnestoneparkgardens.co.uk, www.goodnestoneparkgardens.co.uk. *6m SE of Canterbury. Village lies S of B2046 from A2 to Wingham. Brown tourist signs off B2046. Use CT3 1PJ for satnav.* **For NGS: Sun 20 Feb, Sun 11 Sep (10-5). Adm £8, chd £2. Light refreshments at The Old Dairy Cafe. Café tel: 01304 695098. For other opening times and information, please phone, email or visit garden website.**
One of Kent's outstanding gardens and the favourite of many visitors. 14 acres with views over parkland. Something special year-round from snowdrops and spring bulbs to the famous walled garden with old fashioned roses and kitchen garden. Outstanding trees and woodland garden with cornus collection and hydrangeas later. Two arboretums and a contemporary gravel garden.

49 GRAVESEND GARDEN FOR WILDLIFE
68 South Hill Road, Windmill Hill, Gravesend, DA12 1JZ. Judith Hathrill, 07810 550991, judith.hathrill@live.com. *On Windmill Hill 0.6m from Gravesend town centre. 1.8m from A2. From A2 take A227 towards Gravesend. At T-lights with Cross Lane turn R then L at next T-lights, following yellow NGS signs. Park in Sandy Bank Rd or Leith Park Rd.* **Sun 3 July (12-5). Adm £5, chd free. Home-made teas. Visits also by arrangement Apr to Aug for groups of up to 10.**
Features and planting designed to attract and feed wildlife with borders containing a colourful mix of trees, shrubs, perennials, annuals, herbs, grasses, wildflowers, fruit and vegetables. Three wildlife ponds. Containers of fruit, flowers and vegetables on the terraces. Small lawn with seating, summerhouse and arbour to sit and enjoy the tranquillity. Information and leaflets about gardening for wildlife always available.

Hever Castle & Gardens

50 ♦ GREAT COMP GARDEN

Comp Lane, Platt, nr Borough Green, Sevenoaks, TN15 8QS. Great Comp, 01732 885094, office@greatcompgarden.co.uk, www.greatcompgarden.co.uk. *7m E of Sevenoaks. 2m from Borough Green Station. Accessible from M20 & M26 motorways. A20 at Wrotham Heath, take Seven Mile Lane, B2016; at 1st Xrds turn R; garden on L ½ m.* **For NGS: Sun 27 Mar, Sun 30 Oct (10-5). Adm £8.50, chd free. For other opening times and information, please phone, email or visit garden website.**
Skilfully designed 7 acre garden of exceptional beauty. Spacious setting of well maintained lawns and paths lead visitors through plantsman's collection of trees, shrubs, heathers and herbaceous plants. Early C17 house (not open). Magnolias, hellebores and snowflakes (leucojum), hamamellis and winter flowering heathers are a great feature in the spring. A great variety of perennials in summer inc salvias, dahlias and crocosmias. Tearoom open daily for morning coffee, home-made lunches and afternoon teas. Most of garden accessible to wheelchair users. Disabled WC.

51 GREAT MAYTHAM HALL

Maytham Road, Rolvenden, Tenterden, TN17 4NE. The Sunley Group, 07751 539097, gmh@greatmaythamhall.co.uk. *3m from Tenterden. Maytham Rd off A28 at Rolvenden Church, ½ m from village on R. Designated parking for visitors.* **Wed 25 May, Wed 22 June (1-4). Adm £7, chd free. Visits also by arrangement May to Dec.**
Lutyens designed gardens famous for having inspired Frances Hodgson Burnett to write The Secret Garden (pre Lutyens). Parkland, woodland with bluebells. Walled garden with herbaceous beds and rose pergola. Pond garden with mixed shrubbery and herbaceous borders. Interesting specimen trees. Large lawned area, rose terrace with far reaching views.

52 HAMMOND PLACE

High Street, Upnor, Rochester, ME2 4XG. Paul & Helle Dorrington. *3m NE of Strood or at A2. J1 take A289 twds Grain at r'about follow signs to Gillingham. After 2nd r'about take 1st L following signs to Upnor & Upnor Castle. Park in the free car park & continue by foot to the High St.* **Sat 25, Sun 26 June, Sat 16, Sun 17 July (11-5). Adm £4, chd free. Home-made teas.**
A small village garden around a Scandinavian style house growing an eclectic mix of fruit, vegetables and flowers. Greenhouse, Pond, Sauna Hut.

53 HAVEN

22 Station Road, Minster, Ramsgate, CT12 4BZ. Robin Roose-Beresford, 01843 822594, robin.roose@hotmail.co.uk. *Off A299 Ramsgate Rd, take Minster exit from Manston r'bout, straight rd, R fork at church Station Rd.* **Sun 6, Sun 27 Mar, Fri 15, Mon 18 Apr, Sun 1, Mon 2, Sun 22 May, Sun 5, Mon 6, Sun 19 June, Sun 10, Sun 31 July, Mon 1, Sun 28, Mon 29 Aug, Sun 18 Sept, Sun 16 Oct (10-4). Adm £5, chd free. Visits also by arrangement Mar to Oct for groups of up to 20. Any time or day with 24 hours notice by phone.**
Award winning 300ft garden, designed in the Glade style, similar to Forest gardening but more open and with use of exotic and unusual trees, shrubs and perennials, with wildlife in mind, devised and maintained by the owner, densely planted in a natural style with stepping stone paths. Two ponds (one for wildlife, one for fish with water lilies), gravel garden, rock garden, fernery, Japanese garden, cactus garden, hostas and many exotic, rare and unusual trees, shrubs and plants inc tree ferns and bamboos and year-round colour. Refreshment venues throughout the village. Greenhouse cactus garden. Collection of Bromeliads.

54 ♦ HEVER CASTLE & GARDENS

Edenbridge, TN8 7NG. Hever Castle Ltd, 01732 865224, info@hevercastle.co.uk, www.hevercastle.co.uk. *3m SE of Edenbridge. Between Sevenoaks & East Grinstead off B2026. Signed from J5 & J6 of M25, A21, A264.* **For NGS: Tue 15 Mar (10.30-4.30). Adm £15.85, chd £9.95. see website for details. For other opening times and information, please phone, email or visit garden website.**
Romantic double-moated castle, the childhood home of Anne Boleyn, set in 125 acres of formal and natural landscape. Topiary, Tudor herb garden, magnificent Italian garden with classical statuary, sculpture and fountains. 38 acre lake, yew and water mazes. Walled rose garden with over 4000 roses, 110 metre-long herbaceous border. Fine Daffodil displays in Mar and Tulip displays in Apr. Partial wheelchair access.

55 HOATH HOUSE

Chiddingstone Hoath, Edenbridge, TN8 7DB. Mr & Mrs Richard Streatfeild, 07973 842139, richard@hoathhouse.com, www.hoathhouse.com. *4m SE of Edenbridge via B2026. At Queens Arms Pub turn E to Markbeech. Approx 1m E of Markbeech.* **Visits by arrangement Feb to Oct for groups of 10 to 40. Adm £7.50, chd free.**
Mediaeval/Tudor family house surrounded by mature and unusual young trees, knot garden, shaded garden, herbaceous borders, yew hedges. Situated in the Kentish High Weald there are many stunning viewpoints across the surrounding countryside. This fine old garden beginning to show the effect of new ideas. Refreshments available and family will be on hand to give a brief description of the house and their long connection with it. Steps, a gravel drive and uneven paving stones may cause difficulty for wheelchairs.

Our 2021 donations mean that 12,478 unpaid carers have been supported through funding for Carers Trust

56 ◆ HOLE PARK

Benenden Road, Rolvenden, Cranbrook, TN17 4JB. Mr & Mrs Edward Barham, 01580 241344, info@holepark.com, www.holepark.com. *4m SW of Tenterden. Midway between Rolvenden & Benenden on B2086. Follow brown tourist signs from Rolvenden.* **For NGS: Sun 10 Apr, Wed 11 May, Wed 15 June, Sun 16 Oct (11-6). Adm £10, chd £2. Home-made teas. Picnics only in picnic site and car park please. For other opening times and information, please phone, email or visit garden website.**

Hole Park is proud to stand amongst the group of gardens which first opened in 1927 soon after it was laid out by my great grandfather. Our 15 acre garden is surrounded by parkland with beautiful views and contains fine yew hedges, large lawns with specimen trees, walled gardens, pools and mixed borders combined with bulbs, rhododendrons and azaleas. Massed bluebells in woodland walk, standard wisterias, orchids in flower meadow and glorious autumn colours make this a garden for all seasons. Wheelchairs are available for loan and may be reserved.

Ġ ⁂ ❀ ➡ ♨

57 NEW HOPPICKERS EAST

Hogbens Hill, Selling, Faversham, ME13 9QZ. Katherine Pickering. *Signs from HogbensHill. From A251 signed Selling 1m, then NGS signs.* **Wed 27 July (11-5). Combined adm with Norham House £6, chd free.**

A new garden, started in autumn 2020 on the edge of a field. No dig principles. Emphasis on plants for pollinators and other insects. White Lion pub nearby for lunches and refreshments. Adjoining organic forest farm offering guided tours. Flat grass paths.

Ġ ⁂ ❀ ➡ ♨ 🌳

58 HURST HOUSE

Waltham Road, Hastingleigh, Ashford, TN25 5JD. Mrs Lynn Smith, 01233 750120, btclynn@aol.com. *On the top of the downs above Wye Village, between Ashford and Canterbury, 10 mins from A28. From A28 go through Wye towards Hastingleigh. Follow rd over Downs to x-roads, L towards Waltham. Second turning on the R (first is a road), look out for NGS*

Signs. **Daily Mon 25 July to Fri 29 July (1.30-5). Sat 30, Sun 31 July (11.30-5). Adm £5, chd free. Pre-booking essential, please visit www.ngs.org.uk for information & booking. Home-made teas. Visits also by arrangement July & Aug for groups of 5+.**

3 acre idyllic garden surrounded by bluebell woods. Winner Kent Life garden of the year 2019. Mature borders, winding beds, ponds, planting designed for year-round colour. Damp shady borders/dry sunny borders, unusual plants, huge pieris and unusual trees. Stumpery planted with ferns/shade loving plants – woodland walk/painted forest with artwork on trees, intriguing features and sculptures. A massive owl mural, painted trees and many sculptures in the woods, with interest for all the family. Curving beds with huge variety of plants, flowing grasses and sculptural plants. Gravel garden with winding borders planted for colour throughout the year. Colourful displays of flowering pots. Is possible to use a wheelchair - gravel drive and muddy paths.

Ġ ⁂ ❀ ➡ ♨

59 ◆ IGHTHAM MOTE

Mote Road, Ivy Hatch, Sevenoaks, TN15 0NT. National Trust, 01732 810378, ighthammote@nationaltrust.org.uk, www.nationaltrust.org.uk/ightham-mote. *Nr Ivy Hatch: 6m E of Sevenoaks; 6m N of Tonbridge; 4m SW of Borough Green. E from Sevenoaks on A25 follow brown sign R along coach road. W from Borough Green on A25 follow brown sign L along coach rd. N from Tonbridge on A227 follow brown sign L along High Cross rd.* **For NGS: Thur 31 Mar, Thur 13 Oct (10-4). Adm £16, chd £8. A range of refreshments are available on site at the Mote Café. For other opening times and information, please phone, email or visit garden website.**

Lovely 14 acre garden surrounding a picturesque medieval moated manor house c1320, open for NGS since 1927. Herbaceous borders, lawns, C18 cascade, fountain pools, courtyards and a cutting garden provide formal interest; while the informal lakes, stream, pleasure grounds, stumpery, dell, fernery and orchard contribute to the sense of charm and tranquillity. Garden open 363 days of year. Children's trails usually available in school holidays. No dogs in main garden Mar to Oct

but can enter Nov to Feb or visit south lake area when open. Estate walks open to dogs all year. Please check NT Ightham Mote website for access details, opening times, prices and last admission. Access guide available at visitor reception.

Ġ ⁂ ➡ ➡ ♨ 🌳

60 IVY CHIMNEYS

Mount Sion, Tunbridge Wells, TN1 1TW. Laurence & Christine Smith. *At the end of Tunbridge Wells High St, with Pizza Express on the corner, turn L up Mount Sion. Ivy Chimneys is a red brick Queen Anne house at the top of the hill on the R.* **Sat 11 June (11-5). Adm £5, chd free. Pantiles cafes nearby.**

Town centre garden with herbaceous borders and masses of roses set on three layers of lawns enclosed in an old walled garden. This property also boasts a large vegetable garden with flowers for cutting and chickens for eggs! The property dates back to the late 1600's. Parking in public carparks near the Pantiles. Winner of best back garden in Tunbridge Wells in Bloom competition.

♨

61 KENFIELD HALL

Kenfield, Petham, Canterbury, CT4 5RN. Barnaby & Camilla Swire, kenfieldhallgarden@gmail.com. *Petham near Canterbury. Continue along Kenfield Road, down the hill and up the other side. Pass the farm and look out for the signs.* **Visits by arrangement May to July for groups of up to 30. Adm £10, chd free.**

The 8 acre gardens benefit from views within the AONB and its diverse wildlife, consisting of a sunken formal garden, lawns, mixed borders, herbaceous borders, spring bulbs, a Japanese water garden, orchards, an organic vegetable garden with glasshouses, a wildflower meadow, a rose garden and woodland garden.

➡ ♨

62 ◆ KNOLE

Knole, Sevenoaks, TN15 0RP. Lord Sackville, 01732 462100, knole@nationaltrust.org.uk, www.nationaltrust.org.uk/knole. *1½m SE of Sevenoaks. Leave M25 at J5 (A21). Park entrance S of Sevenoaks town centre off A225 Tonbridge Rd (opp St Nicholas Church). For SatNav use TN13*

1HX. **For NGS: Fri 15 July (11-4). Adm £5, chd £2.50. For other opening times and information, please phone, email or visit garden website.**
Lord Sackville's private garden at Knole is a magical space, featuring sprawling lawns, a walled garden, an untamed wilderness area and a medieval orchard. Access is through the beautiful Orangery, off Green Court, where doors open to reveal the secluded lawns of the 26 acre garden and stunning views of the house. Last entry at 3.30pm and closes at 4pm. Please book in advance using Knole's website. Refreshments are available in the Brewhouse Café. Bookshop and shop in Green Court. Wheelchair access via the bookshop into the Orangery. Some paths may be difficult in poor weather. Assistance dogs are allowed in the garden.

&. 💬

63 THE KNOLL FARM
Giggers Green Rd, Aldington, Ashford, TN25 7BY. Lord & Lady Aldington. *The Postcode leads to Goldenhurst, our drive entrance is opp & a little further down hill.* **Sat 23 Apr (12-5). Adm £8, chd free. Donation to Bonnington Church.**
10 acres of woodland garden with over 100 camellias, acer japonica, young specimen pines and oaks; bluebell wood; formal elements; Flock of Jacob Sheep around lake; long views across Romney Marsh. Picnics welcome by the lake. Paths throughout but the whole garden is on a slope.

&. 🐏 ✳ 🎋))

64 KNOWLE HILL FARM
Ulcombe, Maidstone, ME17 1ES. The Hon Andrew & Mrs Cairns, 01622 850240, elizabeth@knowlehillfarm.co.uk, www.knowlehillfarmgarden.co.uk. *7m SE of Maidstone. From M20 J8 follow A20 towards Lenham for 2m. Turn R to Ulcombe. After 1½ m, L at Xrds, after ½ m 2nd R into Windmill Hill. Past Pepper Box Pub, ½ m 1st L to Knowle Hill.* **Sat 5, Sun 6, Mon 7 Feb (11-3). Light refreshments. Sat 3, Sun 4, Mon 5 Sept (12-4). Home-made teas. Adm £6, chd free. Visits also by arrangement Feb to Sept.**
2 acre garden created over 35 years on South facing slope below the Greensand Ridge. Spectacular views. Snowdrops and hellebores, many tender plants, china roses,

agapanthus, verbenas, salvias and grasses flourish on light soil. Topiary continues to evolve with birds at last emerging. Lavender ribbons hum with bees. Pool enclosed in small walled white garden. A green garden completed in 2018. Access only for 35 seater coaches. Some steep slopes.

&. 🐏 ✳ 🚗 💬))

65 LADHAM HOUSE
Ladham Road, Goudhurst, TN17 1DB. Guy & Nicola Johnson. *8m E of Tunbridge Wells. On NE of village, off A262. Through village towards Cranbrook, turn L at The Goudhurst Inn. 2nd R into Ladham Rd, main gates approx 500yds on L.* **Sun 15 May (2-5). Adm £6, chd free.**
10 acres of garden with many interesting plants, trees and shrubs, inc rhododendrons, camellias, azaleas and magnolias. A beautiful rose garden, arboretum, an Edwardian sunken rockery, ponds, a vegetable garden and a woodland walk leading to bluebell woods. There is also a spectacular 60 metre twin border designed by Chelsea Flower Show Gold Medal winner, Jo Thompson. Small Classic Car Display.

💬))

66 NEW LAMPKYNS
School House Lane, Horsmonden, Tonbridge, TN12 8BJ. Mr & Mrs Jonathan Lyne, 07791 860928, deborahlyne58@gmail.co.uk. *From Horsmonden village, take Goudhurst Rd out of the village with green on your L. After 1½ m turn L into Grovehurst Rd. After another mile the road becomes Schoolhouse Lane.* **Sat 9, Sun 10 July (2-5). Adm £7, chd free. Home-made teas. Visits also by arrangement June & July for groups of 10+.**
3½ acre country garden evolving over 20 years. Yew topiary, vegetable and cut flower garden, pond, wild flower beds and walks and more formal flower beds. Hazel and willow constructed bird hide and bug house. Mature trees.

💬))

67 LEYDENS
Hartfield Road, Edenbridge, TN8 5NH. Roger Platts, www.rogerplatts.com. *1m S of Edenbridge. On B2026 towards Hartfield (use Nursery entrance & car park).* **Sun 7 Aug (12-5). Adm £6, chd free. Home-made teas.**

Private garden of garden designer, nursery owner and author who created NGS Garden at Chelsea in 2002, winning Gold and Best in Show, and in 2010 Gold and People's Choice for the M&G Garden and Gold in 2013. A wide range of roses, shrubs and perennials adjoining wild flower hay meadow and plant nursery. Kitchen garden and orchard. Plants clearly labelled and fact sheet available.

&. ✳ 🚗 💬))

68 LINTON PARK
Heath Road, Linton, Maidstone, ME17 4AB. Linton Park Plc, www.camellia.plc.uk. *ME17 4AJ is the post code for North Lodge at the top of drive on the main road. Visitors need to come down the drive for around ½ m to reach the main house & garden. Parking available.* **Sun 3 Apr, Sun 7 Aug (10.30-4). Adm £8.50, chd free. Home-made teas.**
Overlooking the Weald of Kent this south facing, hillside garden is set in 450 acres of parkland. Re-imagined over the last 35 years, using original J C Loudon plans and historic maps, it boasts wonderful mature tree specimens, amongst others, Copper Beech, Cedars, Limes and Oaks crowned by a magnificent avenue of Wellingtonia planted in the mid 19th century.

💬))

69 LITTLE GABLES
Holcombe Close, Westerham, TN16 1HA. Mrs Elizabeth James. *Centre of Westerham. Off E side of London Rd A233, 200yds from The Green. Please park in public car park. No parking available at house.* **Sat 21, Sun 22 May, Sat 11, Sun 12 June (1.30-4.30). Adm £5, chd free. Home-made teas.**
¾ acre plant lover's garden extensively planted with a wide range of trees, shrubs, perennials etc, inc many rare varieties. Collection of climbing and bush roses. Large pond with fish, water lilies and bog garden. Fruit and vegetable garden. Large greenhouse.

 💬

70 LORDS
Sheldwich, Faversham,
ME13 0NJ. John Sell CBE &
Barbara Rutter, 01795 536900,
john@sellwade.co.uk. *On A251
4m S of Faversham & 3½ m N of
Challock Xrds. From A2 or M2 take
A251 towards Ashford. ½ m S of
Sheldwich church find entrance
lane on R adjacent to wood.* Sun
12 June (2-5). Adm £6, chd free.
Home-made teas. Visits also
by arrangement Apr to July for
groups of 10 to 30.
C18 walled garden. Mediterranean
terrace and citrus standing. Flowery
meadow under apples, pears, quince,
crab apple and medlar. Grass tennis
court. A cherry orchard grazed by
Jacob sheep. Pleached hornbeams,
clipped yew hedges and topiary,
lawns, ponds and wild area. Fine
old sweet chestnuts, planes, copper
beech and 120ft tulip tree. Herb and
salad bed, garden sculpture. Some
gravel paths.
& ☕ ›))

71 MEADOW WOOD
Penshurst, TN11 8AD. Mr & Mrs
James Lee. *1¼ m SE of Penshurst,
5m SW of Tonbridge. On B2176 in
direction of Bidborough.* Sun 8 May
(11-5). Adm £7, chd free. Home-
made teas.
Mature 1920s garden, on edge of
woods, originally part of the Victorian
Swaylands Estate. Long southerly
views over the Weald, and interesting
mature trees and shrubs, azaleas,
rhododendrons, naturalised bulbs and
bluebells in woodlands with mown
walks. New lake.
& 🐴 ❀ ☕ 🎋 ›))

72 12 THE MEADOWS
Chelsfield, Orpington, BR6 6HS.
Mr Roger & Mrs Jean Pemberton.
*3m from J4 on M25. 10 mins walk
from Chelsfield station. Exit M25
at J4. At r'about 1st exit for A224,
next r'about 3rd exit - A224, ½ m,
take 2nd L, Warren Rd. Bear L into
Windsor Drive. 1st L The Meadway,
follow signs to garden.* Sun 12 June
(11-5). Adm £5, chd free. Home-
made teas.
Front garden Mediterranean style
gravel with sun loving plants. Rear
¾ acre garden in two parts. Semi-
formal Japanese style area with tea
house, two ponds, one Koi and one
natural (lots of spring interest). Acers,
grasses, huge bamboos etc and
semi wooded area, children's path
with 13ft high giraffe, Sumatran tigers

and lots of points of interest. Children
and well behaved dogs more than
welcome. Designated children's area.
Adults only admitted if accompanied
by responsible child! Silver award
for garden with the LGS. Winner of
first prize for our back garden from
Bromley in Bloom. Wheelchair access
to all parts except small stepped area
at very bottom of garden.
& 🐴 ❀ ☕

73 THE MOUNT
Haven Street, Wainscott,
Rochester, ME3 8BL.
Marc Beney & Susie Challen,
challensusie@gmail.com. *3½ m
N of Rochester. At M2 J1, take
A289 twds Grain. At r'bout, R into
Wainscott. Co-op ahead, turn R into
Higham Rd. R into Islingham Farm
Rd. Follow road up slight hill. House
first on L, through white gate.* Visits
by arrangement May & June for
groups of 10 to 20. Adm £5, chd
free. Home-made teas.
2 acres surround the house and inc
a renovated walled kitchen garden
with fruit trees, roses, vegetable beds
and a colourful herbaceous border;
old grass tennis court with a mown
labyrinth and a small nuttery around a
wildlife pond; white and yellow terrace
garden above a pleached lime path
with iris and lavender and below,
remains of Victorian glasshouses.
Lovely countryside views. Mature
specimen trees.
🐴 ❀ ☕

74 ◆ MOUNT EPHRAIM GARDENS
Hernhill, Faversham, ME13 9TX.
Mr & Mrs E S Dawes & Mr
W Dawes, 01227 751496,
info@mountephraimgardens.co.uk,
www.mountephraimgardens.co.uk.
*3m E of Faversham. From end
of M2, then A299 take slip rd 1st
L to Hernhill, signed to gardens.*
For NGS: Sun 27 Mar, Thur 16
June, Sun 25 Sept (11-5). Adm
£7, chd £2.50. Cream teas in
West Wing Tea Room. For other
opening times and information,
please phone, email or visit garden
website.
Mount Ephraim is a privately-
owned family home set in 10 acres
of terraced Edwardian gardens
with stunning views over the
Kent countryside. Highlights inc a
Japanese rock and water garden,
arboretum, unusual topiary and a
spectacular grass maze plus many
mature trees, shrubs and spring

bulbs. Partial wheelchair access; top
part manageable, but steep slope.
Disabled WC. Full access to tea
room.
& 🐴 ❀ ☕ 🛏 ☕ ☕

75 NETTLESTEAD PLACE
Nettlestead, Maidstone,
ME18 5HA. Mr & Mrs Roy Tucker,
www.nettlesteadplace.co.uk.
*6m W/SW of Maidstone. Turn S
off A26 onto B2015 then I m on
L, Nettlestead Court Farm after
Nettlestead Church.* Sun 12 June,
Sun 2 Oct (1.30-4.30). Adm £7,
chd free. Home-made teas.
C13 manor house in 10 acre
plantsman's garden. Large formal
rose garden. Large herbaceous
garden of island beds with rose and
clematis walkway leading to a recently
planted garden of succulents. Fine
collection of trees and shrubs; sunken
pond garden, a maze of Thuja,
terraces, bamboos, glen garden,
Acer lawn. Young pinetum adjacent
to garden. Sculptures. Wonderful
open country views. Maze. Gravel
and grass paths. Most of garden
accessible (but not sunken pond
garden). Large steep bank and lower
area accessible with some difficulty.
& 🐴 ☕ ☕ 🎋 ›))

76 NEW NORHAM HOUSE
Selling, Faversham, ME13 9RL.
Liz Bradley. *Off A251 to Selling,
past White Lion, house on corner of
road to Shottenden & Perry Wood.*
Wed 27 July (11-5). Combined
adm with Hoppickers East £6,
chd free.
2 acre country garden with
herbaceous beds, vegetable garden,
chickens and interesting plants. White
Lion pub nearby for lunches and
refreshments.
& 🐴 ❀ ☕

77 NORTON COURT
Teynham, Sittingbourne, ME9 9JU.
Tim & Sophia Steel, 07798 804544,
sophia@nortoncourt.net. *Off A2
between Teynham & Faversham. L
off A2 at Esso garage into Norton
Lane; next L into Provender Lane; L
signed Church for car park.* Mon 6,
Tue 7 June (2.30-5). Adm £5, chd
free. Home-made teas. Visits also
by arrangement June & July for
groups of 10 to 30.
10 acre garden within parkland
setting. Mature trees, topiary, wide
lawns and clipped yew hedges.
Orchard with mown paths through

wildflowers. Walled garden with mixed borders and climbing roses. Pine tree walk. Formal box and lavender parterre. Treehouse in the Sequoia. Church open, adjacent to garden. Flat ground except for 2 steps where ramp is provided.

 ♿ ☕ ᵃᵃ

78 OAK COTTAGE AND SWALLOWFIELDS NURSERY

Elmsted, Ashford, TN25 5JT. **Martin & Rachael Castle.** *6m NW of Hythe. From Stone St (B2068) turn W opp the Stelling Minnis turning. Follow signs to Elmsted. Turn L at Elmsted village sign. Limited parking at house, further parking at Church (7mins walk).* **Wed 13, Thur 14 Apr, Fri 27, Sat 28 May (11-4). Adm £5, chd free. Cream teas.**
Get off the beaten track and discover this beautiful ½ acre cottage garden in the heart of the Kent countryside. This plantsman's garden is filled with unusual and interesting perennials, inc a wide range of salvias. There is a small specialist nursery packed with herbaceous perennials. Auriculas displayed in traditional theatres in April.

 ❄ ☕

79 OLD BLADBEAN STUD

Bladbean, Canterbury, CT4 6NA. **Carol Bruce, www.oldbladbeanstud.co.uk.** *6m S of Canterbury. From B2068, follow signs into Stelling Minnis, turn R onto Bossingham Rd, then follow yellow NGS signs through single track lanes.* **Sun 5, Sun 19 June, Sun 3, Sun 17, Sun 31 July (2-6). Adm £6, chd free. Pre-booking essential, please visit www.ngs.org.uk for information & booking. Home-made teas.**
Five interlinked gardens all designed and created from scratch by the garden owner on 3 acres of rough grassland between 2003 and 2011. Romantic walled rose garden with over 90 old fashioned rose varieties, tranquil yellow and white garden, square garden with a tapestry of self sowing perennials and Victorian style greenhouse, 300ft long colour schemed symmetrical double borders and an organic fruit garden. The gardens are maintained entirely by the owner and were designed to be managed as an ornamental ecosystem with a large number of perennial species encouraged to set seed, and with staking, irrigation, mulching and chemical use kept an absolute minimum. Please see the garden website at www.

oldbladbeanstud.co.uk to read published articles, see photos of what's currently in bloom and for more visitor information.

 ❄ ☕

81 THE OLD RECTORY, FAWKHAM

Valley Road, Longfield, DA3 8LX. **Karin & Christopher Proudfoot, 01474 707513, keproudfoot@gmail.com.** *1m S of Longfield. Midway between A2 & A20, on Valley Rd 1½m N of Fawkham Green, 0.3m S of Fawkham church, opp sign for Gay Dawn Farm/ Corinthian Sports Club. Parking on drive only. Not suitable for coaches.* **Visits by arrangement in Feb for groups of up to 15. Also open by arrangement Feb 2023. Adm £5, chd free. Home-made teas.**
1½ acres with impressive display of long-established naturalised snowdrops and winter aconites; over 100 named snowdrops added more recently. Garden developed around the snowdrops over 35yrs, inc hellebores, pulmonarias and other early bulbs and flowers, with foliage perennials, shrubs and trees, also natural woodland. Gentle slope, gravel drive, some narrow paths.

 ♿ ❄ ☕ ᵃᵃ

54 Athelstan Road, Faversham Gardens

80 NEW **THE OLD RECTORY, OTTERDEN**
Bunce Court Road, Faversham, ME13 0BY. Mrs Gry Iverslien, 07734 538272, gry@iverslien.com. *North Downs. Postcode take you to a property called Bunce Ct. we are 600 yds further on just past Cold Harbour lane.* **Tue 30, Wed 31 Aug (11-4). Adm £5, chd free. Pre-booking essential, please visit www.ngs.org.uk for information & booking. Light refreshments. Visits also by arrangement Apr to Sept for groups of 6 to 16.**
4 acre woodland garden with numerous large Rhododendrons and Camellias, mass of spring bulbs with a formal rose garden, cutting garden and large hydrangea beds throughout the garden. The garden also has a large wildlife pond and a variety of trees of interest.
  ♿ ☕

82 **THE OLD VICARAGE**
Dully Road, Tonge, Sittingbourne, ME9 9NP. Sarah Varley. *Off A2 between Sittingbourne & Faversham. Please note location is Old Vicarage, & not Old Vicarage Bungalow. Parking available in field on corner of Dully rd & A2.* **Sun 26 June (11-5). Adm £5, chd free. Home-made teas. Open nearby Pheasant Barn.**
A delightful mature garden of just under 3 acres, inc an arboretum with some unusual trees, for example a tulip tree, a magnificent cedar, and ancient yews. Gravel paths meander through the wood and onto lawns where they pass formal hedging, mixed herbaceous borders, an active dovecote, a cut flower garden, a potager, a herb garden and more.
  ♿ ☕

83 **THE ORANGERY**
Mystole, Chartham, Canterbury, CT4 7DB. Rex Stickland & Anne Prasse, 01227 738348, rex.mystole@btinternet.com. *5m SW of Canterbury. Turn off A28 through Shalmsford St. In 1½m at Xrds turn R downhill. Continue, ignoring roads on L & R. Ignore drive on L (Mystole House only). At sharp R bend in 600yds turn L into private drive.* **Sun 15 May (1-6); Sat 30, Sun 31 July (1-5). Adm £5, chd free. Home-made teas. Visits also by arrangement Mar to Sept for groups of 10+.**
1½ acre gardens around C18 orangery, now a house (not open). Magnificent extensive herbaceous border and impressive ancient wisteria. Large walled garden with a wide variety of shrubs, mixed borders and unusual specimen trees. Water features and intriguing collection of modern sculptures in natural surroundings. Splendid views from the terrace over ha-ha to the lovely Chartham Downs. Ramps to garden.
  ♿ 🐕 ❀ 🚐 ☕

84 **OUDEN**
Brogdale Road, Ospringe, Faversham, ME13 8XY. Frances & Paul Moskovits. *Close to Faversham. From A2 in Faversham turn S along Brogdale Rd for ¾m, Ouden is on R. Parking on roadside.* **Sun 17, Thur 21 July (12-4). Adm £5, chd free.**
A variety of mature shrubs and trees form the backbone of this ¼ acre garden. The front garden features a shrubbery and cottage planting. The rear garden has a well-stocked colourful long border leading to two greenhouses. Exotic planting intermingles with traditional garden favourites. Small paths allow time for a closer look. Situated close to Belmont House & Gardens, The National Fruit Collection at Brogdale Farm and market town of Faversham. Has been featured in the Middle-sized garden youtube blog.

85 **PARSONAGE OASTS**
Hampstead Lane, Yalding, ME18 6HG. Edward & Jennifer Raikes, 01622 814272, jmraikes@ parsonageoasts.plus.com. *6m SW of Maidstone. On B2162 between Yalding village & stn, turn off at Boathouse Pub. over lifting bridge, cont 100 yds up lane. House & car park on L.* **Visits by arrangement Mar to Oct for groups of up to 20. Adm £5, chd free. Cream teas.**
Our garden has a lovely position on the bank of the River Medway. Typical

Topgallant

Oast House (not open) often featured on calendars and picture books of Kent. 70yr old garden now looked after by grandchildren of its creator. ³/₄ acre garden with walls, daffodils, crown imperials, shrubs, clipped box and a spectacular magnolia. Small woodland on river bank. Best in spring, but always something to see. Local Boathouse pub (5mins) and several nice places for a picnic in the garden. Unfenced river bank. Gravel paths. Bee hives.

&♿ 🚗 💷 🍽

86 ◆ PENSHURST PLACE & GARDENS
Penshurst, TN11 8DG. Lord & Lady De L'Isle, 01892 870307, contactus@penshurstplace.com, www.penshurstplace.com. *6m NW of Tunbridge Wells. SW of Tonbridge on B2176, signed from A26 N of Tunbridge Wells.* For NGS: Wed 14 Sept (10-5). Adm £11, chd £6.50. Light refreshments at The Porcupine Pantry at the visitor entrance. For other opening times and information, please phone, email or visit garden website.
11 acres of garden dating back to C14. The garden is divided into a series of rooms by over a mile of yew hedge. Profusion of spring bulbs, formal rose garden and famous peony border. Woodland trail and arboretum. Year-round interest. Toy museum. Some paths not paved and uneven in places; own assistance will be required. 2 wheelchairs available for hire.

&♿ ✳ 🚗 💷 🍽 »)

87 PHEASANT BARN
Church Road, Oare, ME13 0QB. Paul & Su Vaight, 07843 739301, suvaight46@gmail.com. *2m NW of Faversham. Entering Oare from Faversham, turn R at Three Mariners pub towards Harty Ferry. Garden 400yds on R, before church. Parking on roadside.* Sun 26 June (11-4), open nearby The Old Vicarage. Tue 28, Wed 29, Thur 30 June, Sat 2, Sun 3, Tue 5, Wed 6 July (11-4). Adm £7, chd free. Pre-booking essential, please visit www.ngs.org.uk for information & booking. Visits also by arrangement May to July for groups of up to 8.
Series of smallish gardens around award-winning converted farm buildings in beautiful situation overlooking Oare Creek. Main area is nectar-rich planting in formal design with a contemporary twist inspired

by local landscape. Also vegetable garden, dry garden, water features, wildflower meadow and labyrinth. July optimum for wildflowers. Kent Wildlife Trust Oare Marshes Bird Reserve within 1m. Two village inns serving lunches/dinners, booking recommended. Regional Finalist The English Garden's The Nation's Favourite Gardens 2021

🐕 »)

88 NEW 50 PINE AVENUE
Gravesend, DA12 1QZ. Tony Threlfall. *10 mins from the A2. Leave the A2 at the Gravesend East exit and continue on Valley Drive to the T junction at the end of Valley Drive where you turn L onto Old Rd East. The next turn on the R is Pine Ave.* Sat 6 Aug (11-4). Adm £5, chd free. Light refreshments.
The property sits on a steep ¼ acre plot with a swimming pool to the rear surrounded by tropical planting. Steps lead down to the lawn with mixed borders, and on to the middle patio with more tropical planting. Steps then lead down to the woodland area and then out to the pond. Not suitable for small children due to deep water.

🐕 ✳ 💷 🍽 »)

89 NEW POSTILLIONS
2 Hastings Road, Pembury, Tunbridge Wells, TN2 4PD. Mrs Daphne Males. *In the centre of Pembury village. White house next to St Peter's Church opposite the green near the Camden Arms. Gravel drive. No off road parking, except in the drive for disabled visitors only.* Sat 30 Apr, Sun 1, Mon 2 May (10.30-4.30). Adm £5, chd free. Home-made teas.
1 acre garden on three levels with herbaceous borders, small orchard, large vegetable and cutting garden. Second World War gun emplacement. Gravel drive. Slopes in garden.

&♿ ✳ 💷

90 POTMANS HEATH HOUSE
Wittersham, TN30 7PU. Dr Alan & Dr Wilma Lloyd Smith, 01797 270221, wilmalloydsmith@gmail.com. *1½m W of Wittersham. Between Wittersham & Rolvenden, 1m from junction with B2082. 200yds E of bridge over Potmans Heath Channel.* Sun 27 Mar, Sun 24 Apr (2-6). Adm £5, chd free. Home-made teas. Visits also by arrangement Apr to Oct for groups of 6 to 30.

Large country garden divided into compartments each with a different style. Daffodils, tulips and many blossoming ornamental cherry and apple trees in Spring, often spectacular. Many and varied rose species; climbers a speciality. Early summer beds and borders. Orchards, some unusual trees, lawns, part walled vegetable garden, two greenhouses. House not open. Nearest WC at Wittersham Church. Some awkward slopes but generally accessible.

&♿ 🐕 💷 »)

91 ◆ QUEX GARDENS
Quex Park, Birchington, CT7 0BH. Powell-Cotton Museum, 01843 842168, enquiries@powell-cottonmuseum.org, www.powell-cottonmuseum.org. *3m W of Margate. Follow signs for Quex Park on approach from A299 then A28 towards Margate, turn R into B2048 Park Lane. Quex Park is on L.* For NGS: Sun 17 July (10-4). Adm £5, chd free. Light refreshments in Felicity's Café and Quex Barn. For other opening times and information, please phone, email or visit garden website.
10 acres of woodland and gardens with fine specimen trees unusual on Thanet, spring bulbs, wisteria, shrub borders, old figs and mulberries, herbaceous borders. Victorian walled garden with cucumber house, long glasshouses, cactus house, fruiting trees. Peacocks, dovecote, chickens, Bees, woodland walk, wildlife pond, children's maze, croquet lawn, picnic grove, lawns and fountains. Head Gardener and team will be available on the day for a chat and to answer questions. Felicity's Café (outside museum) serving breakfast, lunch and cakes. Quex Barn farmers market selling local produce and serving breakfasts to evening meals. Picnic sites available. Garden almost entirely flat with tarmac paths. Sunken garden has sloping lawns to the central pond.

&♿ ✳ 🚗 💷

'National Garden Scheme donations have funded four of our gardens in regional NHS spinal injury centres supporting nearly 8,500 patients and their visitors.' *Horatio's Garden*

GROUP OPENING

92 RAMSGATE GARDENS
Ramsgate, CT11 9PX. Anne-Marie Nixey. *Enter Ramsgate on A299, continue on A255. At r'about take 2nd exit London Rd. Continue for less than 1m to the r'about and turn L onto Grange Rd or straight ahead down West Cliff Rd.* **Sun 11 Sept (12-5). Combined adm £5, chd free. Home-made teas.**

6 EDITH ROAD
Nicolette McKenzie.

104 GRANGE ROAD
Anne-Marie Nixey.

12 WEST CLIFF ROAD
Brian Daubney.

Evolving gardens in the beautiful, yet windy, coastal town of Ramsgate showing different sized plots and how to make unique gardens out of them. Varied planting from traditional roses and bedding plants to a range of vegetables and fruit trees, as well as use of recycled and sustainable materials and incorporating traditional family areas. Wheelchairs can access parts of 6 Edith Road and 104 Grange Road.

♿ ❉ ☕ ⇽

93 43 THE RIDINGS
Chestfield, Whitstable, CT5 3QE. David & Sylvie Buat-Menard, 01227 500775, sylviebuat-menard@hotmail.com. *Nr Whitstable. From M2 heading E cont onto A299. In 3m take A2990. From r'about on A2990 at Chestfield, turn onto Chestfield Rd, 5th turning on L onto Polo Way which leads into The Ridings.* **Sat 14, Sun 22 May (11-4). Adm £5, chd free. Home-made teas. Visits also by arrangement Apr to Sept for groups of 8 to 20.**
Delightful small garden brimming with interesting plants both in the front and behind the house. Many different areas. Dry gravel garden in front, raised beds with alpines and bulbs and borders with many unusual perennials and shrubs. The garden ornaments are a source of interest for visitors. The water feature will be of interest for those with a tiny garden as planted with carnivorous plants. Many alpine troughs and raised beds as well as dry shade and mixed borders all in a small space.

⇽ ❉ ♿ ☕

94 ♦ RIVERHILL HIMALAYAN GARDENS
Riverhill, Sevenoaks, TN15 0RR. The Rogers Family. *2m S of Sevenoaks on A225. Leave A21 at A225 & follow signs for Riverhill Himalayan Gardens.* **For NGS: Tue 10 May (9-5). Pre-booking essential, please phone 01732 459777, email info@riverhillgardens.co.uk or visit www.riverhillgardens.co.uk for information & booking. Wed 15 June (9-5). Adm £8, chd £8. Light refreshments in Riverhill Collective Cafe onsite. For other opening times and information, please phone, email or visit garden website.**
Beautiful hillside garden, privately owned by the Rogers family since 1840. Spectacular rhododendrons, azaleas and fine specimen trees. Edwardian Rock Garden with extensive fern collection, Rose Walk and Walled Garden with sculptural terracing. Bluebell walks. Extensive views across the Weald of Kent. Hedge maze, adventure playground, den building and Yeti spotting. Café serves speciality coffee, brunch, light lunches and cakes. Plant sales and quirky shed shop selling beautiful gifts and original garden ornaments. Disabled parking. Wheelchair access to Walled Garden and Rock Garden. Easy access to café, shop and tea terrace. Accessible WC.

♿ ⛳ ❉ ☕ 🍽 ⇽

95 18 ROYAL CHASE
Tunbridge Wells, TN4 8AY. Eithne Hudson. *Situated at the top of Mount Ephraim & The Common. Leave A21 at Southborough, follow signs for Tunbridge Wells. After St John's Rd take R turn at junction on Common & sharp R again. From S, follow A26 through town up over Common. Last turn on L.* **Wed 8 June (12-5). Adm £5, chd free. Tea.**
Town garden of a ¼ of an acre on sandy soil which was originally Common and woodland. Large lawn with island beds planted with roses and herbaceous perennials and a small pond with lilies and goldfish.The owner is a florist and has planted shrubs and annuals specifically with flower arranging in mind. Roses in semi woodland setting in central Tunbridge Wells. Access through right hand side gate.

♿ ⛳ ☕ ⇽

96 ST CLERE
Kemsing, Sevenoaks, TN15 6NL. Mr Simon & Mrs Eliza Ecclestone, www.stclere.com. *6m NE of Sevenoaks. 1m E of Seal on A25, turn L signed Heaverham. In Heaverham turn R signed Wrotham. In 75yds straight ahead marked Private Rd; 1st L to house.* **Sun 22 May (2-5). Adm £5, chd free. Home-made teas in the Garden Room.**
4 acre garden, full of interest. Formal terraces surrounding C17 mansion (not open), with beautiful views of the Kent countryside. Herbaceous and shrub borders, productive kitchen and herb gardens, lawns and rare trees. Some gravel paths and small steps.

♿ ⛳ ☕

97 ♦ SCOTNEY CASTLE
Lamberhurst, TN3 8JN. National Trust, 01892 893820, scotneycastle@nationaltrust.org.uk, www.nationaltrust.org.uk/ scotneycastle. *6m SE of Tunbridge Wells. On A21 London - Hastings, brown tourist signs. Bus: (Mon to Sat) Tunbridge Wells - Wadhurst, alight Lamberhurst Green.* **For NGS: Tue 17 May (10-5). Adm £12, chd £6. Light refreshments. For other opening times and information, please phone, email or visit garden website.**
The medieval moated Old Scotney Castle lies in a peaceful wooded valley. In C19 its owner Edward Hussey III set about building a new house, partially demolishing the Old Castle to create a romantic folly, the centrepiece of his picturesque landscape. From the terraces of the new house, sweeps of rhododendron and azaleas cascade down the slope in summer, mirrored in the moat. In the house three generations have made their mark, adding possessions and character to the homely Victorian mansion which enjoys far reaching views out across the estate. Wheelchairs available for loan.

♿ ⛳ ❉ ☕ ⇽ 🍽

98 THE SILK HOUSE
Lucks Lane, Rhoden Green, nr Paddock Wood, Tunbridge Wells, TN12 6PA. Adrian & Silke Barnwell, www.silkhousegarden.com. *Rhoden Green. The Silk House is ½ m from Queen St; on a sharp bend nr Lucks Ln Fishery. Can also be approached from Maidstone Rd. Disabled parking only at the house. All other parking in Lucks Ln.* **Sat**

14 May, Sat 20, Sun 21 Aug, Sun 16 Oct (10-4). Adm £7.50, chd £3. Light refreshments in garden.
A calm and gentle, Japanese stroll garden, Koi and wildlife ponds, unusual evergreen trees and bamboos, small woodland walk, kitchen garden, Mediterranean dry bank, new cloud garden, almost 2 acres overall, begun 2016. Designed, built and maintained entirely by owners. Main attraction is Japanese stroll garden. Lots of acers (spectacular in autumn especially) and cherry blossom in Spring. The structural planting looks good year-round. Picnics welcome for an additional charitable donation of £10, please take all your litter home. Disabled parking only at the house. Wheelchair users access via the oak framed outbuildings area to avoid steps. Some areas have steps and banks.

&. ✿ ☕ 🛈 🛋

99 SIR JOHN HAWKINS HOSPITAL
High Street, Chatham, ME4 4EW. Susan Fairlamb, www.hawkinshospital.org.uk. On the N side of Chatham High St, on the border between Rochester & Chatham. Leave A2 at J1 & follow signs to Rochester. Pass Rochester Station & turn L at main junction T-lights, travelling E towards Chatham. Sat 25, Sun 26 June (11-5). Adm £3, chd free. Cream teas. Additional light refreshments.
Built on the site of Kettle Hard - part of Bishop Gundulph's Hospital of St Bartholomew, the Almshouse is a square of Georgian houses dating from the 1790s. A delightful small secluded garden overlooks the River Medway, full of vibrant and colourful planting. A lawn with cottage style borders leads to the riverside and a miniature gnome village captivates small children and adults alike. Disabled access via stairlift, wheelchair to be carried separately.

&. 🐕 ✿ 🛈 »)

100 ♦ SISSINGHURST CASTLE GARDEN
Biddenden Road, Sissinghurst, Cranbrook, TN17 2AB. National Trust, 01580 710700, sissinghurst@nationaltrust.org.uk, www.nationaltrust.org.uk/sissinghurst-castle-garden. 2m NE of Cranbrook, 1m E of Sissinghurst on Biddenden Rd (A262), see our website for more information. For

NGS: Sun 18 Sept (11-5.30). Adm £15, chd £7.50. Light refreshments in Coffee Shop or Restaurant at Sissinghurst Castle Garden. For other opening times and information, please phone, email or visit garden website.
Historic, poetic, iconic; a refuge dedicated to beauty. Vita Sackville-West and Harold Nicolson fell in love with Sissinghurst Castle and created a world renowned garden. More than a garden, visitors can also find Elizabethan and Tudor buildings, find out about our history as a Prisoner of War Camp and see changing exhibitions. Picnic spot in the vegetable garden, picnics are not allowed in the formal garden. Free welcome talks and estate walks leaflets. Café, restaurant, gift, secondhand book and plant shops are open from 10am-5.30pm. Some areas unsuitable for wheelchair access due to narrow paths and steps.

&. ✿ 🛈 🛋 🛋

101 SMITHS HALL
Lower Road, West Farleigh, ME15 0PE. Mr S Norman. 3m W of Maidstone. A26 towards Tonbridge, turn L into Teston Lane B2163. At T-junction turn R onto Lower Rd B2010. Opp Tickled Trout pub. Sun 26 June (11-5). Adm £5, chd free. Home-made teas. Donation to Heart of Kent Hospice.
Delightful 3 acre gardens surrounding a beautiful 1719 Queen Anne House (not open). Lose yourself in numerous themed rooms: sunken garden, iris beds, scented old fashioned rose walk, formal rose garden, intense wild flowers, peonies, deep herbaceous borders and specimen trees. Gravel paths.

&. 🐕 ☕ 🛋 »)

102 SPRING PLATT
Boyton Court Road, Sutton Valence, Maidstone, ME17 3BY. Mr & Mrs John Millen, 01622 843383, carolyn.millen1@gmail.com, www.kentsnowdrops.com. 5m SE of Maidstone. From A274 nr Sutton Valence follow yellow NGS signs. Wed 19, Sun 23, Sun 30 Jan, Thur 3, Wed 9 Feb (11-3). Adm £5, chd free. Light refreshments. Visits also by arrangement Jan & Feb for groups of 8 to 50.
1 acre garden under continual development with panoramic views of the Weald. Over 650 varieties of snowdrop grown in tiered display beds with spring flowers in borders. An extensive collection of alpine plants in a large greenhouse. Vegetable garden, natural spring fed water feature and a croquet lawn.

🐕 ✿ 🚗 🛈

103 STABLE HOUSE, HEPPINGTON
Street End, Canterbury, CT4 7AN. Charlie & Lucy Markes. Stable House, Heppington, CT4 7AN. 2m S of Canterbury, off B2068. 1st R after Bridge Rd if coming from Canterbury, 400m after Granville pub on the L if coming towards Canterbury. Sat 16, Sun 17 July (1.30-5.30). Adm £4, chd free. Home-made teas.
Approx 2 acres of relaxed, informal interlinked gardens surrounding converted Edwardian stable block in lovely setting with views towards the North Downs. Mixed borders with mature shrubs and perennials. Climbing roses, honeysuckle and clematis. Gravel garden, veg garden and walkthrough garden room beneath clocktower. Adjoining 5 acre wildflower meadow and 15 acre vineyard. Large wildflower meadow. Disabled parking by arrangement close to garden. Not all areas wheelchair accessible.

&. 🐕 🛈 🛋 »)

In 2021 the National Garden Scheme donation helped support Perennial's caseworkers, who helped over 250 people and their families in crisis to receive a wide range of support including emergency food parcels and accommodation, energy payments and expert advice and information

104 STONEWALL PARK
Chiddingstone Hoath, nr Edenbridge, TN8 7DG. **Mr & Mrs Fleming.** *4m SE of Edenbridge. Via B2026. ½ way between Markbeech & Penshurst. Plenty of parking which will be signed.* **Sun 13 Mar, Sun 8 May (2-5). Adm £6, chd free. Home-made teas in the conservatory at the house. Donation to Sarah Matheson Trust & St Mary's Church, Chiddingstone.**
Even from the driveway you can see a vast amount of self-seeded daffodils, leading down to a romantic woodland garden in historic setting, featuring species such as rhododendrons, magnolias, azaleas and bluebells. You can see them in full flower on our May opening day. You can also discover a range of interesting trees, sandstone outcrops, wandering paths and lakes. The woods can be very wet and muddy, please don't forget your boots!

105 SWEETBRIAR
69 Chequer Lane, Ash, nr Sandwich, CT3 2AX. **Miss Louise Dowle & Mr Steven Edney.** *8m from Canterbury, 3m from Sandwich. Turn off A257 into Chequer Lane, 100 metres from junction on the L.* **Sun 17 July, Sun 21 Aug, Sun 25 Sept (10.30-4.30). Adm £5, chd free. Home-made teas.**
Exotic jungle garden of Steve Edney and Louise Dowle, multi gold medal winners at RHS Chelsea and Hampton court flower shows. Gold award from Kent wildlife trust. As seen as BBC Gardeners' World (Sept 2018, 2020).

GROUP OPENING

106 TANKERTON GARDENS
Tankerton, CT5 2EP. *The gardens are in a triangle, either on Northwood Rd or directly off it, or parallel to it.* **Sat 11 June (10-5). Combined adm £6, chd free. Local cafes are available in Tankerton High Street, Tower Parade and the Sea Front, within easy reach of all six gardens.**

17A BADDLESMERE ROAD
Mr Derek Scoones.

[NEW] 25 BADDLESMERE ROAD
Steve Grix & Dawn Lyon.

14 NORTHWOOD ROAD
Philippa Langton.

16 NORTHWOOD ROAD
Mr Simon Courage.

12 STRANGFORD ROAD
Sarah Yallop.

18 STRANGFORD ROAD
Mia Young.

Six very different gardens within a mile of the sea, enjoying a mild climate. 17a Baddlesmere Road featuring roses and densely planted for colour. The Strangford Road gardens are more traditional but with quirky and wildlife elements. The Northwood Road gardens are more contemporary. 25 Baddlesmere Road is new for 2022 and has been newly developed in the last three years.

107 TOPGALLANT
5 North Road, Hythe, CT21 5UF. **Mary Sampson.** *M20 exit 11, take A259 to Hythe, then going towards Folkestone at r'about, take 2nd L up narrow hill signed to Saltwood. L at junction with North Rd. House on L. See 'Vergers'.* **Sat 4, Sun 5 June (2-5). Combined adm with Vergers £6, chd free.**
Opening with Vergers, two very different hillside gardens, both terraced and developed to cope with the prevailing winds and the slope. Topgallant is a secluded Sculptors' garden, with mature trees and shrubs, a wildlife pond. Decking and grass paths wind down through the garden giving glimpses of the sea. Relaxed planting for year-round interest and to encourage wildlife. Ceramics studio open.

108 TORRY HILL
Frinsted/Milstead, Sittingbourne, ME9 0SP. **Lady Kingsdown,** 01795 830258, **lady.kingsdown@btinternet.com.** *5m S of Sittingbourne. M20 J8, A20, B2163 (Hollingbourne). R at Xrds (Ringlestone Rd). Frinsted-Doddington, NGS signs. M2 J5, A249 (Maidstone), 1st L (Bredgar), L (Bredgar), R at War Memorial, 1st L (Milstead), NGS signs.* **Sun 12 June, Sun 24 July (2-5). Adm £5, chd free. Home-made teas. Picnics welcome on cricket ground. Visits also by arrangement May to Aug for groups of 10 to 30. Please discuss refreshments at booking. Donation to St. Dunstan's Church, Frinsted.**

8 acres; large lawns, specimen trees, flowering cherries, rhododendrons, azaleas and naturalised daffodils; walled gardens with lawns, shrubs, herbaceous borders, rose garden inc shrub roses, wildflower areas and vegetables. Extensive views to Medway and Thames estuaries. Some shallow steps. No wheelchair access to rose garden due to very uneven surface but can be viewed from pathway.

109 TRAM HATCH
Barnfield Road, Charing Heath, Ashford, TN27 0BN. **Mrs P Scrivens,** 07835 758388, **Info@tramhatch.com, www.tramhatchgardens.co.uk.** *10m NW of Ashford. A20 towards Pluckley, over motorway then 1st R to Barnfield. At end, turn L past Barnfield, Tram Hatch ahead.* **Sun 5 June, Sun 3 July, Sun 14 Aug (1-5.30). Adm £5, chd free. Home-made teas. Visits also by arrangement Apr to Sept for groups of 15 to 40.**
Meander your way off the beaten track to a mature, extensive garden changing through the seasons. You will enjoy a garden laid out in rooms - what surprises are round the corner? Large selection of trees, vegetable, rose and gravel gardens, colourful containers. The River Stour and the Angel of the South enhance your visit. Please come and enjoy, then relax in our lovely garden room for tea. The garden is totally flat, apart from a very small area which can be viewed from the lane.

110 TROUTBECK
High Street, Otford, Sevenoaks, TN14 5PH. **Mrs Jenny Alban Davies, albandavies@me.com.** *3m N of Sevenoaks. At W end of village.* **Visits by arrangement in June for groups of 8 to 20. Adm inc light refreshments. Adm £10, chd free.**
3 acre garden surrounded by branches of River Darent which has been developed over 30 years. It combines the informal landscape of the river, a pond and an area of wild meadow with views to the North Downs. The garden has extensive structural planting using box and yew. Knots and topiary shapes are displayed throughout. All main areas of the garden can be accessed by wheelchair.

Great Maytham Hall

UPPER PRYORS
Butterwell Hill, Cowden, TN8 7HB. Mr & Mrs S G Smith. *4½ m SE of Edenbridge. From B2026 Edenbridge-Hartfield, turn R at Cowden Xrds & take 1st drive on R.* **Wed 15 June (11-6). Adm £5, chd free. Home-made teas.**
10 acres of English country garden surrounding C16 house - a garden of many parts; colourful profusion, interesting planting arrangements, immaculate lawns, mature woodland, water and a terrace on which to appreciate the view, and tea!

VERGERS
Church Road, Hythe, CT21 5DP. Nettie & John Wren. *Hythe 6 mins walk from Topgallant. M20 Exit 11, take A259 to Hythe. Take directions as for Topgallant. L at junc into North Rd, then 1st L into Church Rd, Vergers is next door to St Leonards Church. Parking in Church car park.* **Sat 4, Sun 5 June (2-5). Combined adm with Topgallant £6, chd free. Cream teas in St Leonard's Church next to Vergers.**
South facing hillside garden which has been reclaimed and developed over the past five years by the present owners. Steps from car park lead up to the garden terrace, goldfish pond and lawn. Winding paths slope up to many seating areas with spectacular views of the town and Channel. Kitchen garden, wildlife area and pond, bug hotels, mixed planting for year-round interest. Church and Ossuary open. Wheelchair access to lower garden only.

GROUP OPENING

WALMER GARDENS
Walmer, Deal, CT14 7SQ. *Yellow signs from A258. Dover Rd.* **Sat 18 June; Sun 19 June (11-4). Combined adm £5, chd free. Home-made teas at Pembroke Lodge and Woodlea.**

196 DOWNS ROAD
Sue Turner.

OLD CHURCH HOUSE, 26A CHURCH STREET
Christine Symons.

PEMBROKE LODGE, 140 DOVER ROAD
Mrs Jo & Mr Steve Hammond, PembrokeLodge140@gmail.com. Visits also by arrangement June to Sept for groups of 10 to 20. Tea/coffee and home-made cake available on request.

NEW WOODLEA
Mr John & Mrs Liz Lellow, 07774367105, liz@lellow.co.uk. Visits also by arrangement May to Sept for groups of 10 to 15.

The coastal gardens at Walmer showcase a wide variety of horticultural knowledge and garden maturity: newer gardens in their early years of development demonstrating how planning and design takes shape in a newer garden as well as more established gardens that continue to deliver the beauty and grace that maturity brings. A wide variety of plants can be seen in all gardens each with it's own microclimate.

WEST COURT LODGE
Postling Court, The Street, Postling, nr Hythe, CT21 4EX. Mr & Mrs John Pattrick, 01303 863285, pattrickmalliet@gmail.com. *2m NW of Hythe. From M20 J11 turn S onto A20. Immed 1st L. After ½ m on bend take rd signed Lyminge. 1st L into Postling.* **Visits by arrangement Apr to Sept. Combined admission £8 with Churchfield. Adm £4, chd free. Home-made teas.**
South facing 1 acre walled garden at the foot of the North Downs, designed in two parts: main lawn with large sunny borders and a romantic woodland glade planted with shadow loving plants and spring bulbs, small wildlife pond. Lovely C11 church will be open next to the gardens.

GROUP OPENING

115 WEST MALLING EARLY SUMMER GARDENS

West Malling, ME19 6LW. *On A20, nr J4 of M20. Park (Ryarsh Lane & Station) in West Malling. Please start your visit either at Brome House or Went House Parking available at New Barns Cottages.* **Sun 12 June (12-5). Combined adm £8, chd free. Home-made teas at New Barns Cottages only. Donation to St Mary's Church, West Malling.**

ABBEY BREWERY COTTAGE
Dr David & Mrs Lynda Nunn.

BROME HOUSE
John Pfeil & Shirley Briggs.

LUCKNOW, 119 HIGH STREET
Ms Jocelyn Granville.

NEW BARNS COTTAGES
Mr & Mrs Anthony Drake.

TOWN HILL COTTAGE
Mr & Mrs P Cosier.

WENT HOUSE
Alan & Mary Gibbins.

West Malling is an attractive small market town with some fine buildings. Enjoy six lovely gardens that are entirely different from each other and cannot be seen from the road. Brome House and Went House have large gardens with specimen trees, old roses, mixed borders, attractive kitchen gardens and garden features inc a coach house, Roman temple, fountain and parterre. Town Hill Cottage is a walled town garden with mature and interesting planting. Abbey Brewery Cottage is a recent jewel-like example of garden restoration and development. Wheelchair access to Brome House and Went House only.

GROUP OPENING

116 WHITSTABLE JOY LANE GARDENS

Tickets and map from 19 Joy Lane, Whitstable, CT5 4LT. www.facebook.com/whitstableopengardens. *Off A299, or A290. Down Borstal Hill, L by garage into Joy Lane.* **Sun 22 May (10-5). Combined adm £6, chd free. Tea at 96 Joy Lane CT5 4DF.** Enjoy a day visiting a dozen or so eclectic gardens along Joy Lane and neighbourhood by the sea. From Arts & Crafts villas to mid century bungalows, some productive, others wildlife friendly, large or compact, we garden on heavy clay, are prone to northerly winds and hope to inspire those new to gardening with our ingenuity and style. To find out more: visit Whitstable Gardens on Facebook. Plant stalls at 19 Joy Lane.

Knowle Hill Farm

GROUP OPENING

117 NEW WHITSTABLE TOWN GARDENS

Tickets & map available at Stream Walk Community Garden, Whitstable, CT5 1HJ. www.facebook.com/ whitstableopengardens. *Start at Stream Walk Community Garden, off Cromwell Rd.* **Sun 3 July (10-5). Combined adm £6, chd free. Tea.**
From fishermen's yards to formal gardens, the residents of Whitstable are making the most of the mild climate. Enjoy contemporary gardens, seaside gardens, rose gardens, gravel gardens, designers' gardens and wildlife friendly plots, both large and small. Stream Walk is at the heart of our community, ideal for those without gardening space of their own. We toil on heavy clay soils and are prone to northerly winds. By opening, we hope to encourage those new to gardening with our ingenuity and style, rather than rolling acres. To find out more see Whitstable Gardens on Facebook. Refreshments at Stream Walk Community Garden.
✿ 🍵 ᐧ))

118 NEW WINDMILL COTTAGE

Forge Lane, Leeds, Maidstone, ME17 1RT. Wendy Jennings, 07813 597740, wendyjennings@me.com. *Coming from the A20 at J8 M20 follow signs to Leeds Castle proceed then along the B2163 towards Leeds village, as you enter village turn R into Forge Ln.* **Fri 10 June (11-3). Evening opening Sat 11 June (5-8). Adm £5, chd free. Light refreshments. Visits also by arrangement May to Aug.**
The garden enjoys south facing sun all day, and consists of a formal circular garden of box and yew topiary from there leading into smaller garden rooms , where you finally arrive at the tranquil oak garden. An oasis of tranquillity set amongst the Kent country side. This year the theme is "cars in the garden" where a collection of Aston Martin and Jaguar cars will be on display.
🍵 🪑 ᐧ))

119 12 WOODS LEY

Ash, Canterbury, CT3 2HF. Philip Oostenbrink. *20 mins from Canterbury. From A257 turn into Chequer Lane. Go down Chequer Ln & turn L into Chilton Field. Turn the 2nd L into Woods Ley.* **Sat 6 Aug (1-5). Adm £3, chd free. Donation to Plant Heritage.**
A jungle style garden, showing what can be achieved in the smaller modern garden, filled with unusual foliage. The side garden has a selection of ferns and shade loving plants. The back garden is full of densely planted jungle plants. Indoors you will find the National Collection of Aspidistra elatior and sichuanensis. A plant lover's garden full of unusual plants. Private garden of the Head Gardener of Walmer Castle and Gardens, author of 'The Jungle Garden'. NGS garden owners' passes not accepted.
✿ NPC

120 ♦ THE WORLD GARDEN AT LULLINGSTONE CASTLE

Eynsford, DA4 0JA. Mrs Guy Hart Dyke, 01322 862114, info@lullingstonecastle.co.uk, www.lullingstonecastle.co.uk. *1m from Eynsford. Over Ford Bridge in Eynsford Village. Follow signs to Roman Villa. Keep Roman Villa immed on R then follow Private Rd to Gatehouse.* **For NGS: Sun 19 June (11-5). Adm £10, chd £5. Light refreshments. For other opening times and information, please phone, email or visit garden website.**
The World Garden is located within a two acre, C18 Walled Garden in the stunning grounds of Lullingstone Castle, where heritage meets cutting-edge horticulture. The garden is laid out in the shape of a miniature map of the world. Thousands of species are represented, all planted out in their respective beds. The World Garden Nursery offers a host of horticultural and homegrown delights, to reflect the unusual and varied planting of the garden. Wheelchairs available upon request.
♿ ✿ 🚗 NPC 🍵 🪑

GROUP OPENING

121 WYE GARDENS

Ashford, TN25 5BP. coulson.el@gmail.com. *3m NE of Ashford. From A28 take turning signed Wye.* **Sun 26 June (2-6). Combined adm £5, chd free. Home-made teas at Wye Church.**
A diverse selection of gardens in historic Wye, all very different in character; inc a wild experimental garden buzzing with wildlife; a large country garden full of colour featuring a lake, pond and gravel garden; a wildlife garden featuring a wildflower meadow, green-roofed shed, raised vegetable beds and worm composting; a large garden with sweeping views featuring wildlife images, vegetable garden, woodland and wildlife areas and pond; a modest garden packed with plants and features (rose arches, benches, raised beds), designed for year-round interest. Gravel paths and steps in some gardens.
♿ 🍵

122 YOKES COURT

Coal Pit Lane, Frinsted, Sittingbourne, ME9 0ST. Mr & Mrs John Leigh Pemberton, 01795 830210, leighpems@btinternet.com. *2.4m from Doddington. Turn off Old Lenham Rd to Hollingbourne. 1st R at Torry Hill Chestnut Fencing, then 1st L to Torry Hill. 1st L into Coal Pit Ln.* **Visits by arrangement June to Aug. Adm £4.50, chd free.**
3 acre garden surrounded by countryside. Hedges and herbaceous borders set in open lawns. Rose beds. New prairie planting. Serpentine walkway through wildflowers. Walled vegetable garden.
✿

National Garden Scheme funding helped support the provision of horticultural-related assistance to soldiers, veterans and their immediate families, providing education, training and employment opportunities along with supporting the recovery, health and wellbeing of individuals

LANCASHIRE
Merseyside, Greater Manchester

CUMBRIA

oughton Furness

YORKSHIRE

A593 · Kendal · Sedbergh · Bainbridge · Leyburn
Newby Bridge · Windermere · Hawes · Aysgarth
Millom · Ulverston · Milnthorpe · Kirkby Lonsdale · Horton in Ribblesdale · Kettlewell
Dalton-in-Furness · Arnside · Ingleton · Clapham · Grassington
Barrow-in-Furness · Grange-over-Sands · Carnforth · Hornby · Settle
Morecambe Bay · Morecambe · Heysham · Lancaster · Long Preston · Hetton · Skipton · Ilkley
Isle of Walney · Cockerham · Slaidburn · Barnoldswick · Earby · Silsden · Keighley
Fleetwood · Preesall · Garstang · Barnoldswick · Glusburn
Cleveleys · Poulton-le-Fylde · LANCASHIRE · Clitheroe · Colne · Haworth
Blackpool · Longridge · Nelson · Burnley · Queensbury · Halifax
Great Marton · Kirkham · Accrington · Todmorden · Hebden Bridge
Blackpool · Preston · Blackburn · Littleborough
Lytham St Anne's · Lytham · Leyland · Darwen · Rawtenstall · Bacup · Rochdale
Southport · Tarleton · Withnell · Ramsbottom · Heywood · Uppermill
Formby · Ormskirk · Chorley · Bradshaw · Bury · Oldham
Maghull · Skelmersdale · Standish · Bolton · Farnworth · Middleton · Ashton-under-Lyne
Crosby · Kirkby · Wigan · Hindley · Salford · Manchester · Glossop
Bootle · St Helens · Leigh · Stretford · Sale · Stockport
Wallasey · Prescot · Newton-le-Willows · Altrincham · Cheadle · DERBYSHIRE
Hoylake · Liverpool · Warrington · Widnes
Birkenhead · Runcorn · Knut
Heswall · Frodsham
Holywell · Ellesmere Port · Weaverham · Northwich
Flint · CHESHIRE

0 · 10 · 20 kilometres
0 · 10 miles
© Global Mapping / XYZ Maps

The gardens of the Red Rose County of Lancashire offer a wide range of horticultural excellence and inspiration.

Hidden behind walls, hedges and fences lie some of the most exquisite private gardens in the country; a range of expertly tended plots full of colour, innovation and seasonal interest. There is something here to inspire all the family, whether it be allotments, wildlife sanctuaries, rows of back to back terrace gardens, inner city sanctuaries with water features or rolling acres with lakes.

So, whatever size your own patch, why not visit some of our stunning gardens and maybe take away a few brilliant ideas to copy at home- all with the added pleasure of home- made cakes and tea, and often plants for sale too.

Our gardeners look forward to welcoming you!

Below: 1 Osborne Street

Volunteers

County Organiser
Marian & Brian Jones 01695 574628
marianandbrian.jones@ngs.org.uk

County Treasurer
Peter Curl 01704 893713
peter.curl@ngs.org.uk

Publicity
Christine Ruth 07740 438994
caruthchris@aol.com

Social Media
Carole Ann & Stephen Powers
01254 824903
chows3@icloud.com

Photographers
Norman Rigby 01704 840329
norman.rigby@ngs.org.uk

Laurie Lissett 07786 631280
laurielissett@hotmail.co.uk

Booklet Co-ordinator & Distribution
Barbara & Richard Farbon
01772 600750
barbaraandrichard.farbon@ngs.org.uk

Visits by Arrangement
Heather Sidebotham 01704 543389
alansidebotham@yahoo.co.uk

Assistant County Organisers

Margaret & Geoff Fletcher
01704 567742
margaret.fletcher@ngs.org.uk

Sandra Curl 01704 893713
peter.curl@btinternet.com

Deborah Jackson
debs136@icloud.com

Susan & Neil Kinsella 01942 889036
susanandneil.kinsella@ngs.org.uk

John & Jennifer Mawdsley
01704 564708

Eric & Sharon Rawcliffe 01253 883275
ericrawk@talktalk.net

Claire Spendlove 01524 727770
claire@lavenderandlime.co.uk

OPENING DATES

All entries subject to change. For latest information check www.ngs.org.uk

Map locator numbers are shown to the right of each garden name.

February

Snowdrop Festival

Sunday 13th
Weeping Ash Garden 63

Sunday 20th
Weeping Ash Garden 63

April

Sunday 3rd
Derian House Children's Hospice 17

Saturday 16th
Dale House Gardens 15

Sunday 17th
Dale House Gardens 15

Saturday 23rd
Jack Green Cottage 34

Sunday 24th
NEW Booths Farm 3
NEW The Haven Garden 30
Jack Green Cottage 34

May

Monday 2nd
◆ The Ridges 51

Saturday 21st
Halton Park House 29
Willow Wood Hospice Gardens 65

Sunday 22nd
Halton Park House 29
194 Mottram Old Road 43
Parkers Lodges 46

Sunday 29th
Bretherton Gardens 4
Kington Cottage 35
Turton Tower Kitchen Garden 59

June

Thursday 2nd
◆ Clearbeck House 11

Friday 3rd
◆ Clearbeck House 11

Saturday 4th
136 Buckingham Road 7
Mill Barn 40

Sunday 5th
NEW Ainsdale & Birkdale Gardens 1
136 Buckingham Road 7
45 Grey Heights View 26
NEW Holly House 33
Mill Barn 40

Monday 6th
Lytham Hall 37

Saturday 11th
Mill Barn 40
Old Hollows Farm 44

Sunday 12th
31 Cousins Lane 12
79 Crabtree Lane 13
Didsbury Village Gardens 18
Mill Barn 40
Old Hollows Farm 44
NEW Sefton Park June Gardens 54

Saturday 18th
Dale House Gardens 15
Giles Farm 21
Higher Bridge Clough House 32

Sunday 19th
Bretherton Gardens 4
NEW Canning Georgian Quarter 8
Dale House Gardens 15
Giles Farm 21
Green Farm Cottage 24
Higher Bridge Clough House 32
Mill Croft 41
Raw Ridding House 50

Saturday 25th
5 Crib Lane 14
Hale Village Gardens 28
NEW Victoria House 60
Willow Wood Hospice Gardens 65

Sunday 26th
Bridge Inn Community Farm 5
◆ Clearbeck House 11
5 Crib Lane 14
Dutton Hall 19
Hale Village Gardens 28
Kington Cottage 35
NEW Victoria House 60
Woolton Village June Gardens 67

July

Saturday 2nd
Jack Green Cottage 34
4 Roe Green 52

Sunday 3rd
NEW Booths Farm 3
79 Crabtree Lane 13
Freshfield Gardens 20
Jack Green Cottage 34

Sunday 10th
Gorse Hill Nature Reserve 23
◆ Hazelwood 31
72 Ludlow Drive 36
Parkers Lodges 46
NEW Sefton Park July Gardens 53

Saturday 16th
Warton Gardens 61

Sunday 17th
NEW Ainsdale & Birkdale Gardens 1
33 Greenhill Road 25
146 Mather Avenue 39
Mill Croft 41
Moss Park Allotments 42
Southlands 55
Warton Gardens 61

Sunday 24th
Derian House Children's Hospice 17
Glynwood House 22
Maggie's, Manchester 38
Wigan & Leigh Hospice 64
Woolton Village July Gardens 66

Saturday 30th
The Growth Project 27

Sunday 31st
6 Cannock Drive 9
NEW Chorlton Gardens 10
Kington Cottage 35
1 Osborne Street 45
5 Parkfield Road South, Flat 1 47
NEW 36 Queens Drive 49

August

Sunday 7th
Plant World 48

Sunday 14th
Weeping Ash Garden 63

Sunday 21st
45 Grey Heights View 26

Sunday 28th
Bretherton Gardens 4
Kington Cottage 35

Monday 29th
◆ The Ridges 51

5 West Lane, Freshfield Gardens

September

Saturday 3rd
Stanhill Exotic Garden 56

Sunday 4th
Stanhill Exotic Garden 56

Sunday 11th
Weeping Ash Garden 63

Saturday 24th
Ashton Walled
Community Gardens 2

October

Sunday 30th
Weeping Ash Garden 63

By Arrangement

Arrange a personalised garden visit with your club, or group of friends, on a date to suit you. See individual garden entries for full details.

Ashton Walled Community Gardens	2
Bridge Inn Community Farm	5
4 Brocklebank Road	6
79 Crabtree Lane	13
Dent Hall	16
Giles Farm	21
45 Grey Heights View	26
The Growth Project	27
Hazel Cottage, Bretherton Gardens	4
Kington Cottage	35

Mill Barn	40
Owl Barn, Bretherton Gardens	4
14 Saxon Road, Ainsdale & Birkdale Gardens	1
Southlands	55
5 Tolsey Drive	58
10 Tolsey Drive	57
8 Water Head	62

THE GARDENS

GROUP OPENING

1 NEW AINSDALE & BIRKDALE GARDENS
14 Saxon Road, Southport, PR8 2AX. Mrs Margaret Fletcher. *S of Southport. Gardens signed from A565 & A5267.* Sun 5 June, Sun 17 July (11-5). Combined adm £6, chd free. Home-made teas at 14 Saxon Rd, 45 Stourton Rd & 115 Waterloo Rd.

23 ASHTON ROAD
PR8 4QE. John & Jennifer Mawdsley.
Open on Sun 17 July

22 HARTLEY CRESCENT
PR8 4SG. Sandra & Keith Birks.
Open on all dates

14 SAXON ROAD
PR8 2AX. Margaret & Geoff Fletcher, 01704 567742, margaret.fletcher@ngs.org.uk.
Open on all dates
Visits also by arrangement May to Aug for groups of 10 to 50.

45 STOURTON ROAD
PR8 3PL. Pat & Bill Armstrong.
Open on all dates

115 WATERLOO ROAD
PR8 4QN. Antony & Rebecca Eden.
Open on all dates

A new group formed to showcase some of the beautiful gardens to visit around the Victorian seaside town of Southport. They range in size and design from a walled garden opening for its 20th year, a flower arranger's garden of infinite detail and surprises and a recently redesigned family garden rescued from neglect. In addition 2 old favourites: a plantswoman's garden full of colour and interest and a garden of rooms leading to a spectacular fruit and vegetable plot. Not all gardens are wheelchair friendly due to narrow paths or gravel.

  ⌖ ✿ ☕

2 ASHTON WALLED COMMUNITY GARDENS
Pedders Lane, Ashton-On-Ribble, Preston, PR2 1HL.
Annie Wynn, 07535 836364, letsgrowpreston@gmail.com, www.letsgrowpreston.org. *W of Preston. From M6 J30 head towards Preston turn R onto Blackpool Rd, continue for 3.4m, turn L onto Pedders Lane & next R onto the park. Entrance to walled garden is 50 metres on L.* Sat 24 Sept (10-3). Adm £4, chd free. Light refreshments. Visits also by arrangement Apr to Oct for groups of 6 to 25.
Formal raised beds within a walled garden, a peace garden and an edible garden. The formal part of the garden

uses plants predominantly from just 3 families, rose, geranium and aster. It is punctuated by grasses and has been designed to demonstrate how diverse and varied plants can be from just the one family. Live musical entertainment.

  ⌖ 🐕 ✿ ☕

3 NEW BOOTHS FARM
Booths Lane, Aughton, Ormskirk, L39 7HE. Mr & Mrs Boyle. *From Ormskirk, take 1st R after Christ Church onto Gaw Hill Lane, follow until you reach junction of Small Lane & Booths Lane, take Booths Lane & yellow signs will start half way up lane.* Sun 24 Apr, Sun 3 July (11-5). Adm £5, chd free. Cream teas, wine and cakes.
Booths Farm, built in 1780 as a working farm, moved to a fuchsia growers and is now a family home. The garden is a large country garden circling the property, backing onto agricultural fields with open views of the nature reserve, Aughton and up to the Lake District. The garden is a diverse mix of plants and garden objects with highlights being the mature roses and small woodland area.

☕))

31 Cousins Lane

GROUP OPENING

4 BRETHERTON GARDENS
Bretherton, Leyland, PR26 9AD.
8m SW of Preston. Between Southport & Preston, from A59, take B5247 towards Chorley for 1m. Gardens signed from South Rd (B5247) & North Rd (B5248). **Sun 29 May, Sun 19 June (12-5). Combined adm £6, chd free. Sun 28 Aug (12-5). Combined adm £5, chd free. Home-made teas at Bretherton Congregational Church from 12 noon on all dates, also light lunches on 19 June.**

HAZEL COTTAGE
PR26 9AN. John & Kris Jolley, 01772 600896, jolley@johnjolley.plus.com.
Open on all dates
Visits also by arrangement May to Oct.

◆ HAZELWOOD
PR26 9AY. Jacqueline Iddon & Thompson Dagnall.
Open on Sun 29 May, Sun 19 June
(See separate entry)

OWL BARN
PR26 9AD. Richard & Barbara Farbon, 01772 600750, barbaraandrichard.farbon@ngs.org.uk.
Open on all dates
Visits also by arrangement June to Aug for groups of 8 to 20.

PALATINE, 6 BAMFORDS FOLD
PR26 9AL. Alison Ryan.
Open on all dates

PEAR TREE COTTAGE
PR26 9AS. John & Gwenifer Jackson.
Open on all dates

A group of contrasting gardens spaced across an attractive village with conservation area. Hazelwood is a 1½ acre plant lover's paradise with herbaceous and mixed borders, kitchen and cutting garden, alpine house, sculpture gallery, pond, plant nursery. Hazel Cottage's former Victorian orchard plot has evolved into a series of themed spaces, while the adjoining land has a natural pond, meadow and developing native woodland. Owl Barn has herbaceous borders filled with cottage garden and hardy plants, productive kitchen garden with fruit, vegetables and cut flowers, two ponds with fountains and secluded seating area. Palatine is a garden of 3 contrasting spaces started in 2019 around a modern bungalow to attract wildlife and give year-round interest. Pear Tree Cottage has informal beds featuring ornamental grasses, a solar-powered greenhouse watering system, a profusion of fruits, a pond, mature trees, and a fine backdrop of the West Pennine Moors. At Hazelwood: plant nursery, sculpture gallery, sculpture demonstrations at 2pm; at Pear Tree Cottage: live music. Full wheelchair access to Palatine, majority of Hazelwood accessible, varying degrees of access at the other gardens due to narrow or uneven paths.

Gorse Hill Nature Reserve

5 BRIDGE INN COMMUNITY FARM

Moss Side, Formby, Liverpool, L37 0AF. Bridge Inn Community Farm, 01704 830303, bridgeinnfarm@talktalk.net, www.bridgeinncommunityfarm.co.uk. *7m S of Southport. Formby bypass A565, L onto Moss Side.* **Sun 26 June (11-4). Adm £3.50, chd free. Light refreshments. Visits also by arrangement June to Sept.**
Bridge Inn Community Farm was established in 2010 in response to a community need. Our farm sits on a beautiful 4 acre smallholding with views looking out over the countryside. We provide a quality service of training in a real life work environment and experience in horticulture, conservation and animal welfare.

6 4 BROCKLEBANK ROAD

Southport, PR9 9LP. Heather Sidebotham, 01704 543389, alansidebotham@yahoo.co.uk. *1¼ m N of Southport. Off A565 Southport to Preston Rd, opp North entrance to Hesketh Park.* **Visits by arrangement May to Aug for groups of 8 to 40. Adm £4, chd free. Home-made teas.**
A walled garden landscaped with reclaimed materials from local historic sites. There are several water features, an extensive herbaceous border and areas of differing planting. Described by Matthew Wilson of Gardeners Question Time as a lovely garden with beautiful vistas at every turn. Designer and creator of the Large Gold Medal award winning NGS garden at Southport Flower Show 2019.

7 136 BUCKINGHAM ROAD

Maghull, L31 7DR. Debbie & Mark Jackson. *7m N of Liverpool. End M57/M58, take A59 towards Ormskirk. Turn L after car superstore onto Liverpool Rd Sth, cont' on past Meadows pub, 3rd R into Sandringham Rd, L into Buckingham Rd.* **Sat 4, Sun 5 June (12-5). Adm £3, chd free. Home-made teas. Donation to Epilepsy Society.**
A small suburban garden overflowing with cottage garden plants, complemented by a wisteria covered pergola and roses. Features a pond and water feature with plenty of seating.

GROUP OPENING

8 NEW CANNING GEORGIAN QUARTER

Canning Street, Liverpool, L8 8NN. Ms Waltraud Boxhall. *No 86 bus runs every 12 mins from city centre. Ask for bus stop Back Canning St. By car from city centre follow A562, L onto Hope St R onto Huskisson St, L into Back Percy St for the Gambier Terr then L onto Canning Street R onto Hope St and R onto Back Canning St. Parking is Pay & Display.* **Sun 19 June (11-4). Combined adm £6, chd free. Light refreshments and teas will be available in both Canning Street and Gambier Terrace.**

NEW 7 CANNING STREET
L8 7NN. Mr Sam Harry.

NEW 25 CANNING STREET
L8 7NN. Mr Miles Falkingham.

NEW 27 CANNING STREET
L8 7NN. Mrs Waltraud Boxall.

NEW 29 CANNING STREET
L8 7NN. Mrs Erin O'Neil.

NEW 10 GAMBIER TERRACE
L1 7BG. Mr Paul Murphy.

This is a rare opportunity to see 5 very interesting Georgian walled gardens amongst the outstanding architecture of this historic area of Liverpool. There is a wide variety of styles and planting, something for every taste. This group of gardens is within the Georgian Quarter of Liverpool with many important and historic buildings inc Liverpool Cathedral, the largest cathedral and religious building in Britain. There is disabled access from the rear of the property for all of the 5 gardens.

9 6 CANNOCK DRIVE

Heaton Mersey, Stockport, SK4 3JB. Andrea & Stefan Schumacher. *5m S of Manchester. A5154 (Didsbury Rd). The rd takes a slight ascent & you need to turn in Lodge Court, then next L is Cannock Drive.* **Sun 31 July (12-5). Combined adm with 36 Queens Drive £5, chd free. Home-made teas.**
A large atmospheric woodland garden containing an idyllic lake, sweeping lawns and well-stocked borders planted according to principles of colour energy. Snaking path to the central circular seating area, through a wooded area and alongside the waters edge. Summerhouse, fire pit and historic former glasshouse wall are some of the other features of this surprising and secluded garden.

GROUP OPENING

10 NEW CHORLTON GARDENS

Chorlton, Manchester, M21 8UZ. Ms Emma Dibb. *We recommend you use public transport or park centrally in the Chorlton precinct & walk from there to the houses.* **Sun 31 July (11-4). Combined adm £5, chd free.**

NEW 20 DARTMOUTH ROAD
M21 8XJ. Ms Sarah Rycroft.

NEW 30 HAMPTON ROAD
M21 9LA. Mr Phil Facey.

NEW 22 HARTINGTON ROAD
M21 8UY. Mrs Rebecca Norris.

NEW 23 HARTINGTON ROAD
M21 8UZ. Ms Emma Dibb.

NEW 51 WHITELOW ROAD
M21 9HG. Mr Percy Dean.

Chorlton is a suburb of Manchester with great food shops, bars, cafes and a bohemian atmosphere. Our 5 gardens reflect what you can do with smaller urban spaces. A British tropical garden complete with chandelier. A Victorian semi with sunny rear garden, terrace, greenhouse, shallow pool and gazebo. A small, well-proportioned, lawned garden with established borders, espaliered fruit trees, containers and a small water feature. A family garden with sculptural hard landscaping, softened by grasses and prairie style planting, or a temperate jungle complete with unusual plants.

Around 1,050 people living with Parkinson's - and their families - have been helped by Parkinson's nurses thanks to funding from the National Garden Scheme

◫ ◆ CLEARBECK HOUSE
Mewith Lane, Higher Tatham,
Lancaster, LA2 8PJ. Peter &
Bronwen Osborne, 01524 261029,
bronwenmo@gmail.com,
www.clearbeckgarden.org.uk.
*13m E of Lancaster. Signed from
Wray (M6 J34, A683, B6480) & Low
Bentham.* For NGS: Thur 2, Fri 3,
Sun 26 June (11-5). Adm £4, chd
free. Light refreshments. For other
opening times and information,
please phone, email or visit garden
website.
At the entrance gate to this 'Secret
Garden', visitors are astonished to
see an eye-catcher, Don Quixote,
a Tuscan Temple and the long vista
past the herbaceous borders down to
the lake. Exploring the garden there
follows a surprise round every corner.
Painting studio open. Children-friendly
inc quiz. Artists and photographers
welcome by arrangement.
Explanatory garden leaflet on sale.
Wheelchair access -many grass
paths, some sloped.
& 🐄 ✿ 🚌 ☕ 🔊

◩ 31 COUSINS LANE
Ardilea 31 Cousins Lane, Rufford,
Ormskirk, L40 1TN. Brenda & Roy
Caslake. *From M6 J27, follow signs
for Parbold then Rufford. Turn L onto
the A59. Turn R at Hesketh Arms
Pub. 4th turn.* Sun 12 June (10-4).
Adm £3.50, chd free. Cream teas
at Rufford Cricket Club adjacent
to garden.
Rooms within rooms, discreet corners
punctuated with an open vista to the
cricket ground. This cottage garden
welcomes the bees and butterflies.
Frogs, toads and newts are resident
and the blackbird and thrush lead
a vocal chorus whilst wren and
robin flit. A potpourri of planting with
scents pleasing to the senses. A
small, tranquil oasis. Take time to re-
energise with a glass of prosecco and
a cream tea whilst enjoying the best
of English pastimes.
✿ ☕ 🔊

◳ 79 CRABTREE LANE
Burscough, L40 0RW. Sandra
& Peter Curl, 01704 893713,
peter.curl@btinternet.com, www.
youtube.com/watch?v=CW7S8nB_
iX8. *3m NE of Ormskirk. A59 Preston
- Liverpool Rd. From N before bridge
R into Redcat Lane signed for Martin
Mere. From S over 2nd bridge L
into Redcat Lane after ¾ m L into
Crabtree Lane.* Sun 12 June, Sun
3 July (11-5). Adm £4, chd free.

Home-made teas. Visits also by
arrangement June & July.
¾ acre all year-round plantsperson's
garden with many rare and unusual
plants. Herbaceous borders and
island beds, pond, rockery, rose
garden, and autumn hot bed
Many stone features built with
reclaimed materials. Shrubs and
rhododendrons, Koi pond and
waterfall, hosta and fern walk. Gravel
garden with Mediterranean plants.
Patio surrounded by shrubs and
raised alpine bed. Trees giving areas
for shade loving plants. Many beds
replanted recently. Flat grass and bark
paths.
& 🐄 ✿ 🚌 ☕ 🔊

◪ 5 CRIB LANE
Dobcross, Oldham, OL3 5AF.
Helen Campbell. *5m E of Oldham.
From Dobcross village head towards
Delph on Platt Lane, Crib Lane
opp Dobcross Band Club - about
100 metres up. Limited parking for
disabled visitors only opp double
green garage door, signed NGS.* Sat
25, Sun 26 June (12-4). Combined
adm with Victoria House £5, chd
free. Light refreshments.
A well loved and well used family
garden - challenging as on a high
terraced hillside and visited by deer,
hares and the odd cow! Additional
interests are wildlife ponds, wildflower
areas, vegetable garden, a polytunnel,
four beehives with 250,000 bees and
an art gallery and garden sculptures.
Areas re thought annually, dug up
and changed depending on time and
aged bodies aches and pains! Local
honey for sale.
✿ ☕ 🔊

◱ DALE HOUSE GARDENS
off Church Lane, Goosnargh,
Preston, PR3 2BE. Caroline & Tom
Luke. *2½ m E of Broughton. M6
J32 signed Garstang Broughton,
T-lights R at Whittingham Lane,
2½ m to Whittingham. At PO turn L
into Church Lane. Garden between
nos 17 & 19.* Sat 16, Sun 17 Apr,
Sat 18, Sun 19 June (10-4). Adm
£3.50, chd free. Donation to St
Francis School, Goosnargh.
½ acre tastefully landscaped gardens
comprising of limestone rockeries,
well-stocked herbaceous borders,
raised alpine beds, well-stocked koi
pond, lawn areas, greenhouse and
polytunnel, patio areas, specialising in
alpines, rare shrubs and trees, large
collection of unusual bulbs, Secret
Garden. Year-round interest. Large

indoor budgerigar aviary with 300+
budgies. Gravel path, lawn areas.
& 🐄 ✿ 🚌 ☕

◰ DENT HALL
Colne Road, Trawden,
Colne, BB8 8NX. Mr Chris
Whitaker-Webb & Miss
Joanne Smith, 01282 861892,
denthall@tiscali.co.uk. *10 min
from end of M65. Turn L and
from end of M65. Follow A6068 for 2m; just after
3rd r'about turn R down B6250.
After 1½ m, in front of church, turn
R, signed Carry Bridge. Keep R,
follow road up hill, garden on R after
300yds.* Visits by arrangement
June to Sept. Adm £6, chd free.
Home-made teas. Donation to
MIND.
Nestled in the oldest part of Trawden
villllage and rolling Lancashire
countryside, this mature and
evolving country garden surrounds
a 400 yr old grade II listed hall (not
open); featuring a parterre, lawns,
herbaceous borders, shrubbery,
wildlife pond with bridge to seating
area and a hidden summerhouse in
a woodland area. Plentiful seating
throughout. Some uneven paths and
gradients.
✿ ☕ 🪑 🔊

**◷ DERIAN HOUSE
CHILDREN'S HOSPICE**
Chancery Road, Chorley,
PR7 1DH. Gareth Elliott,
www.derianhouse.co.uk/. *2m from
Chorley town centre. From B5252
pass Chorley Hospital on L, at
r'about 1st exit to Chancery Lane.
Hospice on L after 0.4 m. Parking
is available around the building &
on the road. SatNav directions not
always accurate.* Sun 3 Apr, Sun 24
July (10-4.30). Adm £3, chd free.
Home-made teas.
The Chorley-based children's hospice
provides respite and end-of-life care
to more than 400 children and young
people from across the North West
and South Cumbria. The gardens
at the hospice help to create an
atmosphere of relaxation, tranquillity
and joy. Distinct areas inc the seaside
garden, the sensory garden, the
memorial garden and the Smile
Park adventure playground. Family
activities. Homemade cakes and plant
sale. Gardens and refreshments area
are wheelchair friendly, accessible
parking and WC facilities also
available.
& 🐄 ✿ ☕ 🔊

72 Ludlow Drive

GROUP OPENING

⅃8 DIDSBURY VILLAGE GARDENS

Tickets from 68 Brooklawn Drive M20 3GZ or any garden, Didsbury, Manchester, M20 6RW. *5m S of Manchester. From M60 J5 follow signs to Northenden. Turn R at T-lights onto Barlow Moor Rd to Didsbury. From M56 follow A34 to Didsbury.* **Sun 12 June (12-5). Combined adm £6, chd free. Home made teas at Moor Cottage and 68 Brooklawn Drive.**

68 BROOKLAWN DRIVE

M20 3GZ. Anne & Jim Britt, www.annebrittdesign.com.

3 THE DRIVE

M20 6HZ. Peter Clare & Sarah Keedy, www.theshadegarden.com.

MOOR COTTAGE

M20 6RW. William Godfrey.

40 PARRS WOOD AVENUE

M20 5ND. Tom Johnson.

38 WILLOUGHBY AVENUE

M20 6AS. Simon Hickey.

Didsbury is an attractive South Manchester suburb which retains its village atmosphere. There are interesting shops, cafes and restaurants, well worth a visit in themselves. This year we have 5 gardens demonstrating a variety of beautiful spaces, to inc a stylish contemporary cottage garden with a strong organic ethos, a soft country garden with fabulous planting and a large walled family garden surrounding a Georgian cottage, divided into several enchanting areas with towering echiums and free range chickens. Another is an expertly planted shade garden with many choice rarities, whilst another reflects the charm of the cottage garden ethos with rose covered pergola, old fashioned perennials and tranquil raised pool. Our smaller gardens show beautifully how suburban plots, with limited space, can be packed full of interesting features and a range of planting styles. Dogs allowed at most gardens. Wheelchair access to some gardens.

3 The Drive, Didsbury Village Gardens

© Fiona Lea

19 DUTTON HALL

Gallows Lane, Ribchester, PR3 3XX. Mr & Mrs A H Penny, www.duttonhall.co.uk. *2m NE of Ribchester. Signed from B6243 & B6245 also directions on website.* **Sun 26 June (1-5). Adm £5, chd free. Home-made teas. Donation to Plant Heritage.**

An increasing range of unusual trees and shrubs have been added to the existing collection of old fashioned roses, inc rare and unusual varieties and Plant Heritage National Collection of Pemberton Hybrid Musk roses. Formal garden at front with backdrop of C17 house (not open). Analemmatic Sundial, pond, meadow areas all with extensive views over Ribble Valley. Plant Heritage plant stall with unusual varieties for sale.

GROUP OPENING

20 FRESHFIELD GARDENS

West Lane, Freshfield & Formby, Formby, L37 7BA. *6m S of Southport. Brewery Lane, Kenton Close & both West Lane gardens are close together in Freshfield. Buttermere Close is off Ennerdale Rd in Formby approx 1m away from the other gardens.* **Sun 3 July (11-5). Combined adm £6, chd free. Home-made teas at Kenton Close & at Buttermere Close (light refreshments).**

33 BREWERY LANE
L37 7DY. Sue & Dave Hughes.

NEW 4 BUTTERMERE CLOSE
L37 2YB. Marilyn & Alan Tippett.

NEW 18 KENTON CLOSE
L37 7EA. Mrs Alex Reed.

5 WEST LANE
L37 7AY. Ian & Kathy Taphouse.

6 WEST LANE
L37 7BA. Laurie & Sue Lissett.

5 coastal suburban gardens near to Formby sand dunes and NT Nature Reserve, home to the red squirrel. Soil is sandy and well drained. All the gardens feature colourful herbaceous borders with a mixture of shrubs and perennials, and inc many roses and hydrangeas. The group gardens demonstrate a variety of styles and designs and some inc fruit and vegetables areas. Features inc raised beds, greenhouses, rockeries, ponds, arches, pergolas and basket/container displays.

21 GILES FARM

Four Acre Lane, Thornley, Preston, PR3 2TD. Kirsten & Phil Brown, 07925 603246, phil.brown32@aol.co.uk. *3m NE of Longridge. Pass through Longridge & follow signs for Chipping. After 2m turn R at the old school up Hope Lane. Turn L at the top and continue to the farm where there is ample parking.* **Sat 18, Sun 19 June (12-5). Adm £4.50, chd free. Light refreshments. A selection of sandwiches & home baked cakes. Visits also by arrangement June & July for groups of 10+.**

Nestled high on the side of Longridge Fell, with beautiful long-reaching views across the Ribble Valley, the gardens surround the old farmhouse and buildings. The gardens are ever evolving and inc an acre of perennial wildflower meadows, wildlife pond, woodland areas and cottage gardens. There are plentiful areas to sit and take in the views. There are steps and uneven surfaces in the gardens.

22 GLYNWOOD HOUSE

Eyes Lane, Bretherton, Leyland, PR26 9AS. Terry & Sue Riding. *Once in Bretherton, turn onto Eyes Lane by the War Memorial. After 50 yds take the R fork, after 100 yds follow the road around to the L. Glynwood House is a further 200 yds on the L.* **Sun 24 July (11-5). Adm £4, chd free. Home-made teas.**

Set in a peaceful rural location with spectacular views, highlights of this ¾ acre garden inc colour themed mixed borders, wildlife pond with dry stone wall, water feature, a woodland walk with meandering railway sleeper paths, a patio garden with raised beds and flower-adorned pergola. Access available to most of the garden apart from sleeper paths in the woodland walk area.

23 GORSE HILL NATURE RESERVE

Holly Lane, Aughton, Ormskirk, L39 7HB. Jonathan Atkins (Reserve Manager), www.nwecotrust.org.uk. *1½ m S of Ormskirk. A59 from L'pool past Royal Oak pub take 1st L Gaw Hill Lane turn R Holly Lane. From Preston follow A59 across T-lights at A570 J & at r'about. After Xing lights turn R Gaw Hill Lane turn R Holly Lane.* **Sun 10 July (11-4). Combined adm with 72 Ludlow Drive £5, chd free.**

Light refreshments. Situated on a sandstone ridge offering spectacular views across the Lancashire Plain, our wildflower meadow in summer is brimming with a wide variety of wildflowers and grasses. The meadow's wildlife pond is patrolled by dragonflies and damselflies and the air is full of butterflies and bees. Mown grassy paths take you through the meadow to enable close views of the flowers and insects.

24 GREEN FARM COTTAGE

42 Lower Green, Poulton-le-Fylde, FY6 7EJ. Eric & Sharon Rawcliffe. *500yds from Poulton-le-Fylde village. M55 J3 follow A585 Fleetwood. T- lights turn L. Next lights bear L A586. Poulton 2nd set of lights turn R Lower Green. Cottage on L.* **Sun 19 June (10-5). Adm £4, chd free. Light refreshments.**

½ acre well established formal cottage garden. Featuring a koi pond and paths leading to different areas. Lots of climbers and rose beds. Packed with plants of all kinds. Many shrubs and trees. Well laid out lawns. Collections of unusual plants. A surprise round every corner. Said by visitors to be a real hidden jewel.

25 33 GREENHILL ROAD

Mossley Hill, Liverpool, L18 6JJ. Tony Rose. *From L lane at end of M62 follow Ring Road A5058 (S). Follow A5058 through 1st island. Keep to L lane through 2nd island then take B5180 for about ½ m to signage.* **Sun 17 July (12-5). Combined adm with 146 Mather Avenue £5, chd free.**

The central attraction in the garden is a raised water stream over cobbles running into a raised pond (reservoir). On two sides planted into the ground are mature bamboo and other plants around a golden Buddha statue. The remainder of the garden is hard paved in varying materials. There is no lawn. Throughout the garden the embellishment is with many types of plants in pots, exotic and unusual.

26 45 GREY HEIGHTS VIEW

Off Eaves Lane, Chorley, PR6 0TN. Barbara Ashworth, 07941 339702. *From Wigan/Coppull B5251. At town centre Xrds straight across. At r'about across to Lyons Ln and follow NGS signs. From M61, J8 follow signs A6 Town Centre to Lyons Ln signed from here.* **Sun 5 June, Sun 21 Aug (10-5). Adm £3, chd free. Visits also by arrangement June to Aug for groups of 10 to 30.**
A small suburban garden with cottage garden style planting inc fruit trees. Heavily planted with a profusion of perennials, roses and clematis. No repeat planting. Inc a greenhouse, small vegetable and fruit area. An abundance of recycling and space saving ideas. Backdrop of Healey Nab, and a stone's throw from the Leeds - Liverpool Canal.

27 THE GROWTH PROJECT

Kellett Street Allotments, Rochdale, OL16 2JU. Karen Hayday, 07464 546962, k.hayday@hourglass.org.uk, www. rochdalemind.org.uk/growth-project. *From A627M. R A58 L Entwistle Rd then R Kellett St.* **Sat 30 July (11.30-3.30). Adm £3.50, chd free. Home-made lunches & afternoon tea served in the Victorian style 'Woodland Green' railway station and signal box. Visits also by arrangement June to Oct. Donation to The Growth Project.**
The project covers over an acre and inc a huge variety of organic vegetables, a wildlife pond, insect hotels, formal flower and wildflower borders, potager and enchanted woodland garden. See the mock Elizabethan straw bale build and station, stroll down the pergola walk to the wildflower meadow and orchard. Jams and preserves, flowers, craft items and cakes to buy. The new attraction this year is the Japanese garden. The Growth Project is a partnership between Hourglass and Rochdale and District Mind. Guides are on hand to give horticultural advice and show you round. No disabled WC, ground can be uneven.

GROUP OPENING

28 HALE VILLAGE GARDENS

Liverpool, L24 4BA. *6m S of M62 J6. Take A5300, A562 towards L'pool, then A561, L for Hale opp the old RSPCA inn. From S L'pool head for the airport then L sign for Hale. The 82A bus from Widnes/Runcorn to L'pool has village stops.* **Sat 25, Sun 26 June (12-5). Combined adm £5, chd free. Home-made teas at 66 Church Road & cold drinks at 33 Hale Road.**

33 ARKLOW DRIVE
L24 5RW. Rebecca & Ross Firman.

4 CHURCH ROAD
L24 4BA. Mrs Chesters.

66 CHURCH ROAD
L24 4BA. Liz Kelly-Hines & David Hines.

2 PHEASANT FIELD
L24 5SD. Roger & Tania Craine.

 WHITECROFT, 33 HALE ROAD
L24 5RB. Mrs Donna Richards.

The delightful village of Hale is set in rural South Merseyside between Widnes and Liverpool Airport. It is home to the cottage, sculpture and grave of the famous giant known as the Childe of Hale. Five gardens of various sizes have been developed by their present owners. There are 3 gardens (a large skilfully landscaped one and two beautiful contemporary ones) to the west of the village and 2 gardens in Church Rd to the east of the village, one colourful herbaceous and the other mixed planting with substantial vegetable plot. Optional off-road parking for 33 Hale Rd on Hale Service Station forecourt.

29 HALTON PARK HOUSE

Halton Park, Halton, Lancaster, LA2 6PD. Mr & Mrs Duncan Bowring. *7min drive from both J34 & 35 M6. On Park Lane, approx 1½m from Halton or Caton. Park Lane accessed either from Low Rd or High Rd out of Halton. From Low Rd turn into Park Lane through pillars over cattle grid.* **Sat 21, Sun 22 May (10.30-6). Adm £5, chd free. Home-made teas. Barbecue over lunch time.**
Approx 6 acres of garden, with gravel paths leading through large

mixed herbaceous borders, terraces, orchard and terraced vegetable beds. Wildlife pond and woodland walk in dell area, extensive lawns, greenhouse and herb garden. Plenty of places to sit and rest! Gravel paths (some sloping) access viewing points over the majority of the garden. Hard standing around the house.

30 NEW THE HAVEN GARDEN

Snow Hill Lane, Scorton, Preston, PR3 1BA. Mrs Nikki Cookson, www.woodcroftcrafts.co.uk. *Between Preston & Lancaster. Leave A6 follow signs to Scorton. From village centre, go up Snowhill Lane & cross the motorway bridge. Entrance is via Woodcroft Crafts. Parking in the village with 10 min walk.* **Sun 24 Apr (11-4). Adm £6, chd £2.**
Situated in the beautiful Forest of Bowland, the Haven Garden is set in 4 acres of private woodland. There is magic around every corner and something for all the family inc stickmen, fairy houses, a wishing well, 30ft high train bridge, waterwheel and a labyrinth prayer walk. The garden was originally landscaped over 100 yrs ago and has been developing ever since. At the entrance to the garden is Woodcroft Crafts, a little shop-in-a-shed selling handmade gifts and Christian crafts made from natural or recycled materials.

31 ◆ HAZELWOOD

North Road, Bretherton, Leyland, PR26 9AY. Jacqueline Iddon & Thompson Dagnall, 01772 601433, jacquelineiddon@gmail.com, www.jacquelineiddon.co.uk. *8m SW of Preston. Between Southport & Preston, from A59, take B5247 for 1m then L onto B5248. Garden signed from North Rd.* **For NGS: Sun 10 July (12-5). Adm £4, chd free. Cream teas in Coach House. Opening with Bretherton Gardens on Sun 29 May, Sun 19 June. For other opening times and information, please phone, email or visit garden website.**
Alpine House, cutting and vegetable garden. 1½ acre garden and hardy plant nursery, gravel garden with pots and seating area, shrubs, herbaceous borders, stream-fed pond with woodland walk. Oak-framed, summerhouse, log cabin sculpture gallery fronted by cottage garden beds. Sculpture demonstration at 2 pm. Beach area. Extensive sculpture

collection, the work of Thompson Dagnall Printmaking Studio with prints and cards By Tilly Dagnall. Majority of the garden is accessible to wheelchairs.

& 🐎 ✿ 🚐 ☕

32 HIGHER BRIDGE CLOUGH HOUSE

Coal Pit Lane, Rossendale, BB4 9SB. Karen Clough. *4m from Rawtenstall. Take A681 into Waterfoot. Turn L onto the B6238. Approx ½ m turn R onto Shawclough Rd. Follow the road up until you reach the yellow signs.* **Sat 18, Sun 19 June (12-6). Adm £4, chd free. Cream tea, selection of cakes and drinks available.**

Nestled within Rossendale farmland in an exposed site the garden is split by a meandering stream. There are raised mixed borders with shrubs and perennials enclosed by a stone wall, with loose planting of shrubs and water loving plants around the stream. A local farmer once told me 'you won't grow 'owt up 'ere...' so the challenge is on. The Rossendale area provides some excellent walking and rambling sites. Rawtenstall has the famous East Lancashire railway, which is worth a visit.

🐎 ✿ ☕

33 [NEW] HOLLY HOUSE

Moor Road, Croston, Leyland, PR26 9HP. Mrs Elaine Raper. *Situated on the A581, approx 200 metres after the Highfield pub if coming from Leyland area.* **Sun 5 June (11-5). Adm £4, chd free. Light refreshments.**

Large garden, approx an acre of perennial beds with mature trees. Pond with decking area leading to wooded area beyond with rill. Two wisteria clad pergolas, parterre with adjacent gazebo. Mostly accessible to the main parts of the garden. Wood behind pond not accessible.

& 🐎 ☕ ᵔ⁾

34 JACK GREEN COTTAGE

Mill House Lane, Brindle, Chorley, PR6 8NS. Aurelia & Peter McCann. *5m N Chorley. From Chorley A6 turn R at r'about on B5256 Westwood Rd then L at r'about on B5256 Sandy Lane through Brindle for 2m, then L on Hill House Lane for ¾ m. Turn L on Oram Rd for 200yd.* **Sat 23, Sun 24 Apr, Sat 2, Sun 3 July (11-4). Adm £5, chd free. Light refreshments.**

This 2¾ acre garden has been lovingly restored, developed and improved in the last 11 yrs. With long borders of cottage style plants, Japanese style garden, herb garden, parterre, orchards, fruit cage and vegetable plots, there is a surprise around every corner. Chicken pen, secluded BBQ area, greenhouse and children's play area with willow tunnel and den are but few of the delights awaiting. Not all areas are suitable for wheelchair use, users should ideally be accompanied as some parts of the garden may be difficult to navigate.

& 🐎 ✿ ☕ ᵔ⁾

35 KINGTON COTTAGE

Kirkham Road, Treales, Preston, PR4 3SD. Mrs Linda Kidd, 01772 683005. *M55 J3. Take A585 to Kirkham, exit Preston St, L into Carr Lane to Treales village. Cottage on L in front of Derby Arms. Parking here by kind permission of owner.* **Sun 29 May, Sun 26 June, Sun 31 July, Sun 28 Aug (10-5). Adm £4, chd free. Home-made teas. Visits also by arrangement May to Sept for groups of 8 to 30. Escorted tour by garden owner.**

Nestling in the beautiful village of Treales this generously sized Japanese garden has many authentic and unique Japanese features, alongside its 2 ponds linked by a stream. The stroll garden leads down to the tea house garden. The planting and the meandering pathways blend together to create a tranquil meditative garden in which to relax. New additions complete four Japanese garden styles. Wheelchair access to some areas, uneven paths.

& 🐎 ✿ ☕

36 72 LUDLOW DRIVE

Ormskirk, L39 1LF. Marian & Brian Jones. *½ m W of Ormskirk on A570. From M58 J3 follow A570 to Ormskirk town centre. Continue on A570 towards Southport. At A570 junction with A59 cross T-lights after ½ m turn R at Spar garage onto Heskin Lane then 1st R Ludlow Drive.* **Sun 10 July (11-4). Combined adm with Gorse Hill Nature Reserve £5, chd free. Home-made teas. Gluten free & vegan cake also provided. Caffeine free tea & coffee on request.**

A town garden overflowing with a wide variety of bee friendly planting. Developed over 16 yrs it inc a gravel garden and jewel garden to the

front. The back garden has a raised shade border and sunny borders with perennials, roses and clematis. A new Victorian greenhouse has been added with a collection of pelargoniums, succulents and cacti. There is also a raised pond and alpine troughs. Wheelchair access to front and rear garden.

& ✿ ☕ ᵔ⁾

37 LYTHAM HALL

Ballam Rd, Lytham, Lytham St Annes, FY8 4JX. Paul Lomax. *Follow the brown tourist signs for Lytham Hall. For SatNav use postcode FY8 4TQ.* **Mon 6 June (10-4.30). Adm £4.50, chd free. Light refreshments. Picnic tables on the East Lawn.**

Lytham Hall is a C18 Georgian house set in 78 acres of historic woodlands, with a parterre, herbaceous border, south aspect garden and two wildlife ponds. A mount, that can be climbed with views over the parkland and 4km of paths. There is a RHS Gold award winning vegetable garden and potager. Farmland animals, apiary and garden nursery. 1m drive from the main gates to the Hall. There is a separate designated path for pedestrians past fields and through woodland. An outside catering vehicle will be available for hot drinks and snacks in addition to the Lytham Hall cafe. Wheelchair access available to most areas. Gravel paths in woodland. Coaches by appointment only.

& 🐎 ✿ 🚐 ☕ ᵔ⁾

In the first six months of operation at Maggie's Southampton, which was part funded by the National Garden Scheme, the team has supported people affected by cancer more than 2,300 times

38 MAGGIE'S, MANCHESTER
Kinnaird Road, Manchester,
M20 4QL. Jessica Ruth.
www.maggies.org/manchester.
At the end of Kinnaird Rd which is off Wilmslow Rd opp the Christie Hospital. **Sun 24 July (12-3). Adm by donation. Tea.**
The architecture of Maggie's Manchester, designed by world-renowned architect Lord Foster, is complemented by gardens designed by Dan Pearson, Best in Show winner at Chelsea Flower Show. Combining a rich mix of spaces, inc the working glasshouse and vegetable garden, the garden provides a place for both activity and contemplation. The colours and sensory experience of nature becomes part of the Centre through micro gardens and internal courtyards, which relate to the different spaces within the building. Wheelchair access to most of the garden from the front entrance.

⭐ 🅳 ☕ ⋅))

39 146 MATHER AVENUE
Allerton, Liverpool, L18 7HB.
Barbara Peers. *3m S from end of M62. On the R of Mather Ave heading out of town: on the same side as Tesco and 800 metres beyond.* **Sun 17 July (12-5). Combined adm with 33 Greenhill Road £5, chd free. Tea and home-made cake.**
A small tree fringed town garden with two ponds, one for fish and one for wildlife. A large woodpile is left to encourage insects as are the nettles along the back wall. One bed allowed to self seed with wildflowers. No pesticides and only home-made compost used. A multitude of plants encroach on the ever decreasing patch of lawn. Paths around give access.

🐕 ✿ ☕

40 MILL BARN
Goosefoot Close, Samlesbury,
Preston, PR5 0SS. Chris Mortimer, 07742 924124,
millbarnchris@gmail.com. *6m E of Preston. From M6 J31 2½m on A59/A677 B/burn. Turn S. Nabs Head Lane, then Goosefoot Lane.* **Sat 4, Sun 5, Sat 11, Sun 12 June (1-5). Adm £5, chd free. Cream teas. Picnics welcome. Visits also by arrangement May to July. Hot drinks & biscuits only unless other arrangements have been made.**
The unique and quirky garden at Mill Barn is a delight, or rather a series of delights. Along the River Darwin,

through the tiny secret grotto, past the suspension bridge and view of the fairytale tower, visitors can stroll past folly, sculptures, lily pond, and lawns, enjoy the naturally planted flowerbeds, then enter the secret garden and through it the pathways of the wooded hillside beyond. A garden developed on the site of old mills gives a fascinating layout which evolves at many levels. The garden jungle provides a smorgasbord of flowers to attract insects throughout the season. Children enjoy the garden very much. Partial wheelchair access.

⭐ 🐕 ✿ 🚗 ☕ 🎪 ⋅))

41 MILL CROFT
Wennington, Lancaster, LA2 8NX.
Linda Ashworth. *From J34 of M6 take A683 towards Kirkby Lonsdale. Turn R on B6480 towards Bentham.* **Sun 19 June (10-4). Combined adm with Raw Ridding House £6, chd free. Sun 17 July (10-4). Adm £4, chd free. Home-made cakes, including gluten-free and vegan options, hot and cold drinks.**
A rural garden extending to about 3¼ acres with a summer flowering meadow, stream, trees, shrubs, herbaceous planting, vegetable plot and stumpery. Various seating areas to rest and enjoy local wildlife and the surrounding views. An ongoing experiment to discover what will thrive in heavy clay with occasional flooding, exposure to wind and in a frost pocket. New projects always underway.

✿ ☕ ⋅))

42 MOSS PARK ALLOTMENTS
Lesley Road, Stretford,
Manchester, M32 9EE. Allison Sterlini. *3m SW of Manchester. From M60 J7 (Manchester), A56 (Manchester), A5181 Barton Rd, L onto B5213 Urmston Lane, ½m L onto Lesley Rd signed Stretford Cricket Club. Parking at 2nd gate.* **Sun 17 July (11-4). Adm £5, chd free. Gorgeous array of home-made cakes.**
Moss Park is a stunning, award winning allotment site in Stretford, Manchester. Wide grass paths flanked by pretty flower borders give way to a large variety of well-tended plots bursting with ideas to try at home, from insect hotels to unusual fruits and vegetables. Take tea and cake on the lawn outside the quirky society clubhouse that looks like a beamed country pub. WC facilities. Partial wheelchair access.

⭐ 🐕 ✿ 🚗 ☕

43 194 MOTTRAM OLD ROAD
Gee Cross, Hyde, SK14 3BA.
Mrs Anne Dickinson. *10m SE of Manchester on M60, M67. Leave M67 at r'about (motorway terminates) take exit for Gee Cross.* **Sun 22 May (11-4). Adm £5, chd free. Light refreshments.**
A terraced garden on several levels with far reaching views over Manchester and the Pennines. Created by the owner's late husband Harry. Acers and rhododendrons feature alongside many species of perennials. A meandering naturalistic water feature constructed from locally sourced stone cascades down to the pond. Woodland garden leads to a vegetable garden and work area. Many seating areas to enjoy.

☕ ⋅))

44 OLD HOLLOWS FARM
Old Hollow Lane, Banks,
Southport, PR9 8DU. Janet Baxter. *5m N of Southport. A565 r'about take turning for Banks. Straight through Banks. New Lane Pace Rd ends on bend turn L on farm rd into Old Hollow Lane. Parking in yard at lane end.* **Sat 11, Sun 12 June (11-5). Adm £4.50, chd free. Home-made teas.**
Old Hollow Cottage Garden open in memory of my late husband Alec Baxter, whose straw hat was always popping up somewhere. Waste ground and pit 18 yrs ago - now a peaceful tranquil garden on the edge of the Ribble Estuary. Patio area garden room, large lawned areas, trees, large herbaceous border and arboretum. The wildlife pond has a large reed bed. Walks along the estuary embankment. Display of vintage bicycles and driftwood. Bee demonstration. Local Crafts and Artisans. No disabled WC facilities. Level in main area only.

⭐ 🐕 ✿ 🚗 ☕ ⋅))

45 1 OSBORNE STREET
Didsbury, Manchester, M20 2QZ.
Richard & Teresa Pearce-Regan. *5m S of Manchester. From M60 J5 follow signs to Northenden. Turn R at T-lights onto Barlow Moor Rd to Didsbury. From M56 follow A34 to Didsbury.* **Sun 31 July (12-5). Combined adm with Flat 1, 5 Parkfield Road South £5, chd free.**
A new garden with a stylish contemporary feel. Pale porcelain paving provides a cool foil for rich planting, raised brick beds and two

23 Ashton Road, Ainsdale & Birkdale Gardens

water features- one flowing into a pool via a steel water shute, the other at ground level with fish and step over. Pleached trees and hedges provide privacy and divide the space, whilst black Philippe Stark sofas add to the contemporary look.

🐕 ✿))

46 PARKERS LODGES
28 Lodge Side, Bury, BL8 2SW. Keith Talbot. *2m W of M66 J2. From A58 then B6196 Ainsworth Rd turn R onto Elton Vale Rd, drive past the sports club onto a small estate, & follow the road round to car park.* **Sun 22 May, Sun 10 July (10-5). Adm £5, chd free. Light refreshments.**
Parkers Lodges is set on the site of a demolished Victorian Mill that was used for bleaching. Since the houses were completed in 2014 a small group of volunteers have been working to transform what was a jungle into a manicured wild space that still allows the local wildlife to flourish. Set in 12 acres with 2 lakes with 50 percent of them open for a leisurely stroll round.

☕ 🐕

47 5 PARKFIELD ROAD SOUTH, FLAT 1
Didsbury, Manchester, M20 6DA. Kath & Rob Lowe. *From M60 J5 follow signs to Northenden. Turn R at T-lights onto Barlow Moor Rd to Didsbury. From M56 follow A34 to Didsbury.* **Sun 31 July (12-5). Combined adm with 1 Osborne Street £5, chd free.**
A large, stylish, contemporary garden divided by raised white rendered beds, pleached trees and hedges into three distinct rooms, packed with lush planting detail. The artisan owners have forged the ironwork features and sculptural elements. A hidden garden is a surprise to be discovered. The gardens, planted by The Matthew Ludlam Foundation, open in memory of Matthew Ludlam.

♿ 🐕))

48 PLANT WORLD
Myerscough College, St Michaels Road, Bilsborrow, Preston, PR3 0RY. Myerscough College, 01995 642264, tmelia@myerscough.ac.uk, www.myerscough.ac.uk/commercial-services-equine-events/plant-world-gardens/. *From M6 take J32 and head N for 5m up the A6. Turn L onto St Michaels Rd take 2nd entrance into the college signed Plant World.* **Sun 7 Aug (10.30-3). Adm £3.50, chd free. Light refreshments.**
A gardener's paradise with an acre of RHS Gold Award winning gardens and glasshouses, including tropical, temperate and desert zones. Themed and herbaceous borders, pinetum, fruit garden, bog garden, pond and woodland garden. Many plants labelled for identification purposes. Plant sales with many rare and unusual specimens. Myerscough Tearooms overlook the stunning gardens serving a wide range of delicious locally produced cakes and sandwiches. Indoor and outdoor seating. Guided tours throughout the day. Dogs welcome in the gardens, sales area and the café.

🐕 ✿ 🚌 🛋 ☕ 🪑))

49 NEW **36 QUEENS DRIVE**
Heaton Mersey, Stockport,
SK4 3JW. Joanna Wilson. *6m S
of Manchester. Queens Drive is
off Didsbury Rd, but is not directly
accessible from it by car. Go via
Mauldeth Rd or Bankhall Rd. SatNav
directions for the postcode should
be correct.* **Sun 31 July (12-5).
Combined adm with 6 Cannock
Drive £5, chd free.**
A tiny 'avenue' of crab apple trees
and a walled courtyard make an
interesting entrance to a generous
family garden. Flower beds filled
with lush planting wrap around the
shady side of the house, whilst in the
sunshine, a traditional brick wall and
beech hedging provide a backdrop
for a wide variety of shrubs, climbers
and herbaceous borders.
& 🐄 ☕

50 RAW RIDDING HOUSE
Monk's Gate, Tatham, Lancaster,
LA2 8NH. Rebecca & Richard
Sanderson. *10m from J34 M6. Off
the B6480 between Wennington
& Wray. 1m E of Wray, turn L onto
Monk's Gate, signed for Tatham
Church. Park at church unless
disabled.* **Sun 19 June (10-4).
Combined adm with Mill Croft
£6, chd free. Light refreshments.
Gluten free cake available.**
A blend of contemporary design
with relaxed planting with decks
and terraces to accommodate the
sloping site without compromising
the amazing views. Large herbaceous
beds, lawns, a small wildlife pond
and wildflower meadow. Hidden
seating areas. Parking at church with
a 5min walk to garden. No steps but
sloping gravelled or bark chip paths
to all areas may require assistance to
navigate.
& 🐄 ☕))

51 ◆ **THE RIDGES**
Weavers Brow (cont. of
Cowling Rd), Limbrick,
Chorley, PR6 9EB. Mr & Mrs
J M Barlow, 01257 279981,
barbara@barlowridges.co.uk,
www.bedbreakfast-gardenvisits.
com. *2m SE of Chorley town
centre. From M6 J27. From M61
J8. Follow signs for Chorley A6
then signs for Cowling & Rivington.
Passing Morrison's up Brook St,
mini r'about 2nd exit, Cowling Brow.
Pass Spinners Arms on L. Garden
on R.* **For NGS: Mon 2 May, Mon
29 Aug (11-5). Adm £5, chd free.
Light refreshments. For other**

opening times and information,
please phone, email or visit garden
website.
3 acres, inc old walled orchard
garden, cottage-style herbaceous
borders, with perfumed rambling
roses and clematis through fruit trees.
Arch leads to formal lawn, surrounded
by natural woodland, shrub borders
and specimen trees with contrasting
foliage. Woodland walks and dell.
Natural looking stream, wildlife ponds.
Walled water feature with Italian
influence, and walled herb garden.
Classical music played. Some gravel
paths and woodland walks not
accessible.
& 🐄 ❄ 🛏 ☕

52 4 ROE GREEN
Worsley, Manchester, M28 2JB.
Geoff & Pauline Ogden. *5m W of
Manchester. Roe Green is adjacent
to J14 of M60. Please park on Old
Clough Lane.* **Sat 2 July (12-5).
Adm £4, chd free. Home-made
teas. Cordial and biscuits for
children.**
A 300 yr old cottage located on
the edge of the village green in the
picturesque conservation area of
Roe Green. This is a plantswoman's
quintessential cottage garden, packed
with many unusual perennials and
mixed wildflowers that thrive in this
sheltered walled space. In addition
to a woodland area, there is an old
bothy which adds to the delightful
atmosphere of this garden.
🐄 ❄ ☕))

GROUP OPENING

53 NEW **SEFTON PARK JULY
GARDENS**
Liverpool, L17 1AS. Sefton Park
Allotments Society. *From end of
M62 take A5058 Queens Drive S
through Allerton to Sefton Park.
Circle the park and follow yellow
signs. Maps available at all gardens.*
**Sun 10 July (12-5). Combined
adm £6, chd free. Home-made
teas. Refreshments at all venues.**

**FERN GROVE COMMUNITY
GARDEN**
L8 0RY. Liverpool City Council.

PARKMOUNT
L17 3BP. Jeremy Nicholls.

37 PRINCE ALFRED ROAD
L15 8HH. Jane Hammett.

SEFTON PARK ALLOTMENTS
L17 1AS. Sefton Park Allotments
Society.

Two stunning private gardens full
of peak summer colour, plus nearly
100 productive allotments, and the
urban oasis of a community garden
are splendid examples of gardening
in the city. Plants and produce for
sale, a bee demonstration plus lots
of family fun for locals and visitors
alike. Children's activities and
bee demonstration at Fern Grove
Community Garden. Classical music
2-4pm at Sefton Park Allotments.
Plants for sale at Park Mount.
❄ ☕

GROUP OPENING

54 NEW **SEFTON PARK JUNE
GARDENS**
Liverpool, L8 3SA. *From end of
M62 take A5058 Queens Drive S to
Sefton Park. Circle the Park to find
yellow signs for gardens.* **Sun 12
June (12-5). Combined adm £6,
chd free.**

**THE COMMUNITY ORCHARD
AND WILDLIFE GARDEN**
L17 2AT. The Society of Friends,
www.tann.org.uk.

6 CROXTETH GROVE
L8 3SA. Stuart Speeden.

SEFTON VILLA
L8 3SD. Patricia Williams.

17 SYDENHAM AVENUE
L17 3AU. Fatima Aabbar-
Marshall.

Three stunning private gardens at
the height of their early summer
colour, plus the Community Orchard
and Wildlife garden - a hidden oasis
of nature in the urban landscape.
The gardens are just two miles from
Liverpool City Centre in the nearest
area of parkland in South Liverpool.
Excellent planting and original ideas
are inspirational for garden visitors.
❄ ☕))

55 SOUTHLANDS
12 Sandy Lane, Stretford,
M32 9DA. Maureen Sawyer &
Duncan Watmough, 0161 283
9425, moe@southlands12.com,
www.southlands12.com. *3m S of
Manchester. Sandy Lane (B5213) is
situated off A5181 (A56) ¼m from*

M60 J7. **Sun 17 July (12-5.30). Adm £5, chd free. Home-made teas. Cake-away service (take a slice of your favourite cake home). Visits also by arrangement June to Aug for groups of 5+.**
Opening for its 20th year, described by visitors as 'totally inspirational', this artists' multi-award winning garden unfolds into a series of beautiful spaces including Mediterranean, ornamental and woodland gardens. Organic kitchen garden with large glasshouse containing vines. Recently redesigned herbaceous borders, hanging baskets and stunning container plantings throughout the garden. Artist's work on display.

56 STANHILL EXOTIC GARDEN

19 Stanhill Street, Oswaldtwistle, Accrington, BB5 4QE. Tez Donnelly, www.facebook.com/stanhillgarden. *From M65 J5 take A6077 towards Shadsworth, first R to B623. 2.3m, L at Black Dog pub, 0.2m R into Thwaites Rd for parking. Then cross rd to Stanhill St on foot. Garden at rear.* **Sat 3, Sun 4 Sept (12.30-4.30). Adm £4, chd free. Home-made teas.**
Behind a row of terraced houses lies a hidden gem. A lush exotic style garden containing palms, tree ferns, bananas, and many other unusual plants. A mixture of paving and bark chipping paths takes you on a journey round the tropical garden, encountering a pond and an aviary along the way.

The National Garden Scheme searches the length and breadth of England, Channel Islands, Northern Ireland and Wales for the very best private gardens

58 5 TOLSEY DRIVE

Hutton, Preston, PR4 5SH. Marilyn & James Woods, 07973 794136, malwoods@hotmail.co.uk. *2m SW of Preston. Head out of Preston on the A59 towards Southport, at the r'about head towards Longton on Liverpool Rd, Tolsey Dr situated 100 yds on the L. Gardens signed from A59.* **Visits by arrangement July to Sept for groups of 8 to 16. Combined admission with 10 Tolsey Drive. Adm £5, chd free. Home-made teas at 10 Tolsey Drive.**
An informal, peaceful garden with structure and cottage garden planting developed from scratch over the past 4 years. The winding path weaves down the interestingly shaped lawn and colourful borders. There are many places to sit and high hedges that nesting birds enjoy. There is also a small wildlife pond, areas of nettles and wood stacks to encourage wildlife.

57 10 TOLSEY DRIVE

Hutton, Preston, PR4 5SH. Heather & John Lund, 07947 603289, heather.lund@icloud.com. *2m SW of Preston. Head out of Preston on the A59 towards Southport, at the r'about head towards Longton on Liverpool Rd, Tolsey Dr situated 100 yds on the L. Gardens signed from A59.* **Visits by arrangement July to Sept for groups of 8 to 16. Combined admission with 5 Tolsey Drive. Adm £5, chd free. Home-made teas.**
A long, eclectic garden divided into sections. There are large borders full of flowers, trees and shrubs with some unusual plants, greenhouses with vegetables and exotic plants and a large fruit cage. Water features, a quiet, shady secret garden and features built from recycled materials all add to the quirkiness. Plenty of seating areas where afternoon tea is served. There is a 'Wonky Wall' with a moon gate over the path, a water feature made from a recycled hot water cistern, a paving stone from an old septic tank and there are bamboos planted in old cisterns. A Gabion bench inserted into a dry stone wall adds character to the Secret Garden.

59 TURTON TOWER KITCHEN GARDEN

Tower Drive, Turton, Bolton, BL7 0HG. Anna Harvey. *1½m from Edgeworth. Turton Tower is signposted off the B6391 between Bolton and Edgeworth.* **Sun 29 May (11-4). Adm £3, chd free. Light refreshments in The Woodland Cafe.**
Set in the tranquil gardens of Turton Tower the Kitchen Garden is set on a sloping site, with 4 large beds and borders which have been subdivided for vegetables, herbaceous perennials, summer annuals, soft fruit and a variety of fruit trees. The garden was established in Victorian times but fell into disuse and became badly overgrown in the 20th century, though it was worked for a few years during and shortly after WW2. The project to restore it began in 2008 by a committed enthusiastic group of volunteers. The garden was completely covered with brambles, ferns, old bushes and trees – unrecognisable as a garden. It took the volunteers 2 yrs to clear it; a lot of sweat and tears included! The Kitchen Garden is now an attractive, functioning garden which continues to develop to retain and increase both interest and structure.

60 NEW VICTORIA HOUSE

Standedge, Delph, Oldham, OL3 5LT. Mrs Hanna Simpson. *Huddersfield Road (A62). What3words app - thinking.licks. married.* **Sat 25, Sun 26 June (12-4). Combined adm with 5 Crib Lane £5, chd free. Home-made cakes, sandwiches & Saddleworth honey produce.**
Visit our wild hillside garden. With various immature trees, and local grasses. Follow the grass paths through the trees to the lawned area, beehives and stunning views of the Pennine valley. 3 acre rural garden, most areas accessed over grass, areas of sloping land. With areas for picnics. Hosts of local 'Saddleworth honey hives' and garden flock of hens.

GROUP OPENING

61 WARTON GARDENS

Warton, LA5 9PJ. 01524 727770, claire@lavenderandlime.co.uk. 1½ m N of Carnforth. From M6 J35 take A601 NW for 1m, then N on A6 for 0.7m, turn L signed Warton Old Rectory. Warton village 1m down Borwick Lane. From Carnforth pass train stn & follow signs Warton & Silverdale. Park at bottom of village (LA5 9NU) or car park next to Old School Brewery (LA5 9PL). **Sat 16, Sun 17 July (11-5). Combined adm £6, chd free. Home-made teas at 109/111 Main Street.**

BRIAR COTTAGE
LA5 9PT. Mr Bendall.

2 CHURCH HILL AVENUE
LA5 9NU. Mr & Mrs J Street.

NEW 9 MAIN STREET
LA5 9NR. Mrs Sarah Baldwin.

NEW 80 MAIN STREET
LA5 9PG. Mrs Yvonne Miller.

107 MAIN STREET
LA5 9PJ. Becky Hindley, www.pickingposies.co.uk.

111 MAIN STREET
LA5 9PJ. Mr & Mrs J Spendlove, 01524 727 770, claire@lavenderandlime.co.uk.

WARTON ALLOTMENT HOLDERS
LA5 9QU. Mrs Jill Slaughter.

The 6 gardens and allotments are spread across the village and offer a wide variety of planting and design ideas. Our group offers a contemporary garden skilfully planted on limestone pavement, a flower picking garden, a mature cottage style garden with unusual herbaceous planting, trees and productive vegetable/soft fruit section, 21 allotments, a large garden comprised of a series of rooms each with a different atmosphere and 2 new gardens which have been created in the last year and are 'work in progress'. Warton is the birthplace of the medieval ancestors of George Washington, the family coat of arms can be seen in St Oswald's Church. The ruins of the Old Rectory (English Heritage) is the oldest surviving building in the village. Ascent of Warton Crag (AONB), provides panoramic views across Morecambe Bay to the Lakeland hills beyond.

Dale House Gardens

62 8 WATER HEAD
Fulwood, Preston,
PR2 3TU. Phil Parkinson,
philinterfaith@gmail.com. *3m N of
Preston. 2m from M6 J32. A6 into
Preston, R at Black Bull Lane. At
2nd r'about, R, Cadley Causeway. R
at T junction r'about. Signage after
the bend. Parking in Hollins Grove
please.* **Visits by arrangement Mar
to Oct for groups of up to 16.
Solo visitors welcome. Adm £4,
chd free.**
A medium sized, rigorously
structured, suburban garden in 5
rooms with a canal bank for extras.
Over 70 roses, entirely crimson and
white in the first room, a large fernery
with rare specimens, *Iris germanica*,
rudbeckia, hosta, hellebore, canna,
and tree collections, Langdale slate
paving, and an imaginative use of
levels and height, the whole being
suffused with a contemplative,
centred energy.

63 WEEPING ASH GARDEN
Bents Garden & Home, Warrington
Road, Glazebury, WA3 5NS. John
Bent, www.bents.co.uk. *15m W of
Manchester. Next to Bents Garden &
Home, just off the A580 East Lancs
Rd at Greyhound r'about nr Leigh.
Follow brown 'Garden Centre' signs.*
**Sun 13, Sun 20 Feb, Sun 14 Aug,
Sun 11 Sept, Sun 30 Oct (11-4).
Adm £5, chd free.**
Created by retired nurseryman and
photographer John Bent, Weeping
Ash is a garden of year-round
interest with a beautiful display of
early snowdrops. Broad sweeps of
colour lend elegance to this stunning
garden which is much larger than
it initially seems with hidden paths
and wooded areas creating a sense
of natural growth. Bents Garden
& Home offers a choice of dining
destinations including The Fresh
Approach Restaurant, Caffe nel Verde
and a number of al fresco dining
options.

64 WIGAN & LEIGH HOSPICE
Kildare Street, Hindley, Wigan,
WN2 3HZ. Wigan & Leigh Hospice,
thehospicegardener.com. *1½m
SW of Wigan. From Wigan on A577
Leigh/Manchester Rd. In Hindley turn
R at St Peter's Church onto Liverpool
Rd A58. After 250 metres turn R into
Kildare St.* **Sun 24 July (11-4). Adm
£4, chd free. Home-made teas.**

Large attractive gardens surround the
Hospice creating a place of tranquillity.
At the front are beautiful raised beds
and a courtyard garden, at the rear 3
large ponds and a 'rainbow' bridge.
Outside patients' rooms are colourful
flower beds. A memorial daisy
garden. A wildflower garden has been
created - 'The Amberswood Garden'.
They are a haven for wildlife. Garden
awarded 'Gold' in NW in Bloom. Fully
accessible, including WC.

**65 WILLOW WOOD HOSPICE
GARDENS**
Willow Wood Close, Mellor
Road, Ashton-Under-Lyne,
OL6 6SL. Willow Wood Hospice,
www.willowwood.info. *3mins
from J23 M60. Exit onto A6140
towards Ashton-u-Lyne turn R onto
Manchester Rd/A635 then slight
R onto Park Parade/A635 keep R,
stay on A635 turn L onto Mellor Rd
L onto Willow Wood Close.* **Sat 21
May, Sat 25 June (11-4). Adm £5,
chd free. Cakes, light snacks, hot
and cold beverages, Pimms, wine
and cocktails.**
The sensory gardens, redesigned and
maintained by two former National
Trust gardeners and a wonderful
team of volunteers, comprise
a series of formal and informal
gardens. These spaces contain
lush, romantic planting design, filled
with scent, texture, studies in colour
combinations and sculptural form,
water features, a kitchen garden,
wildlife friendly planting and two
woodland areas. The Sensory and
Tranquil gardens are wheelchair
accessible. Please check the Willow
Wood website for further information.

GROUP OPENING

**66 WOOLTON VILLAGE JULY
GARDENS**
Woolton, Liverpool, L25 8QF. *7m
S of Liverpool. Woolton Rd B5171
or Menlove Ave A562 follow signs
for Woolton.* **Sun 24 July (12-5).
Combined adm £5, chd free. Light
refreshments at Layton Close, 1
The Riffle, 89 Oakwood.**

16 LAYTON CLOSE
L25 9NJ. Bob Edisbury.

71 MANOR ROAD
L25 8QF. John & Maureen Davies.

89 OAKWOOD ROAD
L26 1XD. Sean Gargan.

NEW 1 THE RIFFEL
L25 6DR. Mr Mark & Mrs Sue
Thompson.

Woolton village has won multiple
Britain in Bloom and North West
in Bloom awards. The gardens are
all different reflecting their owners'
individuality and style. All within a
short walk or drive from each other.
Wheelchair access to some gardens.

GROUP OPENING

**67 WOOLTON VILLAGE JUNE
GARDENS**
Speke Road, Woolton, Liverpool,
L25 0LA. Paul & Helen Ekoku.
*Gardens are best accessed by car
although Hunts Cross train stn is
very close to one garden and others
can be accessed using frequent
bus services.* **Sun 26 June (12-5).
Combined adm £5, chd free.
Home-made teas.**

**GREEN RIDGES, RUNNYMEDE
CLOSE**
L25 5JU. Sarah & Michael
Beresford.

23 HILLSIDE DRIVE
L25 5NR. Bruce & Fiona Pennie.

231 SPEKE ROAD
L25 0LA. Paul & Helen Ekoku,
07765 379967,
iekoku@yahoo.co.uk.

Three suburban gardens located
in the beautiful historic village of
Woolton featuring C17 buildings that
act as a backdrop to the public space
plant displays maintained by Woolton
in Bloom, for whom the gardens
also open. The gardens feature
herbaceous borders, water features,
tropical plants, greenhouses, kitchen
garden and garden sculptures. 231
Speke Road fully accessible, others
partially accessible.

LEICESTERSHIRE & RUTLAND

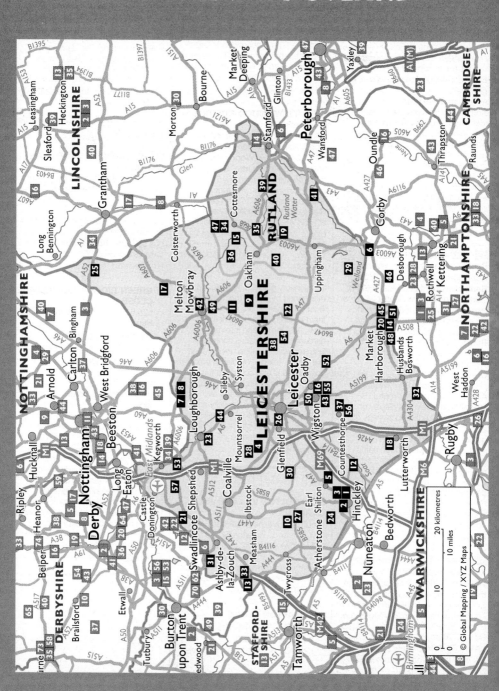

Leicestershire is a landlocked county in the Midlands with a diverse landscape and fascinating heritage providing a range of inspiring city, market town and village gardens.

Our gardens include Victorian terraces that make the most of small spaces and large country houses with historic vistas. We have an arboretum with four champion trees and a city allotment with over 100 plots. We offer something for everyone, from the serious plants person to the casual visitor.

You'll receive a warm welcome at every garden gate. Visit and get ideas for your own garden or to simply enjoy spending time in a beautiful garden. Most gardens sell plants and offer tea and cake, many are happy to take group bookings. We look forward to seeing you soon!

'Much in Little' is Rutland's motto. They say small is beautiful and never were truer words said.

Rutland is rural England at its best. Honey-coloured stone cottages make up pretty villages nestling amongst rolling hills; the passion for horticulture is everywhere you look, from stunning gardens to the hanging baskets and patio boxes showing off seasonal blooms in our two attractive market towns of Oakham and Uppingham.

There's so much to see in and around Rutland whatever the time of year, including many wonderful National Garden Scheme gardens.

Below: Silver Birches

f @NGSLeicestershire
@leicestershire_ngs
f @rutlandngs

@LeicsNGS
@rutlandngs

Volunteers

Leicestershire

County Organiser
Pamela Shave 01858 575481
pamela.shave@ngs.org.uk

County Treasurer
Martin Shave 01455 556633
martin.shave@ngs.org.uk

Publicity
Carol Bartlett 01616 261053
carol.bartlett@ngs.org.uk

**Booklet Co-ordinator
(Leicestershire & Rutland)**
Sharon Maher 01162 711680
sharon.maher@ngs.org.uk

Social Media
Zoe Lewin 07810 800 007
zoe.lewin@ngs.org.uk

Twitter
Donna Smith 07905 297766
donna.smith@ngs.org.uk

Talks
Karen Gimson 07930 246974
k.gimson@btinternet.com

**Local Groups
Communication Officer**
Donna Smith (as above)

Assistant County Organisers
Janet Rowe 01162 597339
janetnandrew@btinternet.com

Gill Hadland 01162 592170
gillhadland1@gmail.com

Roger Whitmore &
Shirley Jackson 07837579672
whitmorerog@hotmail.co.uk

Rutland

County Organisers
Sally Killick 07799 064565
sally.killick@ngs.org.uk

Lucy Hurst 07958 534778
lucy.hurst@ngs.org.uk

County Treasurer
Sandra Blaza 01572 770588
sandra.blaza@ngs.org.uk

Publicity
Lucy Hurst (as above)

Social Media
Nicola Oakey 07516 663358
nicola.oakey@ngs.org.uk

OPENING DATES

All entries subject to change. For latest information check www.ngs.org.uk
Extended openings are shown at the beginning of the month.
Map locator numbers are shown to the right of each garden name.

February

Snowdrop Festival

Saturday 19th
Hedgehog Hall 22
Westview 52

Sunday 20th
The Acers 1
Hedgehog Hall 22
Westview 52

Sunday 27th
Tresillian House 49

March

Sunday 27th
Gunthorpe Hall 19

April

Saturday 9th
Oak Cottage 31

Sunday 10th
Oak Cottage 31

Sunday 24th
The Old Hall 34
Tresillian House 49

May

Sunday 1st
Hedgehog Hall 22
Westbrooke House 51
Westview 52

Monday 2nd
Hedgehog Hall 22
Westview 52

Sunday 8th
Burrough Hall 9

Sunday 15th
1 The Dairy, Hurst Court 13
The Old Vicarage, Whissendine 36
◆ Whatton House 53

Sunday 22nd
NEW Fox Cottage 15

Saturday 28th
88 Brook Street 7
109 Brook Street 8

Sunday 29th
88 Brook Street 7
109 Brook Street 8
The Old Vicarage, Burley 35

June

Every Wednesday
Stoke Albany House 46

Thursday 2nd
Mountain Ash 28
Redhill Lodge 41

Friday 3rd
Mountain Ash 28

Saturday 4th
28 Gladstone Street 16

Sunday 5th
28 Gladstone Street 16
4 Packman Green 37

Saturday 11th
Goadby Marwood Hall 17
The New Barn 30
The Secret Garden at Wigston Framework Knitters Museum 43

Sunday 12th
The New Barn 30
The Secret Garden at Wigston Framework Knitters Museum 43
Snowdrop Ridge 45

Wednesday 15th
Thorpe Lubenham Hall 48

Saturday 18th
Oak Tree House 32

Sunday 19th
44 Fairfield Road 14
Nevill Holt Hall 29

Sunday 8th
Oak Tree House 32
Silver Birches 44
59 Thistleton Road 47

Friday 24th
NEW Brickfield House 6

Saturday 25th
The Old Barn 33

Sunday 26th
Market Bosworth Gardens 27
The Old Barn 33
4 Packman Green 37
Westbrooke House 51
15 The Woodcroft 57

Tuesday 28th
NEW The LOROS Hospice Gardens 26

Wednesday 29th
The Old Vicarage, Burley 35

July

Every Wednesday
Stoke Albany House 46

Saturday 2nd
8 Hinckley Road 24

Sunday 3rd
NEW Carlton Gardens 10
12 Hastings Close 21
8 Hinckley Road 24
Tresillian House 49

Saturday 9th
Wigston Gardens 55

Sunday 10th
Wigston Gardens 55

Saturday 16th
The Secret Garden at Wigston Framework Knitters Museum 43

Sunday 17th
Green Wicket Farm 18
Prebendal House 39
The Secret Garden at Wigston Framework Knitters Museum 43
Willoughby Gardens 56

Wednesday 20th
Green Wicket Farm 18

Wednesday 27th
NEW The LOROS Hospice Gardens 26

Sunday 31st
44 Fairfield Road 14
119 Scalford Road 42

August

Every Sunday
Honeytrees Tropical Garden 25

Every Thursday
Redhill Lodge 41

Sunday 7th
28 Ashby Road 2
NEW 182 Ashby Road 3

Saturday 20th
The Old Barn 33

Sunday 21st
The Old Barn 33
Quaintree Hall 40

Thursday 25th
NEW The LOROS Hospice Gardens 26

Sunday 28th
Tresillian House 49

September

Saturday 3rd
8 Hinckley Road 24

Sunday 4th
8 Hinckley Road 24
Washbrook Allotments 50

Saturday 10th
Oak Tree House 32

Sunday 11th
Oak Tree House 32
Westview 52

Saturday 24th
The New Barn 30

Sunday 25th
The New Barn 30

October

Sunday 9th
Hammond Arboretum 20

Sunday 30th
Tresillian House 49

By Arrangement

Arrange a personalised garden visit with your club, or group of friends, on a date to suit you. See individual garden entries for full details.

Bank Cottage	4
Barracca	5
88 Brook Street	7
109 Brook Street	8
Dairy Cottage	12
1 The Dairy, Hurst Court	13
Farmway, Willoughby Gardens	56
Goadby Marwood Hall	17
Green Wicket Farm	18
134 Herrick Road	23
Honeytrees Tropical Garden	25
Mountain Ash	28
The Old Barn	33
The Old Vicarage, Burley	35
The Paddocks	38
4 Priory Road, Market Bosworth Gardens	27
Redhill Lodge	41
The Secret Garden at Wigston Framework Knitters Museum	43
59 Thistleton Road	47
Tresillian House	49
Westview	52
The White House Farm	54

THE GARDENS

1 THE ACERS
10 The Rills, Hinckley, LE10 1NA. Mr Dave Baggott. *Off B4668 out of Hinckley. Turn into Dean Rd then 1st on the R.* **Sun 20 Feb (10-4). Adm £5, chd free. Home-made teas.** Medium sized garden, with a Japanese theme inc a zen garden, Japanese tea house, koi pond, more than 20 different varieties of Acers, many choice alpines, Trilliums, Cyclamen, Erythroniums, Cornus, Hamamelis and dwarf conifers. Over 150 different varieties of Snowdrops in spring. Large greenhouse.

2 28 ASHBY ROAD
Hinckley, LE10 1SL. Stan & Carol Crow. *Hinckley is SW of Leicester with easy access off the M69 or A5. Ashby Rd is on the A447 running N from Hinckley to Ibstock. Easy parking in road.* **Sun 7 Aug (11-5). Combined adm with 182 Ashby Road £6, chd free. Home-made teas.**
Behind the post war house lies a garden packed full of colour and interesting planting combinations. Approximately 150 feet long. Natural sculptures and pots abound. Wildlife area with pond and wildflowers to attract bees and butterflies into the garden. Plenty of hideaway seating to view the garden at your leisure. Vegetable garden with cut flower area. Eco friendly as much as possible.

3 NEW 182 ASHBY ROAD
Hinckley, LE10 1SW. Ms Lynda Blower. *Hinckley is SW Leicestershire near to the border with Warwickshire, with access off the M69 or A5. from Hinckley town centre on the B4667 on*
R 400yds before the A47/A447 junction. Parking in the road nearby and walking distance from partner garden (28 Ashby Rd). **Sun 7 Aug (11-5). Combined adm with 28 Ashby Road £6, chd free. Light refreshments.**
120ft cottage style garden packed with perennials and a small pond to attract frogs and other wildlife. A bog garden area complete with irrigation system. Kitchen garden with a selection of seasonal vegetables. Greenhouse and potting shed and plenty of seating to sit and view different aspects of the garden.

4 BANK COTTAGE
90 Main Street, Newtown Linford, Leicester, LE6 0AF. Jan Croft, 01530 244865, gardening91@icloud.com. *6m NW Leicester. 2½ m from M1 jct 22. From Leicester on L after Markfield Ln. Just before a public footpath sign if coming via Markfield Ln or Anstey or on the R just after public footpath sign if coming via Warren Hill.* **Visits by arrangement Apr & May for groups of up to 20. Refreshments available for groups up to 8. Adm by donation.**
Traditional cottage garden set on different levels leading down to the River Lin. Providing colour all year-round but at its prettiest in the Spring. Aconites, snowdrops, blue and white bells, primroses, alliums, aquilegia, poppies, geraniums, roses, honeysuckle, Philadelphia, acers, wisteria, autumn crocus, perennial sweet pea, perennial sunflowers, some fruit trees, small pond. Full of wildlife.

5 BARRACCA
Ivydene Close, Earl Shilton, LE9 7NR. Mr John & Mrs Sue Osborn, 01455 842609, susan.osborn1@btinternet.com, www.barraccagardens.co.uk.
10m W of Leicester. From A47 after entering Earl Shilton, Ivydene Close is 4th on L from Leicester side of A47. **Visits by arrangement Feb to July for groups of 10+. Adm £8, chd free. Home-made teas. Adm inc refreshments.**
1 acre garden with lots of different areas, silver birch walk, wildlife pond with seating, apple tree garden, Mediterranean planted area and lawns surrounded with herbaceous plants and shrubs. Patio area with climbing roses and wisteria. There is also a utility garden with greenhouse, vegetables in beds, herbs and perennial flower beds, lawn and fruit cage. Part of the old gardens owned by the Cotton family who used to open approx 9 acres to the public in the 1920's. Partial wheelchair access.

6 NEW BRICKFIELD HOUSE
Rockingham Road, Cottingham, Market Harborough, LE16 8XS. Simon & Nicki Harker. *If using SatNav, postcode will take you into Cottingham Village but garden is ½ a mile from Cottingham on Rockingham Rd/B670 towards Rockingham.* **Fri 24 June (11-4). Adm £5, chd free. Home-made teas.**
Lovely views overlooking the Welland Valley, this 2 acre garden has been developed from a sloping brickyard rubbish plot over 35 years. There is a kitchen garden, orchard, herbaceous borders filled with roses, perennials and shrubs, paths and many pots, filled with succulents, herbs and colourful annuals. Steps abound so sadly not wheelchair friendly.

7 88 BROOK STREET

Wymeswold, LE12 6TU. Adrian & Ita Cooke, 01509 880155, itacooke@btinternet.com. *4m NE of Loughborough. From A6006 Wymeswold turn S by church onto Stockwell, then E along Brook St. Roadside parking on Brook St.* **Sat 28, Sun 29 May (2-5). Combined adm with 109 Brook Street £6, chd free. Visits also by arrangement May & June for groups of 10 to 40 in conjunction with 109 Brook Street. Evening or day time visits welcome.**

The ½ acre garden is set on a hillside, which provides lovely views across the village, and comprises three distinct areas: firstly, a cottage style garden; then a series of water features inc a stream and a 'champagne' pond; and finally at the top there is a vegetable plot, small orchard and wildflower meadow. The ponds attract great crested and common newts, frogs, toads and grass snakes.

8 109 BROOK STREET

Wymeswold, LE12 6TT. Maggie & Steve Johnson, 07973 692931, steve@brookend.org, www.brookend.org. *4m NE of Loughborough. From A6006 Wymeswold turn S onto Stockwell, then E along Brook St. Roadside parking along Brook St. Steep drive with limited disabled parking at house.* **Sat 28, Sun 29 May (2-5). Combined adm with 88 Brook Street £6, chd free. Home-made teas inc gluten free option. Visits also by arrangement May & June for groups of 10 to 40. Evening or day time visits welcome.**

South facing, ¾ acre, gently sloping garden with views to open country. Modern garden with mature features. Patio with roses and clematis, wildlife and fish ponds, mixed borders, vegetable garden, orchard, hot garden and woodland garden. Something for everyone! Optional tour of rain water harvesting. Some gravel paths.

9 BURROUGH HALL

Burrough on the Hill, LE14 2QZ. Richard & Alice Cunningham. *Somerby Rd, Burrough on the Hill. Close to B6047. 10 mins from A606. 20 mins from Melton Mowbray.* **Sun 8 May (2-5). Adm £4, chd free. Home-made teas.**

Burrough Hall was built in 1867 as a classic Leicestershire hunting lodge. The garden, framed by mature trees and shrubs, was extensively redesigned by garden designer George Carter in 2007. The garden continues to develop. This family garden designed for all generations to enjoy is surrounded by magnificent views across High Leicestershire. In addition to the garden there will be a small collection of vintage and classic cars on display. Gravel paths and lawn.

GROUP OPENING

10 NEW CARLTON GARDENS

Congerstone Lane, Carlton, Nuneaton, CV13 0BU. Dr Liz Alun-Jones. *Carlton is 2m N of Market Bosworth & 5m S of Ibstock. All the gardens are either on or very close to Main Street. Free parking & refreshments, toilets & plant sales in the church in village centre where visitors are recommended to start their tour.* **Sun 3 July (11-4). Combined adm £6, chd free. Home-made teas in St Andrew's Parish Church, Main Street, Carlton.**

NEW **BUMBLE COT**
Murray & Pat Lockwood.

NEW **FIELD VIEW**
Dr Rashmi Shukla & Professor Vinod Patel.

NEW **HILLSDON**
Veronica & John Storer.

HOME FARM HOUSE, 7 MAIN STREET
Mr & Mrs C J Peat.

KIRKFIELD, 34 MAIN STREET
Mr & Mrs W R Sharp.

NEW **64 MAIN STREET**
Paul & Judith Boston.

NEW **WOODMILL**
Tom & Liz Alun-Jones.

Seven very different and interesting gardens. A wide variety of gardening styles on show in this small village. Bumble Cot is a small cottage style garden, Field View an eastern inspired garden. Home Farm is a large garden with a spacious vegetable plot and a 1½ acre woodland of indigenous trees planted in 2000. 64, Main Street is planted to encourage wildlife with views to open countryside and Hillsdon is a family friendly garden containing a secret area. Woodmill is a recently redeveloped garden with areas planted in both traditional and modern styles. Kirkfield was planted as a florist's garden with flower and vegetable beds and also has an interesting woodland area. The garden at Kirkfield has access through an outhouse with a small sill around the door. The other gardens are wheelchair accessible.

12 DAIRY COTTAGE

15 Sharnford Road, Sapcote, LE9 4JN. Mrs Norah Robinson-Smith, 01455 272398, nrobinsons@yahoo.co.uk. *9m SW of Leicester. Sharnford Rd joins Leicester Rd in Sapcote to B4114 Coventry Rd. Follow NGS signs at both ends.* **Visits by arrangement May to July for groups of 10 to 30. Adm £4, chd free. Home-made teas. Tea & cakes £2.00.**

From a walled garden with colourful mixed borders to a potager approached along a woodland path, this mature cottage garden combines extensive perennial planting with many unusual shrubs and specimen trees. More than 90 clematis and 30 climbing roses are trained up pergolas, arches and into trees – so don't forget to look up! Also a Hornbeam hedge covered with varieties of viticella clematis. Featured in Garden Answers June 2021 Featured in Garden News May 2020.

13 1 THE DAIRY, HURST COURT

Netherseal Road, Chilcote, Swadlincote, DE12 8DU. Alison Dockray, alisondockray56@gmail.com. *3m from J11 of the M42. 10m from Tamworth & Ashby de la Zouch. Hurst Court is situated on Netherseal Rd but SatNav show it as Church Rd. Due to limited parking it is advisable to park on Netherseal Rd. Chilcote is on the border of four counties.* **Sun 15 May (1-5). Adm £5, chd free. Light refreshments. Visits also by arrangement May to Sept.**

Developed over the last 15 years from a muddy ¼ acre patch attached to a barn conversion, the garden now contains a large Japanese Koi Carp pond, goldfish pond and a stream with planting having a Japanese connection viewed from winding

paths. With many rhododendrons, camellias and azaleas combined with cloud pruning and a variety of other plants, an air of peace pervades the garden.

⁴ 44 FAIRFIELD ROAD
Market Harborough, LE16 9QJ. Steve Althorpe & Judith Rout. *Opp the primary school.* **Sun 19 June, Sun 31 July (12-4.30). Adm £3.50, chd free. Home-made teas.** This wildlife friendly, ⅓ acre plot in the heart of Market Harborough, is a garden in which you can relax. There are large borders informally planted with a good variety of perennials and shrubs, a substantial pond full of amphibians and invertebrates and a copse. There's also plenty of seating at which you can enjoy all the container planting and home-made refreshments. Block paved drive and patio with gentle slope down on to lawn.

⁵ NEW FOX COTTAGE
Woodside, Ashwell, Oakham, LE15 7LX. Mr & Mrs D Pettifer. *No access via Woodside. Follow signs for parking.* **Sun 22 May (11.30-4.30). Adm £5, chd free. Home-made teas. Light lunches.**
A 2 acre country garden on the edge of the village with sweeping views across the surrounding open fields. Walks through the wonderful ancient oaks and ash underplanted with spring bulbs and lawns surrounded by rampant cow parsley. South facing terrace with seasonal planting.

⁶ 28 GLADSTONE STREET
Wigston Magna, LE18 1AE. Chris & Janet Huscroft. *4m S of Leicester. Off Wigston by-pass (A5199) follow signs off McDonalds r'about.* **Sat 4, Sun 5 June (11-5). Adm £3.50, chd free. Home-made teas. Opening with Wigston Gardens on Sat 9, Sun 10 July.**
Our mature 70'x15' town garden is divided into rooms and bisected by a pond with a bridge. It is brimming with unusual hardy perennials, inc collections of ferns and hostas. David Austin roses chosen for their scent feature throughout, inc a 30' rose arch. A shade house with unusual hardy plants and a Hosta Theatre. Regular changes to planting. Wigston Framework Knitters Museum and

garden nearby - open Sunday afternoons. Hosta theatre featured in Garden News.

⁷ GOADBY MARWOOD HALL
Goadby Marwood Hall, Goadby Marwood, Melton Mowbray, LE14 4LN. Mr & Mrs Westropp, 01664 464202, vwestropp@gmail.com. *4m NW of Melton Mowbray. Between Waltham-on-the-Wolds & Eastwell, 8m S of Grantham. Plenty of parking space available.* **Sat 11 June (10.30-5). Adm £5, chd £1. Home-made teas in Village Hall. Visits also by arrangement Apr to Oct.**
Redesigned in 2000 by the owner based on C18 plans. A chain of five lakes (covering 10 acres) and several ironstone walled gardens all interconnected. Lakeside woodland walk. Planting for year-round interest. Landscaper trained under plantswoman Rosemary Verey at Barnsley House. Beautiful C13 church open. Water, Walled gardens. Appeared on Castles in the Country and Best Gardens in England. Gravel paths and lawns.

The New Barn

18 GREEN WICKET FARM

Ullesthorpe Road, Bitteswell, Lutterworth, LE17 4LR.
Mrs Anna Smith, 01455 552646, greenfarmbitt@hotmail.com. *2m NW of Lutterworth J20 M1. From Lutterworth follow signs through Bitteswell towards Ullesthorpe. Garden situated behind Bitteswell Cricket Club. Use this as a landmark rather than relying totally on SatNav.* Sun 17, Wed 20 July (2-4.30). Adm £5, chd free. Light refreshments. Gluten free options available.
Visits also by arrangement June to Sept for groups of up to 30.
A fairly formal garden on an exposed site surrounded by open fields. Mature trees enclosing the many varied plants chosen to give all round year interest. Many unusual hardy plants grown along side good reliable old favourites present a range of colour themed borders. Grass and gravel paths allow access to the whole garden. Disabled parking areas.

& ❀ ☕))

19 GUNTHORPE HALL

Gunthorpe, Oakham, LE15 8BE. Tim Haywood, 01572 737514 ask for lettings. *A6003 between Oakham & Uppingham; 1½ m S of Oakham, up drive between lodges.* Sun 27 Mar (2-5). Adm £5, chd free. Tea. Large garden in a country setting with extensive views across the Rutland landscape with the carpets of daffodils being a key seasonal feature. The Stable Yard has been transformed into a series of parterres. The kitchen garden and borders have all been rejuvenated over recent years. Gravel path allows steps to be avoided.

& 🐾 ❀ 🛏 ☕))

20 HAMMOND ARBORETUM

Burnmill Road, Market Harborough, LE16 7JG. The Robert Smyth Academy, www.hammondarboretum.org.uk. *15m S of Leicester on A6. From High St, follow signs to The Robert Smyth Academy via Bowden Lane to Burnmill Rd. Park in 1st entrance on L.* Sun 9 Oct (2-4.30). Adm £5, chd free. Home-made teas provided by the Academy Parents Association. A site of just under 2½ acres containing an unusual collection of trees and shrubs, many from Francis Hammond's original planting dating from 1913 to 1936 whilst headmaster of the school. Species from America, China and Japan with malus and philadelphus walks and a moat. Proud owners of three champion trees identified by national specialist. Walk plans available. Some steep slopes.

& 🐾 ☕

21 12 HASTINGS CLOSE

Breedon-On-The-Hill, Derby, DE73 8BN. Mr & Mrs P Winship. *5m N from Ashby de la Zouch. Follow NGS signs in the Village. Parking around the Village Green. Please do not park in the close due to limited parking.* Sun 3 July (1-5). Adm £3, chd free.
A medium sized prairie garden, organically managed and planted in the Piet Oudolf style. Also many roses and a wide range of perennials. The back garden has a small 'white' garden with box hedging and more colourful style perennial borders. The garden has narrow paths and steps so is not suitable for wheelchairs.

❀))

22 HEDGEHOG HALL

Loddington Road, Tilton on the Hill, LE7 9DE. Janet & Andrew Rowe. *8m W of Oakham. 2m N of A47 on B6047 between Melton & Market Harborough. Follow yellow NGS signs in Tilton towards Loddington.* Sat 19, Sun 20 Feb (11-4). Sun 1, Mon 2 May (11-4). Light refreshments in May only. Adm £5, chd free. Open nearby Westview. ½ acre organically managed plant lover's garden. Steps leading to three stone walled terraced borders filled with shrubs, perennials, bulbs and a patio over looking the valley. Lavender walk, herb border, beautiful spring garden, colour themed herbaceous borders. Courtyard with collection of hostas and acers and terrace planted for year-round interest with topiary and perennials. Snowdrop collection. Regret, no wheelchair access to terraced borders. Disabled parking in the road outside the White House.

& ❀))

Prebendal House

23 134 HERRICK ROAD

Loughborough, LE11 2BU. Janet Currie, janet.currie@me.com, www.thesecateur.com. *1m SW of Loughborough centre. From M1 J23 take A512 Ashby Rd to L'boro. At r'about R onto A6004 Epinal Way. At Beacon Rd r'about L, Herrick Rd 1st on R.* **Visits by arrangement June to Aug for groups of 6 to 12. Adm £3.50, chd £1. Light refreshments. Dietary requirements catered for, please contact to discuss.**

A small garden brimming with texture, colour and creative flair. Trees, shrubs and climbers give structure. A sitting area surrounded by lilies, raised staging for herbs and alpines. A lawn flanked with deeply curving and gracefully planted beds of perennials growing through willow structures made by Janet. A shaded area under the Bramley apple tree, small greenhouse and potting area.

24 8 HINCKLEY ROAD

Stoke Golding, Nuneaton, CV13 6DU. Mr John & Mrs Stephanie Fraser. *3m NW of Hinckley. Approach from any direction into village then follow NGS signs. Please park roadside with due consideration to other residents properties.* **Sat 2 July (12-4); Sun 3 July (12-3); Sat 3, Sun 4 Sept (12-4). Adm £3.50, chd free. Light refreshments.**

A small SSW garden with pond/ water features to add interest to the colourful and some unusual perennials inc climbers to supplement the trees and shrubs in July and September. Garden established and recently re-established by current owner to provide seating for a variety of views of the garden. Many perennials in the garden are represented in the plants for sale.

25 HONEYTREES TROPICAL GARDEN

85 Grantham Road, Bottesford, NG13 0EG. Julia Madgwick & Mike Ford, 01949 842120, Julia_madgwick@hotmail.com. *7m E of Bingham on A52. Turn into village. Garden is on L on slip road behind hedge going out of village towards Grantham. Parking on grass opposite property.* **Every Sun 7 Aug to 28 Aug (11-4). Adm £4, chd free. Home-made teas. Vegan and gluten free cakes. Visits also by arrangement July & Aug for**

groups of 10+.

Tropical and exotic with a hint of jungle! Raised borders with different themes from lush foliage to arid cacti. Exotic planting as you enter the garden gives way on a gentle incline to surprises, inc glasshouses dedicated to various climatic zones interspersed with more exotic planting, ponds and a stream. A representation of in excess of 20 years plant hunting. Garden of the week in Garden News. Radio 103 The Eye. There are steps and ramps and some gravel but access by wheelchair to most parts of the garden.

26 NEW THE LOROS HOSPICE GARDENS

Duncombe Road, off Groby Road, Leicester, LE3 9QE. Richard Hill. *2½ m NE of Leicester City Centre & just 350 yds from the nearest bus stop. Follow A50 N from Leicester, or A50 S from J22 on the M1.* **Tue 28 June, Wed 27 July, Thur 25 Aug (9-5). Adm £3.50, chd free. Pre-booking essential, please visit www.ngs.org.uk for information & booking. Light refreshments.**

Our gardens are specifically designed and planted for the enjoyment of our patients. They consist of a series of mixed shrub and herbaceous beds, and a productive polytunnel providing produce for the kitchens and therapy for our patients. Highlights inc rambling roses, agapanthus and creamy-white Hydrangea Paniculata. Refreshments freshly made in our kitchens. Our gardens are fully accessible to wheelchair users along paved paths.

GROUP OPENING

27 MARKET BOSWORTH GARDENS

Market Bosworth, CV13 0LE. *13m W of Leicester; 8m N of Hinckley. 1m off A447 Coalville to Hinckley Rd, 3m off A444. Burton to Nuneaton Rd.* **Sun 26 June (12-6). Combined adm £7.50, chd free. Light refreshments at 13 Spinney Hill and 10 Weston Drive. Donation to Bosworth in Bloom.**

NEW 3 CHESTNUT CLOSE
Mrs Sue Styche.

GLEBE FARM HOUSE
Mr Peter Ellis & Ms Ginny Broad.

4 LANCASTER AVENUE
Mr Peter Bailiss.

26 NORTHUMBERLAND AVENUE
Mrs Kathy Boot.

NEW 22 PARK STREET
Mr John Henderson.

30 PARK STREET
Lesley Best.

4 PRIORY ROAD
Mrs Margaret Barrett, 01455 290112, info@margaretbarrett.co.uk. Visits also by arrangement May to Sept for groups of 5 to 15.

5 PRIORY ROAD
David & Linda Chevell.

RAINBOW COTTAGE
Mr David Harrison.

13 SPINNEY HILL
Mrs J Buckell.

17 STATION ROAD
Carol Thomas.

3 WARWICK CLOSE
Mrs Margaret Birch.

NEW 10 WESTON DRIVE
Ms Diane Shepherd.

Market Bosworth is an attractive market town, with an enviable record for the quality of its regular entry in the annual East Midlands in Bloom competition. There are a number of gardens open, all within walking distance of the Market Square. The gardens show various planting styles and different approaches to small and intimate spaces in the historic town centre, as well as larger plots in more recent developments. Tickets and descriptive maps obtainable in the Market Place, with refreshments available there and at some of the gardens. Plants will be on sale at a number of gardens. A proportion of the proceeds from the Gardens Open Day will be used to support Bosworth in Bloom, the voluntary group responsible for the town's floral displays; see www.bosworthinbloom. co.uk. Farmers' Market in town centre (9-2) local produce, hot and cold food.

In 2021 the National Garden Scheme donated £3 million to our beneficiary charities

28 MOUNTAIN ASH

140 Ulverscroft Lane, Newtown Linford, LE6 0AJ. Mike & Liz Newcombe, 01530 242178, mjnew12@gmail.com. *7m SW of Loughborough, 7m NW of Leicester, 1m NW of Newtown Linford. Head ½m N along Main St towards Sharpley Hill, fork L into Ulverscroft Ln & Mountain Ash, is about ½m along on the L. Parking is along the opp verge.* Thur 2, Fri 3 June (11-5). Adm £6, chd free. Home-made teas. Visits also by arrangement May to Sept for groups of 15+.

2 acre garden with stunning views across Charnwood countryside. Near the house are patios, lawns, water feature, flower and shrub beds, fruit trees, soft fruit cage, greenhouses and vegetable plots. Lawns slope down to a gravel garden, large wildlife pond and small areas of woodland with walks through many species of trees. Several places to sit and relax around the garden. Many statues and ornaments. On the Open Days we have stalls by Wildwater Ponds offering sales and advice and others selling quality plants from a local nursery, gift stationery, vintage tools and books. Only the top part of the garden around the house is reasonably accessible by wheelchair.

29 NEVILL HOLT HALL

Drayton Road, Nevill Holt, Market Harborough, LE16 8EG. Mr David Ross. *5m NE of Market Haborough. Signed off B664 at Medbourne.* Sun 19 June (12-4). Adm £6, chd free. Light refreshments.

As well as being a private home, the C13 estate of Nevill Holt Hall is also home to Nevill Holt Opera. In addition to having an award winning theatre, the grounds also boast 3 walled gardens and an impressive modern sculpture collection. When we open in June this year the opera festival will be in full swing - the gardens climaxing - the perfect backdrop to Nevill Holts' country summerhouse opera. Nevill Holt Opera Event partner with the RHS.

30 THE NEW BARN

Newbold Road, Desford, Leicester, LE9 9GS. A Nichols & R Pullin. *8m from J21 M1 and 12m from J22 M1.* Sat 11, Sun 12 June, Sat 24, Sun 25 Sept (11-4). Adm £5, chd free.
A large, sloping garden of ¾ acre with wonderful views. Entering via a side gate you will follow a narrow path which opens up into what feels like a large secret garden, different levels and spaces add to this illusion enabling you to admire the planting and views. This is a well-established plantsman's garden with many unusual plants, inc a collection of Asters, Benton irises and collection of geranium phaeum. A kitchen garden and small orchard with newly planted Leicestershire heritage fruit trees provide additional interest. A wide range of asters, chrysanthemums and architectural grasses provide extensive autumn colour. Pub in village. Cafe open on Sat only.

31 OAK COTTAGE

Well Lane, Blackfordby, Swadlincote, DE11 8AG. Colin & Jenny Carr. *Blackfordby, just over 1m from (and between) Ashby-de-la-Zouch or Swadlincote. From Ashby-de-la-Zouch take Moira Rd, turn R on Blackfordby Ln. As you enter Blackfordby, turn L to Butt Ln and quickly R to Strawberry Ln. Park then it's a 2 min walk to Well Ln entrance.* Sat 9, Sun 10 Apr (10-4.30). Adm £4.50, chd free. Light refreshments.

½ acre garden set around Blackfordby's "hidden" listed thatched cottage, which itself is more than 300 years old. In total there are 3.4 acres of paddocks, front and rear gardens to explore with extensive displays of Hellebores, Snakes Heads and mature Magnolias in Spring. The lower paddock has been planted with 450 native trees as part of the National Forest Freewoods scheme, with a drainage pond created at its base. The central swathe is being developed with wildflowers. At the top of the rear garden there is a chicken run, old and new orchards and a peach house.

32 OAK TREE HOUSE

North Road, South Kilworth, LE17 6DU. Pam & Martin Shave. *15m S of Leicester. From M1 J20, take A4304 towards Market Harborough. At North Kilworth turn R, signed South Kilworth. Garden on L after approx 1m.* Sat 18 June (11-4); Sun 19 June (11-2); Sat 10 Sept (11-4); Sun 11 Sept (11-2). Adm £5, chd free. Home-made teas.

⅔ acre beautiful country garden full of colour, formal design, softened by cottage style planting. Modern sculptures. Large herbaceous borders, vegetable plots, pond, greenhouse, shady area, colour-themed borders. Extensive collections in pots, home to everything from alpines to trees. Trees with attractive bark. Many clematis and roses. Dramatic arched pergola. Constantly changing garden. Appeared twice in the Harborough Mail. Access to patio and greenhouse via steps.

33 THE OLD BARN

Rectory Lane, Stretton-En-Le-Field, Swadlincote, DE12 8AF. Gregg & Claire Mayles, 07870 160318, greggmayles@gmail.com. *On A444, 1½m from M42/A42 J11. Rectory Lane is a concealed turn off the A444, surrounded by trees. Look out for brown 'church' signs. Postcode in SatNav usually helps.* Sat 25, Sun 26 June, Sat 20, Sun 21 Aug (11-5). Adm £4.50, chd free. Light refreshments. Visits also by arrangement May to Sept for groups of up to 50.

2 acres in leafy hamlet, lots of interest. Main garden has lawns, many colourful shrubs and tree-lined cobbled paths. Walled garden with fishpond, pergola with climbers and cottage garden planting. Orchard, meadow with paths and open views. Lots of wildlife, inc our Peafowl. Plenty of drinks, cakes and seats to enjoy them! Redundant medieval church close, open to visitors. WI stall and a treasure hunt around the garden for children. Main garden fully wheelchair accessible. Walled garden partial access due to gravel. Orchard and meadow is accessible, but slightly uneven.

34 THE OLD HALL

Main Street, Market Overton, LE15 7PL. Mr & Mrs Timothy Hart. *6m N of Oakham. 6m N of Oakham; 5m from A1via Thistleton. 10m E from Melton Mowbray.* Sun 24 Apr (1-5). Adm £6, chd free. Home-made teas inc Hambleton Bakery cakes.

Set on a southerly ridge. Stone walls and yew hedges divide the garden into enclosed areas with herbaceous borders, shrubs, and young and mature trees. There are interesting plants flowering most of the time. In 2020 a Japanese Tea House was added at the bottom of the garden.

Partial wheelchair access. Gravel and mown paths. Return to house is steep. It is, however, possible to just sit on the terrace.

♿ 🐎 ☕ 🍵 ✽

35 THE OLD VICARAGE, BURLEY
Church Road, Burley, Oakham, LE15 7SU. Jonathan & Sandra Blaza, 01572 770588, sandra.blaza@googlemail.com, www.theoldvicarageburley.com. *1m NE of Oakham. In Burley just off B668 between Oakham & Cottesmore. Church Rd is opp village green.* **Sun 29 May (10.30-5). Home-made teas. Evening opening Wed 29 June (5-9). Wine. Adm £5, chd free. Visits also by arrangement May & June for groups of 15+.**
The Old Vicarage is a relaxed country garden, planted for year-round interest and colour. There are lawns and borders, a lime walk, rose gardens and a sunken rill garden with an avenue of standard wisteria. The walled garden produces fruit, herbs, vegetables and cut flowers. There are two orchards, an acer garden and areas planted for wildlife inc woodland, a meadow and a pond. Regional Finalist, The English Garden's The Nation's Favourite Gardens 2019. Some gravel and steps between terraces.

♿ 🐎 ✽ ☕ 🍵 ✽

36 THE OLD VICARAGE, WHISSENDINE
2 Station Road, Whissendine, LE15 7HG. Prof Peter & Dr Sarah Furness, www.pathology.plus.com/Garden. *Up hill from St Andrew's church, first L in Station Road.* **Sun 15 May (1-4.30). Adm £5, chd free. Home-made teas in St Andrew's Church, Whissendine (next door!).**
²⁄₃ acre packed with variety. Terrace with topiary, a formal fountain courtyard and raised beds backed by gothic orangery. Herbaceous borders surround main lawn. Wisteria tunnel leads to raised vegetable beds and large ornate greenhouse, four beehives, Gothic hen house plus rare breed hens. Hidden white walk, unusual plants. New Victorian style garden room. Featured on BBC Gardeners' World in 2019. The gravel drive is hard work for wheelchair users. Some areas are accessible only by steps.

♿ 🐎 ✽ 🍵 ✽

National Garden Scheme gardens are identified by their yellow road signs and posters. You can expect a garden of quality, character and interest, a warm welcome and plenty of home-made cakes!

Wigston Framework Knitters Museum

37 4 PACKMAN GREEN

Countesthorpe, Leicester, LE8 5WS.
Roger Whitmore & Shirley Jackson.
*Countesthorpe. 5m S of Leicester.
Garden is close to village centre pass
bank of shops off Scotland way.* **Sun
5, Sun 26 June (10-4). Adm £2, chd
free. Home-made teas.**
A small town house garden packed
with hardy perennials surrounded by
climbing roses and clematis. A pond
and rose arch complete the picture to
make it an enclosed peaceful haven
filled with colour and scent. Lots of
inexpensive plants for sale besides a
refreshing cuppa and slice of cake.

38 THE PADDOCKS

Main Street, Hungarton, LE7 9JY.
Helen Martin, 01162 595230,
Michael.c.martin@talk21.com. *8m
E of Leicester. Follow NGS signs in
village.* **Visits by arrangement May
to Aug for groups of 20 to 40.
Adm £5, chd free. Tea.**
2 acre garden with mature and
specimen trees, rhododendrons,
azaleas, magnolia grandiflora,
wisterias. Two lily ponds and stream.
Three lawn areas surrounded by
herbaceous and shrub borders.
Woodland walk. Pergola with clematis
and roses, hosta collection and
two rockeries, fern bed. Large well
established semi permanent plant
stall in aid of local charities. Huge
magnolia grandiflora and hydrangea
petiolaris. Rhododendron spinney.
Partial wheelchair access due to
steep slopes at rear of garden. Flat
terrace by main lawn provides good
viewing area.

39 PREBENDAL HOUSE

Crocket Lane, Empingham,
LE15 8PW. Matthew & Rebecca
Eatough. *5m E of Oakham. Facing
church in Church Street, large gates
on R.* **Sun 17 July (1.30-5). Adm
£6, chd free. Home-made teas.**
There has been a house on the site
since the C11. The present house was
built in 1688 owned by the diocese
of Lincoln until the mid C19 and then
absorbed into the Normanton Park
Estate. The present owners have been
in residence since 2016. The garden is
a combination of open parklands, yew
tree walks, herbaceous borders and a
large formal C18 walled garden. The
majority of the garden is accessible by
wheelchair.

40 QUAINTREE HALL

Braunston, LE15 8QS.
Mrs Caroline Lomas. *Braunston, nr
Oakham. 2m W of Oakham, in the
centre of the village of Braunston
in Rutland on High St.* **Sun 21 Aug
(12-5). Adm £6, chd free. Light
refreshments.**
An established garden surrounding
the medieval hall house (not open) inc
a formal box parterre to the front of
the house, a woodland walk, formal
walled garden with yew hedges, a
small picking garden and terraced
courtyard garden with conservatory. A
wide selection of interesting plants can
be enjoyed, each carefully selected for
its specific site by the knowledgeable
garden owner. The gravel drive can
cause difficulty for wheelchairs

41 REDHILL LODGE

Seaton Road, Barrowden,
Oakham, LE15 8EN.
Richard & Susan Moffitt,
www.m360design.co.uk.
*Redhill Lodge is 1m from village
of Barrowden along Seaton Rd.*
**Evening opening Thur 2 June
(6.30-9). Adm £10, chd free. Light
refreshments. Every Thur 4 Aug
to 25 Aug (1-5). Adm £5, chd free.
Home-made teas. Visits also by
arrangement Apr to Oct for groups
of 10+.**
Bold contemporary design with
formal lawns, grass amphitheatre
and turf viewing mound, herbaceous
borders and rose garden. Prairie style
planting showing vibrant colour in
late summer. Also natural swimming
pond surrounded by Japanese style
planting, bog garden and fernery. New
for 2022 Japanese style stroll garden,
natural swimming pond, prairie style
planting. House & Garden 2020
November; Garden's Illustrated 2019
November; Rutland Pride June 2021.

42 119 SCALFORD ROAD

Melton Mowbray, LE13 1JZ.
Richard & Hilary Lawrence. *½m
N of Melton Mowbray. Take Scalford
Rd from town centre past Cattle
Market. Garden 100yds after 1st
turning on L (The Crescent). Some
parking available on the drive but
The Crescent is an easy walk.* **Sun
31 July (11-5). Adm £5, chd free.
Home-made teas.**
Larger than average town garden
which has evolved over the last 30
yrs. Mixed borders with traditional and
exotic plants, enhanced by container

planting particularly begonias.
Vegetable parterre and greenhouse.
Various seating areas for viewing
different aspects of the garden. Water
features inc ponds. New additions to
the garden are a White Border and a
Succulents bed.

43 THE SECRET GARDEN AT WIGSTON FRAMEWORK KNITTERS MUSEUM

42-44 Bushloe End, Wigston,
LE18 2BA. 07814 042889,
chris.huscroft@tiscali.co.uk,
www.wigstonframeworkknitters.org.
uk. *4m S of Leicester. On A5199
Wigston bypass, follow yellow signs
to Paddock St public car park.
yellow signs onto Long St to All
Saints Church turn R onto Bushloe
End, Museum on R.* **Sat 11, Sun 12
June, Sat 16, Sun 17 July (11-5).
Adm £3.50, chd free. Home-made
teas. Visits also by arrangement
June to Aug for groups of 10 to 20.**
Victorian walled garden approx
70'x80' with traditional cottage garden
planting. Managed by a group of
volunteers and is undergoing a 2 year
restoration, some replanting started
in autumn 2020. Garden located in
the grounds of a historic museum, (an
extra charge applies). A unique garden
in the centre of Wigston which still
retains an air of tranquillity. Featured on
BBC East Midlands news and Radio
Leicester. Cobbled area before garden,
gravel paths through main parts of the
garden.

*The National Garden
Scheme searches the
length and breadth
of England, Channel
Islands, Northern
Ireland and Wales
for the very best
private gardens*

44 SILVER BIRCHES

82A Leicester Road, Quorn, Loughborough, LE12 8BB. Ann & Andrew Brown. *400m from Quorn Village centre on Leicester Rd. The property is down a gravel drive between 80 & 82 Leicester Rd. Park on Leicester Rd. Please do not bring your car down the drive.* Sun 19 June (11-5). Adm £4, chd free. Home-made teas.

A tree framed garden of nearly ½ an acre leading down to the River Soar. The formal area with an attractive summerhouse has well-stocked borders, specifically planted for year-round interest for both people and wildlife. The rest of the garden inc a vegetable plot, fruit trees, chickens, a wild riverside area and fernery. Plenty of nectar rich flowers and food plants for bees and birds. Wheelchair access not easy on main gravel driveway. Some paths too narrow for wheelchairs.

& ❀ 🍵 ♥

45 SNOWDROP RIDGE

35 The Ridgeway, Market Harborough, LE16 7HG. Donna & Steve Smith. *15m S of Leicester on A6. From High St follow signs to Robert Smyth Academy via Bowden Lane to Burnmill Rd & take R turn to Ridgeway West which becomes The Ridgeway.* Sun 12 June (10-3). Adm £3, chd free. Light refreshments.

A garden reclaimed over the last four years and still a work in progress, constantly changing and evolving. The 320 sqm garden is on three levels and predominantly a cottage style garden where self seeding is encouraged to give a natural effect. The planting inc many traditional cottage plants and is interspersed with gravel areas, barrel ponds, a greenhouse and lawns with colourful borders. Cake, second hand books and handmade crafts for sale.

 ❀ 🍵 ♥

46 STOKE ALBANY HOUSE

Desborough Road, Stoke Albany, Market Harborough, LE16 8PT. Mr & Mrs A M Vinton, www.stokealbanyhouse.co.uk. *4m E of Market Harborough. Via A427 to Corby, turn to Stoke Albany, R at the White Horse (B669) garden ½ m on the L.* Every Wed 1 June to 27 July (2-4.30). Adm £6, chd free. Donation to Marie Curie Cancer Care.

4 acre country house garden; fine trees and shrubs with wide herbaceous borders and sweeping striped lawn. Good display of bulbs

in spring, roses June and July. Walled grey garden; nepeta walk arched with roses, parterre with box and roses. Mediterranean garden. Heated greenhouse, potager with topiary, water feature garden and sculptures.

& 🐄 ❀ 🚌 🥤

47 59 THISTLETON ROAD

Market Overton, Oakham, LE15 7PP. Wg Cdr Andrew Stewart JP, 07876 377397, stewartaj59@gmail.com. *6m NE of Oakham.* Sun 19 June (12-5). Adm £5, chd free. Visits also by arrangement June to Dec for groups of 5 to 20. Teas at local Bowls club.

Over the last 15 years, the owners have transformed 1.8 acres of bare meadow into a wildlife friendly garden full of colour and variety. Against a backdrop of mature trees, the garden inc a small kitchen garden, rose pergola, large pond, shrubbery with 'Onion Day Bed', orchard, wildflower meadow, a small arboretum, a woodland walk and large perennial borders a riot of colour. Small area of shingle to access main path, woodland walk inaccessible to wheelchairs

& ❀ 🍵 ♥

48 THORPE LUBENHAM HALL

Farndon Road, Lubenham, LE16 9TR. Sir Bruce & Lady MacPhail. *2m W of Market Harborough. From Market Harborough take 3rd L off main rd, down Rushes Lane, past church on L, under old railway bridge & straight on up private drive.* Wed 15 June (10.30-4.30). Adm £6, chd free. Cream teas. 15 acres of mature gardens. Formal hedging, topiary and water features give an Italianate feel yet the abundant cottage style planting in herbaceous and shrub borders with Wisteria and Roses scrambling over walls are quintessentially English. Wilderness walks offer opportunity to be close to some magnificent trees, inc well over 100 years old Wellingtonia. Spectacular views to open country. Gravel paths, some steep slopes and steps.

& 🐄 ❀ 🍵 ♥

49 TRESILLIAN HOUSE

67 Dalby Road, Melton Mowbray, LE13 0BQ. Mrs Alison Blythe, 01664 481997, alisonblythe@tresillianhouse.com, www.tresillianhouse.com. *Situated on B6047 Dalby Rd, S of Melton town centre. (Melton to Gt Dalby/ Market Harborough rd). Parking on site.* Sun 27 Feb, Sun 24 Apr, Sun 3 July, Sun 28 Aug, Sun 30 Oct (11-4). Adm £5, chd free. Light refreshments. Visits also by arrangement Feb to Oct for groups of 6 to 30.

¾ acre garden re-established by current owner. Beautiful blue cedar trees, specimen tulip tree. Variety of trees, plants and bushes reinstated. Original bog garden and natural pond. Koi pond maturing well; glass garden room holds exhibitions and recitals. Vegetable plot. Cowslips and bulbs in Springtime. Unusual plants, trees and shrubs. Contemporary area added 2020. Quiet and tranquil oasis. Small Art Exhibition hosted by local artists. Wild Water Ponds will be at the garden. They are specialists in pond set ups, maintenance and planting and have replanted the natural pond at Tresillian House. Relax in August with cream tea whilst listening to traditional jazz with Springfield Ensemble. Keep warm in October with stew and dumplings or soup. Radio Leicester, Radio 101 The Eye and Melton Times all publicise events. Slate paths, steep in places but manageable.

& 🐄 ❀ 🚌 🚍 ♥ 🪑 �»

50 WASHBROOK ALLOTMENTS

Welford Road (opposite Brinsmead Rd), Leicester, LE2 6FP. Sharon Maher. *Approx 2½ m S of Leicester, 1½ m N of Wigston. No onsite parking. Welford Rd (opposite Brinsmead Rd) difficult to park on. Please use nearby side rds & Pendlebury Drive (LE2 6GY).* Sun 4 Sept (11-3). Adm £3.50, chd free. Home-made teas.

A hidden oasis. There are over 100 whole, half and quarter plots growing a wide variety of fruit, vegetables and flowers. Meadows, Anderson shelters and a composting toilet. Circular route around the site is uneven in places but is suitable for wheelchairs and mobility scooters.

& 🐄 ❀ ♥ »

51 WESTBROOKE HOUSE

52 Scotland Road, Little Bowden, Market Harborough, LE16 8AX. Bryan & Joanne Drew. ½ m *S Market Harborough. From Northampton Rd follow NGS arrows & park in designated car park or on nearby roads - NOT on the road directly opp the entrance. There is no disabled parking on the property.* **Sun 1 May, Sun 26 June (10.30-5). Adm £5, chd free. Cream teas.** Westbrooke House is a late Victorian property built in 1887. The gardens comprise 6 acres in total and are approached through a tree lined driveway of mature limes and giant redwoods. Key features are walled flower garden, walled kitchen garden, fernery, lower garden, wildlife pond, spring garden, lawns, woodland paths and a meadow with a wildflower area, ha-ha and hornbeam avenue. Alan Titchmarsh's "Love your garden"in August 2019 on ITV. Regional Finalist The English Garden's The Nation's Favourite Gardens 2021 The English Garden (April 2021) Homes and Gardens (June 2021).

🐕 ✻ 🄳 ☕ 🪑

52 WESTVIEW

1 St Thomas's Road, Great Glen, Leicester, LE8 9EH. Gill & John Hadland, 01162 592170, gillhadland1@gmail.com. *7m S of Leicester. Take either r'about from A6 into village centre then follow NGS signs. Please park in Oaks Rd.* **Sat 19, Sun 20 Feb, Sun 1, Mon 2 May (11-4), open nearby Hedgehog Hall. Sun 11 Sept (11-4). Adm £3, chd free. Home-made teas. Hot soup and home-made bread rolls also available in February. Visits also by arrangement Feb to Sept for groups of 5 to 20.** Organically managed small walled cottage garden with year-round interest. Rare and unusual plants, many grown from seed. Formal box parterre, courtyard garden, alpines, herbaceous borders, woodland areas with unusual ferns, small wildlife pond, greenhouse, vegetables, fruit and herbs. Collection of Snowdrops. Recycled materials used to make quirky garden ornaments and water feature. Restored Victorian outhouse functions as a garden office and houses a collection of old garden tools and ephemera.

✻ ☕

The Old Vicarage, Burley

53 ◆ **WHATTON HOUSE**
Long Whatton, Loughborough,
LE12 5BG. The Crawshaw
Family, 01509 431193,
hello@whattonhouse.co.uk,
www.whattonhouse.co.uk. *4m NE
of Loughborough. On A6 between
Hathern & Kegworth; 2½m SE of
M1J24.* For NGS: Sun 15 May
(10-5). Adm £5, chd under 8 free.
Light refreshments. For other
opening times and information,
please phone, email or visit garden
website.
Come explore our tranquil gardens.
Often described by visitors as a
hidden gem, this 15 acre C19
Country House garden is a relaxing
experience for all the family. Listen to
the birds, and enjoy walking through
the many fine trees, spring bulbs and
shrubs, large herbaceous border,
traditional rose garden, ornamental
ponds and lawns. Gravel paths.

54 **THE WHITE HOUSE FARM**
Ingarsby, Houghton-on-the-
Hill, LE7 9JD. Pam & Richard
Smith, 0116 259 5448,
Pamsmithwhf@aol.com. *7m E of
Leicester. 12m W of Uppingham.
Take A47 from Leicester through
Houghton-on-the-Hill towards
Uppingham. 1m after Houghton,
turn L (signed Tilton). After 1m turn
L (signed Ingarsby), garden is 1m
further on.* Visits by arrangement
May to Sept for groups of 20 to
40. Adm £5, chd free. Home-
made teas.
Former Georgian farm in 2 acres
of country garden. Beautiful views.
Box, yew and beech hedges divide
a cottage garden of gaily coloured
perennials and roses; a formal herb
garden; a pergola draped with
climbing plants; an old courtyard with
roses, shrubs and trees. Herbaceous
borders lead to pools with water lilies
and informal cascade. Orchard, wild
garden and lake. Home for lots of
wildlife.

GROUP OPENING

55 **WIGSTON GARDENS**
Wigston, LE18 3LF. Zoe Lewin.
Just south of Leicester off A5199.
Sat 9, Sun 10 July (11-5).
Combined adm £6, chd free.
Home-made teas at Little Dale
Wildlife Garden, 28 Gladstone
Street and 9 Wicken Rise.

28 GLADSTONE STREET
Chris & Janet Huscroft.
(See separate entry)

2A HOMESTEAD DRIVE
Mrs Sheila Bolton.

**LITTLE DALE WILDLIFE
GARDEN**
Zoe Lewin & Neil Garner,
www.facebook.com/
zoesopengarden.

**'VALLENVINA' 6 ABINGTON
CLOSE**
Mr Steve Hunt.

NEW **9 WICKEN RISE**
Sharon Maher & Michael Costall.

Wigston Gardens consists of five
relatively small gardens all within a
2m radius of each other. There is
something different to see at each
garden from traditional and formal to
a taste of the exotic via wildflowers,
upcycling and interesting artefacts,
prairie style planting and our new
garden this year with a wildlife pond,
borders, fruit and vegetable area
and patio bedding. A couple of the
gardens are within walking distance
of one another but you will need to
travel by car to visit all of the gardens
in the group or it will make for quite a
long walk and you'll need your comfy
shoes.

GROUP OPENING

56 **WILLOUGHBY GARDENS**
Willoughby Waterleys, LE8 6UD.
*9m S of Leicester. From A426
heading N turn R at Dunton
Bassett lights. Follow signs to
Willoughby. From Blaby follow
signs to Countesthorpe. 2m S to
Willoughby.* Sun 17 July (11-5).
Combined adm £6, chd free. Light
refreshments in the Village Hall.

2 CHURCH FARM LANE
Valerie & Peter Connelly.

FARMWAY
Eileen Spencer, 01162 478321,
eileenfarmway9@msn.com.
Visits also by arrangement June
to Aug for groups of up to 25.

HIGH MEADOW
Phil & Eva Day.

JOHN'S WOOD
John & Jill Harris.

KAPALUA
Richard & Linda Love.

3 YEW TREE CLOSE
Emma Clanfield.

Willoughby Waterleys lies in the
South Leicestershire countryside. 6
gardens will be open. John's Wood
is a 1½ acre nature reserve planted
to encourage wildlife. 2 Church
Farm Lane has been professionally
designed with many interesting
features. Farmway is a plant lovers
garden with many unusual plants
in colour themed borders. High
Meadow has been evolving over
13yrs. Inc mixed planting and
ornamental vegetable garden.
Kapalua has an interesting planting
design incorporating views of open
countryside. 3 Yew Tree Close is a
wrap around garden that naturally
creates a series of rooms with cottage
garden style borders.

57 **15 THE WOODCROFT**
Diseworth, Derby, DE74 2QT.
Nick & Sue Hollick. *The Woodcroft
is off The Green, parking on The
Woodcroft.* Sun 26 June (11-5).
Adm £4, chd free. Home-made
teas.
⅓ acre garden developed over 42
yrs with mature choice trees and
shrubs, old and modern shrub roses,
fern garden, wildlife garden inc barrel
pond, alpine troughs, seasonal
containers and mixed herbaceous
borders, planted with a garden
designer's eye and a plantsman's
passion. Three steps from the upper
terrace to the main garden.

LINCOLNSHIRE

Lincolnshire is a county shaped by a rich tapestry of fascinating heritage, passionate people and intriguing traditions; a mix of city, coast and countryside.

The city of Lincoln is dominated by the iconic towers of Lincoln Cathedral. The eastern seaboard contains windswept golden sands and lonely nature reserves. The Lincolnshire Wolds is a nationally important landscape of rolling chalk hills and areas of sandstone and clay, which underlie this attractive landscape.

To the south is the historic, religious and architectural heritage of The Vales, with river walks, the fine Georgian buildings of Stamford and historic Burghley House. In the east the unqiue Fens landscape thrives on an endless network of waterways inhabited by an abundance of wildlife.

Beautiful gardens of all types, sizes and designs are cared for and shared by their welcoming owners. Often located in delightful villages, a visit to them will entail driving through quiet roads often bordered by verges of wild flowers.

Lincolnshire is rural England at its very best. Local heritage, beautiful countryside walks, aviation history and it is the home of the Red Arrows.

Volunteers

County Organisers
Lesley Wykes
01673 860356
lesley.wykes@ngs.org.uk

County Treasurer
Helen Boothman
01652 628424
helen.boothman@ngs.org.uk

Publicity
Margaret Mann
01476 585905
marg_mann2000@yahoo.com

Erica McGarrigle
01476 585909
ericamcg@hotmail.co.uk

Assistant County Organisers

Tricia Elliot 01427 788517
t.elliott575@gmail.com

Sally Grant 01205 750486
sallygrant50@btinternet.com

Stephanie Lee 01507 442151
marigoldlee@btinternet.com

Jenny Leslie 01529 497317
jenny@collegefarmbraceby.com

Sylvia Ravenhall 01507 526014
sylvan@btinternet.com

Jo Rouston 01673 858656
jo@rouston-gardens.co.uk

 @LincolnshireNGS
 @LincsNGS

Left: West Syke

OPENING DATES

All entries subject to change. For latest information check www.ngs.org.uk

Map locator numbers are shown to the right of each garden name.

Extended openings are shown at the beginning of each month.

March

Saturday 26th
The Manor House 22

April

Saturday 9th
◆ Burghley House Private
South Gardens 6

Sunday 10th
◆ Burghley House Private
South Gardens 6

Friday 15th
◆ Easton Walled
Gardens 8

Sunday 17th
Ashfield House 1
Woodlands 42

Sunday 24th
◆ Goltho House 11

May

Sunday 1st
Dunholme Lodge 7

Sunday 8th
66 Spilsby Road 36

Saturday 14th
Oasis Garden - Your
Place 25

Sunday 15th
Fydell House 10
Oasis Garden - Your
Place 25
Woodlands 42

Saturday 21st
Willoughby Road
Allotments 41

Saturday 28th
St Andrews Hospice 32

Sunday 29th
Pottertons Nursery 31

June

Saturday 11th
Kings Hill Lodge 16

Sunday 12th
Manor Farm 21
The Old Vicarage 27

Old White House 28
Springfield 37
West Syke 39

Sunday 19th
Gosberton Gardens 12
Little Ponton Hall 17
Ludney House Farm 20
◆ Mill Farm 24
Woodlands 42

Saturday 25th
Home Farm 14

Sunday 26th
Aubourn Hall 4
Home Farm 14
Shangrila 35
Wildwood 40

July

**Every Thursday
and Sunday from
Thursday 21st**
The Secret Garden of
Louth 33

Sunday 3rd
Dunholme Lodge 7
The Fern Nursery 9
Ludney House Farm 20
The Old House 26
Walnut Tree Cottage 38

Sunday 17th
Ballygarth 5

Sunday 24th
Ludney House Farm 20

Sunday 31st
19 Low Street 18
21 Low Street 19

August

**Every Thursday and
Sunday**
The Secret Garden of
Louth 33

Sunday 7th
The Fern Nursery 9
Fydell House 10

Sunday 21st
Willoughby Road
Allotments 41
Woodlands 42

September

Saturday 17th
Inley Drove Farm 15

Sunday 18th
◆ Goltho House 11
Inley Drove Farm 15
Woodlands 42

By Arrangement

Arrange a personalised garden visit with your club, or group of friends, on a date to suit you. See individual garden entries for full details.

Ashfield House 1
Aswarby House 2
Aswarby Park 3
Fydell House 10
23 Handley Street 13
Inley Drove Farm 15
Little Ponton Hall 17
Ludney House Farm 20
Manor Farm 21
Marigold Cottage 23
The Old Vicarage 27
Overbeck 29
The Plant Lover's
Garden 30
4 Salem Street,
Gosberton Gardens 12
The Secret Garden of
Louth 33
Sedgebrook Manor 34
West Syke 39

The Fern Nursery

THE GARDENS

1 ASHFIELD HOUSE

Lincoln Road, Branston, Lincoln, LN4 1NS. John & Judi Tinsley, 07977 505682, john@tinsleyfarms.co.uk. *3m S of Lincoln on B1188. Northern outskirts of Branston on the B1188 Lincoln Rd. Signed 'Tinsley Farms - Ashfield'. Near bus stop, follow signs down drive.* **Sun 17 Apr (11-4). Adm £4, chd free. Light refreshments. Visits also by arrangement Apr to Oct for groups of 20 to 30. Refreshments inc in adm.**
See 140 Flowering Cherries, 30 Magnolias. Many thousands of spring bulbs, sweeping lawns, a lake and a fascinating arboretum.

2 ASWARBY HOUSE

Aswarby, Sleaford, NG34 8SE. Penny & James Herdman, 07714 690199, penherdman@aol.com. *Past church on R of road. 300 yds from the gates of Aswarby Park. Plenty of parking available on the roadside & gravel paths around the garden.* **Visits by arrangement. Adm £7, chd free. Home-made teas in Aswarby Park.**
New garden of an acre planted 3 years ago in the grounds of a handsome C18 house and Coachhouse. It has a partial walled garden, wildflower meadow surrounded by ornamental grasses and a 30 metre long herbaceous border. With two box parterres, and woodland shrubs, it has stunning views over ancient ridge and furrow grassland. This garden would complement your visit to Aswarby Park. Gravel paths.

3 ASWARBY PARK

Aswarby, Sleaford, NG34 8SD. Mr & Mrs George Playne, 01529 455222/07770 721646, cplayne1@gmail.com, www.aswarbyestate.co.uk. *5m S of Sleaford on A15. Take signs to Aswarby. Entrance is straight ahead by Church through black gates.* **Visits by arrangement Mar to Sept for groups of 10 to 30. Adm £7, chd free. Home-made teas.**
Formal and woodland garden in a parkland setting of approx 20

acres. Yew Trees form a backdrop to borders and lawns surrounding the house which is a converted stable block. Walled garden contains a greenhouse with a Muscat vine, which is over 300 yrs old. Large display of daffodils, snowdrops and climbing roses in season. Partial wheelchair access on gravel paths and drives.

4 AUBOURN HALL

Harmston Road, Aubourn, Lincoln, LN5 9DZ. Mr & Mrs Christopher Nevile, www.aubourngardens.com. *7m SW of Lincoln. Signed off A607 at Harmston & off A46 at Thorpe on the Hill.* **Sun 26 June (2-5). Adm £6, chd free. Home-made refreshments available.**
Approx 9 acres. Lawns, mature trees, shrubs, roses, mixed borders, rose garden, large prairie and topiary garden, spring bulbs, woodland walk and ponds. C11 church adjoining. Access to garden is fairly flat and smooth. Depending on weather some areas may be inaccessible to wheelchairs. Parking in field not on tarmac.

5 BALLYGARTH

Post Office Lane, Whitton, Scunthorpe, DN15 9LF. Joanne & Adrian Davey. *From Scunthorpe on A1077 follow signs to West Halton. Through West Halton approx 3m to Whitton. Follow signs for parking at Village Hall.* **Sun 17 July (11-4). Adm £3.50, chd free. Home-made teas in Whitton Village Hall.**
Set in the rural village of Whitton end terraced house has approx $\frac{1}{3}$ acre garden with large herbaceous and grass borders and two water features. Seating areas overlooking the garden, countryside. Many home-made garden artifacts using recycled materials inc a small folly. Everything in wood, brick and metal has been made by us. Drop off for those with limited mobility but parking is at village hall.

6 ♦ BURGHLEY HOUSE PRIVATE SOUTH GARDENS

Stamford, PE9 3JY. Burghley House Preservation Trust, 01780 752451, burghley@burghley.co.uk, www.burghley.co.uk. *1m E of Stamford. From Stamford follow signs to Burghley via B1443.* **For**

NGS: Sat 9, Sun 10 Apr (10.30-3.30). Adm £5, chd free. Pre-booking essential, please visit www.ngs.org.uk for information & booking. Light refreshments in The Orangery Restaurant and Garden Café. For other opening times and information, please phone, email or visit garden website.**
The Private South Gardens at Burghley House will open for the NGS with spectacular spring bulbs in park like setting with magnificent trees and the opportunity to enjoy Capability Brown's famous lake and summerhouse. Entry via Garden Kiosks. Fine Food Market. Adm charge is a special pre-book price only. Visitors paying at the gate on the day will be charged £13.50. Gravel paths.

7 DUNHOLME LODGE

Dunholme, Lincoln, LN2 3QA. Hugh & Lesley Wykes. *4m NE of Lincoln. Turn off A46 towards Welton at the r'about. After ½m turn L up long private road. Garden at top.* **Sun 1 May, Sun 3 July (11-5). Adm £4.50, chd free. Light refreshments.**
5 acres. Spring bulb area, shrub borders, fern garden, natural pond, wildflower area, orchard and vegetable garden. Developing 2 acre arboretum. RAF Dunholme Lodge Museum and War Memorial within the grounds. Craft stalls. Music. Most areas wheelchair accessible but some loose stone and gravel.

During 2020 – 2021 National Garden Scheme funding supported over 1,400 Queen's Nurses to deliver virtual and hands-on, community care across England, Wales and Northern Ireland

Ashfield House

⑧ ◆ EASTON WALLED GARDENS

Easton, NG33 5AP. Sir Fred & Lady Cholmeley, 01476 530063, info@eastonwalledgardens.co.uk, www.visiteaston.co.uk. *7m S of Grantham. 1m from A1, off B6403.* For NGS: Fri 15 Apr (11-4). Adm £8, chd £4. Light refreshments. For other opening times and information, please phone, email or visit garden website.

A 400 yr old, restored, 12 acre garden set in the heart of Lincolnshire. Home to snowdrops, sweet peas, roses and meadows. The River Witham meanders through the gardens, teeming with wildlife. Other garden highlights include a yew tunnel, turf maze and cut flower gardens. The Courtyard offers shopping, plant sales, a coffee room offering a selection of teas and coffees and beauty salon. Applestore Tearoom offers hot and cold drinks, savoury snacks, cakes and ice creams. Regret no wheelchair access to lower gardens but tearoom, shop, upper gardens and facilities are all accessible.

&. ✿ 🚐 🛏 🍵

⑨ THE FERN NURSERY

Grimsby Road, Binbrook, Market Rasen, LN8 6DH. Neil Timm, www.fernnursery.co.uk. *On B1203 from Market Rasen. On the Grimsby rd from Binbrook Square 400 Metres.* Sun 3 July, Sun 7 Aug

(11-4). Adm £3, chd free. Light refreshments in the bowling pavilion.

The garden has been designed as a wildlife garden with a number of features of interest to both visitors and wildlife, helped by having a natural stream running through the garden, which supplies water to a pond and water features. Visitors can also enjoy rock features, acid beds, and a sheltered winter garden with a sundial at its centre. From which a path leads to a small wood with the main fern collection. In addition there is a semi formal garden and bowling green, where they will often see a game being played, large shrubs, a bank of drought tolerant plants and herbaceous perennials, while steps, seats, a gazebo, bridge and many other features add interest to the garden. Partial wheelchairs access, gravel paths. WC.

&. 🐎 ✿ 🍵 🎪

⑩ FYDELL HOUSE

South Square, Boston, PE21 6HU. Boston Preservation Trust, 01205 351520, info@fydellhouse.org.uk, www.bostonpreservationtrust. com/fydell-garden.html. *Central Boston down South St. Through the Market Square, past Boots the Chemist. One way street. by Guildhall. There are three car parks within 200 yds of the house. Disabled parking in council car park opp the house.* Sun 15 May, Sun 7 Aug (10-4). Adm £4, chd free. Cream teas. Visits also by arrangement May to Dec.

Within three original red brick walls a formal garden was been created in 1995. Yew buttresses, arbours and four parterres use dutch themes. The borders contain herbaceous plants and shrubs. The north facing border holds shade loving plants. There is a mulberry and walnut tree The astrolabe was installed in 1997. A Victorian rockery is built from slag from ironworks in Boston. Walled garden Astrolabe Parterres formal borders topiary of box and yew. Wheelchair access is along the south alleyway from the front to the back garden.

&. ✿ 🍵

⑪ ◆ GOLTHO HOUSE

Lincoln Road, Goltho, Wragby, Market Rasen, LN8 5NF. Mr & Mrs S Hollingworth, 01673 857768, bookings@golthogardens.com, www.golthogardens.com. *10m E of Lincoln. On A158, 1m before Wragby. Garden on L (not in Goltho Village).* For NGS: Sun 24 Apr, Sun 18 Sept (12-4). Adm £7.50, chd free. Light refreshments. For other opening times and information, please phone, email or visit garden website.

4½ acre garden started in 1998 but looking established with long grass walk flanked by abundantly planted

herbaceous borders forming a focal point. Paths and walkway span out to other features inc nut walk, prairie border, wildflower meadow, rose garden and large pond area. Snowdrops, hellebores and shrubs for winter interest.

GROUP OPENING

12 GOSBERTON GARDENS
Gosberton, Spalding, PE11 4NQ. *Entering Gosberton on A152, from Spalding, Salem St on L & Mill Ln on R opp the War Memorial.* Sun 19 June (12-5). Combined adm £5, chd free. Home-made teas at Salem Street.

MILLSTONE HOUSE
Mrs J Chatterton.

4 SALEM STREET
Roley & Tricia Hogben, pahogben@live.co.uk. Visits also by arrangement Apr to Sept for groups of up to 12.

The village of Gosberton welcomes visitors to two private houses to view their gardens. We hope that everyone will find interesting features during their tour and enjoy the two locations. Millstone House. Colourful herbaceous borders are hidden by a privet hedge. Dappled shade creates a feeling of relaxation at the rear of the house. 4 Salem Street. Delightful secluded garden. Mixed borders inc a small water feature lead to a productive vegetable plot. Partial wheelchair access.

13 23 HANDLEY STREET
Heckington, nr Sleaford, NG34 9RZ. Stephen & Hazel Donnison, 01529 460097, donno5260@gmail.com. *A17 from Sleaford, turn R into Heckington. Follow rd to the Green. L, follow rd past Church, R into Cameron St. At end of this rd L into Handley St.* Visits by arrangement May to Sept for groups of 10 to 25. Adm £3, chd free. Home-made teas. Compact, quirky garden, large fish pond. Further five small wildlife ponds. Small wooded area and Jurassic style garden with tree ferns. Densely planted flower borders featuring penstemons. Large patio with seating.

14 HOME FARM
Little Casterton Road, Ryhall, Stamford, PE9 4HA. Steve & Karen Bourne. *1½ m N of Stamford. Off A6121 at mini-r'about, towards Little Casterton & Tolethorpe Hall.* Sat 25, Sun 26 June (1-5). Adm £5, chd free. Home-made teas.
A colourful, scented garden designed to encourage wildlife. Herbaceous and shrub borders, fruit cage and vegetable garden and orchard of old local varieties of top fruit. Show stoppers in mid summer are the roses and honeysuckle. Recent planting are being modified to suit dry conditions with very successful Mediterranean border. Woodland walk makes up the 9 acre site.

15 INLEY DROVE FARM
Inley Drove, Sutton St James, Spalding, PE12 0LX. Francis & Maisie Pryor, 01406 540088, maisietaylor7@gmail.com, www.pryorfrancis.wordpress.com. *Just off rd from Sutton St James to Sutton St Edmund. 2m S of Sutton St James. Look for yellow NGS signs on double bend.* Sat 17, Sun 18 Sept (11-5). Adm £5, chd free. Home-made teas. Visits also by arrangement June & July for groups of 10 to 30.
Over 3 acres of Fenland garden and meadow plus 6½ acre wood developed over 20yrs. Garden planted for colour, scent and wildlife. Double mixed borders and less formal flower gardens all framed by hornbeam hedges. Unusual shrubs and trees, inc fine stand of Black Poplars, vegetable garden, woodland walks and orchard. Wheelchair access, some gravel and a few steps but mostly flat grass.

16 KINGS HILL LODGE
Gorse Hill Lane, Caythorpe, Grantham, NG32 3DY. Tim & Carol Almond. *Off the A607 approx 10m from Grantham towards Lincoln. From S turn L into Church Ln (R from N) at Xrds. Pass church on R, after 100m turn R onto Waterloo Rd. Then sharp L, drive 150m then L into Gorse Hill Ln with Lodge on R.* Sat 11 June (12.30-5). Adm £4, chd free. Home-made teas.
A garden of about 1000sq metres, developed over 8 yrs from 800sq metres of neglected lawn and 200sq metres overgrown, boggy shrubbery. Now consists of 250sq

metres of managed lawn with the remainder put to over twenty mixed herbaceous beds, seven large raised vegetable beds, cedar greenhouse, summerhouse, four sitting out areas, water feature with fifteen different climbing roses around the house. There is a circular path around the house which is wide enough for a wheelchair with care. Wide-wheeled chairs would be able to use the lawn.

17 LITTLE PONTON HALL
Grantham, NG33 5BS. Bianca & George McCorquodale, 01476 530145, george@ stokerochfordestate.co.uk, www.littlepontonhallgardens.org. uk. *2m S of Grantham. ½ m E of A1 at S end of Grantham bypass.* Disabled parking. Sun 19 June (11-4). Adm £5, chd free. Light refreshments. Visits also by arrangement in June.
3 to 4 acre garden. River walk. Spacious lawns with cedar tree over 200 yrs old. Formal walled kitchen garden and listed dovecote, with herb garden. Victorian greenhouses with many plants from exotic locations. Wheelchair access on hard surfaces, unsuitable on grass. Disabled WC.

18 19 LOW STREET
Winterton, DN15 9RT. Jane & Allan Scorer. *Winterton is on A1077 4m N of Scunthorpe & 7m S of the Humber Bridge. Garden signed from A1077. Parking on Low St & nearby Market Place (2 mins walk from Low St).* Sun 31 July (10-4). Combined adm with 21 Low Street £5, chd free.
A ½ acre garden with an emphasis on dense sub tropical planting, although there are other distinct areas too, inc an arid bed, greenhouses, an extensive variety of pots and planters, ornamental pond, wildlife pond set in informal area, soft fruit, cut flower garden and seating areas. The village tearoom will be open where refreshments are available. Wheelchair access is difficult but not impossible as areas of the garden have bark or gravel paths.

19 21 LOW STREET
Winterton, Winterton, DN15 9RT.
Brian Dale & Nigel Bradford.
Garden is in the centre of the village & parking is limited. A short walk from the parking area near the church & Coop. **Sun 31 July (10-4). Combined adm with 19 Low Street £5, chd free.**
The garden is approx ½ acre and when we moved into the house several years ago, it mainly consisted of shrubs that had been allowed free rein. We have enlarged the existing beds and created new beds and borders which are now mostly planted with herbaceous perennials. There is a large area given over to vegetables and soft fruits which is now producing successfully. 19 Low St is a short distance away, walk or drive. The village tearoom will be open where refreshments are available. They have parking facilities but opening may be later than garden times.

20 LUDNEY HOUSE FARM
Ludney, Louth, LN11 7JU.
Jayne Bullas, 07733 018710,
jayne@theoldgatehouse.com.
Between Grainthorpe & Conisholme. **Sun 19 June, Sun 3, Sun 24 July (1.30-4). Adm £6.50, chd free. Home-made teas and cakes inc in adm. Visits also by arrangement June & July. Home-made teas inc in adm.**
A beautiful garden lovingly developed over the last 20 yrs with several areas of formal and informal planting inc a pond which attracts a wonderful variety of wildlife. There is an excellent mix of trees, shrubs, perennials, rose garden and wildflower area. There are plenty of seats positioned around to sit and enjoy a cuppa and piece of cake! Wheelchair access to most parts.

21 MANOR FARM
Horkstow Road, South Ferriby, Barton-upon-Humber, DN18 6HS. Geoff & Angela Wells, 01652 635214,
wells.farming@btinternet.com.
3m from Barton-upon-Humber on A1077, turn L onto B1204, opp Village Hall. **Sun 12 June (11-4). Combined adm with Springfield £6, chd free. Home-made teas. Visits also by arrangement June to Aug.**
A garden which is much praised by visitors. Set within approx 1 acre

with mature shrubberies, herbaceous borders, gravel garden and pergola walk. Rose bed, white garden and fernery. Many old trees with preservation orders. Wildlife pond set within a paddock.

22 THE MANOR HOUSE
Manor House Street, Horncastle, LN9 5HF. Mr Michael & Dr Marilyn Hieatt. *Manor House St runs off the Market Square in middle of Horncastle, beside St Mary's Church. The Manor House is approx 100 metres from the Market Square (on R).* **Sat 26 Mar (1-4.30). Adm £4, chd free.**
An informal spring garden and orchard bordered by the River Bain, hidden in the middle of Horncastle. The garden includes a short section of the C3/4 wall that formed part of a Roman fort (Scheduled Ancient Monument) with the remnants of an adjacent medieval well. Restricted wheelchair access (some parts not accessible).

23 MARIGOLD COTTAGE
Hotchin Road, Sutton-on-Sea, LN12 2NP. Stephanie Lee & John Raby, 01507 442151,
marigoldlee@btinternet.com,
www.rabyley.uk/marigold. *16m N of Skegness on A52. 7m E of Alford on A1111. 3m S of Mablethorpe on A52. Turn off A52 on High St at Cornerhouse Cafe. Follow rd past playing field on R. Rd turns away from the dunes. House 2nd on L.* **Visits by arrangement Apr to Sept. Refreshments may be available if requested at time of booking. Adm by donation.**
Slide open the Japanese gate to find secret paths, lanterns, a circular window in a curved wall, water lilies in pots and a gravel garden, vegetable garden and propagation area. Take the long drive to see the sea. Back in the garden, find a seat, enjoy the birds and bees. We face the challenges of heavy clay and salt ladened winds but look for unusual plants not the humdrum for these conditions. Most of garden accessible to wheelchairs along flat, paved paths.

24 ◆ MILL FARM
Caistor Road, Grasby, Caistor, DN38 6AQ. Mike & Helen Boothman, 01652 628424,
boothmanhelen@gmail.com,
www.millfarmgarden.co.uk. *3m NW of Caistor on A1084. Between Brigg & Caistor. From Cross Keys pub towards Caistor for approx 200yds. Do not go into Grasby village.* **For NGS: Sun 19 June (11-4). Adm £5, chd free. Home-made teas. For other opening times and information, please phone, email or visit garden website.**
A much loved garden by visitors, which continues to be developed and maintained to a high standard by the owners. Over 3 acres of garden with many diverse areas. Formal frontage with shrubs and trees. The rear is a plantsman haven with a peony and rose garden, specimen trees, vegetable area, old windmill adapted into a fernery, alpine house and shade house with a variety of shade loving plants. Herbaceous beds with different grasses and hardy perennials. Small nursery on site with homegrown plants available. Open by arrangement for groups. Wheelchair access, mainly grass, but with some gravelled areas.

25 OASIS GARDEN - YOUR PLACE
Rear of Your Place, 236 Wellington Street, Grimsby, DN32 7JP. Grimsby Neighbourhood Church, www.yourplacegrimsby.com. *Enter Grimsby (M180) over flyover, along Cleethorpes Rd. Turn R into Victor St, Turn L into Wellington St. Your Place is on R on junction of Wellington St & Weelsby St.* **Sat 14, Sun 15 May (11-3). Adm £3, chd free. Light refreshments.**
The multi award winning Oasis Garden, Your Place, recently described by the RHS as the 'Most inspirational garden in the six counties of the East Midlands', is approximately 1½ acres and nestles in the heart of Great Grimsby's East Marsh Community. A working garden producing 15k plants per year, grown by local volunteers of all ages and abilities. Lawns, fruit, vegetable, perennial and annual beds.

The Plant Lover's Garden

26 THE OLD HOUSE
1 The Green, Welbourn, Lincoln, LN5 0NJ. Mr & Mrs David Close. *11m S of Lincoln or 12m N of Grantham on A607. From Newark A17 then A607. Turn off A607 into S end of village, on village green opp red phone box.* Sun 3 July (12-6). Combined adm with Walnut Tree Cottage £5, chd free. Home-made teas at Welbourn Village Hall, LN5 0LZ. Ice creams at The Old House.

The formal front garden of this listed Georgian house was redesigned by Guy Petheram. Gravel, paving and pebble mosaics provide hard landscaping around beds with box hedging, clipped Portuguese laurel, lavender and roses. Herbaceous border, white hydrangea bed, and small enclosed paved garden. As featured in Lincolnshire Life magazine. Welbourn Blacksmiths shop and forge dating from 1864 and still in full working order open with Friends of Forge on hand to answer questions. Plant stall by Plantazia of Lincoln, artisan honey and bee products, metal sculpture, will have stands within the gardens. Wheelchair access, some gravel.

&. ⛹ ✿ D ☕

27 THE OLD VICARAGE
Low Road, Holbeach Hurn, PE12 8JN. Mrs Liz Dixon-Spain, 01406 424148, lizdixonspain@gmail.com. *2m NE of Holbeach. Turn off A17 N to Holbeach Hurn, past post box in middle of village, 1st R at war memorial into Low Rd. Old Vicarage is on R approx 400yds Parking in grass paddock.* Sun 12 June (1-5). Combined adm with Old White House £5, chd free. Visits also by arrangement Mar to Sept for groups of up to 30.

2 acres of garden with 150yr old tulip, plane and beech trees: borders of shrubs, roses, herbaceous plants. Shrub roses and herb garden in old paddock area, surrounded by informal areas with pond and bog garden, wildflowers, grasses and bulbs. Small fruit and vegetable gardens. Kids love exploring winding paths through the wilder areas. Garden is managed environmentally. Fun for kids! Wheelchair access, gravel drive, some paths, mostly grass access.

&. ⛹ ✿ 🚗 ☕

28 OLD WHITE HOUSE
Baileys Lane, Holbeach Hurn, PE12 8JP. Mrs A Worth. *2m N of Holbeach. Turn off A17 N to Holbeach Hurn, follow signs to village, cont through, turn R after Rose & Crown pub at Baileys Ln.* Sun 12 June (1-4). Combined adm with The Old Vicarage £5, chd free. Home-made teas.

1½ acres of mature garden, featuring herbaceous borders, roses, patterned garden, herb garden and walled kitchen garden. Large catalpa, tulip tree that flowers, ginko and other specimen trees. Flat surfaces, some steps, wheelchair access to all areas without using steps.

&. ⛹ ☕

29 OVERBECK
46 Main Street, Scothern, LN2 2UW. John & Joyce Good, 01673 862200, jandjgood@btinternet.com. *4m E of Lincoln. Scothern signed from A46 at Dunholme & A158 at Sudbrooke. Overbeck is E end of Main St.* Visits by arrangement May to July for groups of 10 to 30. Adm £5, chd free. Light refreshments.

Situated in an attractive village this approx ⅔ acre garden is a haven for wildlife. Long herbaceous borders and colour themed island beds with some unusual perennials. Hosta border, gravel bed with grasses, fernery, interesting range of trees, numerous shrubs, small stumpery, climbers inc roses and clematis, recently developed parterre and large prolific vegetable and fruit area.

&. ✿ 🚗 ☕

30 THE PLANT LOVER'S GARDEN
Bourne, PE10 0XF. Danny & Sophie, 07850 239393, plantloversgarden@outlook.com. *Situated on the edge of beautiful South Lincolnshire close to the borders of Cambridgeshire & Rutland in the East of England.* Visits by arrangement Mar to Aug for groups of up to 30. Refreshments by prior arrangement only. No WC. Adm £3.50, chd free.

The Plant Lovers Garden is a verdant space of colour, form and style, with brimming raised beds and packed herbaceous borders, peppered throughout with clipped topiary balls. With an ever changing interest and a variety of blooms throughout it's opening months of March to August. This inspirational garden is a plant

lover's delight. Private visits to larger groups welcomed. Plant sales. Most areas accessible by wheelchair.

&. ✿ ☕ ›)

31 POTTERTONS NURSERY
Moortown Road, Nettleton, Caistor, LN7 6HX. Rob & Jackie Potterton, www.pottertons.co.uk. *1m W of Nettleton. From A46 at Nettleton turn onto B1205 (Moortown). Nursery 1¼m, turn R edge of wood.* Sun 29 May (9-4). Adm £3, chd free. We will be offering excellent cream teas and home-made light refreshments & drinks.

5 acre garden of alpine rockeries, pool and waterfall, raised beds, troughs, tufa bed, crevice garden, woodland beds, extensively planted with alpines, bulbs and woodland plants, which will be at their flowering peak. On the day we have invited Plant Hunters Fairs to the garden, with 10 specialist nurseries offering a range inc acers, shrubs, alpines, rare perennials and cottage garden plants. Wheelchair access mostly on mixed grass surfaces.

&. ⛹ ✿ 🚗 ☕ 🏕

32 ST ANDREWS HOSPICE
Peaks Lane, Grimsby, DN32 9RP. Emily Aitken. *Follow Signs for St Andrews Hospice.* Sat 28 May (10-4). Adm £5, chd free. Light refreshments.

The St Andrews gardens are beautifully landscaped spaces which focus on the lovely nature that surrounds us. They are suitable for all ages providing all with a tranquil and calm environment. The gardens are fully accessible with plenty of room for all to enjoy the outdoors together. Herbaceous beds and ample seating areas.

&. ⛹ 🚗 ☕ ›)

33 THE SECRET GARDEN OF LOUTH
68 Watts Lane, Louth, LN11 9DG. Jenny & Rodger Grasham. *½m S of Louth town centre. For SatNav & to avoid opening/ closing gate on Watts Ln, use postcode LN119DJ this is Mount Pleasant Ave, leads straight to our house front.* Sun 21 July to 28 Aug (11-4). Adm £3, chd free. Pre-booking essential, please phone 07977 318145, email sallysing@hotmail. co.uk or visit www.facebook.

19 Low Street

com/thesecretgardenoflouth for information & booking. Home-made teas. Visits also by arrangement July & Aug. Open every Thu and Sun from 21 July. Booking only.

Blank canvas of ⅕ acre in early 90s. Developed into lush, colourful, exotic plant packed haven. A whole new world on entering from street. Exotic borders, raised exotic island, long hot border, ponds, stumpery. Intimate seating areas along garden's journey. Facebook page - The Secret Garden of Louth. Children, find where the frogs are hiding! Butterflies and bees but how many different types? Feed the fish, find Cedric the spider, Simon the snake, Colin the Crocodile and more.

34 SEDGEBROOK MANOR
Church Lane, Sedgebrook, Grantham, NG32 2EU. Hon James & Lady Caroline Ogilvy,

01949 842337. *2m W of Grantham on A52. In Sedgebrook village by church.* Visits by arrangement Feb to Oct for groups of 10 to 30. Adm by donation. Home-made teas.

Yew and box topiary surround this charming Manor House (not open). Croquet lawn, herbaceous border and summerhouse. Bridge over small pond and two larger ponds. Ancient mulberry tree. Tennis court, vegetable garden. Swimming pool in enclosed garden. Wheelchair access to most areas. Dogs on leads.

35 SHANGRILA
Little Hale Road, Great Hale, Sleaford, NG34 9LH. Marilyn Cooke & John Knight. *On B1394 between Heckington & Helpringham.* Sun 26 June (11-5). Adm £4.50, chd free. Home-made teas.

Approx 3 acre garden with sweeping lawns long herbaceous borders,

colour themed island beds, hosta collection, lavender bed with seating area, topiary, acers, small raised vegetable area, three ponds and new exotic borders new Japanese zen garden. Wheelchair access to all areas.

36 66 SPILSBY ROAD
Boston, PE21 9NS. Rosemary & Adrian Isaac. *From Boston town take A16 towards Spilsby. On L after Trinity Church. Parking on Spilsby Rd.* Sun 8 May (11-4). Adm £5, chd free. Home-made teas.

1⅓ acre with mature trees, moat, Venetian Folly, summerhouse and orangery, lawns and herbaceous borders. Children's Tudor garden house, gatehouse and courtyard. Wide paths most paths suitable for wheelchairs.

Home Farm

37 SPRINGFIELD

**Main Street, Horkstow, Barton-Upon-Humber, DN18 6BL.
Mr & Mrs G Allison.** *4m from Barton on Humber. Take the A1077 towards Scunthorpe & in South Ferriby bear L onto the B1204, after 2m Springfield is on the hillside on L.* **Sun 12 June (11-4). Combined adm with Manor Farm £6, chd free. Home-made teas in Manor Farm South Ferriby.**
This beautiful hillside garden on the edge of the Wolds was renovated and redesigned in 2011 from an overgrown state. It features many shrubs and perennials with a rose pergola and stunning views over the Ancholme Valley.

38 WALNUT TREE COTTAGE

6 Hall Lane, Welbourn, Lincoln, LN5 0NN. Nina & Malcolm McBeath. *Approx 11m S of Lincoln, 12m N of Grantham on A607. From Newark A17 then A607. On A607 from Lincoln turn R into Hall Lane by Welbourn Hall Nursing Home. From Leadenham take L turn after W Hall Nursing Home. Garden is 3rd gate on L. Parking at Village Hall, Beck St please.* **Sun 3 July (12-6). Combined adm with The Old House £5, chd free. Home-made teas at Welbourn Village Hall, Beck Street, LN5 0LZ. Ice Cream available at The Old House.**
A peaceful ½ acre garden full of interesting perennials planted in long, curved and colour themed borders. Winding paths surrounded by shrubs and climbing roses provide varied vistas and secluded seating areas. Many old varieties of roses feature throughout, with spectacular displays in June of Paul's Himalayan Musk, and Adelaide d'Orleans climbing through trees. Plant stall by Plantazia, Lincoln, and Artisan honey and bee products for sale in this garden. Nearby, Welbourn Blacksmith's shop and forge, dating from 1864 and still in full working order (open 2pm until 4.30pm), with the fire lit and Friends of the Forge on hand to answer questions. Wheelchair access, gravel drive to front of house, with some steps and some narrow paths at the rear.

39 WEST SYKE

38 Electric Station Road, Sleaford, NG34 7QJ. Ada Trethewey, 07873 444420, ada.trethewey@dtseeds.com. *From A17, A15 & A153 take bypass exit at r'about to Sleaford Town centre. At HSBC & Nationwide turn R into Westgate. Turn R, on to Electric Station Rd, 38 at end of rd. Ample parking.* **Sun 12 June (12-5). Adm £5. Light refreshments. Visits also by arrangement May to Aug for groups of 6 to 20.**
Over 1 acre, comprising bog gardens, rockeries, three large ponds, wildflower meadow, lawns and cottage garden planting. Rambling roses a feature. Designed for wildlife habitats; sustainable principles and a wealth of native species inc six species of orchids. Lawned paths. WC wheelchair accessible.

40 WILDWOOD

Aisby, Grantham, NG32 3NE. Paul & Joy King. *Halfway between Grantham & Sleaford. Off A52 for Dembelby or Oasby. Follow signs to Aisby. In village take track with a footpath sign on the west side of the green opp the village hall. Plenty of parking on site.* **Sun 26 June (11-5). Adm £5, chd free. Home-made teas.**
Created over 10 yrs from fields and existing hard landscaping. Windbreaks protect the garden which is heavy clay, wet in winter, dry in summer. There are many borders (some sloping) planted with unusual and rare trees, shrubs, climbers, perennials, bulbs and alpines. This is a wildlife friendly garden with a bee orchid patch and fruit and vegetable areas. Grass, gravel and paving provide access. A modern glass Huf Haus, the only one in Lincolnshire, and one of the few in the country open as part of the NGS scheme. There are over 250 Huf Haus in the UK, most in the south. Wheelchair access, most paths are grass or gravel.

41 WILLOUGHBY ROAD ALLOTMENTS

Willoughby Road, Boston, PE21 9HN. Willoughby Road Allotments Association. *Entrance is adjacent to 109 Willoughby Rd. Street Parking only.* **Sat 21 May, Sun 21 Aug (10.30-4). Adm £4, chd free. Light refreshments.**
Set in 5 acres the allotments comprise 60 plots growing fine vegetables, fruit, flowers and herbs. There is a small orchard and wildflower area and a community space adjacent. Grass paths run along the site. Several plots will be open to walk round. There will be a seed and plant stall. Artwork created by Bex Simon situated on site. Small orchard and wildflower beds Community area with kitchen and disabled WC. Large Polytunnel with raised beds inside and out. Accessible for all abilities.

42 WOODLANDS

Peppin Lane, Fotherby, Louth, LN11 0UW. Ann & Bob Armstrong, www.woodlandsplants.co.uk. *2m N of Louth off A16 signed Fotherby. Please park on R verge opp allotments & walk approx 350 yds to garden. If full please park considerately elsewhere in the village. No parking at garden. Please do not drive beyond designated area.* **Sun 17 Apr, Sun 15 May, Sun 19 June, Sun 21 Aug, Sun 18 Sept (10.30-4.30). Adm £4, chd free. Home-made teas.**
A lovely mature woodland garden where a multitude of unusual plants are the stars, many of which are available from the well-stocked RHS listed nursery. During 2021 several small areas have been redesigned and a great deal of fresh planting has taken place. Award winning professional artist's studio/gallery open to visitors. Specialist collection of Codonopsis for which Plant Heritage status has been granted. Wheelchair access possible to some areas with care. We leave space for parking at the house for those who cannot manage the walk from the car park.

You can make a difference! Join our Great British Garden Party fundraising campaign and raise money for some of the best-loved nursing and health charities. Visit ngs.org.uk/gardenparty to find out how you can get involved

LONDON

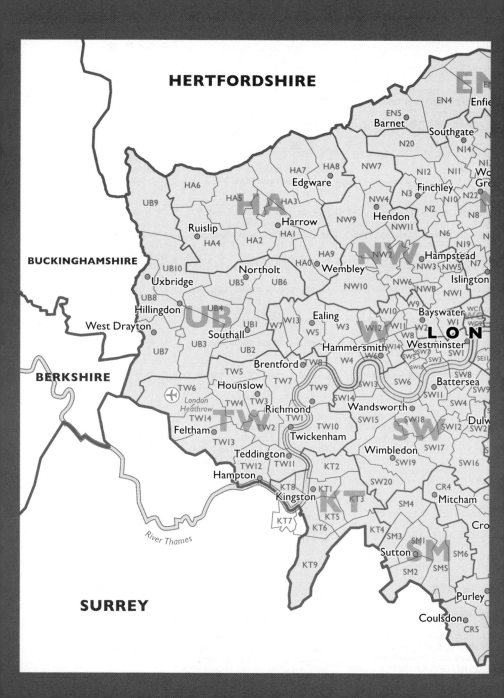

ESSEX

ld EN1 EN3

N9 Chingford
Edmonton E4
N18 Woodford IG7 RM4
od Green IG8 RM5 RM1 RM3
en Tottenham N17 E17 IG5 RM6 RM2
N15 Walthamstow E18 IG4 IG2 IG Romford RM7 RM11 RM
N16 E11 Ilford IG3 RM8 Upminster RM14
N5 E10 E5 IG1 RM12 RM11
NI E8 E9 E7 E12 RM10
E2 Stratford E15 Barking IG11
EC1 E1 E3 E13 E6 RM9 Rainham
SE17 EC2 E14 E16 London City RM13
DON SE1 SE16 SE28 Thamesmead
SE17 SE10 SE7 SE2 DA18
SE5 SE8 SE18 DA17
SE15 SE14 Greenwich SE3 DA8
Peckham SE3 DA16 DA7 Bexleyheath
E24 SE4 SE13 Lewisham DA6 DA1
ich SE22 Eltham DA DA5
SE21 SE23 SE12 SE9 DA15 Bexley
SE27 SE26 SE6 Sidcup
SE19 Chislehurst DA14
SE20 BR1 BR7
BR3 Bromley
R7 SE25 BR5
BR2 BR
ydon CR0 BR4
Addington Orpington
CR BR6
CR2 BR2

KENT

River Thames

TN14
Biggin Hill TN16 TN

| 0 | | 5 | | 10 kilometres |
| 0 | | | 5 miles | |

© Global Mapping / XYZ Maps

Volunteers

County Organiser
Penny Snell
01932 864532
pennysnellflowers@btinternet.com

County Treasurer
Joanna Gray
joanna.gray@ngs.org.uk

Publicity
Sonya Pinto
07779 609715
sonya.pinto@ngs.org.uk

Booklet Co-ordinator
Sue Phipps
07771 767196
sue@suephipps.com

Booklet Distributor
Joey Clover
020 8870 8740
joey.clover@ngs.org.uk

Social Media
Sue Phipps (as above)

Mary Oner
07376 739560
oasisgarden1@gmail.com

Assistant County Organisers

Central London
Eveline Carn
07831 136069
evelinecbcarn@icloud.com

Clapham & surrounding area
Sue Phipps (as above)

Croydon & outer South London
Christine Murray and **Nicola Dooley**
07889 888204
christineandnicola.gardens@gmail.com

Dulwich & surrounding area
Clive Pankhurst
07941 536934
alternative.ramblings@gmail.com

E London
Teresa Farnham
07761 476651
farnhamz@yahoo.co.uk

Finchley & Barnet
Debra Craighead 07415 166617
dcraighead@icloud.com

Hackney
Philip Lightowlers
020 8533 0052
plighto@gmail.com

Hampstead
Joan Arnold
020 8444 8752
joan.arnold40@gmail.com

Islington
Penelope Darby Brown
020 7226 6880
penelope.darbybrown@ngs.org.uk

Gill Evansky
020 7359 2484
gevansky@gmail.com

Northwood, Pinner, Ruislip & Harefield
Hasruty Patel
07815 110050
hasruty@gmail.com

NW London
Susan Bennett & Earl Hyde
020 8883 8540
suebearlh@yahoo.co.uk

Outer NW London
James Duncan Mattoon
07504 565612

Outer W London
Julia Hickman
020 8339 0931
julia@hickmanweb.co.uk

SE London
Janine Wookey
07711 279636
j.wookey@btinternet.com

SW London
Joey Clover (as above)

W London, Barnes & Chiswick
Siobhan McCammon
07952 889866
siobhan.mccammon@gmail.com

From the tiniest to the largest, London gardens offer exceptional diversity. Hidden behind historic houses in Spitalfields are exquisite tiny gardens, while on Kingston Hill there are 9 acres of landscaped Japanese gardens.

The oldest private garden in London boasts 5 acres, while the many other historic gardens within these pages are smaller – some so tiny there is only room for a few visitors at a time – but nonetheless full of innovation, colour and horticultural excellence.

London allotments have attracted television cameras to film their productive acres, where exotic Cape gooseberries, figs, prizewinning roses and even bees all thrive thanks to the skill and enthusiasm of city gardeners.

The traditional sit comfortably with the contemporary in London – offering a feast of elegant borders, pleached hedges, topiary, gravel gardens and the cooling sound of water – while to excite the adventurous there are gardens on barges and green roofs to explore.

The season stretches from April to October, so there is nearly always a garden to visit somewhere in London. Our gardens opening this year are the beating heart of the capital just waiting to be visited and enjoyed.

LONDON GARDENS LISTED BY POSTCODE

Inner London postcodes

E and EC London

26 Arlington Avenue, N1
25 Arlington Square, N1
Arlington Square Gardens, N1
Barnsbury Group, N1
4 Canonbury Place, N1
12 Cloudesley Square, N1
De Beauvoir Gardens, N1
58 Halliford Street, N1
57 Huntingdon Street, N1
King Henry's Walk Garden, N1
2 Lonsdale Square, N1
5 Northampton Park, N1
St Paul's Place, N1
19 St Peter's Street, N1
131 Southgate Road, N1
6 Thornhill Road, N1
66 Abbots Gardens, N2
7 Deansway, N2
12 Lauradale Road, N2
24 Twyford Avenue, N2
18 Park Crescent, N3
32 Highbury Place, N5
Southwood Lodge, N6
9 View Road, N6
5 Blackthorn Av, Apartment 5, N7
9 Furlong Road, N7
10 Furlong Road, N7
33 Huddleston Road, N7
1a Hungerford Road, N7
19 Coolhurst Road, N8
12 Fairfield Road, N8
11 Park Avenue North, N8
77 Muswell Road, Flat 1, N10
Princes Avenue Gardens, N10
5 St Regis Close, N10
25 Springfield Avenue, N10
33 Wood Vale, N10
Golf Course Allotments, N11
20 Hemingford Close, N12
9 Shortgate, N12
11 Shortgate, N12
70 Farleigh Road, N16
15 Norcott Road, N16

36 Ashley Road, N19
24 Langton Avenue, N20
21 Oakleigh Park South, N20
20 Hillcrest, N21
Railway Cottages, N22
Wolves Lane Horticultural Centre, N22
13 Agar Grove, Flat A, NW1
2 Camden Mews, NW1
19 Camden Mews, NW1
The Gable End Gardens, NW1
Garden of Medicinal Plants, Royal College of Physicians, NW1
70 Gloucester Crescent, NW1
36 Park Village East, NW1
28a St Augustine's Road, NW1
93 Tanfield Avenue, NW2
Marie Curie Hospice, Hampstead, NW3
1A Primrose Gardens, NW3
Tudor Herbalist Garden, NW3
The Mysteries of Light Rosary Garden, NW5
Torriano Community Garden, NW5
Highwood Ash, NW7
48 Erskine Hill, NW11
92 Hampstead Way, NW11
100 Hampstead Way, NW11
74 Willifield Way, NW11

SE and SW London

Garden Barge Square at Tower Bridge Moorings, SE1
The Garden Museum, SE1
Lambeth Palace, SE1
33 Weyman Road, SE3
24 Grove Park, SE5
41 Southbrook Road, SE12
13 Waite Davies Road, SE12
15 Waite Davies Road, SE12
Choumert Square, SE15
Lyndhurst Square Garden Group, SE15
4 Becondale Road, SE19
103 & 105 Dulwich Village, SE21
Gardens of Court Lane, SE21
38 Lovelace Road, SE21
174 Peckham Rye, SE22
45 Underhill Road, SE22
86 Underhill Road, SE22

58 Cranston Road, SE23
Forest Hill Garden Group, SE23
39 Wood Vale, SE23
5 Burbage Road, SE24
28 Ferndene Road, SE24
South London Botanical Institute, SE24
Stoney Hill House, SE26
Cadogan Place South Garden, SW1
Eccleston Square, SW1
Spencer House, SW1
31 Trelawn Road, SW2
9 Trinity Rise, SW2
51 The Chase, SW4
Royal Trinity Hospice, SW4
152a Victoria Rise, SW4
The Hurlingham Club, SW6
1 Fife Road, SW14
40 Chartfield Avenue, SW15
325 Leigham Court Road, SW16
10 Streatham Common South, SW16
36 Melrose Road, SW18
61 Arthur Road, SW19
97 Arthur Road, SW19
123 South Park Road, SW19
11 Ernle Road, SW20
Paddock Allotments & Leisure Gardens, SW20

W and WC London

Hyde Park Estate Gardens, W2
Avenue Road & Mill Hill Road Gardens, W3
34 Buxton Gardens, W3
Zen Garden at Japanese Buddhist Centre, W3
Chiswick Mall Gardens, W4
The Orchard, W4
56 Park Road, W4
Maggie's West London, W6
27 St Peters Square, W6
Temple Lodge Club, W6
1 York Close, W7
Edwardes Square, W8
Balfour & Burleigh Kitchen Garden, W10
57 St Quintin Avenue, W10
Arundel & Elgin Gardens, W11
Arundel & Ladbroke Gardens, W11
12 Lansdowne Road, W11
49 Loftus Road, W12

Outer London postcodes

81 Baston Road, BR2
37 Crescent Road, BR3
40 Greenways, BR3
Tudeley House, BR7
109 Riddlesdown Road, CR8
West Lodge Park, EN4
190 Barnet Road, EN5
45 Great North Road, EN5
55 College Road, HA3
42 Risingholme Road, HA3
31 Arlington Drive, HA4
4 Manningtree Road, HA4
39 Glover Road, HA5
470 Pinner Road, HA5
4 Ormonde Road, HA6
Horatio's Garden, HA7
Hornbeams, HA7
53 Lady Aylesford Avenue, HA7
34 Barn Rise, HA9
26 Hillcroft Crescent, HA9
74 Glengall Road, IG8
7 Woodbines Avenue, KT1
40 Ember Lane, KT10
9 Imber Park Road, KT10
The Watergardens, KT2
The Circle Garden, KT3
52A Berrylands Road, KT5
15 Catherine Road, KT6
6 Church Walk, KT7
3 Elmbridge Lodge, KT7
Hampton Court Palace, KT8
5 Pemberton Road, KT8
61 Wolsey Road, KT8
239a Hook Road, KT9
Maggie's, SM2
7 St George's Road, TW1
Ormeley Lodge, TW10
Petersham House, TW10
Stokes House, TW10
16 Links View Road, TW12
106 Station Road, TW12
9 Warwick Close, TW12
Wensleydale Road Gardens, Hampton, TW12
20 Beechwood Avenue, TW9
Kew Green Gardens, TW9
Marksbury Avenue Gardens, TW9
Swakeleys Cottage, 2 The Avenue, UB10
Dragon's Dream, UB8
Silverwood, WD3

OPENING DATES

All entries subject to change. For latest information check www.ngs.org.uk

February

Snowdrop Festival

Sunday 20th
Hornbeams, HA7

March

Sunday 27th
74 Glengall Road, IG8

April

Saturday 2nd
NEW 9 Trinity Rise, SW2

Sunday 3rd
4 Canonbury Place, N1
Royal Trinity Hospice, SW4
NEW 9 Trinity Rise, SW2

Sunday 10th
Edwardes Square, W8
39 Wood Vale, SE23

Wednesday 13th
39 Wood Vale, SE23

Sunday 17th
33 Wood Vale, N10

Thursday 21st
◆ Hampton Court Palace, KT8

Sunday 24th
Arundel & Ladbroke Gardens, W11
51 The Chase, SW4
19 Coolhurst Road, N8
58 Halliford Street, N1
Maggie's West London, W6
Petersham House, TW10
South London Botanical Institute, SE24
The Watergardens, KT2
7 Woodbines Avenue, KT1

Tuesday 26th
51 The Chase, SW4

May

Sunday 1st
5 St Regis Close, N10

Monday 2nd
King Henry's Walk Garden, N1

Saturday 7th
239a Hook Road, KT9

Sunday 8th
7 Deansway, N2
Eccleston Square, SW1
239a Hook Road, KT9
The Orchard, W4
27 St Peters Square, W6

Wednesday 11th
57 Huntingdon Street, N1

Thursday 12th
12 Lansdowne Road, W11

Saturday 14th
NEW 12 Cloudesley Square, N1
The Hurlingham Club, SW6
Maggie's, SM2
9 View Road, N6

Sunday 15th
Highwood Ash, NW7
84 Lavender Grove, E8
Princes Avenue Gardens, N10
42 Risingholme Road, HA3
Stoney Hill House, SE26
86 Underhill Road, SE22
West Lodge Park, EN4

Monday 16th
Lambeth Palace, SE1

Saturday 21st
The Circle Garden, KT3

Sunday 22nd
61 Arthur Road, SW19
Arundel & Elgin Gardens, W11
190 Barnet Road, EN5
The Circle Garden, KT3
9 Furlong Road, N7
10 Furlong Road, N7
Garden Barge Square at Tower Bridge Moorings, SE1

32 Highbury Place, N5
Kew Green Gardens, TW9
21 Oakleigh Park South, N20

Saturday 28th
Cadogan Place South Garden, SW1
5 Northampton Park, N1
NEW St Paul's Place, N1

Sunday 29th
NEW 40 Chartfield Avenue, SW15
Kew Green Gardens, TW9
Lower Clapton Gardens, E5
NEW 43 Roding Road, E5
80 Roding Road, E5
Royal Trinity Hospice, SW4
Stokes House, TW10
31 Trelawn Road, SW2

June

Friday 3rd
16 Links View Road, TW12

Saturday 4th
36 Ashley Road, N19
NEW 34 Barn Rise, HA9
16 Links View Road, TW12
41 Southbrook Road, SE12
10 Streatham Common South, SW16
Wensleydale Road Gardens, Hampton, TW12
Zen Garden at Japanese Buddhist Centre, W3

Sunday 5th
31 Arlington Drive, HA4
36 Ashley Road, N19
NEW 2 Camden Mews, NW1
NEW 19 Camden Mews, NW1
19 Coolhurst Road, N8
De Beauvoir Gardens, N1
Dragon's Dream, UB8
Forest Hill Garden Group, SE23
36 Melrose Road, SW18
174 Peckham Rye, SE22
12 Western Road, E13

61 Wolsey Road, KT8
Zen Garden at Japanese Buddhist Centre, W3

Wednesday 8th
26 Arlington Avenue, N1
25 Arlington Square, N1
19 St Peter's Street, N1

Friday 10th
Chiswick Mall Gardens, W4

Saturday 11th
Hyde Park Estate Gardens, W2
The Mysteries of Light Rosary Garden, NW5
Spitalfields Gardens, E1

Sunday 12th
66 Abbots Gardens, N2
Amwell Gardens, EC1R
97 Arthur Road, SW19
Barnsbury Group, N1
Chiswick Mall Gardens, W4
Choumert Square, SE15
26 College Gardens, E4
55 College Road, HA3
Court Lane Group, SE21
NEW 37 Crescent Road, BR3
The Gable End Gardens, NW1
70 Gloucester Crescent, NW1
37 Harold Road, E11
1a Hungerford Road, N7
NEW 325 Leigham Court Road, SW16
49 Loftus Road, W12
London Fields Gardens, E8
2 Lonsdale Square, N1
Lyndhurst Square Garden Group, SE15
Marksbury Avenue Gardens, TW9
4 Ormonde Road, HA6
36 Park Village East, NW1
5 Pemberton Road, KT8
123 South Park Road, SW19
41 Southbrook Road, SE12
13 Waite Davies Road, SE12
15 Waite Davies Road, SE12

Tuesday 14th
The Inner and Middle
  Temple Gardens, EC4

Wednesday 15th
5 Burbage Road, SE24
239a Hook Road, KT9

Saturday 18th
Zen Garden at Japanese
  Buddhist Centre, W3

Sunday 19th
103 & 105 Dulwich
  Village, SE21
11 Ernle Road, SW20
NEW 39 Glover Road,
  HA5
NEW 92 Hampstead Way,
  NW11
NEW 100 Hampstead
  Way, NW11
11 Park Avenue North,
  N8
18 Park Crescent, N3
NEW Torriano Community
  Garden, NW5
Zen Garden at Japanese
  Buddhist Centre, W3

Saturday 25th
NEW 26 Hillcroft Crescent,
  HA9
Marie Curie Hospice,
  Hampstead, NW3
Paddock Allotments &
  Leisure Gardens, SW20
Victoria Lodge, E18

Sunday 26th
51 The Chase, SW4
40 Ember Lane, KT10
NEW 1 Fife Road, SW14
40 Greenways, BR3
NEW 229 Hackney Road,
  E2
20 Hillcrest, N21
NEW 26 Hillcroft Crescent,
  HA9
9 Imber Park Road, KT10
38 Lovelace Road, SE21
5 St Regis Close, N10
NEW 65 Shrubland Road,
  E8
Silverwood, WD3
NEW 6 Thornhill Road, N1
152a Victoria Rise, SW4
33 Weyman Road, SE3

July

Sunday 3rd
Aldersbrook Gardens,
  E12
Arlington Square
  Gardens, N1
NEW Balfour & Burleigh
  Kitchen Garden, W10
NEW 6 Church Walk, KT7
3 Elmbridge Lodge, KT7
Ormeley Lodge, TW10
Railway Cottages, N22
57 St Quintin Avenue,
  W10
9 Shortgate, N12
11 Shortgate, N12
Tudor Herbalist Garden,
  NW3
74 Willifield Way, NW11

Sunday 10th
190 Barnet Road, EN5
5 Blackthorn Av,
  Apartment 5, N7
28 Ferndene Road, SE24
131 Southgate Road, N1
Swakeleys Cottage, 2
  The Avenue, UB10

Tuesday 12th
Garden of Medicinal
  Plants, Royal College of
  Physicians, NW1

Saturday 16th
33 Huddleston Road, N7
NEW 109 Riddlesdown
  Road, CR8

Sunday 17th
NEW Balfour & Burleigh
  Kitchen Garden, W10
81 Baston Road, BR2
20 Beechwood Avenue,
  TW9
NEW 52A Berrylands
  Road, KT5
15 Catherine Road, KT6
83 Cowslip Road, E18
NEW 20 Hemingford
  Close, N12
NEW 53 Lady Aylesford
  Avenue, HA7
24 Langton Avenue, N20
25 Mulberry Way, E18
NEW 1A Primrose
  Gardens, NW3
NEW 109 Riddlesdown
  Road, CR8
57 St Quintin Avenue,
  W10

24 Twyford Avenue, N2
45 Underhill Road, SE22
7 Woodbines Avenue,
  KT1

Sunday 24th
NEW 13 Agar Grove, Flat
  A, NW1
12 Fairfield Road, N8
70 Farleigh Road, N16
18 Park Crescent, N3
56 Park Road, W4
NEW 28a St Augustine's
  Road, NW1
87 St Johns Road, E17

Monday 25th
87 St Johns Road, E17

Saturday 30th
4 Becondale Road, SE19
34 Buxton Gardens, W3
NEW 106 Station Road,
  TW12

Sunday 31st
4 Becondale Road, SE19
34 Buxton Gardens, W3
58 Cranston Road, SE23
NEW 68 Derby Road, E18
45 Great North Road,
  EN5
NEW 77 Muswell Road,
  Flat 1, N10
5 St Regis Close, N10
NEW 106 Station Road,
  TW12
93 Tanfield Avenue, NW2

August

Sunday 7th
70 Gloucester Crescent,
  NW1
45 Great North Road,
  EN5
4 Manningtree Road,
  HA4

Sunday 14th
NEW 20 Hemingford
  Close, N12
9 Warwick Close, TW12
NEW 28a Worcester
  Road, E17

Saturday 20th
1 York Close, W7

Sunday 21st
NEW Avenue Road & Mill
  Hill Road Gardens, W3

NEW Horatio's Garden,
  HA7
Royal Trinity Hospice,
  SW4
1 York Close, W7

Sunday 28th
10 Streatham Common
  South, SW16

September

Sunday 4th
51 The Chase, SW4
Golf Course Allotments,
  N11
24 Grove Park, SE5
Hornbeams, HA7
15 Norcott Road, N16
42 Risingholme Road,
  HA3
NEW Tudeley House, BR7
152a Victoria Rise, SW4

Saturday 10th
♦ The Garden Museum,
  SE1
NEW Temple Lodge Club,
  W6

Sunday 11th
12 Lauradale Road, N2
4 Ormonde Road, HA6
25 Springfield Avenue,
  N10

Saturday 17th
Wolves Lane Horticultural
  Centre, N22

Sunday 25th
470 Pinner Road, HA5

October

Sunday 16th
The Watergardens, KT2

Sunday 30th
West Lodge Park, EN4

*Our 2021 donations
mean that 69,000
people were helped
by our Support for
Marie Curie*

By Arrangement

Please change wording to read:
Arrange a personalised garden visit on a date to suit you. See individual garden entries for full details.

NEW 15 Arlington Avenue, Arlington Square Gardens, N1
36 Ashley Road, N19
NEW Avenue Road & Mill Hill Road Gardens, W3
190 Barnet Road, EN5
NEW 52A Berrylands Road, KT5
5 Blackthorn Av, Apartment 5, N7
5 Burbage Road, SE24
51 The Chase, SW4
7 Deansway, N2
NEW 68 Derby Road, E18
3 Elmbridge Lodge, KT7
40 Ember Lane, KT10
48 Erskine Hill, NW11
70 Gloucester Crescent, NW1
45 Great North Road, EN5
17 Greenstone Mews, E11
NEW 20 Hemingford Close, N12
1a Hungerford Road, N7
Hyde Park Estate Gardens, W2
9 Imber Park Road, KT10
69 Kew Green, Kew Green Gardens, TW9
71 Kew Green, Kew Green Gardens, TW9
84 Lavender Grove, E8
49 Loftus Road, W12
53 Mapledene Road, London Fields Gardens, E8
The Mysteries of Light Rosary Garden, NW5
470 Pinner Road, HA5
NEW 28a St Augustine's Road, NW1
7 St George's Road, TW1
87 St Johns Road, E17
27 St Peters Square, W6
57 St Quintin Avenue, W10
5 St Regis Close, N10
9 Shortgate, N12
41 Southbrook Road, SE12
131 Southgate Road, N1
Southwood Lodge, N6
Stokes House, TW10
93 Tanfield Avenue, NW2
NEW 6 Thornhill Road, N1
NEW Torriano Community Garden, NW5
24 Twyford Avenue, N2
152a Victoria Rise, SW4
West Lodge Park, EN4
74 Willifield Way, NW11
33 Wood Vale, N10
NEW 28a Worcester Road, E17

5 St Regis Close

THE GARDENS

66 ABBOTS GARDENS, N2
East Finchley, N2 0JH. Stephen & Ruth Kersley. *8 min walk from rear exit East Finchley Underground Stn on Causeway to East End Rd. 2nd L into Abbots Gardens. Buses: 143 stops at Abbots Gardens on East End Rd, 102, 263 & 234 all go to High Rd, East Finchley.* **Sun 12 June (2-6). Adm £4, chd free. Home-made teas.**
Combination of grass and glass. Designed for year-round interest with a calm yet dramatic atmosphere created through plant form, texture, asymmetrical geometry, water features and restricted colour palette. Stephen studied garden design at Capel and Ruth is a stained glass artist. Glass amphorae and mosaics catch the eye amongst grasses, ornamental shrubs and perennials. Rose bedecked archway to quiet space with vegetable plot, silver birches, slate pebble fountain water feature with fish.

NEW 13 AGAR GROVE, FLAT A, NW1
Camden Town, NW1 9SL. Fanny Calder. *On the 274 bus route Agar Grove Estate bus stop. Look out for the enormous plane tree at front of the house. Entrance at side of house at ground level.* **Sun 24 July (2-6). Combined adm with 28a St Augustine's Road £5, chd free. Home-made teas.**
An opportunity to see a work in progress, this garden had been abandoned, its heavy clay soil covered in weeds until it was rescued during lockdown. Two distinct gardens have been created, both with a white theme. The front garden is a sunny, informal explosion of diverse border plants, while the large, shady back garden is more structured though with equally diverse and interesting planting.

The Hurlingham Club

GROUP OPENING

ALDERSBROOK GARDENS, E12

Wanstead, E12 5ES. Empress Ave is a turning off Aldersbrook Rd. Bus 101 from Manor Park or Wanstead Stns. From Manor Park Stn take the 3rd R off Aldersbrook Rd. From Wanstead, drive past St Gabriel's Church, take 6th turning on L. **Sun 3 July (12-5). Combined adm £7, chd free. Home-made teas at 1 Clavering Road, 4 Empress Avenue & 21 Park Road.**

1 CLAVERING ROAD
Theresa Harrison.

4 EMPRESS AVENUE
Ruth Martin.

21 PARK ROAD
Theresa O'Driscoll & Barry Reeves.

NEW 13 ST MARGARET'S ROAD
Mrs Gerti Ashton.

47 ST MARGARET'S ROAD
Jane Karavasili.

Five different gardens situated on the Aldersbrook Estate between Wanstead Park and Wanstead Flats. 21 Park Road is a colour themed garden with evergreen shrubs for year-round structure and a vine covered pergola leading to a vegetable area. 47 St Margaret's Road has a small front south facing garden where as well as off street parking, tomatoes and chillies grow. The back garden is designed with a theme of circles and curves with closely planted borders. 13 St Margaret's Road is a town garden with many interesting reclaimed features. 1 Clavering Road is an end of terrace garden where incremental space to the side has been adapted to create a kitchen garden and chicken coop, excess produce is eagerly received by five resident hens. Borders and beds contain variety of planting. At 4 Empress Avenue a largish garden is divided in two with a vegetable growing area and areas to attract more wildlife inc pond and two mixed borders; one with hot colours and one with white planting.

GROUP OPENING

AMWELL GARDENS, EC1R

South Islington, EC1R 1YE. Tube: Angel, 5 min walk. Buses: 19, 38 to Rosebery Ave; 30, 73 to Pentonville Rd. **Sun 12 June (2-5.30). Combined adm £7, chd free. Home-made teas at 11 Chadwell Street.**

11 CHADWELL STREET
Mary Aylmer & Andrew Post.

LLOYD SQUARE
Lloyd Square Garden Committee.

27 MYDDELTON SQUARE
Sally & Rob Hull.

NEW RIVER HEAD
NRH Residents.

4 WHARTON STREET
Barbara Holliman.

The Amwell Gardens group is in a secluded corner of Georgian Clerkenwell. Contrasting gardens inc Lloyd Square, a mature space with drifting borders in the centre of the Lloyd Baker Estate and the nearby gardens surrounding the historic. New River Head, where a stylish fountain and pergola have replaced the outer pond, which distributed fresh water to London. 27 Myddelton Square is a courtyard garden with lush cottage garden planting, complementing this elegant terraced setting and winning Best Back Garden award for Islington in Bloom competition 2020. New for 2022, 4 Wharton Street demonstrates imaginative planting in a north facing garden. 11 Chadwell Street is a tranquil setting for tea and delicious cakes amongst roses and honeysuckle.

Horatio's Garden

26 ARLINGTON AVENUE, N1
N1 7AX. **Thomas Blaikie.** *South
Islington. Off New North Rd via
Arlington Ave or Linton St. Buses: 21,
76, 141, 271.* **Evening opening Wed
8 June (6-8). Adm £5, chd free.
Wine. Open nearby 25 Arlington
Square. Opening with Arlington
Square Gardens on Sun 3 July.**
A friend once said 'Your garden is like
a tiny corner of some much grander
horticultural vision'. I assume it was a
compliment. Somehow, over 150 plants
(approx) are crammed into the minute
space. Visitors always like my slender
willow tree (*Salix exigua*). In June 'a
roses evening', the highlights should be
a good selection of old roses, climbing
and shrub, big dramatic alliums, lupins
and tall spires of verbascum.

31 ARLINGTON DRIVE, HA4
Ruislip, HA4 7RJ. **John & Yasuko
O'Gorman.** *Tube: Ruislip, then bus
H13 to Arlington Drive, or 15 min
walk up Bury St. Arlington Drive is*
*opp Millar & Carter Steakhouse on
Bury St.* **Sun 5 June (2-5). Adm £4,
chd free. Home-made teas.**
Cottage garden at heart with a
wonderful oriental influence. Traditional
cottage garden favourites have been
combined with Japanese plants, a
reflection of Yasuko's passion for
plants and trees of her native Japan.
Acers, peonies, rhododendrons and
flowering cherries underplanted with
hostas, ferns and hellebores, create
a lush exotic scheme. Emphasis on
structure and texture.

25 ARLINGTON SQUARE, N1
N1 7DP. **Michael Foley.** *South
Islington.* **Evening opening Wed
8 June (6-8). Adm £5, chd free.
Wine. Open nearby 26 Arlington
Avenue. Opening with Arlington
Square Gardens on Sun 3 July.**
Plants are my passion; they pack
the central bed and spill out onto the
other borders. Camelias, hydrangeas,
clematis and roses dominate with
other unusual plants. The exuberance
of the roses, like Compassion,
Ferdinand Pichard, Mutabilis, Rosa
Mundi, Gentle Hermione, Sir John
Mills and the City of York on the arch,
hits you like a painter's palette with
its first flush of the yr. A roses evening.

More than 1,200 people
have been cared for at
Y Bwthyn NGS Macmillan
Specialist Palliative Care
Unit, a unit that would
simply not have been built
without the National Garden
Scheme funding

GROUP OPENING

ARLINGTON SQUARE GARDENS, N1
N1 7DP.
www.arlingtonassociation.org.uk.
South Islington. Off New North Rd via Arlington Ave or Linton St. Buses: 21, 76, 141, 271. **Sun 3 July (2-5.30). Combined adm £10, chd free. Tea at St James' Vicarage, 1A Arlington Square.**

 15 ARLINGTON AVENUE
Armin Eiber & Richard Armit, 07771 740676, armin@eiber.com.
Visits also by arrangement May to Sept for groups of up to 6.

26 ARLINGTON AVENUE
Thomas Blaikie.
(See separate entry)

21 ARLINGTON SQUARE
Alison Rice.

25 ARLINGTON SQUARE
Michael Foley.
(See separate entry)

27 ARLINGTON SQUARE
Geoffrey Wheat & Rev Justin Gau.

30 ARLINGTON SQUARE
James & Maria Hewson.

5 REES STREET
Gordon McArthur & Paul Thompson-McArthur.

ST JAMES' VICARAGE, 1A ARLINGTON SQUARE
John & Maria Burniston.

Behind the early Victorian facades of Arlington Square and Arlington Avenue are eight contrasting town gardens inc new for 2022, 15 Arlington Avenue, a garden featuring flowers, vegetables, fruit and beehives. Seven are plantsmen's gardens and a delightful spacious garden at St James' Vicarage with an impressive herbaceous border created over the last few yrs, and mature London plane trees. The group reflects the diverse tastes and interests of each garden owner, who know each other through the community gardening of Arlington Square. It is hard to believe you are minutes from the bustle of the City of London. Live music at St James' Vicarage, 1A Arlington Square.

61 ARTHUR ROAD, SW19
Wimbledon, SW19 7DN. Daniela McBride. *Tube: Wimbledon Park, then 8 min walk. Mainline: Wimbledon, 18 min walk.* **Sun 22 May (2-6). Adm £5, chd free. Home-made teas.**
This steeply, sloping garden comprises woodland walks, filled with flowering shrubs and ferns. Azaleas, rhododendrons and acers bring early season colour. In early summer the focus is the many roses grown around the garden. Partial wheelchair access to top lawn and terrace only, steep slopes elsewhere.

97 ARTHUR ROAD, SW19
Wimbledon, SW19 7DP. Tony & Bella Covill. *Wimbledon Park Underground Stn, then 200yds up hill on R.* **Sun 12 June (2-6). Adm £5, chd free. Light refreshments. Open nearby 123 South Park Road.**
½ acre garden of an Edwardian house (not open). Garden established for more than 25 yrs, constantly evolving with a large variety of plants and shrubs. It has grown up around several lawns with ponds and fountains, encouraging an abundance of wildlife and a bird haven. A beautiful place with much colour, foliage and texture. New gravel garden, planting to attract butterflies. Wildflower meadow.

ARUNDEL & ELGIN GARDENS, W11
Kensington Park Road, Notting Hill, W11 2JD. Residents of Arundel Gardens & Elgin Crescent. www.arundelandelgingardens.org. *Entrance opp 174 Kensington Park Rd. Nearest tube within walking distance: Ladbroke Grove (5 mins) or Notting Hill (10 mins). Buses: 52, 452, 23, 228 all stop opp garden entrance.* **Sun 22 May (2-6). Adm £4, chd free. Home-made teas.**
A friendly and informal garden square with mature and rare trees, plants and shrubs laid out according to the original Victorian design of 1862, one of the best preserved gardens of the Ladbroke estate. The central hedged garden area is an oasis of tranquillity with extensive and colourful herbaceous borders. The garden inc several topiary hedges, a rare mulberry tree, a pergola and benches from which the vistas can be enjoyed. All looked after by Gardener, Paul

Walsh. Play areas for young children.

ARUNDEL & LADBROKE GARDENS, W11
Kensington Park Road, Notting Hill, W11 2PT. Arundel & Ladbroke Gardens Committee, www.arundelladbrokegardens.co.uk. *Entrance on Kensington Park Rd, between Ladbroke & Arundel Gardens. Tube: Notting Hill Gate or Ladbroke Grove. Buses: 23, 52, 228, 452. Alight at stop for Portobello Market/Arundel Gardens.* **Sun 24 Apr (2-6). Adm £4, chd free. Home-made teas.**
This private communal garden is one of the few that retains its attractive mid Victorian design of lawns and winding paths. A woodland garden at its peak in spring with rhododendrons, flowering dogwoods, early roses, bulbs, ferns and rare exotics. Live music on the lawn during tea. Playground for small children. Wheelchair access with a few steps and gravel paths to negotiate.

36 ASHLEY ROAD, N19
N19 3AF. Alan Swann & Ahmed Farooqui, swann.alan@googlemail.com. *Between Stroud Green & Crouch End. Underground: Archway or Finsbury Park. Overground: Crouch Hill. Buses: 210 or 41 from Archway to Hornsey Rise. W7 from Finsbury Park to Heathville Rd. Car: Free parking in Ashley Rd at weekends.* **Sat 4, Sun 5 June (2-6). Adm £5, chd free. Home-made teas. Visits also by arrangement May to Sept for groups of 8 to 35.**
A lush town garden rich in textures, colour and forms. At its best in late spring as Japanese maple cultivars display great variety of shape and colour whilst ferns unfurl fresh, vibrant fronds over a tumbling stream and alpines and clematis burst into flower on the rockeries and pergola. A number of microhabitats inc fern walls, bog garden, stream and ponds, rockeries, alpines and shade plantings. Young ferns and plants propagated from the garden for sale. Pop-up café with a variety of cakes and biscuits with gluten-free and vegan options. We also offer traditional home-brewed ginger beer. Seating areas around the garden.

GROUP OPENING

NEW **AVENUE ROAD & MILL HILL ROAD GARDENS, W3**
Mill Hill Road, Acton, W3 8JE.
annadargavel@mac.com.
Tube: Acton Town, turn R, down Gunnersbury Ln. **Sun 21 Aug (2-6). Combined adm £6, chd free. Home-made teas at 41 Mill Hill Road & 118b Avenue Road. Visits also by arrangement May to Sept for groups of 5 to 15.**

NEW **118B AVENUE ROAD**
Gareth Sinclair.

41 MILL HILL ROAD
Marcia Hurst.

65 MILL HILL ROAD
Anna Dargavel.

No. 41, a surprisingly secluded original garden with varied selection of plants. Borders, topiary, lavender hedge and large lawn. Adjoining sunny new area from 2019 with meadow, pond and gravel garden. Ample seating. Knowledgeable plantaholic owner selling plants from garden. No. 65, a garden designer's own stylish urban garden with change of levels leading to a studio at the end of the garden. No. 118b is dedicated to encouraging biodiversity and wildlife, this new garden was built on builders rubble, now has a meadow, ponds, 50 trees, and microclimates.
🐄 ✿ 🚗 ☕))

NEW **BALFOUR & BURLEIGH KITCHEN GARDEN, W10**
25 Exmoor Street, North Kensington, W10 6EE. The Lady Lenzie, Lease Holder, www.instagram.com/bnbkitchengarden/. *Opp Carmelite Monastery. Nearest station: Ladbroke Grove, then 7 min walk to North Kensington Fire Stn, take a L at the Eagle pub on St Charles Sq, to Exmoor St, or buses 23, 52, 228, 452 alight (stop F) as above.* **Sun 3, Sun 17 July (2-5.30). Combined adm with 57 St Quintin Avenue £5, chd free. Light refreshments. Home-made teas at 57 St Quintin Avenue.**
Described as 'a mini oasis in an urban concrete jungle', this award-winning kitchen garden is known for growing interesting and unusual heirloom varieties of fruit, vegetables and edible flowers, and forms part of the bee superhighway. The 2022 theme comes with a bit of a twist as the gardeners celebrate the Platinum Jubilee in colourful style. RBKC owned and run by a trio of local residents. We encourage pollinators, insects and birds with bee hotels, bird houses and watering stations around the plot.
♿ 🐄 ✿ 🚗 ☕))

NEW **34 BARN RISE, HA9**
Wembley, HA9 9NJ. Gita Gami.
Coming out of Wembley Park Stn, turn L & head to end of road towards T-lights. Cross at T-lights to a precinct of shops & turn L towards Barn Rise. **Sat 4 June (2-5). Adm £5, chd free. Tea.**
A delightful lush garden, an oasis next to Fryent Country Park, delights the senses of a Mediterranean as well as an English garden, amidst the busy Wembley Park with the view of The Wembley Stadium Arc. Various palms, ferns and *Cornus controversa 'Variegata'*.
☕

Our 2021 donations mean that 72,000 people accessed bereavement support through hospices in the UK

40 Chartfield Avenue

190 BARNET ROAD, EN5

The Upcycled Garden, Arkley, Barnet, EN5 3LF. Hilde Wainstein, 07949 764007, hildewainstein@hotmail.co.uk. *1m S of A1, 2m N of High Barnet Tube Stn. Garden located on corner of A411 Barnet Rd & Meadowbanks cul-de-sac. Nearest tube: High Barnet, then 107 bus, Glebe Ln stop. Ample unrestricted roadside parking. NB Do not park half on pavement.* **Sun 22 May, Sun 10 July (2-6). Adm £5, chd free. Home-made teas & gluten free options. Visits also by arrangement Apr to Sept for groups of 5 to 20.**

The upcycled garden. Garden designer's walled garden, 90ft x 36ft. Modern design and year-round interest. Flowing herbaceous drifts around central pond. Trees, shrubs herbaceous, bulbs. Upcycled containers, recycled objects, home-made sculptures. Handmade copper pipe trellis divides space into contrasting areas. Garden continues evolving as planted areas are expanded. Gravel garden. Home-made jams and plants for sale, all propagated from the garden. Wheelchair access with single steps within garden.

&. ✿ ☕))

GROUP OPENING

BARNSBURY GROUP, N1

Barnsbury, N1 1BX. *Tube: King's Cross, Caledonian Rd or Angel. Overground: Caledonian Rd & Barnsbury. Buses: 17, 91, 259 to Caledonian Rd.* **Sun 12 June (2-6). Combined adm £8, chd free. Home-made teas at 57 Huntingdon Street. Open nearby 2 Lonsdale Square.**

◆ BARNSBURY WOOD

London Borough of Islington, ecologycentre@islington.gov.uk.

44 HEMINGFORD ROAD

Peter Willis & Haremi Kudo.

57 HUNTINGDON STREET

Julian Williams.
(See separate entry)

36 THORNHILL SQUARE

Anna & Christopher McKane.

Within Barnsbury's historic Georgian squares and terraces, discover these four contrasting spaces. Barnsbury Wood is London's smallest nature reserve, a hidden secret and Islington's only site of mature woodland, a tranquil oasis of wild flowers and massive trees just minutes from Caledonian Rd. Wildlife info available. The gardens have extensive collections of unusual plants; 44 Hemingford Road has a small, dense composition of trees with shrubs, perennials and small pond. 57 Huntingdon Street is a secluded garden room with an understorey of silver birch and hazel, ferns, native perennials, grasses and two container ponds to encourage wildlife. 36 Thornhill Square, a 120ft garden with a country atmosphere, filled with old and new roses and many herbaceous perennials. A bonsai collection will astound! These gardens have evolved over many yrs and show what can be achieved in differing spaces with the right plants growing in the right conditions, surmounting the difficulties of dry walls and shade. Plants for sale at 36 Thornhill Square.

✿ ☕))

---

81 BASTON ROAD, BR2

Hayes, Bromley, BR2 7BS. Jill & Charles Wimble. *On B265, 2m S of Bromley. 10 min walk from Hayes (Kent) Stn, 146 & 353 bus-stop outside property. Opp Hayes Secondary School. Free on site parking.* **Sun 17 July (2-5.30). Adm £4, chd free. Home-made teas.**

A generous ½ acre plot converted by the owners into a colourful, plant-filled garden with many features of interest. A gravel garden influenced in style by Beth Chatto greets visitors. Detailed paving and brick work give structure to the garden and divide areas of interest inc exotics, vegetable garden, water features and fabulous pebble mosaic. Mainly level wheelchair access with grass, paved paths, a few steps and slopes.

&. ✿ ☕

4 BECONDALE ROAD, SE19

Gipsy Hill, Norwood, SE19 1QJ. Christopher & Wendy Spink. *Off Gipsy Hill. Nearest station Gipsy Hill. Buses 3 & 322. Some parking on Becondale Rd.* **Evening opening Sat 30 July (6-9). Adm £7, chd free. Sun 31 July (2-5). Adm £5, chd free. Wine & canapés (30 July). Home-made teas (31 July).**

This garden takes vertical planting to new heights, but is not for those who are afraid to walk a gangplank. It is packed with a mass of exotic and rich planting with a Mediterranean feel from bougainvillea to bananas and palms to plumbago. Steeply sloping, it maximises every bit of height with plants cascading over high rise balconies and dropping down to a theatrically styled well of a garden. Colourful Mediterranean planting on four levels.

☕))

20 BEECHWOOD AVENUE, TW9

Kew, Richmond, TW9 4DE. Dr Laura de Beden, www.lauradebeden.co.uk. *Within walking distance of Kew Gardens Underground Stn on E side exit.* **Evening opening Sun 17 July (5-7). Adm £6, chd free. Wine. Open nearby 15 Catherine Road.**

Delightful town garden minutes away from Royal Botanic Gardens and Kew Retail Park. Minimalist layout by the designer owner offsets exquisite favourite plant combinations. A writing shed holds pride of place as safe refuge and main idea production centre. Topiary, pots, sculpture, surprises (the latest in the new small fernery) and good humour are all on offer for an inspiring innovative visit. New sitting area amidst scented plants.

✿ ☕))

52A BERRYLANDS ROAD, KT5

Surbiton, KT5 8PD. Dr Tim & Mrs Julia Leunig, t.leunig@gmail.com. *2m E of Kingston-upon-Thames. A3 to Tolworth; A240 (towards Kingston) for approx 1m, then R into Berrylands Rd (after Fire Stn). 52A on R after Xrds.* **Sun 17 July (2-5). Adm £4, chd free. Open nearby 15 Catherine Road & 7 Woodbines Avenue. Visits also by arrangement for groups of 12 to 30.**

Professionally designed. Bold verticality: eucalyptus, ironwood tree, nine bamboos around stream and pond. South shaped lawn, flowing water, tear shaped Indian sandstone patio, clipped hebes, choisya and bay, slender cypress. Exuberance: large tetrapanax leaves, bonkers *Lobelia tupa* flowers, majestic *Magnolia grandiflora*, many climbing roses, day lilies and star jasmine in abundance. Come see!

))

5 BLACKTHORN AV, APARTMENT 5, N7

N7 8AQ. Juan Carlos Cure Hazzi, 07951 661223, juanhazzi@gmail.com. *Barnsbury. 5 min walk from Highbury & Islington Stn. Building is on S side of Arundel Square.* **Sun 10 July (11-6). Adm £5, chd free. Pre-booking essential, please visit www.ngs. org.uk for information & booking. Light refreshments. Visits also by arrangement.**

Small patio garden with beautiful connection with the house. Plenty of colour, texture and year-round interest with lush tropical, subtropical and temperate plants. Featured in BBC Gardeners' World and several gardening magazines. A finalist in the BBC's Small Space category competition.

5 BURBAGE ROAD, SE24

Herne Hill, SE24 9HJ. Crawford & Rosemary Lindsay, 020 7274 5610, rl@rosemarylindsay.com, www.rosemarylindsay.com. *Nr junction with Half Moon Ln. Herne Hill & N Dulwich Train Stns, 5 min walk. Buses: 3, 37, 40, 68, 196, 468.* **Evening opening Wed 15 June (5.30-8). Adm £7.50, chd free. Wine. Visits also by arrangement Mar to July.**

The garden of a member of The Society of Botanical Artists and regular writer for Hortus magazine. 150ft x 40ft with large and varied range of plants, many unusual. Herb garden, packed herbaceous borders for sun and shade, climbing plants, pots, terraces, lawns. Immaculate topiary. Gravel areas to reduce watering. All the box has been removed because of attack by blight and moth and replaced with suitable alternatives to give a similar look. A garden that delights from spring through to summer. Limited plants for sale.

34 BUXTON GARDENS, W3

Black&Bold, Acton, W3 9LQ. Alex Buxton. *10-15 min walk from: Acton Town Stn (Piccadilly Line), Acton Main Overground, Acton Central Overground, West Acton (Central Line).* **Sat 30, Sun 31 July (3-7). Adm £5, chd free. Home-made teas.**

Meet the Black&Bold, a wee wild yet practical. A bold take on the conventional garden loved by each

of its 80 visitors in 2021. More black, purple and copper is to take over the green in 2022. Close your eyes. Hear it. Think the darkest chocolate. Now see it 'spilled and sprayed' all over: the rockery, the cottage garden and the meadow on the banks of its tropical ponds with waterfall. Cascading ponds with goldfish, frogs and water lilies. 'Hanging Rock' an observation platform over the pond. 'Secret Patio'.

CADOGAN PLACE SOUTH GARDEN, SW1

Sloane Street, Chelsea, SW1X 9PE. The Cadogan Estate, www.cadogan.co.uk. *Entrance to garden opp 97 Sloane St.* **Sat 28 May (10-4). Adm £5, chd free. Home-made teas.**

Many surprises, unusual trees and shrubs are hidden behind the railings of this large London square. The first square to be developed by architect Henry Holland for Lord Cadogan at the end of C18, it was then called the London Botanic Garden. Mulberry trees planted for silk production at end of C17. Cherry trees, magnolias and bulbs are outstanding in spring. Beautiful 300 yr old black mulberry tree (originally planted to produce silk, but incorrect variety!). Area of medicinal plants in honor of Sir Hans Sloane. This was once the home of the Royal Botanic Garden. Now featuring a bug hotel and children's playground.

NEW 2 CAMDEN MEWS, NW1

Camden Town, NW1 9DB. Annabel & Beverley Rowe. *Arriving by bus, take 29 or 253 to Murray St. Go N for a couple of mins & turn R on Murray St. Take 1st R on Camden Mews & you will see the yellow signs.* **Sun 5 June (2-6). Combined adm with 19 Camden Mews £6, chd free. Light refreshments.**

20 yrs ago, two long gardens were turned into one. This resulted in a good sized garden, unusually broad for London and very secluded. Established trees, shrubs and flower beds break up the space so you don't see it all at once. A huge magnolia, three lovely tree peonies and a bed of tangerine geums are highlights. Across the mews a small ingeniously designed front garden will open with us. Wheelchair access over paved paths. No steps or narrow spaces.

NEW 19 CAMDEN MEWS, NW1

Camden Town, NW1 9DB. Andy Gilbert. *Buses 29 & 253 up & down Camden Rd, 5 min walk. Camden Road Train Stn, 10 min walk. Camden Town Underground Stn, 15 min walk.* **Sun 5 June (2-6). Combined adm with 2 Camden Mews £6, chd free.**

Secluded front garden, previously off-street parking space, in narrow cobbled mews and now a small but exquisite garden of raised beds, a green roof, herbaceous planting, interesting shrubs and trees. An imaginative layout, closely planted. Opening with a large garden, also beautifully planted and secluded, just across the mews. Wheelchair access with sloping hard path and limestone slabs in seating area. Deep gravel in one part.

4 CANONBURY PLACE, N1

N1 2NQ. Mr & Mrs Jeffrey Tobias. *Canonbury. Highbury & Islington Underground & Overground Stns. Bus 271 to Canonbury Square. Located in old part of Canonbury Place, off Alwyne Villas, in a cul-de-sac.* **Sun 3 Apr (2.30-5.30). Adm £3.50, chd free. Home-made teas.**

Enjoy the romance of early spring flowering in our historic, secluded 100ft garden with its architectural stonework and ancient hidden fountain all echoing the 1780 house. Mostly pots, interesting shrubs and climbers, along with spectacular mature trees and plenty of seating. Artisan pastries and sourdough bread from the legendary Dusty Knuckle Bakery on sale (as supplied to Fortnum & Masons and Ottolenghi). Wonderful home-made cakes.

15 CATHERINE ROAD, KT6

Surbiton, KT6 4HA. Malcolm Simpson & Stefan Gross. *5-10 min walk from Surbiton Stn. Public transport is recommended. Please note limited free car parking in immed area at weekends.* **Sun 17 July (1-5). Combined adm with 7 Woodbines Avenue £7, chd free. Open nearby 52A Berrylands Road.**

A well loved town garden approx 40ft x 70ft with deep borders of shrubs and perennial planting, sculptures, a small folly and a walled area.

40 CHARTFIELD AVENUE, SW15

Putney, SW15 6HG. Sally Graham. *Mainline & Tube: 10 min walk from Putney Train Stn & 15 mins from East Putney Underground Stn. Buses: 14, 37, 93, 85, 39 stop at end of Chartfield Ave on Putney Hill. Some free parking at weekends.* **Sun 29 May (2.30-5). Adm £4, chd free. Light refreshments.**

The garden was built from scratch in 2010 taking inspiration from the borrowed landscape of generous mature trees and the sloping site. Over the last 10 yrs structural evergreens have been added to provide a contrast with swathes of perennials and grasses.

🐾 ☕))

51 THE CHASE, SW4

SW4 0NP. Mr Charles Rutherfoord & Mr Rupert Tyler, 020 7627 0182, charles@charlesrutherfoord.net, www.charlesrutherfoord.net.

Off Clapham Common Northside. Tube: Clapham Common. Buses: 137, 452. **Sun 24 Apr (12-5). Evening opening Tue 26 Apr (5-8). Sun 26 June, Sun 4 Sept (12-5). Adm £4.50, chd free. Light refreshments. Open nearby 152a Victoria Rise on 26 June & 4 Sept. Visits also by arrangement Apr to Sept.**

Member of the Society of Garden Designers, Charles has created the garden over 40 yrs. In 2015 the main garden was remodelled, to much acclaim. Spectacular in spring, when 2000 tulips bloom among camellias, irises and tree peonies. Scented front garden. Rupert's geodetic dome shelters seedlings, succulents and subtropicals. Roses, brugmansia, hibiscus, and dahlias later in the season.

🐾 D ☕))

'In 2021 the generous donation from the National Garden Scheme helped 12,000 unpaid carers to access the support they need, with 50 more receiving crisis grants to support those in dire need.'
Carers Trust

43 Roding Road

GROUP OPENING

CHISWICK MALL GARDENS, W4
Chiswick Mall, Chiswick, W4 2PS.
By car: Hogarth r'about turn down Church St or A4 (W), turn L to Eyot Gardens. Tube: Stamford Brook or Turnham Green, walk under A4 to river. Buses: 110, 190, 237, 267, H91. **Evening opening Fri 10 June (6-8). Combined adm £12.50, chd free. Wine at Field House & Swan House. Sun 12 June (1-5.30). Combined adm £15, chd free.**

NEW **CEDAR HOUSE**
Stephanie & Philippe Camu.
Open on Sun 12 June

FIELD HOUSE
Rupert King,
www.fieldhousegarden.co.uk.
Open on all dates

LONGMEADOW
Charlotte Fraser.
Open on all dates

NEW **MILLER'S COURT**
Miller's Court Tenants Ltd.
Open on Sun 12 June

NEW **THE OLD VICARAGE**
Eleanor Fein.
Open on Sun 12 June

ST PETERS WHARF
Barbara Brown.
Open on Sun 12 June

SWAN HOUSE
Mr & Mrs George Nissen.
Open on all dates

Gardens on or near the River Thames; a riverside garden in an artists' complex, several large walled gardens, a communal garden on the river bank with well planted borders.
))))

CHOUMERT SQUARE, SE15
Choumert Grove, Peckham,
SE15 4RE. The Residents. *Off Choumert Grove. Trains from London Victoria, London Bridge, London Blackfriars, Clapham Junction to Peckham Rye; buses 12, 36, 37, 63, 78, 171, 312, 345. Free car park in Choumert Grove.* **Sun 12 June (1-6). Adm £4, chd free. Home-made teas & Pimms. Donation to St Christopher's Hospice.**
About 46 mini gardens with maxi planting in Shangri-la situation that the media has described as a floral canyon, which leads to small communal secret garden. The day is primarily about gardens and sharing with others our residents' love of this little corner of the inner city, but it is also renowned for its demonstrable community spirit and a variety of stalls and live music. Wheelchair access; one tiny step to raised paved area in the communal garden.
&. ✿ ☕

NEW 6 CHURCH WALK, KT7
Thames Ditton, KT7 0NW. Lesley & Keith Evetts. *Within 5 min walk from Thames Ditton Stn. Car Park Speer Rd on Thames Ditton High St, short walk from here.* **Sun 3 July (2-5). Combined adm with 3 Elmbridge Lodge £6, chd free.**
6 Church Walk celebrates a love of plants, some recondite. Foliage is as important as flowers. Formal fish pond; some twenty varieties of ferns and clematis; hostas, bamboos, hardy geraniums, roses, grasses, heucheras and succulents and a very old apple tree.
☕))))

THE CIRCLE GARDEN, KT3
33 Cambridge Avenue, New Malden, KT3 4LD. Vincent & Heidi Johnson-Paul-McDonnell, www.thecirclegarden.com. *1¼m N of A3 Malden junction. A3 signed for Kingston. 10 min walk from New Malden Train Stn. Bus 213 stops a short distance from end of road, our house is pink!* **Sat 21, Sun 22 May (2-6). Adm £4, chd free. Home-made teas.**
You are welcomed to a traditional cottage front garden and a back garden that offers visionary and sensory rewards.
&. 🐎 ✿ ☕))))

NEW 12 CLOUDESLEY SQUARE, N1
N1 0HT. Rachel Bower. *Barnsbury, Islington. Cloudesley Square is off Liverpool Rd. 10 min walk from Angel Underground Stn.* **Sat 14 May (2-5.30). Adm £4, chd free.**
A high walled corner garden complete with air raid shelter and washhouse in Barnsbury, built on the 'Stoney Fields'. It was flat and barren and the soil is very stony, but we now have a change of levels, hidden corners and a mix of planting. Perennial borders, shrubs and trees. Colourful in spring and autumn it was a haven in the pandemic for family and wildlife, foxes to damsel flies. Enclosed by high walls, a peaceful and private garden.
🐎 ☕))))

26 COLLEGE GARDENS, E4
Chingford, E4 7LG. Lynnette Parvez. *2m from Walthamstow. 15 min walk Chingford Train Stn. Bus 97 from Walthamstow Central Underground Stn, alight at College Gardens, then short walk downhill.* **Sun 12 June (2-5). Adm £4, chd free. Home-made teas.**
Large suburban garden, approx ⅔ acre. Sun terrace leads to established borders and variety of climbing roses. Beyond this, wildlife pond and lawn, small woodland walk with spring plants and orchard. A further garden area was recently uncovered and will be restored and planted over time.
☕))))

55 COLLEGE ROAD, HA3
Harrow Weald, Harrow, HA3 6EF. Jenny Phillips. *Buses 258, 340, 182,140. Nr Waitrose, Harrow Lawn Tennis Club Tube/Train, Harrow & Wealdstone Train Stn (10 min walk or bus). Garden is few steps from tennis club.* **Sun 12 June (2-5). Adm £4, chd free. Tea.**
A delightful garden with mature shrubs and small trees. The current owner has made very clever use of textures, shapes and colour palates to make the garden very charming. It can be enjoyed from many different aspects and the full length of the garden delights. There are lots of places to sit and relax with lots of quirky features. Two loquat trees which are unusual to see in London.

19 COOLHURST ROAD, N8
Hornsey, N8 8EP. Jane Muirhead. *Exit tube at Highgate onto Priory Gardens, L on Shepherd's Hill, R on Stanhope Rd, L on Hurst Ave, R on Coolhurst Rd (15 mins). W7 from Finsbury Park to Crouch End & 5 min walk. Buses 41 & 91 nearby.* **Sun 24 Apr, Sun 5 June (2-6). Adm £4, chd free. Light refreshments.**
Evolving, organic and wildlife garden with dappled sunlight, bees, birds and butterflies. Informal woodland planting under magnificent deciduous trees with interesting shrubs, box shapes and perennials. Small vegetable patch and wildflower garden where knapweed, campion, honesty, wild carrot and sweet rocket have naturalised. Large lawn with seating. Recently created bee and bug hotels. Gravel garden and wildlife pond.
🐎 ✿ ☕

GROUP OPENING

COURT LANE GROUP, SE21
Dulwich Village, SE21 7EA. *Buses: P4, 12, 40, 176, 185 to Dulwich Library 37. Train stn: North Dulwich, then 12 min walk. Ample free parking in Court Ln.* **Sun 12 June (2-5.30). Combined adm £8, chd free. Home-made teas at 122 & 164 Court Lane.**

122 COURT LANE
Jean & Charles Cary-Elwes.

148 COURT LANE
Mr Anthony & Mrs Sue Wadsworth.

164 COURT LANE
James & Katie Dawes.

No. 164 was recently redesigned to create a more personal and intimate space with several specific zones. A modern terrace and seating area leads onto a lawn with abundant borders and a beautiful mature oak. A rose arch leads to the vegetable beds and greenhouse. No. 122 has a countryside feel, backing onto Dulwich Park with colourful herbaceous borders. No.148 a spacious garden, developed over 20 yrs backs on to Dulwich Park. From the wide sunny terrace surrounded by tall, golden bamboos and fan palms, step down into a garden designed with an artist's eye for colour, form, texture and flow, creating intimate spaces beneath mature trees and shrubs with colourful perennials. Live Jazz on the terrace, a children's trail, plant sales and a wormery demonstration at 122 Court Lane.

❀ ☕ ›)

---

83 COWSLIP ROAD, E18
South Woodford, E18 1JN. Fiona Grant. *5 min walk from Central Line tube. Close to exit for A406.* **Sun 17 July (2-6). Adm £5, chd free. Home-made teas. Open nearby 25 Mulberry Way.**
80ft long wildlife friendly garden. On two levels at rear of Victorian semi. Patio has a selection of containers with a step down to the lawn past a pond full of wildlife. Flowerbeds stuffed with an eclectic mix of perennials. Ample seating on patio and under an ancient pear tree.

☕ ›)

---

58 CRANSTON ROAD, SE23
Forest Hill, SE23 2HB. Mr Sam Jarvis & Mr Andres Sampedro. *12 min walk from nearest overground stns Forest Hill or Honor Oak. Nearest bus stops: Stanstead Rd/Colfe Rd (185, 122), Kilmorie Rd (185, 171) or Brockley Rise/Cranston Rd (122, 171).* **Sun 31 July (12-6). Adm £4, chd free. Teas, cakes, tortilla & sangria.**
An exotic style plant lover's garden features a modern landscaped path and carefully curated subtropical planting. Vivid evergreens inc palms, cordylines, loquat and cycad provide structure and year-round interest. Tree ferns, bananas and tetrapanax add to the striking foliage, while cannas, dahlias and agapanthus provide vibrant pops of colour against the black painted boundaries.

❀ ☕ ›)

NEW ## 37 CRESCENT ROAD, BR3
Beckenham, BR3 6NF. Mrs Myra Bright. *15 min walk from Beckenham Junction Stn. 227 bus route from Shortlands Stn. Street parking in adjacent roads.* **Sun 12 June (2-6). Adm £4, chd free. Home-made teas.**
A new, romantic garden which shows a maturity beyond its yrs. An abundance of geraniums, foxgloves and allium fill the border at the front. Past the potting shed, herb bed and under the vine arch you arrive in the main garden filled with herbaceous plants, roses and clematis, a magnet for bees and butterflies. Gravel paths lead to secret corners with seating. Raised planters with vegetables.

❀ ☕ ›)

GROUP OPENING

DE BEAUVOIR GARDENS, N1
158 Culford Road, N1 4HU. *Underground stations: Highbury & Islington, then 30 bus; Angel, then 38, 56 or 73 bus; Bank, then 21, 76 or 141 bus. 10 min walk from Dalston Junction Train Stn. Street parking.* **Sun 5 June (2-6). Combined adm £8, chd free. Home-made teas at 100 Downham Road.**

158 CULFORD ROAD
Gillian Blachford.

✦ 100 DOWNHAM ROAD
Ms Cecilia Darker.

64 LAWFORD ROAD

21 NORTHCHURCH TERRACE
Nancy Korman.

Four gardens to explore in De Beauvoir, a leafy enclave of Victorian villas near to Islington and Dalston. The area boasts some of Hackney's keenest gardeners and a thriving garden club. 100 Downham Road features garden sculpture, giant echiums and two green roofs. The walled garden at 21 Northchurch Terrace has a formal feel with deep herbaceous borders, pond, fruit trees, pergola, patio pots and herb beds. 64 Lawford Road is a small cottage style garden with old fashioned roses, espaliered apples and scented plants. 158 Culford Road is a long narrow garden with a path winding through full borders with shrubs, small trees, perennials and many unusual plants.

❀ ☕ ›)

---

7 DEANSWAY, N2
East Finchley, N2 0NF. Joan Arnold & Tom Heinersdorff, 07850 764543, joan.arnold40@gmail.com. *From East Finchley Underground Stn exit along the Causeway to East End Rd, then L down Deansway. From Bishops Ave, head N up Deansway towards East End Rd, close to the top.* **Sun 8 May (12-6). Adm £5, chd free. Tea & coffee inc. Visits also by arrangement Apr to July for groups of up to 20.**
A garden of stories, statues, shapes and structures surrounded by trees and hedges. Bird friendly, cottage style with scented roses, clematis, mature shrubs, a weeping mulberry and abundant planting. Containers, spring bulbs and grape vine provide year-round colour. Developing secret shady, wild, woodland area with ferns and hostas. Cakes, gluten free cakes and plants for sale (cash preferred).

❀ ☕ ›)

> 'National Garden Scheme donations have funded four of our gardens in regional NHS spinal injury centres supporting nearly 8,500 patients and their visitors.'
> Horatio's Garden

37 Crescent Road

68 DERBY ROAD, E18
South Woodford, E18 2PS.
Mrs Michelle Greene,
greene@btinternet.com. *Nearest
tube: South Woodford (Central Line).
Buses: 20 & 179 to Chelmsford
Rd. Close to Epping Forest & the
Waterworks r'about.* **Sun 31 July
(1-5). Adm £4, chd free. Tea. Visits
also by arrangement.**
Old fashioned summer garden with
two ponds, one for wildlife and one
for goldfish. Tiny orchard, vegetable
beds and rockery. Highlights inc
American pokeweed and Himalayan
honeysuckle. Many unusual plants
with small plants for sale.

DRAGON'S DREAM, UB8
Grove Lane, Uxbridge, UB8 3RG.
Chris & Meng Pocock. *Garden is in
a small lane very close to Hillingdon
Hospital. Parking available next door.
Buses from Uxbridge Underground
Stn: U1, U3, U4, U5, U7. Buses from
West Drayton: U1, U3.* **Sun 5 June
(2-5). Adm £5, chd free. Home-
made teas.**
This is an unusual and secluded
garden with two contrasting sections
divided by a brick shed that has been
completely covered by a rampant
wisteria and a climbing hydrangea
and rose. Other highlights inc rare
dawn redwood tree and a huge
Gunnera manicata. More features
inc a Romneya poppy, ferns, rose
and herb beds, tree peonies, acers
and a pond. Also available Malaysian
curry puffs and café gourmand (tea or
coffee, plus bite-sized cakes).

GROUP OPENING

**103 & 105 DULWICH VILLAGE,
SE21**
SE21 7BJ. *Rail: N Dulwich or W
Dulwich then 10-15 min walk. Tube:
Brixton then P4 bus, alight Dulwich
Picture Gallery stop. Street parking.*
**Sun 19 June (2-5). Combined adm
£10, chd free. Home-made teas
at 103 Dulwich Village. Donation
to Macmillan Cancer Support.**

103 DULWICH VILLAGE
Mr & Mrs N Annesley.

105 DULWICH VILLAGE
Mr & Mrs A Rutherford.

Two Georgian houses with large
gardens, 3 min walk from Dulwich

Picture Gallery and Dulwich Park. 103
Dulwich Village is a country garden
in London with a long herbaceous
border, lawn, pond, roses and fruit
and vegetable gardens. 105 Dulwich
Village is a very pretty garden with
many unusual plants, lots of old
fashioned roses, fish pond and water
garden. Amazing collection of plants
for sale from both gardens. Please
bring your own bags for plants.
Music provided by the Colomb Street
Ensemble Wind Band.

ECCLESTON SQUARE, SW1
SW1V 1NP. The Residents of
Eccleston Square. *Off Belgrave Rd
nr Victoria Stn, parking allowed on
Suns.* **Sun 8 May (2-5). Adm £5,
chd free. Home-made teas.**
Planned by Cubitt in 1828, the 3
acre square is subdivided into mini
gardens with camellias, iris, ferns
and containers. Dramatic collection
of tender climbing roses and 20
different forms of tree peonies.
National Collection of ceanothus inc
more than 70 species and cultivars.
Notable important additions of tender
plants being grown and tested. World
collection of ceanothus, tea roses and
tree peonies.

EDWARDES SQUARE, W8
South Edwardes Square,
Kensington, W8 6HL. Edwardes
Square Garden Committee,
www.edwardes-square-garden.
co.uk. *Tube: Kensington High St
& Earls Court. Buses: 9, 10, 27,
28, 31, 49 & 74 to Odeon Cinema.
Entrance in South Edwardes Square.*
**Sun 10 Apr (12-5). Adm £5, chd
free. Home-made teas.**
One of London's prettiest secluded
garden squares. 3½ acres laid
out differently from other squares
with serpentine paths by Agostino
Agliothe, an Italian artist and
decorator who lived at No.15 from
1814-1820. This quiet oasis is a
wonderful mixture of rolling lawns,
mature trees and imaginative planting.
Children's play area. WC. Wheelchair
access through main gate, South
Edwardes Square.

3 ELMBRIDGE LODGE, KT7
Weston Green Road, Thames
Ditton, KT7 0HY. Mrs Julia
Hickman, 020 8339 0931,

julia@hickmanweb.co.uk. *House
opp Esher College on Weston Green
Rd & 5 min walk from Thames Ditton
Stn.* **Sun 3 July (2-5). Combined
adm with 6 Church Walk £6, chd
free. Home-made teas. Visits also
by arrangement May to Aug for
groups of 10 to 30.**
Mature garden 70' x 35' designed
by Cleve West 6 yrs ago. Sunny
terrace steps lead through to two
oak pergolas festooned with climbing
plants. Gravelled areas feature unusual
and drought tolerant plants. Decorative
glasshouse. Generous perennial
border brims with a kaleidoscope
of plants. Beyond is a productive
vegetable area opp a catalpa with soft
fruit beneath, plus hellebores.

40 EMBER LANE, KT10
Esher, KT10 8EP. Sarah &
Franck Corvi, 07803 111968,
sarah.corvi@ntlworld.com. *½m
from centre of Esher. From the A307,
turn into Station Rd which becomes
Ember Ln.* **Sun 26 June (1-5).
Combined adm with 9 Imber Park
Road £6, chd free. Home-made
teas. Visits also by arrangement
June to Sept for groups of 5 to 20.**
A contemporary family garden
designed and maintained by the
owners with distinct areas for outdoor
living. A 70ft east facing plot where
the lawn has been mostly removed to
make space for the owner's love of
plants and several ornamental trees.

11 ERNLE ROAD, SW20
Wimbledon, SW20 0HH. Theresa-
Mary Morton. *¼m from Wimbledon
Village, 200yds from Crooked Billet
pub. Exit A3 at A238 to Wimbledon,
turning L at Copse Hill. Train:
Wimbledon or Raynes Park. Tube:
Wimbledon. Bus: 200 to High Cedar
Drive, 200yds walk.* **Sun 19 June
(2.30-6). Adm £5, chd free. Home-
made teas.**
Established suburban garden of ⅓
acre on sandy acid soil, spatially
organised into separate sections;
oak pergola framing the main vista,
woodland garden, pool, yew circle,
flower garden and summerhouse.
Wheelchair access with beaten gravel
paths and one step to main garden.

48 ERSKINE HILL, NW11

Hampstead Garden Suburb, NW11 6HG. Marjorie & David Harris, 020 8455 6507, marjorieharris@btinternet.com. Nr A406 & A1. Tube: Golders Green. H2 Hail & Ride bus from Golders Green to garden, or 13, 102 or 460 buses to Temple Fortune (10 min walk). Free street parking. Visits by arrangement May to Sept for groups of up to 21. Adm £8, chd free. Tea & cake inc.

Restful, organic and pesticide free cottage garden. Copious perennials, pots, roses, clematis and trees with new pergola, containerised vegetable plot and greenhouse. Nest box, bee-friendly plants and quirky water feature. Pre-book dairy-free or gluten free cake and soya milk. Wheelchair access over single steps and narrow paths. Handrail and step to lawn.

♿ ❀ 🚗 ☕

12 FAIRFIELD ROAD, N8

N8 9HG. Christine Lane. Tube: Finsbury Park & then W3 (Weston Park stop) or W7 (Crouch End Broadway), alternatively Archway & then 41 bus (Crouch End Broadway, then a short walk). Sun 24 July (2-5.30). Adm £4, chd free.

A tranquil garden created on two levels with flower beds, lawn, cobbled garden and patio on the lower level, a secluded woodland garden with sculptures on the higher one. There are a variety of trees, shrubs and flowers, as well as succulents, palms and bamboos all of which create different atmospheres and the seating provides places to rest and enjoy.

❀ ›)

70 FARLEIGH ROAD, N16

Stoke Newington, N16 7TQ. Mr Graham Hollick. Short walk from junction of Stoke Newington High St & Amhurst Rd. Sun 24 July (10-5.30). Adm £4, chd free. Home-made teas.

A diverse garden in a Victorian terrace with an eclectic mix of plants, many in vintage pots reflecting the owner's interests. A small courtyard leads onto a patio surrounded by pots followed by a lawn flanked by curving borders. At the rear is a paved area with raised beds containing vegetables.

❀ ☕ ›)

28 FERNDENE ROAD, SE24

Herne Hill, SE24 0AB. Mr David & Mrs Lynn Whyte. Buses 68, 468,

42. A 5 min walk from Denmark Hill. Train stns: Herne Hill, Denmark Hill, Loughborough Junction. All 15 min walk. House overlooks Ruskin Park. Free parking. Sun 10 July (2-5). Adm £4, chd free. Home-made teas.

It's all about structure and careful planting in this dramatically sloping SSE facing garden, 30 x 18 metres. A lively blend of perennials and shrubs shows definite Kiwi influences. The kitchen garden with raised beds and soft fruits is wonderfully secluded. Lower level planting has a coastal feel. Upper level has a hot colour border. Borrowed views of mature trees and big skies set it off. The garden office/summerhouse, constructed from sustainably sourced materials, has a rubble roof to attenuate water runoff. Recycling and re-use of materials.

❀ ☕ ›)

NEW 1 FIFE ROAD, SW14

East Sheen, Mortlake, SW14 7EW. Mr & Mrs J Morgan. Bus routes 33, 337 stops are a 15 min walk away on Upper Richmond Rd. Mortlake Train Stn SWT approx 20 mins away. Sun 26 June (1-6). Adm £5, chd free. Home-made teas.

Dominated by two large cedar trees the garden has matured since it was redesigned in 2013. A maturing oak tree stands in the wild garden with fruit trees and 'dead hedge'. A productive vegetable garden and greenhouse is managed with a no dig regime. Lawns and borders with perennials and shrubs, sunny terrace close to the house.

♿ ☕ ›)

GROUP OPENING

FOREST HILL GARDEN GROUP, SE23

Forest Hill, SE23 3DE. Off S Circular Rd (A205) behind Horniman Museum & Gardens. Forest Hill Stn, 10 min walk. Buses 176,185,197, 356, P4. Sun 5 June (1-6). Combined adm £8, chd free. Home-made teas at 53 Ringmore Rise. Donation to St Christopher's Hospice & Marsha Phoenix Trust.

7 CANONBIE ROAD

June Wismayer.

THE COACH HOUSE, 3 THE HERMITAGE

Pat Rae.

27 HORNIMAN DRIVE

Rose Agnew.

NEW 12 NETHERBY ROAD

Ms Alice Hutton.

53 RINGMORE RISE

Valerie Ward.

Five always changing lively gardens in eclectic and differing styles spread around the highest hill in South East London, nr Horniman Museum. Most with stunning views over the Downs and all within a short walk of each other. They inc an intricately planted, sloping woodland garden; a tame robin still demands cheese in the walled courtyard of an artist's C18 coach house; relax and enjoy breathtaking views among vibrant colours; enjoy a fanciful, twisting, turning, sloping garden with views, unusual plants and a dramatic treehouse; unwind in spacious and fragrant surroundings with delicious cakes, while looking out over the vast London skyline. Plants for sale at 7 Canonbie Road and 27 Horniman Drive.

❀ ☕ ›)

9 FURLONG ROAD, N7

Islington, N7 8LS. Nigel Watts & Tanuja Pandit. Tube & Overground: Highbury & Islington, 3 min walk along Holloway Rd, 2nd L. Furlong Rd joins Holloway Rd & Liverpool Rd. Buses: 43, 271, 393. Sun 22 May (2-5.30). Adm £3.50, chd free. Open nearby 10 Furlong Road.

Award-winning small garden designed by Karen Fitzsimon, making clever use of an awkwardly shaped plot. Curved lines are used to complement a modern extension. Raised beds contain a mix of tender and hardy plants to give an exotic feel and inc loquat, banana, palm, cycad and tree fern. Contrasting traditional front garden. Featured in Small Family Gardens and Modern Family Gardens by Caroline Tilston. Refreshments at 10 Furlong Road.

❀ ›)

10 FURLONG ROAD, N7

N7 8LS. Gavin & Nicola Ralston. Tube & Overground: Highbury & Islington, 3 min walk along Holloway Rd, 2nd L. Furlong Rd runs between Holloway Rd & Liverpool Rd. Buses on Holloway Rd: 43, 271, 393; other buses 4, 19, 30. Sun 22 May (2-5.30). Adm £5, chd free. Home-made teas. Open nearby 9 Furlong Road.

A green oasis in the heart of a

densely populated area, 10 Furlong Road is an open, sunny garden of considerable size for its urban location. Its new owners, previously at Canonbury House, extensively remodelled the garden in 2019, building on a foundation of trees, shrubs and roses, adding herbaceous planting, seating, winding brick path, pergola, raised vegetable bed and wildflower circle. Variety of teas and soft drinks with a range of cakes and biscuits, all home-made; plenty of seating dotted around the garden.

THE GABLE END GARDENS, NW1

52 Hawley Road, Camden Town, NW1 8RG. Magda Segal. *Set back off Chalk Farm Rd, opp the Stables Market. On the L approx 600yds down from Chalk Farm Underground Stn. The nearest bus stop is served by the 31, 24, 168 & 88 buses.* **Sun 12 June (2-6). Adm £5, chd free. Home-made teas. Open nearby 70 Gloucester Crescent.**

The Gable End Gardens consists of a series of planted areas that together create a wildlife haven in the heart of Camden Town, within them can be found a colony of sparrows, beehives and ponds. The planting, based around rescued and donated plants, is dominated by a mature fig tree at the front of the property and a willow in the rear garden, providing forage for the bees and cover for the birds. A must see example of what can be achieved to help wildlife in urban environments, plus prize-winning tree pits. The gardens are not wheelchair accessible, the rest can be enjoyed with comparative ease.

GARDEN BARGE SQUARE AT TOWER BRIDGE MOORINGS, SE1

31 Mill Street, SE1 2AX. Mr Nick Lacey, towerbridgemoorings.org. *5 min walk from Tower Bridge. Mill St off Jamaica Rd, between London Bridge & Bermondsey Stns, Tower Hill also nearby. Buses: 47, 188, 381, RV1.* **Sun 22 May (2-5). Adm £5, chd free. Home-made teas.**

Series of seven floating barge gardens connected by walkways and bridges. Gardens have an eclectic range of plants for year-round seasonal interest. Marine environment: suitable shoes and care needed. Small children must be closely supervised.

Cedar House, Chiswick Mall Gardens

✦ THE GARDEN MUSEUM, SE1

5 Lambeth Palace Road, SE1 7LB. The Garden Museum, www.gardenmuseum.org.uk. *Lambeth side of Lambeth Bridge. Tube: Lambeth North, Vauxhall, Waterloo. Buses: 507 Red Arrow from Victoria or Waterloo Train & Tube Stns, also 3, 77, 344, C10.* **For NGS: Sat 10 Sept (10-4). Adm £6.50, chd free. Light refreshments. For other opening times and information, please visit garden website.**

At the heart of the Garden Museum is the Sackler Garden. Designed by Dan Pearson as an 'Eden' of rare plants, the garden is inspired by John Tradescant's journeys as a plant collector. Taking advantage of the sheltered, warm space, Dan has created a green retreat in response to the bronze and glass architecture, conjuring up a calm, reflective atmosphere. Visitors will also see a permanent display of paintings, tools, ephemera and historic artefacts; a glimpse into the uniquely British love affair with gardens. The Garden Cafe is an award-winning lunch venue. Please note your ticket does not inc access to the temporary exhibition. The Museum is accessible for wheelchair users via ramps and access lift (max load 400kg).

GARDEN OF MEDICINAL PLANTS, ROYAL COLLEGE OF PHYSICIANS, NW1

11 St Andrews Place, Regents Park, NW1 4LE. Royal College of Physicians of London, garden.rcplondon.ac.uk. *Opp the SE corner of Regents Park. Tubes: Great Portland St & Regent's Park. Garden is one block N of station exits, on Outer Circle opp SE corner of Regent's Park.* **Tue 12 July (10.30-4.30). Adm £5, chd free.** We have 1,100 different plants connected with the history of plants in medicine: plants named after physicians; plants which make modern medicines; those used for millennia; plants which cause epidemics; plants used in herbal medicine in all the continents of the world and plants from the College's Pharmacopoeia of 1618 on which Nicholas Culpeper based his Herbal. Guided tours by physicians explaining the uses of the plants, their histories and stories about them. Books about the plants in the medicinal garden will be on sale. The entry to the garden is at far end of St Andrews Place. Wheelchair ramps at steps. Wheelchair lift for WC. No parking on site.

&.))

74 GLENGALL ROAD, IG8

Woodford Green, IG8 0DL. Mr & Mrs J Woolliams, 020 8504 1709, jgmwoolliams@outlook.com. *5 min walk from Woodford Underground Stn (Central line), off Snakes Lane West. Buses nearby inc 275, 179, W13 & 20. No parking restrictions on Suns.* **Sun 27 Mar (2-4.30). Adm £4, chd free. Tea.** A secluded, south facing, cottage style garden, developed over 30 yrs for year-round interest and is at its best in spring. Areas inc two lawns, a rock garden, small wildlife pond with bog garden, shade borders and a gravel garden linked by several paths. Throughout the garden there is a mixture of trees, shrubs, perennials, bulbs, bamboos, grasses and climbers.

&. ✿ ☕

70 GLOUCESTER CRESCENT, NW1

NW1 7EG. Lucy Gent, 07531 828752 (texts please), gent.lucy@gmail.com. *Between Regent's Park & Camden Town Underground Stn. Underground: Camden Town, 2 mins, Mornington Crescent, 10 mins. Metered parking in Oval Rd.* **Sun 12 June, Sun 7 Aug (1.30-5). Adm £5, chd free. Open nearby 36 Park Village East on 12 June. Visits also by arrangement Apr to Oct for groups of up to 20.** Here is an oasis in Camden's urban density, full of interest across the yr, 'max formality with max informality'. Resourceful planting outflanks challenges of space and shade and Mrs Dickens, who once lived here, is an amiable ghost. An Aug opening shows how wonderful the month can be in a town garden. Many cafes in nearby Parkway and home-made teas offered at 36 Park Village East (12 June only).

🚗))

11 Ernle Road

© Matthew Bruce

NEW 39 GLOVER ROAD, HA5
Pinner, HA5 1LQ. **Prakash & Joanne Daswani.** *12 min walk/3 min drive from Pinner Underground Stn (Metropolitan line). Turn L into Marsh Rd 350yds, then R into Eastcote Rd 900yds, then L into Rosecroft Walk for 250yds, then R at T-junction. No parking restrictions.* **Sun 19 June (3.30-7). Adm £5, chd free. Light refreshments.**
Newly landscaped compact space, sensitively filled with varied elements that complement one another, to generate a sense of union with nature and an instant welcome to sit and gaze. Range of plants of all types across numerous beds inc long-established, towering trees alongside new specimens. Multiple seating areas, large deck, steel gazebo and octagonal water feature offer alternative vistas. Backs onto parkland. Wheelchair access via 1.2 metre wide side alley with temporary ramps to patio, then lawn and main planting beds.
🚻 ☕))

GOLF COURSE ALLOTMENTS, N11
Winton Avenue, N11 2AR. **GCAA Haringey, www.golfcourseallotments.co.uk.** *Junction of Winton Ave & Blake Rd. Tube: Bounds Green. Buses: 102, 184, 299 to Sunshine Garden Centre, Durnsford Rd. Through park to Bidwell Gardens. Straight on up Winton Ave. No cars on site.* **Sun 4 Sept (1-4.30). Adm £4, chd free. Home-made teas & light lunches.**
Large, long established allotment with over 200 plots, some organic. Maintained by culturally diverse community growing wide variety of fruit, vegetables and flowers enjoyed by the bees. Picturesque corners and quirky sheds, a visit feels like being in the countryside. Autumn Flower and Produce Show features prize-winning horticultural and domestic exhibits and beehives. Tours of best plots. Enjoy healthy fresh allotment produce, chutneys, jams and honey for sale (cash only). Wheelchair access to main paths only. WC inc disabled.
🚻 🐕 ✻ ☕

45 GREAT NORTH ROAD, EN5
Barnet, EN5 1EJ. **Ron & Miriam Raymond, 07880 500617, ron.raymond91@yahoo.co.uk.** *1m S of Barnet High St, 1m N of Whetstone. Tube: Midway between High Barnet & Totteridge & Whetstone Stns. Buses: 34, 234, 263, 326, alight junction Great North Rd & Lyonsdown Rd. 45 Great North Rd is on the corner of Cherry Hill.* **Sun 31 July (1.30-5.30); Sun 7 Aug (1.30-6). Adm £3, chd free. Light refreshments. Visits also by arrangement Aug & Sept for groups of up to 30.**
45 Great North Road is designed to give a riot of colour in late summer. The 90ft x 90ft cottage style front garden is packed with shrubs and perennials. Tiered stands line the side entrance with over 64 pots displaying a variety of flowering and foliage plants. The rear garden inc nearly 100 tubs and hanging baskets. Small pond surrounded by tiered beds. Magnificent named *Tuberous begonia.* Children's fun trail for 3-6yr olds and adult garden quiz with prizes. Partial wheelchair access.
🚻 🐕 ✻ ☕))

17 GREENSTONE MEWS, E11
Wanstead, E11 2RS. **Mrs T Farnham, 07761 476651, farnhamz@yahoo.co.uk.** *Tube: Snaresbrook or Wanstead, 5 min walk. Buses: 101, 308, W12, W14 to Wanstead High St. Greenstone Mews is accessed via Voluntary Place which is off Spratt Hall Rd.* **Visits by arrangement Mar to Oct for groups of 5 to 8. Adm £5. Tea or coffee inc. Sandwiches & cake can be provided.**
Tiny slate paved garden, approx 15ft sq. Sunken reused bath now a fish pond surrounded by climbers clothing fences underplanted with hardy perennials, herbs, vegetables, shrubs and perennials grown from cuttings. Height provided by established palm. Ideas aplenty for small space gardening. Regret garden unsuitable for children. Wheelchair access through garage. Limited turning space.
🚻 ✻ ☕))

40 GREENWAYS, BR3
Beckenham, BR3 3NQ. **N Dooley & C Murray.** *S of Beckenham High St. Nearest train stn Beckenham Junction, a 10 min walk. Clockhouse Stn is a 15 min walk or 227 bus to High St. Garden is located on the corner of Greenways & Uplands, close to the triangular green.* **Sun 26 June (2-5.30). Adm £4, chd free. Home-made teas.**
Two contrasting garden spaces. The tapering 70ft rear garden, redesigned in 2015, has year-round interest

and is wildlife friendly. Features inc a Mediterranean planted bed, climbers, hydrangeas, olive trees, grasses, huge insect hotel, alpine roof garden, pond, sculptures and areas to relax. The hidden front garden has fruit trees and a small meadow, surrounded by borders in coloured rooms.
🚻 🐕 ✻ ☕))

24 GROVE PARK, SE5
Camberwell, SE5 8LH. **Clive Pankhurst, www.alternative-planting.blogspot.com.** *Chadwick Rd end of Grove Park. Peckham Rye or Denmark Hill Stns, both 10 min walk. Good street parking.* **Sun 4 Sept (11-4.30). Adm £5, chd free. Home-made teas.**
An inspiring exotic jungle of lush big leafed plants and Southeast Asian influences. Exuberant plantings transport you to the tropics. Huge hidden garden created from the bottom halves of two neighbouring gardens gives the wow factor and unexpected size. Lawn and lots of hidden corners give spaces to sit and enjoy. Renowned for delicious home-made cake and plant sale.
🐕 ✻ ☕))

NEW 229 HACKNEY ROAD, E2
E2 8NG. **Susanna Grant, www.hellotherelinda.com.** *Buses on Hackney Rd: 26, 55 & on Bethnal Green Rd: 8, 388. Overground: Hoxton, Cambridge Heath, Hagerstown, Shoreditch. Underground: Bethnal Green. Front & back garden on 229 Hackney Rd, back garden access on Scawfell St.* **Sun 26 June (12-4). Adm £3.50, chd free.**
A sun-drenched front garden filled with aromatic, biodiverse, drought-tolerant planting nods to the original Hackney city gardener, Thomas Fairchild, who is buried nearby. In a separate entrance around the corner, a secret, shaded courtyard oasis spills over with grasses, perennials and oversized ferns doubling up as an occasional shop selling shade-loving plants on Suns.
🚻 ✻ ☕))

Our 2021 donations mean that 750 people living with Parkinson's were supported

58 HALLIFORD STREET, N1
N1 3EQ. Jennifer Tripp Black.
*Canonbury. Tube: Highbury &
Islington or Essex Rd. From Essex
Rd, house numbers consecutive
on LH-side by 3rd speed bump.
Overground: Canonbury.* **Sun 24
Apr (2-6). Adm £4, chd free.
Home-made teas. Vegan & full
fat cakes. Donation to The Royal
Marsden Cancer Charity (Katie's
Lymphoedema Fund).**
An English country garden in the
heart of Islington. Lush planting:
Cytisus battandieri 'Yellow Tail' tree,
two apple trees, one quince. Bush
and climbing roses, tulips, clematis,
rhododendrons, exotic palms,
cannas, abutilons, heucheras, salvias,
cordelines and a hosta collection in
pots. Small greenhouse and antique
pergola. In summer the front garden
welcomes with special roses and
agapanthus.

 **92 HAMPSTEAD WAY,
NW11**
Hampstead Garden Suburb,
NW11 7XY. Ann & Tom Lissauer.
*In square set back on Hampstead
Way, between Finchley Rd &
Meadway. Buses 13,102 & 460
on Finchley Rd, getting off at
Temple Fortune Ln & walk down
Hampstead Way to the square.* **Sun
19 June (2-6). Combined adm
with 100 Hampstead Way £8,
chd free. Pre-booking essential,
please visit www.ngs.org.uk for
information & booking. Home-
made teas in the square between
the two gardens.**
An informal garden, interesting year-
round, combining wildlife friendly
planting with a passion for plants.
Different areas provide a variety of
habitats. These inc a wildlife pond
and, where there used to be lawns,
there are now meadows with mown
paths and wild flowers. Shaded
and sunny beds offer opportunities
to grow a wide range of interesting
plants.

 **100 HAMPSTEAD WAY,
NW11**
Hampstead Garden Suburb,
NW11 7XY. S & J Fogel. *In square
set back on Hampstead Way,
between Finchley Rd & Meadway.
Buses 13,102 & 460 on Finchley
Rd, getting off at Temple Fortune
Ln & walk down Hampstead
Way to the square.* **Sun 19 June**

(2-6). Combined adm with
92 Hampstead Way £8, chd
free. Pre-booking essential,
please visit www.ngs.org.
uk for information & booking.
Home-made teas on the square
between the two gardens.
Corner cottage garden with a
variety of viewing perspectives and
featuring sculpture and planting
in recycled objects (pallets, sinks,
dustbins, mattress on wheels, wine
boxes, poles, chimneys). The garden
comprises a number of rooms inc
a formal parterre, wooded area,
walkway, small meadow and formal
lawn.

SPECIAL EVENT

**♦ HAMPTON COURT PALACE,
KT8**
East Molesey, KT8 9AU. Historic
Royal Palaces, www.hrp.org.uk.
*Follow brown tourist signs on all
major routes. Junction of A308 with
A309 at foot of Hampton Court
Bridge. Traffic is heavy around
Hampton Court. Please leave plenty
of time, the tour will start promptly at
6pm & will not be able to wait.* **For
NGS: Evening opening Thur 21
Apr (6-8). Adm £15, chd free. Pre-
booking essential, please visit
www.ngs.org.uk for information &
booking. Wine. For other opening
times and information, please
visit garden website. Donation to
Historic Royal Palaces.**
Take the opportunity to join a special
NGS private tour after the wonderful
historic gardens have closed to
the public. Spring Walk in the the
remarkable gardens of Hampton
Court Palace. Wheelchair access over
some un-bound gravel paths.

&. NPC 🍵

37 HAROLD ROAD, E11
Leytonstone, E11 4QX. Dr
Matthew Jones Chesters. *Tube:
Leytonstone exit L subway, 5 min
walk. Overground: Leytonstone High
Road, 5 min walk. Buses: 257 &
W14. Parking at station or limited on
street.* **Sun 12 June (1-5). Adm £4,
chd free. Home-made teas.**
50ft x 60ft pretty corner garden
arranged around seven fruit trees.
Fragrant climbers, woodland plants
and shade tolerant fruit along north
wall. Fastigiate trees protect raised
vegetable beds and herb rockery.

Long lawn bordered by roses and
perennials on one side, prairie plants
on the other. Patio with raised pond,
palms and rhubarb. Planting designed
to produce fruit, fragrance and lovely
memories. Garden map with plant
names and planting plans inc. Home-
made preserves for sale.

🍵 🔊)

 **20 HEMINGFORD CLOSE,
N12**
off Fenstanton Avenue,
North Finchley, N12 9HF.
Melvyn Rees, 07903 456385,
melvyn.tymel@gmail.com. *From
Woodhouse Rd go R up Fenstanton
Ave; 20 Hemingford Close is to the L
at the end. Buses 134 & 221, alight
Grove Rd. Nearest tube Woodside
Park & Finchley Central, then bus.*
**Evening opening Sun 17 July
(5-9). Adm £6, chd free. Wine. Sun
14 Aug (2-6). Adm £3.50, chd free.
Home-made teas. Visits also by
arrangement Apr to Oct for groups
of up to 20.**
Exotic but frost hardy species such
as tetrapanax, *Dicksonia antarctica,
Aurelia, Hoheria* form a visual block
making this a garden of hidden
corners. The short range view leads
you to concentrate on your immed
surroundings. Hidden at the back of
the garden is a wildlife pond. A small
space by a lengthy path planted with
interesting species. Art trail activity for
children.

🌿 🚗 🍵 🔊)

32 HIGHBURY PLACE, N5
N5 1QP. Michael & Caroline Kuhn.
*Highbury Fields. Highbury & Islington
Tube; Overground & National Rail.
Buses: 4, 19, 30, 43, 271, 393 to
Highbury Corner. 3 min walk up
Highbury Place which is opp station.*
**Sun 22 May (2-5.30). Adm £5, chd
free. Home-made teas. Open
nearby 9 & 10 Furlong Road.**
An 80ft garden behind a C18 terrace
house (not open). An upper York
stone terrace leads to a larger terrace
surrounded by overfilled beds of
cottage garden style planting. Further
steps lead to a lawn by a rill and a
lower terrace. A willow tree dominates
the garden; amelanchiers, fruit trees
and dwarf acers, winter flowering
cherry, lemon trees and magnolia.

HIGHWOOD ASH, NW7
**Highwood Hill, Mill Hill, NW7 4EX.
Mrs P Gluckstein.** *Totteridge & Whetstone on Northern line, then bus 251 stops outside Rising Sun/ Mill Hill stop. By car: A5109 from Apex Corner to Whetstone. Garden located opp The Rising Sun pub.* **Sun 15 May (2-5.30). Adm £5, chd free. Tea.**
Created over the last 56 yrs, this 3¼ acre garden features rolling lawns, two large interconnecting ponds with koi, herbaceous and shrub borders and a modern gravel garden. A country garden in London for all seasons with many interesting plants and sculptures. May should be perfect for the camellias, rhododendrons and azaleas. Partial access for wheelchairs, lowest parts too steep.

20 HILLCREST, N21
Winchmore Hill, N21 1AT. Gwyneth & Ian Williams. *Tube: Southgate then W9 to Winchmore Hill Green followed by a short walk via Wades Hill. Train: Winchmore Hill, turn R towards the Green, then a short walk via Wades Hill.* **Sun 26 June (1.30-6). Adm £4, chd free. Home-made teas. Herbal teas, non-dairy options.**
A pretty hill garden has a terrace with ironwork gazebos, wide stone steps descending to an evergreen pergola, dappled sunlight and quiet water feature. Rose arches, a meandering path and lawn with shrub and tree borders lead to small alpine rockeries, a summerhouse, a miniature wildlife pond and little garden with fruit trees.

NEW 26 HILLCROFT CRESCENT, HA9
Wembley Park, HA9 8EE. Gary & Suha Holmyard. *½m from Wembley Park Stn. From A406 turn in Harrow Rd, drive 1½m then turn R into Wembley Hill. 1st L at r'about, Hillcroft Cres 2nd on R. Wembley Park Underground Stn 7 min walk. Buses 79 & 204, 5-7 min walk from Wembley Hill Rd.* **Sat 25, Sun 26 June (11-5). Adm £4, chd free. Home-made teas & soya option.**
Small cottage front garden with arched entrance inc fuchsias, wisteria, yucca, canna, hydrangeas, roses and lilies. Rear garden approx 70ft x 80ft with summerhouse, arbours and water features. Planting inc fig, apple, pear, plum and soft fruit. Ten different

flower beds each holding its own particular interest inc lilies, unusual evergreen shrubs and several varieties of hydrangeas, clematis and roses. Plenty of seating around the garden. Wheelchair access through side gate via driveway.

239A HOOK ROAD, KT9
**Chessington, KT9 1EQ.
Mr & Mrs D St Romaine, www.gardenphotolibrary.com.** *4m S of Kingston. A3 from London, turn L at Hook underpass onto A243. Garden 300yds on L. Parking opp in park or on road, no restrictions at night. Buses K4, 71, 465 from Kingston & Surbiton to North Star pub.* **Sat 7, Sun 8 May (2-5). Adm £4.50, chd free. Evening opening Wed 15 June (7-10). Adm £6, chd free. Home-made teas (May). Light refreshments & wine (June).**
Patio with raised vegetable bed and garden room. A central path of standard hollies, urns and box balls leads to a water feature at the end of the garden. Rectangular beds with rose covered obelisks form a grid either side of central axis. Enclosed on three sides by sun and shade borders, shrubs and perennials. All cleverly lit to enhance the atmosphere in the evenings. Tulip display in urns late spring. Wheelchair access with one low step.

NEW HORATIO'S GARDEN, HA7
Royal National Orthopaedic Hospital, Brockley Hill, Stanmore, HA7 4LP. Horatio's Garden, www.horatiosgarden.org.uk. *Enter the Hosptial via Wood Ln, Aspire entrance if arriving by car.* **Sun 21 Aug (2-5). Adm £5, chd free. Home-made teas with vegan & gluten free options.**
Opened in Sept 2020, Horatio's Garden London & South East located at the Royal National Orthopaedic Hospital, Stanmore was designed by Tom Stuart-Smith. The garden is on one level with smooth paths throughout ensuring that it is easily accessible to patients in beds and wheelchairs. The essential design features inc a social space, private areas for patients to seek solitude or share with a family member or friend, the calming sound of flowing water, a garden room, a garden therapy area and a greenhouse. Throughout the garden the planting is designed to supply colour all year-round, whilst

wildlife has been encouraged with bird and butterfly boxes. The Head Gardener Ashley Edwards will be on hand to answer any plant questions and give guided tours of this unique sanctuary. The whole site is designed for wheelchairs.

HORNBEAMS, HA7
**Priory Drive, Stanmore, HA7 3HN.
Mrs B Stalbow.** *5m SE of Watford. Tube: Stanmore. Priory Drive, private road off Stanmore Hill (A4140 Stanmore-Bushey Heath Rd).* **Sun 20 Feb, Sun 4 Sept (2-5). Adm £5, chd free. Tea.**
½ acre garden for year-round interest. Wildlife pond and bog. Woodland grove of birches underplanted with cyclamen and dwarf bulbs. Cornus and willow stooled for winter interest. In Sept pots with *Argyranthemum 'Jamaica Primrose'*, spectacular 40' *Hoheria sexstylosa, Zauschneria californica, Salvia uliginosa* and many other unusual herbaceous perennials.

33 HUDDLESTON ROAD, N7
N7 0AD. Gilly Hatch & Tom Gretton. *Underground: 5 mins from Tufnell Park Stn. Buses: 4, 134, 390 to Tufnell Park. Follow Tufnell Park Rd to 3rd road on R.* **Sat 16 July (2-6). Adm £4.50, chd free. Home-made teas.**
The rambunctious front garden weaves together perennials, grasses and ferns, while the back garden makes a big impression in a small space. After 40+ yrs, the lawn is now a wide curving path, a deep sunny bed on one side; mixing shrubs and perennials in an ever changing blaze of colour, on the other; a screen of varied greens and textures. This flowery passage leads to a secluded area.

In the first six months of operation at Maggie's Southampton, which was part funded by the National Garden Scheme, the team has supported people affected by cancer more than 2,300 times

1A HUNGERFORD ROAD, N7

N7 9LA. David Matzdorf, davidmatzdorf@blueyonder.co.uk, growingontheedge.net/index.php. *Between Camden Town & Holloway. Tube: Caledonian Rd. Buses: 17, 29, 91, 253, 259, 274, 390 & 393. Parking free on Suns.* **Sun 12 June (1-6). Adm £3, chd free. Visits also by arrangement Apr to Oct for groups of up to 6.**

Unique eco house with walled, lush front garden in modern exotic and woodland style, densely planted with palms, acacia, bamboo, ginger lilies, bananas, ferns, yuccas, abutilons and unusual understory plants. Floriferous and ambitious green roof resembling Mediterranean or Mexican hillside, planted with yuccas, dasylirions, nolinas, agaves, cacti, aloes, cistus, euphorbias, grasses, sedums and herbs. Sole access to roof is via built in vertical ladder. Garden and roof each 50ft x 18ft (15 metres x 6 metres).

57 HUNTINGDON STREET, N1

Barnsbury, Islington, N1 1BX. Julian Williams. *Overground: Caledonian Rd & Barnsbury. Tube: Kings Cross or Highbury & Islington. Buses: Caledonian Rd 17, 91, 259, 274; Hemingford Rd 153 from Angel.* **Evening opening Wed 11 May (6-8). Adm £4, chd free. Wine. Opening with Barnsbury Group on Sun 12 June (2-6).**

A secluded woodland garden room below an ash canopy and framed by timber palisade supporting roses, hydrangea and ivy. An understorey of silver birch and hazel provides the setting for shade loving ferns, mainly native perennials and grasses. Oak pathways offset the informal planting and lead to a tranquil central space with bench seating and two container ponds to encourage wildlife.

National Garden Scheme funding helped support the provision of horticultural-related assistance to soldiers, veterans and their immediate families, providing education, training and employment opportunities along with supporting the recovery, health and wellbeing of individuals

THE HURLINGHAM CLUB, SW6

Ranelagh Gardens, SW6 3PR. The Members of the Hurlingham Club, www.hurlinghamclub.org.uk. *Main gate at E end of Ranelagh Gardens. Tube: Putney Bridge (110yds). NB: No on site parking. Meter parking on local streets & restricted parking on Sats (9-5).* **Sat 14 May (10-4). Adm £6.50, chd free. Light refreshments.**

Rare opportunity to visit this 42 acre jewel with many mature trees, 2 acre lake with water fowl, expansive lawns and a river walk. Capability Brown and Humphry Repton were involved with landscaping. The gardens are renowned for their roses, herbaceous and lakeside borders, shrubberies and stunning bedding displays. The riverbank is a haven for wildlife with native trees, shrubs and wild flowers. Light refreshments on site at the Napier Servery and Terrace, weather depending. Guided tours at 11am and 2pm, tickets at gate.

GROUP OPENING

HYDE PARK ESTATE GARDENS, W2

Kendal Street, W2 2AN. Church Commissioners for England, hydeparkestate@churchofengland.org, www.hydeparkestate.com. *The Hyde Park Estate is bordered by Sussex Gardens, Bayswater Rd & Edgware Rd. Nearest underground stations inc Marble Arch, Paddington & Edgware Rd.* **Sat 11 June (10.30-4). Combined adm £6, chd free. Pre-booking essential, please visit www.ngs.org.uk for information & booking. Visits also by arrangement May to July for groups of 5 to 15.**

CONISTON COURT

DEVONPORT

THE QUADRANGLE

◆ REFLECTIONS 2020

THE WATER GARDENS

Unique opportunity to visit five Central London gardens usually only seen by residents. These five gardens only open to the public for the NGS. Each garden planted sympathetically to reflect the surroundings and featuring a new garden created during 2020. The gardens on the Hyde Park Estate are owned and managed by the Church Commissioners for

England and play a key part in the environmental and ecological strategy on the Hyde Park Estate. The Estate covers 90 acres of which 12½% is 'green', not only with the garden spaces but by installing planters on unused paved areas, green roofs on new developments and olive trees throughout Connaught Village. Wheelchair access to most gardens. There are some steps to the upper levels of The Water Gardens.

9 IMBER PARK ROAD, KT10

Esher, KT10 8JB. Jane & John McNicholas, jane_mcnicholas@hotmail.com. *½m from centre of Esher. From the A307, turn into Station Rd which becomes Ember Ln. Go past Esher Train Stn on R. Take 3rd road on R into Imber Park Rd.* **Sun 26 June (1-5). Combined adm with 40 Ember Lane £6, chd free. Home-made teas. Visits also by arrangement June to Sept for groups of 5 to 20.**

An established cottage style garden, always evolving, designed and maintained by the owners who are passionate about gardening and collecting plants. The garden is south facing with well-stocked, large, colourful herbaceous borders containing a wide variety of perennials, evergreen and deciduous shrubs, a winding lawn area and a small garden retreat.

SPECIAL EVENT

THE INNER AND MIDDLE TEMPLE GARDENS, EC4

Crown Office Row, Inner Temple, EC4Y 7HL. The Honourable Societies of the Inner & Middle Temples, www.innertemple.org.uk/www.middletemple.org.uk. *Entrance: Main Garden Gate on Crown Office Row, access via Tudor St Gate or Middle Temple Ln Gate.* **Tue 14 June (11.30-3). Adm £55. Pre-booking essential, please visit www.ngs.org.uk for information & booking. Light refreshments.**

Inner Temple Garden is a haven of tranquillity and beauty with sweeping lawns, unusual trees and charming woodland areas. The well known herbaceous border shows off inspiring plant combinations from early spring through to autumn. The award-

winning gardens of Middle Temple are comprised of a series of courtyards. Adm inc conducted tour of the gardens by Head Gardeners. Light lunch in Middle Temple Hall, please advise of any dietary requirements. Please advise in advance if wheelchair access is required.

GROUP OPENING

KEW GREEN GARDENS, TW9

Kew, TW9 3AH. *NW side of Kew Green. Tube: Kew Gardens. Mainline Stn: Kew Bridge. Buses: 65, 110. Entrance via riverside.* **Sun 22 May (2-5). Combined adm £8, chd free. Evening opening Sun 29 May (6-8). Combined adm £10, chd free. Wine.**

65 KEW GREEN
Giles & Angela Dixon.

67 KEW GREEN
Lynne & Patrick Lynch.

69 KEW GREEN
John & Virginia Godfrey, virginiagodfrey69@gmail.com. **Visits also by arrangement in June.**

71 KEW GREEN
Mr & Mrs Jan Pethick, linda@bpethick.co.uk. **Visits also by arrangement in June.**

73 KEW GREEN
Sir Donald & Lady Elizabeth Insall.

The long gardens run for 100yds from the back of historic houses on Kew Green down to the Thames towpath. Together they cover nearly 1½ acres, and in addition to the style and structures of the individual gardens they can be seen as one large space, exceptional in London. The borders between the gardens are mostly relatively low and the trees and large shrubs in each contribute to viewing the whole, while roses and clematis climb between gardens giving colour to two adjacent gardens at the same time.

KING HENRY'S WALK GARDEN, N1

11c King Henry's Walk, N1 4NX. **Friends of King Henry's Walk Garden, www.khwgarden.org.uk.** *Buses: 21, 30, 38, 56, 141, 277. Behind adventure playground on*

KHW, off Balls Pond Rd. **Mon 2 May (2-4.30). Adm £3.50, chd free. Home-made teas. Donation to Friends of KHW Garden.**
Vibrant ornamental planting welcomes the visitor to this hidden oasis leading into a verdant community garden with secluded woodland area, beehives, wildlife pond, wall trained fruit trees, and plots used by local residents to grow their own fruit and vegetables. Disabled access WC.

53 LADY AYLESFORD AVENUE, HA7

Stanmore, HA7 4FG. *Jadon. About 15 min walk from Stanmore Stn, off Uxbridge Rd, close to St John Church. H12 & 340 bus stops are 5 min walk from garden. Limited free parking nearby.* **Sun 17 July (11-5). Adm £5. Pre-booking essential, please visit www.ngs.org.uk for information & booking. Cream teas.**
A compact tropical fusion garden developed over the past 4 yrs, set in a 20 yr old development of a Battle of Britain, RAF base. This delightful gem of a corner garden with water features and a stunning display of plants and flowers, shows what can be achieved, even in a small space. Colours and textures blend effortlessly to create a harmonious space with exceptional attention to detail.

LAMBETH PALACE, SE1

Lambeth Palace Road, SE1 7JU. **The Church Commissioners, www.archbishopofcanterbury.org.** *Entrance via Main Gatehouse (Morton's Tower) facing Lambeth Bridge. Stn: Waterloo. Tube: Westminster, Vauxhall all 10 min walk. Buses: 3, C10, 77, 344, 507.* **Evening opening Mon 16 May (5-8). Adm £6, chd free. Wine.**
Lambeth Palace has one of the oldest and largest private gardens in London. It has been occupied by Archbishops of Canterbury since 1197. Formal courtyard boasts historic White Marseilles fig planted in 1556. Parkland style garden features mature trees, woodland and native planting. There is a formal rose terrace, summer gravel border, scented chapel garden and active beehives. Please note: Gates will open at 5pm, last entry is 7pm and garden closes at 8pm. Garden Tours will be available. Wheelchair access with ramped path to rose terrace. Disabled WC.

24 LANGTON AVENUE, N20

Whetstone, N20 9DA. *Quentin & Xihomara Zentner. Tube: Totteridge. Buses: 263, 125, 234. 10 min walk from Whetstone High St. M&S on R, turn R at Buckingham Ave. House behind conifers, on corner of Langton Ave & Buckingham Ave. Parking in side road.* **Sun 17 July (2-6). Adm £4.50, chd free. Light refreshments.**
Contemporary front and rear garden with a big heart. Designed by Chelsea winner Jilayne Rickards as part of house renovation. With naturalistic planting, it reflects the lives of its owners incorporating Corten steel screens (Arabic motifs), water feature, fire pit and ample covered seating area. The garden is transformed by lighting into an intimate space at night. Corten steel hoop sculpture. Winner of a prestigious BALI Award.

12 LANSDOWNE ROAD, W11

W11 3LW. *The Lady Amabel Lindsay. Tube: Holland Park. Buses: 12, 88, 94, 148, GL711, 715 to Holland Park, 4 min walk up Lansdowne Rd.* **Thur 12 May (3-6.30). Adm £5, chd free.**
A country garden in the heart of London. An old mulberry tree, billowing borders, rambling *Rosa banksiae* and a greenhouse of climbing pelargoniums. Partial wheelchair access to level paved surfaces.

12 LAURADALE ROAD, N2

Fortis Green, N2 9LU. **David Gilbert & Mary Medyckyj, www.sites.google.com/site/davidgilbertportfolio/garden.** *300 metres from 102 & 234 bus stops. 500 metres from 43 & 134 bus stops. 10 min walk from East Finchley Underground Stn. Look for arrows.* **Sun 11 Sept (1-6). Adm £5, chd free. Home-made teas.**
Exotic, huge, featuring tropical and Mediterranean zone plants, now beginning to mature with much recent development. Dramatic, architectural planting inc bananas, large tree ferns and rare palms weave along curving stone paths, culminating in a paradise garden. A modern take on the rockery embeds glacial boulders amid dry zone plants inc many succulents. Sculptures by artist owner.

84 LAVENDER GROVE, E8
Hackney, E8 3LS. Anne Pauleau, 07930 550414, a.pauleau@hotmail.co.uk. *Short walk from Haggerston or London Fields Overground Stns.* **Sun 15 May (2-5). Adm £4, chd free. Home-made teas. Opening with London Fields Gardens on Sun 12 June. Visits also by arrangement Mar to Oct for groups of 8 to 30.** Courtyard garden with tropical backdrop of bamboos and palms, foil to clipped shrubs leading to wilder area, the cottage garden mingling roses, lilies, alliums, grasses, clematis, poppies, star jasmine and jasmine. A very highly scented garden with rampant ramblers and billowing vegetation enchanting all senses. Tulips and daffodils herald spring. Children's quiz offered with prize on completion.

325 LEIGHAM COURT ROAD, SW16
Streatham, SW16 2RX. Mr & Mrs Martin Cook. *Nr junction of Leigham Court Rd & Leaf Grove. Buses: 417 bus stops outside door, 249 bus stops in Crown Ln, 5 min walk. Mainline: W Norwood, Streatham & Streatham Hill Stns, all approx 1m.* **Sun 12 June (2-5). Adm £3, chd free. Light refreshments.** Two large cedars, a catalpa and some rhododendrons are a reminder of the heritage of this beautiful walled Victorian garden. Although mainly planted for shade, there is a big, mixed, sunny border, plus an ornamental pond, vegetable garden, fruit trees and sweeping lawns. There is also a small wildflower meadow and three beehives at the bottom of the garden. There are plenty of seating areas to sit and enjoy a cuppa. Wheelchair access with some gravel areas.

16 LINKS VIEW ROAD, TW12
Hampton Hill, TW12 1LA. Guy & Virginia Lewis. *5 min walk from Fulwell Stn. On 281, 267, 285 & R70 bus routes.* **Fri 3, Sat 4 June (2-4.30). Adm £5, chd free. Home-made teas & gluten free option.** A surprising garden featuring acers, hostas and fern collection and other unusual shade loving plants. Many climbing roses, clematis and herbaceous border. Rockery and folly with shell grotto and waterfall to small pond and bog garden. Lawn and formal pond. Wild area with chickens and summerhouse. Greenhouse with succulent collection. A verandah with pelargonium collection and seating area with exotic plants. Water features. Children's quiz. Two very friendly dogs. Wheelchair access with assistance.

49 LOFTUS ROAD, W12
W12 7EH. Emma Plunket, emma@plunketgardens.com, www.plunketgardens.com. *Shepherds Bush or Shepherds Bush Market underground, train or bus to Uxbridge Rd. Pay for Ringo parking.* **Sun 12 June (3-6). Adm £5, chd free. Light refreshments. Visits also by arrangement June to Aug for groups of 5 to 10.** Professional garden designer Emma Plunket opens her acclaimed walled garden. Richly planted, it is the ultimate hard working city garden with all year structure and colour incorporating fruit and herbs. Set against a backdrop of trees, this city haven is unexpectedly open and peaceful. Garden plan, plant list and advice available.

GROUP OPENING

LONDON FIELDS GARDENS, E8
Hackney, E8 3JW. *7 min walk from 67, 149, 242, 243 bus stop Middleton Rd, 10 mins from 30, 38, 55 stops on Dalston Ln. 7 mins from Haggerston Overground or 10 min walk through London Fields from Mare St buses.* **Sun 12 June (2-5.30). Combined adm £10, chd free. Home-made teas at 61 Mapledene Road.**

84 LAVENDER GROVE, E8
Anne Pauleau.
(See separate entry)

53 MAPLEDENE ROAD
Tigger Cullinan, 020 7249 3754, tiggerine8@blueyonder.co.uk.
Visits also by arrangement May to July for groups of up to 10.

55 MAPLEDENE ROAD
Amanda & Tony Mott.

61 MAPLEDENE ROAD
Ned & Katja Staple.

84 MIDDLETON ROAD
Penny Fowler.

92 MIDDLETON ROAD
Mr Richard & Mrs Louise Jarrett.

A fascinating and diverse collection of gardens in London Fields within easy walking distance of each other. South facing are twin gardens in Lavender Grove, one a courtyard with tropical backdrop, and its other half a highly scented, romantic cottage garden. 92 Middleton Road is an elegant and serene garden with a circular theme inc roses, acers and examples of stone lettering. At No. 84, lies an unusually large secret garden where you can wander down meandering woodland paths and forget you are in London. The Mapledene Road gardens are north facing and have much the same space but totally different styles. No. 53 is an established plantaholic's garden in five sections with not a spare unplanted inch. No. 55 has a Moorish-inspired terrace leading to a wildlife garden with plants chosen to attract birds, bees and butterflies. No. 61 is a family garden with a wide English lawn where teas are served surrounded by roses and a wildflower meadow.

2 LONSDALE SQUARE, N1
N1 1EN. Jenny Kingsley. *Barnsbury. Tube: Highbury & Islington or Angel. Walk along Liverpool Rd, walk up Richmond Ave, 1st R, entrance via passageway on R.* **Sun 12 June (2-6). Adm £3, chd free.** One could describe our garden as a person: small and unpretentious. Attractively formed by yew and box hedges and beds with hellebores, fatsia, hydrangeas, arum lily and scented climbing roses, star jasmine and solanum. Planters with olive trees, lavender and pansies are fine companions, mauve, white and emerald favoured colours. She walks delicately on cobblestones, a fountain calms her soul.

38 LOVELACE ROAD, SE21
Dulwich, SE21 8JX. José & Deepti Ramos Turnes. *Midway between West Dulwich & Tulse Hill Stns. Buses: 2, 3 & 68.* **Sun 26 June (12.30-4.30). Adm £4, chd free. Home-made teas.** This gem of a garden has an all white front and a family friendly back. The garden slopes gently upwards with curving borders, packed with an informal mix of roses, perennials and annuals. The garden is designed to be an easy to maintain oasis of calm at the end of a busy day. There are

several smile inducing features like a dragon, the Cheshire cat and a stream. Here you'll find a brook with stepping stones, wildlife ponds, wide curving borders packed with colourful perennials, plants for shade, some that love full sun and several that thrive on neglect, two mature Japanese acers, raised vegetable beds, fruit trees and a teenagers' hang-out area.

GROUP OPENING

LOWER CLAPTON GARDENS, E5
8 Almack Road, Lower Clapton, E5 0RL. *12 min walk from Hackney Central, Hackney Downs or Homerton Stns. Buses 38, 55, 106, 242, 253, 254 or 425, alight Lower Clapton Rd or Powerscroft Rd.* **Sun 29 May (2-5). Combined adm £5, chd free. Home-made teas at 77 Rushmore Road. Open nearby 43 Roding Road & 80 Roding Road.**

8 ALMACK ROAD
Philip Lightowlers.

77 RUSHMORE ROAD
Penny Edwards.

Lower Clapton is an area of mid Victorian terraces sloping down to the River Lea. These gardens reflect their owner's tastes and interests. 77 Rushmore Road has a fruit and vegetable garden and wildlife pond. 8 Almack Road is a long thin garden with two rooms, one cool and peaceful the other with hot colours, succulents and greenhouse.

GROUP OPENING

LYNDHURST SQUARE GARDEN GROUP, SE15
Lyndhurst Square, SE15 5AR. *Rail & overground services to Peckham Rye Stn. Numerous bus routes.* **Sun 12 June (1.30-5). Combined adm £6, chd free. Home-made teas in Lyndhurst Square. Donation to MIND, Mental Health Charity.**

5 LYNDHURST SQUARE
Martin Lawlor & Paul Ward.

6 LYNDHURST SQUARE
Iain Henderson & Amanda Grygelis.

7 LYNDHURST SQUARE
Pernille Ahlström & Barry Joseph.

Three very attractive gardens open in this small, elegant square of 1840s listed villas located in Peckham, South East London. Each garden, approx 90ft x 50ft, has its own shape and style as the square curves in a U-shape. No. 5, the design combines Italianate and Gothic themes with unusual herbaceous plants and towering echiums. No. 6, the design features architectural plants, pergola, vegetable garden and espalier apple trees. No. 7, simplicity, Swedish style is key with roses and raised beds, framed by yew hedges. Plants for sale at 5 Lyndhurst Square.

MAGGIE'S, SM2
17 Cotswold Road, Sutton, SM2 5NG. Maggie's Centre. *Maggie's at The Royal Marsden is located on the corner of Cotswold Rd via the staff entrance to The Royal Marsden.* **Sat 14 May (11-3.30). Adm £4, chd free. Tea.**
The garden surrounding the centre designed by world-famous Dutch Landscape Architect Piet Oudolf, has many different zones, some enjoying full sun and others in dappled shade, whilst the pathway from the hospital meanders under mature trees. Plant communities are carefully chosen inc 14 different grasses, a palette of 6 hardy ferns and more than 50 different perennials.

MAGGIE'S WEST LONDON, W6
Charing Cross Hospital, Fulham Palace Road, Hammersmith, W6 8RF. Maggie's West London. *Follow Fulham Palace Rd from Hammersmith Stn towards Charing Cross Hospital. The centre is on the corner of St Dunstan's Rd & is painted tomato-orange so is very visible.* **Sun 24 Apr (10-2). Adm £4, chd free. Tea.**
The garden at Maggie's West London was designed by Dan Pearson in 2008. It is now a well-established space offering therapy and peace to those affected by cancer each yr. The gardens surround the vivid orange walls of the centre. The path leading to the centre meanders through scented beds and mature trees. Visitors have access to various courtyards with a wonderful array of flora inc fig trees, grape vines and even a mature pink silk mimosa. Wheelchair access to ground floor gardens and courtyards. Roof gardens not accessible.

4 MANNINGTREE ROAD, HA4
Ruislip, HA4 0ES. Costas Lambropoulos & Roberto Haddon. *Manningtree Rd is just off Victoria Rd, 10-15 min walk from South Ruislip Underground Stn.* **Sun 7 Aug (2-6). Adm £5, chd free. Home-made teas.**
Compact garden with an exotic feel that combines hardy architectural plants with more tender ones. A feeling of a small oasis inc plants like Musa basjoo, Ensete ventricosum 'Montbeliardii', tree ferns, black bamboo. Potted Mediterranean plants on the patio inc a fig tree and two olive trees. Cakes, savouries, home-made jams and biscuits for sale.

MARIE CURIE HOSPICE, HAMPSTEAD, NW3
11 Lyndhurst Gardens, Hampstead, NW3 5NS. Angela Adams. *Nearest tube: Belsize Park. Buses: 46, 268 & C11 all stop nr the hospice.* **Sat 25 June (2-5). Adm £3.50, chd free. Light refreshments.**
This peaceful and secluded two part garden surrounds the Marie Curie Hospice, Hampstead. A garden, tended by dedicated volunteers, makes for a wonderful space for patients to enjoy the shrubs and seasonal colourful flowers. The garden has seating areas for relaxation either in the shade or in the sunshine with great views of the garden and in company with squirrels running through the trees. Step free access to garden and WC.

In 2021 the National Garden Scheme donation helped support Perennial's caseworkers, who helped over 250 people and their families in crisis to receive a wide range of support including emergency food parcels and accommodation, energy payments and expert advice and information

GROUP OPENING

MARKSBURY AVENUE GARDENS, TW9

Richmond, TW9 4JE. *Approx 10 min walk from Kew Gardens tube. Exit westbound platform to North Rd. Take 3rd L into Atwood Ave. Marksbury Ave is 1st R. Buses 190, 419 or R68.* **Sun 12 June (2.30-5.30). Combined adm £7, chd free. Home-made teas in The Barn Church (corner of Marksbury Ave & Atwood Ave).**

26 MARKSBURY AVENUE
Sue Frisby.

34 MARKSBURY AVENUE
Annette Parshotam.

60 MARKSBURY AVENUE
Gay Lyle.

61 MARKSBURY AVENUE
Siobhan McCammon.

62 MARKSBURY AVENUE
Sarah Halaka.

Although of similar size, these five neighbouring gardens are all very different. At No. 26 you will find many NZ natives and fruit trees inc loquat, mulberry and feijoa, alongside a delicate chamomile lawn. No. 34 is a cottage style garden with an emphasis on roses: abundantly cascading over fences, in standard form in beds and rambling amongst other plants. An 'old sink pond' gives shelter to wildlife. No. 60 is a typical town garden where visitors can enjoy a fine display of patio roses, flowering shrubs and climbers, inc over 20 varieties of clematis around a curved lawn. Next door is a family garden, created from scratch in 2018. Opp is a traditional English garden with a touch of wilderness comprising different rooms containing a variety of plants inc hostas and geums. There is a pond with newts while a *Parrotia persica* provides dappled shade for alliums and ferns. All five gardens and The Barn Church, where tea and cake are served, are within 2 mins walk.

36 MELROSE ROAD, SW18
Wandsworth, SW18 1NE. John Tyrwhitt. *¼ m E of A3 Wandsworth. Entrance behind wooden gates is on Viewfield Rd (on corner of Melrose Rd).* **Sun 5 June (2-6). Adm £4.50, chd free. Tea, cake & wine.**
Unusual walled patio garden with

colour and interest Apr through to Oct. Densely planted with roses, architectural plants, shrubs and climbers. Private and not overlooked with backdrop of trees and views. In early June roses, geraniums and geums should be in full flow with acers at their freshest. As summer closes, agapanthus, roses and geraniums are accompanied by exotic cannas and dahlias.

25 MULBERRY WAY, E18
South Woodford, E18 1EB. Mrs Laura Piercy-Farley. *¼m M11, JW. 100 metres from South Woodford Underground Stn (Central line), westbound exit. Cross the pedestrian crossing & turn L. Garden is 100 metres on the R, opp public car park.* **Sun 17 July (2-6). Adm £4, chd free. Light refreshments, home-made cakes, Pimm's & wine.**
A pretty London, Victorian terraced house with a dog friendly Italian patio style garden. The garden has a tranquil white theme with a preference for white hydrangeas. The garden has year-round interest with box hedges, bay trees evergreen shrubs and climbers. There are places to sit, lounge, eat and relax.

NEW 77 MUSWELL ROAD, FLAT 1, N10
Muswell Hill, N10 2BS. Ms Jennifer Granville. *Off Colney Hatch Ln. Highgate tube then 134 or 43 bus to Queens Ave stop; Bounds Green tube then 102 or 144 bus to Roseberry Rd stop; Free on street parking on Muswell Rd.* **Sun 31 July (2-6.30). Adm £4, chd free. Home-made teas. Open nearby 5 St Regis Close.**
A new garden, inspired by the bedtime story 'The Little Green Gate' that opens onto Fairy Land, told to the owner by her grandfather. The garden is comprised of three linked decks, all providing a different mood and experience with a rose arch, wildlife pond and several green gates; you might even catch a glimpse of a fairy. Live music.

THE MYSTERIES OF LIGHT ROSARY GARDEN, NW5
St Dominic's Priory (the Rosary Shrine), Southampton Road, Kentish Town, NW5 4LB. Raffaella Morini on behalf of the

Church & Priory, 07778 526434, garden@raffaellamorini.com. *Entrance to the garden is from Alan Cheales Way on the RHS of the church, next to the school.* **Sat 11 June (1.30-5.30). Adm £4.50, chd free. Home-made teas. Visits also by arrangement Apr to Sept for groups of up to 20.**
A small walled garden behind the Priory Church of Our Lady of the Rosary and St Dominic, commissioned by the Dominican Friars as a spiritual and meditative space representing the 'Mysteries of Light' of the Holy Rosary. The sandstone path marks out a Rosary with black granite beads, surrounded by flowers traditionally associated with the Virgin Mary: roses, lilies, iris, periwinkle, columbine. The garden is fully accessible with a stone path and a wheelchair friendly gravel path.

15 NORCOTT ROAD, N16
Stoke Newington, N16 7BJ. Amanda & John Welch. *Buses: 67, 73, 76, 106, 149, 243, 393, 476, 488. Clapton & Rectory Rd Overground Stns. Be aware of current traffic calming measures.* **Sun 4 Sept (1-5). Adm £3.50, chd free. Home-made teas.**
A large walled garden developed by the present owners over 40 yrs with pond, aged fruit trees and an abundance of herbaceous plants, many available in our plant sale. After last yr's May opening we are going for a more challenging Sept date. We have plenty of room for people to sit, relax and enjoy their tea.

5 NORTHAMPTON PARK, N1
N1 2PP. Andrew Bernhardt & Anne Brogan. *Backing on to St Paul's Shrubbery, Islington. 5 min walk from Canonbury Stn, 10 mins from Highbury & Islington Tube (Victoria Line). Buses: 73, 30, 56, 341, 476.* **Sat 28 May (1-6). Adm £4, chd free. Wine. Open nearby St Paul's Place.**
Early Victorian south facing walled garden (1840s), saved from neglect and developed over the last 28 yrs. Cool North European blues, whites and greys moving to splashes of red and orange Mediterranean influence. The contrast of the cool garden shielded by a small park creates a sense of seclusion from its inner London setting.

21 OAKLEIGH PARK SOUTH, N20

N20 9JS. Carol & Robin Tullo. *Totteridge & Whetstone Underground Stn (Northern Line), 15 min walk or 251 bus. Oakleigh Park Train Stn, 10 min walk. Also buses 34 & 125 from High Rd. Plenty of street parking.* **Sun 22 May (2-6). Adm £4, chd free. Home-made teas.**
A late spring opening. A mature 200ft garden framed by a magnificent 100 yr old ash tree. Path leads to a pond area fed by a natural spring within landscaped terraced paving. Beyond is a herb and vegetable area, orchard with bulbs and wild flowers and the working part of the garden. A mix of sunny borders, pond marginals and woodland shade areas with seating. Level wheelchair access to terrace and lawn. Path to pond area, but raised levels beyond.

THE ORCHARD, W4

40A Hazledene Road, Chiswick, W4 3JB. Vivien Cantor. *10 min walk from Chiswick mainline & Gunnersbury tube. Off Fauconberg Rd. Close to junction of A4 & Sutton Court Rd.* **Sun 8 May (2-5.30). Adm £6, chd free. Home-made teas.**
Informal, romantic ¼ acre garden with mature flowering trees, shrubs and imaginative planting in flowing herbaceous borders. Climbers, fern planting and water features with ponds, a bridge and waterfall in this ever-evolving garden.

ORMELEY LODGE, TW10

Ham Gate Avenue, Richmond, TW10 5HB. Lady Annabel Goldsmith. *From Richmond Park exit at Ham Gate into Ham Gate Ave, 1st house on R. From Richmond A307, after 1½m, past New Inn on R. At T-lights turn L into Ham Gate Ave.* **Sun 3 July (3-6). Adm £5, chd free. Home-made teas.**
Large walled garden in delightful rural setting on Ham Common. Wide herbaceous borders and box hedges. Walk through to orchard with wild flowers. Vegetable garden, knot garden, aviary and chickens. Trellised tennis court with roses and climbers. A number of historic stone family dog memorials. Dogs not permitted.

20 Beechwood Avenue

4 ORMONDE ROAD, HA6

Moor Park, Northwood, HA6 2EL. Hasruty & Yogesh Patel. *Approx 5m from J17 & 18, M25; 6½m from J5, M1. From Batchworth Ln take Wolsey Rd exit at mini r'about. Ormonde Rd is 2nd turning on L. Ample parking on Ormonde Rd & surrounding roads.* **Sun 12 June, Sun 11 Sept (2-5). Adm £6, chd free. Home-made teas.**
Beautifully planted frontage entices visitors to a large rear garden. A calm oasis enclosed by mature hedging. A rare variegated flowering tulip tree provides dappled shade alongside rhododendrons, peonies, magnolias and diverse acers. Lavender hues of phlox foam along the raised patio. Much interest throughout the whole garden due to attention paid to successional planting. New lily pond. There is an area in the garden we are trying to leave alone so it can be rewilded.

The National Garden Scheme searches the length and breadth of England, Channel Islands, Northern Ireland and Wales for the very best private gardens

PADDOCK ALLOTMENTS & LEISURE GARDENS, SW20

51 Heath Drive, Raynes Park, SW20 9BE. Paddock Horticultural Society. *Buses 57, 131, 200 to Raynes Park Stn, then 10 min walk or bus 163. Bus 152 to Bushey Rd, 7 min walk. Bus 413, 5 min walk from Cannon Hill Ln. Street parking.* Sat 25 June (12-5). Adm £4, chd free. Light refreshments.
An allotment site not to be missed, over 150 plots set in 5½ acres. Our tenants come from diverse communities growing a wide range of flowers, fruits and vegetables. Some plots are purely organic, others resemble English country gardens. Winner of London in Bloom Best Allotment on four occasions. Plants and produce for sale. Ploughman's lunch available. Wheelchair access over paved and grass paths, mainly level.

11 PARK AVENUE NORTH, N8

Crouch End, N8 7RU. Mr Steven Buckley & Ms Liz Roberts. *Buses: 144, W3, W7. Underground: Finsbury Park or Turnpike Ln. Train: Hornsey or Alexandra Palace.* Sun 19 June (11.30-5.30). Adm £4, chd

free. Home-made teas.
An award-winning exotic 250ft garden, much developed in 2021. Dramatic foliage, spiky and lush, dominates with the focus on palms, aloes, agaves, dasylirions, aeoniums, tree ferns, nolinas, cycads, bamboos, yuccas, bananas, cacti, puyas and hardy succulents. Trees inc peach, *Cussonia spicata* and Szechuan pepper. Vegetables grow in oak raised beds and a glasshouse.

18 PARK CRESCENT, N3

Finchley, N3 2NJ. Rosie Daniels. *Underground: Finchley Central. Buses: 13 to Victoria Park, also 125, 460, 626, 683. Walk from Ballards Ln into Etchingham Park Rd, 2nd L Park Cres.* Sun 19 June, Sun 24 July (2-6). Adm £5, chd free. Home-made teas.
This charming, constantly evolving 'Secret Garden' is designed and densely planted by Rosie. Tumbling roses and clematis in June, and an extensive collection of clematis and salvias in July. Two very small ponds, tub water features, bird haven. Stepped terrace with lots of pots. Glass installations and sculptures by owner. Have tea for two in newly

created and planted secluded hideaway. Children's treasure hunt, sorry no prizes!

56 PARK ROAD, W4

Chiswick, W4 3HH. Richard Treganowan. *Adjacent to Chiswick House. Chiswick BR: 6 min walk up Park Rd. District Line: Turnham Green, 15 min walk. Buses: E3 & 272 alight Chesterfield Rd, then 4 min walk. Free street parking.* Sun 24 July (2.30-5.30). Adm £5, chd free. Tea.
Screaming exotica from all over the world! Be prepared to be astounded and intrigued by many mature, different and unusual plants not normally encountered in England, all set in a garden approx 40ft x 80ft. Created over 25 yrs by Richard Treganowan and his late wife Diane. Bold and large leaved plants have been introduced which have thrived owing to the creation some yrs ago of a beneficial and effective microclimate and uncompromising attention to soil condition. A mature stumpery provides a sympathetic backdrop to the fern collection.

10 Streatham Common South

© Matthew Bruce

36 PARK VILLAGE EAST, NW1
Camden Town, NW1 7PZ. Christy Rogers. *Tube: Mornington Cres or Camden Town, 7 mins. Opp railway, just S of Mornington St bridge. Free parking all weekend.* **Sun 12 June (2-6). Adm £6, chd free. Home-made teas.**
A large peaceful garden behind a sympathetically modernised John Nash house. Relandscaped in 2014, retaining the original mature sycamores and adding hornbeam hedges dividing a woodland area and orchard from a central large lawn, mixed herbaceous border and rose bank. Children enjoy an artificial grass slide. Musical entertainment is provided by young local musicians. Wheelchair access via grass ramp down from driveway to main garden (steeper than wheelchair regulations).

♿ ⛾ 🏹 •))

174 PECKHAM RYE, SE22
East Dulwich, SE22 9QA. Mr & Mrs Ian Bland. *Stn: Peckham Rye. Buses: 12, 37, 63, 197, 363. Overlooks Peckham Rye Common from Dulwich side.* **Sun 5 June (2.30-5.30). Adm £4.50, chd free. Home-made teas. Donation to St Christopher's Hospice.**
The garden is back after 3 yrs of gentle development in this oasis of calm along Peckham Rye. It is densely planted with a variety of contrasting foliage. Unusual plants with interesting colour and texture combine with old favourites. It is easy care and child friendly. Garden originally designed by Judith Sharpe. Tasty home-made cakes and a great plant sale attracts enthusiasts. Wheelchair access via side alley.

♿ ❄ ⛾ •))

5 PEMBERTON ROAD, KT8
East Molesey, KT8 9LG. Armi Maddison, no5workshops.com. *Please enter the garden down the side path to R of house.* **Sun 12 June (2-5). Adm £4. Light refreshments.**
An artist's sheltered and secluded gravel garden, designed alongside our new build in 2015. Many grasses, pink blue and white planting with occasional 'pops' of bright colour, a galvanised drinking trough with bullrushes and water lilies, a large mature central acer tree, combine with several sitting areas to extend our living space into this fabulous outdoor room. Modern house and artist studio border the garden on

three sides with large sliding doors making the garden our sheltered outside room.

⛾ •))

PETERSHAM HOUSE, TW10
Petersham Road, Petersham, Richmond, TW10 7AA. Francesco & Gael Boglione, www.petershamnurseries.com. *Station: Richmond, bus 65 to Dysart. Entry to garden off Petersham Rd, through Petersham Nurseries. Parking very limited on Church Ln.* **Sun 24 Apr (11-5). Adm £5, chd free. Light refreshments.**
Broad lawn with large topiary and generously planted double borders. Productive vegetable garden with chickens. Adjoins Petersham Nurseries with extensive plant sales, shop and café serving lunch, tea and cake.

🐄 ❄ ⛾

470 PINNER ROAD, HA5
Pinner, HA5 5RR. Nitty Chamcheon, 07582 727645, nittychamcheon@gmail.com. *North Harrow Stn, L to T-lights, L at next T-lights, crossover to Pinner Rd. On L, 3rd house from T-lights. Parking: Pinner Rd & George V Ave, yellow lines stop after 15yds.* **Sun 25 Sept (2-5). Adm £5, chd free. Visits also by arrangement May to Sept for groups of 12+.**
Once (23 yrs ago) a backyard with just a lawn in the first half and the second half a jungle with a very mature apple and pear tree; now a beautiful garden. A path passing through fruit and vegetable garden to the secret log cabin after a bridge over the pond with waterfall in front of a treehouse in the pear tree. An attempt has been made to extend the season as far as possible.

♿ 🐄 ❄ ⛵ ⛾ 🏹 •))

National Garden Scheme gardens are identified by their yellow road signs and posters. You can expect a garden of quality, character and interest, a warm welcome and plenty of home-made cakes!

NEW ### 1A PRIMROSE GARDENS, NW3
Hampstead, NW3 4UJ. Debra Craighead. *Belsize Park. Convenient from Belsize & Chalk Farm Underground Stns (5 mins) or Swiss Cottage (12 mins). Also buses, 168, 268 & C11. Free parking on Suns.* **Sun 17 July (11.30-4.30). Adm £5, chd free. Tea or coffee inc.**
Hidden gem in the heart of Belsize Park, cool and relaxing. Planted with various microclimates owing to surrounding buildings, limited sun and desire for privacy. Mirrors help create sense of intrigue. An oasis of calm, it features grasses, perennial borders and a water feature in a sunny spot while shade loving species reside elsewhere. Bird friendly with a sedum rooftop attracting bees and butterflies. Cakes, desserts and refills for sale.

❄ ⛾ •))

GROUP OPENING

PRINCES AVENUE GARDENS, N10
Muswell Hill, N10 3LS. *Buses: 43 & 134 from Highgate tube; also W7, 102, 144, 234, 299. Princes Ave opp M&S in Muswell Hill Broadway and The Village Green pub in Fortis Green Rd.* **Sun 15 May (12-6). Combined adm £5, chd free. Home-made teas.**

17 PRINCES AVENUE
Patsy Bailey & John Rance.

28 PRINCES AVENUE
Ian & Viv Roberts.

In a beautiful Edwardian avenue in the heart of Muswell Hill Conservation Area, two very different gardens reflect the diverse lifestyles of their owners. The peaceful garden at No. 17 is designed for relaxing and entertaining. Although south facing it is shaded by large surrounding trees, among which is a ginkgo. The garden features a superb hosta and fern display. No. 28 is a well established traditional garden reflecting the charm typical of the era. Mature trees, shrubs, mixed borders and woodland garden creating an oasis of calm just off the bustling broadway. Live music at 17 Princes Avenue by the Secret Life Sax Quartet, from 4.30 to 5.30pm.

♿ 🐄 ❄ ⛾ •))

GROUP OPENING

RAILWAY COTTAGES, N22
2 Dorset Road, Alexandra Palace, N22 7SL. *Underground: Wood Green, 10 min walk. Overground: Alexandra Palace, 3 mins. Buses: W3, 184, 3 mins. Free parking in local streets on Suns.* **Sun 3 July (2-5.30). Combined adm £5, chd free. Home-made teas at 2 Dorset Road.**

2 DORSET ROAD
Jane Stevens.

4 DORSET ROAD
Mark Longworth.

14 DORSET ROAD
Cathy Brogan.

22 DORSET ROAD
Mike & Noreen Ainger.

24A DORSET ROAD
Eddie & Jane Wessman.

A row of historical railway cottages, tucked away from the bustle of Wood Green nr Alexandra Palace, takes the visitor back in time. The tranquil country style garden at 2 Dorset Road flanks three sides of the house. Clipped hedges contrast with climbing roses, clematis, honeysuckle, abutilon, grasses and ferns. Trees inc mulberry, quince, fig, apple and a mature willow creating an interesting shady corner with a pond. There is an emphasis on scented flowers that attract bees and butterflies and the traditional medicinal plants found in cottage gardens. No. 4 is a pretty secluded garden (accessed through the rear of No. 2) and sets off the sculptor owners figurative and abstract work. There are three front gardens open for view. No. 14 is an informal, organic, bee friendly garden, planted with fragrant and useful herbs, flowers and shrubs. No. 22 is nurtured by the grandson of the original railway worker occupant. A lovely place to sit and relax and enjoy the varied planting. No. 24a reverts to the potager style cottage garden with raised beds overflowing with vegetables and flowers. Popular plant sale.

NEW 109 RIDDLESDOWN ROAD, CR8
Purley, CR8 1DH. Mr George Rogai. *Just off Mitchley Ave for visitors by car. Riddlesdown & Purley Stns within a 10 mins, hilly walk. Ample parking is normally available. No parking on grass verges.* **Sat 16, Sun 17 July (2-5). Adm £4, chd free.**
Small front white garden, inspired by classic white gardens. The large, gently sloping back garden has wonderful views of North Downs. It has a lawn with varied borders inc a rose bed, gravel and shady beds and an abundance of colour with dahlias, crocosmia and various shrubs, augmented each yr with annual bedding. An intensively cultivated vegetable area has a wide variety of edibles.

42 RISINGHOLME ROAD, HA3
Harrow, HA3 7ER. Brenda White. *Buses: 258, 340,182,140 Salvatorian College/St. Joseph's Catholic Church, Wealdstone. Tube/train: Harrow & Wealdstone Stn (10 min walk or bus). Road opp the Salvatorian College.* **Sun 15 May, Sun 4 Sept (12-4). Adm £4, chd free. Light refreshments.**
35 metre long, paved, suburban garden divided into different areas inc a Mediterranean themed area, a raised bed vegetable garden, an aviary and summerhouse. Feature plants inc acers, azaleas, camellias, ferns, hydrangeas, rhododendrons, cannas and grasses as well as box hedging and topiary.

NEW 43 RODING ROAD, E5
E5 0DN. Ms Tanya Barrett. *Homerton. 8 min walk from Homerton Overground Stn or buses 236, 276, 308, W15, alight Homerton High St.* **Sun 29 May (2-5.30). Combined adm with 80 Roding Road £6, chd free. Open nearby Lower Clapton Gardens.**
A small west facing Victorian terrace garden with a curved lawn surrounding two mixed borders (one sunny, one shady) of climbers, shrubs, perennials and annuals. Mainly blue, pinks and white inc roses, clematis, salvias and unusual perennial geraniums. Also a patio area with a large number of pots inc scented pelargoniums. A work in progress as only planted 8 yrs ago.

80 RODING ROAD, E5
E5 0DS. Ms Joan Wadge. *8 min walk from Homerton Overground Stn or buses 236, 276, 308, W15, alight Homerton High St.* **Sun 29 May (2-5.30). Combined adm with 43 Roding Road £6, chd free. Cream teas, wine. Open nearby Lower Clapton Gardens.**
A small terraced garden typical in scale to other gardens in this area. It is very much a work in progress. It has a paved area surrounded by mixed borders. The aim is to combine texture with colour and movement. It faces east so the demands of light and shade are the challenge.

ROYAL TRINITY HOSPICE, SW4
30 Clapham Common North Side, SW4 0RN. Royal Trinity Hospice, www.royaltrinityhospice.org.uk. *Tube: Clapham Common. Buses: 35, 37, 345,137 (37 & 137 stop outside).* **Sun 3 Apr, Sun 29 May, Sun 21 Aug (10.30-4.30). Adm £4, chd free. Light refreshments.**
Royal Trinity's beautiful, award-winning gardens play an important therapeutic role in the life and function of Royal Trinity Hospice. Over the yrs, many people have enjoyed our gardens and today they continue to be enjoyed by patients, families and visitors alike. Set over nearly 2 acres, they offer space for quiet contemplation, family fun and make a great backdrop for events. Wheelchair access via ramps and pathways.

NEW 28A ST AUGUSTINE'S ROAD, NW1
Camden Town, NW1 9RN. Ricky Patel, rickypatelfilm@gmail.com. *10-12 min walk from Camden Stn, 15 min walk from Kings Cross Stn, 15 min walk from Caledonian Road Stn.* **Sun 24 July (2-6). Combined adm with 13 Agar Grove, Flat A £5, chd free. Home-made teas. Visits also by arrangement in Sept.**
Step from a wide, quiet street into a tropical paradise! This young garden away from busy Camden is only 4 yrs old, but looking lush and well established thanks to the plants that moved here with the new owner inc bananas, ginger, cannas, tetrapanax and bamboos. A green fingered, self taught plant lover's garden with an emphasis on impressive foliage and interesting texture.

7 Woodbines Avenue

© Matthew Bruce

7 ST GEORGE'S ROAD, TW1
St Margarets, Twickenham, TW1 1QS. Richard & Jenny Raworth, 020 8892 3713, jraworth@gmail.com. *1½m SW of Richmond. Off A316 between Twickenham Bridge & St Margarets r'about.* Visits by arrangement May to July for groups of 10 to 30. Exuberant displays of Old English roses and vigorous climbers with unusual herbaceous perennials. Massed scented *Crambe cordifolia*. Pond with bridge converted into lush bog garden and waterfall. Large north facing luxuriant conservatory with rare plants and climbers. Pelargoniums a specialty. Sunken garden pergola covered with climbing roses and clematis. New white garden. Water feature and fernery. Reading Garden. ♿ ☕

87 ST JOHNS ROAD, E17
Walthamstow, E17 4JH. Andrew Bliss, blisshand@yahoo.co.uk. *15 min walk from Walthamstow Overground/Underground Stn or buses 212 & 275, alight at St Johns Rd stop. 10 min walk from Wood*

St Overground Stn. Very close to N Circular. Sun 24, Mon 25 July (12.30-5). Adm £4, chd £0.50. Home-made teas. Visits also by arrangement. My garden epitomizes what can be achieved with imagination, design and colour consideration in a small, typical terraced outdoor area. Its themes are diverse and inc a fernery, Jardin Majorelle and three individual seating areas. All enhanced with circles, mirrors and over planting to create an atmosphere of tranquillity within an urban environment. ☕))

NEW ST PAUL'S PLACE, N1
Islington, N1 2QE. Mrs Fiona Atkins. *50 metres W & to the N of the junction of St Paul's Rd & Essex Rd in Islington.* Sat 28 May (1-6). Adm £4, chd free. Home-made teas. Open nearby 5 Northampton Park.
The main feature of the walled garden is a pond with natural planting to encourage pollinators and birds. It is a working garden; many of the plants have been grown from seed in the small greenhouse, compost

is made from waste and leaves from surrounding trees and water is collected in water butts for the pond. A large terrace features a white wisteria and container planting inc vegetables. 🐕 ☕))

27 ST PETERS SQUARE, W6
British Grove, W6 9NW. Oliver & Gabrielle Leigh Wood, oliverleighwood@hotmail.com. *Tube to Stamford Brook, exit station & turn S down Goldhawk Rd. At T-lights continue ahead into British Grove. Entrance to garden at 50 British Grove, 100yds on L.* Sun 8 May (2-6). Adm £5, chd free. Home-made teas. Visits also by arrangement Mar to Sept for groups of 10 to 20.
This long, secret space, is a plantsman's eclectic semi-tamed wilderness. Created over the last 12 yrs it contains lots of camellias, magnolias and fruit trees. Much of the hard landscaping is from skips and the whole garden is full of other people's unconsidered trifles of fancy inc a folly and summerhouse.

19 ST PETER'S STREET, N1
N1 8JD. **Adrian Gunning.** *Angel, Islington. Tube: Angel. Bus: Islington Green.* **Evening opening Wed 8 June (6-8). Adm £5, chd free. Wine. Open nearby 25 Arlington Square.**
Charming, secluded town garden with climbing roses, trees, shrubs, climbers, pond, patio with containers and a gazebo with a trompe l'oeil mural.

57 ST QUINTIN AVENUE, W10
W10 6NZ. **Mr H Groffman, 020 8969 8292.** *Less than 1m from Ladbroke Grove or White City Underground Stn. Buses: 7, 70, 220 all to North Pole Rd.* **Sun 3, Sun 17 July (2-5.30). Combined adm with Balfour & Burleigh Kitchen Garden £5, chd free. Home-made teas. Visits also by arrangement July & Aug.**
Award-winning 30ft x 40ft garden with a diverse selection of plants inc shrubs for foliage effects. Patio with colour themed bedding material. Focal points throughout. Clever use of mirrors and plant associations. New look front garden, new rear patio layout, new plantings for 2022 with a good selection of climbers and wall shrubs. This year's special display celebrates H.M. The Queen's Platinum Jubilee.

5 ST REGIS CLOSE, N10
Alexandra Park Road, Muswell Hill, N10 2DE. **Mrs S Bennett & Mr E Hyde, 020 8883 8540, suebearlh@yahoo.co.uk.** *Tube: Bounds Green, then 102 or 299 bus, or East Finchley take 102, alight St Andrews Church. 134 or 43 bus stop at end of Alexandra Park Rd, follow arrows. Parking not restricted. Coaches in side road.* **Sun 1 May, Sun 26 June, Sun 31 July (2-6.30). Adm £4, chd free. Home-made teas, gluten free option & herbal teas. Visits also by arrangement Apr to Oct for groups of 10+. Refreshments on request.**
Cornucopia of sensual delights. Artist's garden famous for architectural features and delicious cakes. Baroque temple, pagodas, Raku tiled mirrored wall conceals plant nursery. American Gothic shed overlooks Liberace Terrace and stairway to heaven. Maureen Lipman's favourite garden; combines colour, humour, trompe l'oeil with wildlife friendly ponds, waterfalls, weeping willow, lawns and abundant planting. A unique experience awaits! Unusual architectural features inc Oriental Tea House overlooking carp pond. Mega plant sale and open studio with ceramics and cards (cash only). Wheelchair access to all parts of garden, unless waterlogged.

9 SHORTGATE, N12
Woodside Park, N12 7JP. **John & Jane Owen, 020 8445 6732, johnjaneowen@gmail.com.** *Bus: 326, alight at the green on Southover, follow signs. Tube: Woodside Park, exit from northbound platform, follow signs. Parking: surrounding roads, not in Shortgate.* **Sun 3 July (1.30-5.30). Combined adm with 11 Shortgate £7, chd free. Home-made teas. Visits also by arrangement June to Aug for groups of 6 to 30. Weekdays only.**
A large, tranquil garden at the end of a quiet cul-de-sac. To avoid using tap water plants are chosen for draught tolerance and watered from 19 water butts. There is a wooded walkway with hidden surprises, a rockery, two small ponds, a vegetable garden, a fruit cage and a herbaceous border where self seeded plants are allowed to mingle.

11 SHORTGATE, N12
North Finchley, N12 7JP. **Jennifer O'Donovan.** *Bus: 326, alight at the green on Southover, follow signs. Tube: Woodside Park, exit from northbound platform, follow signs. Parking: surrounding roads, not in Shortgate.* **Sun 3 July (1.30-5.30). Combined adm with 9 Shortgate £7, chd free. Home-made teas at 9 Shortgate.**
This corner plot is a spacious and elegant garden. It has sunny herbaceous beds, a neat vegetable patch, shade bearing trees with tranquil seating and a greenhouse busy with plants. Developed over 35 yrs, there wasn't even one tree when the owner arrived.

NEW 65 SHRUBLAND ROAD, E8
Hackney, E8 4NL. **Ms Jackie Cahoon.** *Off Queensbridge Rd towards London Fields Park.* **Sun 26 June (2-5). Adm £3.50, chd £1. Cream teas.**
A garden designer's own town garden used for planting, materials, experiments and incorporating three patios, cobbled path, pleached trees, water feature and shade and sun borders. The garden faces north and is overlooked on three sides with large neighbouring trees so its development has been about resolving these challenges and using suitable plants inc shrubs, perennials and annuals.

SILVERWOOD, WD3
London Road, Rickmansworth, WD3 1JR. **Ian & Kumud Gandhi.** *3m from the M25 J18. The property is situated directly opp the Batchworth Park Golf Club on London Rd. Please park at the golf club & walk across the road to the house.* **Sun 26 June (1-5). Adm £6, chd free. Cream teas.**
A well designed wrap around garden of 1 acre backing on to Moor Park Golf Club with beautiful mature oaks dating back 400 yrs and generous borders stocked with a variety of interesting plants. Developed over the last 10 yrs with the addition of many interesting trees and shrubs as well as a herb garden used for medicinal and culinary purposes and three water features. The grounds were formerly part of The Crown Estate used by King Henry VIII for hunting deer at his hunting lodge Moor Park which is now part of the Moor Park Golf Club estate. For wheelchair access only drive into garden and park closest to the side entrance.

SOUTH LONDON BOTANICAL INSTITUTE, SE24
323 Norwood Road, SE24 9AQ. **South London Botanical Institute, www.slbi.org.uk.** *Mainline stn: Tulse Hill. Buses: 68, 196, 322 & 468 stop at junction of Norwood Rd & Romola Rd.* **Sun 24 Apr (2-5). Adm £4, chd free. Home-made teas. Donation to South London Botanical Institute.**
London's smallest botanical garden, densely planted with 500 labelled species grown in themed borders. Spring highlights inc unusual bulbs, ferns and flowering trees. Wild flowers flourish beside medicinal herbs. Carnivorous, scented, native and woodland plants are featured, growing among rare trees and shrubs. Our small cafe will be serving home-made teas.

123 SOUTH PARK ROAD, SW19

SW19 8RX. Susan Adcock.
Mainline & tube: Wimbledon, 10 mins; South Wimbledon tube, 5 mins. Buses: 57, 93, 131, 219 along High St. Entrance in Bridges Rd (next to church hall), off South Park Rd. **Sun 12 June (2-6). Adm £4, chd free. Home-made cake & cordial. Open nearby 97 Arthur Road.**
This small, romantic L-shaped garden has a high treetop deck overlooking a woodland area with a second deck below and small hut. Paving from the garden room with pots and seating, several small water containers, a fish pond and a secluded courtyard with raised beds for flowers and herbs, as well as a discreet hot tub. Lots of ideas for giving a small space atmosphere and interest.

41 SOUTHBROOK ROAD, SE12

Lee, SE12 8LJ. Barbara Polanski, 07818 022983, polanski101@yahoo.co.uk.
Southbrook Rd is situated off S Circular, off Burnt Ash Rd. Train: Lee & Hither Green, both 10 min walk. Bus: P273, 202. Please enter via side access. **Sat 4 June, Sun 12 June (2-6). Adm £4, chd free. Home-made teas. Open nearby 15 Waite Davies Road on 12 June. Visits also by arrangement May to Aug for groups of 10 to 20.**
Developed over 14 yrs, this large garden has a formal layout with wide mixed herbaceous borders full of colour, surrounded by mature trees, framing sunny lawns, a central box parterre and an Indian pergola. Ancient pear trees festooned in June with clouds of white Kiftsgate and Rambling Rector roses. Discover fish and damselflies in two lily ponds. Many sheltered places to sit and relax. Enjoy refreshments in a small classical garden building with interior wall paintings, almost hidden by roses climbing way up into the trees. Orangery, parterre, gazebo and wall fountain. Side access for standard wheelchairs. Gravel driveway and a few steps.

131 SOUTHGATE ROAD, N1

N1 3JZ. John Le Huquet & Vicki Primm-Sexton, john.lehuquet@gmail.com. *E Canonbury. Nearest tube stns Old Street & Angel. Nearest overground stns Canonbury & Dalston Junction (both 10-15 min stroll). Buses 21*
& 141 stop outside (Englefield Rd stop); bus 76 stop 20 yds. **Sun 10 July (12-5). Adm £3.50, chd free. Pre-booking essential, please visit www.ngs.org.uk for information & booking. Light refreshments. Visits also by arrangement in July for groups of up to 6.**
This vivacious tiny walled town garden is densely planted with sun loving perennials, creating an intense visual experience. The lush, naturalistic planting showcases a jamboree of jewel like blooms weaving through softly waving grasses and delicate umbellifers. Commissioned Corten steel wall screens add a contemporary flourish.

SOUTHWOOD LODGE, N6

33 Kingsley Place, Highgate, N6 5EA. Mrs S Whittington, 020 8348 2785, suewhittington@hotmail.co.uk.
Tube: Highgate then 6 min uphill walk along Southwood Ln. 4 min walk from Highgate Village along Southwood Ln. Buses: 143, 210, 214, 271. **Visits by arrangement Apr to July for groups of up to 40. Adm £5, chd free. Home-made teas. Lunch on request for groups of 10+.**
Densely planted garden hidden behind C18 house (not open). Many unusual plants, some propagated for sale. Ponds, waterfall, frogs, toads, newts. Topiary shapes formed from self-sown yew trees. Sculpture carved from three trunks of a massive conifer which became unstable in a storm. Hard working greenhouse!

◆ SPENCER HOUSE, SW1

27 St James' Place, Westminster, SW1A 1NR. RIT Capital Partners, www.spencerhouse.co.uk. *From Green Park Underground Stn, exit on S side, walk down Queen's Walk, turn L through narrow alleyway. Turn R & Spencer House will be in front of you.* **For opening times and information, please visit garden website.**
Originally designed in the C18 by Henry Holland (son-in-law to Lancelot 'Capability' Brown), the garden was among the grandest in the West End. Restored since 1990 under the Chairmanship of Lord Rothschild, the garden with a delightful view of the adjacent Royal Park, now evokes its original layout with planting suggested by early C19 nursery lists.

GROUP OPENING

SPITALFIELDS GARDENS, E1

E1 6QE. *Nr Spitalfields Market. 10 min walk from Aldgate East Tube & 5 min walk from Liverpool St Stn. Overground: Shoreditch High St, 3 min walk.* **Sat 11 June (10-4). Combined adm £15, chd free. Home-made teas at Town House (5 Fournier Street), 29 Fournier Street & 31 Fournier Street.**

20 FOURNIER STREET
Ms Charlie de Wet.

29 FOURNIER STREET
Juliette Larthe.

31 FOURNIER STREET
Tom Holmes.

21 PRINCELET STREET
Marianne & Nicholas Morse.

37 SPITAL SQUARE
Society for the Protection of Ancient Buildings, www.spab.org.uk.

21 WILKES STREET
Rupert Wheeler.

Discover a selection of courtyard gardens, some very small, behind fine C17 French Huguenots merchants' and weavers' houses in Spitalfields. Experience an architect designed garden in Wilkes St, two small courtyards in Fournier St, and a larger imaginatively created garden in Princelet St. Each garden owner has adapted their particular urban space to complement a historic house: vegetables, herbs, vertical and horizontal beds, ornamental pots, statuary and architectural artefacts abound. Plants for sale at SPAB, Spitalfields Square.

During 2020 – 2021 National Garden Scheme funding supported over 1,400 Queen's Nurses to deliver virtual and hands-on, community care across England, Wales and Northern Ireland

28A Worcester Road

© Matthew Bruce

25 SPRINGFIELD AVENUE, N10
Muswell Hill, N10 3SU. Heather
Hampson & Nigel Ragg. *From main
r'about in Muswell Hill, go down
Muswell Hill descending towards
Crouch End. Springfield Ave is 1st on
L.* **Sun 11 Sept (2-6). Adm £4, chd
free. Home-made teas.**
A mystical and secluded garden
packed with take home ideas. Spread
over three atmospheric terraces up to
a backdrop of the trees of Alexandra
Palace. Travel through perennial
planted beds shaded by the old
apple tree. The middle terrace is lawn
surrounded by shrubs and climbers.
The south facing paved terrace
has sunny flower beds, tub water
features and pots. A garden full of
surprises for a small city garden, from
the secluded setting to the sense of
journey. The traditional summerhouse
is somewhere to rest and view the
owners art works which are for sale in
aid of the NGS.
🐕 ❀ ☕ ⦿)

NEW **106 STATION ROAD, TW12**
Hampton, TW12 2AS. Diane
Kermack. *Coming from Hampton
Stn, turn L along Station Rd, past St
Theodore's Church, opp the green.
Access to garden is via the garden*
gate on the adjacent side road
Station Close. **Sat 30, Sun 31 July
(11-5). Adm £4, chd free. Light
refreshments.**
An apiary garden with six busy hives
which will be of special interest to
bee-keepers. Bushy front garden with
vegetable plot and perimeter flower
bed.Walk through past swimming
pool, greenhouses, seating and many
pots. Informal back garden featuring
many beehives. Pond, chickens and
informal flower beds.
❀ ☕ ⦿)

STOKES HOUSE, TW10
Ham Street, Ham, Richmond,
TW10 7HR. Peter & Rachel
Lipscomb, 020 8940 2403,
rlipscomb@virginmedia.com. *2m
S of Richmond off A307. Trains &
tube to Richmond & train to Kingston
which links with the 65 bus, stopping
at Ham Common every 6 mins.*
**Sun 29 May (2-5). Adm £4, chd
£2. Home-made teas. Visits also
by arrangement Apr to Sept for
groups of 10 to 30.**
Originally an orchard, this ½ acre
walled country garden surrounding
Georgian house (not open) is
abundant with roses, clematis
and perennials. There are mature

trees inc ancient mulberries and
wisteria. The yew hedging, pergola
and box hedges allow for different
planting schemes throughout the yr.
Herbaceous borders, brick garden,
wild garden, large compost area and
interesting trees. Teas, garden tour,
history of house and area for group
visits. Wheelchair access via double
doors from street with two wide
steps. Sorry, no access for larger
motorised chairs.
&. 🐕 ❀ ☕ ⦿)

STONEY HILL HOUSE, SE26
Rock Hill, SE26 6SW. Cinzia &
Adam Greaves. *Off Sydenham
Hill. Nearest train stns: Sydenham,
Gipsy Hill or Sydenham Hill. Buses:
To Crystal Palace, 202 or 363
along Sydenham Hill. House at end
of cul-de-sac on L coming from
Sydenham Hill.* **Sun 15 May (2-6).
Adm £6.50, chd free. Home-made
teas. Prosecco. Open nearby 86
Underhill Road.**
Garden and woodland of approx
1 acre providing a secluded secret
green oasis in the city. Paths meander
through mature rhododendron, oak,
yew and holly trees, offset by pieces
of contemporary sculpture. The
garden is on a slope and a number

of viewpoints set at different heights provide varied perspectives. The planting in the top part of the garden is fluid and flows seamlessly into the woodland. Swings and woodland treehouse for entertainment of children and adults alike! Fresalca, a wonderful saxophone quartet, will be playing for the afternoon. Wheelchair access to garden via shallow steps or grassy slope.

10 STREATHAM COMMON SOUTH, SW16

SW16 3BT. Lindy & Mark Cunniffe. *By Streatham Common. Two nearby train stns, Streatham & Streatham Common both about 10 min walk. Buses from Brixton inc 250,109,159, 118 & 133. Free parking in the area.* **Sat 4 June, Sun 28 Aug (2-6). Adm £5, chd free. Light refreshments.** This large south facing garden is organised into naturally separated spaces with many seating areas. There are winding paths, greenhouse, woodland area, traditional lawn, small wildlife area and many trees such as ash, willow and mulberry. The Chinese inspired garden gives a modern twist. There is a small and tranquil sunken garden with koi pond and seating as well as an award-winning front garden.

SWAKELEYS COTTAGE, 2 THE AVENUE, UB10

Ickenham, Uxbridge, UB10 8NP. Lady Singleton Booth. *Take B466 to Ickenham from A40 at Hillingdon Circus. Go 1m into Ickenham village. Coach & Horses pub on R, turn L into Swakeley's Rd. After the shops, 2 The Ave is on L.* **Sun 10 July (2-5). Adm £4, chd free. Home-made teas.** Classic English cottage garden designed by Lady Booth and her late husband Sir Christopher Booth. The garden is charming and wraps around a 600 yr old cottage (not open). It consists of herbaceous borders which are dotted with vegetables, garden herbs and fruit trees. There is an abundance of colour and some very interesting plants incorporating different styles.

93 TANFIELD AVENUE, NW2

Dudden Hill, NW2 7SB. Mr James Duncan Mattoon, 020 8830 7410. *Nearest station: Neasden (Jubilee*

line), then 10 min walk; or various bus routes to Neasden Parade or Tanfield Ave. **Sun 31 July (2-6). Adm £5, chd free. Home-made teas. Visits also by arrangement May to Oct for groups of up to 15.** Intensely exotic Mediterranean and subtropical paradise garden! Sunny deck with implausible planting and panoramic views of Harrow and Wembley, plunges into incredibly exotic, densely planted oasis of delight, with two further seating areas engulfed by flowers, such as, acacia, colocasia, eryngium, hedychium, plumbago, salvias and hundreds more in vigorous competition! Birds and bees love it! Previous garden was Tropical Kensal Rise (Doyle Gardens), featured on BBC 2 Open Gardens and in Sunday Telegraph. Steep steps down to main garden.

TEMPLE LODGE CLUB, W6

51 Queen Caroline Street, Hammersmith, W6 9QL. The Rev. Peter van Breda, 020 8748 8388, Booking@templelodgeclub.com, templelodgeclub.com/about-us/#history. *Queen Caroline St is opp Broadway Shopping Centre which contains tube & bus stns. Piccadilly, District & Hammersmith & City lines. Buses: 9, 10, 27, 33, 419, 72, H91, 190, 211, 220, 267, 283, 295, 391, Fulham Palace Rd exit. Temple Lodge entrance is via Gate Restaurant Courty.* **Sat 10 Sept (11-5). Adm £5. Light refreshments.** Artist Sir Frank Brangwyn's former home, studio and walled garden. Temple Lodge is an oasis in the heart of London. Perennials and grasses with long seasons of interest provide changing colour, movement and structure throughout the yr. Old carved stone unearthed and set aside during recent garden renovations are repurposed and are on display. Explore to the rhythmic sound of the flow form water feature. Temple Lodge Club is also a thriving and unique guesthouse and has a vegetarian restaurant (booking recommended).

NEW 6 THORNHILL ROAD, N1

Islington, N1 1HW. Janis Higgie, 020 7609 0277, Janisjhiggie@gmail.com. *Barnsbury. Tube: Angel or Highbury & Islington. Overground: Caledonian & Barnsbury. Bus: to Liverpool Rd.* **Sun 26 June (12-5). Adm £4, chd**

free. Light refreshments. Visits also by arrangement June to Sept for groups of up to 25. 150ft Islington garden, designed and planted over the last 30 yrs. This fully accessible family garden draws inspiration from the owner's antipodean roots. A brick path guides visitors past lawns, raised beds, a water feature, fire bowl and a creative mix of plants from around the globe (inc kowhai and *Hoheria* trees with many shade tolerant plants). This garden has a lot; even the kitchen sink! Completely wheelchair friendly.

NEW TORRIANO COMMUNITY GARDEN, NW5

Torriano Avenue, NW5 2ST. Mrs Elisa Puentes, 07952 345562, elisa_puentes@icloud.com. *Kentish Town. Overground/Rail: Camden. 10 min walk along Camden Rd to Torriano Ave. Buses: 29, 253. Walk along Torriano Ave & garden is on R opp the Primary School.* **Sun 19 June (2-6). Adm £4, chd free. Home-made teas. Visits also by arrangement in June.** This beautiful 1 acre community garden, designed and built in 2003 by the residents helped by the Army, has amazing features with a variety of flowers. The design of the flower beds have the numbers 2003. This beautiful space is fully wheelchair accessible and open for all to enjoy even if you do not live on the estate. Our garden is maintained and cleaned by residents and is open all year-round.

31 TRELAWN ROAD, SW2

SW2 1DH. Mr M Simmons & Mr D Waddock. *From Brixton Underground Stn, turn L along Effra Rd towards Sainsbury's. Walk past Halfords & Trelawn Rd 2nd road on L. Buses 2, 3, 37, 196, 415.* **Sun 29 May (1-5). Adm £4, chd free. Home-made teas inc gluten free & vegan options.** A small city garden, only 6 yrs old, designed to give the illusion of space, with a winding path and hidden vistas. Crammed with plants, dominated by perennials, roses and exotics. There is no lawn, but several seating areas from which to contemplate the space.

🆕 9 TRINITY RISE, SW2
Brixton, SW2 2QP. Rupert & Monika Linton. *Nr Brockwell Park. Easily accessible from both Herne Hill & Tulse Hill Train Stns & on buses 2, 3, 196, 415, 322, 37 from Brixton Underground Stn.* **Sat 2, Sun 3 Apr (11-3). Adm £4.50, chd free.**
A country garden in South London with a beautiful display of white blossoms on the magnificent magnolia and amelanchiers, dotted about with early spring bulbs. The garden is naturalistic and a bit wild at the edges with the intention of encouraging insects. There is an overgrown stumpery, a pond under construction and a large green roof which is best in summer. Vegetable plot. Quince jam for sale made from the tree in the back garden.
🐾 ✿ ›))

🆕 TUDELEY HOUSE, BR7
Royal Parade, Chislehurst, BR7 6NW. Mrs Bernadette & Mr Colin Katchoff. *1m from the A20 at J3 of M25. A 20 min walk from Chislehurst Stn, or short bus ride. Buses 61, 160, 161,162, 269 & 273 to Chislehurst War Memorial. Limited parking in side roads.* **Sun 4 Sept (11-4.30). Adm £4. Light refreshments.**
The layout of this Victorian town house garden has remained as shown in the original architect's plans of 1896. The current owners have recently restored the house; employing Jo Thompson, an RHS Chelsea Gold winner, to bring the garden up to date, whilst remaining sympathetic to a Victorian era town garden. Phase one of the three sections being restored is complete. Phase two is under construction. The garden is 95% flat. Some older paths (25% of garden) are narrow, so may be difficult for large mobility scooters.
♿ ☕ ›))

TUDOR HERBALIST GARDEN, NW3
37 Christchurch Hill, Hampstead, NW3 1LA. Paul & Hazelanne Lewis. *7 mins from Hampstead Underground Stn, exit L, then L into Flask Walk, continue to Christchurch Hill & R to No. 37. 10 mins from Hampstead Heath Overground Stn, walk uphill bearing L onto South End Rd & Willow Rd at Horse Trough.* **Sun 3 July (1.30-5). Adm £5, chd free. Home-made teas & homegrown herbal teas.**

A narrow, informal garden with a south west aspect, developed to meet the requirements of a Tudor Herbalist re-enactor. The garden is on four levels. The first level is predominantly flower beds with herbs being introduced progressively on the second and third levels. The informal layout means that herbs mix with plants and clematis climb over other plants.
☕ ›))

24 TWYFORD AVENUE, N2
East Finchley, N2 9NJ. Rachel Lindsay & Jeremy Pratt, 07930 632902, jeremypr@blueyonder.co.uk. *Twyford Ave runs parallel to Fortis Green, between East Finchley & Muswell Hill. Tube: Northern line to East Finchley. Buses: 102, 143, 234, 263 to East Finchley. Buses 43, 134, 144, 234 to Muswell Hill. Buses 102 & 234 stop at end of road. Garden signed from Fortis Green.* **Sun 17 July (2-6). Adm £4, chd free. Home-made teas. Visits also by arrangement May to Sept.**
Sunny, 120ft south facing garden, planted for colour. Brick edged borders and overflowing containers packed with masses of traditional herbaceous and perennial cottage garden plants and shrubs. Shady area at rear evolving as much by happy accident as design. Some uneven ground. Water feature. Greenhouse bursting with cuttings. Many places to sit and think, chat or doze. Honey and bee products for sale.
🐾 ✿ ☕ ›))

45 UNDERHILL ROAD, SE22
East Dulwich, SE22 0QZ. Nicola Bees. *Approx 200 metres from Lordship Ln. Train: Forest Hill, 20 min walk. Buses: P13, P4, 63, 176, 185, 197, 363. Car: Off A205 nr junction with Lordship Ln. Free parking.* **Sun 17 July (2-5.30). Adm £4.50, chd free. Home-made teas.**
A restored Victorian garden of tamed disorder with a few modern twists. In summer the flower beds are packed with a variety of perennials with hosts of clematis among the border flowers and hydrangea walk. An elegant corner summerhouse-come-shed provides a tranquil retreat at the bottom of the garden. Teas served in our conservatory tea room come rain or shine. Wheelchair access with three deep steps into the garden and gravel paths.
♿ ☕ ›))

86 UNDERHILL ROAD, SE22
East Dulwich, SE22 0QU. Claire & Rob Goldie. *Between Langton Rise & Melford Rd. Stn: Forest Hill. Buses: P13, 363, 63, 176, 185 & P4.* **Sun 15 May (2-6). Adm £4.50, chd free. Home-made teas. Open nearby Stoney Hill House.**
A generous family garden packed with spring bulbs. The elegant slate terrace leads to a hot gravel area flanked by a small greenhouse and a living willow arbour, the perfect spot for a cuppa and a slice of delicious cake before winding your way down to the cooler part of the garden and the summerhouse. Vegetables and herbs are dotted throughout. Children and the young at heart can join the treasure trail.
✿ ☕ ›))

VICTORIA LODGE, E18
Hermitage Walk, Snaresbrook, E18 2BN. Lucy St Ville. *7 min walk from Snaresbrook Stn (Central line).* **Sat 25 June (2-5). Adm £3, chd £1. Home-made teas.**
Enter this large London garden through a reclaimed iron pergola, past a colourful mixed bed to a relaxed fire pit. Next to a small rill created from cattle troughs, planted with irises and ferns, which leads to a walkway cut through mature rhododendrons. At the far end, sheltered by a high Victorian wall, is a wildlife garden inc a pond, bee friendly planting and secluded seating area. Most of the garden is accessible with gravel, brick and grass paths.
♿ ☕ ›))

152A VICTORIA RISE, SW4
Clapham, SW4 0NW. Benn Storey, bennstorey@gmail.com. *Entry via basement flat. Closest tube Clapham Common.* **Sun 26 June, Sun 4 Sept (1-5). Adm £4.50, chd free. Visits also by arrangement for groups of up to 10.**
In its 6th yr this terraced garden is 21 metres long by 8 metres wide. Planting ranges from the lush greens of the courtyard to the frothy, bee friendly plants of the main level to the espalier fruit trees and vegetables of the productive levels. A copper beech hedge hides a cozy arbour seat and fire pit at the top of the plot out of view from surrounding neighbours.
›))

9 VIEW ROAD, N6
Highgate, N6 4DJ. Paul & Sophia Davison. *9 min walk (½ m) from Highgate Tube. Buses: 134, 43, 263 to Highgate Tube, 143 to North Hill. View Rd is a turning off North Hill. Please enter garden via path to LHS of house.* Sat 14 May (2-5). Adm £4, chd free. Home-made teas.
A well-stocked, informally planted front garden leads to a generous rear garden which has been lovingly coaxed back from its wild, overgrown state by the current owners. Large lawn, beautiful hornbeam hedge spanning the garden, mature trees (inc handkerchief trees), bulbs and perennials. Fruit trees, grasses, raised beds, plus a beautiful greenhouse. A garden which continues to evolve. Wheelchair access to front and terrace part of rear garden. Steps down to lawn and some uneven paths.

13 WAITE DAVIES ROAD, SE12
Lee, SE12 0NE. Janet Pugh. *Lee Train Stn, 11 min walk. Hither Green & Grove Park Stns, 20 min walk. Bus route 261 stops close. Buses 202 & 160 stop nearby. Usually free roadside parking.* Sun 12 June (2-5.30). Combined adm with 15 Waite Davies Road £4.50, chd free. Home-made teas. Open nearby 41 Southbrook Road.
A colourful and welcoming front garden leads you to a bright and peaceful, private maturing garden. The gentle sound of a discreet water feature provides a calming atmosphere with attractive planting in colours of pinks, purples and creams.

15 WAITE DAVIES ROAD, SE12
Lee, SE12 0NE. Will Jennings. *Lee Train Stn, 11 min walk. Hither Green & Grove Park Stns, 20 min walk. Bus route 261 stops close. Buses 202 & 160 stop nearby. Usually free roadside parking.* Sun 12 June (2-5.30). Combined adm with 13 Waite Davies Road £4.50, chd free. Light refreshments. Open nearby 41 Southbrook Road.
Hidden behind a Victorian terrace is a tiny yet immaculately presented English garden. A huge Malvern Hills rambling rose gently billows over a willow-coloured shed, foxgloves spring up beneath a young crab apple and tightly clipped box hedging frames the scene. Nearby, the soft pink, myrrh-scented flowers

of climbing rose 'The Generous Gardener' nod gracefully above a small, sunbaked stone patio.

9 WARWICK CLOSE, TW12
Hampton, TW12 2TY. Chris Churchman. *2m W of Twickehman, 2m N of Hampton Court, overlooking Bushy Park. 100 metres from Hampton Open Air Swimming Pool.* Sun 14 Aug (10.30-5). Adm £3.50, chd free. Home-made teas.
A small suburban garden in South West London. Front garden with espaliered trees featuring roses, lavender and stipa. Shade garden with rare ferns and herbaceous. Rear garden has a simple rectangular lawn with prairie style plantings crossed with subtropical species. Roof top allotment to garage (the garotment).

THE WATERGARDENS, KT2
Warren Road, Kingston-upon-Thames, KT2 7LF. The Residents' Association. *1m E of Kingston. From Kingston take A308 (Kingston Hill) towards London; after approx ½m turn R into Warren Rd. No. 57 bus along Coombe Lane West, alight at Warren Rd. Roadside parking only.* Sun 24 Apr, Sun 16 Oct (1.30-4). Adm £5, chd free.
Japanese landscaped garden originally part of Coombe Wood Nursery, planted by the Veitch family in the 1860s. Approx 9 acres with ponds, streams and waterfalls. Many rare trees, which in spring and autumn provide stunning colour. For the tree lover this is a must see garden. Gardens attractive to wildlife. Major renovation and restoration has taken place over the past yr revealing a hitherto lost lake and waterfall. Restoration work at the garden is ongoing.

GROUP OPENING

WENSLEYDALE ROAD GARDENS, HAMPTON, TW12
Wensleydale Road, Hampton, TW12 2LX. *For SatNav use TW12 2LX.* Sat 4 June (12-5). Combined adm £5, chd free. Tea at Parke House.

PARKE HOUSE
Mr Mike & Mrs Andrea Harris.

68 WENSLEYDALE ROAD
Julie Melotte.

70 WENSLEYDALE ROAD
Mr Steve Pickering.

Three suburban gardens, all different. No. 68 is a charming garden with abundant and colourful planting and interesting found objects. A round lawn with roses and evergreen borders, leading to wildlife pond and bog garden. No. 70 is a traditional garden with classic layout. Greenhouse, summerhouse, pergola and a rockery. Parke House at No. 74 is a large traditional garden laid to lawn. Mixed flower borders and shrubs. Feature ginkgo tree. Wheelchair access to No. 70 and No. 74 only.

WEST LODGE PARK, EN4
Cockfosters Road, Hadley Wood, EN4 0PY. Beales Hotels, 020 8216 3904, headoffice@bealeshotels.co.uk, www.bealeshotels.co.uk/westlodgepark/. *1m S of Potters Bar. On A111. J24 from M25 signed Cockfosters.* Sun 15 May (2-5); Sun 30 Oct (1-4). Adm £6, chd free. Light refreshments. **Visits also by arrangement Apr to Oct for groups of 10+.**
Open for the NGS for over 30 yrs, the 35 acre Beale Arboretum consists of over 800 varieties of trees and shrubs inc National Collection of Hornbeam cultivars (*Carpinus betulus*) and National Collection of Swamp Cypress (*Taxodium distichum*). Network of paths through good selection of conifers, oaks, maples and mountain ash, all specimens labelled. Beehives and two ponds. Stunning collection within the M25. Guided tours available. Breakfasts, morning coffee and biscuits, restaurant lunches, light lunches, dinner all served in the hotel. Please see website for details.

In 2021 the National Garden Scheme donated £500,000 to Marie Curie enabling us to continue providing our vital services and be there, caring for people on the frontline of the Coronavirus pandemic

12 WESTERN ROAD, E13

Plaistow, E13 9JF. Elaine Fieldhouse. *Nearest stn: Upton Park, 3 min walk. Buses: 58, 104, 330, 376. No parking restrictions on Suns.* **Sun 5 June (1-5). Adm £4, chd free. Home-made teas. Gluten free & vegan options.**
Urban oasis, 85ft garden designed and planted by owners. Relying heavily on evergreen, ferns, foliage and herbaceous planting. Rear of garden leads directly onto a 110ft allotment with half allotment adjoining it; part allotment, part extension of the garden featuring topiary, medlar tree, mulberry tree, two ponds, small fruit trees, raised beds and small iris collection.

33 WEYMAN ROAD, SE3

Blackheath, SE3 8RY. Kevin & Cosetta Lawlor. *Weyman Rd is off Shooters Hill Rd. Stns: Kidbrooke or Blackheath. Bus: 178 from Kidbrooke Stn, 89 from Blackheath Stn, 386 from Greenwich. Free parking in Weyman Rd.* **Sun 26 June (12-6). Adm £5, chd free. Home-made teas. Sangria, beer & wine.**
A small but immaculate garden, that is as pretty as a picture in a wonderfully colour coordinated mélange of pinks, whites, purples and blues. Divided into rooms to entice the visitor on, this is a couples' joint effort with hard and soft landscaping that offers unexpected delights round every corner. The garden finishes with a stunning display of succulents and an alpine rockery and waterfall.

74 WILLIFIELD WAY, NW11

NW11 6YJ. David Weinberg, 07956 579205, davidwayne@hotmail.co.uk. *Hampstead Garden Suburb. H2 bus from Golders Green will stop outside or take the 102, 13 or 460 to Hampstead Way & walk up Asmuns Hill & turn R.* **Sun 3 July (1.30-5.30). Adm £5, chd free. Cream teas. Visits also by arrangement May to Sept.**
A very peaceful, traditional English country cottage garden. Borders full of herbaceous perennials and hydrangeas with a central rose bed surrounded by a box parterre with plenty of space to sit and take it all in and enjoy afternoon tea. Wheelchair access to patio area only.

61 WOLSEY ROAD, KT8

East Molesey, KT8 9EW. Jan & Ken Heath. *Less than 10 min walk from Hampton Court Palace & station, very easy to find.* **Sun 5 June (2-6). Adm £5, chd free. Tea, coffee, cakes & wine.**
Romantic, secluded and peaceful garden of two halves designed and maintained by the owners. Part is shaded by two large copper beech trees with woodland planting. The second reached through a beech arch with cottage garden planting, pond and wooden obelisks covered with roses. Beautiful octagonal gazebo overlooks pond, plus an oak framed summerhouse designed and built by the owners. Extensive seating throughout the garden to sit quietly and enjoy your tea and cake.

WOLVES LANE HORTICULTURAL CENTRE, N22

Wolves Lane, N22 5JD. Ms Denise Farrell, Site Manager, www.wolveslaneflowercompany.com. *Wood Green. Situated nearest the corner of Woodside Rd & Wolves Ln. Please use the name of the centre to search on Google Maps rather than the postcode.* **Sat 17 Sept (11-3). Adm £5, chd free.**
Wolves Lane, an old horticultural site, a thriving space for sustainable growing, education and community engagement. The $3\frac{1}{2}$ acre site is a complex of 1970s glasshouses and external plots, everything grown organically without chemicals or pesticides. WLFC, a micro urban flower farm, has a 40 metre glasshouse and outside plots. Also on site are Edible London, OrganicLea, Black Rootz and Crop Drop. The centre has a palm house and cacti house. Edible London, Crop Drop and BlackRootz welcome visitors to explain what they grow and why. Free children's activities: Under 5s: 11am-12:30pm, Over 5s: 12pm-2pm. Level access within centre and wheelchair accessible WC. Some of the external site is on a slope and has steps.

33 WOOD VALE, N10

Highgate, N10 3DJ. Mona Abboud, 020 8883 4955, monaabboud@hotmail.com, www.monasgarden.co.uk. *Tube: Highgate, 10 min walk. Buses: W3, W7 to top of Park Rd.* **Sun 17 Apr (1-5). Adm £4, chd free. Light refreshments. Visits also**

by arrangement Apr to Sept for groups of 5+. Donation to Plant Heritage.
This 100 metre long award-winning garden is home to the National Collection of Corokia along with a great number of other unusual Australasian, Mediterranean and exotic plants complemented by perennials and grasses which thrive thanks to 300 tons of topsoil, gravel and compost brought in by wheelbarrow. Emphasis on structure, texture, foliage and shapes brought alive by distinctive pruning. Visit website for more information.

39 WOOD VALE, SE23

Forest Hill, SE23 3DS. Nigel Crawley. *Entrance through Thistle Gates, 48 Melford Rd. Train & overground stns: Forest Hill & Honor Oak. Victoria Stn to West Dulwich, then P4. Buses: 363 Elephant & Castle to Wood Vale/Melford Rd; 176, 185 & 197 to Lordship Ln/ Wood Vale.* **Sun 10 Apr (1-5). Adm £4.50, chd free. Home-made teas. Evening opening Wed 13 Apr (5-7). Adm £6, chd free. Wine.**
Diverse garden dominated by a gigantic perry pear forming part of one of the East Dulwich orchards. The emphasis in the garden is on its inhabitants; white comfrey and pear blossom keeps the bees busy in the spring. Home to a variety of birds inc green woodpecker, dunnock and redwing. The clumps of narcissi around the old apple tree are a sight to see. Surprising green oasis in Forest Hill. Close to Sydenham Woods, Horniman Gardens and Camberwell Old Cemetery. Level wheelchair access, but rough terrain in the lane.

7 WOODBINES AVENUE, KT1

Kingston-upon-Thames, KT1 2AZ. Mr Tony Sharples & Mr Paul Cuthbert. *Take K2, K3, 71 or 281 bus. From Surbiton, bus stop outside Waitrose & exit bus Kingston University Stop. From Kingston, walk or bus from Eden St (opp Heals).* **Sun 24 Apr (12-5). Adm £4, chd free. Sun 17 July (12-5). Combined adm with 15 Catherine Road £7, chd free. Home-made teas. Open nearby 52A Berrylands Road on 17 July.**
We have created a winding path through our 70ft garden with trees,

evergreen structure, perennial flowers and grasses. We are also opening early in 2022 for the tulip season where we plant up at least 30 pots around the garden and also, later in July when the garden becomes our summer paradise.

NEW **28A WORCESTER ROAD, E17**
Walthamstow, E17 5QR. Mark & Emma Luggie, 07970 920019, pipinleshrew@hotmail.com. *12 min walk from Blackhorse Road Underground Stn. Just off Blackhorse Ln. On street parking.* **Sun 14 Aug (11-6). Adm £4, chd free. Pre-booking essential, please visit www.ngs.org.uk for information & booking. Visits also by arrangement Aug & Sept for groups of up to 10.**
Typical Walthamstow terraced back garden, turned into a lush tropical

oasis of foliage with a small stream and pond. Small and large leaves mix with floral accents and varying leaf textures from ferns, colocasia and bananas supported by a framework of larger established trees, jasmine, and tree ferns. A small gravel path leads you to a small seating area to reflect, or sit on the patio and enjoy.

1 YORK CLOSE, W7
Hanwell, W7 3JB. Tony Hulme & Eddy Fergusson. *By road only, entrance to York Close via Church Rd. Nearest stn Hanwell mainline.* **Buses E3, 195, 207. Sat 20, Sun 21 Aug (2-6). Adm £7, chd free. Wine.**
Tiny, quirky, prize-winning garden extensively planted with eclectic mix inc hosta collection, many unusual and tropical plants. Plantaholics paradise. Many surprises in this unique and very personal garden.

ZEN GARDEN AT JAPANESE BUDDHIST CENTRE, W3
Three Wheels, 55 Carbery Avenue, Acton, W3 9AB. Reverend Prof K T Sato, www.threewheels.org.uk. *Tube: Acton Town, 5 min walk. 200yds off A406.* **Sat 4, Sun 5, Sat 18, Sun 19 June (2-5). Adm £3.50, chd free. Matcha tea ceremony £3.**
Pure Japanese Zen garden (so no flowers) with 12 large and small rocks of various colours and textures set in islands of moss and surrounded by a sea of grey granite gravel raked in a stylised wave pattern. Garden surrounded by trees and bushes outside a cob wall. Oak framed wattle and daub shelter with Norfolk reed thatched roof. Talk on the Zen garden between 3-4pm. Buddha Room open to public.

6 Church Walk

NORFOLK

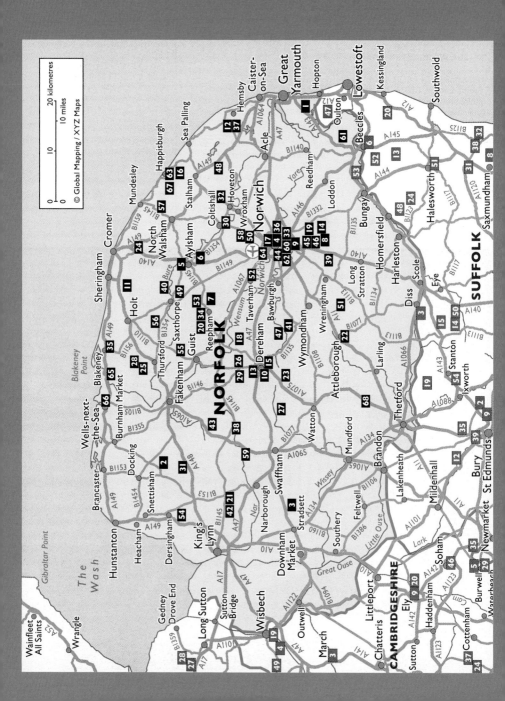

Norfolk is a lovely low-lying county, predominantly agricultural with an abundance of wildlife and a beautiful coastline.

Visitors come here because they are attracted not only to the peaceful and spacious countryside, but also to the medieval churches and historical houses. There is an extensive coastal footpath and a large network of rivers, together with the waterways of the Norfolk Broads. Norwich the capital is a fine city.

We are fortunate to have a loyal group of garden owners; Sandringham was one of the original gardens to open for the scheme in 1927 and has been supporting us continuously ever since.

Whilst many of our gardens have opened their gates for over half a century, others will be opening for the very first time. Located throughout the county, they range from those of the large estates and manor houses, to the smaller cottages, courtyards and town gardens, accommodating different styles of old and traditional, newly constructed and contemporary, designed and naturalistic.

So why not come and experience for yourself the county's rich tapestry of big skies, open countryside, attractive architecture and delightful gardens.

Below: Hoe Hall

Volunteers

County Organiser
Julia Stafford Allen
01760 755334
julia.staffordallen@ngs.org.uk

County Treasurer
Andrew Stephens OBE
07595 939769
andrew.stephens@ngs.org.uk

Publicity
Carol Allen 07368 238528
carol.allen@ngs.org.uk

Social Media
Kenny Higgs 07791 429052
kenny.higgs@ngs.org.uk

Photographer
Simon Smith 01362 860530
simon.smith@ngs.org.uk

Booklet Co-ordinator
Juliet Collier 07986 607170
juliet.collier@ngs.org.uk

New Gardens Organiser
Fiona Black 01692 650247
fiona.black@ngs.org.uk

Assistant County Organisers
Jenny Clarke 01508 550261
jenny.clarke@ngs.org.uk

Nick Collier 07733 108443
nick.collier@ngs.org.uk

Sue Guest 01362 858317
guest63@btinternet.com

Sue Roe 01603 455917
sueroe8@icloud.com

Retty Wace 07876 648543
retty.wace@ngs.org.uk

Graham Watts 01362 690065
graham.watts@ngs.org.uk

OPENING DATES

All entries subject to change. For latest information check www.ngs.org.uk

Map locator numbers are shown to the right of each garden name.

February

Snowdrop Festival

Sunday 13th
Lexham Hall   38

Saturday 19th
Horstead House   30

Sunday 20th
Bagthorpe Hall   2

Saturday 26th
◆ Hindringham Hall   25

Sunday 27th
Chestnut Farm   11

March

Saturday 19th
◆ East Ruston Old
  Vicarage   16

April

Sunday 3rd
Gayton Hall   21

Sunday 10th
◆ Mannington Estate   40

Sunday 17th
Wretham Lodge   68

Monday 18th
Wretham Lodge   68

Sunday 24th
The Old Rectory,
  Catfield   48

May

Sunday 8th
Quaker Farm   50

Wednesday 18th
◆ Stody Lodge   56

Sunday 22nd
Chestnut Farm   11
Lexham Hall   38
The Old Rectory,
  Brandon Parva   47

Saturday 28th
Blickling Lodge   5

Sunday 29th
Bolwick Hall   6
Manor Farmhouse,
  Gayton   42
Warborough House   65

June

Saturday 4th
Home Farmhouse   28

Sunday 5th
Barton Bendish Hall   3
Elsing Hall Gardens   18
NEW Hoe Hall   26
Home Farmhouse   28
Oulton Hall   49

Saturday 11th
Church Cottage   12
La Foray   37

Sunday 12th
Booton Hall   7
Church Cottage   12
Holme Hale Hall   27
La Foray   37
NEW Unthank Road
  Gardens   62

Saturday 18th
Kettle Hill   35

Sunday 19th
NEW Ferndale   19
High House Gardens   23
NEW 57 Ketts Hill   36
Manor House Farm,
  Wellingham   43
27 St Edmunds Road   52
Wells-Next-The-Sea
  Gardens   66

Sunday 26th
Bishop's House   4
Broadway Farm   10
Highview House   24

July

Sunday 3rd
◆ Hoveton Hall
  Gardens   32
NEW Two Eaton
  Gardens   60

Walcott House   63

Saturday 9th
Swafield Hall   57

Sunday 10th
NEW Rags Folgate   51
Swafield Hall   57
Tyger Barn   61
NEW The White House   67

Sunday 17th
Dunbheagan   15
NEW Ferndale   19

Wednesday 20th
Lexham Hall   38

Sunday 24th
Dale Farm   13
26 Ipswich Road   33
Salle Park   53

Sunday 31st
30 Hargham Road   22
The Long Barn   39
61 Trafford Way   58

August

Wednesday 3rd
NEW Fiddian's Folly   20
Honeysuckle Walk   29

Friday 5th
Honeysuckle Walk   29

Sunday 7th
Brick Kiln House   8
NEW Kerdiston Manor   34
North Lodge   44
33 Waldemar Avenue   64

Monday 8th
Honeysuckle Walk   29

Wednesday 10th
Honeysuckle Walk   29

Sunday 14th
68 Elm Grove Lane   17
NEW Ferndale   19
North Lodge   44
◆ Severals Grange   55

Saturday 20th
NEW 47 Norwich Road   45
NEW 51 Norwich Road   46

Sunday 21st
Tudor Lodgings   59

Saturday 27th
Blickling Lodge   5

Sunday 28th
Acre Meadow   1

Monday 29th
Acre Meadow   1

September

Sunday 4th
33 Waldemar Avenue   64

Sunday 11th
High House Gardens   23
Holme Hale Hall   27

October

Saturday 15th
◆ East Ruston Old
  Vicarage   16

By Arrangement

Arrange a personalised garden visit with your club, or group of friends, on a date to suit you. See individual garden entries for full details.

Blickling Lodge   5
Brick Kiln House   8
21 Broadhurst Road   9
Broadway Farm   10
Chestnut Farm   11
Dale Farm   13
Dove Cottage   14
Dunbheagan   15
NEW Ferndale   19
NEW Fiddian's Folly   20
Gayton Hall   21
Highview House   24
NEW Hoe Hall   26
Honeysuckle Walk   29
Horstead House   30
Manor Farm, Coston   41
The Old Rectory,
  Brandon Parva   47
The Old Rectory,
  Catfield   48
Tudor Lodgings   59
Walcott House   63
Wretham Lodge   68

THE GARDENS

1 ACRE MEADOW
New Road, Bradwell, Great Yarmouth, NR31 9DU. Mr Keith Knights, www.acremeadow.co.uk. *Between Bradwell & Belton in arable surroundings. Take Belton & Burgh Castle turn (New Rd) from r'about at Bradwell on A143 Great Yarmouth to Beccles rd. Then 400 yds on R drive in very wide gateway. For SatNav use NR31 9JW.* **Sun 28, Mon 29 Aug (10-5). Adm £4, chd free. Pre-booking essential, please visit www.ngs.org.uk for information & booking. Light refreshments.** Exotic and insect attracting plants. A riot of late summer colour with lots of dark foliage, in deep, densely planted borders in an immersive garden on former greenhouses site of currently a tenth of an acre. Separate areas of interest inc pond area and 60 foot border for pollinators.

2 BAGTHORPE HALL
Bagthorpe, Bircham, King's Lynn, PE31 6QY. Mr & Mrs D Morton. *3½ m N of East Rudham, off A148. Take turning opp The Crown in East Rudham. Look for white gates in trees, slightly set back from the road.* **Sun 20 Feb (11-4). Adm £5, chd free. Tea. Home-made soup.** A delightful circular walk which meanders through a stunning display of snowdrops naturally carpeting a woodland floor, and then returning through a walled garden.

3 BARTON BENDISH HALL
Fincham Road, Barton Bendish, King's Lynn, PE33 9DL. The Barton Bendish Gardening Team. *5m E of Downham Market off A1122. On entering Barton Bendish follow yellow signs to field parking.* **Sun 5 June (11-5). Adm £6, chd free.** Traditional country estate garden of 10 acres. Woodland drive, orchard, kitchen garden with soft fruits, espaliered fruit trees, vegetables, glasshouse full of scented pelargoniums. Walled herb and cut flower garden. Herbaceous borders, south facing terrace. Informal area around pond. Sculptures. Some wheelchair access.

&. ❈ ❦

4 BISHOP'S HOUSE
Bishopgate, Norwich, NR3 1SB. The Bishop of Norwich, www. dioceseofnorwich.org/gardens. *City centre. Located in the city centre near the Law Courts & The Adam & Eve Pub. Parking available at Town Centre car parks inc one by the Adam & Eve pub.* **Sun 26 June (1-5). Adm £5, chd free. Home-made teas.** 4 acre walled garden dating back to the C12. Extensive lawns with specimen trees. Borders with many rare and unusual shrubs. Spectacular herbaceous borders flanked by yew hedges. Rose beds, meadow labyrinth, kitchen garden, woodland walk and long border with hostas and bamboo walk. Popular plant sales. Wheelchair access, gravel paths and some slopes.

&. ❈ ❦ ⊞))

5 BLICKLING LODGE
Blickling, Norwich, NR11 6PS. Michael & Henrietta Lindsell, nicky@lindsell.co.uk. *½ m N of Aylsham. Leave Aylsham on Old Cromer rd towards Ingworth. Over hump back bridge & house is on R.* **Sat 28 May, Sat 27 Aug (11-5). Adm £5, chd free. Light refreshments. Visits also by arrangement.** Georgian house (not open) set in 17 acres of parkland inc cricket pitch, mixed border, walled kitchen garden, yew garden, woodland/water garden.

&. ❈ ❦ ❦))

6 BOLWICK HALL
Marsham, NR10 5PU. Mr & Mrs G C Fisher. *8m N of Norwich off A140. From Norwich, heading N on A140, just past Marsham take 1st R after Plough Pub, signed 'By Road' then next R onto private drive to front of Hall.* **Sun 29 May (1-5). Adm £5, chd free. Home-made teas.** Landscaped gardens and park surrounding a late Georgian hall. The original garden design is attributed to Humphrey Repton. The current owners have rejuvenated the borders, planted gravel and formal gardens and clad the walls of the house in old roses. Enjoy a woodland walk around the lake as well as as stroll through the working vegetable and fruit garden with its double herbaceous border. Please ask at gate for wheelchair directions.

&. ❈ ❦))

Fidians Folly

7 BOOTON HALL

Church Road, Booton, Norwich, NR10 4NZ. Piers & Cecilia Willis. *1m E of Reepham. Drive out of Reepham east on Norwich Rd, after 1m turn L into Church Rd. After 500 metres turn L through white wooden gates just after bendy road sign on L.* **Sun 12 June (11-5). Adm £6, chd free. Home-made teas.**
Walled garden with formal layout and tiered lawns re-designed 8 yrs ago and attached to C17/18 hall. Lawns between the house and parkland meadows, shrub beds, pond planting, small orchard and short woodland walk. Parking in one of the meadows close to drive entrance, prior drop-off by house possible in extremis. Wheelchair access, but some gravel quite deep, and some steps, so will require energetic help.

8 BRICK KILN HOUSE

Priory Lane, Shotesham, Norwich, NR15 1UJ. Jim & Jenny Clarke, jennyclarke@uwclub.net. *6m S of Norwich. From Shotesham All Saints church Priory Lane is 200m on R on Saxlingham Rd.* **Sun 7 Aug (10-4).**

Adm £5, chd free. Home-made teas. **Visits also by arrangement June to Sept for groups of up to 40.**
2 acre country garden with a large terrace, lawns and colourful herbaceous borders. There are garden sculptures and a stream running through a diversely planted wood. Parking in field but easy access to brick path.

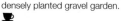

9 21 BROADHURST ROAD

Eaton Rise, Norwich, NR4 6RD. David & Beverly Woods, dwoods054@icloud.com. *1m S of Norwich. Take A140 S from Norwich city centre to outer ring rd T-lights. Stay on A140 & Broadhurst Rd is 3rd turning on R opposite tennis courts.* **Visits by arrangement in July for groups of up to 15. Adm £4, chd free. Home-made teas.**
South facing suburban garden with Mediterranean and Japanese style planting. Japanese maples, pines, tree ferns, olives and palm trees with salvias and lavenders make up this densely planted gravel garden.

10 BROADWAY FARM

The Broadway, Scarning, Dereham, NR19 2LQ. Michael & Corinne Steward, 01362 693286, corinneasteward@gmail.com. *16m W of Norwich. 12m E of Swaffham From A47 W take a R into Fen Rd, opp Drayton Hall Lane. From A47 E take L into Fen Rd, then immed L at T-junction, immed R into The Broadway.* **Sun 26 June (11-5). Adm £4, chd free. Home-made teas. Visits also by arrangement July & Aug for groups of 10 to 40.**
½ acre cottage garden surrounding a C14 clapboard farmhouse. Colourful herbaceous borders with a wide range of perennial and woody plants and a well planted pond, providing habitat for wildlife. A plantswoman's garden!

11 CHESTNUT FARM

Church Road, West Beckham, Holt, NR25 6NX. Mr & Mrs John McNeil Wilson, 01263 822241, judywilson100@gmail.com. *2½m S of Sheringham. From A148 opp Sheringham Park entrance. Take the road signed BY WAY TO*

414 Unthank Road

WEST BECKHAM, about ³/₄ m to the garden. NB SatNav will take you to pub, garden at village sign. **Sun 27 Feb (11-4); Sun 22 May (11-5). Adm £5, chd free. Light refreshments. Visits also by arrangement Feb to Oct. Refreshments by arrangement.**
Mature 3 acre garden with collections of many rare and unusual plants and trees. 100+ varieties of snowdrops, drifts of crocus with seasonal flowering shrubs. Later, wood anemones, fritillary meadow, wildflower walk, pond, small arboretum, croquet lawn and colourful herbaceous borders. In May the Handkerchief tree, Cercis and Camassias should be seen. Good varied selection of spring bulbs. Wheelchair access tricky if wet.

& 🐕 ✿ 🚗 ☕ 🖤

🔢12 CHURCH COTTAGE
57 White Street, Martham, Great Yarmouth, NR29 4PQ. Jo & Nigel Craske. *Approx 9m N of Gt Yarmouth off A149. Take B1152 signed to Martham & Winterton. On White Street pass Village Hall & Bell Meadow. Garden on L down gravel drive before Church & sharp R bend.* **Sat 11, Sun 12 June (12-5). Combined adm with La Foray £5, chd free.**
Delightful small cottage garden attached to 200 yr old house with views of St Mary's Church. Divided into different areas with lots of plants, many typical but others more unusual. Areas inc cool, shady border, hot sunny herbaceous border, small gravel garden, walled garden, sunken area with collection of hostas and greenhouse with pelargoniums and succulents. Unsuitable for wheelchairs.

✿

🔢13 DALE FARM
Sandy Lane, Dereham, NR19 2EA. Graham & Sally Watts, 01362 690065, grahamwatts@dsl.pipex.com. *16m W of Norwich. 12m E of Swaffham. From A47 take B1146 signed to Fakenham, turn R at T-junction, ¼ m turn L into Sandy Ln (before pelican crossing).* **Sun 24 July (11-5). Adm £5, chd free. Home-made teas. Visits also by arrangement June & July for groups of 10 to 50. Adm inc home-made teas.**
2 acre plant lovers' garden with a large spring-fed pond. Over

1000 plant varieties in exuberantly planted borders with sculptures. Also, gravel, vegetable, nature and waterside gardens. Collection of 150 hydrangeas! Music during the day, some grass paths and gravel drive. Wide choice of plants for sale.

🐕 ✿ 🚗 ☕ 🔊

🔢14 DOVE COTTAGE
Wolferd Green, Shotesham All Saints, Norwich, NR15 1YU. Sarah Cushion, 07766 556169, sarah.cushion815@btinternet.com. *From Norwich travel to far end of Poringland, turn R by church into Shotesham rd, continue for approx 2½ m, house pink cottage on L.* **Visits by arrangement May to Aug for groups of up to 30. Tour by owner. Adm £4, chd free. Light refreshments.**
¹/₃ acre densely planted colourful cottage garden inc a small pond, summerhouse, and extensive views across the countryside.

& ☕

🔢15 DUNBHEAGAN
Dereham Road, Westfield, NR19 1QF. Jean & John Walton, 01362 696163, jandjwalton@btinternet.com. *2m S of Dereham. From Dereham turn L off A1075 into Westfield Rd by the Vauxhall garage/Premier food store. Straight ahead at Xrds into lane which becomes Dereham Rd. Garden on L.* **Sun 17 July (1-5). Adm £5, chd free. Home-made teas. Refreshments will be provided on the front lawn by our local day centre for adults with learning difficulties. Visits also by arrangement June & July for groups of 10+. From mid-June.**
Relax and enjoy walking among extensive borders and island beds - a riot of colour all summer. Vast collection of rare, unusual and more recognisable plants in this ever changing plantsman's garden. If you love flowers, you'll love it here. We aim for the WOW factor. Lots of changes made in 2021. Featured in Nick Bailey's book 365 Days of Colour. Wheelchair access, gravel driveway.

& 🐕 ✿ 🚗 ☕

🔢16 ◆ EAST RUSTON OLD VICARAGE
East Ruston, Norwich, NR12 9HN. Alan Gray & Graham Robeson, 01692 650432, erovoffice@btconnect.com, www.eastrustonoldvicarage.co.uk. *3m N of Stalham. Turn off A149 onto B1159 signed Bacton, Happisburgh. After 2m turn R 200yds N of East Ruston Church (ignore sign to East Ruston).* **For NGS: Sat 19 Mar, Sat 15 Oct (12-5.30). Adm £11.50, chd £2. Light refreshments. For other opening times and information, please phone, email or visit garden website.**
Large garden with traditional borders and modern landscapes inc Walled Gardens, Rose Garden, Exotic Garden, Topiary and Box Parterres, Water Features, Mediterranean Garden, a monumental Fruit Cage, Containers to die for in spring and summer. Cornfield and Meadow Gardens, Vegetable and Cutting Gardens, Parkland and Heritage Orchard, in all 32 acres. Rare and unusual plants abound. Regional Finalist, The English Garden's The Nation's Favourite Gardens 2021

& ✿ 🚗 NPC ☕

🔢17 68 ELM GROVE LANE
Norwich, NR3 3LF. Selwyn Taylor, www.selwyntaylorgarden.co.uk. *1³/₄ m N of Norwich city centre. Proceed from Norwich city centre to Magdalen St, to Magdalen Rd, bear L to St Clements Hill turn L into Elm Grove Ln, no 68 is at bottom on R.* **Sun 14 Aug (11-4). Adm £5, chd free. Light refreshments. Hot and cold drinks, a selection of delicious home-made cakes, inc gluten free.**
This extended living/working space is the owner's endeavour to redefine a suburban garden and to provide inspiration when viewed from his studio window. Aesthetic values initially took precedent over gardening know-how, but over 35 yrs a more balanced approach has resulted in an eclectic array of informal planting, rich in colour and form and full of surprises. Semi-exotic mature city garden. Heavily planted, creating layers of tree ferns, tetrapanax, gunnera, fatsia japonica, dahlias, cannas, and gingers.

☕

18 ELSING HALL GARDENS

Elsing Hall, Hall Road, Elsing, NR20 3DX. Patrick Lines & Han Yang Yap, www.elsinghall.com. *6km NW of Dereham. From A47 take the N Tuddenham exit. From A1067 take the turning to Elsing opp the Bawdeswell Garden Centre. Location details can be found on www. elsinghall.com.* Sun 5 June (10-4). Adm £8, chd free.

C15 fortified manor house (not open) with working moat. 10 acre gardens and 10 acre park surrounding the house. Significant collection of old roses, walled garden, formal garden, marginal planting, Gingko avenue, viewing mound, moongate, interesting pinetum and terraced garden. Please note that there are very limited WC facilities available. Picnics allowed in the car park.

19 NEW FERNDALE

14, Poringland Road, Upper Stoke Holy Cross, Norwich, NR14 8NL. Dr Alan & Mrs Sheila Sissons, 01508 494222, asissons@hotmail.com. *4m S of Norwich. From Norwich or Poringland on B1332, take Stoke Rd at Railway Tavern r'about Ferndale is 0.7m on L. Parking is 0.2m further past Xrds at St George's Church Hall NR14 8ND on R.* Sun 19 June, Sun 17 July, Sun 14 Aug (11-5). Adm £4, chd free. Light refreshments. Visits also by arrangement June to Aug for groups of 5 to 10.

⅓ acre garden, paved area with seating surrounded by borders of shrubs and flowers. A pond with water feature. In a second area is more seating plus apple trees, soft fruit, vegetable plot, greenhouse and herb bed. Shingled area with water feature, rose arbour and low semi-circular wall planted with flowers. Wheelchair access, there is a slightly sloping 1 metre wide paved passageway leading to the main garden.

20 NEW FIDDIAN'S FOLLY

Upwood Farm, North Barningham, Norwich, NR11 7LA. Dick & Debbie Fiddian, 07775 621433, dickfid@gmail.com, fiddiansfollies.uk. *North Barningham. Follow SatNav. Gardens will be signed from N.Barningham & Baconsthorpe.* Wed 3 Aug (11-5). Adm £6, chd free. Home-made teas. Visits also by arrangement Jan to Aug.

The garden at Upwood Farm (affectionally known as Fiddian's Follies), has been described as quirky, full of surprises and generally very different to usual herbaceous borders, rosebeds and sweeping lawns. There are several follies, lovingly created with brick and stone elements, in and around what was once an old quarry. The garden, set in 3 acres, boasts wonderful unspoilt views.

21 GAYTON HALL

Gayton, King's Lynn, PE32 1PL. Viscount & Viscountess Marsham, 07776 121438, ciciromney@icloud.com. *6m E of King's Lynn. Off the B1145. At village sign take 2nd exit off Back St to entrance.* Sun 3 Apr (11-4.30). Adm £6, chd free. Home-made teas. Visits also by arrangement Feb to Oct.

This rambling semi-wild 20 acre water garden, has over 2 miles of paths, and contains lawns, lakes, streams, bridges and woodland. Primulas, astilbes, hostas, lysichiton and gunnera. Spring bulbs. A variety of unusual trees and shrubs, many labelled, have been planted over the years. Wheelchair access to most areas, gravel and grass paths.

22 30 HARGHAM ROAD

Attleborough, NR17 2ES. Darren & Karen Spencer. *Turn off A11 at Breckland Lodge, continue 2m into Attleborough, turn R opp Sainsbury's into Hargham Rd garden 200 yds on R.* Sun 31 July (11-5). Adm £4, chd free. Home-made teas.

Step into a vibrant, colourful haven in just under a ⅓ acre. Created from scratch with self built structures and home-made water features. Borders filled with perennials and annuals with a variety of exotics. Follow the pathway round to a modern allotment area.

23 HIGH HOUSE GARDENS

Blackmoor Row, Shipdham, Thetford, IP25 7PU. Sue & Fred Nickerson. *6m SW of Dereham. Take the airfield or Cranworth Rd off A1075 in Shipdham. Blackmoor Row is signed.* Sun 19 June, Sun 11 Sept (12-5). Adm £5, chd free. Home-made teas.

3 acre plantsman's garden developed and maintained by the current owners, over the last 40 years. Garden consists of colour themed herbaceous borders with an extensive range of perennials, box edged rose and shrub borders, woodland garden, pond and bog area, orchard and small arboretum. Plus large vegetable garden. Wheelchair access, gravel paths.

24 HIGHVIEW HOUSE

Norwich Road, Roughton, Norwich, NR11 8NA. Graham & Sarah Last, 07976 066896, grahamrc.last@gmail.com. *On A140 approx ½ m N off Roughton village mini r'abouts. Parking on site is limited & therefore saved for wheelchair access & those with limited walking. Main parking is signed, heading N of house on A140 on L side.* Sun 26 June (12-4). Adm £5, chd free. Light refreshments. Visits also by arrangement July & Aug for groups of 20 to 80.

2 acre garden featuring a large range of herbaceous borders. Long season of interest with a large range of perennial plants maintained by the owners. Over 120 Salvia varieties feature through the planting. Interesting garden structures inc a Japanese pagoda garden and large decked area. Pathways take you through each area of the garden. Suitable in most parts for wheelchair access. Football goals may be used by visitors at their own risk.

25 ♦ HINDRINGHAM HALL

Blacksmiths Lane, Hindringham, NR21 0QA. Mr & Mrs Charles Tucker, 01328 878226, hindhall@btinternet.com, www.hindringhamhall.org. *7m from Holt/Fakenham/Wells. Turn L. off A148 at Crawfish Pub towards Hindringham. L into Blacksmiths Ln after village hall on R.* For NGS: Sat 26 Feb (10-4). Adm £8, chd free. Home-made teas. For other opening times and information, please phone, email or visit garden website.

A garden surrounding a Grade II* Tudor Manor House (not open) enveloped by a complete medieval moat plus 3 acres of fishponds. Working walled vegetable garden, Victorian nut walk, formal beds, bog and stream gardens. Something of interest throughout the year continuing well into autumn. Spring wild garden. Some access for wheelchairs able to cope with gravel paths.

26 NEW **HOE HALL**
Hall Road, Hoe, Dereham,
NR20 4BD. Mr & Mrs James
Keith, 01362 693169,
vrkeith@hoehall.co.uk. *The garden
is next to Hoe church in the village
of Hoe.* **Sun 5 June (2-5). Adm £5,
chd free. Home-made teas. Visits
also by arrangement in June for
groups of up to 15. Narrow paths
may restrict flow in the event of
large numbers.**
The main visual is a walled garden
featuring a long white wisteria
walk. This is set in the grounds of
a Georgian rectory surrounded by
parkland. The garden was redesigned
in 1990 to incorporate climbers and
herbaceous plants, with box parterres
replacing the kitchen garden. There
are espaliered fruit trees, and an
old swimming pool with water lilies.

Seating area and WC available in the
walled garden.

27 **HOLME HALE HALL**
Holme Hale, Swaffham, Thetford,
IP25 7ED. Mr & Mrs Simon Broke.
*2m S of Necton off A47. 1m E of
Holme Hale village.* **Sun 12 June,
Sun 11 Sept (12-4). Adm £7, chd
free. Light refreshments.**
Walled kitchen garden designed
by Arne Maynard and replanted in
2016/17. A soft palette of herbaceous
plants include some unusual varieties.
Topiaries, vegetables, trained fruits
and roses. 130 year old wisteria.
wildflower meadow. Long season
of interest. Wildlife friendly. Historic
buildings and Island Pond. Wildflower
meadow and walks round Island
Pond area. Wheelchair access

available to some areas.

28 **HOME FARMHOUSE**
91 The Street, Hindringham,
NR21 0PS. Rachel & John
Hannyngton. *Hindringham is
between the villages of Binham &
Thursford. From A148 between
Fakenham & Holt, turn N at The
Crawfish pub.* **Sat 4, Sun 5 June
(10-5). Adm £5, chd free. Home-
made teas.**
An imaginative, informal 2 acre
garden, developed over the past 25
years with orchard, working potager,
herbaceous borders, themed beds,
'white' courtyard, Piet Oudolf-style
perennial and grass border, wildflower
meadow and woodland walk.

The White House

29 HONEYSUCKLE WALK
Litcham Road, Gressenhall,
Dereham, NR20 4AR. Simon
& Joan Smith, 01362 860530,
simon.smith@ngs.org.uk. 17m W
of Norwich. Follow B1146 & signs to
Gressenhall Rural Life Museum then
follow Litcham Road into Gressenhall
village. Wed 3, Fri 5, Mon 8, Wed
10 Aug (2-4.30). Adm £10, chd
free. Pre-booking essential,
please visit www.ngs.org.uk for
information & booking. Guided
tour for 15 people starting
at 2pm each day. Afternoon
tea comprising of assorted
sandwiches and cakes inc in
adm. Visits also by arrangement
June to Aug for groups of 10 to 20.
2 acre woodland garden featuring two
ponds, river and stream boundaries,
80 ornamental trees and a collection
of 400 different hydrangeas and 100
hostas. Woodland access is by ¼ m
grass track. Many rare hydrangea and
hosta plants for sale.

30 HORSTEAD HOUSE
Mill Road, Horstead, Norwich,
NR12 7AU. Mr & Mrs Matthew
Fleming. 6m NE of Norwich on
North Walsham Rd, B1150. Down
Mill Rd opp the Recruiting Sergeant
pub. Sat 19 Feb (11-4). Adm £5,
chd free. Pre-booking essential,
please phone 07771 655637 or
email horsteadsnowdrops@gmail.
com for information & booking.
Tea. Visits also by arrangement
in Feb.
Stunning display of beautiful
snowdrops carpet the woodland
setting with winter flowering shrubs.
Another beautiful feature is the
dogwoods growing on a small island
in the River Bure, which flows through
the garden. Small walled garden.
Wheelchair access to main snowdrop
area.

31 ♦ HOUGHTON HALL WALLED GARDEN
Bircham Road, New Houghton,
King's Lynn, PE31 6TY. The
Cholmondeley Gardens
Trust, 01485 528569,
info@houghtonhall.com,
www.houghtonhall.com. 11m W
of Fakenham. 13m E of King's Lynn.
Signed from A148. For opening
times and information, please
phone, email or visit garden
website.

The award-winning, 5 acre walled
garden inc a spectacular double-
sided herbaceous border, rose
parterre, wisteria pergola and
glasshouses. Mediterranean garden
and kitchen garden with arches
and espaliers of fruit trees. Antique
statues, fountains and contemporary
sculptures. Gravel and grass paths.
Electric buggies available in the walled
garden.

32 ♦ HOVETON HALL GARDENS
Hoveton Hall Estate, Hoveton,
Norwich, NR12 8RJ. Mr & Mrs
Harry Buxton, 01603 784297,
office@hovetonhallestate.co.uk,
www.hovetonhallestate.co.uk. 8m
N of Norwich. 1m N of Wroxham
Bridge. Off A1151 Stalham Rd -
follow brown tourist signs. For NGS:
Sun 3 July (10.30-5). Adm £8,
chd £4. Picnics are allowed for
garden patrons only. For other
opening times and information,
please phone, email or visit garden
website.
15 acre gardens and woodlands
taking you through the seasons.
Mature walled herbaceous and
kitchen gardens. Informal woodlands
and lakeside walks. Nature Spy
activity trail for our younger visitors.
A varied events programme runs
throughout the season. Please visit
our website for more details. Light
lunches and afternoon tea from our
on site Garden Kitchen Cafe. The
gardens are approx 75% accessible
to wheelchair users. We offer a
reduced entry price for wheelchair
users and their carers.

33 26 IPSWICH ROAD
Norwich, NR2 2LZ. Pat Adcock.
Parking available opp the garden at
Harford Manor School. Sun 24 July
(11-4). Adm £4, chd free. Tea,
coffee, home-made cakes.
This is no ordinary garden! ½ m from
Norwich City centre this ½ acre
garden is dedicated to sustainability
and biodiversity. Organic and wildlife
friendly there are resident chickens,
bees, a large wildlife pond, fish pond,
vegetables and ornamental plants.
There is a home-made system of
water conservation and storage.
There will be an observational beehive
showing the bees working and a
beekeeper to talk to. The owner is a
Master Composter, and be available

to discuss composting issues and to
give advice.

34 NEW KERDISTON MANOR
Kerdiston, Norwich, NR10 4RY.
Philip & Mararette Hollis. 1m
from Reepham. Turn at Bawdswell
garden centre towards Reepham
after 3.8m turn L Smugglers Rd
leaving Reepham surgery on L. L into
Kerdiston Rd 1½ m house on R. Sun
7 Aug (11-5). Adm £6, chd free.
Home-made teas.
2 acre tranquil garden surrounding
Manor House (not open) that has
been developed by the owners for
over 30 years. Mature trees, colourful
herbaceous borders, dell garden,
potager style vegetable plot, pond,
a 15 acre wild meadow walk and
wonderful thatched C18 barn.

35 KETTLE HILL
The Downs, Langham Road,
Blakeney, NR25 7PN. Mrs R
Winch. ½ m from Blakeney off
B1156 towards Langham Double
white gates on R opp scargills
electric company & campsite which
is on the L. Up the long drive double
white gates at entrance. Sat 18
June (11-5). Adm £6, chd free.
Home-made teas. Tea, coffee,
elderflower and cake.
A garden with herbaceous borders,
wildflower meadows secret garden.
Stunning rose garden. Beautiful
woods. Excellent views across
Morston to sea, framed by lavender,
roses and sky. Gardens have been
developed by owner with design
elements from George Carter to
Tamara Bridge. Wheelchair access,
gravel driveway leading to paths,
flat lawned areas. Partial access to
woods. No disabled WC, nearest is at
Blakeney village hall.

36 NEW 57 KETTS HILL
Norwich, NR1 4EX. Anne & John
Farrow. E of city centre. Follow the
inner ring rd, A147, to the Barrack
Street r'about where it meets the
B1140, Ketts Hill. The garden is
situated 130 yds on L up the hill.
Parking on Ketts Hill. Sun 19 June
(11-5). Adm £4, chd free. Home-
made teas.
A relaxed garden in an historic part of
the City. There is a small lawned area,
shrubs and perennial borders with a
wide variety of plants, terraces and

steep slopes leading to an elevated summerhouse with wonderful views of the cathedrals and city. The garden is approached via a steep gravelled drive and there are steep steps in the garden which means it is only suitable for the able bodied.

37 LA FORAY
White Street, Martham, Great Yarmouth, NR29 4PQ. Ameesha & Alan Williams. *10m N of Gt Yarmouth approx 2m off A149 follow yellow signs at Martham junction. Parking in village.* **Sat 11, Sun 12 June (12-5). Combined adm with Church Cottage £5, chd free. Home-made teas.**
A lovely garden with many interesting and unusual features created and maintained by the owners. Various mixed borders with an array of vintage and unusual items incorporated to add interest. Wildlife retreat, stumpery, collection of hostas and succulents and vintage summerhouse to relax in. Child's gypsy caravan, treehouse birdhide and friendly pet goats.

38 LEXHAM HALL
nr Litcham, PE32 2QJ. Mr & Mrs Neil Foster, www.lexhamestate.co.uk. *6m N of Swaffham off B1145. 2m west of Litcham.* **Sun 13 Feb (11-4). Adm £6, chd free. Sun 22 May, Wed 20 July (11-5). Adm £7.50, chd free. Home-made teas. We regret there will be no refreshments in February.**
Parkland with lake and river walks surround C17/18 Hall (not open). Formal garden with terraces, roses and mixed borders. Traditional working kitchen garden with crinkle-crankle wall. Year-round interest; woods and borders carpeted with snowdrops in February, rhododendrons, azaleas, camellias and magnolias in the 3 acre woodland garden in May and July sees the walled garden borders at their peak.

39 THE LONG BARN
Flordon Road, Newton Flotman, Norwich, NR15 1QX. Mr & Mrs Mark Bedini. *6m S of Norwich along A140. Leave A140 in Newton Flotman towards Flordon. Exit Newton Flotman & approx 150 yds beyond 'passing place' on L, turn L into drive. Note that SatNav does not bring you to destination.* **Sun 31 July (11-4.30). Adm £5, chd free. Home-made teas.**
Beautiful informal garden with new ha-ha creating infinity views across ancient parkland. Strong Mediterranean influence with plenty of seating in large paved courtyard under pollarded plane trees. Unusual wall-sheltered group of four venerably gnarled olive trees, figs and vines, then herbaceous borders, tiered lawns merging northwards into woodland garden. Walks through Parkland the tiny River Tas - serene. Wheelchair drop off at front of house. Gradual lawn slope accesses upper tier of garden. WC requires steps.

40 ◆ MANNINGTON ESTATE
Mannington, Norwich, NR11 7BB. Lady Walpole, 01263 584175, admin@walpoleestate.co.uk, www.manningtonestate.co.uk. *18m NW of Norwich. 2m N of Saxthorpe via B1149 towards Holt. At Saxthorpe/Corpusty follow signs to Mannington.* **For NGS: Sun 10 Apr (11-5). Adm £6, chd free. Light refreshments in the Garden Tearooms. For other opening times and information, please phone, email or visit garden website.**
20 acres feature shrubs, lake and trees. Period gardens. Borders. Sensory garden. Extensive countryside walks and trails. Moated manor house and Saxon church with C19 follies. wildflowers and birds. The tearooms offer home-made locally sourced food with home-made teas. Wheelchair access, gravel paths, one steep slope.

41 MANOR FARM, COSTON
Coston Lane, Coston, Barnham Broom, NR9 4DT. Mr & Mrs J D Hambro, 07554 584471. *10m W of Norwich. Off B1108 Norwich - Watton Rd. Take B1135 to Dereham at Kimberley. After approx 300yds sharp L bend, go straight over down Coston Ln, house & garden on L.* **Visits by arrangement Apr to Oct for groups of 15 to 50. Adm £10, chd free. Home-made teas inc in adm.**
Wonderful 3 acre country garden set in larger estate. Several small garden rooms with both formal and informal planting. Climbing roses, walled kitchen garden, white, grass and late summer themes, classic herbaceous and shrub borders, box parterres

and large areas of wildflowers. Collection of sculptures dotted round the garden. Dogs welcome. Something for everyone. Wheelchair access, some gravel paths and steps. Morning or afternoon visits, tour of garden with head gardener.

42 MANOR FARMHOUSE, GAYTON
Back Street, Gayton, King's Lynn, PE32 1QR. Alistair & Christa Beales. *6m E of King's Lynn. Signed from B1145 & B1153.* **Sun 29 May (1-5.30). Adm £5, chd free. Light refreshments.**
A secret, colourful, densely planted cottage garden created in 2001. Secluded gravel paths meander between double flowerbeds leading through a shady pergola to a sunny, walled courtyard and conservatory. New lawns, flowerbeds, wildflower area and polytunnel were added in 2013 on land bought from a neighbour. Hundreds of pots add colour and texture to the many seating areas around the garden.

43 MANOR HOUSE FARM, WELLINGHAM
Fakenham, Kings Lynn, PE32 2TH. Robin & Elisabeth Ellis, 01328 838227, libbyelliswellingham@gmail.com, www.manor-house-farm.co.uk. *½m off A1065 7m W from Fakenham & 8m E. Swaffham. Nr the Church.* **Sun 19 June (11-5). Adm £6.50, chd free. Home-made teas.**
Charming 4 acre country garden surrounds an attractive farmhouse. Formal quadrants, 'hot spot' of grasses, tree peonies, small arboretum, pleached lime walk, vegetable parterre and rose tunnel. Unusual walled 'Taj' garden with old-fashioned roses, tree peonies, lilies and formal pond. A variety of herbaceous plants. Small herd of Formosan Sika deer. Picnics allowed. Dogs on leads.

Our 2021 donations mean that 1,200 inpatients were supported by the Y Bwthyn NGS Macmillan Specialist Palliative Care unit in Wales since opening

44 NORTH LODGE
51 Bowthorpe Road, Norwich, NR2 3TN. Bruce Bentley & Peter Wilson. *1½ m W of Norwich City Centre. Turn into Bowthorpe Rd off Dereham Rd, garden 150 metres on L. By bus: 21, 22, 23, 23A/B, 24 & 24A from City centre, Old Catton, Heartsease, Thorpe & most of W Norwich. Parking available outside.* Sun 7, Sun 14 Aug (11-5). Adm £4, chd free. Home-made teas. Delightful town garden surrounding Victorian Gothic Cemetery Lodge. Full of follies created by current owners, including a classical temple, oriental water garden and formal ponds. Original 80ft-deep well! Predominantly herbaceous planting. House extension won architectural award. Slide show of house and garden history. Wheelchair access possible but difficult. Sloping gravel drive followed by short, steep, narrow, brickweave ramp. WC not easily wheelchair accessible.
&. ✿ ☕))

45 NEW 47 NORWICH ROAD
Stoke Holy Cross, Norwich, NR14 8AB. Anna & Alistair Lipp. *Heading S through Stoke Holy Cross on Norwich Rd, garden on R down short private drive, no parking at property. Parking at sports ground car park on L of Long Ln, NR14 8LY 500 yds to garden.* Sat 20 Aug (11-5). Combined adm with 51 Norwich Road £6, chd free. Home-made teas.
Medium sized, west facing garden developed over 25 years with views over Tas valley and water meadows. Vine and rose covered pergola, gravel beds, terrace with raised beds and shading magnolias, large greenhouse with exotic plants. Small meadow and informal pond. Gravel driveway to brick paths with slope to raised terrace allows majority of garden to be viewed by wheelchair users.
&. ✿ ☕))

46 NEW 51 NORWICH ROAD
Stoke Holy Cross, Norwich, NR14 8AB. Mrs Vivian Carrington. *5m S of Norwich past Wildebeest restaurant on R, No 51 is on R. 50 yds from the junction with Long Ln. Parking at sports ground car park on L of Long ln NR14 8LY 500 yds to garden.* Sat 20 Aug (11-5). Combined adm with 47 Norwich Road £6, chd free.
The garden consists of a variety of perennials and some annuals at the front with an asparagus bed to the side and a range of vegetables side and rear. There are cold frames and a small greenhouse. Behind the house there are further flower beds and a small lawn. Wheelchair access at the front and rear of garden.
&. ✿))

47 THE OLD RECTORY, BRANDON PARVA
Stone Lane, Brandon Parva, NR9 4DL. Mr & Mrs S Guest, 07867 840149, guest63@btinternet.com. *9m W of Norwich. Leave Norwich on B1108 towards Watton, turn R at sign for Barnham Broom. L at T-junction, stay on rd approx 3m until L next turn to Yaxham. L at Xrds.* Sun 22 May (11-5). Adm £5, chd free. Pre-booking essential, please visit www.ngs.org.uk for information & booking. Home-made teas. Visits also by arrangement May & June for groups of up to 30.
4 acre, mature garden with large collection (70) specimen trees, huge variety of shrubs and herbaceous plants combined to make beautiful mixed borders. The garden comprises several formal lawns and borders, woodland garden inc rhododendrons, pond garden, walled garden and pergolas covered in wisteria, roses and clematis which create long shady walkways. Croquet lawn open for visitors to play.
&. 🐎 ☕ ☕

48 THE OLD RECTORY, CATFIELD
School Road, Catfield, Great Yarmouth, NR29 5DA. Penny Middleditch, 07887 584790, middleditch@catfieldoldrectory.co.uk. *A149 to Catfield. ½ m from Catfield village centre turn R by Post Office & L at T junction opp Church.* Sun 24 Apr (10-5). Adm £5, chd free. Light lunches and teas available on site unless the weather is inclement in which case it will be in the adjoining church. Visits also by arrangement Mar to Sept.
3 acre garden surrounding former Rectory with gate to adjoining C14 Church. A further 15 acres of Glebe land and paddocks providing circular walk beside small lake and through orchards, woodland and extensive cutting garden. Heavily planted for all year interest but in spring masses of different species narcissi, species tulips, hellebores, fritillaries and anemone. Picnics welcome, child friendly. Access from the field into main gardens surrounding the house.
&. 🐎 ✿ 🚗 🛏 ☕ ☕ 🪑

49 OULTON HALL
Oulton, Aylsham, NR11 6NU. Bolton Agnew. *4m NW of Aylsham. From Aylsham take B1354. After 4m turn L for Oulton Chapel, Hall ½ m on R. From B1149 (Norwich/Holt rd) take B1354, next R, Hall ½ m on R.* Sun 5 June (1-5). Adm £5, chd free. Home-made teas.
C18 manor house (not open) and clocktower set in 6 acre garden with lake and woodland walks. Chelsea designer's own garden - herbaceous, Italian, bog, water, wild, verdant, sunken and parterre gardens all flowing from one tempting vista to another. Developed over 25 yrs with emphasis on structure, height and texture, with a lot of recent replanting in the contemporary manner.
&. 🐎 ✿ ☕

50 QUAKER FARM
Quaker Lane, Spixworth, Norwich, NR10 3FL. Mr & Mrs Peter Cook. *3m N of Norwich. From Norwich take Buxton Rd towards Spixworth, through Old Catton. Turning signed Quaker Ln just over the NDR (A1270).* Sun 8 May (11-4). Adm £5, chd free. Light refreshments.
An acre of garden surrounding a traditional Norfolk farmhouse which has evolved over the last 40 plus years. Comprises garden rooms of herbaceous borders, gravel garden, an avenue of shrubs and a more recently created woodland garden. Suitable for wheelchair users - a small area of gravel to negotiate.
&. 🐎 ☕))

51 NEW RAGS FOLGATE
Wattlefield, Wymondham, NR18 9LD. Elizabeth Spearing. *30 min SW of Norwich. From A11 take B1172 Wymondham, Morley, Besthorpe, Spooner Row Follow signs to Spooner Row. Over Xrds at Boars pub, then R at T-junction. Continue to red-tiled roofs on R.* Sun 10 July (2-6). Adm £5, chd free.
Approx 2 acres consisting of garden surrounding Grade II-listed cottage and leading to meadow with wildflowers, mature trees and ponds. Paths mown in the grass twist and turn to give varied views and lead to seating areas.

52 27 ST EDMUNDS ROAD
Taverham, Norwich, NR8 6NY.
Alan Inness & Sue Collins. *6m N
of Norwich, just off the Fakenham
Road A1067. Coming from Norwich
on A1067, drive through the village
of Drayton. Carry on up hill to
Taverham, turn L into Roeditch
Drive. The property will then be on
your R at T-junction.* **Sun 19 June
(11-4). Adm £4, chd free. Light
refreshments. Home made cakes,
quiche and sausage rolls.**
½ acre garden featuring part
woodland setting and view over
the Wensum valley. The garden has
undergone substantial redevelopment
over the past 12 years as it was
originally two separate gardens.
Redevelopment has inc the addition
of vine covered pergola, two
summerhouses, herbaceous borders,
small vegetable plot with greenhouse
and potting shed. Recently added
Island beds. Plant sales.

53 SALLE PARK
Salle, Reepham,
NR10 4SF. **Sir John White,**
www.salleestategardens.com. *1m
NE of Reepham. Off B1145, between
Cawston & Reepham.* **Sun 24 July
(10-4). Adm £5, chd free. Home-
made teas in The Orangery.**

Fully productive Victorian kitchen
garden with original vine houses,
double herbaceous borders, ice
house, and Norfolk Heritage Fruit
orchard. Formal Georgian pleasure
gardens with yew topiary, rose
gardens and lawns and freshly
planted Orangery. Wheelchair access,
some bark chip paths.

54 ♦ SANDRINGHAM GARDENS
Sandringham Estate,
Sandringham, PE35 6EH. **Her
Majesty The Queen, 01485 545408,
visits@sandringhamestate.co.uk,
www.sandringhamestate.co.uk.**
6m NW of King's Lynn. **For opening
times and information, please
phone, email or visit garden
website.**
Set over 25 hectares (60 acres) and
enjoyed by the Royal Family and
their guests when in residence, the
more formal Gardens are open from
April - October. The grounds have
been developed in turn by each
monarch since 1863 when King
Edward VII and Queen Alexandra
purchased the Estate. In 1912, a
charming summerhouse called The
Nest was built for Queen Alexandra
on the rockery, landscaped by James
Pulham using his famous 'Pulhamite'
stone, Queen Alexandra's Nest has a

beautiful vantage point over the lake.
Gravel paths are not deep, some long
distances. Please contact us or visit
the website for an Accessibility Guide.

55 ♦ SEVERALS GRANGE
Holt Road B1110, Wood
Norton, NR20 5BL. **Jane
Lister, 01362 684206,
hoecroft@hotmail.co.uk.** *8m S
of Holt, 6m E of Fakenham. 2m N
of Guist on L of B1110. Guist is
situated 5m SE of Fakenham on
A1067 Norwich rd.* **For NGS: Sun
14 Aug (1-5). Adm £5, chd free.
Home-made teas. For other
opening times and information,
please phone or email.**
The gardens surrounding Severals
Grange are a perfect example of
how colour, shape and form can be
created by the use of foliage plants,
from large shrubs to small alpines.
Movement and lightness are achieved
by interspersing these plants with a
wide range of ornamental grasses,
which are at their best in late summer.
Splashes of additional colour are
provided by a variety of herbaceous
plants. Wheelchair access, some
gravel paths but help can be
provided.

Dale Farm

56 ◆ STODY LODGE

Melton Constable,
NR24 2ER. Mr & Mrs Charles
MacNicol, 01263 860572,
enquiries@stodyestate.co.uk,
www.stodylodgegardens.co.uk.
*16m NW of Norwich, 3m S of Holt. Off
B1354. Signed from Melton Constable
on Holt Rd. For SatNav NR24 2ER.
Gardens signed as you approach.*
For NGS: Wed 18 May (1-5). Adm
£8, chd free. Home-made teas.
For other opening times and
information, please phone, email or
visit garden website.
Spectacular gardens with one
of the largest concentrations of
rhododendrons and azaleas in East
Anglia. Created in the 1920s, the
gardens also feature magnolias,
camellias, a variety of ornamental
and specimen trees, late daffodils
and bluebells. Expansive lawns and
magnificent yew hedges. Woodland
walks and 4 acre Water Garden filled
with over 2,000 vividly-coloured
azalea mollis. Home-made teas
provided by selected local and
national charities. Wheelchair access
to most areas of the garden. Gravel
paths to Azalea Water Gardens with
some uneven ground.

⛔ 🐕 ✿ 🚗 ☕

57 SWAFIELD HALL

Knapton Road, Swafield, North
Walsham, NR28 0RP. Tim
Payne & Boris Konoshenko,
swafieldhall.co.uk. *Swafield Hall is
approx ½ m along Knapton Rd (also
called Mundesley Rd) from its start
in the village of Swafield. You need
to add about 300 yds to the location
given by most SatNavs.* Sat 9, Sun
10 July (10-5). Adm £5, chd free.
Home-made teas.
C16 Manor House with Georgian
additions (not open) set within 4 acres
of gardens inc a parterre and various
rooms inc a summer garden, orchard,
cutting garden, pear tunnel, secret
oriental garden (with nine flower beds
based on a Persian carpet), the Apollo
Promenade of theatrical serpentine
hedging, a duck pond and woodland
walk. The whole garden is accessible
by wheelchair.

⛔ 🐕 ☕ 🪑 🔊

58 61 TRAFFORD WAY

Spixworth, Norwich, NR10 3QL.
Mr & Mrs Colin Ryall. *Park in
Spixworth Community car park
in Crosswick Ln.* Sun 31 July
(10-5). Adm £4, chd free. Light
refreshments.

Small garden showing what can be
achieved with careful planting and
the use of pleached hornbeam trees.
Gravel garden with flower beds and
pot plants. Colourful herbaceous
borders with roses.

⛔ ☕

59 TUDOR LODGINGS

Castle Acre, King's Lynn,
PE32 2AN. Gus & Julia
Stafford Allen, 01760 755334,
jstaffordallen@btinternet.com.
Parking in field below the house. Sun
21 Aug (11-5). Adm £6, chd free.
Visits also by arrangement July
to Sept.
2 acre garden fronts a C15 flint
house (not open), and incorporates
part of the Norman earthworks. C18
dovecote, abstract topiary, lawn and
mixed borders. Ornamental grasses
and hot border. Productive fruit cage
and cutting garden. A natural wild
area includes a shepherd's hut and
informal pond inhabited by ducks and
bantams. Newly planted orchard with
beehive. Partial wheelchair access,
please ask for assistance. Disabled
WC.

⛔ 🐕 ✿ ☕ 🔊

GROUP OPENING

60 NEW TWO EATON GARDENS

15 Waverley Road & 19
Branksome Road, Norwich,
NR4 6SG. *Branksome Rd is off
Newmarket Rd at end of A11
heading into the city turn R after
pedestrian Xing lights. From
the City, 4th L after ring road
r'about. Waverley Rd is 1st L
off Branksome Rd.* Sun 3 July
(10.30-5). Combined adm £7,
chd free. Home-made teas at 19
Branksome Rd.

19 BRANKSOME ROAD
Sue & Chris Pike.

15 WAVERLEY ROAD
Sue & Clive Lloyd.

Two town gardens just 15 minutes
from the City Centre. 19 Branksome
Road, on a corner plot, has been
designed with quite formal shaped
lawns and terraces to fit around
the house and make sunny seating
areas. There are clipped yews, an oak
pergola and swing seat to provide
structure, while the planting is a
relaxed mixture of perennials, shrubs
and trees. A traditional vegetable
plot with fruit cage and greenhouse

is a small but important part of the
garden. 15 Waverley Road has a
long town garden that's pretending
it is in the country. Divided into three
section, it is packed with herbaceous
perennials, roses, native plants and
a large (and growing) collection of
Pelargoniums. Although it is in the
city, it still manages to look natural. It
is gardened with a streak of wildness.
Both gardens have water features
designed and made by the owners.

✿ ☕ 🔊

61 TYGER BARN

Wood Lane, Aldeby, Beccles,
NR34 0DA. Julianne Fernandez,
www.chasing-arcadia.com. *Approx
1m from Toft Monks. From A143
towards Great Yarmouth at Toft
Monks turn R into Post Office Lane
opp White Lion Pub, after ¼ m turn
L into Wood Ln. After ½ m Tyger
Barn is 2nd house on L.* Sun 10 July
(12-4.30). Adm £5, chd free. Light
refreshments.
Featured in The English Garden, EDP
Norfolk and Suffolk magazines, Tyger
Barn is a modern country garden
started in 2007. Extensive borders
with hot, exotic and 'ghost' themes,
a secret cottage garden, wildflower
swathes and colonies of bee orchids.
A traditional hay meadow and ancient
woodland provide a beautiful setting.
Garden is mainly level, but is divided
by a shingle drive which wheelchairs
may find difficult to cross.

⛔ ✿ Ⓓ ☕ 🔊

GROUP OPENING

62 NEW UNTHANK ROAD GARDENS

Norwich, NR4 7QG. *All three
gardens are within walking distance
from each other on Unthank Rd.
Gardens are either side of the
junction of Unthank Rd & Judges
Walk off Newmarket Rd. Turn R for 4
Coach House Court & 414 Unthank
Rd & L for 383 Unthank Rd.* Sun 12
June (11-5). Combined adm £8,
chd free. Home-made teas at 383
Unthank Road.

NEW 4 COACH HOUSE COURT
Jackie Floyd.

NEW 383 UNTHANK ROAD
Carrie Phoenix.

NEW 414 UNTHANK ROAD
Sarah & Peter Scott.

Three different town gardens, 383 and 414 Unthank Road are sizeable gardens with many herbaceous plants, shrubs and trees. Both have highly productive vegetable gardens managed using the 'no-dig' system. 4 Coach House Court is a small courtyard garden packed with plants - roses, herbaceous plants, roses and shrubs. All three feature mature wisteria plants and all three aim to encourage biodiversity.

✿ ☕ ⟿

63 WALCOTT HOUSE

Walcott Green, Walcott, Norwich, NR12 0NU. Nick & Juliet Collier, 07986 607170, julietcollier1@gmail.com. *3m N of Stalham. Off the Stalham to Walcott rd (B1159).* **Sun 3 July (10-5). Adm £5, chd free. Light refreshments. Visits also by arrangement in July for groups of 15 to 30.**

A 12 acre site with over 1 acre of formal gardens based on model C19 Norfolk farm buildings. Woodland and damp gardens, arboretum, vistas with tree lined avenues, woodland walks. Wheelchair access, small single steps to negotiate when moving between gardens in the yards.

ᕕ ☜ ✿ ☕ ⟿

64 33 WALDEMAR AVENUE

Hellesdon, Norwich, NR6 6TB. Sonja Gaffer & Alan Beal, **Visit our facebook page @Hellesdontropicalgarden.** *Waldemar Ave is situated approx 400 yds off Norwich ring road towards Cromer on A140.* **Sun 7 Aug, Sun 4 Sept (10-5). Adm £4, chd free. Light refreshments.**

A surprising and large suburban garden of many parts with an exciting mix of exotic and tropical plants combined with unusual perennials. A quirky palm-thatched Tiki hut is an eye catching feature. There is a wonderful treehouse draped in plants. You can sit by the pond which is brimming with wildlife and rare plants. A large collection of succulents will be on show and there will be plants to buy. Wildlife pond. Wheelchair access surfaces are mostly of lawn and concrete and are on one level. Two entrance gates are 33 and 39 inches wide respectively.

ᕕ ✿ ☕

65 WARBOROUGH HOUSE

2 Wells Road, Stiffkey, NR23 1QH. Mr & Mrs J Morgan. *13m N of Fakenham, 4m E of Wells-Next-The-Sea on A149 in the centre of Stiffkey village. Parking is available & signed at garden entrance. Coasthopper bus stop outside garden. Please DO NOT park on the main road as this causes congestion.* **Sun 29 May (11-4). Adm £6, chd free. Home-made teas.**

7 acre garden on a steep chalk slope, surrounding C19 house (not open) with views across the Stiffkey valley and to the coast. Woodland walks, formal terraces, shrub borders, lawns and walled garden create a garden of contrasts. Garden slopes steeply in parts. Paths are gravel, bark chip or grass. Disabled parking allows access to garden nearest the house and teas.

ᕕ ✿ ☕ ⟿

GROUP OPENING

66 WELLS-NEXT-THE-SEA GARDENS

Wells-Next -The-Sea, NR23 1DP. David & Joolz Saunders. *10m N of Fakenham. All gardens near Coasthopper 'Burnt St' or 'The Buttlands' bus stop. Car parking for all gardens in Market Ln area.* **Sun 19 June (11-5). Combined adm £5, chd free. Light refreshments at Poacher Cottage.**

CAPRICE
Clubbs Lane, Wells-next-the-Sea. David & Joolz Saunders.

HIRAETH
11 Burnt Street, Wells-next-the-Sea. Jen Davies.

7 MARKET LANE
Wells-next-the-Sea. Hazel Ashley.

NORFOLK HOUSE
17 Burnt Street, Wells-next-the-Sea. Katrina & Alan Jackson.

POACHER COTTAGE
15 Burnt Street, Wells-next-the-Sea. Roger & Barbara Oliver.

Wells-next-the-Sea is a small, friendly coastal town on the North Norfolk Coast. Popular with families, walkers and bird watchers. The harbour has shops, cafes, fish and chips. Beach served by a narrow gauge railway. Fine parish church. The five town gardens, though small, demonstrate a variety of design and a wide selection of planting. Wheelchair access to all gardens except Norfolk House which

has limited access.

ᕕ ☕ ⟿

67 NEW THE WHITE HOUSE

The Street, Ridlington, North Walsham, NR28 9NR. Richard & Vanda Barker. *5m E of North Walsham, in village of Ridlington. Can be approached from North Walsham or from the B1159 Stalham to Bacton Rd. Off-road parking 5 minutes walk.* **Sun 10 July (11-4). Adm £4, chd free. Home-made teas.**

1 acre garden of former Rectory, with colour-themed herbaceous and mixed borders, gravel borders, roses, wildlife pond, kitchen garden and fruit garden. Most of the garden is wheelchair-accessible with care. Access is through a gravel courtyard, and there are slopes.

ᕕ ☜ ✿ ☕ ⟿

68 WRETHAM LODGE

East Wretham, IP24 1RL. Mr Gordon Alexander & Mr Ian Salter, 01953 498997, grdalexander@btinternet.com. *6m NE of Thetford. A11 E from Thetford, L up A1075, L by village sign, R at Xrds then bear L.* **Sun 17, Mon 18 Apr (11-5). Adm £5, chd free. Tea at Church. Visits also by arrangement Apr to Sept.**

10 acre garden surrounding former Georgian rectory (not open). In spring masses of species tulips, hellebores, fritillaries, daffodils and narcissi; bluebell walk and small woodland walk. Topiary pyramids and yew hedging lead to double herbaceous borders. Shrub borders and rose beds (home of the Wretham Rose). Traditionally maintained walled garden with fruit, vegetables and perennials.

ᕕ ☜ ☕

You can make a difference! Join our Great British Garden Party fundraising campaign and raise money for some of the best-loved nursing and health charities. Visit ngs.org.uk/gardenparty to find out how you can get involved

NORTH EAST

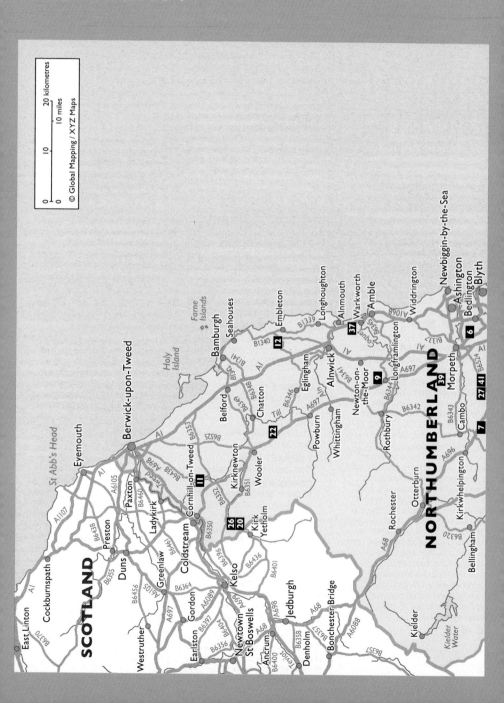

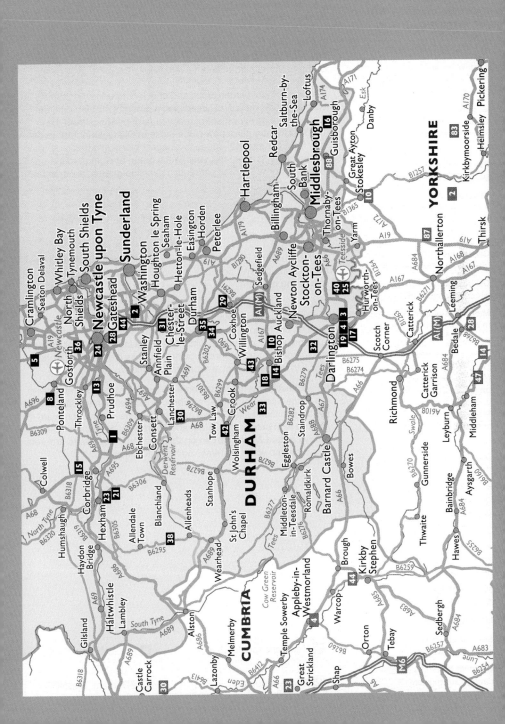

Volunteers

County Durham
County Organiser
Iain Anderson
01325 778446
iain.anderson@ngs.org.uk

County Treasurer
Monica Spencer 01325 286215
monica.spencer@ngs.org.uk

Booklet Co-ordinator
Sheila Walke 07837 764057
sheila.walke@ngs.org.uk

Assistant County Organisers
Sue Douglas 07712 461002
sue.douglas@ngs.org.uk

Helen Jackson
helen.jackson@ngs.org.uk

Aileen Little 01325 356691
aileen.little@ngs.org.uk

Gill Knights 01325 483210
gillianknights55@gmail.com

Gill Naisby 01325 381324
gillnaisby@gmail.com

Margaret Stamper 01325 488911
margaretstamper@tiscali.co.uk

Sue Walker 01325 481881
walker.sdl@gmail.com

Northumberland & Tyne
and Wear County Organiser
& Booklet Coordinator
Maureen Kesteven 01914 135937
maureen.kesteven@ngs.org.uk

County Treasurer
David Oakley 07941 077594
david.oakley@ngs.org.uk

Publicity, Talks Co-ordinator &
Social Media
Liz Reid 01914 165981
liz.reid@ngs.org.uk

Assistant County Organisers
Maxine Eaton 077154 60038
maxine.eaton@ngs.org.uk

Natasha McEwen 07917 754155
natashamcewengd@aol.co.uk

Liz Reid (as above)

Susie White 07941 077594
susie@susie-white.co.uk

David Young 01434 600699
david.young@ngs.org.uk

County Durham: an unsung county.

County Durham lies between the River Wear and River Tees and is varied and beautiful.

Our National Garden Scheme open gardens can be found in the city, high up in the Dales and in the attractive villages of South Durham. Something different every week.

Visit your old favourites again and check out our new gardens such as Eldon Hall Farm Steadings, a group of six very different gardens in a development of rescued farm buildings from the 1800's. Country gardens include those at Old Quarrington, three very different gardens, roses to alpacas! Wolsingham Village is also opening again this year with a group of eight gardens including some unusual gardens, a riverside garden, allotments etc. something for everyone.

Northumberland is a county of ancient castles and wild coastline, of expansive views and big skies.

Northumberland is a big county. Its beautiful landscape, with its picturesque valleys, provides the backdrop for a wide range of interesting gardens.

There is a wide variety of styles, from the walled vegetable gardens and sumptuous borders of large country houses to exciting contemporary planting. An historic manor house has a Lutyens/Jekyll connection while one has a landscape that provides a place of calm to its current owners, just as it did during World War 1 to its then owner, a prominent politician.

An unusual colourful garden on a very steep slope, and another in the rugged country of the Pennines, show you can transform even the most difficult sites. There are city gardens – a tiny courtyard packed with colour; the landscaped garden of a hospice. From a newly created 3 acre garden on the coast to meadows to arboreta and dramatic water features. So much to enjoy.

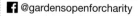 @gardensopenforcharity

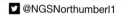 @NGSNorthumberl1

 @ngsnorthumber

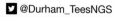 @Durham_TeesNGS

OPENING DATES

All entries subject to change. For latest information check www.ngs.org.uk

Map locator numbers are shown to the right of each garden name.

April

Sunday 10th
Ravensford Farm — 33

May

Sunday 22nd
Blagdon — 5

Sunday 29th
Lilburn Tower — 22

June

Sunday 5th
The Beacon — 1

Saturday 18th
St Oswald's Hospice — 36

Sunday 19th
High Bank Farm — 17
Holmelands — 19
◆ Mindrum Garden — 26

Saturday 25th
NEW Eldon Hall Farm
Steadings — 10
Fallodon Hall — 12
Woodlands — 44

Sunday 26th
NEW Halton Castle — 15
NEW Old Quarrington
Gardens — 29
Oliver Ford Garden — 30
◆ Whalton Manor
Gardens — 41

July

Saturday 2nd
Kirky Cottage — 20
Wolsingham Village
Gardens — 42

Sunday 3rd
The Beacon
Garden and studio
at 67 — 14
Marie Curie Hospice — 24
The Moore House — 27

Saturday 9th
Capheaton Hall — 7

Sunday 10th
2 Briarlea — 6
Capheaton Hall — 7
St Margaret's
Allotments — 35

Saturday 16th
Woodbine House — 43

Sunday 17th
NEW 4 Sparty Lea
Terrace — 38
Stanton Fence — 39

Saturday 23rd
Middleton Hall
Retirement Village — 25
NEW Shortridge Hall — 37

Sunday 24th
Lambshield — 21

Sunday 31st
45 Blackwell — 3
46 Blackwell — 4
Ferndene House — 13
St Cuthbert's Hospice — 34

August

Sunday 7th
Garden and studio
at 67 — 14
Heather Holm — 16

Sunday 28th
NEW Droomveld — 9

October

Sunday 16th
NEW Etal Manor — 11

By Arrangement

Arrange a personalised garden visit with your club, or group of friends, on a date to suit you. See individual garden entries for full details.

The Beacon — 1
24 Bede Crescent — 2
2 Briarlea — 6
Coldcotes Moor
Garden — 8
Fallodon Hall — 12
Ferndene House — 13
2 Hillside Cottage — 18
Kirky Cottage — 20
Lambshield — 21
Lilburn Tower — 22
Loughbrow House — 23
Middleton Hall
Retirement Village — 25
25 Park Road South — 31
Quarry End — 32
Ravensford Farm — 33
28 Washington
Avenue — 40
Woodlands — 44

© Val Corbett

Stanton Fence

THE GARDENS

1 THE BEACON
10 Crabtree Road, Stocksfield, NE43 7NX. Derek & Patricia Hodgson OBE, 01661 842518, patandderek@btinternet.com. *12m W of Newcastle. From A69 follow signs into village. Station & cricket ground on L. Turn R into Cadehill Rd then 1st R into Crabtree Rd (cul-de-sac) Park on Cadehill.* Sun 5 June, Sun 3 July (2-5). Adm £6, chd free. Home-made teas. **Visits also by arrangement June to Sept for groups of 10+.**
This garden illustrates how to make a cottage garden on a steep site with loads of interest at different levels. Planted with acers, roses and a variety of cottage garden and formal plants. Water runs gently through it and there are tranquil places to sit and talk or just reflect. Stunning colour and plant combinations. Wildlife friendly - numerous birds, frogs, newts, hedgehogs. Haven for butterflies and bees. Owner available for entertaining group talks. Comedy/piano recital available at By Arrangement visits (£5 per person in aid of NSPCC).
❀ 🚗 ☕ ⋅))

National Garden Scheme gardens are identified by their yellow road signs and posters. You can expect a garden of quality, character and interest, a warm welcome and plenty of home-made cakes!

3 45 BLACKWELL
Darlington, DL3 8QT. Cath & Peter Proud. *SW Darlington, next to R.Tees. ½ way along Blackwell in Darlington, which links Bridge Rd (on A66 just past Blackwell Bridge) & Carmel Rd South. Alternatively, turn into Blackwell from PO on Carmel Rd South.* Sun 31 July (1-5). Combined adm with 46 Blackwell £5, chd free. Home-made teas.
No. 45 Blackwell rises from the River Tees up to a 1½ acre garden with many mature trees, wildlife meadow, pond with waterfall, herb and Mediterranean garden, vegetable bed, greenhouse, camellia border, lawns and herbaceous borders and containers full of colourful plants inc dahlias, lilies and agapanthus. Refreshments, preserves and plants on sale. Well behaved dogs on leads welcome. Wheelchair access to patios and to lower lawn only with assistance.
♿ 🐕 ❀ ☕ ⋅))

4 46 BLACKWELL
Darlington, DL3 8QT. Christopher & Yvonne Auton. *Please see directions for 45 Blackwell.* Sun 31 July (1-5). Combined adm with 45 Blackwell £5, chd free. Home-made teas.
46 Blackwell is a plantsman's garden - compact, but full of unusual specimens and collections of plants and trees, with a pond and summerhouse in the back garden. Wheelchair access to front garden and partial access to back garden.
♿ 🐕 ❀ ☕ ⋅))

5 BLAGDON
Seaton Burn, NE13 6DE. Viscount Ridley. *5m S of Morpeth on A1. 8m N of Newcastle on A1, N on B1318, L at r'about (Holiday Inn) & follow signs to Blagdon. Entrance to parking area signed.* Sun 22 May (1-4.30). Adm £6, chd free. Home-made teas.
Unique 27 acre garden encompassing formal garden with Lutyens designed 'canal', Lutyens structures and walled kitchen garden. Valley with stream and various follies, quarry garden and woodland walks. Large numbers of ornamental trees and shrubs planted over many generations. National Collections of Acer, Alnus and Sorbus. Partial wheelchair access.
♿ 🐕 ❀ NPC ☕ ⋅))

6 2 BRIARLEA
Hepscott, Morpeth, NE61 6PA. Richard & Carolyn Torr, 07470 391936, richardtorr6@gmail.com. *Entering Hepscott from A192, Briarlea is 2nd road on R. Please park considerately within the village. Please do not park on Briarlea.* Sun 10 July (11-5). Adm £5, chd free. Refreshments at 7 Thornlea, approx 100 metres away, with further cactus collection and plant stall. **Visits also by arrangement June & July for groups of up to 25.**
A plant lover's garden of just under ½ acre, rejuvenated and redeveloped over the last 5 yrs, featuring gravel areas, stream side planting and many herbaceous borders. Planting features hostas, grasses, roses, penstemons, ferns, a wide range of shrubs and other perennials. A vegetable area with raised beds inc greenhouses with an extensive collection of cacti and other succulents. Good access to most of garden, however, some steps and gravel areas.
♿ 🐕 ❀ ☕

7 CAPHEATON HALL
Capheaton, Newcastle Upon Tyne, NE19 2AB. William & Eliza Browne-Swinburne, 01913 758152, capheatonhall@gmail.com, www.capheatonhall.co.uk/accomodation. *24m N of Newcastle off A696. From S turn L onto Silver Hill rd signed Capheaton. From N, past Wallington/Kirkharle junction, turn R.* Sat 9, Sun 10 July (10-5). Adm £10, chd free. Pre-booking essential, please visit www.ngs.org.uk for information & booking. Home-made teas.
Set in parkland, Capheaton Hall has magnificent views over the Northumberland countryside. Formal ponds sit south of the house which has C19 conservatory and a walk to a Georgian folly of a chapel. The outstanding feature is the very productive walled kitchen garden, mixing colourful vegetables, espaliered fruit with annual and perennial flowering borders. Victorian glasshouse and conservatory.
🐕 ❀ 🏠 ☕ 🧺 ⋅))

Lilburn Tower

⑧ COLDCOTES MOOR GARDEN

Ponteland, Northumberland, Newcastle Upon Tyne, NE20 0DF. Ron & Louise Bowey, 07798 532291, info@theboweys.co.uk. *Off A696 N of Ponteland. From S, leave Ponteland on A696 towards Jedburgh, after 1m take L turn marked 'Milbourne 2m'. After 400yds turn L into drive.* Visits by arrangement June to Aug for groups of 20 to 50. Adm £7, chd free. Home-made teas.

The garden, landscaped grounds and woods cover around 15 acres. The wooded approach opens out to lawned areas surrounded by ornamental and woodland shrubs and trees. A courtyard garden leads to an ornamental walled garden, beyond which is an orchard, vegetable garden, flower garden and rose arbour. To the south the garden looks out over a lake and field walks, with woodland walks to the west. Small children's play area. Mel's Garden Metalwork - 20% to NGS. Most areas are accessible though sometimes by circuitous routes or an occasional step. WC access involves three steps.

  ♿ 🐕 ✿ ☕ 🔊

⑨ NEW DROOMVELD

Christmas Farm, Longframlington, Morpeth, NE65 8DA. Maxine Eaton, 07715 460038, alittleplantcompany@gmail.com, www.alittleplantcompany.co.uk. *At the northern edge of the village on the A697, take the road E with signs for log cabins. After 1m turn L to Christmas Farm (signposted).* Sun 28 Aug (11-4). Adm £5, chd free. Home-made teas. Beth's delicious teas and cakes using fresh produce from the farm.

Begun in 2019 in a beautiful setting, this developing garden is nestled in the Northumberland hills and has numerous borders to showcase different styles - cottage, prairie, naturalistic and woodland with roses and a wildlife pool. Large and abundant organic working kitchen gardens.

  ✿ 🚗 🚌 ☕ 🔊

⑩ NEW ELDON HALL FARM STEADINGS

Old Eldon, Shildon, DL4 2QT. Margaret Clothier. *Located at the junction Xrds in Old Eldon. Sign posted.* Sat 25 June (11-5). Adm £6, chd free. Home-made teas.

This is the first year of opening for this delightful rural development of rescued farm buildings dating back to the 1800s. The sloping elevated site takes full advantage of the spectacular views over fields and woodland. The gardens range from small, medium and large, low and high maintenance, formal and informal all walled in natural stone. Meadow, ponds and woodland area.

  🐐 ✿ ☕ 🔊

⑪ NEW ETAL MANOR

Etal Manor, Etal, Cornhill-on-Tweed, TD12 4TL. Lord and Lady Joicey. *N Northumberland, close to Cornhill-on-Tweed, Coldstream, Berwick-upon-Tweed and Wooler. The garden will be signed from the A697 Wooler to Cornhill-on-Tweed road.* Sun 16 Oct (2-5). Adm £5, chd free. Light refreshments.

A ten acre garden in far N E England managed by the same family since 1910. Developed into a predominantly woodland garden, the acid soil and tough growing environment suits rhododendrons, azaleas, acers and magnolias. In 1969 a new kitchen garden was created. Work continues. The variety of trees in the woodland garden provides very good autumn colour. Mel's Garden Metalwork - 20% to NGS.

  ☕ 🔊

Holmelands

12 FALLODON HALL

Alnwick, NE66 3HF. Mr & Mrs Mark Bridgeman, 01665 576252, luciabridgeman@gmail.com, www.bruntoncottages.co.uk. *5m N of Alnwick, 2m off A1. From the A1 turn onto the B6347 signed Christon Bank & Seahouses. Turn into the Fallodon gates after exactly 2m, at Xrds. Follow drive for 1m. Sat 25 June (2-5). Adm £5, chd free. Home-made teas.* Visits also by arrangement May to Oct for groups of 5 to 20. Please call Lucia Bridgeman on 07765 296197.

Extensive, well established garden, with a hot greenhouse beside the bog garden. The late C17 walls of the kitchen garden surround cutting and vegetable borders and the fruit greenhouse. Natasha McEwen replanted the sunken garden from 1898 and the redesigned 30 metres border was planted in 2019. Woodlands, pond and arboretum with over 10 acres to explore. Grave of Sir Edward Grey, Foreign Secretary during WW1, famous ornithologist and fly fisherman, is in the woods near the pond and arboretum.The walls of kitchen garden contain a fireplace, to heat the fruit trees of the Salkeld family, renowned for their gardening expertise. Partial wheelchair access.

&. 🐕 ✿ 🏛 🍵 ⁙)

13 FERNDENE HOUSE

2 Holburn Lane Court, Holburn Lane, Ryton, NE40 3PN. Maureen Kesteven, 0191 413 5937, maureen.kesteven@ngs. org.uk, www.facebook.com/ northeastgardenopenforcharity/. *In Ryton Old Village, 8m W of Gateshead. Off B6317, on Holburn Lane. Park on street or in Co-op car park on High St, cross rd through Ferndene Park following yellow signs. Sun 31 July (12.30-4.30). Adm £6, chd free. Home-made teas. Pizza & complimentary prosecco.* Visits also by arrangement Apr to Aug for groups of 10+.

The ¾ acre garden is surrounded by trees. Informal areas of herbaceous perennials, more formal box bordered area, sedum roof, wildlife pond, gravel and bog gardens (with boardwalk). Willow work. Early interest - hellebores, snowdrops, daffodils, bluebells and tulips. Summer interest from wide range of flowering perennials and a meadow. 1½ acre mixed broadleaf wood with

beck running through. Driveway, from which main borders can be seen, is wheelchair accessible but phone for assistance.

&. ✿ 🍵 ⁙)

14 GARDEN AND STUDIO AT 67

Manor Road, St Helen Auckland, Bishop Auckland, DL14 9ER. Mitsi B Kral, www.instagram.com/gardenat67/. *From A68 W Auckland, turn on to Station Rd towards St Helen Auckland avoiding the bypass follow the road over the bridge and on to Manor Rd, garden on R by pedestrian crossing. Sun 3 July, Sun 7 Aug (11.30-4.30). Adm £4, chd free. Home-made teas.*

A quirky, bohemian garden, where wildlife comes first. No chemicals used anywhere. Lots of interest and art from the talented Mitsi. Wheelchair access to the main features of the garden, other paths are gravel.

&. 🐕 🐎 ✿ 🚐 🍵 🏕 ⁙)

15 NEW HALTON CASTLE

Corbridge, NE45 5PH. Hugh & Anna Blackett. *2m N of Corbridge turn E off the A68 onto the B6318 (Military Rd) towards Newcastle. Turn R onto drive after ¼ m. Sun 26 June (12-4.30). Adm £5, chd free. Home-made teas. Light lunches from 12.00.*

The terraced garden has stunning views over the Tyne Valley. Massive beech hedges give protection for herbaceous borders, lawns and shrubs. A box parterre is filled with vegetables, roses and sweet peas. Paths lead through a recently created wildflower meadow garden. The Castle (not open) is a C14 Pele tower with Jacobean manor house attached beside a charming chapel with Norman origins. Partial wheelchair access.

&. 🐕 ✿ 🍵 ⁙)

16 HEATHER HOLM

Stanghow Road, Stanghow, Saltburn-By-The-Sea, TS12 3JU. Arthur & June Murray. *Stanghow is 5 km E of Guisborough on A171. Turn L at Lockwood Beck (signed Stanghow) Heather Holm is on the R past the Xrds. Sun 7 Aug (11-4). Adm £4, chd free. Home-made teas.*

Divided into different rooms, this is a garden of different aspects, formal, floral and architectural. The owners have a philosophy of colour

throughout the yr having many different species of lilies flowering from March to October. Sheltered by mature hedges hostas and hydrangeas thrive. There are fruit trees, soft fruit bushes, a greenhouse, summerhouse and a large pond attracting wildlife. No dogs.

✿ 🍵

17 HIGH BANK FARM

Cleasby Road, Stapleton, Darlington, DL2 2QE. Lesley Thompson. *We are located on road leading to Cleasby & Manfield from the Stapleton road. Drive 300 yds, you will see a sign saying 'Nursery on a Farm', take turning and park in the car park. Sun 19 June (1-4). Combined adm with Holmelands £5, chd free. Home-made teas.*

The front garden has an abundance of roses, leading onto the orchard. The back garden has a lovely cottage garden, with a secluded summerhouse to relax in, together with paved area with beautiful pots and you can sit and listen to the trickling water from our lovely fishpond. No dogs.

&. 🍵 ⁙)

18 2 HILLSIDE COTTAGE

Low Etherley, Bishop Auckland, DL14 0EZ. Mrs M Smith, 07789 366702, mary@maryruth.plus.com. *3m W of Bishop Auckland on B6282 and ½ m E of Toft Hill. Follow the B6282 from Bishop Auckland. After the Etherley sign continue along the road for approx ¼ m, the Cottage is down the track on the L near the 2nd footpath sign. Visits by arrangement Feb to Nov. Adm £5, chd free. Light refreshments.*

The large island beds, featuring conifers, heathers and perennials, are bordered by grass paths with views over Weardale. There are interesting shrubs and trees, a greenhouse with tender plants and vegetables, a fruit cage, fruit trees, vegetable beds and herbs. Two ponds and naturally managed areas attract wildlife. Tucked away at the bottom of the garden are beehives. This ½ acre garden is a garden for all season and visitors are welcome throughout the year.

🐕 ✿ 🍵 🏕

19 HOLMELANDS

Cleasby, Darlington, DL2 2QY. **Nicky & Clare Vigors.** *1st open yard on R approaching village from Stapleton.* Sun 19 June (1-4). Combined adm with High Bank Farm £5, chd free. Teas at High Bank Farm.
Semi formal garden with orchard and large vegetable patch. Herbaceous beds and climbing roses as well as standard roses. Laid out in a semi formal design to create a harmonious effect. Attractive mixed borders, formal topiary and lavender at the front of the house.

& ☕ ⋅))

20 KIRKY COTTAGE

12 Mindrum Farm Cottages, Mindrum, TD12 4QN. **Mrs Ginny Fairfax,** 01890 850246, ginny@mindrumgarden.co.uk, mindrumestate.com/mindrum-garden/kirky-cottage-garden/. *6m SW of Coldstream. 9m NW of Wooler on B6352. 4m N of Yetholm village.* Sat 2 July (11-5). Adm £5, chd free. Home-made teas. Visits also by arrangement.
Ginny Fairfax has created Kirky Cottage Garden in the beautiful Bowmont Valley surrounded and protected by the Border Hills. A gravel garden in cottage garden style, old roses, violas and others jostle with favourites from Mindrum. A lovely, abundant garden and, with Ginny's new and creative ideas, ever evolving. Regional finalist in The English Garden's The Nation's Favourite Gardens 2021

❋ ☕ ⋅))

21 LAMBSHIELD

Hexham, NE46 1SF. **David Young,** 07785 310645, david.young@ngs.org.uk. *2m S of Hexham. Take the B6306 from Hexham. After 1.6m turn R at chevron sign. Lambshield drive is 2nd on L after 0.6m.* Sun 24 July (12.30-4.30). Adm £6, chd free. Home-made teas. Visits also by arrangement May to July for groups of 10+.
3 ½ acre country garden begun in 2010 with strong structure and exciting plant combinations. Distinct areas and styles with formal herbaceous, grasses, contemporary planting, cottage garden, pool and orchard. Cloud hedging, pleached trees, and topiary combine with colourful and exuberant planting. Modern sculpture. Oak building and

fencing by local craftsmen. Woodland garden. Mel's Garden Metalwork – 20% to NGS.

❋ 🚗 ☕ ⋅))

22 LILBURN TOWER

Alnwick, NE66 4PQ. **Mr & Mrs D Davidson,** 01668 217291, lilburntower@outlook.com. *3m S of Wooler. On A697.* Sun 29 May (2-5). Adm £6, chd free. Home-made teas. Visits also by arrangement May to Sept for groups of 10+.
10 acres of magnificent walled and formal gardens set above river; rose parterre, topiary, scented garden, Victorian conservatory, wildflower meadow. Extensive fruit and vegetable garden, large glasshouse with vines. 30 acres of woodland with walks. Giant lilies, meconopsis around pond garden. Rhododendrons and azaleas. Also ruins of Pele Tower, and C12 church. Partial wheelchair access.

& 🐎 ❋ 🚗 ☕ ⋅))

23 LOUGHBROW HOUSE

Hexham, NE46 1RS. **Mrs K A Clark,** 01434 603351, patriciaclark351@hotmail.com. *1m S of Hexham on B6306. Dipton Mill Rd. Rd signed Blanchland, ¼m take R fork; then ¼m at fork, lodge gates & driveway at intersection.* Visits by arrangement for groups of 10+. Adm £5, chd free. Home-made teas.
A real country house garden with sweeping, colour themed herbaceous borders set around large lawns. Unique Lutyens inspired rill with grass topped bridges and climbing rose arches. Part walled kitchen garden and paved courtyard. Bog garden with pond. New rose bed. Wildflower meadow with specimen trees. Woodland quarry garden with rhododendrons, azaleas, hostas and rare trees. Home-made jams and chutneys for sale.

🐎 ❋ 🚗 🚌 ☕

24 MARIE CURIE HOSPICE

Marie Curie Drive, Newcastle Upon Tyne, NE4 6SS. **Marie Curie,** www.mariecurie.org.uk/help/hospice-care/hospices/newcastle/about. *In West Newcastle just off Elswick rd. At the bottom of a housing estate. Turning is between MA Brothers & Dallas Carpets.* Sun 3 July (2-4). Adm by donation. Cream teas in our Garden Café.
The landscaped gardens of the

purpose-built Marie Curie Hospice overlooks the Tyne and Gateshead and offers a beautiful, tranquil place for patients and visitors to sit and chat. Rooms open onto a patio garden with gazebo and fountain. There are climbing roses, evergreens and herbaceous perennials. The garden is well maintained by volunteers. Come and see the work NGS funding helps make possible. Plant sale and refreshments available. The Hospice and Gardens are wheelchair accessible.

& ❋ ☕

25 MIDDLETON HALL RETIREMENT VILLAGE

Middleton St. George, Darlington, DL2 1HA. **Middleton Hall Retirement Village,** 01325 332207, www.middletonhallretirementvillage.co.uk. *From A67 D'ton/Yarm, turn at 2nd r'about signed to Middleton St George. Turn L at the mini r'about & immed R after the railway bridge, signed Low Middleton. Main entrance is ¼m on L.* Sat 23 July (10-4). Adm £6, chd £2. Light refreshments. Visits also by arrangement May to July.
Like those in our retirement community, the extensive grounds are gloriously mature, endlessly interesting and with many hidden depths. 45 acres of features beckon; natural woodland and parkland, Japanese, Mediterranean and Butterfly Gardens, putting green, allotments, ponds, wetland and bird hide. For more information please visit our website. All wheelchair accessible and linked by a series of woodland walks.

& 🐎 ❋ ☕ 🎋 ⋅))

26 ✦ MINDRUM GARDEN

Mindrum, TD12 4QN. **Mr & Mrs T Fairfax,** 01890 850634, tpfairfax@gmail.com, www.mindrumestate.com. *6m SW of Coldstream, 9m NW of Wooler. Off B6352. Disabled parking close to house.* For NGS: Sun 19 June (2-5). Adm £6, chd free. Home-made teas. For other opening times and information, please phone, email or visit garden website.
A magical combination of old-fashioned roses and hardy perennials. Lawns surround the house with climbing roses, mature shrubs and trees throughout.Mindrum has evolved into a series of gardens including a rose garden, limestone

Etal Manor

rock garden (steep slope), fishponds with terraced area, a woodland walk with mature pines, and wildflower garden by the river.

🐏 🚗 ☕ ⯈)

27 THE MOORE HOUSE
Whalton, Morpeth, NE61 3UX.
Phillip & Filiz Rodger. *5m W of Morpeth & 4m N of Belsay on B6524. House in middle of village. Park in village. Follow NGS signs.* Sun 3 July (2-5). Adm £5, chd free. Home-made teas.
2½ acre mature garden extensively but sympathetically redesigned by Sean Murray, BBC /RHS Great Chelsea Garden Challenge winner. Garden divided into sections. Wide use and mix of flowering perennials and grasses, also gravel garden and stone rill. Decorative stonework around beds in patio area. Emphasis on scent, colour, texture and form with year-round interest. Mel's Garden Metalwork – 20% to NGS.

❋ ☕ ⯈)

28 ◆ NGS BUZZING GARDEN
East Park Road, Gateshead, NE9 5AX. Gateshead Council, maureen.kesteven@ngs.org.uk, www.gateshead.gov.uk/article/3958/Saltwell-Park. *Between Pets' Corner & Saltwell Towers. Pedestrian entrance from East Park Rd or car park in Joicey Rd. Open all year as part of the 55 acre Saltwell Park, known as The People's Park.* **For opening times and information, please email or visit garden website.**
A unique collaboration between the National Garden Scheme North East, Trädgårdsresan, Region Västra Götaland and Gateshead Council. It was funded by sponsorship. The garden is a tribute to the importance of international friendship. The Swedish design reflects the landscape of West Sweden, with coast, meadow and woodland areas. Many of the plant species grow wild in Sweden, providing a welcoming vision for visitors and a feast for pollinators. Planted in 2019 the

garden is maturing. Visitors can make a donation to the NGS. Wide tarmac path around the garden and mown grass paths through the meadow, but much of the garden is loose gravel.

♿ 🐏 🚗 ☕

The National Garden Scheme donated £500,000 to Hospice UK in 2021, enabling us to continue supporting over 200 hospices in the UK who have been at the forefront of the battle against COVID-19

GROUP OPENING

29 NEW OLD QUARRINGTON GARDENS

The Stables, Old Quarrington, Durham, DH6 5NN.
John Little, facebook.com/ OldQuarringtonGardens. *1m from J61 of A1(M). All Vehicle access from Crow Trees Lane, Bowburn. SatNav maybe misleading.* Sun 26 June (11-4). Combined adm £6, chd free. Home-made teas at The Stables - also picnics and WC.

NEW 13 HEUGH HALL ROW
Jacqueline Robson, facebook. com/OldQuarringtonGardens.

ROSE COTTAGE
Mr Richard & Mrs Ann Cowen.

THE STABLES
John & Claire Little, facebook.com/thestablesOQ.

Three very distinct gardens in the hamlet of Old Quarrington. The Stables is a large family garden full of hidden surprises and extensive views. The main garden is about an acre including gravel garden, vegetable patch, orchard, play area, lawn and woodland gardens. There is a further 4 acres to explore which inc wildlife ponds, woodlands, meadows, hens, ducks and alpacas. Number 13 has been developed over 20 yrs with many small garden rooms inc a rose garden, a white garden, a small link garden which contains ferns, viburnum, birch trees and a *Cercidiphyllum japoniocum*. There is a pond and herbaceous beds which contain perennials and grasses. Many roses can be seen throughout the garden and a greenhouse devoted to a large Brown Turkey fig . The main garden at Rose Cottage is planted with wildlife friendly flowers, has slate paths and a pond that attracts 2 species of newts. To the rear there is a Mediterranean area and a woodland garden with stream beyond. Plant sales at 13 Heugh Hall Road.

♿ 🐕 ❀ ☕ 🌳))

---

30 OLIVER FORD GARDEN
Longedge Lane, Rowley, Consett, DH8 9HG. Bob & Bev Tridgett, www.gardensanctuaries.co.uk. *5m NW of Lanchester. Signed from A68 in Rowley. From Lanchester take rd towards Sately. Garden will be signed as you pass Woodlea Manor.* Sun 26 June (1-5). Adm £4, chd free. Light refreshments.
A peaceful, contemplative 3 acre garden developed and planted by the owner and BBC Gardener of the Year as a space for quiet reflection.

Arboretum specialising in bark, stream, wildlife pond and bog garden. Semi-shaded Japanese maple and dwarf rhododendron garden. Rock garden and scree bed. Insect nectar area, orchard and 1½ acre meadow. Annual wildflower area. Terrace and ornamental herb garden. The garden is managed to maximise wildlife and there are a number of sculptures around the garden.

🐕 🪑 ☕ 🌳))

31 25 PARK ROAD SOUTH
Chester le Street, DH3 3LS. Mrs A Middleton, 0191 388 3225, midnot2@gmail.com. *4m N of Durham. Located at S end of A167 Chester-le-St bypass rd. Precise directions provided when booking visit.* Visits by arrangement May to Aug. Adm £3.50, chd free.
A stunning town garden with year-round interest. Herbaceous borders with unusual perennials, grasses, shrubs surrounding lawn and paved area. Courtyard planted with foliage and small front gravel garden. The garden owner is a very knowledgeable plantswoman who enjoys showing visitors around her inspiring garden. No minimum size of group. Plants for sale.

♿ ❀ ☕

Old Quarrington Gardens

32 QUARRY END

Walworth, Darlington, DL2 2LY. Iain & Margaret Anderson, 01325 778446, quarryend@btinternet.com. *Approx 5m W of Darlington on A68 or ½m E of Piercebridge on A67. Follow brown signs to Walworth Castle Hotel. Just up the hill from the Castle entrance, follow NGS yellow signs down private track. Visits by arrangement May to Aug for groups of 10 to 25. Plenty of parking on site for cars or a small bus. Adm £5, chd free. Home-made teas.*

Woodland garden in an ancient quarry setting. Redeveloped over 21 yrs the garden has a C18 ice house, a wide variety of trees, shrubs and perennials, a fernery and ornamental vegetable plot. Spectacular late summer display but something of interest throughout the year inc an acre of reclaimed naturalised woodland in the adjacent quarry. Extensive views over South Durham. Only partial wheelchair access to woodland area especially if wet. Main garden includes some rough steps and gravel paths.

33 RAVENSFORD FARM

Hamsterley, DL13 3NH. Jonathan & Caroline Peacock, 01388 488305, caroline@ravensfordfarm.co.uk. *7m W of Bishop Auckland. From A68 at Witton-le-Wear turn off W to Hamsterley. Follow village Garden signs or at other times go through village & turn L just before tennis courts at West End. Sun 10 Apr (11-2.30). Adm £5, chd free. Light refreshments. Hot soup and cheese scones. Visits also by arrangement Mar to Oct.*

The garden, with some 40 different varieties of narcissi, early-flowering trees, primroses and wood anemones, is often most beautiful in spring. There will be music, of course, as well as plant sales. Colour, variety, ponds, unusual trees and shrubs. Refreshments under cover in case of inclement weather. Some gravel, so assistance will be needed for wheelchairs. Assistance dogs only, please.

34 ST CUTHBERT'S HOSPICE

Park House Road, Durham, DH1 3QF. Paul Marriott, CEO, www.stcuthbertshospice.com. *1m SW of Durham City on A167. Turn into Park House Rd, the Hospice is on the L after bowling green car park. Parking available. Sun 31 July (11-4). Adm £5, chd free.*

5 acres of mature gardens surround this CQC outstanding-rated Hospice. In development since 1988, the gardens are cared for by volunteers inc a Victorian-style greenhouse and large vegetable, fruit and cut flower area. Lawns surround smaller scale specialist planting, and areas for patients and visitors to relax. Woodland area with walks, sensory garden, and an 'In Memory' garden with stream. Plants and produce for sale. We are active participants in Northumbria in Bloom and Britain in Bloom, with several awards in recent years, inc overall winner in 2015, 2018 & 2019 for the Care/ Residential /Convalescent Homes / Day Centre / Hospices category. Almost all areas are accessible for wheelchairs.

GROUP OPENING

35 ST MARGARET'S ALLOTMENTS

Margery Lane, Durham City, DH1 4QU. *From A1 take A690 to City Centre/Crook. Straight ahead at T-lights after 4th r'about. 10mins walk from bus or rail station. Sun 10 July (1.30-5.30). Combined adm £5, chd free. Pre-booking essential, please visit www.ngs. org.uk for information & booking.*

5 acres of over 100 allotments against the spectacular backdrop of Durham Cathedral. This site has been cultivated since the Middle Ages. Enthusiastic gardeners, many using organic methods, cultivate plots which display a great variety of fruit, vegetables and flowers. booking in advanced required. Visits are by guided tour only.

36 ST OSWALD'S HOSPICE

Regent Avenue, Newcastle Upon Tyne, NE3 1EE. St Oswald's Hospice, www.stoswaldsuk.org/ who-we-are/. *Parking available on site & on street. Sat 18 June (10-2). Adm by donation. Light refreshments.*

Recently redesigned in-patients' garden is a delightful, tranquil breakout space. Adjacent to the new 'family room' and designed around an existing pond, offering plenty of opportunities to sit and reflect on the mix of colours, textures, scents and sounds within it. Also special children's hospice garden. Both planted and maintained by a wonderful team of dedicated volunteers. Wheelchair accessible

37 NEW SHORTRIDGE HALL

Warkworth, Morpeth, NE65 0WJ. Rachael & Mike Wyllie. *Garden about 1½m from Warkworth. Sat 23 July (1.30-5.30). Adm £6, chd free. Home-made teas.*

A newly planted 3½ acre garden based on a design by well-known landscape designer, Adam Frost. The garden surrounds a Victorian Hall and has lots of interest, including wildflower meadows, a woodland garden, herbaceous and mixed shrub borders, mixed rose garden and ornamental ponds. A small walled garden houses the greenhouse and a cutting garden. There are significant, but young hedges. Mel's Garden Metalwork – 20% to NGS.

38 NEW 4 SPARTY LEA TERRACE

Sparty Lea, Hexham, NE47 9UB. Vivian Jackson. *On B6295 Sparty Lea is 17m W of Hexham, 5m W of Allendale & 3m before Allenheads. Sun 17 July (11-4). Adm £5. Pre-booking essential, please visit www.ngs.org.uk for information & booking. Home-made teas.*

This surprisingly lush garden lies at 1,100ft above sea level in the North Pennines AONB. It has evolved over 20 yrs from meadowland to cottage garden with herbaceous border, lawns wildlife pond and abundant half hardy annuals. Mature shrubs and trees surrounded by dry stone walls provide wind protection. The terrace was built in 1850 at the height of lead mining and smelting in the Allen valleys.

4 Sparty Lea

39 STANTON FENCE
Stanton, Morpeth, NE65 8PP. Sir
David Kelly. *5m NW of Morpeth.
Nr Stanton on the C144 between
Pigdon & Netherwitton. OS map
ref NZ 135890.* Sun 17 July (1-5).
Adm £6, chd free. Home-made
teas. Donation to St Giles Church,
Netherwitton.
Contemporary 4.7 acre country
garden designed by Chelsea Gold
Medal winner, Arabella Lennox-Boyd,
in keeping with its rural setting. A
strong underlying design unites the
different areas from formal parterre
and courtyard garden to orchard,
wildflower meadows and woodland.
Romantically planted rose covered
arbours and long clematis draped
pergola walk. Nuttery, kitchen garden
and greenhouse. Delightful views.
Robert Iley, the garden builder, and
Steve Grimwood, the gardener, will
be present. Mel's Garden Metalwork
on sale - 20% to NGS. Wheelchair
access for chairs that can use mown
paths as well as hard paving.

40 28 WASHINGTON AVENUE
Middleton St. George,
Darlington, DL2 1HE. Mrs
Vanessa Hart, 07975 611056,
van2695@msn.com. *Situated
between Middleton St George & Oak
Tree.* Visits by arrangement Apr to
Oct for groups of 5 to 15. Adm by
donation. Light refreshments.
A garden created for the love of
colour, plants and wildlife, filled with
English roses, clematis, jasmines and
passion flowers. Borders are packed
with as many bee, butterfly and insect
loving plants as possible. An eclectic
mix of water features and garden
ornaments add to the quirkiness of
this garden and there is something
to simulate every sense. A beautiful
place to sit in the sun.

**41 ◆ WHALTON MANOR
GARDENS**
Whalton, Morpeth, NE61 3UT.
Mr T R P S Norton,
gardens@whaltonmanor.co.uk,
www.whaltonmanor.co.uk. *5m
W of Morpeth. On the B6524, the
house is at E end of the village & will
be signed.* For NGS: Sun 26 June
(1-5). Adm £5, chd free. Home-
made teas in The Game Larder.
For other opening times and
information, please email or visit
garden website.

The historic Whalton Manor, altered
by Sir Edwin Lutyens in 1908, is
surrounded by 3 acres of magnificent
walled gardens, designed by Lutyens
with the help of Gertrude Jekyll. The
gardens, developed by the Norton
family since the 1920s inc extensive
herbaceous borders, spring bulbs,
30yd peony border, rose garden,
listed summerhouses, pergolas
and walls festooned with rambling
roses and clematis. Mel's garden
metalwork for sale - 20% to NGS.
Partial wheelchair access to main
area but otherwise stone steps and
gravel paths.

GROUP OPENING

**42 WOLSINGHAM VILLAGE
GARDENS**
Wolsingham, Bishop Auckland,
DL13 3AY. Janette Kelly. *Gardens
are spread throughout the village.
Parking is available in village centre
& at the recreation field.* Sat 2 July
(1-5). Combined adm £6, chd
free. Light refreshments at St
Anne's community centre in the
recreation field.
A group of 8 gardens mainly centred
around the recreation field. One is a
short walk/drive to the edge of the
village. They vary between traditional
gardens, more unusual gardens and
allotments. One borders the River
Wear, another has ponds and water
features. Owing to the number of
gardens not all are accessible for
wheelchair users.
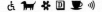

43 WOODBINE HOUSE
22 South View, Hunwick, Crook,
DL15 0JW. Stewart Irwin & Colin
Purvis. *On main rd through the
village opp village green. B6286 off
A689 Bishop Auckland - Crook or
A690 Durham - Crook. On street
parking, entrance to the rear of the
property RHS of house.* Sat 16 July
(1-5). Adm £5, chd free. Home-
made teas.
The garden is approx ¼ of an acre,
divided into two, one half used
as a vegetable garden with large
greenhouse. The other half of the
garden is lawn with well-stocked (and
some unusual planting) herbaceous
borders and small pond. Bees
are kept in the vegetable garden.
All refreshments are home-made.
No dogs. Wheelchair access to

refreshment area but paths in garden
are not wide enough for wheelchairs.

44 WOODLANDS
Peareth Hall Road, Springwell
Village, Gateshead, NE9 7NT.
Liz Reid, 07719 875750,
liz.reid@ngs.org.uk. *3½m N
Washington Galleries. 4m S
Gateshead town centre. On B1288
turn opp Guide Post pub (NE9 7RR)
onto Peareth Hall Rd. Continue for
½m passing 2 bus stops on L. 3rd
drive on L past Highbury Ave.* Sat
25 June (1.30-4.30). Adm £4, chd
free. Home-made teas. Beer &
wine also available. Visits also
by arrangement June to Aug for
groups of 10 to 30.
Mature garden on a site of approx
one seventh acre- quirky, with tropical
themed planting and Caribbean
inspired bar. Also an area of cottage
garden planting. A fun garden with
colour throughout the year, interesting
plants, informal beds and borders and
pond area. On the 25-27 June 2022
Springwell Village plans a 'Forties
Weekend' with many attractions. Eg:
2nd WW battle re-enactments and
a military camp are planned on the
nearby Bowes Railway (SAM) site.
There are also plans for craft and
other stalls and live music throughout
the village.

*In 2021 the National
Garden Scheme
donation helped support
Perennial's caseworkers,
who helped over 250
people and their families
in crisis to receive a
wide range of support
including emergency
food parcels and
accommodation, energy
payments and expert
advice and information*

NORTHAMPTONSHIRE

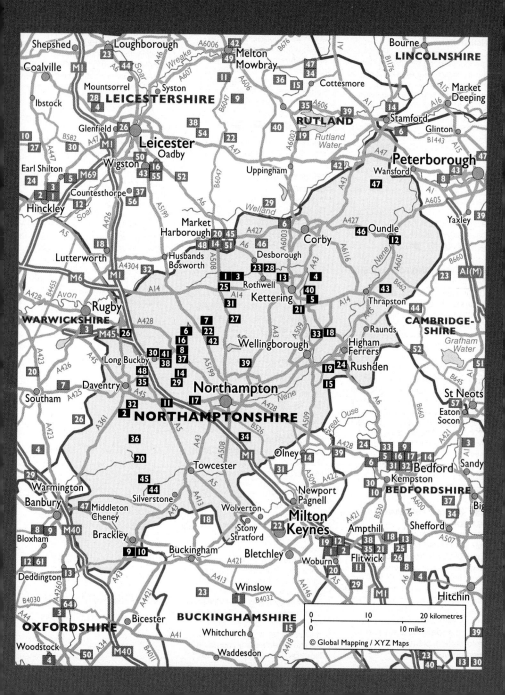

The county of Northamptonshire is famously known as the 'Rose of the Shires', but is also referred to as the 'Shire of Spires and Squires', and lies in the East Midlands area of the country bordered by eight other counties.

Take a gentle stroll around charming villages with thatch and stone cottages and welcoming inns. Wander around stately homes, discovering art treasures and glorious gardens open for the National Garden Scheme at Kelmarsh Hall, Holdenby House, Cottesbrooke Hall and Boughton House. In contrast visit some village groups, which include small imaginatively designed gardens. Explore historic market towns such as Oundle and Brackley in search of fine footwear, antiques and curiosities.

The serenity of our waterways with Woodcote Villa at Long Buckby Wharf will delight, and our winding country lanes and footpaths will guide you around a rural oasis, far from the pressures of modern living, where you can walk knee-deep in bluebells at Boughton House, view hellebores and spring flowers at 67/69 High Street, Finedon or The Old Vicarage at Norton through the seasons, to the late autumn colours of Briarwood.

Our first garden opens in February and the final opening occurs in October, giving a glimpse of gardens throughout the seasons.

Volunteers

County Organisers
David Abbott
01933 680363
david.abbott@ngs.org.uk

Gay Webster
01604 740203
gay.webster@ngs.org.uk

County Treasurer
David Abbott (as above)

Publicity
David Abbott (as above)

Photographer
Snowy Ellson
07508 218320
snowyellson@googlemail.com

Booklet Coordinator
William Portch
01536 522169
william.portch@ngs.org.uk

Talks
Elaine & William Portch
01536 522169
elaine.portch@yahoo.com

Assistant County Organisers
Amanda Bell
01327 860651
amanda.bell@ngs.org.uk

Lindsey Cartwright
01327 860056
lindsey.cartwright@ngs.org.uk

Jo Glissmann-Hill
07725 258755
joanna.glissmann-hill@ngs.org.uk

Philippa Heumann
01327 860142
pmheumann@gmail.com

Elaine & William Portch
(as above)

f @Northants Ngs
@NorthantsNGS
@northantsngs

Left: 136 High Street

OPENING DATES

All entries subject to change. For latest information check www.ngs.org.uk

Map locator numbers are shown to the right of each garden name.

February

Snowdrop Festival

Sunday 27th
♦ Boughton House   4
67-69 High Street   18

March

Sunday 20th
Woodcote Villa   48

April

Friday 1st
Ravensthorpe Nursery   38

Saturday 2nd
Ravensthorpe Nursery   38

Sunday 3rd
Ravensthorpe Nursery   38

Sunday 10th
Flore Gardens   11
Titchmarsh House   43

Sunday 24th
Briarwood   5
♦ Cottesbrooke Hall
Gardens   7
♦ Kelmarsh Hall &
Gardens   25
The Old Vicarage   35
NEW Rosi's Taverna   40

Friday 29th
Ravensthorpe Nursery   38

Saturday 30th
Ravensthorpe Nursery   38

May

Sunday 1st
Great Brington Gardens   14
Ravensthorpe Nursery   38

Sunday 15th
Greywalls   15
♦ Holdenby House &
Gardens   22

Sunday 22nd
Badby Gardens   2
Guilsborough Gardens   16
NEW Maidwell Gardens   31

Saturday 28th
NEW Willow Cottage   46

Sunday 29th
Newnham Gardens   32

June

Thursday 2nd
NEW East Haddon
Gardens   8

Friday 3rd
Ravensthorpe Nursery   38

Saturday 4th
Ravensthorpe Nursery   38

Sunday 5th
Ravensthorpe Nursery   38

Saturday 11th
Titchmarsh House   43

Sunday 12th
Evenley Gardens   9
Foxtail Lilly   12
Harpole Gardens   17
67-69 High Street   18
1 Hinwick Close   21
Spratton Gardens   42

Saturday 18th
Flore Gardens   11

Sunday 19th
Flore Gardens   11
Hostellarie   23
Kilsby Gardens   26
16 Leys Avenue   28
Rosearie-de-la-Nymph   39
Weedon Lois &
Weston Gardens   45

Sunday 26th
Arthingworth Open
Gardens   1
NEW 104 Irchester Road   24
Rosearie-de-la-Nymph   39
Wappenham Gardens   44

July

Sunday 3rd
67-69 High Street   18
NEW Little Brington
Gardens   29

Friday 8th
Ravensthorpe Nursery   38

Saturday 9th
Ravensthorpe Nursery   38

Sunday 10th
Ravensthorpe Gardens   37
NEW Willowbrook House   47

Saturday 16th
♦ Evenley Wood Garden   10

Sunday 17th
Nonsuch   33

Sunday 24th
Long Buckby Gardens   30

August

Sunday 7th
136 High Street   19

Saturday 13th
♦ Lamport Hall   27

Sunday 14th
NEW Highfields   20
NEW Maidwell Gardens   31

Sunday 28th
NEW 104 Irchester Road   24
Old Rectory, Quinton   34

September

Friday 2nd
Ravensthorpe Nursery   38

Saturday 3rd
Ravensthorpe Nursery   38

Sunday 4th
16 Leys Avenue   28
Ravensthorpe Nursery   38

Sunday 11th
Briarwood   5
NEW Rosi's Taverna   40

Saturday 17th
♦ Coton Manor Garden   6

Sunday 25th
4 Skinyard Lane   41
Woodcote Villa   48

Friday 30th
Ravensthorpe Nursery   38

October

Saturday 1st
Ravensthorpe Nursery   38

Sunday 2nd
Ravensthorpe Nursery   38

Sunday 16th
♦ Boughton House   4

February 2023

Sunday 26th
67-69 High Street   18

By Arrangement

Arrange a personalised garden visit on a date to suit you. See individual garden entries for full details.

Bosworth House   3
Briarwood   5
Dripwell House,
Guilsborough Gardens   16
Foxtail Lilly   12
Glendon Hall   13
Greywalls   15
67-69 High Street   18
136 High Street   19
Hostellarie   23
NEW 104 Irchester Road   24
16 Leys Avenue   28
19 Manor Close, Harpole
Gardens   17
The Old Bakery, Flore
Gardens   11
Old West Farm   36
4 Skinyard Lane   41
Titchmarsh House   43
NEW Willowbrook
House   47
Wisteria House, Long
Buckby Gardens   30
Woodcote Villa   48

Our 2021 donations mean that 8,500 patients have been supported across three Horatio's gardens

THE GARDENS

GROUP OPENING

1 ARTHINGWORTH OPEN GARDENS

Arthingworth, nr Market Harborough, LE16 8LA. *6m S of Market Harborough. From Market Harborough via A508, after 4m take L to Arthingworth. From Northampton, A508 turn R just after Kelmarsh. Park cars in Arthingworth village & tickets for sale in the village hall.* **Sun 26 June (1.30-5). Combined adm £7, chd free. Home-made teas by residents of the village at Bosworth House & village hall.**

Arthingworth has been welcoming NGS visitors for a decade. It is a village affair with eight to nine gardens opening and two pop-up tearooms with home baked cakes. We now have some regulars who keep us on our toes and we love it. Come and enjoy the diversity, we aim to give visitors an afternoon of discovery. Our gardens have been chosen because they are all different in spirit and tended by young and weathered gardeners. We have gardens with stunning views, traditional and herbaceous borders and vegetables, walled and artisan. The village is looking forward to welcoming you. St Andrew's Church, Grade II* listed will be open and the village is next to the national cycle path. Wheelchair access to some gardens.

GROUP OPENING

2 BADBY GARDENS

Badby, Daventry, NN11 3AR. *3m S of Daventry on E-side of A361.* **Sun 22 May (1-5). Combined adm £5, chd free. Home-made teas in St Mary's Church.**

CHAPEL HOUSE
Moira & Peter Cooper.

THE OLD HOUSE
Mr & Mrs Robert Cain.

SHAKESPEARES COTTAGE
Jocelyn Hartland-Swann & Pen Keyte.

SOUTHVIEW COTTAGE
Alan & Karen Brown.

Delightful hilly village with attractive old houses of golden coloured Hornton stone, set around a C14 church and two village greens (no through traffic). There are four gardens of differing styles; a wisteria-clad thatched cottage with a sloping garden and modern sculptures; a traditional garden featuring a spectacular view across fields to Badby Wood; an elevated garden with views over the village; and a secluded garden with five distinct areas, pond and fernery, patio, lawn, small orchard and formal vegetable garden. We look forward to welcoming you to our lovely village!

3 BOSWORTH HOUSE

Oxendon Road, Arthingworth, Nr Market Harborough, LE16 8LA. Mr & Mrs C E Irving-Swift, 01858 525202, cirvingswift@gmail.com. *From the phone box, when in Oxendon Rd, take the little lane with no name, 2nd to the R.* **Visits by arrangement Apr to Oct for groups of 10 to 25. One hour tour by the owner. Adm £12, chd free. Home-made teas.** Approx 3 acres, almost completely organic garden and paddock with fabulous panoramic views and magnificent wellingtonia. The garden also inc herbaceous borders, orchard, cottage garden with greenhouse, vegetable garden, herbs and strawberries and spinney. Bring a bag for any cuttings. Partial wheelchair access.

Saddler's Cottage, East Haddon Gardens

4 ♦ BOUGHTON HOUSE

Geddington, Kettering, NN14 1BJ. Duke of Buccleuch & Queensberry, KT. *3m NE of Kettering. From A14, 2m along A43 Kettering to Stamford, turn R into Geddington, house entrance 1½ m on R. What3words app - crispier. sensible.maps.* **For NGS: Sun 27 Feb, Sun 16 Oct (1-5). Adm £6, chd £3. Pre-booking essential, please phone 01536 515731, email info@ boughtonhouse.co.uk or visit www.boughtonhouse.org.uk for information & booking. Tea. For other opening times and information, please phone, email or visit garden website.**

The Northamptonshire home of the Duke and Duchess of Buccleuch. The garden opening inc opportunities to see the historic walled garden and herbaceous border, and the sensory and wildlife gardens. The wilderness woodland will open for visitors to view the spring flowers or the autumn colours. As a special treat the garden originally created by Sir David Scott (cousin of the Duke of Buccleuch) will also be open. Designated disabled parking. Gravel around house, please see our accessibility document for further information.

& ✿ ☷ ☕ ⚘

5 BRIARWOOD

4 Poplars Farm Road, Barton Seagrave, Kettering, NN15 5AF. William & Elaine Portch, 01536 522169, elaine.portch@yahoo.com, www.briarwoodgarden.com. *1½ m SE of Kettering Town Centre. J10 off A14 turn onto Barton Rd (A6) towards Wicksteed Park. R into Warkton Ln, after 200 metres R into Poplars Farm Rd.* **Sun 24 Apr, Sun 11 Sept (10-4). Combined adm with Rosi's Taverna £6.50, chd free. Light refreshments. Visits also by arrangement for groups of 10 to 30.**

A garden for all seasons with quirky original sculptures and many faces. Firstly, a south aspect lawn and borders containing bulbs, shrubs, roses and rare trees with year-round interest; hedging, palms, climbers, a wildlife, fish and lily pond, terrace with potted bulbs and unusual plants in odd containers. Secondly, a secret garden with garden room, small orchard, raised bed potager and greenhouse. Good use of recycled and repurposed materials throughout the garden, inc a unique self-build garden cabin, sculpture and planters.

& ✿ ☕ ⚘

6 ♦ COTON MANOR GARDEN

Coton, Northampton, NN6 8RQ. Mr & Mrs Ian Pasley-Tyler, 01604 740219, pasleytyler@cotonmanor.co.uk, www.cotonmanor.co.uk. *10m N of Northampton, 11m SE of Rugby. From A428 & A5199 follow tourist signs.* **For NGS: Sat 17 Sept (11.30-5). Adm £8, chd £3.50. Light refreshments at Stableyard Cafe. For other opening times and information, please phone, email or visit garden website.**

Winner of The English Garden's The Nation's Favourite Gardens 2019, this 10 acre garden set in peaceful countryside with old yew and holly hedges and extensive herbaceous borders, containing many unusual plants. One of Britain's finest throughout the season, the garden is at its most magnificent in Sept and is an inspiration as to what can be achieved in late summer. Adjacent specialist nursery with over 1000 plant varieties propagated from the garden. Partial wheelchair access as some paths are narrow and the site is on a slope.

& ✿ ☷ ☕ ⚘

7 ♦ COTTESBROOKE HALL GARDENS

Cottesbrooke, Northampton, NN6 8PF. Mr & Mrs A R Macdonald-Buchanan, 01604 505808, welcome@cottesbrooke.co.uk, www.cottesbrooke.co.uk. *10m N of Northampton. Signed from J1 on A14. Off A5199 at Creaton, A508 at Brixworth.* **For NGS: Sun 24 Apr (2-5.30). Adm £10, chd £6. Home-made teas. For other opening times and information, please phone, email or visit garden website. Donation to All Saints Church, Cottesbrooke.**

Award-winning gardens by Geoffrey Jellicoe, Dame Sylvia Crowe, James Alexander-Sinclair and more recently Arne Maynard. Formal gardens and terraces surround Queen Anne house with extensive vistas onto the lake and C18 parkland containing many mature trees. Wild and woodland gardens, a short distance from the formal areas, are exceptional in spring. Partial wheelchair access as paths are grass, stone and gravel. Access map identifies best route.

& ✿ ☷ ☕ ⚘

GROUP OPENING

8 NEW EAST HADDON GARDENS

East Haddon, Northampton, NN6 8BT. *A few hundred yds off the A428 (signed) between M1 J18 (8m) & Northampton (8m). On-road parking. Strictly no parking in Priestwell Court or on the properties.* **Thur 2 June (1-5). Combined adm £6, chd free. Home-made teas at St Mary's Church.**

NEW **BRAEBURN HOUSE**
Judy Darby.

LIMETREES
Barry & Sally Hennessey.

NEW **LINDEN HOUSE**
Hilary Van den Boogard.

NEW **SADDLER'S COTTAGE**
Val Longley.

NEW **THARFIELD**
Julia Farnsworth.

NEW **TOWER COTTAGE**
John Benson.

The pretty village of East Haddon dates back to the Norman invasion. The oldest surviving building is St Mary's, a C12 church. The village has many thatched cottages built in the local honey-coloured ironstone. Other features inc a thatched village pump and fire station which used to house a hand drawn pump and is now used as the bus shelter. The village is less than 10 mins from Coton Manor Gardens. Partial wheelchair access at Tower Cottage.

& ✿ ☕ ⚘

GROUP OPENING

9 EVENLEY GARDENS

Evenley, Brackley, NN13 5SG. *1m S of Brackley off the A43. Gardens situated around the village green & in Church Ln. Follow signs around the village. Tickets available at each garden, to cover entry to all gardens.* **Sun 12 June (2-6). Combined adm £5, chd free. Home-made teas in St George's Church (2.30-5pm).**

15 CHURCH LANE
Carrie & Kevin O'Regan.

FINCH COTTAGE
Cathy & Chris Ellis.

14 THE GREEN
Nic Hamblin.

Evenley is a charming village with a central village green surrounded by many period houses (not open), an excellent village shop and The Red Lion pub which offers first class food and a warm welcome. Evenley gardens are a mix of established gardens and those being developed over the past 5 yrs. They all have mixed borders with established shrubs and trees. There are also orchards and vegetable gardens in some.

◆ EVENLEY WOOD GARDEN
Evenley, Brackley, NN13 5SH.
Whiteley Family, 07788 207428,
alison@evenleywoodgarden.co.uk,
www.evenleywoodgarden.co.uk.
¾ m S of Brackley. Turn off at Evenley r'about on A43 & follow signs within the village to the garden which is situated off the Evenley & Mixbury road. **For NGS: Sat 16 July (10-4). Adm £6, chd free. Light refreshments. For other opening times and information, please phone, email or visit garden website.**
Please come and celebrate summer in the woods when the roses and lillies will have taken over from the azaleas and rhododendrons. A wonderful opportunity to see all that has been developed in the woods since Timothy Whiteley acquired them in 1980 with the continuation of his legacy. Morning tea or coffee, lunch with a glass of wine and home-made cakes will be available in the café. Please take care as all paths are grass.

GROUP OPENING

🔢 FLORE GARDENS
Flore, Northampton, NN7 4LQ. Off the A45 2m W of M1 J16. SatNav NN7 4LS for car park. Coaches advice phone 01327 341225. **Sun 10 Apr (2-6). Combined adm £6, chd free. Sat 18, Sun 19 June (11-6). Combined adm £8, chd free. Home-made teas in Chapel School Room (Apr). Morning coffee & teas in Church & light lunches & teas in Chapel School Room (June). Donation to All Saints Church & United Reform Church, Flore (June).**

24 BLISS LANE
John Miller.
Open on Sun 10 Apr

THE CROFT
John & Dorothy Boast.
Open on all dates

17 THE GREEN
Mrs Wendy Amos.
Open on Sat 18, Sun 19 June

THE OLD BAKERY
John Amos & Karl Jones, 01327 349080, yeolbakery@aol.com, www.johnnieamos.co.uk.
Open on all dates
Visits also by arrangement June to Aug for groups of 15 to 35.

PRIVATE GARDEN OF BLISS LANE NURSERY
Christine & Geoffrey Littlewood.
Open on all dates

ROCK SPRINGS
Tom Higginson & David Foster.
Open on all dates

RUSSELL HOUSE
Peter Pickering & Stephen George, 01327 341734, peterandstephen @btinternet.com, www.RussellHouseFlore.com.
Open on all dates

6 THORNTON CLOSE
William & Lesley Craghill.
Open on Sat 18, Sun 19 June

THE WHITE COTTAGE
Tony & Gill Lomax.
Open on Sun 10 Apr

 **1 YEW TREE GARDENS**
Mr & Mrs Martin Millard.
Open on Sat 18, Sun 19 June

Flore gardens have been open since 1963 as part of the Flore Flower Festival. The partnership with the NGS started in 1992 with openings every yr since, inc 2020 and 2021 following COVID-19 restrictions. Flore is an attractive village with views over the Upper Nene Valley. We have a varied mix of gardens, large and small, inc a new garden this yr. They have all been developed by friendly, enthusiastic and welcoming owners who are in their gardens when open. Our gardens range from the traditional to the eccentric providing year-round interest. Some have been established over many yrs and others have been developed more recently. There are greenhouses, gazebos, summerhouses and seating opportunities to rest while enjoying the gardens. The village Flower Festival is our main event on the same two days as the June opening and garden tickets will be valid for both days. Partial wheelchair access to most gardens, some assistance may be required.

Linden House, East Haddon Gardens

12 FOXTAIL LILLY

41 South Road, Oundle, PE8 4BP. Tracey Mathieson, 01832 274593, foxtaillilly41@gmail.com, www.foxtail-lilly.co.uk. *1m from Oundle town centre. From A605 at Barnwell Xrds take Barnwell Rd, 1st R to South Rd.* **Sun 12 June (10-4). Adm £4.50, chd free. Light salad style lunch. Visits also by arrangement May to July for groups of 10 to 50.**

A cottage garden where perennials and grasses are grouped creatively together amongst gravel paths, complementing one another to create a natural look. Some unusual plants and quirky oddities create a different and colourful informal garden. Lots of flowers for cutting and a shop in the barn. New meadow pasture turned into new cutting garden. Plants, flowers and gift shop.

13 GLENDON HALL

Kettering, NN14 1QE. Rosie Bose, 01536 711732, rosiebose@googlemail.com. *1½m E of Rothwell. A6003 to Corby (A14 J7) W of Kettering, turn L onto Glendon Rd signed Rothwell, Desborough, Rushton. Entrance 1½m on L past turn for Rushton.* **Visits by arrangement for groups of up to 30. Adm £5, chd free.**

Mature specimen trees, topiary, box hedges and herbaceous borders stocked with many unusual plants. Large walled kitchen gardens with glasshouse and a shaded area, well-stocked with ferns. Some gravel and slopes with wheelchair access via longer route.

GROUP OPENING

14 GREAT BRINGTON GARDENS

Northampton, NN7 4JJ. *7m NW of Northampton. Off A428 Rugby Rd. From Northampton, turn 1st L past main gates of Althorp. Details & maps available at free car park.* **Sun 1 May (12-4). Combined adm £7, chd free. Home-made teas.**

FOLLY HOUSE
Sarah & Joe Sacarello.

15 HAMILTON LANE
Mr & Mrs Robin Matthews.

RIDGEWAY HOUSE
Janet & Keith White.

ROSE COTTAGE
David Green & Elaine MacKenzie.

THE STABLES
Mrs J George.

SUNDERLAND HOUSE
Mrs Margaret Rubython.

THE WICK
Ray & Sandy Crossan.

YEW TREE HOUSE
Mrs Joan Heaps.

Great Brington is proud of over 25 yrs association with the NGS and arguably one of the most successful one day scheme events in the county. Eight gardens will open this yr, they are situated in a circular and virtually flat walk around the village. Our gardens provide inspiration and variety; continuing to evolve each yr and designed, planted and maintained by their owners. The village on the Althorp Estate is particularly picturesque and well worth a visit, predominantly local stone with thatched houses, a church of historic interest, and walkers can extend their walk to view Althorp House. Visitors will enjoy a warm welcome with plants for sale, tea, coffee and cake available from 12pm-4pm. There are also secluded spots for artists to draw, sketch and paint. Small coaches for groups welcome by prior arrangement only, please email friends_of_stmarys@btinternet.com. Wheelchair access to some gardens.

15 GREYWALLS

Farndish, Nr Wellingborough, NN29 7HJ. Mrs P M Anderson, 01933 353495, greywalls@dbshoes.co.uk. *2½m SE of Wellingborough. A609 from Wellingborough, B570 to Irchester, turn to Farndish by cenotaph. House adjacent to church.* **Sun 15 May (2-5). Adm £4, chd free. Light refreshments. Visits also by arrangement for groups of 10 to 30.**

Greywalls is an old vicarage set in 2 acres of relaxed country gardens planted for year-round interest, featuring mature specimen trees, an impressive Banksia rose, three large ponds, many stone features, wildflower meadow and a Highgrove inspired stumpery. The borders feature unusual plants and there is an outside aviary.

GROUP OPENING

16 GUILSBOROUGH GARDENS

Guilsborough, NN6 8RA. *10m NW of Northampton. 10m E of Rugby. Between A5199 & A428. J1 off A14. Car parking at Guilsborough Surgery, on West Haddon Rd, NN6 8QE. Please park in the car park to avoid congestion in the village centre.* **Sun 22 May (1-5). Combined adm £7.50, chd free. Home-made teas in the garden at Dripwell House.**

DRIPWELL HOUSE
Mr J W Langfield & Dr C Moss, 01604 740140, cattimoss@gmail.com. **Visits also by arrangement May & June for groups of 10 to 30. Combined visits with Gower House next door.**

FOUR ACRES
Mark & Gay Webster.

FOURWAYS
Phyl & Charles Mynard.

THE GATE HOUSE
Mike & Sarah Edwards.

GOWER HOUSE
Ann Moss.

THE OLD HOUSE
Richard & Libby Seaton Evans.

THE OLD VICARAGE
John & Christine Benbow.

PEACE GARDEN
Guilsborough Church of England Primary School.

Enjoy a warm welcome in this village with its very attractive rural setting of rolling hills and reservoirs. We have a group of eight contrasting gardens for you to visit this yr. Several of us are passionate about growing fruit and vegetables, and walled kitchen gardens and a potager are an important part of our gardening. Plants both rare and unusual from our plantsmen's gardens are for sale, a true highlight here. No wheelchair access at Dripwell House and The Gate House.

GROUP OPENING

17 HARPOLE GARDENS
Harpole, NN7 4BX. *On A45 4m W of Northampton towards Weedon. Turn R at The Turnpike Hotel into Harpole. Village maps given to all visitors.* **Sun 12 June (1-6). Combined adm £6, chd free. Home-made teas at The Close.**

CEDAR COTTAGE
Spencer & Joanne Hannam.

THE CLOSE
Michael Orton-Jones.

5 LARKHALL LANE
Greg Hearne.

19 MANOR CLOSE
Caroline & Eamonn Kemshed, 01604 830512, carolinekemshed@live.co.uk. **Visits also by arrangement in June.**

THE MANOR HOUSE
Mrs Katy Smith.

THE OLD DAIRY
David & Di Ballard.

NEW 7 PARK LANE
Mrs Lorna Julyan.

Harpole is an attractive village nestling at the foot of Harpole Hills with many houses built of local sandstone. Visit us and delight in a wide variety of gardens of all shapes, sizes and content. You will see luxuriant lawns, mixed borders with plants for sun and shade, mature trees, shrubs, herbs, alpines, water features and tropical planting. We have interesting and quirky artifacts dotted around, garden structures and plenty of seating for the weary.

🌼 ☕

18 67-69 HIGH STREET
Finedon, NN9 5JN. Mary & Stuart Hendry, 01933 680414, sh_archt@hotmail.com. *6m SE Kettering. Garden signed from A6 & A510 junction.* **Sun 27 Feb (10.30-3.30); Sun 12 June, Sun 3 July (2-6). Adm £3.50, chd free. Soup & roll in Feb (inc in adm). Home-made teas in June & July. 2023: Sun 26 Feb. Visits also by arrangement Feb to Sept.** ⅓ acre rear garden of C17 cottage (not open). Early spring garden with snowdrops and hellebores, summer and autumn mixed borders, many obelisks and containers, kitchen garden, herb bed, rambling roses and

at least 60 different hostas. All giving varied interest from Feb through to Oct. Large selection of home-raised plants for sale (all proceeds to NGS).

🐕 🌼 🚗 ☕

19 136 HIGH STREET
Irchester, NN29 7AB. Ade & Jane Parker, jane692@btinternet.com. *200yds past the church on the bend as you leave the village going towards the A45. Please park on High St. Disabled parking only in driveway.* **Sun 7 Aug (11-4). Adm £3.50, chd free. Light refreshments. Visits also by arrangement June to Sept.**
Large garden developed by the current owners over the past 20 yrs. Various different planting habitats inc areas designed for shade, sun and pollinator friendly sites. Wildlife pond attracting large range of birds, insects and other creatures into the garden. Alpine houses, planted stone sinks and raised beds. Seasonally planted tubs adding bold summer colour. Wheelchair access mainly over grass with some gravel pathways.

♿ 🌼 ☕ 🔊

20 NEW HIGHFIELDS
Adstone, Towcester, NN12 8DS. Rachel Halvorsen. *The village of Adstone is midway between Banbury & Northampton, about 15m from each.* **Sun 14 Aug (2-5.30). Adm £5, chd free. Cream teas.**
Two sheltered mixed courtyard gardens with vibrant colours; windswept lawn borders and an all-white walled garden with extensive box hedging. Plantsman's garden. Collection of succulents. Cream teas on patio overlooking panoramic views over a ha-ha to 15 miles of unbroken countryside, lake and 100 acre Plumpton wood. Walk down to lake across a couple of fields to see wildlife and waterlilies.

♿ 🌼 ☕ 🔊

21 1 HINWICK CLOSE
Kettering, NN15 6GB. Mrs Pat Cole-Ashton. *J9 A14 A509 Kettering. At Park House r'about take 4th exit to Holdenby. Hinwick Close 3rd exit on R. From Kettering A509, at Park House r'about take the 1st exit to Holdenby, Hinwick Close 3rd exit on R.* **Sun 12 June (12-5). Adm £3.50, chd free. Home-made teas & savouries.**
In the past 10 yrs Pat and Snowy have transformed this space into a wildlife

haven. The garden has numerous influences; seaside, woodland and English country garden. Ponds and waterfalls add to the delights. Vintage signs, numerous figures and seating areas at different vantage points are dotted throughout the garden.

♿ 🐕 🌼 ☕

22 ◆ HOLDENBY HOUSE & GARDENS
Holdenby House, Holdenby, Northampton, NN6 8DJ. Mr & Mrs James Lowther, 01604 770074, office@holdenby.com, www.holdenby.com. *7m NW of Northampton. Off A5199 or A428 between East Haddon & Spratton.* **For NGS: Sun 15 May (11-4). Adm £6, chd £4. Adm subject to change. Cream teas & light refreshments. For other opening times and information, please phone, email or visit garden website.**
Holdenby has a historic Grade I listed garden. The inner garden inc Rosemary Verey's renowned Elizabethan Garden and Rupert Golby's Pond Garden and long borders. There is also a delightful walled kitchen garden. Away from the formal gardens, the terraces of the original Elizabethan Garden are still visible, one of the best preserved examples of their kind. Accessible, but contact garden for further details.

♿ ☕

23 HOSTELLARIE
78 Breakleys Road, Desborough, NN14 2PT. Stella Freeman, 01536 760124, stelstan78@aol.com. *6m N of Kettering. 5m S of Market Harborough. From church & war memorial turn R into Dunkirk Ave, then 3rd R. From cemetery L into Dunkirk Ave, then 4th L.* **Sun 19 June (2-5). Combined adm with 16 Leys Avenue £5, chd free. Home-made teas & a gluten free option. Visits also by arrangement June & July for groups of 10 to 30.**
Town garden that once was an allotment plot. The length has been divided into different rooms; a courtyard garden with a sculptural clematis providing shade, colour themed flower beds, ponds and water features, cottage garden and gravel borders, clematis and roses, all linked by lawns and grass paths. Collection of over 50 different hostas.

🌼 🚗 ☕

24 NEW 104 IRCHESTER ROAD
Rushden, NN10 9XQ. Mr Jason
Richards, 07957 811173,
jrrushden@gmail.com, www.
getrevue.co/profile/jrrushden.
*From Irchester the house is at the
top of the hill just after the green,
by the Welcome Inn on the L. From
Rushden Town Centre the house is
on the R after Knuston Drive.* **Sun 26
June, Sun 28 Aug (2-5.30). Adm
£5, chd free. Light refreshments.
Visits also by arrangement May
to Sept.**
An Edwardian home set in ½ acre
with different levels of patio areas
and surrounded by trees. A rose
garden with English rose varieties
everywhere inc climbers on walls, a
rose frame and a very long pergola
winding its way down to a pear
tree with seating and borders. In
each area of the garden there are
seating places to eat or just enjoy
different perspectives. The owner has
developed an environmentally friendly
rose spray which will be on sale. The
garden is on a hill with wheelchair
access to all main areas with non-slip
ramps. Please contact us for disabled
parking priority.

**25 ◆ KELMARSH HALL &
GARDENS**
Main Road, Kelmarsh,
Northampton, NN6 9LY. The
Kelmarsh Trust, 01604 686543,
marketing@kelmarsh.com,
www.kelmarsh.com. *Kelmarsh
is 5m S of Market Harborough &
11m N of Northampton. From A14,
exit J2 & head N towards Market
Harborough on the A508.* **For NGS:
Sun 24 Apr (10-4). Adm £6, chd
£3.50. Light lunches, cream teas
& cakes in Sweet Pea's Tearoom.
For other opening times and
information, please phone, email or
visit garden website.**
Kelmarsh Hall is an elegant
Palladian house set in glorious
Northamptonshire countryside with
highly regarded gardens, which are
the work of Nancy Lancaster, Norah
Lindsay and Geoffrey Jellicoe. Hidden
gems inc an orangery, sunken garden,
long border, rose gardens and, at the
heart of it all, a historic walled garden.
Highlights throughout the seasons inc
fritillaries, tulips, roses and dahlias.
Beautiful interiors brought together
by Nancy Lancaster in the 1930s,
in a Palladian style hall designed by
James Gibbs. The recently restored

laundry and servant's quarters in the
Hall are open to the public, providing
visitors the incredible opportunity to
experience life 'below stairs'. Blue
badge disabled parking close to
the Visitor Centre entrance. Paths
are loose gravel, wheelchair users
advised to bring a companion.

GROUP OPENING

26 KILSBY GARDENS
Middle Street, Kilsby, Rugby,
CV23 8XT. *5m SE of Rugby. 6m N
of Daventry on A361.* **Sun 19 June
(1-5.30). Combined adm £7, chd
free. Light refreshments at Kilsby
Village Hall (1-5).**
Kilsby's name has long been
associated with Stephenson's famous
railway tunnel and an early skirmish
in the Civil War. The houses and
gardens of the village offer a mixture
of sizes and styles, which reflect
its development through time. We
welcome you to test the friendliness
for which we are renowned. Please
visit www.ngs.org.uk closer to the
opening date to see which gardens
will be opening.

27 ◆ LAMPORT HALL
Northampton, NN6 9HD.
Lamport Hall Preservation
Trust, 01604 686272,
events@lamporthall.co.uk,
www.lamporthall.co.uk. *For SatNav
please use postcode NN6 9EZ. Exit
J2 of the A14. Entry through the
gate flanked by swans on the A508.*
**For NGS: Sat 13 Aug (10-4). Adm
£7, chd £4. Cream teas. For other
opening times and information,
please phone, email or visit garden
website.**
Home of the Isham family for over 400
yrs, the extensive herbaceous borders
complement the Elizabethan bowling
lawns, together with topiary from
the 1700s. In Sept the 2 acre walled
garden is full of colour, with 250 rows
of perennials. Another highlight is the
famous Lamport Rockery, among
the earliest in England and home of
the world's oldest garden gnome.
Wheelchair access on gravel paths
within the gardens.

28 16 LEYS AVENUE
Desborough, NN14 2PY. Keith
& Beryl Norman, 01536 760950,
bcn@stainer16.plus.com. *6m
N of Kettering, 5m S of Market
Harborough. From church & War
Memorial turn R into Dunkirk Ave
& 5th R into Leys Ave.* **Sun 19
June (2-5). Combined adm with
Hostellarie £5, chd free. Sun 4
Sept (2-5). Adm £4, chd free.
Light refreshments. Visits also
by arrangement June to Sept for
groups of 10 to 30.**
A town garden with two water
features, plus a stream and a pond
flanked by a 12ft clinker built boat.
There are six raised beds which are
planted as a shady garden with sweet
peas and dahlias. A patio lined with
acers has two steps down to a gravel
garden with paved paths. Mature
trees and acers give the garden
year-round structure and interest.
Wheelchair access by two steps from
patio to main garden.

GROUP OPENING

**29 NEW LITTLE BRINGTON
GARDENS**
Main Street, Little Brington,
Northampton, NN7 4HS. *Off road
parking can be found at the end of
Folly Ln, Little Brington, NN7 4JR.*
**Sun 3 July (11-5). Combined adm
£7.50, chd £5. Light refreshments.**

NEW CEDAR LEA
Mr Peter & Mrs Lisa Carter.

NEW 1 FOLLY LANE
Nick & Kerstin Banham.

NEW IVY COTTAGE
Mr David & Dirk Toulmin-Van
Sittert.

NEW MANOR COTTAGE
Derek & Carol Bull.

NEW MANOR FARM HOUSE
Rob Shardlow, 07956 254944.

NEW 14 PINE COURT
Chris & Judy Peck.

NEW ROCHE COTTAGE
Malcolm & Susan Uttley.

NEW STONECROFT
Peter Holman.

For the first time eight gardens in
the historic village of Little Brington,
nestled in the Northamptonshire
farmlands will open for the NGS. They
offer a variety of shapes, sizes and

styles, from more formal planting to relaxed cottage gardens, along with a variety of vegetable gardens on show too. Lots of colours on display with a mix of both familiar and unusual plants and flowers. Refreshments will be served and the village pub Saracens Head will also be open, book early as the pub is very popular. Come and enjoy the wonderful gardens and the pretty village setting. Full or partial wheelchair access to most gardens. Some have gravel driveways.

GROUP OPENING

30 LONG BUCKBY GARDENS
Northampton, NN6 7RE. *8m NW of Northampton, midway between A428 & A5. Long Buckby is signed from A428 & A5. 10 mins from J18 M1. Long Buckby Train Stn is ½ m from centre of the village. Free car park at Cotton End on B5385 at the A428 end of village.* **Sun 24 July (1-6). Combined adm £6, chd free. Home-made teas, ice creams & cold drinks.**

25 BERRYFIELD
Mandy Morley & Jane Harrison.

3 COTTON END
Roland & Georgina Wells.

4 COTTON END
Sue & Giles Baker.

NEW 23 COTTON END
Lynnette & Malcolm Cannell.

THE GROTTO
Andy & Chrissy Gamble.

3A KNUTSFORD LANE
Tim & Jan Hunt.

10 LIME AVENUE
June Ford.

THE OLD BOAT
Dawn & Steven Chilvers.

4 SKINYARD LANE
William & Susie Mitchell.
(See separate entry)

WISTERIA HOUSE
David & Clare Croston,
07771 911892,
dad.croston@gmail.com.
Visits also by arrangement May to Sept for groups of 10+. Adm inc combined visit with Woodcote Villa & refreshments.

WOODCOTE VILLA
Sue & Geoff Woodward.
(See separate entry)

Eleven gardens in the historic villages of Long Buckby and Long Buckby Wharf, inc a new garden which features different areas inc a tropical area. The gardeners have been busy creating new borders, features and extensively replanting, offering our visitors something new to enjoy. We welcome visitors old and new to see our wonderful variety of gardens which offer something for everyone. The gardens in the group vary in size and style, from courtyard and canal side to cottage garden, some are established and others evolving. They inc water features, pergolas, garden structures and chickens, but the stars are definitely the plants. Bursting with colour, visitors will find old favourites and the unusual, used in a variety of ways; trees, shrubs, perennials, climbers, annuals, fruit and vegetables. Of course there will be teas and plants for sale to complete the visit. Come and see us for a friendly welcome and a good afternoon out. Full or partial wheelchair access to all gardens, except 4 Skinyard Lane.

GROUP OPENING

31 NEW MAIDWELL GARDENS
Draughton Road, Maidwell, Northampton, NN6 9JF. *From Market Harborough turn L off the A508 (or from Northampton turn R) & look for the yellow signs.* **Sun 22 May, Sun 14 Aug (10-5). Combined adm £6, chd free. Home-made teas at Wyatts.**

NIGHTINGALE COTTAGE
Ken & Angela Palmer.

NEW ROSENHILL
Mr Ivan & Mrs Diana Barrett.

NEW WYATTS
Mr Colin & Mrs Amanda Goddard.

A friendly village with horses exercising daily and often sheep being herded through. The gardens opening are varied from a completely organic garden with many flowering plants and vegetables to an open garden with architectural features, large shrubs and trees, and a small terraced garden with hidden paths, sculptures and obelisks made from prunings. Wheelchair access to two gardens, partial access to Nightingale Cottage.

GROUP OPENING

32 NEWNHAM GARDENS
Newnham, Daventry, NN11 3HF. *2m S of Daventry on B4037 between the A361 & A45. Continue to the centre of the village & follow signs for the car park, just off the main village green.* **Sun 29 May (10.30-5). Combined adm £5, chd free. Light lunches & cakes in village hall.**

THE BANKS
Sue & Geoff Chester.

THE COTTAGE
Jacqueline Minor.

HILLTOP
David & Mercy Messenger.

STONE HOUSE
Pat & David Bannerman.

WREN COTTAGE
Mr & Mrs Judith Dorkins.

Finally open again, we've missed you! Five plant-lover gardens set in a beautiful old village cradled by the gentle hills of south Northamptonshire. The gardens, set around charming traditional village houses, are packed with spring colour. For 2022, we are especially pleased to have a new garden opening. Spend the day with us enjoying the gardens, buying at our large plant sale, strolling around the village lanes and visiting our C14 church. Why not treat yourself to a tasty light lunch, scrumptious cakes and refreshments in the village hall. The old village and gardens are hilly in parts and while most gardens are accessible to wheelchairs, others are more restricted.

33 NONSUCH
11 Mackworth Drive, Finedon, Wellingborough, NN9 5NL. David & Carrie Whitworth. *Off Wellingborough Rd (A510) onto Bell Hill, then to Church Hill, 2nd L after church, entrance on the L as you enter Mackworth Drive.* **Sun 17 July (1-5). Adm £4, chd free. Drinks, cakes & biscuits.**
⅓ acre country garden within a conservation boundary stone wall. Mature trees, enhanced by many rare and unusual shrubs and perennial plants. A garden for all seasons with several seating areas. Wheelchair access on a level site with paved and gravel paths.

SPECIAL EVENT

34 OLD RECTORY, QUINTON
Preston Deanery Road, Quinton, Northampton, NN7 2ED. Alan Kennedy & Emma Wise, www.garden4good.co.uk. *M1 J15, 1m from Wootton towards Salcey Forest. House is next to the church. On-road parking in village. Please note parking on village green is prohibited.* **Sun 28 Aug (10-4). Adm £10, chd free. Pre-booking essential, please visit www.ngs.org.uk for information & booking. Home-made teas. Lunches 11am-2pm to pre-order via garden website.** A beautiful contemporary 3 acre rectory garden designed by multi-award-winning designer, Anoushka Feiler. Taking the Old Rectory's C18 history and its religious setting as a key starting point, the main garden at the back of the house has been divided into six parts; a kitchen garden, glasshouse and flower garden, a woodland menagerie, a pleasure garden, a park and an orchard. Elements of C18 design such as formal structures, parterres, topiary, long walks, occasional seating areas and traditional craft work have been introduced, however with a distinctly C21 twist through the inclusion of living walls, modern planting methods and abstract installations. Pop-up shop selling plants, garden produce, local honey, home-made bread and bath products. Regional Finalist, The English Garden's The Nation's Favourite Gardens 2021. Wheelchair access with gravel paths.
🅖 ❋ 🚗 🄓 ☕ 🍷

35 THE OLD VICARAGE
Daventry Road, Norton, Daventry, NN11 2ND. Barry & Andrea Coleman. *Norton is approx 2m E of Daventry, 11m W of Northampton. From Daventry follow signs to Norton for 1m. On A5 N from Weedon follow road for 3m, take L turn signed Norton. On A5 S take R at Xrds signed Norton, 6m from Kilsby. Garden is R of All Saints Church.* **Sun 24 Apr (1-5). Adm £5, chd free. Home-made teas in orangery.** The vicarage days bequeathed dramatic and stately trees to the modern garden. The last 40 yrs of evolution and the happy accidents of soil-type, and a striking location with lovely vistas have shaped the garden around all the things that makes April so thrilling, inc prodigious sweeps

of primulas of many kinds and the trees in blossom. The interesting and beautiful C14 church of All Saints will be open to visitors.
🐕 ☕ ♪))

36 OLD WEST FARM
Little Preston, Daventry, NN11 3TF. Mr & Mrs G Hoare, caghoare@gmail.com. *7m SW Daventry, 8m W Towcester, 13m NE Banbury. ¾m E of Preston Capes on road to Maidford. Last house on R in Little Preston with white flagpole. Beware, the postcode applies to all houses in Little Preston.* **Visits by arrangement May & June for groups of 10 to 30. Adm £5, chd free. Home-made teas.** Large rural garden developed over the past 40 yrs on a very exposed site, planted with hedges and shelter. Roses, shrubs and borders aiming for year-round interest. Partial wheelchair access over grass.
🅖 ❋ ☕ ♪))

GROUP OPENING

37 RAVENSTHORPE GARDENS
Ravensthorpe, NN6 8ES. *7m NW of Northampton. Signed from A428. Please start & purchase tickets at Ravensthorpe Nursery.* **Sun 10 July (1.30-5.30). Combined adm £6, chd free. Home-made teas in village hall.**

CORNERSTONE
Lorna Jones.

QUIETWAYS
Russ Barringer.

RAVENSTHORPE NURSERY
Mr & Mrs Richard Wiseman.
(See separate entry)

TREETOPS
Ros Smith.

Attractive village in Northamptonshire uplands near to Ravensthorpe reservoir and Top Ardles Wood Woodland Trust which have bird watching and picnic opportunities. Established and developing gardens set in beautiful countryside displaying a wide range of plants, many available from the nursery that now only opens on NGS open days. Offering inspirational planting, quiet contemplation, beautiful views, water features and gardens encouraging wildlife. Disabled WC in village hall.
🅖 🐕 ❋ ☕ ♪))

38 RAVENSTHORPE NURSERY
6 East Haddon Road, Ravensthorpe, NN6 8ES. Mr & Mrs Richard Wiseman. *7m NW of Northampton. First property on L approaching from A428.* **Fri 1, Sat 2, Sun 3, Fri 29, Sat 30 Apr, Sun 1 May, Fri 3, Sat 4, Sun 5 June, Fri 8, Sat 9 July, Fri 2, Sat 3, Sun 4, Fri 30 Sept, Sat 1, Sun 2 Oct (11-5). Adm £4, chd free. Light refreshments. Opening with Ravensthorpe Gardens on Sun 10 July.** Approx 1 acre garden wrapped around the nursery with beautiful views. Planted with many unusual shrubs and herbaceous perennials over the last 20-30 yrs to reflect the wide range of plants produced. Plants for sale. Wheelchair access with gradual slope to garden and nursery.
🅖 🐕 ❋ ☕ 🍷

39 ROSEARIE-DE-LA-NYMPH
55 The Grove, Moulton, Northampton, NN3 7UE. Peter Hughes, Mary Morris, Irene Kay, Steven Hughes & Jeremy Stanton. *N of Northampton town. Turn off A43 at small r'about to Overstone Rd. Follow NGS signs in village. The garden is on the Holcot Rd out of Moulton.* **Sun 19, Sun 26 June (11-5). Adm £5, chd free. Home-made teas & light refreshments.** We have been developing this romantic garden for over 15 yrs and now have over 1800 roses, inc English, French and Italian varieties. Many unusual water features and specimen trees. Roses, scramblers and ramblers climb into trees, over arbours and arches. Collection of 140 Japanese maples. Mostly flat wheelchair access via a standard width doorway.
🅖 🐕 ☕

40 NEW ROSI'S TAVERNA
20 St Francis Close, Barton Seagrave, Kettering, NN15 5DT. Rosi & David Labrum. *Approx 2m from J10 of the A14. Head towards Barton Seagrave, going through 3 sets of T-lights. At the 4th set turn R onto Warkton Ln. At the r'about turn L. Take the next 2 R's into St Francis Close.* **Sun 24 Apr, Sun 11 Sept (10-4). Combined adm with Briarwood £6.50, chd free. Light refreshments at Briarwood.** An established medium south facing town garden. Kitchen garden intermingles with flowers, shrubs, plenty of fruit trees, soft fruits and

vegetables in raised beds. Cacti and succulents hold high importance in the greenhouse. A covered koi carp pond and a pyramid water feature are key elements in the garden. A unique taverna with mosaic flooring offers perfect shelter from sun, wind and drizzle.

41 4 SKINYARD LANE
Long Buckby, Northampton, NN6 7QZ. William & Susie Mitchell, 01327 843426, mitchewi52@gmail.com. *8m NW of Northampton, midway between A428 & A5 Long Buckby is signed from A428 & A5. 10 mins from J18 M1. Take turning off High St into Hall Drive & Skinyard Ln is on the R. Please Note: No parking in lane.* **Sun 25 Sept (11-4). Combined adm with Woodcote Villa £5, chd free. Home-made teas at Woodcote Villa. Opening with Long Buckby Gardens on Sun 24 July (1-6).** Visits also by arrangement May to Sept for groups of 10 to 25. Visits can be combined with another village garden.

Small ever evolving cottage style garden started in 2013. Plantaholics garden crammed with all sorts of plants. Hundreds of different plants from old favourites to the exotic. Replanted borders and new beds and rose arches.

GROUP OPENING

42 SPRATTON GARDENS
Smith Street, Spratton, NN6 8HP. *6½m NNW of Northampton. To find car park, please follow yellow NGS signs from outskirts of village from A5199 or Brixworth Rd.* **Sun 12 June (11-5). Combined adm £7, chd free.**

THE COTTAGE
Mrs Judith Elliott.

DALE HOUSE
Fiona & Chris Cox.

28 GORSE ROAD
Lee Miller.

11 HIGH STREET
Philip & Frances Roseblade.

MULBERRY COTTAGE
Kerry Herd.

NORTHBANK HOUSE
Helen Millichamp.

OLD HOUSE FARM
Susie Marchant.

STONE HOUSE
John Forbear.

VALE VIEW
John Hunt.

As well as attractive cottage gardens alongside old Northampton stone houses, Spratton also has unusual gardens, inc those showing good use of a small area; one dedicated to encouraging wildlife with views of the surrounding countryside; newly renovated gardens and those with new planting; courtyard garden; gravel garden with sculpture; mature gardens with fruit trees and herbaceous borders. Refreshments available in Norman St Andrew's Church. The King's Head Pub will be open, lunch reservations recommended.

23 Cotton End, Long Buckby Gardens

43 TITCHMARSH HOUSE
Chapel Street, Titchmarsh,
NN14 3DA. Sir Ewan &
Lady Harper, 01832 732439,
ewan@ewanh.co.uk,
www.titchmarsh-house.co.uk. *2m
N of Thrapston. 6m S of Oundle.
Exit A14 at junction signed A605,
Titchmarsh signed as turning E
towards Oundle & Peterborough.*
**Sun 10 Apr (2-6); Sat 11 June
(12.30-5). Adm £5, chd free.
Home-made teas at parish
church in Apr. BBQ lunch & teas
at village fete in June. Visits also
by arrangement Apr to June for
groups of 5+.**
4½ acres extended and laid out
since 1972. Special collections of
magnolias, spring bulbs, iris, peonies
and roses with many rare trees and
shrubs. Walled ornamental vegetable
garden and ancient yew hedge. Some
newly planted areas; please refer to
the website. Collections of flowering
trees and other unusual plants such
as rare buddleias, philadelphus,
deutzias and abelias. Wheelchair
access to most of the garden without
using steps. No dogs.

  ♿ ❀ 🚘 ☕

GROUP OPENING

44 WAPPENHAM GARDENS
Wappenham, NN12 8SJ. *4m W of
Towcester, 6m N of Brackley, 8m E
of Banbury. Tickets & map available
at each garden. Limited off street
parking in village.* **Sun 26 June
(2-5). Combined adm £7.50, chd
free. Light refreshments in the
village hall.**

BEECHES HOUSE
Alastair & Kate Judge.

ELM LODGE FARMHOUSE
Charlotte Supple.

HOME FARM
Mr & Mr Robert Tomkinson.

WAPPENHAM MANOR
Mr & Mrs Fordham.

A fabulous collection of diverse gardens
all set around beautiful 17th, 18th and
19th century Northamptonshire stone
houses. Expect packed perennial
borders, topiary, bulging vegetable
gardens and productive orchards. The
gardens range in size from several
acres to ones that offer great ideas for
smaller gardens. Two are designed by
James Alexander-Sinclair.

❀ ☕

Willow Cottage

GROUP OPENING

45 WEEDON LOIS & WESTON GARDENS

Weedon Lois, Towcester, NN12 8PJ. *7m W of Towcester. 7m N of Brackley. Turn off A43 at Towcester towards Abthorpe & Wappenham & turn R for Weedon Lois. Or turn off A43 at Brackley, follow signs to Helmdon & Weston.* Sun 19 June (1-6). Combined adm £6, chd free. Home-made teas at The Chapel, Weston.

THE GARDENER'S COTTAGE
Mrs Sitwell.

NEW 2 THE GREEN
Moira Hillman.

4 HELMDON ROAD
Mrs S Wilde.

NEW 8 HIGH STREET
Jane Kellar.

8A HIGH STREET
Mr & Mrs J Archard-Jones.

MIDDLETON HOUSE
Mark & Donna Cooper.

OLD BARN
John & Iris Gregory.

4 VICARAGE RISE
Ashley & Lindsey Cartwright.

Two adjacent villages set in the rolling south Northamptonshire countryside with a handsome medieval church in Weedon Lois. The extension churchyard contains the grave of the poet, Dame Edith Sitwell who lived in Weston Hall (not open), marked with a gravestone by Henry Moore. We have two new gardens this yr, one a colourful garden with interesting perennials, a cutting bed, fruit and vegetables and the other where an enclosed and peaceful garden has been cleverly created out of a very steep site. There is also a long established plantsman's garden, herbaceous borders, vegetables, roses, woodland planting, a large wildlife pond and much more. So we hope you will join us for our open day, enjoy looking round our gardens, visit the plant stalls and tuck into our famous home-made teas. Not all gardens suitable for wheelchairs.
& ✿ ☕))

46 NEW WILLOW COTTAGE

55 Upper Benefield, Peterborough, PE8 5AL. Mrs Nathalie Tarbuck. *From Oundle on A427 parking is located at Upper Benefield Cricket Club, 1st turning on the L as you enter the village. The garden is located opp Hill Farm. It's a short walk to the garden.* Sat 28 May (10-4). Adm £5, chd free. Home-made teas at Upper Benefield Cricket Club.

Willow Cottage is wrapped in a beautiful cottage style garden. Wander this 1/4 acre site and discover its hidden gems. Planted to be a haven for pollinators and wildlife. Herbaceous borders burst with a wide variety of plants. A large pond, several water features, established and newly planted trees. Meander through rose arches and find a spot to perch to soak up the stunning views. Partial wheelchair access via a slope to enter the garden.
& ✿ ☕))

47 NEW WILLOWBROOK HOUSE

76 Park Street, Kings Cliffe, Peterborough, PE8 6XN. Dr Robert E Stebbings, 03330 116577, bob@stebbing-cons.ndonet.com. *E of village on road to Wansford. Turn off A43 at Bulwick signed Kings Cliffe. Also signed from A47 just W of A1.* Sun 10 July (11-5). Adm £5, chd free. Visits also by arrangement Feb to Sept for groups of up to 8.

Original walled 1/5 acre garden with Victorian fruit trees, is over 250 yrs old. New garden created by ecologist in 2018 to inc native and exotic plants to encourage wildlife. Bulbs and flowering scented shrubs from the New Year and continue through the yr. Garden inc gravel areas with acid and alkaline rockeries and meadow. About 20 magnolia; unusual trees and shrubs; fernery. Wheelchair access to most of garden with some slopes and narrow paths.
&

48 WOODCOTE VILLA

Old Watling Street (A5), Long Buckby Wharf, Long Buckby, Northampton, NN6 7EW. Sue & Geoff Woodward, geoff.and.sue@btinternet.com. *2m NE of Daventry. From M1 J16, take Flore by-pass, turn R at A5 r'about for approx 3m. From Daventry follow Long Buckby signs, but turn L at A5 Xrds. From M1 J18 signed Kilsby, follow A5 S for approx 6m.* Sun 20 Mar (11-5). Adm £4, chd free. Sun 25 Sept (11-4). Combined adm with 4 Skinyard Lane £5, chd free. Home-made teas. Gluten free options. Opening with Long Buckby Gardens on Sun 24 July (1-6). Visits also by arrangement Mar to Sept for groups of 10 to 36. Adm inc home-made teas. Visits can be combined with another village garden.

In a much admired location, this stunning canalside garden has a large variety of plants, styles, structures and unusual bygones. Bulbs and hellebores feature in Mar, colourful planting in July/Sept, many pots, all set against a backdrop of trees and shrubs in themed areas. Places to sit and watch the boats and wildlife. Plants for sale (cash only). Sorry no WC. Wheelchair access via ramp at entrance to garden.
& 🐴 ✿ 🚗 ☕

'National Garden Scheme funding helped support the provision of horticultural-related assistance to soldiers, veterans and their immediate families, providing education, training and employment opportunities along with supporting the recovery, health and wellbeing of individuals'
ABF The Soldiers' Charity

NOTTINGHAMSHIRE

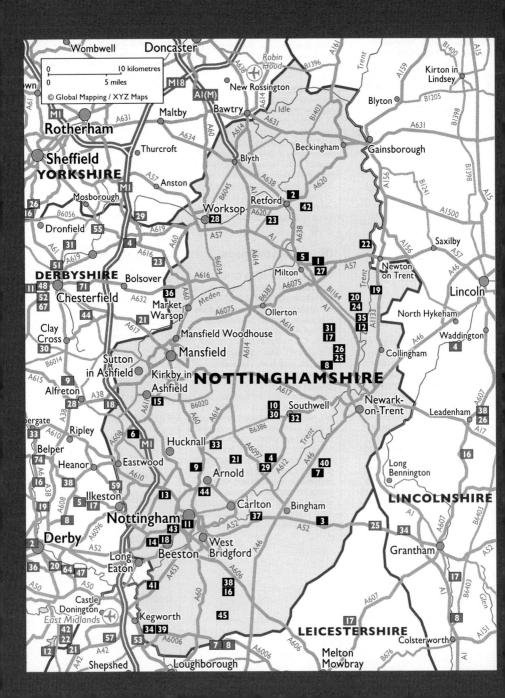

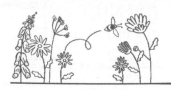

Nottinghamshire is best known as Robin Hood country. His legend persists and his haunt of Sherwood Forest, now a nature reserve, contains some of the oldest oaks in Europe. The Major Oak, thought to be 800 years old, still produces acorns.

Civil War battles raged throughout Nottinghamshire, and Newark's historic castle bears the scars. King Charles I surrendered to the Scots in nearby Southwell after a night at The Saracen's Head, which is still an inn today. Southwell is also home to the famous Bramley apple, whose descendants may be found in many Nottinghamshire gardens.

We have groups of cottage gardens, we have beautiful farmhouse gardens, and we have gardens with special woodland walks. We have gardens with particular concern for environmental issues, we have gardens full of rare exotic imports, and we have artists' gardens of inspiration. All will offer a warm welcome, and most will offer a brilliant tea.

Volunteers

County Organiser
Georgina Denison
01636 821385
georgina.denison@ngs.org.uk

County Treasurer
Nicola Cressey
01159 655132
nicola.cressey@gmail.com

Publicity
Julie Davison
01302 719668
julie.davison@ngs.org.uk

Social Media
Malcolm Turner
01159 222831
malcolm.turner14@btinternet.com

Booklet Co-ordinators
Malcolm & Wendy Fisher
0115 966 4322
wendy.fisher111@btinternet.com.

Assistant County Organisers
Judy Geldart
01636 823832
judygeldart@gmail.com

Beverley Perks
01636 812181
perks.family@talk21.com

Mary Thomas
01509 672056
nursery@piecemealplants.co.uk

Andrew Young
01623 863327
andrew.young@ngs.org.uk

 @National Garden Scheme Nottinghamshire

@nottsngs

Left: Long Acres, Syverston Village Gardens

OPENING DATES

All entries subject to change. For latest information check **www.ngs.org.uk**

Map locator numbers are shown to the right of each garden name.

February

Snowdrop Festival

Sunday 6th
The Poplars 35

Saturday 12th
1 Highfield Road 13

Sunday 13th
Church Farm 5

April

Saturday 16th
◆ Felley Priory 6
Oasis Community
Gardens 28

Saturday 23rd
Capability Barn 4

Sunday 24th
Capability Barn 4
1 Highfield Road 13

May

Sunday 8th
The Old Vicarage 30

Thursday 12th
Rhubarb Farm 36

Sunday 15th
38 Main Street 21

Sunday 22nd
Capability Barn 4
6 Hope Street 18
Ivy Bank Cottage 19
◆ Norwell Nurseries 26

Sunday 29th
NEW Lavender Cottage 20
Normanton Hall 24

June

Saturday 4th
The Old Hall 29
Sutton Bonington
Gardens 39

Sunday 5th
NEW 30 Highgrove
Avenue 14
Sutton Bonington
Gardens 39

Thursday 9th
Rhubarb Farm 36

Saturday 11th
Halam Gardens and
Wildflower Meadow 10

Sunday 12th
Askham Gardens 1
Home Farm House,
17 Main Street 16
Patchings Art Centre 33
Rose Cottage 38

Sunday 19th
Flintham Hall 7
Hollinside 15
Hopbine Farmhouse,
Ossington 17
Ossington House 31
Thrumpton Hall 41
6 Weston Close 44

Sunday 26th
NEW Gaunts Hill 9
Norwell Gardens 25
NEW Wysall Flower
Farm 45

Wednesday 29th
Norwell Gardens 25

July

Sunday 3rd
5 Burton Lane 3

Wednesday 6th
Rhubarb Farm 36

Saturday 16th
The Old Vicarage 30

Sunday 17th
NEW 10 Harlaxton Drive 11
NEW Morton Nurseries 23

Saturday 23rd
Park Farm 32

Sunday 24th
Piecemeal 34
Riseholme,
125 Shelford Road 37

Saturday 30th
Floral Media 8

Sunday 31st
5a High Street 12

August

Thursday 4th
Rhubarb Farm 36

Saturday 6th
The Old Vicarage 30

Sunday 7th
NEW Syerston Village
Gardens 40

Sunday 14th
Meadow Farm 22

Saturday 20th
Oasis Community
Gardens 28

Sunday 21st
University Park
Gardens 43

Monday 29th
5 Burton Lane 3

September

Sunday 11th
Oak Barn Exotic
Garden 27

Sunday 18th
Riseholme,
125 Shelford Road 37

October

Sunday 2nd
◆ Norwell Nurseries 26

By Arrangement

Arrange a personalised garden visit with your club, or group of friends, on a date to suit you. See individual garden entries for full details.

Bolham Manor 2
5 Burton Lane 3
Capability Barn 4
5a High Street 12
Home Farm House,
17 Main Street 16
Meadow Farm 22
Oasis Community
Gardens 28
The Old Vicarage 30
Park Farm 32
Piecemeal 34
Riseholme, 125 Shelford
Road 37
Rose Cottage 38
NEW Thyme House 42

The Old Hall

THE GARDENS

GROUP OPENING

🚻 ASKHAM GARDENS
Markham Moor, Retford,
NG22 0RP. *6m S of Retford. On
A638, in Rockley village turn E to
Askham or on A57 at East Markham
turn N to Askham.* **Sun 12 June
(1-5). Combined adm £6, chd free.
Home-made teas.**

NURSERY HOUSE
Mr & Mrs D Bird.

ORCHARD HOUSE
David Garner & Jane Ball.

NEW ROSE COTTAGE
Paul & Sarah Baker.

THE STABLES
Daniel & Ros Barnes.

VILLOSA
Mr & Mrs Mike Bridge.

Variety of pleasant English village
gardens. Nursery House is a
plantsman's garden, secluded and
private; with an attractive water feature.
Orchard House's back garden contains
flower beds, shrubs, fruit trees, lawns,
fish pond, raised beds with vegetables.
Villosa has a long garden divided into
different rooms with the accent on
sustainability. The Stables incorporates
a fantastic hedged kitchen garden
and large koi pond, herbaceous bed
in the making and new colourful beds
surround the house. Rose Cottage is a
garden full of surprises. Deep gravel at
Nursery House. Long grassy walks at
Villosa and The Stables.
🚻 🐐 🌼 ☕

🚻 BOLHAM MANOR
Bolham Way, Bolham, Retford,
DN22 9JG. Pam & Butch
Barnsdale, 07790 896022,
pamandbutch@hotmail.co.uk. *1m
from Retford. A620 Gainsborough
Rd from Retford, turn L onto Tiln Ln,
signed 'A620 avoiding low bridge'.
At sharp R bend take rd ahead to
Tiln then L Bolham Way.* **Visits by
arrangement Feb to Sept. Visitors
are welcome to bring their own
refreshments or picnic. Adm £4,
chd free.**
This 3 acre mature garden provides
year-round interest. In February,
'Dancing willow Ladies' greet you

amongst swathes of snowdrops,
narcissus and early bulbs. Topiary
features and sculptures guide you
through the different areas of the
garden with its well-planted terraced
and herbaceous borders, ponds and
orchard. Partial wheelchair access to
parts of garden.
🚻 🌼 🛖

🚻 5 BURTON LANE
Whatton in the Vale, NG13 9EQ.
Ms Faulconbridge, 01949 850942,
jpfaulconbridge@hotmail.co.uk,
www.ayearinthegardenblog.
wordpress.com. *3m E of Bingham.
Follow signs to Whatton from A52
between Bingham & Elton. Garden nr
Church in old part of village. Follow
yellow NGS signs.* **Sun 3 July, Mon
29 Aug (11-4). Adm £4, chd free.
Home-made teas. Visits also
by arrangement June to Aug for
groups of up to 30.**
Modern cottage garden which is
productive and highly decorative. We
garden organically and for wildlife. The
garden is full of colour and scent from
spring to autumn. Several distinct
areas, inc fruit and vegetables. Large
beds are filled with over 500 varieties
of plants with paths through so you
can wander and get close. Also
features seating, gravel garden, pond,
shade planting and sedum roof.
Attractive village with walks.
🌼 ☕))

🚻 CAPABILITY BARN
Gonalston Lane, Hoveringham,
NG14 7JH. Malcolm &
Wendy Fisher, 01159 664322,
wendy.fisher111@btinternet.com,
www.capabilitybarn.com. *8m NE of
Nottingham. A612 from Nottingham
through Lowdham. Take 1st R into
Gonalston Lane. Garden is 1m on L.*
**Sat 23, Sun 24 Apr, Sun 22 May
(11-4.30). Adm £4.50, chd free.
Home-made teas. Visits also
by arrangement Apr to June for
groups of 15 to 30.**
Imaginatively planted large country
garden with something new each
year. April brings displays of
Daffodils, Hyacinths and Tulips along
with erythroniums, brunneras and
primulas. Wisteria, Magnolia, Rhodos
and apple blossom greet May. A
backdrop of established trees, shrubs
and shady paths give a charming
country setting. Large vegetable/
fruit gardens with orchard/meadow
completes the picture.
🌼 ☕

🚻 CHURCH FARM
Church Lane, West Drayton,
Retford, DN22 8EB. Robert &
Isabel Adam. *A1 exit Markham
Moor. A638 Retford 500 yds signed
West Drayton. ¾m, turn R, into
Church Lane, 1st R past church.
Ample parking in farm yard.* **Sun 13
Feb (10.30-4). Adm £3.50, chd
free. Light refreshments served
from 11.30am.**
The garden is essentially a spring
garden with a small woodland
area which is carpeted with many
snowdrops, aconites and cyclamen
which have seeded into the adjoining
churchyard, with approx. 180 named
snowdrops growing in island beds,
along with hellebores and daffodils.
Limited amount of snowdrops are
for sale.
🚻 🐐 🌼 ☕

🚻 ✦ FELLEY PRIORY
Underwood, NG16 5FJ. The
Brudenell Family, 01773 810230,
michelle@felleypriory.co.uk,
www.felleypriory.co.uk. *8m SW of
Mansfield. Off A608 ½m W M1 J27.*
**For NGS: Sat 16 Apr (10-4). Adm
£5, chd free. Light refreshments.
For other opening times and
information, please phone, email or
visit garden website.**
Garden for all seasons with yew
hedges and topiary, snowdrops,
hellebores, herbaceous borders and
rose garden. There are pergolas, a
white garden, small arboretum and
borders filled with unusual trees,
shrubs, plants and bulbs. The grass
edged pond is planted with primulas,
bamboo, iris, roses and eucomis.
Bluebell woodland walk. Orchard with
extremely rare daffodils. Regional
Finalist, The English Garden's The
Nation's Favourite Gardens 2021.
🚻 🌼 🚗 ☕))

*'In 2021 the generous
donation from the National
Garden Scheme helped
12,000 unpaid carers
to access the support
they need, with 50 more
receiving crisis grants to
support those in dire need.'*
Carers Trust

Morton Nurseries

⑦ FLINTHAM HALL

Flintham, Newark, NG23 5LE.
Sir Robert & Lady Hildyard. *5m SW of Newark. Flintham is signposted off A46. Follow twisting road past cricket ground & school. At next bend turn R towards church for ample parking.* **Sun 19 June (1-5). Adm £7.50, chd free. Home-made teas in the village hall adjacent to the gardens. Donation to St. Augustine's Church.**

C18 walled gardens with rose borders and espaliered fruit trees. Range of trees and shrubs with a profusion of shrub and rambling roses. Views of Grade I listed house impressively remodelled in 1850s by TC Hine in the Italianate style with an adjoining conservatory said to be the finest of its type in England. Balustraded terrace with views across park and lake. A place of true romance.

⑧ FLORAL MEDIA

Norwell Road, Caunton, Newark, NG23 6AQ. Mr & Mrs Steve Routledge, 01636 636283, info@floralmedia.co.uk, www.floralmedia.co.uk. *Take Norwell Rd from Caunton. Approx ½ m from Caunton on L.* **Sat 30 July (10-4). Adm £4, chd free. Home-made teas.**

A beautifully well maintained country garden. Beds overflowing with a variety of roses, shrubs and flowers. A gravel/oriental garden, cutting gardens, vegetable beds, Flower Farm supplying British grown stems to florists/farm shops. Long sweeping borders surrounding the main lawn leading to the wildflower meadows where you will find an interesting garden retreat. A horticulturists haven. Excellent facilities, refreshments, plenty of parking. Often live music in the garden from a local folk group of musicians. A good range of plants available for sale. Full wheelchair access inc disabled WC.

⑨ NEW GAUNTS HILL

Bestwood Lodge, Arnold, NG5 8NF. Nigel & Penny Lymn Rose. *5m N of Nottingham. Take Bestwood Lodge Dr up to the Bestwood Lodge Hotel, then turn R & continue until you see a sign saying vehicle access to stables only. Then turn R down the drive through the gates.* **Sun 26 June (11-4). Adm £4, chd free. Light refreshments.**

A large country garden with ponds, mature woodlands, greenhouse, borders, lawns and vegetable plot. Car parking available in an adjacent field. Some gravel paths and lawns. There are some steps but these can be avoided.

GROUP OPENING

⑩ HALAM GARDENS AND WILDFLOWER MEADOW

nr Southwell, NG22 8AX. *Village gardens within walking distance of one another. Hill's Farm wildflower meadow is a short drive of ½ m*

towards Edingley village, turn R at brow of hill as signed - plenty parking on tarmac yard. **Sat 11 June (12-4). Combined adm £6.50, chd free. Home-made teas at The Old Vicarage, Halam.**

HILL'S FARM
John & Margaret Hill.

THE OLD VICARAGE
Mrs Beverley Perks.
(See separate entry)

Lovely mix of a very popular beautiful, well-known, organic, rural plant lovers' garden with clematis, striking viburnums amongst herbaceous borders and sweeping lawns; contrasting with small, interesting wrap-around cottage garden and 6 acre wildflower meadow. Part of an organic farm, visitors can be assured of an inspiring discussion with the farmer who is passionate about the benefits of this method of farming for our environment and quality beef. C12 Church open - surrounded by freely planted, attractive churchyard - all welcome to enjoy this peaceful haven in English rural village setting. Old Vicarage - gravel entrance to lower flat garden. Teas on terrace. Hills Farm flat field easy tarmac parking.

  🐕 ✿ 🚗 ☕

11 [NEW] **10 HARLAXTON DRIVE**
Lenton, Nottingham, NG7 1JA.
Jan Brazier. *From M1 J25, take A52 Nottingham & after 7m, 5th R after Savoy cinema. From Nottingham, just outside city centre & off A52 (signed Derby), 2nd L after The Walton Hotel.* **Sun 17 July (10-4.30). Adm £4.50, chd free. Home-made teas.**
A city centre oasis, just a short walk from the city centre. Garden presented on three levels, each separated by steep steps. The top terrace overlooks a large Koi pond surrounded by bog plants, marginals and herbaceous perennials. Seating areas on the second terrace under mature beech trees. On the third level, there is a summerhouse as well as a small pond and densely-planted borders.

🐕 ✿ ☕ 🎪 »)

12 **5A HIGH STREET**
Sutton-on-Trent,
NG23 6QA. Kathryn & Ian Saunders, 07827 920236, kathrynsaunders.optom@gmail.

com. *6m N of Newark. Leave A1 at Sutton on Trent , follow Sutton signs. L at Xrds. 1st R turn (approx 1m) onto Main St. 2nd L onto High St. Garden 50 yds on R. Park on rd.* **Sun 31 July (1-4). Adm £5, chd free. Light refreshments. Visits also by arrangement June & July for groups of 15+.**
Manicured lawns are the foil for this plantsman's garden. Vistas lead past succulents to tropical areas and vibrant herbaceous beds. Ponds run through the plot, leading to woodland walks and a dedicated fernery (180+ varieties, with magnificent tree ferns). Topiary links all the different planting areas to great effect. Around 1000 named varieties of plants with interesting plant combinations.

✿ 🚗 ☕

13 **1 HIGHFIELD ROAD**
Nuthall, Nottingham, NG16 1BQ.
Richard & Sue Bold. *4mins from J26 of the M1- 4m NW of Nottingham City. From J26 of the M1 take the A610 towards Notts, R lane at r'about, take turn-off to Horsendale. Follow rd to Woodland Dr, then 2nd R is Highfield Rd.* **Sat 12 Feb, Sun 24 Apr (10-4). Adm £3, chd free. Light refreshments.**
Visit us in February to see our collection of 500+ snowdrop varieties (280 varieties in the garden) and many others in show benches. Snowdrops for sale. Our spring garden has lots of colour with many rare and unusual plants - miniature narcissus, acers, aconites and magnolias. A good selection of unusual pots and garden ornaments. Plant sales will be available on both dates.

✿ ☕ »)

14 [NEW] **30 HIGHGROVE AVENUE**
Beeston, Nottingham, NG9 4DN.
Sue & Malcolm Turner. *4m West of Nottingham. J25 M1, A52 to Nottm. After 2 r'abouts, turn R for Beeston at The Nurseryman (B6006). After ½m, turn R into Broughton St, continue into Park St, & Bramcote Ave, then turn R into Highgrove Ave.* **Sun 5 June (1-5). Adm £4, chd free.**
Plant collector's garden with many rare and unusual plants. Divided into several rooms. Two ponds and a rill. Contains a collection of species pelargoniums in summer. Large white wisteria late May. Partial wheelchair access.

  ✿ ☕

15 **HOLLINSIDE**
252 Diamond Avenue, Kirkby-In-Ashfield, Nottingham, NG17 7NA.
Sue & Bob Chalkley. *1m E of Kirkby in Ashfield at the Xrds of the A611 & B6020. Please park away from the busy junction.* **Sun 19 June (1-4.30). Adm £3, chd free. Light refreshments.**
A formal front garden with terraced lawns and borders lead to a shaded area with ferns, camellias, roses, hydrangeas and other flowering shrubs. The rear garden has a wildlife pond, a wildflower meadow, a summerhouse and a victorian style greenhouse. There are topiary box and yews and a box parterre planted with roses. Majority of garden is suitable for wheelchairs. Disabled parking near house only by prior arrangement.

  🐕 ✿ ☕

16 **HOME FARM HOUSE, 17 MAIN STREET**
Keyworth, Nottingham,
NG12 5AA. Graham & Pippa Tinsley, 0115 9377122, Graham_Tinsley@yahoo.co.uk, www.homefarmgarden.wordpress. com. *7m S of Nottingham. Follow signs for Keyworth from A60 or A606 & head for church. Garden about 50yds down Main St. Parking on the street or at village hall or Bunny Lane car parks.* **Sun 12 June (12-5). Combined adm with Rose Cottage £5, chd free. Home-made teas. Visits also by arrangement May to Sept for groups of up to 30.**
A large garden behind old farmhouse in the centre of the village. The old orchard, herbaceous and vegetable gardens are preserved and the cart shed has been rebuilt as a pergola. Large areas of unmown grass planted with perennials, ponds, turf mound and many trees. High hedges create hidden areas inc rose and winter gardens. All combine in an intriguing blend of wildness and formality. Interesting and unusual perennials for sale by Piecemeal Plants (www. piecemealplants.co.uk).

✿ ☕ »)

Our 2021 donations mean that 750 people living with Parkinson's were supported

17 HOPBINE FARMHOUSE, OSSINGTON

Hopbine Farmhouse, Main Street, Ossington, NG23 6LJ. Mr & Mrs Geldart. *From A1 N take exit marked Carlton, Sutton-on-Trent, Weston etc. At T-Junction turn L to Kneesall. Drive 2m to Ossington. In village turn R to Moorhouse & park in field.* **Sun 19 June (2-5). Combined adm with Ossington House £6, chd free. Home-made teas in The Hut, Ossington.**

A small garden in separate halves; the southern half has a long herbaceous border with an arbour over which climb honeysuckle, clematis and r. Chinensis mutabilis. A full central bed has many favourite salvias, euphorbia and veronicastrum. The highlight of the intimate walled garden is a "waterfall" of clematis Summer Snow and Wisley, rambling through roses Iceberg and Ghislaine de Feligonde. Some narrow paths.

&. ✿ ☕

18 6 HOPE STREET

Beeston, Nottingham, NG9 1DR. Elaine Liquorish. *From M1 J25, A52 for Nottm. After 2 r'abouts, turn R for Beeston at The Nurseryman (B6006). Beyond hill, turn R into Bramcote Dr. 3rd turn on L into Bramcote Rd, then immed R into Hope St.* **Sun 22 May (1.30-5.30). Adm £4, chd free. Cream teas.**

A small garden packed with a wide variety of plants providing flower and foliage colour year-round. Collections of alpines, bulbs, mini, small and medium size hostas (60+), ferns, grasses, carnivorous plants, succulents, perennials, shrubs and trees. A pond and a greenhouse with subtropical plants. Troughs and pots. Home-made crafts. Shallow step into garden, into greenhouse and at rear. No wheelchair access to plant sales area.

&. ✿ ☕

In the first six months of operation at Maggie's Southampton, which was part funded by the National Garden Scheme, the team has supported people affected by cancer more than 2,300 times

19 IVY BANK COTTAGE

The Green, South Clifton, Newark, NG23 7AG. David & Ruth Hollands. *12m N of Newark. From S, exit A46 N of Newark onto A1133 towards Gainsborough. From N, exit A57 at Newton-on-Trent onto A1133 towards Newark.* **Sun 22 May (1-5). Adm £4, chd free. Home-made teas.**

A traditional cottage garden, with herbaceous borders, fruit trees inc a Nottinghamshire Medlar, vegetable plots and many surprises inc a stumpery, a troughery, dinosaur footprints and even fairies! Many original features: pigsties, double privy and a wash house. Children can search for animal models and explore inside the shepherd's van. Seats around and a covered refreshment area.

✿ ☕

20 NEW LAVENDER COTTAGE

South Street, Normanton-On-Trent, Newark, NG23 6RQ. Margaret Harper. *Leave A1 at Sutton Carlton/Normanton-on-Trent junction. Turn L onto B1164 in Carlton. In Sutton-on-Trent turn R at Normanton sign. Go through Grassthorpe, turn L at Normanton sign.* **Sun 29 May (1-5). Combined adm with Normanton Hall £5, chd free. Home-made teas at Normanton Hall.**

New cottage style garden with herbaceous borders, mixed fruit and ornamental trees, and raised vegetable beds. Started in 2021 and planted with mixed perennial beds, bulbs and patio pots. Hard paving round house with level wide grass path round garden.

&. ☕

21 38 MAIN STREET

Woodborough, Nottingham, NG14 6EA. Martin Taylor & Deborah Bliss. *Turn off Mapperley Plains Rd at sign for Woodborough. Alternatively, follow signs to Woodborough off A6097 (Epperstone bypass). Property is between Park Av & Bank Hill.* **Sun 15 May (1-5). Adm £4, chd free. Home-made teas.**

Varied ⅓ acre. Bamboo fenced Asian species area with traditional outdoor wood fired Ofuro bath, herbaceous border, raised rhododendron bed, vegetables, greenhouse, pond area and art studio and terrace.

✿ ☕

22 MEADOW FARM

Broadings Lane, Laneham, Retford, DN22 0NF. Maureen Hayward, 01777 228284, maureen.hayward@zen.co.uk. *10m E of Retford. From A1, take A57 towards Lincoln 5m, L towards Laneham.Village of Laneham, from Main St, L onto Broading Lane, 2nd on R, parking available past gateway.* **Sun 14 Aug (11-4). Adm £4.50, chd free. Light refreshments. Visits also by arrangement July to Sept.**

A 1 acre garden that takes you through a hosta garden into a jungle with bananas, tree ferns, cannas. Winding path takes you to a parterre with topiary and sequoiadendron giganteum pendula trees and water features. Also into a woodland walk, sculptures, wisteria circular walkway, seating throughout, multiple areas of herbaceous planting and unusual specimen trees and plants with Arctic Cabin. Wheelchair access through separate gate.

&. 🚗 ☕ ♪))

23 NEW MORTON NURSERIES

Mansfield Road, Babworth, Retford, DN22 8HE. Gill McMaster, www.morton-nurseries.co.uk. *Between Retford and A1 on the B6420.* **Sun 17 July (1-5). Adm £3, chd free. Home-made teas.**

A young garden in an open, exposed site started in 2013 by avid plant lovers Gill and Gayle. Flowing walkways through large informal mixed borders with some unusual plants. Sizeable colour co-ordinated herbaceous borders backed by yew and holly hedges. Large ponds attracting lots of interesting wildlife. We were delighted to be televised at the nursery and at RHS Tatton flower show in 2018. Accessible.

&. 🐄 ✿ ☕ 🪑 ♪))

24 NORMANTON HALL

South Street, Normanton-on-Trent, NG23 6RQ. His Honour John & Mrs Machin. *3m SE of Tuxford. Leave A1 at Sutton Carlton/Normanton-on-Trent junction. Turn L onto B1164 in Carlton. In Sutton-on-Trent turn R at Normanton sign. Go through Grassthorpe, turn L at Normanton sign.* **Sun 29 May (1-5). Combined adm with Lavender Cottage £5, chd free. Home-made teas.**

3 acres with mature oak, lime beech and yew and recently planted trees. Vegetable area. New plantings of bulbs, rhododendrons and a camellia

walk. Arboretum planted with unusual, mainly hardwood trees which are between three and twelve years old. Also specimen oaks and beech. New planting of wood anemones. Recently established parkland. All surfaces level from car park.

  ♿ ✿ ☕ 🍴

GROUP OPENING

25 NORWELL GARDENS

Newark, NG23 6JX. *6m N of Newark. Halfway between Newark & Southwell. Off A1 at Cromwell turning, take Norwell Rd at bus shelter. Or off A616 take Caunton turn.* **Sun 26 June (1-5). Evening opening Wed 29 June (6.30-9). Combined adm £5, chd free. Home-made teas in Village Hall (26 June) and Norwell Nurseries (29 June).**

CHERRY TREE HOUSE
Simon & Caroline Wyatt.

FAUNA FOLLIES
Lorraine & Roy Pilgrim.

NORWELL ALLOTMENTS / PARISH GARDENS
Norwell Parish Council.

♦ NORWELL NURSERIES
Andrew & Helen Ward.
(See separate entry)

THE OLD MILL HOUSE, NORWELL
Mr & Mrs M Burgess.

ROSE COTTAGE
Mr Iain & Mrs Ann Gibson.

This is the 26th yr that Norwell has opened a range of different, very appealing gardens all making superb use of the beautiful backdrop of a quintessentially English countryside village. Inc a garden and nursery of national renown and the rare opportunity to walk around vibrant allotments with a wealth of gardeners from seasoned competition growers to plots that are substitute house gardens, bursting with both flower colour and vegetables in great variety. To top it all there are a plethora of breathtaking village gardens showing the diversity that is achieved under the umbrella of a cottage garden description! The beautiful medieval church and its peaceful churchyard with grass labyrinth will be open for quiet contemplation.

  ♿ ✿ 🐕 ☕

26 ♦ NORWELL NURSERIES

Woodhouse Road, Norwell, NG23 6JX. Andrew & Helen Ward, 01636 636337, wardha@aol.com, www.norwellnurseries.co.uk. *6m N of Newark halfway between Newark & Southwell. Off A1 at Cromwell turning, take rd to Norwell at bus stop. Or from A616 take Caunton turn.* **For NGS: Sun 22 May, Sun 2 Oct (2-5). Adm £3.50, chd free.** Home-made teas in Norwell Village Hall, on Sunday 26th June, other dates at the nurseries. Opening with Norwell Gardens on Sun 26, Wed 29 June. For other opening times and information, please phone, email or visit garden website.
Jewel box of over 3,000 different, beautiful and unusual plants sumptuously set out in a one acre plantsman's garden inc shady garden with orchids, woodland gems, cottage garden borders, alpine and scree areas. Pond with opulently planted margins. Extensive herbaceous borders and effervescent colour themed beds. Sand beds showcase Mediterranean, North American and alpine plants. Nationally renowned nursery open with over 1,000 different rare plants for sale. Autumn opening features UK's largest collection of hardy chrysanthemums for sale and the National Collection of Hardy Chrysanthemums. New borders inc the National Collection Of Astrantias. Innovative sand beds. Grass paths, no wheelchair access to woodland paths.

  ♿ ✿ 🐕 NPC ☕

27 OAK BARN EXOTIC GARDEN

Church Street, East Markham, Newark, NG22 0SA. Simon Bennett & Laura Holmes, www.facebook.com/OakBarn1. *From A1 Markham Moor junction take A57 to Lincoln. Turn R at Xrds into E Markham. L onto High St & R onto Plantation Rd. Enter farm gates at T-Junction, garden located on L.* **Sun 11 Sept (1-5). Adm £3.50, chd free. Home-made teas.**
On entering the oak lych-style gate you will be met with the unexpected dense canopy of greenery and tropical foliage. The gravel paths wind under towering palms and bananas which are underplanted with cannas and gingers. On the lowest levels houseplants are bedded out from the large greenhouse to join the summer displays. They surround the Jungle Hut and new raised walkway.

28 OASIS COMMUNITY GARDENS

2a Longfellow Drive, Kilton Estate, Worksop, S81 0DE. Steve Williams, 07795 194957, Stevemark126@hotmail.com, www.oasiscommunitycentre.org. *From Kilton Hill (leading to the Worksop hospital), take 1st exit to R (up hill) onto Kilton Cres, then 1st exit on R Longfellow Dr. Car Park off Dickens Rd (1st R).* **Sat 16 Apr, Sat 20 Aug (10-4). Adm £4, chd free.** Cream teas in Oasis Community Cafe - 'Food for Life'. **Visits also by arrangement Mar to Oct. Meals can be arranged for group bookings by arrangement.**
Oasis Gardens is a community project transformed from abandoned field to an award winning garden. Managed by volunteers the gardens boast over 30 project areas, several garden enterprises and hosts many community events. Take a look in the Cactus Kingdom, the Children's pre-school play village, Wildlife Wonderland or check out a wonderful variety of trees, plants, seasonal flowers and shrubs. The Oasis Gardens hosts the first Liquorice Garden in Worksop for 100 years. The site hosts the 'Flowers for Life' project which is a therapeutic gardening project growing and selling cut flowers and floristry. There is disabled access from Longfellow Drive. From the town end there is a driveway after the first fence on the right next to house number 2.

  ♿ ✿ ☕))

29 THE OLD HALL

Church Lane, Lowdham, Nottingham, NG14 7BQ. Mr & Dr Stewart. *On the R of Church Ln, which is a turning off Ton Ln (same side of the bypass in Lowdham as World's End Pub). The lane is found by following the sign to St Mary's Church - parking sign posted.* **Sat 4 June (12.30-5). Adm £5, chd free. Home-made teas.**
A gorgeous lime tree avenue leads to The Old Hall which is centrally located in this large garden - comprises a mound from the original Ludham Castle left of the drive surrounded on three sides by a moat. Daffodils adorn the drive in Spring. The Hall is Wisteria clad as well as a pergola of late white Wisteria. Vegetable garden with raised beds and formal yew hedges divide our elegant garden.

  ♿ 🐎 ✿ ☕

30 THE OLD VICARAGE

Halam Hill, Halam, NG22 8AX.
Mrs Beverley Perks, 01636 812181,
perks.family@talk21.com. *1m W
of Southwell. Please park diagonally
into beech hedge on verge with
speed interactive sign or in village - a
busy road so no parking on roadside.*
**Sun 8 May, Sat 16 July, Sat 6
Aug (12-4). Adm £5, chd free.
Home-made teas. Opening with
Halam Gardens and Wildflower
Meadow on Sat 11 June. Visits
also by arrangement June to Aug
for groups of 15+.**
An artful eye for design/texture/
colour/love of unusual plants/
trees makes this a welcoming gem
to visit. One time playground for
children, this 2 acre hillside garden
has matured over 25yrs into a much
admired, landscape garden. New
garden planting/design at the bottom.
Beautiful C12 Church open only a
short walk into the village or across
field through attractively planted
churchyard - rare C14 stained glass
window. Gravel drive - undulating
levels as on a hillside - plenty of
cheerful help available.

  ♿ 🐴 ✿ 🚗 ☕ ⟿

31 OSSINGTON HOUSE

Moorhouse Road, Ossington,
Newark, NG23 6LD. Georgina
Denison. *10m N of Newark, 2m
off A1. From A1 N take exit marked
Carlton, Sutton-on-Trent, Weston
etc. At T-junction turn L to Kneesall.
Drive 2m to Ossington. In village
turn R to Moorhouse & park in field
next to Hopbine Farmhouse.* **Sun 19
June (2-5). Combined adm with
Hopbine Farmhouse, Ossington
£6, chd free. Home-made teas in
The Hut, Ossington.**
Vicarage garden redesigned in
1960 and again in 2014. Chestnuts,
lawns, formal beds, woodland walk,
poolside planting, orchard. Terraces,
yews, grasses. Ferns, herbaceous
perennials, roses and a new kitchen
garden. Disabled parking available in
drive to Ossington House.

  ♿ ✿ 🚗 🅳 ☕ ⟿

Gaunts Hill

32 PARK FARM

Crink Lane, Southwell,
NG25 0TJ. Ian & Vanessa
Johnston, 01636 812195,
v.johnston100@gmail.com. *1m SE
of Southwell. From Southwell town
centre go down Church St, turn R on
to Fiskerton Rd & 200yds up hill turn
R into Crink Lane. Park Farm is on
2nd bend.* **Sat 23 July (1-5). Adm
£5, chd free. Home-made teas.
Visits also by arrangement Apr to
Aug for groups of up to 30. Guided
visits available for groups of 10 or
more 50p extra per person.**
3 acre garden noted for its extensive
variety of trees, shrubs and perennials,
many rare or unusual. Long colourful
herbaceous borders, rose arches,
alpine/scree garden, a large wildlife
pond and a maturing area of woodland
and acid loving plants. Spectacular
views of the Minster across a
wildflower meadow and ha-ha.

33 PATCHINGS ART CENTRE

Oxton Road, Calverton,
Nottingham, NG14 6NU.
Chas & Pat Wood,
www.patchingsartcentre.co.uk.
*N of Nottingham city take A614
towards Ollerton. Turn R on to
B6386 towards Calverton & Oxton.
Patchings is on L before turning to
Calverton. Brown tourist directional
signs.* **Sun 12 June (11-3). Adm £3,
chd free. Light refreshments at
Patchings Café.**
Promoting the enjoyment of art.
Established in 1988, Patchings is set
in 50 acres with a visitor centre and
galleries. The grounds are a haven for
artists and a tranquil setting for visitors.
New for 2022 Patchings Artists' Trail
- a walk through art history, famous
paintings within glass take visitors
through the centuries, meeting well
known artists from the past along
the way. SWA (Society of Women
Artists) exhibition in two galleries. New
Farmhouse gift shop, café and art
materials. Grass and compacted gravel
paths with some undulations and uphill
sections accessible to wheelchairs with
help. Please enquire for assistance.

34 PIECEMEAL

123 Main Street, Sutton
Bonington, Loughborough,
LE12 5PE. Mary
Thomas, 01509 672056,
nursery@piecemealplants.co.uk.
*2m SE of Kegworth (M1 J24). 6m
NW of Loughborough. Almost opp*
St Michael's Church at the N end of
the village. **Sun 24 July (2-6). Adm
£4, chd free. Opening with Sutton
Bonington Gardens on Sat 4, Sun
5 June. Visits also by arrangement
June to Aug for groups of 5 to 10.
For 10+ please contact to discuss.**
Tucked behind early C19 cottages,
a tiny walled garden featuring a
wide range of unusual shrubs, many
flowering and most displayed in
around 400 terracotta pots bordering
narrow paths. Also climbers,
perennials and even a few trees!
Focus is on distinctive form, foliage
shape and colour combination.
Collection of ferns around well.
Half-hardy and tender plants fill the
conservatory. Plant list available on
request.

35 THE POPLARS

60 High Street, Sutton-on-Trent,
Newark, NG23 6QA. Sue &
Graham Goodwin-King. *7m N of
Newark. Leave A1 at Sutton/Carlton/
Normanton-on-Trent junction. In
Carlton turn L onto B1164. Turn
R into Hemplands Ln then R into
High St. 1st house on R. Limited
parking.* **Sun 6 Feb (10.30-4). Adm
£4, chd free. Light refreshments.
Home-made soup and rolls will
be offered on snowdrop open day
in February.**
Mature ½ acre garden on the site
of a Victorian flower nursery, now a
series of well planted areas each with
its own character: exotics courtyard,
pond and oriental style gravel garden,
'jungle' with thatched shack, black
and white garden, woodland area,
walled potager and fernery. Lawns,
borders, charming sitting places and
over 400 snowdrop varieties in early
spring for the galanthophiles.

36 RHUBARB FARM

Hardwick Street, Langwith,
nr Mansfield, NG20 9DR.
www.rhubarbfarm.co.uk. *On NW
border of Nottinghamshire in village
of Nether Langwith. From A632 in
Langwith, by bridge (single file traffic)
turn up steep Devonshire Drive. N.B.
Then turn off SatNav. Take 2nd L into
Hardwick St. Rhubarb Farm at end.
Parking to R of gates.* **Thur 12 May,
Thur 9 June, Wed 6 July, Thur 4
Aug (10.30-3.30). Adm £3, chd
free. Cream teas in our on-site
café made by Rhubarb Farm
volunteers.**
This 2 acre horticultural social
enterprise provides training and
volunteering opportunities to 90 ex-
offenders, drug and alcohol misusers,
older people, school students, people
with mental and physical ill health and
learning disabilities. Eight polytunnels,
100 hens, pigs, donkey and a
Shetland pony. Forest school barn,
willow dome and arch, flower borders,
small shop, pond, raised beds,
comfrey bed and comfrey fertiliser
factory, junk sculpture. Chance
to meet and chat with volunteers.
Main path suitable for wheelchairs
but bumpy. Not all site accessible.
Cafe & composting toilet wheelchair-
accessible. Mobility scooter available.

37 RISEHOLME, 125 SHELFORD ROAD

Radcliffe on Trent,
NG12 1AZ. John & Elaine
Walker, 01159 119867,
elaine.walker10@hotmail.co.uk. *4m
E of Nottingham. From A52 follow
signs to Radcliffe. In village centre
take turning for Shelford (by Co-op).
Approx ¾ m on L.* **Sun 24 July, Sun
18 Sept (1.30-4.30). Adm £4, chd
free. Home-made teas. Visits also
by arrangement June to Sept for
groups of 15+.**
Imaginative and inspirational is how
the garden has been described by
visitors. A huge variety of perennials,
grasses, shrubs and trees combined
with an eye for colour and design.
Jungle area with exotic lush planting
contrasts with tender perennials
particularly salvias thriving in raised
beds and in gravel garden with
stream. Unique and interesting
objects complement planting.
Artwork, fairies and dragons feature in
the garden!

The National Garden Scheme searches the length and breadth of England, Channel Islands, Northern Ireland and Wales for the very best private gardens

38 ROSE COTTAGE

81 Nottingham Road, Keyworth, Nottingham, NG12 5GS. Richard & Julie Fowkes, 0115 9376489, richardfowkes@yahoo.co.uk. *7m S of Nottingham. Follow signs for Keyworth from A606. Garden (white cottage) on R 100yds after Sainsburys. From A60, follow Keyworth signs & turn L at church, garden is 400yds on L.* **Sun 12 June (12-5). Combined adm with Home Farm House, 17 Main Street £5, chd free. Home-made teas. Visits also by arrangement May to Sept for groups of 8 to 30.**
Small cottage garden (300sqm) informally designed and packed full with colourful wildlife friendly plants. Sedum roof, mosaics and water features add unique interest. There is a decked seating area and summerhouse. A wildlife stream meanders down between two ponds and bog gardens. Some narrow paths and steps. A woodland area leads to more ponds, fruit, and a herb spiral. Art studio will be open. Paintings and art cards designed by Julie will be on sale.

GROUP OPENING

39 SUTTON BONINGTON GARDENS

Main Street, Sutton Bonington, Loughborough, LE12 5PE. *2m SE of Kegworth (M1 J24). 6m NW of Loughborough. From A6 Kegworth, past University of Nottingham Sutton Bonington campus. From Loughborough, A6 then A6006. From Nottingham, A60 then A6006.* **Sat 4, Sun 5 June (2-6). Combined adm £6, chd free. Home-made teas at Forge Cottage and 118 Main Street.**

FORGE COTTAGE
Judith & David Franklin.

118 MAIN STREET
Alistair Cameron & Shelley Nicholls.

PIECEMEAL
Mary Thomas.
(See separate entry)

All 3 gardens are located at the north end of the village, just a few minutes walk from each other. Piecemeal has a tiny walled garden and small conservatory, both filled with a wide variety of unusual plants. Forge Cottage garden, reclaimed from a

blacksmith's yard and a little larger, has vibrant curved herbaceous borders. 118 Main Street is large with well-established trees and varied planting as well as an orchard/ wildflower meadow. Varied features inc Japanese-inspired seating area, redesigned patio with water feature, as well as more traditional established borders surrounding lawn and pond. Attractive greenhouse.

GROUP OPENING

40 NEW SYERSTON VILLAGE GARDENS

Long Acres, Moor Lane, Syerston, NG23 5NA. Marie Nicholson. *The village is situated ½ way between Bingham & Newark off the A46. Exit A46 either N or S Follow directions to Syerston & then 'Syerston Village Only' Directions given to parking which is available in a field in the centre of the village.* **Sun 7 Aug (1-5). Combined adm £7, chd free. Home-made teas in Syerston village hall.**

THE CROFT HOUSE
Steve & Sarah Walker.

NEW 7 GREENGATE
Jim & Linda Turner.

LONG ACRES
Marie Nicholson.

NEW MOOR HOUSE
David & Jane Tucker.

Syerston is a small rural village with four very contrasting gardens for you to visit. Long Acres is a large traditional cottage garden with an atmospheric walled garden, themed herbaceous borders and a boxed parterre with a dahlia bed and a cutting patch. The Croft House sits in a wonderful setting. With a newly formed large pond, lovely topiary and structure throughout the borders and a productive vegetable garden. 7 Greengates backs onto woods and offers a really interesting variety of plants, many unusual, to suit its setting with a mixture of flowers and foliage that create colour throughout the year. Moor House is an extremely colourful cottage garden with an abundance of pots, a water feature with rockery, herbaceous borders to the front and rear and a compact vegetable garden. The C13 church, with floral displays, will be open to visitors and delicious home-made

cakes available in the village hall. We would love to see you all. Full wheelchair access at Long Acres and The Croft House. Partial access only at Greengates and Moor House due to steps and uneven paths.

&. ✿ ☕))

41 THRUMPTON HALL

Thrumpton, NG11 0AX. Miranda Seymour, www.thrumptonhall.com. *7m S of Nottingham. M1 J24 take A453 towards Nottingham. Turn L to Thrumpton village & cont to Thrumpton Hall.* **Sun 19 June (1.30-4.30). Adm £5, chd free. Home-made teas.**
2 acres inc lawns, rare trees, lakeside walks, flower borders, rose garden, new pagoda, and box-bordered sunken herb garden, all enclosed by C18 ha-ha and encircling a Jacobean house. Garden is surrounded by C18 landscaped park and is bordered by a river. Rare opportunity to visit Thrumpton Hall (separate ticket). Jacobean mansion, unique carved staircase, Great Saloon, State Bedroom, Priest's Hole.

&. ✿ ✿ 🚗 ☕ ⅏

42 NEW THYME HOUSE

Leverton Road, Retford, DN22 0DR. Colin Bowler, 01777948620, kimfbowler@gmail.com. *Go up Spital Hill Retford after the Canalside workshops go over the canal humpback bridge, turn R. House has a brick wall at the gate. Visits by arrangement May to July for groups of 5+. Parking is limited, so please call to discuss for large groups. Adm £5, chd free. Light refreshments.*
An opportunity to see an imaginative 2 acre garden in early development, started in 2018 from an open lawn. The garden consists of islands of unusual shrubs and perennials, with many original features such as a large sunken firepit, a moongate entranced pond area, and sculptures. Plenty of seating in shaded gazebos or sun. All grassed area, but no steps or steep hills.

Thyme House

43 UNIVERSITY PARK GARDENS

Nottingham, NG7 2RD. University of Nottingham, 07779459541, gregory.smith@nottingham.ac.uk, www.nottingham.ac.uk/estates/grounds. *Approx 4m SW of Nottingham city centre & opp Queens Medical Centre.* NGS visitors: Please purchase admission tickets in the Millennium Garden (in centre of campus), signed from N & W entrances to University Park & within internal road network. **Sun 21 Aug (11.30-4). Adm £5, chd free. Light refreshments in the Lakeside Pavilion & Cafe adjacent to the Millennium Garden.**

University Park has many beautiful gardens inc the award-winning Millennium Garden with its dazzling flower garden, timed fountains and turf maze. Also the huge Lenton Firs rock garden, and the Jekyll garden. During summer, the Walled Garden is alive with exotic plantings. In total, 300 acres of landscape and gardens. Picnic area, café, walking tours, information desk, workshop, accessible minibus to feature gardens within campus. Plants for sale in Millennium garden. Some gravel paths and steep slopes.

 ♿ 🐄 ❀ 🚌 🚌 ☕ 🔊

44 6 WESTON CLOSE

Woodthorpe, Nottingham, NG5 4FS. Diane & Steve Harrington. *3m N of Nottingham. A60 Mansfield Rd. Turn R at T-lights into Woodthorpe Dr. 2nd L Grange Rd. R into The Crescent. R into Weston Close. Please park on The Crescent.* **Sun 19 June (1-5). Adm £3, chd free. Home-made teas inc gluten free options.**

Set on a substantial slope with three separate areas surrounding the house. Dense planting creates a full, varied yet relaxed display inc many scented roses, clematis and a collection of over 80 named mature hostas in the impressive colourful rear garden. Walls covered by many climbers. Home propagated plants for sale.

❀ ☕ 🔊

45 NEW WYSALL FLOWER FARM

Widmerpool Rd, Wysall, NG12 5QW. Caroline Onions, wysallflowerfarm.com. *The farm is on the edge of the village, the last drive on the R as you are heading into open fields towards Widmerpool.* **Sun 26 June (1-4). Adm £4, chd free. Home-made teas.**

½ an acre of colourful and productive flower beds filled with a seasonally changing mix of over 150 varieties used for cut flowers and foliage. A wide range of annuals, perennials, roses and shrubs can be seen from country garden classics such as delphiniums and cornflowers to prairie garden grasses creating a unique environment. Buttonhole making during the opening for adults and children. Introduction to the flower farm and cut flower farming at 1.30pm and 2.30pm. One of the few flower farms open to visitors in the UK.

🐄 ❀ ☕ 🔊

OXFORDSHIRE

In Oxfordshire we tend to think of ourselves as one of the most landlocked counties, right in the centre of England and furthest from the sea.

We are surrounded by Warwickshire, Northamptonshire, Buckinghamshire, Berkshire, Wiltshire and Gloucestershire, and, like these counties, we benefit from that perfect British climate which helps us create some of the most beautiful and famous gardens in the world.

Many gardens open in Oxfordshire for the National Garden Scheme between spring and late-autumn. Amongst these are the perfectly groomed college gardens of Oxford University, and the grounds of stately homes and palaces designed by a variety of the famous garden designers such as William Kent, Capability Brown, Rosemary Verey, Tom Stuart-Smith and the Bannermans of more recent fame.

But we are also a popular tourist destination for our honey-coloured mellow Cotswold stone villages, and for the Thames which has its spring near Lechlade. More villages open as 'groups' for the National Garden Scheme in Oxfordshire than in any other county, and offer tea, hospitality, advice and delight with their infinite variety of gardens.

All this enjoyment benefits the excellent causes that the National Garden Scheme supports.

Volunteers

County Organiser
Marina Hamilton-Baillie
01367 710486
marina.hamilton-baillie@ngs.org.uk

Publicity
Priscilla Frost 01608 811818
info@oxconf.co.uk

Social Media
Dr Jill Edwards 07971 201352
jill.edwards@ngs.org.uk

Assistant County Organisers
Lynn Baldwin 01608 642754
elynnbaldwin@gmail.com

Dr David Edwards
07973 129473
david.edwards@ngs.org.uk

Dr Jill Edwards (as above)

Penny Guy 01865 862000
penny.theavon@virginmedia.com

Michael Hougham 01865 890020
mike@gmec.co.uk

Pat Hougham 01865 890020
pat@gmec.co.uk

Lyn Sanders
01865 739486
sandersc4@hotmail.com

Paul Youngson 07946 273902
paulyoungson48@gmail.com

@NGSOxfordshire
@ngs_oxfordshire
@ngs_oxfordshire

Left: Sandy's House, Chadlington Village Gardens

OPENING DATES

All entries subject to change. For latest information check www.ngs.org.uk
Map locator numbers are shown to the right of each garden name.

February

Snowdrop Festival

Sunday 13th
23 Hid's Copse Road 32
Hollyhocks 34
Stonehaven 65

March

Sunday 20th
◆ Waterperry Gardens 68

Sunday 27th
38 Leckford Road 41

April

Sunday 3rd
Ashbrook House 1

Sunday 10th
Buckland Lakes 11
Magdalen College 43

Friday 15th
NEW Sarsden Glebe 58

Monday 18th
Kencot Gardens 37

Wednesday 20th
Claridges Barn 19

Saturday 23rd
◆ Blenheim Palace 4
NEW Central North Oxford Gardens 14

Sunday 24th
NEW Central North Oxford Gardens 14
The Old Vicarage 53

Saturday 30th
NEW Central North Oxford Gardens 14

May

Sunday 1st
◆ Broughton Grange 9
NEW Central North Oxford Gardens 14
Hollyhocks 34

Sunday 8th
Meadow Cottage 45

Wednesday 11th
Claridges Barn 19

Sunday 15th
Westwell Manor 71

Sunday 22nd
Old Boars Hill Gardens 52
NEW 9 Rawlinson Road 57
NEW 11 Rawlinson Road 56

Wednesday 25th
Midsummer House 48

Saturday 28th
Bolters Farm 5
Kings Cottage 39

Sunday 29th
Barton Abbey 3
Bolters Farm 5
Kings Cottage 39
Steeple Aston Gardens 64

June

Sunday 5th
Whitehill Farm 73

Wednesday 8th
Claridges Barn 19

Thursday 9th
Wootton Gardens 75

Friday 10th
NEW Kidmore House Garden & Vineyard 38

Sunday 12th
Brize Norton Gardens 6
NEW Chadlington Village Gardens 15
Failford 25
23 Hid's Copse Road 32
NEW Hid's Copse Road Gardens 33
Iffley Gardens 36
Langford Gardens 40
116 Oxford Road 55

Tuesday 14th
◆ Stonor Park 66

Sunday 19th
◆ Broughton Grange 9
Cumnor Village Gardens 21
Friars Court 27
The Old Vicarage 53
Wheatley Gardens 72

Sunday 26th
◆ Broughton Castle 8
Chalkhouse Green Farm 16
Charlbury Gardens 17
Corpus Christi College 20
Midsummer House 48
Orchard House 54
Sibford Gardens 59
West Oxford Gardens 70
Woolstone Mill House 74

July

Saturday 2nd
NEW Stow Cottage Arboretum & Garden 67

Sunday 3rd
Dorchester Gardens 24
Middleton Cheney Gardens 47

Sunday 24th
◆ Broughton Grange 9
Merton College Oxford Fellows' Garden 46

August

Sunday 7th
Ham Court 31
16 Oakfield Road 51

Sunday 14th
Chivel Farm 18
Manor House 44

Saturday 20th
Aston Pottery 2

Sunday 21st
Aston Pottery 2
113 Brize Norton Road 7
South Hayes 60
NEW Southbank 62

September

Sunday 4th
Ashbrook House 1

Sunday 11th
◆ Broughton Grange 9
Broughton Poggs & Filkins Gardens 10

Sunday 18th
◆ Waterperry Gardens 68

Wednesday 21st
Midsummer House 48

Sunday 25th
Castle End House 13

February 2023

Sunday 12th
Hollyhocks 34

By Arrangement

Arrange a personalised garden visit on a date to suit you. See individual garden entries for full details.

Ashbrook House 1
NEW 57 Besselsleigh Road, Wootton Gardens 75
Bolters Farm 5
Bush House 12
Carter's Yard, Sibford Gardens 59
Chivel Farm 18
Claridges Barn 19
103 Dene Road 22
Denton House 23
Failford 25
Foxington 26
The Grange 28
Greenfield Farm 29
Greyhound House 30
Hollyhocks 34
Home Close 35
86 Hurst Rise Road, West Oxford Gardens 70
NEW Kidmore House Garden & Vineyard 38
Kings Cottage 39
38 Leckford Road 41
Lime Close 42
Meadow Cottage 45
Mill Barn 49
Monks Head 50
Orchard House 54
116 Oxford Road 55

National Garden Scheme gardens are identified by their yellow road signs and posters. You can expect a garden of quality, character and interest, a warm welcome and plenty of home-made cakes!

THE GARDENS

Kidmore House Garden & Vineyard

1 ASHBROOK HOUSE
Westbrook St, Blewbury, OX11 9QA.
Mr & Mrs S A Barrett, 01235 850810,
janembarrett@me.com. *4m SE of Didcot. Turn off A417 in Blewbury into Westbrook St. 1st house on R. Follow yellow signs for parking in Boham's Rd.* Sun 3 Apr, Sun 4 Sept (2-5.30). Adm £5, chd free. Home-made teas. Visits also by arrangement Apr to Sept.
The garden where Kenneth Grahame read Wind in the Willows to local children and where he took inspiration for his description of the oak doors to Badger's House. Come and see, you may catch a glimpse of Toad and friends in this 3½ acre chalk and water garden, in a beautiful spring line village. In spring the banks are a mass of daffodils and in late summer the borders are full of unusual plants.

2 ASTON POTTERY
Aston, Bampton, OX18 2BT.
Mr Stephen Baughan,
www.astonpottery.co.uk. *4m S of Witney. On the B4449 between Bampton & Standlake.* Sat 20, Sun 21 Aug (12-5). Adm £5, chd free. Home-made teas in the café.
Six stunning borders set around Aston Pottery. 72 metre double hornbeam border full of riotous perennials. 80 metre long hot bank of alstroemeria, salvias, echinacea and kniphofia. Quadruple dahlia border with over 600 dahlias, grasses and asters. Tropical garden with bananas, cannas and ricinus. 120 different annuals planted in four giant successive waves of over 6000 plants. Our Hornbeam Walk is planted to give a new experience to the knowing eye every month. If bees and butterflies are your thing, come between July and August for a chance to see our rare Black Bumble Bee *Bombus ruderatus*.

3 BARTON ABBEY
Steeple Barton, OX25 4QS. Mr & Mrs P Fleming. *8m E of Chipping Norton. On B4030, ½m from junction of A4260 & B4030.* Sun 29 May (2-5). Adm £5, chd free. Home-made teas.
15 acre garden with views from house (not open) across sweeping lawns and picturesque lake. Walled garden with colourful herbaceous borders, separated by established yew hedges and espalier fruit, contrasts with more informal woodland garden paths with vistas of specimen trees and meadows. Working glasshouses and fine display of fruit and vegetables.

◆ BLENHEIM PALACE
Woodstock, OX20 1PX. His Grace the Duke of Marlborough, 01993 810530, customerservice@blenheimpalace.com, www.blenheimpalace.com. *8m N of Oxford. The S3 bus runs every 30 mins from Oxford Train Stn & Oxford's Gloucester Green Bus Stn to Blenheim. Oxford Bus Company No. 500 departs from Oxford Parkway & stops at Blenheim.* For NGS: Sat 23 Apr (10-5). Adm £7, chd £5. Light refreshments. For other opening times and information, please phone, email or visit garden website.
Blenheim Gardens, originally laid out by Henry Wise, inc the formal Water Terraces and Italian Garden by Achille Duchêne, Rose Garden, Arboretum, and Cascade. The Secret Garden offers a stunning garden paradise in all seasons. Blenheim Lake, created by Capability Brown and spanned by Vanburgh's Grand Bridge, is the focal point of over 2,000 acres of landscaped parkland. The Walled Gardens complex inc the Herb and Lavender Garden and Butterfly House. Other activities inc the Marlborough Maze, adventure play area, giant chess and draughts. Wheelchair access with some gravel paths, uneven terrain and steep slopes. Dogs allowed in park and East Courtyard only.
👩‍🦽 🐕 ✳ 🚗 ☕ 🪑 ⟩⟩

🖪 BOLTERS FARM
Pudlicote Lane, Chilson, Chipping Norton, OX7 3HU. Robert & Amanda Cooper, art@amandacooper.co.uk. *Centre of Chilson village. On arrival in the hamlet of Chilson, heading N, we are the last in an old row of cottages on R. Please drive past & park considerately on the L in the lane. Limited parking, car sharing recommended.* Sat 28, Sun 29 May (2-5). Combined adm with Kings Cottage £6, chd free. Tea & gluten free options. Visits also by arrangement Apr to Sept for groups of up to 20. Donation to Hands Up Foundation.
A cherished old cottage garden restored over the last 15 yrs. Tumbly moss covered walls and sloping lawns down to a stream with natural planting and character. Running water, weeping willows and a sense of peace.
☕

GROUP OPENING

🖪 BRIZE NORTON GARDENS
Brize Norton, OX18 3LY. www.bncommunity.org/ngs. *3m SW of Witney. Brize Norton Village, S of A40, between Witney & Burford. Parking at Elderbank Hall. Coaches welcome with plenty of parking nearby. Tickets & maps available at* Elderbank Hall & at each garden. Sun 12 June (1-6). Combined adm £7.50, chd free. Home-made teas in Elderbank Village Hall & at Grange Farm.

BARNSTABLE HOUSE
Mr & Mrs P Butcher.

17 CHICHESTER PLACE
Mr & Mrs D Howard.

CHURCH FARM HOUSE
Philip & Mary Holmes.

CLUMBER
Mr & Mrs S Hawkins.

GRANGE FARM
Mark & Lucy Artus.

MIJESHE
Mr & Mrs M Harper.

MILLSTONE
Bev & Phil Tyrell.

PAINSWICK HOUSE
Mr & Mrs T Gush.

ROSE COTTAGE
Brenda & Brian Trott.

95 STATION ROAD
Mr & Mrs P A Timms.

STONE COTTAGE
Mr & Mrs K Humphris.

Doomsday village on the edge of the Cotswold's offering a number of gardens open for your enjoyment. You can see a wide variety of planting inc ornamental trees and grasses,

9 Rawlinson Road

herbaceous borders, traditional fruit and vegetable gardens. Features inc a Mediterranean style patio, courtyard garden, terraced roof garden, water features; plus gardens where you can just sit, relax and enjoy the day. Plants for sale at individual gardens. A Flower Festival will take place in the Brize Norton St Britius Church. Partial wheelchair access to some gardens.

7 113 BRIZE NORTON ROAD
Minster Lovell, Witney, OX29 0SQ. David & Lynn Rogers. *Approx 2½ m W of Witney. On main village road (B4447), ½ m N of A40 Witney Bypass intersection on the R.* Sun 21 Aug (2-5). Adm £5, chd free. Home-made teas.
Mixed variety garden of over 1 acre inc quirky features for added interest. Lawns, meadow grass area, small woodland, native mixed hedging, wildlife pond, fish pond, tree ferns, acers, huge mix of plants and trees with emphasis on year-round colour. The whole garden has been developed with wildlife in mind.

8 ◆ BROUGHTON CASTLE
Banbury, OX15 5EB. Martin Fiennes, 01295 276070, info@broughtoncastle.com, www.broughtoncastle.com. *2½ m SW of Banbury. On Shipston-on-Stour road (B4035).* For NGS: Sun 26 June (2-4.30). Adm £6, chd free. Home-made teas. For other opening times and information, please phone, email or visit garden website.
1 acre; shrubs, herbaceous borders, walled garden, roses, climbers seen against background of C14-C16 castle surrounded by moat in open parkland. House also open (additional charge).

9 ◆ BROUGHTON GRANGE
Wykham Lane, Broughton, Banbury, OX15 5DS. S Hester, www.broughtongrange.com. *¼ m out of village. From Banbury take B4035 to Broughton. Turn L at Saye & Sele Arms Pub up Wykham Ln (one way). Follow road out of village for ¼ m. Entrance on R.* For NGS: Sun 1 May, Sun 19 June, Sun 24 July, Sun 11 Sept (10-5). Adm £9, chd free. Cream teas. For other opening times and information,

please visit garden website.
An impressive 25 acres of gardens and light woodland in an attractive Oxfordshire setting. The centrepiece is a large terraced walled garden created by Tom Stuart-Smith in 2001. Vision has been used to blend the gardens into the countryside. Good early displays of bulbs followed by outstanding herbaceous planting in summer. Formal and informal areas combine to make this a special site inc newly laid arboretum with many ongoing projects.

GROUP OPENING

10 BROUGHTON POGGS & FILKINS GARDENS
Lechlade, GL7 3JH. www.filkins.org.uk. *3m N of Lechlade. 5m S of Burford. Just off A361 between Burford & Lechlade on the B4477. Map of the gardens available.* Sun 11 Sept (2-6). Combined adm £7, chd free. Home-made teas in Filkins Village Hall. Ice creams at village shop.

BROUGHTON POGGS MILL
Charlie & Avril Payne.

3 THE COACH HOUSE
Peter & Brenda Berners-Price.

THE CORN BARN
Ms Alexis Thompson.

THE FIELD HOUSE
Peter & Sheila Gray.

FILKINS ALLOTMENTS
Filkins Allotments.

FILKINS HALL
Filkins Hall Residents.

LITTLE PEACOCKS
Colvin & Moggridge.

PEACOCK FARMHOUSE
Pauline & Peter Care.

PIGEON COTTAGE
Lynne Savege.

PIP COTTAGE
G B Woodin.

THE TALLOT
Ms M Swann & Mr D Stowell.

TAYLOR COTTAGE
Mrs Ronnie Bailey.

Twelve gardens inc flourishing allotments in these beautiful and vibrant Cotswold stone twin villages. Scale and character vary from the grand landscape setting of Filkins

Hall, to the small but action packed Pigeon Cottage, Taylor Cottage and The Tallot. Broughton Poggs Mill has a rushing mill stream with an exciting bridge; Pip Cottage combines topiary, box hedges and a fine rural view. In these and the other equally exciting and varied gardens horticultural interest abounds. Features inc plant stall by professional nursery, home-made teas, Swinford Museum of Cotswolds tools and artefacts, and Cotswold Woollen Weavers. Many gardens have gravel driveways, but most are suitable for wheelchair access. Most gardens welcome dogs on leads.

11 BUCKLAND LAKES
nr Faringdon, SN7 8QW. The Wellesley Family. *3m NE of Faringdon. Buckland is midway between Oxford (14m) & Swindon (15m), just off the A420. Faringdon 3m, Witney 8m. Follow yellow NGS signs which will lead you to driveway & car park by St Mary's Church.* Sun 10 Apr (2-5). Adm £6, chd free. Home-made teas at Memorial Hall. Donation to RWMT (community bus).
Descend down wooded path to two large secluded lakes with views over undulating historic parkland, designed by Georgian landscape architect Richard Woods. Picturesque mid C18 rustic icehouse, cascade with iron footbridge, thatched boathouse and round house, and exedra. Many fine mature trees, drifts of spring bulbs and daffodils amongst shrubs. Norman church adjoins. Cotswold village. Children must be supervised due to large expanse of unfenced open water.

You can make a difference! Join our Great British Garden Party fundraising campaign and raise money for some of the best-loved nursing and health charities. Visit ngs.org.uk/gardenparty to find out how you can get involved

12 BUSH HOUSE

Wiginton Road, South Newington, Banbury, OX15 4JR. Mr John Ainley, 07503 361050, rojoainley@btinternet.com. *In S Newington on A361 from Banbury to Chipping Norton, take 1st R to Wiginton, Bush House 1st house on the L in Wiginton Rd.* Visits by arrangement. Adm £5, chd free. Set in 8 acres, over 10 yrs a 2 acre garden has emerged. Herbaceous borders partner dual level ponds and stream. The terrace leads to a walled parterre framed by roses and wisteria. The orchard is screened by rose and vine covered wrought iron trellis. Kitchen gardens, greenhouses and fruit cage provide organically grown produce. Wild flowers sown in the orchard in Aug 2021. Stream and interconnecting ponds. Walled parterre and knot garden. 1000 native broadleaved trees planted 2006, 2011 and 2014. Gravel drive, a few small steps, and two gentle grass slopes on either side of the garden.

 ♿ 🚗 ☕ 🎋

13 CASTLE END HOUSE

Castle Street, Deddington, Banbury, OX15 0TE. Petra Hoyer Millar. *Castle End House is on Castle St, heading towards Clifton. House is on the R, small gate on the front lawn with ha-ha.* Sun 25 Sept (2-5). Adm £5, chd free.
1 acre dry stone walled garden, consisting of five main areas; formal lawn and herbaceous borders, terraced orchard, woodland garden, herb garden and front lawn with ha-ha and cloud pruned hedge. The centrepiece is a formal lawn with two substantial herbaceous borders, providing interest from early spring through to vibrant new perennial displays in autumn.

»))

GROUP OPENING

14 NEW CENTRAL NORTH OXFORD GARDENS

Leckford Road, Oxford, OX2 6HY. *Three city gardens situated in parallel streets; two in Leckford Rd & one in Plantation Rd. Access from Kingston Rd or Woodstock Rd. Parking in Leckford Rd, Warnborough Rd & Farndon Rd.* Sat 23, Sun 24, Sat 30 Apr, Sun 1 May (2-5). Combined adm £7.50, chd free. Tea at 38 Leckford Road & 50 Plantation Road.

38 LECKFORD ROAD

Dinah Adams.
(See separate entry)

NEW 41 LECKFORD ROAD

Liz & Mark Jennings.

50 PLANTATION ROAD

Philippa Scoones.

Three very different town gardens. The owner of one is a true plant specialist with a wide collection of unusual plants many grown in shade. A second is a surprisingly wide and deep garden in two parts: lovely trees and planting and lots of pots; and an unusual water feature with stepping stones. Many variety of tulips. The third is an exquisitely designed garden for entertaining and relaxing. Plants for sale at 38 Leckford Road and 50 Plantation Road.

♿ ☕ »))

GROUP OPENING

15 NEW CHADLINGTON VILLAGE GARDENS

Bull Hill, Chadlington, Chipping Norton, OX7 3NX. *Between Chipping Norton & Charlbury, from A361 or A44. Postcode for village centre OX7 3NX. Maps will be provided for visitors on arrival.* Sun 12 June (1-5). Combined adm £5, chd free. Home-made teas at Chadlington Manor.

NEW CHADLINGTON MANOR

Alison & George Bailey.

NEW MILLBROOK

Julie & Mark Cummins.

NEW ROSE COTTAGE

Nina Morgan.

NEW SANDYS HOUSE

Jane Bell.

NEW YEW TREE COTTAGE

Isobelle Jaques.

Five gardens in the delightful Cotswold stone village of Chadlington, which lies in the Evenlode Valley. Varying in size and style, these inc formal areas with parterres, topiary and water features, mixed herbaceous and cottage-style borders, and naturalistic planting. Specimen shrubs and trees feature widely, with vantage points to enjoy garden views and the local landscape. Seasonal highlights inc wisterias, roses, orchard blossom and other flowering shrubs and trees. Plant sale at Sandys House.

🐐 ❋ ☕ »))

16 CHALKHOUSE GREEN FARM

Chalkhouse Green, Kidmore End, Reading, RG4 9AL. Mr J Hall, www.chgfarm.com. *2m N of Reading, 5m SW of Henley-on-Thames. Situated between A4074 & B481. From Kidmore End take Chalkhouse Green Rd. Follow NGS yellow signs.* Sun 26 June (2-6). Adm £3, chd free. Home-made teas.
1 acre garden and open traditional farmstead. Herbaceous borders, herb garden, shrubs, old fashioned roses, trees inc medlar, quince and mulberries, walled ornamental kitchen garden and cherry orchard. Rare breed farm animals inc British White cattle, Suffolk Punch horses, donkeys, geese, chickens, ducks and turkeys. Plant and jam stall, donkey rides, swimming in covered pool, grass tennis court, trailer rides, farm trail, WWII bomb shelter, heavy horse and bee display. Partial wheelchair access.

♿ 🐐 ❋ ☕ 💐

GROUP OPENING

17 CHARLBURY GARDENS

Charlbury, OX7 3PP. *6m SE of Chipping Norton. Large Cotswold village on B4022 Witney-Enstone Rd.* Sun 26 June (2-5). Combined adm £6, chd free. Home-made teas at 27 Ditchley Road, Charlbury.

CLOVER PATCH

Dr & Mrs J Goves.

NEW 3 KEARSEY COURT

Dr John & Mrs Liz Waterfall.

THE PRIORY GARDEN

Dr D El Kabir & Colleagues.

Three varied gardens in the centre of this large Cotswold village, in the context of traditional stone houses. Clover Patch, a ½ acre garden with a newly formed cutting garden to the front; a small fruit, vegetable and propagating area with raised beds leading to lawns, a water garden and shady woodland area to the rear. New for 2022, the garden at 3 Kearsey Court is only 4 yrs old. An L-shaped garden with vegetable beds and flower borders. The Priory Garden has 1 acre of formal terraced topiary gardens with Italianate features. Foliage colour schemes, shrubs, parterres with fragrant plants, old roses, water features, sculpture and inscriptions aim to produce a poetic,

wistful atmosphere. Arboretum of over 3 acres borders the River Evenlode and inc wildlife garden and pond.

18 CHIVEL FARM

Heythrop, OX7 5TR. John & Rosalind Sword, 01608 683227, rosalind.sword@btinternet.com. *4m E of Chipping Norton. Off A361 or A44. Parking at Chivel Farm.* Sun 14 Aug (2-5.30). Adm £5, chd free. **Home-made teas. Visits also by arrangement Feb to Sept for groups of 5+.**

Beautifully designed country garden with extensive views, designed for continuous interest that is always evolving. Colour schemed borders with many unusual trees, shrubs and herbaceous plants. Small formal white garden and a conservatory.

19 CLARIDGES BARN

Charlbury Road, Chipping Norton, OX7 5XG. Drs David & Jill Edwards, 07973 129473, drdavidedwards@hotmail.co.uk. *3m SE of Chipping Norton. Take B4026 from Chipping Norton to Charlbury after 3m turn R to Dean, we are 200 metres on the R. Please park on the verge.* Wed 20 Apr, Wed 11 May, Wed 8 June (11-5). Adm £5, chd free. Light refreshments. **Visits also by arrangement Apr to Sept.**

3½ acres of family garden, wood and meadow hewn from a barley field on limestone brash. Situated on top of the Cotswolds, it is open to all weathers, but rewarding views and dog walking opportunities on hand. Large vegetable, fruit and cutting garden, wildlife pond and five cedar greenhouses, all loved by rabbits, deer and squirrel. Herbaceous borders and woodland gardens with gravel and flagged paths, divided by

stone walls. Claridges Barn dates back to the 1600s, the cottage 1860s, converted about 30 yrs ago. Plants for sale.

20 CORPUS CHRISTI COLLEGE

Merton Street, Oxford, OX1 4JF. Domestic Bursar, www.ccc.ox.ac.uk. *Entrance from Merton St.* Sun 26 June (6-10am). Adm £3, chd free. Tea in the Old Lodgings.

As an experiment, after 27 yrs of NGS afternoon openings, we will open for the third time between 6am and 10am! Join us for free tea and coffee in the Old Lodgings and enjoy our informal and beautiful organic garden with the added bonus of great views from the old town wall, across Christ Church gardens, meadows and Cathedral. Wheelchair access with one slope in the garden.

Broughton Castle

© Andrew Lawson

GROUP OPENING

21 CUMNOR VILLAGE GARDENS

Leys Road, Cumnor, Oxford, OX2 9QF. *4m W of central Oxford. From A420, exit for Cumnor & follow B4017 into the village. Parking on road & side roads, behind PO, or behind village hall in Leys Rd.* Sun 19 June (2-6). Combined adm £5, chd free. Home-made teas in United Reformed Church Hall, Leys Road.

19 HIGH STREET
Janet Cross.

10 LEYS ROAD
Penny & Nick Bingham.

41 LEYS ROAD
Philip & Jennie Powell.

43 LEYS ROAD
Anna Stevens.

STONEHAVEN
Dr Dianne & Prof Keith Gull.
(See separate entry)

The gardens feature a wide variety of plants, shrubs, trees, vegetables, fruit and wild flowers. Two of the gardens are cottage style with unusual perennials and many shrubs, trees and vegetables. Another has a Japanese influence exhibiting many plants with black or bronze foliage and gravel areas. The courtyard garden has extremes of light and shade with planting that cleverly reflects the conditions and is easy to maintain. The largest garden has many rooms and features to explore and delight the imagination. Wheelchair access to 19 High Street, 41 and 43 Leys Road and Stonehaven. WC facilities in United Reformed Church Hall.
&. ❀ ☕ ⏶)

22 103 DENE ROAD

Headington, Oxford, OX3 7EQ. Steve & Mary Woolliams, 01865 764153, stevewoolliams@gmail.com. *S Headington, nr Nuffield. Dene Rd accessed from The Slade from the N, or from Hollow Way from the S. Both access roads are B4495. Garden on sharp bend.* Visits by arrangement Apr to Aug for groups of up to 10. Adm £4, chd free. Home-made teas.
A surprising eco-friendly garden with

borrowed view over the Lye Valley Nature Reserve. Lawns, a wildflower meadow, pond and large kitchen garden are inc in a suburban 60ft x 120ft sloping garden. Fruit trees, soft fruit and mixed borders of shrubs, hardy perennials, grasses and bulbs, designed for seasonal colour. This garden has been noted for its wealth of wildlife inc a variety of birds, butterflies and other insects such as the rare Brown Hairstreak butterfly, the rare Currant Clearwing moth and the Grizzled Skipper.

23 DENTON HOUSE

Denton, Oxford, OX44 9JF. Mr & Mrs Luke, 01865 874440, waveney@jandwluke.com. *In a valley between Garsington & Cuddesdon.* Visits by arrangement Apr to Sept for groups of up to 30. Adm £5, chd free. Home-made teas.
Large walled garden surrounds a Georgian mansion (not open) with shaded areas, walks, topiary and many interesting mature trees, large lawns, herbaceous borders and rose beds. The windows in the wall were taken in 1864 from Brasenose College Chapel and Library. Wild garden and a further walled fruit garden.
&. ☕ ☕

GROUP OPENING

24 DORCHESTER GARDENS

Dorchester-On-Thames, Wallingford, OX10 7HZ. *Off A4074 or A415 signed to Dorchester. Parking at Old Bridge Meadow, at SE end of Dorchester Bridge. Disabled parking at 26 Manor Farm Road (OX10 7HZ). Maps available at the car park.* Sun 3 July (2-5). Combined adm £5, chd free. Home-made teas in downstairs tearoom at Abbey Guesthouse. Last orders at 4.30pm.

26 MANOR FARM ROAD
David & Judy Parker.

6 MONKS CLOSE
Leif & Petronella Rasmussen.

7 ROTTEN ROW
Michael & Veronica Evans.

Three contrasting gardens in a historic village surrounding the medieval Abbey and the scene of many Midsomer Murders. 26 Manor Farm

Road (OX10 7HZ) was part of an old larger garden, which now has a formal lawn and planting, vegetable garden, greenhouse and several interesting trees. From the yew hedge down towards the River Thame, which often floods in winter, is an apple orchard underplanted with spring bulbs. 6 Monks Close (OX10 7JA) is idyllic and surprising. A small spring-fed stream and sloping lawn surrounded by naturalistic planting runs down to a monastic fish pond. Bridges over this deep pond lead to the River Thame with steep banks. 7 Rotten Row (OX10 7LJ) is Dorchester's lawless garden, a terrace with borders leads to a lovely geometric garden supervised by a statue of Hebe. Access is from the allotments. Due to deep water at 26 Manor Farm Road and 6 Monks Close children should be accompanied at all times. Wheelchair access to 26 Manor Farm Road, partial access to other gardens. No dogs, please.
&. ☕

25 FAILFORD

118 Oxford Road, Abingdon, OX14 2AG. Miss R Aylward, 01235 523925, aylwardsdooz@hotmail.co.uk. *No. 118 is on the L of Oxford Rd when coming from Abingdon Town, or on the R when approaching from the N. Entrance to this garden is via 116 Oxford Rd.* Sun 12 June (11-4). Combined adm with 116 Oxford Road £5, chd free. Home-made teas. Visits also by arrangement May to Sept for groups of up to 25.
This town garden is an extension of the home divided into rooms both formal and informal. It changes every yr. Features inc walkways through shaded areas, arches, a beach, grasses, fernery, roses, topiaries, acers, hostas and heucheras. Be inspired by the wide variety of planting, many unusual and quirky features, all within an area 570 sq ft.
❀ ☕ ⏶)

26 FOXINGTON

Britwell Salome, Watlington, OX49 5LG. Ms Mary Roadnight, 01491 612418, mary@foxington.co.uk. *At Red Lion Pub take turning to Britwell Hill. After 350yds turn into drive on L.* Visits by arrangement Apr to Oct for groups of 10 to 30. Adm £10, chd free. Adm inc home-made teas. Special

dietary options by prior request. Stunning views to the Chiltern Hills provide a wonderful setting for this impressive garden, remodelled in 2009. Patio, heather and gravel gardens enjoy this view, whilst the back and vegetable gardens are more enclosed. The relatively new planting is maturing well and the area around the house (not open) is full of colour. There is an orchard and a flock of white doves. Well behaved dogs are welcome, but they must be kept on a lead at all times as there are many wild animals in the garden, wildflower meadow, wood and neighbouring fields. Wheelchair access throughout the garden on level paths with no steps.

27 FRIARS COURT

Clanfield, OX18 2SU. Charles Willmer, www.friarscourt.com. *4m N of Faringdon. On A4095 Faringdon to Witney road. ½ m S of Clanfield.* **Sun 19 June (2-5). Adm £4, chd free. Cream teas.**
Over 3 acres of formal and informal gardens with flower beds, borders and specimen trees, lie within the remaining arms of a C16 moat which partially surrounds the large C17 Cotswold stone house. Bridges span the moat with water lily filled ponds to the front whilst beyond the gardens is a woodland walk. A museum about Friars Court is located in the old Coach House. A level path goes around part of the gardens. The museum is accessed over gravel.

28 THE GRANGE

1 Berrick Road, Chalgrove, OX44 7RQ. Mrs Vicky Farren, 01865 400883, vickyfarren@mac.com, thegrangegardener.com. *12m E of Oxford & 4m from Watlington, off B480. The entrance to The Grange is at the grass triangle between Berrick Rd & Monument Rd, by the pedestrian crossing. GPS is not reliable in the final 200yds.* **Visits by arrangement May to Oct for groups of up to 50. Adm £10, chd free. Home-made teas.**
11 acres of gardens inc herbaceous borders and a large expanse of prairie with many grasses and a wildflower meadow. There is a lake with bridges and a planted island, a dry river bed and a labyrinth. A brook runs through the garden with a further pond, arboretum, old orchard and

partly walled vegetable garden. Partial wheelchair access on many grass paths.

29 GREENFIELD FARM

Christmas Common, nr Watlington, OX49 5HG. Andrew & Jane Ingram, 01491 612434, andrew@andrewbingram.com. *4m from J5 M40, 7m from Henley. J5 M40, A40 towards Oxford for ½ m, turn L signed Christmas Common. ¾ m past Fox & Hounds Pub, turn L at Tree Barn sign.* **Visits by arrangement May to Sept for groups of 5 to 30. Adm £5, chd free.**
10 acre wildflower meadow surrounded by woodland, established 25 yrs ago under the Countryside Stewardship Scheme. Traditional Chiltern chalkland meadow in beautiful peaceful setting with 100 species of perennial wild flowers, grasses and five species of orchids. ½ m walk from parking area to meadow. Opportunity to return via typical Chiltern beechwood.

30 GREYHOUND HOUSE

The Street, Ewelme, Wallingford, OX10 6HU. Mrs Wendy Robertson, flowerfrond@gmail.com. *Greyhound House is on the main road at the school end of Ewelme.* **Visits by arrangement June to Sept for groups of 10+. Adm £6, chd free.**
2 acre hillside garden set in historic Chiltern village of Ewelme. Mixed herbaceous borders (inc salvias and unusual plants), ornamental grass walk, walled courtyard with dahlias and late summer flowering perennials, houseplant theatre, fernery, cutting garden, orchard and woodland.

31 HAM COURT

Ham Court Farm, Weald, Bampton, OX18 2HG. Matthew Rice. *Drive through the village towards Clanfield. The drive is on the R, exactly opp Weald St.* **Sun 7 Aug (2-6.30). Adm £5, chd free. Home-made teas.**
Several acres of garden, orchard and paddock surround the last gatehouse fragment of the medieval Bampton Castle, partially moated with a walled kitchen garden, a productive greenhouse and farmyard. This project begun by Emma Bridgewater

and Matthew Rice is 10 yrs old and as trees are growing and buildings are changing it is gradually emerging from its former life as a commercial farm with no garden at all. The teas and vintage tractors are probably better than the borders and there are sheep, pigs, cows and poultry to see as well, so please leave dogs at home.

32 23 HID'S COPSE ROAD

Oxford, OX2 9JJ. Kathy Eldridge. *W of central Oxford, halfway up Cumnor Hill. Turn into Hids Copse Rd from Cumnor Hill. We are the last house on the R before T-junction.* **Sun 13 Feb (2-5). Combined adm with Stonehaven £5, chd free. Sun 12 June (2-6). Combined adm with Hid's Copse Road Gardens £7, chd free. Opening with West Oxford Gardens on Sun 26 June.**
The garden surrounds a house built in the early 30s (not open) on a ½ acre plot. Designed to be wildlife friendly, it has a kitchen garden, two ponds with frogs and newts, a wildflower meadow and woodland areas under many trees. Small winding paths lead to areas to sit and contemplate. The planting is dependent on the area within the garden, but a special treat are the snowdrops in early spring.

In 2021 the National Garden Scheme donation helped support Perennial's caseworkers, who helped over 250 people and their families in crisis to receive a wide range of support including emergency food parcels and accommodation, energy payments and expert advice and information

GROUP OPENING

33 NEW **HID'S COPSE ROAD GARDENS**
Oxford, OX2 9JJ. *From Oxford Train Stn, W along Botley Rd 1⅓m; continue W up Cumnor Hill, 1m to Hid's Copse Rd on R just after bus shelter. A community noticeboard & small postbox are at entrance to Hid's Copse Rd.* **Sun 12 June (2-6). Combined adm with 23 Hid's Copse Road £7, chd free. Home-made teas.**

NEW **11 HID'S COPSE ROAD**
Neil & Valerie Grady.

15 HID'S COPSE ROAD
James & Harriet Bretherton.

NEW **16 HID'S COPSE ROAD**
Jack Bowyer.

NEW **16A HID'S COPSE ROAD**
Kim Ramirez.

NEW **18 HID'S COPSE ROAD**
Nathan Waddington.

NEW **22 HID'S COPSE ROAD**
Adrienne McKenna.

Seven gardens with influences ranging from Edwardian to Mediterranean and family modern. Wildlife friendly, with colourful borders, lawns, ponds, kitchen gardens and a wide range of shrubs and trees, the gardens' other features inc a bog garden, a sunken garden, woodland areas, wildflower plantings and meadow, King Arthur's seat, and several unusual plants. WC available. Wheelchair access to four gardens only.

34 **HOLLYHOCKS**
North Street, Islip, Kidlington, OX5 2SQ. Avril Hughes, 01865 377104, ahollyhocks@btinternet.com. *3m NE of Kidlington. From A34, exit Bletchingdon & Islip. B4027 direction Islip, turn L into North St.* **Sun 13 Feb, Sun 1 May (1.30-5). Adm £3, chd free. Home-made teas. 2023: Sun 12 Feb.** Visits also by arrangement Feb to Sept for groups of up to 30.
Plantswoman's small Edwardian garden brimming with year-round interest, especially planted to provide winter colour, scent and snowdrops. Divided into areas with bulbs, May tulips, herbaceous borders, roses, clematis, shade and woodland planting especially trillium, podophyllum and arisaema, late summer salvias and annuals give colour. Large pots and troughs add seasonal interest and colour.

35 **HOME CLOSE**
29 Southend, Garsington, OX44 9DH. Mrs M Waud & Dr P Giangrande, 01865 361394, m.waud@btinternet.com. *3m SE of Oxford. N of B480, opp Garsington Manor.* Visits by arrangement Apr to Sept for groups of up to 50. Adm £5, chd free. Please discuss refreshments when booking.
2 acre garden with listed house (not open), listed granary and 1 acre mixed tree plantation with fine views. Unusual trees and shrubs planted for year-round effect. Terraces, stone walls and hedges divide the garden and the planting reflects a Mediterranean interest. Vegetable garden and orchard.

GROUP OPENING

36 **IFFLEY GARDENS**
Iffley, Oxford, OX4 4EF. *2m S of Oxford. Within Oxford's ring road, off A4158 Iffley road, from Magdalen Bridge to Littlemore r'about, to Iffley village. Map provided at each garden.* **Sun 12 June (2-6). Combined adm £5, chd free. Home-made teas in church hall & some gardens.**

17 ABBERBURY ROAD
Mrs Julie Steele.

25 ABBERBURY ROAD
Rob & Bridget Farrands.

86 CHURCH WAY
Helen Beinart & Alex Coren.

122 CHURCH WAY
Sir John & Lady Elliott.

6 FITZHERBERT CLOSE
Eunice Martin.

THE MALT HOUSE
Helen Potts.

4A TREE LANE
Pemma & Nick Spencer-Chapman.

Secluded old village with renowned Norman church, featured on cover of Pevsner's Oxon Guide. Visit seven gardens ranging in variety and style from the large Malt House garden to mixed family gardens with shady borders and vegetables. Varied planting throughout the gardens inc herbaceous borders, shade loving plants, roses, fine specimen trees and plants in terracing. Features inc water features, formal gardens, small lake, Thames riverbank and a small Japanese garden. Plant sales at several gardens. Wheelchair access to some gardens.
& ✿ ☕ »))

GROUP OPENING

37 **KENCOT GARDENS**
Kencot, Lechlade, GL7 3QT. *5m NE of Lechlade. E of A361 between Burford & Lechlade.* **Mon 18 Apr (2-6). Combined adm £6, chd free. Light refreshments at village hall.**

THE ALLOTMENTS
Amelia Carter Charity.

BELHAM HAYES
Mr Joseph Jones.

NEW **GREYSTONES**
Mr Tom Valentine.

HILLVIEW HOUSE
Andrea Moss.

IVY NOOK
Gill & Wally Cox.

MANOR FARM
Henry & Kate Fyson.

WELL HOUSE
Janet & Richard Wheeler.

The 2022 Kencot Gardens group will consist of six gardens and The Allotments. The Allotments are tended by eight people and grow a range of vegetables, flowers and fruit. Ivy Nook has spring flowers, shrubs, small pond, magnolia and fruit trees. Belham Hayes is a mature cottage garden with mixed herbaceous borders and two old fruit trees. Emphasis on scent and colour coordination. Manor Farm has a 2 acre walled garden, bulbs, wood anemones, fritillaries in mature orchards, pleached lime walk, 130 yr old yew ball and Black Hamburg vine. Chickens and a pony. Well House is a ⅓ acre garden, mature trees, hedges, wildlife pond, waterfall, small bog area, spring bulbs and rockeries. Hillview House is a 2 acre garden with lime tree drive, established trees, pond, wildflower area, shrubs, perennial borders, daffodils and aconites. Greystones has plentiful stone animals and olive trees with climbers and pots adding colour. At the back of the house, beds and borders frame

a happy family garden focussed around fruit trees and a magnolia. No wheelchair access to The Allotments, other gardens maybe difficult due to gravel and uneven paths.

&. 🐐 🚌 ☕ ᠉)

38 NEW KIDMORE HOUSE GARDEN & VINEYARD
Chalkhouse Green Road, Kidmore End, Reading, RG4 9AR. Mr Stephen & Mrs Niamh Kendall, 07740 290990, www.kidmorevineyard.com. *6m NNW of Reading, Emma Green/ Reading end of the village. Parking in the field through gate signed Kidmore Vineyard.* **Fri 10 June (1-4). Adm £6, chd free. Visits also by arrangement in June for groups of up to 20.**
14 acres set in South Oxfordshire landscaped gardens with features inc ha-ha, walled garden with delphiniums, calla lilies and white wisteria, a rose garden and one hectar of vines. Garden sympathetic with a red-brick Queen Anne house (not open). Anecdotally, the large sweet chestnut in the lawn was planted with the house in 1680. Picnics welcome in the field. Partial wheelchair access with gravel pathways and some steps.

&. 🐐 ✿ ☕ 🪑 ᠉)

39 KINGS COTTAGE
Pudlicote Lane, Chilson, Chipping Norton, OX7 3HU. Mr Michael Anderson, 07771 861928, michaelfanderson66@outlook .com. *S end of Chilson village. Entering Chilson from the S, off the B4437 Charlbury to Burford road, we are the 1st house on the L. Please drive past & park considerately in centre of village.* **Sat 28, Sun 29 May (2-5). Combined adm with Bolters Farm £6, chd free. Light refreshments. Visits also by arrangement Apr to Sept.**
An old row of cottages with mature trees and yew hedging. Over the last 6 yrs a new design and planting scheme has been started to reduce the areas of lawn, bring in planting to complement the house (not open) and setting, introduce new borders and encourage wildlife. A work in progress. Partial wheelchair access via gravel drive. Moderate slopes, grass and some sections of garden only accessible via steps.

&. 🐐 ✿ ☕

GROUP OPENING

40 LANGFORD GARDENS
Lechlade, GL7 3LF. *6m S of Burford A361 towards Lechlade. 1½m E of Filkins. Large free car park in village. Coaches welcome. Map of gardens available.* **Sun 12 June (2-6). Combined adm £7.50, chd free. Home-made teas at Pember House & village hall.**

BAKERY COTTAGE
Mr & Mrs R Robinson.

BAY TREE COTTAGE
Mr & Mrs R Parsons.

BRIDGEWATER HOUSE
Mr & Mrs T R Redston.

CORKSCREW COTTAGE
Fiona Gilbert.

COTSWOLD BUNGALOW
John & Hilary Dudley.

COTSWOLD COTTAGE
Mr & Mrs Tom Marshall.

THE GRANGE
Mr & Mrs J Johnston.

KEMPS YARD
Mr & Mrs R Kemp.

LOWER FARM HOUSE
Mr & Mrs Templeman.

MEADOW VIEW
Linda Moore.

THE OLD BAKERY
Mr & Mrs G Edwards.

PEMBER HOUSE
Mr & Mrs J Potter.

ROSEFERN COTTAGE
Mrs D Lowden.

SPRINGFIELD
Mr & Mrs M Harris.

STONECROFT
Christine Apperley.

THE VICARAGE
Mr & Mrs C Smith.

WELLBANK
Sir Brian & Lady Pomeroy.

WELLBANK COTTAGE
Mr & Mrs S Findlay-Wilson.

WELLBANK HOUSE
Mr & Mrs Robert Hill.

Langford is a charming small Cotswold village with both the important Grade I listed St Matthew's Church and a splendid pub, The Bell Inn where lunch is available. Nineteen gardens will be open with a delightful mix from large formal to small cottage gardens. Ancient Cotswold stone

walls provide a backdrop for many old variety roses. Our plant stall has a large range of local plants and shrubs. Live music in Pember House garden during the afternoon, as well as village teas, and a church floral display add to an enjoyable day for everyone.

🐐 ✿ 🚌 ☕ ᠉)

41 38 LECKFORD ROAD
Oxford, OX2 6HY. Dinah Adams, 01865 511996, dinah_zwanenberg@fastmail.com. *Central Oxford. North on Woodstock Rd take 3rd L. Coming into Oxford on Woodstock Rd, 1st R after Farndon Rd. Some 2 hr parking nearby.* **Sun 27 Mar (2-5). Adm £4, chd free. Tea. Opening with Central North Oxford Gardens on Sat 23, Sun 24, Sat 30 Apr, Sun 1 May. Visits also by arrangement Mar to Sept for groups of up to 15.**
Behind the rather severe facade of a Victorian town house (not open) is a very protected long walled garden with mature trees. The planting reflects the varied levels of shade and inc rare and unusual plants. The trees in the front garden deserve attention. The back garden is divided into three distinct parts, each with a very different character. Amongst other things there is a hornbeam roof.

&. ✿ ☕ ᠉)

42 LIME CLOSE
35 Henleys Lane, Drayton, Abingdon, OX14 4HU. M C de Laubarede, mail@mclgardendesign.com, www.mclgardendesign.com. *2m S of Abingdon. Henleys Ln is off main road through Drayton. Please Note: When visiting Lime Close, please respect local residents & park considerately. Visits by arrangement Feb to Nov for groups of 10+. Adm £5, chd free. Cream teas. Donation to International Dendrology Society.*
4 acre mature plantsman's garden with rare trees, shrubs, roses and bulbs. Mixed borders, raised beds, pergola, topiary and shade borders. Herb garden by Rosemary Verey. Listed C16 house (not open). Cottage garden by MCL Garden Design, planted for colour, an iris garden with 100 varieties of tall bearded irises. Winter bulbs. New arboretum with rare exotic trees and shrubs from Asia and America. The garden is flat and mostly grass with gravel drive and paths.

&. 🐐 ✿ 🚌 ☕ ᠉)

43 MAGDALEN COLLEGE

Oxford, OX1 4AU. Magdalen College, www.magd.ox.ac.uk. *Entrance in High St.* **Sun 10 Apr (10-7). Adm £8, chd under 7 yrs free. Light refreshments in the Old Kitchen Bar.**
60 acres inc deer park, college lawns, numerous trees 150-200 yrs old; notable herbaceous and shrub plantings. Magdalen meadow where purple and white snake's head fritillaries can be found is surrounded by Addison's Walk, a tree lined circuit by the River Cherwell developed since the late C18. Ancient herd of 60 deer. Press bell at the lodge for porter to provide wheelchair access.

44 MANOR HOUSE

Manor Farm Road, Dorchester-on-Thames, OX10 7HZ. Simon & Margaret Broadbent. *8m SSE of Oxford. Off A4074, signed from village centre. Parking at Bridge Meadow 400 metres, disabled parking at house.* **Sun 14 Aug (2.30-4.30). Adm £4, chd free. Home-made teas.**
2 acre garden in beautiful setting around Georgian house (not open) and medieval abbey. Spacious lawn leading to riverside copse of towering poplars with fine views of Dorchester Abbey. Terrace with rose and vine covered pergola around lily pond. Colourful herbaceous borders, small orchard and vegetable garden. Wheelchair access on gravel paths.

45 MEADOW COTTAGE

Christmas Common, Watlington, OX49 5HR. Mrs Zelda Kent-Lemon, 01491 613779, zelda_kl@hotmail.com. *1m from Watlington. Coming from Oxford M40 to J6. Turn R & go to Watlington. Turn L up Hill Rd to top. Turn R after 50yds, turn L into field.* **Sun 8 May (11.30-5.30). Adm £5.50, chd free. Home-made teas. Visits also by arrangement Feb to Oct.**
1¾ acre garden adjoining ancient bluebell woods, created by the owner from 1995 onwards. Many areas to explore inc a professionally designed vegetable garden, many composting areas, wildflower garden and pond, old and new fruit trees, many shrubs, much varied hedging and a tall treehouse which children can climb under supervision. Indigenous trees and C17 barn (not open). For visits by arrangement come and see the wonderful snowdrops in Feb and during the month of May visit the bluebell woodland. Partial wheelchair access over gravel driveway and lawns.

46 MERTON COLLEGE OXFORD FELLOWS' GARDEN

Merton Street, Oxford, OX1 4JD. Merton College, 01865 276310. *Merton St runs parallel to High St about halfway down.* **Sun 24 July (10-5). Adm £6, chd free.**
Ancient mulberry, said to have associations with James I. Specimen trees, long mixed border, recently established herbaceous bed. View of Christ Church meadow.

GROUP OPENING

47 MIDDLETON CHENEY GARDENS

Middleton Cheney, Banbury, OX17 2ST. *3m E of Banbury. From M40 J11 follow A422 signed Middleton Cheney. Parking at nursery school car park, next to 19 Glovers Ln, OX17 2NU. Map available at all gardens.* **Sun 3 July (1-6). Combined adm £7, chd free. Home-made teas at Peartree House. Picnics welcome at Springfield House.**

CROFT HOUSE
Richard & Sandy Walmsley.

19 GLOVERS LANE
Michael Donohoe & Jane Rixon.

NEW **5 LONGBURGES**
Mr D Vale.

38 MIDWAY
Margaret & David Finch.

PEARTREE HOUSE
Roger & Barbara Charlesworth.

14 QUEEN STREET
Brian & Kathy Goodey.

NEW **2A RECTORY LANE**
Debbie Evans.

SPRINGFIELD HOUSE
Lynn & Paul Taylor.

Large village with C13 church (open) with renowned pre-Raphaelite stained glass. Eight open gardens with a variety of sizes, styles and maturity. Of the smaller gardens, one contemporary garden contrasts formal features with colour-filled beds, borders and exotic plants. Another modern garden has flowing curves that create an elegant, serene feeling. A mature small front and back garden is planted profusely with a feel of an intimate haven. A garden that has evolved through family use, features rooms and dense planting. A steeply-pitched garden on three levels has patios, ponds, lawn, herbaceous borders and acer collection. A larger garden new to its owners, is being replanted with cottage-style plants and a vegetable garden. One of the larger gardens continues with the renovation of a long lost garden, along with restoring areas of orchard, beds and borders. Another has an air of mystery with hidden corners and an extensive water feature weaving its way throughout the garden.

48 MIDSUMMER HOUSE

Woolstone, Faringdon, SN7 7QL. Penny Spink. *7m W & 7m S of Faringdon. Woolstone is a small village off B4507, below Uffington White Horse Hill. Take road towards Uffington from the White Horse Pub.* **Wed 25 May (2-6). Adm £5, chd free. Sun 26 June (2-6). Combined adm with Woolstone Mill House £10, chd free. Wed 21 Sept (2-6). Adm £5, chd free. Home-made teas.**
On moving to Midsummer House 6 yrs ago, the owners created the garden using herbaceous plants brought with them from their previous home at Woolstone Mill House. Herbaceous border, parterre with new topiary, and espaliered Malus Everest. The garden designed by owner's son Justin Spink, a renowned garden designer and landscape architect. Plant stall by Mike Collins Plants. Picnics welcome in the field opposite. Wheelchair access over short gravel drive at entrance.

49 MILL BARN

25 Mill Lane, Chalgrove, OX44 7SL. Pat Hougham, 01865 890020, pat@gmec.co.uk. *12m E of Oxford. Chalgrove is 4m from Watlington off B480. Mill Barn is in Mill Ln, W of Chalgrove, 300yds S of Lamb Pub.* **Visits by arrangement May to Sept for groups of 6 to 40. Combined visit with The Manor garden £6. Home-made cream teas.**
Mill Barn has an informal cottage garden with a variety of flowers throughout the seasons. Rose arches

and a pergola lead to a vegetable plot surrounded by a cordon of fruit trees, all set in a mill stream landscape. The Manor garden has a lake and wildlife areas, mixed shrubs and herbaceous beds that surround the C15 Grade I listed Manor House (not open).

50 MONKS HEAD
Weston Road,
Bletchingdon, OX5 3DH.
Sue Bedwell, 01869 350155,
bedwell615@btinternet.com.
Approx 4m N of Kidlington. From A34 take B4027 to Bletchingdon, turn R at Xrds into Weston Rd. Visits by arrangement Jan to Oct.
Plantaholics' garden for year-round interest. Bulb frame and alpine area, greenhouse. Changes evolving all the time, becoming more of a wildlife garden.

51 16 OAKFIELD ROAD
Carterton, OX18 3QN. Karen & Jason. *Off A40 Oxford W bound Carterton & Brize Norton junction. Go past RAF Brize Norton main gate, head for town center. Through T-lights, take 3rd L Foxcroft Dr. Follow road around to T-junction, then turn R into Oakfield Rd.* Sun 7 Aug (12.30-5). Adm £3.50, chd free. Light refreshments.
A small tropical inspired garden that incorporates good use of the small space. Overflowing with palms, bamboo, cannas, tree ferns, hedychiums, *Tetrapanax papyrifera* 'Rex' and colocasia. Small walkway leading to a decked area with hot tub and thatched gazebo with its own Tiki inspired area. Also small pond, lawn, patio area and greenhouse, in an area of 10 x 12 metres. Partial wheelchair access on patio area only.

GROUP OPENING

52 OLD BOARS HILL GARDENS
Jarn Way, Boars Hill, Oxford, OX1 5JF. *3m S of Oxford. From S ring road towards A34 at r'about follow signs to Wootton & Boars Hill. Up Hinksey Hill take R fork. 1m R into Berkley Rd to Old Boars Hill.* Sun 22 May (1.30-5.30). Combined adm £6, chd free. Home-made teas.

TALL TREES
David Clark.

UPLANDS
Lyn Sanders, 01865 739486, sandersc4@hotmail.com.
Visits also by arrangement Apr to Oct for groups of 5 to 25.

WHITSUN MEADOWS
Jane & Nigel Jones,
07500 722722,
mail@jonesoxford.co.uk.
Visits also by arrangement May to Sept for groups of 10 to 30.

YEW COTTAGE
Michael Edwards.

Four delightful gardens in a conservation area. Whitsun Meadows overlooks Oxford and the garden inside gives a whole range of delightful garden areas to explore. Uplands is a southerly facing cottage garden with an extensive range of plants for colour for every season and a new formal area. Tall Trees is providing the plant sale surrounded by pots, rhododendrons and gravel gardens. The garden at Yew Tree Cottage is a delightful mixture of plants to give year-round colour and the owners will display their vintage cars inc one which has been on TV.

22 Hid's Copse Road, Hid's Copse Road Gardens

53 THE OLD VICARAGE
Main Street, Bledington, Chipping Norton, OX7 6UX. Sue & Tony Windsor. *6m SW of Chipping Norton. 4m SE of Stow-on-the-Wold. On the main street B4450 through Bledington. Not next to church.* Sun 24 Apr, Sun 19 June (11-5.30). Adm £5, chd free.
1½ acre garden around an early Victorian vicarage (1843) not open. Borders and beds filled with spring bulbs, hardy perennials, shrubs and trees. Informal rose garden with over 300 David Austin roses. Small pond and vegetable garden. Paddock with trees, shrubs and herbaceous border. Planted for year-round interest.

During 2020 – 2021 National Garden Scheme funding supported over 1,400 Queen's Nurses to deliver virtual and hands-on, community care across England, Wales and Northern Ireland

54 ORCHARD HOUSE
Asthall, Burford, OX18 4HH. Dr
Elizabeth Maitreyi, 07939 111605,
oneconsciousbreath@gmail.com.
*3m E of Burford. 1st house on R as
you come downhill into Asthall from
the A40. There is a small step down
from the pedestrian gate onto the
driveway. Parking in nearby field.*
Sun 26 June (2-6). Adm £5, chd
free. Home-made teas. Visits also
by arrangement for groups of 10
to 20.
A 5 acre garden still in the making.
Formal borders and courtyard. We
are creating an English garden finely
balanced between the formal and
the wild. Beautiful sculptures add to
the planting and there is woodland to
walk in beyond. Rare breed piglets
sometimes to be seen. Dogs on a
lead only. If you need accommodation
in the area our 'dacha' is on Airbnb.
Wheelchair access with small step
onto drive and one step down to
garden.

55 116 OXFORD ROAD
Abingdon, OX14 2AG. Mr &
Mrs P Aylward, 01235 523925,
aylwardsdooz@hotmail.co.uk.
*116 Oxford Rd is on the R if coming
from A34 N exit, or on the L after
Picklers Hill turn if approaching from
Abingdon town centre.* Sun 12
June (11-4). Combined adm with
Failford £5, chd free. Home-made
teas. Visits also by arrangement
May to Sept.
This young town garden brings
alive the imagination of its creators.
It will inspire both the enthusiast
and the beginner. The use of
recycled materials, lots of colour
and architectural plants. A folly/
greenhouse is just one of many quirky
features. Raised beds, rockeries,
specimen plants, beds of roses and
hostas. Pushes the boundaries of
conventional gardening. There is
something for everyone!

57 NEW 9 RAWLINSON ROAD
Oxford, OX2 6UE. Ramnique
Lall, 07803 607112,
ranilall@hotmail.com. *³⁄₄ m N of
Oxford City Centre. Rawlinson Rd
runs between Banbury & Woodstock
roads midway between Oxford City
Centre & Summertown shops.* Sun
22 May (10-5). Adm £3, chd free.
Visits also by arrangement Mar
to Nov.
Townhouse garden with structured
disarray of roses. Terrace of stone
inlaid with brick and enclosed by
Chinese fretwork balustrade, chunky
brick and oak pergola covered
with roses, wisteria and clematis;
potted topiary. Until autumn, garden
delightfully replete with aconites,
lobelias, phloxes, daisies and
meandering clematis.
&

56 NEW 11 RAWLINSON ROAD
Oxford, OX2 6UE. Emma
Chamberlain. *Central N Oxford.
Halfway between Central Oxford &
Summertown, off Banbury Rd.* Sun
22 May (1-6). Adm £3.50, chd free.
A south facing 120ft walled Victorian
town garden created from scratch
since the owners moved there in
2010. The struggle with heavy clay
and poor soil has been instructive.
Interesting mix of herbaceous and
shrubs with particular interest in
late tulips, grasses and unusual
plants. Great emphasis on colour
and succession planting with paths
running through the beds.
))

58 NEW SARSDEN GLEBE
Churchill, Chipping Norton,
OX7 6PH. Mr & Mrs Rupert
Ponsonby. *Situated between
Sarsden and Churchill. Sarsden
Glebe is ¹⁄₄ m S of Churchill on the
road to Sarsden. Turn in to the drive
by a small lodge.* Fri 15 Apr (12-
4.30). Adm £5, chd free. Home-
made teas.
A rectory garden and park laid out
by Humphrey Repton and his son
George. Terraced formal garden; wild
garden with spring bulbs and mature
oaks; and walled kitchen garden. Wild
garden with a sea of blue and white
Anemone blanda interspersed with
fritillaries and daffodils in spring.

Yew Tree Cottage, Chadlington Village Gardens

GROUP OPENING

59 SIBFORD GARDENS
Sibford Ferris, OX15 5RE. *7m W of Banbury. Nr the Warwickshire border, S of B4035, in centre of Sibford Ferris village at T-junction & additional gardens nr the Xrds & Wykham Arms Pub in Sibford Gower. Parking in both villages.* Sun 26 June (2-6). Combined adm £7, chd free. Home-made teas at Sibford Gower Village Hall (opp the church).

CARTER'S YARD
Sue & Malcolm Bannister, 01295 780365, sebannister@gmail.com.
Visits also by arrangement May to Sept.

NEW COPPERS
Mr Andrew & Mrs Chris Tindsley.

HOME CLOSE
Graham & Carolyn White.

THE LONG HOUSE
Jan & Diana Thompson.

In two charming small villages of Sibford Gower and Sibford Ferris, off the beaten track with thatched stone cottages, four contrasting gardens ranging from a truly traditional plants woman's cottage garden, the gardens of an early C20 Arts and Crafts house, to two new entries that have stunning newly designed gardens; one in woodland setting with a shade garden and the last a private garden of a renowned landscape architect. A fantastic collection of gardens bursting with bloom, structural intrigue, interesting planting and some rather unusual plants.

60 SOUTH HAYES
Yarnells Hill, Oxford, OX2 9BG. Mark & Louise Golding. *2m W of Oxford. Take Botley Rd heading W out of Oxford, pass under A34, turn L onto Westminster Way, Yarnells Hill is 2nd road on R. Park at top of hill & walk 100 metres down the lane.* Sun 21 Aug (2-6). Adm £4, chd free. Home-made teas.
1 acre garden transformed to make the most of a steeply sloping site. Formal planting close to the house (not open) and a raised decking area which overlooks the garden. Gravel pathways are retained by oak sleepers and pass through swathes of

hardy perennials and grasses, leading to the lower garden with natural wildlife pond and fruit trees. Garden once owned by the late Primrose Warburg, an Oxford galanthophile.

61 SOUTH NEWINGTON HOUSE
South Newington, OX15 4JW. Mr & Mrs David Swan, 07711 720135, claire_ainley@hotmail.com. *6m SW of Banbury. South Newington is between Banbury & Chipping Norton. Take Barford Rd off A361, 1st L after 100yds in between oak bollards. For SatNav use OX15 4JL.* **Visits by arrangement Mar to Oct. Adm £5, chd free. Home-made teas.**
Meandering tree lined drive leads to 2 acre garden. Herbaceous borders designed for year-round colour. Organic garden with established beds and rotation planting scheme. Orchard full of fruit trees with pond encouraging wildlife. Walled parterre planted for seasonal colour. A family garden with a small menagerie, all beautifully designed to blend seamlessly into the environment; a haven for all. Some gravel paths, otherwise full wheelchair access.

62 NEW SOUTHBANK
Back Lane, Epwell, Banbury, OX15 6LF. Alan Cooper, 01295 780577, alan.cooper2019@gmail.com. *1st bungalow on L after Church Ln on L. Epwell is midway between Banbury & Shipston on Stour. Turn at NGS sign for Epwell, 500yds turn R to village, 1m turn into square. Exit via L corner by church, approx 200yds Southbank.* Sun 21 Aug (2-5). Adm £3.50, chd free. **Visits also by arrangement in Aug for groups of up to 10.**
Front and back garden evolved over 20 yrs with several mature trees. Very densely planted with many rare and unusual plants. The front inc a rockery, mixed herbaceous border, peony and geranium beds. The back has various borders inc a sub-tropical bed, greenhouse, small vegetable plot and wildflower hedgerow.

63 64 SPRING ROAD
Abingdon, OX14 1AN. Janet Boulton, 01235 524514, j.boulton89@btinternet.com, www.janetboulton.co.uk. *S Abingdon from A34 take L turn after police station into Spring Rd. Minute's drive to No. 64 on L.* **Visits by arrangement May to Sept for groups of up to 10. Adm £5.**
A very special small but unique artist's garden (4½ x 30½ metres) behind a Victorian terrace house (not open). Predominantly green with numerous inscribed sculptures relating to art, history and the human spirit. Inspired by gardens the owner has painted, especially Little Sparta in Scotland. Visitors are invited to watch a film about this celebrated garden before walking around the garden itself.

GROUP OPENING

64 STEEPLE ASTON GARDENS
Steeple Aston, OX25 4SF. *14m N of Oxford, 9m S of Banbury. ½m E of A4260. Parking at village hall, OX25 4SF.* Sun 29 May (2-6). Combined adm £7, chd free. Home-made teas in village hall.

NEW THE CHURCH ALLOTMENTS
Mrs R McCready, Chair of Steeple Aston Church Allotments Association.

COMBE PYNE
Chris & Sally Cooper.

KRALINGEN
Mr & Mrs Roderick Nicholson.

THE LONGBYRE
Mr & Mrs V Billings.

NEW THE OLD POST OFFICE
Mr & Mrs John Adriaanse.

THE POUND HOUSE
Mr & Mrs R Clarke.

PRIMROSE GARDENS
Richard & Daphne Preston, 01869 340512, richard.preston5@btopenworld.com.
Visits also by arrangement Apr to July for groups of 10 to 45. 1 hr of interest with optional tour & tea.

Steeple Aston, often considered the most easterly of the Cotswold villages, is a beautiful stone built village with gardens that provide a wide range of interest. A stream meanders down the hill as the landscape changes from sand to

clay. The seven open gardens inc small floriferous cottage gardens, large landscaped gardens, natural woodland areas, ponds and bog gardens, themed borders and allotments. The gardens provide something for everyone from a courtyard garden to a former walled kitchen garden and so much in between. Allotments are wheelchair accessible with care, Primrose Gardens and Longbyre have gravel and Kralingen has slopes to stream and bog garden.

65 STONEHAVEN

6 High Street, Cumnor, Oxford, OX2 9PE. Dr Dianne & Prof Keith Gull. *4m from central Oxford. Exit to Cumnor from the A420. In centre of village opp PO. Parking at back of PO.* Sun 13 Feb (2-5). Combined adm with 23 Hid's Copse Road £5, chd free. Opening with Cumnor Village Gardens on Sun 19 June.
Front, side and rear garden of a thatched cottage (not open). Front is partly gravelled and side courtyard has many pots. Rear garden overlooks meadows with old apple trees underplanted with ferns, wildlife pond, unusual plants, many with black or bronze foliage, planted in drifts and repeated throughout the garden. Planting has mild Japanese influence; rounded, clipped shapes interspersed with verticals. Snowdrops feature in Feb. There are two pubs in the village serving food; The Bear & Ragged Staff and The Vine. Wheelchair access to garden via gravel drive.

66 ◆ STONOR PARK

Stonor, Henley-On-Thames, RG9 6HF. Lady Ailsa Stonor, 01491 638587, administrator@stonor.com, www.stonor.com. *Stonor is located between the M4 (J8/J9) & the M40 (J6) on the B480 Henley-on-Thames to Watlington road. If you are approaching Stonor on the M40 from the E, please exit at J6 only.* For NGS: Tue 14 June (10.30-5). Adm £6.50, chd free. Light refreshments. For other opening times and information, please phone, email or visit garden website.
Surrounded by dramatic sweeping valleys and nestled within an ancient deer park, you will find the gardens at Stonor, which date back to Medieval

times. Visitors love the serenity of the our C17 walled, Italianate Pleasure Garden and herbaceous perennial borders beyond.

67 NEW STOW COTTAGE ARBORETUM & GARDEN

Junction Road, Churchill, Chipping Norton, OX7 6NP. Tom Heywood-Lonsdale. *2½m SW of Chipping Norton, off the B4450. Parking: use postcode OX7 6NP & parking will be signed from William Smith Close.* Sat 2 July (1-6). Adm £5, chd free. Tea.
The arboretum and garden cover approx 15 acres with extensive views towards Stow-on-the-Wold and beyond. Stow Cottage (not open) is surrounded by the garden with trees and large deep borders with many rare shrubs as well as roses and daphnes. The arboretum began in 2009 and has been extensively developed over the yrs. There is an array of 500 trees inc different oaks, sorbus and limes as well as many magnolias, dogwoods, walnuts, birches and liquidambars.

68 ◆ WATERPERRY GARDENS

Waterperry, Wheatley, OX33 1JZ. The School of Philosophy and Economic Science, 01844 339226, office@waterperrygardens.co.uk, www.waterperrygardens.co.uk. *7½m from Oxford city centre. From E M40 J8, from N M40 J8a. Follow brown tourist signs. For SatNav please use OX33 1LA.* For NGS: Sun 20 Mar (10-5); Sun 18 Sept (10-5.30). Adm £9.50, chd free. Light refreshments in the teashop (10-5). For other opening times and information, please phone, email or visit garden website.
Waterperry Gardens are extensive, well-maintained and full of interesting plants. From The Virgin's Walk with its shade-loving plants to the long classical herbaceous border, brilliantly colourful from late May until Oct. The Mary Rose Garden illustrates modern and older roses, and the formal garden is neatly designed and colourful with a small knot garden, herb border and wisteria tunnel. Newly redesigned walled garden, river walk, statues and pear orchard. Riverside walk may be inaccessible to wheelchair users if very wet.

69 WAYSIDE

82 Banbury Road, Kidlington, OX5 2BX. Margaret & Alistair Urquhart, 01865 460180, alistairurquhart@ntlworld.com. *5m N of Oxford. On R of A4260 travelling N through Kidlington.* Visits by arrangement May to Sept for groups of up to 25. Adm £3, chd free. Tea.
¼ acre garden shaded by mature trees. Mixed border with some rare and unusual plants and shrubs. A climber clothed pergola leads past a dry gravel garden to the woodland garden with an extensive collection of hardy ferns. Conservatory and large fern house with a collection of unusual species of tree ferns and tender exotics. Partial wheelchair access.

GROUP OPENING

70 WEST OXFORD GARDENS

Cumnor Hill, Oxford, OX2 9HH. *Take Botley interchange off A34 from N or S. Follow signs for Oxford & then turn R at Botley T-lights, opp MacDonalds & follow NGS yellow signs. Street parking.* Sun 26 June (1-5). Combined adm £5, chd free. Home-made teas at 10 Eynsham Road.

10 EYNSHAM ROAD
Jon Harker.

23 HID'S COPSE ROAD
Kathy Eldridge.
(See separate entry)

86 HURST RISE ROAD
Ms P Guy & Mr L Harris, 07762 342238, penny.theavon@virginmedia.com.
Visits also by arrangement May to July for groups of 10 to 20. Home-made teas by prior request.

6 SCHOLAR PLACE
Helen Ward.

86 Hurst Rise Road, a small garden abounding in perennials, roses, clematis and shrubs displayed in layers and at different levels around a circular lawn and path with sculptural features. Delightful colour. 10 Eynsham Road in Botley, is a New Zealander's take on an English-style garden inc many rose varieties, white garden, herbaceous borders and pond. 23 Hid's Copse Road, a ½ acre, wildlife friendly plot under many trees with two ponds, a

wildflower meadow, kitchen garden and contemplative areas. 6 Scholar Place, an urban garden on a gently upward slope with a selection of small trees, shrubs and perennials. There is a small pond. Steps up from the patio lead to the main garden. There are also planted areas to the front and side of the house. Gravel steps at 6 Scholar Place and pebble path at 86 Hurst Rise Road.

&. ✿ �))

---

71 WESTWELL MANOR
Westwell, Nr Burford, OX18 4JT. Mr Thomas Gibson. *2m SW of Burford. From A40 Burford-Cheltenham, turn L ½ m after Burford r'about signed Westwell. After 1½ m at T-junction, turn R & Manor is 2nd house on L.* **Sun 15 May (2.30-6). Adm £5, chd free. Donation to Aspire.**
7 acres surrounding old Cotswold manor house (not open) with knot garden, potager, shrub roses, herbaceous borders, topiary, earth works, moonlight garden, auricula ladder, rills and water garden.

✿

GROUP OPENING

72 WHEATLEY GARDENS
High Street, Wheatley, OX33 1XX. 07813 339480, echess@hotmail.co.uk. *5m E of Oxford. Leave A40 at Wheatley, turn into High St. Gardens at W end of High St, S side.* **Sun 19 June (2-6). Combined adm £5, chd free. Cream teas. Visits also by arrangement Apr to Sept for groups of up to 30.**

BREACH HOUSE GARDEN
Liz Parry.

THE MANOR HOUSE
Mrs Elizabeth Hess.

THE STUDIO
Ann Buckingham.

Three adjoining gardens in historic Wheatley are: Breach House Garden with many shrubs, perennials, a contemporary reflective space and a wild meadow with ponds; The Studio with walled garden and climbing roses, clematis, herbaceous borders, vegetables and fruit trees; The Elizabethan Manor House (not open) is a romantic oasis with formal box walk, herb garden, rose arches and

old rose shrubbery. Various musical events. Wheelchair access with assistance due to gravel paths, two shallow steps and grass.

&. 🐑 ✿ � 🌲))

---

73 WHITEHILL FARM
Widford, Burford, OX18 4DT. Mr & Mrs Paul Youngson, 01993 822894, paulyoungson48@gmail.com. *1m E of Burford. From A40 take road signed Widford. Turn R at bottom of hill, 1st house on R with ample car parking.* **Sun 5 June (2-6). Adm £5, chd free. Home-made teas. Visits also by arrangement May to Sept.**
2 acres of hillside gardens and woodland with spectacular views overlooking Burford and Windrush valley. Informal plantsman's garden built up by the owners over 25 yrs. Herbaceous and shrub borders, ponds and bog area, old fashioned roses, ground cover, ornamental grasses, bamboos and hardy geraniums. Large cascade water feature, pretty tea patio and wonderful Cotswold views.

🐑 ✿ � 🌲))

---

74 WOOLSTONE MILL HOUSE
Woolstone, Faringdon, SN7 7QL. Mr & Mrs Justin Spink. *7m W of Wantage. 7m S of Faringdon. Woolstone is a small village off B4507, below Uffington White Horse Hill.* **Sun 26 June (2-5). Combined adm with Midsummer House £10, chd free. Home-made teas.**
Redesigned by new owner, garden designer Justin Spink in 2020, this 1½ acre garden has large mixed perennial beds, and small gravel, cutting, kitchen and bog gardens. Topiary, medlars and old fashioned roses. Treehouse with spectacular views to Uffington White Horse and White Horse Hill. C18 millhouse and barn (not open). Partial wheelchair access.

&. 🚗 �))

GROUP OPENING

75 WOOTTON GARDENS
Wootton, OX13 6DP. *Wootton is 3m SW of Oxford. From Oxford ring road S, take turning to Wootton. Parking for all gardens at the Bystander Pub & on the road.* **Thur 9 June (1-5.30). Combined adm £5, chd free. Home-made teas.**

13 AMEY CRESCENT
Sylv & Liz Gleed.

[NEW] **57 BESSELSLEIGH ROAD**
John & Lin Allen, 07443 520565. Visits also by arrangement in June.

[NEW] **3 HOME CLOSE**
Katherine Schomberg.

14 HOME CLOSE
Kev & Sue Empson.

35 SANDLEIGH ROAD
Hilal Baylav Inkersole.

Five inspirational small gardens, all with very different ways of providing personal joy. 13 Amey Crescent is a gravel garden with grasses and prairie plants. The garden has a small wildlife pond, alpine house and troughs. 3 Home Close is laid to lawn with perennial borders, homegrown annuals and a small space for vegetables. Mature shrubs, trees and garden arches give height to the garden. 14 Home Close is a garden containing mainly shrubs with an unusually shaped lawn, a pond, raised bed and a vegetable garden. 57 Besselsleigh Road is a large family garden with many unusual plants alongside shrubs, fruit trees and vegetable plot, with a polytunnel and greenhouse. 35 Sandleigh Road is a mature garden, laid to lawn on two levels. The plants are mainly homegrown from cuttings. The garden is brimming with vibrant flowers, pondside planting and glass art. Partial wheelchair access, some gravel paths.

&. ✿ �))

'In 2021 the National Garden Scheme donated £500,000 to Marie Curie enabling us to continue providing our vital services and be there, caring for people on the frontline of the Coronavirus pandemic.'
Marie Curie

SHROPSHIRE

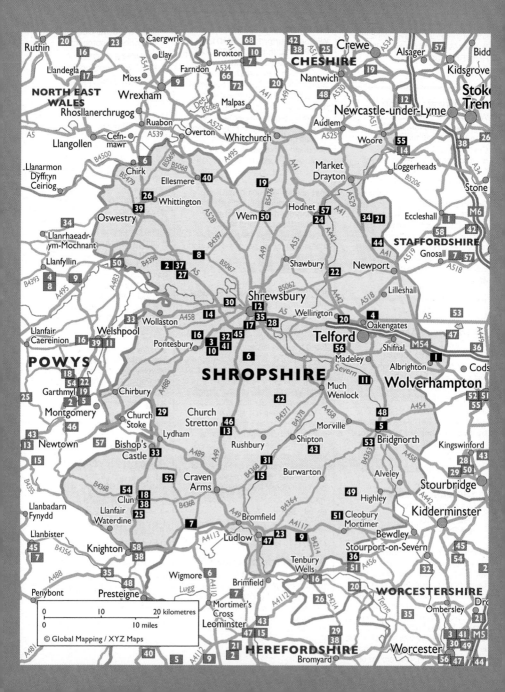

Welcome to Shropshire and our beautiful gardens where our lovely, historical towns (we have no cities within the county) dwell in harmony with the countryside and our farming communities.

Shropshire was also the birthplace of modern industry at Ironbridge near Telford, named after the famous architect Thomas Telford, where many modern businesses flourish.

Our gardens range from small, exquisite cottage and urban gardens to large country estates, several of which opened at the start of the National Garden Scheme in 1927. Our garden history is also unique: Shropshire being the birthplace of the first "celebrity" gardener, Percy Thrower, and the ultimate horticulturist, Charles Darwin.

In 2022 we have 57 gardens opening across the county, several of them for the first time, so there is much to look forward to. Photographs and extended descriptions to help you plan your visits can be found on our website, www.ngs.org.uk. In a few cases the garden entry indicates pre-booking via the website is still necessary; for others you can pre-book if you prefer but it is not essential.

If you love gardens why not become more involved? We are always on the look out for new gardens to open or volunteers to help out with publicity, distributing leaflets or helping on garden open days. For more information please contact Sheila Jones, our New Garden and Volunteer Co-Ordinator.

Thank you for your continued support, it is much appreciated by us and our beneficiaries.

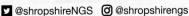

TheNationalGarden SchemeShropshire
@shropshireNGS @shropshirengs

Volunteers

New Garden & Volunteer Coordinator
Sheila Jones
01743 244108
smaryjones@icloud.com

County Treasurer
Elaine Jones
01588 650323
elaine.jones@ngs.org.uk

Publicity
Ruth Dinsdale
01948 710924
ruth.dinsdale@ngs.org.uk

Twitter/Facebook
Vicky Kirk
01743 821429
victoria.kirk@ngs.org.uk

Instagram
Logan Blackburn
l.blackburnissitt@gmail.com

Booklet Co-ordinator
Fiona Chancellor
01952 507675
fiona.chancellor@ngs.org.uk

Assistant County Organisers
Lynne Beavan
lynne.beavan@googlemail.com

Jane & Douglas Wood
07768 058730
jane.liz.wood@gmail.com

Sue Griffiths
sue.griffiths@btinternet.com

Angela Woolrich
angelawoolrich@hotmail.com

And all the other volunteers in Shropshire who help to make the Scheme work in the county

Above: The Secret Gardens at Steventon Terrace

OPENING DATES

All entries subject to change. For latest information check www.ngs.org.uk

Map locator numbers are shown to the right of each garden name.

February

Snowdrop Festival

Sunday 20th
Millichope Park 31

April

Saturday 9th
The Albrighton Trust
Moat & Gardens 1

Sunday 10th
Edge Villa 16

Saturday 23rd
Brownhill House 8

Sunday 24th
Westwood House 53

May

Sunday 1st
The Bramleys 6
Millichope Park 31
Ruthall Manor 43

Monday 2nd
Ruthall Manor 43

Sunday 8th
Henley Hall 23
Oteley 40

Wednesday 11th
Goldstone Hall Gardens 21
NEW Neen View 36

Saturday 14th
Ruthall Manor 43

Sunday 15th
Ruthall Manor 43

Sunday 22nd
NEW Cat's Whiskers 9
Longner Hall 28

Monday 23rd
NEW Cat's Whiskers 9

Tuesday 24th
Brownhill House 8

Wednesday 25th
NEW Neen View 36

Saturday 28th
Beaufort 4

Sunday 29th
The Mount 33
Stanley Hall Gardens 48
Walcot Hall 52

Monday 30th
Walcot Hall 52

June

Friday 3rd
The Gardeners Lodge 20

Saturday 4th
Cruckfield House 14
Kinton Grove 27

Sunday 5th
Broadward Hall 7
Kinton Grove 27
2 School Cottages 45

Saturday 11th
Ruthall Manor 43
Windy Ridge 56

Sunday 12th
NEW Grooms Cottage 22
The Mount 33
Ruthall Manor 43
Sunningdale 50
Windy Ridge 56

Thursday 16th
NEW Four Winds 19

Sunday 19th
♦ Delbury Hall Walled
Garden 15
Preen Manor 42

Wednesday 22nd
Goldstone Hall Gardens 21
NEW 1 Mount Pleasant
Cottages 34

Thursday 23rd
NEW Whitcott Hall 54

Friday 24th
Avocet 3
Cheriton 10

Saturday 25th
The Albrighton Trust
Moat & Gardens 1
The Secret Gardens at
Steventon Terrace 47

Sunday 26th
The Albrighton Trust
Moat & Gardens 1
♦ Hodnet Hall Gardens 24
NEW Horatio's Garden 26

Tuesday 28th
Brownhill House 8

July

Saturday 2nd
48 Bramble Ridge 5
Cruckfield House 14
Ruthall Manor 43

Sunday 3rd
Ruthall Manor 43
2 School Cottages 45
Upper Marshes 51

Wednesday 6th
Goldstone Hall
Gardens 21
NEW 1 Mount Pleasant
Cottages 34

Friday 8th
12 Colley Close 12

Sunday 10th
Lower Brookshill 29
Sambrook Manor 44

Monday 11th
Lower Brookshill 29

Thursday 14th
♦ Delbury Hall Walled
Garden 15

Saturday 16th
153 Willoughbridge 55

Sunday 17th
NEW 4 Cross Bank 13
Esme's Garden 17
Nancy's Garden 35
Stottesdon Village
Open Gardens 49
153 Willoughbridge 55

Wednesday 20th
Merton 30

Thursday 21st
Appledore 2
Offcot 37

Friday 22nd
Appledore 2
Offcot 37

Saturday 23rd
Appledore 2
Offcot 37

Sunday 24th
Oswestry Gatacre
Allotments & Gardens
Association 39

August

Sunday 7th
Merton 30

Saturday 13th
Moat Hall 32

Sunday 14th
♦ Delbury Hall
Walled Garden 15
The Ferns 18

Wednesday 17th
Goldstone Hall
Gardens 21

Sunday 21st
Edge Villa 16

Sunday 28th
Sambrook Manor 44

September

Saturday 3rd
Windy Ridge 56

Sunday 4th
Windy Ridge 56

Wednesday 7th
♦ Wollerton Old Hall 57

Wednesday 14th
Goldstone Hall
Gardens 21

October

Friday 7th
Offcot 37

Saturday 8th
Offcot 37

Saturday 15th
NEW The Paddock 41

Sunday 16th

Millichope Park 31

By Arrangement

Arrange a personalised garden visit with your club, or group of friends, on a date to suit you. See individual garden entries for full details.

THE GARDENS

🏠 THE ALBRIGHTON TRUST MOAT & GARDENS

Blue House Lane, Albrighton, Wolverhampton, WV7 3FL. Stephen Jimson, 01902 372441, moat@albrightontrust.org.uk, albrightontrust.org.uk. *Off A41& adjacent to the motorway network. We are located very close to Albrighton train station & close to the RAF Cosford base.* Sat 9 Apr, Sat 25, Sun 26 June (11-3). Adm £5, chd free. Home-made teas. Visits also by arrangement Apr to June.

The Albrighton Trust gardens are designed around the remains of a C13 fortified manor house and an ancient moat, offering excellent recreational and educational opportunities for anyone wanting to visit and enjoy this award winning outdoor space. The gardens are wheelchair accessible, there are disabled toilets and personal care room with hoist and couch.

🏠 APPLEDORE

Kynaston, Kinnerley, Oswestry, SY10 8EF. Lionel parker. *Just off A5 on Wolfshead r'about (at Oswestry end of Nesscliffe bypass) towards Knockin. Then take the 1st L towards Kinnerley. Follow NGS signs from this road.* Thur 21, Fri 22, Sat 23 July (10-4). Combined adm with Offcot £6, chd free. Home-made teas.

Appledore adjoins neighbouring garden Offcot. It has gone through extensive changes and is managed by Tom Pountney from Offcot. Both gardens are opening together this year so that visitors can see a developing 'edible garden' with 6 large beds for a wide range of fruit and vegetables, all grown organically. To encourage pollinators, the garden also has a wildlife pond and a small wildflower meadow.

🏠 AVOCET

3 Main Road, Plealey, SY5 0UZ. Malc & Jude Mollart, 01743 791743, malcandjude@btinternet.com. *6m SW of Shrewsbury. From A5 take A488 signed Bishops Castle, approx ½m past Lea Cross Tandoori turn L signed Plealey. In ¾m turn L, garden on R. SatNav unreliable.* Fri 24 June (10-4). Combined adm with Cheriton £6, chd free. Pre-booking essential, please visit www.ngs.org.uk for information & booking. Visits also by arrangement May to July for groups of up to 30.

Cottage style garden with modern twists owned by plantaholics, shared with wildlife. Designed round series of garden rooms for year-round interest: wildlife pool, mixed borders, seaside and gravel gardens, succulents, trained fruit, sculpture. Constantly evolving. Opportunity to see two neighbouring gardens of same size, with similar organic principles and for wildlife but different interpretations. Collection of vintage garden tools.

🏠 BEAUFORT

Coppice Drive, Moss Road Wrockwardine Wood, Telford, TF2 7BP. Mike King, www.carnivorousplants.uk.com. *Approx 2m N from Telford town centre. From Asda Donnington, turn L at lights on Moss rd, ⅓m, turn L into Coppice Drive. 4th Bungalow on L with solar panels.* Sat 28 May (10-5). Adm £5, chd free. Light refreshments.

If carnivorous plants are your thing, then come and visit our National Collection of Sarracenia (pitcher plants); also over 100 different Venus flytrap clones (Dionaea muscipula), Sundews (Drosera) and Butterworts (Pinguicula) - over 6000 plants in total. Large greenhouses at Telford's first carbon negative house; a great place to visit - kids will love it! Visitors are asked to wear a face covering in the greenhouses, please. Greenhouses not wheelchair accessible.

🏠 48 BRAMBLE RIDGE

Bridgnorth, WV16 4SQ. Heather, 07572 706706, heatherfran48@gmail.com. *From Bridgnorth N on B4373 signed Broseley. 1st on R Stanley Ln, 1st R Bramble Ridge. From Broseley S on B4373, nr Bridgnorth turn L into Stanley Ln, 1st R Bramble Ridge.* Sat 2 July (11-5). Adm £6, chd free. Light refreshments at 16 Bramble Ridge. Visits also by arrangement Mar to Sept for groups of 15 to 30.

Steep cottage-style garden with many steps; part wild, part cultivated, terraced in places and overlooking the Severn valley with views to High Rock and Queens Parlour. The garden features shrubs, perennials, wildlife pond, summerhouse and, in the wilderness area, wildflowers, fruit trees and a sandstone outcrop. I love my garden very much and am looking forward to sharing it with other people. Another cottage style garden also open at 16 Bramble Ridge.

6 THE BRAMLEYS
Condover, Shrewsbury, SY5 7BH.
Toby & Julie Shaw. *Through
the village of Condover towards
Dorrington. Pass junction by village
hall follow rd round, cross the bridge,
in approx 100 metres there is a drive
on L. Look for NGS signs.* Sun 1
May (11-5). Adm £5, chd free.
Home-made teas.
A large country garden extending to
2 acres with a variety of trees and
shrubs, herbaceous borders and
a woodland with the Cound Brook
flowing through. A courtyard oasis
welcomes you as you enter the
garden with far reaching views over
open countryside. Wheelchair access
around most of the garden, although
not for the woodland area.

7 BROADWARD HALL
Broadward, Clungunford,
SY7 0QA. **Anthony & Caro Skyrme.**
*5m from Craven Arms; 9m from
Ludlow on A49. Turn off nr Ludlow
Food Centre thru Bromfield. Follow
rd towards Leintwardine. Just
before Leintwardine turn R towards
Clungunford before S bend in rd,
turn L, cont along lane, over small
stone bridge; Gate lodge on L.* Sun
5 June (2-6). Adm £6, chd free.
Home-made teas.
The Broadward Hall estate is a site
of special scientific interest (SSSI).
With well established, extensive,
herbaceous borders, ancient trees
and a Victorian walled garden
(undergoing restoration). Other areas
of interest include the magnificent,
giant sequoia trees which line an early
C19 archery walk; Victorian Pump
House. Disabled access to Music
Room via a concrete ramp, disabled
WC.

8 BROWNHILL HOUSE
Ruyton XI Towns, SY4 1LR. **Roger
& Yoland Brown,** 01939 261121,
brownhill@eleventowns.co.uk,
www.eleventowns.co.uk. *9m NW
of Shrewsbury on B4397. On the
B4397 in the village of Ruyton XI
Towns.* Sat 23 Apr, Tue 24 May,
Tue 28 June (10-6.30). Adm £5,
chd free. Pre-booking essential,
please visit www.ngs.org.
uk for information & booking.
Home-made teas. Visits also by
arrangement Apr to July.
A unique 2 acre hillside garden with
many steps and levels bordering
River Perry. Visitors can enjoy a wide

variety of plants and styles from
formal terraces to woodland paths.
The lower areas are for the sure-
footed and mobile while the upper
levels with a large kitchen garden
and glasshouses have many places
to sit and enjoy the views. Kit cars
on show.

9 NEW CAT'S WHISKERS
3 Stone House, Knowbury, Ludlow,
SY8 3LR. **Alan & Mariet Proctor.**
*7m E of Ludlow. From Ludlow
A4117, 2nd turn signed Knowbury,
pass village hall on R. Then 1st L into
Hope Bagot Ln. Go down the hill to
sharp R bend where there will be a
sign directing to property.* Sun 22,
Mon 23 May (2-7). Adm £5, chd
free. Home-made teas.
South facing hillside garden (1000ft)
with panoramic views started in 1994.
Main garden; lawn with shrubs and
herbaceous borders. Features inc:
two wildlife pools, wildlife areas with
walkway through, fruit/vegetable
and herb areas, orchard, courtyard
and aviary. Different levels with some
steep slopes, uneven ground and
gravelled areas. Children's treasure
hunt.

10 CHERITON
Plealey, SY5 0UY. **Vicky Wood.** *6m
SW of Shrewsbury. From A5, take
A488 signed Bishops Castle; approx
1/2 m past Lea Cross Tandoori, turn
L signed to Plealey; in 3/4 m turn L,
garden on R. SatNav unreliable.* Fri
24 June (10-4). Combined adm
with Avocet £6, chd free. Pre-
booking essential, please visit
www.ngs.org.uk for information
& booking.
Family garden where every space
has a function, with annual and
perennial cut flower borders, fruit and
vegetables, polytunnel, chickens,
wildlife pond, outdoor cooking and
green woodworking areas. Full
of colour with stunning borrowed
views to the fields and hill beyond.
Opportunity to see two neighbouring
gardens of same size with similar
organic principles and for wildlife with
different interpretations.

11 CLOVE HITCH
Coalport Road, Broseley,
TF12 5AN. **Nick & Mia
Harrington,** 07957 548240,
mia_armstrong50@hotmail.com.

*1/2 m E of Broseley on Coalport Rd.
From E (Woodbridge Inn) (6'6" height
limit) drive to top of hill - parking on
R, 300m after farm. From Broseley
(W) parking on L, 500m beyond
postcode.* Visits by arrangement
June to Sept for groups of 5 to 20.
Home-made teas.
Award winning Paul Richards
designed garden set in a spectacular
location with ranging views over
the Severn Valley. The 0.3 acres
comprises five areas - small mixed
orchard set to wildflower meadow;
circular main lawn with ha-ha, deep
full borders and sculptures; wildlife
pond with deck that allows visitors
to walk out over the water; circular
elevated patio; working area with
raised beds.

12 12 COLLEY CLOSE
Shrewsbury, SY2 5YN. **Kevin &
Karen Scurry.** *Off Telford Way nr
Shrewsbury police stn. From r'about
by police stn head down Telford
Way at next r'about take 2nd exit
onto Oswell Rd then 1st R into
Colley Close. Parking is very limited
in Colley Close but there are some
spaces in Corinthian Drive, 2 mins
walk away* Evening opening Fri 8
July (4-9). Adm £4, chd free. Light
refreshments.
This garden has three ponds inc
a large koi pond and waterfall,
wildlife pond and goldfish pond all
surrounded by interesting planting. A
large collection of specimen bonsai
trees accent the koi pond giving
an oriental feel to the garden. The
front garden has a large collection
of grasses. The garden has good
wheelchair access and many seating
areas to view the garden from many
different angles.

13 NEW 4 CROSS BANK
Church Stretton, SY6 6QZ. **Andy
& Georgie Morris,** 07971 915430,
georginamorris1996@gmail.com,
www.instagram.com/back_
garden_blooms. *1km SW of Church
Stretton. From Church Stretton
- follow Ludlow Rd towards Little
Stretton. Travel 1km where 'Cross
Bank' lane is found on the R. Don't
take the lane, instead park alongside
the pavement of Ludlow Rd.* Sun
17 July (11-4). Adm £4, chd free.
Home-made teas. Visits also by
arrangement June to Sept for
groups of 5 to 10.
Our terraced garden is located at

the rear of our 1920's home in the foothills of Church Stretton. Featuring raised beds, a self-built greenhouse, terraced mixed borders and a large goldfish pond - there really is something for everyone. Our passion for British cut-flowers is evident - borders brimming full of seasonal blooms. To create more interest, we adorn our many steps with plenty of pots. Covered areas for teas.

◱ CRUCKFIELD HOUSE

Shoothill, Ford, SY5 9NR. Geoffrey Cobley, 01743 850222. *5m W of Shrewsbury. A458 from Shrewsbury, turn L towards Shoothill.* Sat 4 June, Sat 2 July (2-5). Adm £6, chd free. Home-made teas. Visits also by arrangement June & July for groups of 25+.

An artist's romantic 3 acre garden, formally designed, informally and intensively planted with a great variety of unusual herbaceous plants. Nick's garden, with many species trees, shrubs and wildflower meadow, surrounds a large pond with bog and moisture-loving plants. Ornamental kitchen garden. Rose and peony walk. Courtyard fountain garden, large shrubbery and extensive clematis collection Extensive topiary, and lily pond.

◱ ◆ DELBURY HALL WALLED GARDEN

Delbury Hall Estate, Mill Lane, Diddlebury, SY7 9DH. Mr & Mrs Richard Rallings, 01584 841 222, info@myndhardyplants.co.uk, www.myndhardyplants.co.uk. *8m W of Craven Arms. Follow the B4368 to Diddlebury. Drive into village; the entrance to the Walled Garden is on R 300 metres passed St Peter's church.* For NGS: Sun 19 June, Thur 14 July, Sun 14 Aug (10-5).

Adm £5, chd free. Home-made teas. English wine from our own vineyard. For other opening times and information, please phone, email or visit garden website.

A two acre early Victorian Walled Garden with large herbaceous borders, vegetable and herb garden, shrubbery, vines and very old fruit trees. In addition there is a large Penstemon and Hemerocallis collection. A signed walk guides you around the front of Delbury Hall and the lake. Extensive range of perennials and English wine from the vineyard for sale. Please check our website before travelling to ensure that the Hall gardens are open as it may be closed, at short notice, due to a private function. Gravel and grass paths. Dogs are welcome in the Walled Garden but not in the Hall Gardens.

Wollerton Old Hall

16 EDGE VILLA

Edge, nr Yockleton, Shrewsbury, SY5 9PY. Mr & Mrs W F Neil, 01743 821651, billfneil@me.com. *6m SW of Shrewsbury. From A5 take either A488 signed to Bishops Castle or B4386 to Montgomery for approx 6m then follow NGS signs.* **Sun 10 Apr, Sun 21 Aug (2-5). Adm £5, chd free. Home-made teas. Visits also by arrangement Apr to Aug for groups of 10+.**

Two acres nestling in South Shropshire hills. Self-sufficient vegetable plot. Chickens in orchard, foxes permitting. Large herbaceous borders. Dewpond surrounded by purple elder, irises, candelabra primulas and dieramas. Large selection of fragrant roses. Wendy house for children. Extensive plant sale in aid of NGS charities. Book sale in aid of NGS charities. Visitors can stay in the garden for as long as they like. Some German and French spoken. Some gravel paths.

 ♿ 🐕 ✳ 🚌 ☕))

17 ESME'S GARDEN

Church Row, Meole Village, Shrewsbury, SY3 9EX. Nancy Estrey & Peter Alltree. *Through wicker gate by 3 Church Row & follow path to the top. On-street parking on Church Row, Church Rd & Upper Rd* **Sun 17 July (1-5). Combined adm with Nancy's Garden (2½ m away) £6, chd free. Light refreshments in Peace Memorial Hall, Meole Village.**

Esme's Garden is situated in a secluded spot in the centre of Meole Village, with the beautiful Meole Church as a backdrop. Designed purely for its exuberant planting, gravel paths take you on a romantic journey through trees, shrubs and perennials, eventually leading to a central oasis by a tranquil pond. There are also many unexpected features. Both gardens are nurtured by Nancy.

☕

18 THE FERNS

Newport Street, Clun, SY7 8JZ. Andrew Dobbin, 01588 640064, andrew.clun@outlook.com. *Enter Clun from Craven Arms. Take 2nd R signed into Ford St. At T-junction turn R for parking in the Memorial Hall car park (100 yds). Retrace steps to T junction. The Ferns is on L.* **Sun 14 Aug (12-6). Adm £5, chd free. Visits also by arrangement in Aug. Refreshments available in village at the River Cafe and the Malthouse.**

A formal village garden of ¾ acre, approached via a drive lined with crab apple and pear trees. On the right is the autumn garden, giving fine views of the surrounding hills. From the front courtyard garden a path leads through double herbaceous borders full of late summer colour, to further rooms, of yew, beech and box. There is also a rear courtyard with tender exotics. Lily pond and statuary.

🐕 ✳ ☕

Lower Brookshill

19 NEW FOUR WINDS

Gilberts Lane, Whixall, Whitchurch, SY13 2PR. **Lynne Beavan.** *3m N of Wem. B5476 through Quina Brook turn L onto Coton Park/ Gilbert's Lane follow rd bearing L at junction Whitchurch B5476 turn R past Bull & Dog take 1st L past social centre then L Gilbert's Lane.* **Thur 16 June (10.30-5). Adm £5, chd free. Home-made teas.** The traditional garden around the bungalow is backed by 150yr-old oak trees. In the adjoining paddock, a garden is being planted out, now 3-4 yrs old. Fruit tees, ornamental trees silver birches, shrub beds, hedges, pergolas with roses and wisteria, perennial beds, alliums making a delightful garden for wildlife and family. An ongoing evolving project for the owner.

20 THE GARDENERS LODGE

2 Roseway, Wellington, TF1 1JA. **Amanda Goode, www.lovegrowshereweb. wordpress.com.** *1½m (4 mins) from J7 (M54). B5061 Holyhead Rd 2nd L after NT 'Sunnycroft'. (New Church Rd) We are the cream house on corner of NCR & Roseway.* **Fri 3 June (10-4.30). Adm £5, chd free. Light refreshments. Coffee, tea, cake and soft drinks.** There was just one tree in the garden when the current owner purchased The Gardener's Lodge, the ground having been cleared, ready to sell as a building plot. However the owner had other plans for it: the garden is now eclectically divided, arranged and planted into areas: Mediterranean, Cottage, Indian etc but, seamlessly, each section merges and leads into the next developing idea. A small urban garden with seating, water features and shade.

21 GOLDSTONE HALL GARDENS

Goldstone, Market Drayton, TF9 2NA. **John Cushing, 01630 661202, enquiries@goldstonehall.com, www.goldstonehall.com.** *5m N of Newport on A41. Follow brown & white signs from Hinstock. From Shrewsbury A53, R for A41 Hinstock & follow brown & white signs & NGS signs.* **Wed 11 May (12-5). Wed 22 June, Wed 6 July (12-5), open nearby 1 Mount Pleasant Cottages. Wed 17 Aug, Wed 14 Sept (12-5). Adm £6.50, chd free. Home-made teas in award** winning oak framed pavilion in the midst of the garden with cakes created by our talented chef. **Visits also by arrangement Apr to Sept.** 5 acres with highly productive beautiful kitchen garden. Unusual vegetables and fruits - alpine strawberries; heritage tomatoes, salad, chillies, celeriac. Roses in Walled Garden from May; Double herbaceous in front of old English garden wall at its best July and August; sedums and roses stunning in September. Winner of the prestigious 2022 Good Hotel Guide's Editor's Choice Award for Gardens. Lawn aficionados will enjoy the stripes. Majority of garden can be accessed on gravel and lawns.

22 NEW GROOMS COTTAGE

Waters Upton, Telford, TF6 6NP. **Joanne & Andy Harding.** *Waters Upton, Shropshire. There is no parking at the property due to restricted access; parking is available on the verge opp the church or in the village hall car park. The garden will be signed nearby.* **Sun 12 June (11-4). Adm £5, chd free. Teas, coffees, cakes and light snacks will be available.** A cottage garden around ½ an acre in size comprising mixed herbaceous borders and an abundance of English roses. Highlights inc water features, pergolas, oriental garden, hosta garden, alpine and herb beds and a productive vegetable garden and greenhouse. Many established trees and shrubs and shady plant area. Wheelchair access, some gravel areas not accessible. Parking would need to be on the road, with wheeled access down the tarmac drive.

23 HENLEY HALL

Henley, Ludlow, SY8 3HD. **Helen & Sebastian Phillips, www.henleyhallludlow.com.** *2m E of Ludlow. 1½m from A49. Take A4117 signed to Clee Hill & Cleobury Mortimer. On reaching Henley, the gates to Henley Hall are on R when travelling in the direction towards Clee Hill.* **Sun 8 May (10-5). Adm £6, chd free. Home-made teas.** Henley Hall offers a mixture of formal and informal gardens. The historic elements inc formal lawn, stone staircase with balustrades, ha-ha, and a beautiful walled garden created and 'pulmonary' water feature created in 1874. Highlights inc walk ways along the banks of the River Ledwyche with decorative weirs, stone arched bridge, and woodland paths. Some parts of the garden are accessible by wheelchair.

24 ◆ HODNET HALL GARDENS

Hodnet, Market Drayton, TF9 3NN. **Sir Algernon & The Hon Lady Heber-Percy, 01630 685786, secretary@hodnethall.com, www.hodnethallgardens.org.** *5½m SW of Market Drayton. 12m NE Shrewsbury. At junction of A53 & A442. Tickets available on the gate, on the day.* **For NGS: Sun 26 June (11-5). Adm £8.50, chd free. Light refreshments in the C17 tea room. For other opening times and information, please phone, email or visit garden website.** The 60+ acres of Hodnet Hall Gardens are amongst the finest in the country. There has been a park and gardens at Hodnet for many hundreds of years. Magnificent forest trees, ornamental shrubs and flowers planted to give interest and colour from early Spring to late Autumn. Woodland walks alongside pools and lakes, home to abundant wildlife. Productive walled kitchen garden and historic dovecot. For details please see website and Facebook page. Maps are available to show access for our less mobile visitors.

25 THE HOLLIES

Rockhill, Clun, SY7 8LR. **Pat & Terry Badham, 01588 640805, patbadham@btinternet.com.** *10m W of Craven Arms. 8m S of Bishops Castle. From A49 Craven Arms take B4368 to Clun. Turn L onto A488 continue for 1½m. Bear R signed Treverward. After 50 yds turn R at Xrds, property is 1st on L.* **Visits by arrangement June to Sept. Adm £5, chd free.** A garden of 2 acres at 1200ft. Features inc kitchen garden, large island beds, borders with perennials, shrubs, grasses, specimen bamboos and trees. Birch grove and wildlife dingle with stream, rain permitting! Refreshments can be arranged at a local cafe in Clun (daytime hours). We leave signs out on the road so anyone passing can visit on spec! The signs come in if we are out for the day. Wheelchair access is available to the majority of the garden over gravel and grass.

26 NEW HORATIO'S GARDEN

The Robert Jones & Agnes Hunt Orthopaedic Hospital, Gobowen, Oswestry, SY10 7AG. Imogen Jackson, www.horatiosgarden.org.uk. At the spinal unit. From A5 follow signs to Orthopaedic Hospital; park in pay & display car park by hospital. Once parked, & facing main hospital entrance, turn R at mini r'about & walk to end of internal road. Sun 26 June (2-5). Adm £5, chd free. Home-made teas.

Beautifully designed by Bunny Guinness and delightfully planted, this garden opened to great acclaim in September 2019. Part-funded by the National Garden Scheme, the garden offers a place of peace and therapy for patients at the spinal unit. Raised beds, creative use of space, beautiful specimen trees, potting shed, sculpture, all in soothing hues. A pretty rill runs the length of the garden. Very good access throughout.

占 ❀ ☕

27 KINTON GROVE

Kinton, SY4 1AZ. Tim & Judy Creyke, 01743 741263, judycreyke@icloud.com. Off A5, between Shrewsbury & Oswestry, approx 1m from Nesscliffe. Coming from Shrewsbury to Oswestry on the A5, take the 3rd exit off the Wolfshead r'about (at the end of the Nesscliffe bypass) & follow directions to Kinton, approx 1m Sat 4, Sun 5 June (11-5). Adm £5, chd free. Home-made teas. Visits also by arrangement Apr to Oct for groups of 10 to 30.

A garden of ³/₄ acre surrounding a Georgian house. The garden features well-filled herbaceous borders, roses, a gravel area, raised vegetable beds, and a wide range of interesting trees and shrubs. Hedges, inc some as old as the house, divide up the garden. Lovely views across the Breidden hills and plenty of pleasant places to sit, whilst enjoying cream tea and cakes. Wheelchair access is possible, but on uneven, narrow paths.

占 ❀ ☕))

28 LONGNER HALL

Atcham, Shrewsbury, SY4 4TG. Mr & Mrs R L Burton, www.longner.co.uk. 4m SE of Shrewsbury. From M54 follow A5 to Shrewsbury, then B4380 to Atcham. From Atcham take Uffington Rd, entrance ¼ m on L. Sun 22 May (2-5). Adm £6, chd free. Home-made teas.

A long drive approach through parkland designed by Humphry Repton. Walks lined with golden yew through extensive lawns, with views over Severn Valley. Borders containing roses, herbaceous and shrubs, also ancient yew wood. Enclosed 1 acre walled garden open to NGS visitors. Mixed planting, garden buildings, tower and game larder. Short woodland walk around old moat pond which is not suitable for wheelchairs.

占 ☕

29 LOWER BROOKSHILL

Nind, Nr Lydham, SY5 0JW. Patricia & Robin Oldfield, 01588 650137, robin.oldfield@live.com. 3m N of Lydham on A488. Take signed turn to Nind & after ½ m sharp L & follow narrow rd for another ½ m. Drive very slowly & use temporary passing places. Sun 10, Mon 11 July (1-5). Adm £6, chd free. Cream teas.

10 acres of hillside garden and woods at 950ft within the AONB. Begun in 2010 from a derelict and overgrown site, cultivated areas now rub shoulders with the natural landscape using fine borrowed views over and down a valley. Inc brookside walks, a 'pocket' park, four ponds (inc a Monet lily pond), mixed borders and lawns, cottage garden (with cottage) and wildflowers. Lots of lovely picnic spots. Sadly not wheelchair friendly.

🐕 ❀ ☕ 🧺

30 MERTON

Shepherds Lane, Bicton, Shrewsbury, SY3 8BT. David & Jessica Pannett, 01743 850773, jessicapannett@hotmail.co.uk. 3m W of Shrewsbury. Follow B4380 from Shrewsbury past Shelton for 1m Shepherd's Lane turn L garden signed on R or from A5 by pass at Churncote r'about turn towards Shrewsbury 2nd turn L Shepherds Lane. Wed 20 July, Sun 7 Aug (1-5). Adm £5, chd free. Tea. Visits also by arrangement May to Sept.

Mature ½ acre botanical garden with a rich collection of trees and shrubs inc unusual conifers from around the world. Hardy perennial borders with seasonal flowers and grasses plus an award winning collection of hosta varieties in a woodland setting. Outstanding gunneras in a waterside setting with moisture loving plants. Wheelchair access, level paths and lawns.

占 ❀ ☕

31 MILLICHOPE PARK

Munslow, SY7 9HA. Mr & Mrs Frank Bury, www.millichopepark.com. 8m NE of Craven Arms. off B4368 Craven Arms to Bridgnorth Rd. Nr Munslow then follow yellow signs. Sun 20 Feb (2-5); Sun 1 May (1-6); Sun 16 Oct (2-5). Adm £6, chd free.

Historic landscape gardens covering 14 acres with lakes, and cascades dating from C18, woodland walks and wildflowers. Snowdrops feature in February, Bluebells and Violas in May, and Autumn colours in October. The Walled Garden - home of Wildegoose Nursery and restored C19 glasshouses - will open in tandem during the May and October dates. Nursery and café in the Walled Garden will be open (not in aid of the National Garden Scheme).

🐕 ❀ 🚌 🔄

32 MOAT HALL

Annscroft, Shrewsbury, SY5 8AZ. Martin & Helen Davies, 01743 860216, helenatthefarm@hotmail.co.uk. Take the Longden road from Shrewsbury to Hook a Gate. Our lane is 2nd on R after Hook a Gate & before Annscroft. Single track lane for ½ m. Sat 13 Aug (12-5). Adm £5, chd free. Home-made teas. Visits also by arrangement Mar to Sept.

1 acre garden around an old farmhouse within a dry moat which can be walked around. Well organised and extensive kitchen garden, fruit garden and orchard for self-sufficiency. Colourful herbaceous borders; stumpery; many interesting stone items including troughs, cheese weights, staddle stones some uncovered in the garden. Plenty of seating areas on the lawns for enjoying the garden and a homemade tea. Wheelchair access: mostly lawn with one grass ramp and one concrete ramp; kitchen garden has 2' wide paved paths.

占 🐕 ❀ ☕ 🧺))

33 THE MOUNT

Bull Lane, Bishops Castle, SY9 5DA. Heather Willis, 01588 638288, adamheather@btopenworld.com. Off A488 Shrewsbury to Knighton Rd. at top of the town, 130 metres up Bull Lane on R. No parking at property, parking free in Bishops Castle. Sun 29 May, Sun 12 June (1-5.30). Adm £5, chd free. Tea.

The Ferns

Visits also by arrangement Apr to Sept.

An acre of garden that has evolved over 24 years, with 4 lawns, a rosebed in the middle of the drive with pink and white English roses, and herbaceous and mixed shrub borders. There are roses planted throughout the garden and in the spring daffodils and tulips abound. Two large beech trees frame the garden with a view that sweeps down the valley over fields and then up to the Long Mynd. Wheelchair access easy to most parts of the garden itself, but not to WC which is in the house up steps.

34 **NEW** **1 MOUNT PLEASANT COTTAGES**

Lockley Wood, Market Drayton, TF9 2LS. Chris & Clive Brown, 01630 661470, chrisbrownemk@yahoo.co.uk. *Lockley Wood, near Hinstock. Turn off A41 at Hinstock. Follow A529. At Xrds in Lockley Wood turn L. Garden 1st property on R. From Market*

Drayton, A529 towards Newport. In Lockley Wood turn R at Xrds. Parking is limited so car sharing would be encouraged. **Wed 22 June, Wed 6 July (12-5). Adm £5, chd free. Open nearby Goldstone Hall Gardens. Teas at Goldstone Hall. Visits also by arrangement in July for groups of up to 20. Tea, coffee, soft drinks and cakes for by arrangement visits.**

The garden extends to a fifth of an acre, situated in a rural position. The main garden comprises a long border and island beds with cottage style planting, all colour themed to flow throughout the seasons. Box and yew punctuate the planting. Other features inc a fish pond and productive vegetable plot. The back garden is planted predominantly with shade tolerant plants. Refreshments not available 22 June or 6 July.

35 **NANCY'S GARDEN**

11 Elmfield Road, Shrewsbury, SY2 5PB. Nancy Estrey & Peter Alltree. *In Elmfield Rd next to church, off Belvedere Ave. Free Parking in Shire Hall lower car park, adj to garden. Limited on-street parking.* **Sun 17 July (1-5). Combined adm with Esme's Garden (2½ m away) £6, chd free. Light refreshments in Peace Memorial Hall, Meole Village.**

Nancy's garden is a small suburban garden with lots of form, foliage and colour. Winding paths lead you to a circular lawn, patio and pond. A secluded patio at the top of the garden is surrounded by lush planting that gives a sub tropical feel. A summerhouse used throughout the summer is a true outside room. A plantswomen's garden featuring a wealth of plants. Beautifully designed to give colour and form all year-round. Tranquil seating and pond. Both gardens nurtured by Nancy.

36 NEW NEEN VIEW
Neen Sollars, Cleobury Mortimer, DY14 9AB. Ian & Chris Ferguson. *3m from the Market Town of Cleobury Mortimer. From A456 past Mamble, turn R at Neen Sollars, follow lane to Live & Let Live for parking. From Cleobury take the Tenbury Rd, turn L & L again then up the hill to Neen View gardens.* Wed 11, Wed 25 May (12-5). Adm £5, chd free. Pre-booking essential, please visit www.ngs. org.uk for information & booking. Home-made teas in the Live and Let Live Inn.
A woodland garden with stunning panoramic views. Expansive Views, mature trees, azaleas, camellias and wildlife ponds.

37 OFFCOT
Kynaston, Kinnerley, SY10 8EF. Tom Pountney. *Just off A5 on Wolfshead r'about (at Oswestry end of Nesscliffe bypass) towards Knockin. Then take the 1st L towards Kinnerley. Follow NGS signs from this road.* Thur 21, Fri 22, Sat 23 July (10-4). Combined adm with

Appledore £6, chd free. Fri 7, Sat 8 Oct (10-4). Adm £5, chd free. Home-made teas.
A cottage garden with lots of winding pathways leading to different focal points. The garden is packed with a wide range of evergreen and deciduous trees and shrubs and underplanted with herbaceous perennials. There is a natural looking pond with a running stream feeding into it. A haven for wildlife. So many different areas to see and enjoy inc the garden bar.

38 THE OLD VICARAGE, CLUN
Vicarage Road, Clun, SY7 8JG. Peter & Jay Upton, 01588 640775, jay@salopia.plus.com. *16m NW of Ludlow. Over bridge at Clun towards Knighton (parking in public car park by bridge); walk up to church, turn L into Vicarage Rd; house on R next to church. Refreshments in Clun village.* Visits by arrangement May to Sept for groups of up to 30. Adm £5, chd free.
A revived, old vicarage garden: a slow retrieval and recovery

revealing a wealth of features and plants chosen by plantsmen vicars: buddleia globosa fascinates bees and butterflies; glorious oriental poppies fascinate visitors. 'The Tree', an enormous Leyland cypress (5th biggest girth in the world); the most dramatic feature is a formal wisteria allee with alliums - a symphony of mauve and purple.

39 OSWESTRY GATACRE ALLOTMENTS & GARDENS ASSOCIATION
Lloyd Street, Oswestry, SY11 1NL. Graham Mitchell, 01691 654961, gsfmitchell@gmail.com, gatacre.wordpress.com. *2 parts to the allotments either side of Liverpool Road. From Whittington r'about on A5 turn towards Oswestry B4580. In ½ m go across staggered junction (L then R). Continue 100y then bear sharp L. After 200y straight over r'about, then 3rd on L.* Sun 24 July (10-5). Adm £5, chd free. Light refreshments. Tea, coffee and cakes. Visits also by arrangement June to Aug for groups of 5 to 20.
Two adjacent, large allotment communities in the heart of Oswestry; well supported and well-loved by local residents. Vast array of fruit, flowers, vegetables in every shape and form grown on the allotments. Allotment holders will be on-hand to talk about their produce and give advice. Entry ticket covers both sides of the allotments. The site was featured on BBC's Countryfile on Sept 1st 2019. The main pathways are wheelchair friendly, but the small paths tend to be rather steep or narrow. There are disabled WC on one side of the site.

40 OTELEY
Ellesmere, SY12 0PB. Mr RK Mainwaring, www.oteley.com. *1m SE of Ellesmere. Entrance out of Ellesmere past Mere, opp Convent nr to A528/495 junction.* Sun 8 May (11-4). Adm £6, chd free. Light refreshments.
10 acres running down to The Mere. Walled kitchen garden, architectural features, many old interesting trees. Rhododendrons, azaleas, wild woodland walk and views across Mere to Ellesmere. First opened in 1927 when the National Garden Scheme started. Beautiful setting on the Mere. Wheelchair access if dry.

153 Willoughbridge

41 NEW THE PADDOCK
Annscroft, Shrewsbury, SY5 8AN.
Ian Ross. *On road from Annscroft to Hanwood/Plealey 200 yds from the Xrds. Parking is at The Farriers SY5 8AN - on the road from Annscroft to Exfords Green.* **Sat 15 Oct (11-5). Adm £5, chd free. Home-made teas.**
A mini arboretum in which 70 trees are tagged - some of which are rare. The collection inc 12 different acers and a cluster of 6 ginko bilobas. A waterfall cascades through three levels. As the new owner since 2001 I have seen myself as the custodian of an impressive small garden. Wheelchair access is available, by paths and grass, to most of the garden.
&. 🐕 ☕ »))

42 PREEN MANOR
Church Preen, SY6 7LQ. Mr & Mrs J Tanner, 07971 955609, katytanner@msn.com. *6m W of Much Wenlock; For SatNav, please use postcode SY5 6LF. From A458 Shrewsbury to Bridgnorth Rd turn off at Harley and follow signs to Kenley & Church Preen. From B4371 Much Wenlock to Church Stretton Rd go via Hughley to Church Preen.* **Sun 19 June (2-6). Adm £6, chd free. Home-made teas.**
Fine historical and architectural 6 acre garden on site of Cluniac priory and former Norman Shaw mansion. Compartmentalised with large variety of garden rooms, inc kitchen parterre and fernery. Formal terraces with fine yew and hornbeam hedges have panoramic views over parkland to Wenlock Edge. Dell, woodland walks and specimen trees. Gardens also open by appointment (not NGS).
&. ✿ ☕

43 RUTHALL MANOR
Ditton Priors, WV16 6TN. Mr & Mrs G T Clarke, 01746 712698, clrk608@btinternet.com. *7m SW of Bridgnorth. At Ditton Priors Church take road signed Bridgnorth. then 2nd L. Garden 1m.* **Sun 1, Mon 2, Sat 14, Sun 15 May, Sat 11, Sun 12 June, Sat 2, Sun 3 July (12.30-5). Adm £5, chd free. Pre-booking essential, please visit www.ngs. org.uk for information & booking. Home-made teas. Visits also by arrangement May to Sept.**
Offset by a mature collection of specimen trees, the garden is divided into intimate sections, carefully linked by winding paths. The front lawn flanked by striking borders, extends to a gravel, art garden and ha-ha. Clematis and roses scramble through an eclectic collection of wrought-iron work, unique pottery and secluded seating. A stunning horse pond with primulas, iris and bog plants. Lots of lovely shrubs to see. Refreshments. Jigsaw puzzle sale. New viewpoint for Medieval Village with Dovecote Site. Donation to NGS from refreshments. Wheelchair access to most parts.
&. 🐕 🚗 ☕ »))

44 SAMBROOK MANOR
Sambrook, TF10 8AL. Mrs E Mitchell, 01952 550256, eileengran@hotmail.com . *Between Newport & Ternhill, 1m off A41. In the village of Sambrook.* **Sun 10 July, Sun 28 Aug (12-5). Adm £5, chd free. Home-made teas. Visits also by arrangement for groups of 10+.**
Deep, colourful, well-planted borders offset by sweeping lawns surrounding an early C18 manor house (not open). Wide ranging herbaceous planting with plenty of roses to enjoy; the arboretum below the garden, with views across the river, has been further extended with new trees. The waterfall and Japanese garden are now linked by a pretty rill. Lovely garden to visit for all the family. Woodland area difficult for wheelchairs.
&. 🐕 ✿ 🚗 🚌 ☕

45 2 SCHOOL COTTAGES
Hook-a-Gate, Shrewsbury, SY5 8BQ. Andrew Roberts & Dru Yarwood, 07703 558635, andyrobo@hotmail.co.uk. *From B4380 Roman Rd in Shrewsbury by cemetery take the Longden Rd island. 1.8m past schools continue to the village of Hook-a-Gate. Garden is on L past Hill Side Nursery. Parking at Nursery.* **Sun 5 June, Sun 3 July (12-4.30). Adm £5, chd free. Home-made teas. Visits also by arrangement June to Aug for groups of 6 to 40.**
Delights and surprises at every turn and a little oriental mystic. Interest as soon as you enter the property, from little nooks and crannies to fabulous views towards Wales. Combination of sunken garden, borders galore and numerous water features. Woodland walk and specimen trees. Self sufficient veg, fruit, pigs and chickens all in a 3 acre site on an incline. Alterations since 2019.
🐕 ✿ ☕

GROUP OPENING

47 THE SECRET GARDENS AT STEVENTON TERRACE
Steventon Terrace, Steventon New Road, Ludlow, SY8 1JZ. Kevin & Carolyn Wood, 01584 876037, carolynwood2152@yahoo.co.uk. *Gardens are located behind row of terraced cottages. Easily accessible from A49; on-street parking; Park & Ride stops outside the garden.* **Sat 25 June (12.30-4.30). Combined adm £5, chd free. Home-made teas. Ice cream. Visits also by arrangement June to Sept.**
Very secret gardens behind a row of Victorian terraced cottages in Ludlow: ½ acre plot south facing garden developed over 30 years with the love of gardening divided up into different sections rose garden, herbaceous borders, koi fish, chickens, polytunnel, Mediterranean garden. Heart of England in Bloom chairman's award.
&. 🐕 ✿ 🚗 ☕

National Garden Scheme funding helped support the provision of horticultural-related assistance to soldiers, veterans and their immediate families, providing education, training and employment opportunities along with supporting the recovery, health and wellbeing of individuals

Whitcott Hall

48 STANLEY HALL GARDENS

Bridgnorth, WV16 4SP. Mr & Mrs M J Thompson. $\frac{1}{2}$ m N of Bridgnorth. Leave Bridgnorth by N gate B4373; turn R at Stanley Lane. Pass Golf Course Club House on L & turn L at Lodge. **Sun 29 May (2-5.30). Adm £5, chd free. Home-made teas.** Georgian landscaped drive with rhododendrons, fine trees in parkland setting, woodland walks and fish ponds. Restored ice house. Dower House (Mr and Mrs C Wells): 4 acres of specimen trees, contemporary sculpture, walled vegetable garden and potager; South Lodge (Mr Tim Warren) Hillside cottage garden. Wheelchair access to the main gardens.

GROUP OPENING

49 STOTTESDON VILLAGE OPEN GARDENS

Stottesdon, DY14 8TZ. In glorious S Shropshire near Cleobury Mortimer (A4117/B4363). 30m from Birmingham (M5/42), 15m E of Ludlow (A49/4117) & 10m S of Bridgnorth (A458/442) Stottesdon is between Clee Hill & the Severn Valley. NGS Signed from B4363.

SatNav DY14 8TZ. **Sun 17 July (12-4). Combined adm £5, chd free. Home-made teas in the Parish Church.**
Located in unspoilt countryside near the Clee Hills, up to 8 gardens and the heritage church in Stottesdon village are open to visitors. Several places have stunning views. Some gardens feature spaces for outdoor living. Many are traditional or more modern 'cottage gardens', containing fruit, vegetables and livestock. There are contrasting vegetable gardens inc one devoted to permaculture principles and one to growing championship winners. Take teas and refreshments in the Norman church and book on the day to join a unique guided tour of the historic Tower, Bells and Turret Clock. A garden-related competition to be held and be judged by garden visitors. Dogs on leads please. Heritage Church open - tower tours. Lunches may be available at The Fighting Cocks pub - call on 01746 718270 to pre-book (essential). Most gardens have some wheelchair access. Those gardens not suitable for wheelchair access will be listed on our gardens guide.

50 SUNNINGDALE

9 Mill Street, Wem, SY4 5ED. Mrs Susan Griffiths, 01939 236733, sue.griffiths@btinternet.com. Town centre. Wem is on B5476. Parking in public car park Barnard St. The property is opposite the purple house below the church. Some on street free parking on the High St. **Sun 12 June (10.30-3.30). Adm £4, chd free. Light refreshments. Visits also by arrangement Feb to Nov. A free tour if required.**
A good $\frac{1}{2}$ acre town garden. Wildlife haven for a huge variety of birds inc nesting gold crests. A profusion of excellent nectar rich plants means that butterflies and other pollinators are in abundance. Interesting plantings with carefully collected rare plants and unusual annuals means there is always something new to see, in a garden created for year-round viewing. Koi pond and natural stone waterfall rockery. Antique and modern sculpture. Sound break yew walkway. Large perennial borders, with rare plants, unusual annuals, exotic climbers, designed by owner as an all year-round garden. Why not inc a visit by having lunch at the floral Castle Hotel in Wem. Wheelchair access the garden is on the level but with a number of steps mostly around the pond area; paths are mainly gravel or flags; flat lawn.

51 UPPER MARSHES

Catherton Common, Hopton Wafers, nr Kidderminster, DY14 0JJ. Jo & Chris Bargman. *3m NW of Cleobury Mortimer. From A4117 follow signs to Catherton. Property is on Common land 100yds at end of track.* **Sun 3 July (12-5). Adm £5, chd free. Home-made teas.**

Commoner's stone cottage and 3 acre small holding. 800' high. Garden has been developed to complement its unique location on edge of Catherton common with herbaceous borders, vegetable plot, herb garden. Short walk down to a spring fed wildlife pond. Plenty of seats to stop and take in the tranquillity. Optional circular walk across Wildlife Trust common to SSI field. Various animals and poultry.

52 WALCOT HALL

Lydbury North, SY7 8AZ. Mr & Mrs C R W Parish, 01588 680570, enquiries@walcothall.com, www.walcothall.com. *4m SE of Bishop's Castle. B4385 Craven Arms to Bishop's Castle, turn L by The Powis Arms in Lydbury North.* **Sun 29, Mon 30 May (1.30-5). Adm £5, chd free. Home-made teas.**

Arboretum planted by Lord Clive of India's son, Edward in1800. Cascades of rhododendrons and azaleas amongst specimen trees and pools. Fine views of Sir William Chambers' Clock Towers, with lake and hills beyond. Walled kitchen garden, dovecote, meat safe, ice house and mile-long lakes. Russian wooden church, grotto and fountain; tin chapel. Relaxed borders and rare shrubs. Lakeside replanted and water garden at western end re-established. Outstanding Ballroom where excellent teas are served.

53 WESTWOOD HOUSE

Oldbury, Bridgnorth, WV16 5LP. Hugh & Carolyn Trevor-Jones. *Take the Ludlow Road B4364 out of Bridgnorth. Past the Punch Bowl Inn, turn 1st L, Westwood House signed on R.* **Sun 24 Apr (2-5). Adm £5, chd free. Home-made teas.**

A country garden, well designed and planted around the house, particularly known for its tulips. Sweeping lawns offset by deeply planted mixed borders; pool garden and lawn tennis court; productive kitchen and cutting garden, with everything designed to attract wildlife for organic growth. Far reaching views of this delightful corner of the county and woodland walks to enjoy. Reasonable wheelchair access around the house, but gravel paths and some steps.

54 NEW WHITCOTT HALL

Whitcott Keysett, Clun, Craven Arms, SY7 8QE. M Wooldridge & Y Gordon. *Whitcott Keysett. From Clun Bridge; take road to Newcastle, after approx. 2m turn R, Whitcott Keysett, Mardu, & at the T-junction turn L.* **Thur 23 June (11-5). Adm £5, chd free. Light refreshments. Tea, coffee & cake.**

This 2 acre garden features a lily pond with fountain, an old yew tree, and a hornbeam avenue. There are mature shrubs and trees inc walnuts; a small copse plus new orchard inc vines and a cherry. A brook borders one side of the garden. There is a herb garden, vegetables in tubs and courtyard with fig tree. There are plenty of seats to relax in plus beautiful views, especially south. Wheelchair access, a few steps to some small areas, but most can be avoided by an alternative route.

55 153 WILLOUGHBRIDGE

Market Drayton, TF9 4JQ. John Butcher & Sarah Berry, 07817 443837, butchinoz@hotmail.com, www. instagram.com/_thebeegardener_. *Approx ½m from the Dorothy Clive Garden, turn onto Minn Bank from A51, 3rd drive on L. Parking will be signed.* **Sat 16, Sun 17 July (1-5). Adm £5, chd free. Pre-booking essential, please visit www.ngs. org.uk for information & booking. A wide selection of home-made cakes will be available, as well as honey to buy collected from John's bees. Visits also by arrangement May to Oct for groups of up to 20.**

Small and beautiful garden packed full of scented insect friendly plants. The garden inc a long cottage-prairie garden full of climbers, English roses, grasses and herbaceous perennials, a woodland-jungle garden consisting of huge scented tree lilies, tree ferns, acers, bamboo and bananas, two green roofs, three bug hotels and a large Victorian greenhouse full of traditional and exotic plants.

56 WINDY RIDGE

Church Lane, Little Wenlock, TF6 5BB. George & Fiona Chancellor, 01952 507675, fiona.chancellor@ngs.org.uk. *2m S of Wellington. Follow signs for Little Wenlock from N (J7, M54) or E (off A5223 at Horsehay). Parking signed. Do not rely on SatNav.* **Sat 11, Sun 12 June, Sat 3, Sun 4 Sept (12-5). Adm £6, chd free. Home-made teas. Visits also by arrangement June to Sept for groups of 12+.**

Universally admired for its structure, inspirational planting and balance of texture, form and all-season colour, the garden more than lives up to its award-winning record. Developed over 30 years, 'open plan' garden rooms display over 1000 species (mostly labelled) in a range of colour-themed planting styles, beautifully set off by well-tended lawns, plenty of water and fascinating sculpture. Wheelchair access, some gravel paths but help available.

57 ♦ WOLLERTON OLD HALL

Wollerton, Market Drayton, TF9 3NA. Lesley & John Jenkins, 01630 685760, info@wollertonoldhallgarden.com, www.wollertonoldhallgarden.com. *4m SW of Market Drayton. On A53 between Hodnet & A53-A41 junction. Follow brown signs.* **For NGS: Wed 7 Sept (11-5). Adm £8.50, chd free. For other opening times and information, please phone, email or visit garden website.**

4 acre garden created around C16 house (not open). Formal structure creates variety of gardens each with own colour theme and character. Planting is mainly of perennials many in their late summer/early Autumn hues, particularly the asters. Winner of many awards and nationally acclaimed. Ongoing lectures by Gardening Celebrities inc Chris Beardshaw, and other garden designers and personalities. We will suspend the booking system for the NGS day. Partial wheelchair access.

Our 2021 donations mean that 1,200 inpatients were supported by the Y Bwthyn NGS Macmillan Specialist Palliative Care unit in Wales since opening

SOMERSET, BRISTOL AREA
& SOUTH GLOUCESTERSHIRE incl BATH

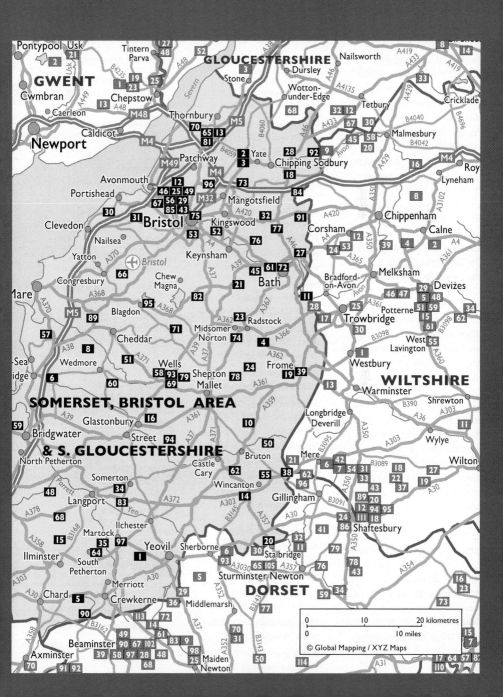

Somerset, Bristol, Bath and South Gloucestershire make up a National Garden Scheme 'county' of captivating contrasts, with castles and countryside and wildlife and wetlands, from amazing cities to bustling market towns, coastal resorts and picturesque villages.

Bristol's stunning location and famous landmarks offer a wonderful backdrop to our creative and inspiring garden owners who have made tranquil havens and tropical back gardens in urban surroundings. The surrounding countryside is home to gardens featuring contrasting mixtures of formality, woodland, water, orchard and kitchen gardens.

Bath is a world heritage site for its Georgian architecture and renowned for its Roman Baths. Our garden visitors can enjoy the secluded picturesque gardens behind the iconic Royal Crescent Hotel in the heart of the city, or venture further afield and explore the hidden gems in nearby villages.

Somerset is a rural county of rolling hills such as the Mendips, the Quantocks and Exmoor National Park contrasted with the low-lying Somerset Levels. Famous for cheddar cheese, strawberries and cider; agriculture is a major occupation. It is home to Wells, the smallest cathedral city in England, and the lively county town of Taunton.

Visitors can explore more than 150 diverse gardens, mostly privately owned and not normally open to the public ranging from small urban plots to country estates.

Somerset Volunteers

County Organiser
Laura Howard 01460 282911
laura.howard@ngs.org.uk

County Treasurer
Jill Wardle 07702 274492
jill.wardle@ngs.org.uk

Publicity
Roger Peacock
roger.peacock@ngs.org.uk

Social Media
Janet Jones 01749 850509
janet.jones@ngs.org.uk

Rae Hick 07972 280083
raehick@gmail.com

Presentations
Dave & Prue Moon 01373 473381
davidmoon202@btinternet.com

Booklet Co-ordinator
John Simmons 07855 944049
john.simmons@ngs.org.uk

Booklet Distributor
Laura Howard (see above)

Assistant County Organisers
Jo Beaumont 07534 777278
jo.beaumont@ngs.org.uk

Marsha Casely 07854 882616
marsha.casely@ngs.org.uk

Kirstie Dalrymple 07772 170537
kirstie.dalrymple@ngs.org.uk

Patricia Davies-Gilbert
01823 412187
pdaviesgilbert@gmail.com

Alison Highnam 01258 821576
allies1@btinternet.com

Janet Jones (as above)

Sue Lewis 07885 369280
sue.lewis@ngs.org.uk

Nicky Ramsay 01643 862078
nicky.ramsay@ngs.org.uk

Judith Stanford 01761 233045
jjudith.stanford@ngs.org.uk

Bristol Area Volunteers

County Organiser
Su Mills 01454 615438
su.mills@ngs.org.uk

County Treasurer
Harsha Parmar 07889 201185
harsha.parmar@ngs.org.uk

Publicity
Myra Ginns 01454 415396
myra.ginns@ngs.org.uk

Booklet Co-ordinator
John Simmons 07855 944049
john.simmons@ngs.org.uk

Booklet Distributor
John Simmons (as above)

Assistant County Organisers
Tracey Halladay
07956 784838
thallada@icloud.com

Christine Healey
01454 612795
christine.healey@uwclub.net

Margaret Jones
01225 891229
ian@weircott.plus.com

Jeanette Parker
01454 299699
jeanette_parker@hotmail.co.uk

Jane Perkins
01454 414570
janekperkins@gmail.com

Irene Randow
01275 857208
irene.randow@sky.com

Karl Suchy 07873 588540
karl.suchy@ngs.org.uk

 @visitsomersetngs

 @SomersetNGS

 @ngs_bristol_s_glos_somerset

OPENING DATES

All entries subject to change. For latest information check www.ngs.org.uk
Map locator numbers are shown to the right of each garden name.

January

Sunday 30th
Rock House   70

February

Snowdrop Festival

Friday 4th
◆ Elworthy Cottage   36

Sunday 6th
Rock House   70

Thursday 10th
◆ East Lambrook Manor Gardens   35

Saturday 12th
NEW Blackmore House   14

Sunday 13th
Greystones   43

Sunday 27th
Algars Manor   2
Algars Mill   3
◆ Elworthy Cottage   36

March

Tuesday 1st
◆ Hestercombe Gardens   47

Saturday 19th
Lower Shalford Farm   55

Sunday 20th
Rock House   70

Sunday 27th
Rock House   70

April

Saturday 2nd
Weir Cottage   91

Sunday 3rd
Weir Cottage   91

Friday 8th
The Downs Preparatory School   31

Saturday 9th
The Downs Preparatory School   31

Sunday 10th
Fairfield   37
Greystones   43
Rose Cottage   71

Tuesday 12th
◆ Elworthy Cottage   36

Saturday 16th
Westbrook House   94

Monday 18th
◆ Elworthy Cottage   36

Wednesday 20th
◆ Greencombe Gardens   42

Saturday 23rd
◆ The Walled Gardens of Cannington   88

Sunday 24th
Algars Manor   2
Algars Mill   3
◆ The Walled Gardens of Cannington   88
Coleford House   24
Watcombe   89
◆ The Yeo Valley Organic Garden at Holt Farm   95

May

Saturday 7th
◆ East Lambrook Manor Gardens   35
Hillcrest   48

Sunday 8th
NEW Glebe Farm   40
Hillcrest   48
◆ Milton Lodge   58
Somerset Street Display Gardens   75

Sunday 15th
Court House   26
4 Haytor Park   46

Lucombe House   56
Watcombe   89
Wayford Manor   90

Tuesday 17th
◆ Elworthy Cottage   36

Saturday 21st
Forest Lodge   38
Lower Shalford Farm   55
NEW The Yews   96

Sunday 22nd
NEW The Yews   96

Thursday 26th
Barford House   9

Saturday 28th
Babbs Farm   6

Sunday 29th
Babbs Farm   6
81 Coombe Lane   25
◆ Elworthy Cottage   36
Holland Farm   50
Somerset Street Display Gardens   75

Tuesday 31st
◆ Elworthy Cottage   36

June

Sunday 5th
Brindham Bungalow   16
◆ Milton Lodge   58
Model Farm   59

Tuesday 7th
◆ Hestercombe Gardens   47

Thursday 9th
Watcombe   89

Friday 10th
Stoneleigh Down   81

Saturday 11th
NEW Badgworth Court Barn   8
The Hayes   45
NEW 1 Steeple View   78

Sunday 12th
NEW Ammerdown House   4
NEW Badgworth Court Barn   8
9 Catherston Close   19
The Hayes   45
NEW 1 Steeple View   78
Stoneleigh Down   81

Wednesday 15th
NEW ◆ Old Down Manor Gardens   65

Thursday 16th
9 Catherston Close   19
◆ Special Plants   77

Saturday 18th
Batcombe House   10
NEW Hillside   49
Lympsham Gardens   57
NEW Mudgley Farm   60

Sunday 19th
Crete Hill House   29
Frome Gardens   39
4 Haytor Park   46
NEW Hillside   49
Lympsham Gardens   57

Saturday 25th
Babbs Farm   6
NEW Beech Cottage   11
NEW Clayhill Arts   22
Forest Lodge   38
John's Corner   53

Sunday 26th
Babbs Farm   6
NEW Beech Cottage   11
NEW Clayhill Arts   22
NEW Dunkery View   33
John's Corner   53
Nynehead Court   63
Penny Brohn UK   67

Monday 27th
John's Corner   53

July

Saturday 2nd
165 Newbridge Hill   61
The Rib   69

Sunday 3rd
NEW Church Farm   21
Honeyhurst Farm   51
◆ Milton Lodge   58
165 Newbridge Hill   61
Stogumber Gardens   80
Yews Farm   97

Monday 4th
◆ Berwick Lodge   12
Honeyhurst Farm   51

Tuesday 5th
◆ Elworthy Cottage   36

Wednesday 6th
9 Catherston Close   19

Thursday 7th
Holland Farm   50

Saturday 9th
◆ East Lambrook Manor Gardens 35

Sunday 10th
Nynehead Court 63
NEW 42 Silver Street 74

Monday 11th
The Royal Crescent Hotel & Spa 72

Tuesday 12th
The Royal Crescent Hotel & Spa 72

Saturday 16th
NEW Vexford Court 87

Sunday 17th
Cox's Hill House 28
Hangeridge Farmhouse 44
Stowey Gardens 82
◆ University of Bristol Botanic Garden 85
NEW Vexford Court 87

Wednesday 20th
◆ Greencombe Gardens 42

Thursday 21st
◆ Special Plants 77

Saturday 23rd
Court View 27
Goathurst Gardens 41

Sunday 24th
Court House 26
Court View 27
◆ Elworthy Cottage 36
Goathurst Gardens 41
Park Cottage 66
Sutton Hosey Manor 83

Tuesday 26th
◆ Elworthy Cottage 36

Saturday 30th
Japanese Garden Bristol 52

Sunday 31st
Japanese Garden Bristol 52
Park Cottage 66

August

Friday 5th
The Downs Preparatory School 31

Badgworth Court Barn

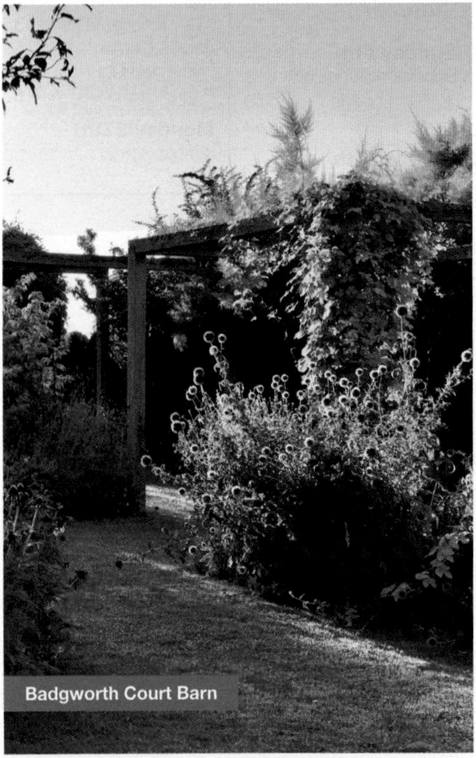

Saturday 6th
The Downs Preparatory School 31

Thursday 18th
◆ Special Plants 77

Saturday 20th
NEW Vexford Court 87

Sunday 21st
NEW Vexford Court 87

Monday 22nd
◆ Stoberry Garden 79

Saturday 27th
Westbrook House 94

Monday 29th
◆ Elworthy Cottage 36

Wednesday 31st
NEW ◆ Old Down Manor Gardens 65

September

Saturday 3rd
NEW Ammerdown House 4
165 Newbridge Hill 61

Sunday 4th
165 Newbridge Hill 61
NEW The Old Dairy House 64
◆ Stoberry Garden 79

Saturday 10th
Babbs Farm 6
Batcombe House 10
The Hayes 45

Sunday 11th
Babbs Farm 6
Coleford House 24
NEW Dunkery View 33
The Hayes 45
Yews Farm 97

Thursday 15th
◆ Special Plants 77

Saturday 17th
NEW Blackmore House 14
◆ The Walled Gardens of Cannington 88

Sunday 18th
◆ The Walled Gardens of Cannington 88

Sunday 25th
The Red Post House 68

October

Thursday 20th
◆ Special Plants 77

By Arrangement

Arrange a personalised garden visit with your club, or group of friends, on a date to suit you. See individual garden entries for full details.

Abbey Farm 1
Avalon 5
NEW Badgers Holt 7
Batcombe House 10
1 Birch Drive 13
Bradon Farm 15
Broomclose 17
Camers 18
Cherry Bolberry Farm 20
Coldharbour Cottage 23
81 Coombe Lane 25
Court View 27
The Dairy, Church Lane 30
Doynton House 32
East End Farm 34
Forest Lodge 38
Hangeridge Farmhouse 44
The Hayes 45
4 Haytor Park 46
Hillcrest 48
Honeyhurst Farm 51
Japanese Garden Bristol 52
Knoll Cottage, Stogumber Gardens 80
Little Yarford Farmhouse 54
Lucombe House 56
Penny Brohn UK 67
Rock House 70
Rose Cottage 71
Serridge House 73
South Kelding 76
Stoneleigh Down 81
Sutton Hosey Manor 83
Tormarton Court 84
Vellacott 86
NEW Vexford Court 87
Watcombe 89
NEW Well Cottage 92
Wellfield Barn 93
Yews Farm 97

THE GARDENS

🚩 ABBEY FARM
Montacute, TA15 6UA. Elizabeth McFarlane, 01935 823556, abbey.farm64@gmail.com. *4m from Yeovil. Follow A3088, take slip rd to Montacute, turn L at T-junction into village. Turn R between church & King's Arms (no through rd).* **Visits by arrangement May & June for groups of 10 to 20. Adm £6, chd free. Light refreshments. Details on request.**
2½ acres of mainly walled gardens on sloping site provide the setting for Cluniac Medieval Priory gatehouse. Interesting plants inc roses, shrubs, grasses, clematis. Herbaceous borders, white garden, gravel garden. Small arboretum. Pond for wildlife - frogs, newts, dragonflies. Fine mulberry, walnut and monkey puzzle trees. Seats for resting.

🚩 ALGARS MANOR
Station Rd, Iron Acton, BS37 9TB. Mrs B Naish. *9m N of Bristol, 3m W of Yate/Chipping Sodbury. Turn S off Iron Acton bypass B4059, past village green & White Hart pub, 200yds, then over level Xing. No access from Frampton Cotterell via lane; ignore SatNav. Parking at Algars Manor.* **Sun 27 Feb (1-4). Light refreshments. Sun 24 Apr (1-5). Home-made teas. Combined adm with Algars Mill £7, chd free.**
2 acres of woodland garden beside River Frome, mill stream, native plants mixed with collections of 60 magnolias and 70 camellias, rhododendrons, azaleas, eucalyptus and other unusual trees and shrubs. Daffodils, snowdrops and other early spring flowers.

🚩 ALGARS MILL
Frampton End Rd, Iron Acton, Bristol, BS37 9TD. Mr & Mrs John Wright. *9m N of Bristol, 3m W of Yate/Chipping Sodbury. (For directions see Algars Manor).* **Sun 27 Feb (1-4); Sun 24 Apr (1-5). Combined adm with Algars Manor £7, chd free. Light refreshments.**
2 acre woodland garden bisected by River Frome; spring bulbs, shrubs; very early spring feature (Feb-Mar) of wild Newent daffodils. 300-400yr-old mill house (not open) through which millrace still runs.

🚩 NEW AMMERDOWN HOUSE
Ammerdown Park, Radstock, BA3 5SH. Mrs Diana Jolliffe. *500 metres from Terry Hill Xrds, A366, A362 & B3139, sharp L to enter park, R fork in drive.* **Sun 12 June, Sat 3 Sept (2-5). Adm £7, chd free. Home-made teas.**
The Ammerdown garden was a brilliant idea by Lutyens who wanted to link the house with the beautiful Orangery. He created 'rooms' of yew, sculptures and parterres. Yew planting creates enclosed formal areas which lead irresistibly from one room to the next. Details inc the clipped Portuguese laurels and honeysuckles trained over wired umbrellas. The kitchen garden is undergoing restoration.

🚩 AVALON
Higher Chillington, Ilminster, TA19 0PT. Dee & Tony Brook, 07506 688191, dee1jones@hotmail.com. *From A30 take turning signed to Chillington opp Swandown Lodges. Take 2nd L down Coley Lane and 1st L Moor Lane. Avalon is the large pink house. Parking limited, so car sharing advised if possible.* **Visits by arrangement June to Aug for groups of up to 20. Max 6 cars or 2 minibuses. Adm £5, chd £2. Home-made teas. Gluten & dairy free cakes available if requested in advance.**
Secluded hillside garden with wonderful views as far as Wales. The lower garden has large herbaceous borders, a sizeable wildlife pond and 2 greenhouses filled with RSA succulents. The middle garden has mixed borders, wild spotted orchids on the lawn, allotment area and a small orchard. The upper garden has a spring fed water course with ponds, plus many terraces with different planting schemes. Partial wheelchair access across lower lawns & side paths. Steep slope & gravel paths. Wheelchairs will require to be pushed & attended at all times.

🚩 BABBS FARM
Westhill Lane, Bason Bridge, Highbridge, TA9 4RF. Sue & Richard O'Brien, www.babbsfarm.co.uk. *1½m E of Highbridge, 1½m SSE of M5 exit 22. Turn into Westhill Lane off B3141 (Church Rd), 100yds S of where it joins B3139 (Wells-Highbridge rd).* **Sat 28, Sun 29 May, Sat 25, Sun 26 June, Sat 10, Sun 11 Sept (2-5). Adm £6, chd free. Home-made teas.**
1½ acre plantsman's garden on Somerset Levels, gradually created out of fields surrounding old farmhouse over last 30 yrs and still being developed. Trees, shrubs and herbaceous perennials planted with an eye for form and shape in big flowing borders. Plants for sale if circumstances allow.

🚩 NEW BADGERS HOLT
Frost Street, Thurlbear, Taunton, TA3 5BA. Mr Neil Jones & Ms Sharon Bradford, 01823 481316, Neil.jones881@gmail.com. *Following SatNav will bring you to parking. House approx 100 yds further along Frost St.* **Visits by arrangement May to July for groups of up to 12. Adm £4, chd free. Tea and cakes will be available.**
Newly created quintessential English Cottage garden, boasting beautiful views over the Blackdown Hills. Wheelchair side access to main garden. Some narrow stone steps and paths.

🚩 NEW BADGWORTH COURT BARN
Notting Hill Way, Stone Allerton, Axbridge, BS26 2NQ. Trish & Jeremy Gibson. *4m SW of Axbridge. Turn off A38 in Lower Weare, signed Wedmore, Weare. Continue 1.1m, pass road on R (Badgworth Arena). Continue 0.1m, car park on L immed before 'No Footway for 600 yds' sign.* **Sat 11, Sun 12 June (2-5). Adm £5, chd free. Home-made teas.**
This 1 acre plot surrounds old stone barn buildings. A small orchard leads to a colourful part-walled garden with areas of perennial meadow and multi-stemmed trees. Gently curving beds are flanked by a more formal oak pergola walk. The planting is a relaxed contemporary mix. In the atmospheric courtyard, planting is more established and leads on to a new flower meadow in front of the barns. Some gravel paths. No disabled WC.

9 BARFORD HOUSE
Spaxton, Bridgwater, TA5 1AG.
Donald & Bee Rice. 4½m W of
Bridgwater. Midway between Enmore
& Spaxton. **Thur 26 May (2-5). Adm
£6, chd free. Home-made teas.**
Formal walled garden and lawns
lead to a 6 acre woodland garden of
camellias, rhododendrons, azaleas
and magnolias. Stream-side gardens
feature candelabra primulas, ferns,
foxgloves and lily-of-the-valley among
veteran pines and oaks, and some
rarer trees. Partial wheelchair access.
Some areas of woodland garden
inaccessible.
  🚹 ✿ ☕

10 BATCOMBE HOUSE
Gold Hill, Batcombe,
Shepton Mallet, BA4 6HF.
Libby Russell, libby@
mazzullorusselllandscapedesign.
com, www.
mazzullorusselllandscapedesign.
com. In centre of Batcombe, 3m
from Bruton. Parking will be between
Batcombe House and church at
centre of village and clearly marked.
**Sat 18 June, Sat 10 Sept (2-6).
Adm £7, chd free. Cream teas.
Visits also by arrangement May to
Sept for groups of 10 to 30.**
Plantswoman's and designer's
garden of two parts – one a riot of
colour through kitchen terraces,
potager leading to wildflower orchard;
the other a calm contemporary
amphitheatre with large herbaceous
borders and interesting trees and
shrubs. Always changing. Dogs are
allowed but on a lead.
  🐕 ✿ Ⓓ ☕))

11 NEW BEECH COTTAGE
Station Road, Freshford, Bath,
BA2 7WQ. Kirstie Sneyd. 6m SE
of Bath. Station Rd is halfway down
The Hill in centre of Freshford.
Parking either at the bottom of The
Hill nr Freshford Inn, or go to end of
Station Rd to stn car park. **Sat 25,
Sun 26 June (2-5). Adm £5, chd
free. Home-made teas.**
Architect designed ¾ acre garden
with stunning views over Somerset
hills. Colour themed borders: white,
purple and lemon, red and lime, hot
border with a wide variety of bee-
friendly plant species. Vegetable and
cutting garden, fruit cage, orchard
and wildflower meadow crescents.
Partial wheelchair access.
  🚹 🐕 ☕))

12 ◆ BERWICK LODGE
Berwick Drive, Bristol, BS10 7TD.
Sarah Arikan, 0117 958 1590,
info@berwicklodge.co.uk,
www.berwicklodge.co.uk. Leave
M5 at J17. A4018 towards Bristol
West. 2nd exit on r'about, straight
on at mini r'about. At next r'about
by Old Crow pub do 360° turn back
down A4018, follow sign saying
BL off to L. **For NGS: Mon 4 July
(11-4). Adm £5, chd free. Cream
teas. For other opening times and
information, please phone, email or
visit garden website.**
Berwick Lodge, named Bristol's
hidden gem by its customers, is
an independent hotel with beautiful
gardens on the outskirts of Bristol.
Built in 1890, this Victorian Arts &
Crafts property is set within 18 acres,
of which 4 acres are accessible
and offer a peaceful garden for use
by its visitors. The gardens enjoy
pretty views across to Wales, and
continue to evolve. Created by Head
Gardener Robert Dunster, an ex Royal
gardener who worked for Prince
Charles at Highgrove, it features an
elegant water fountain, Victorian
summerhouse, orchard, wildflower
meadow, beehives, pond, wisteria
clad pergola plus a thriving house
martin colony.
  🚹 🛏 ☕))

13 1 BIRCH DRIVE
Alveston, Bristol, BS35 3RQ.
Myra Ginns, 01454 415396,
m.ginns1@btinternet.com. 14m N
of Bristol. Alveston on A38 Bristol
to Gloucester. Just before traffic
lights turn left into David's Lane. At
end, L then R onto Wolfridge Ride.
Birch Drive 2nd on R. **Visits by
arrangement in Feb for groups of
up to 8. Adm £5, chd free.**
A newly planted garden with particular
interest in the spring. A wide range
of bulbs will be in flower, along with
unusual named varieties of anemone,
hellebore, hepatica and crocus. The
main feature of the garden are the
snowdrops, collected since 2008.
Many named varieties, flowering
between November and March, will
interest snowdrop collectors. Ramp
to decked area gives a view of the
garden.
  🚹 ✿

14 NEW BLACKMORE HOUSE
Holton Street, Holton, Wincanton,
BA9 8AN. Mrs Lisa Prior. Just off
the Wincanton junction of the A303.
In the centre of Holton village, 2
doors down from Holton Village Hall,
round the corner from The Old Inn.
Limited street parking. **Sat 12 Feb
(11-3). Light refreshments. Sat
17 Sept (12-4). Home-made teas.
Adm £4, chd free.**
A hidden terraced cottage garden
with dry stone walls and gravel paths,
designed for year-round interest
complementing the Georgian listed
house. Wide borders packed full of
perennials and self-seeded surprises.
2 intensely scented 10ft daphnes,
sarcocca, and a plethora of hellebores
in winter invite you outside while most
gardens sleep. Roses, rudbeckia
and helianthus bring bright colours to
autumn.
  🐕 ☕))

15 BRADON FARM
Isle Abbotts, Taunton, TA3 6RX.
Mr & Mrs Thomas Jones,
deborahjstanley@hotmail.com.
Take turning to Ilton off A358. Bradon
Farm is 1½m out of Ilton on Bradon
Lane. **Visits by arrangement June
to Aug for groups of 10+. Adm £6,
chd free. Home-made teas.**
Classic formal garden demonstrating
the effective use of structure with
parterre, knot garden, pleached
lime walk, formal pond, herbaceous
borders, orchard and wildflower
planting.
  🚹 🚗 ☕

16 BRINDHAM BUNGALOW
Wick Lane, Wick, Glastonbury,
BA6 8JR. Ms Elizabeth Anderson.
Foot of Glastonbury Tor. From A39
Tin Bridge R'about take Wells Rd. 1st
L onto Old Wells Rd. 1st L after West
Mendip Hospital into Brindham Lane.
From A361: Wick Lane for 1.7m.
**Sun 5 June (10.30-4). Adm £4,
chd free. Home-made teas. Open
nearby Milton Lodge.**
Very peaceful garden with stunning
views of the Glastonbury Tor and
surrounding countryside. Flower
borders well-stocked with roses,
ceanothus, buddleja, and flowering
cherries to name but a few. Wild area
with bulbs, hydrangeas and cornus.
  ✿ ☕))

Westbrook House

© Heather Edwards

▮17▮ BROOMCLOSE

off the road to Porlock Weir, Porlock, TA24 8NU. David & Nicky Ramsay, 01643 862078, nickyjramsay@googlemail.com. *Off A39 on Porlock Weir Rd, between Porlock and W Porlock. From Porlock take rd signed to Porlock Weir. Leave houses of Porlock behind & after about 500 yds we are 1st drive on L marked Broomclose. NB Some SatNavs direct wrongly from Porlock - so beware.* **Visits by arrangement Apr to Sept for groups of up to 30. Adm £5, chd free. Teas, coffee and cake, gluten-free available.**

Large, varied garden set around early 1900s Arts & Crafts house overlooking Porlock Vale and the sea. Original stone terraces, Mediterranean garden, pond, extensive borders, copse, camellia walk, large orchard with beehives. Maritime climate favours unusual trees, shrubs and herbaceous plants. We are increasingly looking to plant drought tolerant species. Mixed orchard inc 50 apple varieties - many recently grafted from local heritage collections. Wildlife actively encouraged.

🐾 ☕ 🪑

▮18▮ CAMERS

Badminton Road, Old Sodbury, Bristol, BS37 6RG. Mr & Mrs Michael Denman, 01454 327929, jodenman@btinternet.com, www.camers.org. *2m E of Chipping Sodbury. Entrance in Chapel Lane off A432 at Dog Inn. Enter through the field gate and drive to the top of the fields to park next to the garden.* **Visits by arrangement May to Sept for groups of 20+. Refreshments by arrangement.**

Elizabethan farmhouse (not open) set in 4 acres of constantly developing garden and woodland with spectacular views over Severn Vale. Garden full of surprises, formal and informal areas planted with wide range of species to provide year-round interest. Parterre, topiary, Japanese garden, bog and prairie areas, white and hot gardens, woodland walks. Some steep slopes.

♿ ❀ ☕

▮19▮ 9 CATHERSTON CLOSE

Frome, BA11 4HR. Dave & Prue Moon. *15m S of Bath. Town centre W towards Shepton Mallet (A361). R at Sainsbury's r'about, follow lane for ½m. L into Critchill Rd. Over Xrds, 1st L Catherston Close.* **Sun 12, Thur 16 June, Wed 6 July (12-5). Adm £4, chd free. Opening with Frome Gardens on Sun 19 June.**

The unexpected awaits you around the corner. A small town garden which has grown to ⅓ acre! Colour-themed shrub and herbaceous borders, patio, pergolas, pond and evolving wild meadow areas lead to wonderful far reaching views. Productive redesigned 'no dig' vegetable and fruit garden with greenhouse. Exhibition of photography from near and far, by the garden owner, is displayed in the summerhouse. A re-evaluation of two areas has been done, the pergola has been refurbished and replanted with new clematis as well as a redesign of the raised vegetable beds. This is truly a garden of two passionate gardeners which reflects in what you see here. Their garden is a Gold Winner of Frome-in-Bloom. Several shallow steps, gravel paths.

♿ ❀

20 CHERRY BOLBERRY FARM

Furge Lane, Henstridge, BA8 0RN.
Mrs Jenny Raymond, 01963 362177,
cherrybolberryfarm@tiscali.co.uk.
*6m E of Sherborne. In centre of
Henstridge, R at small Xrds signed
Furge Lane. Continue straight up lane,
over 2 cattle grids, garden at top of
lane on R.* **Visits by arrangement in
June for groups of 5+. Adm £5, chd
free. Home-made teas.**
47 yr-old award winning, owner
designed and maintained, 1 acre
garden planted for year-round
interest with wildlife in mind. Colour
themed island beds, shrub and
herbaceous borders, unusual
perennials and shrubs, old roses and
an area of specimen trees. Lots of
hidden areas, brilliant for hide and
seek! Vegetable and flower cutting
garden, greenhouses, nature ponds.
Wonderful extensive views. Garden
surrounded by our dairy farm which
has been in the family for over 100
years.

21 NEW CHURCH FARM

Stanton Prior, Bath, BA2 9HT. Mr &
Mrs A Hardwick. *6 m W of Bath. W
onto A39 from A4 out of Bath. Turn L
in Marksbury.* **Sun 3 July (2-6). Adm
£5, chd free. Light refreshments.**
1 ½ acre garden. Planted with roses,
clematis, foxgloves, lavenders and
mature trees. Beautiful countryside
views. Medieval pond with toads,
newts, ducks and sometimes a swan.
Garden surrounded by our dairy farm
which is part of the Duchy of Cornwall
Estate. Located next to the village
church.

22 NEW CLAYHILL ARTS

Charlynch Lane, Bridgwater,
TA5 2PH. Mike & Debbie Parkes,
www.clayhillarts.co.uk/gardens/.
*On the A39 from Bridgwater to
Cannington, 1st L at r'about to
Charlynch Lane. Continue up hill past
Little Clayhill Farm (black sign) take the
next L & follow lane down to car park.*
**Sat 25, Sun 26 June (10-4). Adm £5,
chd £1. Light refreshments.**

Reclaimed from an old farm, Clayhill
Arts have developed their surrounding
garden spaces to encourage
wildlife and complement the arable
landscape beyond. With a collection
of farm buildings that have been
repurposed to house a residential arts
training space, their garden spaces
sit across 4 acres and inc wildflower,
grasses, and a lake, as well as ponds,
vegetables and edible planters. As
well as providing refreshments on
site, we have a list of local providers
which we can recommend. Access is
available to most of the main garden
spaces (not all) and there is full
wheelchair access in the buildings as
well as WCs.

23 COLDHARBOUR COTTAGE

Radford Hill, Radford, Radstock,
BA3 2XU. Ms Amanda Cranston,
01761 470600,
amanda.cranston@yahoo.co.uk.
*Between Timsbury and Radstock.
8 m S of Bath. Please ask for
directions when booking.*

42 Silver Street

Visits by arrangement May to Sept for groups of up to 15. Please confirm group numbers 2 weeks prior to visit. Adm £6.50. Tea & coffee with biscuits.
Idyllic rural garden set in peaceful countryside. Sublime mix of thoughtful planting, natural areas reflect historical and modern heritage of this secluded acre. Natural hedges and uninterrupted fields form the backdrop to the gentle calm of the design. Glorious spring flowers give way to peonies, lavender and cutting flower plot. Romantic arches with climbing roses, clematis, box hedges and chamomile lawn. Deep herbaceous borders, hidden natural areas frame the lawns, home to old fruit trees. Productive kitchen garden adds practicality to this quiet, sensitive space. Two summerhouses, plenty of seating areas. Wheelchair access to grassed areas weather dependant. Some narrow and uneven paths.
&. ❋ ☕

24 COLEFORD HOUSE
Underhill, Coleford, Radstock, BA3 5LU. Mr James Alexandroff.
Coleford House is opp Kings Head Pub in Lower Coleford with black wrought iron gates just before bridge over river. Parking in field 400 metres away. **Sun 24 April, Sun 11 Sept (10-4). Adm £5, chd free. Home-made teas.**
The River Mells flows through this picturesque garden with large lawns, wildflower planting, ornamental pond, woodland, substantial herbaceous borders, walled garden, arboretum/orchard, kitchen garden, vegetable garden, bat house and orangery. Some art work will be on sale. Most of garden is wheelchair friendly.

25 81 COOMBE LANE
Stoke Bishop, Bristol, BS9 2AT. Karl Suchy, karl.suchy@icloud.com. *4m from Bristol city centre. J17 of M5, then follow A4018, direction Bristol for approx 2m. Turn R onto Canford Rd A4162. After 0.8m turn L onto Coombe Lane. Destination on R.* **Sun 29 May (12-5). Adm £5, chd free. Home-made teas. Visits also by arrangement Apr to Sept for groups of 10 to 30.**
Hidden Victorian walled garden. You'll encounter substantial mixed borders containing traditional and contemporary planting. Large

lawns, numerous seating areas, summerhouse and French inspired patio with coppiced lime trees. Parterre and large raised Koi pond surrounded by bananas and tree ferns. Access to parterre and Koi pond might be difficult for wheelchair due to narrow gravel path, main part of garden is accessible.
&. ☕ ﹚)

26 COURT HOUSE
East Quantoxhead, TA5 1EJ. Mr & Mrs Hugh Luttrell. *12m W of Bridgwater. Off A39, house at end of village past duck pond. Enter by Frog St (Bridgwater/Kilve side from A39). Car park £1 in aid of church.* **Sun 15 May, Sun 24 July (2-5). Adm £6, chd free. Home-made teas.**
Lovely 5 acre garden, trees, shrubs (many rare and tender), herbaceous and 3 acre woodland garden with spring interest and late summer borders. Traditional kitchen garden (chemical free). Views to sea and Quantocks. Gravel, stone and some mown grass paths.
&. 🐄 ❋ ☕

27 COURT VIEW
Solsbury Lane, Batheaston, Bath, BA1 7HB. Maria & Jeremy Heffer, 07786668278, maria.heffer@btinternet.com, www.thebathgreenhouse.com. *3m E of Bath. In Batheaston High St take turning on L signed Northend, St Catherine. At top of rise L into Solsbury Lane. Court View is 2nd driveway on L. Parking for 5 cars. Public car park in the village.* **Sat 23, Sun 24 July (11-5). Adm £5, chd free. Home-made teas. Visits also by arrangement July to Sept for groups of 10 to 30.**
2 acre south facing gardens with ⅓ acre devoted to cut flowers and foliage. Colourful mix of annuals, biennials and perennials. Spectacular views from terraced lawns, box parterre, small orchard and meadow area. A floral experience for garden lovers, artisan florists, flower arrangers and anyone interested in the revival of beautiful, diverse and locally grown British cut flowers.
🐄 ❋ ☕ ﹚)

28 COX'S HILL HOUSE
Horton, Bristol, BS37 6QT. Charles Harman. *Approx 1m W of A46, 4m N of M4 J18. What3words app - giggle.listen.nicer.* **Sun 17 July (2-5.30). Adm £5, chd free. Tea.**
1 acre garden created by current

owners over past 12 yrs and laid out over 2 levels, each backed by a high stone wall, with panoramic views to south and west. Small vegetable/cutting garden and formal lawn flanked by pleached limes on lower level; upper level has herbaceous, shrub and yellow themed borders and orchard with meadow grass and wildflowers.
🐄 ☕ ﹚)

29 CRETE HILL HOUSE
Cote House Lane, Durdham Down, Bristol, BS9 3UW. John Burgess. *2m N of Bristol city centre, 3m S J16 M5. A4018 Westbury Rd from city centre, L at White Tree r'about, R into Cote Rd, continue into Cote House Lane across the Downs. 2nd house on L. Parking on street.* **Sun 19 June (1-5). Adm £4, chd free. Home-made teas. Open nearby 4 Haytor Park.**
C18 house in hidden corner of Bristol. Mainly SW facing garden, 80'x40', with shaped lawn, heavily planted traditional mixed borders - shrub, rose, clematis and herbaceous. Pergola with climbers, terrace with pond, several seating areas. Shady walled garden. Roof terrace (44 steps) with extensive views. A couple of seating areas not accessible by wheelchair as accessed via stepping stones. Whole garden can be viewed.
&. ☕ ﹚)

30 THE DAIRY, CHURCH LANE
Clevedon Road, Weston-in-Gordano, Bristol, BS20 8PZ. Mrs Chris Lewis, 01275 849214, chris@dairy.me.uk. *Weston-in-Gordano is on B3124 Portishead to Clevedon rd. Find Parish Church on main rd and take lane down side of churchyard for 200m. Access by coach involves a walk of 400m.* **Visits by arrangement May to Sept for groups of 10 to 30. Larger groups possible if refreshments not required. Adm £6, chd free. Home-made teas.**
The garden surrounds a barn conversion and has been developed from concrete milking yards and derelict land. Once the site of Weston in Gordano Manor House, the ambience owes much to the use of medieval stone which had lain undiscovered in the land for over 2 centuries.

31 THE DOWNS PREPARATORY SCHOOL
Charlton Drive, Wraxall, Bristol, BS48 1PF. The Downs Preparatory School, thedownsschool.co.uk. *4.3m from J19 of the M5 or 8.3m from the centre of Bristol. Follow signs for Noahs Ark Zoo Farm from motorway or centre of Bristol.* **Fri 8, Sat 9 Apr, Fri 5, Sat 6 Aug (10-4). Adm £6, chd free. Home-made teas.**
65 acres wrap around the Grade II listed Charlton House, once part of a wider estate inc the well known Tyntesfield NT property. Historic garden features inc stumpery, pond and greenhouse. In addition there is an edible and medicinal bed and well presented annual bedding displays framed by beautiful views across open parkland with specimen trees dotted around the estate. Gravel paths and some steps. Majority of garden is wheelchair accessible.
🐕 🚜 🍵 🎐))

32 DOYNTON HOUSE
Bury Lane, Doynton, Bristol, BS30 5SR. Frances & Matthew Lindsey-Clark, Franceslc11@gmail.com. *5m S of M4 J18, 6m N of Bath, 8m E of Bristol. Doynton is NE of Wick (turn off A420 opp Bath Rd) and SW of Dyrham (signed from A46). Doynton House is at S end of Doynton village, opp Culleysgate/Horsepool Lane. Park in signed field.* **Visits by arrangement Apr to Oct for groups of up to 30. Adm £7.50, chd free.**
A variety of garden areas separated by old walls and hedges. Mixed borders, lawns, wall planting, parterre, rill garden, walled vegetable garden, cottage beds, pool garden, dry gardens, peach house and greenhouse. Bees, chickens and meadow area. We can recommend our local pub, the Cross House, just a short stroll across our parking field. Paths are of hoggin, stone and gravel. The grade of the gravel makes it a hard push in places but all areas are wheelchair accessible.
🐕 🌸))

33 NEW DUNKERY VIEW
Brandish Street, Allerford, Minehead, TA24 8HR. Mr M Harris. *4m from Minehead. Off A39 between Minehead & Porlock.* **Sun 26 June, Sun 11 Sept (10-6). Adm £4, chd free.**
½ acre plantsman's garden packed with unusual shrubs, grasses and

perennials laid out in the cottage garden style. Repeat flowering roses, salvias, dahlias and other late season herbaceous plants produce a riot of colour in mid to late summer. A productive vegetable garden adds to the bounty.
🐕 🌸

34 EAST END FARM
Pitney, Langport, TA10 9AL. Mrs A M Wray, 01458 250598. *2m E of Langport. Please telephone for directions.* **Visits by arrangement in June. Refreshments by prior arrangement. Adm £5, chd free.**
Approx ⅓ acre. Timeless small garden of many old-fashioned roses in beautiful herbaceous borders set amongst ancient listed farm buildings. Mostly wheelchair access - some narrow paths.
♿ 🌸 🚜 🍵 🎐

35 ◆ EAST LAMBROOK MANOR GARDENS
Silver Street, East Lambrook, TA13 5HH. Mike & Gail Werkmeister, 01460 240328, enquiries@eastlambrook.com, www.eastlambrook.com. *2m N of South Petherton. Follow brown tourist signs from A303 South Petherton r'about or B3165 Xrds with lights N of Martock.* **For NGS: Thur 10 Feb, Sat 7 May, Sat 9 July (10-5). Adm £6.50, chd free. Tea and cake. For other opening times and information, please phone, email or visit garden website.**
The quintessential English cottage garden created by C20 gardening legend Margery Fish. Plantsman's paradise with contemporary and old-fashioned plants grown in a relaxed and informal manner to create a remarkable garden of great beauty and charm. With noted collections of snowdrops, hellebores and geraniums and the excellent specialist Margery Fish Plant Nursery. Partial wheelchair access.
🐕 🌸 🚜 🎐

36 ◆ ELWORTHY COTTAGE
Elworthy, Taunton, TA4 3PX. Mike & Jenny Spiller, 01984 656427, mike@elworthy-cottage.co.uk, www.elworthy-cottage.co.uk. *12m NW of Taunton. On B3188 between Wiveliscombe & Watchet.* **For NGS: Fri 4, Sun 27 Feb, Tue 12, Mon 18 Apr, Tue 17, Sun 29, Tue 31 May, Tue 5, Sun 24, Tue 26 July, Mon 29 Aug (11-4). Adm £4.50, chd free. Home-made teas. For other**

opening times and information, please phone, email or visit garden website.
1 acre plantsman's garden in tranquil setting. Island beds, scented plants, clematis, unusual perennials and ornamental trees and shrubs to provide year-round interest. In spring, pulmonarias, hellebores and more than 350 varieties of snowdrops. Planted to encourage birds, bees and butterflies. Lots of birdsong, wildflower areas and developing wildflower meadow, decorative vegetable garden, living willow screen. Seats for visitors to enjoy views of the surrounding countryside. Garden attached to plantsman's nursery, open at the same time.
🐕 🌸 🚜 🎐 🪑

37 FAIRFIELD
Stogursey, Bridgwater, TA5 1PU. Lady Acland Hood Gass. *7m E of Williton. 11m W of Bridgwater. From A39 Bridgwater to Minehead road turn N. Garden 1½ m W of Stogursey on Stringston road.* **Sun 10 Apr (2-5). Adm £5, chd free. Home-made teas.**
Woodland garden with many interesting bulbs inc naturalised anemones, fritillaria with roses, shrubs and fine trees. Paved maze. Views of Quantocks. The ground is flat and should be accessible, around half the paths are grass so may be more difficult when wet.
♿ 🎐

38 FOREST LODGE
Pen Selwood, BA9 8LL. James & Lucy Nelson, 07974 701427, lucillanelson@gmail.com. *1½ m N of A303, 3m E of Wincanton. Leave A303 at B3081 (Wincanton to Gillingham rd), up hill to Pen Selwood, L towards church. ½ m, garden on L - low curved wall and sign saying Forest Lodge Stud.* **Sat 21 May, Sat 25 June (10.30-4.30). Adm £7, chd free. Home-made teas. Visits also by arrangement Jan to Sept for groups of 10 to 30. Donation to Heads Up Wells, Balsam Centre Wincanton.**
3 acre mature garden with many camellias and rhododendrons in May. Lovely views towards Blackmore Vale. Part formal with pleached hornbeam allée and rill, part water garden with lake. Wonderful roses in June. Unusual spring flowering trees such as *Davidia involucrata*, many beautiful cornus. Interesting garden sculpture. Wheelchair access to front

Babbs Farm

© Heather Edwards

garden only, however much of garden viewable from there.

GROUP OPENING

39 FROME GARDENS

Frome, BA11 4HR. *9 Catherston Cl signed at r'about A361 W of town, 1 Tucker Cl off A361 E of town onto Wallbridge, R before railway bridge signed. Please park considerately on nearby roads.* **Sun 19 June (12-5). Combined adm £7.50, chd free. Tea at 71 Lynfield Road. Please note 84 Weymouth Rd is open from 1-4pm.**

9 CATHERSTON CLOSE
Dave & Prue Moon.
(See separate entry)

NEW 71 LYNFIELD ROAD
Mr Robert & Mrs Christina Rusbridger.

NEW 61 NUNNEY ROAD
Mrs Caroline Toll.

NEW 1 TUCKER CLOSE
Bev Revie & Tim Cutting.

84 WEYMOUTH ROAD
Amanda Relph.

A warm welcome awaits at 5 differing town gardens. 9 Catherston Close will bowl you over (see separate entry). 61 Nunney Road's new owner has redesigned the garden with a terrace, lawn, shrubs, flowerbeds, old fruit trees, 2 small ponds, wild corner, vegetable patch and greenhouse. From there you can walk to 71 Lynfield Road. The front garden has 'hot' colour, lush planting inc Chusan Palm. Their back garden is restful with seating areas, formal pond and patio. Colourful mixed borders, trees and wildflower area to attract birds and insects. 84 Weymouth Road, designed by Simon Relph in 2015 to celebrate his life. Architectural arches and geometrical raised beds surround a central raised pond. Mature shrubs enhance the walled garden; fern area, roses and camellias add to central courtyard. 1 Tucker Close, a small walled garden with wide beds, exuberant planting with wildlife in mind and small cauldron pond. Although 3 yrs old, it looks mature and abundant with herbaceous borders, fruit trees, decking, pond and slate rather than grass. Catherston Close: few gravel paths, slopes, shallow steps. 71 Lynfield Rd: gravel, steps in back garden; Tucker Close steps, uneven surface.

40 NEW GLEBE FARM
Cheddon Fitzpaine, Taunton, TA2 8JU. Mrs Rhona Ashton. *Glebe Farm is situated at the top of the village street in Cheddon Fitzpaine.* **Sun 8 May (2-5.30). Adm £6, chd free. Cream teas/ cakes inc gluten free.**

Glebe Farm gardens have been recently landscaped over a 2 yr period with work still in progress. The house garden is a typical English walled garden, with a path leading to a vine covered arch opening up to reveal a swimming pool with a Mediterranean themed planting of olive trees and grasses. The outer garden represents different themes - Japanese, Italian, English and nursery beds.

'The National Garden Scheme donated £500,000 to Hospice UK in 2021, enabling us to continue supporting over 200 hospices in the UK who have been at the forefront of the battle against COVID-19.'
Hospice UK

The Yeo Valley Organic at Holt Farm

GROUP OPENING

41 GOATHURST GARDENS
Goathurst, Bridgwater, TA5 2DF.
*4m SW of Bridgwater, 2½ m W of N
Petherton. Close to church in village.
Park in field at N end of village
(signed) 500 yds from gardens.
Disabled parking (3 spaces) available
at The Lodge car port.* **Sat 23, Sun
24 July (2-5). Combined adm £5,
chd free. Home-made teas at The
Lodge.**

THE LODGE
Sharon & Richard Piron.

OLD ORCHARD
Mr Peter Evered.

Only 50 metres apart, 2 beautiful
examples of quintessentially English
cottage gardens in a rural village
setting. Old Orchard: ¼ acre garden
planted with specialist and rare plants
to complement the cottage. Over
100 *Clematis viticella* interplanted
with a range of shrubs, herbaceous
perennials, annuals and summer
bulbs. The Lodge: ¾ acre garden
surrounding a thatched cottage
comprising flower borders packed
with shrubs and perennials. Fruit and
vegetable beds are also a feature.
Both gardens have wheelchair access
to most areas.
&♿

42 ◆ GREENCOMBE GARDENS
Porlock, Minehead,
TA24 8NU. Greencombe
Garden Trust, 01643 862363,
info@greencombe.org,
www.greencombe.org. *W of
Porlock below the wooded slopes
of Exmoor. Take A39 to west end
of Porlock and turn onto B3225
to Porlock Weir. Drive ½ m, turn
L at Greencombe Gardens sign.
Go up drive; parking signed.* **For
NGS: Wed 20 Apr, Wed 20 July
(2-6). Adm £7, chd £1. Cream
teas. For other opening times and
information, please phone, email or
visit garden website. Donation to**
Plant Heritage.
Organic woodland garden of
international renown, Greencombe
stretches along a sheltered hillside
and offers outstanding views over
Porlock Bay. Moss-covered paths
meander through a collection of
ornamental plants that flourish
beneath a canopy of oaks, hollies,
conifers and chestnuts. Camellias,
rhododendrons, azaleas, lilies,
roses, clematis, and hydrangeas
blossom among 4 National
Collections. Champion English
Holly tree (*Ilex aquifolium*), one of
the largest and oldest in the UK.
Giant rhododendrons species
and exceptionally large camellias.
A millennium chapel hides in the
mossy banks of the wood. A moon
arch leads into a walled garden.
Spectacular views onto Porlock Bay.
NPC 🍵

43 GREYSTONES
Hollybush Lane, Bristol, BS9 1JB.
Mrs P Townsend. *2m N of Bristol
city centre, close to Durdham Down
in Bristol, backing onto the Botanic*

Garden. A4018 Westbury Rd, L at White Tree r'about, L into Saville Rd, Hollybush Lane 2nd on R. Narrow lane, parking limited, recommended to park in Saville Rd. **Sun 13 Feb, Sun 10 Apr (11-4). Adm £4, chd free. Light refreshments.** Peaceful garden with places to sit and enjoy a quiet corner of Bristol. Interesting courtyard, raised beds, large variety of conifers and shrubs leads to secluded garden of contrasts - sun drenched beds with olive tree and brightly coloured flowers to shady spots, with acers, hostas and ferns. Snowdrops, hellebores and spring bulbs. Rambling roses, small orchard, espaliered pears. Paved footpath provides level access to all areas.

44 HANGERIDGE FARMHOUSE
Wrangway, Wellington, TA21 9QG. Mrs J M Chave, 07812 648876, hangeridge@hotmail.co.uk. *2m S of Wellington. Off A38 Wellington bypass signed Wrangway. 1st L towards Wellington monument, over motorway bridge 1st R.* **Sun 17 July (1-5). Adm £4, chd free. Home-made teas. Visits also by arrangement July & Aug for groups of 10 to 30.** Rural fields and mature trees surround this 1 acre informal garden offering views of the Blackdown and Quantock Hills. Magnificent hostas and heathers, colourful flower beds, cascading wisteria and roses and a trickling stream. Relax with home-made refreshments on sunny or shaded seating admiring the views and birdsong.

45 THE HAYES
Newton St. Loe, Bath, BA2 9BU. Jane Giddins, 01225 873592, jeturner@btinternet.com. *From the Globe Pub on A4 take Pennyquick which is signed to Odd Down. Take 1st turning R which is just after the bend. At top of hill turn R then L.* **Sat 11, Sun 12 June, Sat 10, Sun 11 Sept (2-5). Adm £6, chd free. Home-made teas. Visits also by arrangement May to Sept for groups of 20+.** Stunning in all seasons. 1 acre garden on edge of Duchy of Cornwall village. Herbaceous borders and formal lawns and terraces; informal garden of trees and long grass, bulbs and meadow flowers; formal potager and greenhouse; small orchard with espalier apple trees. Tulips, wisteria,

alliums, foxgloves, gladioli, dahlias, asters. Wonderful views. All of garden can be accessed in a wheelchair but some grassy inclines.

46 4 HAYTOR PARK
Bristol, BS9 2LR. Mr & Mrs C J Prior, 07779 203626, p.l.prior@gmail.com. *3m NW of Bristol city centre. From A4162 Inner Ring Rd take turning into Coombe Bridge Ave, Haytor Park is 1st on L. Please no parking in Haytor Park.* **Sun 15 May (1.30-5), Sun 19 June (1.30-5).Adm £3.50, chd free. Open nearby Lucombe House (May) & Crete Hill House (Jun). Visits also by arrangement May to Aug for groups of 10 to 30.** A journey of discovery, under many arches, around a lovingly tended plot, full of year-round interest at every turn. Paths, a pond, spaces to sit and quirky features, a bicycle wheel screen, rusty bed trellis so many plants to find and dragons for children to discover and maybe a prize to win.

47 ♦ HESTERCOMBE GARDENS
Cheddon Fitzpaine, Taunton, TA2 8LG. Hestercombe Gardens Trust, 01823 413923, info@hestercombe.com, www.hestercombe.com. *3m N of Taunton, less than 6m from J25 of M5. Follow brown daisy signs. SatNav postcode TA2 8LQ.* **For NGS: Tue 1 Mar (10-3.30); Tue 7 June (10-4.30). Adm £13.75, chd £6.90. Discount/prepaid vouchers not valid on NGS charity days. For other opening times and information, please phone, email or visit garden website.** Magnificent Georgian landscape garden designed by artist Coplestone Warre Bampfylde, a contemporary of Gainsborough and Henry Hoare of Stourhead. Victorian terrace and shrubbery and an exquisite example of a Lutyens/Jeykll designed formal garden; C17 water garden opening 2022. Enjoy 50 acres of woodland walks, temples, terraces, pergolas, lakes and cascades. Restaurant and café, restored watermill and barn, contemporary art gallery. Four centuries of garden design. Gravel paths, steep slopes, steps. An all-access route is shown on the guide map, & visitors can phone to pre-book an all-terrain 'tramper' vehicle.

48 HILLCREST
Curload, Stoke St Gregory, Taunton, TA3 6JA. Charles & Charlotte Sundquist, 01823 490852, chazfix@gmail.com. *At top of Curload. From A358 turn L along A378, then branch L to North Curry & Stoke St Gregory. L ½m after Willows & Wetlands centre. Hillcrest is 1st on R with parking directions.* **Sat 7, Sun 8 May (1-5). Adm £5, chd free. Home-made teas. Visits also by arrangement Apr to Sept for groups of 5 to 30. A guided tour is included in all visits if required.** Boasting stunning views of the Somerset Levels, Burrow Mump and Glastonbury Tor this 6 acre garden offers plenty of interest, inc a standing stone. Enjoy woodland walks, varied borders, flowering meadow and several ponds. There are greenhouses, orchards, a new produce garden and newly built large gravel garden. Garden is mostly level with gentle sloping paths down through meadow.

49 NEW HILLSIDE
35 Westbury Hill, Westbury-on-Trym, Bristol, BS9 3AG. Stephanie Pritchett, hillsideoldstables@gmail.com, www.hillsideoldstables.com/ourgardens. *3 m from Junction 17 M5 or Bristol City Centre. We are next door (downhill) from the Post Office Tavern pub on Westbury Hill. Access via the smaller green garden gate with number 35 sign, not via the larger gates uphill.* **Sat 18, Sun 19 June (11-4). Adm £5, chd free. Home-made teas.** A hidden Grade II listed period gem dating to 1715 with large and established formal walled gardens and family gardens in ½ acre. There are many different areas to explore – magnificent trees c. 500 years old, pond and kitchen herb garden, rockery, rose and cutting gardens, orchard and seasonal interest borders, wildflower meadow and established kitchen garden and fruit bushes.

Our 2021 donations mean that 12,478 unpaid carers have been supported through funding for Carers Trust

50 HOLLAND FARM
South Brewham, Bruton,
BA10 0JZ. Mrs Nickie Gething. *3m
N of Wincanton. From Wincanton:
B3081for 3m toward Bruton. R to S
Brewham. Follow NGS signs. From
Mere: B3092 toward Frome. Under
A303, past Stourhead Hse. L to
Alfred's Tower/Kilmington. Follow
NGS signs.* **Sun 29 May, Thur
7 July (2-5). Adm £8, chd free.
Home-made teas in the Garden
Room.**
The house and garden were created
from a derelict farmyard 15 yrs ago.
Garden now boasts a number of
exquisite rooms, divided by hornbeam
and yew hedging. Some rooms are
tranquil, with a simple water feature
or trees, others burst with a variety
of planting. House frames a stunning
French-style courtyard where the
sound of water echoes. Hornbeam
avenue leads the visitor to a
swimming lake with lakeside planting.
🐄 ✿ D ☕

51 HONEYHURST FARM
Honeyhurst Lane, Rodney Stoke,
Cheddar, BS27 3UJ. Don &
Kathy Longhurst, 01749 870322,
donlonghurst@btinternet.com,
www.ciderbarrelcottage.co.uk. *4m
E of Cheddar. From Wells (A371) turn
into Rodney Stoke signed Wedmore.
Pass church on L and continue
for almost 1m. Car park signed.
From Cheddar (A371) turn R signed
Wedmore, through Draycott to car
park.* **Sun 3, Mon 4 July (2-5). Adm
£4, chd free. Home-made teas.
Visits also by arrangement Apr to
Sept for groups of 10 to 40.**
²⁄₃ acre part walled rural garden with
babbling brook and 4 acre traditional
cider orchard, with views. Specimen
hollies, copper beech, paulownia,
yew and poplar. Pergolas, arbour
and numerous seats. Mixed informal
shrub and perennial beds with many
unusual plants. Many pots planted
with shrubs, hardy and half-hardy
perennials. Level, grass and some
shingle.
🚻 🐄 ✿ 🚗 🛏 ☕

52 JAPANESE GARDEN
BRISTOL
13 Glenarm Walk, Brislington,
Bristol, BS4 4LS. Martin Fitton,
fitton13@outlook.com. *A4 Bristol
to Bath. A4 Brislington, at Texaco
Garage at bottom of Bristol Hill turn
into School Rd and immed R into
Church Parade. Car park 1st turn on
R or proceed to Glenarm Walk.* **Sat
30 July (10-5); Sun 31 July (10-4).
Adm £4, chd free. Pre-booking
essential, please visit www.ngs.
org.uk for information & booking.
Home-made teas. Visits also
by arrangement Apr to Sept for
groups of 10 to 20. Adm £8 inc
home-made teas.**
As you walk through the gate you
will be welcomed by Japanese Koi.
Then take a step to another level to
the relaxing Japanese garden rooms
surrounded by acers and cloud trees.
Walk through the Wisdom of Zen area
where you can embrace the true sound
of Japan. Continue to a Japanese
courtyard then a gate to a peaceful Zen
rock garden. There you will find seating
to enjoy the serene atmosphere.
☕))

53 JOHN'S CORNER
2 Fitzgerald Road, Bedminster,
Bristol, BS3 5DD. John Hodge.
*3m from city centre. S of Bristol, off
St.John's Lane, Totterdown end.
1st house on R, entrance at side of
house. On number 91 bus route.
Parking in residential street.* **Sat 25,
Sun 26, Mon 27 June (1-5). Adm
£4, chd free. Home-made teas.**
Unusual and interesting city garden in
Bedminster with a mixture of exciting
plants and features. Ponds, ferns
and much more. Eden project style
greenhouse with collection of cacti.
Not all areas accessible by wheelchair.
♿ 🐄 ☕

54 LITTLE YARFORD
FARMHOUSE
Kingston St Mary, Taunton,
TA2 8AN. Brian Bradley,
01823 451350,
dilly.bradley@gmail.com. *1½ m
W of Hestercombe, 3½ m N of
Taunton. From Taunton on Kingston
St Mary rd. At 30mph sign turn
L at Parsonage Lane. Continue
1¼ m W, to Yarford sign. Continue
400yds. Turn R up concrete rd.*
**Visits by arrangement Apr to Sept.
Admission inc an informative
guided tour of trees and garden.
Adm £10, chd free. Cream teas/
light refreshments by prior**

arrangement.
Unusual 5 acre garden embracing
C17 house (not open) Natural pond
and 90ft waterlily pond. A plantsman's
garden notable for the aesthetics of
its planting especially its 300+ rare
and unusual tree cultivars: the best
collection of broad leaf and conifer
specimens in Somerset West (listed on
NGS website); those trees not available
to Bampfylde Warre at Hestercombe
in C18. An exercise in landscaping,
contrast planting and creating views
both within the garden and without to
the vale and the Quantock Hills. Mostly
wheelchair access.
♿ 🐄 ✿ 🚗 ☕ 🛏

55 LOWER SHALFORD FARM
Shalford Lane, Charlton Musgrove,
Wincanton, BA9 8HE. Mr & Mrs
David Posnett. *Lower Shalford is
2m NE of Wincanton. Leave A303 at
Wincanton go N on B3081 towards
Bruton. Just beyond Otter Garden
Centre turn R Shalford Lane, garden
is ½ m on L. Parking opp house.*
**Sat 19 Mar (10-3); Sat 21 May
(10-4). Adm £5, chd free. Light
refreshments.**
Fairly large open garden with
extensive lawns and wooded
surroundings with drifts of daffodils
in spring. Small winterbourne stream
running through with several stone
bridges. Walled rose/parterre garden,
hedged herbaceous garden and
several ornamental ponds.
☕

56 LUCOMBE HOUSE
12 Druid Stoke Ave, Stoke Bishop,
Bristol, BS9 1DD. Malcolm
Ravenscroft, 01179 682494,
famrave@gmail.com. *4m NW of
Bristol centre. At top of Druid Hill.
Garden on R 200m from junction.*
**Sun 15 May (1-5). Adm £3.50, chd
free. Home-made teas. Open
nearby 4 Haytor Park. Visits also
by arrangement Apr to Sept.**
For tree lovers of all ages! In addition
to the 255 yr old Lucombe Oak
- registered as one of the most
significant trees in the UK - there are
over 30 mature English trees planted
together with ferns and bluebells to
create an urban woodland - plus a
newly designed Arts & Crafts front
garden. A new path through the
woodland will be completed in time
for the NGS opening. Flautist trio will
be present throughout the afternoon.
Rough paths in woodland area, 2
steps to patio.
♿ ✿ ☕

GROUP OPENING

57 LYMPSHAM GARDENS
Church Road, Lympsham, Weston-super-Mare, BS24 0DT. *5m S of Weston-super-Mare and 5m N of Burnham on Sea. 2m M5 J22. Entrance to all gardens initially from main gates of Manor at junction of Church Rd and Lympsham Rd. Will then receive directions to other gardens.* **Sat 18, Sun 19 June (2-5). Combined adm £6, chd free. Cream teas at Lympsham Manor.**

CHURCH FARM
Andy & Rosemary Carr.

HAWTHORNS
Mrs Victoria Daintree.

LYMPSHAM MANOR
James & Lisa Counsell.

SOMERDOWN FARM
Claire & Martin Sleight.

At the heart of the stunning village of Lympsham next to C15 church are the gardens of 3 of the village's most historic homes. Lympsham Manor, a 200 yr old gothic rectory manor house with 2 octagonal towers, is set in 10 acres of formal/semi-formal garden, surrounded by paddocks and farmland. Fully working Victorian kitchen garden and greenhouse, arboretum of trees from all parts of the world, a large pond and beautiful old rose garden. Church Farm has a ¾ acre informal English country garden with herbaceous borders, shrub-lined paths, raised beds and a small courtyard garden. Somerdown Farm is a Gothic Victorian village house with a meandering garden encircling the house, a long rockery border, curving herbaceous borders with an interesting variety of shrubs, gravelled gardens, rose arches and very unusual swagged roses along the driveway. Hawthorns, a short drive to the hamlet of Eastertown, is an informal cottage garden with colourful borders and an extensive vegetable garden.

&. 🐕 ✿ ☕ »)

58 ◆ MILTON LODGE
Old Bristol Road, Wells, BA5 3AQ. Simon Tudway Quilter, 01749 679341, www.miltonlodgegardens.co.uk. *½m N of Wells. From A39 Bristol-Wells, turn N up Old Bristol Rd; car park 1st gate on L signed.* **For NGS: Sun 8 May, Sun 5 June, Sun 3 July (2-5). Adm £5, chd free. Home-made teas. Discount/prepaid vouchers are not valid on the NGS charity days. For other opening times and information, please phone or visit garden website.**
Architectural terraces transformed from sloping land with profusion of plants capitalising on views of Wells Cathedral and Vale of Avalon. Grade II terraced garden was restored to its former glory by current owner's parents who moved here in 1960, orchard replaced with a collection of ornamental trees. Herbaceous borders and blooming roses, inc Gertrude Jekyll, flourish next to well tended lawns. A serene, relaxing atmosphere within the garden following the ravages of two World Wars. Cross over Old Bristol Rd to our 7 acre woodland garden, The Combe, which is a natural peaceful contrast to the formal garden of Milton Lodge.
✿ ☕

Court View

Lower Shalford Farm

59 MODEL FARM
Perry Green, Wembdon,
Bridgwater, TA5 2BA. **Dave &
Roz Young, 01278 429953,
daveandrozontour@hotmail.com,
www.modelfarm.com.** *4m from
J23 of M5. Follow Brown signs from
r'about on A39 2m W of Bridgwater.*
**Sun 5 June (2-4.30). Adm £5, chd
free. Tea, coffee, squash and
home-made cakes.**
4 acres of flat gardens to S of
Victorian country house. Created
from a field in last 12 yrs and still
being developed. A dozen large
mixed flower beds planted in cottage
garden style with wildlife in mind.
Wooded areas, mixed orchard, lawns,
wildflower meadows and wildlife
pond. Plenty of seating throughout
the gardens with various garden
sculptures by Somerset artists. Lawn
games inc croquet.

60 NEW MUDGLEY FARM
Mudgley, Wedmore, BS28 4TX.
Mr Peter & Mrs Dorothy Wright.
*Take B3151 S out of Wedmore. After
1m at Mudgley Cross take next L,
unnamed lane. Mudgley Farm is
150 yds on R. From Westhay take
B3151 N. Ignore first R to Mudgley,
take second R, unnamed lane.* **Sat
18 June (2-7). Adm £7, chd free.
Wine.**
12 south facing acres with
spectacular views across Glastonbury
Tor and the Polden Hills. The formal
garden has a fine collection of roses,

many rescued from the former Time
Trail of Roses in Wells, topiary and
lavender. Beyond there is wildflower
meadow, pasture, apple, pear and
walnut trees - and the vineyard, with
1,250 vines producing Mowbarton
Estate sparkling wine, available to buy
on site.

☕))

61 165 NEWBRIDGE HILL
Bath, BA1 3PX. **Helen Hughesdon.**
*On the western fringes of Bath
(A431), 100m on L after Apsley Rd.
Several bus routes go to Newbridge
Hill.* **Sat 2, Sun 3 July, Sat 3, Sun
4 Sept (10-5). Adm £5, chd free.
Home-made teas.**
South facing garden with unusual
and exotic plants, vegetable garden,
greenhouse, treehouse, with a sunny
terrace overlooking the garden where
light lunches and home-made cakes
are served. July openings incorporate
'Sculpture to Enhance a Garden' and
in September visitors can enjoy 'In
Celebration of the Arts - All Things
Floral', an exhibition of floral art and
craft.

✳ ☕))

62 NEW ◆ THE NEWT IN SOMERSET
Hadspen, Bruton,
BA7 7NG. **01963 577750,
enquiries@thenewtinsomerset.
com, thenewtinsomerset.com/
garden.** *Located on the A359
between Bruton & Castle Cary,*

*follow the brown tourist signs to the
estate entrance. Upon entry, follow
the 'Gardens' sign for the visitor
car park.* **For opening times and
information, please phone, email or
visit garden website.**
Influenced by thousands of years
of horticultural history and mixing
ornamental and productive elements,
the gardens are a feast for the eyes
and the stomach. At their core sits the
Parabola, a walled garden concealing
an apple tree maze; and at the
edges, diverse woodland provides a
sheltered habitat for native wildlife.

63 NYNEHEAD COURT
Nynehead, Wellington, TA21 0BN.
**Nynehead Care Ltd, 01823 662481,
nyneheadcare@aol.com,
www.nyneheadcare@aol.com.**
*1½ m N of Wellington. M5 J26
B3187 towards Wellington. R on
r'about marked Nynehead & Poole,
follow lane for 1m, take Milverton
turning at fork, turning into Chipley
Rd.* **Sun 26 June, Sun 10 July
(2-5). Adm £5, chd free. Light
refreshments in Orangery.**
Nynehead Court was the home of
the Sandford family from 1590-1902.
The 14 acres of gardens are noted for
specimen trees, and there will be a
garden tour with the Head Gardener
at 2pm. As Nynehead is a private
residential care home, please contact
us before visiting for the latest Covid
precautions. Visitors will need to
wear a face mask and possibly have

temperature taken on arrival. Partial wheelchair access: cobbled yards, gentle slopes, chipped paths, liable to puddle during or after rain. Please wear suitable footwear.

  ☕ 🍵

64 NEW THE OLD DAIRY HOUSE
Compton Durville, South Petherton, TA13 5ET. Mrs Anne Kaile. *Take the Compton Hill road out of S Petherton for approx 1m & turn R into Compton Durville. Continue on road & Old Dairy House is on LH bend on the corner. Entrance down gravel track, 1st on L.* **Sun 4 Sept (2-5). Adm £5, chd free. Home-made teas.**
Main area of the garden is the Arena Garden planted in the prairie style with grasses and autumn flowering herbaceous planting with open countryside beyond. Vegetables, a newly created wildlife pond, a crab apple tree circle, with more formal planting nearer to the house.

🍵

65 NEW ◆ OLD DOWN MANOR GARDENS
Foxholes Lane, Tockington, Bristol, BS32 4PG. Old Down Estate, 03447 769380, Info@olddownestate.co.uk. *Between Olveston and Tockington in S. Glos. Old Down Estate is approx 5 mins from M4 & M5 Almondsbury interchange & 5 mins from Severn Bridge at Aust. 10m N of Bristol.* **For NGS: Wed 15 June, Wed 31 Aug (10-4). Adm £5, chd free. Light refreshments. Tea and cake in the Manor House. For other opening times and information, please phone or email.**
Old Down Manor is a wonderful example of Victorian architecture. A Victorian walled garden contains the kitchen and cut flower gardens, also sumptuous herbaceous borders. Surrounding the manor are a formal rose garden with many old English roses framed by yew hedges, rolling lawns and newly restructured rockery gardens with views across the Severn Valley. Tempting pathways lead through woodland or meadows to a tranquil lake. Walled garden has wheelchair access, the rockery has partial wheelchair access due to some steep paths and steps.

  🐕 ☕ 🚗 🍵 🅿 »))

66 PARK COTTAGE
Wrington Hill, Wrington, Bristol, BS40 5PL. Mr & Mrs J Shepherd. *Halfway between Bristol & Weston S Mare. 10m S of Bristol on A370 at Cleeve turn L onto Cleeve Hill Rd (opp sports field). Continue on Cleeve Hill Rd for 1½ miles. Car park in paddock on R 50m from garden on L.* **Sun 24, Sun 31 July (12-5). Adm £6, chd free.**
Take a colourful journey through 1¼ acres of this 'Alice in Wonderland' garden. Divided by high hedges is an established perennial flower garden developed over 30 yrs. Explore the labyrinth of different areas inc potager, jungle garden, rainbow border, white garden, green gallery, and 90 ft of double herbaceous borders. Large Victorian-style greenhouse displays tender plants. Countryside views and plenty of seating. No WC available. Mostly good wheelchair access, some narrow bark chip paths. Narrow flagstone bridge with steps.

  🐕 ☕ 🍵 🧺 »))

67 PENNY BROHN UK
Chapel Pill Lane, Pill, BS20 0HH. Penny Brohn UK, 01275 370073, fundraising@pennybrohn.org.uk, www.pennybrohn.org.uk. *4m W of Bristol. Off A369 Clifton Suspension Bridge to M5 (J19 Gordano Services). Follow signs to Penny Brohn UK and to Pill/Ham Green (5 mins).* **Sun 26 June (10-4). Adm £4, chd free. Light refreshments. Hot and cold drinks and cakes are available. Visits also by arrangement in June.**
3½ acre tranquil garden surrounds Georgian mansion with many mature trees, wildflower meadow, flower garden and cedar summerhouse. Fine views from historic gazebo overlooking the River Avon. Courtyard gardens with water features. Garden is maintained by volunteers and plays an active role in the Charity's 'Living Well with Cancer' approach. Plants, teas, music and plenty of space to enjoy a picnic. Gift shop. Tours of centre to find out more about the work of Penny Brohn UK. Some gravel and grass paths.

  🐕 ☕ 🚗 🍵 🧺 »))

68 THE RED POST HOUSE
Fivehead, Taunton, TA3 6PX. The Rev Mervyn & Mrs Margaret Wilson. *10m E of Taunton. On the corner of A378 and Butcher's Hill, opp garage. From M5 J25, take A358 towards Langport, turn L at*

T-lights at top of hill onto A378. Garden is at Langport end of Fivehead. **Sun 25 Sept (2-5). Adm £5, chd free. Home-made teas.**
⅓ acre walled garden with shrubs, borders, trees, circular potager, topiary. We combine beauty and utility. Further 1½ acres, lawn, orchard and vineyard. Plums, 40 apple and 20 pear, walnut, quince, medlar, mulberry, fig. Mown paths, longer grass. Views aligned on Ham Hill. Summerhouse with sedum roof, belvedere. Garden in its present form has been developed over last 15 yrs. Paths are gravel and grass, belvedere is not wheelchair accessible. Dogs on leads.

  🐕 ☕ 🍵

69 THE RIB
St. Andrews Street, Wells, BA5 2UR. Paul Dickinson & David Morgan-Hewitt. *Wells City Centre, adjacent to east end of Wells Cathedral and opp Vicars Close. There is absolutely no parking at or very near this city garden. Visitors should use one of the 5 public car parks and enjoy the 10-15 minutes stroll through the city to The Rib.* **Sat 2 July (10-5). Adm £5, chd free.**
The Rib is one of the few houses in England that can boast a cathedral and a sacred well in its garden. Whilst the garden is compact, it delivers a unique architectural and historical punch. Long established trees, interesting shrubs and more recently planted mixed borders frame the view in the main garden. Ancient walled orchard and traditionally planted cottage garden. Lunch, tea and WC facilities available in Wells marketplace or Wells Cathedral. Slightly bumpy but short gravel drive and uneven path to main rear garden. 2-3 steps up to orchard and cottage gardens. Grass areas uneven in places.

  🐕 »))

> 'National Garden Scheme donations have funded four of our gardens in regional NHS spinal injury centres supporting nearly 8,500 patients and their visitors.'
> Horatio's Garden

70 ROCK HOUSE
Elberton, BS35 4AQ. Mr & Mrs
John Gunnery, 01454 413225. *10m
N of Bristol. 3½ m SW Thornbury.
From Old Severn Bridge on M48 take
B4461 to Alveston. In Elberton, take
1st turning L to Littleton-on-Severn
and turn immed R.* Sun 30 Jan, Sun
6 Feb, Sun 20, Sun 27 Mar (11-4).
Adm £5, chd free. Visits also by
arrangement.
2 acre garden. Pretty woodland vistas
with many snowdrops and daffodils,
some unusual. Spring flowers,
cottage garden plants and roses. Old
yew tree and pond.

71 ROSE COTTAGE
Smithams Hill, East Harptree,
Bristol, BS40 6BY. Bev &
Jenny Cruse, 01761 221627,
bandjcruse@gmail.com. *5m N of
Wells, 15m S of Bristol. From B3114
turn into High St in EH. L at Clock
Tower and immed R into Middle St,
up hill for 1m. From B3134 take EH
rd opp Castle of Comfort, continue
1½ m. Car parking in field opp
cottage.* Sun 10 Apr (2-5). Adm £5,
chd free. Home-made teas. Visits
also by arrangement in Apr for
groups of up to 30. Please confirm
group numbers 2 weeks prior to
your visit.
Bordered by a stream and established
mixed hedges, our 1 acre hillside
cottage garden welcomes spring,
carpeted with seasonal bulbs,
primroses and hellebores. The garden
is evolving with new planting. Plenty
of seating areas to enjoy teas, listen
to the Congresbury Brass Band,
whilst admiring panoramic views over
Chew Valley. Wildlife area with pond in
corner of car park field develops with
interest. This hillside cottage garden
is full of spring colour, it is organically
gardened and planted to encourage
wildlife.

**72 THE ROYAL CRESCENT
HOTEL & SPA**
16 Royal Crescent, Bath, BA1 2LS.
Topland Ltd (The Royal Crescent
Hotel and Spa), 01225 823 333,
info@royalcrescent.co.uk,
www.royalcrescent.co.uk/. *Walk
through front door of hotel, carry
straight on, exit via back door to
gardens. Nearest car park is in
Charlotte St. Lansdown P & R bus
stop nearby.* Mon 11, Tue 12 July
(11.30-3). Adm £5, chd free. Light
refreshments. Booking essential

for lunch or afternoon tea.
1 acre of secluded gardens sits
waiting for you behind this iconic
hotel, lovingly curated by our
gardeners. Gently winding lavender
paths take you across the beautiful
lawns, with various stunning floral
displays along the route. Century-
old trees, rescue hedgehogs, rose
bushes, and interesting statues; this
garden has it all. Garden map and
virtual tour available on website.

73 SERRIDGE HOUSE
Henfield Rd, Coalpit Heath,
BS36 2UY. Mrs J Manning,
01454 773188,
janserigehouse@gmail.com. *9m
N of Bristol. On A432 at Coalpit
Heath T-lights (opp church), turn into
Henfield Rd. R at pub, ½ m small
Xrds, garden on corner with Ruffet
Rd. Park on Henfield Rd.* Visits
by arrangement July & Aug for
groups of 10+. Adm inc home-
made scone with jam & cream,
glass of wine evening visits. Adm
£7, chd free.
2½ acre garden with mature trees,
heather and conifer beds, island beds
mostly of perennials, woodland area
with pond. Colourful courtyard with
old farm implements. Lake views and
lakeside walks. Unique tree carvings.
Mostly flat grass and concrete
driveway. Wheelchair access to lake
difficult.

74 NEW 42 SILVER STREET
Midsomer Norton, Radstock,
BA3 2EY. Andrew King & Kevin
Joint. *Parking at Norton Hill School,
Charlton Rd, BA3 4AD. From town
centre, follow the B3355 Silver St
for 0.4m, turn L into Charlton Rd,
School car park is100m on R.* Sun
10 July (12-4). Adm £5, chd £2.50.
Home-made teas.
Half acre plantsman's garden divided
into 7 distinct zones, developed
from scratch by the owners over
the last 10 yrs. Features inc a gravel
garden with formal rill and pond,
mixed/ herbaceous borders in
cool colours, Iris garden (bearded
irises), elliptical lawn with hot colour
planting, informal area with woodland
character and experimental bank
with intermingled mixed herbaceous
planting. Level wheelchair access to
most of the garden, enter via separate
side entrance - please ask at main
entrance on arrival.

**75 SOMERSET STREET
DISPLAY GARDENS**
23-25 Somerset Street,
Kingsdown, Bristol, BS2 8LZ.
John & Heather Frenkel & others.
*At top of St Michael's Hill, 3rd exit
at R'about into Cotham Rd. At end
turn L, then 2nd R into Fremantle Rd.
At far end, turn R into Somerset St.
Parking limited.* Sun 8, Sun 29 May
(1-5). Adm £4, chd free.
A linked row of walled gardens dating
from C18, separated from their
houses by a narrow setted street.
Designed as display gardens for the
enjoyment of passers-by, they form
a welcome green space of shrubs
and perennials between terraces of
Georgian houses. Features inc box
parterre, pleached hornbeam hedge,
fan-trained apple trees, pond, mature
trees and mixed borders.

76 SOUTH KELDING
Brewery Hill, Upton Cheyney,
Bristol, BS30 6LY. Barry &
Wendy Smale, 0117 9325145,
wendy.smale@yahoo.com. *Halfway
between Bristol and Bath. Upton
Cheyney lies ½ m up Brewery Hill off
A431 just outside Bitton. Detailed
directions & parking arrangements
given when appt made. Restricted
access means pre-booking essential.*
Visits by arrangement Mar to Oct
for groups of 6 to 30. Adm price
inc refreshments & tour by owner.
Adm £10, chd free. Home-made
teas.
7 acre hillside garden offering
panoramic views from its upper levels,
with herbaceous and shrub beds,
prairie-style scree beds, orchard,
native copses and small, labelled
arboretum grouped by continents.
Large wildlife pond, boundary stream
and wooded area featuring shade
and moisture-loving plants. In view of
slopes and uneven terrain this garden
is unsuitable for disabled access.

77 ♦ SPECIAL PLANTS
Greenway Lane, Cold
Ashton, SN14 8LA. Derry
Watkins, 01225 891686,
derry@specialplants.net,
www.specialplants.net. *6m N of
Bath. From Bath on A46, turn L into
Greenways Lane just before r'about
with A420.* For NGS: Thur 16
June, Thur 21 July, Thur 18 Aug,
Thur 15 Sept, Thur 20 Oct (11-5).
Adm £5, chd free. Home-made
teas. For other opening times and
information, please phone, email or

visit garden website.
Architect-designed ¾ acre hillside garden with stunning views. Started autumn 1996. Exotic plants. Gravel gardens for borderline hardy plants. Black and white (purple and silver) garden. Vegetable garden and orchard. Hot border. Lemon and lime bank. Annual, biennial and tender plants for late summer colour. Spring fed ponds. Bog garden. Woodland walk. Allium alley. Free list of plants in garden.

🐃 ✿ 🍵 ⁓⁾

78 NEW **1 STEEPLE VIEW**
Stoke St. Michael, Radstock, BA3 5HF. Mr R & Mrs H Wilson.
From A361 turn N at Cranmore signed S-S-M follow road to village at r'about take 2nd exit towards church, Steeple View is 2nd turn on L. Please park considerately on the village roads. **Sat 11, Sun 12 June (10.30-5). Adm £5, chd free. Home-made teas.**
Once a ⅓ acre plot, now an

engaging plantsman's ornamental garden. The approach comprises a mature border, varied range of shrubs and trees giving year-round interest. The garden has recently been partially remodelled with new borders, whilst exploiting the borrowed landscape. Consisting of several areas inc a shady woodland border/fernery, grasses screen, topiary and shrubbery. Mediterranean gravel garden, colour themed herbaceous beds and newly designed rose border with complementary planting. Garden room with small water feature. Several seating areas have been designed to enjoy the garden views of the borrowed landscape. Mainly level paths, some narrow in places, shallow steps.

♿ ✿ 🍵

79 ◆ **STOBERRY GARDEN**
Stoberry Park, Wells, BA5 3LD. Frances & Tim Young, 01749 672906, stay@stoberry-park.co.uk,

www.stoberryhouse.co.uk. *½ m N of Wells. From Bristol - Wells on A39, L into College Rd & immed L through Stoberry Park, signed.* **For NGS: Mon 22 Aug, Sun 4 Sept (12-5.30). Adm £5, chd free. Light refreshments. Discount/ prepaid vouchers not valid on NGS charity days. For other opening times and information, please phone, email or visit garden website.**
With breathtaking views over Wells Cathedral, this 6 acre family garden planted sympathetically within its landscape provides stunning combinations of vistas accented with wildlife ponds, water features, 1½ acre walled garden, gazebo, and lime walk. Colour and interest every season; spring bulbs, irises, salvias, wildflower circles, new wildflower meadow walk and fernery. Interesting sculpture artistically integrated.

✿ 🍵 🍵

Japanese Garden Bristol

GROUP OPENING

80 STOGUMBER GARDENS
Station Road, Stogumber,
TA4 3TQ. *11m NW of Taunton. 3m
W of A358. Signed to Stogumber,
W of Crowcombe. Village maps
given to all visitors.* **Sun 3 July (2-
6). Combined adm £7, chd free.
Home-made teas.**

HIGHER KINGSWOOD
Fran & Tom Vesey.

KNOLL COTTAGE
Elaine & John Leech,
01984 656689,
john@Leech45.com,
www.knoll-cottage.co.uk.
**Visits also by arrangement June
to Sept for groups of 8 to 30.**

ORCHARD DEANE
Brenda & Peter Wilson.

POUND HOUSE
Barry & Jenny Hibbert.

WICK BARTON
Sara & Russ Coward.

5 delightful and very varied gardens
in a picturesque village on the edge
of the Quantocks. 3 surprisingly large
gardens near village centre, plus 2
very large gardens on outskirts of
village, with many rare and unusual
plants. Conditions range from
waterlogged clay to well-drained
sand. Features inc courtyard, ponds,
bog gardens, rockery, extensive
mixed beds, vegetable and fruit
gardens, and a collection of over
80 different roses. Fine views of
surrounding countryside from some
gardens. Wheelchair access to main
features of all gardens.

  ♿ 🐂 ✿ 🚗 ☕

81 STONELEIGH DOWN
Upper Tockington Road,
Tockington, Bristol, BS32 4LQ.
Su & John Mills, 01454 615438,
susanlmills@gmail.com. *12m N of
Bristol. On LH side of Upper Tockington
Rd when travelling from Tockington
towards Olveston. Set back from road
up gravel drive. Parking in village.* **Fri
10, Sun 12 June (1-5). Adm £5,
chd free. Home-made teas. Visits
also by arrangement Apr to Oct for
groups of 16 to 30. Adm for groups
inc refreshments & brief talk by the
owner.**
Approaching ⅔ acre, the south facing
garden has curved gravel pathways
around an S-shaped lawn that
connects themed areas: exotic border;
summer walk; acers; oriental pond;
winter garden; spring garden. On a
level site, it has been densely planted
with trees, shrubs, perennials and
bulbs for year-round interest. Plenty of
places to sit. Steps into courtyard.

🐂 ✿ ☕))

Goathurst Gardens

GROUP OPENING

82 STOWEY GARDENS
Stowey, Bishop Sutton, Bristol, BS39 5TL. *10m W of Bath. Stowey Village on A368 between Bishop Sutton & Chelwood. From Chelwood r'about take A368 to Weston-s-Mare. At Stowey Xrds turn R to car park, 150yds down lane, ample off road parking opp Dormers. Limited disabled parking at each garden which will be signed.* Sun 17 July (2-6). Combined adm £6, chd free. Home-made teas at Stowey Mead.

DORMERS
Mr & Mrs G Nicol.

◆ MANOR FARM
Richard Baines & Alison Fawcett, 01275 332297.

STOWEY MEAD
Mr Victor Pritchard.

A broad spectrum of interest and styles developing year on year. But there is far more than this in these gardens; the visitor's senses will be aroused by the sights, scents and diversity of these gardens in the tiny, ancient village of Stowey. Flower-packed beds, borders and pots, roses, topiary, hydrangeas, exotic garden, many unusual trees and shrubs, orchards, vegetables, ponds, specialist sweet peas, lawns, Stowey Henge, and ha-ha. An abundant collection of mature trees and shrubs. Ample seating areas, wonderful views from each garden. Not to be missed, something of interest for everyone, all within a few minutes walk of car park at Dormers. Plant sales at Dormers. Well behaved dogs on short leads welcome. Wheelchair access restricted in places, many grassed areas in each garden.
  ♿ 🐕 ❀ 🛏 ☕))

83 SUTTON HOSEY MANOR
Long Sutton, Langport, TA10 9NA. Roger Bramble, rbramble@bdbltd.co.uk. *2m E of Langport, on A372. Gates N of A372 at E end of Long Sutton.* Sun 24 July (2.30-6). Adm £6, chd free. Home-made teas. Visits also by arrangement Aug & Sept for groups of 10 to 30.
3 acres, of which 2 are walled. Lily canal through pleached limes leading to amelanchier walk past duck pond; rose and juniper walk from Italian terrace; judas tree avenue; pteiea walk. Ornamental potager. Drive-side shrubbery. Music by players of Young Musicians Symphony Orchestra.
  ♿ ❀ ☕

84 TORMARTON COURT
Church Road, Tormarton, GL9 1HT. Noreen & Bruce Finnamore, home@thefinnamores.com. *3m E of Chipping Sodbury, off A46 at J18 M4. Follow signs to Tormarton from A46 then follow signs for car parking.* Visits by arrangement Mar to July for groups of 15 to 25. Adm £5, chd free. Light refreshments on request.
11 acres of formal and natural gardens in a stunning Cotswold setting. Features inc roses, herbaceous, kitchen garden, Mediterranean garden, mound and natural pond. Extensive walled garden, spring glade and meadows with young and mature trees.
  ☕

85 ◆ UNIVERSITY OF BRISTOL BOTANIC GARDEN
Stoke Park Road, Stoke Bishop, Bristol, BS9 1JG. University of Bristol Botanic Garden, 0117 4282041, botanic-gardens@bristol.ac.uk, botanic-garden.bristol.ac.uk/. *Located in Stoke Bishop ¼m W of Durdham Downs & 1m from city centre. After crossing the Downs to Stoke Hill, Stoke Park Rd is 1st on R.* For NGS: Sun 17 July (10-4.30). Adm £7, chd free. Light refreshments. Provided by local deli. For other opening times and information, please phone, email or visit garden website. Donation to University of Bristol Botanic Garden.
Exciting and contemporary award winning Botanic Garden with dramatic displays illustrating collections of Mediterranean flora, rare native, useful plants (inc European and Chinese herbs) and those that illustrate plant evolution. Large floral displays illustrating pollination in flowering plant and evolution. Glasshouses are home to giant Amazon waterlily, tropical fruit, medicinal plants, orchids, cacti and unique sacred lotus collection. Wheelchair available to borrow from Welcome Lodge on request. Wheelchair friendly primary route through garden inc glasshouses, accessible WCs.
  ♿ ❀ 🚗 ☕ 🍽

86 VELLACOTT
Lawford, Crowcombe, TA4 4AL. Kevin & Pat Chittenden, 01984 618249, patmchittenden@gmail.com. *9m NW of Taunton. Off A358, signed Lawford. For directions please phone.* Visits by arrangement May to Sept for groups of 5 to 12. Adm £4, chd free. Light refreshments. Large informal garden on south facing slope with splendid views of the Quantock and Brendon Hills. Profusely planted with a wide selection of herbaceous perennials, shrubs and trees. Places to sit to enjoy the surroundings.
  ☕

87 NEW VEXFORD COURT
Higher Vexford, Lydeard St. Lawrence, Taunton, TA4 3QF. Dr David Yates, 01984 656735, yatesdavid135@gmail.com. *The best approach is from B3224 into Sheepstealing Lane. Take L after ¼m & continue to the bottom of the hill (0.9m). Turn L up Higher Vexford Farm drive & Vexford Court entrance on the R.* Sat 16, Sun 17 July, Sat 20, Sun 21 Aug (10.30-4.30). Adm £5, chd free. Home-made teas. Visits also by arrangement June to Aug for groups of up to 6. Car parking at the house for 6 cars. Hard standing at stables entrance.
This large garden surrounds 3 converted barns. 1½ acres of grounds slopes gently downhill to a small stream. Roses around the courtyard entrance lead to herbaceous beds and beyond to trees and shrubs. Amongst the interesting trees a large *Liriodendron Tulipa* tree blooms in early summer and there are azaleas, camellias, catalpa, ginko, Wollemi Pine and Persian Ironwood trees.
  🐕 ☕

Around 1,050 people living with Parkinson's - and their families - have been helped by Parkinson's nurses thanks to funding from the National Garden Scheme

88 ◆ THE WALLED GARDENS OF CANNINGTON

Church Street, Cannington, TA5 2HA. Bridgwater College, 01278 655042, walledgardens@btc.ac.uk, www. canningtonwalledgardens.co.uk. *Part of Bridgwater & Taunton College Cannington Campus, 3m NW of Bridgwater. On A39 Bridgwater-Minehead rd - at 1st r'about in Cannington 2nd exit, through village. War memorial, 1st L into Church St then 1st L.* **For NGS: Sat 23, Sun 24 Apr, Sat 17, Sun 18 Sept (10-4). Adm £6, chd free. Light refreshments. For other opening times and information, please phone, email or visit garden website.**
Within the grounds of a medieval priory, the Walled Gardens of Cannington are a gem waiting to be discovered! Classic and contemporary features inc hot herbaceous border, blue garden, sub-tropical walk and Victorian style fernery, amongst others. Botanical glasshouse where arid, sub-tropical and tropical plants can be seen. Tea room, plant nursery, gift shop, also events throughout the year. Gravel paths. Motorised scooter can be borrowed free of charge (only one available).

  ይ ᔭᖦ ✿ 🚐 ☕

89 WATCOMBE

92 Church Road, Winscombe, BS25 1BP. Peter & Ann Owen, 01934 842666, peterowen449@btinternet.com. *12m SW of Bristol, 3m N of Axbridge. 100 yds after yellow signs on A38 turn L, (from S), or R. (from N) into Winscombe Hill. After 1m reach The Square. Watcombe on L after 150yds.* **Sun 24 Apr, Sun 15 May, Thur 9 June (2-5). Adm £5, chd free. Home-made teas. Gluten-free available. Visits also by arrangement Apr to July.**
¾ acre mature Edwardian garden with colour-themed, informally planted herbaceous borders. Strong framework separating several different areas; pergola with varied wisteria, unusual topiary, box hedging, lime walk, pleached hornbeams, cordon fruit trees, 2 small formal ponds and growing collection of clematis. Many unusual trees and shrubs. Small vegetable plot. Some steps but most areas accessible by wheelchair with minimal assistance.

  ይ ᔭᖦ ✿ 🚐 ☕

90 WAYFORD MANOR

Wayford, Crewkerne, TA18 8QG. *3m SW of Crewkerne. Turn N off B3165 at Clapton, signed Wayford or S off A30 Chard to Crewkerne rd, signed Wayford.* **Sun 15 May (2-5). Adm £6, chd £3. Home-made teas.**
The mainly Elizabethan manor (not open) mentioned in C17 for its 'fair and pleasant' garden was redesigned by Harold Peto in 1902. Formal terraces with yew hedges and topiary have fine views over W Dorset. Steps down between spring-fed ponds past mature and new plantings of magnolia, rhododendron, maples, cornus and, in season, spring bulbs, cyclamen and giant echium. Primula candelabra, arum lily and gunnera around lower ponds.

  ᔭᖦ ✿ ☕ ♫

91 WEIR COTTAGE

Weir Cottage, Weir Lane, Marshfield, SN14 8NB. Ian & Margaret Jones. *Opp Weir Farm. 7m NE of Bath. Look for yellow sign on A420 between Cold Ashton & Chippenham. Weir Lane is at the E end of the High St.* **Sat 2, Sun 3 Apr (11-3). Adm £3.50, chd free. Home-made teas in cottage.**
South facing garden of ¼ acre. High stone walls to the north protect against Marshfield weather. Limestone soil. Early spring flowers. Sat 2nd April guided walk led by Cotswold Wardens. Boots advised. Sun 3rd April guided history walk in the village. Both walks meet 10am in Market Place. Dogs on leads welcome.

  ᔭᖦ ☕ 🏕

92 [NEW] WELL COTTAGE

Little Badminton, Tetbury, GL9 1AB. Miranda Beaufort, 01454 218729. *Signs from both ends of Little Badminton. Ignore no entry signs. Parking in Badminton Park.* **Visits by arrangement April, June, July & Sept for groups of 10 to 20. Adm £7, chd free. Home-made teas on request.**
The garden is on 4 levels. The bottom garden was planted 6 yrs ago, helped by the owner's husband, the late Duke of Beaufort. It is mostly planted with David Austin roses, which feature in their catalogue. Also many clematis, which come alive after the first flush of roses have finished. Over the road are wild flowers, picking borders and greenhouses. Wheelchair access on bottom 2 levels and over the road.

  ይ ✿ ☕ 🏕

93 WELLFIELD BARN

Walcombe Lane, Wells, BA5 3AG. Virginia Nasmyth, 01749 675129. *½m N of Wells. From A39 Bristol to Wells rd turn R at 30 mph sign into the narrow Walcombe Lane. Entrance at 1st cottage on R, parking signed.* **Visits by arrangement June & July for groups of 10 to 30. Payment preferred 2 weeks prior to visit. Adm £5.50, chd free. Refreshments available on request.**
A well planned garden created by the owners to provide colour and form around their home for year-round enjoyment. 25 yrs ago this once bustling concrete farmyard began to grow into a tranquil ½ acre garden which is, today, still evolving. Structured design integrates house, lawn and garden with the landscape. Wonderful views, ha-ha, mixed borders, hydrangea bed, hardy geraniums and roses. Formal sunken garden, grass walks with interesting young and semi-mature trees. Now tranquillity, a haven for wildlife, sheep as neighbours, perfect peace. Our collection of hardy geraniums was featured on BBC Gardeners' World with Carol Klein. Moderate slopes in places, some gravel paths.

  ይ ᔭᖦ 🚐 ☕

94 WESTBROOK HOUSE

West Bradley, BA6 8LS. Keith Anderson & David Mendel. *4m E of Glastonbury; 8m W of Castle Cary. From A361 at W Pennard follow signs to W Bradley (2m). From A37 at Wraxall Hill follow signs to W Bradley (2m).* **Sat 16 Apr, Sat 27 Aug (11-5). Adm £5, chd free. Donation to West Bradley Church.**
4 acres comprising 3 distinct gardens around house with mixed herbaceous and shrub borders leading to meadow and orchard with spring bulbs, species roses and lilacs. Planting and layout began 2004 and continues to the present.

  ይ ᔭᖦ

95 ◆ THE YEO VALLEY ORGANIC GARDEN AT HOLT FARM

Bath Road, Blagdon, BS40 7SQ. Mr & Mrs Tim Mead, 01761 258155, visit@yeovalleyfarms.co.uk, www.yeovalley.co.uk. *12m S of Bristol. Off A368. Entrance approx ½m outside Blagdon towards Bath, on L, then follow garden*

signs past dairy. **For NGS: Sun 24 Apr (10-5). Adm £6, chd £2. Light refreshments. For other opening times and information, please phone, email or visit garden website.**
One of only a handful of ornamental gardens that is Soil Association accredited, 6½ acres of contemporary planting, quirky sculptures, bulbs in their thousands, purple palace, glorious meadow and posh vegetable patch. Great views, green ideas. Events, workshops and exhibitions held throughout the year - see website for further details. Winner of People's Choice Award Chelsea 2021.

✿ ☕

96 NEW THE YEWS
Harry Stoke Road, Stoke Gifford, Bristol, BS34 8QH. Dr Barbara Laue & Dr Chris Payne. *From A38/Filton, take A4174 ring road to M32. L turn at Sainsbury R'about. Straight across next R'about. After 200 yds, sharp R turn into Harrystoke Rd. Parking in paddock.* **Sat 21, Sun 22 May (2-5). Adm £5, chd free. Home-made teas.**
Approx 1 acre, developed by present owners since 1987. Part of the old hamlet of Harrystoke, now surrounded by housing development. Formal area with pond, gazebo, herbaceous borders, clipped box and yew. 300 yr old yews, wedding cake tree, magnolias, eucalyptus, Indian bean tree, gingkoes and more. Vegetable garden, greenhouse, orchard and meadow. Spring bulbs and blossom.

✿ ☕))

97 YEWS FARM
East Street, Martock, TA12 6NF. Louise & Fergus Dowding, 01935 822202, fergus.dowding@btinternet.com, instagram.dowdinglouise. *Turn off main road through village at Market House, onto East St, past White Hart & PO on R, Yews Farm 150 yds on R, opp Foldhill Lane. Turn around if you get to Nag's Head.* **Sun 3 July, Sun 11 Sept (1-5). Adm £8, chd free. Home-made teas. Visits also by arrangement May to Sept for groups of 20 to 50.**
Theatrical planting in large south facing walled garden. Sculptural planting for height, shape, leaf and texture. Box topiary. High maintenance pots. Self seeding hugely encouraged. Prolific cracked

concrete garden in farmyard with hens and pigs. Working organic kitchen garden. Greenhouses bursting with summer vegetables. Organic orchard and active cider barn – taste the difference! Hens and pigs are complete waste processors. Large eco bonfire with hedgehogs.

Self seeded flower garden around polytunnel in yard. Orchard planted with heritage apple varieties with cattle grazing. Cider barn viewable and tasting on request. Mostly wheelchair accessible, ring for details.

Barford House

STAFFORDSHIRE
Birmingham & West Midlands

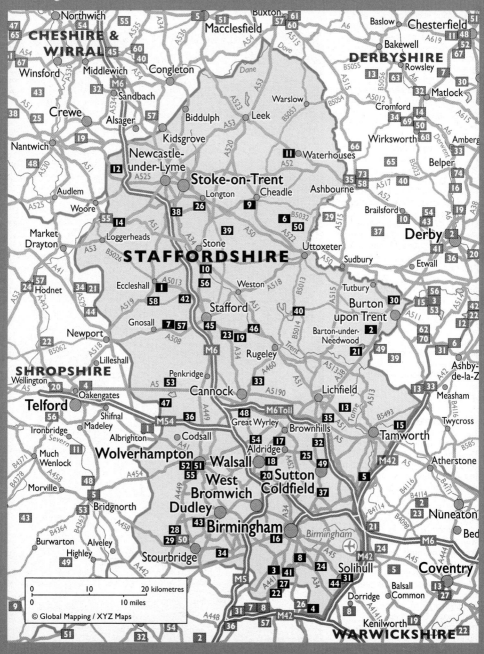

Staffordshire, Birmingham and part of the West Midlands is a landlocked 'county', one of the furthest from the sea in England and Wales.

It is a National Garden Scheme 'county' of surprising contrasts, from the 'Moorlands' in the North East, the 'Woodland Quarter' in the North West, the 'Staffordshire Potteries' and England's 'Second City' in the South East, with much of the rest of the land devoted to agriculture, both dairy and arable.

The garden owners enthusiastically embraced the National Garden Scheme from the very beginning, with seven gardens opening in the inaugural year of 1927, and a further thirteen the following year.

The county is the home of the National Memorial Arboretum, the Cannock Chase Area of Outstanding Natural Beauty and part of the new National Forest.

There are many large country houses and gardens throughout the county with a long history of garden-making and with the input of many of the well known landscape architects.

Today, the majority of National Garden Scheme gardens are privately owned and of modest size. However, a few of the large country house gardens still open their gates for National Garden Scheme visitors.

Volunteers

County Organiser
Anita & David Wright
01785 661182
davidandanita@ngs.org.uk

County Treasurer
Brian Bailey
01902 424867
brian.bailey@ngs.org.uk

Publicity
Ruth & Clive Plant
07591 886921
ruthandcliveplant@ngs.org.uk

Booklet Co-ordinator
Peter Longstaff
01785 282582
peter.longstaff@ngs.org.uk

Assistant County Organisers
Jane Cerone
01827 873205
janecerone@btinternet.com

Ken & Joy Sutton
07791 041189
kenandjoysutton@ngs.org.uk

Alison & Peter Jordan
01785 660819
alisonandpeterjordan@ngs.org.uk

@StaffsNGS

Left: 42 Boden Road, Hall Green Gardens

OPENING DATES

All entries subject to change. For latest information check www.ngs.org.uk

Map locator numbers are shown to the right of each garden name.

February

Snowdrop Festival

Sunday 13th
5 East View Cottages 15

March

Sunday 6th
Millennium Garden 35

Sunday 20th
23 St Johns Road 45

April

Sunday 17th
'John's Garden' at
Ashwood Nurseries 28

Saturday 23rd
NEW Springfield Cottage 47

Sunday 24th
Millennium Garden 35

Thursday 28th
23 St Johns Road 45

May

Sunday 1st
12 Meres Road 34

Saturday 7th
Keeper's Cottage;
Bluebell Wood 29

Sunday 8th
NEW Brackencote 4
Keeper's Cottage;
Bluebell Wood 29

Sunday 15th
Cats Whiskers 8
10 Paget Rise 40

Thursday 19th
The Secret Garden 46

Friday 20th
23 St Johns Road 45

Saturday 21st
NEW The Home Bee
Garden 27

Sunday 22nd
Courtwood House 12

Saturday 28th
33 Gorway Road 20

Sunday 29th
Bridge House 5
Butt Lane Farm 7
Hamilton House 25

June

Saturday 4th
The Old Dairy House 38

Sunday 5th
The Garth 19
The Old Dairy House 38
The Pintles 42
12 Waterdale 51
19 Waterdale 52

Thursday 9th
23 St Johns Road 45

Saturday 11th
Hall Green Gardens 24

Sunday 12th
Ashcroft and Claremont 1
NEW Brackencote 4
Hall Green Gardens 24
3 Marlows Cottages 32
8 Rectory Road 44
91 Tower Road 49

Wednesday 15th
Bankcroft Farm 2

Friday 17th
22 Greenfield Road 23
Monarchs Way 36
Yarlet House 56

Saturday 18th
Colour Mill 11
22 Greenfield Road 23
Monarchs Way 36
The Old Vicarage 39

Sunday 19th
NEW Edgbaston
Gardens 16
49 The Plantation 43
NEW Truckle House,
Croxden 50

Wednesday 22nd
Bankcroft Farm 2

Friday 20th
5 East View Cottages 15

Saturday 25th
NEW Springfield Cottage 47
Yew Trees 58

Sunday 26th
Cheadle Allotments 9
5 East View Cottages 15
The Garth 19
NEW 14 Longbow
Close, Stretton 30
Marie Curie Hospice
Garden 31
15 New Church Road 37
2 Woodland Crescent 55
Yew Trees 58

Wednesday 29th
Bankcroft Farm 2
The Secret Garden 46

July

Saturday 2nd
Cross Roads,
Huddlesford Lane 13

Sunday 3rd
Bournville Village 3
NEW The Bungalow,
Great Gate 6
Cross Roads,
Huddlesford Lane 13
Grafton Cottage 21
12 Waterdale 51
19 Waterdale 52

Thursday 7th
23 St Johns Road 45
Yew Tree Cottage 57

Saturday 9th
Fifty Shades of Green 17

Sunday 10th
NEW The Bungalow,
Great Gate 6
Fifty Shades of Green 17
3 Marlows Cottages 32

Thursday 14th
Yew Tree Cottage 57

Friday 15th
Grafton Cottage 21

Sunday 17th
Grafton Cottage 21
49 The Plantation 43

Wednesday 20th
The Secret Garden 46

Thursday 21st
Yew Tree Cottage 57

Sunday 24th
NEW 76 Station Street 48
The Wickets 53
Yew Tree Cottage 57

Wednesday 27th
The Wickets 53

Saturday 30th
NEW 128 Green Acres
Road 22
NEW The Home Bee
Garden 27

Sunday 31st
Grafton Cottage 21
NEW 25 Wolverhampton
Road 54

August

Sunday 7th
Grafton Cottage 21

Thursday 18th
Colour Mill 11
The Secret Garden 46

Saturday 20th
Hamilton House 25

Sunday 21st
Grafton Cottage 21

Saturday 27th
Fifty Shades of Green 17

Sunday 28th
Fifty Shades of Green 17
The Wickets 53

September

Sunday 4th
8 Rectory Road 44

Friday 9th
NEW Springfield Cottage 47

Sunday 11th
Bridge House 5

Sunday 18th
12 Meres Road 34

October

Saturday 22nd
♦ Dorothy Clive Garden 14
Four Seasons 18

Sunday 23rd
♦ Dorothy Clive Garden 14
Four Seasons 18

February 2023

Sunday 12th
5 East View Cottages 15

By Arrangement

Arrange a personalised garden visit with your club, or group of friends, on a date to suit you. See individual garden entries for full details.

THE GARDENS

GROUP OPENING

1 ASHCROFT AND CLAREMONT
Stafford Road, Eccleshall, ST21 6JP. *7m W of Stafford. J14 M6. At Eccleshall end of A5013 the garden is 100 metres before junction with A519. On street parking nearby. Note: Some SatNavs give wrong directions.* **Sun 12 June (2-5). Combined adm £4.50, chd free. Home-made teas at Ashcroft.**

ASHCROFT
Gillian Bertram.

26 CLAREMONT ROAD
Maria Edwards.

Weeping limes hide Ashcroft, a 1 acre garden of green tranquillity, rooms flow seamlessly around the Edwardian house. Covered courtyard with lizard water feature, sunken herb bed, kitchen garden, greenhouse, wildlife boundaries home to five hedgehogs increasing yearly. Deep shade border, woodland area and ruin with stone carvings and stained glass sculpture. Claremont is a master class in clipped perfection. An artist with an artist's eye has blurred the boundaries of this small Italianate influenced garden. Overlooking the aviary, a stone lion surveys the large pots and borders of vibrant planting, completing the Feng-Shui design of this beautiful all seasons garden. Tickets, teas and plants available at Ashcroft. Partial wheelchair access at Claremont.
&. ✿ ☕

2 BANKCROFT FARM
Tatenhill, Burton-on-Trent, DE13 9SA. Mrs Penelope Adkins. *2m NW of Burton-on-Trent. 1m NW of Burton upon Trent take Tatenhill Rd off A38 on Burton/Branson flyover, 1m 1st house on L after village sign. Parking on farm.* **Wed 15, Wed 22, Wed 29 June (1.30-4.30). Adm £4, chd free.**
Lose yourself for an afternoon in our 1½ acre organic country garden. Arbour, gazebo and many other seating areas to view ponds and herbaceous borders, backed with shrubs and trees with emphasis on structure, foliage and colour. Productive fruit and vegetable gardens, wildlife areas and adjoining 12 acre native woodland walk. Picnics welcome. Gravel paths.
&. 🌲

GROUP OPENING

3 BOURNVILLE VILLAGE
Birmingham, B30 1QY. Bournville Village Trust, www.bvt.org.uk. *Gardens spread across 1,000 acre estate. Walks of up to 30 mins between some. Map supplied on day. Additional parking: Wyevale Garden Centre, (B30 2AE) & Rowheath Pavilion, (B30 1HH).* **Sun 3 July (11-5). Combined adm £6, chd free. Light refreshments at various locations.**

NEW 5 BLACKTHORN ROAD
Mr & Mrs Andrew Christie.

103 BOURNVILLE LANE
B30 1LH. Mrs Jennifer Duffy.

52 ELM ROAD
Mr & Mrs Jackie Twigg.

11 KESTREL GROVE
Mr Julian Stanton.

32 KNIGHTON ROAD
B31 2EH. Mrs Anne Ellis & Mr Lawrence Newman.

MASEFIELD COMMUNITY GARDEN
Mrs Sally Gopsill.

NEW 54 RAMSDEN CLOSE
Ms Lesley Pattenson.

Bournville Village is showcasing seven gardens - two of which are new to the scheme. Bournville is famous for it's large gardens, outstanding open spaces and of course it's chocolate factory in a garden! Free information sheet/map available on the day. Gardens spread across the 1,000 acre estate, with walks of up to 30 minutes between sites. For those with a disability, full details of access are available on the NGS website. Visitors with particular concerns with regards to access are welcome to call Bournville Village Trust on 0300 333 6540 or email: CommunityAdmin@bvt.org.uk. Music, singing and food available across a number of sites. Please check on the day.
&. ✿ ☕))

'In the first six months of operation at Maggie's Southampton, which was part funded by the National Garden Scheme, the team has supported people affected by cancer more than 2,300 times.' *Maggie's*

4 NEW BRACKENCOTE

Forshaw Heath Road, Earlswood, Solihull, B94 5JU. Mr & Mrs Sandy Andrews, 01564 702395 mob: 07710 107000, mjandrews53@hotmail.com. *From J3 M42 take exit signed to Forshaw Heath. At the T junction, turn L onto Forshaw Heath Rd, signed to Earlswood. Garden approx ½ m on the L, before you get to Earlswood Nurseries.* Sun 8 May, Sun 12 June (11-4). Adm £5, chd free. Pre-booking essential, please visit www.ngs.org.uk for information & booking. Teas, coffees, cakes and soft drinks will be available. Visits also by arrangement May to Sept for groups of up to 15.

A beautiful country garden with stunning wildflower meadow, full of orchids in spring and early summer. The 1¼ acre plot is surrounded by mature trees, with herbaceous borders enclosing a large circular lawn. Beyond this, the garden inc a brick and turf labyrinth, a rockery, a pond and bog garden as well as a large raised vegetable plot and garden buildings.

❀ ☕ ⛱ »)

5 BRIDGE HOUSE

Dog Lane, Bodymoor Heath, B76 9JD. Mr & Mrs J Cerone, 01827 873205, janecerone@btinternet.com. *5m S of Tamworth. From A446 at Belfry Island take A4091to Tamworth, after 1m turn R onto Bodymoor Heath Lane & continue 1m into village, parking in field opp garden.* Sun 29 May, Sun 11 Sept (2-5). Adm £4, chd free. Home-made teas. Visits also by arrangement May to Sept for groups of up to 30.

1 acre garden surrounding converted public house. Divided into smaller areas with a mix of shrub borders, azalea and fuchsia, herbaceous and bedding, orchard, kitchen garden with large greenhouse. Pergola walk, arch to formal garden with big fish pool, pond, bog garden and lawns. Some unusual carefully chosen trees. Kingsbury Water Park and RSPB Middleton Lakes Reserve located within a mile.

& �= ❀ ☕ »)

6 NEW THE BUNGALOW, GREAT GATE

Tean, Stoke-On-Trent, ST10 4HF. Mrs Dorothy Hurst. *Arrive in Great Gate and follow yellow signs.* Sun 3, Sun 10 July (11-5). Adm £4, chd free. Home-made teas.

1 acre varied garden with stunning views of the Weaver Hills surrounded by farm land. The garden features large lawns, multiple ponds in a wooded area and water features, with inspiration taken from different countries.

❀ ☕

7 BUTT LANE FARM

Butt Lane, Ranton, Stafford, ST18 9JZ. Pete Gough, 07975 928968, claire-pickering@hotmail.co.uk. *6m W of Stafford. Take A518 to Haughton, turn R Station Rd (signed Ranton) 2m turn L at Butt Ln. Or from Great Bridgeford head W B5405 for 3m. Turn L Moorend Ln, 2nd L Butt Ln.* Sun 29 May (10-4). Adm £4, chd free. Light refreshments inc home-made pizza and BBQ Visits also by arrangement May to July for groups of 20 to 50.

Developing cottage style garden entering from unspoilt farmland through small wooded area onto lawns surrounded by floral beds and productive fruit and vegetable areas. With unusual areas of interest, greenhouse area, well and outside kitchen. Several craft stalls to be in attendance. Lamb petting. Small nature walk (not suitable for wheelchairs)

& ❀ �car ☕

8 CATS WHISKERS

42 Amesbury Rd, Moseley, Birmingham, B13 8LE. Dr Alfred & Mrs Michele White. *Opp back of Moseley Hall Hospital. Past Edgbaston Cricket ground straight on at r'about & up Salisbury Rd. Amesbury Rd, 1st on R.* Sun 15 May (12-5). Adm £5, chd free. Light refreshments.

A plantsman's garden developed over the last 38 years but which has kept its 1923 landscape. The front garden whilst not particularly large is full of interesting trees and shrubs; the rear garden is on three levels with steps leading to a small terrace and further steps to the main space. At the end of the garden is a pergola leading to the vegetable garden and greenhouse.

❀ ☕

9 CHEADLE ALLOTMENTS

Delphouse Road, Cheadle, Stoke-on-Trent, ST10 2NN. Cheadle Allotment Association. *On the A521 1m to the W of Cheadle town centre.* Sun 26 June (1-5). Adm £5, chd free. Home-made teas are inc in the adm price.

The allotments, which were opened in 2015, are located on the western edge of Cheadle (Staffs). There are 29 plots growing a variety of vegetables, fruits and flowers. A new addition in 2019 was a community area, with an adjacent wildlife area. A small orchard is currently being developed. Wheelchair access on all main paths.

& 🐕 ☕

10 CHURCH COTTAGE

Aston, Stone, ST15 0BJ. Andrew & Anne Worrall, 01785 815239, acworrall@aol.com. *1m S of Stone, Staffordshire. N side of St Saviour's Church, Aston. Go S 150 metres on A34 after junction with A51. Turn L at Aston Village Hall. 250 metres down lane into churchyard for parking.* Visits by arrangement June to Aug for groups of 6 to 24. Light refreshments inc in adm price. Adm £6, chd free.

An acre of cottage garden with large pond, waterfall and stream. Trees, sculptures, small orchard and wildflowers. Views across the river Trent. St Saviour's Church and Trent and Mersey Canal nearby.

🐕 ☕ »)

11 COLOUR MILL

Winkhill, Leek, ST13 7PR. Jackie Pakes, 07967 558917, jackie.pakes@icloud.com, www.colourmillbandb.co.uk. *7m E of Leek. Follow A523 from either Leek or Ashbourne, look for NGS signs on the side of the main rd which will direct you down to Colour Mill.* Sat 18 June, Thur 18 Aug (1.30-5). Adm £5, chd free. Home-made teas. Visits also by arrangement June to Sept for groups of 5 to 35.

1½ acre south facing garden, created in the shadow of a former iron foundry, set beside the delightful River Hamps. Informal planting in a variety of rooms surrounded by beautiful 7ft beech hedges. Large organic vegetable patch complete with greenhouse and polytunnel. Maturing trees provide shade for the interesting seating areas. River walk through woodland and willows. Herbaceous borders.

❀ ☕

12 COURTWOOD HOUSE

3 Court Walk, Betley, CW3 9DP.
Mike Reeves. *6m S of Crewe. On
A531 toward Keele & Newcastle
under Lyme or from J16 off M6,
pickup A531 off A500 on Nantwich
rd, into village by Betley Court.* **Sun
22 May (12-5). Adm £4, chd free.
Light refreshments.**
Small L-shaped, walled garden,
which is designed as a walk-through
sculpture. Mainly shrubs with
structures and water features, hidden
spaces and seating areas, with strong
shapes and effects utilising a wide
range of materials, inc a synthetic
lawn. Small art gallery with acrylic
paintings by owner for sale.

13 CROSS ROADS, HUDDLESFORD LANE

Huddlesford Lane, Whittington,
Lichfield, WS14 9NL. **Mike Kinghan
& Julia Spencer.** *3m E of Lichfield,
Staffs. 1m E of the A38 & 1m N of the
A51. Postcode/SatNav takes you to
Back Ln. Park on Back Ln or Chapel
Ln. Walk 30 yds up Huddlesford Ln
(halfway along Back Ln) to house
entrance on L.* **Sat 2, Sun 3 July (12-
5). Adm £4, chd free.**
1.3 acres of stunning wildlife friendly
perennial meadows, (usually full of
bees and butterflies), grass paths, two
ponds, with orchard of 50 heritage
fruit trees, beehives, wild areas,
interesting shrubs, traditional cottage
garden area, polytunnel, small copse.
Not your average garden!

14 ◆ DOROTHY CLIVE GARDEN

Willoughbridge, Market Drayton,
TF9 4EU. **Willoughbridge
Garden Trust, 01630 647237,
info@dorothyclivegarden.co.uk,
www.dorothyclivegarden.co.uk.** *3m
SE of Bridgemere Garden World. From
M6 J15 take A53 W bound, then A51
N bound midway between Nantwich
& Stone, near Woore.* **For NGS: Sat
22, Sun 23 Oct (10-4). Adm £5,
chd £2. Light refreshments in the
Tearooms can be pre-booked
For other opening times and
information, please phone, email or
visit garden website.**
12 informal acres, inc superb
woodland garden, alpine scree, gravel
garden, fine collection of trees and
spectacular flower borders. Renowned
in May when woodland quarry is
brilliant with rhododendrons. Waterfall
and woodland planting. Laburnum
Arch in June. Creative planting has

produced stunning summer borders.
Large Glasshouse. Spectacular
autumn colour. Much to see, whatever
the season. The Dorothy Clive Tea
Rooms will be open throughout
the weekend during winter for
refreshments, lunch and afternoon tea.
Open all week in summer. Plant sales,
gift room, picnic area and children's
play area for a wide age range.
Wheelchairs (inc electric) are available
to book through the tea rooms.
Disabled parking is available. Toilets on
both upper and lower car parks.

15 5 EAST VIEW COTTAGES

School Lane, Shuttington, nr
Tamworth, B79 0DX. **Cathy
Lyon-Green, 01827 892244,
cathyatcorrabhan@hotmail.com,
www.ramblinginthegarden.
wordpress.com.** *2m NE of Tamworth.
From Tamworth, Amington Rd or
Ashby Rd to Shuttington. From
M42 J11, B5493 for Seckington &
Tamworth, 3m L turn to Shuttington.
Pink house nr top of School Ln.
Parking signed, disabled at house.*
**Sun 13 Feb, Wed 22 June (12-4);
Sun 26 June (1-5). Adm £4, chd
free. Home-made teas. 2023: Sun
12 Feb. Visits also by arrangement
June & July for groups of up to
30. Also open by arrangement for
groups in February.**
Deceptive, quirky plantlover's garden,
full of surprises and always something
new. Informally planted themed
borders, cutting beds, woodland
and woodland edge, stream, water
features, sitooterie, folly, greenhouses
and many artefacts. Roses, clematis,
perennials, potted hostas. Snowdrops
and witch hazels in Feb. Seating areas
for contemplation and enjoying home-
made teas. 'Wonderful hour's wander'.

GROUP OPENING

16 NEW EDGBASTON GARDENS

26 Vernon Road, Birmingham,
B16 9SH. *Edgbaston, Birmingham.
The three gardens are all in
Edgbaston. It is 1.3 m from Vernon
House to Metchley Park Rd with
Westfield Rd approx half way between.*
**Sun 19 June (1-5). Combined adm
£7.50, chd free. Light refreshments
at Metchley Park Road & Vernon
House.**

**NEW 15 METCHLEY PARK
ROAD**
Ms Judy Freeman.

VERNON HOUSE
Dr & Mrs Steve & Chris Smith.

NEW 124 WESTFIELD ROAD
Mr & Mrs Helen Fenton.

Vernon House is a large but secluded
city garden framed by mature trees.
There are extensive lawns and
herbaceous borders with a wide
range of planting creating several
distinct areas. Main features inc an
ornamental koi pond, a wildlife pond
with bog garden and a unique holly
hedge. Westfield Road is an oasis of
peace surrounded by many varieties
of trees. It comprises a large Victorian
walled patio with pots and water
features and separate planting areas
over distinct levels. An abundance
of roses, shrubs, perennials and
herbaceous plants add colour and
interest throughout the year. Metchley
Park Road is a medium sized garden
designed to enhance a range of
established trees which inc acer,
cherry, magnolia, tulip, silver birch
and yew. Shrubs inc rhododendron,
hydrangeas, camellias and azaleas.
The sunny perennial border has
many cottage garden favourites. The
dry woodland area has a range of
ferns and hosta. A pergola provides
support for wisteria and clematis.

*The National Garden Scheme searches
the length and breadth of England,
Channel Islands, Northern Ireland and
Wales for the very best private gardens*

17 FIFTY SHADES OF GREEN
20 Bevan Close, Shelfield,
Walsall, WS4 1AB. Annmarie &
Andrew Swift, 07963 041402,
annmarie.1963@hotmail.co.uk.
Walsall. M6 J10 take A454 to Walsall
for 1.6m turn L at Lichfield St for
⅓m, turn L onto A461 Lichfield
Rd for 2m, at Co-op T-lights turn L
onto Mill rd then follow yellow signs.
Sat 9, Sun 10 July (10-6). Adm
£3.50, chd free. Home-made teas.
Sat 27 Aug (1.30-9). Adm £3.50.
Light refreshments. Sun 28 Aug
(11-9.30). Adm £3.50, chd free.
Light refreshments. Visits also
by arrangement May to Oct for
groups of up to 20.
Our garden is 15m x11m taking
several years to create and landscape
one area at a time. We have many
distinctive areas inc two ponds linked
by a stream with a stone waterfall,
many water features, places to sit,
watch and relax. We encourage
and welcome wildlife. Our planting
style is varied and inc architectural
plants for foliage, texture, over 40
trees. A calm garden of surprises,
intrigue and discovery. The garden
has a bridge over a stream and deep
water. Steps to and from some areas.
Gravel pathways. Please note: we
are located in cul-de-sac and parking
is limited, there is some available
in Broad Lane. Please park with
consideration
✿ ☕))

18 FOUR SEASONS
26 Buchanan Road, Walsall,
WS4 2EN. Marie & Tony Newton,
www.fourseasonsgarden.co.uk.
Adjacent to Walsall Arboretum. From
Ring Rd A4148 nr Walsall town
centre. At large junction take A461
to Lichfield. At 1st island 3rd exit
Buchanan Ave, fork R into Buchanan
Rd. Sat 22, Sun 23 Oct (10-5).

Adm £5, chd free. Tea.
Stunning in all seasons. Suburban,
south facing ¼ acre, gently sloping
to arboretum. 120 acers, 450
azaleas, bulbs, hellebores, camellias,
perennials, begonias, bright conifers,
topiary and shrubs. Autumn colours,
bark and berries. Semi-formal,
oriental, woodland-like areas and
jungle. Themes inc contrast of red,
blue and yellow. Pagoda, bridges,
water features, stone ornaments.
Some steps. WC.
🐕 ☕

19 THE GARTH
2 Broc Hill Way, Milford,
Stafford, ST17 0UB. Anita &
David Wright, 01785 661182,
anitawright1@yahoo.co.uk,
www.anitawright.co.uk. *4½m*
SE of Stafford. A513 Stafford to
Rugeley rd; at Barley Mow turn R
(S) to Brocton; L after ½m. Sun 5,
Sun 26 June (2-6). Adm £4, chd

High Trees

free. **Cream teas.** Visits also by arrangement June to Sept for groups of 20+.

½ acre garden of many levels on Cannock Chase AONB. Acid soil loving plants. Series of small gardens, water features, raised beds. Rare trees, island beds of unusual shrubs and perennials, many varieties of hosta and ferns. Varied and colourful foliage, summerhouses, arbours and quiet seating to enjoy the garden. Ancient sandstone caves.

20 33 GORWAY ROAD
Walsall, WS1 3BE. Gillian Brooks, 07972 615501, Brooks.gillian@gmail.com. *M6 J9 turn N onto Bescot Rd, at r'about take Wallows L (A4148), in 2 m at r'about, 1st exit Birmingham Rd, L to Jesson Rd, L to Gorway Rd.* **Sat 28 May (10-3.30). Adm £3.50, chd free. Home-made teas.** Visits also by arrangement May to Sept.

Cottage style Edwardian house garden. Late spring bulbs and roses. Willow tunnel, pond and rockery. Garden viewing is over flat grass and paths. Wheelchair access through garage.

21 GRAFTON COTTAGE
Barton-under-Needwood, DE13 8AL. Margaret & Peter Hargreaves, 01283 713639, marpeter1@btinternet.com. *6m N of Lichfield. Leave A38 for Catholme S of Barton, follow sign to Barton Green, L at Royal Oak, ¼ m.* **Sun 3, Fri 15, Sun 17, Sun 31 July, Sun 7, Sun 21 Aug (12-5). Adm £4.50, chd free. Home-made teas.** Visits also by arrangement June to Aug. Minimum admission £90 if less than 20 people. Donation to Alzheimer's Research UK.

Picturesque cottage garden opening for 30th year. Colour themed borders, amphitheatre, brook, parterre. Old fashioned roses climbing over trellis and arches laden with viticella clematis. Hollyhocks adorn the front of the cottage, perfume from lilies, sweet peas and violas. A wide range of salvias, dahlias and unusual perennials. Foliage seating corner showing many different colours of green. Regional Finalist, The English Garden's The Nation's Favourite Gardens 2021

22 NEW 128 GREEN ACRES ROAD
Kings Norton, Birmingham, B38 8NL. Mr & Mrs Mark Whitehouse. *From the M42 J2 take the A441 towards Birmingham take the 2nd exit at r'about continue along the A441 for 3m Green Acres Rd is on the R next to Spar.* **Sat 30 July (11-4.30). Combined adm with 143 Redditch Road £6. Light refreshments.**

A small garden with lots of character full of interest and abundance of colour, inc various seating areas to enjoy different aspects and views. The garden has many different types of perennials, Hostas, Roses and Dahlias. A fish pond, water feature plus many more points of interest. To access the garden, please follow signs to enter the garden from the rear.

23 22 GREENFIELD ROAD
Stafford, ST17 0PU. Alison & Peter Jordan, 01785 660819, alison.jordan2@btinternet.com. *3m S of Stafford. Follow the A34 out of Stafford towards Cannock. 2nd L onto Overhill Rd.1st R into Greenfield Rd.* **Evening opening Fri 17 June (7-9). Adm £5, chd free. Wine. Sat 18 June (11.30-4.30). Adm £3, chd free. Home-made teas.** Visits also by arrangement May to July for groups of up to 20.

Suburban garden, working towards all round interest. In spring bulbs and stunning azaleas and rhododendrons. June onwards perennials and grasses. A garden that shows being diagnosed with Parkinson's needn't stop you creating a peaceful place to sit and enjoy. You might be able to catch a glimpse of Pete's model railway running. Come in the evening and enjoy a glass of wine and live music. Flat garden but with some gravelled areas.

GROUP OPENING

24 HALL GREEN GARDENS
Hall Green, Birmingham, B28 8SQ. *Off A34, 4m from city centre, 6m from M42, J4. From City Centre start at 120 Russell Rd B28 8SQ . Alternatively, from M42 start at 638 Shirley Rd B28 9LB.* **Sat 11, Sun 12 June (1.30-5.30). Combined adm £6, chd free. Cream teas at 111 Southam Road.**

42 BODEN ROAD
Mrs Helen Lycett.

36 FERNDALE ROAD
Mrs E A Nicholson, 0121 777 4921. Visits also by arrangement Mar to Sept for groups of up to 30. Adm inc home-made teas.

120 RUSSELL ROAD
Mr David Worthington, 07552 993911, hildave@hotmail.com. Visits also by arrangement May to Sept for groups of up to 30.

638 SHIRLEY ROAD
Dr & Mrs M Leigh.

111 SOUTHAM ROAD
Ms Val Townend & Mr Ian Bate.

Five very different large suburban gardens in leafy Hall Green with its beautiful mature trees and friendly residents. Our visitors love the unique atmosphere in each garden. It's such a perfect way to share a relaxing early summer saunter and pause for refreshments served by our brilliant catering team. We look forward to seeing you! 42 Boden Rd: Large restful garden, mature trees, cottage borders, seating areas and small vegetable area. 36 Ferndale Rd: Florist's large suburban garden, ponds and waterfalls, and fruit garden. 120 Russell Rd: Plantsman's garden, formal raised pond and hosta collection and unusual perennials, container planting. 111 Southam Rd: Mature garden with well defined areas inc ponds, white garden, rescue hens and a majestic cedar. 638 Shirley Rd: Large garden with herbaceous borders, vegetables and greenhouses. Unfortunately, there is only partial wheelchair access at some gardens.

National Garden Scheme gardens are identified by their yellow road signs and posters. You can expect a garden of quality, character and interest, a warm welcome and plenty of home-made cakes!

25 HAMILTON HOUSE

Roman Grange, Roman Road, Little Aston Park, Sutton Coldfield, B74 3GA. Philip & Diana Berry, www.hamiltonhousegarden.co.uk. *3m N of Sutton Coldfield. Follow A454 (Walsall Rd) & enter Roman Rd, Little Aston Park. Roman Grange is 1st L after church but enter rd via pedestrian gate.* Sun 29 May (2-5). Home-made teas. Evening opening Sat 20 Aug (7-10). Adm £6, chd free. Wine and canapes (Aug only).

½ acre north facing English woodland garden in a tranquil setting, making the most of challenging shade, providing a haven for birds and other wildlife. Large pond with a stone bridge, pergolas, water features, box garden with a variety of roses. Interesting collection of rhododendrons, clematis, hostas, ferns, old English roses and stunning artworks in the garden. Join us for tea and cakes, listening to live music and admire the art of our garden.

✿ 🍵 ⑴)

26 HIGH TREES

Drubbery Lane, nr Longton Park, Stoke-on-Trent, ST3 4BA. Peter & Pat Teggin, 07979 000349. *5m S of Stoke-on-Trent. Off A5035, midway between Trentham Gardens & Longton. Opp Longton Park.* Visits by arrangement Apr to June weekdays only (10–4). Adm £6, chd free. Home-made teas. Adm inc refreshments.

A delightful, secluded, inspirational garden. Intensively planted mixed herbaceous borders with bulbs in spring, trillium, climbing roses and clematis with an emphasis on scent and colour combinations. Spires, flats and fluffs interwoven with structural planting and focal points. Planted for year-round interest with many unusual plants. Two minutes from a Victorian park.

 🍵

27 NEW THE HOME BEE GARDEN

143 Kings Norton, Birmingham, B38 8RH. Mr & Mrs Zoe Brady, www.thehomebeegarden.co.uk. *We are on the A441, 3m from the M42 Hopwood services or 5.4m from the city centre Birmingham.* Sat 21 May (11-4.30). Adm £4, chd free. Sat 30 July (11-4.30). Combined adm with 128 Green Acres Road £6, chd free. Home-made teas.

The Home Bee Garden is a large family garden, set within historic

---

Kings Norton, Birmingham. Extensive kitchen garden growing a variety of seasonal vegetables, herbs, fruit, with seasonal herbaceous borders, bedding, war effort fruit trees, secret paths, interesting features and resident chickens. Each season offers a unique aspect, spring meadow, summer flowers and autumn colour.

🐄 ✿ 🍵 ⑴)

28 'JOHN'S GARDEN' AT ASHWOOD NURSERIES

Ashwood Lower Lane, Ashwood, nr Kingswinford, DY6 0AE. John Massey, www.ashwoodnurseries.com. *9m S of Wolverhampton. 1m past Wall Heath on A449 turn R to Ashwood along Doctor's Lane. At T-junction turn L. Garden entrance off Main Car Park at Ashwood Nurseries.* Sun 17 Apr (10-4). Adm £6.50, chd free.

A stunning private garden adjacent to Ashwood Nurseries, it has a huge plant collection and many innovative design features in a beautiful canal-side setting. There are informal beds, woodland dells, a stunning rock garden, a unique ruin garden, an Anemone pavonina meadow and wildlife meadow. Fine displays of bulbs and Spring-flowering plants and a notable collection of Malus and Amelanchier. Tea Room, Garden Centre and Gift Shop at adjacent Ashwood Nurseries. Coaches are welcome by appointment only. Disabled access difficult if very wet. Sorry no disabled access to the wildlife garden.

& ✿ NPC 🍵

29 KEEPER'S COTTAGE; BLUEBELL WOOD

24 Greensforge Lane, Stourton, Stourbridge, DY7 5BB. Peter & Jenny Brookes, 07974 454503, peter@brookesmedia.com. *2m NW of Stourbridge. At junction of A449 & A458 at Stourton, take Bridgnorth Rd (A458) westward, after ½m turn R into Greensforge Ln. Keeper's Cottage ½m on R.* Sat 7, Sun 8 May (11-3.30). Adm £4, chd free. Home-made teas on the decking at the rear of the house. Visits also by arrangement in May for groups of up to 12.

This stunning bluebell wood adorns the banks of a river deep in the South Staffordshire countryside, yet only a few miles from the conurbation. In May, the bluebells form a beautiful carpet, sweeping through the natural woodland down to the river,

---

the site of ancient nail making. It is a quintessentially English landscape which can only be glimpsed for a few short weeks of the year.

🐄 🍵

30 NEW 14 LONGBOW CLOSE, STRETTON

Burton upon Trent, DE13 0XY. Debbie & Gavin Richards. *3m from Burton upon Trent in the village of Stretton. From A38 turn off at A5121 (Burton north) Follow signs to Stretton turning into Claymills Road, then L into Church Road, R into Bridge St & R into Athelstan Way. Please park on Athelstan Way.* Sun 26 June (11-4). Adm £3, chd free. Home-made teas with cakes created & served by Stretton & Claymills WI.

The garden is an oasis with a good structure of evergreen planting with some lovely roses, a flower-filled sunny patio where refreshments can be enjoyed and a welcoming front garden. Its design features planting of herbaceous perennials, climbers and evergreen trees with a mauve, pink and purple colour theme. There is good level access to most of the garden with one shallow step.

✿ 🍵

31 MARIE CURIE HOSPICE GARDEN

Marsh Lane, Solihull, B91 2PQ. Mrs Do Connolly, www.mariecurie. org.uk/westmidlands. *Close to J5 M42 to E of Solihull Town Centre. M42 J5, travel towards Solihull on A41. Take slip toward Solihull to join B4025 & after island take 1st R onto Marsh Lane. Hospice is on R. Limited onsite parking - available for blue badge holders.* Sun 26 June (11-4). Adm £4, chd free. Light refreshments at the hospice bistro.

The gardens contain two large, formally laid out patients' gardens, indoor courtyards, a long border adjoining the car park and a wildlife and pond area. The volunteer gardening team hope that the gardens provide a peaceful and comforting place for patients, their visitors and staff.

& 🐄 ✿ 🍵 ⑴)

32 3 MARLOWS COTTAGES

Little Hay Lane, Little Hay, Lichfield, WS14 0QD. Phyllis Davies. *4m S of Lichfield. Take A5127, Birmingham Rd. Turn L at*

Truckle House, Croxden

Park Ln (opp Tesco Express) then R at T junction into Little Hay Ln, ½m on L. **Sun 12 June, Sun 10 July (11-4). Adm £3, chd free. Home-made teas.**
Long, narrow, gently sloping cottage style garden with borders and beds containing abundant herbaceous perennials and shrubs leading to vegetable patch.

33 NEW 13 MAVIS ROAD
Hednesford, Cannock, WS12 4BS. Mr Ryan Hadlington, 07951 747265, rhadlington@live.co.uk.
Hednesford. From Hednesford train stn take 2nd exit at r'about Greenheath Rd, 2nd R High Mount St, 2nd L Heath St, 1st L. **Visits by arrangement June to Sept for groups of up to 10. Adm £3, chd free. Cream teas.**
In the old mining town of Hednesford in the heart of Cannock Chase AONB, we have created a small garden just 15m x 11m in which 13 smaller gardens have been created, from a David Austin inspired garden to, tropical, bee and butterfly, woodland,

and luna garden, even a carnivorous bog garden and more. Our idea was to show even the smallest of gardens could bring beauty and nature for us to enjoy.

34 12 MERES ROAD
Halesowen, B63 2EH. Nigel & Samantha Hopes, 01384 413070, contact@hopesgardenplants.co.uk, www.hopesgardenplants.co.uk.
4m from M5 J3. Follow the A458 out of Halesowen heading W for 2m, L turn onto Two Gates Ln just after Round of Beef pub, this becomes Meres Rd. House is on R. **Sun 1 May, Sun 18 Sept (11-4). Adm £3.50, chd free. Light refreshments. Visits also by arrangement Apr to Oct for groups of 10 to 25.**
A little oasis in the heart of the Black Country, with stunning views across to Shropshire. The borders are filled with interest and colour throughout the year. A small family garden, designed for young children and plantaholics alike, we hold a National Collection of Border Auriculas, with a passion for Snowdrops, Hellebores, Epimedium, Bearded Iris, Roscoea,

Cyclamen and Kniphofia.

35 MILLENNIUM GARDEN
London Road, Lichfield, WS14 9RB. Carol Cooper. *1m S of Lichfield. Off A38 along A5206 towards Lichfield ¼m past A38 island towards Lichfield. Park in field on L. Yellow signs on field post.* **Sun 6 Mar, Sun 24 Apr (1-5). Adm £3.50, chd free. Home-made teas.**
2 acre garden with mixed spring bulbs in the woodland garden and host of golden daffodils fade slowly into the summer borders in this English country garden. Designed with a naturalistic edge and with the environment in mind. A relaxed approach creates a garden of quiet sanctuary with the millennium bridge sitting comfortably, with its surroundings of lush planting and mature trees. Well-stocked borders give shots of colour to lift the spirit and the air fills with the scent of wisterias and climbing roses. A stress free environment awaits you at the Millennium Garden. Park in field then footpath round garden. Some uneven surfaces.

John's Garden at Ashwood Nurseries

36 MONARCHS WAY

Park Lane, Coven,
Wolverhampton, WV9 5BQ. Eileen
& Bill Johnson, 07785 934085,
snappy_eileen@hotmail.com,
www.monarchsway-garden.co.uk.
*From Port Ln (main road between
Codsall & Brewood) turn E onto Park
Ln. Monarchs Way is on the sharp
bend on Park Ln. Limited parking,
(further parking is available at other
end of Park In).* **Fri 17, Sat 18 June
(11-4). Adm £6, chd free. Pre-
booking essential, please visit
www.ngs.org.uk for information &
booking. Home-made teas. Visits
also by arrangement May to Oct
for groups of 5 to 20.**
We bought a 1¾ acre bare, treeless
blank canvas in 2010 with grass
around three feet high! Since then
we have designed a Tudor folly and
jungle hut, built a pergola, excavated
a lily pond with bog garden created

a cottage garden, orchard, and
vegetable garden. We have planted
hundreds of conifer, evergreen,
fruit and flowering trees, roses,
hydrangeas, perennials and designed
numerous flower beds. Wheelchair
access is easy for most of the garden,
on arrival request side gate for
access. Minibuses can be accepted.
♿ ☕

37 15 NEW CHURCH ROAD

Sutton Coldfield, B73 5RT. Owen
& Lloyd Watkins. *4½ m NW of
Birmingham city centre. Take A38M
then A5127 to 6 Ways r'about, take
2nd exit then bear L Summer Rd
then Gravelly Ln over Chester Rd to
Boldmere Rd, 5th R New Church Rd.*
**Sun 26 June (1-5). Adm £4, chd
free. Light refreshments.**
A garden created and evolved over
12 yrs, never standing still. From the
patio an extended pond takes centre

stage. A small stumpery is now well
established. An extended dry shade
area. Herbaceous borders, tree ferns,
bamboo hedging, a rockery and
woodland area. Raised vegetable
beds, chickens and a composting
system. Wheelchair access is
available, although some areas may
not be accessible. Several steps,
portable ramps available.
♿ ✧ ☕ ♩

38 THE OLD DAIRY HOUSE

Trentham Park, Stoke-on-Trent,
ST4 8AE. Philip & Michelle Moore.
*S edge of Stoke-on-Trent. Next to
Trentham Gardens. Off Whitmore Rd.
Please follow NGS signs or signs for
Trentham Park Golf Club. Parking in
church car park.* **Sat 4 June (1-5);
Sun 5 June (1.30-5.30). Adm £5,
chd free. Home-made teas.**
Grade II listed house which originally
formed part of the Trentham Estate

forms backdrop to this 2 acre garden in parkland setting. Shaded area for rhododendrons, azaleas plus expanding hosta and fern collection. Mature trees, 'cottage garden', long borders and stumpery. Narrow brick paths in vegetable plot. Large courtyard area for teas. Wheelchair access - some gravel paths but lawns are an option.

39 THE OLD VICARAGE
Fulford, nr Stone, ST11 9QS. Mike & Cherry Dodson. *4m N of Stone. From Stone A520 (Leek). 1m R turn to Spot Acre & Fulford, turn L down Post Office Terrace, past village green/Pub towards church. Parking signed on L.* **Sat 18 June (11-4.30). Adm £5, chd free. Home-made teas.**
1½ acres of formal sloping garden around Victorian house. Sit on the terrace or in the summerhouse to enjoy home-made cakes and tea amongst mature trees, relaxed herbaceous borders, roses and a small pond. Move to the organic vegetable garden with raised beds, fruit cage and very big compost heaps! In complete contrast, easy walk around the natural setting of a 2 acre reclaimed lake planted with native species designed to attract wildlife. Waterfall, jetty, fishing hut, acer and fern glade plus arboretum provide more interest. Children will enjoy meeting the chickens and horses. A garden of contrasts, with easy formality around the Victorian house and the accent on very natural planting around the lake, managed for wildlife and sustainability. Wheelchair access to most areas.

40 10 PAGET RISE
Paget Rise, Abbots Bromley, Rugeley, WS15 3EF. Mr Arthur Tindle. *4m W of Rugeley 6m S of Uttoxeter & 12m N of Lichfield. From Rugeley: B5013 E. At T junction turn R on B5014. From Uttoxeter take the B5013 S then B5014. From Lichfield take A515 N then turn L on B5234. In Abbots Bromley follow NGS yellow signs.* **Sun 15 May (11-5). Adm £3, chd free. Light refreshments.**
This small two level garden has a strong Japanese influence. Rhododendrons and a wide range of flowering shrubs. Many bonsai-style Acer trees in shallow bowls occupy a central gravel area with stepping stones. The rear of the garden has a woodland feel with a fairy dell under the pine tree. A little gem of a garden!

Arthur hopes visitors will be inspired with ideas to use in their own garden. Arthur is a watercolour artist and will be displaying a selection of his paintings for sale.

41 PAUL'S OASIS OF CALM
18 Kings Close, Kings Heath, Birmingham, B14 6TP.
Mr Paul Doogan, 0121 444 6943, gardengreen18@hotmail.co.uk. *4m from city centre. 5m from M42 J4. Take A345 to Kings Heath High St then B4122 Vicarage Rd. Turn L onto Kings Rd then R to Kings Close.* **Visits by arrangement May to Aug for groups of up to 15. Adm £2.50, chd free. Light refreshments.**
Garden cultivated from nothing into a little oasis. Measuring 18ft x 70ft. It's small but packed with interesting and unusual plants, water features and seven seating areas. It's my piece of heaven. I have cultivated the council land in front of my house which has doubled the pleasure!

42 THE PINTLES
18 Newport Road, Great Bridgeford, Stafford, ST18 9PR. Peter & Leslie Longstaff, 01785 282582, peter.longstaff@ngs.org.uk. *From J14 M6 take A5013 towards Eccleshall, in Great Bridgeford turn L onto B5405 after 600 metres turn L onto Great Bridgeford Village Hall car park The Pintles is opp the hall main doors.* **Sun 5 June (1.30-5). Adm £3.50, chd free. Home-made teas inc gluten free & reduced sugar options. Visits also by arrangement June & July for groups of 10 to 30.**
Located in the village of Great Bridgeford this traditional semi-detached house has a medium sized wildlife friendly garden designed to appeal to many interests. There are two greenhouses, 100s of cacti succulents, vegetable and fruit plot, wildlife pond, weather station and hidden woodland shady garden. Plenty of outside seating to enjoy the home-made cakes and refreshments.

43 49 THE PLANTATION
Pensnett, Brierley Hill, DY5 4RT. Dave & Kath Baker. *From Russells Hall Hospital, take Pensnett High St (A4101) to Kingswinford. After 1½m turn L into The Plantation. Please*

park with consideration. **Sun 19 June, Sun 17 July (11-3). Adm £3, chd free. Home-made teas.**
Small suburban garden 60 ft x 30 ft with lots of roses, hemerocallis, well-stocked borders and fruit trees. Greenhouse with tomatoes, cucumbers and grape vine. Productive vegetable garden.

44 8 RECTORY ROAD
Solihull, B91 3RP. Nigel & Daphne Carter. *Town centre. Located in the town centre: off Church Hill Rd, turn into Rectory Rd, bear L down the rd, house on the R 100 metres down.* **Sun 12 June (11-6). Light refreshments. Evening opening Sun 4 Sept (7-10). Wine. Adm £4, chd free.**
Stunning town garden divided into areas with different features. A garden with unusual trees and intensively planted borders. Walk to the end of the garden and step into a Japanese garden complete with pond, fish and traditional style bridge. Sit on the shaded decking area. A garden to attract bees and butterflies with plenty of places to relax. Japanese themed features and stunning Moon gate.

45 23 ST JOHNS ROAD
Rowley Park, Stafford, ST17 9AS. Colin and Fiona Horwath, 07908 918181, fiona_horwath@yahoo.co.uk. *½m S of Stafford Town Centre. Just a few mins from J13 M6, towards Stafford. After approx 2m on the A449, turn L into St. John's Rd after bus-stop.* **Sun 20 Mar, Thur 28 Apr, Fri 20 May, Thur 9 June (2-5). Home-made teas. Thur 7 July (2-5). Adm £4, chd free. Visits also by arrangement Mar to Sept for groups of 20 to 60.**
Pass through the black and white gate of this Victorian house into a part-walled gardener's haven. Bulbs and shady woodlanders in Spring and masses of herbaceous plants and climbers. Sit and enjoy home-made cakes by the pond or Victorian-style greenhouse. Gardener is keen Hardy Plant Society member and sows far too many seeds, so always something good for sale! Our outdoor kitchen and new revolving summerhouse are great for refreshments! Plenty of places to sit and enjoy the myriad plants. Sensory trail to entertain visitors.

46 THE SECRET GARDEN

3 Banktop Cottages, Little Haywood, ST18 0UL. **Derek Higgott & David Aston, 01889 883473, davidaston1065@yahoo.co.uk.** *5m SE of Stafford. A51 from Rugeley or Weston signed Little Haywood A513 Stafford Coley Ln, Back Ln R into Coley Gr. Entrance 50 metres on L.* **Thur 19 May, Wed 29 June, Wed 20 July, Thur 18 Aug (11-4). Adm £4, chd free. Home-made teas. Visits also by arrangement May to Aug.**

Wander past the other cottage gardens and through the evergreen arch and there before you is a fantasy for the eyes and soul. Stunning garden approx ½ acre, created over the last 30+yrs. Strong colour theme of trees and shrubs, underplanted with perennials, 1000 bulbs and laced with clematis; other features inc water, laburnum and rose tunnel and unique buildings. Is this the jewel in the crown? New water feature and a warm Bothy for inclement days. Most areas have had a complete make-over during Covid lockdown. Wheelchair access difficult - some slopes.

&. 🍵

47 NEW SPRINGFIELD COTTAGE

Kiddemore Green Road, Bishops Wood, Stafford, ST19 9AA. **Mrs Rachel Glover, 07811 342300, Rachelglover1971@gmail.com.** *A5 to Telford from Gailey Island. Turn L at sign for Boscobel House. Follow Ivetsey Bank Rd to Bishop's Wood. Turn 1st L Old Coach Road past church second white cottage on L.* **Sat 23 Apr, Sat 25 June, Fri 9 Sept (11-4). Adm £4, chd free. Home-made teas. Will cater for vegan diets as well. Visits also by arrangement Apr to Sept for groups of up to 25.**

Newly designed and landscaped plant enthusiasts cottage garden with unusual planting in areas, a tropical area inc Gunera's, Cannas, Hedichiums and palms, a rose garden and an established vegetable garden with large greenhouse. Fantastic views of the south Staffordshire countryside from all sides of the garden. Disabled parking for two cars, flat garden area and WC facilities.

&. 🌟 🍵))

48 NEW 76 STATION STREET

Cheslyn Hay, Walsall, WS6 7EE. **Mr Paul Husselbee.** *Located on B4156. Limited on road parking.* **Sun 24 July (11-6). Adm £3, chd free. Home-made teas.**

40 years of gardening on this site has produced a hosta filled courtyard which leads to a Mediterranean patio, steps down to small area with folly, formal gardens area with stream, gated courtyard then finally find the secret garden. A quirky garden with a surprise round every corner.

🐑 🍵 🪑

49 91 TOWER ROAD

Four Oaks, Sutton Coldfield, B75 5EQ. **Heather & Gary Hawkins.** *3m N Sutton Coldfield. From A5127 at Mere Green island, turn onto Mere Green Rd towards Sainsburys, L at St James Church, L again onto Tower Rd.* **Sun 12 June (1.30-5.30). Adm £3, chd free. Cream teas.**

163ft south facing garden with sweeping borders and island beds planted with an eclectic mix of shrubs and perennials. We have made a few changes recently, and removing a tired rockery has given us more room for another seating to enjoy the sunshine. A vast array of home-made cakes will tempt you during your visit. An ideal setting for sunbathing, children's hide and seek and lively garden parties. Large selection of home-made cream teas to eat in the garden or take away. Plant sale on front drive for garden visitors and passers by. More than just an Open Garden, we like to think of it as a garden party!

🐑 🌟 🍵))

50 NEW TRUCKLE HOUSE, CROXDEN

Uttoxeter, ST14 5JD. **Mrs Hilary Hawksworth, 01889 507124, hilaryhawk@outlook.com.** *7m NW of Uttoxeter. From Uttoxeter take B5030 towards Rocester. At the r'about by JCB HQ turn L onto Hollington Rd & follow brown signs to Croxden Abbey (+yellow NGS signs) Parking at Croxden Church 375yds past house.* **Sun 19 June (12-5). Adm £5, chd free. Home-made teas. Visits also by arrangement Apr to July for groups of 6 to 20.**

A truly unique and tranquil setting for this rural ¾ acre garden, set against the impressive remains of Croxden Abbey. Lovingly created over the past 15 years to include mixed herbaceous borders, dozens of roses, trees and shrubs, wildflower meadow, large natural pond with bridge over, vegetable patch. The garden offers a riot of colour and scent in summer but has year-round interest.

🐑 🌟 🍵

51 12 WATERDALE

Compton, Wolverhampton, WV3 9DY. **Colin & Clair Bennett.** *1½m W of Wolverhampton city centre. From Wolverhampton Ring Rd take A454 towards Bridgnorth for 1m. Waterdale is on the L off A454 Compton Rd West.* **Sun 5 June, Sun 3 July (11.30-5). Combined adm with 19 Waterdale £5, chd free.**

A riot of colour welcomes visitors to this quintessentially English garden. The wide central circular bed and side borders overflow with classic summer flowers, inc the tall spires of delphiniums, lupins, irises, campanula, poppies and roses. Clematis tumble over the edge of the decked terrace, where visitors can sit among pots of begonias and geraniums to admire the view over the garden.

🍵

52 19 WATERDALE

Compton, Wolverhampton, WV3 9DY. **Anne & Brian Bailey, 01902 424867, m.bailey1234@btinternet.com.** *1½m W of Wolverhampton city centre. From Wolverhampton Ring Rd take A454 towards Bridgnorth for 1m. Waterdale is on L off A454 Compton Rd West.* **Sun 5 June, Sun 3 July (11.30-5). Combined adm with 12 Waterdale £5, chd free. Home-made teas. Visits also by arrangement June to Aug for groups of 10 to 40.**

A romantic garden of surprises, which gradually reveals itself on a journey through deep, lush planting, full of unusual plants. From the sunny, flower filled terrace, a ruined folly emerges from a luxuriant fernery and leads into an oriental garden, complete with tea house. Towering bamboos hide the way to the gothic summerhouse and mysterious shell grotto. Find us on Facebook at 'Garden of Surprises'.

🌟 🚗 🍵))

53 THE WICKETS

47 Long Street, Wheaton Aston, ST19 9NF. Tony & Kate Bennett, 01785 840233, ajtonyb@talktalk.net. *8m W of Cannock, 10m N of Wolverhampton, 10m E of Telford. M6 J12 W towards Telford on A5; 3m R signed Stretton; 150yds L signed Wheaton Aston; 2m L; over canal, garden on R or at Bradford Arms on A5 follow signs.* Sun 24, Wed 27 July, Sun 28 Aug (1.30-4.30). Adm £4, chd free. Home-made teas. Visits also by arrangement July & Aug.

There's a delight around every corner and lots of quirky features in this most innovative garden. Its themed areas inc a fernery, grasses bed, hidden gothic garden, succulent theatre, cottage garden beds and even a cricket match! It will certainly give you ideas for your own garden as you sit and have tea and cake. Afterwards, walk by the canal and enjoy the beautiful surrounding countryside. Wheelchair access - two single steps in garden and two gravel paths.

54 NEW 25 WOLVERHAMPTON ROAD

Bloxwich, Walsall, WS3 2HB. Mr Mick Carter. *2m S of J11 of M6. Leave J11 of M6 take A462 to Willenhall, Warstone Rd. At first set of T-lights turn L onto B4210 Broad Ln at next set of T-lights turn L A424 then Ist R then 1st L is Wolv Rd.* Sun 31 July (11-4). Adm £3, chd free. Cream teas.

Garden packed with plants, flowering perennials, acers, shrubs, trees, wildlife pond with waterfall. A small Japanese garden with bamboo deer scarer water feature and Torre Gate. Eye catching Gothic Folly adorned with plants and flowers. Hand made raised vegetable beds.

55 2 WOODLAND CRESCENT

Finchfield, Wolverhampton, WV3 8AS. Mr & Mrs Parker, 01902 332392, alisonparker1960@hotmail.co.uk. *2m SW of Wolverhampton City centre. From Inner Ring Rd take A41 W to Tettenhall. At junction with A459 turn L onto Merridale Rd. Straight over Bradwell Xrds then R onto Trysull Rd. 3rd R onto Coppice Rd & 1st R onto Woodland Crescent.* Sun 26 June (11.30-4). Adm £3.50, chd free. Home-made teas. Visits also by arrangement June & July

for groups of 5 to 20.

A semi-detached townhouse garden 120 x 25 ft, every inch packed with perennials, trees, acers, shrubs, roses, hostas and clematis. Wildlife pond and nesting boxes to attract birds. Productive vegetable and fruit garden. Informal style but clipped box and topiary animals add some formality.

56 YARLET HOUSE

Yarlet, Stafford, ST18 9SD. Mr & Mrs Nikolas Tarling. *2m S of Stone. Take A34 from Stone towards Stafford, turn L into Yarlet School & L again into car park.* Fri 17 June (10-1). Adm £4, chd free. Light refreshments. Donation to Staffordshire Wildlife Trust.

4 acre garden with extensive lawns, walks, lengthy herbaceous borders and traditional Victorian box hedge. Water gardens with fountain and rare lilies. Sweeping views across Trent Valley to Sandon. New peaceful Japanese garden for 2021. Victorian School Chapel. 9 hole putting course. Boules pitch. Yarlet School Art Display. Gravel paths.

57 YEW TREE COTTAGE

Podmores Corner, Long Lane, White Cross, Haughton, ST18 9JR. Clive & Ruth Plant, 07591 886925, pottyplantz@aol.com. *4m W of Stafford. Take A518 W Haughton, turn R Station Rd (signed Ranton) 1m, then turn R at Xrds ¼ m on R.* Thur 7, Thur 14, Thur 21 July (11-4); Sun 24 July (2-5). Adm £4, chd

free. Home-made teas. Visits also by arrangement in July for groups of 10+. Donation to Plant Heritage.

Hardy Plant Society member's garden brimming with unusual plants. Year-round interest inc Meconopsis, Trillium. ½ acre inc gravel, borders, vegetables and plant sales. National Collection Dierama featured on BBC Gardeners' World flowering first half July. Facebook 'Dierama Species in Staffordshire'. Covered vinery for tea if weather is unkind, and seats in the garden for lingering on sunny days. Partial wheelchair access, grass and paved paths, some narrow and some gravel.

58 YEW TREES

Whitley Eaves, Eccleshall, Stafford, ST21 6HR. Mrs Teresa Hancock, 07973 432077, hancockteresa@gmail.com. *7m from J14 M6. Situated on A519 between Eccleshall (2.2m) & Woodseaves, (1m). Traffic cones & signs will highlight the entrance.* Sat 25, Sun 26 June (10-4). Adm £4, chd free. Pre-booking essential, please visit www.ngs.org.uk for information & booking. Tea. Visits also by arrangement June to Aug.

1 acre garden divided into rooms by mature hedging, shrubs and trees enjoying views over the surrounding countryside. Large patio area with containers and seating. Other features inc pond, topiary, vegetable plot, hen run and wildlife area. During June and July there are 8 acres of natural wildflower meadow to enjoy before it is cut for hay.

Brackencote

SUFFOLK

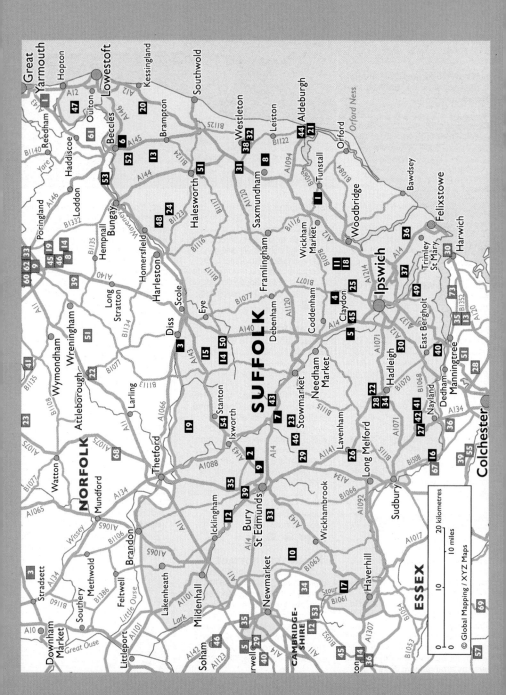

Suffolk has so much to offer – from charming coastal villages, ancient woodlands and picturesque valleys – there is a landscape to suit all tastes.

Keen walkers and cyclists will enjoy Suffolk's low-lying, gentle countryside, where fields of farm animals and crops reflect the county's agricultural roots.

Stretching north from Felixstowe, the county has miles of Heritage Coast set in an Area of Outstanding Natural Beauty. The Suffolk coast was the inspiration for composer Benjamin Britten's celebrated work, and it is easy to see why.

To the west and north of the county are The Brecks, a striking canvas of pine forest and open heathland, famous for its chalky and sandy soils – and one of the most important wildlife areas in Britain.

A variety of gardens to please everyone open in Suffolk, so come along on an open day and enjoy the double benefit of a beautiful setting and supporting wonderful charities.

Volunteers

County Organiser
Jenny Reeve
01638 715289
jenny.reeve@ngs.org.uk

County Treasurer
Julian Cusack
01728 649060
julian.cusack@ngs.org.uk

Publicity
Jenny Reeve
(as above)

Social Media
Barbara Segall
01787 312046
barbara.segall@ngs.org.uk

Booklet Co-ordinator
Michael Cole
07899 994307
michael.cole@ngs.org.uk

Assistant County Organisers
Michael Cole
(as above)

Gillian Garnham 01394 448122
gill.garnham@btinternet.com

Yvonne Leonard 01638 712742
yj.leonard@btinternet.com

Wendy Parkes 01473 785504
wendy.parkes@ngs.org.uk

Barbara Segall
(as above)

Peter Simpson 01787 249845
peter.simpson@ngs.org.uk

@SuffolkNGS
@SuffolkNGS

Left: Leaven Hall

OPENING DATES

All entries subject to change. For latest information check www.ngs.org.uk

Map locator numbers are shown to the right of each garden name.

February

Snowdrop Festival

Sunday 13th
◆ Blakenham Woodland
Garden   5
Gable House   13
Great Thurlow Hall   17

Sunday 20th
The Laburnums   24
Manor House   32

April

Sunday 3rd
Great Thurlow Hall   17

Monday 18th
Helyg   19

Saturday 23rd
Cattishall Farmhouse   9

Sunday 24th
◆ Blakenham Woodland
Garden   5

Magnolia House

◆ The Place for Plants,
East Bergholt Place
Garden   40

May

Sunday 1st
Moat House   33
Paget House   38

Sunday 8th
◆ Fullers Mill Garden   12
◆ The Place for Plants,
East Bergholt Place
Garden   40

Sunday 15th
Finndale House   11
Grundisburgh House   18

Sunday 22nd
The Priory   42

Saturday 28th
◆ Wyken Hall   54

Sunday 29th
Berghersh Place   4
Lavenham Hall   26
◆ Wyken Hall   54

June

Thursday 2nd
◆ The Red House   44

Saturday 4th
NEW Pulham Cottage   43

Sunday 5th
Barton Mere   2
Great Bevills   16

Holm House   23
NEW Longlands Place   30

Wednesday 8th
Leaven Hall   27

Saturday 11th
Magnolia House   31

Sunday 12th
Ashe Park   1
Granary Barn   15
Great Thurlow Hall   17
The Old Rectory,
Nacton   37
Smallwood Farmhouse   46

Wednesday 15th
Leaven Hall   27

Saturday 18th
Brambly Hedge   6

Sunday 19th
Heron House   21
Hillside   22
The Old Rectory,
Kirton   36
Polstead Mill   41

Wednesday 22nd
Leaven Hall   27

Thursday 23rd
NEW Woodland Drive
Gardens   53

Saturday 25th
Larks' Hill   25

Sunday 26th
Lillesley Barn   28
Old Gardens   34
5 Parklands Green   39

July

Saturday 2nd
White House Farm   52

Sunday 10th
Wenhaston Grange   51

Sunday 17th
Helyg   19
Paget House   38
Squires Barn   48

Sunday 24th
Batteleys Cottage   3
The Old Rectory   35
The Rooks   45

August

Tuesday 2nd
◆ Somerleyton Hall
Gardens   47

Saturday 6th
Gislingham Gardens   14

Sunday 7th
Gislingham Gardens   14

Sunday 28th
Bridges   7
Henstead Exotic Garden   20

Monday 29th
◆ The Red House   44

October

Sunday 2nd
◆ Fullers Mill Garden   12

Sunday 9th
◆ The Place for Plants,
East Bergholt Place
Garden   40

By Arrangement

Arrange a personalised garden visit with your club, or group of friends, on a date to suit you. See individual garden entries for full details.

Berghersh Place   4
Brambly Hedge   6
By the Crossways   8
Dip-on-the-Hill   10
Gislingham Gardens   14
Helyg   19
Heron House   21
Hillside   22
Holm House   23
Larks' Hill   25
Lillesley Barn   28
The Lodge   29
Manor House   32
Moat House   33
Old Gardens   34
Paget House   38
5 Parklands Green   39
Polstead Mill   41
NEW Pulham Cottage   43
The Rooks   45
Stone Cottage   49
NEW Thornham Walled
Garden   50
White House Farm   52

THE GARDENS

❶ ASHE PARK
Ivy Lodge Road, Campsea
Ashe, Woodbridge, IP13 0QB.
Mr Richard Keeling. *Using the
postcode in SatNav will bring you
to the entrance to Ashe Park on Ivy
Lodge Rd. Drive through entrance
signed Ashe Park, past the gate
cottage on L & follow signs to car
park.* **Sun 12 June (11-4.30). Adm
£6, chd free.**
In the 400 years of this 12 acre
garden's existence it has gone
through many changes. Gertrude
Jekyll said of it in 1905 that it was
interesting but it had no coherence
of design. Since then the main house
has been destroyed and the gardens
have been re-aligned, however the
bones of the gardens have been
retained namely canals, massive
cedar trees, yew hedges, walled
garden and many more features.
Partial wheelchair access, some
gravel paths and steps.
&. ♨ »)

❷ BARTON MERE
Thurston Road, Great Barton,
IP31 2PR. Mr & Mrs C O
Stenderup. *2m E of Bury St
Edmunds. From Bury St Edmunds
on A143 through Gt Barton turn R at
Bunbury Arms PH. Entrance ½ m on
L. From Thurston take Gt Barton Rd
from railway bridge. Entrance 1½ m
on R.* **Sun 5 June (1-5). Adm £5,
chd free.**
C16 house (not open) with later
Georgian façade, set in 50 acres of
parkland. Extensive lawns with views
over the Mere. Rose garden and
herbaceous borders mostly surrounded
by C16 walls, two courtyards and large
conservatory. Productive vegetable
garden, old orchard and beautiful grass
tennis court. Wheelchair access, gravel
paths.
&. 🐕

❸ BATTELEYS COTTAGE
The Ling, Wortham, Diss,
IP22 1ST. Mr Andy & Mrs Linda
Simpson. *3m W of Diss. Turn signed
from A143 Diss/Bury Rd at Wortham.
By Church turn R at T-junction. At
top of hill turn L. Go down hill &
round sharp L corner.* **Sun 24 July
(11.30-4.30). Adm £5, chd free.
Light lunches, home-made cakes,
tea, coffee and soft drinks.**
A varied one acre garden planted for
abundance in all seasons. Formality
and informality, a mix of winding bark
paths, light and shade, secluded
spots to sit, new vistas at every
turn. Fitting into its rural setting, it
supports a wealth of bird life. There
is a diversity of planting in densely
planted borders as well as pots,
sculptures, meadow, ponds, stream
and vegetable areas to inspire you.
Wheelchair access to most parts of
the garden, gravel, grass and bark
paths.
&. ❆ ♨ »)

❹ BERGHERSH PLACE
Witnesham, Ipswich, IP6 9EZ. Mr
& Mrs T C Parkes, 01473 785504,
wendyparkes@live.com. *N of
Witnesham village, B1077 double
bends. Farm entrance, concrete
drive, approx 1m S of Ashbocking
Xrds. Entrance on sharp bend so
please drive slowly. Turn in between
North Lodge & Berghersh House.*
**Sun 29 May (12-5). Adm £5,
chd free. Light refreshments.
Gluten-free options. Visits also by
arrangement in June.**
Peaceful walled and hedged gardens
surround elegant Regency house (not
open) among fields above the Fynn
Valley. Circular walk from the farm
buildings, around house with lawns
and mature trees to a pretty view of
the valley. Mound, ponds, bog area
and orchard paddock. Informal family
garden with shrub and perennial
beds. Garden created over last 25
years by current owner. Parking for
elderly and disabled available. Most
areas are accessible to disabled
visitors.
&. 🐕 ♨ »)

❺ ◆ BLAKENHAM WOODLAND
GARDEN
Little Blakenham, Ipswich, IP8 4LZ.
M Blakenham, 07917612355,
info@blakenhamfarms.com,
www.blakenhamwoodlandgarden.
org.uk. *4m NW of Ipswich. Follow
signs at Little Blakenham, 1m
off B1113 or go to Blakenham
Woodland Garden web-site.* **For
NGS: Sun 13 Feb, Sun 24 Apr
(10-4). Adm £5, chd £3. Home-
made teas. Tosier Chocolate
Stall. For other opening times and
information, please phone, email or
visit garden website.**
Beautiful 6 acre woodland garden
with variety of rare trees and shrubs,
Chinese rocks and a landscape
spiral form. Lovely in spring with
snowdrops, daffodils and camellias
followed by magnolias and bluebells.
Woodland Garden open from 1 Feb
to 28 June. NGS Openings 13 Feb -
Snowdrops and 24 April - Bluebells
and Magnolias. Suffolk Punches.A
formal vegetable garden open on
NGS days.
❆ 🚌 ♨ »)

❻ BRAMBLY HEDGE
Lowestoft Road, Beccles,
NR34 7DE. Lynton & Teresa
Cooper, 01502 715678,
Bramblyhedgegarden@outlook.
com. *From town centre head
towards Lowestoft, along Ingate -
on R after lights. From Lowestoft
direction head through Worlingham
on L before lights. Roadside parking
Ellough Rd.* **NR34 7AA. Sat 18
June (11-4). Adm £3.50, chd free.
Home-made teas. Visits also by
arrangement June to Aug.**
A garden of contrasts and surprises.
A modern introduction to a quirky
woodland finish, the visitor can
explore a huge variety of shrubs and
trees with many unusual specimens.
Add in a beautiful raised-bed potager
and just when you think you have
seen it all, and relax with tea and
cake on one of the many seats dotted
around, tucked away is a gem you
missed the first time.
❆ ♨

❼ BRIDGES
The Street, Woolpit, Bury St
Edmunds, IP30 9SA. Mr Stanley
Bates & Mr Michael Elles.
*Through green coach gates marked
Deliveries. From A14 take slip rd to
Woolpit, follow signs to centre of
village, road curves to R. Bridges
is on L & covered in Wisteria & opp
Co-op.* **Sun 28 Aug (11-5). Adm £5,
chd free. Home-made teas.**
C15 Grade II terraced house in the
centre of a C12 Suffolk village with
walled garden to the rear of the
property. Additional land was acquired
20 years ago, and this garden was
developed into formal and informal
planting. The main formal feature is
the Shakespeare Garden featuring
the bust of Shakespeare, and the
'Umbrello' a recently constructed
pavillion in an Italianate design. Statue
of Shakespeare, The Umbrello, various
surprises for children of all ages.
Usually a Wind Quintet playing in the
main garden. The Bull in village open
for lunch. Light lunches at Tea Cups.
❆ ♨

Pulham Cottage

8 BY THE CROSSWAYS

Kelsale, Saxmundham, IP17 2PL.
Mr & Mrs William Kendall,
miranda@bythecrossways.co.uk.
*2m NE of Saxmundham, just off
Clayhills Rd. ½ m N of town centre,
turn R to Theberton on Clayhills Rd.
After 1½ m, 1st L to Kelsale, turn L
immed after white cottage.* **Visits by
arrangement in Sept for groups of
up to 10. Adm £5, chd free.**
Three acre wildlife garden designed
as a garden within a working organic
farm where wilderness areas lie next
to productive beds. Large semi-
walled vegetable and cutting garden
and a spectacular crinkle-crankle
wall. Extensive perennial planting,
grasses and wild areas. This garden
is not highly manicured which more
traditionally minded gardeners may
find alarming! The garden is mostly
flat, with paved or gravel pathways
around the main house, a few low
steps and extensive grass paths and
lawns.

& ⊶ ☕ »)

9 CATTISHALL FARMHOUSE

Cattishall, Great Barton,
Bury St Edmunds, IP31 2QT.
Mrs J Mayer, 07738 936496,
joannamayer42@googlemail.com.
*3m NE of Bury St Edmunds.
Approach Great Barton from Bury
on A143 take 1st R turn to church.
If travelling towards Bury take last
L turn to church as you leave the
village. At church bear R & follow
lane to Farmhouse on R.* **Sat 23 Apr
(1-5). Adm £4, chd free. Home-
made teas.**
Approx 2 acre farmhouse garden
enclosed by a flint wall and mature
beech hedge laid mainly to lawns
with both formal and informal planting
and large herbaceous border. There
is an abundance of roses, small
wildlife pond and recently developed
kitchen garden inc a wildflower area
and fruit cages. Chickens, bees and
a boisterous Labrador also live here.
Generally flat with some gravel paths.
The occasional small step.

& ⊶ ⌂ ☕

10 DIP-ON-THE-HILL

Ousden, Newmarket,
CB8 8TW. Geoffrey & Christine
Ingham, 07947 309900,
gki1000@cam.ac.uk. *5m E of
Newmarket; 7m W of Bury St
Edmunds. From Newmarket: 1m
from junction of B1063 & B1085.
From Bury St Edmunds follow signs
for Hargrave. Parking at village hall.*

*Follow NGS sign at the end of the
lane.* **Visits by arrangement June to
Sept for groups of up to 12. Adm
£5, chd free. Tea.**
Approx 1 acre in a dip on a south
facing hill based on a wide range of
architectural/sculptural evergreen
trees, shrubs and groundcover:
pines; grove of Phillyrea latifolia;
'cloud pruned' hedges; palms; large
bamboo; ferns; range of kniphofia
and Croscosmia. Winner: 'Britain's
Best Garden' 2018, Telegraph/
Yorkshire Tea. Visitors may wish to
make an appointment when visiting
gardens nearby.

☕

11 FINNDALE HOUSE

Woodbridge Road, Grundisburgh,
Woodbridge, IP13 6UD. Bryan &
Catherine Laxton. *On B1079, 2m
NW of Woodbridge. Parking in field
(postcode IP13 6PU), blue badge
parking by the house. Short walk
to Grundisburgh House.* **Sun 15
May (11-5). Combined adm with
Grundisburgh House £6, chd free.
Home-made teas.**
A Georgian house surrounded by 10
acres of garden and meadows which
are bisected by a 'Monet' style bridge
over the River Lark. The garden was
designed 30 years ago and has been
refreshed by recent additions. Many
mature trees, colourful herbaceous
borders, thousands of daffodils
followed by tulips and alliums, roses in
the summer and dahlias to round the
year off. Productive kitchen garden.
Wheelchair access, gravel drive.

& ⊶ ✿ ☕ »)

12 ◆ FULLERS MILL GARDEN

West Stow, IP28 6HD.
Perennial, 01284 728888,
fullersmillgarden@perennial.org.uk,
www.fullersmillgarden.org.uk.
*6m NW of Bury St Edmunds. Turn
off A1101 Bury to Mildenhall Rd,
signed West Stow Country Park,
go past Country Park continue for
¼ m, garden entrance on R. Sign
at entrance.* **For NGS: Sun 8 May,
Sun 2 Oct (11-5). Adm £6, chd
free. Home-made teas. For other
opening times and information,
please phone, email or visit garden
website.**
An enchanting 7 acre garden on the
banks of the river Lark. A beautiful
site with light dappled woodland
and a plantsman's paradise of rare
and unusual shrubs, perennials
and marginals planted with great
natural charm. Euphorbias and lilies

are a particular feature with the late
flowering colchicums, inc many rare
varieties, being of great interest in
Autumn. Tea, coffee and soft drinks.
Home-made cakes. Partial wheelchair
access around garden.

& ✿ ⌂ ☕

13 GABLE HOUSE

Halesworth Road, Redisham,
Beccles, NR34 8NE. Brenda
Foster. *5m S of Beccles. Signed
from A12 at Blythburgh & A144
Bungay/Halesworth Rd.* **Sun 13 Feb
(11-4). Adm £4.50, chd free. Light
refreshments.**
We have a large collection of
snowdrops, cyclamen, hellebores
and other flowering plants for the
Snowdrop Day in February. Many
bulbs and plants will be for sale.
Greenhouses contain rare bulbs and
tender plants. Refreshments available.
A 1 acre garden with lawns and
scree with water feature. We have a
wide range of unusual trees, shrubs,
perennials and bulbs collected over
the last fifty years.

& ✿ ☕

GROUP OPENING

14 GISLINGHAM GARDENS
Mill Street, Gislingham, IP23 8JT. 01379 788737, alanstanley22@gmail.com. *4m W of Eye. Gislingham 2½ m W of A140. 9m N of Stowmarket, 8m S of Diss. Disabled parking at Ivy Chimneys. Parking limited to disabled parking at Chapel Farm Close.* **Sat 6, Sun 7 Aug (11-4.30). Combined adm £5, chd free. Light refreshments at Ivy Chimneys.** Visits also by arrangement June to Aug.

12 CHAPEL FARM CLOSE
Ross Lee.

IVY CHIMNEYS
Iris & Alan Stanley.

2 varied gardens in a picturesque village with a number of Suffolk timbered houses. Ivy Chimneys is planted for year-round interest with ornamental trees, some topiary, exotic borders and fishpond set in an area of Japanese style. Wisteria draped pergola supports a productive vine. Also a separate ornamental vegetable garden. Small orchard on front lawn. New 12 Chapel Farm Close is a tiny garden, exquisitely planted and an absolute riot of colour. Despite the garden's size, the owner has planted a Catalpa, a Cornus Florida Rubra and many unusual plants. It is a fine example of what can be achieved in a small space. Tea, coffee, fruit teas, squash, savouries, cake, vegetarian option, and gluten free options Wheelchair access to Ivy Chimneys. Access for smaller wheelchairs only at 12 Chapel Farm Close.

& ⛺ ☕

15 GRANARY BARN
Little Green, Burgate, Diss, IP22 1QQ. Wendy Keeble. *23m NE of Bury St Edmunds; 6m SW of Diss; 1m S of A143. On A143 between Wortham & Botesdale, take turning signed Burgate Little Green (Buggs Ln) & follow NGS signs to car park 200 yd walk from garden. No parking on verges or common please.* **Sun 12 June (11-4). Adm £4, chd £2. Tea and cake.**
If re-wilding is the latest trend, we must be high fashion! From 2 acres of closely mown grass 11 yrs ago, the garden now has formal planting near the house, box parterre and pergola, herbaceous borders, a productive orchard, vegetable and soft fruit gardens and a large perennial wildflower meadow with 120 native trees and pond. Our aim is to attract and sustain wildlife during every season. Tea and cakes are offered for sale. Partial wheelchair access can be organised on arrival.

& ⛺ ☕

16 GREAT BEVILLS
Sudbury Road, Bures, CO8 5JW. Mr & Mrs G T C Probert. *4m S of Sudbury. Just N of Bures on the Sudbury rd B1508.* **Sun 5 June (2-5.30). Adm £5, chd free. Home-made teas.**
Overlooking the Stour Valley the gardens surrounding an Elizabethan manor house are formal and Italianate in style with Irish yews and mature specimen trees. Terraces, borders, ponds and woodland walks. A short drive away from Great Bevills visitors may wish to also see the C13 St Stephen's Chapel with wonderful views of the Old Bures Dragon recently re-created by the owner. Woodland walks give lovely views over the Stour Valley. Gravel paths.

& ⛺ ☕

17 GREAT THURLOW HALL
Great Thurlow, Haverhill, CB9 7LF. Mr George Vestey. *12m S of Bury St Edmunds, 4m N of Haverhill. Great Thurlow village on B1061 from Newmarket; 3½ m N of junction with A143 Haverhill/Bury St Edmunds rd.* **Sun 13 Feb (1-4) No refreshments. Sun 3 Apr, Sun 12 June (2-5). Home-made teas in the Church. Adm £5, chd free.**
13 acres of beautiful gardens set around the River Stour. Masses of snowdrops in late winter are followed by daffodils and blossom around the riverside walk in spring. Herbaceous borders, rose garden and extensive shrub borders come alive with colour from late spring onwards, there is also a large walled kitchen garden and arboretum

& ⛺ ☕

18 GRUNDISBURGH HOUSE
Woodbridge Road, Grundisburgh, Woodbridge, IP13 6UD. Mrs Linden Hibbert. *Not, as the postcode claims, at the junction but just off B1079. Car parking in field IP13 6PU.* **Sun 15 May (11-5). Combined adm with Finndale House £6, chd free.**
3 acre garden wrapping around classic Georgian house, highlights inc natural swimming pond, formal garden, spring bulbs and fruit blossom, roses, irises and hydrangeas. New projects are on-going but inc planting more hedging, ornamental trees and pleaching. There is a pop-up art gallery in the old coach house which is open intermittently throughout the year. The Grundisburgh Dog serves hot food. Also several cafes in the village, though hours vary. 3m from Woodbridge with numerous restaurants and cafes. Wheelchair access paved terrace and path in the formal garden, decking with two steps on swimming pond terrace. Remainder is gravel path.

& ⛻ ⛺ ☕))

19 HELYG
Thetford Road, Coney Weston, Bury St Edmunds, IP31 1DN. Jackie & Briant Smith. *From Barningham Xrds/shop turn off the B1111 towards Coney Weston & Knettishall Country Park. After approx 1m Helyg will be found on L behind some large willow trees.* **Mon 18 Apr, Sun 17 July (11-4). Adm £5, chd free. Pre-booking essential, please phone 01359 220106 or email briant.broadsspirituality@gmail.com for information & booking. Home-made teas.** Visits also by arrangement Apr to Sept for groups of 10 to 25.
A garden that combines planting and novel ideas to stimulate interest, with many seats providing tranquillity and relaxation. There are different areas with their own character, inc naturalised spring bulbs, hundreds of hostas, roses, rhododendrons, camellias, irises, buddleias, fuchsias, azaleas, herbs, vegetables and exotics. Raised beds, three ponds and four water features supplement the plants. Many varied, colourful and inspirational areas as above in descriptions. Most of the garden is wheelchair accessible.

& ☕))

20 HENSTEAD EXOTIC GARDEN
Church Road, Henstead, Beccles, NR34 7LD. Andrew Brogan. www.hensteadexoticgarden.co.uk. *Equal distance between Beccles, Southwold & Lowestoft approx 5m. 1m from A12 turning after Wrentham (signed Henstead) very close to B1127.* **Sun 28 Aug (11-4). Adm £5, chd £1. Choice of top quality**

The Rooks

local delicatessen cakes as well as home made cheese scones & sausage rolls.
2 acre exotic garden featuring 100 large palms, 20+ bananas and giant bamboo, some of biggest in the UK. Streams, 20ft tiered walkway leading to Thai style wooden covered pavilion. Mediterranean and jungle plants around 3 large ponds with fish. Winner Britains best garden 2015 on itv as voted by Alan Titchmarsh. Unique garden buildings, streams, waterfalls, rock walkways, different levels, Victorian grotts, giant compost toilet etc. Wheelchair access, can gain access to the garden but not the whole garden admittedly.

21 HERON HOUSE
Priors Hill Road, Aldeburgh, IP15 5EP. Mr & Mrs Jonathan Hale, 01728 452200, jonathanrhhale@aol.com. *At the southeastern junction of Priors Hill Rd & Park Rd. Last house on Priors Hill Rd on south side, at the junction where it rejoins Park Rd.* Sun 19 June (2-5). Adm £5, chd free. Light refreshments in conservatory. Visits also by arrangement Apr to Oct.

2 acres with superb views over the North Sea, River Alde and marshes. Unusual trees, herbaceous beds, shrubs and ponds with a waterfall in large rock garden, and a stream and bog garden. Some half hardy plants in the coastal microclimate. Partial wheelchair access.

22 HILLSIDE
Union Hill, Semer, Ipswich, IP7 6HN. Mr & Mrs Neil Mordey, 07753 332022, Mordeysue@gmail.com. *Car park through field gate off A1141.* Sun 19 June (11-4). Adm £5, chd free. Light refreshments. Visits also by arrangement May to Aug for groups of 10 to 30.
This garden in its historic setting of 10½ acres has sweeping lawns running down to a spring fed carp pond. The formal garden has island beds of mixed planting for a long season of interest. The wild area of meadow has been landscaped with extensive tree planting to complement the existing woodland. There is also a small walled kitchen garden and raised beds in the stable yard. Wheelchair access, most areas are accessible although the fruit and

vegetable garden is accessed over a deep gravel drive.

23 HOLM HOUSE
Garden House Lane, Drinkstone, Bury St Edmunds, IP30 9FJ. Mrs Rebecca Shelley, Rebecca.shelley@hotmail.co.uk. *7m SE of Bury St Edmunds. Coming from the E exit A14 at J47, from W J46. Follow signs to Drinkstone, then Drinkstone Green. Turn into Rattlesden Rd & look for Garden House Lane on L. 1st house on L.* Sun 5 June (10-5). Adm £7, chd free. Home-made teas. Visits also by arrangement May to Sept for groups of 12+.
Approx 10 acres inc orchard and lawns with mature trees and clipped Holm Oaks; formal garden with topiary, parterre and mixed borders; rose garden; woodland walk with hellebores, camellias, rhododendrons and bulbs; lake, woodland planting and wildflower meadow; cut flower garden with greenhouse; large kitchen garden with impressive greenhouse; Mediterranean courtyard with mature olive tree. Extensive kitchen garden. Lake and wildflower meadow created in 2017.

24 THE LABURNUMS

The Street, St James South Elmham, Halesworth, IP19 0HN. Mrs Jane Bastow. *6m W of Halesworth, 7m E of Harleston & 6m S of Bungay. Parking at nearby village hall. For disabled parking please phone to arrange. Yellow signs from 8m out in all directions.* Sun 20 Feb (11-4). Adm £4.50, chd free. Home-made teas, cakes & hot soup with crusty bread. Gluten free will be available.

Again open for Snowdrops, but also the beautiful Hellebores and other flowering plants and shrubs. More snowdrops will be added to the 20,000 odd Snowdrops already planted in the last few years. The herbaceous beds and borders are always being added to by the 'plantaholic' owner. A garden for wildlife with a large variety of birds and creatures. A haven to relax in and enjoy nature in all forms. Plant stall with a variety of plants and bulbs. Newly restored pond and sunken garden. Thousands of Snowdrops complementing the Hellebores and other plants. Conservatory packed with tender plants. Large glasshouse. Gravel drive. Partial wheelchair access to front garden. Steps to sunken garden. Concrete path in back garden.

25 LARKS' HILL

Clopton Road, Tuddenham St Martin, IP6 9BY. Mr John Lambert, 07906 614705, lordtuddenham@gmail.com. *3m NE of Ipswich. From Ipswich take B1077, go through village, take the Clopton Rd to the L, after 300 metres at the brow of the hill you will see the house. Follow the car parking signs.* Sat 25 June (2-6). Adm £5, chd free. Home-made teas. Visits also by arrangement May to Sept for groups of 20+.

The gardens of eight acres, comprise woodland, a newly planted conifer garden and formal areas, which fall away from the house to the valley floor. A hill within a garden and in Suffolk at that! Hilly garden with a modern castle keep with an interesting and beautiful site overlooking the gentle Fynn valley and the village beyond. A fossil of a limb bone from a Pliosaur that lived at least sixty million years ago was found in the garden in 2013. The discovery was reported in the national press but its importance has been recognised

world-wide. A booklet is available to purchase giving all the details. Our Big Shed Café can comfortably seat thirty or so and there is additional seating outside. Sit and talk and plan what to do next.

26 LAVENHAM HALL

Hall Road, Lavenham, Sudbury, CO10 9QX. Mr & Mrs Anthony Faulkner, www.katedenton.com. *Next to Lavenham's iconic church & close to High St. From church turn off the main road down the side of church (Potland Rd). Go down hill. Car Park on R after 100 metres.* Sun 29 May (10-4.30). Adm £5, chd free.

5 acre garden built around the ruins of the original ecclesiastical buildings on the site and the village's fishpond. Deep borders of herbaceous planting with sweeping vistas provide the perfect setting for the sculptures which Kate makes in her studio at the Hall and exhibits both nationally and internationally under her maiden name of Kate Denton. 40 garden sculptures by Kate Denton on display. There is a gallery in the grounds which displays a similar number of indoor sculptures and her working drawings. Mostly wheelchair accessible. Note gravel paths / slopes may limit access to certain areas. Follow signs for separate disabled parking.

27 LEAVEN HALL

Nayland Road, Leavenheath, Colchester, CO6 4PU. Mrs Holly Armour. *8m from Colchester, 7m S of Sudbury. Off A134 in Leavenheath between church & Hare and Hounds Pub.* Wed 8, Wed 15, Wed 22 June (11-5). Adm £7, chd free. Light refreshments.

Gravel drive leading to wisteria and rose covered C17 Farm House (not open). Garden extends over 15 acres. Highlights inc meadow, woodland, fruit cages, walled and cut flower gardens, established pond/bog garden. Additionally orchards with beehives. Nectarine, apricots and peach trees adjacent to swimming pool. Wheelchair access, gravel paths, some steps to the pond and woodchips in woodland areas.

28 LILLESLEY BARN

The Street, Kersey, Ipswich, IP7 6ED. Mr Karl & Mrs Bridget Allen, 07939 866873, bridgetinkerseybarn@gmail.com. *In village of Kersey, 2m NW Hadleigh. Driveway is 200 metres above 'The Bell' pub. Lillesley Barn is situated behind 'The Ancient Houses'.* Sun 26 June (11-5). Combined adm with Old Gardens £5, chd free. Home-made teas. Visits also by arrangement May to Aug.

Dry gravel garden (inspired by the Beth Chatto Garden) inc variety of mediterranean plants, ornamental grasses, herbs and collection of succulents. Large herbaceous borders, rose arbours and small orchard with poultry. The garden contains various species of birch, elder, amelanchier and willow in less than an acre of garden bordered on two sides by fields. Meals available at The Bell Inn.

29 THE LODGE

Bury Road, Bradfield St Clare, Bury St Edmunds, IP30 0ED. Christian & Alice Ward-Thomas, 07768 347595, alice.baring@btinternet.com. *4m S of Bury St Eds. From N turn L up Water Lane off A134, at Xrds, turn R & go exactly 1m on R. From S turn R up Ixer Lane, R at T-junction, ½m on R. Before post box on R & next door to Lodge Farm.* Visits by arrangement Apr to Sept for groups of up to 30. Please discuss refreshments when booking.

A self-made country garden, surrounded by beautiful parkland established from blank canvass over 20yrs but recently remodelled. New gravel garden inc alpines and rockery, Herbaceous border, Rose garden, veg garden, tulip and wildlife meadows, extensive grassland with mown paths. Life is busy and help is minimal so please don't expect immaculacy! Parking on gravel but wheelchair access is possible.

30 NEW LONGLANDS PLACE

Wenham Road, Washbrook, Ipswich, IP8 3EZ. Christopher Haines. *On A12 S of Ipswich take turning to Washbrook/Copdock, approx 1m L to Elm Ln. After approx 150 yds L to Wenham Rd. After 1m the garden is on R.* Sun 5 June (11-5). Adm £5, chd free. Home-made teas.

The garden surrounds an early C17 farmhouse (not open). It extends over 10 acres and inc lovely trees and avenues as well as roses and a developing arboretum with wide views over open farmland.

31 MAGNOLIA HOUSE
Yoxford, IP17 3EP. Olivia Laing. *4m N of Saxmundham. Centre of Yoxford on A1120, next to Griffin pub.* **Sat 11 June (11-4). Adm £5, chd free. Home-made teas.**
Small romantic walled garden, originally designed by Mark Rumary, tucked behind a pretty C18 village house (not open). Arranged in a series of rooms and planted to provide year-round colour, scent and horticultural interest. Inc King James Mulberry, raised Moorish-style pond and newly planted library garden.

32 MANOR HOUSE
Leiston Road, Middleton, Saxmundham, IP17 3NS. Mandy Beaumont & Steve Thorpe, mandshome@btinternet.com. *Manor House is an 8 minute fieldside walk (signed) from parking area. A12 at Yoxford take B1122 to Leiston. Turn L after 1.2m at Middleton Moor. After 1m enter Middleton - drive straight ahead into Back Rd. Turn 1st R into Fletchers Ln for Playing Field Car Park.* **Sun 20 Feb (10-3). Adm £4.50, chd free. Light refreshments. Home-made soup. Visits also by arrangement Feb to Apr for groups of 6 to 24. Guided visits can be arranged.**
Just over an acre of garden on a triangular plot which was once the northern tip of a medieval green. Started from a wilderness in 2015 - now an ambulatory garden with seating to enjoy many new tree plantings, borders, meadows and a vegetable garden all created from scratch. We have focussed on interest for all seasons and there are many winter/spring flowering trees, shrubs and bulbs to enjoy. An area of the garden has been designated a 'Silent Space' with https://silentspace.org.uk/garden/manor-house/.

33 MOAT HOUSE
Little Saxham, Bury St Edmunds, IP29 5LE. Mr & Mrs Richard Mason, 01284 810941, suzanne@countryflowerssuffolk.com. *2m SW of Bury St Edmunds. Leave A14 at J42 – leave r'about towards Westley. Through Westley Village, at Xrds R towards Barrow/Saxham. After 1.3m turn L down track. (follow signs).* **Sun 1 May (1-6). Adm £5, chd free. Home-made teas. Visits also by arrangement Apr to July for groups of 20 to 60. Plenty of parking.**
Set in a 2 acre historic and partially moated site. This tranquil mature garden has been developed over 20yrs. Bordered by mature trees the garden is in various sections inc a sunken garden, rose and clematis arbours, herbaceous borders with hydrangeas and alliums, small arboretum. A Hartley Botanic greenhouse erected and partere have been created. Each year the owners enjoy new garden projects. Secluded and peaceful setting, each year new additions and wonderful fencing.

34 OLD GARDENS
The Street, Kersey, Ipswich, IP7 6ED. Mr & Mrs David Anderson, 01473 828044, davidmander15@gmail.com. *10m W of Ipswich. Up hill, approx 100 metres from The Bell Inn Pub. On the same side of the road.* **Sun 26 June (11-5). Combined adm with Lillesley Barn £5, chd free. Home-made teas at Lillesley Barn. Visits also by arrangement May to Aug.**
Entered from The Street, a natural garden with wildflowers under a copper beech tree. To the rear, a formal garden designed by Cherry Sandford with a sculpture by David Harbour. Meals available at The Bell Inn in the village.

35 THE OLD RECTORY
Ingham, Bury St Edmunds, IP31 1NQ. Mr J & Mrs E Hargreaves. *5m N of Bury St Edmunds & A14. The garden is on R immed as you come into Ingham, coming N on A134 from Bury St Edmunds, just before the church.* **Sun 24 July (11-5). Adm £4, chd free. Tea.**
A large garden in a lovely setting surrounding an early Victorian Rectory. We are developing a vibrant colourful flower display inc dahlias, geraniums, insect-friendly borders and lawns. Lavender walk and parterre. Wide variety of mature trees inc weeping willows. Children friendly. Wheelchair access through 1m wide gate.

36 THE OLD RECTORY, KIRTON
Church Lane, Kirton, Ipswich, IP10 0PT. Mr & Mrs N Garnham. *Adjacent to Kirton parish church on corner of Church Lane & Burnt House Lane. Car parking available in Church Hall car park next door.* **Sun 19 June (12-6). Adm £5, chd free. Home-made teas.**
This traditional English garden contains mixed flower borders for both sun and shade providing year-round colour, fragrance and succour for bees and butterflies. The 3 acre garden contains many mature trees, including varieties of oak, which give it a park-like feel. Many plants are labelled. Delicious teas served by rose and lavender border. Plant stall. Refreshments in aid of Falkenham Church.

37 THE OLD RECTORY, NACTON
Nacton, IP10 0HY. Mrs Elizabeth & Mr James Wellesley Wesley. *The garden is down the road to Nacton from the first A14 turn off after Orwell bridge going N/E. Parking on Church Rd opp Old Rectory driveway. This will be signed.* **Sun 12 June (10-4.30). Adm £5, chd free. Home-made teas.**
Just under 2 acres of garden divided into areas for different seasons: mature trees and herbaceous borders, herb/picking garden, rose garden. Light soil so many self sown flowers. Damp area with emphasis on foliage (Rheum, Darmera, Rodgersia, Hydrangea. Still a work in progress after 31 years, looking at how to bring in more butterflies and deal with very dry conditions in most of the garden. The Ship Inn is 2m up road in Levington and does good pub lunches. Lovely walks on the Orwell Estuary with extensive bird life especially at low tide. Nacton is very accessible from Ipswich and surrounding areas. Most areas are accessible for disabled visitors, however several grassy slopes and various different levels so some energy needed to get everywhere!

38 PAGET HOUSE

Back Road, Middleton, Saxmundham, IP17 3NY. Julian & Fiona Cusack, 01728 649060, julian.cusack@btinternet.com. *From A12 at Yoxford take B1122 towards Leiston. Turn L after 1.2m at Middleton Moor. After 1m enter Middleton & drive straight ahead into Back Rd. Turn 1st R on Fletchers Ln for car park.* Sun 1 May, Sun 17 July (11-5). Adm £5, chd free. Light refreshments. Gluten free & vegan options. Visits also by arrangement May to Sept for groups of up to 30.

The garden is designed to be wildlife friendly with wild areas meeting formal planting.There is an orchard and vegetable plot. There are areas of woodland, laid hedges, pond supporting amphibians and dragonflies, wildflower meadow and an abstract garden sculpture by local artist Paul Richardson. We record over 40 bird species each year and a good showing of butterflies, dragonflies and wildflowers including orchids. Wheelchair access, gravel drive and mown paths. Parking on drive by prior arrangement.

39 5 PARKLANDS GREEN

Fornham St Genevieve, Bury St Edmunds, IP28 6UH. Mrs Jane Newton, newton.jane@talktalk.net. *2m Northwest of Bury St Edmunds off B1106. Plenty of parking on the green.* Sun 26 June (11-4). Adm £5, chd free. Home-made teas. Visits also by arrangement May to Sept.

1½ acres of gardens developed since the 1980s for all year interest. There are mature and unusual trees and shrubs and riotous herbaceous borders. Explore the maze of paths to find four informal ponds, a treehouse, the sunken garden, greenhouses and woodland walks.

40 ◆ THE PLACE FOR PLANTS, EAST BERGHOLT PLACE GARDEN

East Bergholt, CO7 6UP. Mr & Mrs Rupert Eley, 01206 299224, sales@placeforplants.co.uk, www.placeforplants.co.uk. *2m E of A12, 7m S of Ipswich. On B1070 towards Manningtree, 2m E of A12. Situated on the edge of East Bergholt.* For NGS: Sun 24 Apr, Sun 8 May (2-5). Adm £7, chd free. Sun 9 Oct (1-5). Adm £6, chd free. Home-made teas. For other opening times and information, please phone, email or visit garden website.

20 acre woodland garden originally laid out at the turn of the last century by the present owner's great grandfather. Full of many fine trees and shrubs, many seldom seen in East Anglia. A fine collection of camellias, magnolias and rhododendrons, topiary, and the National Collection of deciduous Euonymus. Partial Wheelchair access in dry conditions - it is advisable to telephone before visiting.

  NPC

41 POLSTEAD MILL

Mill Lane, Polstead, Colchester, CO6 5AB. Mrs Lucinda Bartlett, 07711 720418, lucyofleisure@hotmail.com. *Between Stoke by Nayland & Polstead on the River Box. From Stoke by Nayland take rd to Polstead - Mill Ln is 1st on L & Polstead Mill is 1st house on R.* Sun 19 June (2-5). Adm £7, chd free. Home-made teas. Visits also by arrangement May to Sept for groups of 10 to 50.

The garden has been developed since 2002, it has formal and informal areas, a wildflower meadow and a large productive kitchen garden. The River Box runs through the garden and there is a mill pond, which gives opportunity for damp gardening, while much of the rest of the garden is arid and is planted to minimise the need for watering. Range of refreshments available inc full cream teas and light lunches. Featured in Secret Gardens of East Anglia. Partial wheelchair access.

42 THE PRIORY

Stoke by Nayland, Colchester, CO6 4RL. Mrs H F A Engleheart. *5m SW of Hadleigh. Entrance on B1068 to Sudbury (NW of Stoke by Nayland).* Sun 22 May (2-5). Adm £5, chd free. Home-made teas.

Interesting 9 acre garden with fine views over Constable countryside; lawns sloping down to small lakes and water garden; fine trees, rhododendrons and azaleas; walled garden; mixed borders and ornamental greenhouse. Wide variety of plants. Plant stall. Wheelchair access over most of garden, some steps.

43 NEW PULHAM COTTAGE

Wetherden, Stowmarket, IP14 3LQ. Susanne Barker, 07882 849379, susanne@evolution-planning.co.uk. *Take the track signed 'Mutton Hall' & we are the red house on L.* Sat 4 June (11-5). Adm £5, chd free. Pre-booking essential, please visit www.ngs.org.uk for information & booking. Home-made teas. Visits also by arrangement May to Sept for groups of up to 20. Parking is limited to 6 cars.

A relaxed cottage garden set in 1½ acres, created over the last 5 yrs. Divided into rooms using mixed hedging, hazel fencing and vintage iron gates and fencing. A Clipped box parterre, a kitchen garden with flowers for cutting, orchard and wildflower areas to explore. Areas left for re-wildng to encourage moths, butterflies and bees. Lots of seating to relax and enjoy the vistas and views. Victorian style greenhouse, orchard and free range chickens. The Kings Arms is a lovely pub in Haughley with a garden.

44 ◆ THE RED HOUSE

Golf Lane, Aldeburgh, IP15 5PZ. Britten Pears Arts, brittenpearsarts.org. *Top of Aldeburgh, approx. 1m from the sea. From A12, take A1094 to Aldeburgh. Follow the brown sign directing you towards the r'about, take 1st exit: B1122 Leiston Road. Golf Lane is 2nd L, follow sign to 'The Red House'.* For NGS: Thur 2 June (11-5). Adm £10, chd free. In celebration of Queen Elizabeth II's Platinum Jubilee, entry inc to the Benjamin Britten Exhibition, the Archives & the Museum. Mon 29 Aug (11-4). Adm £5, chd free. Light refreshments. August opening Garden only. For other opening times and information, please visit garden website.

The former home of the renowned British composer Benjamin Britten and partner, the tenor Peter Pears. The 5 acre gardens provide an atmospheric setting for the house they shared and contain many plants loved by the couple. Mixed herbaceous borders, kitchen garden, contemporary planting and a new summer tropical border. For 2 June the house and garden will be open, for 29 August, the garden only. The Red House inc the collections left by the two men, inc their Archive

The Laburnums

which holds an extraordinary wealth of material documenting their lives. The garden offers a peaceful setting to this beautiful corner of Suffolk. For Museum opening times, see website. Wheelchair access, brick, concrete, gravel paths and grass. Some areas are uneven, may require effort to navigate. Wheelchair available upon request.

45 THE ROOKS
Old Paper Mill Lane, Claydon, Ipswich, IP6 0AL. Mrs Marilyn Gillard, 07900 271267, marilyng2010@hotmail.co.uk. *Off A14 at J52. From r'about turn in Claydon & take 1st available R, into Old Ipswich Rd where parking is available. The Rooks is 200m,*

1st house in Old Paper Mill Ln with thatched roof. **Sun 24 July (11-4). Adm £5, chd free. Home-made teas. Visits also by arrangement in July.**
The garden surrounds a thatched cottage built c1600. The garden has been divided into rooms to give different feelings of interest, with seating in most areas. There are two ponds, mixed borders, trees, statues and features.

46 SMALLWOOD FARMHOUSE
Smallwood Green, Bradfield St George, Bury St Edmunds, IP30 0AJ. Mr & Mrs P Doe. *On Hessett/Felsham rd, S of A14, E of A134 on Bradfield St George to Felsham rd. On main rd between*

Hessett & Felsham, ignore sign to Smallwood Green & follow NGS signage. **Sun 12 June (11-5). Adm £5, chd free.**
The garden is a combination of traditional cottage planting and contemporary styles. At its heart, a C16 farmhouse provides the backdrop to a number of old English roses, a profusion of clematis and honeysuckle, and a variety of perennials. There are two natural ponds and a more recently planted gravel garden, whilst paths wind through an ancient meadow and orchard. Partially wheelchair accessible, although not suitable in damp or wet weather.

Lillesley Barn

47 ◆ SOMERLEYTON HALL GARDENS

Somerleyton, NR32 5QQ. Lord Somerleyton, 01502 734901, visitors@somerleyton.co.uk, www.somerleyton.co.uk. *5m NW of Lowestoft. From Norwich (30mins) - on the B1074, 7m SE of Great Yarmouth (A143). Coaches should follow signs to the rear west gate entrance.* For NGS: Tue 2 Aug (11-3). Adm £7.95, chd £5.25. Light refreshments in Cafe, check website for opening hours. For other opening times and information, please phone, email or visit garden website.

12 acres of beautiful gardens contain a wide variety of magnificent specimen trees, shrubs, borders and plants providing colour and interest throughout the year. Sweeping lawns and formal gardens combine with majestic statuary and original Victorian ornamentation. Highlights inc the Paxton glasshouses, pergola, walled garden and yew hedge maze. House and gardens remodelled in 1840s by Sir Morton Peto. House created in Anglo-Italian style with lavish architectural features and fine state rooms. All areas of the gardens are accessible, path surfaces are gravel/stone and can be difficult. Wheelchairs available on request.

♿ ✿ 🚗 ☕ 🏕

48 SQUIRES BARN

St. Cross South Elmham, Harleston, IP20 0PA. Stephen & Ann Mulligan. *6m W of Halesworth, 6m E of Harleston & 7m S of Bungay. On New Rd between St Cross & St James. Parking in field opp. Yellow signs from 8m out in all directions.* Sun 17 July (10.30-4). Adm £5, chd free. Home-made teas on lawn inc gluten free options.

A young and evolving garden of some 3 acres, inc an orchard, cutting and kitchen garden with greenhouse and fruit cage, large ornamental pond with water lilies, fish and waterfall, wildflower area, willow spiral, island beds of mixed planting and a growing range of trees .Views over surrounding countryside. Gravel drive with pool. Plant stall. Wheelchair access, garden is largely grass, some slight slopes. Seating is available across the garden. One single flight of steps can be bypassed.

♿ ✿ ☕

49 STONE COTTAGE

34 Main Road, Woolverstone, Ipswich, IP9 1BA. Mrs Jen Young, 01473 780156, j_s_young@icloud.com. *Take B1456 towards Shotley. When leaving Woolverstone Village the yellow signs will direct you to Stone Cottage.* Visits by arrangement Apr to June for groups of up to 20. Adm £3, chd free. Home-made teas.

An idyllic Suffolk Country cottage, surrounded by a garden created and maintained by the owner from a derelict space into a beautiful, calming garden. Over a hundred roses, unusual delphiniums, irises, spring bulbs and many more are planted together in interesting colour combinations that provide year-round interest and perfume. A lovely space to sit and relax. Areas of gravel paths.

♿ ✿ ☕

51 WENHASTON GRANGE

Wenhaston, Halesworth, IP19 9HJ. Mr & Mrs Bill Barlow. *Turn SW from A144 between Bramfield & Halesworth. Take the single track rd (signed Walpole 2) Wenhaston Grange is approx ½m, at the bottom of the hill on L.* Sun 10 July (11-4). Adm £5, chd free. Home-made teas.

Over 3 acres of varied gardens on a long established site which has been extensively landscaped and enhanced over the last 15 yrs. Long herbaceous borders, old established trees and a series of garden rooms created by beech hedges. Levels and sight lines have been carefully planned. The vegetable garden is now coming on nicely and there is also a wildflower meadow and woodland garden.

 ☕ �))

52 WHITE HOUSE FARM

Ringsfield, Beccles, NR34 8JU. Jan Barlow, Justin (gardener) 07780 901233, coppertops707@aol.com. *2m SW of Beccles. From Beccles take B1062 to Bungay, after 1¼ turn L signed Ringsfield. Continue for approx 1m. Parking opp church. Garden 300yds on L. NB parking at house* Sat 2 July (10-4.30). Adm £6, chd free. Light refreshments. Visits also by arrangement Apr to Aug for groups of 10 to 30.

Tranquil park-type garden approx 30 acres, bordered by farmland and with fine views. Comprising formal areas, copses, natural pond, woodland walk, vegetable garden and orchard. Picnickers welcome. The pond and beck are unfenced. Uneven paving around house. Partial wheelchair access to the areas around the house.

♿ 🐕 ✿ ☕ 🏕

GROUP OPENING

53 NEW WOODLAND DRIVE GARDENS

Woodland Drive, Bungay, NR35 2PT. 01986 896016. *Woodland drive is opposite Three Willows garden centre on Flixton Rd, B1062. (Near Fen farm dairy).* Thur 23 June (11-4). Combined adm £5. Home-made teas.

NEW 7 WOODLAND DRIVE
Mr Richard Pietrzak.

NEW 8 WOODLAND DRIVE
Mrs Ann Woolston, 01986896016, woolstonann@aol.com.

NEW 9 WOODLAND DRIVE
Mrs Val Whyte.

The gardens at Woodland Drive are situated in a quiet cul-de-sac on the outskirts of Bungay. They are next door to each other and while quite different in style and planting, all share wonderful views over the Waveney Valley. This also means that they share steep sections of garden, but all have patios to sit and admire the view.

 ☕

54 ◆ WYKEN HALL

Stanton, IP31 2DW. Sir Kenneth & Lady Carlisle, 01359 250262, kenneth.carlisle@wykenvineyards.co.uk, www.wykenvineyards.co.uk. *9m NE of Bury St Edmunds. Along A143. Follow signs to Wyken Vineyards on A143 between Ixworth & Stanton.* For NGS: Sat 28, Sun 29 May (10-5). Adm £5, chd free. For other opening times and information, please phone, email or visit garden website.

4 acres around the old manor. The gardens inc knot and herb gardens, old-fashioned rose garden, kitchen and wild garden, nuttery, pond, gazebo and maze; herbaceous borders and old orchard. Woodland walk and vineyard nearby. Restaurant (booking 01359 250287), shop and vineyard. Farmers' Market Sat 9 - 1.

♿ ✿ ☕ �))

SURREY

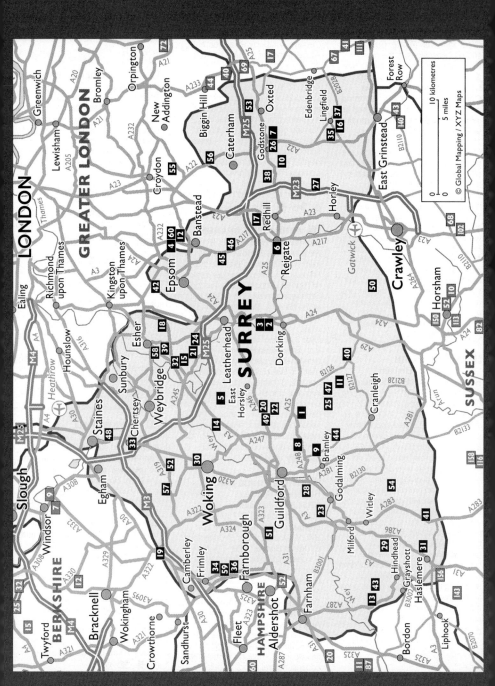

As a designated Area of Outstanding Natural Beauty, it's no surprise that Surrey has a wealth of gardens on offer.

With its historic market towns, lush meadows and scenic rivers, Surrey provides the ideal escape from the bustle of nearby London.

Set against the rolling chalk uplands of the unspoilt North Downs, the county prides itself on extensive country estates with historic houses and ancient manors.

Surrey is the heartland of the National Garden Scheme at Hatchlands Park and the RHS at Wisley, both promoting a precious interest in horticulture. Surrey celebrates a landscape coaxed into wonderful vistas by great gardeners such as John Evelyn, Capability Brown and Gertrude Jekyll.

With many eclectic gardens to visit, there's certainly plenty to treasure in Surrey.

Volunteers

County Organiser
Margaret Arnott
01372 842459
margaret.arnott@ngs.org.uk

County Treasurer
Nigel Brandon
020 8643 8686
nbrandon@ngs.org.uk

Booklet Co-ordinator
Annabel Alford-Warren
01483 203330
annabel.alford-warren@ngs.org.uk

Publicity
Susanna Edwards
07879 815160
susanna.edwards@ngs.org.uk

Social Media
Annette Warren
07790 045354
annette.warren@ngs.org.uk

Assistant County Organisers
Anne Barnes
01306 730196
spurfold@btinternet.com

Clare Bevan
01483 479963
clare.bevan@ngs.org.uk

Jan Brandon
020 8643 8686
janmbrandon@outlook.com

Penny Drew
01252 792909
penelopedrew@yahoo.co.uk

Joy Greasley
01342 837369
joy.greasley@ngs.org.uk

Di Grose
01883 742983
di.grose@ngs.org.uk

Annie Keighley
01252 838660
annie.keighley12@btinternet.com

Jean Thompson
01483 425633
norney.wood@btinternet.com

Below: 5 Lydele Close

© Leigh Clapp

OPENING DATES

All entries subject to change. For latest information check **www.ngs.org.uk**
Extended openings are shown at the beginning of the month.

Map locator numbers are shown to the right of each garden name.

January

Every Wednesday from Wednesday 12th
Timber Hill 52

February

Snowdrop Festival

Every Monday to Monday 21st
Timber Hill 52

Sunday 13th
♦ Gatton Park 17

Sunday 20th
Shieling 46

Wednesday 23rd
♦ The Sculpture Park 43

March

Every Monday from Monday 21st
Timber Hill 52

Sunday 20th
Albury Park 1

Sunday 27th
Timber Hill 52

April

Sunday 3rd
Coverwood Lakes 11

Saturday 9th
11 West Hill 55

Sunday 10th
Coverwood Lakes 11
11 West Hill 55

Tuesday 12th
♦ Dunsborough Park 14

Sunday 17th
Caxton House 6
Coverwood Lakes 11

Monday 18th
Shieling 46

Sunday 24th
♦ Hatchlands Park 20
Timber Hill 52

Wednesday 27th
Little Orchards 27

May

Sunday 1st
♦ Crosswater Farm 13
The Garth Pleasure Grounds 16

Monday 2nd
Coverwood Lakes 11
♦ Crosswater Farm 13
Fairmile Lea 15
Moleshill House 32

Sunday 8th
The Garth Pleasure Grounds 16
Westways Farm 57

Friday 13th
♦ Ramster 41

Sunday 15th
Little Orchards 27

Wednesday 18th
Little Orchards 27

Thursday 19th
Lower House 29

Saturday 21st
Hall Grove School 19

Sunday 22nd
21 Glenavon Close 18
Knowle Grange 25
Lower House 29
The Therapy Garden 51
♦ Titsey Place Gardens 53

Friday 27th
Chauffeur's Flat 7

Saturday 28th
15 The Avenue 4
Chauffeur's Flat 7

Sunday 29th
15 The Avenue 4
Chauffeur's Flat 7
Little Orchards 27
Monks Lantern 33

Monday 30th
Chauffeur's Flat 7

Tuesday 31st
Woodland 60

June

Wednesday 1st
Little Orchards 27

Thursday 2nd
Woodland 60

Saturday 4th
57 Westhall Road 56

Sunday 5th
Chilworth Manor 8
57 Westhall Road 56

Sunday 12th
40 The Crescent 12
Little Orchards 27
♦ Loseley Park 28
The Old Rectory 38

Tuesday 14th
♦ Dunsborough Park 14
♦ The Sculpture Park 43

Wednesday 15th
Little Orchards 27

Saturday 18th
Bridge End Cottage 5
40 The Crescent 12
Leigh Place 26

Sunday 19th
Leigh Place 26
NEW The Oast House 37
Shieling 46

Wednesday 22nd
NEW The White House 58

Friday 24th
Chauffeur's Flat 7
NEW The White House 58

Saturday 25th
Chauffeur's Flat 7
16 Hurtmore Chase 23
NEW The White House 58

Sunday 26th
Chauffeur's Flat 7
16 Hurtmore Chase 23
NEW 5 Lydele Close 30
The Manor House 31

♦ Titsey Place Gardens 53
NEW The White House 58

Monday 27th
Chauffeur's Flat 7

Wednesday 29th
Ashleigh Grange 3
NEW The White House 58

July

Friday 1st
Ashcombe 2
Ashleigh Grange 3
NEW The White House 58

Saturday 2nd
Ashcombe 2
NEW The White House 58

Sunday 3rd
Ashcombe 2
Ashleigh Grange 3
Pratsham Grange 40
NEW Staines Gardens 48
NEW The White House 58

Saturday 9th
NEW 5 Lydele Close 30

Sunday 17th
High Clandon Estate Vineyard 22
41 Shelvers Way 45
Tanhouse Farm 50
♦ Titsey Place Gardens 53

Sunday 24th
Heathside 21

August

Sunday 14th
♦ Titsey Place Gardens 53

Sunday 21st
Pratsham Grange 40
41 Shelvers Way 45

Saturday 27th
NEW 26 Rowden Road 42

Sunday 28th
NEW 26 Rowden Road 42

September

Sunday 4th
Little Orchards 27
NEW 5 Lydele Close 30

During 2020 – 2021 National Garden Scheme funding supported over 1,400 Queen's Nurses to deliver virtual and hands-on, community care across England, Wales and Northern Ireland

THE GARDENS

1 ALBURY PARK
Albury, GU5 9BH. Trustees of Albury Estate. *5m SE of Guildford. From A25 take A248 towards Albury for ¼m, then up New Rd, entrance to Albury Park immed on L.* **Sun 20 Mar, Sun 2 Oct (2-5). Adm £5, chd free. Home-made teas.**
14 acre pleasure grounds laid out in 1670s by John Evelyn for Henry Howard, later 6th Duke of Norfolk. ¼m terraces, fine collection of trees, lake and river. Access over gravel path and slight slope.

2 ASHCOMBE
Chapel Lane, Westhumble, Dorking, RH5 6AY. Vivienne & David Murch. *2m N of Dorking. From A24 at Boxhill/Burford Bridge follow signs to Westhumble. Through village & take L drive by ruined chapel (1m from A24).* **Evening opening Fri 1 July (6-8.30). Combined adm with Ashleigh Grange £10, chd free. Wine. Sat 2 July (2-5.30). Adm £5, chd free. Sun 3 July (2-5.30). Combined adm with Ashleigh Grange £8, chd free. Home-made teas, wine & Pimms.**
Plantaholics 1½ acre wildlife friendly sloping garden on chalk and flint. Enclosed ⅓ acre cottage garden with large borders of roses, delphiniums and clematis. Amphibian pond. Secluded decking and patio area with colourful acers and views over garden and Boxhill. Gravel bed of salvia and day lilies. House surrounded by banked flower beds and lawn leading to bee and butterfly garden.

3 ASHLEIGH GRANGE
off Chapel Lane, Westhumble, RH5 6AY. Clive & Angela Gilchrist, 01306 884613, ar.gilchrist@btinternet.com. *2m N of Dorking. From A24 at Boxhill/ Burford Bridge follow signs to Westhumble. Through village & L up drive by ruined chapel (1m from A24).* **Wed 29 June (2-5.30). Adm £5, chd free. Home-made teas. Evening opening Fri 1 July (6-8.30). Combined adm with Ashcombe £10, chd free. Wine. Sun 3 July (2-5.30). Combined adm with Ashcombe £8, chd free. Home-made teas. Visits also by arrangement May to July. Sorry, no access for coaches.**
Plant lover's chalk garden on 3½ acre sloping site in charming rural setting with delightful views. Many areas of interest inc rockery and water feature, raised ericaceous bed, prairie style bank, foliage plants, woodland walk, fernery and folly. Large mixed herbaceous and shrub borders planted for dry alkaline soil and widespread interest.
& ⚬ ✿ ☕

4 15 THE AVENUE
Cheam, Sutton, SM2 7QA. Jan & Nigel Brandon, 020 8643 8686, janmbrandon@outlook.com. *1m SW of Sutton. By car; exit A217 onto Northey Av, 2nd R into The Ave. By train; 10 min walk from Cheam Stn. By bus; use 470.* **Evening opening Sat 28 May (5.30-9). Adm £8, chd £3. Wine. Sun 29 May (1-5). Adm £5, chd free. Home-made teas. Visits also by arrangement May to July for groups of 10+. Adm inc refreshments.**
A contemporary garden designed by RHS Chelsea Gold Medal Winner, Marcus Barnett. Four levels divided into rooms by beech hedging and columns; formal entertaining area, contemporary outdoor room, lawn and wildflower meadow. Over 100 hostas hug the house. Silver birch, cloud pruned box, ferns, grasses, tall bearded irises, contemporary sculptures. Partial wheelchair access, terraced with steps; sloping path provides view of whole garden.
& 🚗 ☕ ⚬))

5 BRIDGE END COTTAGE

Ockham Lane, Ockham, GU23 6NR. Clare & Peter Bevan, 07956 307546, clare.bevan@ngs.org.uk. *Nr RHS Gardens, Wisley. At Wisley r'about turn L onto B2039 to Ockham/ Horsley. After ½m turn L into Ockham Ln. House ½m on R. From Cobham go to Blackswan Xrds.* Evening opening Sat 18 June (5.30-9.30). Adm £8, chd free. Wine in the garden room. Visits also by arrangement May to Sept for groups of up to 35.

A 2 acre country garden with different areas of interest inc perennial borders, mature trees, pond and streams, small herb parterre, fruit trees and a vegetable patch. An adjacent 2 acre field was sown with perennial wildflower seed in May 2013 and has flowered well each summer and will be of interest to anyone establishing a wildflower garden. Partial wheelchair access.

6 CAXTON HOUSE

67 West Street, Reigate, RH2 9DA. Bob Bushby, 01737 243158/07836 201740, bob.bushby@sky.com. *On A25 towards Dorking, approx ¼m W of Reigate. Parking on road or past Black Horse on Flanchford Rd.* Sun 17 Apr (2-5). Adm £5, chd free. Cream teas. Visits also by arrangement Apr to Sept for groups of 10 to 50.

Lovely large spring garden with arboretum, two well-stocked ponds, large collection of hellebores and spring flowers. Pots planted with colourful displays. Interesting plants. Small Gothic folly built by owner. Herbaceous borders with grasses, perennials and spring bulbs, parterre, bed with wild daffodils and prairie style planting in summer, and new wildflower garden in arboretum. Wheelchair access to most parts of the garden.

7 CHAUFFEUR'S FLAT

Tandridge Lane, Tandridge, RH8 9NJ. Mr & Mrs Richins, 01883 742983. *2m E of Godstone. 2m W of Oxted. Turn off A25 at r'about for Tandridge. Take 2nd drive on L past church. Follow arrows to circular courtyard. Do not use Jackass Ln even if your SatNav tells you to do so.* Fri 27, Sat 28, Sun 29, Mon 30 May, Fri 24, Sat 25, Sun 26, Mon 27 June (10-5). Adm £5, chd free. Home-made teas (Sats & Suns only). Visits also by arrangement May to Sept.

Enter a 1½ acre tapestry of magical secret gardens with magnificent views. Touching the senses, all sure footed visitors may explore the many surprises on this constantly evolving exuberant escape from reality. Imaginative use of recycled materials creates an inspired variety of ideas, while wild and specimen plants reveal an ecological haven.

8 CHILWORTH MANOR

Halfpenny Lane, Chilworth, Guildford, GU4 8NN. Mia & Graham Wrigley, www.chilworthmanorsurrey.com. *3½m SE of Guildford. From centre of Chilworth village turn into Blacksmith Ln. 1st drive on R on Halfpenny Ln.* Sun 5 June (11-5). Adm £7.50, chd free. Home-made teas.

The grounds of the C17 Chilworth Manor create a wonderful tapestry, a jewel of an C18 terraced walled garden, topiary, herbaceous borders, sculptures, mature trees and stew ponds that date back a 1000 yrs. A fabulous, peaceful garden for all the family to wander and explore or just to relax and enjoy! Perhaps our many visitors describe it best, 'Magical', 'a sheer delight', 'elegant and tranquil', 'a little piece of heaven', 'spiffing!'.

9 2 CHINTHURST LODGE

Wonersh Common, Wonersh, Guildford, GU5 0PR. Mr & Mrs M R Goodridge, 01483 535108, michaelgoodridge@ymail.com. *4m S of Guildford. From A281 at Shalford turn E onto B2128 towards Wonersh. Just after Waverley sign, before village, garden on R, via stable entrance opp Little Tangley.* Visits by arrangement May to July for groups of 10+. Adm £6, chd free. Home-made teas.

1 acre enthusiast's atmospheric and

tranquil garden divided into rooms with year-round interest. Herbaceous borders, dramatic white garden, specimen trees and shrubs, gravel garden with new water feature, small kitchen garden, fruit cage, two wells, ornamental ponds, herb parterre and millennium parterre garden. Wheelchair access with some avoidable gravel paths.

10 COLDHARBOUR HOUSE

Coldharbour Lane, Bletchingley, Redhill, RH1 4NA. Mr Tony Elias, 01883 742685, eliastony@hotmail.com. *Coldharbour Ln off Rabies Heath Rd, ½m from A25 at Bletchingley & 0.9m from Tilburstow Hill Rd. Park in field & walk down to house.* Visits by arrangement Apr to Oct for groups of 10+.

This 1½ acre garden offers breathtaking views to the South Downs. Originally planted in the 1920s, it has since been adapted and enhanced. Several mature trees and shrubs inc a copper beech, a Canadian maple, magnolias, azaleas, rhododendrons, camellias, wisterias, *Berberis georgii, Vitex agnus-castus*, fuchsias, hibiscus, potentillas, mahonias, a fig tree and a walnut tree.

11 COVERWOOD LAKES

Peaslake Road, Ewhurst, GU6 7NT. The Metson Family, 01306 731101, farm@coverwoodlakes.co.uk, www.coverwoodlakes.co.uk. *7m SW of Dorking. From A25 follow signs for Peaslake; garden ½m beyond Peaslake on Ewhurst Rd.* Sun 3, Sun 10, Sun 17 Apr, Mon 2 May, Sun 16 Oct (11-5). Adm £7, chd free. Light refreshments. Visits also by arrangement Apr to Sept for groups of 20+.

14 acre landscaped garden in stunning position high in the Surrey Hills with four lakes and bog garden. Extensive rhododendrons, azaleas and fine trees. 3½ acre lakeside arboretum. Marked trail through the 180 acre working farm with Hereford cows and calves, sheep and horses, extensive views of the surrounding hills. Light refreshments inc home produced beef burgers, gourmet coffee and home-made cakes from the Fillet & Bean Cafe (outdoor mobile kitchen).

12 40 THE CRESCENT

Belmont, Sutton, SM2 6BJ. Mrs Barbara Welch. *Off B2230 Brighton Rd. By car, exit A217 L onto The Cres. Train: 5 mins from Belmont Stn. Bus: 280 from Sutton to Belmont, Station Rd bridge, 1st L into The Cres. No. 40 halfway on L. Street parking.* **Sun 12 June (1-5). Adm £5, chd free. Home-made teas. Evening opening Sat 18 June (5-8). Adm £6, chd free. Wine.**

Densely planted rectangular garden, 80' x 50' on chalk with formal borders, island beds surrounded by clipped box hedges, box and yew topiary, many different shrubs inc philadelphus, deutzias, weigela, lilacs, roses, interwoven with cottage style perennials. Discrete paths dissect borders from central lawn leading to enclosed areas, some with seating inc a circular tree seat; water feature and rose covered pergola. Terrace with second water feature, many pots for tender fuchsias, ericaceous and seasonal planting.

❀ 🍷 ›))

13 ◆ CROSSWATER FARM

Crosswater Lane, Churt, Farnham, GU10 2JN. David & Susanna Millais, 01252 792698, sales@rhododendrons.co.uk, www.rhododendrons.co.uk. *6m S of Farnham, 6m NW of Haslemere. From A287 turn E into Jumps Rd ½m N of Churt village centre. After ¼m turn acute L into Crosswater Ln & follow signs for Millais Nurseries.* **For NGS: Sun 1, Mon 2 May (10-5). Adm £5, chd free. Home-made teas. For other opening times and information, please phone, email or visit garden website.**

Idyllic 5 acre woodland garden. Plantsman's collection of rhododendrons and azaleas inc rare species collected in the Himalayas and hybrids raised by the family. Everything from alpine dwarfs to architectural large leaved trees. Ponds, stream and companion plantings inc sorbus, magnolias and Japanese acers. Recent new plantings and wildflower meadows. Woodland garden and specialist rhododendron, azalea and magnolia plant centre. Grass paths may be difficult for wheelchairs after rain.

♿ ❀ 🚗 🍷 ›))

The White House

◆ DUNSBOROUGH PARK

Ripley, GU23 6AL. Baron & Baroness Sweerts de Landas Wyborgh. *6m NE of Guildford. Entrance via Newark Ln, Ripley through Tudor-style gatehouses & courtyard up drive. Car park signposted. For SatNav use GU23 6BZ.* **For NGS: Tue 12 Apr, Tue 14 June, Tue 13 Sept (9.30-12 & 1.30-4). Adm £8, chd free. Pre-booking essential, please email events@ dunsboroughpark.com or visit www.dunsboroughpark.com for information & booking. Charity teas for sale when possible. For other opening times and information, please email or visit garden website.** 6 acre garden redesigned by Penelope Hobhouse and Rupert Golby. Garden rooms, lush herbaceous borders, standard wisteria, 70ft ginkgo hedge, potager and 300 yr old mulberry tree. Rose Walk, Italian Garden and Water Garden with folly bridge. April Tulip Festival: Formal borders and colourful informal display in meadow under oaks. June: Mid-summer herbaceous and roses. Sept: Autumn colour and dahlia displays. Wheelchair access over gravel paths and grass, cobbled over folly bridge.

& ✿ ☺ ☕

FAIRMILE LEA

Portsmouth Road, Cobham, KT11 1BG. Steven Kay. *2m NE of Cobham. On Cobham to Esher Road. Access by lane adjacent to Moleshill House & car park for Fairmile Common woods.* **Mon 2 May (2-5). Combined adm with Moleshill House £7, chd free. Home-made teas.** Victorian sunken garden fringed by rose beds and lavender with a pond in the centre. An old acacia tree stands in the midst of the lawn. Interesting planting on a large mound camouflages an old underground air raid shelter. Caged vegetable garden. Formality adjacent to wilderness.

& 🐕 ☕

THE GARTH PLEASURE GROUNDS

The Garth, Newchapel Road, Lingfield, RH7 6BJ. Mr Sherlock & Mrs Stanley, ab_post@yahoo.com, www.oldworkhouse.webs.com. *From A22 take B2028 by the Mormon Temple to Lingfield. The Garth is on the L after 1½m, opp Barge Tiles. Parking: Gun Pit Rd in Lingfield & limited space for disabled at Barge Tiles.* **Sun 1, Sun 8 May (1-5). Adm £7, chd free. Home-made teas. Visits also by arrangement June & July for groups of 5 to 40.** Mature 9 acre Pleasure Grounds

Orchard House

created by Walter Godfrey in 1919, present an idyllic setting surrounding the former parish workhouse refurbished in Edwardian style. The formal gardens, enchanting nuttery, a spinney with many mature trees and a pond attract wildlife. Wonderful bluebells in spring. The woodland gardens and beautiful borders are full of colour and fragrance for year-round pleasure. Many areas of interest, large specimen plants inc 500yr old oak, many architectural features designed by Walter H Godfrey. Picnics are welcome. Partial wheelchair access in woodland, iris and secret gardens.

  ♿ 🐑 🚌 🚐 ☕ 🪑))

17 ◆ GATTON PARK
Reigate, RH2 0TW. Royal Alexandra & Albert School. *3m NE of Reigate. 5 mins from M25 J8 (A217) or from top of Reigate Hill, over M25 then follow sign to Merstham. Entrance off Rocky Ln accessible from Gatton Bottom or A23 Merstham.* For NGS: Sun 13 Feb (12-5). Adm £6, chd free. Pre-booking essential, please phone 01737 649068, email events@gatton-park.org.uk or visit www.gattonpark.co.uk for information & booking. Light refreshments. For other opening times and information, please phone, email or visit garden website.
Historic 260 acre estate in the Surrey Hills AONB. Capability Brown parkland with ancient oaks. Discover the Japanese garden, Victorian parterre and breathtaking views over the lake. Seasonal highlights inc displays of snowdrops and aconites in Feb. Ongoing restoration projects by the Gatton Trust. Bird hide open to see herons nesting. Free guided tours. A selection of hot and cold drinks, cakes and snacks. Plants for winter interest for sale. Adm £6 is a pre-book price only, tickets on the gate on the day will be £7.

🐑 ❀ 🚌 ☕

18 21 GLENAVON CLOSE
Claygate, Esher, KT10 0HP. Selina & Simon Botham, www.designsforallseasons.co.uk. *2m SE of Esher. From A3 S exit Esher, R at T-lights. Continue straight through Claygate village, bear R at 2 mini r'abouts. Past church & rec. Turn L at bollards into Causeway. At end straight over to Glenavon Close.* Sun 22 May, Sun 11 Sept (1.30-5.30). Adm £5, chd free. Home-made teas.

Enjoy a taste of 'Forest bathing', which promotes wellbeing and relaxation in nature, in this suburban garden designed by the owner, an RHS Gold medal winning designer. An awkward shaped plot has been transformed to create interest through all the seasons and a relaxing environment. Swathes of grasses and perennials, spacious lawn and inviting paths, pond and wildlife-friendly design. Guided tours by the designer, exhibit of private garden design work and RHS show garden concepts.

☕))

19 HALL GROVE SCHOOL
London Road (A30), Bagshot, GU19 5HZ. Mr & Mrs A R Graham, www.hallgrove.co.uk. *6m SW of Egham. M3 J3, follow A322 1m until sign for Sunningdale A30, 1m E of Bagshot, opp Longacres Garden Centre, entrance at footbridge. Ample car parking.* Sat 21 May, Sat 1 Oct (2-5). Adm £5, chd free. Home-made teas.
Formerly a small Georgian country estate, now a co-educational preparatory school. Grade II listed house (not open). Mature parkland with specimen trees. Historical features inc ice house, recently restored walled garden, lake, woodland walks, rhododendrons and azaleas. Live music at 3pm.

  ♿ ❀ ☕))

20 ◆ HATCHLANDS PARK
East Clandon, Guildford, GU4 7RT. National Trust, 01483 222482, hatchlands@nationaltrust.org.uk, www.nationaltrust.org.uk/hatchlands-park. *4m E of Guildford. Follow brown signs to Hatchlands Park (NT).* For NGS: Sun 24 Apr (10-5). Adm £10.50, chd £5.30. Adm subject to change. For other opening times and information, please phone, email or visit garden website.
Garden and park designed by Repton in 1800. Follow one of the park walks to the stunning bluebell wood in spring (2½ km round walk over rough and sometimes muddy ground). In autumn enjoy the changing colours on the long walk. Partial wheelchair access to parkland with rough and undulating terrain, grass and gravel paths, dirt tracks and cobbled courtyard. Mobility scooter booking essential.

  ♿ 🐑 🚌 ☕ 🪑

21 HEATHSIDE
10 Links Green Way, Cobham, KT11 2QH. Miss Margaret Arnott & Mr Terry Bartholomew, 01372 842459, margaret.arnott@ngs.org.uk. *1½m E of Cobham. Through Cobham A245, 4th L after Esso garage into Fairmile Ln. Straight on into Water Ln. Links Green Way 3rd turning on L.* Sun 24 July (11-5). Adm £5, chd free. Home-made teas. Visits also by arrangement Jan to Dec. Morning coffee, afternoon tea or wine & canapés.
Terraced, plants persons garden, designed for year-round interest. Gorgeous planting all set off by harmonious landscaping. Many urns and pots give seasonal displays. Several water features add tranquil sound. Topiary shapes provide formality. Stunning colour combinations excite. Dahlias and begonias a favourite. Beautiful Griffin Glasshouse housing the exotic. Many inspirational ideas. Situated 5 miles from RHS Wisley.

❀ 🚌 ☕))

22 HIGH CLANDON ESTATE VINEYARD
High Clandon, Off Blakes Lane, East Clandon, GU4 7RP. Mrs Sibylla Tindale, www.highclandon.co.uk. *A3/Wisley junction, L for Ockham/Horsley for 2m to A246. R for Guildford for 2m, then 100yds past landmark Hatchlands NT, turn L into Blakes Ln, straight up hill through gates High Clandon to vineyard entrance. Extensive parking in our woodland area.* Sun 17 July (11-4). Adm £6, chd free. Cream teas & home-made teas. Gold awarded English sparkling wine by the glass & bottle.
Vistas, gardens, 1 acre wildflower meadow with rare butterflies, multi-gold award-winning vineyard, all set in 12 acres of beautiful Surrey Hills, AONB. Panoramic views to London, water features, Japanese garden, truffière and apiary. English sparkling wine, High Clandon Cuvée sold from atmospheric glass barn. Twice winner Cellar Door of Year. Sculptures exhibition with over 150 works of art on show in gardens and vineyard. 4 metres of gravel, otherwise access on lawned paths on firm ground.

  ♿ 🐑 ☕))

23 16 HURTMORE CHASE
Hurtmore, Godalming, GU7 2RT. Mrs Ann Bellamy, 01483 421274. *4m SW of Guildford. From Godalming follow signs to Charterhouse & continue about ¼m beyond Charterhouse School. From A3 take Norney, Shackleford & Hurtmore turn off & proceed E for ½m.* **Sat 25 June (11-5); Sun 26 June (1-5). Adm £5, chd free. Home-made teas. Visits also by arrangement May to Aug for groups of 8 to 15.**

A secluded medium sized (approx ¼ acre) garden comprised mainly of a large lawn divided into discrete areas by shrubs, trees and colourful flower beds. On the bungalow side of the lawn there is a patio area with hanging baskets, troughs and planted pots. In the opp corner there is a shaded arbour bordered by hostas. Award-winner of Godalming in Bloom 2019. Cash only for refreshments. Kerb height step from patio to lawn, so minor assistance may be required for wheelchairs.

&. ✿ ☕))

24 2 KNOTT PARK HOUSE
Wrens Hill, Oxshott, Leatherhead, KT22 0HW. Joanna Nixon, 07463 343303, Joannanixon@hotmail.co.uk. *10 mins from Oxshott village centre. From A244, which is off the A3, or S from Leatherhead take Wrens Hill, next to Bear Pub, continue c200 metres, take R fork, part of 1st big house on L.* **Visits by arrangement Apr to Oct for groups of 10 to 20. Adm £4, chd free. Home-made teas.**

A south facing terrace with far-reaching views is planted with herbs and lavender. Steps lead down to a lower area extending to ¼ acre. Wildlife friendly and maintained without pesticides. On four levels, it features pollinator loving plants, trees and shrubs. These inc irises, alliums, sedum, geums, acers, flowering currant and succulents. Scented flowering shrubs and climbers attract bees. Beehive.

✿ ☕))

25 KNOWLE GRANGE
Hound House Road, Shere, Guildford, GU5 9JH. Mr P R & Mrs M E Wood, 01483 202108, prmewood@hotmail.com. *8m S of Guildford. From Shere (off A25), through village for ¾m. After*

railway bridge, continue 1½m past Hound House on R (stone dogs on gateposts). After 100yds turn R at Knowle Grange sign, go to end of lane. **Sun 22 May (11-4.30). Adm £6, chd free. Home-made teas on front lawn. Visits also by arrangement May to Sept for groups of 20+. No large coaches.**

80 acres undulating landscape. 7 acre gardens. New features recently added. Small knot garden. Double herbaceous border. About seven various garden rooms with French, Japanese and English inspiration. A new clock tower garden. The one mile bluebell valley unicursal path which snakes through two valleys and a hill and inc the labyrinth upon a labyrinth.

☕

26 LEIGH PLACE
Leigh Place Lane, Godstone, RH9 8BN. Mike & Liz McGhee. *Take B2236 Eastbourne Rd from Godstone village. Turn 2nd L onto Church Ln. Follow parking directions.* **Sat 18, Sun 19 June (10-4). Adm £5, chd free. Tea.**

Leigh Place garden has 25 acres on greensand. Part of the Godstone Pond's with SSSI and lakeside paths, walled garden inc cutting garden, orchard and vegetable quadrant with greenhouses. Orchard, beehives and large rock garden. WC available. The walled garden has Breedon gravel paths suitable for wheelchairs and pushchairs.

&. 🐄 ☕ 🛏))

27 LITTLE ORCHARDS
Prince Of Wales Road, Outwood, Redhill, RH1 5QU. Nic Howard, 01883 744020, info@we-love-plants.co.uk. *A few hundred metres N of the Dog & Duck Pub.* **Wed 27 Apr (12-4); Sun 15 May (11-5); Wed 18 May (12-4); Sun 29 May (11-5); Wed 1 June (12-4); Sun 12 June (11-5); Wed 15 June (12-4); Sun 4 Sept (11-5); Wed 7 Sept (12-4). Adm £5, chd free. Home-made teas. Visits also by arrangement Apr to Sept for groups of 10 to 30.**

Garden designer's contemporary cottage garden that has been planted for year-round interest using a tapestry of foliage textures as well as flower interest. The garden is arranged as a series of connected garden areas that flow between the old gardener's cottage and the old stables. The small spaces are

full of character with paved areas, brick walls and vintage garden paraphernalia.

✿ 🚗 Ⓓ ☕))

28 ◆ LOSELEY PARK
Guildford, GU3 1HS. Mr & Mrs A G More-Molyneux, 01483 304440/405112, pa@loseleypark.co.uk, www.loseleypark.co.uk. *4m SW of Guildford. For SatNav please use GU3 1HS, Stakescorner Ln.* **For NGS: Sun 12 June (11-4). Adm by donation. Tea. For other opening times and information, please phone, email or visit garden website.**

Delightful 2½ acre walled garden. Award-winning rose garden (over 1000 bushes, mainly old fashioned varieties), extensive herb garden, fruit and flower garden, white garden with fountain and spectacular organic vegetable garden. Magnificent vine walk, herbaceous borders, moat walk, ancient wisteria and mulberry trees.

&. ✿ 🚗 ☕

29 LOWER HOUSE
Bowlhead Green, Godalming, GU8 6NW. Georgina Harvey. *1m from A3 leaving at Thursley/Bowlhead Green junction. Follow Bowlhead Green signs. Using A286 leave at Brook (6m from Haslemere & 3m from Milford). Follow NGS signs for approx 2m. Good parking.* **Thur 19, Sun 22 May (11-5). Adm £6, chd free. Home-made teas.**

Unusual rare trees and shrubs shape the layout of the garden creating many stunning vistas and quiet areas. The sandy soil accommodates azaleas, rhododendrons, camelias and magnolias followed by roses to continue the colour until the herbaceous plants bloom. The white topiary garden and pond brings calm and the kitchen garden, greenhouses, orchard and fruit cage bring seasonal changes. Alternative routes to avoid steps for wheelchair users and some narrow paths.

&. 🐄 ✿ ☕))

30 NEW 5 LYDELE CLOSE
Woking, GU21 4ER. Mr Alan Rio. *Situated off Woodham Rd, Horsell, nr Woking. 4⅓m from J11, M25 (10 mins). Free parking on Woodham Rd.* **Sun 26 June, Sat 9 July, Sun 4 Sept (12-6). Adm £7.50, chd free. Pre-booking essential, please email alanrio8@gmail.com for information & booking.**

Adm inc cream teas. Visits also by arrangement June to Sept for groups of up to 6. Individual visitors also welcome.

At the heart of this naturalistic garden are long lived, durable perennial plants that support a rich biodiversity over a long flowering period. The garden weaves elegant grasses within the perennial planting combinations effortlessly. This inspirational garden shows how the deep emotional combinations of the Dutch designer Piet Oudolf might be created.

31 THE MANOR HOUSE
Three Gates Lane, Haslemere, GU27 2ES. Mr & Mrs Gerard Ralfe. *NE of Haslemere. From Haslemere centre take A286 towards Milford. Turn R after Museum into Three Gates Ln. At T-Junction turn R into Holdfast Ln. Car park on R.* **Sun 26 June (12-5). Adm £5, chd free.**

Described by Country Life as 'The Hanging Gardens of Haslemere', the well-established Manor House gardens are tucked away in a valley of the Surrey Hills. Set in 6 acres, it was one of Surrey's inaugural NGS gardens with fine views, an impressive show of azaleas, wisteria, beautiful trees underplanted with bulbs, enchanting water gardens and a magnificent rose garden.

Our 2021 donations mean that 12,478 unpaid carers have been supported through funding for Carers Trust

26 Rowden Road

32 MOLESHILL HOUSE

The Fairmile, Cobham, KT11 1BG. Penny Snell, pennysnellflowers@ btinternet.com, www.pennysnellflowers.co.uk. *2m NE of Cobham. On A307 Esher to Cobham Rd next to free car park by A3 bridge, at entrance to Waterford Close.* **Mon 2 May (2-5). Combined adm with Fairmile Lea £7, chd free. Home made teas at Fairmile Lea. Visits also by arrangement Apr to Sept for groups of 10+.**
Romantic garden. Short woodland path leads from dovecote to beehives. Informal planting contrasts with formal topiary box and garlanded cisterns. Colourful courtyard and pots, conservatory, pond with fountain, pleached avenue, circular gravel garden replacing most of the lawn. Gipsy caravan garden, green wall and stumpery. Espaliered crab apples. Chickens and bees. Garden 5 mins from Claremont Landscape Garden, Painshill Park and Wisley, also adjacent to excellent dog walking woods.

33 MONKS LANTERN

Ruxbury Road, Chertsey, KT16 9NH. Mr & Mrs J Granell, 01932 569578, janicegranell@hotmail.com. *1m NW from Chertsey. M25 J11, signed A320/Woking. At r'about take 2nd exit A320/Staines, straight over next r'about. L onto Holloway Hill, R Hardwick Ln. ½ m, R over motorway bridge, on Almners then Ruxbury Rd.* **Sun 29 May (2-5.30). Adm £6, chd free. Light refreshments. Visits also by arrangement June to Sept for groups of up to 20.**
A delightful garden with borders arranged with colour in mind: silvers and white, olive trees blend together with nicotiana and senecio. A weeping silver birch leads to the oranges and yellows of a tropical bed with large bottle brush, hardy palms and *Fatsia japonica*. Large rockery and an informal pond. There is a display of hostas, *Cytisus battandieri* and a selection of grasses in an island bed. Aviary with small finches. Workshop with handmade guitars, and paintings. Pond with ornamental ducks and fish. Music and wine.

34 NEW THE NUTRITION GARDEN

156A Frimley Green Road, Frimley Green, Camberley, GU16 6NA. Dr Trevor George RNutr, 07914 911410, t-george@hotmail.co.uk. *2m (5 mins) from J4 of the M3. Follow signs for A331 towards Farnborough from M3 & then follow signs to Frimley Green (B3411). Approach to house directly opp the recreation ground.* **Sun 4 Sept (1-5). Adm £5, chd free. Pre-booking essential, please visit www.ngs.org. uk for information & booking. Light refreshments. Open nearby Wildwood. Visits also by arrangement June to Sept for groups of up to 12.**
A garden designed by a registered nutritionist to produce and display a wide variety of edible plants inc fruits, vegetables, herbs and plants for infusions. There are trees, shrubs, tubers, perennials and annual plants. Over 100 types of edible plants and over 200 varieties are grown throughout the yr. These inc unusual food plants, heritage varieties and unusual coloured varieties. Tea, coffee and the option of trying an infusion from plants in the garden, along with snacks made with homegrown produce. Wheelchair access on paved paths around fruit and vegetable beds. Other areas are step free around uneven grass lawn.

&. ✿ ☕ ⋅))

35 OAKLANDS

Eastbourne Road, Blindley Heath, Lingfield, RH7 6LG. Joy & Justin Greasley, 01342 837369, joy@greasley.me.uk. *S of Blindley Heath Village. From M25 take A22 to East Grinstead. Go straight on at Blindley Heath T-lights & after 800yds take sign on L to Nestledown Boarding Kennels. Oaklands is down the lane on the L. Limited parking.* **Visits by arrangement May to Sept for groups of 8 to 30. Adm £5, chd free. Light refreshments.**
A spacious garden of approx ½ acre surrounded by natural woodland featured in Surrey Life. Specimen trees, area of large planted pots, pond, folly, colourful herbaceous planting and various areas of interest. Long curved pergola complemented by many climbing plants and hanging baskets with plenty of seating areas. Level access on paths to main features.

&. ☕ ⋅))

36 OAKLEIGH

22 The Hatches, Frimley Green, GU16 6HE. Angela O'Connell, 01252 668645, angela.oconnell@icloud.com. *100 metres from village green. Street parking.* **Visits by arrangement in June for groups of 10 to 20. Open with a neighbouring garden: Wildwood. Adm £10, chd free. Home-made teas at Wildwood.**
A magical long garden with a few surprises. There are plenty of colours and textures with a great variety of different plants. Wander past the long borders and under a rose arch and you will find the garden opens up to two large colour themed mixed beds. The style is naturalistic with just a hint of elegance. Fruit and vegetables grow by the summerhouse and pots adorn the top patio.

☛ ✿ ☕ ⋅))

37 NEW THE OAST HOUSE

Station Road, Lingfield, RH7 6EF. Mrs Andrea Watson. *In Station Rd look for sign to New Place Farm on the L. Park in field opp the drive entrance & walk 100 metres down the lane to The Oast House where a young man will welcome you.* **Sun 19 June (11-5). Adm £6, chd free. Home-made teas.**
Traditional country garden with large croquet lawn, borders, old brick walls, courtyard garden, beds, rambling roses, vines, topiary and mature trees inc 35 yr old ginkgo. Approx 1½ acres. Views of Grade II* manor house and Grade I church. The Oast House itself is a building of local interest. Level wheelchair access with gravel paths.

&. ✿ ☕

'National Garden Scheme funding helped support the provision of horticultural-related assistance to soldiers, veterans and their immediate families, providing education, training and employment opportunities along with supporting the recovery, health and wellbeing of individuals.'
ABF The Soldiers' Charity

38 THE OLD RECTORY

Sandy Lane, Brewer Street,
Bletchingley, RH1 4QW.
Mr & Mrs A Procter,
01883 743388 or 07515 394506,
trudie.y.procter@googlemail.com.
Top of village nr Red Lion pub, turn R into Little Common Ln, then R at Cross Rd into Sandy Ln. Parking nr house, disabled parking in courtyard. **Sun 12 June (11-4). Adm £5, chd free. Home-made teas. Visits also by arrangement Apr to Sept.**
Georgian Manor House (not open). Quintessential Italianate topiary garden, statuary, box parterres, courtyard with columns, water features, antique terracotta pots. New sunken water garden. Much of the 4 acre garden is the subject of ongoing reclamation. This inc the ancient moat, woodland with fine specimen trees, one of the largest tulip trees in the country. New water garden. Wheelchair access with gravel paths.

&. 🐕 🌺 ☕

39 NEW ORCHARD HOUSE

5 The Mount, Esher, KT10 8LQ.
Kathy & Richard Goode. *Outskirts of Esher, off the A307. From the A307 Portsmouth Rd turn into Hawkshill Way, opp the entrance to Claremont School. Take 2nd turning R into The Mount. Orchard House is on L nr the top of the road.* **Sun 11 Sept (2-6). Adm £6, chd free. Home-made teas.**
Set on a steep hill with a surprising 30 mile view towards Windsor. Almost an acre of terraced cottage garden style planting with year-round colour and interest. Terraces and banks of late summer flowering perennials and grasses together with roses and some tropical interest. Steep paths and lots of steps.

🌺 ☕ •))

40 PRATSHAM GRANGE

Tanhurst Lane, Holmbury St Mary,
RH5 6LZ. Alan & Felicity Comber.
12m SE of Guildford, 8m SW of Dorking. From A25 take B2126, after 4m turn L into Tanhurst Ln. From A29 take B2126, before Forest Green turn R on B2126 then 1st R to Tanhurst Ln. **Sun 3 July, Sun 21 Aug (12.30-4.30). Adm £6, chd free. Home-made teas.**
5 acre garden overlooked by Holmbury Hill and Leith Hill. Features inc two ponds joined by cascading stream, extensive scented rose and blue hydrangea beds. Also herbaceous borders, cutting flower garden and

two white beds. Partial wheelchair access with some steps, steep slopes (slippery when wet) and gravel paths. Deep ponds and a drop from terrace.

&. 🌺 ☕

41 ◆ RAMSTER

Chiddingfold, GU8 4SN.
Mrs R Glaister, 01428 654167,
office@ramsterhall.com,
www.ramsterevents.com. *Ramster is on A283 1½m S of Chiddingfold, large iron gates on R, the entrance is signed from the road.* **For NGS: Fri 13 May (10-5). Adm £8, chd £2. Light refreshments. For other opening times and information, please phone, email or visit garden website.**
A stunning, mature woodland garden set in over 20 acres, famous for its rhododendron and azalea collection and its carpets of bluebells in spring. Enjoy a peaceful wander down the grass paths and woodland walk, explore the bog garden with its stepping stones, or relax in the tranquil enclosed tennis court garden. The teahouse, by the entrance to the garden, serves sandwiches, home-made soup, cakes and drinks and is open every day while the garden is open. The teahouse is wheelchair accessible, some paths in the garden are suitable for wheelchairs.

&. 🐕 🌺 🚌 ☕ •))

42 NEW 26 ROWDEN ROAD

Epsom, KT19 9PN.
Mr Robert Stacewicz,
robstacewicz@hotmail.com. *At Ruxley Ln take the turning at the Co-op on to Cox Ln. At the end of road, take a R on to Rowden Rd. The garden is on the R.* **Sat 27 Aug (12-5); Sun 28 Aug (12-4). Adm £8. Pre-booking essential, please visit www.ngs.org. uk for information & booking. Home-made teas. Visits also by arrangement May to Oct for groups of 5 to 10.**
A small 19 x 8 metre south facing garden, transformed from a plain lawn in spring 2020 to a plant lovers paradise. The owner is a garden designer and the space is carefully planted with hardy exotics. Inspiration has come from world travels, in particular SE Asia and Indonesia. A large circular pond dominates the main garden, while raised beds home a succulent collection. Cactus and succulent border, wildlife pond, tropical water lilies, hardy banana plants, palm collection, planted

succulent/alpine house, hardy bromeliads, exotic aquatic plants, small garden inspiration, exotic garden, unusual ferns. 15 min drive from Wisley. Sorry, no children due to deep water.

☕ •))

43 ◆ THE SCULPTURE PARK

Tilford Road, Churt,
Farnham, GU10 2LH. Eddie Powell, 01428 605453,
sian@thesculpturepark.com,
www.thesculpturepark.com.
Corner of Jumps & Tilford Rd, Churt. Directly opp Bell & The Dragon pub. Use our car park or the pub, where refreshments are available. **For NGS: Wed 23 Feb, Tue 14 June (10-5). Adm £5, chd £3. For other opening times and information, please phone, email or visit garden website.**
This garden sculpture exhibition is set within an enchanting arboretum and wildlife inhabited water garden. You should set aside between 2-4 hrs for your visit as there are 2 miles of trail within 10 acres. Our displays evolve and diversify as the seasons pass with vivid and lush colours of the rhododendrons in May and June, to the enchanting frost in the depths of winter. Approx one third of The Sculpture Park is accessible to wheelchairs. Disabled WC.

&. 🐕 🎋

44 SHAMLEY WOOD ESTATE

Woodhill Lane, Shamley Green,
Guildford, GU5 0SP. Mrs Claire Merriman, 07595 693132,
claire@merriman.co.uk. *5m (15 mins) S of Guildford in village of Shamley Green. Entrance is approx ¼ m up Woodhill Ln from centre of Shamley Green.* **Visits by arrangement Feb to Nov. Adm by donation. Home-made teas. Gluten free options.**
A relative newcomer, this garden is worth visiting just for the setting! Sitting high on the North Downs, the garden enjoys beautiful views of the South Downs and is approached through a 10 acre deer park. Set within approx 3 acres, there is a large pond and established rose garden. More recent additions inc fire pits, vegetable patch, stream, tropical pergola and terraced wildflower lawn. Wheelchair access to most of garden. Step to access ground level WC.

&. 🐕 🚌 Ⓓ ☕ •))

The Oast House

45 41 SHELVERS WAY

Tadworth, KT20 5QJ. Keith & Elizabeth Lewis, 01737 210707, kandelewis@ntlworld.com. *6m S of Sutton off A217. 1st turning on R after Burgh Heath T-lights heading S on A217. 400yds down Shelvers Way on L.* **Sun 17 July, Sun 21 Aug (2-5.30). Adm £5, chd free. Home-made teas. Visits also by arrangement Apr to Aug for groups of 10+.**
Visitors say 'one of the most colourful gardens in Surrey'. In spring, a myriad of small bulbs with specialist daffodils and many pots of colourful tulips. Choice perennials follow. Cobbles and shingle support grasses and self-sown plants with a bubble fountain. Annuals and herbaceous plants ensure colour well into Sept. A garden for all seasons.

46 SHIELING

The Warren, Kingswood, Tadworth, KT20 6PQ. Drs Sarah & Robin Wilson, 01737 833370, sarahwilson@doctors.org.uk. *Kingswood Warren Estate. Off A217, gated entrance just before church on S-bound side of dual carriageway after Tadworth r'about . ³⁄₄ m walk from station. Parking on The Warren or by church on A217.* **Sun 20 Feb (1-3); Mon 18 Apr (11-4); Sun 19 June (2-5). Adm £5, chd free. Home-made teas. Visits also by arrangement May to July for groups of 10+.**
1 acre garden restored to its original 1920s design. Formal front garden with island beds and shrub borders. Unusual large rock garden and mixed borders with collection of beautiful slug free hostas and uncommon woodland perennials. The rest is an interesting woodland garden with acid loving plants, a new shrub border and a stumpery. Plant list provided for visitors. Lots for children to do. Many hostas for sale in June plant sale. Some narrow paths in back garden. Otherwise resin drive, grass and paths easy for wheelchairs.

47 SPURFOLD

Radnor Road, Peaslake, Guildford, GU5 9SZ. Mr & Mrs A Barnes, 01306 730196, spurfold@btinternet.com. *8m SE of Guildford. A25 to Shere then through to Peaslake. Pass village stores & L up Radnor Rd.* **Visits by arrangement May to Aug for groups of 10 to 35. Adm £6, chd free. Home-made teas or evening wine & nibbles.**
2¹⁄₂ acres, large herbaceous and shrub borders, formal pond with Cambodian Buddha head, sunken gravel garden with topiary box and water feature, terraces, beautiful lawns, mature rhododendrons, azaleas, woodland paths, and gazebos. Garden contains a collection of Indian elephants and

other objets d'art. Topiary garden created in 2010 and new formal lawn area created in 2012.

GROUP OPENING

48 NEW STAINES GARDENS
Thames Side, Staines-Upon-Thames, TW18 2HF. *From B376 Staines Rd turn L into Wheatsheaf Ln. After ½ m turn L into Thames Side. Limited parking, use nearby roads.* **Sun 3 July (12-5). Combined adm £6, chd free. Home-made teas.**

NEW **31 CARLYLE ROAD**
Pauline Thomas.

NEW **33 CARLYLE ROAD**
Sanda Connolly.

NEW **87 THAMES SIDE**
Mrs Gulbin Chaworth-Musters.

Three charming gardens with distinctly different styles within walking distance of each other. 87 Thames Side has a colourful front garden with a panoramic view of the Thames. Beautiful wisteria, hanging baskets and window boxes. Densely planted allotment garden showcasing fruit and vegetables. Excellent example of maximising space with a vast range of varieties. 31 Carlyle Road is a contemporary garden with a Mediterranean feel. Beautifully landscaped with a *magnolia grandiflora*, olive tree, phormium and water feature. 33 Carlyle Road is a compact walled garden showcasing how to maximise space with containers and living walls. Emphasise on year-round greenery and colour.

49 STUART COTTAGE
Ripley Road, East Clandon, GU4 7SF. John & Gayle Leader, 01483 222689, gayle@stuartcottage.com, www.stuartcottage.com. *4m E of Guildford. Off A246 or from A3 through Ripley until r'about, turn L & continue through West Clandon until T-lights, then L onto A246. East Clandon 1st L.* **Visits by arrangement May to Sept for groups of 10+. Home-made teas on request.**
Walk in to this tranquil partly walled ½ acre garden to find an oasis of calm. Beds grouped around the central

fountain offer floral continuity through the seasons with soft harmonious planting supported by good structure with topiary, a rose/clematis walk and wisteria walk. Outside the wall is the late border with its vibrant colours and fun planting. The decorative kitchen garden with raised beds edged with tiles is always of interest to visitors, many say it is one of the best gardens that they visit and just a lovely place to be.

50 TANHOUSE FARM
Rusper Road, Newdigate, RH5 5BX. Mrs N Fries, 01306 631334. *8m S of Dorking. On A24 turn L at r'about at Beare Green. R at T-junction in Newdigate, 1st farm on R approx ⅔ m. Signed Tanhouse Farm Shop.* **Sun 17 July (1-5). Adm £5, chd free. Visits also by arrangement June to Aug for groups of up to 30.**
Country garden created by owners since 1987. 1 acre of charming rambling gardens surrounding a C16 house (not open). Herbaceous borders, small lake and stream with ducks and geese. Orchard with wild garden and meadow walk with plentiful seats and benches to stop for contemplation.

51 THE THERAPY GARDEN
Manor Fruit Farm, Glaziers Lane, Normandy, Guildford, GU3 2DT. The Centre Manager, www.thetherapygarden.org. *SW of Guildford. Take A323 travelling from Guildford towards Aldershot, turn L into Glaziers Ln in centre of Normandy village, opp War Memorial. The Therapy Garden is 200yds on L.* **Sun 22 May, Sun 11 Sept (10-4). Adm £5, chd free. Light refreshments.**
The Therapy Garden is a horticulture and education charity that uses gardening to have a positive and significant impact on the lives of people facing challenges in life. In our beautiful and tranquil 2 acre garden we work to change lives for the better and we do this by creating a safe place to enjoy the power of gardening and to connect with nature. We are a working garden full of innovation with an on site shop selling plants and produce. BBQ, salads and sandwiches, teas, coffees and cakes also available. Wheelchair access over paved pathways throughout most of garden, many with substantial handrails.

52 TIMBER HILL
Chertsey Road, Chobham, GU24 8JF. Nick & Lavinia Sealy, www.timberhillgarden.com. *4m N of Woking. 2½ m E of Chobham & ⅓ m E of Fairoaks aerodrome on A319 (N side). 1¼ m W of Ottershaw, J11 M25. (If approaching from Ottershaw the A319 is the Chobham Rd). See garden website for more detail.* **Every Wed 12 Jan to 26 Jan (11.30-2.30). Every Mon 7 Feb to 21 Feb, Mon 21 Mar to 28 Mar (11.30-2.30). Sun 27 Mar, Sun 24 Apr (1.30-4.30). Adm £7, chd free. Pre-booking essential, please visit www.ngs.org.uk for information & booking. Self service refreshments (Mons & Weds). Home-made teas (Suns).**
16 acres of garden, park and woodland giving an undulating walk with views to North Downs. Stunning winter garden to enjoy winter walks on Weds in Jan, then Mons in Feb and Mar. Winter honeysuckle and witch hazel walk, abundant snowdrops, aconites and a sea of crocuses, spectacular camellias (featured in Surrey Life) followed by magnolias and wild cherries. Nature and wildlife trails for adults and children. For other information, pop-up openings and events, see Timber Hill website or please telephone 01932 873875.

In 2021 the National Garden Scheme donation helped support Perennial's caseworkers, who helped over 250 people and their families in crisis to receive a wide range of support including emergency food parcels and accommodation, energy payments and expert advice and information

33 Carlyle Road, Staines Gardens

© Leigh Clapp

53 ◆ **TITSEY PLACE GARDENS**
Titsey, Oxted, RH8 0SA. The
Trustees of the Titsey Foundation,
07889 052461, office@titsey.org,
www.titsey.org. *3m N of Oxted.
A25 between Oxted & Westerham.
Follow brown heritage signs to Titsey
Estate from A25 at Limpsfield or see
website for directions.* **For NGS:
Sun 22 May, Sun 26 June, Sun
17 July, Sun 14 Aug (1-5). Adm
£6, chd £2. Light refreshments.
Pre-book your ticket through
Titsey Place Gardens website
book.titsey.org. Card payments
& cash also accepted on the
door. For other opening times and
information, please phone, email or
visit garden website.**
One of the largest surviving historic
estates in Surrey. Magnificent
ancestral home and gardens of
the Gresham family since 1534.
Walled kitchen garden restored early
1990s. Golden Jubilee rose garden.
Etruscan summerhouse adjoining
picturesque lakes and fountains.
15 acres of formal and informal
gardens in an idyllic setting. Highly
Commended in the 2019 Horticulture
Week Custodian Awards. Tea room
serving delicious home-made cakes
and selling local produce open from
12.30-5.00pm on open days. Walks
through the estate woodland are
open year-round. Pedigree herd of
Sussex Cattle roam the park. Last
admission to gardens at 4pm. Dogs
on leads allowed in picnic area, car
park and woodland walks. Disabled
car park alongside tearooms.

&. 🐄 🚗 ☕

54 ◆ **VANN**
Hambledon, Godalming,
GU8 4EF. Caroe Family,
01428 683413, vann@caroe.com,
www.vanngarden.co.uk. *6m S
of Godalming. A283 to Lane End,
Hambledon. On NGS days only,
follow yellow Vann signs for 2m.
Please park in the field as signed,
not in the road. At other times
follow the website instructions.* **For
opening times and information,
please phone, email or visit garden
website.**
5 acre, 2* English Heritage registered
garden surrounding house dating
back to 1542 with Arts and Crafts
additions by W D Caröe inc a Bargate
stone pergola. At the front, brick
paved original cottage garden; to
the rear a lake, yew walk with rill
and Gertrude Jekyll water garden.
Snowdrops and hellebores, spring

bulbs, spectacular fritillaria in Feb/March. Island beds, crinkle crankle wall, orchard with wild flowers. Vegetable garden. Also open for by arrangement visits for individuals or groups. Some paths not suitable for wheelchairs due to uneven stone walkways. Please ring prior to visit to request disabled parking.

& ✿ 🚗 ☕

55 11 WEST HILL
Sanderstead, CR2 0SB. Rachel & Edward Parsons. *M25 J6, A22, 2.9m r'about 4th exit to Succombs Hill, R to Westhall Rd, at r'about 2nd exit to Limpsfield Rd, r'about 2nd exit on Sanderstead Hill 0.9m, sharp R to West Hill. Please park on West Hill.* **Sat 9, Sun 10 Apr (2-5). Adm £5, chd free. Home-made teas. Donation to British Hen Welfare Trust.**
A hidden gem tucked away. A beautiful country cottage style garden set in ½ acre, designed by Sam Aldridge of Eden Restored. The garden flows through pathways, lawn, vegetable and play areas. Flower beds showcase outstanding tulips, informal seating areas throughout the garden allows you to absorb the wonderful garden, whilst observing our rescued chickens and rabbits!

& ☕

56 57 WESTHALL ROAD
Warlingham, CR6 9BG. Robert & Wendy Baston. *3m N of M25. M25, J6, A22 London, at Whyteleafe r'about, take 3rd R, under railway bridge, turn immed R into Westhall Rd.* **Sat 4, Sun 5 June (11-5). Adm £5, chd free. Home-made teas. Donation to Warlingham Methodist Church.**
Reward for the sure footed, many steps to three levels! Mature kiwi and grape vines. Mixed borders. Raised vegetable beds. Box, bay, cork oak and yew topiaries. Amphitheatre of potted plants on lower steps. Stunning views of Caterham and Whyteleafe from top garden. Olive tree floating on a circular pond of white and pink flowers. Flint walls, water spilling onto pebbles in secluded lush setting, vegetable borders, summerhouse, apple tree with child swing, gravel garden.

🐾 ✿ ☕ 🛏 ⑅

57 WESTWAYS FARM
Gracious Pond Road, Chobham, GU24 8HH. Paul & Nicky Biddle, 01276 856163, nicolabiddle@rocketmail.com. *4m N of Woking. From Chobham Church proceed over r'about towards Sunningdale, 1st Xrds R into Red Lion Rd to junction with Mincing Ln.* **Sun 8 May (11-5). Adm £5, chd free. Home-made teas. Visits also by arrangement Apr to June for groups of up to 50.**
6 acre garden surrounded by woodlands planted in 1930s with mature and some rare rhododendrons, azaleas, camellias and magnolias, underplanted with bluebells, lilies and dogwood; extensive lawns and sunken pond garden. Working stables and sand school. Lovely Queen Anne House (not open) covered with listed *Magnolia grandiflora*. Victorian design glasshouse. New planting round garden room.

& 🐾 ✿ 🚗 ☕

58 NEW THE WHITE HOUSE
21 West End Lane, Esher, Surrey, KT10 8LB. Lady Peteranne Hunt & Mr David John, 07850 367600, peajaya@btinternet.com. *Nr Garsons Farm. On the Old Portsmouth Rd, leading towards Cobham, from Esher, turn R into West End Ln. At T-junction turn R. We are the 5th house on the R. The White House has 2 eyebrow windows in the roof.* **Evening opening Wed 22 June (5-9). Adm £12.50. Wine. Fri 24, Sat 25, Sun 26, Wed 29 June, Fri 1, Sat 2, Sun 3 July (11-5). Adm £4.50, chd free. Light refreshments. Visits also by arrangement June & July for groups of 5 to 15.**
Recently landscaped. Although our garden is compact and is on several levels it is dominated by a large beautiful very old oak tree. The garden is full of colour with interesting plants and grasses. Modern water feature and a few sculptures, plus an art exhibition. There is a perfect peaceful spot to sit in the evening for a drink in the late sun. Patio access only for wheelchairs.

& 🐾 ☕ ⑅

59 WILDWOOD
34 The Hatches, Frimley Green, Camberley, GU16 6HE. Annie Keighley, 01252 838660, annie.keighley12@btinternet.com. *3m S of Camberley. M3 J4 follow A325 to Frimley Centre, towards Frimley Green for 1m. Turn R by the green, R into The Hatches for on street parking.* **Sun 4 Sept (1-5). Adm £4.50, chd free. Pre-booking essential, please visit www.ngs.org.uk for information & booking. Home-made teas. Open nearby The Nutrition Garden. Visits also by arrangement in June for groups of up to 20. Visits can be combined with Oakleigh.**
Groups love the hidden surprises in this romantic cottage garden with tumbling roses, topiary and scented *Magnolia grandiflora*. Enjoy discovering a sensory haven of sun and shade with wildlife pond, hidden dell, fernery and loggia. Secret cutting garden with raised beds, vegetables, fruit trees and potting shed patio.

☕ ⑅

60 WOODLAND
67 York Rd, Cheam, Sutton, SM2 6HN. Sean Hilton. *York Rd runs parallel to Belmont Rise, main A217 from Sutton to Banstead. From A217 turn L (from N) or R (from S) at T-lights into Dorset Rd. York Rd is 1st L.* **Evening opening Tue 31 May, Thur 2 June (5.30-8). Adm £6, chd free. Wine.**
Woodland is a suburban walled garden of approx ⅕ acre with a range of plants shrubs and young trees. Landscaped to terraces, two lawns and four levels from the upward incline of the garden. Good selection of shrubs, perennials, hostas, bamboos and ferns. Around 20 different varieties of plectanthrus. Features of the garden are a pond with pergola, a weeping copper beech and a Victorian plant house. Wheelchair access with exception of top level.

& ✿ ☕ ⑅

Our 2021 donations mean that 72,000 people accessed bereavement support through hospices in the UK

SUSSEX

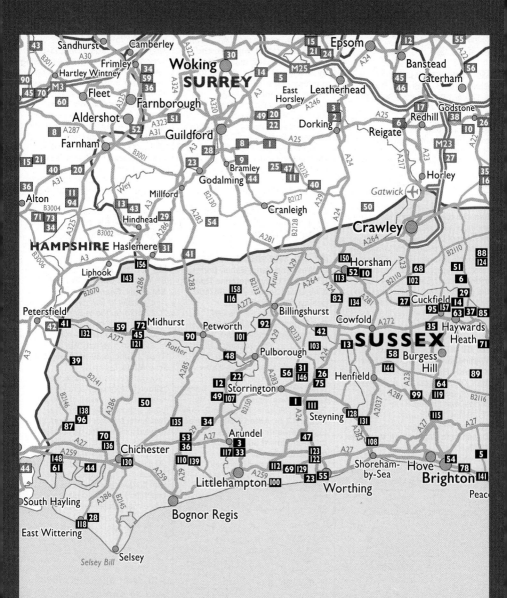

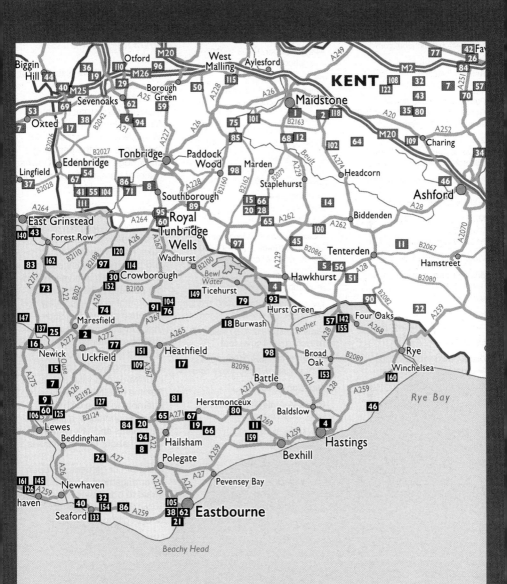

East & Mid Sussex Volunteers

County Organiser, Booklet & Advertising Co-ordinator
Irene Eltringham-Willson
01323 833770
irene.willson@btinternet.com

County Treasurer
Andrew Ratcliffe 01435 873310
andrew.ratcliffe@ngs.org.uk

Publicity & Social Media
Geoff Stonebanks 01323 899296
sussexeastpublicity@ngs.org.uk

Booklet Distributor
Dr Denis Jones 01323 899452
sweetpeasd49@gmail.com

Assistant County Organisers
Jane Baker 01273 842805
jane.baker@ngs.org.uk

Michael & Linda Belton
01797 252984
belton.northiam@gmail.com

Victoria Brocklebank

Shirley Carman-Martin
01444 473520
shirleycarmanmartin@gmail.com

Isabella Cass 07908 123524
oaktreebarn@hotmail.co.uk

Linda Field

Diane Gould 01825 750300
lavenderdgould@gmail.com

Aideen Jones 01323 899452
sweetpeasa52@gmail.com

Dr Denis Jones
(as above)

Susan Laing 01892 770168
splaing@btinternet.com

Sarah Ratcliffe 01435 873310
sarah.ratcliffe@ngs.org.uk

David Wright 01435 883149
david.wright@ngs.org.uk

West Sussex Volunteers

County Organiser, Booklet & Advertising Co-ordinators
Meryl Walters 07766 761926
meryl.walters@ngs.org.uk

Maggi Hooper 07793 159304
maggi.hooper@ngs.org.uk

County Treasurer
Philip Duly 07789 050964
philipduly@tiscali.co.uk

Publicity
Position Vacant, for details please contact Maggi Hooper (as above)

Social Media
Claudia Pearce 07985 648216
claudiapearce17@gmail.com

Photographer
Judi Lion 07810 317057
judi.lion@ngs.org.uk

Assistant County Organisers
Teresa Barttelot 01798 865690
tbarttelot@gmail.com

Sanda Belcher 01428 723259
sandambelcher@gmail.com

Lesley Chamberlain 07950 105966
chamberlain_lesley@hotmail.com

Patty Christie 01730 813323
pattychristie49@gmail.com

Elizabeth Gregory 01903 892433
elizabethgregory1@btinternet.com

Judi Lion (as above)

Carrie McArdle 01403 820272
carrie.mcardle@btinternet.com

Ann Moss 01243 370048
ann.moss@ngs.org.uk

Claudia Pearce (as above)

Fiona Phillips 07884 398704
fiona.h.phillips@btinternet.com

Susan Pinder 07814 916949
nasus.rednip@gmail.com

Diane Rose 07789 565094
dirose8@me.com

Sussex is a vast county with two county teams, one covering East and Mid Sussex and the other covering West Sussex.

Over 80 miles from west to east, Sussex spans the southern side of the Weald from the exposed sandstone heights of Ashdown Forest, past the broad clay vales with their heavy yet fertile soils and the imposing chalk ridge of the South Downs National Park, to the equable if windy coastal strip.

Away from the chalk, Sussex is a county with a largely wooded landscape with imposing oaks, narrow hedged lanes and picturesque villages. The county offers much variety and our gardens reflect this. There is something for absolutely everyone and we feel sure that you will enjoy your garden visiting experience - from rolling acres of parkland, country and town gardens, to small courtyards and village trails. See the results of the owner's attempts to cope with the various conditions, discover new plants and talk with the owners about their successes.

Many of our gardens are open by arrangement, so do not be afraid to book a visit or organise a visit with your local gardening or U3A group.

Should you need advice, please e-mail sussexeastpublicity@ngs.org.uk for anything relating to East and Mid Sussex or maggi.hooper@ngs.org.uk for anything in West Sussex.

f @SussexNGSEast
🐦 @SussexNGS
📷 @ngseastsussex

f @Sussexwestngs
🐦 @SussexWestNGS
📷 @sussexwestngs

OPENING DATES

All entries subject to change. For latest information check **www.ngs.org.uk**
Extended openings are shown at the beginning of the month.
Map locator numbers are shown to the right of each garden name.

January

Tuesday 25th
5 Whitemans Close   157

Thursday 27th
5 Whitemans Close   157

Saturday 29th
5 Whitemans Close   157

February

Snowdrop Festival

By Arrangement
Mitchmere Farm   96

Every Thursday from Thursday 10th
The Old Vicarage   111

Every Tuesday to Friday from Thursday 10th
Pembury House   119

Tuesday 1st
5 Whitemans Close   157

Thursday 3rd
5 Whitemans Close   157

Saturday 5th
5 Whitemans Close   157

Sunday 6th
Manor of Dean   90

Monday 7th
5 Whitemans Close   157

Wednesday 9th
5 Whitemans Close   157

Tuesday 15th
5 Whitemans Close   157

Wednesday 16th
◆ Highdown Gardens   69

Thursday 17th
5 Whitemans Close   157

Saturday 19th
◆ Denmans Garden   36

Sunday 20th
◆ Bates Green   8

March

Every Thursday
The Old Vicarage   111

Every Tuesday to Friday to Friday 11th
Pembury House   119

Sunday 6th
Manor of Dean   90

Sunday 20th
◆ Bates Green   8
The Old Vicarage   111

Monday 21st
47 Denmans Lane   37

Tuesday 22nd
Manor of Dean   90

Saturday 26th
Down Place   39
Limekiln Farm   84

Sunday 27th
Down Place   39
◆ King John's Lodge   79
Limekiln Farm   84

April

Every Wednesday from Wednesday 20th
Fittleworth House   48

Every Thursday
The Old Vicarage   111

Saturday 2nd
Butlers Farmhouse   19

Sunday 3rd
Butlers Farmhouse   19

Monday 4th
47 Denmans Lane   37

Tuesday 5th
◆ Borde Hill Garden   14

Friday 8th
NEW 33 The Plantation 122

Sunday 10th
Penns in the Rocks   120

Saturday 16th
Winchelsea's Secret Gardens   160

Monday 18th
47 Denmans Lane   37
The Old Vicarage   111

Wednesday 20th
Cupani Garden   32

Saturday 23rd
The Garden House   54
The Oast   104
NEW Warnham Park   150

Sunday 24th
Cupani Garden   32
NEW Eastfield Cottage   44
The Garden House   54
Manor of Dean   90
Newtimber Place   99
The Oast   104
Peelers Retreat   117

Tuesday 26th
Peelers Retreat   117

Wednesday 27th
Fairlight End   46

Saturday 30th
Banks Farm   7
◆ Denmans Garden   36

May

Every Wednesday to Wednesday 11th
Fittleworth House   48

Every Thursday
The Old Vicarage   111

Every Monday
Peelers Retreat   117

Sunday 1st
Banks Farm   7
Copyhold Hollow   29
Stanley Farm   143

Monday 2nd
47 Denmans Lane   37
The Old Vicarage   111

Tuesday 3rd
Bignor Park   12

Friday 6th
NEW Telscombe Manor 145

Saturday 7th
Cookscroft   28
◆ King John's Lodge   79
St Mary's Hospital   130

NEW Telscombe Manor 145
NEW The Warren, Crowborough Gardens   152

Sunday 8th
Hammerwood House   59
◆ King John's Lodge   79
Mountfield Court   98
NEW The Warren, Crowborough Gardens   152

Tuesday 10th
Manor of Dean   90

Wednesday 11th
Cookscroft   28

Saturday 14th
96 Ashford Road   4
Forest Ridge   51
Holly House   73
◆ Nymans   102

Sunday 15th
Champs Hill   22
Forest Ridge   51
NEW Foxwood Barn   53
Holly House   73
28 Larkspur Way   82
Legsheath Farm   83
Penns in the Rocks   120

Monday 16th
47 Denmans Lane   37

Wednesday 18th
Balcombe Gardens   6

Saturday 21st
96 Ashford Road   4
54 Elmleigh   45
NEW Hollymount   74
Wych Warren House 162

Sunday 22nd
54 Elmleigh   45
Holford Manor   71
NEW Hollymount   74

Wednesday 25th
Kemp Town Enclosures: South Garden   78

Friday 27th
Holford Manor   71

Saturday 28th
96 Ashford Road   4
◆ The Priest House   124
Skyscape   141

Clinton Lodge

Wednesday 13th
Fittleworth House 48
Foxglove Cottage 52

Friday 15th
Cupani Garden 32
◆ St Mary's House
Gardens 131

Saturday 16th
Bagotts Rath 5
54 Elmleigh 45
Grovelands 58
[NEW] Hollymount 74
Oaklands Farm 103
144 Rodmell Avenue 126
◆ St Mary's House
Gardens 131
[NEW] Westham & Stone
Cross Trail 154

Sunday 17th
Bagotts Rath 5
D & S Haus 33
54 Elmleigh 45
Foxglove Cottage 52
Grovelands 58
4 Hillside Cottages 70
[NEW] Hollymount 74
144 Rodmell Avenue 126

Wednesday 20th
Fittleworth House 48
Knightsbridge House 81

Thursday 21st
Bramley 16
Cumberland House 31
[NEW] 33 The Plantation 122
Thakeham Place Farm 146

Friday 22nd
Bramley 16
Five Oaks Cottage 49

Saturday 23rd
Five Oaks Cottage 49
The Hundred House 77
Knightsbridge House 81

Sunday 24th
The Beeches 9
Cumberland House 31
Five Oaks Cottage 49
The Folly 50
The Hundred House 77
3 Normandy Drive 100
Thakeham Place Farm 146
Whitehanger 156

Wednesday 27th
◆ Herstmonceux Castle
Estate 66

Friday 29th
◆ Charleston 24

Saturday 30th
Hoopers Farm 76
33 Wivelsfield Road 161

Sunday 31st
East Grinstead Gardens 43
Hoopers Farm 76
33 Wivelsfield Road 161

August

Every Thursday
The Old Vicarage 111

**Every Tuesday
from Tuesday 16th**
Peelers Retreat 117

Thursday 4th
Kitchenham Farm 80
Rose Cottage 127

Saturday 6th
Kitchenham Farm 80
Rose Cottage 127

Sunday 7th
Penns in the Rocks 120
Whitehanger 156

Wednesday 10th
Fittleworth House 48

Thursday 11th
Findon Place 47

Saturday 13th
Camberlot Hall 20
54 Elmleigh 45

Sunday 14th
Camberlot Hall 20
Champs Hill 22
Colwood House 27
54 Elmleigh 45

Wednesday 17th
Colwood House 27
◆ Merriments Gardens 93

Friday 19th
[NEW] Abbots Barn 1

Saturday 20th
Butlers Farmhouse 19
D & S Haus 33
Holly House 73

Sunday 21st
Butlers Farmhouse 19
Cloud Cottage 26
The Folly 50
Holly House 73
Hollyoaks 75

Malthouse Farm 89
Whitehanger 156

Tuesday 23rd
St Mary's Hospital 130

Wednesday 24th
Malthouse Farm 89

Monday 29th
47 Denmans Lane 37
Durrance Manor 42
Lindfield Jungle 85
The Old Vicarage 111

September

Every Thursday
The Old Vicarage 111

Every Tuesday
Peelers Retreat 117

Saturday 3rd
54 Elmleigh 45
South Grange 142

Sunday 4th
East Grinstead Gardens 43
54 Elmleigh 45
Parsonage Farm 116
South Grange 142

Wednesday 7th
Knightsbridge House 81
◆ Sheffield Park and
Garden 137

Thursday 8th
Findon Place 47
[NEW] Hollist House 72

Friday 9th
Five Oaks Cottage 49
Holford Manor 71

Saturday 10th
Five Oaks Cottage 49
Knightsbridge House 81
Limekiln Farm 84

Sunday 11th
Five Oaks Cottage 49
Limekiln Farm 84
◆ Sussex Prairies 144

Tuesday 13th
Bignor Park 12

Friday 16th
Holford Manor 71

Saturday 17th
Holford Manor 71
◆ King John's Lodge 79

Sunday 18th
[NEW] Hamsey House 60

Sunday 25th
The Old Vicarage 111

October

**Every Thursday
to Thursday 13th**
The Old Vicarage 111

**Every Tuesday to
Tuesday 11th**
Peelers Retreat 117

Sunday 2nd
◆ High Beeches
Woodland and Water
Garden 68

Saturday 29th
◆ Denmans Garden 36

By Arrangement

Arrange a personalised
garden visit on a date to
suit you. See individual
garden entries for full
details.

[NEW] Abbots Barn 1
4 Ben's Acre 10
Black Barn 13
Brightling Down Farm 17
Butlers Farmhouse 19
Camberlot Hall 20
Champs Hill 22
Channel View 23
Colwood House 27
Cookscroft 28
Copyhold Hollow 29
Cosy Cottage, Seaford
Gardens 133
Cupani Garden 32
Dale Park House 34
47 Denmans Lane 37
Dittons End 38
Down Place 39
Driftwood 40
Durrance Manor 42
[NEW] Eastfield Cottage 44
Fairlight End 46
Fittleworth House 48
The Folly 50
Foxglove Cottage 52
The Garden House 54
[NEW] Hamsey House 60
Harbourside 61
Hardwycke 62
4 Hillside Cottages 70
Holford Manor 71
Holly House 73

Bignor Park

THE GARDENS

❶ NEW ABBOTS BARN

Washington Road, Storrington, RH20 4AF. Emma & Alistair Broda, emma.broda@gmail.com. *On A283 1m outside Storrington village. On A283 Washington Rd between the turns for Barns Farm Ln & Water Ln. Opp sign for Greenacres Farm.* Sun 10 July, Fri 19 Aug (11-5). Adm £6, chd free. Pre-booking essential, please visit www.ngs. org.uk for information & booking. Home-made teas. Visits also by arrangement July & Aug for groups of 5 to 15.

A 1 acre garden backing on to Sandgate Park incorporating part of the original kitchen garden wall. This newly created garden aims to attract wildlife with informal wild flowering slopes, pond and shaded area, plus a fruit cage and vegetable patch. Drought tolerant plants and grasses are found throughout the garden with lots of seating areas to sit and relax.

❷ ALPINES

High Street, Maresfield, Uckfield, TN22 2EG. Ian & Cathy Shaw. *1½ m N of Uckfield. Garden approx 150 metres N of Budletts r'about towards Maresfield. Blue Badge parking at garden, other parking in village.* Sat 9, Sun 10 July (11-4). Adm £5, chd free. Home-made teas.

A 1 acre garden with large and rampant mixed borders, each loosely following a limited colour palette of unusual combinations. Numerous new trees, orchard with beehives and meadow grasses. Wildlife pond with bog garden, developing stumpery and fernery. Vegetable patch with raised beds, fruit cage, pretty greenhouse and bee garden. Wheelchair access largely on one level with a few steps round greenhouse and gravel paths.

❸ ◆ ARUNDEL CASTLE & GARDENS

Arundel, BN18 9AB. Arundel Castle Trustees Ltd, 01903 882173, visits@arundelcastle.org, www.arundelcastle.org. *In the centre of Arundel, N of A27.* For opening times and information, please phone, email or visit garden website.

Ancient castle, family home of the Duke of Norfolk. 40 acres of grounds and gardens which inc hot subtropical borders, English herbaceous borders, stumpery, wildflower garden, two glasshouses with exotic fruit and vegetables, walled flower and organic kitchen gardens. C14 Fitzalan Chapel white garden.

❹ 96 ASHFORD ROAD

Hastings, TN34 2HZ. Lynda & Andrew Hayler. *From A21 (Sedlescombe Rd N) towards Hastings, take 1st exit on L about A2101, then 3rd on L (approx 1m).* Sat 14, Sat 21, Sat 28 May (1-4.30). Adm £3, chd free.

Small (100ft x 52ft) Japanese inspired front and back garden. Full of interesting planting with many acers, azaleas and bamboos. Over 100 different hostas, many miniature. Lower garden with greenhouse and raised beds. Also an attractive Japanese Tea House.

❺ BAGOTTS RATH

5 Crescent Drive North, Woodingdean, BN2 6SP. Stephen McDonnell & Den Daly. *A bus service from Brighton Stn & Brighton seafront stops outside the house, otherwise follow NGS signs & park in adjoining streets.* Sat 16, Sun 17 July (12-5). Combined adm with 144 Rodmell Avenue £6, chd free. Home-made teas.

A small garden on the Downs, near Brighton. Created on a challenging site with shallow chalk soil. The garden looks more mature than its 7 yrs of planning. The garden inc many of the elements that were needed to win the owner eight Chelsea Gold Medals and twice Best in Show for floral design. Water features, topiary, carnivorous plants, succulents and many pieces of sculptures.

GROUP OPENING

❻ BALCOMBE GARDENS

Follow B2036 N from Cuckfield for 3m. ¼ .m N of Balcombe Stn, turn L immed before Balcombe Primary School. From N, take J10A from M23 & follow S for 2½ m. Gardens signed within village. NB A fair walk down lane to 46 Westup Farm Cottages. Wed 18 May, Sat 18 June (12-5). Combined adm £7.50, chd free.

Home-made teas at Stumlet.

STUMLET
Oldlands Avenue, RH17 6LW. Max & Nicola Preston Bell.

46 WESTUP FARM COTTAGES
London Road, RH17 6JJ. Chris Cornwell, 01444 811891, chris.westup@btinternet.com. Visits also by arrangement Apr to Sept.

WINTERFIELD
Oldlands Avenue, RH17 6LP. Sue & Sarah Howe, 01444 811380, sarahjhowe_uk@yahoo.co.uk. Visits also by arrangement Apr to July for groups of up to 30.

Within the Balcombe AONB there are three quite different gardens that are full of variety and interest, which will appeal to plant lovers. Set amidst the countryside of the High Weald, No. 46 is a classic cottage garden with unique and traditional features linked by intimate paths through lush and subtle planting with pollinators and wildlife in abundance. In the village, Winterfield is a country garden packed with uncommon shrubs and trees, herbaceous borders, a summerhouse, pond and wildlife area. At nearby Stumlet the garden is restful, there are places to sit and enjoy a little peace, scent and colour. Redesigned to inc interesting plants for lasting enjoyment by different generations. A garden to watch develop in the future.

❼ BANKS FARM

Boast Lane, Barcombe, Lewes, BN8 5DY. Nick & Lucy Addyman. *From Barcombe Cross follow signs to Spithurst & Newick. 1st road on R into Boast Ln towards the Anchor Pub. At sharp bend carry on into Banks Farm.* Sat 30 Apr, Sun 1 May (11-4). Adm £5, chd free. Home-made teas.

9 acre garden set in rural countryside. Extensive lawns and shrub beds merge with the more naturalistic woodland garden set around the lake. An orchard, vegetable garden, ponds and a wide variety of plant species add to an interesting and very tranquil garden. Refreshments served outside, so may be limited during bad weather. Wheelchair access to the upper part of garden. Sloping grass paths in the lower part.

8 ◆ BATES GREEN
Tye Hill Road, Arlington,
BN26 6SH. John McCutchan,
01323 485151,
john@bluebellwalk.co.uk,
www.batesgreengarden.co.uk.
*3½m SW of Hailsham & A22. Midway
between the A22 & A27, 2m S of
Michelham Priory. Bates Green is in Tye
Hill Rd (N of Arlington village), 350yds
S of Old Oak Inn. Ample parking on
hard-standing verges.* **For NGS: Sun
20 Feb, Sun 20 Mar (10.30-4). Adm
£6, chd £3. Pre-booking essential,
please visit www.ngs.org.uk for
information & booking. Home-
made soup, cakes & scones, plus
light lunches in a large insulated
barn. For other opening times and
information, please phone, email or
visit garden website.**
A welcome return to this
plantswoman's 2 acre tranquil garden
of interest through the seasons.
Woodland garden created around
a majestic oak tree. Middle garden
peaks in late summer. Courtyard
gardens with seasonal container
displays. Front garden a winter and
spring joy with narcissi, primroses,
violets, early tulips and coloured stems
of cornus and salix. Wildlife pond and
conservation meadow. Gardened for
nature. NGS visitors will be able to
walk through the daffodil glade leading
to a 24 acre ancient oak woodland.
This wood has been owned by the
McCutchan family for 100 yrs and
is managed for conservation and
diversity. Wheelchair access to most
areas. Mobility scooters available to
borrow free of charge. Accessible WC.
&. 🍵

9 THE BEECHES
Church Road, Barcombe,
Lewes, BN8 5TS. Sandy
Coppen, 01273 401339,
sand@thebeechesbarcombe.com,
www.thebeechesbarcombe.com.
*From Lewes, A26 towards Uckfield
for 3m, turn L signed Barcombe.
Follow road for 1½m, turn L signed
Hamsey & Church. Follow road for
approx ½m & parking in field on R.*
**Sun 24 July (1-5). Adm £6, chd
free. Home-made teas.**
C18 walled garden with cut flowers,
vegetables, salads and fruit. Separate
orchard and rose garden. Herbaceous
borders, a hot border and extensive
lawns. A hazel walk is being
developed and a short woodland
walk. An old ditch has been made
into a flowing stream with gunnera,
ferns, tree ferns, hostas and a few

flowers going into a pond. Wheelchair
access without steps, but some
ground is a little bumpy.
&. 🐕 ❀ 🛏 🍵

10 4 BEN'S ACRE
Horsham, RH13 6LW.
Pauline Clark, 01403 266912,
brian.clark8850@yahoo.co.uk. *E
of Horsham. A281 via Cowfold, after
Hilliers Garden Centre, turn R by
Tesco on to St Leonards Rd, straight
over r'about to Comptons Ln, next R
Heron Way, 2nd L Grebe Cres, 1st L
Ben's Acre.* **Visits by arrangement
June to Aug for groups of 12 to
30. Adm £9, chd free. Home-made
teas inc. Call to discuss wine and
canapé options.**
Described as inspirational, a visual
delight on different levels with
ponds, rockery, summerhouse
and arbours, all interspersed with
colourful containers and statuettes.
The compartmentalised layout of the
garden lies at the heart of the design.
Small themed sections nest within
borders full of harmonising perennials,
climbers, roses and more. See what
a diverse space can be created on a
small scale. Seating throughout the
garden. 5 mins from Hilliers Garden
Centre, 15 mins from Leonardslee
and NT Nymans. Visit us on YouTube
Pauline & Brian's Sussex Garden.
🐕 ❀ 🛏 🍵 🎍

GROUP OPENING

11 BEXHILL-ON-SEA TRAIL
*Bexhill & Little Common. Follow
individual NGS signs to gardens
from main roads. Tickets & maps at
all gardens.* **Sun 12 June (12-5).
Combined adm £6, chd free.
Home-made teas & light lunch at
Westlands.**

NEW THE CLINCHES
Collington Lane East, TN39 3RJ.
Val Kemm.

64 COLLINGTON AVENUE
TN39 3RA. Dr Roger & Ruth Elias.

NEW DE WILP
Collington Lane East, TN39 3RJ.
Stuart & Hazel Wood.

WESTLANDS
36 Collington Avenue, TN39 3NE.
Madeleine Gilbart & David Harding.

Westlands with mature shrubs in the
front and a large walled rear garden
with shrubs, trees, lawn, fruit and
vegetables. 64 Collington Avenue is

a bit of a surprise as it incorporates
the garden next door too. 34 yrs in
the making, it has a beautiful mix of
herbaceous planting with structural
shrubs, vegetables, planting to
encourage wildlife and stunning roses.
New to the trail this yr is De Wilp, a
beautiful garden laid to lawn with beds
containing a large variety of perennial
and annual plants, vegetables, mature
trees and shrubs. The Clinches, also
new to the trail, is a mature cottage
garden surrounded by trees, pond with
fish, toads and newts. Adjacent to De
Wilp. Plant sale at Westlands. Partial
wheelchair access to some gardens.
&. ❀ 🍵 🎵

12 BIGNOR PARK
Pulborough, RH20 1HG.
The Mersey Family,
www.bignorpark.co.uk. *5m S of
Petworth & Pulborough. Well signed
from B2138. Nearest villages Sutton,
Bignor & West Burton. Approach
from the E, directions & map
available on website.* **Tue 3 May,
Tue 14 June, Tue 13 Sept (2-5).
Adm £5, chd free. Home-made
teas.**
11 acres of peaceful garden to
explore with magnificent views of
the South Downs. Interesting trees,
shrubs, wildflower areas with swathes
of daffodils in spring. The walled
flower garden has been replanted
with herbaceous borders. Temple,
Greek loggia, Zen pond and unusual
sculptures. Former home of romantic
poet Charlotte Smith, whose sonnets
were inspired by Bignor Park.
Spectacular cedars of Lebanon
and rare Lucombe oak. Wheelchair
access to shrubbery and croquet
lawn. Gravel paths in rest of garden
and steps in stables quadrangle.
&. 🐕 🍵

13 BLACK BARN
Steyning Road, West Grinstead,
Horsham, RH13 8LR.
Jane Gates, 07774 980819,
jane.er.gates@gmail.com. *Between
Partridge Green & A24 on Steyning
Rd at West Grinstead. From A24
follow Steyning Rd signed West
Grinstead for 1m, passing Park
Ln & Catholic Church on the L,
continue round 2 bends, Black
Barn is on L. Parking limited so car
share would be appreciated.* **Visits
by arrangement Apr to Sept for
groups of up to 20. Adm £5, chd
free. Home-made teas.**
Black Barn Garden was designed and

planted in Jan 2018. The site was cleared and only the mature trees remained. A hedgerow separating the garden from the field was removed and a large pond has been created in the southwest corner. A large gravel garden was created to the south of the barn and a terrace laid. The existing terrace at the back was increased and a large bed was created. Wheelchair access over grass only.

  ᵔ 🐕 🍵 ⚑

14 ◆ BORDE HILL GARDEN

Borde Hill Lane, Haywards Heath, RH16 1XP. Borde Hill Garden Ltd, 01444 450326, info@bordehill.co.uk, www.bordehill.co.uk. *1½ m N of Haywards Heath. 20 mins N of Brighton, or S of Gatwick on A23 taking exit 10a via Balcombe.* **For NGS: Tue 5 Apr (10-5). Adm £11, chd £7.40. For other opening times and information, please phone, email or visit garden website.**
Rare plants and stunning landscapes make Borde Hill Garden the perfect day out for horticultural enthusiasts, families and those who love beautiful countryside. Enjoy tranquil outdoor rooms, woodland and parkland walks, playground, picnic areas, home-cooked food and events throughout the season. Wheelchair access to 17 acres of formal garden.

  ᵔ 🐕 ✿ 🚐 🍵 ⛲

15 BRADNESS GALLERY

Spithurst Road, Spithurst, Barcombe, BN8 5EB. Michael Cruickshank & Emma Burnett, www.bradnessgallery.com. *5m N of Lewes. Bradness Gallery lies midway between Barcombe & Newick in Spithurst. Free parking in field. Disabled parking will be available outside the gallery.* **Sat 4, Sun 5 June (1-5). Adm £5, chd free. Home-made teas.**
A welcome return to this delightful and tranquil mature, wild, wildlife garden with trees, scented shrubs, old roses, herbaceous borders and wild garden planting. A wooded stream flows along the bottom and two large ponds are home to wild ducks, dragonflies and frogs. Also raised beds for vegetables, herbs and cut flowers. Surrounded by fields and cows. Bradness Gallery will be open showing original paintings, prints, cards by the artists Michael Cruickshank and Emma Burnett.

🍵 ⠐⠻

16 BRAMLEY

Lane End Common, North Chailey, Lewes, BN8 4JH. Marcel & Lee Duyvesteyn. *From A272 North Chailey mini r'abouts take NE turn to A275 signed Bluebell Railway, after 1m turn R signed Fletching. Bramley is 300yds on R. Free car park opp & roadside parking.* **Thur 21, Fri 22 July (12.30-4.30). Adm £5, chd free. Cream teas.**
Rural 1 acre garden. Planting began in 2006 and inc an orchard avenue with wild flowers and long grassed areas and beehives. Vegetable garden, numerous formal and informal ornamental flowerbeds and borders. Planted for strong seasonal effect and structure. Interesting planting and design. SSSI nearby.

✿ 🍵 ⠐⠻

17 BRIGHTLING DOWN FARM

Observatory Road, Dallington, TN21 9LN. Val & Pete Stephens, 07770 807060, valstephens@icloud.com. *1m from Woods Corner. At Swan Pub, Woods Corner, take road opp to Brightling. Take 1st L to Burwash & almost immed, turn into 1st driveway on L.* **Visits by arrangement on 9 June, 10 June & 23 Sept for groups of 18 to 30. Adm £12, chd free. Home-made teas inc.**
The garden has several different areas inc a Zen garden, water garden, walled vegetable garden with two large greenhouses, herb garden, herbaceous borders and a new woodland walk. The garden makes clever use of grasses and is set amongst woodland and stunning countryside views. Winner of the Society of Garden Designers award. Most areas of garden can be accessed with the use of temporary ramps.

  ᵔ 🅳 🍵

'National Garden Scheme donations have funded four of our gardens in regional NHS spinal injury centres supporting nearly 8,500 patients and their visitors.'
Horatio's Garden

GROUP OPENING

18 BURWASH HIDDEN GARDENS

Burwash, TN19 7EN. *In Burwash village on A265. All gardens in centre of village. Dedicated parking at Swan Meadow, entry via Ham Ln. Detailed map available on the day.* **Sat 25, Sun 26 June (11-4.30). Combined adm £7, chd free. Home-made teas in Swan Meadow Sports Pavilion, Ham Lane.**

NEW BRAMBLY COTTAGE
Ms Cas Connor.

BRAMDEAN
Fiona & Paul Barkley.

IVY HOUSE
Susan & Dom Beddard.

LONGSTAFFES
Dorothy Bysouth.

MANDALAY
David & Vivienne Wright, 01435 883149, david.wright@ngs.org.uk, www.mandalaygarden.co.uk. **Visits also by arrangement June to Aug for groups of 6 to 16.**
🅳

Our focus this yr is on smaller village gardens located in and around the picturesque High St in Burwash at the heart of the High Weald AONB, and home for so many yrs of Rudyard Kipling who lived at nearby Bateman's. Within easy walking distance of each other, you'll find five gardens with a diversity of character and styles. Bramdean is a hillside garden with winding paths and extensive views over the Rother valley; Ivy House is south facing with heavily planted twin borders and views over the River Dudwell; Longstaffes has a small formal entrance garden, and elsewhere is extensively terraced; Mandalay is a contemporary cottage garden with an interesting mix of hard and soft landscaping. Newcomer, Brambly Cottage has a south facing Mediterranean influenced garden.

✿ 🍵 ⠐⠻

19 BUTLERS FARMHOUSE

Butlers Lane, Herstmonceux, BN27 1QH. Irene Eltringham-Willson, 01323 833770, irene.willson@btinternet.com, www.butlersfarmhouse.co.uk. *3m E of Hailsham. Take A271 from Hailsham, go through village of Herstmonceux, turn R signed Church Rd, then approx 1m turn R. Do not use SatNav!* Sat 2, Sun 3 Apr, Tue 14, Wed 15 June (2-5). Adm £5, chd free. Sat 20, Sun 21 Aug (2-5). Adm £6, chd free. Home-made teas. Visits also by arrangement Mar to Oct. Call to discuss refreshment options.

Lovely rural setting for 1 acre garden surrounding C16 farmhouse with views of South Downs. Pretty in spring with daffodils, hellebores and primroses. Come and see our meadow in June and perhaps spot an orchid or two. Quite a quirky garden with surprises round every corner inc a rainbow border, small pond, Cornish inspired beach corners, a poison garden and secret jungle garden. Plants for sale. Picnics welcome in June and Aug. Live jazz in Aug. Most of garden accessible by wheelchair.

&. ❀ 🚗 🚐 ☕ 🍴 ◁))

20 CAMBERLOT HALL

Camberlot Road, Lower Dicker, Hailsham, BN27 3RH. Nicky Kinghorn, 07710 566453, nickykinghorn@hotmail.com. *500yds S of A22 at Lower Dicker, 4½m N of A27 Drusillas r'about. From A27 Drusilla's r'about through Berwick Stn to Upper Dicker & L into Camberlot Rd after The Plough pub, we are 1m on L. From A22 we are 500yds down Camberlot Rd on R.* Sat 13, Sun 14 Aug (2-5). Adm £6, chd free. Home-made teas. Visits also by arrangement June to Aug for groups of 8 to 20.

A 3 acre country garden with a lovely view across fields and hills to the South Downs. Created from scratch over the last 9 yrs with all design, planting and maintenance by the owner. Lavender lined carriage driveway, naturalistic border, vegetable garden, shady garden, 30 metre white border and exotic garden. New part-walled garden and summerhouse with new planting. Wheelchair access over gravel drive and some uneven ground.

&. ❀ ☕ ◁))

21 51 CARLISLE ROAD

Eastbourne, BN21 4JR. E & N Fraser-Gausden. *200yds inland from seafront (Wish Tower), close to Congress Theatre.* Sat 4, Sun 5 June (2-5). Adm £4, chd free. Home-made teas.

Small walled, south facing garden (82ft x 80ft) with small pool and mixed beds intersected by stone paths. Profuse and diverse planting. Wide selection of shrubs, old roses, herbaceous plants and perennials mingle with specimen trees and climbers. Constantly revised planting to maintain the magical and secluded atmosphere.

🍴 ❀ ☕

22 CHAMPS HILL

Waltham Park Road, Coldwaltham, Pulborough, RH20 1LY. Mrs Mary Bowerman, info@thebct.org.uk, www.thebct.org.uk. *3m S of Pulborough. On A29 turn R to Fittleworth into Waltham Park Rd, garden 400 metres on R.* Sun 15 May, Sun 14 Aug (2-5). Adm £5, chd free. Tea. Visits also by arrangement Apr to Aug for groups of 10+.

A natural landscape, the garden has been developed around three disused sand quarries with far-reaching views across the Amberley Wildbrooks to the South Downs. A woodland walk in spring leads you past beautiful sculptures, against a backdrop of colourful rhododendrons and azaleas. In summer the garden is a colourful tapestry of heathers, which are renowned for their abundance and variety.

&. ☕ ☕

23 CHANNEL VIEW

52 Brook Barn Way, Goring-by-Sea, Worthing, BN12 4DW. Jennie & Trevor Rollings, 01903 242431, tjrollings@gmail.com. *1m W of Worthing, nr seafront. Turn S off A259 into Parklands Ave, L at T-junction into Alinora Cres. Brook Barn Way is immed on L.* Visits by arrangement May to Sept for groups of up to 30. Adm £5, chd free. Home-made teas.

A seaside Tudor cottage garden, cleverly blending the traditional, antipodean and subtropical with dense planting, secret rooms and intriguing sight-lines. Sunny patios, insect friendly flowers and unusual structures supporting numerous roses, clematis and other climbers, as well as brick and flint paths

radiating from a wildlife pond. Countless planted hanging baskets and containers, sinuous beds packed with flowers and foliage, with underplanting to ensure a 3D experience. Please visit www.ngs. org.uk for pop-up openings. Partial wheelchair access.

&. 🍴 🐄 ❀ ☕

SPECIAL EVENT

24 ◆ CHARLESTON

Firle, Lewes, BN8 6LL. The Charleston Trust, 01323 811626, www.charleston.org.uk. *Charleston is on the A27 signed halfway between Brighton & Eastbourne. From A27 follow narrow lane with deep ditches either side. Parking 200 metres from House entrance. Blue badge only parking 50 metres from house.* For NGS: Evening opening Fri 29 July (6-8). Adm £12.50, chd free. Pre-booking essential, please visit www.ngs.org.uk for information & booking. The café will be open with a rustic Italian menu. For other opening times and information, please phone or visit garden website.

The Bloomsbury artists Vanessa Bell and Duncan Grant moved to Charleston in 1916. They transformed the walled vegetable plot into a quintessential painters' garden mixing Mediterranean influences with cottage garden planting. The garden is full of surprises inc a variety of sculpture, from classical forms to works by Quentin Bell, mosaics and tiled pools, an orchard and tranquil pond. The event inc after-hours access to the garden and talk by Head Gardener, Harry Hoblyn about the history of the garden, how Bell and Grant used the garden to inspire their art, how they chose the plants, and how Harry maintains and develops the garden today. Garden and grounds partially accessible. Gravel pathways, some uneven and narrow.

&. ☕

5 ◆ CLINTON LODGE

Fletching, TN22 3ST. Lady Collum, 01825 722952, garden@clintonlodge.com, www.clintonlodgegardens.co.uk. *4m NW of Uckfield. Clinton Lodge is situated in Fletching High St, N of The Griffin Inn. Off road parking provided, weather permitting. It is important visitors do not park in street. Parking available from 11am.*

For NGS: Thur 16 June (11-5).
Adm £7, chd free. Home-made
teas from 12pm. No lunches.
For other opening times and
information, please phone, email or
visit garden website. Donation to
local charities.
6 acre formal and romantic garden
overlooking parkland with old roses,
William Pye water feature, double
white and blue herbaceous borders,
yew hedges, pleached lime walks,
medieval style potager, vine and rose
allée, wildflower garden, small knot
garden and orchard. Caroline and
Georgian house (not open).

26 CLOUD COTTAGE
Ivy Close, Ashington, Pulborough,
RH20 3LW. Ian & Elizabeth Gregory.
*At northern end of Ashington village.
1st turning L on London Rd, off
B2133 r'about. Cloud Cottage is at
bottom of close on L.* Sun 21 Aug (2-
5). Combined adm with Hollyoaks
£5, chd free. Home-made teas.
A garden created over the past 4
yrs to provide year-round interest. At
the front is a sycamore underplanted
with shade loving plants and bulbs,
inc epimediums, hostas and ferns.
The side and rear garden has a series
of rooms with a large terrace, pond,
mixed shrub and herbaceous beds,
a Japanese style garden, a fruit and
vegetable cage, greenhouses and
further shrub and mixed borders.
Some gravel paths not suitable for
powered wheelchairs.

27 COLWOOD HOUSE
Cuckfield Lane, Warninglid,
RH17 5SP. Mrs Rosy Brenan,
01444 461352. *6m W of Haywards
Heath, 6m SE of Horsham. Entrance
on B2115 Cuckfield Ln. From E, N &
S, turn W off A23 towards Warninglid
for ¾ m. From W come through
Warninglid village.* Sun 14, Wed 17
Aug (12.30-4.30). Adm £7, chd
free. Visits also by arrangement
May to Sept for groups of 10 to
30. Tea, coffee & cake. Donation to
Seaforth Hall, Warninglid.
12 acres of garden with mature and
specimen trees from the late 1800s,
lawns and woodland edge. Formal
parterre, rose and herb gardens.
100ft terrace and herbaceous border
overlooking flower rimmed croquet
lawn. Cut turf labyrinth and forsythia
tunnel. Water features, statues and
gazebos. Pets' cemetery. Giant
chessboard. Lake with island and

temple. Wheelchair access with gravel
paths and some slopes.

28 COOKSCROFT
Bookers Lane, Earnley,
Chichester, PO20 7JG. Mr &
Mrs J Williams, 01243 513671,
john@cookscroft.co.uk,
www.cookscroft.co.uk. *6m S
of Chichester. At end of Birdham
Straight A286 from Chichester, take
L fork to East Wittering B2198.
1m before sharp bend, turn L
into Bookers Ln, 2nd house on L.
Parking available.* Sat 7, Wed 11
May (11-4). Evening opening
Sat 25 June (5-9). Adm £5, chd
free. Light refreshments (May).
Wine & cheese (June). Visits also
by arrangement Apr to Dec for
groups of up to 30.
A garden for all seasons which
delights the visitor. Started in 1988,
it features cottage, woodland and
Japanese style gardens, water
features and borders of perennials
with a particular emphasis on
southern hemisphere plants. Unusual
plants for the plantsman to enjoy,
many grown from seed. The differing
styles of the garden flow together
making it easy to wander anywhere.
Wheelchair access over grass or bark
paths and unfenced ponds.

Telscombe Manor

29 COPYHOLD HOLLOW

Copyhold Lane, Borde Hill, Haywards Heath, RH16 1XU. Frances Druce, 01444 413265, frances.druce@yahoo.com. *2m N of Haywards Heath. Follow signs for Borde Hill Gardens. With Borde Hill Gardens on L over brow of hill, take 1st R signed Ardingly. Garden ½ m. Please park in the lane.* Sun 1 May, Fri 3 June (11-4). Adm £4, chd free. Home-made teas. Visits also by arrangement May & June.

A different NGS experience in two north facing acres. The cottage garden surrounding C16 house (not open) gives way to steep slopes up to woodland garden, a challenge to both visitor and gardener. Species primulas a particular interest of the owner. Stumpery. Not a manicured plot, but with a relaxed attitude to gardening, an inspiration to visitors.

✿ 🍽 ☕

GROUP OPENING

30 CROWBOROUGH GARDENS

Pine Grove, Crowborough, TN6 1FE. *Crowborough is 10m S of Tunbridge Wells on A26. Four gardens close to town centre,* please park in public car parks, nr Pine Grove. Thur 16, Wed 22 June (2-5). Combined adm £6, chd free. Home-made teas at Crowborough Community Centre.

HOATH COTTAGE
Frances Arrowsmith.

8 MILL LANE
Brenda Smart.

 OVERHILL
Mrs Fiona Cattermole.

SWEET SPRINGS
Janet Gamba.

Four gardens are opening all of which are within easy walking distance of the town centre. Please use central car parks as parking near these gardens is difficult. Hoath Cottage is an informal garden dedicated to supporting wildlife. 8 Mill Lane is a compact garden with clematis walk and well-stocked borders. Sweet Springs has an extensively planted, large garden wrapped around the cottage (not open) with vastly different soil conditions throughout. Overhill on London Road has a cottage style garden with a rewilding area.

✿ ☕

31 CUMBERLAND HOUSE

Cray's Lane, Thakeham, Pulborough, RH20 3ER. George & Jane Blunden. *At junction of Cray's Ln & The Street, nr the church.* Thur 21, Sun 24 July (2-5.30). Combined adm with Thakeham Place Farm £8, chd free. Home-made teas at Thakeham Place Farm.

A Georgian village house (not open), next to the C12 church with a beautiful, mature, ¾ acre English country garden comprising a walled garden laid out as a series of rooms with well-stocked flower beds, two rare ginkgo trees and yew topiary, leading to an informal garden with vegetable, herb and fruit areas, pleached limes and a lawn shaded by a copper beech tree. Wheelchair access through gate at right-hand side of house.

♿ ☕))

32 CUPANI GARDEN

8 Sandgate Close, Seaford, BN25 3LL. Dr D Jones & Ms A Jones OBE, 01323 899452, sweetpeasa52@gmail.com, www.cupanigarden.com. *From A259 follow signs to Alfriston, E of Seaford. R off the Alfriston Rd*

 33 The Plantation

onto Hillside Ave, 2nd L,1st R & 1st R. Park in adjoining streets. Bus 12A Brighton/Eastbourne, get off Millberg Rd stop & walk down alley to the garden. **Wed 20, Sun 24 Apr (1-4); Sun 19, Wed 29 June, Sat 9, Fri 15 July (2-5). Adm £5, chd free. Home-made teas. Lunch (pre-booked only). Opening with Seaford Gardens on Sun 29 May. Visits also by arrangement Apr to July for groups of 6 to 20. Bookings must be confirmed & paid 2 weeks prior to visit.**
Cupani is a small tranquil haven with a delightful mix of trees, shrubs and perennial borders in different themed beds. Courtyard garden, gazebo, summerhouse, water features, sweet pea obelisks and a huge range of plants. See TripAdvisor reviews. The garden has undergone a major renovation in 2020 and 2021 and now inc a dry/gravel garden and some more tropical planting.

33 D & S HAUS
41 Torton Hill Road, Arundel, BN18 9HF. Darrell Gale & Simon Rose. *1m SW of Arundel town square. From A27 Ford Rd/ Chichester Rd r'about, take exit to Ford & immed turn R into Torton Hill Rd. Continue uphill & at large oak tree, keep L & we are on L going down the hill.* **Sun 17 July, Sat 20 Aug (1-5.30). Adm £5, chd free. Home-made teas.**
A lush suburban garden, 25ft x 200ft, which the owners have transformed over the yrs. Both front and rear gardens contain a mass of palms, bananas, bamboos and all manner of spiky and large luxuriant foliage. Rules are not followed, as the delights of colour, shape and texture have driven its design with desert plants next to bog plants, a pond, stream and raised flint bed. Tropical planting with lots of unusual plants, quirky sculptures and features.

34 DALE PARK HOUSE
Madehurst, Arundel, BN18 0NP. Robert & Jane Green, 01243 814260, robertgreenfarming@gmail.com. *4m W of Arundel. Take A27 E from Chichester or W from Arundel, then A29 (London) for 2m, turn L to Madehurst & follow red arrows.* **Visits by arrangement May to July for groups of 10+. Adm £5, chd free. Home-made teas.**

Set in parkland, enjoying magnificent views to the sea. Come and relax in the large walled garden which features an impressive 200ft herbaceous border. There is also a sunken gravel garden, mixed borders, a small rose garden, dreamy rose and clematis arches, an interesting collection of hostas, foliage plants and shrubs, and an orchard and kitchen garden.

GROUP OPENING

35 DEAKS LANE GARDENS
Deaks Lane, Ansty, Haywards Heath, RH17 5AS. *3m W of Haywards Heath on A272. 1m E of A23. At r'about at junction of A272 & B2036 take exit A272 Bolney, then take immed R onto Deaks Ln. Park at Ansty Village Centre on R, where tickets for gardens are purchased.* **Sun 12 June (12-4). Combined adm £6, chd free. Light refreshments at Ansty Village Centre.**

BUTTERFLY HOUSE
Cindy & Roger Edmonston.

3 LAVENDER COTTAGES
Derry Baillieux.

NUTBOURNE
David Miller.

THICKETS
Becky & Matt Morgan.

All four gardens are close together on Deaks Lane, each bringing different designs and feel, but all united in attracting bees and wildlife. Plenty of flowers and interest to see and enjoy.

36 ◆ DENMANS GARDEN
Denmans Lane, Fontwell, BN18 0SU. Gwendolyn van Paasschen. *5m from Chichester & Arundel. Off A27, ½ m W of Fontwell r'about.* **For NGS: Sat 19 Feb, Sat 30 Apr, Sat 29 Oct (10-4). Adm £9, chd £7. Pre-booking essential, please phone 01243 278950, email office@denmans. org or visit www.denmans. org for information & booking. Light refreshments. For other opening times and information, please phone, email or visit garden website.**
Created by Joyce Robinson, a brilliant pioneer in gravel gardening and

former home of influential landscape designer, John Brookes MBE. Denmans is a Grade II listed post-war garden renowned for its curvilinear layout and complex plantings. Enjoy year-round colour, unusual plants, structure and fragrance in the gravel gardens, faux riverbeds, intimate walled garden, ponds and conservatory. On site there is a plant centre with unusual plants for sale, a gift shop and treat shop offering refreshments.

37 47 DENMANS LANE
Lindfield, Haywards Heath, RH16 2JN. Sue & Jim Stockwell, 01444 459363, jamesastockwell@aol.com, www. lindfield-gardens.co.uk/47denmans-lane. *Approx 1½ m NE of Haywards Heath town centre. From Haywards Heath Train Stn follow B2028 signed Lindfield & Ardingly for 1m. At T-lights turn L into Hickmans Ln, then after 100 metres take 1st R into Denmans Ln.* **Mon 21 Mar, Mon 4, Mon 18 Apr, Mon 2, Mon 16 May (10-5). Adm £5, chd free. Pre-booking essential, please visit www.ngs. org.uk for information & booking. Mon 29 Aug (1-5). Combined adm with Lindfield Jungle £6, chd free. Home-made teas. Visits also by arrangement Mar to Sept for groups of 5+. Visits can be combined with Lindfield Jungle garden.**
This beautiful and tranquil 1 acre garden was described by Sussex Life as a 'Garden Where Plants Star'. Created by the owners, Sue and Jim Stockwell, over the past 20 yrs, it is planted for interest throughout the yr. Spring bulbs are followed by azaleas, rhododendrons, roses and herbaceous perennials. The garden also has ponds, vegetable and fruit gardens. Most of the garden accessible by wheelchair with some steep slopes.

Around 1,050 people living with Parkinson's - and their families - have been helped by Parkinson's nurses thanks to funding from the National Garden Scheme

38 DITTONS END

Southfields Road, Eastbourne, BN21 1BZ. Mrs Frances Hodkinson, 01323 647163. *Town centre, ⅓m from train stn. Off A259 in Southfields Rd. House directly opp Dittons Rd. 3 doors from Hardwycke.* **Sun 29 May (11-4). Combined adm with Hardwycke £5, chd free. Home-made teas. Visits also by arrangement Apr to Sept.** Lovely, well maintained, small town garden. At the back, a very pretty garden (35ft x 20ft) with small lawn area, patio surrounded by a selection of pots and packed borders with lots of colour. In the front a compact lawn with colourful borders (25ft x 18ft).

39 DOWN PLACE

South Harting, Petersfield, GU31 5PN. Mrs David Thistleton-Smith, 01730 825374, selina@downplace.co.uk. *1m SE of South Harting. B2141 to Chichester, turn L down unmarked lane below top of hill.* **Sat 26, Sun 27 Mar, Sun 19, Mon 20 June (1.30-5.30). Adm £5, chd free. Home-made teas & cream teas. Visits also by arrangement Apr to July for groups of 15+.** Set on the South Downs with panoramic views out to the undulating wooded countryside. A garden which merges seamlessly into its surrounding landscape with rose and herbaceous borders that have been moulded into the sloping ground. There is a well-stocked vegetable garden and walks shaded by beech trees, which surround the natural wildflower meadow where various native orchids flourish. Substantial top terrace and borders accessible to wheelchairs.

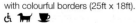

'In the first six months of operation at Maggie's Southampton, which was part funded by the National Garden Scheme, the team has supported people affected by cancer more than 2,300 times.'
Maggie's

40 DRIFTWOOD

4 Marine Drive, Bishopstone, Seaford, BN25 2RS. Geoff Stonebanks & Mark Glassman, 01323 899296, visitdriftwood@gmail.com, www.driftwoodbysea.co.uk. *A259 between Seaford & Newhaven. Turn L into Marine Drive from Bishopstone Rd, 2nd on R. Only park same side as house please, not on bend beyond the drive.* **Visits by arrangement June & July for individuals, couples or groups of up to 14. Adm £6, chd free. Discuss catering options upon booking.** Monty Don introduced Geoff's garden on BBC Gardeners' World saying, a small garden by the sea, full of character with inspired planting and design. Francine Raymond wrote in her Sunday Telegraph feature, Geoff's enthusiasm is catching, he and his amazing garden deserve every visitor that makes their way up his enchanting garden path. Over 130 5-star TripAdvisor visitors comments, three successive Certificates of Excellence and 2020 Travellers Choice Award. Selection of Geoff's home-made cakes, all served on vintage china, on trays, in the garden.

41 DURFORD ABBEY BARN

Petersfield, GU31 5AU. Mr & Mrs Lund. *3m from Petersfield. Situated on the S side of A272 between Petersfield & Rogate, 1m from the junction with B2072.* **Sat 18, Sun 19 June (1-5.30). Adm £5, chd free. Home-made teas.** A 1 acre plot with areas styled with cottage garden, prairie and shady borders and set in the South Downs National Park with views of the Downs. Plants for sale. Partial wheelchair access due to quite steep grass slopes.

42 DURRANCE MANOR

Smithers Hill Lane, Shipley, RH13 8PE. Gordon Lindsay, 01403 741577, galindsay@gmail.com. *7m SW of Horsham. A24 to A272 (S from Horsham, N from Worthing), turn W towards Billingshurst. Approx 1¾m, 2nd L Smithers Hill Ln signed to Countryman Pub. Garden 2nd on L.* **Mon 29 Aug (12-6). Adm £6, chd free. Home-made teas. Visits also by arrangement May to Sept.** This 2 acre garden surrounding a medieval hall house (not open) with Horsham stone roof, enjoys uninterrupted views over a ha-ha of the South Downs and Chanctonbury Ring. There are many different gardens here, Japanese inspired gardens, a large pond, wildflower meadow and orchard, colourful long borders and vegetable garden. There is also a Monet style bridge over a pond with waterlilies.

GROUP OPENING

43 EAST GRINSTEAD GARDENS

7m E of Crawley on A264 & 14m N of Uckfield on A22. Tickets & maps at each garden. Imberhorne Ln, Allotments Car Park 75yds, disabled parking on site. No parking in Chapmans Ln, use Crossways Ave with easy footpath to Jasmine Cottage. **Sun 31 July (12-5); Sun 4 Sept (1-5). Combined adm £6, chd free.**

NEW 35 BLOUNT AVENUE
RH19 1JJ. Nicki Conlon.
Open on all dates

NEW 26 CROSSWAYS AVENUE
RH19 1HZ. Philip & Caroline Barry.
Open on Sun 31 July

IMBERHORNE ALLOTMENTS
RH19 1TX. Imberhorne Allotment Association, www.imberhorneallotments.org.
Open on Sun 31 July

NEW JASMINE COTTAGE
RH19 1JB. Margaret & Laurie Lawrence.
Open on Sun 31 July

27 MILL WAY
RH19 4DD. Jeff Dyson.
Open on all dates

29 MILL WAY
RH19 4DD. Dee & Richard Doyle.
Open on all dates

16 MUSGRAVE AVENUE
RH19 4BS. Carole & Bob Farmer.
Open on Sun 31 July

5 NIGHTINGALE CLOSE
RH19 4DG. Carole & Terry Heather.
Open on all dates

7 NIGHTINGALE CLOSE
RH19 4DG. Gail & Andy Peel.
Open on Sun 4 Sept

Gardens to lift the spirits and make you smile! Established gardens, displaying a mix of planting inc

shrubs, perennials, dahlias and annuals, tubs and baskets. Some gardens are past winners of East Grinstead in Bloom. The gardens all have quite different styles. 16 Musgrave Avenue is a cottage style garden with a thriving vegetable patch. 7 Nightingale Close is on heavy clay in a frost pocket going down to a stream, plus a potager and collection of bonsai. The garden at 35 Blount Avenue has a more modern image for the younger gardener. Imberhorne Allotments consist of 80 plots with a diverse mix of planting inc grape vines, fruit, flowers and a community orchard. All the enthusiastic garden owners are keen propagators, growing from seed, cuttings and plugs, sharing their surplus plants.

Plenty of gardening advice available and homegrown plants for sale at several gardens. The Town Council hanging baskets and planting in the High St are not to be missed and have achieved a Gold Medal from South and South East in Bloom. For steam train fans, the Bluebell Railway starts nearby.

✿ ☕))

---

44 NEW **EASTFIELD COTTAGE**
Taylors Lane, Bosham, Chichester, PO18 8QQ. Mrs Jenifer Fox, 01243 572479, jenifox@waitrose.com. *3m W of Chichester. At Bosham r'about, take Delling Ln to T-junction, then take L turn, then 1st R into Taylors Ln. Eastfield Cottage is located on the R.* **Sun 24 Apr, Fri 10 June (1.30-5). Adm £4.50, chd free. Home-made teas.** Visits also by arrangement May & June for groups of up to 12. Year-round garden featuring tulips, wisteria and spring colour, and twenty rose varieties flower in June. Many other interesting shrubs and plants. The design inc a number of zones such as rose pergola, gravel garden, wild area and well planted herbaceous borders. Restful and tranquil. Views to South Downs and within walking distance to Bosham waterfront. Garden designed for owner's wheelchair access.

♿ ✿ ☕

Herstmonceux Castle Estate

Five Oaks Cottage

© Judi Lion

45 54 ELMLEIGH

Midhurst, GU29 9HA. Wendy
Liddle. ¼ m W of Midhurst off A272.
*Reserved disabled parking at top
of drive, please phone on arrival for
assistance. Other visitors off road
parking on marked grass area.* **Sat
21, Sun 22 May, Sat 18, Sun 19
June, Sat 16, Sun 17 July, Sat
13, Sun 14 Aug, Sat 3, Sun 4
Sept (11-5). Adm £4, chd free.
Home-made teas. Donation to
Chestnut Tree House, Raynaud's
Association, Canine Partners.**
⅓ acre property with terraced front
garden, leading to a heavily planted rear
garden with majestic 120 yr old black
pines. Shrubs, perennials, packed
with interest around every corner,
providing all season colours. Many
raised beds, numerous sculptures,
vegetables in boxes, a greenhouse,
pond and hedgehogs in residence. A
large collection of tree lilies, growing
8-10ft. Child friendly. Come and enjoy
the peace and tranquillity in this award-
winning garden, our little bit of heaven.
Not suitable for electric buggies.

&. 🐐 ✳ ☕ 🎪 🏕

46 FAIRLIGHT END

Pett Road, Pett, Hastings,
TN35 4HB. Chris & Robin
Hutt, 07774 863750,
chrishutt@fairlightend.co.uk,
www.fairlightend.co.uk. *4m E of
Hastings. From Hastings take A259
to Rye. At White Hart Beefeater turn
R into Friars Hill. Descend into Pett
village. Park in village hall car park,
opp house.* **Wed 27 Apr, Sun 12
June (11-5). Adm £6, chd free.
Home-made teas. Visits also
by arrangement May to Sept for
groups of 10+. Donation to Pett
Village Hall.**
Gardens Illustrated said 'The 18th
century house is at the highest point
in the garden with views down the
slope over abundant borders and
velvety lawns that are punctuated
by clusters of specimen trees and
shrubs. Beyond and below are the
wildflower meadows and the ponds
with a backdrop of the gloriously
unspoilt Wealden landscape'.
Wheelchair access with steep paths,
gravelled areas and unfenced ponds.

&. 🐐 ✳ 🚗 🅳 ☕

47 FINDON PLACE

Findon, Worthing, BN14 0RF.
Miss Caroline Hill,
www.findonplace.com. *Directly
off A24 N of Worthing. Follow signs
to Findon Parish Church & park
through the 1st driveway on LH-side.*
**Evening opening Thur 9 June,
Thur 7 July, Thur 11 Aug, Thur
8 Sept (4-8). Adm £7, chd under
12 free. Pre-booking essential,
please visit www.ngs.org.uk for
information & booking. Light
refreshments.**
Stunning grounds and gardens
surrounding a Grade II listed Georgian
country house (not open), nestled
at the foot of the South Downs. The
most glorious setting for a tapestry of
perennial borders set off by Sussex
flint walls. The many charms inc a yew
allee, cloud pruned trees, espaliered
fruit trees, a productive ornamental
kitchen garden, rose arbours and
arches, and a cutting garden.

🐐 ✳ 🚗 ☕ 🔊

48 FITTLEWORTH HOUSE

Bedham Lane, Fittleworth, Pulborough, RH20 1JH. Edward & Isabel Braham, 01798 865074, marksaunders66.com@gmail.com, www.racingandgreen.com. *2m E, SE of Petworth. Midway between Petworth & Pulborough on the A283 in Fittleworth, turn into lane by sharp bend signed Bedham. Garden is 50yds along on the L. Plenty of car parking space.* **Every Wed 20 Apr to 11 May (2-5). Wed 8, Wed 15 June, Wed 13, Wed 20 July, Wed 10 Aug (2-5). Adm £5, chd free. Home-made teas. Visits also by arrangement Apr to Aug for groups of 10 to 40. Garden tours between 1-2 hrs.**

3 acre tranquil, romantic, country garden and walled kitchen garden growing a wide range of fruit, vegetables and flowers. Large glasshouse and old potting shed, mixed flower borders, roses, rhododendrons and lawns. Magnificent 115ft tall cedar overlooks wisteria covered Grade II listed Georgian house (not open). Wild garden, long grass areas and pond, stream and rock garden. The garden sits on a gentle slope, but is accessible for wheelchairs and buggies.

   🐕 ✿ ☕ 》)

49 FIVE OAKS COTTAGE

Petworth, RH20 1HD. Jean & Steve Jackman. *5m S of Pulborough. SatNav does not work! To ensure best route, we provide printed directions, please email jeanjackman@hotmail.com or call 07939 272443.* **Fri 22, Sat 23, Sun 24 July, Fri 9, Sat 10, Sun 11 Sept (10-4). Adm £5, chd free. Pre-booking essential, please visit www.ngs.org.uk for information & booking.**

An acre of delicate jungle surrounding an Arts and Crafts style cottage (not open) with stunning views of the South Downs. Our unconventional garden is designed to encourage maximum wildlife with a knapweed and hogweed meadow on clay attracting clouds of butterflies in July, plus two small ponds and lots of seating. An award-winning, organic garden with a magical atmosphere. Refreshments can be taken at nearby Amberley Tea Rooms (10 min drive), or The Café at The Old Workshop, Sullington Manor Farm (20 min drive).

50 THE FOLLY

Charlton, Chichester, PO18 0HU. Joan Burnett & David Ward, 07711 080851, joankeirburnett@gmail.com, www.thefollycharlton.com. *7m N of Chichester & S of Midhurst off A286 at Singleton, follow signs to Charlton. Follow NGS parking signs. No parking in lane, drop off only. Parking nr pub 'Fox Goes Free'.* **Sun 24 July, Sun 21 Aug (2-5). Adm £5, chd free. Home-made teas. Visits also by arrangement July & Aug for groups of 10 to 30.**

Colourful cottage garden surrounding a C16 period house (not open), set in pretty downland village of Charlton, close to Levin Down Nature Reserve. Herbaceous borders well-stocked with a wide range of plants. Variety of perennials, grasses, annuals and shrubs to provide long season of colour and interest. Old well. Busy bees. Art Studio open to visitors. Partial wheelchair access with steps from patio to lawn. No dogs.

   ♿ ✿ 🛏 ☕

51 FOREST RIDGE

Paddockhurst Lane, Balcombe, RH17 6QZ. Philip & Rosie Wiltshire, 07900 621838, rosiem.wiltshire@btinternet.com. *3m from M23, J10a. M23 J10a take B2036 to Balcombe. After ²/₃m take 1st L onto B2110. After Worth School turn R into Back Ln. After 2m it becomes Paddockhurst Ln. Forest Ridge on R after 2¹/₄m. Ignore SatNav to track!* **Sat 14, Sun 15 May (2-6). Adm £5, chd free. Home-made teas.**

A charming 4¹/₂ acre Victorian garden with far-reaching views, boasting the oldest Atlantic cedar in Sussex. The owners themselves are currently undertaking a major restoration: felling, planting and redesigning areas. Within the garden there is formal and informal planting, woodland dell and mini arboretum. Azaleas, rhododendrons and camellias abound, rare and unusual species. The major restoration project has opened up new vistas. A garden to watch over the coming yrs as the new plantings develop and the newly designed areas grow and flourish. A garden to explore!

   🐕 🛏 ☕

52 FOXGLOVE COTTAGE

29 Orchard Road, Horsham, RH13 5NF. Peter & Terri Lefevre, 01403 256002, teresalefevre@outlook.com. *From Horsham Stn, over bridge, at r'about take 3rd exit (signed Crawley), 1st R Stirling Way, at end turn L, 1st R Orchard Rd. From A281, take Clarence Rd, at end turn R, at end turn L. Street parking.* **Sun 29 May, Wed 13, Sun 17 July (1-5). Adm £5, chd free. Home-made teas. Vegan, gluten & dairy free cake. Visits also by arrangement June & July for groups of 10+. Smaller groups please ask to join another group.**

A ¹/₄ acre plantaholic's garden, full of containers, vintage finds and quirky elements. Paths intersect both sun and shady borders bursting with colourful planting and salvias in abundance! A beach inspired summerhouse and deck are flanked by a water feature in a pebble circle. Two small ponds encourage wildlife. The end of the garden is dedicated to plant nursery, cut flowers and fruit growing. Plenty of seating in both sun and shade throughout the garden. Member of the Hardy Plant Society. A large selection of unusual plants for sale.

   🐕 ✿ ☕ 》)

53 NEW FOXWOOD BARN

Little Heath Road, Fontwell, Arundel, BN18 0SR. Stephen & Teresa Roccia, 07867 383753, foxwoodcottage@outlook.com. *At the junction of Little Heath Rd & Dukes Rd, follow the signs.* **Sun 15 May (11-4). Adm £5, chd free. Home-made teas.**

From a green field site 3 yrs ago, this 1 acre garden has been developed into different areas inc a wildlife pond, rose and gravel garden, patio areas and a dry riverbed. There are herbaceous borders, wildflower areas and a small orchard and allotment. Picnic area adjacent to a paddock with donkeys and ponies. Separate drop off area for wheelchair access.

   ♿ ✿ 🛏 ☕ 🪑 》)

The National Garden Scheme searches the length and breadth of England, Channel Islands, Northern Ireland and Wales for the very best private gardens

54 THE GARDEN HOUSE

5 Warleigh Road, Brighton, BN1 4NT. Bridgette Saunders & Graham Lee, 07729 037182, contact@ gardenhousebrighton.co.uk, www.gardenhousebrighton.co.uk. *1½m N of Brighton pier, Garden House is 1st L after Xrds, past the open market. Paid street parking. London Road Stn nearby. Buses 26 & 46 stopping at Bromley Rd.* **Sat 23, Sun 24 Apr (11-4). Adm £5.50, chd free. Home-made teas. Visits also by arrangement Mar to Sept for groups of 10 to 25.**

One of Brighton's secret gardens. We aim to provide year-round interest with trees, shrubs, herbaceous borders and annuals, fruit and vegetables, two glasshouses, a pond and rockery. A friendly garden, always changing with a touch of magic to delight visitors, above all it is a slice of the country in the midst of a bustling city. Plants for sale.

✿ 🐛))

55 GORING FOLLY

29 Harvey Road, Goring-by-Sea, Worthing, BN12 4DS. Tim & Jean Blewitt. *Just W of Worthing, nr to coast. Turn S off A259 into Parklands Ave. Harvey Rd is 3rd on L.* **Sat 18, Sun 19 June (2-5). Adm £5, chd free.**

An artist's south facing garden designed by the owner to have something of interest from all viewpoints throughout the yr. A medium sized garden in a suburban area that underwent a major replanting during the lockdown of 2020. A main feature is a folly built by the owner to celebrate the Millennium, along with a garden shrine. There will be a children's trail, for adults too perhaps! Sorry, no refreshments available, but you are welcome to bring your own. Wheelchair access via side of house, please ask on arrival.

♿ 🐛

National Garden Scheme gardens are identified by their yellow road signs and posters. You can expect a garden of quality, character and interest, a warm welcome and plenty of home-made cakes!

56 GORSELANDS

Common Hill, West Chiltington, Pulborough, RH20 2NL. Philip Maillou. *12m N of Worthing, approx 1m N of Storrington. Take either School Hill or Old Mill Drive from Storrington. 2nd L on to Fryern Rd to West Chiltington & continue on to Common Hill. Gorselands is on the R. Roadside parking.* **Sun 26 June, Sun 3 July (2-5). Adm £5, chd free. Home-made teas.**

Approx ¾ acre garden featuring mature mixed borders, dahlia garden, fruit area, woodland area with giant redwood, camellias, azaleas, rhododendrons and two ponds. On display will be sculptures for sale by Uckfield sculptur Allan Mackenzie. Wheelchair access on sloping garden with short grass.

♿ 🐛 🍵))

57 ◆ GREAT DIXTER HOUSE, GARDENS & NURSERIES

Northiam, TN31 6PH. Great Dixter Charitable Trust, 01797 253107, groupbookings@greatdixter.co.uk, www.greatdixter.co.uk. *8m N of Rye. Off A28 in Northiam, follow brown signs.* **For opening times and information, please phone, email or visit garden website.**

Designed by Edwin Lutyens and Nathaniel Lloyd. Christopher Lloyd made the garden one of the most experimental and constantly changing gardens of our time, a tradition now being carried on by Fergus Garrett. Clipped topiary, wildflower meadows, the famous long border, pot displays, exotic garden and more. Spring bulb displays are of particular note. Please see garden website for accessibility information.

♿ ✿ 🚗 🍵

58 GROVELANDS

Wineham Lane, Wineham, Henfield, BN5 9AW. Mrs Amanda Houston. *8m SW Haywards Heath. From Haywards Heath A272 W approx 6m, then L into Wineham Ln. House 1¾m on L after Royal Oak Pub. 3m NE Henfield N on A281, R onto B2116 Wheatsheaf Rd, L into Wineham Ln. House ½m on R.* **Sat 16, Sun 17 July (10.30-4). Adm £6, chd free. Home-made teas.**

A South Downs view welcomes you to this rural garden set in over an acre in the hamlet of Wineham. Created and developed by local landscape designer Sue McLaughlin and the owners, it is designed to delight throughout the seasons. Features inc

mixed borders, mature shrubs and orchard. A vegetable garden with greenhouse and pond hide behind a tall clipped hornbeam hedge.

🐕 🍵))

59 HAMMERWOOD HOUSE

Iping, Midhurst, GU29 0PF. Mr & Mrs M Lakin. *3m W of Midhurst. Take A272 from Midhurst, approx 2m outside Midhurst turn R for Iping. From A3 leave for Liphook, follow B2070, turn L for Milland & Iping.* **Sun 8 May (1.30-5). Adm £6, chd free. Home-made teas.**

Large south facing garden with lots of mature shrubs inc camellias, rhododendrons and azaleas. An arboretum with a variety of flowering and fruit trees. The old yew and beech hedges give a certain amount of formality to this traditional English garden. Tea on the terrace is a must with the most beautiful view of the South Downs. For the more energetic there is a woodland walk. Partial wheelchair access as garden is set on a slope.

♿ 🐕 ✿ 🍵))

60 NEW HAMSEY HOUSE

Hamsey, Lewes, BN8 5TD. Mrs Amy Bell, 07740 203265, amy@hamseybelle.co.uk, www.hamseybelle.co.uk. *2m N of Lewes. Turn off the A275 at Offham Church. Over the level crossing, turn R at Ivors Ln. Parking is at Old Hamsey Church. The garden is a 10 min walk. Walk over the bridge, turn R & follow signs along Whitfeld Ln.* **Sun 18 Sept (1-5). Adm £6, chd free. Home-made teas. Visits also by arrangement July to Sept for groups of 10 to 20.**

Nestled within the South Downs National Park, just a few miles from Lewes, Hamsey House was built in 1849. The country garden incorporates an orchard with a wildflower patch, a vegetable and cut flower garden, large herbaceous border, a parterre and many established trees and shrubs. Recently planted willow beds in the orchard will grow willow for garden structures. Sussex Succulents will be selling plants in the vegetable patch. Wheelchair access across uneven lawns. Blue Badge only parking at Hamsey House. Non-accessible WC.

♿ ✿ 🍵))

61 HARBOURSIDE

Prinsted Lane, Prinsted, Southbourne, PO10 8HS.
Ann Moss, 01243 370048, ann.moss@ngs.org.uk. *6m W of Chichester, 1m E of Emsworth. Turn onto Prinsted Ln off A259. Follow lane until forced to the R past the Scout Hut car park. Harbourside is the next house. Old blue boat & buoy with house name in front garden.* **Visits by arrangement for groups of up to 25. Adm £6, chd free. Various refreshments options, discuss upon booking.**
Award-winning coastal garden takes you on a journey through garden styles from around the world. Visit the Mediterranean, France, Holland, New Zealand and Japan. Enjoy tree ferns, topiary, shady area, secret woodland parlour, potager, containers, unusual shrubs and plants, silver birch walk, herbaceous borders, art and crafts, wildlife, seaside garden, blue and white area. Year-round colour and interest. Guided and explanatory tour of garden. Piped music and welcoming fire. Plants and gardening items for sale. Lovely waterside location. Wheelchair access to most of the garden via 10ft of gravel at entrance.

&. ✽ 🍵

62 HARDWYCKE

Southfields Road, Eastbourne, BN21 1BZ.
Lois Machin, 01323 729391, loisandpeter@yahoo.co.uk. *Centre of Eastbourne, Upperton. A259 towards Eastbourne, Southfields Rd on R just before junction with A2270 (Upperton Rd). Limited parking, public car park (pay) in Southfields Rd.* **Sun 29 May (11-4). Combined adm with Dittons End £5, chd free. Home-made teas. Visits also by arrangement.**
Delightful south facing town garden, mainly of chalky soil with many usual and unusual plants and small new summerhouse. Smart front garden with sunken patio. Wide selection of shrubs inc 50 types of clematis. Square garden at rear 70ft x 50ft. Wheelchair access with care, two slight steps to rear garden.

&. 🐴 ✽ 🍵

GROUP OPENING

63 HARLANDS GARDENS

Penland Road, Haywards Heath, RH16 1PH. *Follow yellow signs from Balcombe Rd or Milton Rd &*

Hoopers Farm

© Leigh Clapp

Bannister Way (Sainsbury's). Bus stop on Bannister Way (Route 30, 31, 39 & 80). Gardens within 5 min easy walk from train station & bus stop. **Sun 12 June (10-5). Combined adm £5, chd free. Home-made teas in the front garden of 52 Penland Road.**

55 PENLAND ROAD
Steve & Lisa Williams.

72 PENLAND ROAD
Sarah Gray & Graham Delve.

5 SUGWORTH CLOSE
Lucy & Brian McCully.

27 TURNERS MILL ROAD
Sam & Derek Swanson.

Opening a little later in the 2022 season, our eclectic mix of town gardens continue to inspire and delight our visitors. We comprise awkward shapes and differing gradients, our gardens are designed with relaxation and socialisation in mind. We offer rich cottage style planting schemes, varied ponds, pretty courtyards, practical kitchen gardens and habitats for wildlife. Look out for interesting pots and carnivorous plants. Please check our Facebook page 'Harlands Gardens' for updated information. Our home-made cakes are always a joy inc a contribution from a 'Bake-off' contestant. Roadside parking is readily available. Park once to visit all gardens. Plants sales of our popular 'Harlands Gardens' varieties from the gardens. The quaint English villages of Cuckfield and Lindfield are worthy of a visit. Nymans (NT) and Wakehurst (Kew) are also nearby. Partial wheelchair access to most gardens, no access to No. 72.

&. ✽ 🍵 »)

Sussex Prairies

© Leigh Clapp

GROUP OPENING

64 HASSOCKS GARDEN TRAIL
Hassocks, BN6 8EY. *6m N of Brighton, off A273. Gardens are between Stonepound Xrds & Keymer, N & S of B2116. Park on road or in free car parks in Hassocks. No parking in Parklands Rd. Trail walkable from Hassocks Stn.* **Sun 12 June (1-5). Combined adm £6, chd free. Home-made teas at the United Reform Church (1.15-5).**

13 CHANCELLORS PARK
Steve Richards & Pierre Voegeli.

NEW THE OLD THATCH
Melville Moss & Julie Latham.

PARKLANDS ROAD ALLOTMENTS
Tony Copeland & Jeannie Brooker.

The two gardens on this trail are 1m apart and quite different, but each has a range of unusual plants and shrubs. Both are examples of use of space to inc seating places, winding paths and a good selection of plants. The 55 allotments are not to be missed, a range of classic vegetables inc some exotic ones are grown. The allotmenteers will show you their plots and answer questions. There are spectacular views across to the Downs to Jack and Jill Windmills. Ancient woodland lies along the north side of the allotments. One of the few remaining chalk streams, the Herring Stream, flows through the village, where flash floods have occurred. Whilst on the trail, you can visit the rain gardens in Adastra Park, BN6 8QH and find out more about them, public WC available. Dogs permitted at allotments only.
✿ ☕))

GROUP OPENING

65 HELLINGLY PARISH TRAIL
Follow yellow signs. Bus 51 from Eastbourne. Once parked in the village all gardens are in walking distance of each other. **Sun 10 July (1-5). Combined adm £6, chd free. Home-made teas will be served in St Peter & St Paul's Parish Church.**

BROADVIEW
BN27 4EX. Gill Riches.

MAY HOUSE
BN27 4FA. Lynda & David Stewart.

PRIORS COTTAGE
BN27 4EZ. Pat Booth.

PRIORS GRANGE
BN27 4EZ. Sylvia Stephens.

Four very different gardens ranging from formal structured gardens to naturalistic and wildlife friendly planting schemes. Trail tickets can be bought on the green near the church and at May House with maps available. May House is the furthest from the village centre and has the Cuckoo Trail Car Park across the road. Plant sale at Priors Grange.
✿ ☕))

66 ◆ HERSTMONCEUX CASTLE ESTATE
Hailsham, BN27 1RN. **Bader International Study Centre, Queen's University (Canada), 01323 833816, c_harber@bisc.queensu.ac.uk, www.herstmonceux-castle.com.**

Located between Herstmonceux & Pevensey on Wartling Rd. From Herstmonceux take A271 to Bexhill, 2nd R signed Castle. Do not use SatNav. **For NGS: Wed 27 July (10-7). Adm £8, chd £3.50. Light refreshments. For other opening times and information, please phone, email or visit garden website.**

The Herstmonceux Castle Estate has formal gardens, woodland trails, meadows and lakes set around a majestic C15 moated castle. Features inc an avenue of ancient sweet chestnut trees and lakeside folly in the style of a Georgian house with a walled cottage garden. The gardens and grounds first opened for the NGS in 1927. Partial wheelchair access to formal gardens.

GROUP OPENING

67 HERSTMONCEUX PARISH TRAIL
4m NE of Hailsham. See directions in individual entries. All gardens are signed from the A271. NB not a walking trail. **Sun 26 June (12-5). Combined adm £6, chd free. Home-made teas at Rewa. Teas (12-5) & BBQ lunch (12-2) at The Windmill.**

THE ALLOTMENTS, STUNTS GREEN
BN27 4PP. Nicola Beart.

COWBEECH HOUSE
BN27 4JF. Mr Anthony Hepburn.

1 ELM COTTAGES
BN27 4RT. Audrey Jarrett.

MERRIE HARRIERS BARN
BN27 4JQ. Lee Henderson.

NEW REWA
BN27 1QG. Trudy Gower.

THE WINDMILL
BN27 4RT. Windmill Hill Windmill Trust, windmillhillwindmill.org/.

Five gardens inc a historic windmill and allotments. Cowbeech House, a place to linger, has an exciting range of water features and sculpture in the garden dating back to 1731. Vintage car collection on site to view. Merrie Harriers Barn is a garden with sweeping lawn and open countryside beyond. Colourful herbaceous planting and a large pond with places to sit and enjoy the view. A developing garden that 6 yrs ago was agricultural land. The Allotments comprise 54 allotments growing a huge variety of traditional and unusual crops. Park in the pub across the road from 1 Elm Cottages for this garden and the Windmill. 1 Elm Cottages is a lovely cottage garden packed full of edible and flowering plants you cannot afford to miss. From here a short stroll back towards the village will take you to the historic windmill that will be one of the venues for refreshments and plant sale. Rewa is new to the trail and has stunning views over the Pevensey Marshes with island beds that wrap around the house.

---

68 ◆ HIGH BEECHES WOODLAND AND WATER GARDEN
High Beeches Lane, Handcross, Haywards Heath, RH17 6HQ. High Beeches Gardens Conservation Trust, 01444 400589, gardens@highbeeches.com, www.highbeeches.com. 5m NW of Cuckfield. On B2110, 1m E of A23 at Handcross. **For NGS: Sun 29 May, Sun 2 Oct (1-5). Adm £9, chd free. For other opening times and information, please phone, email or visit garden website. Donation to Plant Heritage.**

25 acres of enchanting landscaped woodland and water gardens with spring daffodils, bluebells and azalea walks, many rare and beautiful plants, an ancient wildflower meadow and glorious autumn colours. Picnic area. National Collection of Stewartias.

69 ◆ HIGHDOWN GARDENS
33 Highdown Rise, Littlehampton Road, Goring-by-Sea, Worthing, BN12 6FB. Worthing Borough Council, 01273 263060, highdown. gardens@adur-worthing.gov.uk, www.highdowngardens.co.uk. 3m W of Worthing. Off the A259 approx 1m from Goring-by-Sea Train Stn. **For NGS: Wed 16 Feb (10-4.30); Wed 1 June (10-9). Adm by donation. For other opening times and information, please phone, email or visit garden website.**

Curated by Sir Frederick Stern, these unique chalk gardens are home to rare plants and trees, many from seed collected by Wilson, Farrer and Kingdon-Ward. New visitor centre, supported by National Lottery Heritage Fund, sharing stories of the plants and people behind the gardens. Also new accessible paths, a project to propagate and protect rare plants and a sensory garden with a secret sea view. Refreshments available at nearby Highdown Tea Rooms. Accessible top pathway and lift to visitor centre. Go to garden website for further details.

&

70 4 HILLSIDE COTTAGES
Downs Road, West Stoke, Chichester, PO18 9BL. Heather & Chris Lock, 01243 574802, chlock@btinternet.com. 3m NW of Chichester. From A286 at Lavant, head W for 1½m, nr Kingley Vale. **Sun 12 June, Sun 17 July (11-4). Adm £5, chd free. Home-made teas. Visits also by arrangement June to Aug.**

In a rural setting this stunning garden is densely planted with mixed borders and shrubs. Large collection of roses, clematis, fuchsias and dahlias, a profusion of colour and scent in a well maintained garden. Please visit www. ngs.org.uk for pop-up openings in June, July and August.

71 HOLFORD MANOR
Holford Manor Lane, North Chailey, Lewes, BN8 4DU. Martyn Price, 01444 471714, martyn@holfordmanor.co.uk, www.chailey-iris.co.uk. 4½m SE of Haywards Heath. SE From Scaynes Hill on A272, after 1¼m turn R onto Holford Manor Ln. **Sun 22, Fri 27 May, Sat 11, Sun 12 June, Fri 9, Fri 16, Sat 17 Sept (11-4). Adm £7, chd free. Home-made teas. Visits also by arrangement May to Sept for groups of 10+.**

5 acre garden for all seasons, surrounding a C16 Manor (not open) with far-reaching views over the ha-ha to open fields with rare breed sheep and geese. Designed and laid out by the current owners with extensive herbaceous borders, iris beds and formal parterre rose garden. Features inc a secret Chinese garden, tropical beds, cutting garden and a wildflower meadow. An ornamental pond and a landscaped 'horse pond' with water lilies as well as a 2 acre lake and swamp garden with walking track. Brick or gravel paths give wheelchair access to most of the garden.

72 NEW **HOLLIST HOUSE**
Hollist Lane, Easebourne, Midhurst, GU29 9RS. **Mrs Caro & Mr Gavin Darlington.** *Coming from Midhurst towards Petworth take 1st L on r'about at bottom of town signed Haslemere. Then follow large yellow NGS arrow signs.* **Sat 25 June, Thur 8 Sept (2-5.30). Adm £5, chd free. Home-made teas.** Tradional English garden with natural spring pond and the River Rother running through acres of lawns, woods, herbaceous borders and kitchen garden.
✿ ☕ •))

73 **HOLLY HOUSE**
Beaconsfield Road, Chelwood Gate, Haywards Heath, RH17 7LF. **Mrs Deirdre Birchell,** 01825 740484, db@hollyhousebnb.co.uk, **www.hollyhousebnb.co.uk.** *7m E of Haywards Heath. From Nutley village on A22 turn off at Hathi Restaurant signed Chelwood Gate 2m. Chelwood Gate Village Hall on R, Holly House is opp.* **Sat 14, Sun 15 May, Sat 20, Sun 21 Aug (2-5). Adm £6, chd free. Home-made teas. Visits also by arrangement May to Aug for groups of 10 to 30.** An acre of English garden providing views and cameos of plants and trees round every corner with many different areas giving constant interest. A fish pond and a wildlife pond beside a grassy area with many shrubs and flower beds. Among the trees and winding paths there is a cottage garden which is a profusion of colour and peace. Exhibition of paintings and cards by owner. Garden accessible by wheelchair in good weather, but it is not easy.
& 🐾 � 🏠 ☕ •))

You can make a difference! Join our Great British Garden Party fundraising campaign and raise money for some of the best-loved nursing and health charities. Visit ngs.org.uk/gardenparty to find out how you can get involved

74 NEW **HOLLYMOUNT**
Burnt Oak Road, High Hurstwood, Uckfield, TN22 4AE. **Jonathan Hughes-Morgan,** 07717 706520, rebeccamarchtaylor@gmail.com. *Exactly halfway between Uckfield & Crowborough, just off the A26. From A26 S of Crowborough or A272 between Uckfield & Buxted, follow sign to High Hurstwood. From N approx 2m down Chillies Ln take L, from S 1½m up Hurstwood Rd take R, ½m on L.* **Sat 21, Sun 22 May, Sat 11, Sun 12 June, Sat 16, Sun 17 July (11-5). Adm £7, chd free. Home-made teas. Visits also by arrangement Apr to Oct for groups of 10+.**
A new 7 acre garden on sloping hillside. Four large ponds, a stream, waterfalls, terraced beds, interesting planting, some tropical, large rhododendrons, wildlife; alpacas, chickens, ducks, fish. The garden has a great variety of trees, two greenhouses, shepherds hut, summerhouse, gravel paths, kitchen garden, many decks and wildflower terracing to the rear. Very peaceful setting with great views.
✿ 🚻 🏠 ☕ •))

75 **HOLLYOAKS**
London Road, Ashington, Pulborough, RH20 3JR. **Pam & Bill Whittaker.** *Enter Ashington from N of village, take 1st l into Ivy Close, garden on L.* **Sun 21 Aug (2-5). Combined adm with Cloud Cottage £5, chd free. Home-made teas at Cloud Cottage.**
A small cottage style garden with specimen trees, heavily planted borders with shrubs, perennials, roses, clematis, dahlias and fuchsias. A pond and a variety of containers surround the patio. At the front is a scree bed and borders with roses, shrubs and perennials. Climbing roses and climbing hydrangeas clothe the front of the house and baskets and containers overflow.
& ☕ •))

76 **HOOPERS FARM**
Vale Road, Mayfield, TN20 6BD. **Andrew & Sarah Ratcliffe.** *10m S of Tunbridge Wells. Turn off A267 into Mayfield. Parking in the village & field parking at Hoopers Farm.* **Sat 30, Sun 31 July (11-5). Adm £5, chd free. Home-made teas. Opening with Mayfield Gardens on Sat 11, Sun 12 June.**
Large south facing garden with colour

themed mixed herbaceous planting. Mature trees, flowering shrubs, rose arbour, rock garden, secret garden and vegetable plot. New planted area with lots of late season colour developed from existing sand school. Lovely views. Plant sales by Rapkyns Nursery. Wheelchair access to most of the garden.
& 🐾 ✿ ☕ •))

77 **THE HUNDRED HOUSE**
Pound Lane, Framfield, TN22 5RU. **Dr & Mrs Michael Gurney.** *4m E of Uckfield. From Uckfield take B2102 through Framfield. 1m from centre of village turn L into Pound Ln, then ¾m on R. Disabled parking close by the entrance gate to the garden.* **Sat 23, Sun 24 July (2-5.30). Adm £6, chd free. Home-made teas.**
Delightful garden with panoramic views, set in the grounds of the historic The Hundred House (not open). Fine stone ha-ha. 1½ acre garden with mixed herbaceous borders, productive vegetable garden, greenhouse, ancient yew tree, pond area with some subtropical plants, secret woodland copse and orchard. Beech hedge, field and butterfly walk, silver birch (jacquemontii) grove under development. Homegrown plants, vegetables and fruit for sale.
& 🐾 ✿ ☕ 🧺 •))

SPECIAL EVENT

78 **KEMP TOWN ENCLOSURES: SOUTH GARDEN**
Lewes Crescent, Brighton, BN2 1FH. **Kemp Town Enclosures Ltd,** kte.org.uk. *On S coast, 1m E of Brighton Palace Pier, ½m W of Brighton Marina. 2m from Brighton Stn. Bus No. 7, stop St Mary's Hall. M23/A23 to Brighton Palace Pier; L on A259. 5m S A27 on B2123, R on A259.* **Wed 25 May (12-5). Adm £7.50, chd free. Pre-booking essential, please visit www.ngs.org.uk for information & booking. Tours every 30 mins from 12pm to 3.30pm (2 groups of 15 per tour) inc. No refreshments, good coffee shops nearby.**
Unique historic Grade II listed Regency private town garden in a spectacular seaside location. Enduring strong salty winds and thin chalk soil, the garden balances naturalistic planting and a more ordered look, relaxed not manicured. With several distinctive areas, this wonderful 5 acre garden combines

open lawns, winding paths, trees, herbaceous and shrub borders and a shaded woodland garden. Designed by Henry Phillips in 1820s, the garden was a central feature of the Regency development of the Kemp Town Estate. Queen Victoria and Edward VII walked in these gardens. Lewis Carroll visited many times and the garden tunnel is said to have inspired the rabbit hole in 'Alice in Wonderland'. Ramped gate entry. Gravel winding paths give access to most of the garden. Relatively steep slopes on main lawn and in the garden tunnel.

&

---

79 ◆ KING JOHN'S LODGE
Sheepstreet Lane, Etchingham, TN19 7AZ. Jill Cunningham, 01580 819220, harry@kingjohnsnursery.co.uk, www.kingjohnsnursery.co.uk. *2m W of Hurst Green. Off A265 nr Etchingham. From Burwash turn L before Etchingham Church, from Hurst Green turn R after church, into Church Ln, which leads into Sheepstreet Ln after ½ m, then L after 1m.* **For NGS: Sun 27 Mar, Sat 7, Sun 8 May, Sat 18, Sun 19 June, Sat 17 Sept (11-5). Adm £5, chd free. Home-made teas. For other opening times and information, please phone, email or visit garden website.**
4 acre romantic garden for all seasons. An ongoing family project since 1987 with new areas completed in 2020. From the eclectic shop, nursery and tearoom, stroll past wildlife pond through orchard with bulbs, meadow, rose walk and fruit according to the season. Historic house (not open) has broad lawn, fountain, herbaceous border, pond and ha-ha. Explore secret woodland with renovated pond and admire majestic trees and 4 acre meadows. Garden is mainly flat. Areas with steps can usually be accessed from other areas. Disabled WC.

80 KITCHENHAM FARM
Kitchenham Road, Ashburnham, Battle, TN33 9NP. Amanda & Monty Worssam. *S of Ashburnham Place from A271 Herstmonceux to Bexhill Rd, take L turn 500 metres after Boreham St. Kitchenham Farm is 500 metres on L.* **Tue 7, Thur 9 June, Thur 4, Sat 6 Aug (2-5). Adm £5, chd free. Home-made teas.**

1 acre country house garden set amongst traditional farm buildings with stunning views over the Sussex countryside. Series of borders around the house and Oast House (not open). Lawns and mixed herbaceous borders inc roses and delphiniums. A ha-ha separates the garden from the fields and sheep. The garden adjoins a working farm. Wheelchair access to the garden. One step to WC.

& 🐑 ✿ ☕))

81 KNIGHTSBRIDGE HOUSE
Grove Hill, Hellingly, Hailsham, BN27 4HH. Andrew & Karty Watson. *3m N of Hailsham, 2m S of Horam. From A22 at Boship r'about take A271, at 1st set of T-lights turn L into Park Rd, new road layout here, so you need to take a L turn approx 150 metres from the lights & drive for 2²/₃ m, garden on R.* **Wed 20, Sat 23 July, Wed 7, Sat 10 Sept (2-5). Adm £6, chd free. Home-made teas.**
Mature landscaped garden set in 5 acres of tranquil countryside surrounding Georgian house (not open). Several garden rooms, spectacular herbaceous borders planted in contemporary style in traditional setting. Opening July and Sept for visitors to enjoy a very different experience. Lots of late season colour with grasses and some magnificent specimen trees; also partly walled garden. Wheelchair access to most of garden with gravel paths. Ask to park by house if slope from car park is too steep.

& 🐑 ✿ 🏠 ☕))

82 28 LARKSPUR WAY
Southwater, Horsham, RH13 9GR. Peter & Marjorie Cannadine. *From A24 take Worthing Rd signed Southwater, at 2nd r'about take 1st exit Blakes Farm Rd. At T-junction turn R, follow road round into Larkspur Way. At T-junction turn L, then R, No. 28 is on the L.* **Sun 15 May, Sun 26 June (2-5). Adm £3.50, chd free. Light refreshments.**
Created for a new build this small garden is packed with big ideas for those looking for inspiration. A small front garden with pond, Mediterranean area and well-stocked border. The back garden being approx 15 x 10 metres, backing onto woodland is filled with cottage garden plants, containers, ornaments and more to inspire.

✿ ☕))

83 LEGSHEATH FARM
Legsheath Lane, nr Forest Row, RH19 4JN. Mr & Mrs M Neal. *4m S of East Grinstead. 2m W of Forest Row, 1m S of Weirwood Reservoir.* **Sun 15 May (2-4.30). Adm £5, chd free. Home-made teas. Donation to Holy Trinity Church, Forest Row.**
Legsheath was first mentioned in Duchy of Lancaster records in 1545. It was associated with the role of Master of the Ashdown Forest. Set high in the Weald with far-reaching views of East Grinstead and Weirwood Reservoir. The garden covers 11 acres with a spring fed stream feeding ponds. There is a magnificent davidia, rare shrubs, embothrium and many different varieties of meconopsis and abutilons.

& 🐑 ✿ ☕

84 LIMEKILN FARM
Chalvington Road, Chalvington, Hailsham, BN27 3TA. Dr J Hester & Mr M Royle. *10m N of Eastbourne. Nr Hailsham. Turn S off A22 at Golden Cross & follow the Chalvington Rd for 1m. The entrance has white gates on LH-side. Disabled parking space close to house, other parking 100 metres further along road.* **Sat 26, Sun 27 Mar, Sat 10, Sun 11 Sept (2-5). Adm £6, chd free. Home-made teas in the oast house.**
The garden was designed in the 1930s when the house was owned by Charles Stewart Taylor, MP for Eastbourne. It has not changed in basic layout since then. The planting aims to reflect the age of the C17 property (not open) and original garden design. The house and garden are mentioned in Virginia Woolf's diaries of 1929, depicting a particular charm and peace that still exists today. Flint walls enclose the main lawn, herbaceous borders and rose garden. Nepeta lined courtyard, Physic garden with talk at 3pm about medicinal plants, informal pond and specimen trees inc a very ancient oak. Many spring flowers and tree blossom. Mostly flat access with two steps up to main lawn and herbaceous borders.

& 🐑 ✿ ☕))

85 LINDFIELD JUNGLE

16 Newton Road, Lindfield, Haywards Heath, RH16 2ND. Tim Richardson & Clare Wilson, 01444 484132, info@lindfieldjungle.co.uk, www.lindfieldjungle.co.uk. *Approx 1½ m NE of Haywards Heath town centre. Take B2028 into Lindfield. Turn onto Lewes Rd (B2111), then Chaloner Rd & turn R into Chaloner Close (no parking in close or at garden). Garden is located at far end, use postcode RH16 2NH.* **Mon 29 Aug (1-5). Combined adm with 47 Denmans Lane £6, chd free. Visits also by arrangement July to Sept for groups of 5 to 10. Visits can be combined with 47 Denmans Lane.**
A surprising, intimate garden, 17 x 8 metres. Transformed since 1999 into an atmospheric jungle oasis planted for tropical effect. Lush and exuberant with emphasis on foliage and hot colours. From the planter's terrace enjoy the winding path through lillies, cannas, ginger and bamboo, to the tranquil sundowner's deck over hidden pools.

86 THE LONG HOUSE

The Lane, Westdean, nr Seaford, BN25 4AL. Robin & Rosie Lloyd, 01323 870432, rosiemlloyd@gmail.com, www.thelonghousegarden.co.uk. *3m E of Seaford, 6m W of Eastbourne. From A27 follow signs to Alfriston then Litlington, Westdean 1m on L. From A259 at Exceat, L on Litlington Rd, ¼ m on R. Free parking in village. Coach parties go to Friston Forest car park.* **Visits by arrangement May to July for groups of 10+. Adm £8, chd free. Home-made teas.**
The Long House's 1 acre garden has become a favourite for private group visits, being compared for romance, atmosphere and cottage garden planting to Great Dixter and Sissinghurst. Lavenders, hollyhocks, roses, a wildflower meadow, a long perennial border, water folly and pond are just some of the features, and everyone says Rosie's home-made cakes are second to none. Situated on the South Downs Way in the South Downs National Park within the medieval village of Westdean and a stones throw from the Seven Sisters Country Park. Wheelchair access over gravel forecourt at entrance, some slopes and steps.

&. ✿ ⌂ ☕

87 LORDINGTON HOUSE

Lordington, Chichester, PO18 9DX. Mr & Mrs John Hamilton, 01243 375862, hamiltonjanda@btinternet.com. *7m W of Chichester. On W side of B2146, ½ m S of Walderton, 6m S of South Harting. Enter through white railings on bend.* **Sat 4, Sun 5 June (2-5). Adm £5, chd free. Home-made teas. Visits also by arrangement June to Oct for groups of up to 30.**
Early C17 house (not open) and walled gardens in South Downs National Park. Clipped yew and box, lawns, borders and fine views. Vegetables, fruit and poultry in the kitchen garden. 100+ roses planted since 2008. Trees both mature and young. Lime avenue planted in 1973 to replace elms. Wildflowers in field outside walls, accessible from garden. Gardens overlook Ems Valley, farmland and wooded slopes of South Downs, all in AONB. Wheelchair access is possible, but challenging on gravel paths, uneven paving and slopes. No disabled WC.

&. ⛏ ✿ 🚌 ☕ 🪑

88 LUCTONS

North Lane, West Hoathly, East Grinstead, RH19 4PP. Drs Hans & Ingrid Sethi, 01342 810085, ingrid@sethis.co.uk. *4m SW of East Grinstead, 6m E of Crawley. In centre of West Hoathly village, nr church, Cat Inn & Priest House. Car parks in village.* **Sat 25, Sun 26, Tue 28 June (1-5). Adm £5, chd free. Home-made teas. Visits also by arrangement June to Sept for groups of 10+. Groups pay by number booked, rather than number attending.**
A peaceful 2 acre Gertrude Jekyll style garden with box parterre, topiary, acclaimed herbaceous borders, swathes of spotted orchids, wildflower orchard, pond, greenhouses, large vegetable, herb and fruit gardens, croquet lawn, and a huge variety of plants, especially salvias. Admired by overseas garden tour visitors, U3A groups and featured in Caroline Holmes book 'The English Garden Celebrated'.

&. ✿ ☕

89 MALTHOUSE FARM

Streat Lane, Streat, Hassocks, BN6 8SA. Richard & Helen Keys, 01273 890356, helen.k.keys@btinternet.com. *2m SE of Burgess Hill. From r'about between B2113 & B2112 take Folders Ln & Middleton Common Ln E (away from Burgess Hill); after 1m R into Streat Ln, garden is ½ m on R. Please park carefully as signed/ directed.* **Sun 21, Wed 24 Aug (2-5.30). Adm £6, chd free. Pre-booking essential, please visit www.ngs.org.uk for information & booking. Home-made teas. Visits also by arrangement May to Sept for groups of 10 to 30.**
Rural 5 acre garden with stunning views to South Downs. Garden divided into separate rooms; box parterre and borders with glass sculpture, herbaceous and shrub borders, mixed border for seasonal colour and kitchen garden. Orchard with newly planted wild flowers leading to partitioned areas with grass walks, snail mound, birch maze and willow tunnel. Wildlife farm pond with planted surround. Plants for sale. Wheelchair access mainly on grass with some steps (caution if wet).

&. ✿ ☕))

90 MANOR OF DEAN

Tillington, Petworth, GU28 9AP. Mr & Mrs James Mitford, 07887 992349, emma@mitford.uk.com. *3m W of Petworth. From Petworth towards Midhurst on A272, pass Tillington & turn R onto Dean Ln following NGS signs. From Midhurst on A272 towards Petworth, past Halfway Bridge, turn L following NGS signs.* **Sun 6 Feb (2-4); Sun 6 Mar (2-5); Tue 22 Mar (10.30-1); Sun 24 Apr (2-5); Tue 10 May (10.30-1). Adm £5, chd free. Home-made teas. Visits also by arrangement Feb to Sept for groups of 20+. Excluding school holidays.**
Approx 3 acres of traditional English garden with extensive views of the South Downs. Herbaceous borders, early spring bulbs, bluebell woodland walk, walled kitchen garden with fruit, vegetables and cutting flowers. NB some parts of the garden may be affected by building work.

 ))

Cleveland Place, Winchelsea Gardens

© Suzie Gibbons

GROUP OPENING

91 MAYFIELD GARDENS
Mayfield, TN20 6AB. *10m S of Tunbridge Wells. Turn off A267 into Mayfield. Parking in the village, TN20 6BE & field parking at Hoopers Farm, TN20 6BD. A detailed map available at each garden.* **Sat 11, Sun 12 June (11-5). Combined adm £7, chd free. Home-made teas at Hoopers Farm & The Oast.**

ABBOTSBURY
Rob & Becky Morris.

HOOPERS FARM
Andrew & Sarah Ratcliffe.
(See separate entry)

MULBERRY
M Vernon.

OAKCROFT
Nick & Jennifer Smith.

THE OAST
Mike & Tessa Crowe.
(See separate entry)

SOUTH STREET PLOTS
Val Buddle.

SUNNYBANK COTTAGE
Eve & Paul Amans.

Mayfield is a beautiful Wealden village with tearooms, an old pub and many interesting historical connections.

The gardens to visit are all within walking distance of the village centre. They vary in size and style inc colour themed, courtyard and cottage garden planting, wildlife meadows and fruit and vegetable plots. There are far-reaching, panoramic views over the beautiful High Weald.

🐓 ✿ 🍵))

92 MEADOW FARM
Blackgate Lane, Pulborough, RH20 1DF. Charles & Vanessa Langdale. *5m N of Pulborough. From Pulborough take A29 N. Just outside Pulborough L into Blackgate Ln signed to Toat. Continue on road for 1½ m. At sign for Scrase Farms keep going straight. Signed parking on R.* **Sun 19 June (2.30-5.30). Adm £4, chd free. Home-made teas.**

Approx 1 acre garden built from scratch over the last 14 yrs; designed and planted by current owners. Colour themed beds inc double borders, formal pond and green and white shady garden. A pleached hornbeam avenue out to the Sussex countryside. A walled garden provides fruit, cut flowers and vegetables. Extensive orchard with a hazelnut walk. Wildlife swimming pond, a work in progress.

🍵))

93 ◆ MERRIMENTS GARDENS
Hawkhurst Road, Hurst Green, TN19 7RA. Lucy Cross, 01580 860666, info@merriments.co.uk, www.merriments.co.uk. *Off A21, 1m N of Hurst Green. On A229 Hawkhurst Rd. Situated between Hurst Green & Hawkhurst 300yds on R from A21/A229 junction.* **For NGS: Wed 17 Aug (9-5). Adm £9, chd free. For other opening times and information, please phone, email or visit garden website.**

Our beautiful 4 acre garden with its colour themed borders is set amongst the rolling countryside of East Sussex. Seamlessly blending, its large borders of inspiring planting evolve through the seasons from spring pastels to the fiery autumn hues of the many trees, all on a gently sloping south facing site with good parking and easy access. There are a number of benches to allow visitors to enjoy the atmosphere of this special ever-evolving garden. Many unusual plants, most sold in the plant centre. A great shop and restaurant serving home-made lunches and teas (a donation to the NGS from café sales on the day). Wheelchairs can be pre-booked from the shop.

♿ 🐓 🐕 ✿ 🚗 🍵

Harbourside

© Judi Lion

and stunning sunsets. Deep pond. Sloping bumpy lawn and no hard paths. No wheelchair access to WC.

👌 ✿ NPC 🍵 🪑

96 MITCHMERE FARM

Stoughton, Chichester, PO18 9JW. Neil & Sue Edden, 02392 631456, sue@mitchmere.co.uk. *5½m NW of Chichester. Turn off the B2146 at Walderton towards Stoughton. Farm is ¾m on L, ¼m beyond the turning to Upmarden. Please do not park on verge, follow signs for parking.* **Visits by arrangement Feb to Nov for groups of up to 20. Adm £5, chd free. Min charge per group £50. Tea, coffee & biscuits.**

1½ acre garden in lovely downland position. Unusual trees and shrubs growing in dry gravel, briefly wet most yrs when the Winterbourne rises and flows through the garden. Coloured stems, catkins, drifts of snowdrops and crocuses. Small collection of special snowdrops. Optional 10 min walk down the long field beside the river, across the sleeper bridge, take the path through the copse with snowdrops up the steps into the new wood, then into the meadow and back to the garden. Wellies advisable. Dogs on short leads. Wheelchair access over gravel and grass.

👌 🐕 ✿ 🍵 🪑

94 ◆ MICHELHAM PRIORY

Upper Dicker, Hailsham, BN27 3QS. Sussex Archaeological Society, 01323 844224, propertymich@sussexpast.co.uk, www.sussexpast.co.uk. *3m W of Hailsham. A22 N from Eastbourne, exit L to Arlington Rd W. 1⅙m turn R, Priory on R after approx 300yds.* **For opening times and information, please phone, email or visit garden website.**

The stunning 7 acre gardens at Michelham Priory (open to the public) are enclosed by England's longest water-filled moat, which teams with wildlife and indigenous waterlilies. Cloister and Physic gardens weave together features of medieval gardening. Over 40 yrs of developments have created a variety of features inc herbaceous borders, orchard, kitchen garden and tree lined moat walk. The gardens have 80,000 daffodils that create a blaze of colour from early spring onwards.

👌 ✿ 🚗 🍵

95 MILL HALL FARM

Whitemans Green, Cuckfield, Haywards Heath, RH17 5HX. Kate & Jonathan Berry, 07974 115658, katehod@gmail.com. *2½m E of A23, junction with B2115. Please ignore SatNav. From S & E take Staplefield Rd. After 300 metres R into Burrell Cottages, then L. From W or A23 Warninglid exit follow signs to Cuckfield. After 30mph sign, L at end of hedge into Burrell Cottages.* **Sat 4 June (1-5.30). Adm £5, chd free. Home-made teas. Visits also by arrangement Mar to Oct for groups of up to 40. Donation to Plant Heritage.**

A 2½ acre, north facing garden, now 9 yrs old with long view sloping down to maturing pond with lilies, irises and sanguisorba, dragonflies and other wildlife. Long border with ornamental trees, herbaceous plants inc cornus, acer, peonies, daylily, phlox, hollyhock, brunnera, geum and potentillas, climbing and shrub roses and part of the National Collection of Noel Burr daffodils. Victorian underground water cistern guarded by a nymph and used for our watering system. Yr long changing colour enhanced by morning light

97 NEW MOORLANDS

Friars Gate, Crowborough, TN6 1XF. Calum Love, 01892 611546, calumlove@hotmail.co.uk. *2m N of Crowborough. St Johns Rd to Friar's Gate. Or turn L off B2188 at Friar's Gate signed Horder Hospital.* **Visits by arrangement Mar to Oct for groups of up to 30. Adm £5, chd free. Light refreshments.**

4 acres set in lush valley deep in Ashdown Forest. The many special trees planted 50 yrs ago make this garden an arboretum. Also a water garden with ponds, streams and river; primulas, rhododendrons and azaleas. River walk with grasses and bamboos.

🐑 ✿ 🍵 🪑 ⸩⸩

98 MOUNTFIELD COURT

Robertsbridge, TN32 5JP. Mr & Mrs Simon Fraser. *3m N of Battle. On A21 London-Hastings; ½m NW from Johns Cross.* **Sun 8 May (2-5). Adm £5, chd free. Home-made teas.**

3 acre wild woodland garden; bluebell

lined walkways through exceptional rhododendrons, azaleas, camellias, and other flowering shrubs; fine trees and outstanding views. Stunning paved herb garden. Recently restored unique C18 walled garden.

99 NEWTIMBER PLACE

Newtimber, BN6 9BU. **Mr & Mrs Andrew Clay, 01273 833104, andy@newtimberholidaycottages. co.uk, www.newtimberplace.co.uk.** *7m N of Brighton. From A23 take A281 towards Henfield. Turn R at small Xrds signed Newtimber in approx ½ m. Go down Church Ln, garden is on L at end of lane.* **Sun 24 Apr (2-5.30). Adm £5, chd free. Home-made teas.**
Beautiful C17 moated house (not open). Gardens and woods full of bulbs and wild flowers in spring. Herbaceous border and lawns. Moat flanked by water plants. Mature trees, wild garden, ducks, chickens and fish. Wheelchair access across lawn to parts of garden, tearoom and WC.

100 3 NORMANDY DRIVE

East Preston, BN16 1LT. **Sarah Chandler, 07903 400543, sarahchandler@live.co.uk.** *From A280/A259 r'about, follow sign to East Preston on B2140. Over railway crossing, take immed L on North Ln, leading into Sea Rd. Pass shops on L, then Normandy Drive is 2nd R.* **Thur 23 June, Sun 24 July (1-5). Adm £5, chd free. Home-made teas. Visits also by arrangement June to Sept for groups of 10 to 20.**
A self-confessed plantaholic's garden, 45' x 65', just 5 mins from the sea and a true delight. Still in its infancy, designed around a large pergola providing seating areas, borders are full of pretty herbaceous perennials, cutting flowers, climbers and a little bit of fruit and vegetables for good measure. Further interest inc a small wildlife pond, corten steel planters, obelisks, pots, water feature and greenhouse.

101 NORTH SPRINGS

Bedham, nr Fittleworth, RH20 1JP. **Mr & Mrs R Haythornthwaite.** *Between Fittleworth & Wisborough Green. From Wisborough Green take A272 towards Petworth. Turn L into Fittleworth Rd signed Coldharbour &* *proceed 1½ m. From Fittleworth take Bedham Ln off A283 & proceed for approx 3m NE. Limited parking.* **Sun 19 June (1-5). Adm £5, chd free. Home-made teas.**
Hillside garden with beautiful views surrounded by mixed woodland. Focus on structure with a wide range of mature trees and shrubs. Stream, pond and bog area. Abundance of roses, clematis, hostas, rhododendrons and azaleas.

102 ◆ NYMANS

Staplefield Road, Handcross, RH17 6EB. **National Trust, 01444 405250, nymans@nationaltrust.org.uk, www.nationaltrust.org.uk/nymans.** *4m S of Crawley. On B2114 at Handcross signed off M23/A23 London-Brighton road. Metrobus 271 & 273 stop nearby.* **For NGS: Sat 14 May (10-5). Adm £15, chd £7.50. Adm subject to change. Light refreshments. For other opening times and information, please phone, email or visit garden website. Donation to Plant Heritage.**
One of NT's premier gardens with rare and unusual plant collections of national significance. In spring see blossom, bulbs and a stunning collection of subtly fragranced magnolias. The Rose Garden, inspired by Maud Messel's 1920s design, is scented by layers of old fashioned roses. The comfortable yet elegant house, a partial ruin, reflects the personalities of the creative Messel family. Some level pathways. See full access statement on Nymans website.

103 OAKLANDS FARM

Hooklands Lane, Shipley, Horsham, RH13 8PX. **Zsa & Stephen Roggendorff, 01403 741270, zedrog@roggendorff.co.uk.** *S of Shipley village. Off the A272 towards Shipley, R at Countryman Pub, follow yellows signs. Or N of A24 Ashington, off Billingshurst Rd, 1st R signed Shipley, garden 2m up the lane.* **Thur 2 June, Sat 16 July (10.30-5). Adm £6, chd free. Home-made teas. Visits also by arrangement Apr to Oct for groups of up to 25.**
Country garden designed by Nigel Philips in 2010. Oak lined drive leading to the house and farm opens out to an enclosed courtyard with pleached hornbeam and yew. The herbaceous borders are colourful throughout the yr. Vegetable garden with raised beds and greenhouse with white peach and vine. Wild meadow leading to orchard and views across the fields, full of sheep and poultry. Mature trees. Lovely Louise will be here with her special perennials for sale. Picnics welcome. Wheelchair access over gravel and brick paths, large lawn area and grassy paths.

104 THE OAST

Fletching Street, Mayfield, TN20 6TN. **Mike & Tessa Crowe.** *10m S of Tunbridge Wells. Turn off A267 into Mayfield. Parking along East St & in the village public car parks. Please do not park outside The Oast in Fletching St as it is a very narrow road.* **Sat 23, Sun 24 Apr (11-5). Adm £5, chd free. Home-made teas. Opening with Mayfield Gardens on Sat 11, Sun 12 June.**
A south facing, gently sloping 1 acre garden with a lovely view, herbaceous borders and a ½ acre wildflower meadow. There is an interesting and varied selection of hardy and half-hardy plants, trees and shrubs, vegetables and fruit. Lots of colour with imaginative planting, a fine display of tulips and spring flowers. Homegrown plants for sale. Local nursery Rapkyns will also be selling plants.

105 OCKLYNGE MANOR

Mill Road, Eastbourne, BN21 2PG. **Wendy & David Dugdill, 01323 734121, ocklyngemanor@hotmail.com, www.ocklyngemanor.co.uk.** *Close to Eastbourne District General Hospital. Take A22 (Willingdon Rd) towards Old Town, turn L into Mill Rd by Hurst Arms Pub. Visits by arrangement May & June for groups of up to 15.*
A hidden oasis behind an ancient flint wall. Informal and tranquil, ½ acre chalk garden with sunny and shaded places to sit. Use of architectural and unusual trees. Rhododendrons, azaleas and acers in raised beds. Garden evolved over 20 yrs, maintained by owners. Georgian house (not open), former home of Mabel Lucie Attwell. Wheelchair access via short gravel path before entering garden. Brick path around perimeter.

106 OFFHAM HOUSE
The Street, Offham, Lewes,
BN7 3QE. Mr & Mrs P Carminger &
Mr S Goodman. *2m N of Lewes on
A275. Offham House is on the main
road (A275) through Offham between
the filling station & Blacksmiths Arms.*
**Sun 5 June (1-5). Adm £6, chd
free. Home-made teas.**
Romantic garden with fountains,
flowering trees, arboretum, double
herbaceous border and long peony
bed. 1676 Queen Anne house (not
open) with well knapped flint facade.
Herb garden and walled kitchen
garden with glasshouses, coldframes,
chickens, guinea fowl, sheep and
ducks. A selection of pelargoniums
and other plants for sale.
🐐 ✤ ☕ •))

107 OLD CROSS STREET FARM
West Burton, Pulborough,
RH20 1HD. Belinda & David
Wilkinson, 01798 839373,
belinda@westburton.com. *If
travelling S on A29, continue & turn
off at the signs for Bignor, Roman
Villa. The house is in the centre of
West Burton, not as indicated by the
postcode! Parking in bottom of field.*
**Visits by arrangement May to Oct
for groups of 10 to 30. Adm £6,
chd free. Light refreshments.**
A modern garden with a nod to
traditional planting nestled in the
ancient landscape of the South
Downs. Despite its ancient buildings
the garden was only designed and
planted 14 yrs ago and enjoys many
of the contemporary twists not
usually found in such a landscape.
An abundance of mass planting
demonstrates the advantages of a
limited planting palate. An enormous
circular lawn, cloud hedging, an
orchard, cutting garden, transformed
farmyard, modern mass planting,
year-round interest, a cottage garden,
use of hedging, a raised formal pond,
uses of different hard landscaping
materials and planting of over 40
trees. Sorry, no picnics and WC.
✤ Ⓓ ☕

108 OLD ERRINGHAM COTTAGE
Steyning Road, Shoreham-
By-Sea, BN43 5FD. Fiona &
Martin Phillips, 07884 398704,
fiona.h.phillips@btinternet.com.
*2m N of Shoreham-By-Sea. From
A27 Shoreham flyover take A283
towards Steyning. Take 2nd R into
private lane. Follow sharp LH-
bend at top, house on L.* **Visits by**

arrangement in June for groups of
10 to 25. Home-made teas.
Plantsman's garden set high on the
South Downs with panoramic views
overlooking the Adur valley. 1⅓
acres with flower meadow, stream,
bed and ponds, formal and informal
planting areas with over 600 varieties
of plants. Very productive fruit and
vegetable garden with glasshouses.
Many plants grown from seed and
coastal climate gives success with
tender plants.
☕

109 THE OLD HOUSE
Waldron, Heathfield, TN21 0QX.
Jennifer Graham. *In centre of village
opp The Star Inn & War Memorial.*
**Fri 17 June (11-4). Combined
adm with Warren Cottage £6, chd
free. Home-made teas in Waldron
Village Hall.**
Total renovation was required on
my arrival in 2004. Apart from a
long hedge the garden was cleared
and levels changed. My plan was
to conceal the ordinariness of the
garden's shape through a strong
landscape plan of my own design,
and good structural planting. I wanted
numerous pathways, plenty of
seating, strong perfume and a formal
water feature. Those key elements are
still critical today.
☕

110 THE OLD RECTORY
97 Barnham Road,
Barnham, PO22 0EQ.
Peter & Alexandra Vining,
theoldrectory97@gmail.com. *8m
E of Chichester. Between Arundel &
Chichester at A27 Fontwell junction,
take A29 road to Bognor Regis. Turn
L at next r'about onto Barnham Rd.
30 metres after speed camera arrive
at garden.* **Visits by arrangement
June to Aug for groups of up to
20. Combined adm £5 with The
Shrubbery opp. Home-made teas.**
Scratch built in June 2019 after the
300m² garden was removed down to
40cm, then new topsoil and returfed.
By summer 2021 the garden was well
established. Some formal areas and
a range of plants with acers, salvias,
lilies, roses, cypresses and boxes. We
strive for a range of changing hues
rather than blocks of colour. Please
visit www.ngs.org.uk for pop-up
open days. No steps and wheelchair
access through 90cm wide entrance,
please advise when booking.
♿ ✤ ☕

111 THE OLD VICARAGE
The Street, Washington,
RH20 4AS. Sir Peter & Lady
Walters, 07766 761926,
meryl.walters@ngs.org.uk. *2½ m
E of Storrington, 4m W of Steyning.
From Washington r'about on A24
take A283 to Steyning. 500yds R to
Washington. Pass Frankland Arms,
R to St Mary's Church.* **Every Thur
10 Feb to 13 Oct (10.30-4). Pre-
booking essential, please visit
www.ngs.org.uk for information
& booking. Sun 20 Mar, Mon 18
Apr, Mon 2 May, Mon 29 Aug,
Sun 25 Sept (10.30-4). Home-
made teas. Adm £7, chd free. Self
service refreshments on Thurs
or picnics welcome. Visits also
by arrangement Mar to Oct for
groups of 10 to 30.**
Gardens of 3½ acres set around
1832 Regency house (not open).
The front is formally laid out with
topiary, wide lawn, mixed border and
contemporary water sculpture. The
rear features new and mature trees
from C19, herbaceous borders, water
garden and stunning uninterrupted
views of the North Downs. The
Japanese garden with waterfall and
pond leads to a large copse, stream,
treehouse and stumpery. Each yr
2000 tulips are planted for spring
as well as another 2000 snowdrops
and mixed bulbs throughout the
garden. Regional Finalist, The English
Garden's The Nation's Favourite
Gardens 2021. WC available.
Wheelchair access to front garden,
but rear garden is on a slope.
♿ 🐐 ☕ 🪑 •))

112 NEW OLD WELL COTTAGE
High Street, Angmering,
Littlehampton, BN16 4AG. Mr
N Waters. *We are situated nr
Angmering Manor Hotel & almost
adjacent to the top of Weavers Hill in
the High St. Look for the 'mushroom'
shape tree! On road parking only,
please be mindful of residents.* **Fri 1
July (10-2). Adm £5, chd free. Tea,
soft drinks & cakes will be served
from our sunroom.**
⅓ acre plot featuring topiary, formal
areas and perennial borders. Framed
within flint walls and surrounding the
C16 to C18 cottage (not open) in
the Angmering Conservation Area.
Splendid Holm oak and bay topiary
trees, large espalier apple trees and a
small kitchen garden. Lots of purples,
whites and pinks.
✤ ☕ •))

📶🄳 28 OLIVER ROAD

Horsham, RH12 1LH. **Mary & Ian Sharp.** *Off the Worthing road. 1½m from A24 Hop Oast r'about, L off Worthing Rd into Blackbridge Ln, 2nd L into Longfield Rd, L into Oliver Rd, No. 28 is at the end.* **Sun 12 June (1-5); Fri 17 June (2-5). Adm £4, chd free. Home-made teas.**
A ¼ acre garden on the fringe of Horsham, secluded by mature trees and wildlife friendly hedges. Bespoke garden structures and buildings inc a rose pergola and small cabin called Poets Corner, made by the family. No dig vegetable beds and flower borders, greenhouses and cottage garden planting. There is small pond, bee hotels and log piles with an established willow tree.
☕ 🔊

🄸🄳 NEW ORCHARD COTTAGE

Boars Head Road, Boarshead, Crowborough, TN6 3GR. **Jane Collins, 01892 653444, collinsjane1@hotmail.co.uk.** *6m S of Tunbridge Wells, off A26. At T-junction, don't follow SatNav. Turn L down dead end. Orchard Cottage is at the bottom of the hill on LHS.* **Fri 17, Sat 18 June (11-4). Adm £5, chd £3. Home-made teas. Visits also by arrangement Jan to Oct for groups of up to 30.**
Mature 1½ acre plantaholic's garden with a large variety of trees and shrubs, perennials and bulbs, many unusual. Gardened organically. Mainly colour themed beds, planted informally. Small woodland, meadow and deep pond to encourage wildlife. Kitchen garden with raised beds. Hardy Plant Society member. Access via gravel drive with wide gently sloping grass paths suitable for wheelchairs and mobility scooters. Drop-off in drive by prior arrangement.
♿ ❀ 🚗 ☕ 🔊

🄸🄳 PANGDEAN FARM

London Road, Pyecombe, Brighton, BN45 7FJ. **Ian & Nicky Currie.** *Leave A23 at Pyecombe, take A273 towards Hassocks. Pangdean signed on E of A23. Please use postcode BN45 7FN for entry to garden.* **Sun 5, Mon 6 June (12-5). Adm £10, chd £4. Children under 5 free. Adm inc home-made teas.**
This delightful sunny walled garden dating from the C17 nestles in the South Downs National Park. Featuring herb garden which supplies the kitchen, an extensive herbaceous

border which gives interest over a long period, roses and a 400 yr old James I mulberry tree. It is very much the late Sue Currie's garden: whenever she entered her garden she smiled! Home-made teas will be served in the garden or the stunning 300 yr old Grade II listed Sussex Barn. Wonderful plant sale (cash only).
♿ 🐕 ❀ ☕ 🔊

🄸🄶 PARSONAGE FARM

Kirdford, RH14 0NH. **David & Victoria Thomas.** *5m NE of Petworth. From centre of Kirdford before church, turn R through village towards Balls Cross, past Foresters Pub on R. Entrance on L, just past R turn to Plaistow. For SatNav use RH14 0NG.* **Fri 24 June, Sun 4 Sept (2-6). Adm £7, chd free. Home-made teas.**
Major garden in beautiful setting developed over 30 yrs with fruit theme and many unusual plants. Formally laid out on grand scale with long vistas. C18 walled garden with borders in apricot, orange, scarlet and crimson. Topiary walk, pleached lime allée, tulip tree avenue, rose borders and vegetable garden with trained fruit. Turf amphitheatre, informal autumn shrubbery, yew cloisters and jungle walk.
♿ 🚗 ☕

🄸🄿 PEELERS RETREAT

70 Ford Road, Arundel, BN18 9EX. **Tony & Lizzie Gilks, 01903 884981, timespan70@tiscali.co.uk, www.timespanhistoricalpresentations.co.uk.** *1m S of Arundel. At Chichester r'about take exit to Ford & Bognor Regis onto Ford Rd. We are situated close to Maxwell Rd, Arundel.* **Sun 24, Tue 26 Apr (2-5). Every Mon 2 May to 30 May (2-5). Every Tue 7 June to 28 June, 12 July to 26 July, 16 Aug to 30 Aug, 6 Sept to 11 Oct (2-5). Adm £5, chd free. Home-made teas. Visits also by arrangement Apr to Oct for groups of 5 to 20.**
Stunning garden and gift shop with imaginative woodland sculptures and a flare for the unusual. This inspirational space is a delight in which to sit and relax, enjoying delicious teas. Interlocking beds packed with year-round colour and scent, shaded by specimen trees, pebbled stream and fish pond.
🐕 🚗 ☕ 🔊

During 2020 - 2021 National Garden Scheme funding supported over 1,400 Queen's Nurses to deliver virtual and hands-on, community care across England, Wales and Northern Ireland

🄸🄼 33 PEERLEY ROAD

East Wittering, PO20 8PD. **Paul & Trudi Harrison, 01243 673215, stixandme@aol.com.** *7m S of Chichester. From A286 take B2198 to Bracklesham. Turn R into Stocks Ln, L at Royal British Legion into Legion Way. Follow road round to Peerley Rd. No. 33 is halfway along.* **Sun 3 July (12-4). Adm £3, chd free. Visits also by arrangement May to Oct.**
Small seaside garden 65ft x 32ft, 110yds from the sea. Packed full of ideas and interesting plants using every inch of space to create rooms and places for adults and children to play. A must for any suburban gardener. Specialising in unusual plants that grow well in seaside conditions with advice on coastal gardening.
❀

🄸🄽 PEMBURY HOUSE

Ditchling Road, Clayton, BN6 9PH. **Nick & Jane Baker, www.pemburyhouse.co.uk.** *6m N of Brighton, off A23. No parking at house. Use village green, BN6 9PJ. Then follow signs across playing field to footpath by railway to back gate. Good public transport.* **Every Tue to Fri 10 Feb to 11 Mar (10.30-12.30). Adm £10, chd free. Pre-booking essential, please visit www.ngs.org.uk for information & booking. Adm inc home-made teas.**
Depending on the vagaries of the season, hellebores and snowdrops are at their best in Feb and March. It is a country garden, tidy but not manicured. Work always in progress on new areas. Winding paths give a choice of walks through 3 acres of garden, which is in and enjoys views of the South Downs National Park. Wellies, macs and winter woollies advised. A German visitor observed 'this is the perfect woodland garden'. Year-round interest. Plants for sale.

120 PENNS IN THE ROCKS
Groombridge, Tunbridge Wells, TN3 9PA. Mr & Mrs Hugh Gibson, 01892 864244, www.pennsintherocks.co.uk. *7m SW of Tunbridge Wells. On B2188 Groombridge to Crowborough road, just S of Xrd to Withyham. For SatNav use TN6 1UX which takes you to the white drive gates, through which you should enter the property.* **Sun 10 Apr, Sun 15 May, Sun 7 Aug (2-6). Adm £7, chd free. Home-made teas. Visits also by arrangement Apr to July for groups of 10 to 50.**
Large garden with spectacular outcrop of rocks, 140 million yrs old. Lake, C18 temple and woods. Daffodils, bluebells, azaleas, magnolia and tulips. Old walled garden with herbaceous borders, roses and shrubs. Stone sculptures by Richard Strachey. Part C18 house (not open) once owned by William Penn of Pennsylvania. Cash only on the day please. Restricted wheelchair access. No disabled WC.
&. ✿ 🍵

121 1 PEST COTTAGE
Carron Lane, Midhurst, GU29 9LF. Jennifer Lewin. *W edge of Midhurst behind Carron Lane Cemetery. Free parking at recreation ground at top of Carron Ln. Short walk on woodland track to garden, please follow signs.* **Fri 10 June (2-7); Sun 12 June (2-6). Adm £4, chd free.**
This edge of woodland, architect's studio garden of approx ¾ acre sits on a sloping sandy site. Designed to support wildlife and bio-diversity, a series of outdoor living spaces connected with informal paths through lightly managed areas, creates a charming secret world tucked into the surrounding common land. The garden spaces have made a very small house (not open) into a hospitable family home. Exhibition of architect's projects.
🐕 🏕

122 NEW 33 THE PLANTATION
Worthing, BN13 2AE. Mrs Judy Gordon, 07766 011706, mudandflowers@btinternet.com. *A24 meets A27 at Offington r'about. Turn into Offington Ln, 1st R into The Plantation.* **Fri 8 Apr, Fri 10 June, Thur 21 July (1-5). Adm £5, chd free. Home-made teas. Visits also by arrangement May to July for groups of up to 10.**
A medium sized town garden with

something of interest all year-round. The garden has several mature trees creating a feeling of seclusion. The informal beds contain a mixture of shrubs, perennials, cottage garden plants and spring bulbs. There are little hidden areas to enjoy, a small fish pond and other water features. There is also a pretty log cabin overlooking the garden.
✿ 🍵

123 6 PLANTATION RISE
Worthing, BN13 2AH. Nigel & Trixie Hall, 01903 262206, trixiehall008@gmail.com. *2m from seafront on outskirts of Worthing. A24 meets A27 at Offington r'about. Turn into Offington Ln, 1st R into The Plantation, 1st R again into Plantation Rise. Parking on The Plantation only, short walk up to 6 Plantation Rise.* **Visits by arrangement Mar to Sept for groups of 5 to 30. Adm £7, chd free. Adm inc home-made teas. Please advise of specific dietary requirements upon booking.**
Clever use is made of evergreen shrubs, azaleas, rhododendrons and acers enclosing our 70' x 80' garden, enhancing the flower decked pergolas, folly and summerhouse, which overlooks the pond. Planting inc nine silver birches 'Tristis', which are semi pendula, plus a lovely combination of primroses, anemones and daffodils in spring and a profusion of roses, clematis and perennials in summer. Wheelchair access to patios only with a good view of the garden.
&. 🐕 🍵

124 ◆ THE PRIEST HOUSE
North Lane, West Hoathly, RH19 4PP. Sussex Archaeological Society, 01342 810479, priest@sussexpast.co.uk, www.sussexpast.co.uk. *4m SW of East Grinstead, 6m E of Crawley. In centre of West Hoathly village, nr church, the Cat Inn & Luctons. Car parks in village.* **For NGS: Sat 28 May, Sat 25 June (10.30-5.30). Adm £2, chd free. Home-made teas. Open nearby Luctons on 25 June. For other opening times and information, please phone, email or visit garden website.**
C15 timber framed farmhouse with cottage garden on acid clay. Large collection of culinary and medicinal herbs in a small formal garden and mixed with perennials and shrubs in exuberant borders. Long established yew topiary, box hedges and espalier apple trees provide structural

elements. Traditional fernery and stumpery, recently enlarged with a small secluded shrubbery and gravel garden. Be sure to visit the fascinating Priest House Museum, adm £1 for NGS visitors.
🐕 ✿ 🍵 🏕

125 144 RODMELL AVENUE
Saltdean, Brighton, BN2 8PJ. Sue & Ray Warner. *A259 between Rottingdean & Telscombe, turn into Saltdean (Longridge Ave) at T-lights. Rodmell Ave last turning on R, house ½ m on R. Parking on the road outside the house or adjoining streets.* **Sat 16, Sun 17 July (12-5). Combined adm with Bagotts Rath £6, chd free. Home-made teas.**
A fun jungle garden, created in 2012, but completely revamped in 2021 and returning to the NGS after a 3 yr break. Measuring 65ft x 36ft, but appearing larger with winding paths that lead you through lush jungle and insect friendly planting, listen out for jungle sounds. Tea and home-made cakes served overlooking the garden. Exquisite planting of exotic plants.
🍵 ♪))

126 ROSE COTTAGE
Laughton, Lewes, BN8 6BX. Paul Seaborne & Glenn Livingstone, www.pelhamplants.co.uk. *5m E of Lewes; 6m W of Hailsham. Signed from junction of Common Ln & Shortage Ln, ½ m N of Roebuck Pub, Laughton.* **Thur 4, Sat 6 Aug (1-5). Adm £6, chd £3. Pre-booking essential, please visit www.ngs.org.uk for information & booking. Home-made teas.**
Rare opportunity to access nurseryman's private garden packed with unusual examples of herbaceous perennials and grasses. Informally planted 1 acre garden subdivided by strong structural shaped hedging and surrounding an old cottage (not open). Multiple densely planted borders with new plantings each yr. Specialist nursery forms part of the 2 acre woodland edge site.
🐕 ✿ 🍵 ♪))

128 SAFFRONS

Holland Road, Steyning, BN44 3GJ. Tim Melton & Bernardean Carey, 07850 343516, tim.melton@btinternet.com, www.thetransplantedgardener.uk. *6m NE of Worthing. Exit r'about on A283 at S end of Steyning bypass into Clays Hill Rd. 1st R into Goring Rd, 4th L into Holland Rd. Park in Goring Rd & Holland Rd.* **Visits by arrangement June to Aug for groups of 10 to 30. Home-made teas.**

Planted with an artist's eye for contrasts and complementary colours. Vibrant late summer flower beds of salvias, eryngiums, agapanthus, grasses and lilies attract bees and butterflies. A broad lawn is surrounded by borders with maples, rhododendrons, hydrangeas and mature trees interspersed with ferns and grasses. The large fruit cage and vegetable beds comprise the productive area of the garden. One level garden with good access, except in very wet conditions.

&. 🐑 ❀ ☕ 🍱

129 ST BARNABAS HOUSE

2 Titnore Lane, Goring-By-Sea, Worthing, BN12 6NZ. www.stbh.org.uk. *W of Worthing & just N of the r'about between A259 & A2032. Titnore Ln can be accessed via A27 from N, the A259 from W (Littlehampton) or the A2032 from E (Worthing).* **Sun 12, Sat 18 June (11-4). Adm £5, chd free. Pre-booking essential, please visit www.ngs.org.uk for information & booking. Home-made teas.** Please arrive at the start of your 1hr time slot to join the accompanied tour through the patient gardens. After which, take a relaxing wander through the grounds, which have a central courtyard garden like an exotic atrium with seating, water features and abundant foliage from tree ferns, magnolias and katsura trees. Outside a large pond with fountain-aerator adds tranquillity with the sound of running water. Lavender maze, meadow and productive vegetable plot. In 2021, we were delighted to be gifted five cherry trees from the Sakura Cherry Tree Project, through Sir Peter Bottomley MP and the Japanese Embassy. We now have three prunus 'Tai-haku' in the meadow, a prunus 'Beni-yutaka' in the centre of the lavender maze and one on the adjacent bank. Good access to the site, central courtyard, main surrounding gardens and car park. Paths in the pond area can be affected by heavy rain.

&. 🐑 ❀ ☕

130 ST MARY'S HOSPITAL

St Martins Square, Chichester, PO19 1NR. St Mary's Trust, www.chichestercathedral.org.uk/about-us/st-marys-hospital. *Central Chichester. From East St, turn into St Martin's St adjacent to M&S Food, follow road round RH-bend & you will see the hospital entrance in the corner.* **Sat 7 May, Sat 2, Tue 5 July, Tue 23 Aug (11-3). Adm £5, chd free. Light refreshments.**

A large formal garden, opened by HRH Princess Alexandra, comprising large rose beds, traditional fruit trees, herb garden and large lawn. Four impressive knot gardens designed by Mr Ray Winnett, our Gardener who based them on medieval designs and planted them in 2014. Visitors can also visit the C13 hospital building, not usually open to the public. The only Almshouse in the country where residents still live in the ancient hospital, as well as in purpose built flats nearby. A hidden gem in the heart of Chichester. Wheelchair access to garden and hospital, but assistance may be required for small ridges on site.

&. 🐑 ❀ ☕ 🍱))

131 ◆ ST MARY'S HOUSE GARDENS

Bramber, BN44 3WE. Roger Linton & Peter Thorogood, 01903 816205, info@stmarysbramber.co.uk, www.stmarysbramber.co.uk. *1m E of Steyning. 10m NW of Brighton in Bramber village, off A283.* **For NGS: Fri 15, Sat 16 July (2-5.30). Adm £7, chd free. Light refreshments. For other opening times and information, please phone, email or visit garden website.**

5 acres inc formal topiary, large prehistoric *Ginkgo biloba* and magnificent *Magnolia grandiflora* around enchanting timber-framed medieval house (not open for NGS). Victorian Secret Gardens inc splendid 140ft fruit wall with pineapple pits, Rural Museum, Terracotta Garden, Jubilee Rose Garden, King's Garden and circular Poetry Garden. Woodland walk and Landscape Water Garden. In the heart of the South Downs National Park. WC facilities. Wheelchair access with level paths throughout.

&. ❀ �car ☕

132 SANDHILL FARM HOUSE

Nyewood Road, Rogate, Petersfield, GU31 5HU. Rosemary Alexander, 07551 777873, rosemary@englishgardeningschool.co.uk, www.rosemaryalexander.co.uk. *4m SE of Petersfield. From A272 Xrds in Rogate take road S signed Nyewood & Harting. Follow road for approx 1m over small bridge. Sandhill Farm House on R, over cattle grid.* **Sat 11, Sun 12 June (2-5). Adm £6, chd free. Home-made teas. Visits also by arrangement Apr to Sept for groups of 10 to 30.**

Front and rear gardens broken up into garden rooms inc small kitchen garden. Front garden with small woodland area, planted with early spring flowering shrubs, ferns and bulbs. White garden, large leaf border and terraced area. Rear garden has rose borders, small decorative vegetable garden, red border and grasses border. Home of author and principal of The English Gardening School.

❀ Ⓓ ☕))

In 2021 the National Garden Scheme donation helped support Perennial's caseworkers, who helped over 250 people and their families in crisis to receive a wide range of support including emergency food parcels and accommodation, energy payments and expert advice and information

GROUP OPENING

133 SEAFORD GARDENS

As there are several gardens on the trail, they will be signed from the A259 as the gardens are N & S of this road. 6 gardens N of A259 & 4 are S. NB Not a walking trail. **Sun 29 May (12-5). Combined adm £7, chd free. Sun 12 June (12-5). Combined adm £8, chd free. Home-made teas at various gardens, see map on the day.**

2 BARONS CLOSE
BN25 2TY. Diane Hicks.
Open on Sun 12 June

BURFORD
Cuckmere Road, BN25 4DE. Chris Kilsby.
Open on all dates

34 CHYNGTON ROAD
BN25 4HP. Dr Maggie Wearmouth & Richard Morland.
Open on Sun 12 June

5 CLEMENTINE AVENUE
BN25 2UU. Joanne Davis.
Open on Sun 12 June

COSY COTTAGE
69 Firle Road, BN25 2JA. Ernie & Carol Arnold, 07763 196343, ernie.whitecrane@gmail.com.
Open on all dates
Visits also by arrangement May to July.

CUPANI GARDEN
8 Sandgate Close, BN25 3LL. Dr D Jones & Ms A Jones OBE.
Open on Sun 29 May
(See separate entry)

LAVENDER COTTAGE
69 Steyne Road, BN25 1QH. Christina & Steve Machan.
Open on all dates

MADEHURST
67 Firle Road, BN25 2JA. Martin & Palo.
Open on all dates

SEAFORD ALLOTMENTS
Sutton Drove, BN25 3NQ. Peter Sudell, seafordallotment.com.
Open on Sun 12 June

SEAFORD COMMUNITY GARDEN
East Street, BN25 1AD.
Seaford Community Garden, www.seaford-sussex.co.uk/scg/.
Open on Sun 29 May

On 29 May, six gardens open. Cosy Cottage, a cottage garden over three levels with ponds, flowers, vegetables and shrubs. Lavender Cottage a flint walled garden with a coastal and kitchen garden. Madehurst is a garden on different levels with interesting planting and seasonal interest. Burford, a mature garden with a mix of flowers, vegetables and an auricula theatre. The Community Garden provides an interesting space with flower and vegetable beds for members of the community to come together to share their gardening experience. Cupani garden is rejoining the trail to provide the main refreshments venue. On 12 June, seven gardens will open inc four of the above, plus 5 Clementine Avenue where the garden slopes upwards over three levels and opens out onto the downs and a nice collection of succulents. Seaford Allotments offer a unique chance to see a variety of planting and colour. A site of 189 well maintained plots with a wildlife area, a dye bed and a compost WC. 2 Barons Close provides a delightful mix of flower and vegetable planting with a structure of glorious roses.
✿ 🍵 ♫)

134 SEDGWICK PARK HOUSE
Sedgwick Park, Horsham, RH13 6QQ. Clare Davison, 01403 734930, clare@sedgwickpark.com, www.sedgwickpark.co.uk. *1m S of Horsham off A281. A281 towards Cowfold, Hillier Garden Center on R, then 1st R into Sedgwick Ln. At end of lane enter N gates of Sedgwick Park or W gate via Broadwater Ln, from Copsale or Southwater, off A24.* **Visits by arrangement Apr & May for groups of 10+. Adm £6, chd free.**
Last chance to see before sold. Parkland, meadows and woodland. Formal gardens by Harold Peto featuring 20 interlinking ponds, impressive water garden known as The White Sea. Large Horsham stone terraces and lawns look out onto clipped yew hedging and specimen trees. One of the finest views of the South Downs, Chanctonbury Ring and Lancing Chapel. Turf labyrinth and organic vegetable garden. Garden has uneven paving, slippery when wet; unfenced ponds and swimming pool.
🚐 🐕 🍵 ﹅

135 SELHURST PARK
Halnaker, Chichester, PO18 0LZ. Richard & Sarah Green, 01243 839310, mail@selhurstparkhouse.co.uk. *8m S of Petworth. 4m N of Chichester on A285.* **Sun 12 June (2-5). Adm £6, chd free. Home-made teas. Visits also by arrangement June & July for groups of up to 30.**
Come and explore the varied gardens surrounding a beautiful Georgian flint house (not open), approached by a chestnut avenue. The flint walled garden has a mature 160ft herbaceous border with unusual planting along with rose, hellebore and hydrangea beds. Pool garden with exotic palms and grasses divided from a formal knot and herb garden by Espalier apples. Kitchen and walled fruit garden. Wheelchair access to walled garden, partial access to other areas.
🚐 ✿ 🍵

136 SENNICOTTS
West Broyle, Chichester, PO18 9AJ. Mr & Mrs James Rank, 07950 324181, ngs@sennicotts.com, www.sennicotts.com. *2m NW of Chichester. White gates diagonally opp & W of the junction between Salthill Rd & the B2178. Large buses cannot enter our gates.* **Visits by arrangement for groups of 20 to 30. Please call to discuss refreshment options.**
Historic gardens set around a Regency villa (not open) with views across mature Sussex parkland to the South Downs. Working walled kitchen and cutting garden. Lots of space for children and a warm welcome for all.
🚐 🐎 🍵

137 ◆ SHEFFIELD PARK AND GARDEN
Uckfield, TN22 3QX. National Trust, 01825 790231, sheffieldpark@nationaltrust.org.uk, www.nationaltrust.org.uk/sheffieldpark. *10m S of East Grinstead. 5m NW of Uckfield; E of A275.* **For NGS: Wed 7 Sept (11-5). Adm £13.30, chd free. Last entry 4pm. For other opening times and information, please phone, email or visit garden website.**
Magnificent landscaped garden laid out in C18 by Capability Brown and Humphry Repton covering 120 acres (40 hectares). Further development in the early yrs of this century by its

owner Arthur G Soames. Centrepiece is original lakes with many rare trees and shrubs. Beautiful at all times of the yr, but noted for its spring and autumn colours. National Collection of Ghent azaleas. Natural play trail for families on South Park. Large number of champion trees, 87 in total. Garden largely accessible for wheelchairs, please call for information.

NPC

138 SHEPHERDS COTTAGE

Milberry Lane, Stoughton, Chichester, PO18 9JJ. Jackie & Alan Sherling, 07795 388047, milberrylane@gmail.com. *9⅙m NW Chichester. Off B2146, next village after Walderton. Cottage is nr telephone box & beside St Mary's Church. No parking in lane beside house.* **Visits by arrangement Apr to Aug for groups of 10 to 30. Adm £5, chd free.**

A compact terraced garden using the borrowed landscape of Kingley Vale in the South Downs. The south facing flint stone cottage (not open) is surrounded by a Purbeck stone terrace and numerous individually planted and styled seating areas. A small orchard under-planted with meadow, lawns, yew hedges, amelanchier, cercis and drifts of wind grass provide structure and year-round interest. Many novel design ideas for a small garden. Ample seating throughout the garden to enjoy the views.

D

139 NEW THE SHRUBBERY

140 Barnham Road, Barnham, PO22 0EH. John & Ros Woodhead, rosalindwoodhead@hotmail.com. *Between Arundel & Chichester. At A27 Fontwell junction take A29 road to Bognor Regis. Turn L at next r'about onto Barnham Rd. 30 metres after speed camera arrive at garden.* **Visits by arrangement June to Aug for groups of up to 20. Combined adm with The Old Rectory. Adm £5. Home-made teas.**

¼ acre plot with mature trees, shrubs and colourful borders of mixed perennials. Features inc hosta, sculpture and areas of soft fruit. Please visit www.ngs.org.uk for pop-up openings.

140 SIENNA WOOD

Coombe Hill Road, East Grinstead, RH19 4LY. Belinda & Brian Quarendon, 07970 707015, belinda222@hotmail.com. *1m W of East Grinstead. Off B2110 East Grinstead to Turners Hill. Garden is ½m down Coombe Hill Rd on L.* **Sun 29 May (1-5). Adm £6, chd free. Teas. Visits also by arrangement Apr to Aug for groups of 15 to 30.**

Explore our beautiful 4½ acre garden, picturesque lakeside walk and 6 acre ancient woodland behind. Start at the herbaceous borders surrounding the croquet lawn, through the formal rose garden to the lawns and summer borders, then down through the the arboretum to the lake and waterfall and back past the exotic border, orchard and vegetable garden. Many unusual trees and shrubs. Possible sighting of wild deer inc white deer. Many interesting statues. Partial wheelchair access to many parts of the garden.

141 SKYSCAPE

46 Ainsworth Avenue, Ovingdean, Brighton, BN2 7BG. Lorna & John Davies. *From Brighton take A259 coast road E, passing Roedean School on L. Take 1st L at r'about to Greenways & 2nd R into Ainsworth Ave. Skyscape at the top on R. No. 52 bus on Sat & No. 57 on Sun.* **Sat 28, Sun 29 May (1-5). Adm £5, chd free. Tea & cake served on the patio.**

250ft south facing rear garden on a sloping site with fantastic views of the South Downs and the sea. Garden created by owners over past 9 yrs. Orchard, flower beds and planting with bees in mind. Small protected apiary in orchard. Full access to site via purpose built sloping path.

Malthouse Farm

© Carole Drake

142 SOUTH GRANGE

Quickbourne Lane, Northiam, Rye, TN31 6QY. Linda & Michael Belton, 01797 252984, belton.northiam@gmail.com. *Between A268 & A28, approx ½ m E of Northiam. From Northiam centre follow Beales Ln into Quickbourne Ln, or Quickbourne Ln leaves A286 approx ½ m S of A28 & A286 junction. Disabled parking at front of house.* **Sat 3, Sun 4 Sept (11-5). Adm £6, chd free. Teas & light lunches made to order. Visits also by arrangement Apr to Oct for groups of 5+.**
Hardy Plant Society members' garden with wide variety of trees, shrubs, perennials, grasses and pots arranged into a complex garden display for year-round colour and interest. Raised vegetable beds, wildlife pond, water features, orchard, rose arbour, soft fruit cage and living gazebo. House roof runoff diverted to storage and pond. Small area of wild wood. An emphasis on planting for insects. We try to maintain nectar and pollen supplies and varied habitats for most of the creatures that we share the garden with, hoping that this variety will keep the garden in good heart. Home propagated plants for sale. Wheelchair access over hard paths through much of the garden, but steps up to patio and WC.

🕭 ❀ 🚗 🚐 🍵

143 STANLEY FARM

Highfield Lane, Liphook, GU30 7LW. Bill & Emma Mills. *For SatNav please use GU30 7LN, which takes you to Highfield Ln & then follow NGS signs. Track to Stanley Farm is 1m.* **Sun 1 May (12-5). Adm £5, chd free. Home-made teas.**
1 acre garden created over the last 15 yrs around an old West Sussex farmhouse (not open), sitting in the midst of its own fields and woods. The formal garden inc a kitchen garden with heated glasshouse, orchard, espaliered wall trained fruit, lawn with ha-ha and cutting garden. A motley assortment of animals inc sheep, donkeys, chickens, ducks and geese. Bluebells flourish in the woods, so feel free to bring dogs and a picnic, and take a walk after visiting the gardens. Wheelchair access via a ramp to view main part of the garden. Difficult access to woods due to muddy, uneven ground.

🕭 🐄 ❀ 🍵 ›))

144 ✦ SUSSEX PRAIRIES

Dutch Barn Morlands Farm, Wheatsheaf Road (B2116), Henfield, BN5 9AT. Paul & Pauline McBride, 01273 495902, morlandsfarm@btinternet.com, www.sussexprairies.co.uk. *2m NE of Henfield on B2116 Wheatsheaf Rd (also known as Albourne Rd). Follow Brown Tourist signs indicating Sussex Prairie Garden.* **For NGS: Sun 11 Sept (1-5). Adm £10, chd free. Home-made teas. For other opening times and information, please phone, email or visit garden website.**
Exciting prairie garden of approx 8 acres planted in the naturalistic style using 60,000 plants and over 1,600 different varieties. A colourful garden featuring a huge variety of unusual ornamental grasses. Expect layers of colour, texture and architectural splendour. Surrounded by mature oak trees with views of Chanctonbury Ring and Devil's Dyke on the South Downs. Permanent sculpture collection and exhibited sculpture throughout the season. Rare breed sheep and pigs. New tropical entrance garden planted in 2018. Picnics welcome, but please take rubbish away. Woodchip pathway at entrance. Soft woodchip paths in borders not accessible, but flat garden for wheelchairs and mobility scooters. Disabled WC.

🕭 🐄 ❀ 🚗 🍵 🍴

145 NEW TELSCOMBE MANOR

Telscombe, Lewes, BN7 3HY. Matthew & Helen Brumsen. *Off C7 Lewes-Newhaven road (no access from A259 coast road). Turn S into Gorham's Ln between Rodmell & Southease & follow single track road (with passing places) for 1½ m.* **Fri 6, Sat 7 May (2-5). Adm £7, chd free. Home-made teas in Telscombe Village Hall.**
A Grade II listed manor house (not open) and separately listed C18 barn set in a 2 acre garden in the South Downs National Park. Series of garden rooms and herbaceous borders structured by hedges and flint walls. Wildflower meadow, roses, tree peony, acers, water feature, pond, Tudor sundial, vegetable garden. Stunning views, framed by garden features of the Downs landscape. Wheelchair access is possible to most of the garden, but there are slopes and uneven paving/cobbles.

🕭 🐄 🍵 ›))

146 THAKEHAM PLACE FARM

The Street, Thakeham, Pulborough, RH20 3EP. Mr & Mrs T Binnington. *In the village of Thakeham, 3m N of Storrington. The farm is at the E end of The Street, where it turns into Crays Ln. Follow signs down farm drive to Thakeham Place.* **Thur 21, Sun 24 July (2-5.30). Combined adm with Cumberland House £8, chd free. Home-made teas.**
Set in the middle of a working dairy farm, the garden has evolved over the last 30 yrs. Taking advantage of its sunny position on free draining greensand, the borders are full of sun loving plants and grasses with a more formal area surrounding the farmhouse (not open). Lovely views across the farm to Warminghurst from the orchard.

🐄 🍵 ›))

147 TOWN PLACE

Ketches Lane, Freshfield, Sheffield Park, RH17 7NR. Anthony & Maggie McGrath, 01825 790221, mcgrathsussex@hotmail.com, www.townplacegarden.org.uk. *5m E of Haywards Heath. From A275 turn W at Sheffield Green into Ketches Ln for Lindfield. 1¾ m on L.* **Sun 12, Thur 16, Thur 23, Sun 26 June, Sun 3, Sun 10 July (2-5). Adm £7.50, chd free. Visits also by arrangement June & July.**
A stunning 3 acre garden with a growing international reputation for the quality of its design, planting and gardening. Set round a C17 Sussex farmhouse (not open), the garden has over 800 roses, herbaceous borders, herb garden, topiary inspired by the sculptures of Henry Moore, ornamental grasses, an 800 yr old oak, potager, and a unique ruined Priory Church and Cloisters in hornbeam. There are steps, but all areas can be viewed from a wheelchair.

🕭 ❀ 🍴 ›))

148 TUPPENNY BARN

Main Road, Southbourne, PO10 8EZ. Maggie Haynes, 01243 377780, contact@tuppennybarn.co.uk, tuppennybarn.co.uk. *6m W of Chichester, 1m E of Emsworth. On Main Rd A259, corner of Tuppenny Ln. Disabled parking.* **Visits by arrangement for groups of up to 25. Adm £6, chd free. Cream teas. Food intolerances & allergies catered for.**

An iconic, organic smallholding used as an outdoor classroom to teach children about the environment, sustainability and healthy food. 2½ acres packed with a wildlife pond, orchard with heritage top fruit varieties, two solar polytunnels, fruit cages, raised vegetables, herbs and cut flower garden. Willow provides natural arches and wind breaks. Bug hotel and beehives support vital pollinators. Most of the grounds are accessible for wheelchairs, but undulated areas are more difficult.

& ❀ ☕ �ঃ)

149 WADHURST PARK
Riseden Road, Wadhurst, TN5 6NT. Nicky Browne, wadhurstpark.co.uk. *6m SE of Tunbridge Wells. Turn R along Mayfield Ln off B2099 at NW end of Wadhurst. Then turn L by The Best Beech Inn & L at Riseden Rd.* **Wed 1, Wed 8 June (10-3.30). Adm £6, chd free. Home-made teas in the Common Room.**
The naturalistic gardens, designed by Tom Stuart-Smith, created on a C19 site, situated within a 2000 acre estate managed organically to protect its wildlife, cultural heritage and beauty. The gardens invite the wider landscape in, while meadows and hedgerows, woodland trees and groundcover soften and frame views to hills and lake. We strive to garden with a greater respect for the natural world. Features inc restored Victorian orangery, naturalistic gardens planted with native species, potager, log hives and woodland walks. Due to uneven paths, please wear sensible shoes. Wheelchair access to main features of garden, some surfaces inc grass, cobbles and steps.

& D ☕ ঃ)

150 NEW WARNHAM PARK
Robin Hood Lane, Warnham, Horsham, RH12 3RP. Mrs Caroline Lucas. *Turn in off A24 end of Robin Hood Ln, turn immed R by the large poster & follow signs.* **Sat 23 Apr (2-5.30). Adm £6, chd free. Home-made teas.**
The garden is situated in the middle of a 200 acre Deer Park, which has a very special herd of Red Deer husbanded by the Lucas Family for over 150 yrs. Borders with traditional planting and a kitchen garden that is prolific most of the yr. The rest of the garden comprises different spaces, inc a small white garden, a Moroccan courtyard and a walled garden. There

is also a woodland walk. Disabled WC.

& ☕ ঃ)

151 WARREN COTTAGE
Warren Lane, Cross In Hand, Heathfield, TN21 0TB. Mr & Mrs Allcorn. *2½ m W of Heathfield, 2m E of Blackboys. At junction of B2102 Lewes Rd & Warren Ln. Follow signs for parking nr garden.* **Fri 17 June (11-4). Combined adm with The Old House £6, chd free. Home-made teas in Waldron Village Hall.**
½ acre mature, secluded garden being redeveloped by the owners and using many reclaimed materials. A 60ft herbaceous border with oak frame support, long grass area with specimen shrubs and mown paths, wildlife pond and borders, vegetable patch with raised beds, greenhouses and potting shed, a pub shed and magical fairy and woodland garden.

& ❀ ☕

GROUP OPENING

152 NEW THE WARREN, CROWBOROUGH GARDENS
Rannoch Road, Crowborough, TN6 1RA. *All gardens 1m W of Crowborough town centre. Street parking close to each garden.* **Sat 7, Sun 8 May (2-5). Combined adm £6, chd free. Home-made teas.**

REDRIFF
John Mitchell.

SILVER SPRINGS
Barbara Diamond.

NEW WEAVERS
Mr Graham James.

Three gardens in the Warren area of Crowborough. Redriff is a Japanese influenced, richly planted spring garden; bridge and seating with views overlooking fish pond. Silver Springs is a spring garden, developed by a keen plantswoman over the past 25 yrs from a bare site. Shrubs, perennials, rock garden and bulbs surround the house (not open). Weavers has rhododendrons, azaleas, stumpery and hidden wooded areas with natural and ornamental stone features.

GROUP OPENING

153 WATERWORKS & FRIENDS
Broad Oak & Brede, TN31 6HG. *4 Waterworks Cots, Brede, off A28 by church & opp Red Lion, ¾ m at end of lane. Sculdown, B2089 Chitcombe Rd, W off A28 at Broad Oak Xrds. Start at either garden, a map will be provided.* **Sat 4 June (10.30-4). Combined adm £6, chd free. Light refreshments at Sculdown.**

SCULDOWN
TN31 6EX. Mrs Christine Buckland.

4 WATERWORKS COTTAGES
TN31 6HG. Mrs Kristina Clode, 07950 748097, kristinaclode@gmail.com, www. kristinaclodegardendesign.co.uk. **Visits also by arrangement June to Oct for groups of 10 to 20.** D

An opportunity to visit two unique gardens and discover the Brede Steam Giants 35ft Edwardian water pumping engines, and Grade II listed pump house located behind 4 Waterworks Cottages. Garden designer Kristina Clode has created her wildlife friendly garden at 4 Waterworks Cottages over the last 12 yrs. Delightful perennial wildflower meadow, pond, wisteria covered pergola and mixed borders packed full of unusual specimens with year-round interest and colour. Sculdown's garden is dominated by a very large wildlife pond formed as a result of iron-ore mining over 100 yrs ago. The stunning traditional cottage (not open) provides a superb backdrop for several colourful herbaceous borders and poplar trees. Plants for sale at 4 Waterworks Cottages. At Brede Steam Giants, WC available, but regret no disabled facilities and assistance dogs only (free entry, donations encouraged). Wheelchair access at Sculdown (park in flat area at top of field) and in the front garden of 4 Waterworks Cottages only.

GROUP OPENING

154 NEW WESTHAM & STONE CROSS TRAIL

4m NE of Eastbourne & 4m E of Polegate. 19 & 21 Rattle Rd are next door to each other on road through Westham BN24 5DF. Nuthatch is in Stone Cross BN24 5EU, N off mini r'about by Tesco Express shop. Side street parking only. **Sat 16 July (12-5). Combined adm £6, chd free. Home-made teas at Nuthatch & 21 Rattle Road.**

NUTHATCH
27 St Michaels Close, Stone Cross, BN24 5EU. Annie Reynolds.

NEW 19 RATTLE ROAD
Westham, BN24 5DF. Jennie & Alan Starr.

NEW 21 RATTLE ROAD
Westham, BN24 5DF. Alex & Chris Pedrosa.

19 and 21 Rattle Road are two gardens next door to each other. Both have lovely herbaceous borders, mature trees and shrubs. No. 19 is planted for wildlife with roses climbing through trees; No. 21 has a pergola, a new herbaceous border and a greenhouse. Nuthatch is less than a mile away on the same road going west and is a small unban garden with a summerhouse and borders. WC at 19 Rattle Road. Wheelchair access to 19 and 21 Rattle Road only.
♿ ✿ ☕))

155 NEW WESTWELL HOUSE
Main Street, Northiam, TN31 6NB. John & Patrick. *Down gravel drive, signed Westwell House, on opp side of road to GP Surgery and village car park. Park in village car park or on road only (no vehicles to drive to garden or house).* **Sun 26 June (11-4.30). Adm £5, chd free. Light refreshments.**
Our garden is a multicoloured journey. Wander past the magnolias and azaleas at the entrance and you can start to explore the more intimate areas. Whether finding a shady spot by the pond (perhaps take a seat in the boathouse), gazing at the meandering laburnum and wisteria over the pergola, or sitting under the wellingtonia in the meadow, there are many places to sit and enjoy. We hope you do.
 ☕

156 WHITEHANGER
Marley Lane, Haslemere, GU27 3PY. Lynn & David Paynter, 07774 010901, lynn@whitehanger.co.uk. *3m S of Haslemere. Take A286 Midhurst Rd from Haslemere & after approx 2m turn R into Marley Ln (opp Hatch Ln). After 1m turn into drive shared with St Magnus Nursing & keep bearing L through the nursing home.* **Sun 10, Sun 24 July, Sun 7, Sun 21 Aug (10.30-3.30). Adm £6.50, chd £6.50. Pre-booking essential, please visit www.ngs.org.uk for information & booking. Visits also by arrangement June to Oct for groups of 5 to 30.**
Set in 6 acres on the edge of the South Downs National Park surrounded by NT woodland, this rural garden was started in 2012 when a new Huf house was built on a derelict site. Now there are lawned areas with beds of perennials, a serenity pool with koi carp, a wildflower meadow, a Japanese garden, a sculpture garden, a woodland walk, a large rockery and an exotic walled garden.
♿ 🐕))

157 5 WHITEMANS CLOSE
Cuckfield, Haywards Heath, RH17 5DE. Shirley Carman-Martin. *1m N of Cuckfield. On B2036 signed Balcombe, Whitemans Close is 250yds from r'about on LH-side. No parking in Whitemans Close. Buses stop at Whitemans Green, where there is also a large free car park.* **Tue 25, Thur 27, Sat 29 Jan, Tue 1, Thur 3, Sat 5, Mon 7, Wed 9, Tue 15, Thur 17 Feb (10-4). Adm £8, chd free. Pre-booking essential, please phone 01444 473520 or email shirleycarmanmartin@gmail.com for information & booking. Adm inc home-made teas. Visits also by arrangement Jan & Feb for groups of up to 15.**
A garden visit for snowdrop and plant lovers. A relatively small cottage garden packed full of exciting and unusual winter plants, plus a large snowdrop collection. All snowdrops can be viewed from paths, so you can leave the wellies at home.
✿ ☕

158 WHITHURST PARK
Plaistow Road, Kirdford, nr Billingshurst, RH14 0JW. Mr Richard Taylor & Mr Rick Englert, www.whithurst.com. *7m NW of Billingshurst. A272 to Wisborough*

Green, follow sign to Kirdford, turn R at 1st T-junction through village, then R again, 1m on Plaistow Rd, look for the white Whithurst Park sign at roadside. **Sun 3 July (11-5). Adm £5, chd free. Cream teas.**
11 yr old walled kitchen garden with many espaliered fruit trees. Herb beds, vegetable beds, flower borders and cutting beds. Central greenhouse and potting shed with interesting support buildings behind the wall, inc extensive compost area close to beehives. Sustainability through permaculture principles. We have plenty of open lawn around the walled garden and house which can be used for picnics. There are also footpaths around the woodlands surrounding the house and lake. Plants for sale will be in a self-serve area with honesty box, please bring cash (no change available). Wheelchair access via ramp over 3' step onto garden paths.
♿ ✿ ☕ ⛺))

159 NEW WHYDOWN MANOR
Whydown Road, Bexhill-On-Sea, TN39 4RB. Mr & Mrs Little. *A259 take Pear Tree Ln N at Little Common r'about. Continue 1m turning L into Whydown Rd, follow NGS signs to parking (½m), across the road from Whydown Manor. Parking is limited to 30 spaces.* **Sat 2 July (11-5). Adm £8, chd free. Pre-booking essential, please visit www.ngs.org.uk for information & booking. Home-made teas.**
Exquisitely planted, 3½ acre garden framed by mature trees and shrubs with an accessible path. 2½ mile path meanders through the garden and provides great vistas. Hazel arch, Mediterranean bed with plumbago, dramatic beds of tall cannas and grasses add to the beauty. A series of rooms inc a white garden, orchard, rockery and great sweeps of herbaceous beds. Sculptures strategically incorporated. Wheelchair access to garden. Steps to WC.
♿ ☕))

GROUP OPENING

160 WINCHELSEA'S SECRET GARDENS
Winchelsea, TN36 4EJ. *2m W of Rye, 8m E of Hastings.* **Sat 16 Apr (1-5.30). Combined adm £5, chd free. Sat 18 June (11-5). Combined adm £8, chd free. Home-made teas at Winchelsea New Hall.**

CLEVELAND PLACE
Sally & Graham Rhodda.
Open on all dates

 FIREBRAND
Christopher & Octavia Tancredi.
Open on all dates

GILES POINT
Ant Parker & Tom Ashmore.
Open on Sat 18 June

KING'S LEAP
Philip Kent.
Open on all dates

LOOKOUT COTTAGE
Mary & Roger Tidyman.
Open on Sat 18 June

MAGAZINE HOUSE
Susan Stradling.
Open on Sat 18 June

THE ORCHARDS
Brenda & Ralph Courtenay.
Open on Sat 18 June

PERITEAU HOUSE
Dr & Mrs Lawrence Youlten.
Open on all dates

RYE VIEW
Howard Norton & David Page.
Open on all dates

SOUTH MARITEAU
Robert Holland.
Open on Sat 18 June

THE WELL HOUSE
Alice Kenyon.
Open on Sat 16 Apr

Six gardens will open in April, ten in June. Many styles, large and small, secret walled gardens, spring bulbs, tulips, roses, herbaceous borders and more, in the beautiful setting of the Cinque Port of Winchelsea. Explore the town with its magnificent church. Check winchelsea.com for the latest information on tours of our famous medieval cellars. If you are bringing a coach please contact ryeview@gmail. com, 01797 226524. WC facilities available. Wheelchair access to four gardens in April and six in June; see map provided on the day for details.

---

161 **33 WIVELSFIELD ROAD**
Saltdean, Brighton, BN2 8FP. Chris Briggs & Steve Jenner. *From A259 at Saltdean turn onto Arundel Drive West, continue onto Saltdean Vale. Take the 6th turning on L, Tumulus Rd. Take 1st R onto Wivelsfield Rd, continue up steep hill, 33 is on the R.* Sat 30, Sun 31 July (11-5). Adm £5, chd free.

A new garden that was cleared in 2016, landscaped during 2017 and planting started later that yr. Split over three levels filled with colourful perennials, annuals, grasses, and succulents planted in the ground and in containers. The formal garden leads onto a wildflower meadow extending onto the downs, giving spectacular views of both the ocean and South Downs National Park.

162 **WYCH WARREN HOUSE**
Wych Warren, Forest Row, RH18 5LF. Colin King & Mary Franck. *1m S of Forest Row. Proceed S on A22, track turning on L, 100 metres past 45mph warning triangle sign. Or 1m N of Wych Cross T-lights, track turning on R. Go 400 metres across golf course till the end.* Sat 21 May (2-5). Adm £5, chd free. Home-made teas.
6 acre garden in Ashdown Forest, AONB, much of it mixed woodland. Perimeter walk around property (not open). Delightful and tranquil setting with various aspects of interest providing sensory and relaxing visit. Lovely stonework, specimen trees, tulip display, bluebell woods, three ponds, herbaceous borders, greenhouse and always something new on the go. Plenty of space to roam and explore and enjoy the fresh air. Plants for sale and a great range of chutney and jams. Dogs on leads and children welcome. Partial wheelchair access by tarmac track to the kitchen side gate.

Champs Hill

© Judi Lion

WARWICKSHIRE

For Birmingham & West Midlands see Staffordshire

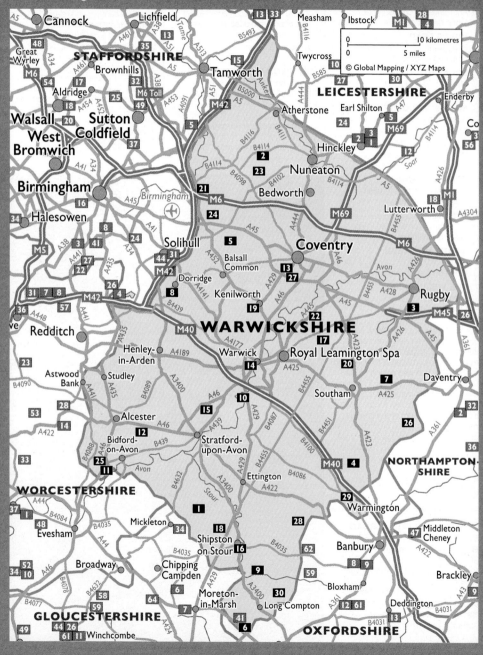

Set in the heart of England, Warwickshire is essentially
a rural county, with many delightful villages and historic
towns, amidst enchanting stretches of unspoilt countryside.

Set in the heart of England. Warwickshire is essentially a rural
county, with many delightful villages and historic towns, amidst
enchanting stretches of unspoilt countryside. In the rolling hills of
the south, Cotswold villages of honey-coloured stone nestle in the
valleys and Stratford-upon-Avon is a mecca for tourists who flock
to see Shakespeare's birthplace and enjoy his plays.

The ancient county town of Warwick with its great castle and
elegant Leamington Spa lie at Warwickshire's centre, with Coventry
and the more industrial landscapes to the north.

The Coventry Canal runs along the county's northern border, and
the towns give way once again to open countryside. Warwickshire's
gardens offer the visitor a tapestry of styles and settings, with
locations ranging from picturesque villages and towns to nurseries
and allotments. Grand country house gardens and charming tiny
village ones are generously opened by their owners to support the
National Garden Scheme Beneficiaries in their vital work.

So do please visit us. You will be assured of a warm welcome
by our Garden Owners who take tremendous pleasure in sharing
their gardens, knowledge and enthusiasm. And, of course, there
is always the promise of a glorious afternoon tea to complete your
day visiting our delightful gardens. delightful gardens.

Below: 11 Priors Crescent

Volunteers

County Organiser
Liz Watson 01926 512307
liz.watson@ngs.org.uk

County Treasurer
Dee Broquard 07773 568317
dee@ngs.org.uk

Publicity
Lily Farrah 07545 560298
lily.farrah@ngs.org.uk

Publicity
Fiona Murphy
07754 943277
fiona.murphy@ngs.org.uk

Talks / Booklet Advertising
Dee Broquard 07773 568317
dee@ngs.org.uk

Booklet Co-ordinator
David Ruffell 01926 316456
de.ruffell@btinternet.com

Assistant County Organisers
Jane Redshaw 07803 234627
jane.redshaw@ngs.org.uk

David Ruffell (as above)

Isobel Somers 07767 306673
ifas1010@aol.com

 @WarwickshireNGS   @WarksNGS

OPENING DATES

All entries subject to change. For latest information check www.ngs.org.uk

Extended openings are shown at the beginning of the month

Map locator numbers are shown to the right of each garden name.

February

Snowdrop Festival

Saturday 19th
◆ Hill Close Gardens   14

April

Every Saturday and Sunday from Saturday 9th
◆ Bridge Nursery   7

Sunday 17th
Broadacre   8

Monday 18th
◆ Bridge Nursery   7

May

Every Saturday and Sunday
◆ Bridge Nursery   7

Monday 2nd
◆ Bridge Nursery   7
Earlsdon Gardens   13

Saturday 14th
6 Canon Price Road   10

Sunday 15th
6 Canon Price Road   10

Saturday 28th
6 Canon Price Road   10
Hunningham Gardens   17
Ilmington Gardens   18

Sunday 29th
6 Canon Price Road   10
Hunningham Gardens   17
Ilmington Gardens   18

June

Every Saturday and Sunday
◆ Bridge Nursery   7

Thursday 2nd
◆ Bridge Nursery   7

Friday 3rd
◆ Bridge Nursery   7

Saturday 4th
Tysoe Gardens   28

Sunday 5th
Tysoe Gardens   28

Sunday 12th
Packington Hall   24
Styvechale Gardens   27

Wednesday 15th
Priors Marston Manor   26

Sunday 19th
Honington Gardens   16
Kenilworth Gardens   19
Maxstoke Castle   21
Whichford & Ascott Gardens   30

Saturday 25th
Admington Hall   1
6 Canon Price Road   10
Long Itchington Village Gardens   20

Sunday 26th
Berkswell Gardens   5
6 Canon Price Road   10
Long Itchington Village Gardens   20
NEW Old Arley Gardens   23
Warmington Gardens   29

July

Every Saturday and Sunday
◆ Bridge Nursery   7

Sunday 3rd
Ansley Gardens   2
Blacksmiths Cottage   6

Saturday 9th
6 Canon Price Road   10

Sunday 10th
Avon Dassett Gardens   4
6 Canon Price Road   10

Saturday 16th
3 Cleeve View   11
NEW 11 Priors Crescent   25

Sunday 17th
3 Cleeve View   11
NEW 11 Priors Crescent   25

Saturday 30th
Anya Court Care Home   3

Sunday 31st
Anya Court Care Home   3

August

Every Saturday and Sunday
◆ Bridge Nursery   7

Monday 29th
◆ Bridge Nursery   7

September

Every Saturday and Sunday to Friday 30th
◆ Bridge Nursery   7

Sunday 11th
Burmington Grange   9

October

Saturday 29th
◆ Hill Close Gardens   14

By Arrangement

Arrange a personalised garden visit with your club, or group of friends, on a date to suit you. See individual garden entries for full details.

Admington Hall   1
10 Avon Carrow, Avon Dassett Gardens   4
Broadacre   8
6 Canon Price Road   10
The Croft House   12
Fieldgate, Kenilworth Gardens   19
The Hill Cottage   15
19 Leigh Crescent, Long Itchington Village Gardens   20
The Motte, Hunningham Gardens   17
Oak House   22

1 Brakeley Cottages, Long Itchington Village Gardens

THE GARDENS

1 ADMINGTON HALL

Admington, Shipston-on-Stour, CV36 4JN. Mark & Antonia Davies, 01789 450279, adhall@admingtonhall.com. *6m NW of Shipston-on-Stour. From Ilmington, follow signs to Admington. Approx 2m, turn R to Admington by Polo Ground. Continue for 1m.* Sat 25 June (11-5). Adm £7.50, chd free. Home-made teas. Visits also by arrangement May to Sept for groups of 20+.
A continually evolving 10 acre garden with an established structure of innovative planning and planting. A wide ranging collection of fine and mature specimen trees provide the essential core structure to this traditional country garden. Features inc a lush broad lawn, orchard, water garden, large walled garden, wildflower meadows and extensive modern topiary. This is a garden in motion. Wheelchair access to most parts of garden.

GROUP OPENING

2 ANSLEY GARDENS

Ansley, CV10 0QR. *Ansley is situated W of Nuneaton, adjacent to Arley. Ansley is directly off the B4114.* Sun 3 July (2-6). Combined adm £6, chd free. Light refreshments, cream teas & home-made cakes in specified gardens.

1A BIRMINGHAM ROAD
Adrian & Heather Norgrove.

NEW 7 BIRMINGHAM ROAD
Mrs Freda Lynex.

25 BIRMINGHAM ROAD
Pat & David Arrowsmith.

NEW 59 BIRMINGHAM ROAD
Joan & Peter McParland.

188 BIRMINGHAM ROAD
Mrs Fiona Robinson.

14 GALLEY VIEW
Joanna Harze.

NEW 1 GOLDSBY CROFT
Mrs Jean Lennon.

35 NUTHURST CRESCENT
Roger & Heather Greaves.

THE OLD POLICE HOUSE
Mike & Hilary Ward.

1 PARK COTTAGES
Janet & Andy Down.

Ansley is a small ex-mining village situated in North Warwickshire. The ten gardens open are a selection of different styles and offerings. This year there are three new gardens opening. They range from a very small traditional cottage garden crammed with flowers and pots to larger gardens maximising the amazing views of the countryside. There is one with a large range of unusual plants, a country garden with mature plants and ancient roses and one new build garden. Nine of the gardens are in the village with the opportunity to walk across the fields on public footpaths to the tenth garden for those who are able. The local Norman church will be open and the Morris Dancing Group will be entertaining visitors during the day.

3 ANYA COURT CARE HOME

286 Dunchurch Road, Rugby, CV22 6JA. Hallmark Care Homes. *Opp Sainsbury's on Dunchurch Rd. If our car park is busy, please use their car park as an alternative. Please go to Anya Court reception, who will guide you to the garden.* Sat 30, Sun 31 July (10.30-3.30). Adm £5, chd free. Entry inc light refreshments & cream teas.
Anya Court has a large wooded wrap around garden consisting of a number of sensory herbaceous perennial planting schemes. There is also a fruit and vegetable garden grown by the residents of the home and a colourful annual bedding and basket display. Due to the number of trees on site the garden is a good example of dry shade and drought tolerant planting for anyone requiring inspiration. Fully accessible to wheelchairs.

'In 2021 the National Garden Scheme donated £500,000 to Marie Curie enabling us to continue providing our vital services and be there, caring for people on the frontline of the Coronavirus pandemic'
Marie Curie

GROUP OPENING

4 AVON DASSETT GARDENS

Avon Dassett, CV47 2AE. *7m N of Banbury. From M40 J12 turn L & L again onto the B4100, following signs to Herb Centre & Gaydon. Take 2nd L into village (signed). Please park in cemetery car park at top of hill or where signed.* Sun 10 July (1-5). Combined adm £7, chd free. Home-made teas at The Thatches.

10 AVON CARROW
Anna Prosser, 01295 690926, annaatthecarrow@btopenworld.com.
Visits also by arrangement Mar to Sept for groups of 5 to 20.

THE EAST WING, AVON CARROW
Christine Fisher & Terry Gladwin.

HILL TOP FARM
Mr D Hicks.

OLD MILL COTTAGE
Mike & Jill Lewis.

THE OLD RECTORY
Lily Hope-Frost.

POPPY COTTAGE
Audrey Butler.

THE SNUG
Mrs Deb Watts.

THE THATCHES
Trevor & Michele Gill.

Pretty Hornton stone village sheltering in the lee of the Burton Dassett hills, well wooded with parkland setting and The Old Rectory mentioned in Domesday Book. Wide variety of gardens inc kitchen gardens, cottage, gravel and tropical gardens. Range of plants inc alpines, herbaceous, perennials, roses, climbers and shrubs. The gardens are on/off the main road through the village. We would be grateful if visitors could avoid parking along the main road in the village, but park where signed. For 2022, we expect to run a shuttle service from top to bottom of the village. Book sale, plant sales, tombola, historic church and lunch available at the Yew Tree village pub, recently purchased by the Community, visit www.theyewtreepub.co.uk for details. Wheelchair access to most gardens.

GROUP OPENING

5 BERKSWELL GARDENS
Berkswell, Coventry, CV7 7BB.
7m W of Coventry. A452 to Balsall Common & follow signs to Berkswell. Tickets & maps available at each garden. Car necessary to visit all gardens. Sun 26 June (11-6). Combined adm £7, chd free. Light refreshments at Yew Tree Barn only.

2 AGRICULTURAL COTTAGES
Mrs Jane Edwards.

NEW BARN LODGE
Joanne & Gerry Rolls.

NEW EMSCOT BARN
Leigh & Sarah Mayers.

HOLLY OAK
Jane Bostock.

115 MEETING HOUSE LANE
Flick & Geoff Wheeler.

SPENCER'S END
Gordon Clark & Nicola Content.

SQUIRRELS JUMP
Brian & Jenny Harris.

YEW TREE BARN
Angela & Ken Shaw.

Berkswell is a beautiful village dating back to Saxon times with a C12 Norman church and has several C16 and C17 buildings inc the pub. In 2014 and 2015 the village was awarded Gold in the RHS Britain in Bloom campaign, plus a special RHS award in 2014 for the Best Large Village in the Heart of England. The gardens provide great variety with fine examples of small and large, formal and informal, wild, imaginatively planted herbaceous borders and productive vegetable gardens. Something for everyone and plenty of ideas to take home. Also open to visitors is the C12 Norman church and garden.

6 BLACKSMITHS COTTAGE
Little Compton, Moreton-in-Marsh, GL56 0SE. Mrs Andrew Lukas.
Garden entrance is opp the village hall car park. Please park at village hall or in Reed College car park nearby. Sun 3 July (2-5.30). Adm £5, chd free. Home-made teas.
A walled garden created in the last 7 years for all seasons with many fine and unusual trees, shrubs, plants and bulbs, set around a large lawn with a beautiful Aqualens fountain at its centre. Unusual varieties of clematis climb through shrubs and up walls. There is a productive vegetable garden, greenhouse and summerhouse. All designed and made by the owners to create a sense of magic.

7 ◆ BRIDGE NURSERY
Tomlow Road, Napton, Southam, CV47 8HX. Christine Dakin & Philip Martino, 01926 812737, chris.dakin25@yahoo.com, www.bridge-nursery.co.uk. *3m E of Southam. Brown tourist sign at Napton Xrds on A425 Southam to Daventry rd.* For NGS: Every Sat and Sun 9 Apr to 30 Sept (10-4). Mon 18 Apr, Mon 2 May, Thur 2, Fri 3 June, Mon 29 Aug (10-4). Light refreshments. Adm £3.50, chd free. For other opening times and information, please phone, email or visit garden website.
Clay soil? Don't despair. Here is an acre of garden with an exciting range of plants which thrive in hostile conditions. Grass paths lead you round borders filled with many unusual plants, a pond and bamboo grove complete with panda! A peaceful haven for wildlife and visitors. A visitor commented 'it is garden that is comfortable with itself.' Tea or coffee and biscuits gladly provided on request. Group visits welcome.

8 BROADACRE
Grange Road, Dorridge, Solihull, B93 8QA. John Woolman, 07818 082885, jw234567@gmail.com, www.broadacregarden.org. *Approx 3m SE of Solihull. On B4101 opp The Railway Inn. Plenty of parking.* Sun 17 Apr (2-6). Adm £5, chd free. Home-made teas. Visits also by arrangement.
Broadacre is a semi-wild garden, managed organically. Attractively landscaped with pools, lawns and trees, beehives, vegetable area and adjoining stream and wildflower meadows. Bring sensible footwear to follow the nature trail. Dorridge Cricket Club is on site (the bar will be open). Lovely venue for a picnic. Dogs and children are welcome. Excellent country pub, The Railway Inn, at the bottom of the drive. Wheelchair access improvement suggestions welcome.

9 BURMINGTON GRANGE
Cherington, Shipston-on-Stour, CV36 5HZ. Mr & Mrs Patrick Ramsay. *2m E of Shipston-on-Stour. Take Oxford Rd (A3400) from Shipston-on-Stour, after 2m turn L to Burmington, go through village & continue for 1m, turn L to Willington & Barcheston, on sharp L bend turn R over cattle grid.* Sun 11 Sept (2-6). Adm £6, chd free. Home-made teas.
Interesting plantsman's garden extending to about 1½ acres, set in the rolling hills of the North Cotswolds with wonderful views over unspoilt countryside. The garden is well developed considering it was planted 18 years ago. Small vegetable garden, beautiful sunken rose garden with herbaceous and shrub borders. Orchard and tree walk with unusual trees.

10 6 CANON PRICE ROAD
Nursery Meadow, Barford, CV35 8EQ. Mrs Marie-Jane Roberts, 07775 584336. *From A429 turn into Barford. Park on Wellesbourne Rd & walk into Nursery Meadow by red phone box. No 6 is R in 1st close. Disabled parking by house.* Sat 14, Sun 15, Sat 28, Sun 29 May (2-4.30). Adm £3, chd free. Sat 25, Sun 26 June, Sat 9, Sun 10 July (2-4.30). Adm £5, chd free. Light refreshments in the garden room. Visits also by arrangement May to Sept.
Unexpectedly large and mature garden with colour themed shrub and perennial plants immaculately grown. Separate areas for cut flowers, dahlias, herbs, vegetables and 19 types of fruit, some fan trained. Spectacularly colourful patio pots, a small delightful rockery, pond and wildlife garden. With many seating areas. Hardy perennials for sale - please bring cash. Access via a single slab path that joins a wide path through the garden. No WC.

11 3 CLEEVE VIEW
Evesham Road, Salford Priors, Evesham, WR11 8UW. Ms Pip Harris. *8m from Stratford upon Avon. Enter Salford Priors from A46 r'about. The Bell will be on your L. We are a few hundred yrds on the R in a red brick terrace. Small car park opp or try the church car park.* Sat 16, Sun 17 July (10-4.30). Combined adm with 11 Priors

34 Clarendon Road, Kenilworth Gardens

Cescent £5, chd free.
Small cottage garden with an abundance of plants, pots and interesting metal features. Beds have been carefully planned to ensure a continuous display of colour. The beds are well-stocked with a mixture of shrubs, perennials and bulbs. There is a small water feature that attracts various wildlife.

12 THE CROFT HOUSE
Haselor, Alcester, B49 6LU. Isobel & Patrick Somers, 07767 306673, ifas1010@aol.com. 6m W of Stratford-upon-Avon, 2m E of Alcester, off A46. From A46 take Haselor turn. From Alcester take old Stratford Rd, turn L signed Haselor, then R at Xrds. Garden in centre of village. Please park considerately. Visits by arrangement May & June for groups of 5 to 30. Adm £4, chd free. Home-made teas.
Wander through an acre of trees, shrubs and herbaceous borders densely planted with a designer's passion for colour and texture. Hidden areas invite you to linger. Gorgeous scented wisteria on two sides of the house. Organically managed, providing a haven for

birds and other wildlife. Frog pond, treehouse, small vegetable plot and a few venerable old fruit trees from its days as a market garden.

GROUP OPENING

13 EARLSDON GARDENS
Coventry, CV5 6FS. *Turn towards Coventry at A45 & A429 T-lights. Take 3rd L into Beechwood Ave, continue ½m to St Barbara's Church at Xrds with Rochester Rd. Maps & tickets at St Barbara's Church Hall.* **Mon 2 May (11-4). Combined adm £5, chd free. Light refreshments at St Barbara's Church Hall.**

43 ARMORIAL ROAD
Gary & Jane Flanagan.

3 BATES ROAD
Victor Keene MBE.

28 CLARENDON STREET
Ruth & Symon Whitehouse.

27 HARTINGTON CRESCENT
David & Judith Bogle.

40 HARTINGTON CRESCENT
Viv & George Buss.

114 HARTINGTON CRESCENT
Liz Campbell & Denis Crowley.

40 RANULF CROFT
Spencer & Sue Swain.

2 SHAFTESBURY ROAD
Ann Thomson & Bruce Walker.

27 SPENCER AVENUE
Helene Devane.

23 SPENCER AVENUE
Susan & Keith Darwood.

Varied selection of town gardens from small to more formal with interest for all tastes inc a mature garden with deep borders bursting with spring colour; a large garden with extensive lawns and an array of rhododendrons, azaleas and large mature trees; densely planted town garden with sheltered patio area and wilder woodland; and a surprisingly large garden offering interest to all ages! There is also a pretty garden set on several levels with hidden aspect; a large peaceful garden with water features and vegetable plot; a large mature garden in peaceful surroundings; and a plantaholic's garden with a large variety of plants, clematis and small trees.

◆ HILL CLOSE GARDENS
Bread and Meat Close,
Warwick, CV34 6HF. Hill Close
Gardens Trust, 01926 493339,
centremanager@hcgt.org.uk,
www.hillclosegardens.com. *Town
centre. Follow signs to Warwick
racecourse. Entry from Friars St
onto Bread & Meat Close. Car park
by entrance next to racecourse. 2
hrs free parking. Disabled parking
outside the gates.* **For NGS: Sat 19
Feb (11-4); Sat 29 Oct (11-5). Adm
£5, chd £1. Cream teas. For other
opening times and information,
please phone, email or visit garden
website. Donation to Plant Heritage.**
Restored Grade II* Victorian
leisure gardens comprising 16
individual hedged gardens, 8 brick
summerhouses. Herbaceous borders,
heritage apple and pear trees,
C19 daffodils, over 100 varieties of
snowdrops, many varieties of asters
and chrysanthemums. Heritage
vegetables. Plant Heritage border,
auricula theatre, and Victorian style
glasshouse. Children's garden. Before
you visit, please see our website for
up-to-date information. Wheelchair
available, please phone to book in
advance.

♿ ✿ 🐕 NPC ☕

THE HILL COTTAGE
Kings Lane, Snitterfield, Stratford-
upon-Avon, CV37 0QA. Gillie &
Paul Waldron, 07895 369387,
info@thehillcottage.co.uk,
www.thehillcottage.co.uk. *5 mins
from M40 J15. Take A46 to Stratford,
after 1m take 2nd exit at r'about,
½m L into Kings Lane, through S
bends, house on R. Or from village,
up White Horse Hill, R at T-junction,
over A46, R Kings Lane, 2nd on L.*
Visits by arrangement Apr to Sept
for groups of up to 30. Adm £6,
chd free. Home-made teas.
High on a ridge overlooking orchards
and golf course with fabulous views
to distant hills, this 2¼ acre garden,
full of surprises, offers varied planting;
sunny gravel with exotic specimens;
cool, shady woodland with relaxed
perennial groups; romantic green
oak pond garden and stone
summerhouse; pool with newts and
dragonflies. Traditional glasshouse
in walled kitchen garden with raised
beds. Bluebell wood best in late April.
Gazebo, pergolas, lavender walk,
pond garden, clematis, walled kitchen
garden and glasshouse and too many
pots to count!

✿ 🏠 ☕

GROUP OPENING

HONINGTON GARDENS
Honington, Shipston-on-Stour,
CV36 5AA. *1½m N of Shipston-
on-Stour. Take A3400 towards
Stratford-upon-Avon, then turn R
signed Honington.* Sun 19 June
(2-5.30). Combined adm £6, chd
free. Home-made teas.

HONINGTON GLEBE
Mr & Mrs J C Orchard.

HONINGTON HALL
B H E Wiggin.

MALT HOUSE RISE
Mr P Weston.

THE OLD HOUSE
Mr & Mrs I F Beaumont.

ORCHARD HOUSE
Mr & Mrs Monnington.

SHOEMAKERS COTTAGE
Christopher & Anne Jordan.

C17 village, recorded in Domesday,
entered by old toll gate. Ornamental
stone bridge over the River Stour and
interesting church with C13 tower and
late C17 nave after Wren. Six super
gardens. 2 acre plantsman's garden
consisting of rooms planted informally
with year-round interest in contrasting
foliage and texture, lily pool and
parterre. Extensive lawns and fine
mature trees with river and garden
monuments. Secluded walled cottage
garden with roses, and a structured
cottage garden formally laid out with
box hedging and small fountain.
Small, developing garden created by
the owners with informal mixed beds
and borders. Wheelchair access to
most gardens.

♿ 🐑 ✿ 🐕 ☕))

1a Birmingham Road, Ansley Gardens

GROUP OPENING

17 HUNNINGHAM GARDENS
Hunningham, Leamington Spa,
CV33 9DS. *6m NE of Leamington
Spa, 8m SW of Rugby, 7m S of
Coventry. Just off the Fosse Way
(B4455), or take B4453 from
Leamington through Weston-
under-Wetherley, then turn R to
Hunningham. Parking in village
at CV33 9DS & at Sandy Acre at
CV47 9QE.* **Sat 28, Sun 29 May
(12.30-5.30). Combined adm £6,
chd free.** Home-made teas in St
Margaret's Church Parish Room
from 1pm.

NEW APPLE TREE COTTAGE
Mr Michael Wall & Ms Leana
Horton.

NEW 3 ELM FARM COTTAGES
Moira Rawlings.

GLENCOVE
Simon & Annabel Shackleton.

HUNNINGHAM HILL FARM
Jonathan Hofstetter.

THE MOTTE
Margaret & Peter
Green, 01926 632903,
margaretegreen100@gmail.com.
Visits also by arrangement May
to Sept for groups of up to 30.

THE OLD HALL
Nicholas & Rona Horler.

Hunningham, a hamlet nestling in
the countryside close to the River
Leam with St Margaret's Church
dating in part to the C13. Six gardens
in varied styles, with more possibly
open on the day. A plant lover's
garden brimming with woodland
plants, tender perennials, unusual
shrubs and trees, fruit and vegetable
plot and plant filled conservatory.
Newly formed garden with pleached
hornbeam avenue, parterre with
feature sculpture, panoramic views,
wooded areas, cut flower garden
and new holm oak circle. Large
partly walled garden with mature
shrubs and trees surrounding the
Old Hall. Hedged cottage garden
with herbaceous perennials, fruit
and vegetable areas. A garden set
high on the hill, with herbaceous
planting, walled vegetable garden,
natural pond, orchard, wildflower
meadow and a rewilding project that
has so far resulted in richer and more
diverse wildlife. New for 2022 are
a bijou cottage front garden ablaze
with colour and a newly created
garden that is still under development.
Panoramic views and views across
the River Leam. Good plant sale.

GROUP OPENING

18 ILMINGTON GARDENS
Ilmington, CV36 4LA. *8m S of
Stratford-upon-Avon. 8m N of
Moreton-in-Marsh. 4m NW of
Shipston-on-Stour off A3400. 3m NE
of Chipping Campden.* **Sat 28, Sun
29 May (12.30-6). Combined adm
£10, chd free.** Home-made teas
in Ilmington Community Shop,
Upper Green (Sat) & at the Village
Hall (Sun). **Donation to Shipston
Home Nursing.**

THE BEVINGTONS
Mr & Mrs N Tustain.

CHERRY ORCHARD
Mr Angus Chambers.

THE DOWER HOUSE
Mr & Mrs M Tremellen.

FOXCOTE HILL
Mr & Mrs Michael Dingley.

FROG ORCHARD
Mr & Mrs Jeremy Snowden.

GRUMP COTTAGE
Mr & Mrs Martin Underwood.

ILMINGTON MANOR
Mr Martin Taylor.

OLD FOX HOUSE
Rob & Sarah Beebee.

RAVENSCROFT
Mr & Mrs Clasper.

STUDIO COTTAGE
Sarah Hobson.

Ilmington is an ancient hillside
Cotswold village 2m from the Fosse
Way with two good pubs. Start at
Ilmington Manor (next to the Red Lion
Pub); wander the 3 acre gardens
with fish pond. Then walk to the
upper green behind the village hall
to Foxcote Hill's large gardens and
Old Fox House, then up Grump St
to Ravenscroft's large sculpture filled
sloping vistas commanding the hilltop.
Walk to nearby Frog Lane, view
cottage gardens of Cherry Orchard
and Frog Orchard. Then to the
Bevingtons many-chambered cottage
garden at the bottom of Valanders
Lane near the church and manor
ponds and beyond to the Dower
House in Back Street.

GROUP OPENING

19 KENILWORTH GARDENS
Kenilworth, CV8 1BT. *Fieldgate
Lane, off A452. Parking available
at Abbey Fields or in town. Street
parking on Fieldgate Lane (limited),
Siddley Ave & Beehive Hill. Tickets
& maps at most gardens. Transport
is necessary to visit all the gardens.*
**Sun 19 June (12-5). Combined
adm £7, chd free.** Home-made
teas at St Nicholas Parochial Hall
from 1pm.

BEEHIVE HILL ALLOTMENTS
Kenilworth Allotment Association.

NEW 30 CLARENDON ROAD
Mr & Mrs Craddock.

NEW 34 CLARENDON ROAD
Barrie & Maggie Rogers.

FIELDGATE
Liz & Bob Watson, 01926 512307,
liz.watson@ngs.org.uk.
Visits also by arrangement May
to Sept for groups of 5 to 30.

65 RANDALL ROAD
Mrs Jan Kenyon.

2 ST NICHOLAS AVENUE
Mr Ian Roberts.

**ST NICHOLAS PAROCHIAL
HALL**
St Nicholas Church.

1 SIDDELEY AVENUE
Clare Wightman.

TREE TOPS
Joanna & George Illingworth.

NEW 14 WHITEHEAD DRIVE
James Coleman.

Kenilworth was historically a very
important town in Warwickshire. It has
one of England's best castle ruins,
Abbey Fields and plenty of pubs
and good restaurants. The gardens
open this year are very varied. There
are small and large gardens, formal,
contemporary and cottage styles
with trees, shrubs, herbaceous
borders, ponds and more intimate,
wildlife friendly areas, plus plenty of
vegetables at the allotments. Several
of the gardens have won Gold in
the Kenilworth in Bloom garden
competition. Partial wheelchair access
to many of the gardens.

GROUP OPENING

20 LONG ITCHINGTON VILLAGE GARDENS

Long Itchington, nr Southam, CV47 9PD. *Long Itchington is on the A423 main trunk road between Coventry & Banbury, less than 3m N of the market town of Southam; Royal Leamington Spa is 7m to the W.* Sat 25, Sun 26 June (12-5). Combined adm £7, chd free. Home-made teas in Holy Trinity Church, Church Road.

BAKEHOUSE COURT
Martyn & Erica Smith.

1 BRAKELEY COTTAGES
Andy & Sue Jack.

CHERRYWOOD
Andy & Rosie Skilbeck.

38 DALE CLOSE
Simon & Jeni Neale.

IFFLEY LODGE
John Glare.

NEW **LAKE VIEW**
Chris & Phil Lawrence.

19 LEIGH CRESCENT
Tony Shorthouse, 01926 817192, Tonyshorthouse19@gmail.com. Visits also by arrangement June to Sept for groups of 5 to 10.

MEADOW COTTAGE
Charlotte Griffin.

3 ODINGSELL DRIVE
Adrienne & Steve Mitchell.

20 ODINGSELL DRIVE
Jean & Gerry Bailey.

SANDY ACRE
David & Janis Tait.

NEW **6 SHORT LANE**
Alan & Jean Huitson.

8 THE SQUARE
Janet Powell.

NEW **THORNFIELD**
Harvey & Margaret Bailey.

THE WILLOWS
Simon & Charlotte Collyer.

Opening its gardens for the second time in 2022, Long Itchington is a large village in south Warwickshire next to the Grand Union Canal. It features a network of waymarked paths and several historic buildings inc a half-timbered Tudor house where Queen Elizabeth I once stayed, a C15 Manor House and a C12/C13 church. It also boasts the biggest village pond in Warwickshire, a village green, six pubs, a Co-op and a public park and playing field with children's playground, picnic area and a wildflower meadow. Gardens of all types are featured inc gravel, tropical, vegetable, cottage and contemporary. These range in size from small/courtyard gardens to an extensive landscaped garden with panoramic countryside views. Plant sales.
✿ 🍵))

21 MAXSTOKE CASTLE

Coleshill, B46 2RD.
Mr G M Fetherston-Dilke. *2½m E of Coleshill. E of Birmingham, on B4114. Take R turn down Castle Lane, Castle drive 1¼m on R.* Sun 19 June (11-5). Adm £8, chd £5. Home-made teas. Tickets available on the day or in advance via www.maxstoke.com. Donation to The NGS & other charities.
Approx 5 acres of garden and grounds with roses, herbaceous plants, shrubs and trees in the courtyard and immediate surroundings of this C14 moated castle. No wheelchair access into the house.
& ✿ 🍵

22 OAK HOUSE

Waverley Edge, Bubbenhall, Coventry, CV8 3LW. Helena Grant, 07731 419685, helena.grant@btinternet.com. *15 mins from Leamington Spa via the Oxford Rd/A423 & the Leamington Rd/A445 & the A46. Spaces for 4 cars only.* Visits by arrangement Apr to Oct for groups of up to 12. Adm £5, chd free. Home-made teas.
Tucked away next to Waverley Woods, Oak House enjoys a walled garden that has been landscaped and extended over 30 years. The garden is split on two levels with seven seating areas allowing for relaxed appreciation of every aspect of the garden, with peaceful places to sit, ponder and enjoy. A focal point is the large terracotta urn, over 60 years old, which delivers vertical interest and the summerhouse and arbour which face each other diagonally across the garden. The curved borders have a wide range of planting creating distinct areas which surround the lawn. There are over 80 different plant varieties giving year-round interest which is a haven for birds and other wildlife. Wheelchair access only on level path which runs round the house.
& ✿ 🍵

GROUP OPENING

23 NEW OLD ARLEY GARDENS

Ansley Lane, Arley, Coventry, CV7 8FT. Mrs Carolyn McKay. *2m off Tamworth Road or ½ m from Birmingham road. Enter Ansley Lane via Birmingham Road or Rectory Road.* Sun 26 June (2-6). Combined adm £4, chd free. Light refreshments.

NEW **7 ST WILFREDS COTTAGES**
Mrs Sarah Shepherd.

NEW **21 ST WILFREDS COTTAGES**
Miss Jo Carter.

NEW **24 ST WILFREDS COTTAGES**
Mrs Carolyn McKay.

NEW **29 ST WILFREDS COTTAGES**
Ms Maggie Eggar.

NEW **30 ST WILFREDS COTTAGES**
Mr Mike Nicholson.

NEW **32 ST WILFREDS COTTAGES**
Mr Ronald Whiting.

NEW **THE SCHOOL HOUSE**
Mrs Pauline McAleese.

Old Arley is an ancient village which appears in the Domesday book. More recently it was a small mining community and St Wilfreds Cottages were built in 1907 to accommodate the mine's supervisors and their families. The gardens vary in style and size and can be easily reached one after the other on the lane. The planting is varied, ranging from traditional cottage gardens to more contemporary.
✿ 🍵))

24 PACKINGTON HALL

Meriden, nr Coventry, CV7 7HF.
Lord & Lady Guernsey, www.packingtonestate.co.uk. *Midway between Coventry & Birmingham on A45. Entrance 400yds from Stonebridge r'about towards Coventry. For SatNav please use CV7 7HE or What3words app - mint.target.statement.* Sun 12 June (2-5). Adm £6, chd free. Home-made teas.
Packington is the setting for an elegant Capability Brown landscape. Designed from 1751, the gardens inc

a serpentine lake, impressive Cedars of Lebanon, Wellingtonias and a 1762 Japanese bridge. There is also a millennium rose garden, wildflower meadow, mixed terrace borders, woodland walks and a newly restored walled garden. Home-made teas on the terrace or in The Pompeiin Room if wet. Wheelchair access is possible but please note there are no paths in the garden. The terrace is easily accessible. WCs are down steep steps.

&. 🐴 🚐 ☕ ⑴))

25 NEW **11 PRIORS CRESCENT**
off School Road, Salford Priors, WR11 8AN. Rob & Diane Cole. *Midway between Evesham & Alcester. Follow signs to Salford Priors from either A46 or B4088. Priors Crescent is off School Rd & fronted by a large public open space. We are open in conjunction with 3 Cleeve View, 10 mins on foot.*

Sat 16, Sun 17 July (10-4.30). **Combined adm with 3 Cleeve View £5, chd free.** The garden was newly created in 2021 by two plant enthusiasts, and demonstrates how hardy perennials can be used to great effect in a short time in a relatively small space (approx. 18m x 18m). Predominantly flower borders, there is also a lawn, an alpine scree bed, greenhouse, and a small nursery area. Potted plants are arranged on the patio with seating, and sculptures are used as ornament.

&. ❀

26 **PRIORS MARSTON MANOR**
The Green, Priors Marston, CV47 7RH. **Dr & Mrs Mark Cecil.** *8m SW of Daventry. Off the A361 between Daventry & Banbury at Charwelton. Follow signs to Priors Marston, approx 2m. Arrive at T-junction with a war memorial on R.*

The manor will be on your L. **Wed 15 June (10-5). Adm £6, chd free.** **Home-made teas.**
This opening inc an indoor Bonhams Valuation Day (11-2) suggested donation £2 per item, proceeds to the NGS. Arrive in Priors Marston village and explore the manor gardens. Greatly enhanced by present owners to relate back to a Georgian manor garden and pleasure grounds. Wonderful walled kitchen garden provides seasonal produce and cut flowers for the house. Herbaceous flower beds and a sunken terrace with water feature by William Pye. Lawns lead down to the lake and estate around which you can walk amongst the trees and wildlife with stunning views up to the house and garden aviary. Sculpture on display. Partial wheelchair access.

&. 🐴 ☕ ⑴))

14 Galley View, Ansley Gardens

Ravenscroft, Ilmington Gardens

GROUP OPENING

27 STYVECHALE GARDENS
The Chesils, Coventry, CV3 6FP.
styvechale-gardens.wixsite.com/
ngs2020. *The gardens are located
on the S side of Coventry close to
A45. Tickets & map available on
the day from the Church Hall, West
Orchard United Reformed Church.*
**Sun 12 June (11-5). Combined
adm £5, chd free. Home-made
teas.**

11 BAGINTON ROAD
Ken & Pauline Bond.

164 BAGINTON ROAD
Fran & Jeff Gaught.

NEW **38 THE CHESILS**
Isobel Woods & Alan Marsden.

59 THE CHESILS
John Marron & Richard Bantock.

NEW **63 THE CHESILS**
Ann & Nick Mills.

NEW **66 THE CHESILS**
Ami Samra & Rodger Hope.

NEW **96 THE CHESILS**
Rebecca & Barry Preston.

16 DELAWARE ROAD
Val & Roy Howells.

2 THE HIRON
Sue & Graham Pountney.

NEW **50 KNOLL DRIVE**
Anita & Barry Hallam.

NEW **54 KNOLL DRIVE**
Ruth & Mark Concannon.

NEW **56 KNOLL DRIVE**
Ginny & Liam McElvenney.

177 LEAMINGTON ROAD
Barry & Ann Suddens.

27 RODYARD WAY
Jon & Karen Venables.
D

An eclectic mix of lovely, mature
suburban gardens. Enjoy their variety
from kitchen garden to a touch of
the exotic, calm white gardens to
a riot of colourful borders. Roses,
water features, ponds, shady areas
and more. Something for everyone
and plenty of ideas for you to take
home. Three of our gardens have
been featured in garden magazines
and one garden was awarded garden
of the year by a national newspaper.
Relax in the gardens where a warm
friendly welcome will await you. Plant
sales and refreshments in some
gardens. 40 Ranulf Croft will also be
open on the day.

GROUP OPENING

28 TYSOE GARDENS

Tysoe, Warwick, CV35 0SE. *W of A422, N of Banbury (9m). E of A3400 & Shipston-on-Stour (4m). N of A4035 & Brailes (3m). Please park on the village Recreation Ground beside the Old Fire Station CV35 0FF.* Sat 4, Sun 5 June (2-6). Combined adm £7, chd free. Home-made teas.

5 AVON AVENUE
Penny & Rob Varley.

NEW CHELMSCOTE HOUSE
Stephanie Schofield.
D

DINSDALE HOUSE
Julia & David Sewell.

GARDEN COTTAGE & WALLED KITCHEN GARDEN
Sue & Mike Sanderson,
www.twkg.co.uk.

IVYDALE
Sam & Malcolm Littlewood.

KERNEL COTTAGE
Christine Duke.

THE OLD POLICE HOUSE
Bridget & Digby Norton.

We would like to invite you to Tysoe to celebrate the Queen's Platinum Jubilee weekend by visiting our gardens. Tysoe, an original Hornton stone village stands on the North East foothills of the Cotswolds, We much look forward to seeing you all again after so much uncertainty this past year and more. There will be a courtesy bus available. You can be sure that Tysoe will offer a happy atmosphere, some terrific gardens, a pleasant walk round the village and a jolly good tea made by the large band of WI bakers and other cooking enthusiasts living in the village. A warm welcome awaits you in this buzzy, energetic, friendly village and gardening community. Come and check us out! Partial wheelchair access.

GROUP OPENING

29 WARMINGTON GARDENS

Banbury, OX17 1BU. *5m NW of Banbury. Take B4100 N from Banbury, after 5m turn R across short dual carriageway into Warmington. From N take J12 off M40 onto B4100.* Sun 26 June (1-5). Combined adm £6, chd free. Home-made teas at village hall.

2 CHAPEL STREET
c/o Tim Stevens Group Coordinator.

GOURDON
Jenny Deeming.

GREENWAYS
Tim Stevens.

HILL COTTAGE, SCHOOL LANE
Mr Mike Jones.

LANTERN HOUSE
Peter & Tessa Harborne.

THE MANOR HOUSE
Mr & Mrs G Lewis.

THE ORCHARD
Mike Cable.

SPRINGFIELD HOUSE
Jenny & Roger Handscombe,
01295 690286,
jehandscombe@btinternet.com.

1 THE WHEELWRIGHTS
Ms E Bunn.

Warmington is a charming historic village, mentioned in the Doomsday Book, situated at the north-east edge of the Cotswolds in a designated AONB. There is a large village green with a pond overlooked by an Elizabethan Manor House (not open). There are other historic buildings including St Michael's Church, The Plough Inn and Springfield House all dating from the C16 or before. There is a mixed and varied selection of gardens to enjoy during your visit to Warmington. These inc the formal knot gardens and topiary of The Manor House, cottage and courtyard gardens, terraced gardens on the slopes of Warmington Hill and orchards containing local varieties of apple trees. Some gardens will be selling homegrown plants. WC at village hall, along with delicious home-made cakes, and hot and cold drinks.

GROUP OPENING

30 WHICHFORD & ASCOTT GARDENS

Whichford & Ascott, Shipston-on-Stour, CV36 5PG. *6m SE of Shipston-on-Stour. For parking please use CV36 5PG. We have a large car park.* Sun 19 June (1.30-5). Combined adm £6, chd free. Home-made teas.

ASCOTT LODGE
Charlotte Copley.

ASCOTT RISE
Carol & Jerry Moore.

BELMONT HOUSE
Robert & Yoko Ward.

THE OLD RECTORY
Peter & Caroline O'Kane.

PLUM TREE COTTAGE
Janet Knight.

WHICHFORD HILL HOUSE
Mr & Mrs John Melvin.

THE WHICHFORD POTTERY
Jim & Dominique Keeling,
www.whichfordpottery.com.

The gardens in this group reflect many different styles. The two villages are in an AONB, nestled within a dramatic landscape of hills, pasture and woodland, which is used to picturesque effect by the garden owners. Fine lawns, mature shrub planting and much interest to plantsmen provide a peaceful visit to a series of beautiful gardens. Many incorporate the inventive use of natural springs, forming ponds, pools and other water features. Classic cottage gardens contrast with larger and more classical gardens which adopt variations on the traditional English garden of herbaceous borders, climbing roses, yew hedges and walled enclosures. Partial wheelchair access as some gardens are on sloping sites.

More than 1,200 people have been cared for at Y Bwthyn NGS Macmillan Specialist Palliative Care Unit, a unit that would simply not have been built without the National Garden Scheme funding

WILTSHIRE

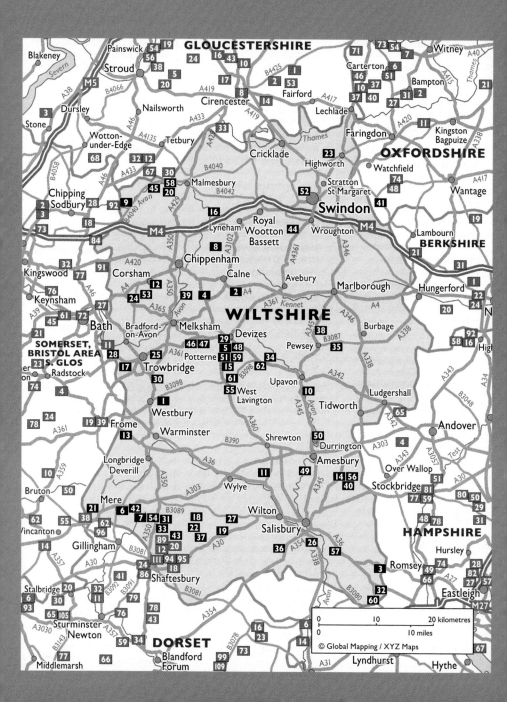

GLOUCESTERSHIRE

Blakeney
Painswick 54 19
56
Stroud 38
5
20
24
16 43
10
17
B4425 1
2 53
Fairford
8
14
A419
Cirencester
71
Carterton 6
46
10 37
37 40
73 54
7
51
37
Witney
Bampton
21

A38
M5
B4066
Nailsworth
A433
A419
A417
Lechlade
27
31 2

Dursley
3
Stone
Wotton-
under-Edge
68
32 12
67 30
45 58
20
92 9
33
Tetbury
B4040
Malmesbury
B4042
Cricklade
Highworth
23
Watchfield
74
48
Faringdon
A420
11
Kingston
Bagpuize
OXFORDSHIRE
Wantage
A417

Chipping
Sodbury
2
3
28
73
18
84
A4058
A46
A433
A4135
B4040 Avon
A419
A350
M4
16
Lyneham
A3102
8
Royal
Wootton
Bassett
52
44
Swindon
Wroughton
A436
A346
M4
41
Lambourn
21
BERKSHIRE
19

Kingswood
76
Keynsham
A39
45
A46
21
SOMERSET,
BRISTOL AREA
S. GLOS
23
Radstock
74
4
32
77
61 72
91
27
Corsham
A4
12
24 53
A365
Avon
Bradford-
on-Avon
11
28
25
A361
Melksham
39 4
2 A4
Avebury
A361 Kennet
WILTSHIRE
Devizes
46 47
29
5 48
51 59
15
61
55 West
Lavington
38
Pewsey
35
B3087
A342
Upavon
10
Marlborough
A4
A346
Burbage
A338
58 92
16
Hungerford
22
20
24
Hig
31
1
N

Trowbridge
30
Potterne
34
62
I
Westbury
Warminster
13
B3098
Frome
19 39
78 24
A361
10
A359
Bruton
62
55
50
21
38
96
42
6
7 54 31
33
89 43
111 94 95
86
Shaftesbury
B3089
18
22
37
20
12
27
19
A30
Wylye
Shrewton
B390
A36
A303
Mere
Gillingham
B3081
Wilton
Salisbury
36 A354 26
57
50
Durrington
49
Amesbury
14 56
40
11
Ludgershall
65
A342
Tidworth
A345
A343
B3048
Andover
Over Wallop
51
A30
Stockbridge
81
77 59
80 50
29
48 78
31
HAMPSHIRE
Hursley
Romsey
3
74
49
66
28
82
27 57
Eastleigh

Stalbridge
20
6
93
65 105
Sturminster
Newton
32
11
B3092
B3091
79
76
41
24
78
43
A354
59 34
DORSET
Blandford
Forum
16
23
14
B3080
Avon
32
60
M27
Middlemarsh
77
66
99
109
B3078
73
A31
Lyndhurst
Hythe
67

0   10   20 kilometres
0   10 miles
© Global Mapping / XYZ Maps

Wiltshire, a predominantly rural county, covers 1,346 square miles and has a rich diversity of landscapes, including downland, wooded river valleys and Salisbury Plain.

Chalk lies under two-thirds of the county, with limestone to the north, which includes part of the Cotswold Areas of Outstanding Natural Beauty. The county's gardens reflect its rich history and wide variety of environments.

Gardens opening for the National Garden Scheme include the grade II listed Edwardian style gardens of Hazelbury Manor and large privately owned gems such as Knoyle Place, Chisenbury Priory and Corsley House, together with more modest properties that are lovingly maintained by the owners, such as 41 Whistley Road in Potterne and 1 Southview in Devizes.

The season opens with snowdrops at Westcroft, daffodils at Fonthill House, fabulous tulips at Blackland House and magnolias in spring at, amongst others, Corsham Court and Oare House.

A wide selection of gardens, large and small, are at their peak in the summer. There are also three village openings which number a total of twenty gardens including a new group at Whaddon, near Salisbury. If you are from a gardening club there are in addition a wide range of gardens open by arrangement totalling twenty one in all. There is something to delight the senses from January to September and one will always have a warm welcome wherever one goes.

Below: Salthrop House

Volunteers

County Organiser
Amelia Tester 01672 520218
amelia.tester@ngs.org.uk

County Treasurer
Tony Roper 01249 447436
tony.roper@ngs.org.uk

Publicity
& Booklet Co-ordinator
Tricia Duncan 01672 810443
tricia.duncan@ngs.org.uk

Social Media
Maud Peters 07595 266299
maudahpeters@gmail.com

Assistant County Organisers
Sarah Coate 01722 782365
sarah.coate@ngs.org.uk

Annabel Dallas 01672 520266
annabel.dallas@btinternet.com

Andy Devey 01672 540078
andy.devey@ngs.org.uk

Ros Ford 01380 722778
ros.ford@ngs.org.uk

Donna Hambly 07760 889277
donna.hambly@ngs.org.uk

Jo Hankey 01722 742472
jo.hankey@ngs.org.uk

Alison Parker 01380 722228
alison.parker@ngs.org.uk

Sue Allen 07785 294153
sue.allen@ngs.org.uk

Alex Graham 07906 146337
alex.graham@ngs.org.uk

f @WiltshireNGS
🐦 @WiltshireNgs
📷 @Wiltshirengs

OPENING DATES

All entries subject to change. For latest information check www.ngs.org.uk

Map locator numbers are shown to the right of each garden name.

Extended openings are shown at the beginning of the month.

January

Every Thursday from Thursday 13th
Westcroft 56

Sunday 30th
Westcroft 56

February

Snowdrop Festival

Every Thursday
Westcroft 56

Sunday 6th
Westcroft 56

Sunday 20th
Westcroft 56

March

Thursday 3rd
Westcroft 56

Sunday 20th
◆ Corsham Court 12
Fonthill House 18

April

Sunday 3rd
◆ Corsham Court 12

Thursday 7th
Cadenham Manor 8

Friday 22nd
Blackland House 2

Saturday 23rd
◆ Iford Manor Gardens 28
The Parish House 42

Sunday 24th
Broadleas House Gardens 5
Cottage in the Trees 14
Foxley Manor 20
Oare House 38

Saturday 30th
Manor Farm House 34

May

Sunday 1st
Blackland House 2
Bush Farm 7
◆ Waterdale House 54

Saturday 7th
NEW Julia's House Children's Hospice 29

Sunday 8th
NEW Julia's House Children's Hospice 29
Lavender Gardens 32

Saturday 14th
Knoyle Place 31
Lower Lye 33

Sunday 15th
Cottage in the Trees 14
Lavender Gardens 32

Sunday 22nd
North Cottage 37
◆ Twigs Community Garden 52

Thursday 26th
Windmill Cottage 61

Friday 27th
Windmill Cottage 61

Sunday 29th
Tristenagh House 51

June

Wednesday 1st
Trantor House 50

Saturday 4th
Fovant House 19
NEW Whaddon Gardens 57

Sunday 5th
Cottage in the Trees 14
The Old Rectory, Boscombe 40
Trantor House 50

Thursday 9th
Cadenham Manor 8
NEW Court Hill House 15

Friday 10th
NEW Salthrop House 44

Saturday 11th
NEW The Old Vicarage 41
NEW Salthrop House 44
West Lavington Manor 55

Sunday 12th
Burton Grange 6
Chisenbury Priory 10
Gold Hill 22
Hannington Village Gardens 23
Hazelbury Manor Gardens 24
Hyde's House 27
Lavender Gardens 32

Tuesday 14th
Whatley Manor 58

Saturday 18th
Hilperton House 25

Sunday 19th
Broadleas House Gardens 5
Dauntsey Gardens 16
Hilperton House 25
North Cottage 37

Thursday 23rd
Windmill Cottage 61

Friday 24th
Windmill Cottage 61

Saturday 25th
NEW The Manor House 35

Sunday 26th
Duck Pond Barn 17
Oare House 38
1 Southview 48

July

Saturday 2nd
Seend House 46
Seend Manor 47
NEW Wadswick Green 53

Sunday 3rd
Teasel 49

Wednesday 6th
Manor House, Stratford Tony 36

Friday 15th
NEW The Old Mill 39

Saturday 16th
NEW The Old Mill 39
NEW Scots Farm 45

Sunday 17th
Cherry Orchard Barn 9
Horatio's Garden 26
The Parish House 42

The Rectory Boscombe

THE GARDENS

1 BEGGARS KNOLL CHINESE GARDEN

Newtown, Westbury, BA13 3ED. Colin Little & Penny Stirling, 01373 823383, silkendalliance@talktalk.net. *1m SE of Westbury. Turn off B3098 at White Horse Pottery, up hill towards the White Horse for ³/₄ m. Parking at end of drive for 10-12 cars.* Visits by arrangement June & July for groups of up to 20. Adm £6, chd free. Tea & cake on request.
New for this year, a tranquil Islamic-style tiled garden influenced by NW China. Remaining garden rooms are Chinese-style, separated by elaborate gateways inc moongate, with mosaic paths winding past pavilions, ponds and many rare Chinese trees, shrubs and flowers. Potager full of flowers and vegetables with chickens. Spectacular views to the Mendips. Map and garden tours by owners inc in ticket. The garden features a 21 yr old specimen of *Toona sinensis* - the 2022 Tree of the Year for the Dendrological Society.

 ❁ 💮

2 BLACKLAND HOUSE

Quemerford, Calne, SN11 8UQ. Polly & Edward Nicholson, www.bayntunflowers.co.uk. *Situated just off A4. Use Google Maps. Enter the grounds through the side entrance signed St. Peter's Church & Blackland Park Deliveries. Opp The Willows on Quemerford.* Fri 22 Apr, Sun 1 May (2.30-4). Adm £10,

chd free. Pre-booking essential, please visit www.ngs.org.uk for information & booking. Home-made teas. Vegan & gluten free cakes. Donation to Dorothy House Hospice.
A wonderfully varied 5 acre garden adjacent to River Marden (house not open). Formal walled productive and cutting garden, traditional glasshouses, rose garden and wide herbaceous borders. Interesting topiary, trained fruit trees, historic tulips and other unusual spring bulbs. Hand-tied bunches of flowers for sale. Partial wheelchair access, steps, grass and cobbles, wooden bridges.

♿ ❁ NPC 💮))

3 BLUEBELLS

Cowesfield, Whiteparish, Salisbury, SP5 2RB. Hilary Mathison, hilary.mathison@icloud.com. *SW of Salisbury. On main A27 road from Salisbury to Romsey. 1¹/₂ SW of Whiteparish, 100-200 metres inside Wiltshire county boundary.* Visits by arrangement Apr to Sept for groups of 5 to 30. Adm £4, chd free. Home-made teas. Wine & savoury bites for evening visits.
Relatively new garden on 1¹/₂ acre plot, with original deciduous woodland inc bluebells in season. Adjoining new-build contemporary house, so rear courtyard reflects this. Other areas inc shady border, winter garden, vegetable and fruit plot, formal and wildlife ponds. Large lawn surrounded by differently styled borders and large feature bed planted with white birch and cornus.

 ❁ 💮

4 ◆ BOWOOD WOODLAND GARDENS

Calne, SN11 9PG. The Marquis of Lansdowne, 01249 812102, houseandgardens@bowood.org, www.bowood.org. *3¹/₂ m SE of Chippenham. Located off J17 M4 nr Bath & Chippenham. Entrance off A342 between Sandy Lane & Derry Hill Villages. Follow brown tourist signs. For SatNav, please use SN11 9PG.* For opening times and information, please phone, email or visit garden website.
This 30 acre woodland garden of azaleas, magnolias, rhododendrons and bluebells is one of the most exciting of its type in the country. From the individual flowers to the breathtaking sweep of colour, this is a garden not to be missed. With two miles of meandering paths, you will find hidden treasures at every corner. The Woodland Gardens are 2m from Bowood House and Garden. Please visit www.ngs.org.uk for details of pop-up openings.

> 'The National Garden Scheme donated £500,000 to Hospice UK in 2021, enabling us to continue supporting over 200 hospices in the UK who have been at the forefront of the battle against COVID-19'
> Hospice UK

5 BROADLEAS HOUSE GARDENS

Devizes, SN10 5JQ. Mr & Mrs Cardiff. *1m S of Devizes. Turn L from Hartmoor Rd onto Broadleas Park. Follow the road until you reach grassed area on R with red brick wall, stone pillars, grey gates & cattle grid, which is the entrance.* Sun 24 Apr, Sun 19 June, Sun 21 Aug (2-5.30). Adm £7, chd free. Home-made teas.

6 acre garden of hedges, perennial borders, walled rose garden, secret garden, bee garden and orchard stuffed with good plants. Well-stocked kitchen and herb garden. Mature collection of specimen trees inc oaks, magnolia, handkerchief, redwood, dogwood. Overlooked by the house and arranged above the valley garden crowded with magnolias, camellias, rhododendrons, azaleas, cornus, hydrangeas etc. Broadleas' professional beekeeper, Graham Davison, sells honey at open days. Wheelchair access to upper garden only, some gravel and narrow grass paths.

6 BURTON GRANGE

Burton, Mere, BA12 6BR. Sue Phipps & Paddy Sumner, www.suephipps.com. *Take lane, signposted to Burton, on A303 just E of Mere bypass. After 400 yds follow rd past pond and round to L. Go past wall on R. Burton Grange entrance is in laurel hedge on R.* Sun 12 June (11-5). Adm £4, chd free. Home-made teas.

1½ acre garden, created from scratch since 2014. Lawns, borders, large ornamental pond, some gravel planting, vegetable garden and pergola rose garden, together with a number of wonderful mature trees. Artist's studio open.

7 BUSH FARM

West Knoyle, Mere, BA12 6AE. Lord & Lady Seaford, www.bisonfarm.co.uk. *From A303 turn off at Esso petrol station (Willoughby Hedge) follow L hand lane to West Knoyle (signed Bush Farm) through to end of village. Entrance on bend through woods to Bush Farm.* Sun 1 May (11-5). Adm £6, chd free. Light refreshments. Bison burgers.

Mature oak woodland glades jungliefied with climbing roses, clematis, honeysuckle and specimen trees. Bog garden with ferns, skunk cabbage and iris. Nearby lakeside walk with farm trail to see the bison and elk. Wildflowers everywhere. Bluebells in May. Flat woodland walks - not paved.

8 CADENHAM MANOR

Foxham, Chippenham, SN15 4NH. Victoria & Martin Nye, garden@cadenham.com, www.cadenham.com. *B4069 from Chippenham or M4 J17, turn R in Christian Malford & L in Foxham. On A3102 turn L from Calne or R from Lyneham at Xrds between Hilmarton & Goatacre. See map https://www.cadenham.com/contact.* Thur 7 Apr, Thur 9 June (2-5). Adm £10, chd free. Pre-booking essential, please email www.ngs.org. uk for information & booking. Home-made teas. Visits also by arrangement Mar to Oct for groups of 15 to 40.

This glorious 4 acre garden surrounds a listed C17 manor house and C16 dovecote. Divided by yew hedges and moats, its many rooms are furnished with specimen trees and fountains and statues to focus the eye. Known for its stunning displays of old roses, it also has bold swathes of spring bulbs, wisteria, bearded iris, a water garden in the old canal, plus extensive vegetable and herb gardens.

9 CHERRY ORCHARD BARN

Luckington, SN14 6NZ. Paul Fletcher & Tim Guard. *Cherry Orchard Barn is ¾ m before the centre of SN14 6NZ, at a T junction. Passing the Barn is ill-advised, as turning rapidly becomes difficult.* Sun 17 July (1-5). Adm £5, chd free. Home-made teas.

Charming 1 acre garden created over past 8 yrs from the corner of a field, with open views of surrounding countryside. Containing 7 rooms, 3 of which are densely planted with herbaceous perennials, each with individual identities and colour themes. The garden is described by visitors as a haven of tranquillity. Largely level access to all areas of garden. Some gravel paths.

10 CHISENBURY PRIORY

East Chisenbury, SN9 6AQ. Mr & Mrs John Manser. *3m SW of Pewsey. Turn E from A345 at Enford then N to E Chisenbury, main gates 1m on R.* Sun 12 June (2-5.30). Adm £5, chd free. Home-made teas.

Medieval Priory with Queen Anne face and early C17 rear (not open) in middle of 5 acre garden on chalk. Mature garden with fine trees within clump and flint walls, herbaceous borders, shrubs, roses. Moisture loving plants along mill leat, carp pond, orchard and wild garden, many unusual plants.

11 COCKSPUR THORNS

Berwick St James, Salisbury, SP3 4TS. Stephen & Ailsa Bush, 01722 790445, stephenjdbush@gmail.com. *8m NW of Salisbury. 1m S of A303, on B3083 at S end of village of Berwick St James.* Visits by arrangement May to July for groups of 5 to 20. Adm £5, chd free. Home-made teas.

2¼ acre garden, completely redesigned 22 yrs ago and developments since, featuring roses (particularly colourful in June), herbaceous border, shrubbery, small walled kitchen garden, secret pond garden, mature and new unusual small trees, fruit trees and areas of wildflowers. Beech, yew and thuja hedgings planted to divide the garden. Small number of vines planted during early 2016.

12 ♦ CORSHAM COURT

Corsham, SN13 0BZ. Lord Methuen, 01249 701610, staterooms@corsham-court.co.uk, www.corsham-court.co.uk. *4m W of Chippenham. Signed off A4 at Corsham.* For NGS: Sun 20 Mar, Sun 3 Apr (2-5.30). Adm £10, chd £5. For other opening times and information, please phone, email or visit garden website.

Park and gardens laid out by Capability Brown and Repton. Large lawns with fine specimens of ornamental trees surround the Elizabethan mansion. C18 bath house hidden in the grounds. Spring bulbs, beautiful lily pond with Indian bean trees, young arboretum and stunning collection of magnolias. Wheelchair (not motorised) access to house, gravel paths in garden.

13 NEW CORSLEY HOUSE

Corsley, Warminster, BA12 7QH. Glen Senk & Keith Johnson. *From Longleat on the A362 turning 1st R on Deep Lane, Corsley House is ¼ m on R. The parkland entrance, where there is parking, is on R beyond the house.* Sun 7 Aug (11-5). Adm £10, chd free. Tea, coffee and home-made cakes.

A garden full of surprises to reflect the eclectic nature of a Georgian home with a secret Jacobean facade. A unique sculpted wave lawn and a truly exceptional walled garden. Many well preserved ancient outbuildings such as a potting and apple storage shed and a granary built on staddle stones. All gloriously overlooking the NT's Cley Hill.

   ♿ 🐄 ✿ 💷

14 COTTAGE IN THE TREES

Tidworth Rd, Boscombe Village, nr Salisbury, SP4 0AD. Karen Robertson, 01980 610921, robertson909@btinternet.com. *7m N of Salisbury. Turn L off A338 just before Social Club. Continue past church, turn R after bridge to Queen Manor, cottage 150yds on R.* Sun 24 Apr, Sun 15 May, Sun 5 June (1.30-5). Adm £4, chd free. Home-made teas. Open nearby The Old Rectory, Boscombe on 5

June. Visits also by arrangement Apr to Sept.

Enchanting ½ acre cottage garden, immaculately planted with water feature, raised vegetable beds, small wildlife pond and gravel garden. Spring bulbs, hellebores and pulmonarias give a welcome start to the season, with pots and baskets, roses and clematis. Mixed borders of herbaceous plants, collection of geraniums, dahlias, grasses and shrubs giving year-round interest. Large variety of cottage plants for sale, grown from the garden.

🐄 ✿ 🚗 💷

15 NEW COURT HILL HOUSE

Court Hill, Potterne, Devizes, SN10 5PN. Janey Ewart. *Potterne is 2m S of Devizes. At George & Dragon Pub, turn up Court Hill. Garden is 250 yds on the R hand side of the 1st L hand bend.* Thur 9 June (1.30-5.30). Adm £8, chd free.

Well-stocked mature garden with mixed borders, shrubberies, mature trees, a rose garden, topiary and vegetable garden. Greenhouse with a colourful display of pelargoniums and tender plants. Good views of the local countryside. Not very suitable for prams or wheelchairs, due to gravel and grass paths.

•))

National Garden Scheme funding helped support the provision of horticultural-related assistance to soldiers, veterans and their immediate families, providing education, training and employment opportunities along with supporting the recovery, health and wellbeing of individuals' ABF The Soldiers' Charity

Gasper Cottage

GROUP OPENING

16 DAUNTSEY GARDENS
Church Lane, Dauntsey, Malmesbury, SN15 4HT. *5m SE of Malmesbury. Approach via Dauntsey Rd from Gt Somerford, 1¼m from Volunteer Inn Great Somerford.* **Sun 19 June (1-5). Combined adm £7.50, chd free. Home-made teas at Idover House.**

THE COACH HOUSE
Col & Mrs J Seddon-Brown.

DAUNTSEY PARK
Mr & Mrs Giovanni Amati, 01249 721777, enquiries@dauntseyparkhouse.co.uk.

THE GARDEN COTTAGE
Miss Ann Sturgis.

IDOVER HOUSE
Mr & Mrs Christopher Jerram.

THE OLD COACH HOUSE
Tony & Janette Yates.

THE OLD POND HOUSE
Mr & Mrs Stephen Love.

This group of 6 gardens, centred around the historic Dauntsey Park Estate, ranges from the Classical C18 country house setting of Dauntsey Park, with spacious lawns, old trees and views over the River Avon, to mature country house gardens and traditional walled gardens. Enjoy the formal rose garden in pink and white, old fashioned borders and duck ponds at Idover House, and the quiet seclusion of The Coach House with its thyme terrace and gazebos, climbing roses and clematis. Here, mop-headed pruned *Crataegus prunifolia* line the drive. The Garden Cottage has a traditional walled kitchen garden with organic vegetables, apple orchard, woodland walk and yew topiary. Meanwhile the 2 acres at The Old Pond House are both clipped and unclipped! Large pond with lilies and fat carp, and look out for the giraffe and turtle. The Old Coach House is a small garden with perennial plants, shrubs and climbers.

17 DUCK POND BARN
Church Lane, Wingfield, Trowbridge, BA14 9LW. Janet & Marc Berlin, 01225 777764, janet@berlinfamily.co.uk. *On B3109 from Frome to Bradford on Avon, turn opp Poplars pub into Church Ln. Duck Pond Barn is at end of lane. Big field for parking.* **Sun 26 June, Sun 7 Aug (10-5). Adm £5, chd free. Visits also by arrangement June to Aug.**
Garden of 1.6 acres with large duck pond, lawns, ericaceous beds, orchard, vegetable garden, big greenhouse, spinney and wild area of grass and trees with many wildflowers. Large dry stone wall topped with flowerbeds with rose arbour. 3 ponds linked by a rill in flower garden and large pergola in orchard. Set in farmland and mainly flat. In August there is an opportunity to see many interesting and rare succulents, eucomis lilies and agapanthus in flower.

18 FONTHILL HOUSE
Tisbury, SP3 5SA. The Lord Margadale of Islay, www.fonthill.co.uk/gardens. *13m W of Salisbury. Via B3089 in Fonthill Bishop. 3m N of Tisbury.* **Sun 20 Mar (12-5). Adm £7, chd free. Sandwiches, quiches & cakes, soft drinks, tea & coffee. Bottled beer & wine.**
Wonderful woodland walks with daffodils, rhododendrons, azaleas, shrubs, bulbs. Magnificent views, formal gardens. The gardens have been extensively redeveloped under the direction of Tania Compton and Marie-Louise Agius. The formal gardens are being continuously improved with new designs, exciting trees, shrubs and plants. Gorgeous William Pye fountain and other sculptures. Partial wheelchair access.

19 FOVANT HOUSE
Church Lane, Fovant, Salisbury, SP3 5LA. Amanda & Noel Flint. *Fovant House is located approx. 6½m W of Wilton and 9.3m E of Shaftesbury. Take A30 to Fovant then head N through village and follow signs to St Georges Church.* **Sat 4 June (2-5). Adm £7, chd free. Home-made teas.**
Fovant House is a former Rectory set in about 3 acres of formal garden (house not open). In 2016 the garden was redesigned by Arabella Lennox

Boyd. Garden inc 60m herbaceous border, terraces and parterre. A range of mature trees inc cedars, copper beech and ash. Majority of garden has easy wheelchair access subject to ground conditions being dry.

20 FOXLEY MANOR
Foxley, Malmesbury, SN16 0JJ. Richard & Louisa Turnor. *2m W of Malmesbury. 10 mins from J17 on M4. Turn towards Malmesbury/ Cirencester, then towards Norton and follow signs for the Vine Tree, yellow signs from here.* **Sun 24 Apr (12-4). Adm £7, chd free. Home-made teas.**
Yew hedges divide lawns, borders, rose garden, lily pond and a newer wild area with a natural swimming pond shaded by a liriodendron. Views through large Turkey oaks to farmland beyond. Small courtyard and gravel garden. Sculptures are sited throughout the gardens.

21 GASPER COTTAGE
Gasper Street, Gasper Stourton, Warminster, BA12 6PY. Bella Hoare & Johnnie Gallop, bella.hoare@icloud.com, www.youtube.com/channel/UCgar2Akygp4j3dWNGMI6i0A. *Near Stourhead Gardens, 4m from Mere, off A303. Turn off A303 at B3092 Mere. Follow Stourhead signs. Go through Stourton. After 1m, turn R after phone box, signed Gasper. House 2nd on R going up hill. Parking past house on L, in field.* **Sun 21 Aug (11-5). Adm £5, chd free. Visits also by arrangement May to Sept for groups of 10 to 20.**
1½ acre garden, with views to glorious countryside. Luxurious planting of dahlias, grasses, asters, cardoons and more, inc new perennial planting combinations. Orchard with wildlife pond. Artist studio surrounded by colour balanced planting and formal pond. Pergola with herb terrace. Several seating areas. Garden model railway.

22 GOLD HILL
Hindon Lane, Tisbury, Salisbury, SP3 6PZ. Anne Ralphs. *On Hindon Lane, 500 yds up on R from top of Tisbury High St. From Hindon, on L 500yds after road narrows. Parking down the lane in field beside the garden.* **Sun 12 June (2-5). Adm £6, chd free. Tea and cake will be available in the sunken garden.**

Overlooking the Fonthill Brook the house and garden, which were designed together and are Arts & Crafts inspired, were created on a 1.2 acre derelict builder's yard and field between 2015 and 2017. Formal garden with mixed shrub and perennial planting give interest throughout the year. Sunken garden, rose garden, fruit trees, white walled garden with pond, fountain and parterre beds.

GROUP OPENING

23 HANNINGTON VILLAGE GARDENS
Hannington, Swindon, SN6 7RP. *Off B4019 Blunsdon to Highworth Rd by the Freke Arms. Park behind Jolly Tar pub, in the street where possible, or opp Lushill House.* **Sun 12 June (11-5.30). Combined adm £8, chd free. Home-made teas in Hannington Village Hall.**

CHESTNUT HOUSE
Mary & Garry Marshall.

CHESTNUT VILLA
David Cornish.

HANNINGTON HALL
Guillaume Molhant-Proost.

LOWER FARM
Mr Piers & Mrs Jenny Martin.

LUSHILL HOUSE
John & Sasha Kennedy.

QUARRY BANK
Paul Minter & Michael Weldon.

22 QUEENS ROAD
Jan & Pete Willis.

ROSE COTTAGE
Mrs Ruth Scholes.

THE BUTLER'S COTTAGE
Mr John & Mrs Karen Mayell.

YORKE HOUSE GARDEN
Mr Miles & Mrs Cath Bozeat.

Hannington has a dramatic hilltop position on a Cotswold ridge overlooking the Thames Valley. A great variety of gardens, from large manor houses to small cottage gardens, many of which follow the brow of the hill and afford stunning views of the surrounding farmland. You will need lots of time to see all that is on offer in this beautiful historic village.

24 HAZELBURY MANOR GARDENS
Wadswick, Box, Corsham, SN13 8HX. Mr L Lacroix, 01225 812952, phylip@mac.com. *5m SW of Chippenham, 5m NE of Bath. From A4 at Box, A365 to Melksham, at Five Ways junction L onto B3109 towards Corsham; 1st L in ¼ m, drive immed on R.* **Sun 12 June (11-5); Wed 14 Sept (10-4); Sun 18 Sept (11-4.30). Adm £7.50, chd free. Home-made teas. Visits also by arrangement May to Sept for groups of 10 to 50.**
The C15 Manor house comes into view as you descend along the drive and into the Grade II landscaped Edwardian gardens. The extensive plantings that surround the house are undergoing considerable redevelopment by the owners and their head gardener. A wide range of organic horticulture is practiced in 8 acres of relaxed gardens.

25 HILPERTON HOUSE
The Knap, Hilperton, Trowbridge, BA14 7RJ. Chris & Ros Brown. *1½ m NE of Trowbridge. Follow A361 towards Trowbridge and turn R at r'about signed Hilperton. House is next door to St Michael's Church in The Knap off Church St.* **Sat 18, Sun 19 June (2-6). Adm £5, chd free. Home-made teas.**
2½ acres well-stocked borders, small stream leading to large pond with fish, ducks, water lilies, waterfall and fountain. Fine mature trees inc unusual specimens. Walled fruit and vegetable garden, small woodland area. Rose walk with roses and clematis. Interesting wood carvings, mainly teak. 170yr old vine in conservatory of Grade II listed house, circa 1705 (not open). Activity sheets for children. Some gravel and lawns. Conservatory not wheelchair accessible. Path from front gate has uneven paving but can be bypassed on lawn.

26 HORATIO'S GARDEN
Duke of Cornwall Spinal Treatment Centre, Salisbury Hospital NHS Foundation Trust, Odstock Road, Salisbury, SP2 8BJ. Horatio's Garden Charity, www.horatiosgarden.org.uk. *1m from centre of Salisbury. Follow signs for Salisbury District Hospital. Please park in car park 10, which will be free to NGS visitors on the day.* **Sun 17 July (2-5). Adm £5, chd free. Tea and delicious cakes - made by Horatio's Garden volunteers - will be served in the Garden Room.**
Award winning hospital garden, opened in Sept 2012 and designed by Cleve West for patients with spinal cord injury at the Duke of Cornwall Spinal Treatment Centre. Built from donations given in memory of Horatio Chapple who was a volunteer at the centre in his school holidays. Low limestone walls, which represent the form of the spine, divide densely planted herbaceous beds. Everything in the garden designed to benefit patients during their long stays in hospital. Garden is run by a Head Gardener and team of volunteers. SW Regional Winner, The English Garden's The Nation's Favourite Gardens 2019. Designer Cleve West has 8 RHS gold medals. At 3pm there will be a short talk from the Head Gardener about therapeutic gardens and the work of Horatio's Garden.

27 HYDE'S HOUSE
Dinton, SP3 5HH. Mr George Cruddas. *9m W of Salisbury. Off B3089 nr Dinton Church on St Mary's Rd.* **Sun 12 June (2-5). Adm £7, chd free. Home-made teas at Thatched Old School Room with outside tea tables.**
3 acres of wild and formal garden in beautiful situation with series of hedged garden rooms. Numerous shrubs, flowers and borders, all allowing tolerated wildflowers and preferred weeds, while others creep in. Large walled kitchen garden, herb garden and C13 dovecote (open). Charming C16/18 Grade I listed house (not open), with lovely courtyard. Every year varies. Free walks around park and lake. Steps, slopes, gravel paths and driveway.

'In 2021 the generous donation from the National Garden Scheme helped 12,000 unpaid carers to access the support they need, with 50 more receiving crisis grants to support those in dire need'
Carers Trust

28 ◆ IFORD MANOR GARDENS

Bradford-on-Avon, BA15 2BA.
Mr Cartwright-Hignett,
01225 863146,
info@ifordmanor.co.uk,
www.ifordmanor.co.uk. *7m S of
Bath. Off A36, brown tourist sign to
Iford 1m. From Bradford-on-Avon
or Trowbridge via Lower Westwood
Village (brown signs). Please note
all approaches via narrow, single
track lanes with passing places.*
For NGS: Sat 23 Apr (11-4). Adm
£7.50. Pre-booking essential,
please phone 01225 863146,
email info@ifordmanor.co.uk
or visit http://www.ifordmanor.
co.uk for information & booking.
Children under 10 will not be
admitted to the garden. For other
opening times and information,
please phone, email or visit garden
website.
Harold Peto's former home, this
2½ acre terraced garden provides
timeless inspiration. Influenced by his
travels, particularly to Italy and Japan,
Peto embellished the garden with a
collection of classical statuary and
architectural fragments. Steep steps
link the terraces with pools, fountains,
loggias, colonnades, urns and figures,
with magnificent rural views across
the Iford Valley. Lunches, cream teas
and cakes all served with a selection
of hot and cold drinks in the on site
cafe. Wine also available.

🐾 ✸ ☕ ☕

29 NEW JULIA'S HOUSE CHILDREN'S HOSPICE

Bath Road, Devizes, SN10 2AT.
Nicky Clack. *Situated just off
A361 Bath Road in Devizes. Please
note there is no parking available
at hospice. Pls use nearby Station
Rd car park. For SatNav use SN10
1BZ.* Sat 7, Sun 8 May (10.30-
3.30). Adm £4, chd free. Light
refreshments.
Julia's House Children's Hospice
provides respite care for children with
life-threatening or limiting conditions.
Our garden has been designed so
the children can experience and
enjoy different sensory elements
and is cared for by our volunteer
gardeners. Explore how our children
use the garden. Hospice tours may
be available.

🚻 ✸ ☕ •))

30 KETTLE FARM COTTAGE

Kettle Lane, West Ashton,
Trowbridge, BA14 6AW. Tim &
Jenny Woodall, 01225 753474,
trwwoodall@outlook.com. *Kettle
Lane is halfway between West
Ashton T-lights and Yarnbrook
r'about on S side of A350. Garden
½m down end of lane.* Visits by
arrangement June to Sept for
groups of up to 20. Limited car
parking. Adm free. chd free.
Home-made teas.
Previously of Priory House, Bradford
on Avon, the garden of which was on
Gardeners' World, September 2017,
we have now created a new cottage
garden, full of colour and style,
flowering from June to Oct. Bring a
loved one/friend to see the garden.
One or two steps.

🚻 🐕 ✸ ☕ ☕

31 KNOYLE PLACE

Holloway, East Knoyle, Salisbury,
SP3 6AF. Lizzie & Herve de la
Moriniere. *Turn off A350 into East
Knoyle and follow signs to parking
at Lower Lye. Walk 5 mins to Knoyle
Place through village following signs.*
Sat 14 May (2-5). Adm £10, chd
free. Home-made teas. Open
nearby Lower Lye.
Very beautiful and elegant garden
created over 60 years by previous
and current owners. Above the
house there are several acres of
mature rhododendron and magnolia
woodland planting. Among the many
different areas in this 9 acre garden
is a box parterre, rose garden,
vegetable garden and, around the
house, a recently planted formal
garden designed by Dan Combes.
Sloping lawns and woodland paths,
stone terrace.

🚻 ☕ •))

32 LAVENDER GARDENS

Giles Lane, Landford, Salisbury,
SP5 2BG. Mr Michael Hayward,
www.newforestlavender.com.
*11m from Southampton, 11m
from Salisbury on A36. Village
landmark on A36 Royal Jaipur Indian
restaurant approx 1m turn L. From
Southampton landmark The Shoe Inn
approx 1m turn R.* Sun 8, Sun 15
May, Sun 12 June (10-3.30). Adm
£6, chd £2. Light refreshments.
Take time to wander through colourful
borders. Be intrigued by plants you
may not have seen before. Step
back and admire a stunning colourful
display of annual and perennial plants.
Find areas en masse and specimens
in mixed borders. Stroll around
themed gardens, dahlia borders, a
white garden along with colourful
grasses. Spring bulbs and lily pond. A
selection of different trees and shrubs.
Wheelchair access from car park to
garden and plant sales area. Gravel
pathway runs through the garden.
Disabled WC.

🚻 🐾 ✸ ☕ ☕ 🗻 •))

33 LOWER LYE

Holloway, East Knoyle, Salisbury,
SP3 6AQ. Belinda & Andrew
Scott. *From A350 exit at East
Knoyle. Lower Lye is at upper
southern end of village, follow signs
to house. Parking on L entrance
field.* Sat 14 May (2-5). Adm £10,
chd free. Pre-booking essential,
please visit www.ngs.org.uk for
information & booking. Open
nearby Knoyle Place.
The gardens at Lower Lye are
exceptional and were completely
reconfigured by the Landscape
architect Michael Balston 24 yrs ago.
An extremely large garden, approx 9
acres placed on the brow of the hill
with wonderful views across the valley
and the magnificent King Alfred's
Tower in the distance. More recently
the gardens have been worked on by
garden designers Tania Compton and
Jane Hurst, both extremely well known
garden designers, they have given
improved structure through replanting
of the various borders. The gardens
have been developed in a simplistic
and modern style, which gives a sense
of elegance whilst respecting the
natural habitat There are numerous
modern sculptures and water features
placed throughout the garden which
are spectacular and provide a number
of individual focal points. The gardens
include herbaceous borders, mature
trees, a meadow area and a vegetable
and cutting garden. Coffee/tea and
light refreshments will be served at the
beautiful gardens just along the road at
Knoyle Place, which will also be open
throughout the afternoon. Some steps
and slopes.

🚻

34 MANOR FARM HOUSE

Manor Farm Lane, Patney,
Devizes, SN10 3RB. Mark & Tricia
Alsop. *Between Pewsey & Devizes.
Take 3rd entrance on L going up
Manor Farm Lane from village green.
Parking available in paddock.* Sat
30 Apr (2-5). Adm £6, chd free.
Home-made teas.
2 acre plantsman's garden designed
by Michael Balston and updated
by us over the past 10 yrs. Lawned
areas with borders surrounded
by yew hedging, long border and

gravel garden by tennis court, formal vegetable garden with buxus parterres and meadow with spring bulbs, box mound and walkway through moist plants garden. Limited wheelchair access due to upward slope and gravel paths. No WC.

35 NEW THE MANOR HOUSE
The Street, Milton Lilbourne, Pewsey, SN9 5LQ. Esther & Jamie Cayzer-Colvin. *3 m E of Pewsey. Turn into the village from the main road. The Manor House is on the R after passing the village hall. Parking in field opp.* **Sat 25 June (11-4). Adm £10, chd free. Pre-booking essential, please visit www.ngs. org.uk for information & booking. Home-made teas.**
When the current owners bought the house, it required a fairly lengthy period of restoration. In 2009 the owners began restoring and developing the gardens to create interest with a series of 'rooms' and interconnecting views, varying in colour scheme and seasonal interest. Charming walled vegetable garden, pleached lime allées, topiary, roses and a spectacular fountain.

36 MANOR HOUSE, STRATFORD TONY
Stratford Tony, Salisbury, SP5 4AT. Mr & Mrs Hugh Cookson, 01722 718496, lucindacookson@ stratfordtony.co.uk, www.stratfordtony.co.uk. *4m SW of Salisbury. Take minor road W off A354 at Coombe Bissett. Garden on S after 1m. Or take minor road off A3094 from Wilton signed Stratford Tony & racecourse.* **Wed 6 July (2-5). Adm £6, chd free. Visitors are welcome to bring a picnic. Visits also by arrangement May to Sept.**
Varied 4 acre garden with year-round interest. Formal and informal areas. Herbaceous borders, vegetable garden, parterre garden, orchard, shrubberies, roses, specimen trees, lakeside planting, winter colour and structure, many original contemporary features and places to sit and enjoy the downland views. Some gravel.

37 NORTH COTTAGE
Tisbury Row, Tisbury, SP3 6RZ. Jacqueline & Robert Baker, 01747 870019, baker_jaci@yahoo.co.uk. *12m W of* Salisbury. From A30 turn N through Ansty, L at T-junction, towards Tisbury. From Tisbury take Ansty road. Car park entrance nr junction signed Tisbury Row.* **Sun 22 May, Sun 19 June (11.30-5). Adm £5, chd free. Home-made teas.**
Leave car park, walk past vegetables and through the paddock to reach house and gardens. Although modest, there is much variety to find. Garden is divided with lots to explore as each part differs in style and feel, augmented with pottery and woodwork handmade by the owners. From the intimacy of the garden go out to see the orchard, ponds, walk the coppice wood and see the rest of the smallholding. As well as the owners' handiwork for sale, there are exciting metalwork sculptures too. Please see website for extra pop-up open days.

38 OARE HOUSE
Rudge Lane, Oare, nr Pewsey, SN8 4JQ. Sir Henry Keswick. *2m N of Pewsey. On Marlborough Rd (A345).* **Sun 24 Apr, Sun 26 June (1.30-6). Adm £8, chd free. Home-made teas in potting shed. Donation to The Order of St John.**
1740s mansion house later extended by Clough Williams Ellis in 1920s (not open). The original formal gardens around the house have been developed over the years to create a wonderful garden full of many unusual plants. Current owner is very passionate and has developed a fine collection of rarities. Garden is undergoing a renaissance but still maintains split compartments each with its own individual charm; traditional walled garden with fine herbaceous borders, vegetable areas, trained fruit, roses and grand mixed borders surrounding formal lawns. The magnolia garden is wonderful in spring with some trees dating from 1920s, together with strong bulb plantings. Large arboretum and woodland with many unusual and champion trees. In spring and summer there is always something of interest, with the glorious Pewsey Vale as a backdrop. Partial wheelchair access.

39 NEW THE OLD MILL
Reybridge, Lacock, Chippenham, SN15 2PF. Trudy Clayton. *Limited parking in nearby field. Alternatively park in the Lacock car park & walk into Reybridge which will take about 20mins. Once there, follow the NGS signs.* **Fri 15, Sat 16 July (10-7). Adm £5, chd free. Home made savouries, home baked cakes & cream teas. Ice creams. Hot & cold drinks.**
The Old Mill dates back to Doomsday and is surrounded by the River Avon. It lies in a very tranquil, picturesque setting, in the heart of beautiful Wiltshire countryside in the hamlet of Reybridge, which is within the parish of the NT village of Lacock. There are lots of areas to wander or to sit and relax, taking in and enjoying the wildlife all around you.

The Old Mill

40 THE OLD RECTORY, BOSCOMBE

Tidworth Road, Boscombe, Salisbury, SP4 0AB. Helen & Peter Sheridan. *7m N of Salisbury on A338. From Salisbury, 2nd L turning after Earl of Normanton pub, just S of Boscombe Social Club & Black Barn.* **Sun 5 June (1.30-5). Adm £4, chd free. Home-made teas. Open nearby Cottage in the Trees.**
The elegant gardens of this period property feature a traditional walled garden with herbaceous borders and vegetable beds, contrasting with a parkland of sweeping lawns, mature trees and flowering shrubs. Wheelchair users note soft ground in places & some gravel paths.

&. 🐕 ❀ 🚘 🍵

41 NEW THE OLD VICARAGE

Church Lane, Ashbury, Swindon, SN6 8LZ. Mr David Astor. *The garden is in the village of Ashbury, next to the church.* **Sat 11 June (10-4). Adm £5, chd free. Light refreshments.**
Within The Vale of the White Horse, Ashbury is a picturesque village with thatched cottages and a friendly atmosphere. Nestled between the village pub and St Mary's church is the garden of The Old Vicarage. The garden surrounds the house and is made up of a floriferous walled garden, a wildflower meadow, an extensive kitchen garden, filled with flowers, as well as vegetables, plus more.

🍵))

42 THE PARISH HOUSE

West Knoyle, Mere, BA12 6AJ. Philip & Alex Davies. *From E on A303 take signpost to West Knoyle at petrol station. Continue down hill and past church, take first R signposted Charnage, continue 1m to end of lane. Parking in field on L.* **Sat 23 Apr, Sun 17 July (2-5). Adm £5, chd free. Home-made teas.**
The garden at The Parish House is small and south facing surrounded by hedges protecting it from the exposure of a high wide open landscape beyond. The garden is laid out with gravel to encourage a self-seeding natural look but there are also roses and herbaceous perennials as well. The look is held together with topiary. Beyond this garden there is a larger area of lawn, trees and developing bulb cover (Camassias in May). Large conservatory greenhouse containing mature Muscat grapevine and pelargoniums. Small vegetable garden. Level but gravel surfaces, some lawn.

&. ❀ 🍵))

43 PYTHOUSE KITCHEN GARDEN

West Hatch, Tisbury, SP3 6PA. Mr Piers Milburn, 07779 616894, info@pythousekitchengarden.co.uk, www.pythousekitchengarden.co.uk. *A350 S of E Knoyle, follow brown signs to Walled Garden approx 3m. From Tisbury take Newtown road past church, stay on it 2½m, garden on R. Check map on garden website.* **Thur 8 Sept (10-3.30). Adm £5, chd free. Light refreshments. Visits also by arrangement May to Oct for groups of up to 30.**
3 acres of walled working kitchen garden, in continuous use since C18, and managed with biodiversity in mind, with fruit-lined walls and gnarled apple trees leading to a glamping orchard (beehives beyond) via rosa rugosa-edged beds of soft fruit, vegetable and cutting garden. A restaurant and shop now occupy the old potting shed, with ancient kiwi and mulberry trees, as well as the deliciously scented 1920s HT rose, Mrs Oakley Fisher growing by the garden entrance. Restaurant opens at 12 for lunch (booking essential see pythousekitchengarden.co.uk). Coffee/tea from 10, served both inside and out on terrace, on open days. Grass paths across slope.

&. 🐕 🚘 🍵))

44 NEW SALTHROP HOUSE

Basset Down, Wroughton, Swindon, SN4 9QP. Sophie Conran. *Driving W on M4, exit at J16, take 1st exit signposted for Butterfly World, drive 2m, passing the golf course on your R, keep going up the hill, Salthrop House is the drive on the L.* **Fri 10, Sat 11 June, Fri 9, Sat 10 Sept (11-4). Adm £5, chd free. Light refreshments.**
Salthrop House is a manor house garden set on the edge of the Marlborough Downs. A tremendous variety of perennials, shrubs, borders and pots unfurl themselves across this romantic garden and surround the sweeping lawn. You can wind your way through the woodland paths, enjoy a moment of peace by the pond or visit the new greenhouse and kitchen garden.

🍵))

45 NEW SCOTS FARM

Pinkney, Malmesbury, SN16 0NZ. Mr & Mrs Martin Barrow, LJikoB@gmail.com. *5m W of Malmesbury on B4040 towards Sherston. Take L at Pinkney Xrds, follow road over a bridge and up a hill.* **Sat 16 July (10-5). Adm £5, chd free. Cream teas. Visits also by arrangement Apr to Sept for groups of up to 12.**
Across 7 acres a colourful perennial border, a white garden, a Japanese garden, a Spanish garden and follow a path through a wildflower meadow to a pottery studio and koi pond in this haven of tranquillity. Garden ware, pottery and sculptures on display.

&. 🐕 ❀ 🍵

46 SEEND HOUSE

High Street, Seend, Melksham, SN12 6NR. Maud Peters. *In Seend village. Nr church & opp PO.* **Sat 2 July (1-6). Combined adm with Seend Manor £10, chd free. Tea.**
Seend House is a Georgian house with 6 acres of gardens and paddocks. Framed with yew and box. Highlights inc cloud and rose garden, stream lavender, view of knot garden from above, fountain with grass border, walled garden as well as formal borders. Amazing view across the valley to Salisbury Plain.

🐕 🍵))

47 SEEND MANOR

High Street, Seend, Melksham, SN12 6NX. Stephen & Amanda Clark. *In centre of village, opp village green with car parking for garden visitors.* **Sat 2 July (1-6). Combined adm with Seend House £10, chd free. Tea.**
Created over 20 yrs, a stunning walled garden with 4 quadrants evoking important parts of the owners lives - England, China, Africa and Italy, with extensive trelliage, hornbeam hedges on stilts, cottage orne, temple, Chinese ting, grotto, fern walk, fountains, parterres, stone loggia and more. Kitchen garden. Folly ruin in woods. Courtyard garden. Extensive walled gardens, water features, garden structures, topiary and hedging and one of the best views in Wiltshire. Many gravel paths, so wheelchairs with thick tyres are best.

&. 🐕 🍵))

48 1 SOUTHVIEW

Wick Lane, Devizes, SN10 5DR.
Teresa Garraud, 01380 722936,
tl.garraud@hotmail.co.uk. *From
Devizes Mkt Pl go S (Long St). At
r'about go straight over, at mini
r'about turn L into Wick Ln. Continue
to end of Wick Ln. Park in road or
roads nearby.* **Sun 26 June, Sun
11 Sept (2-5). Adm £4, chd free.**
**Visits also by arrangement May to
Sept for groups of 5 to 20.**
An atmospheric and very long town
garden, full of wonderful planting
surprises at every turn. Densely
planted with both pots near the
house and large borders further up,
it houses a collection of beautiful and
often unusual plants, shrubs and trees
many with striking foliage. Colour from
seasonal flowers is interwoven with this
textural tapestry. 'Truly inspirational' is
often heard from visitors.

49 TEASEL

Wilsford, Amesbury, Salisbury,
SP4 7BL. Ray Palmer. *2m SW of
Amesbury in the Woodford Valley on
western banks of R Avon which runs
through the gardens.* **Sun 3 July (11-5).
Adm £5, chd free. Home-made teas.**

The gardens at Teasel were originally
laid out in the 1970s by James
Mitchell the publisher who made
his fortune from the worldwide best
seller ' The Joy of Sex '. The gardens
have been the subject of extensive
restoration and new landscaping
during 2020. This includes tropical
gardens around the swimming pool
terrace, long herbaceous borders and
a ½ m riverside walk.

50 TRANTOR HOUSE

Hackthorne Road,
Durrington, SP4 8AS. Mrs
Jane Turner, 01980 655101,
sjcturner@talktalk.net. *9 m N of
Salisbury. Turn off A345 (signed
Village Centre) onto Hackthorne Rd.
Approx 200 yds on L.* **Wed 1 June,
Sun 5 June (12-5).Adm £4, chd
free. Tea. Open nearby Cottage in
the Trees on 5 June. Visits also by
arrangement May to July.**
Border Oak timber framed house on
country lane surrounded by approx
²⁄₃ acre of both formal and informal
gardens. Attractive mixed and
herbaceous colour themed borders,
rose garden, wildlife pond and stream.

Summerhouse, raised vegetable beds
and wildflower meadow. Chickens.
Sloping garden with steps.

51 TRISTENAGH HOUSE

Devizes Road, Potterne,
Devizes, SN10 5LW. Ros Ford,
ros.ford@ngs.org.uk. *Im S of
Devizes on A360. Turn down byway
by postbox and cottage (27 Devizes
Rd) and follow yellow signs to car
park and entrance to the garden.*
**Sun 29 May (1.30-5.30). Adm £6,
chd free. Home-made cakes, inc
gluten free options. Visits also
by arrangement May & June for
groups of 5+.**
Garden of approx 2 acres, created
over the past 20 yrs. Island beds
with a mixture of herbaceous plants,
bulbs, annuals and shrubs. Year-round
structure provided by beech and yew
hedges, box topiary and by mature
beech and Scots pine trees. Some
gravelled areas with containers. Good
views of valley from terrace. Wheelchair
access to most parts of garden on
grass paths. Access to terrace limited
due to gravel. Some steps.

Court Hill House

Corsley House

© Maud Peters

camellias, maples, magnolias, ornamental water, bog garden, herbaceous borders. Bluebell walk. Shrub border created by storm damage, mixed with agapanthus and half-hardy salvias. Difficult surfaces, sensible footwear essential as parts of garden can be very wet. Please keep to raked and marked paths in woodland. Partial wheelchair access.

å ┡ ☕

55 WEST LAVINGTON MANOR
1 Church Street, West Lavington, SN10 4LA. Andrew Doman & Jordina Evins, andrewdoman01@gmail.com. *6m S of Devizes, on A360. House opp White St, where parking is available.* Sat 11 June (11-6). Adm £10, chd free. Lunch & cream teas will be served all day. Visits also by arrangement for groups of 10+. Donation to West Lavington Youth Club and Nestling Trust.
5 acre walled garden first established in C17 by John Danvers who brought Italianate gardens to the UK. Herbaceous border, Japanese garden, rose garden, orchard and arboretum with some outstanding specimen trees all centred around a trout stream and duck pond. Children's activities. Picnics welcome. We will have an even larger artisans market this year after the very popular launch last year which will inc a wide variety of plants and produce for sale. Partial wheelchair access.

å ┡ ✿ 🚗 Ⅾ ☕))

56 WESTCROFT
Boscombe Village, nr Salisbury, SP4 0AB. Lyn Miles, 01980 610877 (evenings), lynmiles@icloud.com, www.westcroftgarden.co.uk. *7m N/E Salisbury. On A338 from Salisbury, just past Boscombe & District Social Club. Park there or in field opp house, or where signed on day. Disabled parking only on drive.* Every Thur 13 Jan to 3 Mar (11-4). Sun 30 Jan, Sun 6, Sun 20 Feb (11-4). Adm £4, chd free. Home-made soups, scrummy teas, inside or outside. Visits also by arrangement Jan & Feb for groups of 15+. Refreshments can be pre-ordered for groups.
Whilst overflowing with roses in June, in Jan and Feb the bones of this ⅔ acre galanthophile's garden on chalk are on show. Brick and flint walls, terraces, rustic arches, gates and pond add character. Drifts of snowdrops carpet the floor whilst throughout is a growing collection of

52 ◆ TWIGS COMMUNITY GARDEN
Manor Garden Centre, Cheney Manor, Swindon, SN2 2QJ. TWIGS, 01793 523294, twigs.reception@gmail.com, www.twigscommunitygardens.org.uk. *From Gt Western Way, under Bruce St Bridges onto Rodbourne Rd. 1st L at r'about, Cheney Manor Industrial Est. Through estate, 2nd exit at r'about. Opp Pitch & Putt. Signs on R to Manor Garden Centre.* For NGS: Sun 22 May, Sun 17 July (12-4). Adm £3.50, chd free. Home-made teas. For other opening times and information, please phone, email or visit garden website.
Delightful 2 acre community garden, created and maintained by volunteers. Features inc 7 individual display gardens, ornamental pond, plant nursery, Iron Age round house, artwork, fitness trail, separate kitchen garden site, Swindon beekeepers and the haven, overflowing with wildflowers. Excellent hot and cold lunches available at Olive Tree café within Manor Garden centre adj to Twigs (pre booking required) 01793 533152. Most areas wheelchair accessible. Disabled WC at Garden Centre.

å ┡ ✿ 🚗 ☕

53 NEW WADSWICK GREEN
Corsham, SN13 9RD. Rangeford Villages, www.wadswickgreen.co.uk. *Signed from Bradford on Avon & Corsham, directions off B3109. Pls use Westwells Rd entrance, Neston, Corsham.* Sat 2 July (9-4). Adm £5, chd free. Light refreshments in The Greenhouse Restaurant.
Wadswick Green Retirement Village's parkland landscape of formal, informal and wild gardens has interest throughout the year. Seasonal bulbs, flowering shrubs and perennial borders contrast with clipped hedges, mature trees and lawns, attracting the welcomed wildlife. Relax in the Italian Terrace Garden.

å ┡ ✿ 🚗 ☕))

54 ◆ WATERDALE HOUSE
East Knoyle, SP3 6BL. Mr & Mrs Julian Seymour, 01747 830262. *8m S of Warminster. N of East Knoyle, garden signed from A350. Do not use SatNav.* For NGS: Sun 1 May (2-5). Adm £5, chd free. Home-made teas. For other opening times and information, please phone.
In the event of inclement weather please check www.ngs.org.uk before visiting. 4 acre mature woodland garden with rhododendrons, azaleas,

well over 400 named varieties. Many hellebores, pulmonarias, grasses and seedheads add interest. Snowdrops (weather dependent) and snowdrop sundries for sale inc greetings cards, mugs, bags, serviettes, also chutneys and free range eggs.

✿ 🚗 💷 ♪)

GROUP OPENING

57 NEW WHADDON GARDENS
Castle Lane, Whaddon, Salisbury, SP5 3EG. *Approx 5m S of Salisbury on the A36 Southampton Rd towards Southampton. Take slip road signposted Alderbury & Whaddon, and turn into Castle Ln opp the PO. Bumpy track.* **Sat 4 June (1-5). Combined adm £5, chd free. Light refreshments in the garden at The Old Cottage.**

NEW CLEARBURY VIEW
Ros & Adam Hughes,

NEW HAND HOUSE
Rachel Eveling.

NEW 2 LADIES COTTAGES
Astrid & Peter Pountney.

NEW THE OLD COTTAGE
Dame Elizabeth Neville.

A group of 4 very different gardens each complementing the other. All situated within the boundary of Castle Lane in the hamlet of Whaddon. Enjoy the wonderfully diverse garden at The Old Cottage with its wildflower areas, natural swimming pond, formal areas planted with roses and herbaceous borders. Fruit trees inc walnut. Enjoy the beautiful summerhouse. Wonderful views over the surrounding countryside. Travel on down the hill in Castle Lane to the child friendly garden at Clearbury View with its fruit trees, herb beds, decking areas and more glorious views over the adjoining fields and countryside with sheep grazing. Back onto the track to Hand House with its interesting collection of trees and a mediterranean style quirky gravel garden and then pop next door to Ladies Cottages to enjoy a traditional small country cottage garden with fruit trees and shrubs, herbaceous borders, perfumed roses and climbers, and small pond tucked away with resident amphibians. Wheelchair acccess available at The Old Cottage, Clearbury View and Hand House but NOT at 2 Ladies Cottages.

&. 🐕 ✿ 💷 ♪)

58 WHATLEY MANOR
Easton Grey, Malmesbury, SN16 0RB. **Christian & Alix Landolt, 01666 822888, reservations@whatleymanor.com, www.whatleymanor.com.** *4m W of Malmesbury. From A429 at Malmesbury take B4040 signed Sherston. Manor 2m on L.* **Tue 14 June (2-6). Adm £6.50, chd free. Light refreshments in The Loggia Garden. Visits also by arrangement.**
12 acres of English country gardens with 26 distinct rooms each with a strong theme based on colour, scent or style. Original 1920s Arts & Crafts plan inspired the design and combines classic style with more contemporary touches, inc specially commissioned sculpture. Dogs must be on a lead at all times. Hotel also open for lunch and full afternoon tea.

&. 🐕 🚌 💷 ♪)

59 NEW 41 WHISTLEY ROAD
Potterne, Devizes, SN10 5QY. **Mike & Linda Kavanagh.** *From Devizes head S towards Salisbury for 2m on A360. In the centre of Potterne turn sharp R signposted Whistley. Continue about 500yds along the narrow road. 41 is on the L.* **Sun 4 Sept (1.30-5). Adm £4, chd free. Home-made teas.**
This garden may surprise you! It's small but packed with colour. Winding gravel paths lead through arches around a lawn bordered with tall perennials. You will discover a wildlife pond where on sunny days we watch newts, dragonflies, bees and butterflies. Archways also lead to a vegetable area with raised beds and a well-stocked greenhouse.

💷 ♪)

60 5 WHITEHORN DRIVE
Landford, Salisbury, SP5 2AX. **Jackie & Barry Candler, 01794 390951, jackie.candler37@gmail.com.** *4m N of M27 J2 & 12m S of Salisbury off A36. Turn off A36 into Landford. Follow road to Xrds. Take Forest Rd towards Nomansland. Whitehorn Dr 2nd R off Forest Rd.* **Visits by arrangement May to Sept for groups of 5 to 15. We can tailor a visit to suit. Cream teas.**
A small garden packed with interest. Underground springs ensure areas across the garden remain damp year-round, flowing to a natural wildlife pond surrounded by bog planting.

Dryer areas ensure a large variety of plant interest throughout the year. Island beds and borders, wild patch and ornamental surprises. Brand new border and greenhouse in 2021.

✿ 💷

61 WINDMILL COTTAGE
Kings Road, Market Lavington, SN10 4QB. **Rupert & Gill Wade, 01380 813527.** *5m S of Devizes. Turn E off A360 1m N of W. Lavington, signed Market Lavington & Easterton. At top of hill turn L into Kings Rd, L into Windmill Lane after 200yds. Limited parking on site, more parking nearby.* **Thur 26, Fri 27 May, Thur 23, Fri 24 June (2-5). Adm £4, chd free. Home-made teas. Visits also by arrangement in June for groups of up to 40.**
1 acre cottage style, wildlife friendly garden on greensand. Mixed beds and borders with long season of interest. Roses on pagoda, large vegetable patch for kitchen and exhibition at local shows, greenhouse, polytunnel and fruit cage. Whole garden virtually pesticide free for last 20 yrs. Small bog garden by wildlife pond. Secret glade with prairie. Grandchildren's little wood and wild place.

🐕 ✿ 🚗 💷 🪑

62 WUDSTON HOUSE
High Street, Wedhampton, Devizes, SN10 3QE. **David Morrison, 07881 943213, djm@piml.co.uk.** *Wedhampton lies on N side of A342 approx 4m E of Devizes. House is set back on E side of village street at end of drive with beech hedge on either side.* **Visits by arrangement June to Sept.**
The garden of Wudston House was started in 2010, following completion of the house. It consists of formal gardens round the house, perennial meadow, pinetum and arboretum. Nick Macer and James Hitchmough, who have pioneered the concept of perennial meadows, have been extensively involved in aspects of the garden, which is still developing.

✿

'National Garden Scheme donations have funded four of our gardens in regional NHS spinal injury centres supporting nearly 8,500 patients and their visitors' *Horatio's Garden*

WORCESTERSHIRE

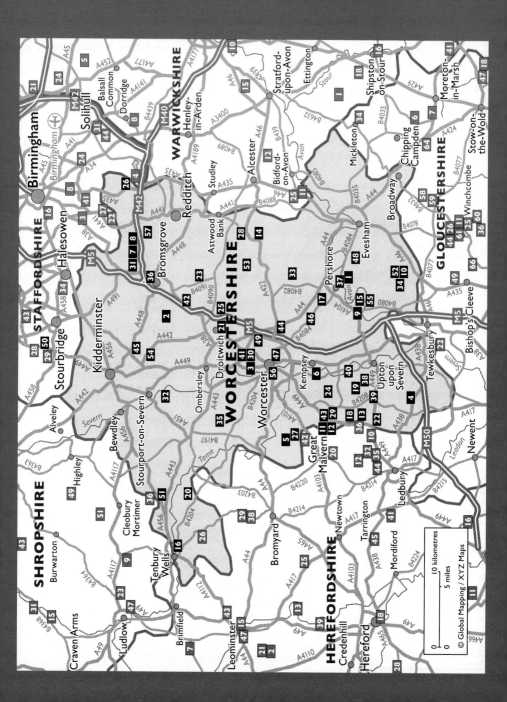

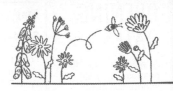

Worcestershire has something to suit every taste, and the same applies to its gardens.

From the magnificent Malvern Hills, the inspiration for Edward Elgar, to the fruit orchards of Evesham which produce wonderful blossom trails in the spring, and from the historic city of Worcester, with its 11th century cathedral and links to the Civil War, to the numerous villages and hamlets that are scattered throughout, there is so much to enjoy in this historic county.

Worcestershire is blessed with gardens created by both amateur and professional gardeners, and the county can boast properties with grounds of many acres to small back gardens of less than half an acre, but all have something special to offer.

There are gardens with significant historical interest and some with magnificent views and a few that are not what you might consider to be a "typical" National Garden Scheme garden! We also have a number of budding artists within the Scheme, and a few display their works of art on garden open days.

Worcestershire's garden owners guarantee visitors beautiful gardens, some real surprises and a warm welcome.

Volunteers

County Organiser
David Morgan
01214 453595
meandi@btinternet.com

County Treasurer
Doug Bright
01886 832200
doug.bright@ngs.org.uk

Publicity
Pamela Thompson
01886 888295
peartree.pam@gmail.com

Social Media
Brian Skeys
01684 311297
brian.skeys@ngs.org.uk

Booklet Co-ordinator
Steven Wilkinson & Linda Pritchard
01684 310150
steven.wilkinson48412@gmail.com

Assistant County Organisers
Andrea Bright
01886 832200
andrea.bright@ngs.org.uk

Brian Bradford
07816 867137
bradf0rds@icloud.com

Lynn Glaze
01386 751924
lynnglaze@cmail.co.uk

Philippa Lowe
01684 891340
philippa.lowe@ngs.org.uk

Stephanie & Chris Miall
0121 445 2038
stephaniemiall@hotmail.com

Alan Nokes
alan.nokes@ngs.org.uk

 @WorcestershireNGS
 @WorcsNGS

Left: The Rest, Withybed Green

OPENING DATES

All entries subject to change. For latest information check www.ngs.org.uk

Map locator numbers are shown to the right of each garden name.

February

Snowdrop Festival

Sunday 6th
Brockamin   6

March

Friday 11th
◆ Little Malvern Court   22

Friday 18th
◆ Little Malvern Court   22

Sunday 20th
Brockamin   6

Friday 25th
◆ Little Malvern Court   22

April

Saturday 2nd
Overbury Court   34
◆ Whitlenge Gardens   54

Sunday 3rd
◆ Whitlenge Gardens   54

Sunday 10th
◆ Spetchley Park
Gardens   44
White Cottage &
Nursery   53

Sunday 17th
Brockamin   6
The Dell House   13

Sunday 24th
Bridges Stone Mill   5

Saturday 30th
The River School   41

May

Sunday 1st
Nimrod, 35 Alexandra
Road   29
Pear Tree Cottage   35
Whitcombe House   52
White Cottage &
Nursery   53

Monday 2nd
◆ Little Malvern Court   22
Nimrod, 35 Alexandra
Road   29
White Cottage &
Nursery   53

Wednesday 4th
NEW The Alpine Garden
Society   1

Saturday 7th
NEW Cowleigh Park
Farm   12
The Walled Garden   47

Sunday 8th
Hiraeth   21

Wednesday 11th
The Walled Garden   47

Saturday 14th
NEW The Alpine Garden
Society   1

Sunday 15th
NEW The Alpine Garden
Society   1
White Cottage &
Nursery   53

Saturday 21st
Oak Tree House   31
Ravelin   38

Sunday 22nd
Madresfield Court   24
Ravelin   38
Rothbury   43
Warndon Court   49

Saturday 28th
1 Church Cottage   9
Eckington Gardens   15
NEW 3 Perryfields
Road   36

Sunday 29th
NEW 2 Brookwood Drive   7
1 Church Cottage   9
Eckington Gardens   15
Oak Tree House   31
Rothbury   43

June

Saturday 4th
Hanley Swan NGS
Gardens   19

Sunday 5th
NEW Cowleigh Park
Farm   12
Hanley Swan NGS
Gardens   19
White Cottage &
Nursery   53

Saturday 11th
NEW The Alpine Garden
Society   1
Pershore Gardens   37

Sunday 12th
NEW The Alpine Garden
Society   1
Birtsmorton Court   4
Pershore Gardens   37
Warndon Court   49
Whitcombe House   52

Wednesday 15th
NEW Highways   20

Saturday 18th
North Worcester
Gardens   30
Rest Harrow   39

Sunday 19th
Brockamin   6
North Worcester
Gardens   30
NEW The Old House   33
Rest Harrow   39
White Cottage &
Nursery   53

Saturday 25th
The Dell House   13
Rhydd Gardens   40
The Walled Garden   47
Walnut Cottage   48
◆ Whitlenge Gardens   54

Sunday 26th
Cowleigh Lodge   11
The Dell House   13
The Firs   17
Hiraeth   21
3 Oakhampton Road   32
Rhydd Gardens   40
Walnut Cottage   48
◆ Whitlenge Gardens   54
Withybed Green   57

Wednesday 29th
The Walled Garden   47

July

Saturday 2nd
The Lodge   23
Wharf House   51

Sunday 3rd
The Folly   18
The Lodge   23
◆ Spetchley Park
Gardens   44
Wharf House   51

Sunday 10th
The Firs   17
NEW The Old House   33

Saturday 16th
NEW Manor Cottage   25

Sunday 17th
NEW Brookwood
Gardens   8
Millbrook Lodge   27

Sunday 24th
Rothbury   43

Thursday 28th
The River School   41

Saturday 30th
5 Beckett Drive   3

Sunday 31st
5 Beckett Drive   3
NEW Cowleigh Park
Farm   12
Hiraeth   21
3 Oakhampton Road   32

August

Wednesday 3rd
NEW Highways   20

Sunday 14th
Cowleigh Lodge   11

Saturday 20th
Rest Harrow   39
Westacres   50

Sunday 21st
Hiraeth   21
Rest Harrow   39
Westacres   50

Saturday 27th
The Dell House   13
◆ Morton Hall
Gardens   28
3 Oakhampton Road   32

Sunday 28th
The Dell House   13

THE GARDENS

1 NEW **THE ALPINE GARDEN SOCIETY**
Avon Bank, Wick, Pershore, WR10 3JP, 01386 554790, ags@alpinegardensociety.net, www.alpinegardensociety.net.
Wick, ½ m from Pershore town. Take the Evesham Road from Pershore over the River Avon, continue for ½ m & turn R for Pershore College, the garden is the 1st entrance on the L. **Wed 4, Sat 14, Sun 15 May, Sat 11, Sun 12 June (11-4). Adm £4, chd free. Light refreshments. Visits also by arrangement Apr to June for groups of 10 to 20.**
Inspirational small garden adjacent to the office of the Alpine Garden Society charity. The garden shows a wide range of alpine plants that are easy to grow in contemporary gardens over a long season. Visitors can see different settings to grow alpines, inc rock and tufa, scree, shade and sunny areas, also a dedicated alpine house, and many pots and troughs with alpines and small bulbs. Volunteers will be on hand on open days to provide more information, and planting demonstrations may be available on some dates.
✿ ☕ ⟡

2 **BADGE COURT**
Purshull Green Lane, Elmbridge, Droitwich, WR9 0NJ. Stuart & Diana Glendenning, 01299 851216, dianaglendenning1@gmail.com.
5m N of Droitwich Spa. 2½ m from J5 M5. Turn off A38 at Wychbold down side of the Swan Inn. Turn R into Berry Ln. Take next L into Cooksey Green Ln. Turn R into Purshull Green Ln. Garden is on L. **Visits by arrangement May to July for groups of 5 to 30. A short history of the C16 house is given as part of the visit. Adm £5, chd free. Home-made teas.**
The 2½ acre garden is set against the backdrop of a C16 house (not open). There is something for all gardeners inc mature specimen trees, huge range of clematis and roses, lake with waterfall, stumpery, topiary garden, walled garden, Mediterranean Garden, specialist borders, long herbaceous border, large potager vegetable garden and Japanese Garden (new for 2022).
♿ ✿ ☕

3 **5 BECKETT DRIVE**
Northwick, Worcester, WR3 7BZ. Jacki & Pete Ager, 01905 451108, agers@outlook.com. *1½ m N of Worcester city centre. A cul-de-sac off the A449 Ombersley Road directly opp Grantham's Autocare Garage.*

1m S of the Claines r'about on A449 & just N of Northwick Cinema on Ombersley Rd. **Sat 30, Sun 31 July (2-5). Adm £4, chd free. Home-made ice cream on sale. Opening with North Worcester Gardens on Sat 18, Sun 19 June. Visits also by arrangement May to July for groups of 10 to 30.**
An extraordinary town garden on the northern edge of Worcester packed with different plants and year-round interest guaranteed to give visitors ideas and inspiration for their own gardens. Over 15 years visitors have enjoyed the unique and surprising features of this garden which has many planting schemes for a variety of situations. Home-made ice cream on sale.

Around 1,050 people living with Parkinson's - and their families - have been helped by Parkinson's nurses thanks to funding from the National Garden Scheme

4 BIRTSMORTON COURT

Birtsmorton, nr Malvern, WR13 6JS. Mr & Mrs N G K Dawes. *7m E of Ledbury. Off A438 Ledbury/Tewkesbury rd.* **Sun 12 June (2-5.30). Adm £7, chd free. Home-made teas.**
10 acre garden surrounding beautiful medieval moated manor house (not open). White garden, built and planted in 1997 surrounded on all sides by old topiary. Potager, vegetable garden and working greenhouses, all beautifully maintained. Rare double working moat and waterways inc Westminster Pool laid down in Henry VII's reign to mark the consecration of the knave of Westminster Abbey. Ancient yew tree under which Cardinal Wolsey reputedly slept in the legend of the Shadow of the Ragged Stone.
🪑 ✺ ☕ ·))

5 BRIDGES STONE MILL

Alfrick Pound, WR6 5HR. Sir Michael & Lady Perry. *6m NW of Malvern. A4103 from Worcester to Bransford r'about, then Suckley Rd for 3m to Alfrick Pound.* **Sun 24 Apr (2-5.30). Adm £7, chd free. Home-made teas.**
Once a cherry orchard adjoining the mainly C19 flour mill, this is now a 2½ acre year-round garden laid out with trees, shrubs, mixed beds and borders. The garden is bounded by a stretch of Leigh Brook (an SSSI), from which the mill's own weir feeds a mill leat and small lake. A rose parterre and a traditional Japanese garden complete the scene. Wheelchair access by car to courtyard.
🪑 ✺ ☕

6 BROCKAMIN

Old Hills, Callow End, Worcester, WR2 4TQ. Margaret Stone, 01905 830370, stone.brockamin@btinternet.com. *5m S of Worcester. ½ m S of Callow End on the B4424, on an unfenced bend, turn R into the car park signed Old Hills. Walk towards the houses keeping R.* **Sun 6 Feb (11-4); Sun 20 Mar, Sun 17 Apr, Sun 19 June, Sun 18 Sept (2-5). Adm £4, chd free. Home-made teas. Visits also by arrangement Feb to Oct for groups of 10+.**
This is a plant specialist's 1½ acre informal working garden, parts of which are used for plant production rather than for show. Situated next to common land. Mixed borders with wide variety of hardy perennials where plants are allowed to self seed. Plant Heritage National Collections of Symphyotrichum (Aster) novae-angliae and some Hardy Geraniums. Open for snowdrops in Feb, daffodils and pulmonarias in March and April, geraniums in June and asters in September. Seasonal pond/bog garden and kitchen garden. Teas with home-made cakes and unusual plants for sale. An access path reaches a large part of the garden.
🪑 ✺ 🚌 [NPC] ☕

7 [NEW] 2 BROOKWOOD DRIVE

Barnt Green, Birmingham, B45 8GG. Mr Mike & Mrs Liz Finlay. *Please park courteously in local roads or in village. Brookwood Drive is on R towards top of Fiery Hill Rd approx. ¼ m from station. Press the Access button to open security gates.* **Sun 29 May (10.30-5). Adm £5, chd free. Home-made teas. Opening as part of Brookwood Gardens on Sun 17 July.**
A multi-themed mature garden with numerous water features and colourful borders. There is a formal white garden, wildlife pond and cutting garden surrounded by large rhododendrons which give a colourful display in late spring. Plant sales on a commecial basis with a % donated to the NGS. Parking on Brookwood Drive for disabled only.
🪑 ✺ ☕ ·))

2 Brookwood Drive

GROUP OPENING

8 NEW **BROOKWOOD GARDENS**
Brookwood Drive, Barnt Green, Birmingham, B45 8GG. *Please park courteously in local roads or in village. Brookwood Drive is on R towards top of Fiery Hill Rd approx. ¼ m from station. Press the Access button to open security gates.* **Sun 17 July (10.30-5). Combined adm £7, chd free. Home-made teas.**

NEW **2 BROOKWOOD DRIVE**
Mr Mike & Mrs Liz Finlay.
(See separate entry)

NEW **5 BROOKWOOD DRIVE**
Mr Charles & Mrs Denise Gregory.

2 Brookwood Drive is a garden overflowing with colour, variety and texture. 5 Brookwood Drive is a working garden with a vegetable area and orchard. Plant sales on commercial basis with % to NGS. Disabled parking only on Brookwood Drive.

  ♿ ✿ ☕ ᵍ⁾

9 **1 CHURCH COTTAGE**
Church Road, Defford, WR8 9BJ. John Taylor & Ann Sheppard, 01386 750863, ann98sheppard@btinternet.com. *3m SW of Pershore. A4104 Pershore to Upton rd, turn into Harpley Rd, Defford. Don't go up Bluebell Lane as directed by SatNav, black & white cottage at side of church. Parking in village hall car park.* **Sat 28, Sun 29 May (1-5). Adm £5, chd free. Home-made teas. Visits also by arrangement Feb to Sept for groups of 10 to 30.**
True countryman's ⅓ acre cottage garden. Japanese style feature with 'dragons den'. Specimen trees, rare and unusual plants, water features, perennial garden, vegetable garden, poultry, streamside bog garden. New features in progress. Wheelchair access to most areas, narrow paths may restrict access to some parts.

  ♿ 🐕 ✿ ☕ ᵍ⁾

10 **CONDERTON MANOR**
Conderton, nr Tewkesbury, GL20 7PR. Mr & Mrs W Carr, 01386 725389, carrs@conderton.com. *5½ m NE of Tewkesbury. From M5 - A46 to Beckford - L for Overbury/ Conderton. From Tewkesbury B4079 to Bredon - then follow signs to Overbury. Conderton from B4077 follow A46 directions from Teddington r'about.* **Visits by arrangement Apr to Nov for groups of up to 30. Individuals welcome. Light refreshments.**
7 acre garden with magnificent views of Cotswolds. Flowering cherries and bulbs in spring. Formal terrace with clipped box parterre; huge rose and clematis arches, mixed borders of roses and herbaceous plants, bog bank and quarry garden. Many unusual trees and shrubs make this a garden for all seasons. Visitors are particularly encouraged to visit in spring and autumn when the trees are at their best. This is a garden/ small arboretum of particular interest for tree lovers. The views towards the Cotswolds escarpment are spectacular and it provides a peaceful walk of about an hour. Some gravel paths and steps - no disabled WC.

  ♿ 🐕 🍴 ☕ ᵍ⁾

11 **COWLEIGH LODGE**
16 Cowleigh Bank, Malvern, WR14 1QP. Jane & Mic Schuster, 01684 439054, dalyan@hotmail.co.uk. *7m SW from Worcester. From Worcester or Ledbury follow the A449 to Link Top. Take North Malvern Rd (behind Holy Trinity Church), follow yellow signs. From Hereford take B4219 after Storridge church, follow yellow signs.* **Sun 26 June, Sun 14 Aug (11-5). Adm £5, chd free. Home-made teas. Visits also by arrangement June to Aug for groups of 10+.**
The now mature but still 'quirky' garden on the slopes of the Malvern Hills has a formal rose garden, grass beds, bamboo walk, colour themed beds, nature path leading to a wildlife pond, Acer bank, chickens. Large vegetable plot and orchard with views overlooking the Severn Valley. Explore the polytunnel and then relax with a cuppa and slice of home-made cake served with a smile. This is the 8th year of opening of this developing and expanding garden - visitors from previous years will be able to see the difference. Lots of added interest with staddle stones, troughs, signs and other interesting artefacts. The garden is definitely now a mature one.

🐕 ✿ ☕ ᵍ⁾

12 NEW **COWLEIGH PARK FARM**
Cowleigh Road, Malvern, WR13 5HJ. John & Ruth Lucas, 01684 566750, info@cowleighparkfarm.co.uk, www.cowleighparkfarm.co.uk. *On the edge of Malvern. Leaving Malvern on the B4219 the driveway for Cowleigh Park Farm is on the R just before the derestrict speed sign.* **Sat 7 May, Sun 5 June, Sun 31 July (1-5). Adm £5, chd free. Home-made teas. Visits also by arrangement Apr to Oct.**
The 1½ acre garden at Cowleigh Park Farm surrounds a Grade II listed timber framed former farmhouse (not open). Whilst no longer a farm, the property has views to adjacent orchards and inc lawns, spring fed ponds, a waterfall and stream. The focus in established beds and borders is to be bee and wildlife friendly. The garden contains multiple seating areas and a summerhouse. The whole garden can be viewed from wheelchair accessible places but some parts contain steep grassy slopes that may not be accessible by wheelchair

  ♿ 🚻 ☕

13 **THE DELL HOUSE**
2 Green Lane, Malvern Wells, WR14 4HU. Kevin & Elizabeth Rolph, 01684 564448, stay@thedellhouse.co.uk, www.dellhousemalvern.uk. *2m S of Gt Malvern. Behind former church on corner of A449 Wells Rd & Green Ln. NB SatNavs/Google don't work with postcode. Small car park.* **Sun 17 Apr (2-6); Sat 25, Sun 26 June, Sat 27, Sun 28 Aug (12-7); Sun 2 Oct (1-5). Adm £5, chd free. Pre-booking essential, please visit www.ngs.org.uk for information & booking. Light refreshments. Visits also by arrangement for groups of up to 20. Short notice possible.**
Two acre wooded hillside garden of the 1830s former rectory, now a B&B. Peaceful and natural, the garden contains many magnificent specimen trees inc a Wellingtonia Redwood. Informal in style with meandering bark paths, historic garden buildings, garden railway and a paved terrace with outstanding views. Spectacular tree carvings by Steve Elsby, and other sculptures by various artists. Featured in 'A survey of Historic Parks & Gardens in Worcestershire'.

🐕 🚻 ☕ 🪑 ᵍ⁾

4 6 DINGLE END

Inkberrow, WR7 4EY. Mr Glenn & Mrs Gabriel Allison, 01386 792039. *12m E of Worcester. A422 from Worcester. At the 30 sign in Inkberrow turn R down Appletree Ln then 1st L up Pepper St. Dingle End is 4th on R of Pepper St. Limited parking in Dingle End but street parking on Pepper St.* **Visits by arrangement Mar to Oct for groups of 5 to 20. Adm £4, chd free. Home-made teas.** Over 1 acre garden with formal area close to the house opening into a flat area featuring a large pond, stream and weir with apple orchard and woodland area. Large vegetable garden inc an interesting variety of fruits. Garden designed for wildlife and attractive to birds on account of water and trees. Named varieties of apple and pear trees. Wheelchair access - slopes alongside every terrace.

GROUP OPENING

5 ECKINGTON GARDENS

Hilltop, Nafford Road, Eckington, WR10 3DH. Group Coordinator Richard Bateman. *3 gardens - 1 in Upper End, 1 close by in Nafford Rd, 3rd about 1m along Nafford Rd. A4104 Pershore to Upton & Defford, L turn B4080 to Eckington. In centre, by war memorial turn L into New Rd (becomes Nafford Rd).* **Sat 28, Sun 29 May (11-5). Combined adm £6, chd free. Home-made teas at Mantoft.**

HILLTOP FARM
Richard & Margaret Bateman, 01386 750667, richard. bateman111@btinternet.com. **Visits also by arrangement May to Sept for groups of 5 to 30.**

MANTOFT
Mr & Mrs M J Tupper, 01386 750819. **Visits also by arrangement May to Nov for groups of 5 to 30.**

NAFFORD HOUSE
George & Joanna Stylianou.

3 very diverse gardens set in/ close to lovely village of Eckington. Hilltop – 1 acre garden with sunken garden/pond, rose garden, herbaceous borders, interesting topiary inc cloud pruning and formal hedging to reduce effect of wind and having 'windows' for views

over the beautiful Worcestershire countryside. Sculptures made by owner. Vegetable yurt (added 2018) has been successful in allowing pollination and preventing damage to young plants. Mantoft - Wonderful ancient thatched cottage with 1½ acres of magical gardens. Fishpond with ghost koi, Cotswold and red brick walls, large topiary, treehouse with seating, summerhouse and dovecote, pathways, vistas and stone statues, urns and herbaceous borders. Featured in Cotswold Life - should not be missed. Nafford House is 2 acre mature natural garden, wood with walk and slopes to River Avon, formal gardens around the house/ magnificent wisteria. Some wheelchair access issues, particularly at Nafford House.

&. 🐾 / ☕

6 FARLANDS

Kyrewood, Tenbury Wells, WR15 8SG. Alan & Frances Eachus, 01584 810288, frances.eachus@btinternet.com. *½m E of Tenbury Wells on B4204. Approaching from Tenbury slow down when you reach the 40mph sign at Kyrewood. The rd bends sharply to the L & the garden entrance is on R through the open timber gates.* **Visits by arrangement in Aug for groups of up to 20. Adm £5, chd free. Home-made teas.** Beech and hornbeam hedges divide the 1 acre garden into separate compartments all linked by a central hedged pathway. There is a mature Atlantic cedar at the centre of the garden but the most striking features are the extensive drifts of herbaceous perennials planted around a naturalised pond and through the kitchen garden. Vegetable garden in a series of raised beds.

'In the first six months of operation at Maggie's Southampton, which was part funded by the National Garden Scheme, the team has supported people affected by cancer more than 2,300 times'
Maggie's

7 THE FIRS

Brickyard Lane, Drakes Broughton, Pershore, WR10 2AH. Ann & Ken Mein, annmmein@googlemail.com. *From J7 M5 take B4084 towards Pershore. At Drakes Broughton turn L to Stonebow Rd. First R into Walcot Ln then second R into Brickyard Ln. The Firs is 200 yds on L.* **Sun 26 June, Sun 10 July (1-5). Adm £4, chd free. Cream teas. Visits also by arrangement July to Sept for groups of 12+.** 2 acre garden with over 200 trees, predominantly Silver Birch. A Rockery and gravel path lead down to the terrace. Informal beds filled with Agapanthus, Sedums, Roses, Hydrangeas and Grasses; a Fruit and Vegetable garden and a Fernery surround the house. The C19 Cider Barn houses the Pottery with a variety of pots for sale. Lots of seating areas with views towards Bredon Hill. Gentle slopes, grassy paths.

&. ☕)))

8 THE FOLLY

87 Wells Road, Malvern, WR14 4PB. David & Lesley Robbins, 01684 567253, lesleycmedley@btinternet.com. *1½m S of Great Malvern & 9m S of Worcester. Approx 8m from M5 via J7 or J8. Situated in Malvern Wells on A449, 0.7m N of B4209 and 0.2m S of Malvern Common. Parking off A449 0.25m N on lay-by or side road, or in 0.1m N turn E on Peachfield Rd which runs by Malvern Common.* **Sun 3 July (1.30-5). Adm £4, chd free. Light refreshments. Visits also by arrangement May & June for groups of 5 to 20.** Steeply sloping garden on Malvern Hills with views over Severn Vale. Three levels accessed by steps, paved/gravel paths and ramps. Potager and greenhouse, courtyard, formal terrace and lawn, pergola, mature cedars, ornaments and sculpture in landscaped beds and borders. Climbers, small trees, shrubs, hostas, grasses and ferns, with new areas developing. Seating on each level. Gravel and rockery gardens, small cottage garden, stumpery and shrubbery linked by winding paths with an intimate atmosphere as views are concealed and revealed.

GROUP OPENING

19 HANLEY SWAN NGS GARDENS

Hanley Swan, WR8 0DJ. Group Co-ordinator Brian Skeys, 01684 311297, brimfields@icloud.com. *5m E of Malvern, 3m NW of Upton upon Severn, 9m S of Worcester & M5. From the B4211 towards Great Malvern & Guarlford (Rhydd Road) turn L to Hanley Swan continue to Orchard Side WR80EA for entrance tickets & maps.* **Sat 4, Sun 5 June (1-5). Combined adm £6, chd free. Home-made teas at 19 Winnington Gardens. Visits also by arrangement June to Sept for groups of 5 to 30. Number of gardens available & entrance costs agreed when booking.**

MEADOW BANK
Mrs Lesley Stroud & Mr Dave Horrobin, 01684 310917, djhorrobin@gmail.com.

ORCHARD SIDE
Mrs Gigi Verlander, 01684 310602, gigiverlander@icloud.com.

THE PADDOCKS
Mr & Mrs N Fowler.

SUNDEW
Mr Nick & Mrs Alison Harper.

19 WINNINGTON GARDENS
Brian & Irene Skeys, 01684 311297, brimfields@icloud.com, www.brimfields.com.
Visits by arrangement June to Sept for groups of 5 to 30.

20 WINNINGTON GARDENS
Mr & Mrs Sauntson.

Entrance tickets from Orchard Side a country garden offering lots of interest of both plants and unusual items dotted around the garden. There is a large koi pond that sits just in front of the peaceful Zen Den where visitors are welcome to sit and contemplate. Sundew sits in a modest plot - since 2016 the owners have added planting, hard landscaping, new borders to a well-stocked garden. The Paddocks is a wildlife garden with ponds, a tadpole nursery, mixed borders and a new greenhouse with cacti and succulents. Meadow Bank is a modern interpretation of a cottage garden, with a hot border, Dahlias grown for show and collections of Iris and Auriculas. 20 Winnington Gardens has an octagonal greenhouse, water features, colourful beds and planters provide year-round colour. 19 Winnington Gardens is a garden of rooms. Mixed borders enclosed with climbing roses, a small oriental garden, fruit trees, raised herb bed with a special standard gooseberry, collection of garden vintage tools. 6 gardens different in size and style. Wildlife photos on display.

20 NEW HIGHWAYS

Hanley William, Tenbury Wells, WR15 8QT. Mr & Mrs K Baker, 01584 781216, annejbaker@outlook.com. *7m from Tenbury Wells, 9m from Bromyard. From Worcester take the A443 to Tenbury, turn L at the turn marked Eastham. From Tenbury take the B4204. From Bromyard take the B4203, turn L to Tenbury at the Xrds.* **Wed 15 June, Wed 3 Aug (10-4). Adm £6, chd free. Pre-booking essential, please visit www.ngs.org.uk for information & booking. Home-made teas. Visits also by arrangement May to Sept for groups of 12 to 30. Parking is limited to 8 cars, so car sharing is advisable.**
A 1 acre garden developed over the last 16 years, with several herbaceous borders, natural stream and wildlife pond. Woodland area with established trees, newly planted arboretum, bog garden and some very impressive gunnera! Vegetable garden, koi pond and pergolas with clematis and climbing roses. Views over the Teme valley. Steps and sloping lawn. Not suitable for wheelchairs.

Highways

21 HIRAETH

30 Showell Road, Droitwich, WR9 8UY. Sue & John Fletcher, 07752 717243 or 01905 778390, sueandjohn99@yahoo.com. *1m S of Droitwich. On The Ridings estate. Turn off A38 r'about into Addyes Way, 2nd R into Showell Rd, 500yds on R. Follow the yellow signs.* **Sun 8 May, Sun 26 June, Sun 31 July, Sun 21 Aug (2-5). Adm £3.50, chd free. Visits also by arrangement Apr to Aug for groups of 10 to 30.** ⅓ acre gardens, front and rear, containing many plant species, cottage, herbaceous, hostas, ferns, acer trees, 300 year old olive tree, pool, waterfall, oak sculptures, metal animals inc giraffes, elephant, birds. New patio in 2019 and rear lawn removed but still an oasis of colours in a garden not to be missed described by visitor as 'A haven on the way to heaven'.

22 ◆ LITTLE MALVERN COURT

Little Malvern, WR14 4JN. Mrs T M Berington, 01684 892988, littlemalverncourt@hotmail.com, www.littlemalverncourt.co.uk. *3m S of Malvern. On A4104 S of junction with A449.* **For NGS: Every Fri 11 Mar to 25 Mar (2-5). Adm £6, chd £1. Mon 2 May (2-5). Adm £8, chd £1. For other opening times and information, please phone, email or visit garden website.** 10 acres attached to former Benedictine Priory, magnificent views over Severn Valley. Garden rooms and terrace around house designed and planted in early 1980s; chain of lakes; wide variety of spring bulbs, flowering trees and shrubs. Notable collection of old fashioned roses. Topiary hedge and fine trees. Regional Finalist, The English Garden's The Nation's Favourite Gardens 2019. The May Bank Holiday - Flower Festival in the Priory Church. Partial wheelchair access.

23 THE LODGE

off Holmes Lane, Dodderhill Common, Hanbury, Bromsgrove, B60 4AU. Mark & Lesley Jackson. *1m N of Hanbury Village. 3½m E from M5 J5, on A38 at the Hanbury Turn Xrds take A4091 S towards Hanbury. After 2½m turn L into Holmes Ln, then immed L again into dirt track. Car Park (Worcs Woodland Trust) on L.* **Sat 2, Sun 3 July (11-4). Adm £4, chd free. Cream teas. including gluten free options.** 1½ acre garden attached to a part C16 black and white house (not open) with three lawned areas, traditional greenhouse, various beds plus stunning views over the North Worcestershire countryside. Small display of classic cars plus other cars of interest. Garden is wheelchair accessible, disabled parking within grounds, toilets not wheelchair accessible. No dogs.

Spetchley Park Gardens

24 MADRESFIELD COURT

Madresfield, Malvern, WR13 5AJ. Trustees of Lord Beauchamp's 1963 Settlement, www.madresfieldestate.co.uk. *2m E of Malvern. Entrance ½m S of Madresfield village.* **Sun 22 May (12-5). Adm £10, chd £4. Tea.** Gardens mainly laid out in 1865, based on three avenues of oak, cedar and lombardy poplar, within and around which are specimen trees and flowering shrubs. Meadows within the avenues covered in daffodils, and later, fritillaries, bluebells, cowslips etc. Recent rhododendron plantings. Holly hedge enclosure with 100m walk of peonies and irises, next to a crescent tunnel of pollarded limes. Overall a parkland garden of approx 60 acres.

♿ 🐎 🍸 🎵

25 NEW MANOR COTTAGE

Hadzor, Droitwich, WR9 7DR. Mr Ian & Mrs Caroline Hancock. *Approx 10 mins from either J5 or J6 from M5. J5: A38 S 1st L B4065 to L, B4090, under M5, R to Hadzor Ln for 1m / J6: A4538 to A38, R to island R on Adoyes Way R at island to Primsland Way R on Tagwell Rd L on Middle Ln 2nd L to Hadzor Ln.* **Sat 16 July (1-6). Adm £4.50, chd free. Home-made teas.** We moved here six years ago to fulfil my desire to develop a garden large enough to keep us busy for years! The plot is just under an acre with borders surrounding the cottage. Large specimen trees and mixed hedges help give the garden structure. The pond is a definite pull to people and nature alike. We have many fruit trees, island beds, vegetables and a small woodland area. We are developing a new outdoor kitchen/patio area with a brick pillar pergola.

🍸 🎵

26 74 MEADOW ROAD

Wythall, B47 6EQ. Joe Manchester, 01564 829589, joe@cogentscreenprint.co.uk. *4m E of Alvechurch. 2m N from J3 M42. On A435 at Becketts Farm r'about take rd signed Earlswood/Solihull. Approx 250 metres turn L into School Dr, then L into Meadow Rd.* **Visits by arrangement May to Aug. Adm £3.50, chd free. Light refreshments.** Has been described as one of the most unusual urban gardens dedicated to woodland, shade-loving plants. 'Expect the unexpected' in

a few tropical and foreign species. Meander through the garden under the majestic pine, eucalyptus and silver birch. Sit and enjoy the peaceful surroundings and see how many different ferns and hostas you can find. As seen on BBC Gardeners' World.

✿ ♿ 🍸

27 MILLBROOK LODGE

Millham Lane, Alfrick, Worcester, WR6 5HS. Andrea & Doug Bright, andreabright@hotmail.co.uk. *11m from M5 J7. A4103 from Worcester to Bransford r'about, then Suckley Rd for 3m to Alfrick Pound. Turn L at sign for Old Storridge - No Through Road.* **Sun 17 July, Sun 4 Sept (1-5). Adm £5, chd free. Home-made teas. Visits also by arrangement Apr to Oct for groups of 10+.** 3½ acre garden and woodland developed by current owners over 25 years. Large informal flowerbeds planted for year-round interest, from spring flowering bulbs, camellias and magnolias through to asters and dahlias. Pond with stream and bog garden. Fruit and vegetable garden and gravel garden. Peaceful setting in an area of outstanding natural beauty and opposite a nature reserve.

✿ 🍸

28 ◆ MORTON HALL GARDENS

Morton Hall Lane, Holberrow Green, Redditch, B96 6SJ. Mrs A Olivieri, www.mortonhallgardens.co.uk. *In centre of Holberrow Green, at a wooden bench around a tree, turn up Morton Hall Ln. Follow NGS signs to gate opposite Morton Hall Farm.* **For NGS: Sat 27 Aug (10-5). Adm £10, chd free. Pre-booking essential, please visit www.mortonhallgardens.co.uk for information & booking. Home-made teas. For other opening times and information, please email or visit garden website.** Perched atop an escarpment with breathtaking views, hidden behind a tall hedge, lies a Georgian country house with a unique garden of outstanding beauty. A garden for all seasons, it features one of the country's largest fritillary spring meadows, sumptuous herbaceous summer borders, a striking potager, a majestic woodland rockery and an elegant Japanese Stroll Garden with tea house. Tulip Festival on first May bank holiday weekend. Visits by appointment from April to September. ALL visits must be pre-booked via

the Morton Hall Garden website. For NGS Open Day, click on the YELLOW BANNER on the Morton Hall Gardens homepage. Pre-booking closes at 5pm on 26.08.22.

♿ 🍸

29 NIMROD, 35 ALEXANDRA ROAD

Malvern, WR14 1HE. Margaret & David Cross, 01684 569019, margaret.cross@ifdev.net. *From A449. From Malvern Link, pass train stn, ahead at T-lights, 1st R into Alexandra Rd. From Great Malvern, go through Link Top T-lights (junction with B4503), 1st L.* **Sun 1, Mon 2 May (10.30-5.30). Adm £4.50, chd free. Light refreshments. Visits also by arrangement May to Sept.** Overlooked by the Malvern Hills, the garden is on two levels with mature horse chestnuts, western red cedars, wildlife pond, small wildflower meadow, shady woodland area, cottage garden, Japanese garden, rockeries and a New Zealand influenced area. An arbour inspired by Geoff Hamilton, also a treehouse and den for accompanied children. Elgar wrote some of the Enigma variations in a bell tent here! With help, the garden can be accessed by wheelchair, there are few steps but gravel paths and gradients. If advised we can offer closer parking.

♿ 🐎 🍸

You can make a difference! Join our Great British Garden Party fundraising campaign and raise money for some of the best-loved nursing and health charities. Visit ngs.org.uk/gardenparty to find out how you can get involved

GROUP OPENING

30 NORTH WORCESTER GARDENS

Northwick, Worcester, WR3 7BZ.
Five town gardens off A449, Ombersley Rd, S of Claines r'about. Look for the Yellow signs from the main road. **Sat 18, Sun 19 June (11-5). Combined adm £6, chd free. Home-made teas in a neighbouring garden in Beckett Drive.**

5 BECKETT DRIVE
Jacki & Pete Ager.
(See separate entry)

14 BECKETT ROAD
Mr Mike & Mrs Julia Roberts.

19 BEVERE CLOSE
Mr Malcolm & Mrs Diane Styles.

10 LUCERNE CLOSE
Mark & Karen Askwith,
01905756870.
Visits also by arrangement.

27 SHELDON PARK ROAD
Mr Alan & Mrs Helen Kirby.

Five town gardens on the northern edge of Worcester each having its own identity. The diversity of this quintet of gardens would satisfy anyone from a dedicated plantsman to an enthusiastic amateur while also offering plenty of ideas for landscaping, planting and structures. The landscaped garden at 5 Beckett Drive inc borders planted at different levels using palettes of harmonising or contrasting colours complemented by innovative features. 10 Lucerne Close is a cottage style garden literally packed with a wide variety of plants with secluded seating areas. 27 Sheldon Park Road is a contemporary style garden planned with low maintenance in mind and expertly planted with many different foliage plants. The hard landscaping set amongst colourful borders with vegetables planted amongst the flowers are significant features at 14 Beckett Road. And by no means least, 19 Bevere Drive with a stunning collection of bonsai trees planted in an oriental setting.

31 OAK TREE HOUSE
504 Birmingham Road, Marlbrook, Bromsgrove, B61 0HS. Di & Dave Morgan, 0121 445 3595, meandi@btinternet.com. *On main A38 midway between M42 J1 & M5 J4. Park in old A38 - R fork 250 yds N of garden or small area in front of Miller & Carter Pub car park 200 yds S or local roads.* **Sat 21, Sun 29 May (1.30-5.30). Adm £4, chd free. Pre-booking essential, please visit www.ngs.org.uk for information & booking. Home-made teas. Visits also by arrangement May to Aug for groups of 10 to 30.**
Plantswoman's cottage garden overflowing with plants, pots and interesting artifacts. Patio with plants and shrubs for spring, small pond and waterfall. Plenty of seating, separate wildlife pond, water features, alpine area, rear open vista. Scented plants, hostas, dahlias and lilies. Conservatory with art by owners. Visitor HS said: "Such a wonderful peaceful oasis". Also: 'Wynn's Patch' - part of next door's garden being maintained on behalf of the owner. Some structural changes are planned over the Autumn/Winter period.

32 3 OAKHAMPTON ROAD
Stourport-On-Severn, DY13 0NR. Sandra & David Traynor, 07970 014295, traynor@clickspeedphotography.co.uk. *Between Astley Cross Inn & Kings Arms. From Stourport take A451 Dunley Rd towards Worcester. 1600 yds turn L into Pearl Ln. 4th R into Red House Rd, past the Kings Arms Pub, & next L to Oakhampton Rd. Extra parking at Kings Arms Pub.* **Sun 26 June, Sun 31 July, Sat 27, Sun 28, Mon 29 Aug (10-6). Adm £5, chd free. Home-made teas. Visits also by arrangement June to Aug for groups of 5 to 20.**
Beginning in March 2016 our plan was to create a garden with a decidedly tropical feel to inc palms from around the world, with tree ferns, bananas and many other strange and unusual plants from warmer climes that would normally be considered difficult to grow here as well as a pond and small waterfall. Not a large garden but you'll be surprised what can be done with a small space. Some narrow paths.

33 THE OLD HOUSE
Naunton Beauchamp, Pershore, WR10 2LQ. Mrs Gayle Rowe, 07977327287, raspberryrowe@gmail.com. *In the centre of Naunton Beauchamp. From A422 in Upton Snodsbury, B4082 1.8m to L turn to village. From A44 in Pinvin B4082 for 2.7m to R turn to village. Garden on R. Park in field in Seaford Ln (follow signs) 300 yd walk.* **Sun 19 June, Sun 10 July, Sun 25 Sept (1.30-5). Adm £5, chd free. Home-made teas. Visits also by arrangement June to Sept for groups of 8 to 12. Parking is limited to 6 spaces.**
A charming 1 acre informal garden with water features, bridges, garden sculptures, orchard, vegetable garden and lawns set around a 300 year old part timber framed house (not open) with beautiful views out over fields of ancient plough and furrow and old orchards. There is partial wheelchair access to the garden, some is on flat lawns some on paths. Limited parking on drive - please book space with garden owner.

34 OVERBURY COURT
Overbury, GL20 7NP. Sir Bruce Bossom & Penelope Bossom, 01386 725111(office), gardens@overburyenterprises.co.uk. *5m NE of Tewkesbury. Overbury signed off A46. Turn off village road beside the church. Park by the gates & walk up the drive. What3words app - cars.blurs.crunches.* **Sat 2 Apr (10-3). Adm £5, chd free. Visits also by arrangement Mar to Sept for groups of 10 to 30.**
A 10 acre historic garden, at the centre of a picturesque Cotswold village, nestled amongst Capability Brown inspired Parkland. The Garden compromises vast formal lawns skirted by a series of rills and ponds which reflect the ancient plane trees that are dotted throughout the garden. The south side of the house has a formal south terrace with mixed borders and yew hedging, overlooking a formal lawn with a reflection pool and yew topiary. Running parallel to the pool is a long mix border which repeats its colours of silver and gold down to the pool house at the end of the garden. Under a grand yew hedge you will find a column garden which was designed by James Alexander-Sinclair in 2005 with its show piece wisteria looking effortlessly elegant in June. On the

Farlands

north side of the house is a woodland grotto first opened in 1903 which has waterfalls and harmonious naturalised planting. Local pubs in Conderton (The Yew Tree) and Kemerton (The Crown) as well as great cafes in Kemerton (Kemerton Coffee House) and Beckford (The Old PO). Some slopes, while all the garden can be viewed, parts are not accessible to wheelchairs.

35 PEAR TREE COTTAGE
Witton Hill, Wichenford, WR6 6YX. Pamela & Alistair Thompson, 01886 888295, peartree.pam@gmail.com, www.peartreecottage.me. *13m NW of Worcester & 2m NE of Martley. From Martley, take B4197. Turn R into Horn Lane then 2nd L signed Witton Hill. Keep L & Pear Tree Cottage is on R at top of hill.* **Sun 1 May (11-5); Wed 31 Aug (2-9.30). Adm £5, chd free. Home-made teas. Sun 31 Aug - Wine**

& Pimms after 6pm. Visits also by arrangement May to Sept. £5 garden entry excludes cost of teas.
A Grade II listed black and white cottage (not open) South West facing gardens with far reaching views across orchards to Abberley Clock Tower. The ¾ acre garden comprises gently sloping lawns with mixed and woodland borders, shade and plenty of strategically placed seating. The garden exudes a quirky and humorous character with the odd surprise and even includes a Shed of the Year Runner Up 2017. 'Garden by Twilight' evenings are very popular. Trees, shrubs and sculptures are softly uplit and the garden is filled with 100s of candles and nightlights (weather permitting). Visitors are invited to listen to the owls and watch the bats whilst enjoying a glass of wine. Regional Winner, The English Garden's The Nation's Favourite Gardens 2021 Partial wheelchair access.

36 NEW 3 PERRYFIELDS ROAD
Bromsgrove, B61 8SY. Mrs Caroline Mytton. *1½ m N of Bromsgrove town centre. Take Stourbridge Rd - B4091 towards Catshill. Take 2nd L past Sainsbury's into Perryfields Rd. Parking on road in King Edward Rd -1st L off Perryfields Rd.* **Sat 28 May, Sat 17 Sept (2-5). Adm £3, chd free. Pre-booking essential, please visit www.ngs.org.uk for information & booking. Light refreshments.**
Relatively small garden but still evolving as a working owner's time and new ideas allow. Originally mainly a lawned garden, areas developed so far inc informal, well-stocked island and long, curved borders with all round interest and colour - a variety of fruit trees, acers, grasses, roses, shrubs, perennials, alpines and spring flowering bulbs within an overall cottage garden theme. Selection of plants for sale.

GROUP OPENING

37 PERSHORE GARDENS

Pershore, WR10 1BG. Group Co-ordinator Jan Garratt, www.visitpershore.co.uk. On B4084 between Worcester & Evesham, & 6m from J7 on M5. There is also a train station to N of town. Sat 11, Sun 12 June (1-5). Combined adm £7.50, chd free. Refreshments at selected gardens as indicated on the map/description sheet.

Most years about twenty gardens open in Pershore. This small town has been opening gardens as part of the NGS for 50 years, almost continuously. In those days the open gardens were in the Georgian heart of the town but now, gardens open from all over the town. Some gardens are surprisingly large, well over an acre, while others are courtyard gardens. All have their individual appeal and present great variety. The wealth of pubs, restaurants and cafes offer ample opportunities for refreshment while the Abbey and the River Avon are some of the many points of interest in this market town. Tickets, which take the form of a map and garden descriptions, are valid for both days. They can be purchased a week before the event at 'Blue' in Broad Street or at the Town Hall. On the weekend they can be bought at Number 8 Community Arts Centre in the High Street and any open garden. Refreshments available in pubs, hotels and cafes in the town, at Holy Redeemer School and in Number 8 Community Arts Centre.

🐕 ✱ 🚻 🚌 🍵

38 RAVELIN

Gilberts End, Hanley Castle, WR8 0AS. Mrs Christine Peer, 01684 310215, cvpeer55@btinternet.com. From Worcester/Callow End B4424 or from Upton B4211 to Hanley Castle. Then B4209 to Hanley Swan. From Malvern B4209 to Hanley Swan. At pond/Xrds turn to Welland. ½m turn L opp Hall to Gilberts End. Sat 21, Sun 22 May, Sat 17, Sun 18 Sept, Sat 8, Sun 9 Oct (1-5). Adm £5, chd free. Home-made teas. Visits also by arrangement Apr to Oct.

Established, yet ever developing ½ acre garden with many unusual plants full of colour and texture whatever the season. Of interest to plant lovers and flower arrangers alike with views overlooking the fields and Malvern Hills. Year-round interest provided by a wide variety of hellebores, hardy geraniums, aconitums, heucheras, Michaelmas daisies, grasses and dahlias and a 50 yr old silver pear tree. Thought to be built on medieval clay works in the royal hunting forest. Garden containing herbaceous and perennial planting with gravel garden, woodland area, pond, summerhouse and plenty of seating areas around the garden. A quiz for children.

🐕 ✱ 🚻 🍵

39 REST HARROW

California Lane, Welland, Malvern, WR13 6NQ. Mr Malcolm & Mrs Anne Garner. 4.6m S of Gt Malvern In un-adopted California Lane off B4208 Worcester Rd. From Gt Malvern A449 towards Ledbury, L onto Hanley Rd/B4209 signed Upton. After about 1m R (Blackmore Park Rd/B4209). After 1m R onto B4208. After ⅓m R (California Lane) - garden 300 yds on L. Sat 18, Sun 19 June, Sat 20, Sun 21 Aug (1.30-5). Adm £5, chd free. Pre-booking essential, please phone 01684 310503 or email anne.restharrow@gmail.com for information & booking. Light refreshments.

1½ acres developed over 15 years with 5 acre wildflower meadow, woodland and stunning views of Malvern Hills. Colourful and diverse flower beds, unusual plants, roses, alstroemeria, stocks and shrubs. Potager kitchen garden, fruit trees and rustic trellis made from our own pollarded trees. Sit, relax, enjoy the views or stroll down through the wildflower meadow to the wooded wetland border area. Wheelchair access in garden but not down in field.

♿ 🍵

40 RHYDD GARDENS

Worcester Road, Hanley Castle, Worcester, WR8 0AB. Bill Bell & Sue Brooks, 01684 311001, NGS@Rhyddgardens.co.uk, www.rhyddgardens.co.uk. 2Km N of Hanley Castle. Gates 200m N of layby on B4211. Sat 25, Sun 26 June (2-6). Adm £5, chd free. Home-made teas. Visits also by arrangement.

Two walled gardens and a 60 foot greenhouse from the early 1800s set in 6 acres with wonderful views of the entire length of the Malvern ridge. One Walled garden is set out with formal paths and borders bounded by box hedging. We are planting fruit trees in espaliers and cordons as they would have been when the garden was first set out and have a nature area with walks and some woodland. Teas and homemade cakes on the lawn. Self-guided tour leaflets available. Wheelchair access to the main walled garden with grass and paving paths. Parking near gates can be arranged in advance.

♿ 🚌 🍵 ♪))

41 THE RIVER SCHOOL

Oakfield House, Droitwich Road, Worcester, WR3 7ST. Christian Education Trust -Worcester, www.riverschool.co.uk. 2.4m N of Worcester City Centre on A38 towards Droitwich. At J6 M5, take A449 signed for Kidderminster, turn off at 1st turning marked for Blackpole. Turn R to Fernhill Heath & at T- junction with A38 turn L. The school is ½m on R. Sat 30 Apr, Thur 28 July (10.30-3.30). Adm £5, chd free. Light refreshments in the Lewis Room near garden entrance.

A former Horticultural College garden being brought back to life. For 35 years after WW2 it was known as Oakfield Teacher Training College for Horticulture. It now features a Forest School, apiary, wildlife pond, and children's vegetable plots within a walled garden. It has many less common trees and shrubs with others coming to light as we develop the Estate.

🍵 ♪))

More than 1,200 people have been cared for at Y Bwthyn NGS Macmillan Specialist Palliative Care Unit, a unit that would simply not have been built without the National Garden Scheme funding

42 ◆ RIVERSIDE GARDENS AT WEBBS
Wychbold, Droitwich, WR9 0DG. Webbs of Wychbold, 01527 860000, www.webbsdirect.co.uk. *2m N of Droitwich Spa. 1m N of M5 J5 on A38. Follow tourism signs from M5.* For opening times and information, please phone or visit garden website.
2½ acres. Themed gardens inc colour spectrum, tropical and dry garden, rose garden, vegetable garden, National Collection of Harvington Hellebores, seaside garden, bamboozeleum and self-sufficient garden. The New Wave garden is a natural wildlife area and inc seasonal interest with grasses and perennials. *New for 2022* Extended pathways and a new woodland walk. There are willow wigwams and wooden tepees made for children to play in, a bird hide, the Hobbit House and beehives which produce honey for our own food hall. Our New Wave Garden and new Woodland Walk (2022) has had new paths installed and wheelchair accessible.

43 ROTHBURY
5 St Peter's Road, North Malvern, WR14 1QS. John Bryson, Philippa Lowe & David. *7m W of M5 J7 (Worcester). Turn off A449 Worcester to Ledbury Rd at B4503, signed Leigh Sinton. Almost immed take the middle rd (Hornyold Rd). St Peter's Rd is ¼m uphill, 2nd R.* **Sun 22, Sun 29 May, Sun 24 July (1-6). Adm £4, chd free. Home-made teas. Gluten free options available.**
Set on slopes of Malvern Hills, ⅓ acre plant-lovers' garden surrounding Arts and Crafts house (not open), created by owners since 1999. Herbaceous borders, rockery, pond, small orchard. Siberian irises in May and magnificent Eucryphia glutinosa in July. A series of hand-excavated terraces accessed by sloping paths and steps. Views and seats. Partial wheelchair access. One very low step at entry, one standard step to main lawn and one to WC. Decking slope to top lawn. Dogs on leads.

44 ◆ SPETCHLEY PARK GARDENS
The Estate Office, Spetchley Park, Worcester, WR5 1RS. Mr Henry Berkeley,

01905 345106, enquiries@spetchleygardens.co.uk, www.spetchleygardens.co.uk. *2m E of Worcester. On A44, follow brown signs.* **For NGS: Sun 10 Apr, Sun 3 July (10.30-5). Adm £8.50, chd £3.50. Home-made teas. For other opening times and information, please phone, email or visit garden website.**
Surrounded by glorious countryside lays one of Britain's best kept secrets. Spetchley is a garden for all tastes and ages, containing one of the biggest private collections of plant varieties outside the major botanical gardens and weaving a magical trail for younger visitors. Spetchley is not a formal paradise of neatly manicured lawns or beds but rather a wondrous display of plants, shrubs and trees woven into a garden of many rooms and vistas. Plant sales, gift shop and coffee shop serving homemade treats, and picnics during the open season. Gravel paths, and grassed areas.

45 ◆ STONE HOUSE COTTAGE GARDENS
Church Lane, Stone, DY10 4BG. Louisa Arbuthnott, 07817 921146, louisa@shcn.co.uk, www.shcn.co.uk. *2m SE of Kidderminster. Via A448 towards Bromsgrove, next to church, turn up drive.* **For opening times and information, please phone, email or visit garden website.**
A beautiful and romantic walled garden adorned with unusual brick follies. This acclaimed garden is exuberantly planted and holds one of the largest collections of rare plants in the country. It acts as a shop window for the adjoining nursery. Open Wed to Sat late March to late August 10-5. Partial wheelchair access.

46 THE TYNINGS
Church Lane, Stoulton, Worcester, WR7 4RE. John & Leslie Bryant, 01905 840189, johnlesbryant@btinternet.com. *5m S of Worcester; 3m N of Pershore. On the B4084 between M5 J7 & Pershore. The Tynings lies beyond the church at the extreme end of Church Ln. Ample parking.* **Visits by arrangement June to Sept. Adm £5, chd free. Light refreshments.**
Acclaimed plantsman's ½ acre garden, generously planted with a large selection of rare trees and shrubs. Features inc specialist

collection of lilies, many unusual climbers and rare ferns. The colour continues into late summer with cannas, dahlias, berberis, euonymus and tree colour. Surprises around every corner. Lovely views of adjacent Norman Church and surrounding countryside. Plants labelled and plant lists available.

47 THE WALLED GARDEN
6 Rose Terrace, off Fort Royal Hill, Worcester, WR5 1BU. William & Julia Scott. *Close to City centre. ½m from Cathedral. Via Fort Royal Hill, off London Rd (A44). Park on 1st section of Rose Terrace & walk 20yds down track.* **Sat 7, Wed 11 May, Sat 25, Wed 29 June (1-5). Adm £4, chd free. Tea.**
This C19 Walled Kitchen Garden, is formal in layout, with relaxed chemical free planting. An outer path connects the camellia walk, soft fruit cordons, compost heaps, an area awaiting archeological investigation, and bees in a new bee garden. The inner walk, leads to topiary, vegetables, flower gardens, cook's herb garden, old and new fruit trees, as well as medlar, mulberry and quince trees. Historic garden with a focus on herbs and their uses.

48 WALNUT COTTAGE
Lower End, Bricklehampton, Pershore, WR10 3HL. Mr Richard & Mrs Janet Williams. *2½ m S of Pershore on B4084, then R into Bricklehampton Lane to T-junction, then L. Cottage is on R.* **Sat 25, Sun 26 June (2-5). Adm £6, chd free. Wine.**
1½ acre garden with views of Bredon Hill, designed into rooms, many created with high formal hedging of beech, hornbeam, copper beech and yew. There is a small 'front garden' with circular gravel path, well-stocked original garden area with pond and arches to the side of the house. Magnolia garden with several species and magnificent tree garden with specimens from around the world. Over 200 roses, in colour themed beds, climbing over a pergola or up trees, greenhouse, raised Koi Carp pond and metal stairway leading to roof-based viewing platform surrounded by roses. The garden continues to evolve and a Japanese garden is planned. Plenty of seating and interesting artefacts.

49 WARNDON COURT

St Nicholas Lane, Worcester, WR4 0SL. Drs Rachel & David Pryke, 07944 854393, rachelgpryke@btinternet.com. *½m from J6 of M5, Worcester N. St Nicholas Ln is off Hastings Drive.* **Sun 22 May, Sun 12 June (12-4). Adm £5, chd free. Home-made teas in St Nicholas Church barn. Visits also by arrangement May to Aug for groups of 10 to 30. Garden and Church visits contact Rachel or Vicar Diane Cooksey 01905 611268.** Warndon Court is a 2 acre family garden surrounding a Grade II* listed farmhouse (not open) featuring a circular route taking in formal rose gardens and terraces, two ponds, pergolas, topiary (inc a scruffy dragon), pretty summerhouse, a potager and woodland walk along the dry moat and through the secret garden. It has bee-friendly wildlife areas and is home to great-crested newts and slow-worms. Grade I listed St Nicholas Church will also be open to visitors. There will be an exhibition of original oil paintings and display of vintage cars. The gardens around the house can be accessed across the lawn. The potager is accessible but the woodland walk is bumpy with slopes at each end.

&. 🐄 ❀ ☕))

50 WESTACRES

Wolverhampton Road, Prestwood, Stourbridge, DY7 5AN. Mrs Joyce Williams. *3m W of Stourbridge. A449 in between Wall Heath (2m) & Kidderminster (6m). Ample parking Prestwood Nurseries (next door).* **Sat 20, Sun 21 Aug (11-4). Adm £4, chd free.**
¾ acre plant collector's garden with unusual plants and many different varieties of acers, hostas, shrubs. Woodland walk, large fish pool. Covered tea area with home-made cakes. Come and see for yourselves, you won't be disappointed. Described by a visitor in the visitors book as 'A garden which we all wished we could have, at least once in our lifetime'. Garden is flat. Disabled parking.

&. 🐄 ❀ 🚐 ☕

51 WHARF HOUSE

Newnham Bridge, Tenbury Wells, WR15 8NY. Gareth Compton & Matthew Bartlett, 01584 781966, gco@no5.com, www.wharfhousegardener.blog. *Off A456 in hamlet of Broombank, between Mamble & Newnham Bridge. Follow signs. Do not rely on*

SatNav. **Sat 2, Sun 3 July (10-5). Adm £5, chd free. Home-made teas. Visits also by arrangement May to Sept for groups of 10+.**
2 acre country garden, set around an C18 house and outbuildings (not open). Mixed herbaceous borders with colour theming: white garden, bright garden, spring garden, canal garden, long double borders, intimate courtyards, a scented border, stream with little bridge to an island, vegetable garden. The garden is on several levels, with some uneven paths and only partial wheelchair access.

🐄 ❀ ☕

52 WHITCOMBE HOUSE

Overbury, Tewkesbury, GL20 7NZ. Faith & Anthony Hallett, 01386 725206, faith.hallett1@gmail.com. *9m S of Evesham, 5m NE Tewkesbury. Leave A46 at Beckford to Overbury (2m). Or B4080 from Tewkesbury through Bredon/Kemerton (5m). Or small lane signed Overbury at r'about junction A46, A435 & B4077. Approx 5m from J9 M5.* **Sun 1 May, Sun 12 June, Sun 28 Aug (1.30-4.30). Adm £5, chd free. Home-made teas. Visits also by arrangement Apr to Sept for groups of up to 35.** Cotswold stone walled shrub and herbaceous garden flanked by mature Beech, Birch, Acer and Catalpa. Spring fed gravel brook bordered by primula, hosta, hydrangea, lavender and rose. Borders of herbaceous, climbers and shrubs. Pastel colours merge with cool white and blue and later mellow yellow. Nooks, arches, vine, fig, vegetable parterre over bridges with terrace and benches on island for peaceful reflection. Plant store open C17 Listed Cotswold stone walled House (not open). Lovely village of Overbury with Norman St Faiths Church Wheelchair access through iron gate at south entrance - signed.

&. 🐄 ❀ 🚐 ☕))

53 WHITE COTTAGE & NURSERY

Earls Common Road, Stock Green, Inkberrow, B96 6SZ. Mr & Mrs S M Bates, 01386 792414, smandjbates@aol.com, whitecottage.garden. *2m W of Inkberrow, 2m E of Upton Snodsbury. A422 Worcester to Alcester, turn at sign for Stock Green by Red Hart Pub, 1½m to T- junction, turn L, 500 yds on the L.* **Sun 10 Apr, Sun 1, Mon 2, Sun 15 May, Sun 5, Sun 19 June**

(11-4.30). Adm £4.50, chd free. Home-made teas.
2 acre garden with large herbaceous and shrub borders, island beds, stream and bog area. Spring meadow with 1000s of snakes head fritillaries. Formal area with lily pond and circular rose garden. Alpine rockery and new fern area. Large collection of interesting trees inc Nyssa sylvatica, Parrotia persica, and Acer 'October Glory' for magnificent Autumn colour and many others. Nursery and Garden open most Thursdays (10.30-5), please check before visiting. For further information please phone, email or visit garden website and Facebook page.

&. ❀ 🚐 ☕

54 ♦ WHITLENGE GARDENS

Whitlenge Lane, Hartlebury, DY10 4HD. Mr & Mrs K J Southall, 01299 250720, keith.southall@creativelandscapes. co.uk, www.whitlenge.co.uk. *5m S of Kidderminster, on A442. A449 Kidderminster to Worcester L at T-lights, A442 signed Droitwich, over island, ¼m, 1st R into Whitlenge Ln. Follow brown signs.* **For NGS: Sat 2, Sun 3 Apr, Sat 25, Sun 26 June, Sat 3, Sun 4 Sept (10-5). Adm £5, chd £2. Light refreshments in the adjacent tea rooms. For other opening times and information, please phone, email or visit garden website.**
3 acre show garden of professional garden designer inc large variety of trees, shrubs etc. Features inc a twisted brick pillar pergola, 2½ metre diameter solid oak moon gate set into reclaimed brickwork, and this year a new four turreted, moated castle folly with vertical wall planter set between two water falls, then walk through giant gunnera leaves to the Fairy Garden. There is a full size Standing Stone Circle, a 400 sq metre turf labyrinth and a children's play/pet corner. Extensive plant nursery and Tea room. Wheelchair access but mix of hard paths, gravel paths and lawn.

&. ❀ 🚐 ☕))

55 WILLOW POND

Pass Street, Eckington, Pershore, WR10 3AX. James Field & Mike Washbourne, 07970 962842, jamesfield@hotmail.com, www.willow-pond.co.uk. *Black & white cottage about half way down Pass St. 4m S of Pershore; 7m N of Tewkesbury. In Eckington, 2nd R off New Rd.* **Visits by arrangement Apr to Sept. Adm £5, chd free.**

Home-made teas.
Colourful and informal village garden of approx 1 acre with a listed black and white cottage (not open). Gardened for wildlife, there are areas of lawn and long grass with well-stocked, herbaceous borders and a vegetable plot. Several water features inc a pond. Rose covered pergola, terrace garden and cottage garden along with large planted pots and choice plants. Lots of places to sit and relax.

GROUP OPENING

57 WITHYBED GREEN
Withybed Green, Alvechurch, Nr Birmingham, B48 7RJ. *3m N of Redditch, 11m SW of Birmingham. By car to Alvechurch (6 mins from J2 of M42.). Take Tanyard Ln or Bear Hill following NGS signs along Snake Ln & Withybed Ln. By rail to Alvechurch Stn then a 10 minute walk along canal towpath.* **Sun 26 June (1-6). Combined adm £6, chd free.** Light refreshments at 'The New Smithy' next to the Crown public house.

FAIRVIEW
Bryan & Angela Haycocks.

5 FORWARD COTTAGES
Mary Green.

2 FRONT COTTAGES
Clive & Ann Southern.

3 FRONT COTTAGES
Sarah & Steve Beddoe.

THE MOUSEHOLE
Lucy Cox.

NEW **THE NEW SMITHY**
Ms Jan Brice.

1 REAR COTTAGES
Mr David & Mrs Serena Saunders.

NEW **2 REAR COTTAGES**
Ms Mary Parsons.

6 REAR COTTAGES
Amelda Brown & John Adams.

NEW **THE REST**
Ms Jo Nind.

SELVAS
Jo & Matt Scriven.

A small hamlet with a canal side pub featuring cottage gardens large and small set in beautiful Worcestershire countryside, with spinneys of ancient woodland. Withybed Green is compact and you can easily walk round all the gardens. Wheelchair access is extremely limited.

Pear Tree Cottage

© Ian Thwaites

YORKSHIRE

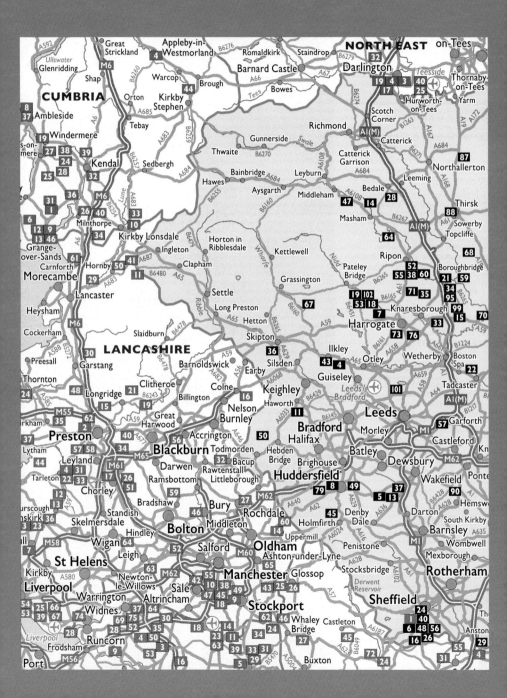

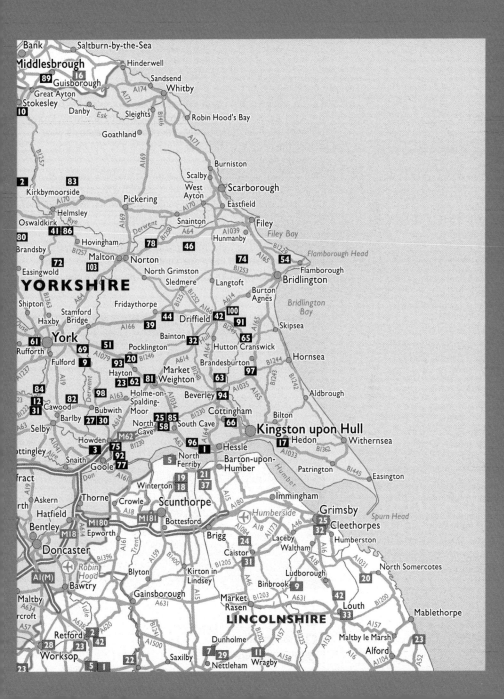

Volunteers

County Organisers

East Yorks
Helen Marsden
01430 860222
helen.marsden@ngs.org.uk

North Yorks
David Lis 01439 788846
david.lis@ngs.org.uk

South & West Yorks
Veronica Brook 01423 340875
veronica.brook@ngs.org.uk

County Treasurer
Angela Pugh 01423 330456
angela.pugh@ngs.org.uk

Publicity & Social Media
Jane Cooper 01484 604232
jane.cooper@ngs.org.uk

Booklet Coordinator
Jane Cooper (as above)

Booklet Advertising
Sally Roberts 01423 871419
sally.roberts@ngs.org.uk

Assistant County Organisers

East Yorks
Ian & Linda McGowan
01482 896492
ianandlinda.mcgowan@ngs.org.uk

Hazel Rowe 01430 861439
hazel.rowe@ngs.org.uk

Natalie Verow 01759 368444
natalieverow@aol.com

North Yorks
Dee Venner 01765 690842
dee.venner@ngs.org.uk

South & West Yorks
Felicity Bowring 01729 823551
felicity.bowring@ngs.org.uk

Jane Hudson 01484 866697
jane.hudson@ngs.org.uk

Elizabeth & David Smith
01484 644320
elizabethanddavid.smith@ngs.org.uk

Peter Lloyd 07958 928698
peter.lloyd@ngs.org.uk

Yorkshire, England's largest county, stretches from the Pennines in the west to the rugged coast and sandy beaches of the east: a rural landscape of moors, dales, vales and rolling wolds.

Nestling on riverbanks lie many historic market towns, and in the deep valleys of the west and south others retain their 19th century industrial heritage of coal, steel and textiles.

The wealth generated by these industries supported the many great estates, houses and gardens throughout the county. From Hull in the east, a complex network of canals weaves its way across the county, connecting cities to the sea and beyond.

The Victorian spa town of Harrogate with the RHS garden at Harlow Carr, or the historic city of York with a minster encircled by Roman walls, are both ideal centres from which to explore the gardens and cultural heritage of the county.

We look forward to welcoming you to our private gardens – you will find that many of them open not only on a specific day, but also by arrangement for groups and individuals - we can help you to get in touch.

f @YorkshireNGS

@YorkshireNGS

@YorkshireNGS

Above: Duncanne House

OPENING DATES

All entries subject to change. For latest information check www.ngs.org.uk
Map locator numbers are shown to the right of each garden name.

February

Snowdrop Festival

Sunday 20th
Devonshire Mill — 20
Millrace Garden — 57

March

Sunday 27th
Fawley House — 25

April

Sunday 3rd
Goldsborough Hall — 33

Sunday 10th
Clifton Castle — 14
Ellerker House — 23

Saturday 23rd
249 Barnsley Road — 5

Sunday 24th
249 Barnsley Road — 5

May

Tuesday 3rd
Markenfield Hall — 55

Saturday 7th
The Cottage — 17

Sunday 8th
The Cottage — 17
Highfield Cottage — 42
Low Hall — 53
◆ RHS Garden Harlow Carr — 73
Thirsk Hall — 88

Sunday 15th
Scape Lodge — 79
◆ Stillingfleet Lodge — 84
Well House — 95
Whixley Gardens — 99

Wednesday 18th
◆ Parcevall Hall Gardens — 67
Primrose Bank Garden and Nursery — 69

Sunday 22nd
◆ Jackson's Wold — 46
Millrace Garden — 57
The Ridings — 74
Rudding Park — 76

Wednesday 25th
5 Hill Top — 43
Pilmoor Cottages — 68

Sunday 29th
NEW Bank Wheel — 3
Firvale Perennial Garden — 29
5 Hill Top — 43
Rewela Cottage — 72
Rosemary Cottage — 75

Monday 30th
115 Millhouses Lane — 56

June

Wednesday 1st
Pilmoor Cottages — 68

Friday 3rd
◆ Shandy Hall Gardens — 80
Thimbleby Hall — 87

Saturday 4th
Frog Hall Barn — 30
The Grange — 35
Old Sleningford Hall — 64
Shiptonthorpe Gardens — 81

Sunday 5th
NEW Firby Hall — 28
Frog Hall Barn — 30
The Grange — 35
Holmfield — 44
Old Sleningford Hall — 64
Shiptonthorpe Gardens — 81
◆ The Yorkshire Arboretum — 103

Wednesday 8th
Holmfield — 44

Thursday 9th
Skipwith Hall — 82

Sunday 12th
Brookfield — 11
Clifton Castle — 14
Cobble Cottage — 15
The Cottage — 16
3 Embankment Road — 24
Grafton Gardens — 34

Tuesday 14th
Markenfield Hall — 55

Wednesday 15th
Primrose Bank Garden and Nursery — 69

Thursday 16th
Arden Hall — 2
Land Farm — 50

Friday 17th
◆ Shandy Hall Gardens — 80

Saturday 18th
Galehouse Barn — 31
NEW Tudor Croft — 89

Sunday 19th
Birstwith Hall — 7
Galehouse Barn — 31
◆ Jackson's Wold — 46
The Old Priory — 62
The Old Vicarage — 65
NEW Tudor Croft — 89
Tythe Farm House — 91
The Villa — 92
NEW Walled Gardens of Beverley — 94

Wednesday 22nd
Saltmarshe Hall — 77

Friday 24th
NEW Prospect House — 71

Sunday 26th
The Cottage — 16
Fernleigh — 26
Havoc Hall — 41
Scape Lodge — 79
Yorke House & White Rose Cottage — 102

Wednesday 29th
Glencoe House — 32

July

Saturday 2nd
NEW 12 Brendon Drive — 8

Sunday 3rd
Cobble Cottage — 15

Grafton Gardens — 34
Highfield Cottage — 42
Myton Grange — 59
23 The Paddock — 66
The Ridings — 74
White Wynn — 98
NEW 5 Wold Road — 100

Wednesday 6th
3 The Barns — 4

Thursday 7th
The Priory, Nun Monkton — 70

Saturday 9th
Cawood Gardens — 12
Ferry House — 27

Sunday 10th
NEW Bridge House — 10
Brookfield — 11
Cawood Gardens — 12
Dacre Banks & Summerbridge Gardens — 19
Honey Head — 45
Sleightholmedale Lodge — 83

Tuesday 12th
Markenfield Hall — 55

Wednesday 13th
NEW Mires Beck Nursery — 58

Saturday 16th
The Cottage — 16
Stonefield Cottage — 85

Sunday 17th
The Nursery — 61
Stonefield Cottage — 85
The Vines — 93

Monday 18th
The Nursery — 61

Tuesday 19th
The Nursery — 61

Wednesday 20th
Jervaulx Hall — 47

Sunday 24th
Goldsborough Hall — 33
NEW 32 West Street — 97

Wednesday 27th
The Grange — 36

Saturday 30th
249 Barnsley Road — 5
Kirkwood Hospice — 49

Sunday 31st
249 Barnsley Road — 5
Fernleigh — 26
Rewela Cottage — 72

Tudor Croft

THE GARDENS

1 🆕 **ANNE TURNER MEMORIAL ALLOTMENTS**
Church Road, North Ferriby, HU14 3AA. Anne Turner Allotments. *From Hull, A63 W from Humber Br to N. Ferriby junction. At village Xrds S towards parish church. Rail stn & cycle access available.* **Sun 7 Aug (11-4). Adm £4, chd free. Light refreshments in nearby Riding For the Disabled cafe 500m from allotments.**
Allotments founded in 1902 by philanthropist Anne Turner for the local community celebrating 120 years of allotment gardening. There are 83 plots cared for by enthusiastic gardeners producing flowers, fruit and vegetables in an attractive setting. Competition sweet peas and dahlias in addition to homegrown produce. A protected woodland copse providing a wildlife sanctuary is currently being restored. Main paths accessible, some paths between plots too narrow for safe access.
🚽 🐕 ✿ 🍵))

2 **ARDEN HALL**
Hawnby, York, YO62 5LS. Victoria Savile. *L at shop in Hawnby, follow road up past church and over bridge.* **Thur 16 June (1-5). Adm £7, chd free. Pre-booking essential, please visit www.ngs.org.uk for information & booking. Home-made teas.**
Historic gardens featuring a 2 acre walled garden with formal stone terraces providing exceptional views over Hawnby Hill and the national park. The planting is an informal mix of shrubs and perennials. A spring fed stream flows through the garden in a series of rills and formal ponds. Other striking features inc magnificent yew topiary, clipped box, a laburnum walk and a sunken greenhouse.
🍵))

3 🆕 **BANK WHEEL**
Ferry Lane, Airmyn, Goole, DN14 8LS. Frank & Angela Meneight. *On E edge of Airmyn village, close to Boothferry Bridge. From M62 Jct 36 or 37 follow signs to Airmyn. Ferry La is a narrow cul-de-sac.* **Sun 29 May (11-4). Adm £4, chd free. Home-made teas.**
One acre mature country garden surrounded by trees including formal and wild areas with plenty of seating

and interesting statuary. Mixed borders, greenhouse, summerhouse, small orchard with meadow. Two ponds, one with stream and waterfall. Woodland area with bluebells.
🚽 ✿ 🍵))

4 **3 THE BARNS**
Ben Rhydding Drive, Ilkley, LS29 8BG. Miss Linda Jones & Mr Allan Shaw. *2m from centre of Ilkley on edge of Ilkley Moor. From A65 turn at T-lights on to Wheatley Lane to Ben Rhydding. Go under railway bridge, as road bears R on corner turn L & then immed L through 4 stone pillars. Garden at top 1 mile.* **Wed 6 July (11.30-4.30). Adm £4, chd free.**
Charming small garden on the edge of Ilkley Moor with mixed herbaceous borders, small pond, oak summerhouse, greenhouse and raised bed area. Roses, hostas, geraniums, alstroemerias, perennials, trees and shrubs. Lovely view of Wharfe valley can be seen on approach to the garden. Limited parking nearby. Coffee, lunch and afternoon tea available in the restaurant or on the terrace at Audley Clevedon next door. 10% discount for NGS garden visitors with their ticket.
✿ 🍵

5 **249 BARNSLEY ROAD**
Flockton, Wakefield, WF4 4AL. Nigel & Anne Marie Booth, 01924 848967, nigel.booth1@btopenworld.com. *On A637 Barnsley Road. M1 J38 or 39 follow the signs for Huddersfield. Parking on Manor House Rd (WF4 4AL) & Hardcastle Lane.* **Sat 23, Sun 24 Apr, Sat 30, Sun 31 July (1-5). Adm £5, chd free. Home-made teas. Visits also by arrangement Apr to Sept for groups of 15+.**
An elevated garden with panoramic views. 1/3 acre south facing garden packed with an abundance of spring colour, created from 1000s of bulbs, perennials, shrubs and trees. Make a return visit in the summer to view a transformation, with up to 60 hanging baskets and over 150 pots, creating the 'wow factor' summer garden. Partial wheelchair access. There will be a ukulele group playing live in the garden at the summer opening. Disabled drop-off point at the bottom of the drive.
🚽 🐕 ✿ 🍵

6 **90 BENTS ROAD**
Bents Green, Sheffield, S11 9RL. Mrs Hilary Hutson, 0114 225 8570, h.hutson@paradiseregained.net. *3m SW of Sheffield. From inner ring road in Sheffield nr Waitrose, follow A625. Bents Rd approx 3m on R.* **Visits by arrangement July & Aug for groups of up to 50. Individuals & groups welcome. Adm £4, chd free. Light refreshments.**
Plantswoman's NE facing garden with many unusual and borderline-hardy species. Patio with alpine troughs for year-round interest and pots of colourful tropical plants in summer. Mixed borders surround a lawn which leads to mature trees underplanted with shade-loving plants at end of garden. Front garden peaks in summer with hot-coloured blooms. Front garden and patio flat and accessible. Remainder of back garden accessed via 6 steps with handrail, so unsuitable for wheelchairs.
🚽 🐕 ✿ 🍵

7 **BIRSTWITH HALL**
High Birstwith, Harrogate, HG3 2JW. Sir James & Lady Aykroyd, 01423 770250, ladya@birstwithhall.co.uk. *5m NW of Harrogate. Between Hampsthwaite & Birstwith villages, close to A59 Harrogate/Skipton road.* **Sun 19 June (2-5). Adm £5, chd free. Home-made teas. Visits also by arrangement Apr to Aug for groups of 10 to 50.**
Charming and varied 4 acre garden nestling in secluded Yorkshire dale. Formal garden and ornamental orchard, extensive lawns leading to picturesque stream and large pond. Walled garden and Victorian greenhouse.
🚽 🐕 🚗 🍵

8 🆕 **12 BRENDON DRIVE**
Birkby, Huddersfield, HD2 2DF. Jon Caddick. *Off Birkby Road.* **Sat 2 July, Sat 10 Sept (11-4). Adm £3, chd free. Pre-booking essential, please visit www.ngs.org.uk for information & booking. Tea.**
The inspiration for this garden is to create a practical family space with an atmosphere of relaxation with many sensory experiences. Practical but packed with striking blooms, colour and interest throughout. Meandering paths and a pond, idyllic views, complemented by the sound of water and wildlife attracted to the garden. Architectural plants and wide borders create colour, drama and interest.
✿ 🍵

9 NEW BRIDGE HOUSE
Main Street, Elvington,
York, YO41 4AA. Mrs W
C Bundy, 01904 608297,
wendy@bundy.co.uk. *6m E from
York ring road (A64). On B1128 from
York, last house on R before bridge.*
Visits by arrangement Apr to Sept
for groups of up to 40.
A 2 acre garden carved out of the
floodplain of the River Derwent
about 40 years ago. The planting is
remarkable as it survives the annual
winter flooding of the river which can
last up to 2 months and is up to 2/3
feet deep. Mixed borders, shrubbery,
large pond with a kitchen garden
and orchard. Hostas and ferns thrive
here. Various devices in the kitchen
garden are used to keep above water
level. Slopes to the main garden are
relatively steep.

10 NEW BRIDGE HOUSE
Station Road, Stokesley, TS9 7AB.
Caroline & Adrian Rathmell. *From
B1257 in Stokesley, ½ m along
Station Rd heading S towards Kirkby.*
Sun 10 July (12-5). Adm £5, chd
free. Home-made teas.
A mature, colourful 1 acre country
garden created by the present owners
over 30 yrs. Many mixed herbaceous
borders planted for all season
interest with consideration for wildlife.
Extensive organic kitchen garden and
poultry. New gravel garden. Paddock
with grazing sheep. Large lawn,
mature trees and long distance views
to the North York Moors. Parking on
site or along the road. All areas are
wheelchair accessible. Some gravel
to cross.

11 BROOKFIELD
Jew Lane, Oxenhope, Keighley,
BD22 9HS. Mrs R L Belsey,
01535 643070. *5m SW of Keighley.
From Keighley take A629 (Halifax).
Fork R onto A6033 towards Haworth
& Oxenhope turn L at Xrds into
village. Turn R (Jew Lane) at bottom
of hill.* Sun 12 June, Sun 10 July
(1.30-5.30). Adm £4, chd free.
Home-made teas. Visits also
by arrangement June to Aug for
groups of 10 to 20.
An intimate 1 acre sloping garden
with steps and paths leading down
to a large pond with an island,
mallards and wild geese. Many
varieties of primula and dactylorrhiza
have seeded into the lower lawn

around a small pond with a stream.
Unusual trees and shrubs in a series
of island beds with many azaleas
and rhododendrons. Charming old
greenhouses and a conservatory.
'Round and round the garden'
children's quiz. Steep narrow paths,
not suitable for wheelchairs.

GROUP OPENING

12 CAWOOD GARDENS
Cawood, nr Selby,
YO8 3UG. 01757 268571,
davidjones051946@gmail.com.
*10m S of York on B1222 5m N of
Selby & 7m SE of Tadcaster. Village
maps given at all gardens.* Sat 9,
Sun 10 July (12-5). Combined
adm £6, chd free. Home-made
teas. Visits also by arrangement
June & July for groups of 10 to 30.

9 ANSON GROVE
Brenda Finnigan, 01757 268888,
beeart@ansongrove.co.uk.

21 GREAT CLOSE
David & Judy Jones,
01757 268571,
davidjones051946@gmail.com.

Two contrasting gardens in an
attractive historic village linked by
a pretty riverside walk to the C11
church and memorial garden and
across the Castle Garth to the
remains of Cawood Castle. 9 Anson
Grove is a small garden with tranquil
pools and secluded seating areas.
Narrow winding paths lead to views
of the oriental-style pagoda, bridge
and Zen garden. 21 Great Close is
a flower arranger's garden designed
and built by the owners. Interesting
trees and shrubs combine with
herbaceous borders inc many types
of grass.Two ponds are joined by a
stream, winding paths lead to the
vegetable garden and summerhouse,
then back to the colourful terrace
for views across the garden and
countryside beyond. Arts and crafts
on sale. Partial wheelchair access.

13 THE CIRCLES GARDEN
8 Stocksmoor Road, Midgley, nr
Wakefield, WF4 4JQ. Joan Gaunt,
veronica.brook@ngs.org.uk.
*Equidistant from Huddersfield,
Wakefield & Barnsley, W of M1. Turn
off A637 in Midgley at the Black*

*Bull Pub (sharp bend) onto B6117
Stocksmoor Rd. Park on road.* Visits
by arrangement Apr to Sept for
groups of 5 to 20. Adm £4, chd
free. Home-made teas.
An organic and self-sustaining
plantswoman's ½ acre garden on
gently sloping site overlooking fields,
woods and nature reserve opposite.
Designed and maintained by owner.
Herbaceous, bulb and shrub
plantings linked by grass and gravel
paths, woodland area with mature
trees, meadows, fernery, greenhouse,
fruit trees, viewing terrace with pots.
About 100 hellebores propagated
from owner's own plants. South
African plants, hollies, and small bulbs
of particular interest.

14 CLIFTON CASTLE
Ripon, HG4 4AB. Lord & Lady
Downshire. *2m N of Masham. On rd
to Newton-le-Willows & Richmond.
Gates on L next to red telephone
box.* Sun 10 Apr, Sun 12 June
(2-5). Adm £5, chd free. Home-
made teas.
Impressive gardens and parkland with
fine views over lower Wensleydale.
Formal walks through the wooded
'pleasure grounds' feature bridges
and follies, cascades and abundant
wildflowers. The walled kitchen
garden is similar to how it was set
out in the C19. Recent wildflower
meadows have been laid out with
modern sculptures. Gravel paths and
steep slopes to river.

15 COBBLE COTTAGE
Rudgate, Whixley, YO26 8AL.
John Hawkridge & Barry
Atkinson, 01423 331419,
cobblecottage@outlook.com. *8m
W of York, 8m E of Harrogate, 6m
N of Wetherby. From High St, L at
Anchor Inn onto Station Rd, on L.*
Sun 12 June, Sun 3 July (11-5).
Adm £4, chd free. Open nearby
Grafton Gardens. Opening with
Whixley Gardens on Sun 15 May.
Visits also by arrangement May to
July for groups of 20+.
Imaginatively designed, constantly
changing, small cottage garden full
of decorative architectural plants and
old family favourites. Interesting water
garden, containers and use of natural
materials. Black and white courtyard
garden and Japanese-style garden
with growing willow screen.

Saltmarshe Hall

16 THE COTTAGE
55 Bradway Road, Bradway,
Sheffield, S17 4QR. Jane Holbrey.
6m S Sheffield City Centre. Follow
Greenhill Parkway (B6054) towards
Derbyshire, cottage set back just
before Dore & Totley Golf Club.
Sun 12, Sun 26 June (12-5). Adm
£3.50, chd free. Cream teas.
Evening opening Sat 16 July
(6-8.30). Adm £15. Pre-booking
essential, please visit www.ngs.
org.uk for information & booking.
Wine.
Stylish cottage garden around
renovated garden buildings with
herbaceous borders, vegetable plot,
wildflower area, and auricula theatre.
Shepherd's hut and pond. Specimen
fruit trees including step-over apples.
Many seating areas. No wheelchair
access possible due to steps and
uneven York stone paving.

17 THE COTTAGE
3 Fletcher Gate, Hedon, Hull,
HU12 8ET. Mr Ian & Mrs Yvonne
Mcfarlane. *6m E of Hull. Take A1033*
to Hedon, L at r'about onto Hull Rd
which joins Fletcher Gate. Garden on
R after the 3rd zebra X. No parking
at the property, 2 free car parks 2
mins walk away. **Sat 7, Sun 8 May**
(1-4). Adm £5, chd free. Light
refreshments.
Mature 1/3 acre suburban secret garden
around Grade II listed cottage. Unusual
planting in hidden areas accessed
via steps, sloping and grassed paths.
Small pond, summerhouse and lots
of seating. Small stream originally
constructed in early 1900s in a gravel
garden. Sitting area in reclaimed
palm house. Many farm and garden
implements. Some small areas may not
be accessible to wheelchairs.

18 COW CLOSE COTTAGE
Stripe Lane, Hartwith, Harrogate,
HG3 3EY. William Moore &
John Wilson, 01423 779813,
cowclose1@btinternet.com. *8m NW*
of Harrogate. From A61(Harrogate-
Ripon) at Ripley take B6165 to Pateley
Bridge. 2m beyond Burnt Yates turn
R, signed Hartwith/ Brimham Rocks
onto Stripe Lane. Parking available.
Visits by arrangement June & July
for groups of 10 to 40. Adm £5,
chd free.
2/3 acre country garden on sloping
site with stream and far reaching
views. Large borders with drifts
of interesting, well-chosen, later

flowering summer perennials and
some grasses contrasting with
woodland shade and streamside
plantings. Gravel path leading to
vegetable area. Courtyard area,
terrace and seating with views of
the garden. Orchard and ha-ha with
steps leading to wildflower meadow.
The lower part of the garden can be
accessed via the orchard.

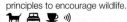

GROUP OPENING

19 DACRE BANKS &
SUMMERBRIDGE GARDENS
Nidderdale, HG3 4EW. *4m*
SE Pateley Bridge, 10m NW
Harrogate,10m N Otley, on B6451 &
B6165. Parking at each garden. Map
available for garden locations. **Sun**
10 July (12-5). Combined adm
£10, chd free. Home-made teas
at Yorke House, Low Hall and
Woodlands Cottage. Visitors are
welcome to picnic in the orchard
at Yorke House.

LOW HALL
Mrs P A Holliday.
(See separate entry)

RIVERSIDE HOUSE
Joy Stanton, 07815 695233,
joy.stanton21@gmail.com.
Visits also by arrangement May
to July for groups of up to 10.

WOODLANDS COTTAGE
Mr & Mrs Stark, 01423 780765,
annstark@btinternet.com, www.
woodlandscottagegarden.co.uk.
Visits also by arrangement May
to Aug for groups of up to 25.

YORKE HOUSE & WHITE
ROSE COTTAGE
Tony & Pat Hutchinson and Mark
& Amy Hutchinson.
(See separate entry)

Dacre Banks and Summerbridge
Gardens are situated in the beautiful
countryside of Nidderdale and
designed to take advantage of the
scenic Dales landscape. The gardens
are linked by attractive walks along
the valley, but each may be accessed
individually by car. Low Hall has a
romantic walled garden set on different
levels around the historic C17 family
home (not open) with herbaceous
borders, shrubs, climbing roses and a
tranquil water garden. Riverside House
is an atmospheric waterside garden on
many levels, supporting shade-loving
plants and features a Victorian folly,

fernery, courtyard and naturalistic
riverside plantings. Woodlands
Cottage is a garden of many rooms,
with exquisite formal and informal
plantings, and an attractive wildflower
meadow which harmonises with
mature woodland. Yorke House has
extensive colour-themed borders and
water features with beautiful waterside
plantings. The newly developed garden
at White Rose Cottage is specifically
designed for wheelchair users.

20 DEVONSHIRE MILL
Canal Lane, Pocklington,
York, YO42 1NN. Sue &
Chris Bond, 01759 302147,
chris.bond.dm@btinternet.com,
www.devonshiremill.co.uk. *1m*
S of Pocklington. Canal Lane, off
A1079 on opp side of the rd from the
canal towards Pocklington. **Sun 20**
Feb (11-4.30). Adm £5, chd free.
Home-made teas.
Drifts of double snowdrops,
hellebores and ferns surround the
historic Grade II listed watermill.
Explore the two acre garden with
mill stream, orchards, woodland,
herbaceous borders, hen run and
greenhouses. The old mill pond is
now a vegetable garden with raised
beds and polytunnel. Over the
past twenty years the owners have
developed the garden on organic
principles to encourage wildlife.

SPECIAL EVENT

21 NEW DUNCANNE HOUSE
Roecliffe Lane, Boroughbridge,
York, YO51 9LN. Colette &
Tom Walker. *Off Roecliffe Lane*
leaving Boroughbridge, on L along
small private drive, just before
Boroughbridge Manor Care Home.
Evening opening Thur 22 Sept
(6-8). Adm £15, chd free. Pre-
booking essential, please visit
www.ngs.org.uk for information
& booking. Wine and canapes
included.
A secluded town garden, which
borrows enclosure from surrounding
gardens. From the front garden,
a birch glade leads to theatrical
rear garden with sculptural grass
bank, lawns, grass paths and two
vistas terminated by treehouse and
rustic tea pavilion. The product of a
landscape architect husband and
garden tour operator wife team, who

have lovingly developed the garden over the last 10 yrs. Accessible via grass paths.

22 EAST WING, NEWTON KYME HALL

Croft Lane, Newton Kyme, nr Boston Spa, LS24 9LR. Fiona & Chris Royffe, 07983 272182, plantsbydesign@btinternet.com, www.plantsbydesign.info. *2m from Tadcaster or Boston Spa. Follow directions for Newton Kyme village from A659.* **Visits by arrangement June & July for groups of 10 to 30. Home-made teas.**
Contemporary designed garden in dramatic, historic setting with views of Kyme Castle, St Andrews Church and C18 Newton Kyme Hall (not open). Sculptural planting, herb and cutting garden, small meadow. The garden emphasises the broad scene and setting for the East Wing and planted areas create a rich variety of visual interest through the seasons as well as attracting wildlife. Garden design exhibition.

23 ELLERKER HOUSE

Everingham, York, YO42 4JA. Mr & Mrs M Wright, www.ellerkerhouse.weebly.com. *15m SE of York. 5½m from Pocklington. Just out of the village towards Harswell on R.* **Sun 10 Apr (10-5). Adm £6, chd free. Home-made teas served all day, savouries at lunchtime.**
5 acre garden with many fine old trees, lawns surrounded by colour themed herbaceous borders planted with old roses, unusual shrubs and herbaceous plants for all year colour. Daffodils, spring bulbs and alpines planted around the lake in a stumpery. 11 acres of woodland, thatched oak hut and several sitting areas. Entry inc Rare Plant Fair with many plant stalls. See website for details. Most of the garden is accessible by wheelchair.

24 3 EMBANKMENT ROAD

Broomhill, Sheffield, S10 1EZ. Charlotte Cummins. *1½m W of city centre. A61 ring rd follow A57 to Manchester. In Broomhill turn R onto Crookes Rd, 1st R on to Crookesmoor Rd. Embankment Rd is 2nd on L.* **Sun 12 June (10.30-4.30). Adm £3.50, chd free. Light refreshments.** Good selection of

home-made cakes.
Immaculate, compact, city garden with cottage style planting. Well-stocked borders of interesting, carefully selected herbaceous perennials. Front garden features clipped box, hostas and a lavender bed. Rear garden with steep steps to small, elevated lawn, herbaceous borders and many pots. Collection of over 50 astrantias and more than 100 varieties of hosta. Homegrown plants for sale.

25 FAWLEY HOUSE

7 Nordham, North Cave, nr Brough, Hull, HU15 2LT. Mr & Mrs T Martin, 01430 422266, louisem200@hotmail.co.uk, www.nordhamcottages.co.uk. *15m W of Hull. Leave M62E at J38. L at '30' & signs: Wetlands & Polo. At L bend, turn R into Nordham. From Beverley, B1230 to N Cave. R past church and over bridge.* **Sun 27 Mar (12-5). Adm £5, chd free. Please check website for availability and venue for refreshments. Visits also by arrangement Feb to June for groups of 10+. Teas included in adm. No visits in May.**
Tiered, 2½ acre garden with lawns, mature trees, formal hedging and gravel pathways. Lavender beds, mixed shrub/herbaceous borders, and hot double herbaceous borders. Apple espaliers, pears, soft fruit, produce and herb gardens. Terrace with pergola and vines. Sunken garden with white border. Woodland with naturalistic planting and spring bulbs. Quaker well, stream and spring area with 3 bridges, ferns and hellebores near mill stream. Beautiful snowdrops and aconites early in year. Treasure hunt for children. Self catering accommodation at Nordham Cottages http://nordhamcottages.co.uk/. Partial wheelchair access to top of garden and terrace on pea gravel, sloping paths thereafter which are not recommended for wheelchairs.

26 FERNLEIGH

9 Meadowhead Avenue, Meadowhead, Sheffield, S8 7RT. Mr & Mrs C Littlewood, 01142 747234, littlewoodchristine@gmail.com. *4m S of Sheffield city centre. From city centre. A61, A6102, B6054 r'about, exit B6054. 1st R Greenhill Ave, 2nd R. From M1 J33, A630 to A6102,*

then as above. **Sun 26 June, Sun 31 July, Sun 28 Aug (11-5). Adm £3.50, chd free. Home-made teas. Visits also by arrangement Apr to Aug.**
Plantswoman's ⅓ acre cottage style suburban garden. Large variety of unusual plants set in different areas provide year-round interest. Several seats to view different aspects of garden. Auricula theatre, patio, gazebo and greenhouse. Miniature log cabin with living roof and cobbled area with unusual plants in pots. Sempervivum, alpine displays, collection of epimedium and wildlife hotel. Wide selection of homegrown plants for sale. Animal Search for children.

27 FERRY HOUSE

Breighton, Selby, YO8 6DH. Group Captain Neil & Mrs Claire Bale, 01757 288538, cyfie@hotmail.co.uk. *4m NW of Howden. From A63 take rd from Loftsome Bridge towards Wressle & Breighton. From Bubwith take Church St then Breighton Rd to Breighton. Street parking available.* **Sat 9 July (2-5). Adm £4, chd free. Home-made teas in a nearby garden. Visits also by arrangement Apr to Sept for groups of 5 to 20.**
Newly landscaped country garden with informal cottage style planting. Colourful herbaceous borders with a variety of perennials. Large pond with Monet style bridge, interesting paths and seating from which to enjoy the garden. Gate through to woodland area with wildflower walk. Greenhouse and vegetable beds.

28 NEW FIRBY HALL

Firby, Bedale, DL8 2PW. Mrs S Page. *½ m along Masham Rd out of Bedale, follow sign to Firby. Hall gates on L after ½ m.* **Sun 5 June (12-5). Adm £7.50, chd free.**
The Hall sits in 4 acres with a walled garden to the north and two lakes to the south, one of which features a folly. The walled garden and greenhouse were restored in 2019. The main garden continues to undergo renovation: the ha-ha was restored during the 2020 lockdown as were the 110m long herbaceous beds. Ongoing work is focused on the main west facing lawns. Some steps but most of the garden is accessible.

29 FIRVALE PERENNIAL GARDEN

Winney Hill, Harthill, nr Worksop, S26 7YN. Don & Dot Witton, 01909 771366, donshardyeuphorbias@btopenworld.com, www.donseuphorbias.webador.co.uk. *12m SE of Sheffield, 6m W of Worksop. M1 J31 A57 to Worksop. Turn R to Harthill. Allotments at S end of village, 26 Casson Drive at N end on Northlands Estate.* Sun 29 May (11-3). Adm £3, chd free. Home-made teas at 26 Casson Drive, Harthill S26 7WA. Visits also by arrangement Apr to July.
Interesting and unusual large allotment with 13 island beds displaying 500+ herbaceous perennials including the National Collection of hardy euphorbias with over 100 varieties flowering between March and October. Organic vegetable garden. Refreshments, WC and plant sales at 26 Casson Drive, a small garden with mixed borders, shade and seaside garden.

❀ 🚗 NPC ☕

30 FROG HALL BARN

Breighton, Selby, YO8 6DH. Mr & Mrs Clarke, sarahclarke100@btinternet.com. *From Bubwith, pass sign for Breighton, 3rd house on R.* Sat 4, Sun 5 June (10.30-4.30). Adm £4, chd free. Light refreshments. Visits also by arrangement June to Aug.
Bee friendly flower and vegetable garden in ¾ acre around a converted threshing barn. At the front, a walled courtyard garden of perennials and annuals. To the rear the garden reaches down to water feeding the River Derwent. Borders full of cottage garden flowers selected to encourage wildlife. A small meadow, fruit trees, beehives and chickens. Kitchen garden with traditional greenhouse.

♿ 🐕 ❀ ☕ ⛱))

31 GALEHOUSE BARN

Bishopdyke Road, Cawood, Selby, YO8 3UB. Mr & Mrs P Lloyd and Madge & Paul Taylor, 07768 405642, junelloyd042@gmail.com. *On B1222 1m out of Cawood towards Sherburn in Elmet.* Sat 18, Sun 19 June (12-5). Adm £3.50, chd free. Home-made teas. Visits also by arrangement Apr to Sept for groups of 6 to 12.
The Barn: A plantaholic's informal cottage garden, created in 2015, to encourage birds and insects. Raised beds with tranquil seating area. The Farm: South facing, partly shaded varied herbaceous border. North facing exposed shaded border redeveloped 2017, ongoing for spring and autumn interest. Small experimental 50 shades of white garden. Raised beds for vegetables. Partial wheelchair access.

♿ 🐕 ❀ ☕

Anne Turner Memorial Allotments

32 GLENCOE HOUSE
Main Street, Bainton, Driffield, YO25 9NE. Liz Dewsbury, 01377 217592, efdewsbury@gmail.com. *6m SW of Driffield on A614. 10m N of Beverley on B1248 Malton Rd. House on W of A614 in centre of the village. Parking around village or in layby 280m N towards Bainton r'about.* Wed 29 June (12-5). Adm £4, chd free. Home-made teas. Visits also by arrangement June & July for groups of 5 to 30.
A tranquil 3 acre garden developed over 40+ years including a cottage and kitchen garden, parkland and wildlife pond. The cottage garden is resplendent with trees, shrubs, roses, clematis and masses of herbaceous perennials. Paths lead to an area of mown grass planted with specimen trees and an orchard. Furthest from the house there is a grove of native and unusual trees and a large wildlife pond. Wheelchair access to paved area in cottage garden but difficult elsewhere.
& ✿ ☕

33 GOLDSBOROUGH HALL
Church Street, Goldsborough, HG5 8NR. Mr & Mrs M Oglesby, 01423 867321, info@goldsboroughhall.com, www.goldsboroughhall.com. *2m SE of Knaresborough. 3m W of A1M. Off A59 (York-Harrogate). Spring gardens parking at Hall top car park. Summer gardens parking E of village in field off Midgley Lane. Disabled parking only at front of Hall.* Sun 3 Apr (11-4); Sun 24 July (11-5). Adm £5, chd free. Light refreshments. Donation to St Mary's Church.
Historic 12 acre garden and formal landscaped grounds in parkland setting around Grade II*, C17 house, former residence of HRH Princess Mary, daughter of George V and Queen Mary. Gertrude Jekyll inspired 120ft double herbaceous borders, rose garden and woodland walk. Large restored kitchen garden and large glasshouse which produces fruit and vegetables for the Hall's commercial kitchens. Quarter-mile Lime Tree Walk planted by royalty in the 1920s, orchard, flower borders featuring 'Yorkshire Princess' rose, named after Princess Mary. Gravel paths and some steep slopes.
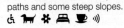

GROUP OPENING

34 GRAFTON GARDENS
Marton Cum Grafton, York, YO51 9QJ. Mrs Glen Garnett. *2½m S of Boroughbridge. Turn off the A168 or B6265 to Marton or Grafton (South of Boroughbridge).* Sun 12 June, Sun 3 July (11-5). Combined adm £6, chd free. Open nearby Cobble Cottage.

NEW PADDOCK HOUSE
Tim & Jill Smith.

WELL HOUSE
Glen Garnett.
(See separate entry)

These two gardens in adjacent rural villages are also connected by a public footpath. Paddock House is on an elevated site with extensive views down a large sloping lawn to a wildlife pond. A plant lover's garden where the house is encircled by a profusion of pots and extensive plant collections combining cottage gardening with the Mediterranean and Tropical. A curved terrace of Yorkshire stone and steps using gravel and wood sleepers leads to many seating areas culminating in a cutting garden and small greenhouse. Well House in Grafton nestles under the hillside, with long views to the White Horse. This 1½ acre garden was begun 40 yrs ago and is constantly changing. A traditional English cottage garden with herbaceous borders, climbing roses and ornamental shrubs with a variety of interesting species. Paths meander through the borders to an orchard with ducks. Refreshments at The Punch Bowl pub, a 5 minute walk from Well House.
🐕 ✿ ♫))

35 THE GRANGE
Wath Lane, Copgrove, Harrogate, HG3 3TA. Peter & Maggie Edwards. *10m N of Harrogate. Between Burton Leonard & Staveley, 200yds E of Copgrove Church, next to business park where parking is available.* Sat 4, Sun 5 June (11-4). Adm £4, chd free. Home-made teas.
Mature 1 acre garden created by the owners over the last 30 years. Special features include an extended laburnum arch, a pleached liquidamber hedge and a rose pergola leading to a formal lily pond. Planting

includes conifer and heather beds, specimen trees and mixed shrub and herbaceous borders, a greenhouse, raised alpine bed and gravel paths. Paths around the pond are narrow. Gravel drive.
& 🐕 ✿ ☕

36 THE GRANGE
Carla Beck Lane, Carleton in Craven, Skipton, BD23 3BU. Mr & Mrs R N Wooler, 07740 639135, margaret.wooler@hotmail.com. *1½m SW of Skipton. Turn off A56 (Skipton-Clitheroe) into Carleton. Keep L at Swan Pub, continue to end of village then R into Carla Beck Lane.* Wed 27 July, Wed 10 Aug (12-4.30). Adm £5, chd free. Home-made teas. Visits also by arrangement July & Aug for groups of 20+. Donation to Sue Ryder Care Manorlands Hospice.
Over 4 acres of garden set in the grounds of Victorian house (not open) with mature trees and panoramic views towards The Gateway to the Dales. The garden has been restored by the owners over the last 3 decades with many areas of interest added to the original footprint. Bountiful herbaceous borders with many unusual species, rose walk, parterre, mini-meadows and water features. Mature trees, topiary and large greenhouse. Extensive vegetable and cut flower beds. Oak seating placed throughout the garden invites quiet contemplation - a place to 'lift the spirits'. Gravel paths and steps in some areas.
& ✿ ♿ ☕

37 GREAT CLIFF EXOTIC GARDEN
Cliff Drive, Crigglestone, Wakefield, WF4 3EN. Kristofer Swaine, www.greatcliffexoticgarden.co.uk. *1m from J39 M1. From M1 (J39) take A636 towards Denby Dale, past Cedar Court Hotel then L at British Oak pub onto Blacker Lane. Parking on Cliff Road motorway bridge a 3 minutes walk from the garden.* Sat 13, Sun 14 Aug (12.30-4.30). Adm £4, chd free.
An exotic garden on a long narrow plot. Possibly the largest collection of palm species planted out in Northern England including a large Chilean wine palm. Colourful and exciting borders with zinnias, cannas, ensete, bananas, tree ferns, agaves, aloes, colcasias and bamboos. Jungle hut, winding paths and a pond that traverses the full width of the garden.
✿ ♫))

38 GREENCROFT

Pottery Lane, Littlethorpe, Ripon, HG4 3LS. David & Sally Walden, 01765 602487, s-walden@outlook.com. *1½ m SE of Ripon town centre. Off A61 Ripon bypass follow signs to Littlethorpe, turn R at church. From Bishop Monkton take Knaresborough Rd towards Ripon then R to Littlethorpe.* **Sun 7 Aug (12-4). Adm £5, chd free. Home-made teas. Visits also by arrangement July & Aug.** ½ acre informal country garden created by the owners. Features long herbaceous borders packed with colourful late summer perennials, annuals and exotics culminating in a circular garden with views through to large wildlife pond and surrounding countryside. Special ornamental features inc gazebo, temple pavilions, formal pool, stone wall with mullions and gate to pergola and cascade water feature.

39 GREENWICK FARM

Huggate, York, YO42 1YR. Fran & Owen Pearson, 01377 288122, greenwickfarm@hotmail.com. *2m W of Huggate. From York on A166, turn R Im after Garrowby Hill at brown sign for picnic area & scenic route. White wind turbine on drive.* **Visits by arrangement June to Aug. Home-made teas.** 1 acre woodland garden created in 2010 from disused area of the farm. Set in a large dell with mature trees. Paths up the hillside borders lead to terrace and woodland planting. Seating areas with spectacular views across wooded valley and the Wolds. Stumpery and hot border. New summerhouse, water feature, brushed steel sculpture and wirework animals. Described by guests as a magical tranquil garden. Access for wheelchairs difficult, but good view of garden from hard standing outside house where teas served.

♿ 🐎 ❀ 🛏 ☕ ❦

40 NEW 138 GREYSTONES ROAD

Sheffield, S11 7BR. Mr Nick Hetherington. *From Sheffield inner Ring Rd, W on A625 (Ecclesall Rd) for 1.8m. R onto Greystones Rd.* **Sun 4 Sept (9-4). Adm £4, chd free. Light refreshments.** This typical, small suburban plot has been developed into a lovely garden over 20 yrs. It features many trees and acers combined with stunning late tender perennials including banana plants, cannas, agapanthus and dahlias. Several sculptures created by the owner are displayed amongst the plants.

❀ ☕ ❦

41 HAVOC HALL

York Rd, Oswaldkirk, York, YO62 5XY. David & Maggie Lis, 01439 788846, davidglis@me.com, www.havochall.co.uk. *21m N of York. On B1363, 1st house on R as you enter Oswaldkirk from S & last house on L as you leave village from N.* **Sun 26 June (1-5). Adm £7.50, chd free. Home-made teas. Visits also by arrangement on 25th May, 16th June and 4th July for groups of 5+.** 12 areas inc knot, herbaceous, mixed shrub and flower gardens, prairie beds, courtyard, vegetable area and orchard, woodland walk and large lawned area with hornbeam topiary and hedging. To the south is a 2 acre wildflower meadow and small lake. Extensive collection of roses, herbaceous perennials and grasses. Wheelchair access: some steps but these can be avoided.

♿ 🐎 ❀ 🛏 ☕ ❦

42 HIGHFIELD COTTAGE

North Street, Driffield, YO25 6AS. Debbie Simpson, 01377 256562, debbie@simpsonhighfield.karoo. co.uk. *30m E of York. From A614/ A166 into Driffield (York Rd, then North St.) Highfield Cottage is white detached house opp park nr Indian takeaway.* **Sun 8 May (10.30-3.30). Adm £4, chd free. Sun 3 July (10.30-3.30). Combined adm with 5 Wold Road £6, chd free. Home-made teas. Visits also by arrangement Apr to Sept for groups of up to 30.** A ¾ acre suburban garden bordered by mature trees and a stream. Structure provided by numerous yew and box topiary, a pergola and sculptures. Lawns with island beds, mixed shrubs, fruit trees, a shaded fern and hosta area and herbaceous borders. For 2022, weather permitting, there will be some additional garden sculpture on the theme of dance created by the garden owner. Small art workshop. Refreshments are weather dependent.

❀ 🛏 ☕ ❦

43 5 HILL TOP

Westwood Drive, Ilkley, LS29 9RS. Lyn & Phil Short. *½ m S of Ilkley town centre, steep uphill. Turn S at town centre T-lights up Brook St, cross The Grove taking Wells Rd up to the Moors where rd becomes Westwood Drive.* **Wed 25, Sun 29 May (11-4). Adm £4, chd free. Home-made teas.** Delightful ⅔ acre steep garden on edge of Ilkley Moor. Sheltered woodland underplanted with naturalistic, flowing tapestry of foliage, shade-loving flowers, shrubs & ferns amongst large moss-covered boulders. Many Japanese maples, natural rocky stream and bridges. Meandering gravel paths & steps lend magic to 'Dingley Dell'. Lawns, large rockery, & summerhouse with stunning views. Some steep steps.

❀ ☕ ❦

44 HOLMFIELD

Fridaythorpe, YO25 9RZ. Susan & Robert Nichols, 01377 236627, snicholswire@gmail.com. *9m W of Driffield. From York A166 through Fridaythorpe. 1m turn R signed Holmfield. 1st house on lane.* **Sun 5, Wed 8 June (12-5). Adm £5, chd free. Home-made teas. Visits also by arrangement May & June for groups of 8+.** Informal 2 acre country garden on gentle south facing slope, developed from a field since 1988. Family friendly garden with mixed borders, bespoke octagonal gazebo, 'Hobbit House', sunken trampoline, large lawn, tennis court and hidden paths for hide and seek. Productive fruit cage, vegetable and cut flower area. Collection of phlomis. Display of wire sculptures. Bee friendly planting. Some gravel areas, sloping lawns. Wheelchair access possible with help.

♿ ❀ 🛏 ☕ 🎪 ❦

45 HONEY HEAD

33 Wood Nook Lane, Meltham, Holmfirth, HD9 4DU. Susan & Andrew Brass. *6m S of Huddersfield. Turn from A616 to Honley, through village then follow Meltham rd for 1m, turn L on Wood Nook Lane.* **Sun 10 July (10-4). Adm £4, chd free. Home-made teas.** Set high on a Pennine hillside with panoramic views, Honey Head aspires to provide year-round interest whilst attempting to be self sufficient in fruit, vegetables, cut flowers and plants. Formal gardens

12 Brendon Drive

with interconnecting ponds lead to extensive kitchen gardens with greenhouses complemented by areas planted to encourage wildlife. Weather permitting we will have "The Saxpots" playing an assortment of music, a local ensemble who are keen to support our event.

46 ♦ JACKSON'S WOLD
Sherburn, Malton, YO17 8QJ. Mr & Mrs Richard Cundall, 07966 531995, jacksonswoldgarden@gmail.com, www.jacksonswoldgarden.com. *11m E of Malton, 10m SW of Scarborough. Signs from A64. A64 E to Scarborough. R at T-lights in Sherburn, take the Weaverthorpe rd, after100 metres R fork to Helperthorpe & Luttons. 1m to top of hill, turn L at garden sign.* **For NGS: Sun 22 May, Sun 19 June (1-5). Adm £5, chd free. Home-made teas. For other opening times and information, please phone, email or visit garden website.**
Spectacular 2 acre country garden. Many old shrub roses underplanted with unusual perennials in walled garden and woodland paths lead to further shrub and perennial borders. Lime avenue with wildflower meadow. Traditional vegetable garden inc roses and flowers with a Victorian greenhouse. Adjoining nursery. Tours by appointment. Finalist in

The English Garden's The Nation's Favourite Gardens 2021.

47 JERVAULX HALL
Jervaulx, Ripon, HG4 4PH. Mr & Mrs Phillip Woodrow. *Parking in the grounds of Jervaulx Abbey accessed from the A1608.* **Wed 20 July, Wed 10 Aug (12-5). Adm £7, chd free. Home-made teas.**
Eight acre garden undergoing renovation, adjacent to ruins of Jervaulx Abbey and inc Abbey Mill ruins with views of River Ure. Mixed borders and beds, croquet lawn, parterre, glasshouse. A small vegetable garden and fernery. Magnificent older trees and woodland areas with choice trees and shrubs planted in last 7 years, inc magnolia, acer, sorbus and betula. Contemporary sculpture.

48 NEW THE JUNGLE GARDEN
124 Dobcroft Road, Millhouses, Sheffield, S7 2LU. Dr Simon & Julie Olpin, 07710 559189, simonolpin@blueyonder.co.uk. *3m SW of city centre. Dobcroft Rd runs between A625 & A621.* **Visits by arrangement June to Oct for groups of 5 to 25. Adm £12, chd free. Home-made teas. Donation to Sheffield Children's Hospital.**
Fascinating mature garden using mainly

hardy exotics to create a jungle effect. A long (250ft), narrow site densely planted with mature trees and shrubs including many trachycarpus and European fan palms, large bamboos, several tree ferns, mature eucalypts and a number of species of mature sheffleras. Overall much of the planting has a South East Asian theme with specialist interest. A good selection of home-made cakes.

49 KIRKWOOD HOSPICE
21 Albany Road, Dalton, Huddersfield, HD5 9UY. Susan Wood, www.kirkwoodhospice.co.uk. *2m from Huddersfield town centre along A629. (Wakefield Rd.) Follow Kirkwood Hospice signs L onto Dalton Green Rd then R onto Albany Rd.* **Sat 30 July (10-3). Adm £4, chd free. Home-made teas. Cake stall and barbecue.**
Large, mature formal summer garden with seasonal interest. Level access with composite pathways draws the visitor around sweeping bed of prairie planting. Lawns leading to mixed beds, labyrinth and pond. Mature trees and shrubs enclose the garden boundaries. Extensive patio and viewing area. Specimen plants as well as favourites. Small wildflower area and allotment. Kiddies Trail. Complete wheelchair accessibility.

50 LAND FARM

Edge Lane, Colden, Hebden Bridge, HX7 7PJ. Mr J Williams. *8m W of Halifax. At Hebden Bridge (A646) after 2 sets of T-lights take turning circle to Heptonstall & Colden. After 2¾m in Colden village turn R at Edge Lane 'no through rd'. In ¾m turn L down lane.* Thur 16 June (11-5). Adm £5, chd free. Home-made teas.

An intriguing 6 acre upland garden within a sheltered valley, created by the present owner over the past 50 yrs. In that time the valley has also been planted with 20,000 trees which has encouraged a habitat rich in birds and wildlife. Within the garden vistas have been created around thought-provoking sculptures. Moss garden and well established meconopsis and cardiocrinum lilies. Partial wheelchair access, please telephone 01422 842260 for more information.

51 LINDEN LODGE

Newbridge Lane, nr Wilberfoss, York, YO41 5RB. Robert Scott & Jarrod Marsden, 07900 003538, rdsjsm@gmail.com. *Equidistant between Wilberfoss, Bolton & Fangfoss. From York on A1079, ignore signs for Wilberfoss, take nxt turn to Bolton village. After 1m at Xrds, turn L onto Newbridge Lane.* Sat 10, Sun 11 Sept (12-5). Adm £5, chd free. Light lunches, sandwiches, cakes & cream teas in the Bothy. Visits also by arrangement Aug & Sept for groups of 20+. Home-made cream teas or wine, juice & nibbles.

A 1 acre garden with 5 acres of developing meadow, trees, pathways, hens and vegetable garden. Owner designed and constructed since 2000. Gravel paths edged with brick or lavender, many borders with unusual mixed herbaceous perennials, shrubs and feature trees. Wildlife pond, summerhouse, nursery, glasshouse and fruit cage. Orchard and woodland area. Formal garden with pond/water feature. Far reaching views towards the Yorkshire Wolds. Gravel paths and shallow steps.

52 LITTLETHORPE MANOR

Littlethorpe Road, Littlethorpe, Ripon, HG4 3LG. Mrs J P Thackray, www.littlethorpemanor.com. *Outskirts of Ripon nr racecourse. Ripon bypass A61. Follow Littlethorpe Rd from Dallamires Lane r'about to stable block with clock tower. Map supplied on application.* Sun 11 Sept (1.30-5). Adm £7, chd free. Home-made teas in marquee.

11 acres. Walled garden with herbaceous planting, roses and gazebo. Sunken garden with ornamental plants and herbs. Brick pergola with wisteria, blue and yellow borders. Formal lawn with fountain pool, hornbeam towers, yew hedging. Box-headed hornbeam drive with Aqualens. Large pond with classical pavilion and boardwalk. New contemporary physic garden with rill, raised beds and medicinal plants. Wheelchair access - gravel paths, some steep steps.

53 LOW HALL

Dacre Banks, Nidderdale, HG3 4AA. Mrs P A Holliday, 01423 780230, 1pamelaholliday@gmail.com. *10m NW of Harrogate. On B6451 between Dacre Banks & Darley.* Sun 8 May (1-5). Adm £5, chd free. Home-made teas. Opening with Dacre Banks & Summerbridge Gardens on Sun 10 July. Visits also by arrangement May to Sept for groups of 5 to 30.

Romantic walled garden set on differing levels designed to complement historic C17 family home (not open). Spring bulbs, rhododendrons and azaleas round tranquil water garden. Asymmetric rose pergola underplanted with auriculas and lithodora links the orchard to the garden. Vegetable garden and conservatory. Extensive herbaceous borders, shrubs and climbing roses give later interest. Bluebell woods, lovely countryside and farmland all around, overlooking the River Nidd. 80% of garden can be seen from a wheelchair but access involves three stone steps.

54 MANSION COTTAGE

8 Gillus Lane, Bempton, Bridlington, YO15 1HW. Polly & Chris Myers, 01262 851404, chrismyers0807@gmail.com. *2m NE of Bridlington. From Bridlington take B1255 to Flamborough. 1st L at T-lights - Bempton Lane, turn 1st R into Short Lane then L at end. Continue - L fork at church.* Sat 6, Sun 7 Aug (10-4). Adm £4.50, chd free. Light refreshments. Visits also by arrangement June to Aug for groups of 10 to 30.

Exuberant, lush, vibrant borders with late perennial planting in this peaceful, surprising, hidden garden. Visitors' book says 'A veritable oasis', 'The garden is inspirational'. Globe garden, mini hosta walk, Japanese themed area,100ft border, summerhouse, and art studio, vegetable plot, cuttery, late summer hot border, bee and butterfly border, deck and lawns. Produce, plants and home made soaps.

55 MARKENFIELD HALL

Ripon, HG4 3AD. Lady Deirdre & Mr Ian Curteis, www.markenfield.com. *A61 between Ripon & Ripley. Turning between two low stone gateposts W of main road. Do not follow SatNav.* Tue 3 May, Tue 14 June, Tue 12 July (2-3). Adm £5, chd free. Pre-booking essential, please visit www.ngs.org.uk for information & booking. Home-made teas in the Hall.

By guided tour only - starts 2pm (max 10 people). The work of the Hall's owner Lady Deirdre Curteis and gardener Giles Gilbey. Mature planting combines with newly designed areas, where walls with espaliered apricots and figs frame a mix of hardy perennials. In 2018 the Farmhouse Border was replanted to eventually blend seamlessly with the Hall's main East Border. The gardens surround Markenfield Hall - a moated, medieval manor house - one of the oldest, continuously inhabited houses in the country.

56 115 MILLHOUSES LANE

Sheffield, S7 2HD. Sue & Phil Stockdale. *Approx 4m SW of Sheffield City Centre. Follow A625 Castleton/Dore Rd, 4th L after Prince of Wales pub, 2nd L. OR take A621 Baslow Rd. After Tesco garage take 2nd R, then 1st L.* Mon 30 May (11-4.30). Adm £4, chd free.

Plantswoman's ⅓ acre south facing level cottage style garden with many choice and unusual perennials and bulbs, providing year-round colour and interest. Large collection of 50+ hostas, roses, peonies, iris and clematis with many tender and exotic plants inc aeoniums, echeverias, bananas and echiums. Seating areas around the garden. Many home-propagated plants for sale. Most of the garden is accessible for wheelchairs.

57 MILLRACE GARDEN
84 Selby Road, Garforth, Leeds, LS25 1LP. Mr & Mrs Carthy, 07966 450876, carolcarthy.millrace@gmail.com. *5m E of Leeds. On A63 in Garforth. 1m from M1 J46, 3m from A1.* Sun 20 Feb, Sun 22 May, Sun 21 Aug (1-5). Adm £5, chd free. Home-made teas. Visits also by arrangement Feb to Aug.
Overlooking a secluded valley, garden inc large herbaceous borders containing over 3000 varieties of perennials, shrubs and trees, many of which are unusual and drought tolerant. Ornamental pond, vegetable garden and walled terraces lead to wildflower meadow, small woodland and bog garden. This will be the last year that our garden will open so we hope you can join us. Propagation opportunity depending on season (cuttings, seeds, divisions). Art exhibition and The Illuminate Choir at some of our openings. Most of the garden is accessible for wheelchairs. Although there are steps in places there is generally an alternative ramp.
& 🐕 ✿ 🚐 ☕

58 NEW MIRES BECK NURSERY
Low Mill Lane, North Cave, Brough, HU15 2NR. Graham Elliot, www.miresbeck.co.uk. *Between N & S Cave. Do not follow SatNav if entering N Cave from the A63/ M62. Take rd to S Cave, turn R 400 yds after leaving the village. From S Cave, turn 1st L after prison.* Wed 13 July (10.30-4). Adm £4, chd free. Light refreshments.
A registered charity that provides horticultural work experience for adults with learning disabilities. The 14 acre site features herbaceous borders, rose garden, vegetable beds, wildflower woodland walk & Hull's official Garden of Sanctuary. We grow over 300 herbaceous perennials, 50 herbs & 100 Yorkshire provenance wildflowers for garden centres in Yorks & Lincs. Plants for sale. Compressed gravel paths.
& 🐕 ✿ 🚐))

59 MYTON GRANGE
Myton On Swale, York, YO61 2QU. Nick & Annie Ramsden. *15m N of York. From the N go through Helperby on York Rd. After ½m follow yellow signs towards Myton. From the S leave A19 through Tollerton & Flawith. Turn L at Xrds.* Sun 3 July (10-5). Adm £7, chd free.

This garden, attached to a Victorian farmhouse, once formed part of the Myton Estate. Extending to ¾ acre, the site is adjacent to the River Swale and inc a paved terrace garden, formal parterre, circular garden with mixed shrub and herbaceous border and lawn with topiary borders. There will be a guided tour, and a talk about the recently restored Victorian Stud Farm buildings at 11am and 3pm.
🐕 ✿ ☕

60 ◆ NEWBY HALL & GARDENS
Ripon, HG4 5AE. Mr R C Compton, 01423 322583, info@newbyhall.com. www.newbyhall.com. *4m SE of Ripon. (HG4 5AJ for Sat Nav). Follow brown tourist signs from A1(M) or from Ripon town centre.* For opening times and information, please phone, email or visit garden website.
40 acres of extensive gardens and woodland laid out in 1920s. Full of rare and beautiful plants. Formal seasonal gardens and stunning double herbaceous borders slope down to River Ure. National Collection of cornus. Newly refurbished rock garden. Miniature railway and adventure gardens for children. Sculpture exhibition June-Sept. Free parking. Licensed restaurant, shop and plant nursery. Wheelchair map available. Disabled parking. Manual and electric wheelchairs available on loan, please call to reserve.
& ✿ 🚐 NPC ☕

61 THE NURSERY
15 Knapton Lane, Acomb, York, YO26 5PX. Tony Chalcraft & Jane Thurlow, 01904 781691, janeandtonyatthenursery@hotmail.co.uk. *2½m W of York. From A1237 take B1224 towards Acomb. At r'about turn L (Beckfield Ln.). After 150 metres turn L.* Sun 17, Mon 18, Tue 19 July (1-6). Adm £4, chd free. Light refreshments. Visits also by arrangement May to Sept for groups of 10+.
A former suburban commercial nursery, now an attractive and productive 1 acre organic, private garden. Over 100 fruit trees, many in trained form. Many different vegetables grown both outside and under cover in 20m greenhouse. Productive areas interspersed with informal ornamental plantings provide colour and habitat for wildlife. The extensive planting of different forms and varieties of fruit trees make this

an interesting garden for groups to visit by arrangement at blossom and fruiting times in addition to the main summer openings. Plants will be on sale from Summerfields Nursery.
✿ ☕

62 THE OLD PRIORY
Everingham, YO42 4JD. Dr J D & Mrs H J Marsden, 01430 860222, helen.marsden@ngs.org.uk. *15m SE of York, 6m from Pocklington. 2m S of A1079. On E side of village. Parking at village hall opp.* Sun 19 June (10.30-5). Adm £6, chd free. Home-made teas in Everingham Village Hall. Visits also by arrangement May & June. Wine and beer offered for evening visits.
2 acre rural garden reflecting surrounding countryside. Created in 1990s to enable self-sufficiency in vegetables, meat, most fruit, logs and timber for furniture. Walled vegetable garden with polytunnel. Borders and lawn near house are on dry sandy loam. Garden slopes down to bog. Roughly mown pathway through woodland, along lakeside and lightly grazed pasture. Please drive up gravel driveway for drop off if necessary.
& ✿ 🚐 ☕))

63 THE OLD RECTORY
Arram Road, Leconfield, Beverley, HU17 7NP. David Baxendale, 01964 502037, davidbax@newbax.co.uk. *Garden entrance on L 80yds along Arram Rd next to double bend sign before the church.* Visits by arrangement Jan to May for groups of up to 10. Adm £5.
Approx 3 acres of garden and paddock. The garden is particularly attractive from early spring until mid summer. Notable for aconites, snowdrops, crocuses, daffodils and bluebells. Later hostas, irises, lilies and roses. There is a small wildlife pond with all the usual residents inc grass snakes. Well established trees and shrubs, with new trees planted when required. No refreshments available but visitors are welcome to bring a picnic.
🏕

The National Garden Scheme searches the length and breadth of England, Channel Islands, Northern Ireland and Wales for the very best private gardens

64 OLD SLENINGFORD HALL

Mickley, nr Ripon, HG4 3JD. Jane & Tom Ramsden. *5m NW of Ripon. Off A6108. After N Stainley turn L, follow signs to Mickley. Gates on R after 1½m opp cottage.* **Sat 4, Sun 5 June (12-4). Adm £7.50, chd free. Home-made teas. Donation to other charities.**

A large English country garden and award winning permaculture forest garden. Early C19 house (not open) and garden with original layout. Wonderful mature trees, woodland walk and Victorian fernery, romantic lake with islands, watermill, walled kitchen garden, beautiful long herbaceous border, yew and huge beech hedges. Several plant and other stalls. Picnics around the mill pond very welcome. Of particular interest to anyone interested in permaculture. Reasonable wheelchair access to most parts of garden. Disabled WC at Old Sleningford Farm next to the garden.

65 THE OLD VICARAGE

North Frodingham, Driffield, YO25 8JT. Professor Ann Mortimer. *From Driffield take B1249 E for approx 6m. Garden on R opp church. Entrance is on T-junction of rd to Emmotland & B1249. From North Frodingham take the B1249 W for ½m. Park in farmyard opp.* **Sun 19 June (10.30-4.30). Adm £4.50, chd free. Home-made teas. Open nearby Tythe Farm House.**

1½ acre plantsman's garden, owner developed over 25 years. Many themed areas e.g. rose garden, jungle, desert, fountain, scented, kitchen gardens, glasshouses. Numerous classical statues, unusual trees and shrubs, large and small ponds, orchard, water feature. Children's interest with 'Jungle Book' dinosaur and wild animal statues. Neo-Jacobean revival house, built 1837, mentioned in Pevsner (not open). The land now occupied by the house and garden was historically owned by the family of William Wilberforce. Some areas of the garden, including the nuttery, jungle, rose and desert gardens, are not wheelchair accessible.

66 23 THE PADDOCK

Cottingham, HU16 4RA. Jill & Keith Stubbs, 07932 713281, keith@cottconsult.karoo.co.uk. *Between Beverley & Hull. From Humber Bridge A164 towards Beverley. R onto Castle Rd, past hospital. From Beverley A164 towards Humber Bridge, L onto Harland Way 1st r'about. Garden at S end of village.* **Sun 3 July (10.30-4.30). Adm £4, chd free. Cream teas. Visits also by arrangement June to Sept for groups of 10 to 25.**

A secret garden behind a small mixed frontage. Archway to themed areas within the garden including Japanese, Mediterranean, fairy and mixed herbaceous areas with patios and lawns. Two ponds, ornamental and tree sculptures and a recent water feature. Plants and blacksmith's garden ornaments and sculptures for sale. Assisted access for disabled through front gate.

67 ◆ PARCEVALL HALL GARDENS

Skyreholme, Skipton, BD23 6DE. Walsingham College, 01756 720311, parcevallhall@btconnect.com, www.parcevallhallgardens.co.uk. *9m N of Skipton. Signs from B6160 Bolton Abbey-Burnsall rd or off B6265 Grassington-Pateley Bridge & at A59 Bolton Abbey r'about.* **For NGS: Wed 18 May (10-5). Adm £8, chd free. For other opening times and information, please phone, email or visit garden website.**

The only garden open daily in the Yorkshire Dales National Park. 24 acres on a sloping south facing hillside in Wharfedale sheltered by mixed woodland. Terrace garden, rose garden, rock garden and ponds. Mixed borders, spring bulbs, tender shrubs and autumn colour.

68 PILMOOR COTTAGES

Pilmoor, nr Helperby, YO61 2QQ. Wendy & Chris Jakeman, 01845 501848, cnjakeman@aol.com. *20m N of York. From A1M J48. From B'bridge follow rd towards Easingwold. From A19 follow signs to Hutton Sessay then Helperby. Garden next to mainline railway.* **Wed 25 May, Wed 1 June, Sun 28 Aug (11-5). Adm £5, chd free. Light refreshments.**

Visits also by arrangement May to Sept.
A year-round garden for rail enthusiasts and garden visitors alike. A ride on the 7¼' gauge railway runs through 2 acres of gardens and gives you the opportunity to view the garden from a different perspective. The journey takes you across water, through a little woodland area, past flower filled borders, and through a tunnel behind the rockery and water cascade. 1½ acre wildflower meadow and pond. Clock-golf putting green.

69 PRIMROSE BANK GARDEN AND NURSERY

Dauby Lane, Kexby, York, YO41 5LH. Sue Goodwill & Terry Marran, www.primrosebank.co.uk. *4m E of York. At J of A64 & A1079 take rd signed to Hull. After 3m, just as entering Kexby, turn R onto Dauby Lane, signed for Elvington. From the E travel on A1079 towards York. Turn L in Kexby.* **Wed 18 May, Wed 15 June (1-5). Adm £5, chd free. Home-made teas.**

2 acres of rare and unusual plants, shrubs and trees. Bulbs, hellebores and flowering shrubs in spring, followed by planting for year-round interest. Extensive eranthis collection. Courtyard garden, mixed borders, summerhouse and pond. Lawns, contemporary rock garden, shade and woodland garden with pond, stumpery, and shepherd's hut. Adjoining award-winning nursery. Poultry and Hebridean sheep. Dogs allowed on a short lead in car park and at designated tables outside the tearoom. CL Caravan Site (CAMC members only) adjoining the nursery. Most areas of the garden are level and are easily accessible for wheelchairs. Accessible WC.

70 THE PRIORY, NUN MONKTON

York, YO26 8ES. Mrs K Harpin. *9m W of York, 12 E of Harrogate. E of A1M J47 off A59 signed Nun Monkton.* **Thur 7 July (11-5). Adm £6, chd free. Home-made teas.**

Large country garden surrounding William and Mary house (not open), at the confluence of the River Nidd and River Ouse. Featuring species trees, calm swathes of lawn, clipped yew, beech and box, formal rose garden and mixed borders. New

Prospect House

area of soft perennial planting and informal parkland. Kitchen gardens with greenhouse and swimming pool where teas will be served. The Nun Monkton Ferryboat will be running a special service on this day, connecting Nun Monkton with Beningbrough and Moor Monkton, from the riverbank next to The Priory 11am - 4pm www.nunmonktonferryboat.org. Gravel paths.

SPECIAL EVENT

71 NEW PROSPECT HOUSE
Scarah Lane, Burton Leonard, Harrogate, HG3 3RS. Cathy Kitchingman, 07989 195773, cathyrk@icloud.com. *5 m S of Ripon 5½ m from A1, junction 48. Exit A61 signed Burton Leonard. From Station Ln, 1st R right onto narrow Scarah Ln. Drop off only.* **Fri 24 June (10.30-2). Adm £35, chd free. Pre-booking essential, please visit www.ngs.org.**

uk for information & booking. Light refreshments. **Visits also by arrangement May to Sept for groups of 15 to 40. Weekdays only.**
A limited number of tickets have been made available for this special event. Following a welcome by the owner, there will be talks on the development of the garden, the creation of a cutting garden and colour-themed borders plus demonstration of cut flower arrangements in the potting shed. Buffet lunch included. One acre walled, landscaped garden with ornamental pond, pergola, large oval lawned area, cutting and vegetable beds. Colour-themed herbaceous long border, 'hot' borders, and a physic bed. Also mature hedging, trees and seasonal interest throughout. Additional new planting areas are being established. A renovated outhouse now converted into a potting area used for garden workshops.

72 REWELA COTTAGE
Skewsby, YO61 4SG. John Plant & Daphne Ellis, 01347 888125, rewelacottage@gmail.com, www.rewelahostas.com. *4m N of Sheriff Hutton, 15m N of York. After Sheriff Hutton, towards Terrington, turn L towards Whenby & Brandsby. Turn R just past Whenby to Skewsby. Turn L into village. 500yds on R.* **Sun 29 May, Sun 31 July (11-5). Adm £5, chd free. Light refreshments. BBQ. Visits also by arrangement May to July for groups of 10+.**
Situated in a lovely quiet country village, Rewela Cottage was designed from an empty paddock to be as labour saving as possible using unusual trees and shrubs for year-round interest. Their foliage, bark and berries enhance the well-designed structure of the garden. The garden owner now specialises in growing and selling hostas. Over 200 varieties of hosta for sale, as well as heucheras, heucherellas, tiarellas and ferns. Some gravel paths may make assistance necessary.

Thimbleby Hall

73 ♦ **RHS GARDEN HARLOW CARR**

Crag Lane, Harrogate, HG3 1QB. Royal Horticultural Society, 01423 565418, harlowcarr@rhs.org.uk, www.rhs.org.uk/harlowcarr. *1½ m W of Harrogate town centre. On B6162 (Harrogate - Otley).* For NGS: Sun 8 May (9.30-6). Adm £12.15, chd £6.10. Adm subject to change. For other opening times and information, please phone, email or visit garden website.

Harlow Carr offers a variety of growing landscapes, from running and still water, to woodland and wildflower meadows. Highlights include the lavish main borders, bursting with generous prairie-style planting and the lush, moisture-loving plants around Streamside. Betty's Cafe Tearooms, gift shop, plant centre and children's play area inc treehouse and log ness monster. Wheelchairs and mobility scooters available, advanced booking recommended.

  も ✿ ♿ ☕

74 **THE RIDINGS**

South Street, Burton Fleming, Driffield, YO25 3PE. Roy & Ruth Allerston, 01262 470489. *11m NE of Driffield. 11m SW of Scarborough. From Driffield B1249, before Foxholes turn R to Burton Fleming. From Scarborough A165 turn R to Burton Fleming.* Sun 22 May, Sun 3 July (12-4). Adm £4, chd free. Home-made teas. Visits also by arrangement Apr to July.

Secluded cottage garden with colour-themed borders surrounding neat lawns. Grass and paved paths lead to formal and informal areas through rose and clematis covered pergolas and arbours. Box hedging defines well-stocked borders with roses, herbaceous plants and trees. Seating in sun and shade offer vistas and views. Greenhouse and summerhouse. Terrace with water feature. Indoor model railway. Terrace, tea area and main lawn accessible via ramp.

も 🐂 ✿ ☕

75 **ROSEMARY COTTAGE**

163 High Street, Hook, Goole, DN14 5PL. Justine Dixon, www.rosemarycottagehook.co.uk. *Between Goole, Howden & Airmyn, close to M62 J36. Approach Hook from Boothferry Rd r'about 300yds S of Boothferry Bridge. Follow signs for Hook at Xrds turn L. Garden is 550yds on L. Garden entry is from rear through car park.* Sun 29 May (12-4). Adm £4, chd free. Light refreshments. Also cakes for sale.

Delightful combination of traditional cottage garden with themed planting overlooking open fields. Garden 'rooms' link to a small orchard and on through a living willow arch to herbaceous perennial borders and an edible garden. Variety of stalls for local organisations inc beekeepers, hedgehog rescue and gardening club. Wheelchair access is available to most of the garden (from rear carpark) albeit ground a little uneven. One part of the garden has stepped access.

も 🐂 ✿ ♿ ☕

76 RUDDING PARK
Follifoot, Harrogate, HG3 1JH. Mr & Mrs Simon Mackaness, 01423 871350, www.ruddingpark.co.uk. *3m S of Harrogate off the southern bypass A658. Follow brown tourist signs. Use hotel entrance.* **Sun 22 May (1-5). Adm £5, chd free. Light refreshments.**
20 acres of attractive formal gardens, kitchen gardens and lawns around a Grade I Regency House extended and now used as an hotel. Humphry Repton parkland. Formal gardens designed by Jim Russell with extensive rhododendron and azalea planting. Recent designs by Matthew Wilson, contemporary look with grasses and perennials.

77 SALTMARSHE HALL
Saltmarshe, Howden, DN14 7RX. Claire Connely, 01430 434920, info@saltmarshehall.com, www.saltmarshehall.com. *6m E of Goole. From Howden (M62, J37) follow signs to Howdendyke & Saltmarshe. Hall in park W of Saltmarshe village.* **Wed 22 June (12-4). Adm £4.50, chd free. Light refreshments available outside. Afternoon teas in Hall and picnic hampers available via pre-booking. Visits also by arrangement for groups of 5 to 99.**
17 acre estate surrounding Regency house set on the banks of the River Ouse. Walled garden, herbaceous borders of shrubs, climbers, perennials, annuals and roses. Lawns, fine old trees, pond, orchard, courtyards, river and countryside views. Wheelchair to the house via a ramp. Garden is accessed via gravel paths, narrow walkways and shallow steps.

78 ◆ SCAMPSTON WALLED GARDEN
Scampston Hall, Scampston, Malton, YO17 8NG. The Legard Family, 01944 759111, info@scampston.co.uk, www.scampston.co.uk/gardens. *5m E of Malton. 0.5m N of A64, nr the village of Rillington & signed Scampston only.* **For opening times and information, please phone, email or visit garden website.**
An exciting modern garden designed by Piet Oudolf. The 4 acre walled garden contains a series of hedged enclosures designed to look good throughout the year. The garden contains many unusual species and is a must for any keen plant lover. The Walled Garden is set within the grounds and parkland surrounding Scampston Hall. The Hall opens to visitors for a short period during the summer months. A restored Richardson conservatory is at the heart of the Walled Garden and is used as a Heritage and Learning Centre. The Walled Garden, cafe and facilities are accessible by wheelchair. Some areas of the parkland and the first floor of the Hall are harder to access.

79 SCAPE LODGE
11 Grand Stand, Scapegoat Hill, Golcar, Huddersfield, HD7 4NQ. Elizabeth & David Smith, 01484 644320, elizabethanddavid.smith@ngs.org.uk. *5m W of Huddersfield. From J23 or 24 M62, follow signs to Rochdale. From Outlane village, 1st L. At top of hill, 2nd L. Park at Scapegoat Hill Baptist Church (HD7 4NU) or in village. 5 mins walk to garden. 303/304 bus.* **Sun 15 May, Sun 26 June (1.30-4.30). Adm £5, chd free. Home-made teas. Visits also by arrangement May to July. Donation to Mayor of Kirklees Charity Appeal.**
1/3 acre contemporary country garden at 1000ft in the Pennines on a steeply sloping site with far-reaching views. Gravel paths lead between mixed borders on many levels. Colour themed informal planting chosen to sit comfortably in the landscape and give year-round interest. Steps lead to terraced kitchen and cutting garden. Gazebo, pond, shade garden, collection of pots and tender plants. Featured in Episode 2 of the Dec 2021 Gardeners' World Winter Special.

80 ◆ SHANDY HALL GARDENS
Thirsk Bank, Coxwold, York, YO61 4AD. The Laurence Sterne Trust, 01347 868465, info@laurencesternetrust.org.uk, www.laurencesternetrust.org.uk. *N of York. From A19, 7m from both Easingwold & Thirsk, turn E signed Coxwold. Park on road.* **For NGS: Evening opening Fri 3, Fri 17 June (6.30-8). Adm £4, chd free. For other opening times and information, please phone, email or visit garden website.**
Home of C18 author Laurence Sterne. 2 walled gardens, 1 acre of unusual perennials interplanted with tulips and old roses in low walled beds. In old quarry another acre of trees, shrubs, bulbs, climbers and wildflowers encouraging wildlife, inc nearly 450 recorded species of moths. Moth trapping demonstration. Partial wheelchair access. Gravel car park, steps down to Wild Garden.

GROUP OPENING

81 SHIPTONTHORPE GARDENS
Shiptonthorpe, York, YO43 3PQ. *2m NW of Market Weighton. Both gardens are in the main village on the N of A1079.* **Sat 4, Sun 5 June (11-5). Combined adm £5, chd free. Light refreshments in the village hall.**

6 ALL SAINTS DRIVE
Mr & Mrs Thompson.

WAYSIDE
Susan Sellars.

Two contrasting gardens with different gardening styles. 6 All Saints Drive, 'Langdale End' is an eclectic maze-like garden with a mix of contemporary and cottage garden styles, featuring a 'hidden corner' with tropical plants and greenhouse, a Japanese /Asian inspired garden with water features and a pond. Wayside has interesting planting in a variety of garden areas and developing vegetable and fruit growing areas with greenhouse. Wheelchairs possible with help at Wayside.

National Garden Scheme gardens are identified by their yellow road signs and posters. You can expect a garden of quality, character and interest, a warm welcome and plenty of home-made cakes!

82 SKIPWITH HALL

Skipwith, Selby, YO8 5SQ.
Mr & Mrs C D Forbes
Adam, 07976 821903,
rosalind@escrick.com,
www.escrick.com/hall-gardens.
9m S of York, 6m N of Selby. From York A19 Selby, L in Escrick, 4m to Skipwith. From Selby A19 York, R onto A163 to Market Weighton, then L after 2m to Skipwith. **Thur 9 June (1-4). Adm £5, chd free. Home-made teas. Visits also by arrangement in June for groups of 10 to 50.**
4 acre walled garden of Queen Anne house (not open). Mixture of historic formal gardens (in part designed by Cecil Pinsent), wildflower walks and lawns. 'No-dig' kitchen garden with herb maze, Italian garden, collection of old-fashioned shrub roses and climbers. Orchard with espaliered and fan-trained fruit and small arboretum cum woodland. Gravel paths.

83 SLEIGHTHOLMEDALE LODGE

Fadmoor, YO62 7JG. Patrick & Natasha James. *6m NE of Helmsley. Parking can be limited in wet weather. Garden is 1st property in Sleightholmedale, 1m from Fadmoor.* **Sun 10 July (1-5.30). Adm £5, chd free. Home-made teas.**
A glorious south facing, 3 acre hillside garden with views over a peaceful valley in the North York Moors. Cultivated for over 100 years, wide herbaceous borders and descending terraces lead down the valley with beautiful, informal planting within the formal structure of walls and paths. In July, the garden features roses, delphiniums and other classic English country garden perennials.

84 ◆ STILLINGFLEET LODGE

Stewart Lane, Stillingfleet, York, YO19 6HP. Mr & Mrs J Cook, 01904 728506, vanessa.cook@stillingfleetlodgenurseries.co.uk, www.stillingfleetlodgenurseries.co.uk. *6m S of York. From A19 York-Selby take B1222 towards Sherburn in Elmet. In village turn opp church.* **For NGS: Sun 15 May, Sun 18 Sept (1-5). Adm £6, chd £1. Home-made teas. For other opening times and information, please phone, email or visit garden website.**
Organic, wildlife garden subdivided into smaller gardens, each based on a colour theme with emphasis on use of foliage plants. Wildflower meadow, natural pond, 55yd double herbaceous borders and modern rill garden. Rare breeds of poultry wander freely in garden. Adjacent nursery. Garden courses run all summer - see website. Art exhibitions in the cafe. Gravel paths and lawn. Ramp to cafe if needed. No disabled WC.

85 STONEFIELD COTTAGE

27 Nordham, North Cave, Brough, HU15 2LT. Nicola Lyte. *15m W of Hull. M62 E, J38 towards N Cave. Turn L towards N Cave Wetlands, then R at LH bend. Stonefield Cottage is on R, ¼m along Nordham.* **Sat 16, Sun 17 July (10-5). Adm £5, chd free. Home-made teas.**
A hidden and surprising 1 acre garden, with an emphasis throughout on strong, dramatic colours and sweeping vistas. Rose beds, mixed borders, vegetables, a riotous hot bed, boggy woodland, wildlife pond and jacquemontii underplanted with red hydrangeas. Collections of hellebores, primulas, ferns, astilbes, hostas, heucheras, dahlias, hemerocallis and hydrangeas.

GROUP OPENING

86 THE TERRACE GARDENS

Oswaldkirk, York, YO62 5XZ. Bridget Hannigan. *20m N of York, 4m S of Helmsley. Single track road on bend of B1363 in the centre of Oswaldkirk. Parking in Main St opp.* **Sun 7 Aug (1-5). Combined adm £6, chd free. Home-made teas in the village hall.**
Collection of four gardens nestled along a south facing hillside known as The Hag. All with stunning views of the Coxwold-Gilling Gap and Howardian Hills beyond. Bramleys: plantswoman's garden with winding paths through naturalistic planting and wildflower orchard. Sunday Telegraph 'Six of the Best Small Gardens 2021'. Orchard House: beekeepers' garden with an emphasis on wildlife and fruit & vegetable production. Ewe Cote: neat traditional cottage garden full of roses and perennial favourites and a small orchard. Pavilion House: terraced garden, creating different 'rooms' and planting themes. There is no vehicular access to The Terrace but parking is available nearby.

87 THIMBLEBY HALL

Thimbleby, Northallerton, DL6 3PY.
Mr & Mrs A Shelley. *From A19, follow signs for Osmotherly then R in village centre onto South End Rd towards Thimbleby.* **Fri 3 June (1-5). Adm £7, chd free. Home-made teas.**
Country estate on the western edge of the North York Moors. A number of formal garden areas inc terraced gardens, herbaceous garden and lake within an extensive parkland setting with sweeping views of the surrounding countryside. The gardens have been substantially extended by the owner with formal planting and a large banked area to the west of the house with spring flowering shrubs featuring azaleas and cornus. Mature trees feature on the estate and especially impressive is an avenue of redwoods framing views across the lake to the south of the Hall.

88 THIRSK HALL

Kirkgate, Thirsk, YO7 1PL.
Willoughby & Daisy Gerrish,
020 3764 2470,
info@thirskhall.com,
www.thirskhall.com. *In the centre of Thirsk. on Kirkgate, next to St Mary's Church.* **Sun 8 May (11-5). Adm £6, chd free. Home-made teas.**
Thirsk Hall is a Grade II* listed townhouse completed by John Carr in 1777 (not open). Behind the house the unexpected 20 acre grounds inc lawns, herbaceous borders, kitchen gardens, walled paddocks and parkland. The present layout and planting are the result of a sensitive restoration, blending formal and informal beds, shrubbery, and mature trees. Wheelchair access. Sculpture Park.

89 NEW TUDOR CROFT

Stokesley Road, Guisborough, TS14 8DL. Mike Heagney. *9m E of Teesside, next to northern edge of N York Moors. From Teesside: A171 to Guisborough, R at T lights, 400 metres on L, park on rd. Additional large car park a further 400m on L. From South: A19, A172, A173 then A171 to Guisborough as above.* **Sat 18, Sun 19 June (11-4). Adm £7.50, chd free. Home-made afternoon teas available, plus wine etc.**
A very beautiful 1930s Arts & Crafts garden, immaculately maintained with many features including a stone fernery, walled and water gardens, rose gardens & pergola and trout

stream. This plantsman's paradise covers 5 acres and is a haven full of surprises. Large plant nursery. Featured on BBC Gardeners' World and in many magazines. Plant and craft sales. A great garden for children, with nooks and crannies, arbours, secret places, stepping stones across the stream and even a revolving summerhouse!

 ♿ 🐾 ✻ 🚗 🍵

90 NEW 94 TURNBERRY AVENUE

Ackworth, Pontefract, WF7 7FB. Mr Chris Ensell, www.instagram. com/theyorkshirejunglegarden/. *Ackworth. Off A638. Follow rd round the bend to green on L Garden 50m further on R.* **Sun 28 Aug, Tue 6, Sun 11 Sept (12-3). Adm £3, chd free. Pre-booking essential, please visit www.ngs.org.uk for information & booking. Tea.**
Set on a new-build estate and only 3 yrs old, this compact garden features an array of tropical and unusual plants along with some more recognisable flora. Bananas, gingers, cannas, colocasia, bamboo and other subtropical plants feature in a typical new-build plot, very densley planted with statement plants. Access and garden size requires pre-booking to accommodate visitors.

✻ 🍵))

91 TYTHE FARM HOUSE

Carr Lane, Wansford, Driffield, YO25 8NP. Terry & Susanne Hardcastle, 07951 126588, susanannhardcastle@gmail.com, tythefarmgardens.com. *3m E of Driffield on B1249. Turn L at mini r'about onto Nafferton Rd. Carr Lane is opposite the church. Approx 600 yds on R.* **Sun 19 June (10-5). Adm £5, chd free. Light refreshments. Visits also by arrangement Apr to Sept for groups of 10+.**
Terry and Susanne welcome you to their secret garden that extends to 10 acres. Deciduous woodlands, orchards, lake, courtyard garden, herbaceous, rose garden and Italian sculptures. Formerly a working farm with traditional buildings now renovated. Mature garden developed over 25 years. Excavation of the lake and landscaping projects have created something very special. Ample parking space on site and easy access to most areas. An optional short hike through the woods will prepare you for home-made refreshments in the courtyard garden

or the garden room as the weather dictates. Access to many parts of the garden is via paved paths and level lawns.

 ♿ 🐾 ✻ 🚗 🍵))

92 THE VILLA

High Street, Hook, Goole, DN14 5PJ. Penny & John Settle. *Close to M62 J36 & J37. Approaching Hook from A614 Boothferry Rd along Westfield Ln around 'z' bend to Xrds at village hall. Turn L, garden approx. 300yds on R. Park on High St.* **Sun 19 June (11.30-4.30). Adm £3.50, chd free.**
Acquired by the current owners in 2011 in a derelict state, the garden now offers a stunning variety of different areas inc a Mediterranean Garden, an extensive bonsai display, an oriental area featuring Asian sculptures, pergola walkway, paved terrace and large lawned area. The garden also features a collection of statues, alongside a large variety of perennial shrubs, bamboos and ornamental grasses, bearded irises and hostas. The garden offers plenty of seating for visitors to sit and take in the tranquillity of this hidden gem. Sorry, no wheelchair access.

93 THE VINES

Waplington Hall, Allerthorpe, York, YO42 4RS. Penny & Bill Simmons. *Leave A1079 at Pocklington r'about, SW through Allerthorpe, turn R signed 'Waplington only'. Coming from Melbourne turn L at start of Allerthorpe village.* **Sun 17 July (12-5). Adm £5, chd free. Home-made teas at Allerthorpe Village Hall.**
This spacious 1¾ acre English country garden is traditionally planted with varied herbaceous borders of perennials, shrubs and climbers. Walk through an unusual vine house full of fruiting grapevines to a thriving walled kitchen garden with fruit trees, vegetables, soft fruit and a productive greenhouse. Also an informal garden featuring extensive grassed areas with mature and ornamental trees. Most areas of the garden, apart from greenhouses, are grassed and mainly level and accessible for wheelchairs.

 ♿ ✻ 🍵))

GROUP OPENING

94 NEW WALLED GARDENS OF BEVERLEY

North Bar Without, Beverley, HU17 7AG. Rosie Ryan. *From E, turn R at North Bar (brick gatehouse) lights. From N gardens on R north of North Bar. From S gardens on L through North Bar. Street parking.* **Sun 19 June (10-4). Combined adm £5, chd free. Home-made teas at No 45.**

NEW 33 NORTH BAR WITHOUT
Sally McDonald.

NEW 35 NORTH BAR WITHOUT
Michele Barker.

39 NORTH BAR WITHOUT
Mr & Mrs C Ryan.

NEW 43 NORTH BAR WITHOUT
Dr Richard and Dr Gwen Turner.

45 NORTH BAR WITHOUT
John & Jill Edmond.

33 and 35 are small tranquil gardens made in old terraced cottage backyards with quirky conversion of garages. 33 has random planting for sun and shade, lots of pots and rustic seating. Pass through to 35 to find ivy covered walls, borders, pots and lawn. 43 is larger and partly shaded by a magnificent copper beech. Borders contain a wide selection of small trees, shrubs and perennials which give colour all year. Wildflowers for bees and insects. Small pond. 39 and 45 are larger. 39 is a traditional townhouse garden, artistically planted for all year interest, winding paths through borders of perennials and roses. Paths continue through fruit trees and into a hidden plot with vegetables, cutting flowers and beehives. 45 has several compartments, the walls of which are believed to be the remains of old malt houses. Lawns surrounded by borders lead onto an orchard and more. Behind another wall is a kitchen garden, greenhouse, gravel and herb garden. Nos 33, 35 & 43 have full access. 39 & 45 partial wheelchair access, but can see the main parts of each garden.

 ♿ 🍵

95 WELL HOUSE

Grafton, YO51 9QJ. Glen Garnett, 01423 322884. *2½ m S of Boroughbridge. Turn off B6265 or A168 S of Boroughbridge.* Sun 15 May (11-5). Adm £4, chd free. Open nearby Whixley Gardens. Opening with Grafton Gardens on Sun 12 June, Sun 3 July. Visits also by arrangement May to July. On the outskirts of Grafton village, nestling under a hillside with long views to the White Horse and Hambleton hills, extending to 1½ acres, this garden was begun 40 yrs ago and is constantly changing. A traditional English cottage garden, with herbaceous borders, climbing and rambling roses, and ornamental shrubs with a variety of interesting species. Paths lead to orchard with ducks.

96 WELTON LODGE

Dale Road, Welton, Brough, HU15 1PE. Brendon Swallow. *11 m W of Hull nr A63. From A63 take exit for Welton, Elloughton & Brough. Immed turn R junction. Garden on R just after Xrds.* Sun 4 Sept (10-4). Adm £4, chd free. Home-made teas.
Welton Lodge is a Grade II listed house occupying 1½ acres in the beautiful village of Welton and features a series of tiered gardens. The top lawn features topiary bay balls, leading to a tranquil formal pond with box hedging and shaded semi-circular seating. The renovated walled kitchen gardens have espaliers of fruit trees and vines around formal lawns and flower beds and a 20m orangery. Block paved ramp leading to gravelled access to lower and upper gardens without steps. Steep upper garden.

97 NEW 32 WEST STREET

Leven, HU17 5LF. Mrs Janet Phillips. *8.5 miles NE of Beverley. Turn off Main St by the Hare & Hounds pub & follow yellow signs.* Sun 24 July (10-4). Adm £4, chd free.
A quirky garden with themed areas inc tropical jungle planting, fairies and dinosaurs, an oriental style nook and rockery. This family garden was begun 9 yrs ago and has gradually evolved into a wonderfully chaotic mix of themes with some unusual plants and features inc a glass bottle wall. Street parking.

98 WHITE WYNN

Ellerton, York, YO42 4PN. Cindy & Richard Hutchinson, 01757 289495, richardahutchinson@btinternet.com. *From York B1228 through Sutton, turn R towards Howden. From Selby A19 N turn R along A163 towards Market Weighton. Turn L at Bubwith Xrds. ½ m up Shortacre Ln (no through road).* Sun 3 July (1.30-5.30). Adm £4.50, chd free. Light refreshments. Visits also by arrangement Apr to Aug for groups of 5 to 30.
1½ acre country garden with many mature trees. Lawns and patios adjoin 60m long border, heather bed, orchard, rose garden with arbour. Vegetable beds, woodland, wildflower meadow and shade beds. Secret garden contains less usual plantings to give a tropical feel. Wildlife-friendly with 2 ponds, blackthorn and damson copses and stored logs providing shelter for hedgehogs and toads. Very good, level access, mostly on grass.

GROUP OPENING

99 WHIXLEY GARDENS

York, YO26 8AR. *8m W of York, 8m E of Harrogate, 6m N of Wetherby. 3m E of A1(M) off A59 York-Harrogate. Signed Whixley.* Sun 15 May (11-5). Combined adm £7, chd free. Light refreshments at The Old Vicarage. Open nearby Well House.

COBBLE COTTAGE
John Hawkridge & Barry Atkinson.
(See separate entry)

THE OLD VICARAGE
Mr & Mrs Roger Marshall, biddymarshall@btinternet.com.
Visits also by arrangement May to July.

Attractive rural yet accessible village nestling on the edge of the York Plain with beautiful historic church and Queen Anne Hall (not open). The gardens are at opposite ends of the village with good footpaths. A plantsman's and flower arranger's garden at Cobble Cottage, has views to the Hambleton Hills. Close to the church, The Old Vicarage, with a ¾ acre walled flower garden, overlooks the old deer park. The walls, house and various structures are festooned with climbers. Gravel and old brick paths lead to hidden seating areas creating the atmosphere of a romantic English garden. Finalist in The English Garden's The Nation's Favourite Gardens 2021. Wheelchair access only to The Old Vicarage.

100 NEW 5 WOLD ROAD

Nafferton, Driffield, YO25 4LB. Peter & Jennifer Baker, 01377 255224. *Follow directions rather than SatNav: From Driffield bypass to Nafferton on A614. Then 1st L & 1st L on Wold Rd. Park on street.* Sun 3 July (10.30-3.30). Combined adm with Highfield Cottage £6, chd free. Home-made teas at Highfield (weather permitting). Sun 7 Aug (10.30-5). Adm £4, chd free. Visits also by arrangement June to Aug for groups of 5 to 20. Teas on request.
Designed and developed by owners since 2019. A small garden made to feel spacious. 50+ ferns mingle with many other plants in borders, a pond, many quirky containers, up trellises and walls. Two greenhouses, one full of ferns and a living wall. Seats to view different aspects of a constantly evolving garden.

101 ♦ YORK GATE

Back Church Lane, Adel, Leeds, LS16 8DW. Perennial, 0113 267 8240, yorkgate@perennial.org.uk, www.yorkgate.org.uk. *5m N of Leeds. A660 to Adel, turn R at lights before 'Mio Modo' restaurant. L on to Church Lane. After church, R onto Back Church Ln. Garden on L.* For opening times and information, please phone, email or visit garden website.
An internationally acclaimed 1 acre jewel of a garden with 14 individual garden rooms. Many unusual plants and architectural topiary. 2020 saw an extension to the garden with new facilities inc a new cafe and gift shop as well as exciting new gardens, plant nursery and heritage exhibition. Owned by Perennial, the charity that looks after horticulturists and their families in times of need. Narrow gravel and cobbled paths make most of the original garden inaccessible to wheelchairs. The new gardens, tea room, shop and WC are accessible.

102 YORKE HOUSE & WHITE ROSE COTTAGE
Dacre Banks, Nidderdale, HG3 4EW. Tony & Pat Hutchinson and Mark & Amy Hutchinson, 01423 780456, pat@yorkehouse.co.uk, www.yorkehouse.co.uk. *4m SE of Pateley Bridge, 10m NW of Harrogate, 10m N of Otley. On B6451 near centre of Dacre Banks. Car park.* Sun 26 June (11-5). Adm £5, chd free. Cream teas. Visitors welcome to use picnic area in orchard. Opening with Dacre Banks & Summerbridge Gardens on Sun 10 July (12-5). **Visits also by arrangement June & July for groups of 10+.**
Award-winning English country garden in the heart of Nidderdale. A series of distinct areas flowing through 2 acres of ornamental garden. Colour-themed borders, natural pond and stream with delightful waterside plantings. Secluded seating areas and attractive views. Adjacent cottage has a recently developed garden designed for wheelchair access. Large collection of hostas. Orchard picnic area. All main features accessible to wheelchair users.

103 ◆ THE YORKSHIRE ARBORETUM
Castle Howard, York, YO60 7BY. The Castle Howard Arboretum Trust, 01653 648598, marketing@ yorkshirearboretum.org, www.yorkshirearboretum.org. *15m NE of York. Off A64. Follow signs to Castle Howard then Yorkshire Arboretum signs at the obelisk r'about.* For NGS: Sun 5 June (10-4). Adm £10, chd free. Arboretum Cafe. **For other opening times and information, please phone, email or visit garden website. Donation to Plant Heritage.**
A glorious, 120 acre garden of trees from around the world set in a stunning landscape of parkland, lakes and ponds. Walks and lakeside trails, tours, family activities. We welcome visitors of all ages wanting to enjoy the space, serenity and beauty of this sheltered valley as well as those interested in our extensive collection of trees and shrubs. Internationally renowned collection of trees in a beautiful setting, accompanied by a diversity of wildflowers, birds, insects and other wildlife. Not suitable for wheelchairs. Motorised all-terrain buggies are available on loan, please book 24hrs in advance on 01653 648598.

York Gate

CHANNEL ISLANDS

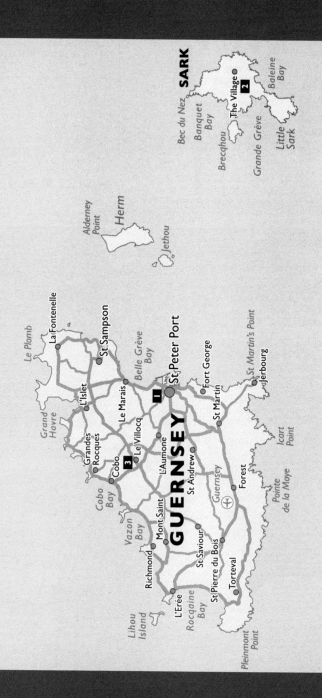

SARK

Bec du Nez

Banquet Bay

Brecqhou

The Village **2**

Grande Grève

Baleine Bay

Little Sark

Alderney Point

Herm

Jethou

Le Plomb

LaFontenelle

St Sampson

Belle Grève Bay

St Peter Port

Fort George

St Martin's Point

Jerbourg

L'Islet

Le Marais

1

Le Villocq

Grandes Rocques

Cobo

3

L'Aumone

St Martin

GUERNSEY

Icart Point

Grand Havre

Cobo Bay

Vazon Bay

Mont Saint

St Andrew

Guernsey

Forest

Pointe de la Moye

Richmond

St Saviour

St Pierre du Bois

Torteval

L'Erée

Rocqaine Bay

Lihou Island

Pleinmont Point

5 kilometres

3 miles

0

0

© Sparrow Publishing

North of Saint-Malo and west of the Cotentin Peninsula, the spectacular beaches and rugged coastline of the Channel Islands have a definite subtropical feel.

The mild winters and endless summer sunshine see a stream of visitors and islanders enjoy the peace and tranquillity offered in Guernsey, along with many scenic cliff top walks, prehistoric remains, woodland valleys, idyllic parish gardens, secluded town gardens and the garden gems of our neighbouring islands of Sark and Herm.

Three Gardens join the National Garden Scheme this year offering glasshouses, walled gardens, sculpture and much more!

Volunteers

Area Organiser
Patricia McDermott
patricia.mcdermott@ngs.org.uk

Treasurer
Liz Bell
elizabeth.bell@ngs.org.uk

Publicity
Alison Carney
alison.carney@ngs.org.uk

Booklet Coordinator
Ellie Phillips
ellie.phillips@ngs.org.uk

THE GARDENS

1 NEW **CASTLE CAREY**
L'hyvreuse, St Peter Port, Guernsey, GY1 1UX. Mr Royston Clegg. *Turn R at top of The Grange, go along Brock Rd, turn R at T-lights, L at Candie Stores, 1st R onto L'hyvreuse. Garden entrance at end of road. No onsite parking.* **Sat 25 June (12-5). Adm £5, chd free. Home-made teas.**
The Gardens have stunning views over St Peter Port. Set in 4 acres, the upper garden is mainly lawned and is surrounded by herbaceous borders. There are many statues adding further interest. The Lower Garden has a fine example of a Victorian glasshouse in which can be found vines and a selection of cactus. Moving on from here is the vegetable garden and fruit trees. Jazz band.
☕

2 NEW **LE GRAND DIXCART**
Sark, Guernsey, GY10 1SD. Helen Magell, 01481832943, helen@horse.gg. *Next to Stocks Hotel. Take the boat from Guernsey to Sark & follow the signs to Stocks Hotel. Once at the hotel continue up Dixcart Ln towards La Coupee & Le Grand Dixcart will be on your R.* **Sat 25, Sun 26 June, Sat 2, Sun 3 July (11-3). Adm £4, chd £2. Home-made teas.**
The gardens surround an old farmhouse and date from 1565. They are formed into five distinct areas over 2 acres and are cultivated for

beauty, wildlife and food. There is a large mandala style permaculture area providing many different vegetables and cutting flowers alongside habitats for wildlife, ponds, lawns, herbaceous borders, two glasshouses, woodland, sculptures and an orchard. Wheelchair access around Sark can be difficult but once you are actually at the gardens there are just grassy slopes and paths.

3 NEW **♦ VICTORIAN WALLED GARDEN**
Saumarez Park, La Route De Saumarez, Guernsey, GY5 7UJ. Jill Tetlaw, walledgarden.gg. *41/42 bus from St Peter Port or follow signs to the W. The entrance is within Saumarez Park.* **For NGS: Sat 25 June, Sat 2 July (2-5). Adm £5, chd free. Light refreshments. For other opening times and information, please visit garden website.**
Visit Guernsey's hidden gem at the uniquely restored Garden, inc 170 feet of period glasshouses. Since 2006 volunteers have lovingly reclaimed a derelict site to become a thriving, productive garden. Rest awhile in the tranquil environment where insects buzz amongst over 300 Heritage fruit, flowers and vegetable plants all available in Queen Victoria's reign from 1837 to 1901. A newly built Education and visitor centre. 'La Choppe' selling produce, heritage seeds and locally made arts and crafts.

OPENING DATES

All entries subject to change. For latest information check **www.ngs.org.uk**
Map locator numbers are shown to the right of each garden name.

June

Saturday 25th
NEW Castle Carey   1
NEW Le Grand Dixcart   2
NEW ♦ Victorian Walled Garden   3

Sunday 26th
NEW Le Grand Dixcart   2

July

Saturday 2nd
NEW Le Grand Dixcart   2
NEW ♦ Victorian Walled Garden   3

Sunday 3rd
NEW Le Grand Dixcart   2

NORTHERN IRELAND

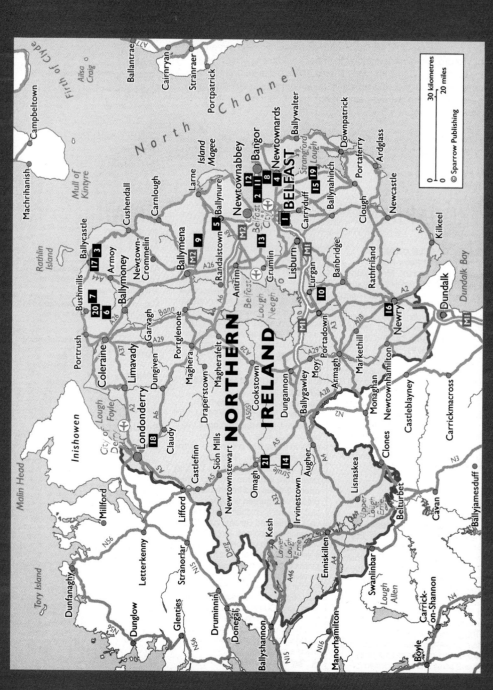

Northern Ireland is the most recent area to join the National Garden Scheme – not just one County but six.

Northern Ireland has had a long and successful history of an open gardens scheme and the Organising Team are thrilled to be able to continue the tradition by joining the National Garden Scheme.

An interesting and varied twenty-one friendly private garden owners will open in this inaugural season. Our program will start in February for snowdrops running through to late summer.

The region is exposed to the ameliorating effects of the North Atlantic current, a north eastward extension of the Gulf Stream. These mild and humid climatic conditions allow the growth of many tender garden plants and have, in sum, made Northern Ireland a green country in all seasons.

Northern Ireland boasts some of the best public gardens in Europe. The six counties also offer a wealth of large and small private gardens. Please plan to visit as many of the gardens as possible with the assurance of the renowned Northern Ireland warm welcome.

Left: Billy Old Rectory

Volunteers

Area Organiser
Trevor Edwards
07860 231115
trevor.edwards@ngs.org.uk

Area Treasurer
Jackie Harte
028 9754 2418
jackie.harte@ngs.org.uk

Assistant Area Organisers

Trevor Browne
028 9061 3878
trevor.browne@ngs.org.uk

Pat Cameron
07866 706825
pat.cameron@ngs.org.uk

Fionnuala Cook
028 4066 9669
fionnuala.cook@ngs.org.uk

Ann Fitzsimmons
07706 110367
ann.fitzsimmons@ngs.org.uk

Rosslind McGookin
028 2587 8848
rosslind.mcgookin@ngs.org.uk

Sally McGreevy
028 9181 5699
sally.mcgreevy@ngs.org.uk

Margaret Orr

🇫 @ngsnorthernireland
📷 @ngsnorthernireland

OPENING DATES

All entries subject to change. For latest information check **www.ngs.org.uk** Map locator numbers are shown to the right of each garden name.

February

Snowdrop Festival

Saturday 12th
NEW Benvardin Gardens 6
NEW Billy Old Rectory 7

Sunday 13th
NEW Benvardin Gardens 6
NEW Billy Old Rectory 7

April

Saturday 23rd
NEW Tattykeel House Garden 21

Sunday 24th
NEW Tattykeel House Garden 21

May

Saturday 7th
NEW Guincho 11

Sunday 8th
NEW Guincho 11

Saturday 21st
NEW Grovehill 10

Sunday 22nd
NEW Grovehill 10

Sunday 29th
NEW Clandeboye Estate 8

Monday 30th
NEW Clandeboye Estate 8

June

Saturday 4th
NEW Guincho 11

Sunday 5th
NEW Guincho 11

Saturday 11th
NEW Ardreigh House 2

Sunday 12th
NEW Ardreigh House 2

Saturday 18th
NEW Holly House Garden 13

Sunday 19th
NEW Holly House Garden 13

July

Saturday 2nd
NEW Clayburn 9
NEW Oak Gardens 18

Sunday 3rd
NEW Clayburn 9
NEW Oak Gardens 18

Saturday 16th
NEW Billy Old Rectory 7

Sunday 17th
NEW Billy Old Rectory 7

Saturday 23rd
NEW Beechmount House Garden 5

Sunday 24th
NEW Beechmount House Garden 5

Saturday 30th
NEW Tattykeel House Garden 21

Sunday 31st
NEW Tattykeel House Garden 21

August

Saturday 6th
NEW Kilcootry Barn 14

Sunday 7th
NEW Kilcootry Barn 14

Saturday 13th
NEW Billy Old Rectory 7

Sunday 14th
NEW Billy Old Rectory 7

September

Saturday 10th
NEW Clayburn 9
NEW Helen's Bay Organic 12

Sunday 11th
NEW Clayburn 9
NEW Helen's Bay Organic 12

By Arrangement

Arrange a personalised garden visit with your club, or group of friends, on a date to suit you. See individual garden entries for full details.

NEW Adrian Walsh Belfast Garden 1
NEW 13 Ballynagard Road 3
NEW Barley House 4
NEW Clayburn 9
NEW Linden 15
NEW The McKelvey Garden 16
NEW Mitreicari 17
NEW Old Balloo House and Barn 19
NEW 10 Riverside Road 20

Benvardin Gardens

THE GARDENS

1 NEW ADRIAN WALSH BELFAST GARDEN
59 Richmond Park, Stranmillis, Belfast, BT9 5EF. Adrian Walsh, 07808 156856. *Travelling from the r'about at Stranmillis College & going along the Stranmillis Rd towards Malone Rd, Richmond Park is the 2nd exit on the L. No 59 is on the L.* Visits by arrangement June to Oct. Adm £5, chd free.
Inc in 'The Open Gardens of Ireland' by Shirley Lanigan, this is an imaginatively designed naturalistic city garden that combines a vibrant mix of perennials, grasses, shrubs and trees set within a formal layout.

2 NEW ARDREIGH HOUSE
33 Cultra Avenue, Holywood, BT18 0AY. Mr & Mrs Trevor Marshall. *A2 Belfast towards Bangor pass Holywood after Maxol Station turn left into Cultra Ave. A2 Belfast towards Bangor pass H/w after Maxol St. turn L into Cultra Ave. Bangor - H/w on A2 after Culloden Hotel @ Traffic lights turn R - Cultra Station Rd - L into Circular Rd W - L Ailsa Rd.* Sat 11, Sun 12 June (2-5). Adm £5, chd free. Light refreshments.
The house and garden were restored about 15 yrs ago. A new walled garden with a corner Belvedere was created using old Belfast clay brick and houses a lawn surrounded by herbaceous plants, shrubs and climbers. Outside offers a woodland walk, wisteria arch, pleached lime and a Folly building with sunken garden and pond.
☕))

3 NEW 13 BALLYNAGARD ROAD
Ballyvoy, Ballycastle, BT54 6PW. Tom & Penny McNeill, 07754190687, pennymcneill@yahoo.co.uk. *3m outside Ballycastle. Drive through Ballycastle, pass hotel on L, 2nd exit at r'about to Cushendall. From Ballyvoy drive 0.75m, Ballynagard Rd is on R. Drive 0.75m. Arrive at 1st bungalow on R.* Visits by arrangement June to Sept for groups of up to 8. Adm by donation.
A challenging ½ acre site 400 ft above sea level with stunning rural and sea views. Designed to meet prevailing environmental conditions and to protect each section from severe winds. Seasonal planting with mature shrubs and rockery on a terraced site create cosy contrasting rooms with seating area.

4 NEW BARLEY HOUSE
3 Brooklands Park, Newtownards, BT23 4XY. Miss Gillian Downing, 028 9181 5263, downingoriginals@gmail.com. *Newtownards, Co. Down. From Dundonald follow A20 to the r'about at Ards Shopping Centre. Take the 1st exit onto Blair Mayne Rd N. Turn L onto Manse Rd. Continue until you reach Brooklands Pk on the L.* Visits by arrangement May to Aug. Adm £5, chd free.
A constantly evolving garden with emphasis on roses, trees, shrubs and herbaceous perennials grown to attract birds, bees and butterflies. It has an extensive range of plants and the garden areas have features aimed to enhance and intrigue. It has been artistically planted to give year-round interest. Most of the garden is wheelchair accessible.
& ✿ ⊟

5 NEW BEECHMOUNT HOUSE GARDEN
85 Ballyalbanagh Road, Ballyclare, BT39 9SP. Mr David Henderson. *North of Ballyeaston nr Ballyclare. From Ballyclare town centre take the Rashee Rd after 1.8m at 5 Corners Guest House fork R onto the Sawmill Rd at junction turn R. Ballyalbanagh Rd is next R.* Sat 23, Sun 24 July (2-5). Adm £5, chd free. Pre-booking essential, please visit www.ngs.org.uk for information & booking.
A large country garden on three sides of house with herbaceous plants, mixed shrub borders and trees. Lawns and a large elevated rockery offer stunning views of the surrounding Co Antrim countryside.
))

6 NEW BENVARDIN GARDENS
Benvardin Road, Ballybogy, Ballymoney, BT53 6NN. Mr Hugh Montgomery, www.benvardin.com. *From Ballymoney head toward Portrush, in the village of Ballybogey turn R into the Benvardin Rd after ½m (before the River Bush) the Gardens are on your R.* Sat 12, Sun 13 Feb (12-4). Combined adm with Billy Old Rectory £8, chd free. Light refreshments.
The garden at Benvarden enclosed since the C17, when it was most probably a semi-fortified Bawn, built for the purpose of protecting livestock from roaming thieves. Bought by the Montgomery family in the late C18, it was transformed into a modern, for those days, walled garden with the bawn wall faced with brick, the height raised to the present 16 ft. and paths and beds laid out. From the Pond, paths lead to the banks of the river Bush, well-known as the river which leads to the Bushmills Distillery, the world's oldest whiskey, and here the river is spanned by a splendid bridge, built by Robert James Montgomery, who survived the charge of the Heavy Brigade in the Crimean war.
☕))

7 NEW BILLY OLD RECTORY
5 Cabragh Road, Castlecat, Bushmills, BT57 8YH. Mrs Meta Page. *B/money bypass straight at Kilraughts Rd take 2nd R to B66 sign Dervock turn L (B66) sign Bushmills thro Derrykeighan after 2.3m at Castlecatt - R sign Billy ½m & L - Haw Rd at Church R -Cabragh Rd.* Sat 12, Sun 13 Feb (12-4). Combined adm with Benvardin Gardens £8, chd free. Sat 16, Sun 17 July, Sat 13, Sun 14 Aug (12-5). Adm £5, chd free. Home-made teas. Limited refreshments during Snowdrop Opening.
A mature 3 acre garden on an historic site. Front of the Georgian rectory is a large lawn with mature trees, an ancient well and a developing woodland garden with a small fernery. Rear has another large lawn with contrasting borders of roses, herbaceous, shrubs and pond area. Also kitchen, greenhouse, herb, vegetable and fruit gardens - an large old orchard and area with wildflowers and annuals.
✿ ☕))

During 2020 - 2021 National Garden Scheme funding supported over 1,400 Queen's Nurses to deliver virtual and hands-on, community care across England, Wales and Northern Ireland

8 [NEW] **CLANDEBOYE ESTATE**
Bangor, BT19 1RN. Mrs Karen
Kane, www.clandeboye.co.uk.
Main entrance is off the main Belfast
to Bangor A2 circa 2m before
Bangor. **Sun 29, Mon 30 May (2-5).**
Adm £10, chd free. Pre-booking
essential, please visit www.ngs.
org.uk for information & booking.
Light refreshments.
A series of intimate walled gardens
adjoin the courtyard and house.
These inc the delightful Bee Garden,
the Chapel Walk and the intimate
Conservatory Garden.

✿ ♿ ☕

Our 2021 donations mean
that 69,000 people were
helped by our Support for
Marie Curie

9 [NEW] **CLAYBURN**
30A Ballynulto Road, Glenwherry,
Ballymena, BT42 4RJ. Judith &
Hugh Jackson, 07539 712991.
What3words app - schematic.
composers.remedy. From the A36
Ballymena to Larne Rd, ½m E of its
junction with the B94, turn L onto
Ballynulto Rd. The garden is 0.8m
on the R. **Sat 2, Sun 3 July, Sat 10,**
Sun 11 Sept (2-5). Adm £3.50, chd
£3.50. Light refreshments. Visits
also by arrangement June to Sept
for groups of 5 to 10.
This prairie-style garden is nestled in
a fold of moorlands south of Slemish
Mountain. Taking advantage of the
surrounding landscape, the mass
planting of native trees and layers of
colourful herbaceous plants add to
the spectacular views from the site:
the retained and extended dry stone
walls helping to protect the planting in
a location that is, somewhat 'off the
beaten track'.

☕

10 [NEW] **GROVEHILL**
101 Dunkirk Road, Lurgan,
Craigavon, BT66 7AR. Mr Brian
& Mrs Shirley McKnight. *From*
Lurgan signposted Waringstown,
Banbridge & Gilford take B3. Follow
sign to Waringstown (Dunkirk Road).
After ½m arrive Grovehill' – large
house on hill on L. **Sat 21, Sun 22**
May (2-5). Adm £5, chd free. Light
refreshments.
This delightful garden started its
development in 1996 when the lawns
were completed with the first planting
of whip trees / shrubbery taking
place that Autumn. Varieties of trees
planted were Oak, Beech, Birch,
Lime and Ash. Since then many other
features have been established inc
a Follies Garden, an Arboretum, an
Italian Garden, a Japanese Garden,
an Arizona Garden and much, much
more.

♿ ✿ ☕))

Beechmount House Garden

1 NEW GUINCHO
69 Craigdarragh Road, Helen's
Bay, Bangor, BT19 1UB. Mr & Mrs
Eric Cairns. *On the Craigdarragh
Rd, Helen's Bay, Co Down. 10m from
Belfast City centre take the A2 towards
Bangor proceed past Culloden Hotel
for a further 2m then turn L into
Craigdarragh Rd sign posted Helen's
Bay. Garden is on the L.* Sat 7, Sun
8 May, Sat 4, Sun 5 June (2-5).
Adm £10, chd free. Pre-booking
essential, please visit www.ngs.
org.uk for information & booking.
Light refreshments.
A 12 acre garden surrounding an
unusual Portuguese style house is
a place to experience unforgettable
sights, scents and sounds. Worth
a visit for gorgeous hydrangea
'Sea Foam' alone, glimmering with
flowers in dappled shade or to meet
the original of the elder Sambucus
'Guincho Purple' or to the rock pool
fringed with primula. Laid out in the
1930s but planted by Mrs Frazer
Mackie 1948-1979.
♿ ☕

**2 NEW HELEN'S BAY
ORGANIC**
Coastguard Avenue, Helen's Bay,
BT19 1JY. Mr John McCormick,
www.helensbayorganic.com.
*Coastguard Ave. off Craigdarragh
Rd, Helen's Bay, Co Down. Coming
from A2 (Main Belfast-Bangor Road).
Drive 200m past the railway bridge
on Craigdarragh Rd then turn L
Coastguard Ave. Go over 2 speed
bumps & enter first farm gate on L.*
Sat 10, Sun 11 Sept (2-5). Adm £5,
chd free.
An urban market garden, established
in 1991, producing over 50 varieties
of organic vegetables for direct
retailing. Also hosts a community
garden and allotments which include
an extensive range of fruit and
vegetables. An ideal space to get
ideas to combine flowers, fruit, food
and biodiversity in your garden.
🐕))

**3 NEW HOLLY HOUSE
GARDEN**
3 Ballyutoag Hill, Nutts
Corner, Crumlin, BT29 4UH.
Mr Will Hamilton,
www.hollyhousegardens.com. *In
the hills over looking West Belfast.
Belfast > Crumlin Rd, following signs
for Crumlin/Int Airport (A52). After 3m
Horse Shoe Bend, 4m turn L onto
Ballyutoag Hill & the garden is the 1st*

entrance on the R. Sat 18, Sun 19
June (2-5). Adm £5, chd free.
Holly House Garden is an area of six
acres created out of farmland over the
past 20+ yrs. The garden comprises
woodlands, herbaceous borders
and an iris garden where thousands
of spring and summer bulbs have
been planted. There is an alpine bed,
wildlife ponds and a newly planted
shrub and woodland garden. Also, in
contrast to the traditional parts there
is a modern contemporary garden.
Partially wheelchair friendly.
♿ 🚗 ☕ 🌿

4 NEW KILCOOTRY BARN
Fintona, Omagh, BT78 2JF.
Miss Anne Johnston, 07761 918951,
annejohnston678@btinternet.com.
*Situated 2m from Fintona on the A5
& approx 6m from Omagh on the L.
Google map directions can found by
searching for Kilcootry Barn.* Sat 6,
Sun 7 Aug (10-5). Adm £5, chd free.
Home-made teas. Refreshments
provided by Pandora's box.
A 2½ acre mature cottage garden
featuring herbaceous seasonal
perennials, water feature, fruit trees,
vegetable garden, children's play
area, alpacas and ponies in delightful
surroundings. Some areas have
uneven surfaces.
♿ 🐑 🌿 🚗 🛏 ☕ 🪑))

5 NEW LINDEN
24 Raffrey Road, Killinchy,
Newtownards, BT23 6SF.
Mr Alan & Mrs Margaret McAteer,
07770 773611. *From Comber
r'about take A22 towards Killyleagh,
R at Saintfield Rd, after 1.8m L to
Raffery Rd. From the Saintfield Xrds
take Todds Hill Rd onto Station Rd
for 1.6m then L bend. After 1m go R
& then L at the staggered junction.
Go along road signed Killinchy 4 for
1.6m, Raffrey Rd is on the R.* Visits
by arrangement Apr to June and
September for groups of up to
8. Tuesdays & Thursdays after
midday. Adm £5, chd free.
A new 2 acre country garden with
formal and informal areas. Year-round
colour from perennials and grasses
plus a large, rose covered pergola, a
small parterre, an orchard in perennial
flower meadow, soft fruit, vegetables,
a greenhouse, woodland planting
and experimental growing area.
A pleached lime 'hedge' is being
developed. Wheelchair access most
areas
♿

**6 NEW THE MCKELVEY
GARDEN**
7 Mount Charles North,
Bessbrook, Newry, BT35 7DW.
Mr William & Mrs Hilary McKelvey,
02830 838006. *In the village of
Bessbrook. Enter village from
junction beside Morrow's Garage,
300yds up hill past terraced houses
turn L through gate.* Visits by
arrangement May to Aug for
groups of up to 40. Adm £5.
A connoisseurs garden situated in a
village setting containing snowdrops,
alpine crevice beds, salvias and a
large collection of clematis planted
among herbaceous and shrub
borders. Can be accessed by a side
entrance.
♿ ✿ 🚌 🚗

7 NEW MITREICARI
3 Whitepark Road, Ballycastle,
BT54 6HH. Dr Tricia &
Dr Mike Colohan, 028 2076 8798,
triciacolohan@gmail.com.
*Approx 1.3m or 5min drive from
Ballycastle. Take main A44 from
Belfast @ Frosses R'about take
A44 Drones Rd drive straight thro
Armoy, At T-junction turn R onto
B67 Moyarget Rd after ½m turn L
into Whitepark Rd the house is on R.*
Visits by arrangement June & July
for groups of up to 40. Adm by
donation.
A 1 acre garden with views towards
Fair Head and Scotland. Created in
2002 with areas of different interest
sheltered by hawthorn, griselinia
and escallonia hedges. Lawns are
bordered by herbaceous, heather
and herb planting. Paths lead past
rhododendrons to the rose garden. A
wildlife pond can be viewed from the
timber deck.
♿ ✿

'The National Garden
Scheme donated £500,000
to Hospice UK in 2021,
enabling us to continue
supporting over 200
hospices in the UK who have
been at the forefront of the
battle against COVID-19'
Hospice UK

18 NEW OAK GARDENS

219 Glenshane Road, Derry,
Londonderry, BT47 3EW.
Mr & Mrs Kelly. *4m from Derry,
Belfast bound on the A6 , take
Tamnaherin junction following
brown signs for Faughan Valley to
Woodlands & Oakfire Adventure.* **Sat
2, Sun 3 July (9.30-6). Adm £5,
chd free. Light refreshments.**
Our family garden has been
developing on a 2 acre site since
2014.The gardens offer an array of
different graded areas encompassing
everything from the humble vegetable
garden through to the formal gardens
with its neoclassical statues and
reflective pond. Salvaged pieces
sit in unison with a diverse range
of planting to create harmonious
schemes within each garden area.
Flat grass paths.

  🚻 🚗 🍷 ♪))

19 NEW OLD BALLOO HOUSE AND BARN

15 - 17 Comber Road, Killinchy,
Newtownards, BT23 6PB.
**Ms Lesley Simpson / Miss Moira
Concannon,** 07484 649767,
lsimpsonballoo@gmail.com.
*Balloo, Killinchy, Co. Down. Between
Comber & Killyleagh on the A22. On
the Xrds opp Sofaland shop.* **Visits
by arrangement May & June. 21st
May - 5th June. Adm £5, chd free.**
Restored and newly created gardens
around late Georgian house.
Wide range of planting inc bulbs,
perennials, shrubs, roses and trees in
the original garden and fields down to
the river Blackwater and old mill race.
Part of the garden is not accessible
to everyone due to the steep incline.
Unsuitable for young children and
wheelchairs.

20 NEW 10 RIVERSIDE ROAD

Bushmills, BT57 8TP.
Mrs Pam Traill, 02820731219,
pmtraill@gmail.com. *1½ m from
Bushmills on Riverside rd, off the
B66. Turn L by Drum Lodge, 100 yds
further on R beware ramps.* **Visits by
arrangement Feb to Aug. There is
only parking for 6 cars. Adm £5,
chd free.**
Rambling cottage garden
with unusual shrubs,deep
borders,woodland spring walk,rockery
and arboretum. Springtime is a sea
of snowdrops and aconites and May/
June see the perennials in the borders
at their best.

  ✿

21 NEW TATTYKEEL HOUSE GARDEN

115 Doogary Road, Omagh,
BT79 0BN. **Mr Hugh & Mrs
Kathleen Ward,** +44 (0) 28 8224
9801, info@tattykeelhouse.com,
tattykeelhouse.com/gardens.
*Tattykeel House is approx 2½ m
from Omagh on the S side of the A5
Omagh to Ballygawley Rd. There's a
sign outside the entrance Tattykeel
House & Studio.* **Sat 23, Sun 24
Apr, Sat 30, Sun 31 July (2-5).
Adm £5, chd free.**
A country garden of approximately
1½ acres created over a 30 year
period, planted with conifers, shrubs,
roses and perennials. There is a
sheltered seating area, a Japanese
influenced area, interesting features
and a collection of well grown
climbers on the house. The garden
recently underwent numerous
improvements.

  🚻 🛏 ♪))

In 2021 the National Garden Scheme donation helped support Perennial's caseworkers, who helped over 250 people and their families in crisis to receive a wide range of support including emergency food parcels and accommodation, energy payments and expert advice and information

Linden

Llanllyr

WALES

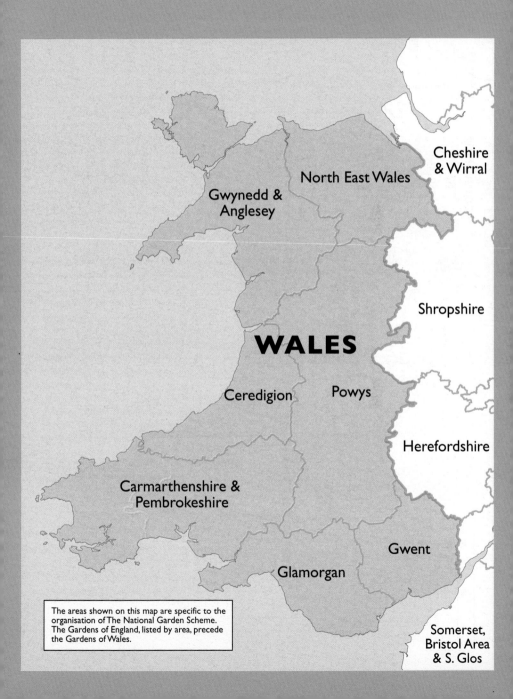

Cheshire & Wirral

North East Wales

Gwynedd & Anglesey

Shropshire

WALES

Ceredigion

Powys

Herefordshire

Carmarthenshire & Pembrokeshire

Gwent

Glamorgan

The areas shown on this map are specific to the organisation of The National Garden Scheme. The Gardens of England, listed by area, precede the Gardens of Wales.

Somerset, Bristol Area & S. Glos

CARMARTHENSHIRE & PEMBROKESHIRE

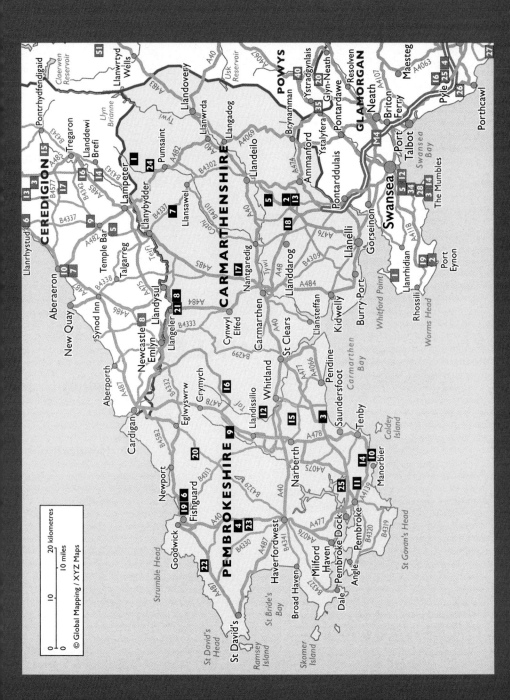

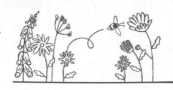

From the rugged Western coast and beaches to the foothills of the Brecon Beacons and Black Mountain, these counties offer gardens as varied as the topography and weather.

Look out for new gardens this year: Cefn Amlwg and Moelfryn (Llandeilo Road, Gorslas), two gardens opening jointly By Arrangement; and Cold Comfort Farm, Wolfscastle. After a break, often due to Covid, some gardens are returning: The Grange, Colby Woodland Garden, Upton Castle and Rhyd y Groes. Each of our gardens has something different to offer the visitor and many welcome dogs as well as their owners!

Several fascinating gardens have limited parking and so are only open 'By Arrangement'; the owners will be delighted to see you, but please do telephone first to arrange a visit. Most of our gardens also offer teas and what better way to enjoy an afternoon in a garden, where there is no weeding or washing up for you to do! We look forward to welcoming you to our gardens again and hoping no restrictions will impair our enjoyment.

Volunteers

County Organisers
Jackie Batty
01437 741115
jackie.batty@ngs.org.uk

County Treasurer
Brian Holness
01437 742048
brian.holness@ngs.org.uk

Assistant County Organisers
Elena Gilliatt
01558 685321
elenamgilliatt@hotmail.com

Liz and Paul O'Neill
01994 240717
lizpaulfarm@yahoo.co.uk

Brenda Timms
01558 650187
brendatimmsuk@gmail.com

Social Media
Mary-Ann Nossent
07985077022
maryann.nossent@ngs.org.uk

@CarmsandPembsNGS
carmsandpembsngs

Left: Lamphey Walled Garden

OPENING DATES

All entries subject to change. For latest information check **www.ngs.org.uk**
Map locator numbers are shown to the right of each garden name.

April

Sunday 17th
Llwyngarreg   12
Sunday 24th
Pen-y-Garn   18

May

Sunday 1st
Treffgarne Hall   23
Sunday 8th
◆ Dyffryn Fernant   6
Saturday 14th
◆ Colby Woodland
Garden   3
Sunday 15th
◆ Colby Woodland
Garden   3
Saturday 21st
Dwynant   5

Sunday 22nd
Dwynant   5
Llwyngarreg   12
Sunday 29th
NEW Cold Comfort
Farm   4

June

Wednesday 1st
Pont Trecynny   19
Saturday 4th
Skanda Vale Hospice
Garden   21
Sunday 12th
Norchard   14
◆ Upton Castle
Gardens   25
Saturday 18th
Rhyd-y-Groes   20
Sunday 19th
NEW Cold Comfort
Farm   4
Rhyd-y-Groes   20
Saturday 25th
Dwynant   5
◆ Lamphey Walled
Garden   11
Sunday 26th
Dwynant   5
NEW ◆ The Grange   10
◆ Lamphey Walled
Garden   11

July

Saturday 2nd
Pen-y-Garn   18
Wednesday 6th
Pont Trecynny   19
Sunday 10th
Llwyngarreg   12
Saturday 16th
Skanda Vale Hospice
Garden   21
Saturday 23rd
Rhyd-y-Groes   20
Sunday 24th
Pentresite   17
Rhyd-y-Groes   20

August

Saturday 13th
Glyn Bach Gardens   9
Sunday 14th
◆ Dyffryn Fernant   6
Glyn Bach Gardens   9
Wednesday 17th
Pont Trecynny   19

September

Saturday 3rd
◆ Lamphey Walled
Garden   11
Sunday 4th
NEW ◆ The Grange   10

◆ Lamphey Walled
Garden   11
Saturday 24th
◆ Colby Woodland
Garden   3
Sunday 25th
◆ Colby Woodland
Garden   3

By Arrangement

Arrange a personalised garden visit with your club, or group of friends, on a date to suit you. See individual garden entries for full details.

Bwlchau Duon   1
NEW Cefn Amlwg   2
NEW Cold Comfort
Farm   4
Dwynant   5
Gelli Uchaf   7
Glandwr   8
Llwyngarreg   12
NEW Moelfryn   13
Norchard   14
The Old Rectory   15
Pencwm   16
Pentresite   17
Pen-y-Garn   18
Pont Trecynny   19
Rhyd-y-Groes   20
Stable Cottage   22
Treffgarne Hall   23
Ty'r Maes   24

Cold Comfort Farm

THE GARDENS

1 BWLCHAU DUON

Ffarmers, Llanwrda,
SA19 8JJ. Brenda & Allan
Timms, 01558 650187,
brendatimmsuk@gmail.com. *7m
SE Lampeter, 8m NW Llanwrda.
From A482 turn to Ffarmers. In
Ffarmers, take lane opp Drovers
Arms pub. After caravan site on L,
turn L at small Xrds into single track
lane & follow NGS arrows.* **Visits
by arrangement June to Aug for
groups of up to 20. Individuals
welcome. Teas on request when
booking. Adm £4.50, chd free.**
1 acre, ever evolving garden
challenge, set in the foothills of the
Cambrian Mountains at 1100ft. This
is a plantaholics haven where borders
are full of many unusual plants and
lots of old favourites. There are
raised vegetable gardens, a 100ft
herbaceous border, natural bog areas,
small wildlife pond, new rose borders
and winding pathways through semi-
woodland.

2 NEW CEFN AMLWG

Llandeilo Road, Gorslas,
Llanelli, SA14 7LU. Ann &
Collin Wearing, 01269 842754,
collin.wearing@yahoo.co.uk.
*Approx 2m from Cross Hands
r'about heading to Llandeilo, From
Llandeilo towards Cross Hands
on A476 go through Carmel
village into Castell y Rhingyll. 1st
& 2nd properties on R.* **Visits
by arrangement June to Aug.
Combined opening with Moelfryn.
Adm £6, chd free. Teas on
request when booking.**
The garden provides a mix of
neat and tidy manicured lawn and
ornamental beds with colour planted
to attract bees and butterflies. A
large fish pond, raised vegetable
beds, fruit cage and seating areas. A
summerhouse allows you to sit and
soak in the delights, the lawn leads
your eyes to explore the beautifully
laid out garden, cleverly designed
structures add interest. See separate
entry for description of Moelfryn.

3 ◆ COLBY WOODLAND GARDEN

Amroth, Narberth, SA67 8PP.
National Trust, 01646 623 110,
colby@nationaltrust.org.uk,
www.nationaltrust.org.uk/colby-
woodland-garden. *6m N of Tenby,
5m SE of Narberth. Follow brown
tourist signs on coast rd & A477. NT
car park - charges apply.* **For NGS:
Sat 14, Sun 15 May, Sat 24, Sun
25 Sept (10-5). Adm by donation.
For other opening times and
information, please phone, email or
visit garden website.**
8 acre woodland garden in a
secluded valley with fine collection
of rhododendrons and azaleas.
Wildflower meadow and stream
with stepping stones for children to
explore and play. Ornamental walled
garden inc unusual gazebo, designed
by Wyn Jones, with internal trompe
l'oeil. Inc in the Register of Historic
Parks and Gardens: Pembrokeshire.
Children's play encouraged, inc den
building and climbing. Seasonal family
trails provided. Wooden sculptures
and features dotted around the
garden. Full range of refreshments in
the Bothy Tearoom. Partial wheelchair
access.

4 NEW COLD COMFORT FARM

Wolfscastle, Haverfordwest,
SA62 5PA. Judy & Paul
Rumbelow, 07809 560409,
judy.rumbelow@gmail.com,
www.facebook.com/Cold-
Comfort-Plants. *7m N of
Haverfordwest signed off A40 at
Wolfscastle. Turn towards Hayscastle
at Wolfe Inn. 1m along lane on L.*
**Sun 29 May, Sun 19 June (11-5).
Adm £3.50, chd free. Home-made
teas. Visits also by arrangement
Apr to Aug for groups of 2 to 6.
Teas on request when booking.**
2 acres of developing wildflower
meadow alongside wrap around
farm garden and small plant nursery.
Perennial beds, showcasing nursery
stock, rockery, gravel garden, raised
beds, greenhouses, polytunnel and
compost. Welcoming garden under
development on sloping plot, full of
planting ideas. Outstanding views of
the Preseli Mountains.

5 DWYNANT

Golden Grove, Carmarthen,
SA32 8LT. Mrs Sian Griffiths,
www.airbnb.co.uk/rooms/31081717.
*14m east of Carmarthen, 3m from
Llandeilo. Take B4300 Llandeilo to
Carmarthen. Take L turning to Gelli
Aur, pass church & vicarage then
1st R onto Old Coach Rd. Dwynant
is approximately ¼m on R.* **Sat 21,
Sun 22 May, Sat 25, Sun 26 June
(11-4). Adm £4, chd free. Pre-
booking essential, please phone
01558 668727, or email sian.41@
btinternet.com for information
& booking. Home-made teas on
request when booking. Visits also
by arrangement May to Aug for
groups of 2 to 10.**
A ¾ acre garden set on a steep slope
designed to sit comfortably within
a verdant countryside environment
with beautiful scenery and tranquil
woodland setting. A spring garden
with lily pond, selection of plants and
shrubs inc azaleas, rhododendrons,
rambling roses set amongst a carpet
of bluebells. Seating in appropriate
areas to enjoy the panoramic view
and flowers. (For accommodation see
garden website above).

6 ◆ DYFFRYN FERNANT

Llanychaer, Fishguard,
SA65 9SP. Christina Shand &
David Allum, 01348 811282,
christina@dyffrynfernant.co.uk,
www.dyffrynfernant.co.uk. *3m E
of Fishguard, then ½m inland. A487
E, 2m from Fishguard turn R towards
Llanychaer. Follow lane for ½m, entrance
on L. Look for yellow garden signs.* **For
NGS: Sun 8 May, Sun 14 Aug (11-5).
Adm £7, chd free. For other opening
times and information, please phone,
email or visit garden website.**
A modern, 6 acre garden which, over
two decades, has grown out of the
ancient landscape. Distinctly different
areas inc a lush bog garden, exotic
courtyard, and a field of ornamental
grasses combine to create a garden
that unfolds as you journey though it.
Abundant sitting places and a garden
library invite visitors to take their
time. RHS Partner Garden. Scented
azaleas and peonies in May. Dahlias,
ornamental grasses and exotics in
August. Tickets may also be purchased
through garden's own website.

7 GELLI UCHAF

Rhydcymerau, Llandeilo, SA19 7PY. Julian & Fiona Wormald, 01558 685119, thegardenimpressionists@gmail.com, www.thegardenimpressionists.com. *See garden website for detailed directions. 5m SE of Llanybydder. 1m NW of Rhydcymerau. From the B4337 in Rhydcymerau take minor road opp bungalows. After 300yds turn R up track. Parking very limited: essential to phone or email first* **Visits by arrangement Feb to Oct for individuals & groups of up to 20. Teas on request when booking. Adm £5, chd free.** Complementing a C17 Longhouse and 11 acre smallholding this 1½ acre garden is mainly organic. Trees and shrubs are underplanted with hundreds of thousands of snowdrops, crocus, cyclamen, daffodils, woodland shrubs, clematis, rambling roses, hydrangeas and autumn flowering perennials. Extensive views, shepherd's hut and seats to enjoy them. Year-round flower interest with naturalistic plantings. 6 acres of wildflower meadows, two ponds and stream.

8 GLANDWR

Pentrecwrt, Llandysul, SA44 5DA. Jo Hicks, 01559 363729, leehicks@btinternet.com. *15m N of Carmarthen, 2m S of Llandysul, 7m E of Newcastle Emlyn. On A486. At Pentrecwrt village, take minor rd opp Black Horse pub. After bridge keep L for ¼ m. Glandwr is on R.* **Visits by arrangement June to Aug. Teas on request when booking. Just a phone call! Small groups welcome. Adm £3.50, chd free.** Delightful 1 acre enclosed mature garden, with a natural stream. Inc a rockery, various flower beds (some colour themed), many clematis and shrubs. Do spend time in the woodland with interesting trees, shade loving plants and ground cover, surprise paths, and secluded places to hear the bird song.

9 GLYN BACH GARDENS

Efailwen, SA66 7JP. Peter & Carole Whittaker. *8m N of Narberth, 15m S of Cardigan. About 1m N of Efailwen turn W off A478 at Glandy Cross square, follow signs for 1m towards Llangolman & Pont Hywel Bridge. Glyn Bach is situated on L before 'road narrows' sign.* **Sat 13, Sun 14 Aug (10-6). Adm £5, chd free. Pre-booking essential,** please phone 01994 419104, email carole_whittaker@hotmail.com or visit www.glynbachgardens.co.uk for information & booking. Home-made teas on request when booking. **Donation to Plant Heritage.** 3 acres of garden with numerous perennial borders, alpine walls, tropical beds, large pond, bog garden, rose garden, grass beds, cottage garden, polytunnels, greenhouse and succulent bed, surrounded by 3 acres of mixed woodland and grassland. Featured on BBC Gardeners' World and in RHS The Garden, The English Garden, Garden News, and Countryside Magazine. Holders of a National Collection of Monarda. Wheelchair access on grass pathways.

10 NEW ◆ THE GRANGE

Manorbier, Tenby, SA70 7TY. Joan Stace, 01834 871311, www.grangegardensmanorbier.com. *4m W of Tenby. From Tenby, take the A4239 for Pembroke. ½ m after Lydstep, The Grange is on L, at the Xrds. Parking limited.* **For NGS: Sun 26 June, Sun 4 Sept (11-4.30). Adm £4, chd free. Home-made teas. Also open Lamphey Walled Garden. For other opening times and information, please phone or visit garden website.** 5 acre country garden of two parts. Older established garden around Grade II listed house (not open) has colourful herbaceous borders, rose garden, outdoor chess set and swimming pool (private). Newer garden was reclaimed from a heavy clay bog field which was drained and now consists of a lake with islands, ponds and dry river bed, newly-planted with wide variety of grasses as a 'prairie' garden. Sorry, wheelchair access difficult but walking frames manageable.

11 ◆ LAMPHEY WALLED GARDEN

Lamphey, Pembroke, SA71 5PD. Mr Simon Richards, 07503 976766, ullapoolsi@hotmail.co.uk, www.facebook.com/lowerlampheypark. *½ m from Lamphey village off the Ridgeway at Lower Lamphey Park. Turn off A477 at Milton towards Lamphey for 1m. At T-junction, turn R to Lamphey (signposted), after 1m take R up farm track signed Lower Lamphey Park. Parking behind cottages.* **For NGS: Sat 25 June (10-4). Sun 26 June (10-4). Sat 3 Sept (10-4). Sun 4 Sept (10-4). Open nearby The Grange (Sundays only). Adm £5, chd free. Home-made teas. For other opening times and information, please phone or email. Donation to The Bumblebee Conservation Trust.** Built in late 1700's an acre with 12 ft-high walls. Renovated 2005, extensive plantings from 2015. Several hundred different species, a plantsperson's garden with a natural feel. Over 40 Salvia species, old roses, lavender, sunflowers, grasses and ferns. Espalier apples and pears plus fan-trained stone fruit. Heritage vegetable garden. Organic and wildlife-friendly planting. Grassed paths slope gently uphill and allow wheelchair access to the majority of garden.

12 LLWYNGARREG

Llanfallteg, Whitland, SA34 0XH. Paul & Liz O'Neill, 01994 240717, lizpaulfarm@yahoo.co.uk, www.llwyngarreg.co.uk. *19m W of Carmarthen. A40 W from Carmarthen, turn R at Llandewi Velfrey, 2½ m to Llanfallteg. Go through village, garden ½ m further on: 2nd farm on R. Disabled car park in bottom yard on R.* **Sun 17 Apr, Sun 22 May, Sun 10 July (1-5). Adm £6, chd free. Home-made teas. Visits also by arrangement Jan to Nov. Please phone first, even for last minute visits.** Llwyngarreg is always changing, delighting plant lovers with its many rarities inc species Primulas, many huge bamboos with Roscoeas, Hedychiums and Salvias extending the season through to riotous autumn colour. Trees and rhododendrons are underplanted with perennials. The exotic sunken garden and gravel gardens continue to mature. Springs form a series of linked ponds across the main garden, providing colourful bog gardens. Spot the subtle mobiles and fun constructions hidden around the 4 acre garden. Wildlife ponds, fruit and vegetables, composting, numerous living willow structures, mobiles, swing, chickens, goldfish. Partial wheelchair access.

13 NEW MOELFRYN

Llandeilo Road, Gorslas, Llanelli, SA14 7LU. Elaine & Graeme Halls, revelainehalls@gmail.com. *Approx 2m from Cross Hands r'about heading to Llandeilo. From Llandeilo towards Cross Hands on A476 go through Carmel village into Castell y Rhingyll. 1st & 2nd properties on R.* **Visits by arrangement June to Aug. Combined opening with Cefn Amlwg (please book with Cefn Amlwg). Adm £6, chd free. Home-made teas at Cefn Amlwg, please discuss at booking.** Organic, environmentally friendly and recycling concerns have moulded our garden of a herb labyrinth, asparagus patch, cottage garden borders, vegetable beds, polytunnel, brassica tunnel, fruit cage, a small orchard and small wildflower meadow area, shrubs, small wooded/wild patch, free ranging hens, hedgehog house, bug hotels, small pond, compost bins and water butts. Sitting areas and views. Home-made organic ice-cream. See separate entry for description of Cefn Amlwg.

14 NORCHARD

The Ridgeway, Manorbier, Tenby, SA70 8LD. Ms H Davies, 07790 040278, h.norchard@hotmail.co.uk. *4m W of Tenby. From Tenby, take A4139 for Pembroke. ½ m after Lydstep, take R at Xrds. Proceed down lane for ¾ m. Norchard on R.* **Sun 12 June (1-5). Adm £6, chd free. Open nearby Upton Castle Gardens. Visits also by arrangement Apr to June for groups of 20+.** Historic gardens at medieval residence. Nestled in tranquil and sheltered location with ancient oak woodland backdrop. Strong structure with formal and informal areas inc early walled gardens with restored Elizabethan parterre and potager. 1½ acre orchard with old (many local) apple varieties. Mill and millpond. Range of wildlife habitats. Extensive collections of roses, daffodils and tulips. Regional Finalist The English Garden's The Nation's Favourite Gardens 2021 Partial wheelchair access. Access to potager via steps only.

15 THE OLD RECTORY

Lampeter Velfrey, Narbeth, SA67 8UH. Jane & Stephen Fletcher, 01834 831444, jane_e_fletcher@hotmail.com. *3m E of Narbeth. Next to church in Lampeter Velfrey. Parking in church car park.* **Visits by arrangement Feb to Sept Teas on request when booking. Even 1 or 2 people welcome! Adm £3.50, chd free.** Historic approx 2 acre garden, sympathetically redesigned and replanted since 2009 and still being restored. Many unique trees, some over 300yrs old, wide variety of planting and several unique, architecturally designed buildings. Formal beds, mature woodland surrounding an old quarry with recently planted terraces and rhododendron bank. Meadow, fernery and orchard.

Cefn Amlwg

16 PENCWM

Hebron, Whitland, SA34 0JP. Lorna Brown, 07967 274830, lornambrown@hotmail.com. *10m N of Whitland. From A40 take St Clears exit & head N to Llangynin then on to Blaenwaun. Through village, after speed limit signs take 1st L. Over Xrds, 1¼m then 2nd lane on L marked Pencwm.* **Visits by arrangement Mar to Nov for groups of up to 25. Individuals also welcome. Teas on request when booking. Adm £4, chd free.** A secluded garden of about 1 acre set among large native trees, designed for year-round interest and for benefit of wildlife. A wide variety of exotic specimen trees and shrubs inc magnolias, rhododendrons, hydrangeas, bamboos and acers. Drifts of bluebells and other spring bulbs and good autumn colour. Inc boggy area and pond with appropriate planting. Wellies recommended at most times.

17 PENTRESITE

Rhydargaeau Road, Carmarthen, SA32 7AJ. Gayle & Ron Mounsey, 01267 253928, gayle.mounsey@gmail.com. *4m N of Carmarthen. Take A485 heading N out of Carmarthen, once out of village of Peniel take 1st R to Horeb & cont for 1m. Turn R at NGS sign,* 2nd house down lane. **Sun 24 July (11-5). Adm £4, chd free. Home-made teas. Visits also by arrangement June to Sept for groups of up to 20. Individuals also welcome. Teas on request when booking.**
Approx. 2 acre garden developed over the last 16 years with extensive lawns, colour filled herbaceous and mixed borders, on several levels. A bog garden and magnificent views of the surrounding countryside. There is now a new area planted with trees and herbaceous plants. This garden is south facing and catches the south westerly winds from the sea.

18 PEN-Y-GARN

Foelgastell, Cefneithin, Carmarthen, SA14 7EU. Mary-Ann Nossent & Mike Wood, 07985 077022, maryann.nossent@ngs.org.uk, tinyurl.com/r4ry8va7. *10m SE Carmarthen, A48 N from Cross Hands. take 1st L to Foelgastell R at T-junction 300 metres sharp L, 300 metres 1st gateway on L. A48 S Bot. Gdns turning r'about R to Porthythyd 1st L before T junction. 1m 1st R & 300 metres on L.* **Sun 24 Apr, Sat 2 July (11-4). Adm £4, chd free. Home-made teas. Visits also by arrangement June to Aug for groups of 2 to 12. Teas for groups** on request.
1½ acres unusual setting within former limestone quarry, the garden is on several levels with slopes and steps. Sympathetically developed to sit within the landscape, there are five distinct areas with a mixture of wild and cultivated plants. A shady area with woodland planting and wild ponds; no dig kitchen garden; terraced borders with shrubs and herbaceous planting; lawns and pond; and a wild garden. Areas of no mow lawns. Steep in places.

19 PONT TRECYNNY

Garn Gelli Hill, Fishguard, SA65 9SR. Wendy Kinver. *1½m N of Fishguard. Driving up the hill from Fishguard to Dinas turn R ½ way up the rd & follow signs. SatNav will take you to a lay-by opp the garden. Parking v limited.* **Wed 1 June, Wed 6 July, Wed 17 Aug (11-4). Adm £5, chd free. Pre-booking essential, please phone 01348 873040 or email wendykinver@icloud.com for information & booking. Visits also by arrangement June to Aug for groups of 10 to 30.**
A diverse garden of 3½ acres. Meander through the meadow planted with native trees, pass the pond and over a bridge which takes you along a path, through

Moelfryn

an arboretum, orchard and gravel garden and into the formal garden full of cloud trees, exotic plants and pots,which then leads you to the stream and vegetable garden.

🐐 ✳ ⁓))

20 RHYD-Y-GROES
Brynberian, Crymych, SA41 3TT. Jennifer & Kevin Matthews, 01239 891363, rhydygroesgardeners@gmail.com. *12m SW of Cardigan. 5m W of Crymych, 16m NE of Haverfordwest, on B4329, ³/₄ m downhill from cattlegrid (from Haverfordwest) & 1m uphill from signpost to Brynberian (from Cardigan).* **Sat 18, Sun 19 June, Sat 23, Sun 24 July (1-5). Adm £5, chd £1.50. Light refreshments. Visits also by arrangement May to Aug for groups of 12+. (Minimum charge £60 irrespective of numbers on the day).**
Upland garden with extensive views over boggy moor and barren hillside. A 4 acre oasis of abundant, diverse planting to suit varied growing conditions. Mixed borders, shrubbery, boggy corner, and prairie planting. Wildflower meadow that is better in June. Woodland and shade areas featuring many hydrangeas best in July. Ample seating. Beautiful, mollusc-proof planting demonstrates what can be achieved without using slug killer, pesticides and fungicides, resulting in a garden that is full of wildlife.

🐐 ✳ 🚗 ☕

21 SKANDA VALE HOSPICE GARDEN
Saron, Llandysul, Carmarthen, SA44 5DY. Skanda Vale Hospice, 07967 245912, brotherfrancis@skandavale.org, www.skandavalehospice.org. *On A484, in village of Saron, 13m N of Carmarthen. Between Carmarthen & Cardigan.* **Sat 4 June, Sat 16 July (11-4.30). Adm £4, chd free. Home-made teas.**
A tranquil garden of approx 1acre, built for therapy, relaxation and fun. Maintained by volunteers, the lawns and glades link garden buildings with willow spiral, wildlife pond, colourful borders, sculptures and stained glass. Planting schemes of blue and gold at entrance inspire calm and confidence, leading to brighter red, orange and white. Hospice facilities open for visitors to view. A garden for quiet contemplation, wheelchair friendly,

with lots of small interesting features. Craft stall. For accommodation please visit: www.skanda-hafan.com or phone 01559 384566.

♿ 🐐 ✳ 🛏 ☕

22 STABLE COTTAGE
Rhoslanog Fawr, Mathry, Haverfordwest, SA62 5HG. Mr Michael & Mrs Jane Bayliss, 01348 837712, michaelandjane1954@ michaelandjane.plus.com. *Between Fishguard & St David's. Head W on A487 turn R at Square & Compass sign. ¹/₂ m, at hairpin take track L. Stable Cottage on L with block paved drive.* **Visits by arrangement May to Aug. 2-20 visitors welcome! Teas on request when booking. Adm £3.50, chd free.**
Garden extends to approx ¹/₃ of an acre. It is divided into several smaller garden types, with a seaside garden, small orchard and wildlife area, scented garden, small vegetable/kitchen garden, and two Japanese areas - a stroll garden and courtyard area.

🐐 ✳ ☕

23 TREFFGARNE HALL
Treffgarne, Haverfordwest, SA62 5PJ. Martin & Jackie Batty, 01437 741115, jmv.batty@gmail.com, www. facebook.com/jackiebatty.3344. *7m N of Haverfordwest, signed off A40. Proceed up through village & follow rd round sharply to L, Hall ¹/₄ m further on L.* **Sun 1 May (1-5). Adm £5, chd free. Check website for pop up opening in July. Picnic boxes as refreshments: Please reserve by phone, email or Facebook PM or bring your own! Visits also by arrangement Mar to Oct. Teas for groups on request.**
Stunning hilltop location with panoramic views: handsome Grade II listed Georgian house (not open) provides formal backdrop to garden of 4 acres with wide lawns and themed beds. A walled garden, with double rill and pergolas, planted with a multitude of borderline hardy exotics. Also large scale sculptures, summer boardwalk, meadow patch, gravel garden, heather bed and stumpery. Planted for year-round interest. The planting schemes seek to challenge the boundaries of what can be grown in Pembrokeshire.

🐐 ✳ 🚗 ☕ 🪑 ⁓))

24 TY'R MAES
Ffarmers, Llanwrda, SA19 8JP. John & Helen Brooks, 01558 650541, johnhelen140@gmail.com. *7m SE of Lampeter. 8m NW of Llanwrda. 1¹/₂ m W of Pumsaint on A482, opp turn to Ffarmers (please ignore SatNav).* **Visits by arrangement Apr to Oct Even just 1or 2 people welcome. Adm £5, chd free. Home-made teas on request when booking**
4 acre garden with splendid views. Herbaceous and shrub beds – formal design, exuberantly informal planting, full of cottage garden favourites and many unusual plants. Small arboretum with over 200 types of tree; wildlife and lily ponds; pergola, gazebos, post and rope arcade covered in climbers. Gloriously colourful from early spring till late autumn. Wheelchair note: Some gravel paths.

♿ 🐐 ✳ 🚗 ☕

25 ◆ UPTON CASTLE GARDENS
Cosheston, Pembroke Dock, SA72 4SE. Prue & Stephen Barlow, 01646 689996, info@uptoncastle.com, www.uptoncastlegardens.com. *4m E of Pembroke Dock. 2m N of A477 between Carew & Pembroke Dock. Follow brown signs to Upton Castle Gardens through Cosheston.* **For NGS: Sun 12 June (10-4.30). Adm £6, chd free. Home-made teas. Open nearby Norchard. For other opening times and information, please phone, email or visit garden website.**
Privately owned listed historic gardens with an exceptional collection of mature trees and plants extending to over 35 acres. Rare rhododendrons, camellias and magnolias abound. Formal rose garden contains over 150 roses of many varieties and colours. Fully stocked herbaceous borders provide constant interest. Traditional walled, productive kitchen garden. Arboretum with 15 champion trees. Walk on the Wild Side: Woodland walks funded by C.C.W. and Welsh Assembly Government. Medieval chapel as featured on Time Team. Partial wheelchair access.

♿ 🐐 ✳ 🚗 🛏 ☕ 🪑

CEREDIGION

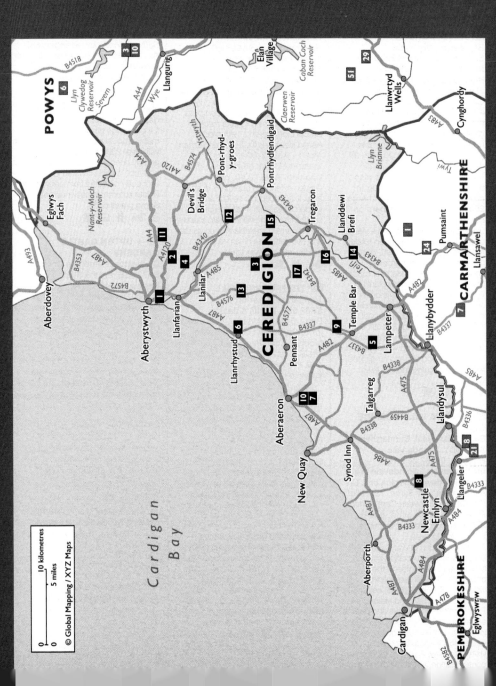

Ceredigion is essentially a rural county, the second most sparsely populated in Wales devoid of any large commercial area.

Much of the land is elevated, particularly towards the east of the county. There are steep sided wooded valleys, fast flowing rivers and streams, acres of moorland and a dramatic coastline with some lovely sandy beaches. From everywhere in the county there are breath taking views of the Cambrian Mountains and from almost everywhere glimpses of the stunning Cardigan Bay are visible. The gardens in Ceredigion reflect this natural beauty and sit comfortably in the rugged scenery.

As you would expect from this varied landscape, the gardens that open for the National Garden Scheme are equally diverse. Bwlch y Geuffordd Gardens is particularly family friendly and will provide children all ages and adults too with hours of interest, adventure and fun. There are a number of dedicated vegetable growers and you can see the fruits of their labours at Yr Efail, Aberystwyth Allotments and Melindwr Valley Bees – which as its name implies, is also a bee farm. Whether your preference is for traditional rolling acres around a grand manor house, cottage gardens, woodland gardens or water gardens you will find something to inspire you, and you can be sure of receiving a warm welcome from the garden owners, and some delicious home-made refreshments to complete a perfect day out.

Volunteers

County Organiser
Position vacant
For details please
contact hello@ngs.org.uk

County Treasurer
Elaine Grande
01974 261196
e.grande@zoho.com

Booklet Co-ordinator
Shelagh Yeomans
01974 299370
shelagh.yeomans@ngs.org.uk

Assistant County Organisers
Gay Acres
01974 251559
gayacres@aol.com

Brenda & Norman Jones
01974 261737
tobrenorm@gmail.com

f @Ceredigion Gardens

Below: Tanffordd

OPENING DATES

All entries subject to change. For latest information check www.ngs.org.uk

Map locator numbers are shown to the right of each garden name.

May

Saturday 14th
Bryngwyn   2

Monday 16th
Bryngwyn   2

Sunday 22nd
Bwlch y Geuffordd   4

June

Sunday 5th
Rhos Villa   14

Saturday 11th
Bryngwyn   2

Sunday 12th
Ffynnon Las   7
Marlais   10

Monday 13th
Bryngwyn   2

Sunday 19th
Llanllyr   9

Sunday 26th
Ysgoldy'r Cwrt   17

July

Sunday 10th
♦ Cae Hir Gardens   5

Saturday 16th
The Flower Meadow   8

Sunday 17th
Aberystwyth Allotments   1
The Flower Meadow   8

Sunday 24th
Yr Efail   16

August

Monday 29th
Bryngwyn   2

Wednesday 31st
Bryngwyn   2

By Arrangement

Arrange a personalised garden visit with your club, or group of friends, on a date to suit you. See individual garden entries for full details.

Bryngwyn   2
Bwlch y Geuffordd Gardens   3
NEW Felin Ganol Watermill   6
Ffynnon Las   7
Llanllyr   9
Melindwr Valley Bees, Tynyffordd Isaf   11
Penybont   12
NEW Tanffordd   15
Yr Efail   16
Ysgoldy'r Cwrt   17

Llanllyr

© Helen Harrison

THE GARDENS

1 ABERYSTWYTH ALLOTMENTS

5th Avenue, Penparcau, Aberystwyth, SY23 1QT. Aberystwyth Town Council. *On S side of R.Rheidol on Aberystwyth by-pass. From N or E, take A4120 between Llanbadarn & Penparcau. Cross bridge then take 1st R into Minyddol. Allotments ¼ m on R.* **Sun 17 July (1-5). Adm £4, chd free. Home-made teas.**
There are 37 plots in total on two sites just a few yards from each other. The allotments are situated in a lovely setting alongside River Rheidol close to Aberystwyth. Wide variety of produce grown, vegetables, soft fruit, top fruit, flowers, herbs and a newly created wildlife pond. Car parking available. For more information contact Brian Heath 01970 617112. Sample tastings from allotment produce. Grass and gravel paths.
👩 🐎 ☕

2 BRYNGWYN

Capel Seion, Aberystwyth, SY23 4EE. Mr Terry & Mrs Sue Reeves, 01970 880760, sueterr02@btinternet.com. *On the A4120 between the villages of Capel Seion & Pant y Crug. Parking for up to 12 cars available on site.* **Sat 14, Mon 16 May, Sat 11, Mon 13 June, Mon 29, Wed 31 Aug (1.30-5.30). Adm £4, chd free. Home-made teas. Visits also by arrangement May & June for groups of up to 40.**
Bluebells in May. Traditional wildflower-rich hay meadows managed for wildlife. As a result of conservation grazing, hedgerow renovation and tree planting, habitat has been restored such that numbers and diversity of wild flowers and wildlife have increased. Pond for wildlife. Meander along mown paths through the meadows. Small orchard containing Welsh heritage apples and pears. Wild flower seed sales.
🐎 ☕ 🪑 •))

3 BWLCH Y GEUFFORDD GARDENS

Bronant, Aberystwyth, SY23 4JD. Mr & Mrs J Acres, 01974 251559, gayacres@aol.com, bwlch-y-geuffordd-gardens.myfreesites.net. *12m SE of Aberystwyth, 6m NW of Tregaron off A485. Take turning opp village school in Bronant for 1½ m then L up ½ m uneven track.* **Visits by arrangement. Maximum bus size 25 seater. Adm £5, chd £2.50. Tea. Please discuss refreshments at booking.**
1000ft high, 3 acre, constantly evolving wildlife and water garden. An adventure garden for children. There are a number of themed gardens, inc Mediterranean, cottage garden, woodland, oriental, memorial and jungle. Plenty of seating. Unique garden sculptures and buildings, inc a cave, temple, gazebo, jungle hut, treehouse and willow den. Children's adventure garden, musical instruments, pond dipping, treasure hunt, beautiful lake, temple and labyrinth, treehouse, sculptures, wildlife rich, particularly insects and birds. Sadly, no dogs allowed. For a Mad Hatter's Tea Party, please see details on website.
🐷 🪑

4 BWLCH Y GEUFFORDD

New Cross, Aberystwyth, SY23 4LY. Manuel & Elaine Grande. *5m SE of Aberystwyth. Off A487 from Aberystwyth, take B4340 to New Cross. Garden on R at bottom of small dip. Parking in lay-bys opp house.* **Sun 22 May (10.30-4.30). Adm £4, chd free. Home-made teas.**
Landscaped hillside 1½ acre garden, fine views of Cambrian mountains. Embraces its natural features with different levels, ponds, mixed borders merging into carefully managed informal areas. Banks of rhododendrons, azaleas, bluebells in spring. Full of unusual shade and damp-loving plants, flowering shrubs, mature trees, clematis and climbing roses scrambling up the walls of the old stone buildings. Choice rhododendrons in May. Partial wheelchair access only to lower levels around house. Some steps and steep paths further up the hillside.
♿ 🐎 ✿ ☕ •))

5 ◆ CAE HIR GARDENS

Cribyn, Lampeter, SA48 7NG. Julie & Stuart Akkermans, 01570 471116, caehirgardens@gmail.com, caehirgardens.com. *5m W of Lampeter. Take A482 from Lampeter towards Aberaeron. After 5m turn S on B4337. Garden on N side of village of Cribyn.* **For NGS: Sun 10 July (10-5). Adm £6, chd £2. Home-made teas. For other opening times and information, please phone, email or visit garden website.**
A Welsh Garden with a Dutch History, Cae Hir is a true family garden of unassuming beauty, made tenable by its innovative mix of ordinary garden plants and wild flowers growing in swathes of perceived abandonment. At Cae Hir the natural meets the formal and riotous planting meets structure and form. A garden not just for plant lovers, but also for design enthusiasts. 5 acres of fully landscaped gardens. Tea room serving a selection of homemade cakes and scones and a 'Soup of the Day'. Limited wheelchair access.
🐎 ✿ 🚗 ☕ •))

6 NEW FELIN GANOL WATERMILL

Llanrhystud, SY23 5AL. Andrew & Anne Parry, 01974 202272, miller@felinganol.co.uk, www.felinganol.co.uk. *8m S of Aberystywyth in Llanrhystud. Approx 8m S of Aberystywyth on the A487 turn L just after the Llanrhystud Village sign. 1st L after the sch, narrow lane (unsuitable for heavy vehicles). Felin Ganol in 200 metres.* **Visits by arrangement Mar to Oct for groups of up to 10. Adm £4.**
Informal and relaxed garden bounded by the river Wyre, incorporating lawns, flower borders, herb garden, no-dig vegetable beds surrounding a working watermill. There is a mill pond and orchard and an area of woodland with paths running through. Stone ground flour produced by the mill will be for sale.
•))

> 'In 2021 the generous donation from the National Garden Scheme helped 12,000 unpaid carers to access the support they need, with 50 more receiving crisis grants to support those in dire need'
> Carers Trust

7 FFYNNON LAS
Ffosyffin, Aberaeron, SA46 0HB.
Liz Roberts, 01545 571687,
lizhomerent@hotmail.co.uk. *A
short distance off the A487. 1m S
of Aberaeron. Turn off A487 opp
The Forge Garage in Ffosyffin, 300m
up the road take the L turn at the
T junction.* **Sun 12 June (12-5).
Adm £5, chd free. Home-made
teas. Open nearby Marlais. Visits
also by arrangement June & July.
Donation to Pancreatic Cancer
Research.**
A 2 acre garden that has been in the
making for over 15 yrs, Ffynnonlas
is a beautiful area that delivers on
many different aspects of gardening.
There are large lawns, several beds
of mature shrubs and flowers. A
small lake and two smaller ponds
that are separated by a Monet style
bridge with lilies. There is a wildflower
meadow as a work in progress
that has spectacular wild orchids
in spring. Lake with water lilies and
other aquatic plants. Wild meadow
with spectacular wild orchids in
spring. A rockery with water cascade,
vegetable garden with raised beds.
Grass paths, level ground.

8 THE FLOWER MEADOW
Llain Manal, Rhydlewis, Llandysul,
SA44 5QH. Mrs Sara Redman,
www.theflowermeadow.co.uk.
*We are located on the B4571. From
Newcastle Emlyn we are the last
house in Penrhiwpal before the Xrd
with the coach garage on it. From
Ffostrasol we are the 1st house after
Xrd.* **Sat 16, Sun 17 July (10-4). Adm
£5, chd free. Home-made teas.**
3 acre small holding specialising in
growing both exotic and wild flowers
for cutting. Large hay meadow
with many different native species,
vegetable garden, greenhouse and
polytunnel for more tender vegetables
and fruit. Interesting and attractive
courtyard garden with herbaceous
perennials, shrubs and young trees.
Extensive views over beautiful
countryside. Terrain is level. Grass
paths.

9 LLANLLYR
Talsarn, Lampeter, SA48 8QB.
Mrs Loveday Gee and Mr Patrick Gee,
01570 470900, lgllanllyr@aol.com.
*6m NW of Lampeter. On B4337
to Llanrhystud. From Lampeter,
entrance to garden on L, just before
village of Talsarn.* **Sun 19 June (2-6).**

Adm £5, chd free. Home-made
teas. Visits also by arrangement
Apr to Oct.
Large early C19 garden on site of
medieval nunnery, renovated and
replanted since 1989. Large pool,
bog garden, formal water garden,
rose and shrub borders, gravel
gardens, rose arbour, allegorical
labyrinth and mount, all exhibiting fine
plantsmanship. Year-round appeal,
interesting and unusual plants.
Spectacular rose garden planted
with fragrant old fashioned shrub and
climbing roses. Specialist Plant Fair
by Ceredigion Growers Association.

10 MARLAIS
Ffosyffin, Aberaeron, SA46 0EY.
Dr & Mrs David Shepherd. *From
Aberaeron take A487 S to Henfynyw
& bear L at green past bus stop, then
L again past single storey cottages.
Marlais is 2nd bungalow on R at
junction of Parc Ffos.* **Sun 12 June
(12-5). Adm £3, chd free. Open
nearby Ffynnon Las where you can
enjoy your tea on the patio.**
The garden at Marlais was designed
for easy access and maintenance
to suit more mature gardeners with
some disability. To the front we have
planted a mini orchard with many
varieties of top fruit on dwarfing
rootstocks and shrub and perennials
as edging. The rear garden has raised
flower beds with an exceptional
variety of unusual plants. The raised
vegetable and soft fruit beds are
screened by trellis with tayberry,
loganberry, blackberry and wineberry
giving over 40 varieties of fruit. There
will be a garden themed tombola with
interesting and varied items. Only
central part of rear garden accessible
by wheelchair.

**11 MELINDWR VALLEY BEES,
TYNYFFORDD ISAF**
Capel Bangor, Aberystwyth,
SY23 3NW. Vicky Lines &
Jim Palmer, 01970 880534,
vickysweetland@googlemail.com.
*Capel Bangor. From Aberystwth
take L turn off A44 at E end of Capel
Bangor. Follow this rd round to R
until you see sign with Melindwr
Valley Bees.* **Visits by arrangement
May to Aug for groups of up to
10. Please email or phone before
visiting. Adm £4, chd free. Cream
teas.**
A bee farm dedicated to wildlife with
permaculture and forest garden

ethos. Fruit, vegetables, culinary and
medicinal herbs and bee friendly plants
within our wildlife zones. Beehives are
situated in dedicated areas and can be
observed from a distance. Ornamental
and wildflower areas in a cottage
garden theme. Formal and wildlife
ponds. Grass paths, not suitable for
wheelchairs. Vintage tractors and other
machinery. Subtropical greenhouse
with carnivorous plants, orchids, exotic
fruits.

12 PENYBONT
Llanafan, Aberystwyth,
SY23 4BJ. Norman & Brenda
Jones, 01974 261737,
tobrenorm@gmail.com. *9m SE of
Aberystwyth. Ystwyth Valley. 9m SE
of Aberystwyth. B4340 via Trawscoed
towards Pontrhydfendigaid. Over
stone bridge. 1/4 m up hill. Lane on R
by row of ex Forestry houses.* **Visits
by arrangement May to Aug. Adm
£4, chd free. Home-made teas on
request.**
Carefully designed hillside garden
backed by Ystwyth Forest and
overlooking the beautiful valley.
An acre of heavenly beauty and
continuity of interest from Spring
bulbs May Rhododendrons and
Azaleas, Roses from June, July
brings a Mediterranean feel with large
swathes of Lavender, grapevines,
olives followed by Hydrangeas in
bright blue, and whites turning to
pink. Loads of varied foliage. Original
design, maturing fast. Seats with
stunning views over the borrowed
landscape, forest, valley, hills. Kites
and buzzards. Sloping ground, gravel
paths. Partial wheelchair access.

14 RHOS VILLA
Llanddewi Brefi, Tregaron,
SY25 6PA. Andrew & Sam
Buchanan. *From Lampeter take
the A485 towards Tregaron. After
Llangybi turn R opp junction for
Olmarch. The property can be
found on the R after 1½ m.* **Sun 5
June (11-4.30). Adm £4, chd free.
Home-made teas.**
A ¾ acre garden creatively utilising
local materials. Secret pathways
meander through sun and shade, dry
and damp. A variety of perennials
and shrubs are inter-planted to
create interest throughout the year. A
productive vegetable and fruit garden
with semi-formal structure contrasts
the looser planting through the rest of
the garden. Interesting and beautifully

crafted paths and walls constructed from local materials.

15 NEW **TANFFORDD**
Swyddffynnon, Ystrad Meurig,
SY25 6AW. Jo Kennaugh &
Stuart Bradley, 07872 451821,
stustart53@outlook.com.
*Swyddffynnon. 1m W of Ystrad
Meurig. 5m E of Tregaron. Tanffordd
is ¼m from Swyddffynnon village
on the rd to Tregaron. Please
do not follow SatNav.* **Visits by
arrangement May to Sept for
groups of up to 20. Teas on
request when booking. Adm £4,
chd free.**
Wildlife garden, rich in biodiversity,
set in a 5 acre smallholding with
large pool. There is a small woodland
area and various beds of shrubs and
herbaceous planting containing some
more unusual plants. Vegetables,
polytunnel and poultry enclosures with
chickens and ducks. Wander along to
meet the friendly donkeys and ponies
who share a buttercup filled field in
late spring and early summer. Large
natural pond with an island. Some
unusual shrubs and trees.

16 **YR EFAIL**
Llanio Road, Tregaron,
SY25 6PU. Mrs Shelagh
Yeomans, 07796 285003,
shelagh.yeomans@ngs.org.uk. *3m
SW of Tregaron. On B4578 between
Llanio & Stag's Head.* **Sun 24 July
(10.30-5.30). Adm £4, chd free.
Home-made teas. Visits also by
arrangement Feb to Oct.**
Savour one of the many quiet
spaces to sit and reflect amongst the
informal gardens of relaxed perennial
planting, inc a wildlife pond, shaded
areas, bog and gravel gardens. Be
inspired by the large productive
vegetable plots, three polytunnels
and greenhouse. Wander along grass
paths through the maturing, mostly
native, woodland. Enjoy home-made
teas incorporating homegrown fruit
and vegetables. Bilingual quiz sheet.
Seasonal vegetables, flowers and
plants for sale. Gravel and grass
paths accessible to wheelchairs with
pneumatic wheels.

17 **YSGOLDY'R CWRT**
Llangeitho, Tregaron, SY25 6QJ.
Mrs Brenda Woodley,
01974 821542. *1½m N of*

Llangeitho. *From Llangeitho, turn
L at sch signed Penuwch. Garden
1½m on R. From Cross Inn take
B4577 past Penuwch Inn, R after
brown sculptures in field. Garden
¾m on L.* **Sun 26 June (11-5).
Adm £4, chd free. Home-made
teas. Visits also by arrangement
Apr to Aug.**
1 acre hillside garden, with four natural
ponds which are a magnet for wildlife
plus a fish pond. Areas of wildflower
meadow, rockery, bog, dry and
woodland gardens. Established rose
walk. Rare trees, large herbaceous
beds with ornamental grasses. Azalea
and Acer collection in shade bed,
bounded by a mountain stream, with
two natural cascades and magnificent
views. Large Iris ensata and Iris
laevigata collections in a variety of
colours. Regional Finalist in The
English Garden's competition 'The
Nation's Favourite Gardens 2019'.

Ffynnon Las

GLAMORGAN

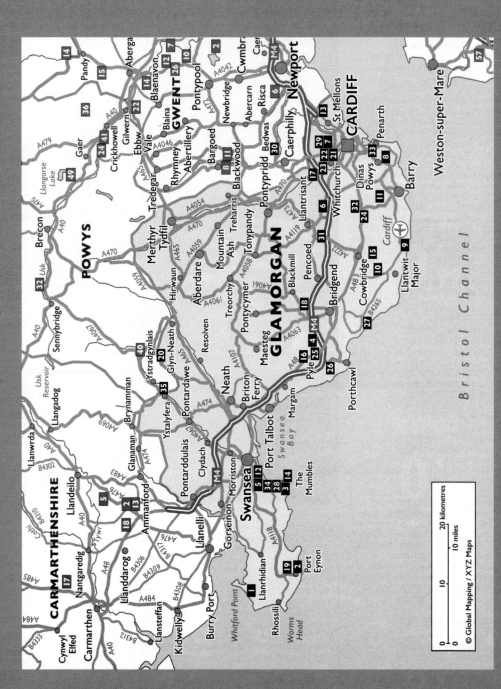

Glamorgan is a large county stretching from the Brecon Beacons in the north to the Bristol Channel in the south, and from the city of Cardiff in the east to the Gower Peninsula in the west. The area has a natural divide where the hills rise from the vale in a clear line of demarcation.

There are gardens opening for the National Garden Scheme throughout the county, and in recent years the number of community openings has greatly increased and have been very successful.

A number of gardens open in villages or suburbs, often within walking distance of each other, providing a very pleasant afternoon for the visitors. Each garden has its own distinct character and the locality is full of hospitality and friendliness.

Gardens range from Mediterranean-style to gardens designed to encourage wildlife. Views from our coastal gardens are truly spectacular.

Our openings start around Easter with a woodland and spring bulbs garden and continue through to mid-September.

So just jump in the car – *Garden Visitors Handbook* book in hand – and head west on the M4. The gardens in Wales are waiting for you!

Below: Parc y Fro

Volunteers

County Organiser
Rosamund Davies
01656 880048
rosamund.davies@ngs.org.uk

County Treasurer
Steven Thomas 01446 772339
steven.thomas@ngs.org.uk

Publicity
Rhian James 07802 438299
rhian.james@ngs.org.uk

Social Media
Rhian Rees 01446 774817
rhian.rees@ngs.org.uk

Booklet Co-ordinator
Lesley Sherwood 02920 890055
lesley.sherwood@ngs.org.uk

Talks Co-ordinator
Frances Bowyer
02920 892264
frances.bowyer@ngs.org.uk

Health and Gardens Co-ordinator
Miranda Workman 02920 766225
miranda.parsons@talktalk.net

Assistant County Organisers
Dr. Isabel Graham
isabelgraham84@gmail.com

Trevor Humby 02920 512709
trevor.humby@ngs.org.uk

Sol Blytt Jordens 01792 391676
sol.blyttjordens@ngs.org.uk

Tony Leyshon 07896 799378
anthony.leyshon@icloud.com

Ceri Macfarlane 01792 404906
ceri@mikegravenor.plus.com

 @GlamorganNGS
 @GlamorganNGS
 @ngsglamorgan

OPENING DATES

All entries subject to change. For latest information check www.ngs.org.uk
Map locator numbers are shown to the right of each garden name.

February

Snowdrop Festival

Sunday 13th
Slade 27

Sunday 20th
Slade 27

April

Sunday 3rd
The Cedars 3

Saturday 23rd
Slade 27

Sunday 24th
Slade 27

Saturday 30th
110 Heritage Park 13

May

Saturday 14th
9 Willowbrook Gardens 34

Sunday 15th
9 Willowbrook Gardens 34

Saturday 28th
Plas y Coed 24

Sunday 29th
Plas y Coed 24

June

Saturday 4th
17 Maes y Draenog 17
NEW Ystalyfera Gardens 35

Sunday 5th
6 The Boarlands 2
Gileston Manor 9
17 Maes y Draenog 17
3 Monksland Road 19
NEW Ystalyfera Gardens 35

Friday 10th
NEW 19 Coed Celyn Road 5

Saturday 11th
NEW 19 Coed Celyn Road 5

Sunday 12th
NEW 185 Pantbach Road 21

Friday 17th
NEW 100 Pendwyallt Road 23

Saturday 18th
Dinas Powys 8
NEW 100 Pendwyallt Road 23
Sunny Cottage 30

Sunday 19th
Big House Farm 1
22 Dan-y-Coed Road 7
Dinas Powys 8
28 Slade Gardens 28
Sunny Cottage 30

Saturday 25th
Hafod y Fro 10

Sunday 26th
Cefn Cribwr Garden Club 4
Hen Felin & Swallow Barns 11

July

Saturday 2nd
38 South Rise 29

Sunday 3rd
38 South Rise 29
NEW 12 Uplands Crescent 33

Saturday 9th
Uplands 32

Sunday 10th
Creigiau Village Gardens 6
NEW 12 Uplands Crescent 33

Sunday 17th
4 Hillcrest 14
50 Pen y Dre 22

Saturday 23rd
Maes-y-Wertha Farm 18

Sunday 24th
16 Hendy Close 12

Saturday 30th
NEW 2 Llys Castell 16

Sunday 31st
NEW 2 Llys Castell 16

August

Saturday 6th
NEW Pwyllygarth Farm 25
NEW Swn y Coed 31

Sunday 7th
NEW Pwyllygarth Farm 25
NEW Swn y Coed 31

Sunday 14th
NEW 12 Uplands Crescent 33

Sunday 21st
Creigiau Village Gardens 6
Gileston Manor 9
NEW 12 Uplands Crescent 33

September

Saturday 10th
Uplands 32

Friday 16th
Llandough Castle 15

Saturday 17th
Llandough Castle 15

Sunday 18th
Llandough Castle 15

February 2023

Sunday 19th
Slade 27

By Arrangement

Arrange a personalised garden visit with your club, or group of friends, on a date to suit you. See individual garden entries for full details.

22 Dan-y-Coed Road 7
Gileston Manor 9
17 Maes y Draenog 17
Nant Melyn Farm 20
NEW Sandville Court 26
NEW 12 Uplands Crescent 33

Gileston Manor

THE GARDENS

1 BIG HOUSE FARM
Llanmadoc, Gower, Swansea, SA3 1DE. Mark & Sheryl Mead. *15m W of Swansea. M4 J47, L A483 for Swansea, 2nd r'about R, A484 Llanelli 3rd r'about L, B4296 Gowerton T-lights, R B4295, pass Bury Green R to Llanmadoc.* Sun 19 June (1-5.30). Adm £5, chd free. Home-made teas.
Multi awarded inspirational garden of around 1 acre at this lovely listed property combines colour form and texture, described by visitors as 'the best I've seen', 'a real gem'. 'better than Chelsea and Gardeners' World, should visit'. Large variety of interesting plants and shrubs, with ambient cottage garden feel, Victorian glasshouse with rose garden potager. Beautiful views over sea and country. Located on the Gower Peninsular, Britain's first designated Area of Outstanding Natural Beauty. Majority of garden accessible to wheelchairs.

2 6 THE BOARLANDS
Porteynon, Swansea, SA3 1NX. Robert & Annette Dyer. *16.8m W of Swansea on Gower Peninsula. Follow A4118 until it starts to descend towards the sea. Take R turn signposted Overton & then L turn over cattlegrid into small estate of bungalows. Proceed to bottom of the estate to No 6.* Sun 5 June (2-5.30). Combined adm with 3 Monksland Road £5, chd free.
Small plantsmans garden with enchanting views over Port Eynon Bay. Rare and unusual plants and bulbs with many from the Southern Hemisphere, inc proteas,banksias and eucalyptus. Formal pond with wildlife area. Decking area overlooking view, small woodland area, many climbers, herbaceous/shrub borders and scree/rockery. Two front gardens with rare bulbs and alpine plants. Several seating areas with panoramic views of Port Eynon Bay.

3 THE CEDARS
20A Slade Road, Newton, Swansea, SA3 4UF. Mr Ian & Mrs Madelene Scott. *Take the A4067 to Oystermouth, turn R at White Rose pub continue along Newton Rd keeping R at fork to T-junction, turn R & 1st R into Slade Rd, follow yellow signs.* Sun 3 Apr (2-5). Adm £5, chd free. Home-made teas.
South facing garden on a sloping site consisting of rooms subdivided by large shrubs and trees. Small kitchen garden with greenhouse. Ornamental pond. Herbaceous perennials, number of fruit trees. It is a garden which affords all year interest with azalea, camellias, rhododendrons, magnolias and hydrangeas.

GROUP OPENING

4 CEFN CRIBWR GARDEN CLUB
Cefn Cribwr, Bridgend, CF32 0AP. www.cefncribwrgardeningclub. com. *5m W of Bridgend on B4281.* Sun 26 June (11-5). Combined adm £5, chd free. Home-made teas.

13 BEDFORD ROAD
Mr John Loveluck.

2 BRYN TERRACE
Alan & Tracy Birch.

CEFN CRIBWR GARDEN CLUB ALLOTMENTS
Cefn Cribwr Garden Club.

CEFN METHODIST CHURCH
Cefn Cribwr Methodist Church.

77 CEFN ROAD
Peter & Veronica Davies & Mr Fai Lee.

25 EAST AVENUE
Mr & Mrs D Colbridge.

15 GREEN MEADOW
Tom & Helen.

HILL TOP
Mr & Mrs W G Hodges.

6 TAI THORN
Mr Kevin Burnell.

NEW 3 TY-ISAF ROAD
Mr Ryland & Mrs Claire Downs.

Cefn Cribwr is an old mining village atop a ridge with views of Swansea to the west, Somerset to the south and home to Bedford Park and the Cefn Cribwr Iron Works. The village hall is at the centre with teas, cakes and plants for sale. The allotments are to be found behind the hall. Children, art and relaxation are just some of the themes to be found in the gardens besides the flower beds and vegetables. There are also water features, fish ponds, wildlife ponds, summerhouses and hens adding to the diverse mix in the village. Themed colour borders, roses, greenhouses, recycling, composting and much more. The chapel grounds are peaceful with a meandering woodland trail. Visitors may travel between gardens courtesy of the Glamorgan Iron Horse Vintage Society.

5 NEW 19 COED CELYN ROAD
Derwen Fawr, Swansea, SA2 8DS. Ms Lynette Pothecary. *Approx 3m W of Swansea. A4067 Mumbles Rd, follow sign for Singleton Hospital. Then R onto Sketty lane at mini r'about turn L ,then 4th L, Follow yellow NGS signs. Park on Derwen Fawr rd if possible.* Fri 10, Sat 11 June (1-5). Adm £4, chd free. Light refreshments.
Woodpecker Wood. Backed by mature woodland this long narrow town garden is full of surprises and interest. The garden is divided into 'rooms', all are charming and inspiring with seating to enjoy the details. It is fascinating to see what can be achieved in a rectangular garden.

'National Garden Scheme funding helped support the provision of horticultural-related assistance to soldiers, veterans and their immediate families, providing education, training and employment opportunities along with supporting the recovery, health and wellbeing of individuals' *ABF The Soldiers' Charity*

GROUP OPENING

6 CREIGIAU VILLAGE GARDENS
Maes Y Nant, Creigiau, CF15 9EJ.
W of Cardiff (J34 M4). From M4 J34 follow A4119 to T-lights, turn R by Castell Mynach Pub, pass through Groes Faen & turn L to Creigiau. Follow NGS signs. Sun 10 July (11-5). Combined adm £6, chd free. Sun 21 Aug (11-5). Combined adm £5, chd free. Home-made teas at 28 Maes y Nant (July opening) and at Waunwyllt (August opening).

NEW THE BARN HOUSE
Mr Stephen & Mrs Mary Davies.
Open on Sun 10 July

28 MAES Y NANT
Mike & Lesley Sherwood.
Open on all dates

NEW 26 PARC Y FRO
Mr Daniel Cleary.
Open on Sun 10 July

WAUNWYLLT
John Hughes & Richard Shaw.
Open on all dates

Creigiau Village Gardens inc four vibrant and innovative gardens – two of which are new for 2022. Each quite different, they combine some of the best characteristics of design and planting for modern town gardens as well as cottage gardens. Each has its own forte; Waunwyllt has incorporated next door's garden; 28 Maes y Nant, cottage garden planting reigns; 26 Parc y Fro is newly planted with wildlife at its heart; The Barn House has a newly planted garden. The back garden has interesting hard landscaping features and a Japanese planting theme, whilst the front garden is a more traditional planting scheme with seasonal colour and interest year-round. Anyone looking for ideas for a garden in an urban setting will not go away disappointed; enjoy a warm welcome, home-made teas (July - Maes y Nant, August - Waunwyllt) and plant sales.

✿ 🍵

7 22 DAN-Y-COED ROAD
Cyncoed, Cardiff,
CF23 6NA. Alan & Miranda Workman, 029 2076 6225,
miranda.parsons@talktalk.net.
Dan y Coed Rd leads off Cyncoed Rd at the top & Rhydypenau Rd at the bottom. No 22 is at the bottom
of Dan y Coed Rd. There is street parking & level access to the R of the property.* Sun 19 June (2-6). Adm £4.50, chd free. Home-made teas. Visits also by arrangement Apr to Sept for groups of 5 to 20.
A medium sized, much loved garden. Owners share a passion for plants and structure, each year the lawn gets smaller to allow for the acquisition of new plants and features. Hostas, ferns, Acers and other trees form the central woodland theme as a backdrop is provided by the Nant Fawr woods. Year-round interest has been created for the owner's and visitor's greater pleasure. There is a wildlife pond, many climbing plants and a greenhouse with a cactus and succulent collection.

✿ 🍵

GROUP OPENING

8 DINAS POWYS
Dinas Powys, CF64 4TL. *Approx 6m SW of Cardiff. Exit M4 at J33, follow A4232 to Leckwith, onto B4267 & follow to Merry Harrier T-lights. Turn R & enter Dinas Powys. Follow yellow NGS signs.* Sat 18, Sun 19 June (11-5). Combined adm £5, chd free. Light refreshments at Ashgrove & the Community Gardens, inc gluten free and vegan cakes. Donation to Dinas Powys Voluntary Concern and Dinas Powys Community Library.

1 ASHGROVE
Sara Bentley.

NEW 69 HEOL-Y-FRENHINES
Mrs Penny Jones.

30 MILLBROOK ROAD
Mr & Mrs R Golding.

32 MILLBROOK ROAD
Mrs G Marsh.

NIGHTINGALE COMMUNITY GARDENS
Keith Hatton.

NEW 5 SIR IVOR PLACE
Ceri Coles.

There are many gardens to visit in this small friendly village, all with something different to offer, plus the village church. The gardens at 1 Ashgrove have a large variety of different plants and trees in sweeping beds, with many hidden nooks and places to sit. The community garden features lovely displays of vegetable and fruit. 30 Millbrook Road, a large and beautiful garden, established over 25 years, with
lovely pond and waterfall. 32 Millbrook Road is a lovely family garden with interesting touches. Our village church, St Peters, is also opening with displays of flowers, classic cars and other attractions. There will also be plants for sale in the different gardens. There are many restful and beautiful areas to sit and relax. Good wheelchair access at the community gardens. Partial access elsewhere.

& ✿ 🍵 »)

9 GILESTON MANOR
Gileston, Vale of Glamorgan,
CF62 4HX. Lorraine & Joshua, 07794611105,
enquiries@gilestonmanor.co.uk,
www.gilestonmanor.co.uk. *From Cardiff airport take B4265 to Llantwit Major. After 3m turn L at petrol station. Go under bridge, turn R follow yellow NGS signs. No turning at Cenotaph.* Sun 5 June, Sun 21 Aug (11-4). Adm £6, chd free. Tea, coffee, cakes & cocktails at the garden bar. Visits also by arrangement June to Sept.
Surrounded by beautiful Welsh countryside with breathtaking views across the jurassic coast, you will find our historic 9 acre estate. Gileston Manor, in the Vale of Glamorgan, has been loved and lived in since 1320 and recently, lovingly renovated and restored by the current owners. There is so much to see and explore and will definitely delight any keen gardener - a perfect blend of old and new. From the parking area we have flat gravel pathways to access the Walled Garden and The Rookery.

& 🐕 ✿ 🏠 🍵

10 HAFOD Y FRO
Sigingstone, Cowbridge,
CF71 7LP. Rhodri & Kathy Williams. *3m SW of Cowbridge. W. along A48 passing Cowbridge. L at Pentre Meyrick on B4268 (signed Sigingstone Llysworney/Llantwit Major). 1m after Llysworney turn L (signed Sigingstone/Victoria Inn).* Sat 25 June (2-6). Adm £5, chd free. Home-made teas.
Pretty courtyard surrounded by barn conversions covered by climbers, pond and bog areas. Lawn leading to raised terrace. Summerhouse and waterfall. Annual, herbaceous, rose and shrub border sheltered by evergreens. Woodland and orchard.

🍵 »)

The Barn House

GROUP OPENING

▣ HEN FELIN & SWALLOW BARNS

Vale of Glamorgan, Dyffryn, CF5 6SU. 02920 593082, rozanne.lord@blueyonder.co.uk. *3m from Culverhouse. Cross r'about.* **Sun 26 June (10-5). Combined adm £5.50, chd free. Home-made teas.**

Dyffryn hamlet is a hidden gem in the Vale of Glamorgan; despite the lack of a pub there is a fantastic community spirit. Yr Hen Felin: Beautiful cottage garden with stunning borders, breathtaking wildflower meadows, oak tree with surrounding bench, 200 year old pig sty, wishing well, secret garden with steps to river, lovingly tended vegetable garden and chickens. Mill stream running through garden with adjacent wildflowers. Swallow Barns: Cross the bridge over the river and pass under the weeping ash to enter Swallow Barns garden, a mature garden with packed herbaceous borders - formal and informal, orchard, hens, herb garden, lavender patio, willow arches leading to woodland walk and deep secluded pond. We welcome all visitors - old and new. Wheelchair access possible to most of the two gardens. Unprotected river access, children must be supervised in both gardens. Home-made jams, Pimm's at the pond, cheese and wine, artists' stall, face painting, white elephant stall, jewellery stall and plant stall.

▣ 16 HENDY CLOSE

Derwen Fawr, Swansea, SA2 8BB. Peter & Wendy Robinson. *Approx 3m W of Swansea. A4067 Mumbles Rd follow sign for Singleton Hospital. Then R onto Sketty Lane at mini r'about, turn L then 2nd R onto Saunders Way. Follow yellow NGS signs. Please park on Saunders Way if possible.* **Sun 24 July (2-5). Adm £7, chd free. Light refreshments. Tea/coffee/soft drinks & cake is included in the price.**

Originally the garden was covered with 40ft conifers. Cottage style, some unusual and mainly perennial plants which provide colour in spring, summer and autumn. Hopefully the garden is an example of how to plan for all seasons. Visitors say it is like a secret garden because there are a number of hidden places. Plants to encourage all types of wildlife in to the garden.

🔢 110 HERITAGE PARK
St Mellons, Cardiff, CF3 0DS.
Sarah Boorman. *Leave A48 at St Mellons junction, take 2nd exit at r'about. Turn R to Willowdene Way & R to Willowbrook Drive. Heritage Park is 1st R. Park outside the cul-de-sac.* Sat 30 Apr (1-5)..Adm £4, chd free. Gluten free options available.
An unexpected gem within a modern housing estate. Evergreen shrubs, herbaceous borders, box topiary and terracotta pots make for a mix between cottage garden and Italian style. With numerous seating areas and a few quirky surprises this small garden is described by neighbours as a calm oasis. The garden would be able to be viewed from the patio area.
& ✿ ☕))

🔢 4 HILLCREST
Langland, Swansea, SA3 4PW.
Mr Gareth & Mrs Penny Cross.
Approach from L, turn at Langland corner on Langland Rd Mumbles; take first L. off Higher Lane; take 3rd L. up Worcester Rd & bungalow faces you at top. Sun 17 July (1.30-5). Adm £5, chd free. Home-made teas.
Redesigned and developed over the last 7 years, our hilltop garden backs onto woodland overlooking Swansea bay and attracts many birds. We have planted large herbaceous borders with mainly perennial plants/shrubs to provide interest and colour through the seasons. A wildlife pond and fruit/vegetable garden add to interest.
✿ ☕))

🔢 LLANDOUGH CASTLE
Llandough, Cowbridge, CF71 7LR.
Mrs Rhian Rees. *1½ m outside Cowbridge. At the T- lights in Cowbridge turn onto the St Athan Rd. Continue then turn R to Llandough. Drive into the village follow the car park signs. Walk up a short lane & into the gardens.* Fri 16, Sat 17, Sun 18 Sept (10.30-4.30). Adm £6.50, chd free. Home-made teas.
Set within castle grounds and with a backdrop of an ancient monument, the 3½ acres of garden inc a potager with a hint of the Mediterranean, formal lawns and herbaceous beds, a wildlife pond with waterfall and a woodland garden with stumpery and sculpture. Over 60,000 Spring bulbs have been planted inc snowdrops, narcissi and tulips. Potager, wildlife pond, formal borders, stumpery.
✿ ☕))

🔢 NEW 2 LLYS CASTELL
Coed Hirwaun, Port Talbot, SA13 2UX. Mrs Mair Jones. *Coed Hirwaun is situated on the A48, between Margam Country Park & Pyle, please follow yellow signs.* Sat 30, Sun 31 July (11-5). Adm £5, chd free. Home-made teas.
Approx. ⅓ acre featuring raised beds planted with a mix of cottage style plants. There are vegetable beds and soft fruit beds along side a small ornamental fish pond. The garden is split into two parts by a stream, the second part is a woodland containing mature trees, accessed by a bridge or pathway. New this year is a gabion wall with raised herbaceous planting leading to a wildlife pond. Partial access available, the woodland area has some steps.
& 🐎 ✿ ☕))

🔢 17 MAES Y DRAENOG
Maes Y Draenog, Tongwynlais, Cardiff, CF15 7JL. Mr Derek Price, 07717462295. *N of M4, J32. From S: M4 , J32, take A4054 into village. R at Lewis Arms pub, up Mill Rd. 2nd R into Catherine Drive, park in signed area (no parking in Maes y draenog). Follow signs to 17 Maes y draenog.* Sat 4, Sun 5 June (12-5). Adm £4, chd free. Light refreshments. Teas, coffees, variety of cakes and pastries. Visits also by arrangement May & June for groups of up to 16.
A hidden gem of a garden, in the shadow of Castell Coch, fed by a natural mountain stream having a wooden footbridge to naturalised areas and woodland area. Set against a woodland backdrop. Developed over 15 years with a wide variety of plants, lavender beds and four herbaceous borders, front/rear with plants for spring and summer displays. There is a stream, summerhouse, patios, greenhouse and vegetable area. A good variety of plants in different borders around house. Rear of house is set against woodland and fields, while front areas have mature roses and herbaceous plants, borders.
✿ 🚗 ☕

🔢 MAES-Y-WERTHA FARM
Bryncethin, CF32 9YJ. Stella & Tony Leyshon. *3m N of Bridgend. Follow sign for Bryncethin, turn R at Masons Arms. Follow sign for Heol-y-Cyw garden about 1m outside Bryncethin on R.* Sat 23 July (12-7). Adm £5.50, chd free. Home-made

teas. Pimms. Live music all day.
A 3 acre hidden gem outside Bridgend. Entering the garden you find a small Japanese garden fed by a stream, this leads you to informal mixed beds and enclosed herbaceous borders. Ponds and rill are fed by a natural spring. A meadow with large lawns under new planting gives wonderful vistas over surrounding countryside. Mural in the summerhouse by contemporary artist Daniel Llewelyn Hall. His work is represented in the Royal Collection and House of Lords. Fresh hand made sandwiches available.
& 🐎 🚗 ☕ ☕ 🪑))

🔢 3 MONKSLAND ROAD
Scurlage, Reynoldston, Swansea, SA3 1AY. Mrs Vhairi Cotter, vhairi.cotter@btinternet.com. *From Swansea follow A4118 signed to Port Eynon. Continue until turning R onto B4247 signed to Rhossili. At Medical Centre on the L, turn into Monksland Rd, continue to 3rd house along on R.* Sun 5 June (1.30-6). Combined adm with 6 The Boarlands £5, chd free. Home-made teas.
This small garden, formerly mostly grass, is just 7 years old and still evolving. However it has surprisingly mature and diverse planting that, within seven distinct areas, features everything from coastal varieties and grasses to roses, perennials and shrubs. Water features encourage wildlife, while plants and shrubs attract bees and butterflies as well as providing year-round interest. Pergola, several seating areas. An ornamental bee hunt for children.
✿ ☕))

🔢 NANT MELYN FARM
Nant Melyn Farm, Seven Sisters, Neath, SA10 9BW. Mr Craig Pearce, cgpearce@hotmail.co.uk. *From J43 on M4 take A465 towards Neath. Exit for Seven Sisters at r'about take 3rd exit, 6m for Seven Sisters you come to Pantyffordd sign, turn L under low bridge.* Visits by arrangement June to Sept for groups of up to 20. Adm £3.50, chd free. Light refreshments.
A spacious interesting garden with many features which inc a stunning natural waterfall, a meandering woodland stream covered by a canopy of entwined trees, a picturesque Japanese garden, beautiful lawned areas with winding pathways.
& 🐎 ✿ ☕ ☕

21 NEW 185 PANTBACH ROAD

Rhiwbina, Cardiff, CF14 6AD. Kate & Glynn Canning. *Situated ½ m from Heol-y -Deri in the heart of Rhiwbina.* **Sun 12 June (11.30-5). Adm £4.50, chd free. Cream teas.** An Urban Retreat...quite literally a brand new garden in the heart of Cardiff. The garden, once overgrown wasteland, turned into an ongoing lockdown' project in 2020 for owners Kate and Glynn. Although still in its infancy, the garden features raised beds, a formal rose garden and a central water feature. The winding path is framed by standard roses, borders and lawns.

&. ☕ ᐧ))

22 50 PEN Y DRE

Rhiwbina, Cardiff, CF14 6EQ. Ann Franklin. *N Cardiff. M4 J32, A470 to Cardiff, 1st L to mini r'about, turn R. At T-lights in village, turn R to Pen-y-Dre.* **Sun 17 July (11-4.30). Adm £3, chd free. Home-made teas in the conservatory.** Situated in the heart of the conservation area of Rhiwbina Garden Village, this north facing garden features deep herbaceous borders with a variety of cottage garden style plants and shrubs, some rare and unusual. Small pond for wildlife and vegetable plot. It provides a peaceful haven with year-round interest. Plants for sale by the vegetable plot.

✿ ☕

23 NEW 100 PENDWYALLT ROAD

Whitchurch, Cardiff, CF14 7EH. *Cul-de-sac across rd from The Village Hotel. Narrow turn nr T-lights. Proceed uphill in cul-de-sac past 3 blocks of flats.* **Fri 17, Sat 18 June (12-5). Adm £4, chd free.** Lose yourself in this ⅓ of an acre 5 year old garden divided into three parts. There are no lawns and the garden is entirely given over to plants and ponds to encourage wildlife. There are narrow informal routes between densely packed trees, shrubs, grasses and bamboos and two huge ponds, one with koi. Tarmac and coarse gravel allow partial access but good views of the garden.

&. ✿

24 PLAS Y COED

Bonvilston, CF5 6TR. Hugh & Gwenda Child. *Plas y Coed is just off the A48 at Bonvilston. Find the Church & you will find us. Parking will be clearly marked at the Reading Rooms.* **Sat 28, Sun 29 May (10-6). Adm £5, chd free. Home-made teas.** The garden at Plas y Coed has become more than 'just a garden' in the seventeen years we have lived here. The field that extends beyond the pond and folly is now an arboretum with close on sixty trees - trees chosen for their form, bark and colour. The garden is an interesting marriage of architecture, artwork and landscape.

☕ ᐧ))

'National Garden Scheme donations have funded four of our gardens in regional NHS spinal injury centres supporting nearly 8,500 patients and their visitor' *Horatio's Garden*

19 Coed Celyn Road

Uplands

25 NEW **PWYLLYGARTH FARM**
Garth Street, Kenfig Hill, Bridgend,
CF33 6EU. Cheryl Bass. *In Kenfig
Hill. Farmhouse directly off main
road in Kenfig Hill. At the Spar follow
yellow signs.* Sat 6 Aug (10-5); Sun
7 Aug (11-4). Adm £5, chd free.
Light refreshments.
Pwllygarth Farm was built by Welsh
heiress Emily Charlotte Talbot in 1904
as a working farm. The front and side
gardens are a mix of rose gardens,
sedum planted walls, raised rockery
beds, small woodland garden and
a landscaped paved area. The rear
garden offers a Japanese garden,
butterfly rockery, summerhouse,
reading corner and and a creative
central shrub bed around an upcycled
tree trunk. To the rear of the property
is a car park area that will feature
some classic cars. The garden is
accessible via a wheelchair and there
are no steps that split the garden
areas.

26 NEW **SANDVILLE COURT**
Kenfig, Bridgend,
CF33 4PU. Sandville Self
Help Centre, 01656743344,
info@sandville.org.uk,
www.sandville.org.uk. *3m N of
Porthcawl, CF33 4PU. Situated
between Cornelly & Porthcawl,
adjacent to the Pyle & Kenfig Golf
Club, sat in the ground of Sandville*

Self Help foundation. Visits by
arrangement. Garden is open
when the Centre is open, please
check the website. Adm by
donation.
Relaxing Sensory Garden, filled with
seasonal plants. Very tranquil, with
seating area. Adjacent to a small
stone built church. On the grounds
of Sandville Self Help Centre. Fully
accessible for wheelchair and
disabled users.
&

27 **SLADE**
Southerndown, CF32 0RP.
Rosamund & Peter
Davies, 01656 880048,
rosamund.davies@ngs.org.uk,
www.sladeholidaycottages.co.uk.
*5m S of Bridgend. M4 J35 Follow
A473 to Bridgend. Take B4265 to
St. Brides Major. Turn R in St. Brides
Major for Southerndown, then follow
yellow NGS signs.* Sun 13, Sun 20
Feb (2-5); Sat 23, Sun 24 Apr (11-
5). Adm £6, chd free. Home-made
teas. 2023: Sun 19 Feb.
Hidden away Slade garden is an
unexpected jewel to discover next to
the sea with views overlooking the
Bristol Channel. The garden tumbles
down a valley protected by a belt of
woodland. In front of the house are
delightful formal areas a rose and
clematis pergola and herbaceous
borders. From terraced lawns great

sweeps of grass stretch down the
hill enlivened by spring bulbs and
fritillaries. Heritage Coast wardens
will give guided tours of adjacent
Dunraven Gardens with slide shows
every hour from 2pm (Apr opening
only). Partial wheelchair access.

28 **28 SLADE GARDENS**
West Cross, Swansea, SA3 5QP.
Peter & Helen Sheterline. *At
the end of Slade Gardens facing
Oystermouth Cemetery. Wheelchair
drop off only in Slade Gdns. Parking
in cemetery car park at top of lane
from Newton Rd indicated with white
sign. Approx 150 metres level walk
on tarmac. Additional parking on
Bellevue Rd.* Sun 19 June (1.30-
5.30). Adm £5, chd free. Home-
made teas.
This is a renovation of the old garden
of the original Lodge to Oystermouth
Cemetery. It is tucked under the steep
limestone woodland at the eastern
end of the cemetery valley and faces
south overlooking the Victorian part of
the cemetery. It is planted in cottage
garden style with perennials and
selected shrubs on the side of the hill
separated from a lawn by a limestone
wall. The garden can be enjoyed from
the terrace of the house which is
reached without climbing steps and
where tea and cakes can be enjoyed.
The view over the garden and 'hidden

Valley' of the cemetery is a lovely surprise even for those who know Mumbles well. The scented roses should be in full bloom.

29 38 SOUTH RISE
South Rise, Llanishen, Cardiff, CF14 0RH. Dr Khalida Hasan. *N of Cardiff, from Llanishen Village Station Rd past Train Stn go R down The Rise or further down onto S Rise directly. Following yellow signs.* Sat 2, Sun 3 July (11-5). Adm £5, chd free. Home-made teas. Cakes and South Asian savouries (e.g. samosa, chick pea chaat, pakora) available.
A relatively new garden backing on to Llanishen Reservoir gradually establishing with something of interest and colour all year-round. Herbaceous borders, vegetables and fruit plants surround central lawn. Wildlife friendly; variety of climbers and exotics. In front shrubs and herbaceous borders to a lawn. Stepping stones leading to children's play area and vegetable plot also at the back. Wheelchair access to rear from the side of the house.

30 SUNNY COTTAGE
Mountain Road, Bedwas, Caerphilly, CF83 8ES. Mr Paul & Mrs Carol Edwards. *Head E from Caerphilly to Bedwas on A468. Turn L at T-lights into village onto Church St follow rd up to St Barrwgs Church. Turn R after bridge then 1st I onto Mountain Rd. Follow NGS signs.* Sat 18, Sun 19 June (11-4). Adm £4, chd free. Light refreshments.
Terraced garden surrounded by wildlife friendly hedges. Hidden areas on the terraces are linked by paths and arches. Each level is very well-stocked with a multitude of flowers, shrubs and trees. Something of interest for every season. Two lawn areas provide a welcome splash of green. One is shaded by two mature apple trees. Seating areas to relax and enjoy the vistas can be found on most levels.

31 NEW SWN Y COED
Tyla Garw, Pontyclun, CF72 9HD. Mair & Owen Hopkin. *N. of Pontyclun. Talbot Green A473 towards Llanharan. On r'about take exit for Trecastell. Over railway Xing. Turn R Boar's Head pub on L, pass*

forestry entrance on R, garden is first house on R. Sat 6, Sun 7 Aug (11-4). Adm £4, chd free. Light refreshments inc gluten free options.
This family friendly garden started from a blank canvas 5 years ago, initially laid to lawn. Raised vegetable beds were installed and a 75m natural hedge planted along the side boundary to encourage wildlife. This was supplemented with fruit trees, flower and herb borders to attract insects. The lawn provides a clearing to the surrounding forestry attracting a variety of birds. Disabled parking on drive. Ramped access to rear patio and WC. Path adjacent to herb border.

32 UPLANDS
Gwern-y-Steeple, Peterston Super Ely, CF5 6LG. David Richmond. *From the A48 between St Nicholas & Bonvilston take the Peterston Super Ely turning & follow yellow NGS arrow, park at small green near Gwern-y-Steeple sign.* Sat 9 July, Sat 10 Sept (12-5). Adm £4, chd free.
Uplands has a rustic heart within a cottage garden design. The front is vegetables and currant bushes. The back was planted in 2019, on once all grass. There are four main herbaceous borders, young fruit trees, ornamental grasses, ferns, shrubs and roses, with many places to relax and enjoy the garden. Medium sized greenhouse with citrus and fig tree. Several sculptures located around the garden.

33 NEW 12 UPLANDS CRESCENT
Llandough, Penarth, CF64 2PR. Mr Dean Mears, 07910638682, dean.mears@ntlworld.com. *Head for Llandough Hospital & follow the sign to a small cul-de-sac with a Weeping Willow clearly visible in the front garden. Follow NGS signs.* Sun 3, Sun 10 July, Sun 14, Sun 21 Aug (2-4.30). Adm £4, chd free. Light refreshments. Visits also by arrangement June to Sept for groups of up to 5.
An exotic medium size garden full of variety, unusual and big plants, an unusual fern collection and a pond. Banana plants and Gunnera fill the corners and Tree Ferns, Phormium, Tetrapanax, Cordyline and Giant Reed add height to the garden. An area of

potted tropical plants, Brugmansia, Canna, Alocasia, Strelitzia and palms add further interest.

34 9 WILLOWBROOK GARDENS
Mayals, Swansea, SA3 5EB. Gislinde Macphereson. *Nr Clyne Gardens. Go along Mumbles Rd to Blackpill. Turn R at Texaco garage up Mails Rd. 1st R along top of Clyne Park, at mini r'about into Westport Ave. 1st L into Willowbrook gardens.* Sat 14, Sun 15 May (1-5). Adm £5, chd free.
Informal ½ acre mature garden on acid soil, designed to give natural effect with balance of form and colour between various areas linked by lawns; unusual trees suited to small suburban garden, especially conifers and maples; rock and water garden. Sculptures, ponds and waterfall.

GROUP OPENING

35 NEW YSTALYFERA GARDENS
Ystalyfera, Swansea, SA9 2AJ. *13m N of Swansea. M4 J45 take A4067. Follow signs for Dan yr Ogof caves across 5 r'abouts. After T-lights follow yellow NGS signs.* Sat 4, Sun 5 June (12-5). Combined adm £5, chd free. Home-made teas at Rhosybedw and 4 Clyngwyn Road. Gluten free option available at Rhosybedw.

4 CLYNGWYN ROAD
Paul Steer,
www.artinacorner.blogspot.com.

RHOS Y BEDW
Robert & Helen Davies.

Inspiring and eclectic duo of village gardens. Each with something different to offer visitors: a mature hillside plot with hidden treasures in every corner and a green and peaceful oasis for relaxation Majestic views of the Darren Mountain and the Brecon National Park in the backgrounds. Teas and refreshments available to be enjoyed in restful and beautiful surroundings. Plant sales are also an attraction. Limited access for those with mobility issues at Rhosybedw due to hillside location. Home made Crafts and Art work for sale a donation will be made to the NGS.

698

GWENT

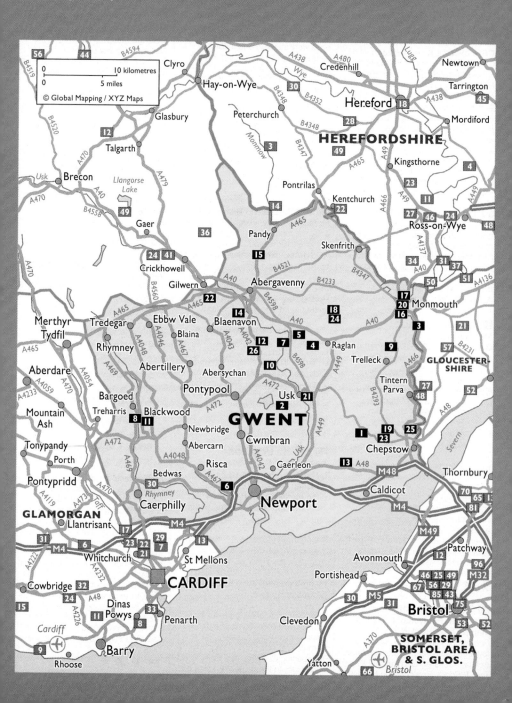

Welcome to Gwent! It is a county of valleys and hills, of castles and farms, of country lanes yet very accessible main roads, easily reached from Cardiff, Bristol or Hereford.

Some of our gardens are clustered around the delightful market towns of Monmouth and Abergavenny, many with breathtaking panoramic views. The historic small town of Usk opens around 20 varied gardens over a June weekend. Our Gwent gardens range from small jewels of town gardens to gracious estates, from manicured lawns to hillside gardens that blend into the landscape. Look out for some lovely gardens opening for the first time - marked clearly in the book as New.

A very warm welcome to our gardens and thank you for your support.

Left: Woodhaven

Volunteers

County Organiser
Cathy Davies
01291 672625 / 07976 633743
cathydavies127@gmail.com

County Treasurer
David Warren
01873 880031
wdavid270@aol.com

Publicity
Cathy Davies
(as above)

Penny Reeves
01873 880355
penny.reeves@ngs.org.uk

Social Media
Roger Lloyd 01873 880030
droger.lloyd@btinternet.com

Assistant County Organiser
Cherry Taylor
07803 853681
cherry.taylor@dynamicmarkets.co.uk

Sue Torkington
01873 890045
sue.torkington@ngs.org.uk

Veronica Ruth
07967 157806 / 01873 859757
veronica.ruth@ngs.org.uk

Jenny Lloyd
01873 880030 / 07850 949209
jenny.lloyd@ngs.org.uk

Booklet Co-Ordinator
Veronica Ruth (as above)

🅕 @gwentngs
🅧 @GwentNGS
🅞 @gwentngs

OPENING DATES

All entries subject to change. For latest information check www.ngs.org.uk

Extended openings are shown at the beginning of the month.

Map locator numbers are shown to the right of each garden name.

March

Sunday 27th
Llanover   12

April

Every day from Saturday 9th to Friday 22nd
Woodlands Farm   24

Sunday 17th
The Old Vicarage   18

Saturday 23rd
Glebe House   7

Sunday 24th
Glebe House   7

May

Sunday 1st
High Glanau Manor   9

Friday 6th
The Alma   1

Saturday 7th
The Alma   1
Park House   19
Woodhaven   23

Sunday 8th
The Alma   1

Sunday 15th
Middle Ninfa Farm & Bunkhouse   14

Saturday 28th
Hillcrest   11
The Nelson Garden   16
North Parade House   17

Sunday 29th
Hillcrest   11
The Nelson Garden   16
North Parade House   17
Wenallt Isaf   22

Monday 30th
Hillcrest   11

June

Thursday 2nd
Hillcrest   11

Friday 3rd
Hillcrest   11

Saturday 4th
◆ Wyndcliffe Court   25

Sunday 5th
NEW Lynbrook   13

Sunday 12th
NEW April House   2
Highfield Farm   10

Sunday 19th
Mione   15
Rockfield Park   20

Saturday 25th
Usk Open Gardens   21

Sunday 26th
Usk Open Gardens   21

July

Every Sunday
Hillcrest   11

Sunday 3rd
Mione   15

Saturday 9th
14 Gwerthonor Lane   8

Sunday 10th
NEW April House   2
14 Gwerthonor Lane   8
Mione   15

Sunday 17th
Clytha Park   5

Sunday 24th
Highfield Farm   10

August

Every Sunday
Hillcrest   11

Sunday 7th
Birch Tree Well   3

Sunday 14th
Highfield Farm   10

Sunday 21st
Croesllanfro Farm   6

Sunday 28th
Wenallt Isaf   22

September

Sunday 11th
Highfield Farm   10

By Arrangement

Arrange a personalised garden visit with your club, or group of friends, on a date to suit you. See individual garden entries for full details.

The Alma   1
Birch Tree Well   3
Bryngwyn Manor   4
Croesllanfro Farm   6
Glebe House   7
Highfield Farm   10
Hillcrest   11
Llanover   12
Middle Ninfa Farm & Bunkhouse   14
Wenallt Isaf   22
Woodhaven   23
NEW Y Bwthyn   26

Croesllanfro Farm

THE GARDENS

1 THE ALMA

Bully Hole Bottom, Usk Road,
Shirenewton, NP16 6SA.
Dr Pauline Ruth, 01291 641902,
pmruth@hotmail.co.uk. *B4235 Usk
to Chepstow signposted Bully Hole
Bottom. Down hill over bridge up to
T junction. Drive straight ahead along
track signposted The Alma. Parking
in meadow on L.* Fri 6, Sat 7, Sun
8 May (12-5). Adm £5, chd free.
Home-made teas. Visits also by
arrangement May to Sept.
Large sheltered south west facing
garden, uncommon trees, wisteria,
roses and acid loving shrubs. Long
border, hot border, productive
vegetable garden, old brick
outbuildings, fruit cage and vines,
wildlife pond, sunset arbour and
stream side walk. Drive packed with
native daffodils, snowdrops and
bluebells in the spring. Wildflower
meadow and orchard in development.
Sunny terrace for teas. Children's
play area and picnics welcome.
Wheelchair access to level terrace.

2 NEW APRIL HOUSE

Coed y Paen, Usk, NP15 1PT.
Charlotte Fleming. *2m W of Usk.
From Usk bridge go S towards
Caerleon. Take 1st R towards Coed y
Paen and go uphill for 1.9m. Garden
is on L. SatNav gets you here.*
Sun 12 June, Sun 10 July (11-5).
Adm £5, chd free. Pre-booking
essential, please visit www.ngs.
org.uk for information & booking.
Home-made teas.
Long ½ acre site with glorious views
over the Usk Valley and Wentwood
forest. Garden developed over past
5 yrs from bramble thicket. Low
maintenance shrub and prairie-style
and herbaceous borders. Fruit and
vegetables.

3 BIRCH TREE WELL

Upper Ferry Road, Penallt,
Monmouth, NP25 4AN. Jill
Bourchier, 01600 775327,
gillian.bourchier@btinternet.com.
*4m SW of Monmouth. Approx 1m
from Monmouth on B4293, turn L for
Penallt & Trelleck. After 2m turn L to
Penallt. On entering village turn L at
Xrds & follow yellow signs.*
Sun 7 Aug (2-5.30). Adm £4, chd

free. Home-made teas. **Visits also
by arrangement Apr to Sept for
groups of up to 25.**
Situated in the heart of the Lower
Wye Valley, amongst the ancient
habitat of woodland, rocks and
streams these 3 acres are shared
with deer, badgers and foxes. A
woodland setting with streams and
boulders which can be viewed from a
lookout tower and a butterfly garden
planted with specialist hydrangeas inc
many plants to also attract bees and
insects. Children are very welcome
(under supervision).

4 BRYNGWYN MANOR

Bryngwyn, Raglan, Usk,
NP15 2JH. Peter & Louise
Maunder, 01291 691485,
louiseviola@live.co.uk. *2m W of
Raglan. Turn S (between the two
garden centres) off B4598 (old A40)
Abergavenny-Raglan rd at Croes
Bychan. House ¼m up lane on L.*
**Visits by arrangement Feb to
Sept for groups of up to 25. Adm
£5, chd free. Home-made teas.
Picnics welcome if preferred.
If booking a group visit please
contact us to discuss your
requirements.**
3 acres. Winter snowdrops, daffodil
walk, mature trees, walled parterre
garden, mixed borders, lawns,
ponds and shrubbery. Family
friendly afternoon out, with children's
activities, loads of space to run
about, and scrumptious teas. A series
of practical, small group garden
workshops is being held – for details
please see website. All areas of the
garden can be accessed without
using the steps, however, ground is
uneven and consist mainly of grass
paths.

5 CLYTHA PARK

Abergavenny, NP7 9BW. Jack
& Susannah Tenison. *Between
Abergavenny (5m) & Raglan (3m).
The main Clytha gate is shut for
repairs. Please follow the signs on
the old A40 Raglan-Abergavenny rd,
& turn off 500 yds E of the Clytha
Arms.* Sun 17 July (2-5). Adm £5,
chd free. Home-made teas.
Large C18/19 garden around lake
with wide lawns and specimen trees,
original layout by John Davenport,
with C19 arboretum, and H. Avray
Tipping influence. Visit the 1790
walled garden and the newly restored

greenhouses. Gravel and grass paths.

6 CROESLLANFRO FARM

Groes Road, Rogerstone,
Newport, NP10 9GP. Barry
& Liz Davies, 07957694230,
lizplants@gmail.com. *3m W of
Newport. From M4 Junction 27 take
B4591 towards Risca. Take 3rd R,
Cefn Walk (also signed 14 Locks
Canal Centre). Proceed over bridge,
continue ½m to island in middle of
lane.* Sun 21 Aug (1.30-5). Adm £5,
chd free. Home-made teas. **Visits
also by arrangement June to Sept
for groups of 6 to 30.**
An informal 2 acre garden featuring
mass planted perennials, grasses,
wildflower meadow and exotic
garden. Spring and early summer is
a tapestry of green concentrating on
leaf form and texture. Late summer,
early autumn brings the the garden
to a finale with an explosion of colour.
A formal garden designed on six
different levels for easy maintenance.
Some gravel paths and shallow
steps. Large barn open to the public,
'fabulous folly' and grotto. Owner is
a Garden Designer and co-author
of 'Designing Gardens on Slopes'.
Some gravel paths and shallow steps
to main area of garden.

7 GLEBE HOUSE

Llanvair Kilgeddin, Abergavenny,
NP7 9BE. Mr & Mrs Murray
Kerr, 01873 840422,
joanna@amknet.com. *Midway
between Abergavenny (5m) & Usk
(5m) on B4598.* Sat 23, Sun 24
Apr (2-6). Adm £6, chd free.
Home-made teas. **Visits also by
arrangement Apr to Sept. Only
accessible to small coaches.**
Borders bursting with spring colour
inc tulips, narcissi and camassias.
South facing terrace with wisteria and
honeysuckle, decorative vegetable
garden and orchard underplanted
with succession of bulbs. Some
topiary and formal hedging in 1½
acre garden set in AONB in Usk
valley. Old rectory of St Mary's,
Llanfair Kilgeddin will also be open
to view famous Victorian scraffito
murals. Some gravel and gently
sloping lawns.

🖪 14 GWERTHONOR LANE
Gilfach, Bargoed, CF81 8JT.
Suzanne & Philip George. *8m N of Caerphilly. A469 to Bargoed, through the T-lights next to sch then L filterlane at next T-lights onto Cardiff Rd. First L into Gwerthonor Rd, 4th R into Gwerthonor Lane.* Sat 9, Sun 10 July (11-6). Adm £4, chd free. Light refreshments.
The garden has a beautiful panoramic view of the Rhymney Valley. A real plantswoman's garden with over 800 varieties of perennials, annuals, bulbs, shrubs and trees. There are numerous rare, unusual and tropical plants combined with traditional and well loved favourites (many available for sale). A pond with a small waterfall adds to the tranquil feel of the garden.
& 🐄 ✳ ☕

🖪 HIGH GLANAU MANOR
Lydart, Monmouth, NP25 4AD. Mr & Mrs Hilary Gerrish, 01600 860005, helenagerrish@gmail.com, www.highglanaugardens.com. *4m SW of Monmouth. Situated on B4293 between Monmouth & Chepstow. Turn R into private rd, ¼ m after Craig-y-Dorth turn on B4293.* Sun 1 May (2-5.30). Adm £6, chd free. Home-made teas.
Listed Arts and Crafts garden laid out by H Avray Tipping in 1922. Original features inc impressive stone terraces with far reaching views over the Vale of Usk to Blorenge, Skirrid, Sugar Loaf and Brecon Beacons. Pergola, herbaceous borders, Edwardian glasshouse, rhododendrons, azaleas, tulips, orchard with wildflowers. Originally open for the NGS in 1927. Garden guidebook by owner, Helena Gerrish, available to purchase. Gardens lovers cottage to rent.
✳ 🚗 🏠 ☕))

🖪 HIGHFIELD FARM
Penperlleni, Goytre, NP4 0AA. Dr Roger & Mrs Jenny Lloyd, 01873 880030, jenny.plants@btinternet.com, www.instagram.com/jenny.plants. *4m W of Usk, 6m S of Abergavenny. Turn off the A4042 at the Goytre Arms, over railway bridge, bear L. Garden ½ m on R. From Usk off B4598, turn L after Chain Bridge, then L at Xrds. Garden 1m on L.* Sun 12 June, Sun 24 July, Sun 14 Aug, Sun 11 Sept (11-4). Adm £6, chd free. Home-made teas. Visits also by arrangement May to Sept. By arrangement admission inc guided

tour plus refreshments.
This is a garden defined by its plants. There are over 1200 cultivars, with many rarities, densely planted over 3 acres to generate an exuberant display across the seasons. It provides an intimate, immersive experience with this diverse array of herbaceous, shrubs and trees. New garden area open in 2022. Huge sale of plants from the garden. Over 1200 plant varieties. Live music. Art sale. Access to almost all garden without steps.
& ✳ 🚗 ☕ 🎋))

🖪 HILLCREST
Waunborfa Road, Cefn Fforest, Blackwood, NP12 3LB. Mr M O'Leary, 01443 837029, olearymichael18@gmail.com. *3m W of Newbridge. B4254/A469 at T/L head to B'wood. At X take lane ahead,1st on L at top of hill. A4048/B4251 cross Chartist Bridge, 2nd exit on next 2 r'abouts. End of road turn L & immed R onto Waunborfa. 400m on R.* Sat 28, Sun 29, Mon 30 May, Thur 2, Fri 3 June (11-6). Every Sun 3 July to 28 Aug (11-5). Adm £5, chd free. Light refreshments. Visits also by arrangement Apr to Oct for groups of up to 30.
A cascade of secluded gardens of distinct character over 1½ acres. Magnificent, unusual trees, interesting shrubs, perennials and annuals. Choices at every turn, visitors are well rewarded as hidden delights and surprises are revealed. Well placed seats encourage a relaxed pace to fully appreciate the garden's treasures. Tulips in April, glorious blooms of the Chilean Firebushes, Handkerchief Tree and cornuses in May and many trees in their autumnal splendour in October. Regional Winner, The English Garden's The Nation's Favourite Gardens 2021. Lowest parts of garden not accessible to wheelchairs.
& 🐄 ✳ ☕

🖪 LLANOVER
Abergavenny, NP7 9EF. Mr & Mrs M R Murray, 07753 423635, elizabeth@llanover.com, www.llanovergarden.co.uk. *4m S of Abergavenny, 15m N of Newport, 20m SW Hereford. On A4042 Abergavenny - Cwmbran Rd, in village of Llanover.* Sun 27 Mar (2-5). Adm £7, chd free. Home-made teas. Visits also by arrangement May to Oct for groups of up to 6.

Benjamin Waddington, the direct ancestor of the current owners, purchased the house and land in 1792. Subsequently he created a series of ponds, cascades and rills which form the backbone of the 15 acre garden as the stream winds its way from its source in the Black Mountains to the River Usk. There are herbaceous borders, a drive lined with narcissi, spring bulbs, wild flowers, a water garden, champion trees and two arboreta. The house (not open) is the birthplace of Augusta Waddington, Lady Llanover, C19 patriot, supporter of the Welsh language and traditions. Gwerinyr Gwent will be performing Welsh folk dances during the afternoon in traditional Welsh costume. Gravel and grass paths and lawns. No disabled WC.
& 🐄 🚗 ☕ 🎋))

🖪 NEW LYNBROOK
20A Castle Rise, Llanvaches, Caldicot, NP26 3BS. Gaynor & Andy Sinton. *In the village of Llanvaches. The house is ½ m N of Penhow on the A48. From Newport turn L off A48 at the Rock & Fountain pub. From Chepstow turn R off A48 by the Tabernacle Church. After the church take the next L.* Sun 5 June (11-4). Adm £4, chd free. Tea.
Situated in about ⅓ acre this garden has been transformed over the last 18 yrs from a simple rectangular lawn totally surrounded by conifers to one with many contrasting features in colour, texture and shape. It has numerous shrubs and flowers some of which are quite rare, a variety of stone and metal sculptures, winding pathways, a gazebo and a cascading waterfall. Access down the drive to the back garden and then onto the lawn.
& 🐄 ☕

🖪 MIDDLE NINFA FARM & BUNKHOUSE
Llanelen, Abergavenny, NP7 9LE. Richard Lewis, 01873 854662, richard@middleninfa.co.uk, www.middleninfa.co.uk. *2½ m SSW Abergavenny. At A465/ B4246 junction, S for Llanfoist, L at mini r'about, B4269 towards Llanelen, ½ m R turn up steep lane, over canal. ¾ m to Middle Ninfa on R.* Sun 15 May (1-5.30). Adm £5, chd free. Pre-booking essential, please visit www.ngs.org. uk for information & booking. Home-made teas. Visits also

by arrangement May & June for groups of up to 12.
Large terraced eco-garden on east slopes of the Blorenge mountain. Vegetable beds, polytunnel, three greenhouses, orchard, flower borders, wild flowers. Great views, woodland walks, cascading water and ponds with ducks. Paths steep in places, unsuitable for less able. Campsite and small bunkhouse on farm. 5 mins walk uphill to scenic Punchbowl Lake and walks on the Blorenge.

15 MIONE
Old Hereford Road, Llanvihangel Crucorney, Abergavenny, NP7 7LB. Yvonne & John O'Neil. *5m N of Abergavenny. From Abergavenny take A465 to Hereford. After 4.8m turn L - signed Pantygelli. Mione is ½ m on L.* Sun 19 June, Sun 3, Sun 10 July (10.30-5). Adm £5, chd free. Home-made teas.
Beautiful garden with a wide variety of established plants, many rare and unusual. Pergola with climbing roses and clematis. Wildlife pond with many newts, insects and frogs. Numerous containers with diverse range of planting. Several seating areas, each with a different atmosphere. Enjoy our new benches in a secret hideaway under the pergola. Lovely home-made cakes, biscuits and scones to be enjoyed sitting in the garden or pretty summerhouse.

16 THE NELSON GARDEN
Blestium Street, Monmouth, NP25 3ER. The Nelson Garden Monmouth (Registered Charity), www.nelsongarden.org.uk. *Chippenham Mead. Garden accessed from Monnow St. car park via Blestium St. Follow yellow NGS signs. Also tourist signs indicating the Nelson Garden. Tunnel entrance from Chippenham Mead.* Sat 28, Sun 29 May (2-6). Combined adm with North Parade House £7, chd free. Home-made teas at North Parade House.
This ancient town garden has a history dating back to Roman and Norman times; remains lie deep beneath the lawn. In 1802 when Lord Nelson visited the garden, it was the garden of the town clerk. The charming retreat where Nelson and the Hamilton's took tea after the civic dinner was demolished, but Nelson's Seat was saved and installed in the present memorial pavilion thought to

date from 1840. By arrangement with the Nelson Garden Trust via a private local access point.

17 NORTH PARADE HOUSE
12 Hereford Road, Monmouth, NP25 3PB. Tim Haynes & Lisa O'Neill. *5mins walk from the centre of town. Take the sign to Monmouth off the A40 r'about by the town. At the T-lights, turn R on to the A466 & the house is on the R after about 300 yds. Parking is on the street.* Sat 28, Sun 29 May (2-6). Combined adm with The Nelson Garden £7, chd free. Home-made teas.
A secluded town walled garden of ⅔ acre which is in the process of restoration. Inc a kitchen garden, mature specimen trees, shrubs, spring bulbs and herbaceous border.

18 THE OLD VICARAGE
Penrhos, Raglan, Usk, NP15 2LE. Mrs Georgina Herrmann. *3m N of Raglan. From A449 take Raglan exit, join A40 & move immed into R lane & turn R across dual carriageway. Follow yellow NGS signs.* Sun 17 Apr (2-6). Adm £5, chd free. Light refreshments.
A Victorian Gothic house set in a traditional vicarage garden in rolling Monmouthshire countryside. Lovely all year, but best in spring with camellias, hellebores, magnolias and a wide range of spring bulbs, as well as unusual trees, all set off by sweeping lawns. A parterre with charming gazebo, kitchen garden, wildlife areas and natural ponds make this a garden well worth visiting and revisiting.

Y Bwthyn

Highfield Farm

19 PARK HOUSE

School Lane, Itton, Chepstow, NP16 6BZ. Professor Bruce & Dr Cynthia Matthews. *From M48 take A466 Tintern. At 2nd r'about turn L B4293 After blue sign Itton turn R Park House is at end of lane. Parking 200m before house. From Devauden B4293 1st L in Itton.* **Sat 7 May (10-5). Combined adm with Woodhaven £6, chd free.** Approx 1 acre garden with large vegetable areas and many mature trees, rhododendrons, azaleas, camellias in a woodland setting. Bordering on Chepstow Park Wood. Magnificent views over open country. A few small steps. and irregular paths too narrow for wheelchairs. Disabled parking adjacent to house.

♿ 🐑 ♪))

20 ROCKFIELD PARK

Rockfield, Monmouth, NP25 5QB. Mark & Melanie Molyneux. *On arriving in Rockfield village from Monmouth, turn R by phone box. After approx 400yds, church on L. Entrance to Rockfield Park on R, opp church, via private bridge over river.* **Sun 19 June (10.30-4.30). Adm £5, chd free. Home-made teas.** Rockfield Park dates from C17 and is situated in the heart of the Monmouthshire countryside on the banks of the River Monnow. The extensive grounds comprise formal gardens, meadows and orchard, complemented by riverside and woodland walks. Possible to picnic on riverside walks. Main part of gardens can be accessed by wheelchair but not steep garden leading down to river.

♿ 🐑 ❄ ☕ 🧺 ♪))

GROUP OPENING

21 USK OPEN GARDENS

Maryport Street, Usk, NP15 1BH. www.uskopengardens.com. *Main car park postcode is NP15 1AD. From M4 J24 take A449 8m N to Usk exit. Free parking signposted around town. Blue badge parking in main car parks. Map of gardens provided with ticket.* **Sat 25, Sun 26 June (10-5). Combined adm £7.50, chd free. Donation to local charities.** Usk's floral public displays are a wonderful backdrop to the gardens. Around ten private gardens opening, inc the private gardens around the ramparts at Usk Castle. Gardeners' Market with interesting plants. Great day out for all the family with lots of

places to eat and drink inc places to picnic. Sorry but NGS discretionary entry tickets are not accepted at this event. Various cafes, pubs and restaurants available for refreshments, plus volunteer groups offering teas and cakes. Wheelchair accessible gardens and gardens allowing well-behaved dogs on leads noted on passport/map available from the ticket desks at the free car park at Usk Memorial Hall (NP15 1AD). Some gardens/areas of gardens are partially wheelchair accessible. Accessibility noted on ticket/map.

  ♿ ✿ 🚗 ☕ 🍴

22 WENALLT ISAF
Twyn Wenallt, Gilwern, Abergavenny, NP7 0HP. Tim & Debbie Field, 01873 832753, wenalltisaf@gmail.com. *3m W of Abergavenny. Between Abergavenny & Brynmawr. Leave the A465 at Gilwern & follow yellow NGS signs through the village. Do not follow SatNav.* **Sun 29 May, Sun 28 Aug (2-5.30). Adm £5, chd free. Home-made teas inc gluten free and lactose free options. Visits also by arrangement Apr to Sept for groups of 10+.**
An everchanging garden of nearly 3 acres designed in sympathy with its surroundings and the challenges of being 650ft up on a North facing hillside. Far reaching views of the magnificent Black Mountains, mature trees, rhododendrons, viburnum, hydrangeas, borders, vegetable garden, small polytunnel, orchard, pigs (even years), chickens, beehives. Child friendly with plenty of space to run about.

☕ ♫)

23 WOODHAVEN
Itton, Chepstow, NP16 6BX. Mr & Mrs Kelly, 01291 641219, lesley@classics.co.uk. *Take the B4293 at Chepstow Racecourse r'about at Itton Common triangle, turn L at red telephone box, and then L along the the rd to Shirenewton, Woodhaven is on the L.* **Sat 7 May (10-5). Combined adm with Park House £6, chd free. Cream teas. Visits also by arrangement May to Oct for groups of up to 30. Parking is limited so please use as few cars as possible.**
A modern house built on the site of a former sawmills for the Itton Court Estate. Garden of ⅔ of an acre

developed over the last 20 years for year-round colour and interest. Level front garden and gently sloping rear garden with extensive views over the valley. Lots of seating areas to enjoy the views. Meadow area with bulbs. Display of tulips in spring, fruit trees and wild flowers.

🐕 ✿ ☕ 🍴

24 WOODLANDS FARM
Penrhos, NP15 2LE. Craig Loane & Charles Horsfield, www.woodlandsfarmwales.com. *3m N of Raglan. From A449 take Raglan exit, join A40 & move immed into R lane & turn R across dual carriageway towards Tregare. Follow NGS signs or check website for directions.* **Daily Sat 9 Apr to Fri 22 Apr (11-3). Adm £5. Picnics welcome. Tea and coffee will be available.**
A design led garden, built to entertain, which has opened for 13 yrs under the NGS. The 4 acre garden contains rooms and hidden spaces with buildings, ponds, viewing platform, jetty, hard landscaping, sculptures and Pygmy goats. Lovely in spring, with many white-blossomed cherry trees and carpets of bulbs.

☕ 🍴

25 ◆ WYNDCLIFFE COURT
St Arvans, NP16 6EY. Mr & Mrs Anthony Clay, 07710 138972, sarah@wyndcliffecourt.com, www.wyndcliffecourt.com. *3m N of Chepstow. Off A466, turn at Wyndcliffe signpost coming from the Chepstow direction.* **For NGS: Sat 4 June (1-6). Adm £10. Pre-booking essential, please visit www.ngs. org.uk for information & booking. Home-made teas in the house. For other opening times and information, please phone, email or visit garden website.**
Exceptional and unaltered garden designed by H. Avray Tipping and Sir Eric Francis in 1922. Arts and Crafts 'Italianate' style. Stone summerhouse, terracing and steps with lily pond. Yew hedging and topiary, sunken garden, rose garden, bowling green and woodland. Walled garden and double tennis court lawn under refurbishment. Rose garden completely replanted to a new design by Sarah Price in 2017. Not suitable for children under 12.

☕

26 NEW Y BWTHYN
Pencroesoped, Llanover, Abergavenny, NP7 9EL. Jacqui & David Warren, warrens.ybwthyn@gmail.com. *6m S of Abergavenny, just outside Llanover. Detailed directions provided ahead of visit.* **Visits by arrangement July and Aug for groups of 10 to 30. Limited parking so group size constrained by number of cars. Home-made teas.**
Beautifully varied 1½ acre garden. Sweeping herbaceous, mixed and prairie-style borders, gravel garden, lawns, pond and bog garden, ornamental kitchen garden and greenhouse, wildflower banks, and a magnificent veteran oak. Lovely views of the surrounding hills and countryside and a fascinating house history too. Some steep grass slopes and narrow gravel paths. Most routes are step-free. No wheelchair access to the WC.

  ♿ ✿ ☕

'In the first six months of operation at Maggie's Southampton, which was part funded by the National Garden Scheme, the team has supported people affected by cancer more than 2,300 times' *Maggie's*

GWYNEDD & ANGLESEY

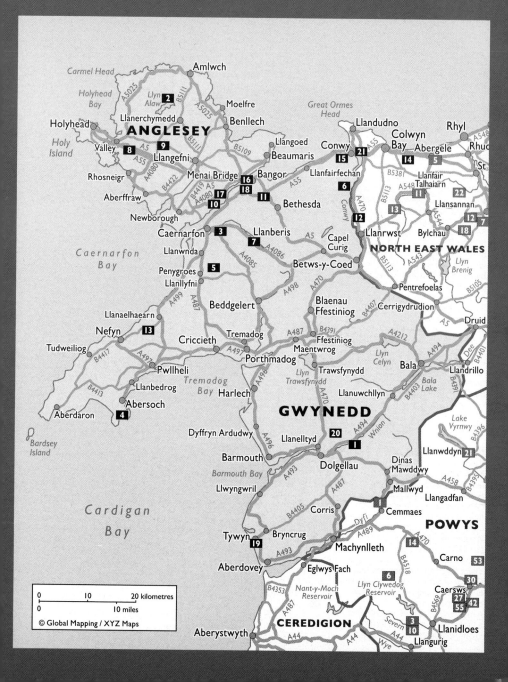

Gwynedd is a county rich in history and outstanding natural beauty. Bordered by the Irish Sea and home to Snowdonia National Park, Gwynedd can boast some of the most impressive landscapes in the UK.

The mountains in Gwynedd are world famous, and have attracted visitors for hundreds of years – the most famous perhaps, was Charles Darwin in 1831. As well as enjoying the tallest peaks in the UK, Gwynedd has fine woodland – from hanging oak forests in the mountains to lush, riverside woods.

Holiday-makers flock to Gwynedd and Anglesey to take advantage of the sandy beaches, and many can enjoy sightings of dolphins and porpoises off the coast.

The gardens of Gwynedd and Anglesey are just as appealing an attraction for visitors. A variety of gardens open for Gwynedd National Garden Scheme, ranging from Crowrach Isaf a two-acre garden with views of Snowdonia and Cardigan Bay to Ty Capel Ffrwd, a true cottage garden in the Welsh mountains.

So why not escape from the hustle and bustle of everyday life and relax in a beautiful garden? You will be assured of a warm welcome at every garden gate.

Below: Pensychnant

Volunteers

County Treasurer
Nigel Bond
01407 831354
nigel.bond@ngs.org.uk

Publicity
Rebecca Andrews
07901 878009
rebecca.andrews@ngs.org.uk

Assistant County Organisers
Hazel Bond
07378 844295
hazelcaenewydd@gmail.com

Janet Jones
01758 740296
janetcoron@hotmail.co.uk

Delia Lanceley
01286 650517
delia@lanceley.com

Kay Laurie
07971 083361
kay.laurie@ngs.org.uk

Sue Macdonald
sue.macdonald@ngs.org.uk

f @gwyneddandangleseyngs

OPENING DATES

All entries subject to change. For latest information check **www.ngs.org.uk**
Map locator numbers are shown to the right of each garden name.

April

Saturday 23rd
Llanidan Hall — 10

Sunday 24th
Maenan Hall — 12

Wednesday 27th
◆ Plas Cadnant Hidden Gardens — 16

May

Sunday 1st
Gilfach — 6

Saturday 14th
Glan Llyn — 7
Mynydd Heulog — 13

Sunday 15th
◆ Gardd y Coleg — 5
Mynydd Heulog — 13

Saturday 21st
Ty Capel Ffrwd — 20

Sunday 22nd
Bryn Gwern — 1
Ty Capel Ffrwd — 20

Saturday 28th
Gwaelod Mawr — 8

Sunday 29th
Gwaelod Mawr — 8
Llys-y-Gwynt — 11

June

Saturday 4th
Cae Newydd — 2

Sunday 5th
Cae Newydd — 2
Gilfach — 6
◆ Pensychnant — 15

Sunday 12th
Ty Cadfan Sant — 19

Llanidan Hall

Saturday 18th
Crowrach Isaf — 4

Sunday 19th
Crowrach Isaf — 4

Saturday 25th
Llanidan Hall — 10

Sunday 26th
Gwyndy Bach — 9

July

Saturday 2nd
NEW Penrallt — 14

Sunday 3rd
NEW Penrallt — 14

Saturday 9th
NEW Cae Rhydau — 3
Llanidan Hall — 10

Sunday 10th
Bryn Gwern — 1
NEW Cae Rhydau — 3

Sunday 17th
◆ Pensychnant — 15

Sunday 24th
Maenan Hall — 12

August

Sunday 7th
Cae Newydd — 2

Sunday 14th
41 Victoria Drive — 21

September

Saturday 10th
Treborth Botanic Garden, Bangor University — 18

Sunday 18th
◆ Gardd y Coleg — 5

Sunday 25th
Llys-y-Gwynt — 11

By Arrangement

Arrange a personalised garden visit with your club, or group of friends, on a date to suit you. See individual garden entries for full details.

Crowrach Isaf — 4
Gilfach — 6
Llanidan Hall — 10
Llys-y-Gwynt — 11
Mynydd Heulog — 13
Ty Capel Ffrwd — 20

The National Garden Scheme searches the length and breadth of England, Channel Islands, Northern Ireland and Wales for the very best private gardens

THE GARDENS

1 BRYN GWERN
Llanfachreth, Dolgellau, LL40 2DH.
H O Nurse. *5m NE of Dolgellau. Do not go to Llanfachreth, stay on Bala rd, A 494, 5m from Dolgellau, 14m from Bala, look for NGS signs.* Sun 22 May (10-5), open nearby Ty Capel Ffrwd. Sun 10 July (10-5). Adm £5, chd free. Cream teas.
Sloping 2 acre garden in the hills overlooking Dolgellau with views to Cader Idris, originally wooded but redesigned to enhance its natural features with streams, ponds and imaginative and extensive planting and vibrant colour. The garden is now a haven for wildlife with hedgehogs and 26 species of birds feeding last winter as well as being home to ducks, dogs and cats. Dogs must be on a lead.

2 CAE NEWYDD
Rhosgoch, Anglesey, LL66 0BG.
Hazel & Nigel Bond. *3m SW of Amlwch. A5025 from Benllech to Amlwch, follow signs for leisure centre & Lastra Farm. Follow yellow NGS signs (approx 3m), car park on L.* Sat 4, Sun 5 June, Sun 7 Aug (11-4). Adm £5, chd free. Light refreshments.
A mature country garden of 2½ acres which blends seamlessly into the open landscape with stunning views of Snowdonia and Llyn Alaw. Variety of shrubs, trees and herbaceous areas, large wildlife pond, polytunnel, greenhouses, raised beds. Collections of fuchsia, pelargonium, cacti and succulents. An emphasis on gardening for wildlife throughout the garden. Hay meadow. Lots of seating throughout the garden, visitors are welcome to bring a picnic. Garden area closest to house suitable for wheelchairs.

3 NEW CAE RHYDAU
Caeathro, Caernarfon, LL55 2TN.
Ms Lieneke van der Veen & Mr Victor van Daal. *4m E of Caernarfon. Take A4086 from Caernarfon to Llanberis. After narrow bridge take R to Bontnewydd & then immed L. Follow signs Lieneke's Flowers. Take the 2nd track on R.* Sat 9, Sun 10 July (11-4.30). Adm £4, chd free. Home-made teas.

A Dutch couple started in 2000 redesigning the gardens of a 14 acre smallholding, formerly a dairy mill. 1 acre garden and a vegetable garden is accessed along an 800 metres track (partly public) footpath. The land is bordered on one side by a stream. Very peaceful and rural.

4 CROWRACH ISAF
Bwlchtocyn, LL53 7BY. Margaret & Graham Cook, 01758 712860, crowrach_isaf@hotmail.com.
1½m SW of Abersoch. Follow road through Abersoch & Sarn Bach, L at sign for Bwlchtocyn for ½m until junction & no-through road sign. Turn R, parking 50 metres on R. Sat 18, Sun 19 June (1.30-4). Adm £5, chd free. Cream teas. Visits also by arrangement June to Sept for groups of 10+.
2 acre plot developed from 2000, inc island beds, windbreak hedges, vegetable garden, wildflower area and wide range of geraniums, unusual shrubs and herbaceous perennials. Views over Cardigan Bay and Snowdonia. Grass and gravel paths, some gentle slopes. Parking at garden for disabled visitors.

5 ◆ GARDD Y COLEG
Carmel, LL54 7RL. Pwyllgor Pentref Carmel Village Committee. *Garden at Carmel village centre. Parking on site.* For NGS: Sun 15 May, Sun 18 Sept (11-3). Adm £3, chd free. Light refreshments.
Approx ½ acre featuring raised beds planted with ornamental and native plants mulched with local slate. Benches and picnic area, wide pathways suitable for wheelchairs. Spectacular views. Garden created and maintained by volunteers. Development of the garden is ongoing. Ramped access.

6 GILFACH
Rowen, Conwy, LL32 8TS.
James & Isoline Greenhalgh, 01492 650216, isolinegreenhalgh@btinternet.com. *4m S of Conwy. At Xrds 100yds E of Rowen S towards Llanrwst, past Rowen School on L, turn up 2nd drive on L.* Sun 1 May, Sun 5 June (2-5.30). Adm £4, chd free. Home-made teas. Visits also by arrangement Apr to Aug.
1 acre country garden on south facing slope with magnificent views of the

River Conwy and mountains; set in 35 acres of farm and woodland. Collection of mature shrubs is added to yearly; woodland garden, herbaceous border and small pool. Spectacular panoramic view of the Conwy Valley and the mountain range of the Carneddau. Classic cars. Large coaches can park at bottom of steep drive, disabled visitors can be driven to garden by the owner.

7 GLAN LLYN
Llanberis, Caernarfon, LL55 4EL.
Mr Bob Stevens. *On A4086, ½m from Llanberis village. Next door to the Galty-Glyn Hotel (Pizza & Pint Restaurant) opp DMM factory.* Sat 14 May (11-6). Adm £4, chd free. Tea.
A 3 acre woodland edge garden inc 2 acres of woodland, wildlife ponds, stream, wildflower area, raised sphagnum bog garden, two green roofs, three glasshouses for cacti and succulents, Australasian and South African beds, sand bed, many unusual trees, shrubs and herbaceous perennials. The garden is on fairly steep sloping ground, no wheelchair access to the woodland.

8 GWAELOD MAWR
Caergeiliog, Anglesey, LL65 3YL.
Tricia Coates. *6m E of Holyhead. ½m E of Caergeiliog. From A55 J4. r'about 2nd exit signed Caergeiliog. 300yds, Gwaelod Mawr is 1st house on L.* Sat 28, Sun 29 May (11-4). Adm £5, chd free. Light refreshments.
2 acre garden created by owner over 20 yrs with lake, large rock outcrops and palm tree area. Spanish style patio and laburnum arch lead to sunken garden and wooden bridge over lily pond with fountain and waterfall. Peaceful Chinese orientated garden offering contemplation. Separate Koi carp pond. Abundant seating throughout. Mainly flat, with gravel and stone paths, no wheelchair access to sunken lily pond area.

Mynydd Heulog

9 GWYNDY BACH

Llandrygarn, Tynlon, Anglesey, LL65 3AJ. Keith & Rosa Andrew. *5m W of Llangefni. From Llangefni take B5109 towards Bodedern, cottage exactly 5m out on L. Postcode good for SatNav.* **Sun 26 June (11-4.30). Adm £4, chd free. Home-made teas.**
¾ acre artist's garden, set amidst rugged Anglesey landscape. Romantically planted in informal intimate rooms with interesting rare plants and shrubs, box and yew topiary, old roses and Japanese garden with large Koi pond (deep water, children must be supervised). Gravel entrance to garden.

& 🚌 ♨

10 LLANIDAN HALL

Brynsiencyn, LL61 6HJ. Mr J W Beverley (Head Gardener), 07759 305085, work.beverley@btinternet.com. *5m E of Llanfair Pwll. From Llanfair PG follow A4080 towards Brynsiencyn for 4m. After Hooton's farm shop on R take next L, follow lane to gardens.* **Sat 23 Apr, Sat 25 June, Sat 9 July (10-4). Adm £4, chd free. Refreshments (weather dependant) are served outside. Visits also by arrangement Mar to Sept. Donation to CAFOD.**
Walled garden of 1¾ acres. Physic and herb gardens, ornamental vegetable garden, herbaceous borders, water features and many varieties of old roses. Sheep, rabbits and hens to see. Children must be kept under supervision. Well behaved dogs on leads welcome. Llanidan Church will be open for viewing. Hard gravel paths, gentle slopes.

& 🐐 ♨

Around 1,050 people living with Parkinson's - and their families - have been helped by Parkinson's nurses thanks to funding from the National Garden Scheme

11 LLYS-Y-GWYNT

Pentir Road, Llandygai, Bangor, LL57 4BG. Jennifer Rickards & John Evans, 01248 353863, mjrickards@gmail.com. *3m S of Bangor. 300yds from Llandygai r'about at J11, A5 & A55, just off A4244. Follow signs for services (Gwasanaethau). Turn off at No Through Rd sign, 50yds beyond. Do not use SatNav.* **Sun 29 May, Sun 25 Sept (11-4). Adm £5, chd free. Home-made teas. Visits also by arrangement Feb to Nov. By arrangement price includes tea, coffee, biscuits.**
Interesting, harmonious and very varied 2 acre garden inc magnificent views of Snowdonia. An exposed site inc Bronze Age burial cairn. Winding paths and varied levels planted to create shelter, year-round interest, microclimates and varied rooms. Ponds, waterfall, bridge and other features use local materials and craftspeople. Wildlife encouraged, well organised compost. Good family garden. Share with us the joy of gardening in old age.

& ❄ 🚌 ♨))

12 MAENAN HALL

Maenan, Llanrwst, LL26 0UL. The Hon Mr & Mrs Christopher Mclaren. *2m N of Llanrwst. On E side of A470, ¼m S of Maenan Abbey Hotel.* **Sun 24 Apr, Sun 24 July (10.30-4.30). Adm £5, chd free. Light refreshments. Donation to Ogwen Valley Mountain Rescue Organisation.**
A superbly beautiful 4 hectares on the slopes of the Conwy Valley, with dramatic views of Snowdonia, set amongst mature hardwoods. Both the upper part, with sweeping lawns, ornamental ponds and retaining walls, and the bluebell carpeted woodland dell contain copious specimen shrubs and trees, many originating at Bodnant. Magnolias, rhododendrons, camellias, pieris, cherries and hydrangeas, amongst many others, make a breathtaking display. Upper part of garden accessible but with fairly steep slopes.

& 🐐 ❄ ♨ 🎪

13 MYNYDD HEULOG

Llithfaen, Pwllheli, LL53 6PA. Mrs Christine Jackson, 01758 750400, christine.jackson007@btinternet. com. *From A499 take B4417 road at r'about signed Nefyn, approx 3m enter Llithfaen, 1st R turn opp chapel. Follow NGS signs, garden*

last property on R, limited parking. **Sat 14, Sun 15 May (10-4). Adm £3.50, chd free. Cream teas. Visits also by arrangement Apr to July. Donation to Dog's Trust.**
Mynydd Heulog is an C18 stone cottage set in approx 1 acre of sloping garden with amazing views over the Lleyn and Cardigan Bay. Gradually being developed over 25 years, the garden is now an eclectic mix of mature trees, shrubs, perennials and exotics. Features inc arches, statues, bridges, summerhouse and shepherds hut. Large terrace and veranda with views and secret seating areas. Narrow paths.

& 🐐 🚌 ♨

14 NEW PENRALLT

Bron Y Llan Road, Llysfaen, Colwyn Bay, LL29 8TP. Mrs Louise Henson. *2m SE of Colwyn Bay. No parking at the garden, parking available at the top of Bron y Llan in the Mynydd Marian Nature Reserve car park, 5 min walk to Penrallt from there.* **Sat 2, Sun 3 July (11-4). Adm £5, chd free. Home-made cakes, scones, teas, coffees and cold drinks.**
Penrallt sits on an elevated position within the Mynydd Marian nature reserve with far reaching views across Snowdonia National Park. The garden is just under ½ acre and divided up in to smaller areas and inc herbaceous, shady, exotic, Japanese, patio and vegetable gardens. Flat and paved wheelchair access to the lower tiers of garden and refreshment area only.

& ❄ ♨

15 ◆ PENSYCHNANT

Sychnant Pass, Conwy, LL32 8BJ. Pensychnant Foundation; Warden Julian Thompson, 01492 592595, jpt.pensychnant@btinternet.com, www.pensychnant.co.uk. *2½m W of Conwy at top of Sychnant Pass. From Conwy: L at Lancaster Sq. into Upper Gate St; after 2½m, Pensychnant's drive signed on R. From Penmaenmawr: fork R by shops, up Sychnant Pass; after walls at top of Pass, U turn L into drive.* **For NGS: Sun 5 June, Sun 17 July (11-5). Adm £3.50, chd free. Home-made teas & FairTrade cakes. For other opening times and information, please phone, email or visit garden website.**
Wildlife Garden. Diverse herbaceous cottage garden borders surrounded by mature shrubs, banks of rhododendrons, ancient and Victorian woodlands. 12 acre woodland walks

with views of Conwy Mountain and Sychnant. Woodland birds. Picnic tables, archaelogical trail on mountain. A peaceful little gem. Large Victorian Arts and Crafts house (open) with art exhibition. Partial wheelchair access, please phone for advice.

16 ◆ **PLAS CADNANT HIDDEN GARDENS**
Cadnant Road, Menai Bridge, LL59 5NH. Mr Anthony Tavernor, 01248 717174, plascadnantgardens@gmail.com, www.plascadnantgardens.co.uk. *½ m E of Menai Bridge. Take A545 & leave Menai Bridge heading for Beaumaris, then follow brown tourist information signs. SatNav not always reliable.* **For NGS: Wed 27 Apr (12-5). Adm £9, chd free. Light refreshments in traditional Tea Room. For other opening times and information, please phone, email or visit garden website. Donation to Wales Air Ambulance; Anglesey Red Squirrel Trust; Menai Bridge Community Heritage Trust.**
Early C19 picturesque garden undergoing restoration since 1996. Valley gardens with waterfalls, large ornamental walled garden, woodland and early pit house. Also Alpheus water feature and Ceunant (Ravine) which gives visitors a more interesting walk featuring unusual moisture loving Alpines. Restored area following flood damage. Guidebook available. Visitor centre open. Partial wheelchair access to parts of gardens. Some steps, gravel paths, slopes. Access statement available. Accessible Tea Room and WC.

18 **TREBORTH BOTANIC GARDEN, BANGOR UNIVERSITY**
Treborth, Bangor, LL57 2RQ. Natalie Chivers, treborth.bangor.ac.uk. *On the outskirts of Bangor towards Anglesey. Approach Menai Bridge either from Upper Bangor on A5 or leave A55 J9 & travel towards Bangor for 2m. At Antelope Inn r'bout turn L just before entering Menai Bridge.* **Sat 10 Sept (10-1). Adm £4, chd free. Home-made teas inc vegan and gluten free options.**
Owned by Bangor University and used as a resource for teaching, research, public education and enjoyment. Treborth comprises

planted borders, species rich natural grassland, ponds, arboretum, Chinese garden, ancient woodland, and a rocky shoreline habitat. Six glasshouses provide specialised environments for tropical, temperate, orchid and carnivorous plant collections. Partnered with National Botanic Garden of Wales to champion Welsh horticulture, protect wildlife and extol the virtues of growing plants for food, fun, health and wellbeing. Glasshouse and garden Q&As. Wheelchair access to some glasshouses and part of the garden. Woodland path is surfaced but most of the borders only accessed over grass.

19 **TY CADFAN SANT**
National Street, Tywyn, LL36 9DD. Mrs Katie Pearce. *A493 going S & W. L into one way, garden ahead. Bear R, parking 2nd L. A493 going N, 1st R in 30mph zone, L at bottom by garden, parking 2nd L.* **Sun 12 June (9.30-4.30). Adm £5, chd free. Cream teas.**
Large eco friendly garden. In the front, shrubbery, mixed flower beds and roses surround a mature copper beech. Up six steps the largely productive back garden has an apiary in the orchard, fruit, vegetables, flowers and a polytunnel, plenty of seating. Special diets catered for. Seasonal produce, honey, plants and crafts. Partial wheelchair access due to steps to rear garden.

20 **TY CAPEL FFRWD**
Llanfachreth, Dolgellau, LL40 2NR. Revs Mary & George Bolt, 01341 422006, maryboltminstrel@gmail.com. *4m NE of Dolgellau, 18m SW of Bala. From Dolgellau 4m up hill to Llanfachreth. Turn L at War Memorial. Follow lane ½ m to chapel on R. Park & walk down lane past chapel to cottage.* **Sat 21, Sun 22 May (12-5.30). Adm £4, chd free. Home-made teas. Visits also by arrangement May to Sept for groups of up to 15. Individuals welcome.**
True cottage garden in Welsh mountains. Azaleas, rhododendrons, acers; large collection of aquilegia. Many different hostas give added strength to spring bulbs and corms. Stream flowing through the garden, 10ft waterfall and on through a small woodland bluebell carpet. For

summer visitors there is a continuous show of colour with herbaceous plants, roses, clematis and lilies, inc Cardiocrinum giganteum. Harp will be played in the garden.

21 **41 VICTORIA DRIVE**
Llandudno Junction, LL31 9PF. Allan & Eirwen Evans. *A55 J18. From Bangor 1st exit, from Colwyn Bay 2nd exit, A546 to Conwy. Next r'about 3rd exit then 1st L.* **Sun 14 Aug (1.30-4.30). Adm £4, chd free. Home-made teas.**
A very interesting small urban garden, offering so many creative ideas inc growing sweet peas and dahlias in a small garden. Come along to see the large selection of bedding plants shrubs and herbaceous plants. Great hosts with a lovely tea and cake stall.

You can make a difference! Join our Great British Garden Party fundraising campaign and raise money for some of the best-loved nursing and health charities. Visit ngs. org.uk/gardenparty to find out how you can get involved

Glan Llyn

NORTH EAST WALES

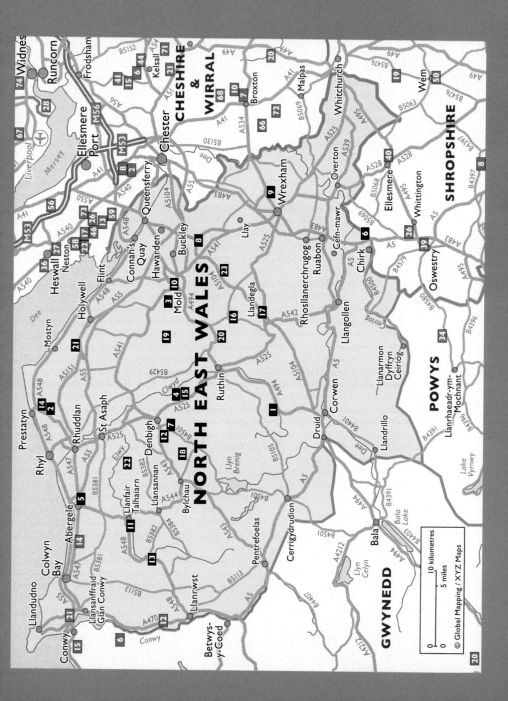

With its diversity of countryside from magnificent hills, seaside vistas and rolling farmland, North East Wales offers a wide range of gardening experiences.

Our gardens offer a wealth of designs and come in all shapes and sizes, ranging from large old parks offering a good walk, to the compact town gardens. Visitors will have something to see from the frost-filled days of February through till the magnificent colourful days of autumn.

The majority of our gardens are within easy reach of North West England, and being a popular tourist destination make an excellent day out for all the family.

Come and enjoy the beauty and the variety of the gardens of North East Wales with the added bonus of a delicious cup of tea and a slice of cake. Our garden owners await your visit.

Volunteers

County Organiser
Jane Moore
07769 046317
jane.moore@ngs.org.uk

County Treasurer
Iris Dobbie
01745 886730
iris.dobbie@ngs.org.uk

Booklet Co-ordinator
Position vacant
Please email hello@ngs.org.uk
for details

Assistant County Organisers
Fiona Bell
07813 087797
bell_fab@hotmail.com

Kate Bunning
01978 262855
kate.bunning@ngs.org.uk

Lesley Callister
01824 705444
lesley.callister@ngs.org.uk

Anne Lewis
01352 757044
anne.lewis@ngs.org.uk

Pat Pearson
01745 813613
pat.pearson@ngs.org.uk

Helen Robertson
01978 790666
helen.robertson@ngs.org.uk

Left: Fron Haul

OPENING DATES

All entries subject to change. For latest information check www.ngs.org.uk
Map locator numbers are shown to the right of each garden name.

February

Snowdrop Festival

Wednesday 9th
Aberclwyd Manor   1

Wednesday 23rd
Aberclwyd Manor   1

March

Wednesday 9th
Aberclwyd Manor   1

Wednesday 23rd
Aberclwyd Manor   1

April

Wednesday 6th
Aberclwyd Manor   1

Wednesday 20th
Aberclwyd Manor   1

May

Wednesday 4th
Aberclwyd Manor   1

Wednesday 18th
Aberclwyd Manor   1

Thursday 26th
Brynkinalt Hall   6

June

Wednesday 1st
Aberclwyd Manor   1
NEW Plas Newydd   19

Thursday 2nd
Garthewin   11

Saturday 4th
Hafodunos Hall   13
The Laundry   15

Sunday 5th
The Laundry   15

Wednesday 8th
NEW Plas Newydd   19

Saturday 11th
Bryn Dyfnog   4

Sunday 12th
Bryn Dyfnog   4

Wednesday 15th
Aberclwyd Manor   1
NEW Plas Newydd   19

Sunday 19th
Gwaenynog   12

Wednesday 22nd
NEW Plas Newydd   19

Sunday 26th
NEW Mysevin   18

Wednesday 29th
Aberclwyd Manor   1
NEW Plas Newydd   19

July

Sunday 3rd
Tal-y-Bryn Farm   22

Saturday 9th
Llanarmon-yn-Ial Village Gardens   16

Wednesday 13th
Aberclwyd Manor   1

Sunday 17th
NEW Llandegla Village Gardens   17

Wednesday 27th
Aberclwyd Manor   1

August

Wednesday 10th
Aberclwyd Manor   1

Sunday 21st
Tyn Rhos   23

Wednesday 24th
Aberclwyd Manor   1

September

Wednesday 7th
Aberclwyd Manor   1

Thursday 8th
Brynkinalt Hall   6

Sunday 11th
◆ Erlas Victorian Walled Garden   9

Wednesday 21st
Aberclwyd Manor   1

Saturday 24th
The Laundry   15

Sunday 25th
The Laundry   15

By Arrangement

Arrange a personalised garden visit with your club, or group of friends, on a date to suit you. See individual garden entries for full details.

Aberclwyd Manor	1
5 Birch Grove	2
Bryn Bellan	3
33 Bryn Twr and Lynton	5
Dolhyfryd	7
Dove Cottage	8
NEW Fron Haul	10
Garthewin	11
The Laundry	15
NEW Plas Newydd	19
Plas Y Nant	20
Saith Ffynnon Farm	21
Tal-y-Bryn Farm	22

Brynkinalt Hall

National Garden Scheme gardens are identified by their yellow road signs and posters. You can expect a garden of quality, character and interest, a warm welcome and plenty of home-made cakes!

THE GARDENS

Mysevin

1 ABERCLWYD MANOR

Derwen, Corwen, LL21 9SF.
Miss Irene Brown & Mr G
Sparvoli, 01824 750431,
irene662010@live.com. *7m from
Ruthin. Travelling on A494 from Ruthin
to Corwen. At Bryn SM Service
Station turn R, follow sign to Derwen.
Aberclwyd gates on L before Derwen.
Do not follow SatNav directions* **Wed
9, Wed 23 Feb, Wed 9, Wed 23 Mar,
Wed 6, Wed 20 Apr, Wed 4, Wed 18
May, Wed 1, Wed 15, Wed 29 June,
Wed 13, Wed 27 July, Wed 10, Wed
24 Aug, Wed 7, Wed 21 Sept (10-4).
Adm £4, chd free. Cream teas.
Visits also by arrangement Feb to
Sept for groups of 10 to 30.**
4 acre garden on a sloping hillside
overlooking the Upper Clwyd Valley.
The garden has many mature trees
underplanted with snowdrops, fritillaries
and cyclamen. An Italianate garden
of box hedging lies below the house
and shrubs, ponds, perennials, roses
and an orchard are also to be enjoyed
within this cleverly structured area.
Mass of cyclamen in Sept. Abundance
of spring flowers. Cyclamen in August/
September. Snowdrops in February.
Scones, jam and cream and tea are
available. Mostly flat with some steps
and slopes.

2 5 BIRCH GROVE

Woodland Park, Prestatyn,
LL19 9RH. Mrs Iris
Dobbie, 01745 886730,
iris.dobbie@ngs.org.uk. *A547
from Rhuddlan turn up The Avenue,
Woodland Park after railway bridge
1st R into Calthorpe Dr, 1st L Birch
Gr. 10 mins walk from town centre
- at top of High St, turn R & L onto
The Avenue.* **Visits by arrangement
May to Sept for groups of 5 to 20.
Adm £4, chd free.**
The gardens consist of a variety
of borders inc woodland, grass,
herbaceous, alpine, shrub, drought,
tropical and a simulated bog garden
with a small pond. The more formal
front lawned garden has borders
of mixed colourful planting and box
balls. A small greenhouse is fully
used for propagation. Gravel drive
with few steps. Plenty of parking and
not far from the beach, Offa's Dyke,
town centre. A variety of borders and
planting.

✿

3 BRYN BELLAN

Bryn Road, Gwernaffield,
CH7 5DE. Gabrielle Armstrong
& Trevor Ruddle, 01352 741806,
gabrielle@indigoawnings.co.uk.
*2m W of Mold. Leave A541 at Mold
on Gwernaffield Rd (Dreflan), ½ m
after Mold derestriction signs turn
R to Rhydymwyn & Llynypandy.
Bryn Bellan is 300yds along on R.
Parking is available in courtyard.*
**Visits by arrangement Apr to Sept
for groups of 10+. Adm £7, chd
free. Light refreshments. Please
discuss refreshments when
making arrangements to visit.**
A tranquil, elegant garden, perfect
for morning coffee, afternoon tea or
evening glass of wine with nibbles.
A partly walled upper garden with
circular sunken lawn featuring a
Sequoia and white and green themed
mixed borders. The lower garden
has an ornamental cutting garden,
two perennial borders, an orchard
and bijou potting shed. spring bulbs,
iris, peonies, roses, hydrangeas and
cyclamen. A very photogenic garden,
pre shoot visits and shoots by
appointment. Some gravel paths.

4 BRYN DYFNOG

Llanrhaeadr, Denbigh, LL16 4NL.
Clare & Richard Argent. *3m S of
Denbigh. 5m N of Ruthin. Take A525
from Denbigh or Ruthin. Follow signs
at Llanrhaeadr.* **Sat 11, Sun 12 June
(12-5). Adm £4, chd free. Home-
made teas.**

Beautiful gardens, approx ⅔ of
an acre, with some steps. Winding
paths leading to hidden corners, lots
of seating areas and a gazebo and
summerhouse with beautiful views
of the Clwydian Hills. Feature trees
inc many acers. There is a mature
Woodland front garden, A secret
garden, Japanese planting, wild
flowers, ponds and a wildlife stream,
lawns and mature shrubs. Front
gardens are accessible, many steps
in the back garden.

5 33 BRYN TWR AND LYNTON

Lynton, Highfield Park, Abergele,
LL22 7AU. Mr & Mrs Colin
Knowlson & Bryn Roberts & Emma
Knowlson-Roberts, 07712 623836,
apk@slaters.ltd. *From A55 heading
W take slip road into Abergele town
centre. Turn L at 2nd set of T-lights
signed Llanfair TH, 3rd road on L.
For SatNav use LL22 8DD.* **Visits by
arrangement June to Aug. Adm £5,
chd free. Home-made teas.**
Bryn Twr is a family garden with
chickens, shrubs, roses, pots and
lawn. Lynton completely different,
intense cottage style garden:
vegetables, trees, shrub, roses,
ornamental grasses and lots of
pots. Garage with interesting fire
engine; classic cars and memorabilia;
greenhouse over large water capture
system that was part of an old
swimming pool.

6 BRYNKINALT HALL
Brynkinalt, Chirk, Wrexham, LL14 5NS. Iain & Kate Hill-Trevor, www.brynkinalt.co.uk. 6m N of Oswestry, 10m S of Wrexham. Come off A5/A483 & take B5070 into Chirk village. Turn into Trevor Rd (beside St Mary's Church). Continue past houses on R. Turn R on bend into Estate Gates. N.B. Do not use postcode with SatNav. Thur 26 May, Thur 8 Sept (11-4.30). Adm £5, chd free. Home-made teas.
5 acre ornamental woodland shrubbery, overgrown until recently, now cleared and replanted, rhododendron walk, historic ponds, well, grottos, ha-ha and battlements, new stumpery, ancient redwoods and yews. Also 2 acre garden beside Grade II* house (see website for opening), with modern rose and formal beds, deep herbaceous borders, pond with shrub/mixed beds, pleached limes and hedge patterns. Home of the first Duke of Wellington's grandmother and Sir John Trevor, Speaker of House of Commons. Stunning rhododendrons and formal West Garden.

🚻 🐕 🚗 ☕))

7 DOLHYFRYD
Lawnt, Denbigh, LL16 4SU. Captain & Mrs Michael Cunningham, 01745 814805, virginia@dolhyfryd.com. 1m SW of Denbigh. On B4501 to Nantglyn, from Denbigh - 1m from town centre. Visits by arrangement Jan to Oct for groups of up to 50. Adm £6, chd free. Light refreshments.
Established garden set in small valley of River Ystrad. Acres of crocuses in late Feb/early Mar. Paths through wildflower meadows and woodland of magnificent trees, shade loving plants and azaleas; mixed borders; walled kitchen garden. Many woodland and riverside birds, inc dippers, kingfishers, grey wagtails. Many species of butterfly encouraged by new planting. Much winter interest, exceptional display of crocuses. Gravel paths, some steep slopes.

🚻 🐕 ☕ 🧺 🎪

8 DOVE COTTAGE
Rhos Road, Penyffordd, Chester, CH4 0JR. Chris & Denise Wallis, 01244 547539, dovecottage@supanet.com. 6m SW of Chester. Leave A55 at J35 take A550 to Wrexham. Drive 2m, turn R from A541 Wrexham/Mold Rd in Pontblyddyn take A5104 to Chester. Garden opp train stn. Visits by arrangement July & Aug for groups of 5 to 30. Adm £4, chd free. Tea.
Approx 1½ acre garden, shrubs and herbaceous plants set informally around lawns. Established vegetable area, two ponds (one wildlife), summerhouse and woodland planted area. Raised board walk. Gravel paths.

🚻 ❀ 🚗 🛏 ☕ 💷

5 Birch Grove

9 ♦ ERLAS VICTORIAN WALLED GARDEN
Bryn Estyn Road, Wrexham, LL13 9TY. Erlas Victorian Walled Garden, 01978 265058, info@erlas.org, www.erlas.org. *From A483 follow signs for the Wrexham Ind Est. From A5156 follow signs to Wrexham on A534 (Holt Rd). At 2nd r'about on Holt Rd take 1st L on to Brynestyn Rd, for ½ m.* **For NGS: Sun 11 Sept (10.30-3.30). Adm £4, chd free. Light refreshments. For other opening times and information, please phone, email or visit garden website.** Home of the Erlas Victorian Walled Garden charity, this is a place of work, solace and inspiration for adults of all abilities. A garden of four parts: The Walled Garden has many delights inc a centuries-old mulberry tree; The West Garden is full of fruit, vegetables, herbs and our Roundhouse; The Orchard has a mixture of Apple and Pear varieties. Our ecology area is a haven for flora and fauna. We have wheelchair access throughout the garden, however it is on a slope, but the gradient is not too extreme.

  👌 🐃 🌼 ☕

10 NEW FRON HAUL
Denbigh Road, Mold, CH7 1BL. Mr David & Mrs Hilary Preece, 07966 080032, dglynnep@gmail.com. *We are a Yellow house, opp the entrance to Bailey Hill. If using SatNav it is better to input 'Shire View, Mold' rather than the postcode.* **Visits by arrangement Apr to Sept for groups of up to 15. Adm £4, chd free. Light refreshments.** A garden of approximately ½ acre, laid out around 1870, possibly under Edward Kemp's guidance. The general lay out and some original features remain. It comprises herbaceous borders, a small orchard, lawns and a Wisteria covered walkway. There is also a wooded area with a number of old yew trees. Disabled parking available, please phone first. Access to garden via terraced area, some paths are uneven.

  👌 🐃 🌼 ☕

11 GARTHEWIN
Llanfairtalhaiarn, LL22 8YR. Mr Michael Grime, 01745 720288, michaelgrime12@btinternet.com. *6m S of Abergele & A55. From Abergele take A548 to Llanfair TH & Llanrwst. Entrance to Garthewin 300yds W of Llanfair TH on A548 to Llanrwst. SatNav misleading.* **Thur 2 June (2-6). Adm £5, chd free. Home-made teas.** Visits also by arrangement Apr to Nov for groups of up to 30. Valley garden with ponds and woodland areas. Much of the 8 acres have been reclaimed and redesigned providing a younger garden with a great variety of azaleas, rhododendrons and young trees, all within a framework of mature shrubs and trees. Teas in old theatre. Chapel open.

  🐃 ☕

12 GWAENYNOG
Denbigh, LL16 5NU. Major & Mrs Tom Smith. *1m W of Denbigh. On A543, Lodge on L, ¼ m drive.* **Sun 19 June (2-5.30). Adm £5, chd free. Cream teas.** 2 acres inc the restored walled garden where Beatrix Potter wrote and illustrated the Tale of the Flopsy Bunnies. Also a small exhibition of some of her work. C16 house (not open) visited by Dr Samuel Johnson during his Tour of Wales. Herbaceous borders some recently replanted, espalier fruit trees, rose pergola and vegetable area. Grass paths.

  👌 🌼 ☕

13 HAFODUNOS HALL
Llangernyw, Abergele, Conwy, LL22 8TY. Dr Richard Wood, www.hafodunoshall.co.uk. *1m W of Llangernyw. ½ way between Abergele & Llanrwst on A548. Signed from opp Old Stag Public House. Parking available on site.* **Sat 4 June (12-5). Adm £5, chd free. Light refreshments in Victorian conservatory.** Historic garden undergoing restoration after 30 years of neglect surrounds a Sir George Gilbert Scott Grade I listed Hall, derelict after arson attack. Unique setting. ½ m tree-lined drive, formal terraces, woodland walks with ancient redwoods, laurels, yews, lake, streams, waterfalls and a gorge. Wonderful rhododendrons. Uneven paths, steep steps. Children must have adult supervision. Most areas around the hall accessible to wheelchairs by gravel pathways. Some gardens are set on slopes.

  👌 🐃 🌼 🚗 ☕ 🪑))

15 THE LAUNDRY
Llanrhaeadr, Denbigh, LL16 4NL. Mr & Mrs T Williams, 01745 890515, hello@thelaundryretreat.co.uk, thelaundryretreat.co.uk. *3m SE of Denbigh. Entrance off A525 Denbigh to Ruthin Rd.* **Sat 4, Sun 5 June (2-6); Sat 24, Sun 25 Sept (12-4). Adm £6, chd free. Home-made teas.** Visits also by arrangement May to Oct for groups of 10 to 40. Terraced courtyard garden developed since 2009 surrounded by old stone walls enclosing cottage style planting and formal hedging. 9 years ago work started on the old kitchen walled garden with a view to incorporating it within the whole garden plan. A chance to see a new garden evolving within an old setting. Woodland walk, roses, pleached limes, peonies and herbaceous planting. Some deep gravel areas, may prove difficult for wheelchair users.

  👌 🌼 🚗 🚌 ☕ 🪑))

You can make a difference! Join our Great British Garden Party fundraising campaign and raise money for some of the best-loved nursing and health charities. Visit ngs.org.uk/gardenparty to find out how you can get involved

GROUP OPENING

16 LLANARMON-YN-IAL VILLAGE GARDENS

Ffordd Rhiw Ial, Llanarmon-Yn-Ial, Mold, CH7 4QE. *6m S of Mold. From Mold/Ruthin Rd (A494) turn into B5430. After 2m turn R to B5431to Llanarmon. From A525 & A5104, join B5430 & turn L to Llanarmon. Drop off possible at Raven Inn then follow car park signs.* **Sat 9 July (11-4). Combined adm £6, chd free. Home-made teas at The Old Schoolroom behind St. Garmon's Church. Donation to Church of St Garmon.**

ARDWYN
Gill & Pete Hodson.

BRONALLT
Brenda & Tony Rigby.

CRUD-Y-GWYNT
Elaine & Gareth Jones.

NEW FIELDFARE
Peter & Vicky O'Neill.

NEW 5 MAES IAL
Viv Bennion.

12A MAES IAL
Beryl Campbell.

Enter Llanarmon-yn-Ial from the B5430 then drive over the ancient stone bridge, up the hill to The Old Schoolroom - Yr Hen Ysgoldy. Tickets and refreshments are available here and limited disabled parking. Tickets also available at the main car park. There is some parking in the village or follow signs for the main car park 350 yards out of the village on Llandegla Road. A map of the gardens is included with the ticket. The gardens are all close to the heart of the village. The people of Llanarmon-yn-Ial have been successfully running the Raven Inn and Village Shop as community ventures for many years now.

✿ ☕))

GROUP OPENING

17 NEW LLANDEGLA VILLAGE GARDENS

Llandegla, LL11 3AW. *Please follow NGS signs for parking in Llandegla village. Mini bus available from car park to take visitors to out-lying gardens.* **Sun 17 July (1-5). Combined adm £6, chd free. Home-made teas.**

BRYN EITHIN
Mr & Mrs A Fife.

NEW BRYNIAU MANOR
Mrs Hilary Berry.

THE GATE HOUSE, RUTHIN ROAD
Rod & Shelagh Williams.

6 MAES TEG
Martin & Norma Weston.

Llandegla is a small Welsh village on the banks of the River Alyn in North East Wales. Nestling below the Clwydian Hills, the village lies in an Area of Outstanding Natural Beauty. Our village gardens offer a wide variety of features such as colourful bedding, mature trees, shrubs and herbaceous borders, water features, orchards, vegetable and fruit plots. A number of the gardens have extensive views over the Clywdian Hills.

🐕 ✿ ☕ 🐾

18 NEW MYSEVIN

Nantglyn, Denbigh, LL16 5PG. Miss Alex Kerr-Wilson. *4½m SW of Denbigh. From Denbigh B4501 to Nantglyn. Mysevin entrance on R opp footpath sign. What3words app - stay.denoting.hips. Stone gate pillars to 8ft wide drive & bridge.* **Sun 26 June (2-5.30). Adm £5, chd free. Home-made teas.**

Situated on a wooded hillside over looking lawned gardens, a little rose garden, meadows, interesting herbaceous borders running down to the river Ystrad. To the rear of the house is a green bank inc white garden and ornamental woodland garden. The garden is the essence of peace and serenity, with rare plants and a shell house by Blott Kerr-Wilson. Some steps and gravel paths. Shell House by Blott Kerr- Wilson. Wheelchair access to front garden on gravel paths.

♿ ✿ ☕ 🐾

19 NEW PLAS NEWYDD

Pen Line Road, Cilcain, Mold, CH7 5NZ. Mrs Eileen Bigglestone, 01352 740082, plasnewydd.teagarden@mail.com. *Cilcain. If you enter Plas Newydd tea garden on Google maps, it will bring you directly to the garden or ask on booking.* **Every Wed 1 June to 29 June (11-5). Adm by donation. Home-made teas. Visits also by arrangement in June for groups of up to 8.**

Small country garden located

opposite Moel Famau with spectacular views and established herbaceous borders created over the last 15 years. It has been described by several of our tea garden customers as a hidden gem nestled amongst the Welsh Hills.

🐕 ☕

20 PLAS Y NANT

Llanbedr Dyffryn Clwyd, Ruthin, LL15 1YF. Lesley & Ian, 01824 705444, lesleycallister@icloud.com. *From A494 turn onto B5429 Graigfechan, approx 1m, 4th turning L private rd. If using SatNav follow postcode LL15 2YA. Proceed through farmyard continue & keep L, uphill to cottage on R, go straight onto forest track. Travel 0.8m on track, drive on R.* **Visits by arrangement Apr to Sept. Adm £4, chd free. Light refreshments. Refreshments to be discussed when booking.**

Listed Gothic Villa in a serene upland valley (AONB) amid seven acres of gardens, bluebell woods and stream. Rhododendrons, magnolia and specimen trees abound, formal parterre of clipped box and yew. Embryonic Dragon's Head rose garden and trelliage. Procession of seasonal colour led by snowdrops, primroses and daffodils. Other aspects inc water features, loggia, summer and greenhouses, beehives. Dragon Head carved into fallen tree trunk that has formed an archway over Ha-Ha.

☕

21 SAITH FFYNNON FARM

Downing Road, Whitford, Holywell, CH8 9EN. Mrs Jan Miller-Klein, 01352 711198, Jan@7wells.org, www.7wells.co.uk. *1m outside Whitford village. from Holywell follow signs for Pennant Park Golf Course. Turn R just past the Halfway House. Take 2nd lane on R (signed for Downing & Trout Farm) & Saith Ffynnon Farm is the 1st house on R.* **Visits by arrangement Sept & Oct for groups of 5 to 10. Adm £4, chd £2. Tea. Donation to Plant Heritage.**

Wildlife garden 1 acre and re-wilded meadows of 8 acres, inc ponds, woods, wildflower meadows, butterfly and bee gardens, Medieval herbal, natural dye garden and the Plant Heritage National Collection of Eupatorium. Garden at it's best early September - early October. Guided walks with the owner. Other displays may be possible depending

Tyn Rhos

on Covid restrictions at the time of opening. Hard surface from gate to patio and two sections of the garden. No wheelchair access on the damp meadows.

22 TAL-Y-BRYN FARM

Llannefydd, Denbigh, LL16 5DR. Mr & Mrs Gareth Roberts, 01745 540208, falmai@villagedairy.co.uk, www.villagedairy.co.uk. 3m W of Henllan. From Henllan take rd signed Llannefydd. After 2½m turn R signed Llaeth y Llan. Garden ½m on L. **Sun 3 July (2-5.30). Adm £5, chd free. Home-made teas. Visits also by arrangement Mar to Oct. Refreshments to be discussed at booking.**
Medium sized working farmhouse cottage garden. Ancient farm machinery. Incorporating ancient privy festooned with honeysuckle, clematis and roses. Terraced arches,

sunken garden pool and bog garden, fountains and old water pumps. Herb wheels, shrubs and other interesting features. Lovely views of the Clwydian range. Water feature, new rose tunnel, vegetable tunnel and small garden summerhouse.

23 TYN RHOS

Ffordd Y Rhos, Treuddyn, Mold, CH7 4NJ. Karen & Robert Waight. 4m S of Mold. On A541 at Pontblyddyn, turn onto A5104 toward Corwen. After 2.3m turn R onto Ffordd-y-Llan, signed for Treuddyn. After 0.4m turn L at Xrds onto Ffordd-y-Rhos. After 0.2m take farm track on R. **Sun 21 Aug (1-5). Adm £5, chd free. Home-made teas. Gluten free options available.**
1 acre garden, 2 acre wood (Waight's Wood), orchard, vegetable plot. Main garden planning by Jenny Hendy, laid to herbaceous planting, enhanced

during summer with homegrown annuals. Path winds past the natural pond, stream and under planting to the British woodland containing native bulbs, leading to paddocks and hives. Newly planted orchard contains Denbigh plum trees. A graveled yard and small steps (2 inch) need to be negotiated. For the intrepid wheelchair user the woodland walk is a possibility.

National Garden Scheme gardens are identified by their yellow road signs and posters. You can expect a garden of quality, character and interest, a warm welcome and plenty of home-made cakes!

POWYS

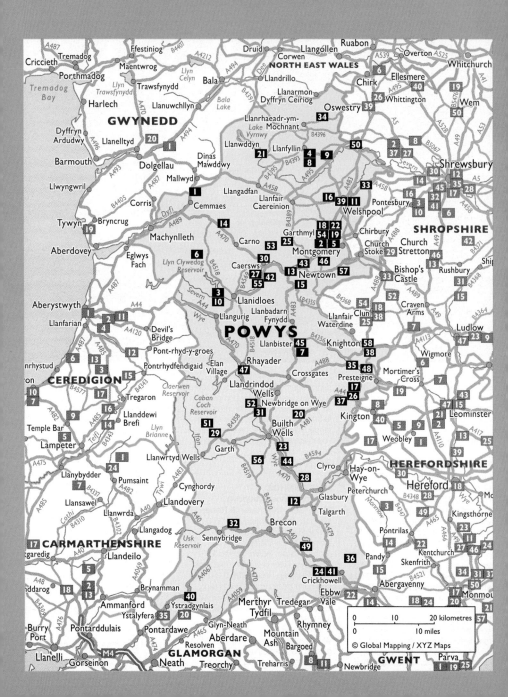

A three hour drive through Powys takes you through the spectacular and unspoilt landscape of Mid Wales, from the Berwyn Hills in the north to south of the Brecon Beacons.

Through the valleys and over the hills, beside rippling rivers and wooded ravines, you will see a lot of sheep, pretty market towns, half-timbered buildings and houses of stone hewn from the land.

The stunning landscape is home to many of the beautiful National Garden Scheme gardens of Powys. Gardens nestling in valleys, gardens high in the hills, wild-life gardens, riverside gardens, walled gardens, grand gardens, cottage gardens, gardens in picturesque villages, gardens in towns... they can all be found in Powys!

Here in Powys all is the spectacular, the unusual, the peaceful and the enchanting all opened by generous and welcoming garden owners.

Below: Lower Wernfigin Barns

Volunteers

North Powys County Organiser
Susan Paynton 01686 650531
susan.paynton@ngs.org.uk

County Treasurer
Jude Boutle 07702 061623
jude.boutle@ngs.org.uk

Publicity
Helen Anthony 07986 061051
helen.anthony@ngs.org.uk

Sue McKillop 07753 289701
sue.mckillop@ngs.org.uk

Social Media
Roo Nicholls 07989788640
roo.nicholls@ngs.org.uk

Nikki Trow 07958 958382
nikki.trow@ngs.org.uk

Booklet Co-ordinator
Liz childerley 07734 383510
liz.childerley@ngs.org.uk

Assistant County Organisers
Ann Thompson 07979 645489
ann.thompson@ngs.org.uk

South Powys County Organiser
Christine Carrow 01591 620461
christine.carrow@ngs.org.uk

County Treasurer
Steve Carrow 01591 620461
steve.carrow@ngs.org.uk

Publicity Officer
Gail Jones 07974 103692
gail.jones@ngs.org.uk

Assistant County Organisers
Bob & Andrea Deakin
01982 551718
bandeak@googlemail.com

f @powysngs
🐦 @PowysNGS
📷 @powysngs

OPENING DATES

All entries subject to change. For latest information check www.ngs.org.uk

Map locator numbers are shown to the right of each garden name.

Extended openings are shown at the beginning of each month

Evancoyd Court

© Miguel Flores Vianna

Brookside

THE GARDENS

GROUP OPENING

1 NEW **ABERANGELL VILLAGE GARDENS**
Aberangell, Aberangell, Machynlleth, SY20 9ND. *Just off A470 midway between Dolgellau & Machynlleth. From Mallwyd r'about to Cemmaes Rd turn R at Aberangell sign. From Machynlleth, come through Cemmaes & Cwm Llinau, turn L at Aberangell sign.* Sat 2, Sun 3 July (11-4). Combined adm £6, chd free. Home-made teas at Ger Y Llyn & Pen Pentre. WC facilities in village hall at top of village & Pen Pentre.

ABERANGELL, PEN PENTRE
Jacqueline Parsons.

NEW **BETHANIA CHAPEL**
John Linden.

NEW **GER Y LLYN**
Janet Twigg.

NEW **INNISFREE TY HEBRON**
Linda Rogers, 01650 511463,
isfryn@2spoons.co.uk.

The beautiful village of Aberangell is on the River Angell on edge of Snowdonia National Park with forest tracks and mountains providing backdrop. Four very different gardens: Ger y Llyn, small newly designed and thoughtfully developed garden, beautiful borders, vegetable plot, originally designed water feature, wild area: Innisfree terraced garden built into steep hillside with viewpoint, raised beds and innovative ideas: Pen Pentre on site of old station many railway artefacts displayed in original waiting room; cottage garden style planting with vegetable plot and wildflower bed situated on what was the railway line. Slate steps lead down to seating area by river: Bethania Chapel full of salvaged and upcycled artefacts used to provide planters and interest, espaliered fruit trees grow along chapel walls and reclaimed slate and Victorian railings are given new purpose in this sculptor's garden.

2 ABERNANT
Garthmyl, SY15 6RZ. Mrs B M Gleave, 01686 640494. *1½ m S of Garthmyl. On A483 midway between Welshpool & Newtown (both 8m). Approached over steep humpback bridge with wooden statue of workman. Straight ahead to house & parking.* Visits by arrangement Apr to July for groups of up to 12. Adm £4, chd free. Light refreshments.
3 acres: stunning cherry blossom orchard. Knot garden, box hedging, formal rose garden, rockery, pond, shrubs, ornamental trees, archaic sundials, fossilised wood and stone heads. Additional woodland of 9 acres borrowed views of the Severn Valley. 85 cherry trees in blossom in late April. Roses in late June.

3 NEW **ASH AND ELM HORTICULTURE**
Cae Felyn, Old Hall, Llanidloes, SY18 6PW. Emma Maxwell, www.ashandelmhorticulture.co.uk. *3m from Llanidloes on the River Severn. At Market Hall turn R on Shortbridge St over River Severn & stay on this road for 3m.* Sat 2, Sun 3 July (10.30-4). Adm £5, chd free. Home-made teas.
Diverse 5 acre market garden; flowers, vegetables, fruit, nuts and plants grown using agroecological techniques that nurture nature. Enjoy wandering through the extensive cut flower garden or explore the 1 acre orchard home to a family of barn owls. See wide range of seasonal vegetables growing in the polytunnels, glasshouse and in the field or just relax by one of the wildlife pools. Flower cutting garden, vegetable garden, orchard, nuttery. Talks through the day on growing principles. Grass paths.

4 BACHIE UCHAF
Bachie Road, Llanfyllin, SY22 5NF. Glyn & Glenys Lloyd. *S of Llanfyllin. Going towards Welshpool on A490 turn R onto Bachie Rd after Llanfyllin primary school. Keep straight for 0.8m. Take drive R uphill at cottage on L.* Sat 28, Sun 29 May (12.30-4.30). Adm £5, chd free. Home-made teas.
Inspiring, colourful hillside country garden. Gravel paths meander around extensive planting and over streams cascading down into ponds. Specimen trees, shrubs and vegetable garden. Enjoy the

wonderful views from one of the many seats; your senses will be rewarded.

5 BRON HAFREN
Garthmyl, Montgomery, SY15 6RT. Rod & Debbie Kent. *5m S Welshpool. A483 Opp Nags Head turn on B4835 towards Montgomery. After 600 metres L through double gates diagonally opp Kings Nursery & park in field. Enter garden through wooden gate nr barn.* Sat 25, Sun 26 June (2-5). Adm £5, chd free. Home-made teas in log cabin.
1½ acre mature garden on banks River Severn. Riverside walk with view of ornate Grade II listed bridge. Surrounding the Victorian house are lawns, orchard, mixed borders, shrubbery, raised beds, spinney and large redwood. Interesting mature specimen trees, outbuildings inc original Ty Bach. Uneven surface in paddock parking area. Wheelchair access to refreshments over gravel.

6 NEW **BRON Y LLYS**
Dylife, Llanbrynmair, SY19 7BW. Maya & John Bimson. *10m NW of Llanidloes, on mountain road between Staylittle & Machynlleth. From Llanidloes, take B4518 to Staylittle & Llanbrynmair - 1m after Staylittle, take L to Machynlleth & Dylife. From Machynlleth, take mountain road opp Hennigans Fish & Chips to Dylife.* Sat 9, Sun 10 July (2-5). Adm £4.50, chd free. Home-made teas. Dietary needs catered for.
At 1400' possibly the highest NGS garden. Come and see what can be achieved despite the challenging conditions. A beautiful wild garden shared with birds, bees and other wildlife. We grow a variety of vegetables and fruit and lots of flowers for pollinators. Weeds are organically managed, not eliminated. A peaceful haven with winding paths to different levels and views to the hills all around. Bring your garden tools to the 'Sharpening Shed' where volunteers will sharpen them.

7 NEW **BROOKSIDE**
Llanbister, Llandrindod Wells, LD1 6TW. Mr Adam & Mrs Elizabeth Fairhead. *Head N from Crossgates on A483. After 7m turn R onto minor road signed Llanbister Rd, after 1m turn R signed*

Heartsease. After approx 1m garden is on R immed before bridge. **Sat 23, Sun 24 July (11-5.30). Adm £5, chd free. Light refreshments.**
A stream side garden in the Maelienydd. Approx 1 acre, inc species rich meadow with mown paths to wander through, colourful herbaceous beds and borders, vegetable plot with small apiary, wetland and woodland plantings. Pollinators, butterflies, birds and amphibians in abundance. The garden combines peace, beauty and colour with rich wildlife in the midst of glorious scenery.

8 BRYNCELYN
Lluest Lane, Cwmnantymeichaid, Llanfyllin, SY22 5NE. Rosemary Clarke. *Going towards Welshpool on A490 turn R onto Bachie Rd after Llanfyllin primary school. Follow NGS signs, keep on Bachie Road for 1½ m. Turn L where the road widens at top of rise.* **Sat 4, Sun 5 June (1-5). Adm £5, chd free. Home-made teas.**
3 acre country garden and paddocks. Spectacular backdrop of near hills with views to Cefn Coch & Berwyns. Deep beds of perennial planting with mature trees and shrubs chosen to attract birds and insects; circular walk beside the lake and stream. Meet the resident donkeys and peacocks, find a seat, indulge in your own thoughts and lose yourself in the tranquillity of this achingly special place. Children's play area (supervision required) and children's garden quiz. Partial wheelchair access over gravel area then brick path and grass; excellent views.

9 NEW BRYNGWYN HALL
Bwlch-y-Cibau, Llanfyllin, SY22 5LJ. Auriol Marchioness of Linlithgow, www.bryngwyn.com. *3m SE Llanfyllin. From Llanfyllin take A490 towards Welshpool for 3m turn L up drive just before Bwlch-y-Cibau.* **Sun 3 Apr (10-4). Adm £7.50, chd free. Home-made teas.**
Stunning grade II* listed 9 acre garden with 60 acres parkland design inspired by William Emes. Prunus subhirtella 'Autumnalis', varieties of hamamelis, mahonia, early flowering daphnes, corylopsis and chimonanthus. Woodland garden carpeted with snowdrops then stunning show of thousands of daffodils, camassias and fritillaries in

the long grass down to serpentine lake. Unusual trees, shrubs and unique Poison Garden.

10 CEUNANT
Old Hall, Llanidloes, SY18 6PW. Sharon McCready, 01686 412345, sharon.mccready@yahoo.co.uk. *2m W of Llanidloes. Leave Llanidloes over Shortbridge St, turn L along Pen y Green Rd, approx ½ m turn L signposted Llangurig, Glyn Brochan. Follow signs property is on R.* **Visits by arrangement May to Sept. Adm £5, chd free. Light refreshments.**
4 acre riverside garden started in 2013 in beautiful setting on River Severn just 7m from source. Wooded wildlife area, two wildlife ponds, orchard, ornamental garden, herbaceous borders, scented seating areas, Hobbit House, riverside path, meadow and vegetable plot. Full of unusual features. Planting aimed at pollinators and encouraging wildlife. Sleeping mud maid, clay oven and brook home to Indian Runner ducks, lots of seating areas and recycled features. Accommodation available in shepherd's hut and Hobbit house. www.holidaycottages.co.uk/cottage/56492-severn-way.

11 1 CHURCH BANK
Welshpool, SY21 7DR. Mel & Heather Parkes, 01938 559112, melandheather@live.co.uk. *Centre of Welshpool. Church Bank leads onto Salop Rd from Church St. Follow one way system, use main car park then short walk. Follow yellow NGS signs.* **Visits by arrangement Apr to Aug for groups of 5 to 30. Adm £3.50, chd free. Home-made teas.**
An intimate jewel in the town. C17 barrel maker's cottage with museum of tools and motor memorabilia. Gothic arch leads to shell grotto with mystic pool of smoke and sounds, bonsai garden, fernery, many interesting plants and unusual features.

12 CHURCH HOUSE
Llandefalle, Brecon, LD3 0ND. Chris & Anne Taylor, 01874754330, Chris.n.t@hotmail.com. *Between Brecon & Llyswen, off A470, signposted Llandefalle, then single track lane for ½ m. Parking is next to Church.* **Sat 23, Sun 24 July (2-5.30). Adm £5, chd free. Home-made teas. Visits also by arrangement Apr to Sept.**

1 acre garden, subdivided into different areas, each with its own character inc orchard. Skilfully landscaped in the 1980s to provide terraces, generous borders and year-round interest. New owners have added small pond, herb garden, Stumpery and rill. Tranquil places to sit with fine views to Black Mts. Next to St Matthew's Church, C15 with notable earlier features. Some steps. Wheelchair access to terraces over sloping lawns but only if ground is dry.

13 NEW CULTIVATE COMMUNITY GARDEN
Llanidloes Road, Newtown, SY16 4HX. www.cultivate.uk.com. *A489 W from Newtown adjacent to Newtown College & Theatre Hafren.* **Sun 10 July (1-5). Adm £4.50, chd free. Home-made teas.**
Thriving 2 acre community garden run by the local food cooperative Cultivate. Extensive range of vegetables, herbs and fruit growing on communal plots and 'micro-allotments'. Two polytunnels, small hydroponic unit and lots of compost heaps! Lawns to relax on and wildlife area with pond. Managed by Cultivate volunteers with help from college students and Montgomery Wildlife Trust. Look out for the turf-roofed roundhouse, amazing colourful mural, and trained apple trees. Wheelchair access to main parts of garden, although surfaces may be soft or uneven. Accessible compost toilet.

14 CWM CARNEDD ISAF
Dolfach, Llanbrynmair, SY19 7AF. Jenny Hall, 07952 195605, gingermumma@gmail.com. *1.75m SE Llanbrynmair. From Llanbrynmair take A470 to Dolfach, then 1st L & follow road up hill passing cemetery & chapel, after ¾ m take R fork for house/ From Newtown take A470 to Dolfach, 1st R follow yellow signs.* **Visits by arrangement June to Aug for groups of 5 to 20. Adm £4.50, chd free. Light refreshments.**
Quiet country garden of approx 1 acre surrounding recently renovated barn. Newly created garden enclosed in stone walls, inc herbaceous and mixed borders, gravel garden with pots, garden train track, raised vegetable beds, soft fruit cage, paddock with orchard, wildflower meadow and wildlife pond.

Ger Y Llyn, Aberangell Village Gardens

15 CWM-WEEG

Dolfor, Newtown, SY16 4AT.
Dr W Schaefer & Mr K D
George, 01686 628992,
wolfgang@cwmweeg.co.uk,
www.cwmweeg.co.uk. *4½m SE
of Newtown. Off Bypass, take A489
E from Newtown for 1½m, turn
R towards Dolfor. After 2m turn L
down asphalted farm track, signed
at entrance. Do not rely on SatNav.
Also signed from Dolfor village on
NGS days.* **Sun 26 June (2-5). Adm
£6, chd free. Home-made teas.**
2½ acre garden set within 24 acres
of wildflower meadows and bluebell
woodland with stream centred
around C15 farmhouse (open by
prior arrangement). Formal garden
in English landscape tradition with
vistas, grottos, sculptures, stumpery,
lawns and extensive borders terraced
with stone walls. Translates older
garden vocabulary into an innovative
C21 concept. Extensive under cover
seating area in the new Garden
Pavilion. Partial wheelchair access.

For further information please see
garden website.
&. ⛲ 🚌 ☕

16 ◆ DINGLE NURSERIES & GARDEN

Welshpool, SY21 9JD. Mr & Mrs
D Hamer, 01938 555145, info@
dinglenurseriesandgarden.co.uk,
www.dinglenurseries.co.uk.
*2m NW of Welshpool. Take A490
towards Llanfyllin & Guilsfield. After
1m turn L at sign for Dingle Nurseries
& Garden. Follow signs & enter the
Garden from adjacent plant centre.*
**For NGS: Sat 14, Sun 15 May, Sat
8, Sun 9 Oct (9-5). Adm £3.50, chd
free. Tea and coffee. For other
opening times and information,
please phone, email or visit garden
website.**
4½ acre internationally acclaimed
RHS partner garden on south facing
site, sloping down to lakes. Huge
variety of rare and unusual trees,
ornamental shrubs and herbaceous
plants give year-round interest. Set

in the hills of mid Wales this beautiful
well known garden attracts visitors
from Britain and abroad. Plant
collector's paradise. Open all yr
except 24 Dec - 2 Jan.
🐕 ✿ 🚌 ☕

17 NEW EVANCOYD COURT

Evancoyd, Presteigne, LD8 2PA.
Mr & Mrs Guy Morrison. *5m W
Presteigne. From Presteigne B4356
W for 3½m then turn L on B4357
for 1.4m.* **Sat 30, Sun 31 July (11-
5). Adm £6, chd free. Home-made
teas.**
Impressive tree lined drive with large
box balls leads to 9 acres landscaped
grounds around Grade II listed house
(not open). Large walled garden
divided into rooms with kitchen
garden, tennis court and swimming
pool. Two lakes form focal point below
raised garden terrace. Grounds extend
to around 70 acres inc approx 50
acres mature woodland featuring many
specimen trees. Spectacular views.

GROUP OPENING

 FELINDRE GARDENS
Felindre, Berriew, Welshpool,
SY21 8BE. *6m S Welshpool. From
Welshpool A483 for approx 4m. Turn
R on B4390 straight through Berriew.
After1m fork L, cross bridge & take
road to R. Follow NGS signs to car
park.* **Sun 7 Aug (1-5). Combined
adm £5, chd free. Home-made
teas at Rivermead.**

> **NEW 2 FELINDRE COTTAGE**
> Wendy & Richard Rossiter.
>
> **NEW RIVERMEAD**
> Kathleen & Mark Harvey.
>
> **NEW SPINDLE COTTAGE**
> Denise & Simon Garfield.

Three different gardens in hamlet of
Felindre with its old corn mill on River
Rhiew. Spot dippers, kingfishers and
otters. Spindle Cottage new garden
in progress with mixed beds and
beautiful arbour; 2 Felindre Cottage
compact garden on banks of river
with hanging baskets and pots;
Rivermead large riverside garden with
dense planting, quirky features and
driftwood sculptures.

GARTHMYL HALL
Garthmyl, Montgomery, SY15 6RS.
Julia Pugh, 07716 763567,
hello@garthmylhall.co.uk,
www.garthmylhall.co.uk. *On A483
midway between Welshpool &
Newtown (both 8m). Turn R 200yds
S of Nag's Head Pub.* **Mon 11 July
(12-5). Adm £5, chd free. Home-
made teas.**
Grade II listed Georgian manor
house (not open) surrounded by
5 acres of grounds. 100 metre
herbaceous borders, newly restored
1 acre walled garden with gazebo,
circular flowerbeds, lavender beds,
wildflower meadow, pond, two fire
pits and gravel paths. Fountain, three
magnificent Cedar of Lebanon and
giant redwood. Partial wheelchair
access. Accessible WC.

GLANOER
Bettws, Hundred House,
Llandrindod Wells, LD1 5RP.
Dave & Sue Stone, 07771767246,
stone@glanoer.co.uk. *Centre of
postcode area. Use postcode for*

---

*SatNav. From A481 take turning to
Bettws & Franksbridge by Hundred
House Inn. Take L fork signposted
Bettws. Glanoer is 1m further along
lane on L (past St Mary's Church).*
**Sun 24 July (12-5). Adm £5, chd
free. Home-made teas. Picnics
welcome on the field.**
Just over an acre in an alder valley
with running brook. Numerous
'rooms' throughout providing seating,
vistas and interest. Inc an allotment,
bluebell wood, wildlife pond, secret
garden and water features. Planting
for colour and pollination throughout
the year for resident bees with over
50 varieties of rose. A young garden
created since 2015 on boulder
clay from open space. Free-range
chickens, beehives, allotment,
terraces.

1 GLANRAFON
Llanwddyn, Oswestry, SY10 0LU.
Margaret Herbert. *24m W of
Oswestry. From Llanfyllin, follow
brown signs to Lake Vyrnwy.
Through village of Llanwddyn & turn
L across dam then L past Artisans
Cafe & park in public car park by
playground. Follow yellow signs to
garden.* **Sat 16, Sun 17 July (11-
4.30). Adm £4.50, chd free.**
1 acre secluded garden under
development. As a keen
plantsperson, I have been establishing
this steeply sloping, densely planted
wildlife garden with hundreds of
varieties of shrubs and perennials
over the past 5 years. Very productive
raised vegetable beds, fruit cages
and polytunnels, large pond. Large
greenhouse with ornamental and
edible crops. Fruit trees, bushes
and vegetables, many of which are
unusual varieties. Yard with chickens
and ducks. Wheelchairs can access
the upper & lower levels via the
access road & separate gates.
Carparking strictly for disabled people
at the sculpture park.

**◆ GLANSEVERN HALL
GARDENS**
Berriew, Welshpool, SY21 8AH.
Jem Skelding & Julia Pugh. *5m
SW of Welshpool. On A483 midway
between Newtown & Welshpool.* **For
NGS: Sat 30, Sun 31 July (12-5).
Adm £6, chd free. Home-made
teas in Potting Shed Cafe or
courtyard.**

Beautiful Greek revival house (not
open) set in mature parkland with
rare and ancient trees. 25 acres of
gardens inc walled garden of rooms,
vegetable garden, original potting
shed, Victorian grotto and orangery.
Wysteria scented fountain walk, 4
acre lake with shady seating areas,
folly island and wildfowl. Birdhide on
banks of River Severn and River Rhiw.
Some parts of the garden will be
difficult for wheelchairs.

GLANWYE
Builth Wells, LD2 3YP. Mr & Mrs H
Kidston. *2m SE Builth Wells. From
Builth Wells on A470, after 2m R
at Lodge Gate. From Llyswen on
A470, after 6m L at Lodge Gate. Will
be signposted. Suggest not using
SatNav as unreliable.* **Sun 29 May
(2-5). Adm £5, chd free. Home-
made teas.**
Large Victorian garden, spectacular
rhododendrons, azaleas. Herbaceous
borders, extensive yew hedges,
lawns, long woodland walk with
bluebells and other woodland flowers.
Magnificent views of upper Wye
Valley.

**GLIFFAES COUNTRY HOUSE
HOTEL**
Gliffaes Rd, Crickhowell,
NP8 1RH. Mrs N Brabner & Mr
& Mrs J C Suter, 01874 730371,
calls@gliffaeshotel.com,
www.gliffaes.com. *3½m W of
Crickhowell. From Crickhowell, drive
W for 2½ m, L off A40 & continue
for 1m.* **Sun 23 Oct (1.30-4.30).
Adm £5, chd free. Cream teas.**
Gliffaes Hotel has, within its 33 acres
of grounds, one of the best small
arboretums in Wales with an enviable
collection of specimen trees from
around the globe planted by far
sighted Victorian collectors. It also
has numbers of much older trees
shedding light on how the woodlands
were used and managed in past
times. There will be a guided Autumn
colours Tree Walk at 2pm. Gliffaes is
a country house hotel and is open for
lunch, bar snacks, afternoon tea and
dinner to non residents and garden
visitors. Wheelchair ramp to the west
side of the hotel. In dry weather main
lawns accessible, but more difficult
if wet.

25 ◆ GREGYNOG HALL & GARDEN

Tregynon, Newtown, SY16 3PL. Gregynog Trust, 01686 650224, russell.roberts@gregynog.org, www.gregynog.org. *5m N of Newtown. From Newtown A483 turn L B4389 for Llanfair Caereinion (£2.50 car parking charge applies).* **For NGS: Sat 7, Sun 8 May, Sat 15, Sun 16 Oct (10-4). Adm by donation. Light refreshments at Courtyard Cafe. For other opening times and information, please phone, email or visit garden website.**
Gardens are Grade I Listed due to association with the C18 landscape architect William Emes. Set within 750 acres, a designated National Nature Reserve with SSSI. Parkland with small lake and traces of a water garden. A mass display of rhododendrons, azaleas and unique yew hedge surround the sunken lawns. Unusual trees, woodland walks and arboretum. Good autumn colour. Some gravel paths.

&.

26 THE HYMNS

Walton, Presteigne, LD8 2RA. E Passey, 07958 762362, thehymns@hotmail.com, www.thehymns.co.uk. *5m W of Kington. Take A44 W, then 1st R for Kinnerton. After approx 1m, at the top of small hill, turn L (W).* **Sat 25, Sun 26 June (10.30-5). Adm £5, chd free. Home-made teas. Visits also by arrangement May to July.**
In a beautiful setting in the heart of the Radnor valley, the garden is part of a restored C16 farmstead, with long views to the hills, and The Radnor Forest. It is a traditional garden reclaimed from the wild, using locally grown plants and seeds, and with a herb patio, wildflower meadows and a short woodland walk. It is designed for all the senses: sight, sound and smell.

27 LITTLE HOUSE

Llandinam, nr Newtown, SY17 5BH. Peter & Pat Ashcroft, 07443 524128, littlehouse1692@gmail.com, www.littlehouse1692.uk. *1m from Llandinam Village Hall. Cross river at statue of David Davies on A470 in Llandinam. Follow rd for just under 1m (ignore GPS), Little House is black & white cottage on roadside. Limited parking.* **Sun 12**

June (1-4.30). Adm £4.50, chd free. Home-made teas. Visits also by arrangement June & July for groups of 5 to 20.
⅓ acre plantswoman's garden on a quiet lane surrounded by fields, woodland and stream. Slate and bark paths give access to the many features inc fish and wildlife ponds, conifer, azalea, grass and mixed beds, vegetable garden, woodland, mini meadow, sensory garden, carnivorous plant and grotto water features, auricula theatre and alpine/cactus house. 500+ different plants, many propagated for sale. Summer garden in full bloom and sensory garden alive with colour and wonderful scents.

✿ ☕

28 LLANSTEPHAN HOUSE

Llanstephan, Llyswen, LD3 0YR. Lord & Lady Milford. *10m SW of Builth Wells. Leave A470 at Llyswen onto B4350. 1st L after crossing river in Boughrood. From Builth Wells leave A470, Erwood Bridge, 1st L. Follow signs.* **Sat 4 June (1-5). Adm £5, chd free. Visitors are welcome to bring a picnic.**
20 acre garden, first laid out almost 200 years ago and in the present owner's family for more than a century, featuring a Victorian walled kitchen garden and greenhouses, 100 year old wisteria, woodland walks punctuated by azaleas and rhododendrons, specimen trees and immaculate lawns. Beautiful and celebrated views of Wye Valley and Black Mountains.

&. ⊨ ✿ ☕ ⊨

29 LLWYN MADOC

Beulah, Llanwrtyd Wells, LD5 4TT. Patrick & Miranda Bourdillon, 01591 620564, miranda.bourdillon@gmail.com. *8m W of Builth Wells. On A483 at Beulah take rd towards Abergwesyn for 1m. Drive on R. Parking on field below drive - follow signs.* **Sun 29 May (2-5.30). Adm £5, chd free. Cream teas.**
Terraced garden in attractive wooded valley overlooking lake; yew hedges; rose garden with pergola; azaleas and rhododendrons.

⊨ ⊨ ☕

30 LLYS CELYN

Llanwnog, Caersws, SY17 5JG. Lesley & Tony Geary, 01686 688476, lesley_geary@hotmail.com. *9m W of Newtown. From Newtown A489 W to A470, turn R to Machynlleth & Caersws. After 3m turn R on B4589. Follow signs. Alternative route: from Newtown B4589 from McDonalds direct to Llanwnog.* **Sat 23, Sun 24 July (2-5). Home-made teas. Visits also by arrangement July & Aug for groups of 10 to 20. Weekdays only.**
An evolving 1 acre garden with extensive vegetable garden which inc fruit cage, polytunnel and greenhouse. Large intensively planted herbaceous borders. Wildlife areas inc bog garden, ponds and habitats, a haven for re-homed rescue hedgehogs. Secluded courtyard garden and rockery. Fabulous views of the surrounding countryside and village church steeple.

&. ☕

31 LLYSDINAM

Newbridge-on-Wye, LD1 6NB. Sir John & Lady Venables-Llewelyn & Llysdinam Charitable Trust, 01597 860190/07748492025, llysdinamgardens@gmail.com, llysdinamgardens.co.uk. *5m SW of Llandrindod Wells. Turn W off A470 at Newbridge-on-Wye; turn R immed after crossing R Wye; entrance up hill.* **Thur 2 June (2-5). Adm £5, chd free. Cream teas. Visits also by arrangement.**
Llysdinam Gardens are among the loveliest in mid Wales, especially noted for a magnificent display of rhododendrons and azaleas in May. Covering some 6 acres, they command sweeping views down the Wye Valley. Successive family members have developed the gardens over the last 150 years to inc woodland with specimen trees, large herbaceous and shrub borders and a water garden, all of which provide varied, colourful planting throughout the year. The Victorian walled kitchen garden and extensive greenhouses grow a wide variety of vegetables, hothouse fruit and exotic plants. Gravel paths.

Tyn y Graig

32 NEW LOWER WERNFIGIN BARNS

Trallong, Brecon, LD3 8HW. Mark Collins & Alan Loze, 01874 638259, markinpowys@roughwood.net. *Trallong, Nr Sennybridge, Brecon. A40 W from Brecon, 2nd signpost to Trallong (R). Down, over river, up to Trallong Common then follow yellow signs. A40 E from Sennybridge take 1st sign to Trallong then the same.* **Sat 2, Sun 3 July (11-5). Adm £5, chd free. Home-made teas. Visits also by arrangement Apr to Sept for groups of 5 to 20.**

A terraced south facing garden with dense planting of herbaceous perennials and shrubs. Rear garden planted with hydrangeas, azaleas and rhododendrons. A newly planted area of woodland and field walk. A small orchard, vegetable and fruit garden, all managed, like the flower garden without chemicals. In front of the house is a large courtyard with formal rill, fishpond and seating areas.

33 MAESFRON HALL AND GARDENS

Trewern, Welshpool, SY21 8EA. Dr & Mrs TD Owen, 01938 570600, maesfron@aol.com, www.maesfron.co.uk. *4m E of Welshpool. On N side of A458 Welshpool to Shrewsbury Rd.* **Visits by arrangement Apr to Sept for groups of 10+. Adm £5, chd free. Home-made teas. Wide range of refreshments available by prior arrangement.**

Largely intact Georgian estate of 6 acres. House (partly open) built in Italian villa style set in south facing gardens on lower slopes of Moel-y-Golfa with panoramic views of The Long Mountain. Terraces, Walled Kitchen Garden, Chapel, Restored Victorian Conservatories, Tower, Shell Grotto and Hanging Gardens below tower. Explore ground floor, wine cellar, old kitchen and servants quarters. Parkland walks with wide variety of trees. Refreshments served in reception rooms or on terrace. Some gravel, steps and slopes.

34 MOEL Y GWELLTYN UCHA

Llansilin, Oswestry, SY10 7QX. Mr Nick & Mrs Sue Roberts. *8m W of Oswestry. Follow yellow NGS signs from St Silin's Church Llansilin. Garden 2.3m W of Llansilin on B4580 towards Llanrhaeadr-ym-Mochnant. Garden ¼ m from parking area accessed via a farm track.* **Sat 6, Sun 7 Aug (1.30-5.30). Adm £5, chd free. Home-made teas.**

South facing terraced cottage garden at 900ft on steep hillside in stunning location; fabulous views towards Rodney's Pillar and Long Mountain. Colourful, floriferous: roses, shrubs, pots and herbaceous perennials; garden and pond offer a haven for birds, insects, wildlife. Vegetable plot. Some steps. Seats enable you to pause, relax and enjoy views.

Waen

GROUP OPENING

37 NEW RADNOR GARDENS

New Radnor, Presteigne, LD8 2SS. *Situated on the A44, 6m W of Kington & 12m E from Llandrindod Wells. Tickets & Map from The Hub in School Ln, (nr the monument.) Parking at the end of School Ln.* Sun 26 June (10.30-4.30). Combined adm £6, chd free. Cream teas at The Old School Hub and Garden. The Conservation Village of New Radnor, formally the county town of Radnorshire and strategic site of a Motte and Bailey Castle, whose mound now dominates the village, lies in the beautiful Radnor Valley, cradled between the two high hills of The Smatcher and The Wimble. New for 2022, a pop-up Garden Centre and a new garden a rather steep walk away but giving magnificent views and a wonderful bonsai collection.

38 NO 2 THE OLD COACH HOUSE

Church Road, Knighton, LD7 1ED. Mr Richard & Mrs Jenny Vaughan, 01547 520246. *Out of Knighton on the A488 road to Clun, take 1st L into Church Rd, enter by courtyard of 1 Ystrad House.* Sat 25, Sun 26 June (1-5). Combined adm with 1 Ystrad House £5, chd free. Home-made teas at 1 Ystrad House. Visits also by arrangement June to Aug. The garden at the Old Coach House is a green haven of rooms as you move along a winding path edged by the top borders of shrubs, colourful perennials and circular lawns. An archway of Clematis and Passiflora leads to the lower lawn, flanked by beech hedging, apple trees, a greenhouse, shrubs, hostas and ferns, arriving at a private quiet riverside and woodland glade. The garden can be accessed through the side gate for wheelchair users, where the lawns are generally level.

39 OAK COTTAGE

23 High Street, Welshpool, SY21 7JP. Tony Harvey. *Entered from back of house via Bowling Green Lane parallel to the High Street in centre of Welshpool.* Sun 27 Mar, Mon 18, Sun 24 Apr, Mon 2 May (2-5). Adm £3.50, chd free. Home-made teas. Intimate garden continues to be

35 MONAUGHTY MILL

Monaughty, Knighton, LD7 1SH. Peter & Shelley Lane. *5m SW Knighton. From Knighton take A488 towards Llandrindod Wells. After 4m turn R B4356 Garden 400m on L.* Sun 31 July (11.30-5). Adm £4.50, chd free. Home-made teas. C17 converted mill (not open) with approx 2 acre garden set on banks of River Lugg in stunning position with lovely views of Glogg Hill. Informal herbaceous and shrub borders, pond, small woodland areas, riverside, shady and bog plantings, unusual rusted iron 'church' sculpture laden with climbers and shrubs.

36 THE NEUADD

Llanbedr, Crickhowell, NP8 1SP. Robin & Philippa Herbert, 01873 812164, philippahherbert@gmail.com. *1m NE of Crickhowell. Leave Crickhowell by Llanbedr Rd. At junction with*

Great Oak Rd bear L, cont up hill for approx 1m, garden on L. Ample parking. Sun 5 June (2-6.30). Adm £5, chd free. Home-made teas in the courtyard. Visits also by arrangement June to Sept for groups of 6 to 12. Robin and Philippa Herbert have worked on the restoration of the garden at The Neuadd since 1999 and have planted many unusual trees and shrubs in the dramatic setting of the Brecon Beacons National Park. One of the major features is the walled garden, which has both traditional and decorative planting of fruit, vegetables and flowers. There is also a woodland walk with ponds and streams and a formal garden with flowering terraces. Spectacular views, water feature, rare trees and shrubs and a plant stall. The owner uses a wheelchair and most of the garden is accessible, but some steep paths.

developed but is still an oasis of green in the town centre. Gravel paths and stepping stones meander through a wide variety of plants, inc unusual species, and make the garden seem much larger than it is. Alpines are still a favourite as are the insectivorous plants. Modern representation of a Wardian cabinet, with hepaticas. Places to sit and enjoy garden views. Gravel paths and steps or steep slope at entrance.

ઙ 🐄 ☕

40 OSPREY STUDIOS

57 Ynyswen, Penycae, Swansea, SA9 1YT. Rebecca Buck, 07913743457, osprey.studios@btinternet.com, www.ospreystudios.org. *20m from Swansea. M4 exit 45, 15m on A4067 towards Brecon. L after Ynyswen rd sign. L at T junction, Blue house on R, no. 57. 13m from A40/A4067 junction, Sennybridge.* Visits by arrangement May to Sept for groups of up to 10. Adm £4, chd free. Tea.
Wildlife, sculpture and fruit in front and back gardens. Blending into the wet meadow at the base of Cribarth, Sleeping Giant Mountain on the SW corner of the Brecon Beacons National Park. Specialising in slug-proof planting! Ceramic sculpture studio on site, sculptures and planters for sale. Teas and home-made cake. WC. Easy parking in front. Unique Sculpture for sale or commission. A varied selection of 'Seconds' starting at £1! Lovely walks and great pubs in this area.

🐄 ❀ 🚌 ☕ 🪑

41 PENMYARTH HOUSE - GLANUSK ESTATE

Crickhowell, NP8 1SH. Mr Harry Legge-Bourke, 01873 810414, info@glanuskestate.com, www.glanuskestate.com. *2m NW of Crickhowell. Please access the Glanusk Estate via the Main Entrance (NP8 1SH) on the A40 and follow signs to car park. There is no access for this event from the B4558 Cwm Crawnon Rd.* Sun 15 May (11-4). Adm £7.50, chd free. Light refreshments. Family Tea Tent, locally sourced food and drink stands, licensed bar.
The garden, adorned with many established plant species such as Rhododendrons, Azaleas, Acers, Camelia, Magnolia, Prunus, Dogwood and 300 cultivars of Oak, give a vast array of colour in the spring and summer months. Stunning views of

the River Usk and the majestic Black Mountains. We will also be holding our annual Estate Fayre with over 30 artisan stands and locally sourced and produced food and drink. Penmyarth Church will be open. For more information see our website and socials. Historic gardens, Oaks, Cottage Orné, Artisan stands, home made cakes, coffee, tea and locally sourced and produced catering, licensed bar, talks, garden tours, plant sale, activities and demonstrations. The gardens contain some historic features, including paths and steps which are not suitable for access by wheelchairs or pushchairs.

ઙ 🐄 ❀ 🚌 🚍 ☕

42 PLAS DINAM

Llandinam, Newtown, SY17 5DQ. Eldrydd Lamp, 07415 503554, eldrydd@plasdinam.co.uk, www.plasdinamcountryhouse. co.uk. *7½m SW Newtown. on A470.* Visits by arrangement Apr to Nov for groups of 10+. Adm £8 inc tea, coffee and cake.
12 acres of parkland, gardens, lawns and woodland set at the foot of glorious rolling hills with spectacular views across the Severn Valley. A host of daffodils followed by one of the best wildflower meadows in Montgomeryshire with 36 species of flowers and grasses inc hundreds of wild orchids; Glorious autumn colour with parrotias, liriodendrons, cotinus etc. Millennium wood. From 1884 until recently the home of Lord Davies and his family (house not open).

ઙ 🐄 🚍 🚌 ☕

43 PONTHAFREN

Long Bridge Street, Newtown, SY16 2DY. Ponthafren Association, www.ponthafren.org.uk. *Park in main car park in town centre, 5 mins walk. Turn L out of car park, turn L over bridge, garden on L. Limited disabled parking, please phone for details.* Sat 23 July (10-4.30). Adm by donation. Home-made teas.
Ponthafren is a registered charity that provides a caring community to promote positive mental health and well-being for all. Open door policy so everyone is welcome. Interesting community garden on banks of River Severn run and maintained totally by volunteers: sensory garden with long grasses, herbs, scented plants and shrubs, quirky objects. Productive vegetable plot. Lots of plants for sale. Covered seating areas positioned around the garden to enjoy the views.

Partial wheelchair access.

ઙ 🐄 ❀ 🚍 ☕

44 PONTSIONI HOUSE

Aberedw, Builth Wells, LD2 3SQ. Mr & Mrs Jonathan Reeves. *5m SE of Builth Wells. On B4567 between Erwood Bridge & Aberedw on Radnorshire side of R Wye.* Sun 8, Sun 15 May (2.30-6). Adm £5, chd free. Home-made teas.
With a background of old ruins and steep rocky woodland, this Wye Valley garden with herbaceous, shrub borders, terraces and natural rockery merge with lawns. Recently constructed small walled vegetable and fruit garden. Walks through wildflower meadow along a mile of old railway line with bluebell woods and walks up to the Aberedw Rocks. Dogs welcome along old railway line. Spectacular rocky and woody situation. Extensive bluebells.

ઙ ❀ ☕

45 THE ROCK HOUSE

Llanbister, LD1 6TN. Jude Boutle & Sue Cox. *10m N of Llandrindod Wells. Off B4356 just above Llanbister village.* Sat 4, Sun 5 June (12-5). Adm £5, chd free. Home-made teas. We will have gluten free and vegan cakes available.
About an acre of informal hillside garden, 1000ft up with views over the Radnorshire Hills. Wildlife ponds, bluebell meadow and a laburnum arch. It's a bit of a battle with nature so come and visit and see who you think is winning! The Cwtch - an epic summerhouse and a new fern area created for 2022.

❀ ☕))

During 2020 – 2021 National Garden Scheme funding supported over 1,400 Queen's Nurses to deliver virtual and hands-on, community care across England, Wales and Northern Ireland

46 ROCK MILL

Abermule, Montgomery,
SY15 6NN. Rufus & Cherry
Fairweather, 01686 630664,
fairweathers66@btinternet.com.
*1m S of Abermule on B4368
towards Kerry. Best approached
from Abermule village as there is an
angled entrance into field for parking.*
**Sat 21, Sun 22 May (2-5). Adm £6,
chd free. Home-made teas.** Visits
also by arrangement in May for
groups of 10 to 30.
A river runs through this magical
3 acre garden in a beautiful
wooded valley. Colourful borders
and shrubberies, specimen trees,
terraces, woodland walks, bridges,
extensive lawns, fishponds, orchard,
herb and vegetable beds, beehives,
thatched roundhouse, remnants of
industrial past (corn mill and railway
line) offer much to explore. Child
friendly activities (supervision required)
inc croquet, animal treasure hunt,
wilderness trails, cockleshell tunnel.
Sensible shoes and a sense of fun/
adventure recommended. Much to
explore.

GROUP OPENING

47 SOUTH STREET GARDENS

South Street, Rhayader,
LD6 5BH. Gwyneth Rose &
Steve Harvey, 01597 811868,
info@penralleyhouse.com. *All
gardens are 100 metres S of the
centre of Rhayder on A470. Parking
in public car park in St Harmon Rd,
by sports centre. Penralley House
& Beechcroft gardens are in South
St on the R & the Toll house is opp,
approx 100 metres from town clock.*
**Sun 3 July (1-4.30). Combined
adm £5, chd free. Tea in Penralley
garden.**
Three very different gardens close to
the centre of town. The Toll House
shows what can be done in a tiny
space, with raised beds of annuals,
troughs and traditional roses around
the door. Penralley House has a large
terraced garden with flower borders,
mature trees, orchard, chicken coop,
fruit garden and lawns. Beechcroft,
the largest of the three, has an
herbaceous border, fruit garden
with greenhouse and compost area,
raised vegetable garden, pond and
wildflower meadow. Below is a sloped
woodland garden with zig zag paths
and natural spring at the bottom.
All gardens have views of the lovely
Gwastedyn Hill at the edge of town.

Tea and cake available in Penralley
garden. Plant sales and open textile
studio in Beechcroft garden. Both
Beechcroft and Penralley gardens
are accessible. The Toll house is
restricted. Blue badge only Disabled
parking in Beechcroft.

48 TRANQUILITY HAVEN

7 Lords Land, Whitton,
Knighton, LD7 1NJ. Val Brown,
01547 560070,
valerie.brown1502@gmail.com.
*approx 3m from Knighton & 5m
Presteigne. From Knighton take
B4355 after approx. 2m turn R on
B4357 to Whitton. Car park on L by
yellow NGS signs.* **Sat 18, Sun 19
June (2-5). Evening opening Wed
13 July, Wed 17 Aug (6-8). Sat 15,
Sun 16 Oct (2-4). Evening opening
Sat 17, Sun 18 Dec (4-6). Adm
£4.50, chd free. Home-made teas
at daytime openings only.** Visits
also by arrangement Apr to Dec
for groups of up to 30.
Amazing Japanese inspired Garden
with borrowed views to Offa's Dyke.
Winding paths pass small pools and
lead to Japanese bridges over natural
stream with dippers and kingfishers.
Sounds of water fill the air. Enjoy
peace and tranquillity from one of the
seats or the Japanese Tea House.
Dense oriental planting with Cornus
kousa satomi, acers, azaleas, unusual
bamboos and wonderful cloud
pruning.

49 TREBERFYDD HOUSE

Llangasty, Bwlch, Brecon,
LD3 7PX. David Raikes & Carla
Rapoport, www.treberfydd.com.
*6m E of Brecon. From Abergavenny
on A40, turn R in Bwlch on B5460.
Take 1st turning L towards Pennorth
& cont 2m along lane. From Brecon,
turn L off A40 in Llanhamlach
towards Pennorth. Go through
Pennorth, 1m on.* **Sun 3 July (1-
5.30). Adm £5.50, chd free. Home-
made teas.**
Grade I listed Victorian Gothic house
with 10 acres of grounds designed
by W A Nesfield. Magnificent Cedar
of Lebanon, avenue of mature
Beech, towering Atlantic Cedars,
Victorian rockery, herbaceous border
and manicured lawns ideal for a
picnic. Wonderful views of the Black
Mountains. Plants available from
Commercial Nursery in grounds -
Walled Garden Treberfydd. Easy

wheelchair access to areas around
the house, but herbaceous border
only accessible via steps.

50 TREMYNFA

Carreghofa Lane,
Llanymynech, SY22 6LA. Jon
& Gillian Fynes, 01691 839471,
gillianfynes@btinternet.com. *Edge
of Llanymynech village. From N leave
Oswestry on A483 to Welshpool.
In Llanymynech turn R at Xrds (car
wash on corner). Take 2nd R then
follow yellow NGS signs. 300yds
park signed field, limited disabled
parking nr garden.* **Sat 18, Sun 19
June (1-5). Adm £5, chd free.
Cream teas inc gluten free
option.** Visits also by arrangement
13-24 June for groups of 10 to
35. Afternoon or evening visits
welcome.
South facing 1 acre garden developed
over 15 yrs. Old railway cottage set
in herbaceous and raised borders,
patio with many pots of colourful
and unusual plants. Garden slopes
to productive fruit and vegetable
area, ponds, spinney, unusual trees,
wild areas and peat bog. Patio and
seats to enjoy extensive views inc
Llanymynech Rocks. Pet ducks
on site, Montgomery canal close
by. 100s of homegrown plants and
home-made jams for sale.

51 TYN Y CWM

Beulah, Llanwrtyd Wells,
LD5 4TS. Steve & Christine
Carrow, 01591 620461,
steve.carrow@ngs.org.uk. *10m W
of Builth Wells. On A483 at Beulah
take rd towards Abergwesyn for
2m. Drive drops down to L.* **Sun 21
Aug (2-5.30). Adm £5, chd free.
Home-made teas.** Visits also by
arrangement June to Sept for
groups of up to 30.
Garden started 20 years ago, lower
garden has spring/woodland area,
raised beds mixed with vegetables,
fruit trees, fruit and flowers. Perennial
borders, summerhouse gravel paths
through rose and clematis pergola.
Grass and Dahlia beds. Upper
garden, partly sloped, inc bog and
water gardens. Perennial beds with
unusual slate steps. Beautiful views.
Property bounded by small river.
Children's quiz.

52 TYNRHOS
Newbridge-On-Wye, Llandrindod Wells, LD1 6ND. Clare Wilkinson.
1 mile NW Newbridge-on-Wye. From A470 take B4518 (signed Beulah) after 400yds cross bridge, turn R for Llysdinam. Proceed up the hill for 1m, Tynrhos is on L. **Sun 10 July (1.30-5.30). Adm £5, chd free. Home-made teas.**
A ¾ acre family cottage garden lying at approx 800' with views over the Wye Valley. Mainly herbaceous planting with summer annuals and pots. Vegetable plot with small greenhouse leading to orchard, fields and wildlife pond. Cobbled area to terrace. Access to rear garden area over grass. Paths are gravel/grass, maybe slippery if wet.
&. ❀ ☕

53 NEW TYN-Y-GRAIG
Bwlch y Ffridd, Newtown, SY16 3JB. Simon & Georgina Newson. *4m N Caersws. B4568 from Newtown Turn R after Aberhafesp. At fork bear L past community centre. At xrds turn R. At fork bear L. After cattle grid take first R onto rough track.* **Sat 2, Sun 3 July (11-4). Adm £4.50, chd free. Home-made teas.**
A garden at 300m with views of surrounding hills, variety of borders and areas inc hectare of meadow managed for biodiversity. Garden planted to achieve different moods inc a herb area, bright, white and pastel borders, rose garden, farmyard borders, fernery, fruit trees and vegetable beds. Meadow with woodland and large pond. Open studio. Rough track to parking and short walk to the garden. Partial wheelchair access. Grass paths, some steps, most can be avoided. Disabled visitors may be dropped off at house.
&. ❀ ☕ 🥪

54 VAYNOR PARK
Berriew, Welshpool, SY21 8QE.
Mr & Mrs William Corbett-Winder.
Leave Berriew going over bridge & straight up the hill on the Bettws rd. Entrance to Vaynor Park is on R ¼m from the speed derestriction sign. **Sun 4 Sept (1-5). Adm £6, chd free. Home-made teas.**
Beautiful C17 house (not open) with 5 acre garden. Stunning herbaceous borders with late flowering salvias, penstemons and dahlias, box edged rose parterre, banks of hydrangeas; topiary yew birds, box buttresses

and spires bring formality. Courtyard with lime green hydrangea paniculata and Annabelle. Woodland garden. Orangery. Spectacular views. Home to the Corbett-Winder family since 1720.
&. ❀ ☕

55 NEW WAEN
Waen Lane, Llandinam, Newtown, SY17 5BH. Mike & Rachael Harris, 07790 026201, rachaelfrankland@yahoo.co.uk.
1m E Llandinam. Cross river at David Davies statue on A470 in Llandinam. Turn L at Waen Lane continue up lane to farm gate. Through gate & up track where track splits bear R. **Visits by arrangement Apr to Aug for groups of up to 15. Adm £5, chd free. Light refreshments.**
Secret 2½ acre cottage garden at 1100ft with perennial beds, wildlife lake with ducks and geese, raised vegetable beds, small woodland area, A stream runs through garden and small meadow is inhabited by two Alpaca. In spring the woodland is full of native bluebells, the garden has a wild/natural/cottage garden vibe.
❀ 🏠 ☕ 🥪

56 ◆ WELSH LAVENDER
Cefnperfedd Uchaf, Maesmynis, Builth Wells, LD2 3HU. Nancy Durham & Bill Newton-Smith, 01982 552467, farmers@welshlavender.com, www.welshlavender.com. *Approx 4½m S of Builth Wells & 13m N from Brecon Cathedral off B4520. The farm is 1⅓m from turn signed Farmers' Welsh Lavender.* **For NGS: Every Fri 17 June to 24 June (10-4). Every Fri 15 July to 19 Aug (10-4). Adm £5, chd free. Pre-booking essential, please visit www.ngs. org.uk for information & booking. Light refreshments. For other opening times and information, please phone, email or visit garden website.**
Jeni Arnold's stylish wild planting of the steep bank above the ever popular wild swimming pond is a riot of colour best seen in June. Fields of blue lavender peak from mid July to mid August. Walk in the lavender fields, learn how the distillation process works, and visit the farm shop to try body creams and balms made with lavender oil distilled on the farm. Swim in the pond before enjoying coffee, tea and light refreshments. Partial wheelchair

access. Large paved area adjacent to teas and shop area easy to negotiate.
&. 🐕 ❀ ☕

57 WHITE HOPTON FARM
Wern Lane, Sarn, Newtown, SY16 4EN. Claire Austin, www. claireaustin-hardyplants.co.uk.
From Newtown A489, E towards Churchstoke for 7m & turn R in Sarn follow yellow NGS signs. **Fri 17 June (10-4). Adm £7, chd free. Pre-booking essential, please visit www.ngs.org.uk for information & booking.**
Horticulturist and author Claire Austin's private 1½ acre plant collector's garden designed along the lines of a cottage garden with hundreds of different perennials. Front garden mainly full of May blooming perennials, back garden, which is split into various areas, has a June and July garden, a small woodland walk, a Victorian fountain and mixed rose borders. Fabulous views over the Kerry Vale. Stunning Peony and Iris fields. Wide range of Claire Austin's Hardy Plants for sale at the nursery. Toilet facilities on site.
&. 🐕 ❀ NPC ☕))

58 1 YSTRAD HOUSE
1 Church Road, Knighton, LD7 1EB. John & Margaret Davis, 01547 528154, jamdavis@ystradhouse.plus.com.
At junction of Church Rd & Station Rd. Take the turning opp Knighton Hotel (A488 Clun) travel 225yds along Station Rd. Yellow House, red front door, at junction with Church Rd. **Sat 25, Sun 26 June (1-5). Combined adm with No 2 The Old Coach House £5, chd free. Home-made teas inc gluten free cakes. Visits also by arrangement June to Aug.**
A town garden behind a Regency Villa of earlier origins. A narrow entrance door opens revealing unexpected calm and timelessness. A small walled garden with box hedging and greenhouse lead to broad lawns, wide borders with soft colour schemes and mature trees. More intimate features: pots, urns and pools add interest and surprise. The formal areas merge with wooded glades leading to a riverside walk. Croquet on request. Lawns and gravelled paths mostly flat, except access to riverside walk.
&. 🐕 ❀ � ☕

Early Openings 2023

Plan your garden visiting well ahead – put these dates in your diary!

Gardens across the country open early – before the next year's guide is published – with glorious displays of colour including hellebores, aconites, snowdrops and carpets of spring bulbs.

Bedfordshire
Sun 26 February (2-4)
King's Arms Garden

Cheshire & Wirral
Sun 26 February (12.30-4)
Bucklow Farm

By Arrangement in February
Rosewood
The Well House

Devon
Fri 3, Fri 10, Sat 18
February (2-5)
Higher Cherubeer

Essex
Sun 22 January (10-5)
Green Island

Glamorgan
Sun 19 February (2-5)
Slade

Gloucestershire
Sun 29 January, Sun 12
February (11-4)
Home Farm

Sun 12, Sun 19 February
(11-4.30)
Trench Hill

Herefordshire
Sun 12, Sun 26 February (11-4)
The Picton Garden

Kent
Sat 11, Sun 19 February (12-4)
Copton Ash

By arrangement in February
The Old Rectory

Northamptonshire
Sun 26 February (10.30-3.30)
67-69 High Street

Oxfordshire
Sun 12 February (1.30-5)
Hollyhocks

Somerset, Bristol & South Gloucestershire
By arrangement in February
1 Birch Drive

Staffordshire, Birmingham & West Midlands
Sun 12 February (12-4)
5 East View Cottages

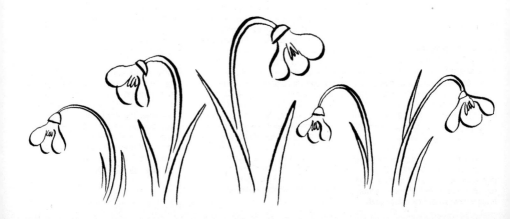

Visit Scottish gardens open for charity
Explore secret gardens and hidden gems

scotlandsgardens.org
Charity no SC049866

Scotland's
GARDENS
Scheme
OPEN FOR CHARITY

Photo © Armadale Castle,
Gardens & Museum

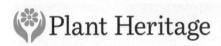Plant Heritage

Nearly 70 gardens that open for the National Garden Scheme are holders of a Plant Heritage National Plant Collection although this may not always be noted in the garden description. These gardens carry the NPC symbol.

Plant Heritage, 12 Home Farm, Loseley Park, Guildford, Surrey GU3 1HS.
01483 447540 www.plantheritage.org.uk

Acer (excl. palmatum cvs.)
Blagdon, North East

Alnus
Stone Lane Gardens, Devon
Blagdon, North East

Anemone nemorosa cvs.
Kingston Lacy, Dorset

Araliaceae (excl. Hedera)
Meon Orchard, Hampshire

Aspidistra elatior &
sichuanensis cvs.
12 Woods Ley, Kent

Aster & related genera
(autumn flowering)
The Picton Garden, Herefordshire

Aster (Symphyotrichum)
novae-angliae
Brockamin, Worcestershire

Astrantia
Norwell Nurseries, Norwell Gardens,
Nottinghamshire

Betula
Stone Lane Gardens, Devon

Camellia (autumn and
winter flowering)
Green Island, Essex

Camellias & Rhododendrons
introduced to Heligan pre-1920
The Lost Gardens of Heligan,
Cornwall

Carpinus
Sir Harold Hillier Gardens, Hampshire

Carpinus betulus cvs.
West Lodge Park, London

Catalpa
West Lodge Park, London

Ceanothus
Eccleston Square, London

Cercidiphyllum
Sir Harold Hillier Gardens, Hampshire
Hodnet Hall Gardens, Shropshire

Chlorophytum comosum cvs.
52 Cobblers Bridge Road, Kent

Chrysanthemum (Hardy) Dispersed
Norwell Nurseries, Norwell Gardens,
Nottinghamshire

Chrysanthemum Hardy (Dispersed
collection)
Hill Close Gardens, Warwickshire

Clematis viticella
Longstock Park Water Garden,
Hampshire

Clematis viticella cvs.
Roseland House, Cornwall

Codonopsis & related genera
Woodlands, Lincolnshire

Colchicum
East Ruston Old Vicarage, Norfolk

Convallaria
12 Woods Ley, Kent

Cornus
Sir Harold Hillier Gardens, Hampshire

Cornus (excl. C. florida cvs.)
Newby Hall & Gardens, Yorkshire

Corokia
33 Wood Vale, London

Corylus
Sir Harold Hillier Gardens, Hampshire

Cotoneaster
Sir Harold Hillier Gardens, Hampshire

Cyclamen (excl. persicum cvs.)
Higher Cherubeer, Devon

Daboecia
Holehird Gardens, Cumbria

Daffodil Dispersed Noel Burr
Cultivars
Mill Hall Farm, Sussex

Dahlia (dark leaved)
Sweetbriar, Kent

Dierama spp.
Yew Tree Cottage, Staffordshire

Erica & Calluna –
Sussex heather cvs.
Nymans, Sussex

Erythronium
Greencombe Gardens,
Somerset & Bristol

Eucalyptus
Meon Orchard, Hampshire

Eucalyptus spp.
The World Garden at Lullingstone
Castle, Kent

Eucryphia
Whitstone Farm, Devon

Euonymus (deciduous)
The Place for Plants, East Bergholt
Place Garden, Suffolk

Eupatorium
Saith Ffynnon Farm, North East Wales

Euphorbia (hardy)
Firvale Perennial Garden, Yorkshire

Fraxinus
The Lovell Quinta Arboretum,
Cheshire & Wirral

Galanthus
127 Stoke Road, Bedfordshire

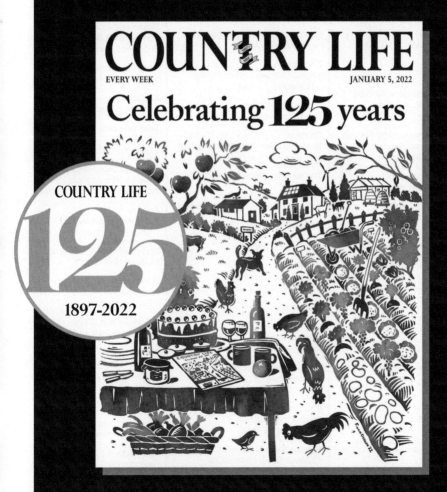

Gaultheria (incl Pernettya)
Greencombe Gardens,
Somerset & Bristol

Geranium sanguineum,
macrorrhizum & x cantabrigiense
Brockamin, Worcestershire

Geum
1 Brickwall Cottages, Kent

Hakonechloa macra & cvs.
12 Woods Ley, Kent

Hamamelis
Sir Harold Hillier Gardens, Hampshire

Hamamelis cvs.
Green Island, Essex

Heliotropium
Hampton Court Palace, London

Helleborus (Harvington hybrids)
Riverside Gardens at Webbs,
Worcestershire

Hemerocallis (cvs bred by RH Coe,
LW Brummitt & HJ Randall)
Broadward Hall, Shropshire

Hilliers (Plants raised by)
Sir Harold Hillier Gardens, Hampshire

Hoheria
Abbotsbury Gardens, Dorset

Hypericum
Sir Harold Hillier Gardens, Hampshire

Hypericum sect. Androsaemum
& Ascyreia spp.
Holme for Gardens, Dorset

Iris (Bearded)
White Hopton Farm, Powys

Juglans
Upton Wold, Gloucestershire

Lapageria rosea (& named cvs)
Roseland House, Cornwall

Lewisia
'John's Garden' at Ashwood
Nurseries, Staffordshire

Ligustrum
Sir Harold Hillier Gardens, Hampshire

Lithocarpus
Sir Harold Hillier Gardens, Hampshire

Magnolia spp. in ect. Buergeria,
Magnolia, Oyama, Rhytidospermum,
Tulipastrum & Yulania
Caerhays Castle, Cornwall

Malus (ornamental)
Barnards Farm, Essex

Meconopsis (large perennial spp.
& hybrids)
Holehird Gardens, Cumbria

Metasequoia
Sir Harold Hillier Gardens, Hampshire

Monarda
Glyn Bach Gardens, Carmarthenshire
& Pembrokeshire

Ophiopogon japonicus cvs.
12 Woods Ley, Kent

Paeonia (hybrid herbaceous)
White Hopton Farm, Powys

Pennisetum spp. & cvs. (hardy)
Knoll Gardens, Dorset

Penstemon
Kingston Maurward Gardens and
Animal Park, Dorset

Persicaria virginiana
Sweetbriar, Kent

Photinia
Sir Harold Hillier Gardens, Hampshire

Picea spp.
The Yorkshire Arboretum, Yorkshire

Pinus (excl dwarf cvs.)
Sir Harold Hillier Gardens, Hampshire

Pinus spp.
The Lovell Quinta Arboretum,
Cheshire & Wirral

Plants named after
Sir Winston Churchill
Churchill College, Cambridgeshire

Plectranthus
Sweetbriar, Kent

Podocarpaceae
Meon Orchard, Hampshire

Podocarpus & related
Pocarpaceae
Caerhays Castle, Cornwall

Polystichum
Greencombe Gardens,
Somerset & Bristol

Primula auricula (Border)
12 Meres Road, Staffordshire

Pseudopanax
Sweetbriar, Kent

Pterocarya
Upton Wold, Gloucestershire

Quercus
Chevithorne Barton, Devon
Sir Harold Hillier Gardens, Hampshire

Quercus (Sir Bernard Lovell
collection)
The Lovell Quinta Arboretum,
Cheshire & Wirral

Rhododendron (Ghent Azaleas)
Sheffield Park and Garden, Sussex

Rhododendron (Kurume Azalea
Wilson 50)
Trewidden Garden, Cornwall

Rhus
The Place for Plants, East Bergholt
Place Garden, Suffolk

Rosa - Hybrid Musk intro by
Pemberton & Bentall 1912-1939
Dutton Hall, Lancashire

Rosa (rambling)
Moor Wood, Gloucestershire

Sarracenia
Beaufort, Shropshire

Saxifraga sect. Ligulatae:
spp. & cvs.
Waterperry Gardens, Oxfordshire

Saxifraga sect. Porphyrion
subsect. Porophyllum
Waterperry Gardens, Oxfordshire

Sorbus
Ness Botanic Gardens,
Cheshire & Wirral

Sorbus (British endemic spp.)
Blagdon, North East

Stewartia - Asian spp.
High Beeches Woodland and Water
Garden, Sussex

Taxodium spp. & cvs.
West Lodge Park, London

Toxicodendron
The Place for Plants, East Bergholt
Place Garden, Suffolk

Tulbaghia
Marwood Hill Garden, Devon

Tulipa (historic tulips)
Blackland House, Wiltshire

Vaccinium
Greencombe Gardens, Somerset
& Bristol

Verbena spp. & cvs
9 Chalfield Close, Cheshire & Wirral

Yucca
Spring View, Burwell Village Gardens,
Cambridgeshire
Renishaw Hall & Gardens, Derbyshire

Traditionally...
The Gardener's Glasshouse

Griffin has been designing bespoke glasshouses since the early 1960s. With a history of innovating glasshouse design for the commercial sector, Griffin continues to be the choice of many estate managers and discerning professional gardeners today, with glasshouses installed in the UK and worldwide.

Each Griffin glasshouse is individually created for you, tailored to your individual requirements and unique surroundings whilst being both a pleasure for you to use and an enhancing feature of your property. Manufactured from powder coated aluminium in any colour of your choice, your glasshouse will have all the appeal of a traditional wooden structure but without the maintenance issues.

Unreservedly distinct Glasshouses, Greenhouses and Orangeries

For more information please call or visit our website.

GRIFFIN GLASSHOUSES
GREENHOUSES OF DISTINCTION
www.griffinglasshouses.com
01962 772512

Partnering National Garden Scheme with our select range of free standing glasshouses

Society of Garden Designers

The 🔲 symbol at the end of a garden description indicates that the garden has been designed by a Fellow, Member, Pre-Registered Member or Student of the Society of Garden Designers.

Fellow of the Society of Garden Designers (FSGD) is awarded to Members for exceptional contributions to the Society or to the profession

Rosemary Alexander FSGD
Roderick Griffin FSGD
Sarah Massey FSGD
Nigel Philips FSGD
David Stevens FSGD
Julie Toll FSGD
Malcolm Veitch FSGD

Member of the Society of Garden Designers (MSGD) is awarded after passing adjudication

James Alexander Sinclair MSGD
Marian Boswall MSGD
Lisa Cox MSGD
Jill Fenwick MSGD
Fiona Harrison MSGD
Phil Hirst MSGD
Thomas Hoblyn MSGD
Nic Howard MSGD
Barbara Hunt MSGD (retired)
Anne Keenan MSGD
Ian Kitson MSGD
Arabella Lennox-Boyd MSGD
Robert Myers MSGD
Chris Parsons MSGD
Dan Pearson MSGD
Joe Perkins MSGD
Emma Plunket MSGD
Paul Richards MSGD

Jilayne Rickards MSGD
Debbie Roberts MSGD
Libby Russell MSGD
Charles Rutherfoord MSGD
Ian Smith MSGD
Lorenzo Soprani-Volpini MSGD
Tom Stuart-Smith MSGD
Joe Swift MSGD
Sue Townsend MSGD
Cleve West MSGD
Matthew Wilson MSGD
Rebecca Winship MSGD

Pre-Registered Member is a member working towards gaining Registered Membership

Tamara Bridge
Alasdair Cameron
Kristina Clode
Linsey Evans
Anoushka Feiler
Claire Merriman
Sarah Naybour
Guy Petheram
Anne-Marie Powell
Faith Ramsay
Caz Renshaw
Judy Shardlow
Julia Whiteaway
Ruth Willmott

Students
Susanne Barker
Jackie Cahoon
Julianne Fernandez
Tom Gadsby
Will Jennings
Paul Kimberley
Jonathan Venables

Acknowledgements

Each year the National Garden Scheme receives fantastic support from the community of garden photographers who donate and make available images of gardens: sincere thanks to them all. Our thanks also to our wonderful garden owners who kindly submit images of their gardens.

Unless otherwise stated, photographs are kindly reproduced by permission of the garden owner.

The 2022 Production Team: Vicky Flynn, Louise Grainger, Vince Hagan, Lucy Hooper, Kay Palmer, Christina Plowman, Helena Pretorius, George Plumptre, Jane Sennett, Gail Sherling-Brown, Catherine Swan, Georgina Waters, Anna Wili.

A CIP catalogue record for this book is available from the British Library.

ISBN: 978-1-4087-1689-2

Designed by Level Partnership
Maps by Mary Spence © Global Mapping and XYZ Maps
Typeset in Helvetica Neue
Printed and bound in Italy by Rotolito S.p.A.

Constable
An imprint of Little, Brown Book Group
Carmelite House, 50 Victoria Embankment,
London EC4Y 0DZ

An Hachette UK Company
www.hachette.co.uk www.littlebrown.co.uk

If you require this information in alternative formats, please telephone 01483 211535 or email hello@ngs.org.uk